Judicial Politics

Judicial Politics

Readings from *Judicature*

Elliot E. Slotnick, Editor
Ohio State University

Third Edition

CQ PRESS

A Division of Congressional Quarterly Inc.
Washington, D.C.

CQ Press
1255 22nd St., N.W., Suite 400
Washington, D.C. 20037

Phone, 202-729-1900
Toll-free, 1-866-4CQ-PRESS (1-866-427-7737)

www.cqpress.com

Cover design: Auburn Incorporated
Interior design: Octavio
Composition: BMWW

Printed and bound in the United States of America
09   08   07   06   05   5   4   3   2   1

Library of Congress Cataloging-in-Publication Data

Judicial politics : readings from Judicature / Elliot E. Slotnick, Editor.—3rd ed.
    p. cm.
  ISBN 1-56802-944-6 (alk. paper)
   1. Judicial process—United States.   2. Political questions and judicial power—United States.   3. Justice, Administration of—United States.   I. Slotnick, Elliot E.   II. American Judicature Society.   III. Judicature. IV. Title.

  KF8775.A7J8   2005
  347.73′1—dc22   2004028475

CONTENTS

Contributors

Shirley S. Abrahamson is chief justice of the Supreme Court of Wisconsin.

Arlin M. Adams is a retired judge of the U.S. Court of Appeals for the Third Circuit and a lecturer at the University of Pennsylvania School of Law.

Larry Aspin is professor and chair of the Department of Political Science at Bradley University.

James Austin is executive director of the JFA Institute.

Hugo Adam Bedau is professor emeritus, Department of Philosophy, Tufts University.

Susan M. Behuniak is a professor of political science and the 2004–2007 Francis J. Fallon, S. J. Endowed Professor at Le Moyne College, Syracuse, New York.

Larry C. Berkson served as director of educational programs for the American Judicature Society from 1976 to 1982. He is currently in private business in New Hampshire.

Greg Berman is director of the Center for Court Innovation.

Robert Boatright is an assistant professor of government and international relations at Clark University.

Terry Bowen was an associate professor of political science at the University of North Florida.

William J. Bowers is principal research scientist at the Criminal Justice Research Center, College of Criminal Justice, Northeastern University.

Michael L. Boyer is an assistant professor of law sciences at the University of Alaska, Southeast.

Kathleen A. Bratton is an assistant professor of political science at Louisiana State University.

William J. Brennan Jr. was an associate justice of the U.S. Supreme Court from 1956 to 1990.

Susan W. Brenner is NCR Distinguished Professor of Law and Technology at the University of Dayton School of Law.

J. Louis Campbell III is an associate professor of speech communication at Pennsylvania State University, Altoona.

Bradley C. Canon is a professor of political science at the University of Kentucky.

Robert A. Carp is a professor of political science at the University of Houston.

John Clark is deputy director of the Pretrial Services Resource Center in Washington, D.C.

Avern Cohn is a senior judge on the U.S. District Court for the Eastern District of Michigan.

Beverly Blair Cook is emeritus professor of political science at the University of Wisconsin–Milwaukee.

John W. Cooley is adjunct professor at Northwestern University School of Law. He is a former U.S. magistrate who has served as a settlement master, mediator, and arbitrator.

David Crump is a professor of law at the University of Houston.

Sue Davis is a professor of political science at the University of Delaware.

Rebecca E. Deen is an associate professor of political science at the University of Texas at Arlington.

Rhett DeHart is former special counsel at the Heritage Foundation.

Brannon P. Denning is an associate professor at Samford University's Cumberland School of Law.

Shari Seidman Diamond is Howard J. Trienens Professor of Law and a professor of psychology at Northwestern University and senior research fellow at the American Bar Foundation.

Michael Esler is a professor of politics and government at Ohio Wesleyan University.

Kevin M. Esterling is an assistant professor of political science at the University of California, Riverside.

Bruce Fein is a constitutional lawyer and international consultant in Washington, D.C., at Bruce Fein and Associates and the Lichfield Group.

John Feinblatt is criminal justice coordinator of New York and founding director of the Center for Court Innovation.

Jason S. Fleming is assistant county attorney for Christian County, Hopkinsville, Kentucky.

Barry Friedman is Jacob D. Fuchsberg Professor of Law at the New York University School of Law.

Stephen B. Goldberg is a professor of law at Northwestern University School of Law.

Sheldon Goldman is a professor of political science at the University of Massachusetts, Amherst.

John M. Greacen is a court consultant.

Eric D. Green is a professor of law at Boston University.

Kimberly Greenfield is co-owner of Trinity Health Care in Lexington, Kentucky.

Gordon M. Griller is vice president in the justice practice group with ACS, Inc.

Gerard Gryski is a professor of political science at Auburn University.

Diane S. Gutmann is an attorney in Madison, Wisconsin.

Susan Haire is an associate professor of political science at the University of Georgia.

Edward A. Hartnett is the Richard J. Hughes Professor for Constitutional and Public Law and Service at Seton Hall University School of Law.

Arthur D. Hellman is a professor of law at the University of Pittsburgh School of Law.

D. Alan Henry is executive director of the Pretrial Services Resource Center in Washington, D.C.

Robert M. Howard is an associate professor of political science at Georgia State University.

Ronald J. Hrebenar is professor and chair of the Department of Political Science, University of Utah, and interim director of the Hinckley Institute of Politics.

Mark S. Hurwitz is an assistant professor in the Department of Political Science at the University at Buffalo, SUNY.

Joseph Ignagni is an associate professor of political science at the University of Texas at Arlington.

Elissa Krauss is a research coordinator in the Office of Court Research in the New York State Unified Court System and a founding member of the National Jury Project.

Herbert M. Kritzer is a professor of political science and law at the University of Wisconsin–Madison

Drew Noble Lanier is an associate professor of political science at the University of Central Florida.

Stefanie A. Lindquist is an associate professor of political science and law at Vanderbilt University.

Edmund V. Ludwig is a judge on the U.S. District Court for the Eastern District of Pennsylvania.

William Lyons is a professor of political science at the University of Tennessee, Knoxville.

George Mace is an emeritus faculty member at Southern Illinois University, Carbondale, and is currently on the faculty of John A. Logan College in Carterville, Illinois.

Kenneth L. Manning is an associate professor of political science at the University of Massachusetts, Dartmouth.

Thomas R. Marshall is a professor of political science at the University of Texas at Arlington.

James Meernik is chair of the Department of Political Science at the University of North Texas.

Edwin Meese III served as U.S. attorney general from 1985 to 1988 and is now the Ronald Reagan Fellow at the Heritage Foundation.

Albert P. Melone is a professor of political science at Southern Illinois University, Carbondale.

Mark C. Miller is associate professor and chair of the Department of Government and director of the Law and Society Program at Clark University.

Roger J. Miner is a senior judge of the U.S. Court of Appeals for the Second Circuit.

Norval Morris was the Julius Kreeger Professor of Law and Criminology Emeritus at the University of Chicago.

Robert D. Myers is chief counsel of the Arizona Department of Corrections.

Laura Natelson is a former Ph.D. candidate in the School of Public Affairs at American University.

Burt Neuborne is the John Norton Pomeroy Professor of Law at New York University School of Law and director of the Brennan Center for Justice.

David M. O'Brien is the Leone Reaves and George W. Spicer Professor of Government at the University of Virginia.

Zoe M. Oxley is an associate professor of political science at Union College.

Kimberlianne Podlas is an assistant professor of media law in the Department of Broadcasting and Cinema at the University of North Carolina at Greensboro.

Nathan L. Posner was a partner in the Philadelphia law firm of Fox, Rothschild, O'Brien, and Frankel and served as chancellor of the Philadelphia Bar Association from 1975 to 1976.

D. Marie Provine is director of the School of Justice and Social Inquiry at Arizona State University.

Ronald S. Reinstein is a judge of the Arizona Superior Court in Maricopa County.

Wm. Bradford Reynolds was assistant attorney general for the Civil Rights Division, U.S. Department of Justice, from 1981 to 1988 and counselor to the attorney general of the United States from 1987 to 1988.

Jack E. Rossotti is a professor in the School of Public Affairs at American University.

Frank E. A. Sander is Bussey Professor at Harvard Law School.

John M. Scheb II is a professor of political science at the University of Tennessee, Knoxville.

Nancy Scherer is an assistant professor in the Department of Political Science at Ohio State University.

Sara Schiavoni is a doctoral candidate in political science at Ohio State University.

Jeffrey A. Segal is a professor of political science at State University of New York, Stony Brook.

Jennifer A. Segal is an assistant professor in the Department of Government at American University.

Jeffrey M. Shaman is St. Vincent de Paul Professor of Law at DePaul University.

Elliot E. Slotnick, editor of *Judicial Politics: Readings from Judicature,* is a professor of political science at Ohio State University and associate dean of the graduate school.

Christopher E. Smith is a professor of criminal justice at Michigan State University.

Donald R. Songer is a professor of political science at the University of South Carolina.

Peter Sperlich is professor emeritus of political science at the University of California, Berkeley.

Rorie L. Spill is an assistant professor of political science at Oregon State University.

John Paul Stevens is an associate justice of the Supreme Court of the United States.

Ronald Stidham is a professor of political science and criminal justice at Appalachian State University.

John Stookey is a member of the law firm Osborn Maledon and a former professor of political science at Arizona State University.

Raymond Tatalovich is a professor of political science at Loyola University Chicago.

Clifford Taylor is a Michigan Supreme Court justice.

Clive S. Thomas is a professor of political science at the University of Alaska, Southeast.

Michael Tonry is Marvin J. Sonosky Professor of Law and Public Policy at the University of Minnesota and a professor of law and public policy and director of the Institute of Criminology, University of Cambridge.

J. Clifford Wallace is a judge on the U.S. Court of Appeals for the Ninth Circuit.

Stephen L. Wasby is professor emeritus of political science, University at Albany, SUNY, and visiting scholar, University of Massachusetts, Dartmouth.

George Watson is a political science professor in the Walter Cronkite School of Journalism at Arizona State University.

Alissa Worden is a professor in the School of Criminal Justice at the University at Albany, SUNY.

David Yalof is an associate professor of political science at the University of Connecticut.

Gary Zuk was a professor of political science at Auburn University.

Preface

In the preface for the first edition of *Judicial Politics,* I wrote that editing this volume has been, from the outset, a labor of love. Instructors of courses on judicial politics have long recognized that a wealth of the most important, interesting, current, and accessible research in our domain has appeared in the pages of *Judicature,* the journal of the American Judicature Society (AJS). These sentiments are as true today, perhaps even more so, than when they were initially written.

The first edition of *Judicial Politics* was published by AJS in 1992, followed by a second edition in 1999. This project has been a bit unusual for a textbook venture from the start. For one, an edited anthology is seldom a collection of readings from a single source. Given the excellence of work found in *Judicature* this has been a virtue to the reader. Just as unusual has been the in-house production of a textbook by an organization not in the commercial publishing business.

The production of previous editions of this reader was a challenge well met by David Richert and his colleagues at AJS. Marketing and distributing were, perhaps, less easily accomplished. When discussions began about a revised third edition, it turned out to be fortuitous that we would need a new distributor for the volume. What we found was a good deal more.

This third edition is long overdue and represents what we hope is the beginning of a long-term partnership and collaboration between AJS and CQ Press. For me, it is the perfect culmination of established relationships with several individuals associated with CQ Press—including James Headley and former editor Jean Woy—a culmination that needed just the right alignment of the stars to allow this pursuit to come to pass. The book will benefit greatly from the resources CQ Press brings to it, such as a more extensive marketing effort and wider distribution to potential users across a range of courses, including those in Judicial Processes and Behavior, the American Legal System, Law and Society, and Introduction to the American Judiciary.

Users of the previous editions will note the trimmer size and new interior design, both of which have been accomplished while maintaining the same extensive content. A good deal more changed in this revision as well. More than a third of the articles are new to the collection. Wholesale changes have occurred in several sections, including in "Judges: Judicial Selection Systems and Their Consequences," in which every selection save for one is new (and even that one, "Judicial selection in the United States: a special report," has been updated). Much of the material in this section now focuses on judicial selection during the presidency of George W. Bush, viewed in the context of previous administrations.

In "The American Judiciary and the Politics of Representation," new readings incorporate interesting comparative temporal data on the diversity of the nation's appellate benches; they also present a targeted view of how one president, Bill Clinton, aggressively pursued diversity through judicial appointments. A new reading on problem-solving justice has been added to "States and State Courts," and a challenging assessment of the state of state courts is also offered. The volume's concluding section, "Judicial Policy Making and Judicial Independence in the United States," now includes a provocative collaborative essay from Bruce Fein and Burt Neuborne, strange bedfellows in that Fein served in the Reagan administration's Justice Department whereas Neuborne has a long association with the American Civil Liberties Union.

Acknowledgments

The most difficult task in putting together a volume such as this is the selection of the "right" articles given the constraints of limited space and the numerous topic areas that stake claims for coverage. I had an unusual amount of excellent guidance and advice when making what often were very difficult choices. In the initial stages of this revision Aaron Spielman, a graduate student at Ohio State, provided me with extensive memos and cogent arguments about why each of the pieces I was considering made (or didn't make) sense for inclusion. His assistance was much appreciated. David Richert of the American Judicature Society used a somewhat different set of critical eyeglasses to offer several gentle suggestions about the content and structure of this anthology that have, without question, resulted in a better book. For that, and David's editorial talents, his shepherding of this project from start to finish, and his long-term friendship, I owe him my gratitude. My thanks are also owed to Nichole Collier for her excellent work in typing large portions of the manuscript.

Finally, special thanks are owed to James Headley, Charisse Kiino, Colleen Ganey, and Lorna Notsch of CQ Press for their belief in and encouragement of this revision and for their efforts at making it better, including their administration of a very helpful survey instrument to more than two dozen judicial politics colleagues whose thoughts have informed the contents of the book before you. In no particular order, I would like to thank Tom Hansford, University of South Carolina; Albert Melone, Southern Illinois University, Carbondale; Philip A. Dynia, Loyola University New Orleans; Larry Baum, Ohio State University; Susan Gluck Mezey, Loyola University Chicago; Rorie L. Spill, Oregon State University; Steven Puro, Saint Louis University; Amy Steigerwalt, University of California, Berkeley; Stephen L. Wasby, University at Albany, SUNY; Steven Peterson, Pennsylvania State University, Harrisburg; Charles Anthony Smith, University of Miami; Drew Nobel Lanier, University of Central Florida; Roger E. Hartley, University of Arizona; Mark Hurwitz, University at Buffalo, SUNY; Justin Crowe, Princeton University; David Weiden, Fort Hays State University; Gerald N. Rosenberg, University of Chicago; Priscilla Zotti, U.S. Naval Academy; Sara C. Benesh, University of Wisconsin, Milwaukee; Paul Wahlbeck, George Washington University; Barbara Hayler, University of Illinois, Springfield; Diane E. Wall, Mississippi State University; Jeremy Buchman, Long Island University; Jan P. Vermeer, Nebraska Wesleyan University; Frederick S. Wood, Michigan State University; Beau Breslin, Skidmore College; and Mark Kemper, Bridgewater State College. While acknowledging all of this assistance is a pleasant task, I alone bear full responsibility for any remaining errors of inclusion or exclusion in this volume.

The ultimate test of this volume's success will be its utility in the classroom. As in the earlier editions, that still remains the measure by which it should be judged. Looking toward the future, I continue to urge colleagues and students to drop me a note about those selections that work well and those (hopefully few) that are less successful. Perhaps most important, I look forward to hearing from colleagues as we collectively monitor future editions of *Judicature* for articles we would like our students to read in the years to come. Please feel free to e-mail me at Slotnick.1@osu.edu if and when you have such suggestions to make. The responsibility is ours to continue the kind of scholarly work that, under David Richert's editorial direction, has contributed to *Judicature*'s excellence.

As before, I must underscore that this book has been prepared for our students, and it is my hope that these readings will give them a great deal to think about regarding the system of justice in the United States. It is to our students—past, present, and future—and their efforts to both understand and to improve that system, that this book is dedicated.

The American Judicature Society

The American Judicature Society was founded in 1913 as an independent, non-partisan organization of judges, lawyers, and members of the lay public who seek "to improve the justice system through efforts to support an independent judiciary, increase public understanding and appreciation of the justice system, and build knowledge through research on judicial issues."

Judicature, the society's refereed bimonthly journal, has been published continuously since 1917. It serves as a forum for fact and opinion relating to all aspects of the administration of justice and its improvement.

The American Constitutional System and the Role of the Supreme Court in the American Polity

Every society has established some mechanism for adjudicating disputes and performing judicial functions. In the United States, the judiciary is a uniquely powerful one from a policymaking perspective. Much of the unusual authority of U.S. courts stems from their exercise of the power of judicial review, the ability to invalidate the acts and actions of other governmental entities because of their failure to meet the guidelines set by the U.S. Constitution, the fundamental charter of American government. Judicial review may give the courts the final say in legitimating policy choices made elsewhere; however, it is a power that has always been exercised amid great controversy. Considerable historical scholarship exists that debates the fundamental question of whether judicial review was actually intended by the framers of the Constitution, since this potentially awesome power is not explicitly mentioned within the written document itself.

This first section of readings examines several facets of the dilemma of judicial review and judicial authority within the fabric of American democracy. In "The place of judicial review in the American tradition: the emergence of an eclectic power," Elliot Slotnick takes the reviewing power as a given and examines why the American political context was a uniquely hospitable one for such an extraordinary judicial prerogative to take hold.

In addition to their debating the underlying concepts of the historical legitimacy of judicial review and its place in the American scheme of things, it has been commonplace for analysts to ponder the question of judicial review's consistency with democracy. After all, critics contend, isn't there something fundamentally undemocratic in a group of nine justices—appointed for life and held largely unaccountable—invalidating, sometimes by a 5–4 vote, the will of popular majorities enacted into law by representative legislative bodies? Others are quick to respond that American democracy means more than simply majority rule and that it is equally concerned about questions of minority rights. For such analysts, judicial review is a bulwark in the protection of minority rights. In "Judicial review: the usurpation and democracy questions," puzzles such as these are explored by Albert Melone and George Mace. The authors recognize that one cannot turn back the clock and that judicial review is a fact of American life. Further, they argue, concern over whether judicial review is democratic or undemocratic begs an equally important question, the compatibility of judicial review with a "good" democracy, one that "operates to guard against threats to liberty and human happiness."

While scholarly questions about the legitimacy of judicial review and its relationship to democracy are interesting and important, their exploration does not solve the problem faced by judges who must come to grips with their reviewing authority and make decisions about the scope of its exercise. This section offers four selections that frame the two alternative solutions posed for this dilemma. In "The judiciary is too powerful," Justice Clifford Taylor argues that today's judiciary is muscling out the legislature, imposing judge-made law in place of the policies established by the people's legislative representatives. Government by the judiciary has foiled the intent of the Constitution's framers. Judge J. Clifford Wallace's article, "The case for judicial restraint," complements Taylor's presentation by making an argument for judges' reliance on interpretivism, "the principle that judges, in resolving constitutional questions, should rely on the express provisions of the Constitution or upon those norms that are clearly implicit in its text."

Countering these views, Judge Avern Cohn notes in "Judicial review is exercised properly" that the post–Civil War amendments created a new Constitution with new interpretive responsibilities for judges. "Hard cases," often those handled by appellate courts such as the U.S. Supreme Court, yield no single, clear answer and often involve elements of political choice. Law professor Jeffrey Shaman adds in "The Supreme Court's proper and historic function" that interpretivism, as espoused by Judge Wallace, is both impossible and unwise. Indeed, "the court's role, when all is said and done, is to create meaning for a Constitution that otherwise would be a hollow document."

In reading the articles in this section, one is struck by the frequent use of terms such as strict construction, interpretivism, non-interpretivism, judicial restraint, judicial activism, and others in the parlance of authors making a case for the "appropriate" exercise of judicial power. Such terms often are ill defined or, even worse, not defined at all. When reading pieces on the issue of the exercise and scope of judicial power, one must examine the arguments with a critical and cautious eye.

The place of judicial review in the American tradition: the emergence of an eclectic power

Elliot E. Slotnick

Whether judicial review was "intended" by the framers or not, it developed as a pragmatic response to the American experience, consistent with main currents of our political history.

Traditionally, historical analyses of the American doctrine of judicial review have gone through a series of elaborate manipulations of memoirs and documents in an effort to decide whether judicial review was "intended" by the framers of the Constitution. The question of whether such "intentions" existed could be viewed as a peripheral one having little contemporary importance, except for the reality that emerges whenever there is any discussion of the role of the Supreme Court. As one scholar has noted:

> A doubt that the whole package of present judicial power was legitimately conferred . . . lurks in the background of American politics and emerges to help convert grievance into passion when any sector of the population is greatly disappointed with the behavior of the Supreme Court in Constitutional cases.[1]

The question of the validity of judicial review has not been solely academically inspired, but was a great concern of many of the Constitution's framers and their contemporaries. The precedent for judicial review was established in the landmark case of *Marbury v. Madison* in an opinion by Chief Justice John Marshall. Yet the precedent was not, in reality, actively supported by all or even the great majority of his contemporaries. Thomas Jefferson raised what has since become a common argument against the judiciary's "proud preeminence."

> . . . Yet this case of Marbury and Madison is continually cited by bench and bar as if it were settled law without any animadversion on its being merely an *obiter* dissertation of the Chief Justice.[2]

Despite the arguments of Jefferson and others, judicial review was here to stay. The inability of its critics to eliminate judicial review has traditionally been traced to two major factors: the contemporary political situation, and Marshall's judicial craftsmanship. While establishing a precedent for judicial review in *Marbury*

v. Madison, Marshall did, in fact, decide the case as the Jeffersonians wanted. What better means of obtaining acquiescence in the *entire* decision? While the Jeffersonians won the case, the price they paid was substantially greater than they had anticipated.

> . . . This decision bears many of the earmarks of a deliberate partisan coup. The court was bent on reading the President a lecture on his legal and moral duty to recent Federalist appointees to judicial office, whose commissions the last Administration had not had time to deliver, but at the same time hesitated to (initiate opposition) by actually asserting jurisdiction of the matter. It therefore took the engaging position of declining to exercise power which the Constitution withheld from it by making the occasion an opportunity to assert a far more transcendent power.[3]

The role of Marshall in this coup has rarely been underestimated.

> The problem was given no answer by the Constitution. A hole was left where the Court might drive in the peg of judicial supremacy if it could. And this is what John Marshall did. He drove it in, so firmly that no one yet has been able to pull it out.[4]

While the question of whether judicial review was "provided" for by the framers is an interesting one, our verdict shall not be added to the countless others already in. Rather, for the most part, the existence of judicial review will be accepted as a "given." Beginning with the existence of judicial review, we shall attempt to relate what was a peculiarly American phenomenon to a number of undercurrents in American political thought.

Several facets of the American political experience are, at least, consistent with the Court's review power. Among these factors we shall examine the following: precedents relating to judicial review, colonial notions about the "common law," colonial notions about "natural law," limited government and constitutionalism, American pragmatism and the fear of legislative omnipotence, and the prevalence of "magical" conceptions of the judicial function and the role of justices.

Finally, we shall attempt to relate the ambivalence of many of these factors to the emergence of an American tradition of "judicial self-restraint." In essence, we shall attempt to view judicial review as a "composite" power and take an eclectic approach. Judicial review may be seen as consistent with a number of modes of constitutional thought which otherwise have not been seen as consistent with each other. Although Hamilton and Jefferson stood on opposite sides of the judicial review question, there was no inherent reason why both Hamiltonians and Jeffersonians could not support the power. The foundations of judicial review were simply that broad.

> The primary principles formulated as a basis for the American doctrine were: first, that a written Constitution is fundamental and paramount and therefore superior to common and statutory law; second, that the powers of the legislature are limited, a written constitution being in the nature of a commission to the legislature by which its powers are delegated and its limitations defined; third, that judges are the special guardians of the provisions of written constitutions which are in the nature of mandatory instructions to the judges, who must uphold these provisions and refuse to enforce any legislative enactment in conflict therewith. To understand the nature of these principles it is necessary to examine the notion of a higher law . . . During the seventeenth and eighteenth centuries this idea of a higher law became the basis in England and France for laws which were held to be fundamental and unalterable and for a theory of the supremacy of courts.[5]

It is to a consideration of these and other themes and their relationship to judicial review that the bulk of this article will be addressed. First, we shall consider some of the precedents pointed to by the "headcounters" of the Constitutional Convention as evidence of the "intention " of the framers.

Not a new doctrine

The enunciations of the doctrine of judicial review by Marshall in *Marbury v. Madison* was not the first time that America was confronted with its existence. The review power had previously been recognized numerous times by colonial and state practices, debates held in the Constitutional and state conventions, and by specific clauses in state constitutions. Clearly, the notion of judicial review was not foreign to the American ear. Jefferson, it may be asserted, opposed judicial review, but he clearly recognized its existence in states other than his native Virginia.

> In Virginia, where a great proportion of the legislature considers the constitution but as other acts of legislation, laws have been frequently passed which controlled its effects. I have not heard that in the other states they have ever infringed their Constitutions, and I suppose they have not done it, as the judges would consider any law void which was contrary to the Constitution.[6]

Jefferson is attesting to the existence of conceptions of judicial review in states other than his own. Yet, for an earlier period, there even exists evidence of judicial review in Jefferson's Virginia.

> In Virginia . . . the Supreme Court of the colony, having been put the question, early in 1766, whether officers of the law would incur a penalty if they did not use stamped paper in conformance with the prescription of the Stamp Act, answered that the act did not bind the inhabitants of Virginia, "inasmuch as they conceived" it "to be unconstitutional." [7]

Similar words were used in many of the state courts and courts of the colonies. On the very eve of the Declaration of Independence, Judge Cushing, later one of the original members of the Supreme Court of the United States, charged a Massachusetts jury to ignore certain acts of Parliament as "void" and "inoperative." [8] Further, it is interesting to note that many of the opponents of the federal Constitution, and particularly its provisions relating to the judiciary, were critics simply because they felt that the power of judicial review, exercised so well by the state courts, would be weakened by the new system. Patrick Henry's remarks stand out.

> The honorable gentleman did our judiciary honor in saying that they had the firmness to counteract the legislature in some cases. Yes, sir, our judges opposed the acts of the legislature. We have this landmark to guide us. They had fortitude to declare that they were the judiciary, and would oppose unconstitutional acts. Are you sure that your federal judiciary will act thus?[9]

It is obvious that the framers knew of precedents for courts exercising an authority analogous to judicial review. There even exists a great deal of evidence to support the view that many people felt that judicial review had, in fact, been *included* in the federal Constitution. The Convention spent much time on a proposal for a Council of Revision that would review constitutionality. When discussing the court's role in such a council, there was a general fear of giving the courts a *double* power.

> It is clear, then, that one of the reasons why the Council of Revision proposal was rejected was that some of the members assumed that the courts would exercise the power of judicial review, and they doubted the wisdom of conferring any further power of a similar character upon the judiciary.[10]

And, discussing the Council of Revision, Elbridge Gerry expressed his doubts.

> . . . Whether the Judiciary ought to form a part of it, as they will have a sufficient check against encroachments . . . by their exposition of the laws which involved a power of deciding on their constitutionality.[11]

Other pronouncements by various framers can also serve as further evidence for the fact that judicial review, in their eyes, was not unprecedented. Rufus King simply stated in the Convention that, ". . . Judges will have the expounding of those Laws when they come before them, and they will, no doubt, stop the operation of such as shall appear repugnant to the Constitution." [12] Similar remarks were made at state ratifying conventions. When George Nicholas was asked in the Virginia convention who would determine the extent of legislative powers, he replied directly, ". . . the same power which, in all well-regulated communities determines the extent of legislative powers. If they exceed these powers, the judiciary will declare it void." [13]

Similarly, in the Massachusetts convention, Samuel Adams said that, "any law . . . beyond the power granted by the proposed constitution . . . (will be) adjudged by the courts of law to be void." Oliver Ellsworth told the Connecticut convention that if the general legislature should at any time overlap their limits, the judicial department is a constitutional check; "a law which the constitution does not authorize is 'void,' and the judges 'will declare it to be void.' " Similar statements were made by Wilson in Pennsylvania and by John Marshall in Virginia.[14]

A few remarks made by Wilson can serve to illustrate the extent to which judicial review, in some minds, was regarded as an integral part of the judicial function.

When the suggestion arose in the Pennsylvania ratification convention that judges might be impeached if they were to "decide against the law," Wilson retorted, "The judges are to be impeached because they decide an act null and void, that was made in defiance of the Constitution! What House of Representatives would dare to impeach, or Senate to commit, judges for performance of their duty?" [15]

Supporters of judicial review often relied on more than simply their word as evidence of its existence. Specifically, two clauses in the Constitution, the "arising under" clause and the "supremacy clause," were cited as "proof" of the framers' intentions. Admittedly, these clauses do not, in and of themselves, furnish undeniable proof of the intended existence of judicial review. But our purpose in this survey of precedents is not to "prove" the "intention" of the framers but, rather, to show that, at worst, the power was not unheard of and inconceivable. To a certain extent, we can readily endorse Corwin's view of *Marbury v. Madison* as a logical culmination of events preceding it in the American experience.

> Upon the latent talent the problem of the time acted as incentive and stimulant, eliciting from it suggestion after suggestion which it needed but the ripe occasion to erect into institutions composing a harmonious whole.[16]

Common law and Coke

In discussing the relationship between judicial review and the American experience we may take as a starting point the American conception of the English common law and our particular reverence of the juridical philosophy of Sir Edward Coke. In part, Coke's doctrine, pronounced in the *Dr. Bonham's Case,* was seen as a precedent of judicial review; in part, it served as inspiration for it. In Coke's view, adjudication was a very special function, with the common law courts standing above all else, including the Crown, in matters of law. According to Haines, Coke sought "to erect the judges into a tribunal of arbitration between the king and the nation." [17] At bottom, Coke attempted to revive what he conceived were the limits imposed upon all authority by the Magna Carta. In his view, sovereignty had little meaning in England because "Magna Carta is such a fellow that he will have no sovereign." As a result, parliamentary acts that were "contrary to common right and reason" were to be declared "void." [18] The common law, however, and "common right and reason" were the peculiar province of judges.[19]

Coke's conception of judicial function as pronounced in *Dr. Bonham's Case* would be echoed in almost identical form in many arguments raised by American colonial judges. As early as 1688, during the short reign of the Stuart despotism, there is evidence that "the men of Massachusetts ... did much quote Lord Coke." [20] In 1761, allegedly on Coke's authority, James Otis at Boston—in the Writs of Assistance case—plunged at once into the most fundamental issues. His argument was, that whether such writs were warranted by Act of Parliament or not, was a matter of indifference, since such Act of Parliament would be "against the Constitution" and "against natural equity" and therefore "void." [21]

Others followed Coke even more closely.

> Governor Hutchinson, referring to the opposition to the Stamp Act, wrote, "The prevailing reason at this time is that the Act of Parliament is against Magna Carta, and the natural rights of Englishmen, and therefore according to Lord Coke, null and void." As late, indeed, as 1766, Judge Cushing, who was destined to become 20 years later a member of the first bench of the United States Supreme Court, charged a Massachusetts jury to ignore certain acts of Parliament as void and inoperative, and was felicitated by John Adams for his courage in doing so.[22]

Coke's doctrine had quite a different status in England than it did in the colonies, and this is the source of an interesting paradox related to the American readiness to accept judicial review. "The conception of a fundamental law as a rule to guide common law courts whose duty it is to keep both King and Parliament within bounds seems to have existed, so far as England is concerned, chiefly in the mind of Coke and a few of his very willing followers." [23]

Yet acceptance of Coke in America could be seen as a pragmatic coup; a means of accepting the common law and at the same time rejecting Great Britain. As Carr notes,

> Coke's thesis was never really accepted in England, ... but the *Dr. Bonham Case* was known in the American colonies ... Accordingly, when in the second half of the 18th century the great controversy between the colonies and England began, and became centered in opposition in Parliament, Americans could not resist the temptation to use Coke's reasoning in the *Dr. Bonham's Case*. ... Thus, on the eve of the writing of the American constitution, and long after England had repudiated the idea of a legislature's dependence upon

a higher law enforced by the Courts, the idea was known and accepted in this country, in part at least, for a very practical reason.[24]

What better method could the colonies employ than invoking a doctrine which had had its birth in the mother country? No argument was likely to be as persuasive for the colonies as the accusation that England no longer subscribed to limitations she, herself, had formulated. Unquestionably, "At the moment when Americans were beginning to lay about them for weapons with which to resist the pretensions of Parliament," Coke's doctrine "met with a degree of success— enough at least to make it a permanent memory with the men of the time." [25] It would be difficult for a country professedly founded in idealism not to adopt this doctrine as its own.

A reductionist view

The relationship between Coke's doctrine and American development has even been extended into a reductionist explanation of the American revolution itself. Such a view goes far beyond merely using Coke to justify opposition to Britain. According to Boudin, the theory is "nothing less than the assertion that the American Revolution was but a lawyers' revolution, designed to revive and perpetuate in America Lord Coke's doctrine of Judicial Power which seems to have fallen upon evil days in England just about that time." The theory "first took definite form in the special committee appointed by the New York State Bar Association." As stated in the Committee Report, "In short, the American Revolution was a lawyer's revolution to enforce Lord Coke's theory of the invalidity of Acts of Parliament in derogation of common right and the rights of Englishmen." [26]

We need not accept such an obviously incomplete and simplistic explanation of the Revolution to assert simply that the views held of Coke's jurisprudence in America were consistent with the development of the power of judicial review in this country. When Perry Miller speaks of the "ambivalence" in the American experience towards the common law, to a certain extent this ambivalence may be viewed simply as an acceptance of Coke (who was rejected in Britain) and a xenophobia towards and rejection of things that were British. This corresponds to the paradox already noted.

> Indeed, it is fascinating to consider how, during these and subsequent decades, the ambivalence persisted between hostility to the intricacy of the Common Law

and at the same time reluctance to abandon it as constituting the bulwark of rights and liberties.[27]

Miller's "ambivalence" seems less of a paradox, and is more understandable when we trace back our acceptance of the "bulwark of rights and liberties" to Coke, and our rejection of the remaining intricacies of the common law to our xenophobia towards basically British accoutrements.

Natural law thinking

A second factor which may be seen as totally consistent with the American doctrine of judicial review and as related to our conception of the common law is the prevalence of natural law thinking in America at the time of the country's founding. Natural law reasoning, in fact, emerges as the basic argument for why judicial review was consistent with Jeffersonian thought and could be supported by his followers even while Jefferson himself opposed the doctrine. The natural law thinking of the era was not, in any sense, a contemporary invention, but reverted back to an earlier mode of thought. "The enthusiasm which manifested itself in the fight for human rights on both sides of the Atlantic gave new life and vigor to the Roman and medieval conception of a law of nature." [28] According to this regeneration of natural law thought, there were certain things which even government could not do, and the judiciary would serve as an overseer to guard against unwarranted governmental usurpation. Thus, according to Corwin, the idea of a "universally valid code of justice which is knowable to all men in the form given it in seventeenth century England by Locke and others, of a code of individual rights prior to government and available against it, this idea is basic to all . . . conceptions of judicial review." [29]

There is much evidence that serves to link natural law thinking with judicial review, including even the somewhat questionable assertion that the very reasoning used by Marshall in *Marbury v. Madison* stemmed from ideas about natural law.

> Like Marshall in *Marbury v. Madison,* (Gouverneur) Morris believed that judicial authority to void such legislation was "derived from higher authority than this Constitution. They derive it from the Constitution of man, from the nature of things, from the necessary progress of human affairs." [30]

Perhaps Dewey does stretch a point unnecessarily when he cites Morris to make an assertion about Mar-

shall. Nevertheless, we are satisfied by the notion that judicial review (or some form of review) was, indeed, linked by some with natural law thinking. Further, this linkage was by no means limited to Morris.

> The influence of the notion of an overruling law of nature is clearly apparent at an early period in the American colonies . . . George Mason in a Virginia case argued: "The laws of nature are the laws of God, whose authority can be superseded by no power on earth . . . All human constitutions which contradict his laws we are in conscience bound to disobey." Basing its judgement on a similar doctrine, a Connecticut court said: "The fundamental law which God and nature have given to the people cannot be infringed . . ." The analytical theory which deems positive law an independent of moral consideration and as based on a sovereign will, was not accepted at the time; in fact the colonies were so impressed with the idea of an overruling law of nature that the laws of God and so-called natural laws were regarded "As the true law, and all temporal legislation was to be considered binding only insofar as it was an expression of this natural law." [31]

Natural law doctrine did not simply appeal to the Americans on an intellectual level, but was also used from a pragmatic standpoint, sometimes serving to bring an end to troublesome debates. As Perry Miller notes, "it was in order that the first efforts to manufacture a doctrine of American law after the Revolution should devote long sections to the law of nature, particularly because in 1790 . . . there was so little accurate information about what constituted law in America." [32] It is unnecessary to assert that all justices or adherents of judicial review justified it on the basis of natural law, yet such an argument could and did certainly aid in adding a mystical aura to the function which removed it, to a certain degree, from reproach.

In reality, strict natural law doctrine was in no sense the major thrust of specific judicial review arguments, but natural law did serve to bolster judicial review in the abstract. Essentially, natural law arguments were used most often in the formative stages of the development and ascendance of judicial review, and served to make the judicial power a bit more palatable to a wider spectrum of citizens. As Haines notes, "The idea of rejecting laws contrary to natural justice or as infractions of the law of nature though frequently repeated by justices was, in the beginning of judicial review, seldom regarded as sufficient grounds to declare legislative acts void." [33] Nevertheless, natural law did place a cloak of idealism over the judicial function, and could serve as ample incentive to mobilize one line of support for judicial review.

Other justifications

Closely linked to natural law thought supporting judicial review were various strands of thought centering upon constitutionalism and limited government as the justification for the doctrine.

> It may be remarked here that the doctrine of declaring legislative Acts void as being contrary to the Constitution was probably helped into existence by a theory . . . that Courts might disregard such acts if they were contrary to the fundamental maxims of morality, or . . . the laws of nature.[34]

Arguments for judicial review based on constitutionalism and limited government would appeal to a somewhat different segment of the population than did assertions based solely on the "mystical" natural law. The Constitution loomed as something more concrete than the heavens and the soul of man.

> One of the most important principles which led to the acceptance of the American doctrine was the theory that a Constitution is a fundamental or paramount enactment. At the same time that the idea of a superior law of nature was prevalent the conception that a written constitution is a fundamental act was acquiring new meaning . . . in America.[35]

At the same time, however, judicial review's natural law constituency remained enticed by the apparent congruence between natural law, limited government, and constitutionalism.

> Many historians have felt that in favoring judicial review the men of the Convention were influenced by a strong belief in certain fundamental principles . . . Accordingly they established a written constitution as the fundamental law and authorized judges to act as guardians of this Constitution by enforcing it against the improper laws which the legislature might enact.[36]

Written constitutions were alleged to be reflections of the natural law and, consequently, were viewed as fundamental, fixed, immutable, and permanent. Linking natural law with constitutionalism we are faced with, in Cahn's terms, "A change from higher-than-positive law to higher, positive law."

This, of course, is the very change that Marshall consummated in *Marbury v. Madison;* by legitimizing the appeal to the Courts he presumedly bastardized any possible "appeal to heaven" . . . "Appeal to heaven" having served its historic purpose, had nothing to offer toward meeting the need of a new era, i.e., the day to day enforcement of a written constitution.[37]

Once constitutions replace natural law, upholding the documents becomes as serious a task as meeting the earlier moral code.

> It is easy to smile at the vagaries of ancient political practice, and to reflect with pleasure on modern superiority—but perhaps not wholly justified. For we are about to see a strange phenomenon: the typical political theorist of seventeenth century England proceeds in a sensible fashion to secularize and naturalize the process of drafting a fundamental law; he transmutes the obsolete supernatural code into a product of human ingenuity and intellect; yet—the moment the draft has been formulated—incontinently he assumes the prostrate attitude of the ancients, invests the document with the same reverential awe he declares for its source, and declares . . . that every part and the whole of it shall remain immutable forever and in perpetuity![38]

The general notion of written constitutions as a reflection of basic fundamental law can be traced to several threads in the American fabric. Haines attributes such a notion primarily to the French, and to the English conception of Magna Carta. Even in the very early American experience we have evidence of the theme repeatedly; it appears in Puritan writings where, perhaps, notions of the primacy or importance of secular law would be expected to be muted. Winthrop writes, however,

> The deputies having conceived great danger to our State, we regard that our magistrates, for want of positive laws, in many cases, might proceed according to their discretions, it was agreed that some men should be appointed to frame a body of grounds of laws, in resemblance to a Magna Carta, which, being allowed by some of the ministers, and the general Court, should be received for fundamental laws.[39]

Thus, charters were written in the early Pilgrim settlements and these served as useful precedents for the American colonies. The courts were to play a significant role in elucidating the charters.

These charters were in the strict sense written law: As their restraints upon the colonial legislatures were enforced by the English Courts of last resort, so might they be enforced through the colonial courts, by disregarding as null what went counter to them.[40]

These charters were also significant in that they were self-imposed by "the people." What greater reason could exist for treating them as "fundamental?"

> . . . there was no longer an external sovereign. Our conception now was that "the people" took his place . . . So far as existing institutions were left untouched they were construed by translating the name and style of the English sovereign into that of our new rules—ourselves, the People. After this the charters, and still more obviously the new constitutions, were not so many orders from without, backed by an organized outside government, which simply performed an ordinary function enforcing them; they were precepts from the people themselves who were to be governed, addressed . . . especially to those who were charged with the duty of conducting the government.[41]

Thus, judicial review emerges as being consistent with theories of constitutionalism aimed at establishing the rule of law over the rule of men. "The basic antithesis . . . remains substantially what it was in the period between Coke and Locke, that is, the antithesis between . . . legal precept and executive prerogative, between wise rules and exercise of wide discretion . . ."[42]

The link between judicial review and constitutionalism only maintains clarity and consistency if, somehow, judges are a different breed than executives and legislators, and adjudication does not imply wide discretion and the "rule of men," but, rather, reinforces a rule of law. We will return to this point later but, for the moment, can conclude with Andrew McLaughlin that judicial review was consistent with and was an extension of American views on constitutionalism and limited government.

> The doctrine of what is now called "judicial review" is the last word, logically and historically speaking, in the attempt of a free people to establish and maintain a non-autocratic government. It is the culmination of the essentials of Revolutionary thinking and, indeed, of the thinking of those who a hundred years or more before the Revolution called for a government of laws and not men.[43]

John Marshall incorporated these views of constitutionalism in *Marbury v. Madison*. Between the lines one can read of "the Constitution" as "fundamental" law, but there remains a sense of linkage with natural law as well. Marshall, like McLaughlin, skirts the issue of why judges alone can "know" the Constitution and, as will be developed, this becomes a crucial point in the American genesis of judicial review.

> Between the alternatives there is no middle ground. The constitution is either a superior paramount law, unchangeable by ordinary means, or it is on a level with ordinary legislative acts, and, like other acts, is alterable when the legislature shall please to alter it. If the former part of the alternative be true, then a legislative act, contrary to the Constitution, is not law; if the latter part be true then written constitutions are absurd attempts on the part of the people to limit a power, in its own nature, illimitable. Certainly, all those who have framed written constitutions contemplate them as forming the fundamental and paramount law of the nation, and consequently, the theory of every such government must be, that an act of the legislature, repugnant to the Constitution is void.[44]

The fear of legislative omnipotence has been a major part of the American political tradition, and this is another crucial area where judicial review served as a doctrine which could be supported by both Federalists and Jeffersonians. While the followers of Hamilton and Jefferson were rarely found on the same side of basic constitutional questions, it is crucial to an understanding of the place of judicial review in the American tradition to see how politically antagonistic groups could support the same doctrine for essentially diametrically opposed reasons. Thus, it can be demonstrated that the Hamiltonian Federalists feared that the popularly elected legislatures might not respect the prerogatives of property rights; the Jeffersonian conception, on the other hand, stressed the threat of legislatures to other minorities with the assertion that a multitude of despots were as bad as one. Approaching the problem of legislative omnipotence from different perspectives, it is instructive that judicial review was a doctrine that could serve several masters. According to Haines, "The right of the judiciary to declare law invalid, and thus to check the rapacity of legislative assemblies, was in the opinion of many to be the chief cornerstone of a governmental structure planned with particular reference to preserving property rights inviolate and to assuring special sanction for individual liberties." [45] In its utility for the preservation of property rights, judicial review became a primary Federalist doctrine; similarly, the stress on individual liberties made it acceptable to the Jeffersonians.

State legislative power

Federalist support for the doctrine of judicial review and fear of the legislature grew out of two closely related phenomena observable under the Articles of Confederation: the vast scope of state legislative power, and the use of that power against the interests of private property rights. In their framework for a new federal government, the Federalists' view of state legislatures would be instrumental in the call for both a separation and a division of powers emphasizing a new balance. Clearly, their view of the state legislatures was not a benevolent one. As Corwin notes of the "constitutional reaction" culminating in the formation of a new government, "The reaction embraced two phases, that of nationalism against State sovereignty, that of private rights against uncontrolled legislative power; but the point of attack in both instances was the State legislature." [46]

Suspicion of the post–1776 legislatures arose, in large part, as a result of their nearly unlimited powers. With virtually unchecked power in their possession, abuses followed and, as Madison noted, "Experience in all the States had evinced a powerful tendency in the Legislature to absorb all power into its real vortex. This was the real source of danger to the American Constitution, and suggested the necessity of giving every defensive authority to the other departments that was consistent with republican principles." [47] Hamilton raises a similar argument in *Federalist* No. 78 in presenting his rationale for the judicial power.

> The complete independence of the courts of justice is peculiarly essential in a limited constitution. By a limited constitution I understand one which contains certain specified exceptions to the legislative authority; ... Limitations of this kind can be preserved in practice no other way than through the medium of courts of justice, whose duty it must be to declare all acts contrary to the manifest tenor of the Constitution void. Without this, all the reservations of particular rights or privileges would amount to nothing. [48]

The insistence upon further checks on Congress became the rallying cry of the Constitutional Convention for many Federalists. Yet by and large the checks they sought were not to protect the populace but, rather, to seek protection *from* the popularly elected legislatures. Much of this argument is articulated in the work of Charles Beard.

> This very system of checks and balances, which is undeniably the essential element of the Constitution, is built upon the doctrine that the popular branch of the government cannot be allowed full sway, and least of all in the enactment of laws touching the rights of property. [49]

In seeking to avert "legislative tyranny" the Federalists sought a judiciary which would be the bastion of property, in Gouverneur Morris' words, "aristocracy, men who from pride will support consistency and permanency ... Such an aristocratic body will keep down the turbulence of democracy." [50] Thus, as Paul notes, "The right wing Federalists ... led by Hamilton and later by Marshall, had early regarded the judiciary as potentially the key bulwark of conservative defense." [51] Yet just as judicial review could serve the propertied Federalist interests, the doctrine could also be found in the arguments of anti-Federalists. Fear of legislatures was clearly a two-edged sword.

> One who would understand the significance of judicial review for the Founders does well to start from the fact that in 1787 there was widespread fear of oppression by a remote federal government centered largely in dread of "legislative despotism." [52]

Jeffersonian support

Support for judicial review by Jeffersonians can trace its roots to the existence of natural law doctrine and its espousal by the Puritans as seen in the work of Winthrop. Winthrop notes the deficiencies of positive law as pronounced by *legislatures*.

> Those who make laws ... are also men subjecte to Temptations, and may also miscarrye through Ignorance, headlessnesse, or sinister respects: And it is not hard, to prove, that the Lawe makers, in all States, have Committed more and more pernitious errors than the Judges. [53]

Winthrop's characterization of the unique features of the judiciary are central to any understanding of judicial review in the American political tradition, and while Jefferson himself did not support judicial review, he often echoed the bulk of Winthrop's argument.

All of the powers of government, legislative, executive and judiciary, result to the legislative body. The concentrating of these in the same hands is precisely the definition of despotic government. It will be no alleviation that these powers will be exercised by a plurality of hands ... 173 despots would surely be as oppressive as one ... An elective despotism was not the government we fought for.[54]

To the extent that Jeffersonians could subscribe to Winthrop's conception of the nature of judicial power, judicial review could serve as a means to avert despotic government. Clearly Jefferson himself was not "mystified" by the judicial robes, yet "judicial magic" did serve to ingratiate judicial review to many Jeffersonians. Thus, the doctrine created strange bedfellows, serving as a rallying cry for both Federalists and Jeffersonians; the former supporting the doctrine as a protection from the excesses of mass democracy, and the latter supporting it as the very means by which to maintain such a mass democracy.

Pragmatic support

That judicial review could serve so many masters attests to the underlying pragmatic nature of support for the doctrine. Such "pragmatism" may, in fact, be seen as a manifestation of the seemingly "theoretical" American approach to politics, particularly as demonstrated during the formative years of our constitutional development. The basic pragmatism inherent in the doctrine of judicial review follows directly from the consequences of possible judge-made errors as compared to the much more severe societal consequences of legislative errors. Thus, John Winthrop noted,

> If a Judge should sometymes erre in his Sentence; through misprision, or Temptation; the error or fault is his owne: and the injurye or damage extends not farr: but an error in the Lawe resteth upon the Ordinance it selfe, and the hurt of it may reach far, even to posteritye, there is more unrighteousness, and dishonor, in one unjust Lawe than in many unjust Sentences.[55]

Further, it was legislative despotism the founders feared, and not necessarily the despotism of courts. The work of Charles Beard becomes instructive in viewing judicial review as a pragmatic, nondoctrinaire response to the need the founders saw for a firmly founded, economically based government. In Beard's formulation, judicial review was just one of several bulwarks against populism. In a similar vein, Corwin notes that "judicial review was expedient, since the judiciary had control of neither the purse nor the sword; it was the substitute offered by political wisdom for the destructive right of revolution."[56] Some authoritative organ was clearly needed to interpret the meaning of the vague formulations of the Constitution and, in large measure, judicial review can be seen as a "peculiarly" pragmatic, non-ideological American response to a glaring need.

> What is the basis of this power ... of ... no limit save self-restraint? Why did the country let the court—let it?—insist that it should have this power? What is the magic? There is no magic. It is the most commonplace of situations. When a great people finds that there are certain things they want done, and no one specifically appointed to do the work, a job to be done and no one named to do it, they look around. When an applicant appears, shovel on his shoulder, they take him. He proves quiet, industrious, and discreet. What if he does go on a drunk now and then? He sobers off and goes to work again. Before you know it, John is a fixture. He likes his job. He is a good worker. He's a member of the family. No one else seems to know how to do the work so well.[57]

Curtis aptly portrays the importance of tradition and the basic pragmatism inherent in delineating a constitutional system out of a largely unspecified constitutional framework. Yet pragmatism cannot be the whole answer, for pragmatic men could have looked elsewhere to delegate a reviewing authority in governmental affairs. Such was, in fact, the reasoning behind demands for a Council of Revision in the original constitutional convention. While Chief Justice Marshall argued against the wisdom of allowing the legislature to be limited by limits they set for themselves, Bickel has noted that the Constitution limits "the power of the Courts as well, and it may be equally absurd, therefore, to allow the courts to set the limits."[58]

We are finally ready to address the question, then, of why *judicial* review? To this point we have attempted to demonstrate that review of some sort followed in the tradition of several different strands of American political thought. Yet to more fully understand the implications of and for *judicial* review, we must begin to view the peculiar role played by courts, judges, and the gloss of legality in American political thought.

A necessary principle

The principle of fundamental and superior constitutions, as well as defined and limited legislative powers, was necessary but not sufficient for the establishment of the American doctrine of judicial review. The role of "judicial magic" and the American conception of "the people" were both crucial to the assertion of the judicial review power in America. For the origin of the review power and its special relationship with the judiciary we may return again to the common law view of courts as outlined by Lord Coke. In his doctrine, the source of judicial power was not strictly based on or limited by constitutionalism but, rather, was inherent in the judicial office itself. "Common right and reason" were talents peculiarly held by judges and enforceable by them. That law was the special province of judges went far towards legitimizing judicial review.

> As the law derives a semblance of eternal stability from this idea of Coke's that the law is over all government, so tradition lends a feeling of ancient stability to the Court. As the laws we enact are felt to be only a part of Law itself, so the Court feels that it belongs in a judicial lineage that is far older than the Constitution which it is interpreting and expounding. The Court, in fact, was already sitting and had been sitting for centuries before the Constitution was entrusted to its keeping, and Marshall's announcement of the doctrine of judicial review was, in one sense, the most natural thing in the world.[59]

Behind the common law conception of the judicial function there often lay an implicit intricate interrelationship between the role of the judge, and his position on earth as a representative of God; this corresponds to the natural law input of the common law. As early as the work of John Winthrop in America we get a clear portrayal of the place of the judiciary. Winthrop writes of special "parts and gifts, as the word of God requires in a judge,"[60] and implores, ". . . may we not . . . trust him (God) to give . . . muche wisdom . . . to such Judges as he shall sett up after us?"[61] While American legality is not simply the reflection of the common law, as we have argued, it is clear that the "religious" nature of the judicial calling survived well beyond the era of our Constitution's framing, and served for many as sufficient justification for the legitimacy of judicial review. Thus, Perry Miller notes of the legal profession in general that it "operated under a religious sanction, even when engaged in the most hairsplitting disputation."[62]

For some, the connection between religion and adjudication has been quite a direct link. Theodore Dwight Woolsey, an ex-President of Yale, said in the post–Civil War period that, "Judges . . . are in no sense representatives of the people or the king, or of any will whatever . . . In a higher sense they are not representatives of the community nor of its chief magistrates, but of justice and of God! . . . They are in fact more immediately servants of God than any other men who manage the affairs of a country."[63] Similarly, Perry Miller cites the words of Jesse Bledsoe in 1827. "An able and upright judge does, among men, perform the office of God's vicegerent. The ministers of religion, as is their duty, may show the divine anathema pointed against crime and unrighteousness; but it is the sword of law, wielded by the judge, which, from its nearness and immediate effect, operates most strongly to deter from their commission."[64]

We need not assert that all of America saw judges as the representatives of God on earth to make the more important and general point that judges have been viewed, in a sense, as a special breed of men. The "high priest" status of members of the Bar may, in part, be traced to the use of complex legalisms and "mystical" Latin phraseologies by judges and lawyers. While not accepting the "divine" element of judging, most Americans have at least been willing to grant the judicial process a peculiarly nonpolitical status.

> This is a country that has most emphatically rejected the divine origin of government . . . To tell the truth, this leaves a void, which we seek somehow to fill, disguising what we are doing under different names . . . Likewise the Court's power seems to be more than can rationally be ascribed to its competence in its work. There seems to be some undisclosed factor in the equation, and its presence is indicated by excessive admiration.[65]

In the American conception, "men" were viewed as subject to acts that were arbitrary and capricious, yet "law" was seen as stable and enduring. " 'Equal Justice Under Law,' we read as we enter the . . . home of the United States Supreme Court . . . In our minds takes shape a picture of impartial, impersonal judges applying traditional and immutable principles of law so as to render absolute justice to all men. Here there is no uncertainty, no mere whim or caprice, no arbitrary edict by man over man."[66] We need not look very far before seeing countless instances of the "peculiar" role of the American judiciary in our system of government.

Hamilton, for example, asserts in *Federalist* No. 78 that the Court, "may truly be said to have neither Force nor Will, but merely judgment." [67] Similarly, Madison stated in the Virginia convention, "Were I to select a power which might be given with confidence, it would be the judicial power." [68] Largely due to a mysticism of their own making, judges and lawyers were able to take a unique place in the American scheme of things. As Miller notes, "The figure of John Marshall loomed as the paragon of reason, as vivid a symbol to the American imagination as Natty Bumppo." [69]

Miller also notes that:

Again and again the lawyers impressed upon the democracy the idea that to attain distinction at the Bar required so severe an intellectual discipline that few could ever even hope to measure up to it. They devised a litany in which the awesome terms were regularly flung out. The law "demands the energies of the most powerful minds, and exhausts all the stores of learning." The profession is allied to every department of human knowledge: it must with the metaphysician explore the mysterious powers of the mind, with the logician it must master the rules of evidence, with the moral philosophers ascertain the duties and obligations of men, with the artisan it must learn methods and processes. In short, said Warren Dutton, "it calls to its aid all that the wisdom and experience of past times has recorded, and, in its highest exercises, becomes a model of all that is captivating or powerful in eloquence." [70]

In the landmark case of *Marbury v. Madison* Chief Justice Marshall asserted that it was "emphatically the province and duty of the judicial department to say what the law is," [71] and we may cite with great understanding John Randolph's reaction to another of Marshall's opinions: "All wrong, all wrong, but no man in the United States can tell why or wherein." [72]

Thus, in large part, the acceptance of judicial review and the unique potential of America for the development of the doctrine rested upon "an act of faith" that judges alone "knew" the law. As evidence that this was indeed the case Americans relied upon a myriad of diverse authorities from the common law to the founding fathers themselves.

Says Montesquieu: "Judges are no more than the mouth that pronounces the words of the Law." Mr. Pope in his article in the Harvard Law Review . . . insists upon the belief in 1787 that judges knew the law, while others had only opinions on it. [73]

Further, as Daniel Webster noted:

The president may say a law is unconstitutional, but he is not the judge . . . If it were otherwise, then there would be not a government of law, but we should all live under the government, the rule, the caprices of individuals. [74]

And, finally, we return to Hamilton in *Federalist* 22: "Laws are a dead letter without Courts to expound and define their true meaning and operation." [75]

The final link

Only one more link remains to be established to answer the question, why *judicial* review? While we have demonstrated that judges were invested by the populace with God-like qualities, it would be oversimplistic to equate them directly with God's will on earth. (Although this reasoning process was practiced by some.) The "missing link" may be found in the place of "the people" in American political thought and the acceptance of the judiciary as the representative not necessarily of God on earth but, perhaps more importantly, as the surrogate for "the people." Like so many other constructs, the importance of "the people" in the American system may be traced to the common law whose very name notes the locus of sovereignty in lawmaking. Sovereignty in America was identified with "the people" who were viewed both as the source of, as well as the location of, ultimate governing power. When Jefferson critiques judicial review, the role of "the people" becomes his primary argument. "But the Chief Justice says, 'there must be an ultimate arbiter somewhere.' True, there must, but does that prove it is either party? The ultimate arbiter is the people of the Union . . ." [76] Yet in his opposition to judicial review, Jefferson fails to take note of the ultimate coup which the Court has accomplished; that is, the identification of its pronouncements with the will of "the people." Bickel notes the apparent paradox involved.

The root difficulty is that judicial review is a countermajoritarian force in our system. There are various ways of sliding over this ineluctable reality. Marshall did so when he spoke of enforcing, in behalf of "the people," the limits that they have ordained for the institution of a limited government. [77]

Marshall, and several other justices, simply exercised the potential of the mystique that contemporary attitudes toward the judiciary afforded them. He disavowed any desire for judicial supremacy nor, alternatively did he support legislative supremacy. Rather, the will of "the people" was superior to both and the judges were the "oracles" of this "will." This theme is not unique to Marshall, but was widely echoed in the constitutional era and has reappeared with regularity ever since. Byrce states, "the Supreme Court is the living voice of the Constitution . . . that is, of the will of the people expressed in the fundamental law they have enacted." [78] The argument was stated most precisely in its pre–*Marbury v. Madison* form by Hamilton in *Federalist* 78.

> It is not . . . to be supposed that the Constitution could intend to enable the representatives of the people to substitute their will to that of their constituents. It is far more rational to suppose that the Courts were designed to be an intermediate body between the people and the legislature, in order, among other things, to keep the latter within the limits assigned to their authority. The interpretation of the laws is the proper and peculiar province of the courts. A Constitution is, in fact, and must be regarded by the judges as a fundamental law . . . That which has superior obligation and validity ought, of course, to be preferred . . . The Constitution ought to be preferred to the statute. The intention of the people to the intention of their agents. Nor does this conclusion by any means suppose a superiority of the judicial to the legislative power. It only supposes that the power of the People is superior to both; and that when the will of the legislature, declared in its statutes, stands in opposition to that of the people, declared in the Constitution, the judges ought to be governed by the latter rather than the former.[79]

Hamilton's argument, and its virtual repetition by Marshall in *Marbury v. Madison,* successfully performed an admirable "sleight of hand." Until their pronouncements, the representatives of the people were, by and large, viewed as "the people." Yet as the judicial version of the Constitution became accepted as "the Constitution," likewise did the judiciary substitute itself as "the people." Alpheus T. Mason succinctly states the essence of the "judicial magic" through which the Court interposed itself as the representatives of "the people" of 1789, a position which it apparently still holds in the eyes of many Americans.

> The fiction is that constitutional interpretation consists in finding meanings that can be clear only to judges. To them the purport of the Constitution is obvious; to the

President and Congress, its meaning is hidden and obscure. The only final and authoritative voice of the Constitution is a majority of the Supreme Court, and its every version, gleaned from a sort of brooding omnipresence, has the special virtue of never mangling, distorting, or changing the original instrument. The continuing myth is that the Court does not govern, nor does it affect those who do. What really controls is the immortal, unchanging instrument of 1789.[80]

In the final analysis, the American concept of the judicial function was and is a somewhat more "acceptable" version of the earlier Puritan conception. "The Puritan covenant had been that of God with his elect; the American covenant was an act of the people" speaking with their original, collective voice.[81] For the Puritans, "Judges are Gods upon earthe: Therefore, in the Administrations, they are to holde forthe the wisdome and mercye of God." [82] While not necessarily the manifestation of God on earth, early on the American judiciary interposed itself between "the people" who had ratified the American covenant and the current government. In such a way the judiciary became the living voice of "the people." In asserting this role, opposition to the judicial branch strong enough to deny it its coup could never be mounted. Largely, this could be credited to the unique position that judges were able to command in the American mind, traceable to the Common Law, the Puritans, and the trappings of legality in early American society. The consequences of this for the American doctrine of judicial review are telling, as the doctrine could be more readily accepted, and more easily legitimized and justified when the substantial powers were held by a body lacking both "force" and "will."

A continuing role

We have demonstrated that American pragmatism played a key part in the genesis of the doctrine of judicial review. Such pragmatism has also played a critical role in the doctrine's exercise and continued legitimacy. In a government based on separation of powers and checks and balances, the need arises for checking the potentially awesome power of judicial review. Yet any external check on this aspect of judicial power would fly in the face of the entire rationale for the legitimacy of judicial review. If justices were a "peculiar" breed of men how could an external check be justified? American pragmatism again supplies what has proven to be, at most times, a workable answer. In balancing the checks, the Court must simply check itself. As Justice Iredell stated, "That such a power in the Judge may be abused is very certain; that it will be, is not very probable." [83]

Advocates of "judicial supremacy" have often criticized the Court for what they feel is excessive exercise of judicial self-restraint. Such arguments stress that it is the Constitution, and not the questionable statute that should be given the benefit of the doubt. Some have gone so far as to say that judicial self-restraint is, "Plainly a betrayal of the very basis on which the whole doctrine of judicial review has been based. A betrayal of the rights of the litigant, and the judicial duty owed him by the Court." [84] Nevertheless, it is essential to any discussion of judicial review to recognize that judicial self-restraint has had a long and honored history, and to the extent that judicial review was, and has been legitimized, its limits have always been implicitly recognized.

> An essential maneuver in the exquisite strategy by which the Courts maintained their cause, despite the rising tide of democracy, was a prolongation of their advocacy of the Common Law into fervent adherence to the principle of judicial restraint. As long as they insisted upon this self-limitation, who could attack them? [85]

In the very next breath, after advocates had argued for the necessity of judicial review, they argued coincidingly for judicial self-restraint. Indeed, Hamilton himself, for example, stressed the importance of precedents for the courts, the very touchstone of judicial self-restraint.

> To avoid an arbitrary discretion in the Courts, it is indispensable that they should be bound down by strict rules and precedents which serve to define and point out their duty in every particular case that comes before them.[86]

The same theme was continually sounded by a majority of the early members of the American judiciary.

> Justice Iredell said in 1798 that because the authority to declare a legislative act, federal or state, "void, is of a delicate and awful nature, the Court will never resort to that authority but in a clear and unjust case." "A very clear case," said Justice Chase. In McCulloch v. Maryland, Marshall indicated that something like a "bold and plain usurpation, to which the Constitution gave no countenance," was required to invoke the exercise

of judicial annulment. In Fletcher v. Peck . . . Marshall said, "The question whether a law be void for its repugnancy to the Constitution, is, at all times, a question of much delicacy which ought seldom, if ever, to be decided in the affirmative, in a doubtful case . . . The opposition between the Constitution and the law should be such that the judge feels a clear and strong conviction of their incompatibility with each other." This attitude carried over, as is evidenced by the remark of Justice Bushrod Washington in 1827, "It is but a decent respect due to the wisdom, the integrity, and the patriotism of the legislative body by which any law is passed to presume in favor of its validity until its violation of the Constitution is proved beyond all reasonable doubt." (Ogden v. Saunders)[87]

What is demonstrated by the above statements is the final pragmatic thrust at making the doctrine of judicial review a palatable one. In essence, the logic of the doctrine itself has been turned around and the ultimate question being addressed becomes one not of ascertaining the "true" meaning of the Constitution, but rather of deciding whether specific legislation can be sustained. Judicial review when aligned with the doctrine of judicial self-restraint becomes primarily a "negative" and/or defensive power, as opposed to a much more problematical and less acceptable positive initiating power. When viewed from this perspective, the review power can be seen as amenable to several opposing schools of governmental philosophy in America.

> *Marbury v. Madison* has proved to be one of those very special occurrences that mark an epoch in the life of the republic. Culminating the great achievements of the Constitutional Period, it accomplished the transition from perpetuity to efficacy, from immutability to adaptation, and from heavenly to judicial sanction. Finally, it introduced an unending colloquy between the Supreme Court and the people of the United States, in which the Court continually asserts, "You live under a Constitution but the Constitution is what we say it is," and the people incessantly reply, "As long as your version of the Constitution enables us to live with pride in what we consider a free and just society, you may continue exercising this august, awesome and altogether revocable authority." [88]

These remarks are instructive in emphasizing the crucial interrelationship between judicial review and judicial self-restraint. We need only casually scan the periods during which the most severe Court curbing activity has occurred (i.e., the New Deal period, post-*Brown* decision Warren Court, etc.) to recognize that such efforts have coincided with periods during which a philosophical commitment to judicial self-restraint, even on the most abstract level, has been abandoned by the Court. Indeed, historical perspective helps us to understand the contemporary controversies about the appropriate scope of the judicial role as played out in the contemporary dialogue between the William Brennan and Edwin Meese jurisprudential camps.

Conclusion

We have attempted to demonstrate that judicial review was able to develop in America as a consequence of several distinct facets of American political thought which, while often in opposition to each other, were mutually amenable to and supportive of judicial review. This is not to say that all Americans of every persuasion welcomed the doctrine with open arms and gave it full sway. Rather, we have argued that the doctrine itself is such a multifaceted one that virtually all in America could support it because of at least one of its facets or, at worst, that a significant and vigorous opposition to the doctrine could not be mustered. Corwin has most completely captured the eclectic nature of the American experience which led to the ability of the landmark case of *Marbury v. Madison* to serve as the culmination of several distinct trends.

> Upon this latent talent the problems of the times acted as incentive and stimulant, eliciting from it suggestion after suggestion which it needed but the ripe occasion to erect into institutions composing a harmonious whole . . .
>
> 1. from Massachusetts and New Hampshire came the idea of this ordered and regular procedure for making constitutions, with the result . . . of furthering the idea . . . of the legal character of the constitution.
> 2. from New Jersey, Connecticut, Virginia, Rhode Island and perhaps New Hampshire came the idea of judicial review, partly on the basis of the doctrine of the right of revolution and partly on the basis of the doctrine of certain principles fundamental to the Common Law that had found recognition in the State constitutions.
> 3. from North Carolina . . . came the idea of judicial review based squarely on the written constitution and the principle of the separation of powers.
> 4. from various sources came the idea that legislative power, instead of being governmental power in general, is a peculiar kind of power.
> 5. from various sources came the idea that judicial power exercised as it habitually was under the guiding influence of Common Law principles was naturally conservative of private rights.
> 6. from various sources came the idea that the judiciary must be put in a position to defend its prerogative against the legislative tendency to absorb all powers, and this idea was connected with the idea of judicial review both in the relation of means and of ends.
> 7. from the Congress of the Confederation came the idea that the Articles of Confederation and treatises made under them were rightfully to be regarded as part and parcel of the law of every State paramount, moreover, to conflicting acts of the State legislatures and enforceable by the State Courts.

Probably no one public man of the time shared all these ideas when the Philadelphia Convention met. But the able membership of that famous body was in a position to compare views drawn from every section of the country. Slowly, by a process of discussion and conversation, these men . . . discovered the intrinsic harmony of the ideas just passed in review; discovered, in other words, that the acceptance of the others also, that each implied a system embracing all.[89]

Perhaps Corwin has overidealized the "intrinsic harmony" of the American experience in a misplaced effort to prove that the American outcome was, somehow, "natural." Such an approach is not really necessary and is, to some extent, misleading. In examining the peculiar American phenomenon of judicial review we have chosen to emphasize its eclectic nature. Post–revolutionary America was the site of numerous conflicts which often became serious points of contention in the general and ongoing Federalist/Democratic-Republican debate.

We have argued, however, that several facets of the judicial review doctrine enabled *all* people to at least *accept*, if not actually support the power. While Jefferson clearly opposed judicial review, it seems equally clear that a Jeffersonian could, in good conscience, support the doctrine because of its natural law and limited government orientation. Staunch Federalists, on the other hand, could support the doctrine for distinctly different reasons; namely its alleged tendency to control popular majorities. Two further tendencies served to make the doctrine acceptable in the American context. First was the entire dimension of "judicial magic" whereby all aspects of legalism possessed a mystique allowing the doctrine of judicial review to appear both less dangerous and more "natural." Judges, after all, were not "creating" the law, but were simply "midwives" lacking "force" and "will." Yet despite all of this, the American experience was a particularly pragmatic one, and "judicial magic" only appears to be functional when the judiciary has adhered to narrow limits self-imposed on judicial review, the adherence to judicial self-restraint.

We have argued that in addressing the seemingly unanswerable question of whether judicial review was part of the framers' "intentions" an equally important question has been largely ignored. We have attempted to demonstrate not that judicial review was "intended," but, rather, that it is clearly consistent with several facets of American political thought and that it emerged in America, whether strictly "intended" or not, in a peculiarly amenable and ripe environment.

Notes

This article originally appeared in Volume 71, Number 2, August–September 1987, pages 68–79. It is dedicated to Alpheus T. Mason whom I had the good fortune to serve as a Graduate Teaching Assistant a decade and a half ago. His love for and deep commitment to American constitutionalism kindled my interests and the legacy of his scholarship well informs our bicentennial celebration.

1. Hyneman, *The Supreme Court on Trial* (New York: Atherton Press, 1964), 114.

2. Dumbauld, (ed.), *The Political Writing of Thomas Jefferson* (New York: Liberal Arts Press, 1955), 147.

3. Corwin, *The Doctrine of Judicial Review* (Princeton: Princeton University Press, 1914), 9.

4. Curtis, *Lions Under the Throne* (Boston: Houghton Mifflin Co., 1947), 12.

5. Haines, *The American Doctrine of Judicial Supremacy* (New York: Macmillan Company, 1914), 18.

6. Dumbauld, *supra* n. 2, at 107.

7. Corwin, *supra* n. 3, at 31–32.

8. Ibid. at 32.

9. Berger, *Congress v. the Supreme Court* (Cambridge: Harvard University Press, 1969), 251.

10. Carr, *The Supreme Court and Judicial Review* (New York: Holt, Rinehart, and Winston, 1942), 45.

11. Berger, *supra* n. 9, at 50.

12. Ibid. at 53.

13. Ibid. at 15–16.

14. Ibid. at 15–16.

15. Ibid. at 43.

16. Corwin, *supra* n. 3, at 38.

17. Haines, *supra* n. 5, at 27.

18. Corwin, *supra* n. 3, at 18–19.

19. Berger, *supra* n. 9, at 182.

20. Corwin, *Court Over Constitution* (Princeton: Princeton University Press, 1938), 22.

21. Corwin, *supra* n. 3, at 29–30.

22. Corwin, *supra* n. 20, at 22–23.

23. Haines, *supra* n. 5, at 34.

24. Carr, *supra* n. 10, at 41–43.

25. Corwin, *supra* n. 3, at 29–31.

26. Boudin, *Government by Judiciary,* vol. 1 (New York: William Goodwin, Inc., 1932), 11–12.

27. Miller, *The Life of the Mind in America* (New York: Harcourt, Brace, and World, Inc., 1965), 241.

28. Haines, *supra* n. 5, at 21.

29. Corwin, *supra* n. 20, at 5.

30. Dewey, *Marshall versus Jefferson: The Political Background of Marbury v. Madison* (New York: Alfred A. Knopf, 1970), 65.

31. Haines, *supra* n. 5, at 23–24.

32. Miller, *supra* n. 27, at 165.

33. Haines, *supra* n. 5, at 177.

34. Levy, (ed.), *Judicial Review and the Supreme Court* (New York: Harper Torchbooks, 1967), 46.

35. Haines, *supra* n. 5, at 24.

36. Carr, *supra* n. 10, at 47.

37. Cahn, (ed.), *Supreme Court and Supreme Law* (New York: New York University Press, 1954), 16.

38. Ibid. at 4.

39. Morgan, *Puritan Political Man* (New York: Bobbs-Merrill Company, Inc., 1965), 101.

40. Levy, *supra* n. 34, at 44–45.

41. Ibid. at 45.

42. Cahn, *supra* n. 37, at 2.

43. Carr, *supra* n. 10, at 48.

44. *Marbury v. Madison,* 1 Cranch 137 (1803).

45. Carr, *supra* n. 10, at 49.

46. Corwin, *supra* n. 3, at 37.

47. Berger, *supra* n. 9, at 72.

48. Fairfield, (ed.), *The Federalist Papers* (New York: Doubleday and Company, Inc., 1961), 228.

49. Beard, *The Supreme Court and the Constitution* (New York: Macmillan Company, 1916), 95.

50. Ibid. at 91.

51. Paul, *Conservative Crisis and the Rule of Law* (Ithaca: Cornell University Press, 1960), 231.

52. Berger, *supra* n. 9, at 8.

53. Morgan, *supra* n. 39, at 156.

54. Dumbauld, *supra* n. 2, at 222–224.

55. Morgan, *supra* n. 39, at 157.

56. Corwin, *supra* n. 3, at 59.

57. Curtis, *supra* n. 4, at 46.

58. Berger, *supra* n. 9, at 183.

59. Curtis, *supra* n. 4, at 64.

60. Morgan, *supra* n. 9, at 123.

61. Ibid. at 153.

62. Miller, *supra* n. 27, at 186.

63. Curtis, *supra* n. 4, at 53–54.

64. Miller, *supra* n. 27, at 186.

65. Curtis, *supra* n. 4, at 53–54.

66. Carr, *supra* n. 10, at 1–2.

67. Fairfield, *supra* n. 48, at 227.

68. Berger, *supra* n. 9, at 185.

69. Miller, *supra* n. 27, at 119–120.

70. Ibid. at 136.

71. *Marbury v. Madison, supra* n. 44.

72. Rostow, *The Sovereign Prerogative: The Supreme Court and the Quest for Law* (New Haven: Yale University Press, 1962), 87.

73. Corwin, *supra* n. 3, at 63–64.

74. Ibid. at 22.

75. Fairfield, *supra* n. 48, at 55.

76. Dumbauld, *supra* n. 2, at 148.

77. Bickel, *The Least Dangerous Branch* (New York: Bobbs-Merrill Company, 1962), 16.

78. Rostow, *supra* n. 73, at 122–123.

79. Fairfield, *supra* n. 48, at 229.

80. Mason and Beaney, *American Constitutional Law,* 4th ed. (Englewood Cliffs, N.J.: Prentice-Hall, Inc., 1968), 18.

81. Miller, *supra* n. 27, at 217.

82. Morgan, *supra* n. 39, at 152.

83. Haines, *supra* n. 5, at 181.

84. Curtis, *supra* n. 4, at 25.

85. Miller, *supra* n. 27, at 236.

86. Fairfield, *supra* n. 48, at 232–233.

87. Berger, *supra* n. 9, at 338–339.

88. Cahn, *supra* n. 37, at 25.

89. Corwin, *supra* n. 3, at 38–41.

Judicial review: the usurpation and democracy questions

Albert P. Melone and George Mace

Whatever its origins, judicial review is a fact of political life. Debate continues, however, as to whether or not it is consistent with the spirit and form of democratic government.

It is emphatically the province and duty of the judicial department, to say what the law is . . .

—John Marshall in *Marbury v. Madison*

Although it may be inferred, there is no explicit mention of judicial review in the Constitution. The only "express wording" that supports that power is the oath of office, the same oath taken by other members of the national government.[1] Therefore, the justification for judicial review requires more than an inspection of the wording of the basic document. Indeed, the justification in *Marbury v. Madison* (1803)[2] rests not only upon an *interpretation* of words, but equally upon an interpretation of a much more nebulous *intent* of the entire document.

The first issue explored in this article concerns the establishment of judicial review, which has been questioned from Jefferson's time by many who insist that the Court usurped power when claiming this function. For them, there is no constitutional justification— implicit or explicit. They insist that the founding fathers never intended to invest the judiciary with such power. Thus, we will seek to answer the question best phrased by historian Charles A. Beard: "The Supreme Court—'Usurper or Grantee?'"[3]

The second part of this article concerns the matter of Court rulings which, in the final analysis, seem to be legislative mandates emanating from *lawmakers* who are not directly accountable through the electoral process. This has led some to charge that such a power wielded by the judiciary is not consistent with the spirit and form of democratic government.

These two problems are closely linked. Those who believe judicial review is not democratic portray the judiciary, not as the unambiguous spokespersons of the Constitution, but as so many individuals who express their own personal attitudes or group interests. To them, the judiciary is little more than an outrageous oligarchy masquerading in the black robes of constitutional impartiality. The history of these issues forms the foundation for the analysis that follows.

Those interested in other issues such as the judicial capacity[4] and interpretivism[5] debates necessarily must face the fundamental questions explored in this article. If the federal judiciary may not legitimately exercise review and if that power is incompatible with democracy, then no amount of interpretation, selective use of power or its carefully considered timing may excuse its exercise.

The usurpation question

Judge John B. Gibson's 1825 dissenting opinion in the Pennsylvania Supreme Court case of *Eakin v. Raub*[6] is the classic statement addressing the usurpation of power issue. It is considered by many the most effective answer given to John Marshall's famous arguments in support of judicial review.[7] Judge Gibson weaves at least six related points.

First, he states that the ordinary and essential powers of the judiciary do not extend to the annulling of an act of the legislature.[8] In other words, the everyday duty of courts is to interpret the meaning of laws. Today, we would call this the duty of statutory interpretation; and indeed, courts spend considerable time and effort in deciding what the legislature meant when it enacted a given piece of legislation, and how the legislation should be interpreted, given the facts of the particular case or controversy before it. This task, argues Gibson, is the ordinary and essential aspect of judicial power.

Secondly, Judge Gibson argues that what is good for one co-equal branch of the government should be good for the others. He claims that it would be viewed as a usurpation of judicial power if the legislature should attempt to reverse a Supreme Court decision. Yet, it is not regarded as a usurpation of legislative power when the judiciary holds a statute unconstitutional.[9] This argument is all the more cogent in the light of twentieth century experience. Interest groups have attempted, and sometimes succeeded, in reversing controversial Supreme Court decisions by proposing the rewriting of statutes to avoid previously held unconstitutional provisions, removing appellate jurisdiction or even campaigning for constitutional amendments. Defenders of Court decisions will often appeal to a sense of deep commitment to the Court as the guardian of the Constitution.[10] Though reason may require equal regard for the authority of the legislative branch, as Gibson points out, the judiciary occupies a special status within the governmental system, unaffected by the rules of logic.

Third, Gibson argues that the concept of checks and balances does not include the idea of a judicial veto. Within the legislative branch itself, a proposal must pass through two legislative chambers. If the framers intended to impose the judiciary as an additional barrier, they would have explicitly granted to the judges the power, instead of leaving the matter in doubt.[11]

Fourth, Gibson takes up the matter of the oath, which John Marshall regarded as a high moral duty. For Gibson, the oath of office taken by judicial officers, or for that matter any government official, extends only to supporting the Constitution as far as it extends to official conduct. If one's duty does not entail excursions into the legislative realm, neither does one's oath.[12] This conclusion gives rise to a rhetorical question that we may treat as Gibson's fifth point.

Does a judge violate the Constitution when he permits an unconstitutional legislative act to stand? "No!" Gibson says. The enactment and the interpretation of a legislative act are not concurrent. In other words, the judge does not adopt unconstitutional legislation as his own simply because he interprets it. Members of the legislative branch enact legislation, not the judiciary.[13]

The sixth major point states that if the legislature enacts an unconstitutional law, the people may petition their elected representatives to repeal it. If the judiciary makes a mistake, then a constitutional amendment is needed. The former remedy is clearly preferable to the latter one, given the relatively drastic and cumbersome process of amending a constitution.[14]

The remainder of Gibson's famous dissent is an exposition of the authority of state courts under the Constitution. However, what is of lasting value is his contribution to the debate over judicial review. Interestingly, Gibson later recanted his bold view because

the Pennsylvania legislature had "sanctioned the pretensions of the courts to deal freely with the acts of the legislature, and from experience of the necessity of the case." [15]

Judicial self-restraint

Forty years after Gibson's death, James B. Thayer stood before the Congress on Jurisprudence and Law Reform on August 9, 1893, to read one of the most influential papers ever delivered on the subject of judicial review.[16] After noting with favor Judge Gibson's dissent, he went on to argue for the view he had adopted early in life. If the Supreme Court exercised judicial review at all, he said, it must be with great restraint; it may declare acts void only when their constitutionality was beyond all reasonable doubt.

The Harvard law professor reviewed carefully the historical antecedents to the establishment of judicial review. He came to the skeptical conclusion: "[t]he judiciary may well reflect that if they had been regarded by the people as the chief protection against legislative violation of the constitution, they would not have been allowed . . . incidental and postponed control." [17] Yet, Thayer accepts judicial review as a legitimate judicial function, and not a per se usurpation of legislative power. What is unacceptable is the employment of judicial review in those instances in which reasonable persons may disagree. Judicial review should be reserved for those cases where there is no "reasonable doubt" that the legislature enacted an unconstitutional law.[18]

Thayer counsels for judicial self-restraint because the very independence of the judiciary may be jeopardized without it. He argues that repeated and unnecessary use of the judicial veto could excite institutional jealousy and diminish public reverence for the laws. He acknowledges that judges are part of the political process and therefore should ". . . apply methods and principles that befit their task." [19] It is this view of the Court's relationship with the other branches of government that clearly distinguishes advocates of judicial self-restraint from others—whether these be mechanistic rule-oriented absolutists on the one hand, or, on the other hand, activist judges committed to using courts to right the many wrongs abroad in the land in the manner of a superlegislature.

This famous essay is the foundation on which Justices Holmes, Brandeis, and Frankfurter constructed their judicial philosophies. All three were associated with Harvard and connected with Thayer as faculty member or student. All three acknowledged the intellectual impact of Thayerism upon their own thinking. The three justices represent the most articulate spokespersons for judicial self-restraint from 1902 to 1962. While all three made unique contributions to constitutional law, reading the judicial opinions of each provides scholar and practitioner alike with the finest primer available in any form on the doctrine of judicial self-restraint. Consider the dissent from the Supreme Court's social Darwinist activist era at the turn of the century through the mid-1930s. Also reflect on the opposition to the writing of the Bill of Rights into the Constitution as a prohibition against state power through the 1950s and early 1960s and beyond. The legacy of Holmes, Brandeis, and Frankfurter is unmistakable.[20]

The timelessness of the Thayer article is evident when considering contemporary criticisms of the Supreme Court. The charge that the Supreme Court has become a policy-making institution, with little regard for popular opinion and proper deference toward the legislature, is one that modern conservative ideologues, including those in the Reagan administration, have trumpeted with great resonance. Yet, the political noise directed against the Court is not limited to this age. The same arguments were directed against the Court by liberals in an earlier age who opposed the Court's tendency to strike down social and economic legislation designed to protect the masses against economic wealth and power.

Without intending undue cynicism, we must point out from a historical perspective that positions on judicial activism versus restraint often turn on whose ox is being gored. Yesterday's liberals often criticized the Court for its activism; today, it is the conservatives who condemn the Court for the same sin. Though this fact does not alter the validity, if any, of Professor Thayer's views, it nonetheless reinforces his basic underlying assumption of the Supreme Court as a political institution.

Judicial review as obligation

In the face of rising controversy surrounding the Court's activism in apparent opposition to government regulation of the economy, Associate Justice Horace H. Lurton in 1911 defended the institution against its critics.[21] Few men were more suitable for the task, whether from conviction or deed.

Justice Lurton argues that public opinion and the oath of office are not sufficient guarantees insuring that legislators will stay within constitutional boundaries when promulgating laws. Lurton proceeds from the premises first enunciated by Montesquieu in *The Spirit of the Laws* (1748). The great French scholar of the eighteenth century concluded that liberty could not be maintained without a separation of powers between the legislative, executive and judicial functions. Lurton argues that American history supports the contention that the exercise of judicial review is an obligation of the judiciary as a guarantor of liberty.[22]

Not only is early case law presented in support of judicial review, but Lurton asserts also that its practice was accepted by the people in the early years of the republic. Unfortunately, however, the enormous mass of new immigrants, "unaccustomed to democratic government," consider the judicial veto as a usurpation of legislative authority.[23] Justice Lurton then proceeds to instruct that in a government of laws there is no such thing as unlimited power. Rather, all power is delegated.

Thus, when courts exercise judicial review they are not legislating or employing uncontrolled political power; they are applying the elementary principle that ". . . the acts of an agent in excess of his authority do not bind his principal." Judges in such instances have no choice but to " . . . enforce the constitution as the law of highest obligation." [24]

There is an unstated premise in Lurton's argument. It is that law and politics are somehow separate and distinct; the judges' role is simply to find the law, not to make it. Indeed, the widespread belief that legal rules are superior to individual choice is the genesis of the phrase: a nation of laws, not of men. The ideology of legalism summarized in this phrase has as much attraction today as it did when Lurton wrote his article over three-quarters of a century ago. The search for neutral principles of law and objectivity in decision making is a recurring theme in American law. The current so-called interpretivism or intentionalism debate championed by Attorney General Edwin Meese and Robert Bork, among others, is but the latest variation on an old theme. As long as humans believe that their decisions should be based upon principles transcending self-interest and subjectivity, essays such as Lurton's will be written. Yet, how we believe we ought to behave is not always how we *in fact* behave. The confusion of a value prescription for a factual description is as common to judges as it is to ordinary mortals.

Rebutting judicial review

Justice Lurton's vigorous defense of judicial review was answered contemporaneously with an equally spirited essay. Louis Boudin, a New York labor lawyer and prominent member of the American Labor Party during the early part of this century, challenged Lurton's arguments.[25] The debate reached well beyond cloistered academic halls. The fact is the Supreme Court deployed constitutional concepts, such as substantive due process and liberty of contract, to strike down legislation designed to protect working persons. Organized labor and progressives viewed the Supreme Court at the turn of the century as an important force of reaction and opposition.

Boudin sets out to make two major points. First, he presents evidence to discredit Justice Lurton's claim that judicial review was intended by the framers of the Constitution. Second, he argues that as a matter of fact, the power of judicial review as exercised by the turn of the century Supreme Court is nothing less than revolutionary.

The author maintains that judicial review was not a recognized power at the time of the American revolution. He argues that the authority was not recognized in England, and that Lurton's reliance on the writings of Montesquieu is misplaced. The failure of John Marshall to cite so-called existing precedents from state courts was wise because, according to Boudin, the "precedents" do not demonstrate opinion in favor of judicial review, but its very opposite.[26]

Boudin examines evidence concerning the framers' intent. He concludes that although some who gathered at Philadelphia favored judicial review, given their explicit silence on the subject, " . . . the great majority of the Framers never suspected a general power of the judiciary to control legislation could be interpreted into the new constitution." [27]

Citing Judge Gibson's dissent approvingly, Marshall's decision in *Marbury v. Madison* is characterized by Boudin in the first instance as "amazing." [28] Boudin also makes two additional points worthy of consideration. First, the *Marbury* decision related particularly to judicial power, and not to general legislation. It is one thing for the Supreme Court to defend the judicial branch against legislative encroachment; it is quite another to claim the Court is the sole and binding interpreter of the Constitution. Second, Jefferson won the immediate battle because Marbury was denied the commission he sought. Thus, the unpopular Federalist attempt to stack the judiciary with the party faithful was spoiled. The decision in *Marbury* provoked no extended public debate because it had no practical importance. The lack of a huge public outcry should therefore not be interpreted as acceptance of judicial review.[29]

If one line of reasoning fails to convince judge and jury, try another. This is true even if the two arguments proceed from different premises. This typical lawyer tactic is employed by Boudin in his "brief" against the then contemporary Supreme Court. He first makes the case that there is nothing in the pre-convention history, court precedents, intent of the framers and Supreme Court decisions to justify judicial review. Boudin then argues, in essence, that if all the arguments just presented are rejected, and one accepts the exercise of judicial review as a legitimate authority, the contemporary Court has nonetheless employed the power improperly.[30] In short, a posture of self-restraint is prescribed. Let the policy judgments of the legislatures stand, Boudin says. If the legislative branch violates the Constitution, the best protection against such abuse is the people, not the courts. At this point in the essay, Boudin reads very much like Thayer.

Boudin ends his argument with a consideration of how the Supreme Court abused its power in a number of important recent cases. Boudin argues that the Court's conservative majority substituted their personal policy views for that of legislatures. The Court's famous decisions in *Lochner v. New York* (1905), *Adair v. United States* (1908), and others are pointed to as proof that there are not "plain and simple" rules of constitutional interpretation as claimed by Justice Lurton. "On the contrary, there are now practically no rules at all," [31] said Boudin. Once again, we are reminded of contemporary criticism. The principal difference is that since the mid-1950s, the critical voices come from the political right, instead of the political left.

The intent of the framers

Mr. Boudin's accusations and those of his fellow doubters did not pass unnoticed. A popular Columbia University professor, later to become president of both the American Historical Association and the American Political Science Association, answered the complaint.[32] Through an examination of the direct and indirect declarations of certain members of the Philadelphia Convention and the "general purpose and spirit of the federal Constitution," Charles A. Beard concludes that judicial review was not usurped; it was intended by the framers. The evidence adduced in support of his conclusion, and the assumptions underlying his research methodology, not only shed light upon the usurpation question, but also point to the many difficulties inherent in constitutional interpretation.

Beard begins his argument by conceding that the delegates to the Constitutional Convention did not consider a proposition to grant the judicial branch veto power over legislative acts. In fact, none was submitted. A council of revision was proposed that would have joined a number of judges with the executive to revise laws passed by Congress.[33] According to Beard, however, that is a different proposition from judicial review. It may be legitimately asked whether this difference is sufficiently dissimilar to sustain Beard's point. Later in the article, Beard cites the apparent support of certain delegates for the revisionary council proposition as persuasive evidence of their belief in judicial review. Logic militates against arguing on the one hand that judicial review and the revisionary proposition were not the same; and then, on the other hand, suggesting that if a delegate favored the revisionary proposition, he probably also favored judicial review. In any event, Beard claims the "question of judicial control . . . did not come squarely before the Convention, in such form that a vote could be taken."[34]

The bulk of Beard's article is devoted to the difficult question of what the framers intended. He prefaces this research approach with the caution that any such inquiry must be incomplete because new research could uncover additional information. However, the search for intent is fraught with even greater difficulties, not the least of which are its underlying assumptions. These are succinctly outlined by Professors Walter Murphy and C. Herman Pritchett in their standard modern text.[35]

The first assumption is that future generations should be bound by the specific intentions of the framers, not the general principles that guided their actions. If the assumption is accepted, then Americans will be constitutionally mired in the eighteenth century. In this view, the Constitution must be interpreted as a set of rules that can be clearly understood as articulated by the framers. In fairness, both Beard and his intellectual antagonist, Boudin, silently accept this questionable assumption. Yet given the nature of the argument, it is reasonable for Beard to search for specific intent. It is Boudin and others who claim that, because the framers were silent on the matter of judicial review, they

could not have intended to make it a part of the Constitution. Beard uses evidence of the specific intent of the individual framers to counter this point.

The second assumption underlying the search for the framers' intent is more difficult to defend. It is that the framers had a single intention. In fact, it is probable that they had many different, sometimes contradictory and even irreconcilable "intentions." Indeed, the Philadelphia Convention was not an exercise in ascertaining the "general will" or Confucian harmony. Rather, it was a matter of compromise, logrolling and negotiation about matters that do not lend themselves to simple solutions. The politics of such a setting renders the ascertainment of a solid and unified group intention difficult at best.

Beard mitigates the problem of intent by breaking the group down into its constituent parts, namely, each individual delegate. He does this by examining the debates at the Convention, public comments made after Philadelphia, congressional votes and the letters and private documents of many of the delegates.

He does not examine the views of all 55 delegates to the Philadelphia Convention. Rather, Beard first investigates the views of what he calls the leading or the most influential members of the Convention.[36] He concludes that, of these, not less than 13 believed that judicial power extended to the nullification of an act of Congress. He adds four more delegates to his total by virtue of their subsequent votes in support of the Judiciary Act of 1789.[37] Of the less influential delegates, six either expressed themselves in favor of judicial review or approved of it by virtue of their votes on the 1789 act.[38] [Beard's reference to the Judiciary Act is to that part of the law dealing with federal-state relations under the Constitution's Supremacy Clause. The argument supposes that favoring judicial review of state actions is the equivalent of support for judicial control over congressional acts. Though the two are related, one should consider whether it is reasonable to support the federalism principle without favoring third branch veto over congressional enactments. Finally, with respect to the Judiciary Act, it must be pointed out that the methodological problems inherent in ascertaining legislative intent are, in principle, similar to those met when studying constitutional intent.]

We are not persuaded that the evidence presented for each delegate's position on judicial review is clear and convincing. Beard's best case argument does not add up to even a majority of the delegates favoring judicial review. He finds that 23 were for judicial review, 5 were against review, and the views of the remaining 27 are unknown. Edward S. Corwin, whose authority ranks with that of Beard's, found only 17 in favor of judicial review.[39] Nevertheless, both scholars insist that the framers intended judicial review. It is troublesome nonetheless that as influential as the 23 or 17 delegates may have been, it requires considerable faith in their leadership abilities to conclude that all, most, or even a majority of the delegates would have voted for judicial review if the proposition were presented squarely to them.

However, as one progresses through Beard's presentation, it is discovered that numbers are not everything. Beard's fall back position is clear enough: ". . . the Constitution was not designed to be perfectly explicit on all points and to embody definitely the opinions of a majority of the Convention . . . .[40] If this is true, then why did Beard make the case for the specific intent of as many convention delegates as he could? Beard does not rest his case with the submission of evidence on the framers' intentions. He continues the "brief" against Boudin and other named and unnamed opposing counsels by addressing the remaining usurpation charges and evidence.

Constitutions are not only framed, they are also ratified. Beard presents admittedly fragmentary evidence on this point. He offers information from the debates in 4 of 13 state ratifying conventions in support of his argument that those who ratified the Constitution favored judicial review.[41] Beard is also unimpressed by arguments that state judicial opinions do not serve as adequate precedents for judicial review.[42] Finally, Beard defends John Marshall against the charge that he created judicial review out of whole cloth. Beard points out that the concept was known within legal circles at the time of the founding; indeed, before the decision in *Marbury,* the Supreme Court had alluded to judicial review in a number of decisions.[43]

Reasonable persons may disagree on the usurpation question. It may be true, as former Chief Justice Warren Burger has stated, "[i]t is now accepted that the original assertion of the power was not judicial usurpation as Jefferson considered it." [44] However, whether that acceptance is based upon reasoned analysis or political reality is another matter altogether.

The compatibility question

Behind the usurpation of power question lurks the equally difficult issue of the compatibility of judicial review with democratic values. Democratic sensibilities

are offended by nine persons voiding acts of popularly selected representatives of the people. Moreover, the judiciary is independent of the people and their elected representatives. The result is a third branch free from popular control. Is judicial review a menace to popular democracy? Alternatively, is review a way to perfect democratic government? In essence, is there any way to reconcile the practice of judicial review with democratic theory?

We first consider the arguments of Robert Yates, a leading opponent of the ratification of the proposed constitution crafted at Philadelphia. Yates, Alexander Hamilton and John Lansing had composed the New York delegation to the Constitutional Convention. Yates and Lansing walked out on the Convention some two and one-half months before its work was completed. The two joined other Americans in making speeches, writing pamphlets, essays and letters. Collectively, they came to be called Antifederalists. The other side of the debate was represented successfully by the Federalists.

As is often the case for winners and losers, much is widely known about Federalist thought, but little is understood about Antifederalist thinking. Fundamentally, this loosely knitted group believed the great choice facing humankind was either despotism or republicanism. The latter is based on consent of the governed or self-government, and the former is insured by force. Antifederalists believed the proposed constitution granted too much power to the people's representatives without providing an effective counter check. They reasoned that privileged people would benefit from the proposed constitution at the expense of ordinary people. Unless restrictions could be placed on all three constitutional branches of the central government, they feared, the potential for despotism would become a reality. Though they lost the ratification debate, Antifederalist ideology was largely responsible for the addition of the Bill of Rights to our constitutional structure.[45]

Writing under the pseudonym of "Brutus," Robert Yates, then a judge of the New York Supreme Court, makes the case against the excesses of Article III. In the process of showing why the new government would prove destructive of political happiness, he argues that due to the nature of judicial review, members of the Court have such overwhelming power they could " . . . mould the government into almost any shape they please." [46]

For the most part, this follows from two facts. First, there was no limit to the amount of power the Court could imply from the Constitution since interpretation would not be restricted to the "letter" of the Constitution, that is, to the "words in their common acception." Thus, the Court could build through implication from nebulous "spirit" and "intent" of the document. Second, and even more to be feared, the Court was not held accountable to either the people or their representatives. As such, the Court constituted a will, independent of society, which could be "controlled" only by an appeal to the sword.[47]

Yates was one delegate to the Philadelphia Convention who had no doubt the proposed constitution contained within its meaning the power of judicial review. He finds it particularly alarming because the judges are " . . . rendered totally independent, both of the people and the legislature, both with respect to their offices and salaries. No errors they may commit can be corrected by any person above them, if any such power there be . . . ." [48]

The probable impact of the federal judiciary upon the States' rights was central to Antifederalist republican principles and concerns. Every enlargement of national power will restrict state power, Yates believed. This will happen, he said, because the necessary and proper clause of Article I, section 8, may be interpreted by the federal judiciary to permit the Congress to do ". . . which in their best judgement is best." [49] To be sure, the employment of the "elastic clause" has been a source of continuing controversy over the 200-year history of the Constitution.

Though Yates approves of judicial independence, he argues that the type of independence contained in the proposed constitution was unknown anywhere in the world, including England. Judges in both England and under the proposed constitution hold office during good behavior and possess fixed salaries. In England, Parliament may override judicial decisions but no such analogous power was contemplated for the would-be Congress of the United States.[50]

Yates' interpretation of history is important. English judges were given life tenure and salary guarantees so that the king would no longer influence them to support royal claims to the detriment of the liberties of the people. The great difference is that in the United States, there is no hereditary monarch with a vested interest in maintaining power at the expense of liberty. Government officials are elected in this country by the people and are consequently controlled by them. There is no need, according to Yates, to create uncontrolled power unless the goal is autonomy, not from a despotic king, but from the democratic tendencies of a free people.[51] Alexander Hamilton addresses this very point.

The Federalist papers

As with the Antifederalists, ratification proponents of the proposed constitution published their arguments. These appeared in New York newspapers from October 27, 1787, to August 16, 1788. Alexander Hamilton, James Madison and John Jay, writing under the name "Publius," prepared 85 short essays referred to as *The Federalist*.

The influential constitutional scholar Edward S. Corwin noted:

> Hamilton's later argument in *Federalist* 78 and 81 seems to have been inspired by the effort of Yates, an opponent of the Constitution to inflate judicial review to the dimensions of a bugaboo, and thereby convert the case for it into an argument against the constitution.[52]

This seems all the more apparent when we look to *Federalist* 29, published in the *Daily Advertiser* on January 19, 1778, coincidently with the Brutus letters. Hamilton observed:

> In reading many of the publications against the Constitution, a man is apt to imagine that he is perusing some ill-written tale or romance, which, instead of natural and aggreable images, exhibits to the mind nothing but frightful and distorted shapes—"Gorgons, hydras, and chimeras dire"; discoloring and disfiguring whatever it represents, and transforming everything it touches into a monster.

Returning to this theme in *Federalist* 78, Hamilton wrote of his constitutional adversaries', ". . . rage for objection, which disorders their imaginations and judgments." He proposed, nevertheless, to discuss those unreasoned objections in the light of constitutional provision for the appointment and tenure of judges, the partition of authority to various courts and the relation of those courts to one another. Of all these, the major objection was ". . . the tenure by which the judges are to hold their places: this chiefly concerns their duration in office; the provisions for their support; and the precautions for their responsibility."

The crux of the matter lay in the constitutional provision for responsibility. Hamilton's argument is precisely what we would expect it not to be. Rather than showing the accountability of the judiciary to the people or how their will is not insulated from or independent of society, Hamilton instead showed a lack of direct responsibility, and why this should be celebrated and not dreaded. The reason, as Madison had observed in *Federalist* 48, is that tyranny should be feared from the legislative branch more than any other, due to our form of government. The sort of despotism most likely in a democratic republic would follow from " . . . the encroachments and oppressions of the representative body."

If it were most likely that tyranny were to stem from the branch of government most responsible to the very source of that tyranny, the people, then it would hardly seem wise to make the judiciary responsible to that tyrannical majority when its purpose is to check it. Thus, the criticism in "Brutus" is well-founded; judicial power may be used to check the will of the people's elected representatives.

It should be understood that Hamilton is reflecting in part the views of the commercial class in America. During the preceding decade (1777–1787), they experienced to their horror and detriment the practice of state legislatures giving in to the demands of the debtor classes. The excesses of the majority were at least one reason for scrapping the Articles of Confederation in favor of the Philadelphia proposal. Though clearly admitting that the judiciary may not be accountable to the elected representatives of the people, Hamilton argued there is no cause for alarm since the judiciary has " . . . neither FORCE nor WILL, but merely judgment; and must ultimately depend upon the executive arm even for the efficacy of its judgments." [53]

It can be discerned why the judiciary lacks force. Obviously, the judiciary must depend upon the executive branch for enforcement of its will. However, it is not so easy to understand why judicial will is only "judgment" and therefore not will. After all, if the judiciary is to check the legislative branch, it must have a will of its own, regardless of whether the success of that check depends upon executive cooperation. What Hamilton means is, insofar as the judiciary must depend upon the executive, the federal courts have no *meaningful will.*

The Court's will is not enforced unless it is also the will of the executive. Thus, while the Court and its determination of will remain independent of society in terms of responsibility, the application of that will is never independent since it occurs through the executive who is accountable. Though the judiciary can at times have a will independent of society, which differs from the will of the executive, it may not be applied, and thus is not to be feared.

Federalist 81 reinforces the view expressed in *Federalist* 78. Hamilton answers the charge " . . . the errors and usurpations of the Supreme Court . . . will be uncontrollable and remediless."

First, it is argued that the powers of the federal judiciary are no different in principle from those enjoyed by the state judiciaries. The power of courts to limit legislative acts stems from the general theory of limited government, and does not follow directly from a novel authority granted to the federal bench in the proposed constitution. Second, it is not true, as some have claimed, that state legislatures or the English Parliament may correct an undesirable court decision. In this sense, the federal judiciary under the proposed constitution would be no more uncontrollable than those in Britain and the states. The final point is a reiteration of the least dangerous branch argument made in *Federalist* 78, with an additional point. Hamilton doubts whether judicial encroachment upon legislative prerogatives would ever become extensive. If, per chance, it does, the impeachment power can be employed: "[t]his alone is a complete security." Whatever might be the merits of Hamilton's first two arguments, historical experience points to the dubious quality of the last.

Neither Robert Yates nor Alexander Hamilton believed judicial review is democratic. Yates condemned it for that reason, while Hamilton applauded it as a necessary check on the majority. There is a third view. It is best expressed by former Yale Law School Dean Eugene V. Rostow. He argues judicial review is in fact democratic.[54]

Judicial review as democratic

It is not surprising that Rostow prefaces his seminal 1952 article by acknowledging widespread "uneasiness, and even guilt" about judicial review.[55] Certainly by the end of World War II the activist posture of the Supreme Court, which resulted in striking down state and federal government economic regulation during the first third of the twentieth century, was thoroughly discredited. Judicial self-restraint had become part of the liberal credo. However, by the late 1940s and early 1950s the difficult issues reaching the Supreme Court were no longer government regulation of the economy. Rather, issues such as First Amendment questions involving communist control, religious freedom, minority rights and the application of the Bill of Rights to the states through the Due Process Clause of the Fourteenth Amendment became salient. The liberal impulse is to come to the aid of the political minority and under-represented in society. But how could the Supreme Court justify its intervention without renouncing the lessons of the past? Rostow attempts to show the way.

Rostow maintains that it is erroneous to define democracy solely in terms of people voting directly on every issue. The real task is to assure that both elected and appointed officials are ultimately responsible to the people for their acts. Moreover, Supreme Court justices are not the only governmental officers not held accountable through the electoral process. Other unelected officials such as admirals, generals and members of the independent regulatory agencies are not perceived to be acting undemocratically. Why then should Court justices be considered undemocratic?

Besides, Rostow continues,

> . . . the final responsibility of the people is appropriately guaranteed by the provisions for amending the Constitution itself, and by the benign influence of time, which changes the personnel of courts. Given the possibility of constitutional amendment, there is nothing undemocratic in having responsible and independent judges act as important constitutional mediators.[56]

Article V of the Constitution, the amendment provision, requires a two-thirds and three-fourths vote depending upon the procedures employed; and thus, Rostow has not so subtly substituted simple majority rule with extraordinary majority rule. Also note that most recent U.S. presidents have usually appointed no more than two justices to the nine-member high court, thereby requiring special patience and faith in the "benign influence of time."

For the sake of argument, one may concede Rostow's point that the Supreme Court is ultimately responsible to the people. However, this proves only that our governmental system is based on popular sovereignty. It does not prove that the Supreme Court's use of judicial review to strike down acts of representative bodies is democratic.

Among the most important ideas contributed by Rostow to the judicial review debate is the notion that the Supreme Court may contribute to democracy by helping maintain a pluralistic equilibrium in society. It can mediate conflict between political institutions to insure the maintenance of rights for all citizens.[57] One way to judge how democratic institutions may be is to study what they do. That is, the substance of decisions may be at least as important as the procedures employed to make those decisions. Rostow attacks what he regards as the over-reliance upon judicial self-restraint as a failure to ensure the democratic character of U.S. society.[58]

Thus, democracy entails more than procedural majority rule; it also entails the protection of minority rights. Indeed, for Rostow, judicial review is not only compatible with democracy, it is, in fact, democratic.

Rostow would have been more correct had he written of the compatibility of the Supreme Court's exercise of judicial review with democracy, rather than "The Democratic Character of Judicial Review." Judicial review is neither democratic nor undemocratic; rather, it is anti-democratic.

Ironically, it is precisely the anti-democratic character of judicial review that imparts a major and beneficial contribution to the democratic system of which it is a part. In Aristotelian terms, judicial review contributes to our "good democracy."

The classic distinction between bad and good democracies is crucial to a justification of judicial review. To be sure, process plays a central role in any democracy. However, it is not the whole of the matter. A good democracy is directed to the interests of the whole people, including both majorities. The Supreme Court must resist the other branches or divisions of government when they act tyrannically, whether against majorities or minorities. When the Court exercises a check against a tyrannical majority it acts in an anti-democratic fashion. But it is precisely this anti-democratic feature, known as judicial review, that makes our governmental system a good democracy.[59]

Conclusion

The exercise of judicial review has often placed the court at the heart of political controversies, and this has resulted in the posing of serious questions concerning that role.

The first concerns the origins of judicial review. Many have insisted the Court usurped law-making power when claiming this function. The writings of Judge Gibson and Louis Boudin are illustrative of this viewpoint. Others, including Justice Lurton and Charles Beard, argue there is sufficient justification to support the conclusion that the Constitution framers intended judicial review and, together with other historical evidence, point to the conclusion that it is a desirable feature of our governmental system. Still others, such as James B. Thayer, accept judicial review as an authority properly possessed, but nonetheless, counsel restraint in its employment.

It is difficult to make a case one way or the other with absolute certitude. However, judicial review is a fact of political life, usurpation or not! The Supreme Court has exercised the authority and has gotten away with it. Albeit, the use of the judicial veto has from time to time in U.S. history generated serious opposition for the Court. Yet through it all, the high bench has been able to maintain its extraordinary authority, a power masterfully seized by John Marshall in *Marbury v. Madison.*

There is a second great and difficult query surrounding the exercise of judicial review; is judicial review compatible with democracy? Unlike the first question, the answer is less doubtful, though far from definitive and unqualified.

It is significant that both Robert Yates and Alexander Hamilton agreed that judicial review is inconsistent with the democratic principle that government ought to be accountable to the people. Yet, of course, they each came to different conclusions about its desirability. Yates, the Antifederalist, argued against the proposed constitution and judicial review because the Court would constitute a will independent of society. Hamilton applauds review because the Court's independence of society would serve as a safeguard against tyranny inflicted by the elected representatives of the people.

A third view is best expressed by Eugene Rostow. It is an argument positively proclaiming the democratic character of judicial review. According to this view, the judiciary is accountable to the people for its decisions. Further, judicial review must not be assessed solely in procedural terms; it also most be judged in terms of the ends it serves. Therefore, to the extent judicial review protects precious rights and liberties, it is consistent with democratic theory, and the justices of the Supreme Court should feel no guilt about its use.

There is at least one additional view. Judicial review is neither democratic nor undemocratic. Rather, it is anti-democratic. Because it is anti-democratic, it is consistent with the Aristotelian notion of a "good democracy." Therefore, we applaud judicial review as a functional tool in the service of important democratic values. While review is anti-democratic, it is nonetheless compatible with democracy; it operates to guard against threats to liberty and human happiness.

Whatever the legitimacy of its origins, judicial review may be justified in terms of democratic theory. It is also clear that many proponents of judicial supremacy find it difficult to defend. This is especially true when Court decisions seem removed from prevailing public opinion. Obviously, not all exercises of judicial review have placed the Court under severe attack. The justices themselves have attempted to protect the Court from attack through the exercise of judicial self-restraint. However, rational political calculation is not the only explanation for this behavior. No doubt, as Eugene Rostow explained, there is a sense of guilt surrounding the use of the judicial veto. It is an uneasiness that does not seem to disappear, despite repeated usage and the passing of time.

Supreme Court justices, judges of other courts, constitutional scholars, bar association representatives, members of Congress, the executive branch and others, have felt compelled to justify the Court's power. Though no responsible public figure has in recent years called for the end to judicial review, there have been forcefully presented criticisms of its uses and alleged misuses.

Contemporary conservatives such as Chief Justice William Rehnquist and Judge Robert Bork have written and spoken about the importance of exercising judicial self-restraint. Justice William Brennan and Judge Frank Johnson, who many would characterize as liberals, are representative of those arguing for the importance of an activist posture. Courts must function to articulate and protect valuable constitutional rights, so goes the refrain. President Ronald Reagan's Justice Department speaks of the Jurisprudence of Original Intention when interpreting constitutional provisions.[60] At the same time, there have been recurrent calls for Court curbing, including the introduction of legislation that would remove appellate jurisdiction from the Supreme Court to hear cases involving certain controversial issues.[61]

We believe the recurring debate about the Court's role is traceable to the fundamental question of legitimacy centering around the usurpation and compatibility issues. However, what is rarely acknowledged, and will be denied by many, is an underlying uncertainty about whether ordinary Americans can understand the intellectual justification for judicial review without coming to a conclusion that may contribute to the instability of the political system. A recently reported empirical study found that public confidence in the incumbents of the Court is related to judicial activism. The conventional wisdom that the Court skates on thin ice when it invalidates federal statutes is substantiated by the data.[62] However, confidence in particular justices of the Supreme Court is probably different from support for the Court as an institution. Empirical studies demonstrate that while specific support for Court decisions may wane from time to time, diffuse support for the Supreme Court remains relatively high and favorable.[63] It is also true that political elites have a tendency to come to the aid of the Court when direct institutional attacks are made upon its authority.[64] We do not have convincing empirical evidence linking a diminution of public confidence in Supreme Court justices or in the exercise of judicial review with a drastic decline in diffuse support. Nevertheless, it is conceivable that at some point public acquiescence may turn to intolerance, resulting in the removal of the deep reservoir of public support necessary for the Court to continue its historic role in U.S. politics.

Paradoxically, because the judicial review debate refuses to disappear, the use of that power is made more secure. Proponents and opponents of the judicial veto are compelled to carefully assess and reassess its costs against its benefits. The debate serves as a reminder to all that in a democratic society all power must be limited.

Notes

This article originally appeared in Volume 71, Number 4, December–January 1988, pages 202–210. It is based on the authors' book, *Judicial Review and American Democracy*, published in 1988 by Iowa State University Press; reprinted by Beard Book in 2004.

1. *See* Judge Gibson's argument in *Eakin v. Raub*, 12 S.&R. 330 (Pa. 1825).

2. 5 U.S. (Cranch) 137, 2 L. Ed. 60.

3. Beard, "The Supreme Court—Usurper or Grantee?" *Pol. Sci. Q.* 27 (1912), 1.

4. Horwitz, *The Courts and Social Policy* (Washington, D.C.: Brookings Institution, 1977).

5. Grey, "Do We Have an Unwritten Constitution?", 27 *Stan. L. Rev.* 703–718 (1975); Berger, *Government by Judiciary: The Transformation of the Fourteenth Amendment* (Cambridge, Mass.: Harvard University Press, 1977); Ely, *Democracy and Distrust* (Cambridge, Mass.: Harvard University Press, 1981); The Federalist Society, *The Great Debate: Interpreting Our Written Constitution* (Washington, D.C.: The Federalist Society, 1986).

6. 12 S.&R. at 343–381 (Pa. 1825).

7. Mason, Beaney, and Stephenson, *American Constitutional Law: Introductory Essays and Selected Cases*, 7th ed. (Englewood Cliffs, N.J.: Prentice-Hall, 1983), 50.

8. *Eakin v. Raub*, 12 S.&R. at 346.

9. Ibid. at 347.

10. Melone, "System Support Politics and the Congressional Court of Appeals," *N.D.L. Rev.* 51 (1975), 597–613; also see special issue of 69 *Judicature* (October 1981).

11. *Eakin v. Raub*, 12 S.&R. at 351–352.

12. Ibid. at 352–353.

13. Ibid. at 353–354.

14. Ibid. at 354–355.

15. Mason, Beaney and Stephenson, *supra* n. 7.

16. Published as: Thayer, "The Origin and Scope of the American Doctrine of Constitutional Law," *Harv. L. Rev.* 7 (1896), 129–156.

17. Ibid. at 136.

18. Ibid. at 151.

19. Ibid. at 152.

20. Mendelson, *Supreme Court Statecraft: The Rule of Law and Men* (Ames: Iowa State University Press, 1985), 5–17.

21. Lurton, "A Government of Law Or A Government of Men?" *N. Am. Rev.* 193 (1911), 9–25.

22. Ibid. at 13.

23. Ibid. at 17.

24. Ibid. at 19.

25. Boudin, "Government by Judiciary," *Pol. Sci. Q.* 26 (1911), 238–270.

26. Ibid. at 243–247.

27. Ibid. at 248.

28. Ibid. at 253.

29. Ibid. at 254–256.

30. Ibid. at 264.

31. Ibid. at 267.

32. Beard, *supra* n. 3.

33. Ibid. at 3.

34. Ibid.

35. *Courts, Judges, & Politics*, 4th ed. (New York: Random House, 1986), 485–486.

36. Beard, *supra* n. 3, at 3–4.

37. Ibid. at 19.

38. Ibid.

39. *The Doctrine of Judicial Review* (Gloucester, Mass.: Peter Smith, 1963), 11 .

40. Beard, *supra* n. 3, at 24.

41. Ibid. at 24–28.

42. Ibid. at 22.

43. Ibid. at 32–34.

44. Berger, "The Doctrine of Judicial Review: Mr. Marshall, Mr. Jefferson and Mr. Marbury," in Cannon and O'Brien (eds.), *Views From the Bench: The Judiciary and Constitutional Politics* (Chatham, N.J.: Chatham House, 1985), 8.

45. Allen and Lloyds, eds., *The Essential Anti–Federalist* (Washington, D.C.: University Press of America, 1985), viii–xiv.

46. *Brutus* XI.

47. Ibid.

48. *Brutus* XII.

49. Ibid.

50. *Brutus* XV.

51. Ibid.

52. *Court Over Constitution* (Glouster, Mass.: Peter Smith, 1957), 45–46.

53. *Federalist* 78.

54. Rostow, "The Democratic Character of Judicial Review," *Harv. L. Rev.* 66 (1952), 193–224.

55. Ibid. at 193.

56. Ibid. at 197.

57. Ibid. at 203–210.

58. Ibid. at 210–223.

59. Mace, "The Anti–Democratic Character of Judicial Review," *Cal. L. Rev.* 60 (1972), 1140–1149.

60. For a convenient compilation of recent speeches, see, *The Great Debate, supra* n. 5, especially speeches by Attorney General Edwin Meese and Justice William J. Brennan Jr.

61. *Supra* n. 10.

62. Caldeira, "Neither the Purse Nor the Sword: Dynamics of Public Confidence in the Supreme Court," *Am. Pol. Sci. Rev.* 80 (1986), 1222.

63. Murphy and Tanenhaus, "Public Opinion and the United States Supreme Court: A Preliminary Mapping of Some Prerequisites for Court Legitimation of Regime Changes," *L. & Soc'y Rev.* 2 (1968), 357–382; Murphy, Tanenhaus and Kastner, *Public Evaluations of Constitutional Courts: Alternative Explanations* (Beverly Hills: Sage Publications, 1973); Tanenhaus and Murphy, "Patterns of Public Support for the Supreme Court: A Panel Study," *J. of Pol.* 43 (1981), 24–39.

64. Melone, *supra* n. 10.

The judiciary is too powerful

Clifford Taylor

In overturning the actions of the people's elected representatives, are judges undermining America's republican form of government?

We are living through a period of an unprecedented decline in legislative power to set public policy. The reason for this is that the judiciary has increasingly muscled legislatures out of the way.

To appreciate the import of this, it is important to recall that our government, as established, was one where the people, speaking though their representatives in the legislature, established laws, the executive carried them out, and the judiciary had the modest role of adjudicating disputes that arose under the statutes.

At no time was it contemplated, much less claimed by the most zealous advocates of judicial power, that the courts should be in the policy-making role. That was for the legislature. There, with robust debate, few rules of evidence, and easy entry of unpopular and poorly financed views, the people could be sovereign.

The Constitution made only a few areas off limits to the will of the majority. They are set forward, for the most part, in the Bill of Rights.

While this separation of powers still exists, few could doubt that much of the power to set policy has shifted from the legislative arena into the judicial. The courts have done this by the use of an ancient tool, judicial review of legislation, used in a new and quite undisciplined fashion, with the result being that courts, not legislatures, are now in control of important agendas of American life.

It has been accurately said that more public policy is determined on an average Monday in June by the U.S. Supreme Court when it issues its decisions than by Congress during an entire session. This is a remarkable development, one that should concern not only those with legislative responsibilities, but also each of us as citizens who speak through our legislators and, thus, wish to preserve legislative policy making.

Properly understood, judicial review derives from the necessity to decide a case or controversy in which one party is relying on the law and the other is relying on the Constitution, and where the law and the Constitution are in conflict. In that rare situation, the Constitution prevails over the statute. This is an American law concept that was developed by Chief Justice John Marshall in the famous case of *Marbury v. Madison* in 1803. It was needed to establish supremacy of our written Constitution (the first in the world) over legislative enactments.

In exercising judicial review, the Constitution was to be read in a common-sense fashion, and the courts were deferential to the elected representatives of "we the people." The goal was to attempt to determine the understanding of the words used in the Constitution at the time of adoption. This wasn't an exercise that was intended to be complicated. The dictionary or common-law tradition was the principal tool to determine meaning, just as one would with a contract or a bill of sale. The idea was that the Constitution was a document meant to be understood by the people, not just by lawyers. And, at the end of the consideration of the statute, the statute was not to be held to be in conflict with the Constitution if, by any construction, it could be held to be harmonious.

Eroded restraint

This restraint or discipline has been, in this century, greatly eroded. On the basis of highly debatable and novel theories, courts read into the Constitution their own ideas about what constitutes wise policy and strain to find statutes that offend their notion of what the people should want unconstitutional. To get an idea of this, the most recent theory set forward by the U.S. Supreme Court in *Planned Parenthood v. Casey* says that our Constitution, which you will recall was a late 18th century document, notwithstanding no words to this effect, was written to establish the liberty to "define one's own concept of existence, of meaning, of the universe, and of the mystery of human life."

The result of judicial review gone astray has been that, increasingly, many important areas of American cultural or political life are no longer in control of the people through their elected representatives, but are more and more controlled by judges. For example, if the legislature decides that it wishes to move in the areas of welfare rights, term limits, crime, punishment, and prisons, the courts are almost invariably invited, by those who lost in the political arena, to replace the pol-

Judicature Volume 82, Number 1, pp. 28, 30–32

icy of the legislature with a policy that is more congenial to the petitioners and, hopefully, the judges.

Similarly, the courts seem disposed to displace legislative determinations on moral questions such as who can and cannot get married, or what lifestyle forms are acceptable or unacceptable. Indeed, when the people, either through the legislature or by referendum, act in areas such as homosexual rights, vagrancy, homelessness, panhandling, nude dancing, pornography, and other forms of explicit sexual activity they feel produce moral chaos, the courts, on what seems to be in some cases highly debatable constitutional grounds, step in to displace the people's choices with the court's.

Of those who are alarmed by this trend toward judicial supremacy, few are more outspoken than Harvard law professor Mary Anne Glendon, who traces it, simply stated, to the notion among certain well-educated individuals that the educated are better equipped to govern than the masses. She argues that these elites have a disdain for ordinary politics and the legislative process.

It is hard to read the scholarly legal defenses of this growth of judicial power and not agree. This issue was also put forward with great force by Judge Andrew Kleinfeld of the U.S. Court of Appeals for the Ninth Circuit in his dissent in the "right to die" litigation when he said, "That a question is important does not imply that it is constitutional. The Founding Fathers did not establish the United States as a democratic republic so that elected officials would decide trivia, while all great questions would be decided by the judiciary."

Government by judiciary

Frequently, when this is pointed out and even acknowledged, the response is to assert that the alarm giver just doesn't like the thrust of the decisions—that is, that he or she would simply prefer different outcomes. This is a red herring and an unfortunate trivialization of a significant constitutional issue. Indeed, I want to go so far as to suggest that the outcomes of these cases are not what should be alarming: Rather, what is most disturbing is that we are witnessing a movement to, as Robert Bork describes it, government by judiciary with decisions further and further removed from the moorings of original meaning and the intent of the drafters of the Constitution.

This means that we are moving in a direction to deprive each and every one of us in our capacities as citizens of our right to self-government. The issue is not liberal or conservative policy results, but who is entitled to make decisions about the direction of our society. After all, when something is declared a constitutional right, it simply means that the people and those holding their voice—the legislators—are forever silenced on the topic (unless, of course, a constitutional amendment can be effected, which is so difficult to do that it isn't much of a remedy). This precludes effective debate, discussion, and compromise. The issue goes in the constitutional deep-freeze and is off limits to the people. This has many effects.

The first, as I've mentioned, is a reduction of the ability of the people to set their own agenda.

The second effect, which is also alarming, has been to change the judiciary and how it is perceived. When the judiciary simply accepted the policy choices of the legislature, the importance of a judge's political and policy views were nearly irrelevant. However, when the courts could displace a policy they disliked with one perceived to be more enlightened or beneficial on the claimed basis that the policy violated the Constitution, it became clear that the politics of the judge were all important. After all, if judges are to determine issues like abortion, school prayer, homosexual rights, and the death penalty, it suddenly makes a difference what they think about these issues. Thus, the sad spectacle of the Bork and Thomas confirmation hearings that took place at the federal level.

In Michigan, as in other states such as Florida, Alabama, and Texas, the last several supreme court races have become, for all intents and purposes, partisan political races. Special interests on both sides increasingly spend huge sums in an effort to elect persons with whom they expect to share policy positions. Both these developments are recent and traceable, I believe, to the expanded power the courts have assumed. After all, with power comes, reasonably enough, an interest by those affected in how it is exercised. Judges, rather than being seen as having no ax to grind, will be, and are increasingly seen as, practicing politics by another name.

Further, judicial decisions are different from legislative decisions. There are no compromises, no half-loaves, no give-and-take. It's all or nothing, and one can't, unlike a legislative decision, modify it if it doesn't work, absent the court overruling itself or the people utilizing the constitutional amendment process, which is very rare.

This point was well made by U.S. Supreme Court Justice Antonin Scalia in his dissent in the Virginia Military Institute case. He said, "A virtue of the democratic system with a First Amendment is that it readily enables the people, over time, to be persuaded that what they took for granted is not so, and to change their laws accordingly. That system is destroyed if the smug assurances of each age are removed from the democratic process and written into the Constitution."

Currently, legislatures seem passive, even apologetic, when the courts aggressively enter the political arena. Witness the legislative reaction to the Michigan courts' handling of emergency assistance, general assistance, campaign finance reform, teacher strike legislation, charter schools, executive branch reorganizations, and liability reform, to name but several recent exercises of judicial review. While some of these rulings may have been legitimate exercises of judicial power, the legislature, almost always, accepts each arrogation of power with resignation, rather than with perplexity or even outrage.

Indeed, it is enough to cause the suspicion that some legislators seem to appreciate having "tough" decisions made by the judiciary. Perhaps, aware of what is at stake institutionally, a little less comity and toleration would be appropriate in view of courts' disinterest in separation of powers.

Restoring the balance

What is to be done? I would modestly suggest that legislative staff should monitor court decisions. When a court oversteps, there could be legislative reaction in the form of thoughtful press comment and, also, if possible, appropriate formal legislative action so as to undo the judicial usurpation. This should not be merely a reflexive irritation at every exercise of judicial review because, as is obvious, there are occasions when we would all agree that it has been appropriately exercised, but on those occasions where that cannot be said, the comment would be justified.

Further, legislation could be considered to require notification of the leaders of both chambers of the legislature, as well as the governor and attorney general, when an issue of a statute's constitutionality has been raised, or if that is too onerous, to require a trial court to notify them when a statute has been declared unconstitutional. Intervention by the legislature with amicus briefs could then be contemplated, and the fate of the statute on appeal may not be left to the vicissitudes of the representation that the parties might chose. Such parties may, and likely would, have little interest in the preservation of the constitutional prerogatives of the legislature.

Also, I believe that the legislature could require the appellate courts to give docket priority to appeals of statute constitutionality so that they are decided with dispatch. In addition, the legislature could consider limiting the time that stays or injunctions of a statute can be in place without a final adjudication, so as to effectively accomplish the same result.

Similarly, citizens' and other groups should pay attention. This also may require a formal monitoring of decisions and focusing public attention on offending decisions and judges who authored them. There is little of this now. It can be seen in the puzzling endorsements many judicial candidates secure. What could be more curious than groups supporting judges, and even endorsing them, with no knowledge that they have an agenda that is perhaps hostile to the groups' interests, to say nothing of being dismissive of the virtues of the democratic process.

Over time, perhaps judges will take note of these forms of scrutiny and hopefully, having been chastened or even embarrassed, be less inclined to undertake unwarranted incursions into judicial activism in the future.

While doubts can be raised on the basis of the federal court experience that, having secured power, courts will be willing to yield it up, we can only rely on the intellectual strength of an understood separation-of-powers jurisprudence to appeal to the future members of the judiciary. Plus, such a restrained understanding of the role of the courts in the current electoral environment of many states, with its temptations to assume power so as to assuage political allies, is an unlikely environment in which such an approach will flourish.

Finally, I believe that we have an obligation to those who come after us to understand and begin to address this issue because it affects a most basic right—the right, guaranteed by the Constitution, to live under a republican form of government. The legislature's role, regrettably, is much diminished from a generation or two ago. It will be further diminished a generation or two from now if people don't assert themselves. As a result, American self-government and self-determination will also be diminished.

This article originally appeared in Volume 82, Number 1, July–August 1998, pages 28, 30–32. It was reprinted with permission of the Michigan Bar Journal.

Interpreting the Constitution: the case for judicial restraint

J. Clifford Wallace

Our constitutional plan was never meant to allow judges to impose their values instead of the original intent of the framers.

This year we celebrate the 200th anniversary of our Constitution. This remarkable document has structured our government and secured our liberty as we have developed from 13 fledgling colonies into a mature and strong democracy. Without doubt, the Constitution is one of the grandest political achievements of the modern world.

In spite of this marvelous record, we will celebrate our nation's charter in the midst of a hotly contested debate on the continuing role that it should have in our society. Two schools of constitutional jurisprudence are engaged in a long-running battle. Some contend that the outcome of this conflict may well determine whether the Constitution remains our vital organic document or whether it instead becomes a curious historical relic. The competing positions in this constitutional battle are often summarized by a variety of labels: judicial restraint versus judicial activism, strict construction versus loose construction, positivism versus natural law, conservative versus liberal, interpretivism versus noninterpretivism.

In large measure, these labels alone are of little assistance in analyzing a complex problem. Ultimately, what is at stake is what Constitution will govern this country. Will it be the written document drafted by the framers, ratified by the people, and passed down, with amendments, to us? Or will it be an illusive parchment upon which modern-day judges may freely engrave their own political and sociological preferences?

In this article, I intend to outline and defend a constitutional jurisprudence of judicial restraint.[1] My primary thesis is that a key principle of judicial restraint—namely, interpretivism—is required by our constitutional plan. I will also explore how practitioners of judicial restraint should resolve the tension that can arise in our current state of constitutional law between interpretivism and a second important principle, respect for judicial precedent.

Interpretivism vs. noninterpretivism

What is the difference between "interpretivism" and "noninterpretivism"? This question is important because I believe interpretivism to be the cornerstone of a constitutional jurisprudence of judicial restraint. By "interpretivism," I mean the principle that judges, in resolving constitutional questions, should rely on the express provisions of the Constitution or upon those norms that are clearly implicit in its text.[2] Under an interpretivist approach, the original intention of the framers is the controlling guide for constitutional interpretation. This does not mean, of course, that judges may apply a constitutional provision only to situations specifically contemplated by the framers. Rather, it simply requires that when considering whether to invalidate the work of the political branches, the judges do so from a starting point fairly discoverable in the Constitution.[3] By contrast, under noninterpretive review, judges may freely rest their decisions on value judgments that admittedly are not supported by, and may even contravene, the text of the Constitution and the intent of the framers.[4]

Interpretivist review

I believe that the Constitution itself envisions and requires interpretivist review. To explore this thesis, we should first examine the Constitution as a political and historical document.

As people read the Constitution, many are struck by how procedural and technical its provisions are. Perhaps on first reading it may be something of a disappointment. In contrast to the fiery eloquence of the Declaration of Independence, the Constitution may seem dry or even dull. This difference in style, of course, reflects the very different functions of the two documents. The Declaration of Independence is an indictment of the reign of King George III. In a flamboyant tone, it is brilliantly crafted to persuade the

Judicature Volume 71, Number 2, pp. 81–84

world of the justice of our fight for independence. The Constitution, by contrast, establishes the basic set of rules for the nation. Its genius lies deeper, in its skillful design of a government structure that would best ensure liberty and democracy.

The primary mechanism by which the Constitution aims to protect liberty and democracy is the dispersion of government power. Recognizing that concentrated power poses the threat of tyranny, the framers divided authority between the states and the federal government. In addition, they created three separate and co-equal branches of the federal government in a system of checks and balances.

The framers were also aware, of course, that liberty and democracy can come into conflict. The Constitution, therefore, strikes a careful balance between democratic rule and minority rights. Its republican, representative features are designed to channel and refine cruder majoritarian impulses. In addition, the Constitution's specific individual protections, particularly in the Bill of Rights, guarantee against certain majority intrusions. Beyond these guarantees, the Constitution places its trust in the democratic process—the voice of the people expressed through their freely elected representatives.

Raoul Berger argues persuasively in *Government by Judiciary* that the Constitution "was written against a background of interpretive presuppositions that assured the Framers their design would be effectuated." [5] The importance of that statement may escape us today, when it is easy to take for granted that the Constitution is a written document. But for the framers, the fact that the Constitution was in writing was not merely incidental. They recognized that a written constitution provides the most stable basis for the rule of law, upon which liberty and justice ultimately depend.

As Thomas Jefferson observed, "Our peculiar security is in the possession of a written constitution. Let us not make it a blank paper by construction." [6] Chief Justice John Marshall, in *Marbury v. Madison,* the very case establishing the power of judicial review, emphasized the constraints imposed by the written text and the judicial duty to respect these constraints in all cases raising constitutional questions.[7]

Moreover, the framers recognized the importance of interpreting the Constitution according to their original intent. In Madison's words, if "the sense in which the Constitution was accepted and ratified by the Nation . . . be not the guide in expounding it, there can be no security for a consistent and stable govern-

ment, [nor] for a faithful exercise of its powers." [8] Similarly, Jefferson as president acknowledged his duty to administer the Constitution "according to the safe and honest meaning contemplated by the plain understanding of the people at the time of its adoption—a meaning to be found in the explanations of those who advocated . . . it." [9] It seems clear, therefore, that the leading framers were interpretivists and believed that constitutional questions should be reviewed by that approach.

Next, I would like to consider whether interpretivism is necessary to effectuate the constitutional plan. The essential starting point is that the Constitution established a separation of powers to protect our freedom. Because freedom is fundamental, so too is the separation of powers. But separation of powers becomes a meaningless slogan if judges may confer constitutional status on whichever rights they happen to deem important, regardless of textual basis. In effect, under noninterpretive review, the judiciary functions as a superlegislature beyond the check of the other two branches. Noninterpretivist review also disregards the Constitution's careful allocation of most decisions to the democratic process, allowing the legislature to make decisions deemed best for society. Ultimately, noninterpretivist review reduces our written Constitution to insignificance and threatens to impose a tyranny of the judiciary.

Prudential considerations

Important prudential considerations also weigh heavily in favor of interpretivist review. The rule of law is fundamental in our society. To be effective, it cannot be tossed to and fro by each new sociological wind. Because it is rooted in written text, interpretivist review promotes the stability and predictability essential to the rule of law. By contrast, noninterpretivist review presents an infinitely variable array of possibilities. The Constitution would vary with each judge's conception of what is important. To demonstrate the wide variety of tests that could be applied, let us briefly look at the writings of legal academics who advocate noninterpretivism.

Assume each is a judge deciding the same constitutional issue. One professor seeks to "cement[] a union between the distributional patterns of the modern welfare state and the federal constitution." Another "would guarantee a whole range of nontextually based rights against government to ensure 'the dignity of full membership in society.' " A third argues that the courts should give "concrete meaning and application" to those values that "give our society an identity and inner coherence [and] its distinctive public morality." Yet another professor sees the court as having a "prophetic" role in developing moral standards in a "dialectical relationship" with Congress, from which he sees emerging a "more mature" political morality. One professor even urges that the court apply the contractarian moral theory of Professor Rawls' *A Theory of Justice* to constitutional questions.[10] One can easily see the fatal vagueness and subjectivity of this approach: each judge would apply his or her own separate and diverse personal values in interpreting the same constitutional question. Without anchor, we drift at sea.

Another prudential argument against noninterpretivism is that judges are not particularly well-suited to make judgments of broad social policy. We judges decide cases on the basis of a limited record that largely represents the efforts of the parties to the litigation. Legislators, with their committees, hearings, and more direct role in the political process, are much better equipped institutionally to decide what is best for society.

Noninterpretivist arguments

But are there arguments in favor of non-interpretivism? Let us consider several assertions commonly put forth by proponents. One argument asserts that certain constitutional provisions invite judges to import into the constitutional decision process value judgments derived from outside the Constitution. Most commonly, advocates of this view rely on the due process clause of the Fifth and Fourteenth Amendments. It is true that courts have interpreted the due process clause to authorize broad review of the substantive merits of legislation. But is that what the draftsmen had in mind? Some constitutional scholars make a strong argument that the clause, consistent with its plain language, was intended to have a limited procedural meaning.[11]

A second argument asserts that the meaning of the constitutional text and the intention of the framers cannot be ascertained with sufficient precision to guide constitutional decision making. I readily acknowledge that interpretivism will not always provide easy answers to difficult constitutional questions. The judicial role will always involve the exercise of discretion. The strength of interpretivism is that it channels and constrains this discretion in a manner consistent with the Constitution. While it does not necessarily ensure a cor-

rect result, it does exclude from consideration entire ranges of improper judicial responses.

Third, some have suggested that the Fourteenth Amendment effected such a fundamental revision in the nature of our government that the intentions of the original framers are scarcely relevant any longer. It is, of course, true that federal judges have seized upon the Fourteenth Amendment as a vehicle to restructure federal/state relations. The argument, however, is not one-sided. Berger, for example, persuasively demonstrates that the framers of the Fourteenth Amendment sought much more limited objectives.[12] In addition, one reasonable interpretation of the history of the amendment demonstrates that its framers, rather than intending an expanded role for the federal courts, meant for Congress (under section 5 of the amendment) to play the primary role in enforcing its provisions.[13] Thus, it can be argued that to the extent that the Fourteenth Amendment represented an innovation in the constitutional role of the judiciary, it was by limiting the courts' traditional role in enforcing constitutional rights and by providing added responsibility for the Congress.

Advocates of noninterpretivism also contend that we should have a "living Constitution" rather than be bound by "the dead hand of the framers." These slogans prove nothing. An interpretivist approach would not constrict government processes; on the contrary, it would ensure that issues are freely subject to the workings of the democratic process. Moreover, to the extent that the Constitution might profit from revision, the amendment process of Article V provides the only constitutional means. Judicial amendment under a noninterpretivist approach is simply an unconstitutional usurpation.

Almost certainly, the greatest support for a noninterpretive approach derives from its perceived capacity to achieve just results. Why quibble over the Constitution, after all, if judges who disregard it nevertheless "do justice"? Such a view is dangerously shortsighted and naive. In the first place, one has no cause to believe that the results of noninterpretivism will generally be "right." Individual judges have widely varying conceptions of what values are important. Noninterpretists spawned the "conservative" substantive economic due process of the 1930s as well as the "liberal" decisions of the Warren Court. There is no principled result in noninterpretivism.

But even if the judge would always be right, the process would be wrong. A benevolent judicial tyranny is nonetheless a tyranny. Our Constitution rests on the faith that democracy is intrinsically valuable. From an instrumental perspective, democracy might at times produce results that are not as desirable as platonic guardians might produce. But the democratic process—our participation in a system of self-government—has transcendental value. Moreover, one must consider the very real danger that an activist judiciary stunts the development of a responsible democracy by removing from it the duty to make difficult decisions. If we are to remain faithful to the values of democracy and liberty, we must insist that courts respect the Constitution's allocation of social decision making to the political branches.

Respect for precedent

I emphasized earlier the importance of stability to the rule of law. I return to that theme now to consider a second principle of judicial restraint: respect for precedent. Respect for precedent is a principle widely accepted, even if not always faithfully followed. It requires simply that a judge follow prior case law in deciding legal questions. Respect for precedent promotes predictability and uniformity. It constrains a judge's discretion and satisfies the reasonable expectations of the parties. Through its application, citizens can have a better understanding of what the law is and act accordingly.

Unfortunately, in the present state of constitutional law, the two principles of judicial restraint that I have outlined can come into conflict. While much of constitutional law is consistent with the principle of interpretivism, a significant portion is not. This raises the question how a practitioner of judicial restraint should act in circumstances where respecting precedent would require acceptance of law developed under a noninterpretivist approach.

The answer is easy for a judge in my position, and, indeed, for any judge below the United States Supreme Court. As a judge on the Ninth Circuit Court of Appeals, I am bound to follow Supreme Court and Ninth Circuit precedent even when I believe it to be wrong. There is a distinction, however, between following precedent and extending it. Where existing precedent does not fairly govern a legal question, the principle of interpretivism should guide a judge.

For Supreme Court justices, the issue is more complex. The Supreme Court obviously is not infallible. Throughout its history, the Court has at times rejected its own precedents. Because the Supreme Court has the ultimate judicial say on what the Constitution means, its justices have a special responsibility to ensure that they are properly expounding constitutional law as well as fostering stability and predictability.

Must Supreme Court advocates of judicial restraint passively accept the errors of activist predecessors? There is little rational basis for doing so. Periodic activist inroads could emasculate fundamental doctrines and undermine the separation of powers. Nevertheless, the values of predictability and uniformity that respect for precedent promotes demand caution in overturning precedent. In my view, a justice should consider overturning a prior decision only when the decision is clearly wrong, has significant effects, and would otherwise be difficult to remedy.

Significantly, constitutional decisions based on a noninterpretivist approach may satisfy these three criteria. When judges confer constitutional status on their own value judgments without support in the language of the Constitution and the original intention of the framers, they commit clear error. Because constitutional errors frequently affect the institutional structure of government and the allocation of decisions to the democratic process, they are likely to have important effects. And because constitutional decisions, unlike statutory decisions, cannot be set aside through normal political channels, they will generally meet the third requirement. In sum, then, despite the prudential interests furthered by respect for precedent, advocates of judicial restraint may be justified in seeking to overturn noninterpretivist precedent.

Conclusion

It is obvious that courts employing interpretivist review cannot solve many of the social and political problems facing America, indeed, even some very important problems. The interpretivist would respond that the Constitution did not place the responsibility for solving those problems with the courts. The courts were not meant to govern the core of our political and social life—Article I gave that duty, for national issues, to the Congress. It is through our democratically elected representatives that we legitimately develop this fabric of our life. Interpretivism encourages that process. It is, therefore, closer to the constitutional plan of governance than is noninterpretivist review.

After 200 years, the Constitution is not "broke"—we need not fix it—just apply it.

Notes

This article originally appeared in Volume 71, Number 2, August–September 1987, pages 81–84. It is adapted from an address given at Hillsdale College, Hillsdale, Michigan, on March 5, 1986.

1. I have elsewhere presented various aspects of this jurisprudence. *See, e.g.,* Wallace, "A Two Hundred Year Old Constitution in Modern Society," *Tex. L. Rev.* 61 (1983), 1575; Wallace, "The Jurisprudence of Judicial Restraint: A Return to the Moorings," *Geo. Wash. L. Rev.* 50 (1981), 1.

2. Wallace, "A Two Hundred Year Old Constitution," *supra* n. 1; Ely, *Democracy and Distrust* (Cambridge: Harvard University Press, 1980), 1.

3. Ely, *supra* n. 2, at 2.

4. *See* ibid. at 43–72.

5. Berger, *Government by Judiciary* (Cambridge: Harvard University Press, 1977), 366.

6. Ibid. at 364, *quoting* Letter of Wilson Cary Nicholas (Sept. 7, 1803).

7. *Marbury v. Madison,* 5 U.S. (1 Cranch) 137, (1803), 176–180.

8. Berger, *supra* n. 5, at 364, *quoting The Writings of James Madison* (G. Hunt ed. 1900–1910), 191.

9. Ibid. at 366–367, *citing* 4 Elliot, *Debates in the Several State Conventions on the Adoption of the Federal Constitution* (1836), 446.

10. Monaghan, "Our Perfect Constitution," *N.Y.U. L. Rev.* 56 (1981), 353, 358–360 (summarizing theories of noninterpretivists).

11. *See, e.g.,* Berger, *supra* n. 5, at 193–220.

12. *See* ibid.

13. *See* ibid. at 220–29.

Judicial review is exercised properly

Avern Cohn

The view of some legislators, columnists, and even judges that the judiciary these days has, in Justice Taylor's words, "increasingly muscled the Legislature out of the way" displays a considerable lack of understanding of the institutional role that judges play in our constitutional scheme and reflects little knowledge of history. This view also expresses a lack of confidence in a legislature's ability to maintain its status as a co-equal branch of government, as well as a belief that the people have little knowledge of the judicial branch's daily activities in resolving a myriad of disputes.

It is wrong to suggest that judicial "restraint or discipline has been, in this century, greatly eroded." From the inception of the republic, there have been differing views about the proper scope of judicial authority and the role of judges with conflicting views over what the Constitution says. Justice David Souter, in his concurring opinion in *Washington v. Glucksberg,* canvasses very well the history of the shifting approaches to constitutional interpretation over the last 200 years.

A similar position, that at first "the judiciary had the modest role of adjudicating disputes that arose under the statutes" and "[t]he Constitution made only a few areas off limits to the will of the majority," is also flawed. To begin with, no distinction is made between the Constitution of 1789, which condoned slavery, and the new Constitution created by the Civil War amendments, under which we now live. Further, the view fails to appreciate the important role that the common law has played in establishing the rules of law under which we live.

The real concern with the so-called erosion in judicial restraint is not with how judges go about deciding cases, but with what judges say—that is, with the results reached in the decisions. This is clear from the litany of supposed judicial encroachments: abortion, parental rights, homosexual rights, welfare rights, term limits, the death penalty, prayer in public schools, vagrancy and homelessness, and various forms of explicit sexual activity. Always inexplicably absent from the list, at least in Michigan, is assisted suicide as a judge-made crime. See *People v. Kevorkian* as a classic

example of judges making a public policy pronouncement, and with a real sting.

Often cited as an egregious example of judicial activism is the preliminary injunction against the implementation of California Proposition 209 by U.S. District Judge Thelton E. Henderson in San Francisco in November 1996. Careful examination of the record in the Proposition 209 case points out what a poor example this is, and supports the belief that philippics attacking Judge Henderson are merely disagreements with his initial decision to issue a preliminary injunction.

Proposition 209, which added a provision to the California Constitution prohibiting race- and gender-based affirmative action, was adopted by initiative on November 5, 1996, after a contentious debate in which opponents vigorously argued that it violated federal law and that hence the Supremacy Clause of the U.S. Constitution made it nugatory. Consistent with Alexis de Tocqueville's 1835 observation that there is seldom a political question in America that does not end up as a judicial question, opponents of the proposition went to federal court to enjoin its effectiveness. Judge Henderson issued a preliminary injunction against it becoming effective, reasoning in an extensive opinion that it appeared unconstitutional. Admittedly, the question of the proposition's constitutionality is not easy to answer. Hard cases frequently have no single answer. Judge Henderson clearly decided the case on the facts as he found them and the law as he understood it.

The proponents of Proposition 209, dissatisfied with the district court's decision, exercised their right to go to the U.S. Court of Appeals for the Ninth Circuit in an effort to stay the preliminary injunction. There, on February 10, 1997, the panel of judges to whom the motion for stay was assigned did not immediately rule on the motion. Rather, the panel deferred consideration and ordered the merits of the appeal briefed. Almost two months later, the panel reversed Judge Henderson's decision on the basis of a finding that Proposition 209 did not violate the U.S. Constitution. Only after en banc review was denied, and not without

Judicature Volume 82, Number 1, pp. 29, 32–34

opposition, did Proposition 209 go into effect, on August 28, 1997.

Hard cases

The course of Proposition 209 in court was neither extraordinary nor abusive. Likewise, the disagreement between Judge Henderson, who found Proposition 209 constitutionally flawed, and the panel of the Ninth Circuit, which was of a contrary view, is the kind of disagreement frequently exhibited in hard cases, and most often is a consequence not of personal whim or caprice but, as explained by Chief Justice Aharon Barak of the Israel Supreme Court, of a judge's personal experiences and world view. Lord Goff of Chieveley, the senior law lord in the United Kingdom, explains that a judge's often instinctive feel for the result in a case is no mere hunch:

> [It] is the fruit of an amalgam—an amalgam of his knowledge of legal principle, his experience as a lawyer, his understanding of the subtle restraints with which all judges should work, his developed sense of justice and his innate sense of humanity, and his common sense.

In his 1990 book *The Problems of Jurisprudence,* Chief Judge Richard Posner of the U.S. Court of Appeals for the Seventh Circuit puts it differently in pointing to "a reasonable result in the circumstances" as the "judicial lodestar." Among the circumstances to consider are:

> the facts of the case, legal doctrines, precedents, and such rule-of-law virtues as stare decisis. Bland as this recommendation may seem, it differs from both the orthodox legal view of the judge's task and the various natural law approaches by substituting the humble, fact-bound, policy-soaked, instrumental concept of "reasonableness" for both legal and moral rightness.

Also to the point is U.S. Court of Appeals for the District of Columbia Circuit Chief Judge Harry Edwards's view, as expressed in a 1991 *Wisconsin Law Review* article:

> Five to 15 percent of our cases [are in] the "very hard" category. . . . In this narrow set of cases, careful research and reflection fail to yield conclusive answers. The relevant legal materials, thoroughly studied, show only that the competing arguments advanced by the parties are equally strong, and the judges who must decide are left in a state of equipoise. Disposition of this small

number of cases, then, requires judges to exercise a measure of discretion, drawing to some degree on their own social and moral beliefs. That judges may find themselves in disagreement as the outcome of these "very hard" cases is thus to be expected, and represents something quite different from stark political decision making.

There is nothing really new in the idea that it is particularly important who the judge is in a hard case, as the following passage written in 1931 by Professor Walton Hale Hamilton of Yale Law School reveals:

> It was Marshall and not the law who made the Constitution stand for nationalism instead of a mere "federative union of sovereign states." It was Taney, not the writing on parchment, who made "the police power" an instrument for the control of a rising industrial system. It was Field and his like-minded brethren, not the Fourteenth Amendment, who have accorded to business the protection of "the due process" clause. The replacement of Clark, Day and Pitney by Sutherland, Butler and Sanford in 1922 made the bench more conservative; the elevation of Hughes to the Chief Justiceship in 1929 has already given evidence of a liberalizing trend. It would be strange if it were not so. The law cannot escape life, jurists cannot dwell in a legal realm apart from the world of affairs; underneath legal rites and formulas the issues and values which a man of sense would take into account win consideration. Justices differ in their knowledge and experience, in what appeals and fails to attract; they cannot escape the light of their own understanding. Even as other men, they behave like human beings.

Most recently professors Marvin Zalman and John Strate of Wayne State University have described how constitutional decision making involves elements of political choice—and that there is no single answer in hard cases—as they contrast the different approaches to the right to physician-assisted suicide expressed in the four main opinions from the court of appeals cases that found such a right, and which were reversed by the U.S. Supreme Court's decisions in *Washington v. Glucksberg* and *Vacco v. Quill.* Ronald Dworkin, in a *New York Review of Books* article, posits that the Supreme Court cases are most significant for their discussions of the due process clause, and "the actual protection it offers depends on whether it is read narrowly or expansively":

The words "due process of law" might conceivably have been taken to mean, at one extreme, that government may compromise liberty in any way it likes so long as it follows stipulated procedures of lawmaking in doing so. At the other extreme, the clause might be interpreted to say that judges may strike down any law that offends what they themselves deem to be a requirement of pure justice. But almost every lawyer rejects both those extremes. The due process clause, according to the general understanding, condemns all the laws—and only the laws—that curtail liberties that are, in an often-quoted passage from an earlier Supreme Court decision, "deeply rooted in this Nation's history and tradition." But that historical standard is also very abstract and lawyers disagree about what it means.

Disagreement over this historical standard is less a result of conflicting legal principles than a result of differing values, beliefs, and experiences.

What is ultimately involved is a choice of approaches to the job of being a judge. The late Chief Justice Walter Schaefer of the Illinois Supreme Court, writing in the *University of Chicago Law Review,* best stated it when he said:

> If I were to attempt to generalize, as indeed I should not, I should say that most depends upon the judge's unspoken notion as to the function of his court. If he views the role of the court as a passive one, he will be willing to delegate the responsibility for change, and he will not greatly care whether the delegated authority is exercised or not. If he views the court as an instrument of society designed to reflect in its decisions the morality of the community, he will be more likely to look precedent in the teeth and to measure it against the ideals and the aspirations of his time.

Flawed solutions

Solutions frequently offered to the so-called problem of the powers exercised by judges are also flawed. Most solutions appear to be premised on the assumption that judges make their decisions in secret and it is difficult to ferret them out.

For example, a suggestion frequently offered is that legislatures should monitor court decisions. This suggestion is made in the apparent belief this does not now happen. It does, and always has. Recent activities in the U.S. Congress, contemplating impeachment of

errant judges and proposing an amendment to the Constitution to set time limits on service, are nothing new. In 1861, Senator John P. Hale of New Hampshire introduced a bill to abolish the Supreme Court because of his dissatisfaction with decisions written by Chief Justice Taney. In 1912, President Theodore Roosevelt wrote a laudatory introduction to William L. Ransom's *Majority Rule and the Judiciary,* which discusses the advisability, among other things, of a method to recall ill-advised constitutional decisions of the Supreme Court. In the 1920s, Senator Robert La Follette of Wisconsin suggested election of federal judges and called specific federal district judges who had handed down anti-labor decisions "petty tyrants and arrogant despots." And we are all aware of President Franklin D. Roosevelt's efforts to change the composition of the Supreme Court to achieve the legislative goals that a conservative Supreme Court thwarted in the first years of his presidency.

Lastly, the sometimes-heard suggestion that citizens and other groups should pay attention to court decisions and "focus . . . on offending decisions and judges who author them" is premised on the assumption that legislatures and the Supreme Court in Washington are located on out-of-the-way streets, and that there never existed an "Impeach Earl Warren" bumper sticker.

Georgetown University professor Robert A. Katzmann, a visiting fellow at the Brookings Institution, observes in his book *Courts and Congress* that "our judicial system is the envy of much of the world; indeed, it is the model for nations striving to build a constitutional system," and that "[j]udges may have policy preferences, but in the overwhelming number of cases, they are guided by powerful norms of precedent, deference, procedural regularity, and coherence." Importantly, according to Professor Katzmann, "[j]udicial decision making is an edifice. The vision of freewheeling judges, acting according to their own policy objectives, is faulty."

Critics of judicial activism, I suggest, are lost in a Tennysonian world of single instances. Seen as a coherent whole in the light of judicial decision making, from the early days of the republic down to the present, judges have done reasonably well by all of us. There is no need for judges to change their course.

This article originally appeared in Volume 82, Number 1, July–August 1998, pages 29, 32–34.

Interpreting the Constitution: the Supreme Court's proper and historic function

Jeffrey M. Shaman

The Court's role, when all is said and done, is, and always has been, to create meaning for a Constitution that would otherwise be a hollow document.

Considerable criticism, frequently quite sharp, has recently been directed at the Supreme Court for the way it has gone about its historic function of interpreting the Constitution. In particular, Edwin Meese, the current Attorney General of the United States, has accused the Court of exceeding its lawful authority by failing to adhere strictly to the words of the Constitution and the intentions of the framers who drafted those words.[1]

The attorney general's attack upon the Court echoes a similar one made by Richard Nixon, who, campaigning for the presidency in 1968, denounced Supreme Court justices who, he claimed, twisted and bent the Constitution according to their personal predilections. If elected president, Nixon promised to appoint to the Court strict constructionists whose decisions would conform to the text of the Constitution and the intent of the framers. (Ironically, it is some of the Nixon appointees to the Court that Meese now accuses of twisting and bending the Constitution.)

I hasten to add that it is not only politicians who sing the praises of strict constructionism; there are judges and lawyers, as well as some scholars, who join the song. Among legal scholars, though, the response to strict constructionism has been overwhelmingly negative. There are legal scholars, for instance, who describe strict constructionism as a "misconceived quest,"[2] an "impossibility,"[3] and even a "fraud."[4]

Those who criticize the Court point to rulings during the tenure of Chief Justice Burger, most notably the decision in *Roe v. Wade*[5] legalizing abortion, as examples of illegitimate revision or amendment of the Constitution based upon the personal beliefs of the justices. Some years ago, similar charges were leveled at the Warren Court for its ruling requiring reapportionment along the lines of one person-one vote,[6] its decision striking down school prayer,[7] and other rulings, even including the one in *Brown v. Board of Education* outlawing school segregation.[8]

It should not be supposed, however, that strict constructionism is always on the side of conservative political values. In the 1930s it was the liberals who claimed that the Supreme Court was not strictly construing the Constitution when the justices repeatedly held that minimum wage, maximum hour, and other protective legislation violated the Fourteenth Amendment.[9] As the liberals then saw it, the conservative justices on the Court were illegitimately incorporating their personal values into the Fourteenth Amendment, which had been meant to abolish racial discrimination, not to protect the prerogatives of employers.

History lessons

The lesson of this bit of history seems to be that, whether liberal or conservative or somewhere in between, whoever has an ox that is being gored at the time has a tendency to yell "foul." Whenever the Supreme Court renders a decision that someone doesn't like, apparently it is not enough to disagree with the decision; there also has to be an accusation that the Court's decision was illegitimate, being based upon the justice's personal views and not the words of the Constitution or the intent of the framers.

We can go back much further in history than the 1930s to find the Supreme Court being accused of illegitimacy. In 1810, for instance, Thomas Jefferson condemned Chief Justice John Marshall for "twistifying" the Constitution according to his "personal biases."[10]

History also reveals something else extremely significant about the Court, which is that from its earliest days, the Court has found it necessary in interpreting the Constitution to look beyond the language of the document and the intent of the framers. In the words of Stanford Law Professor Thomas Grey, it is "a matter of unarguable historical fact" that over the years the Court has developed a large body of constitutional law that derives neither from the text of the document nor the intent of the framers.[11]

Judicature Volume 71, Number 2, pp. 80, 84–87, 122

Moreover, this has been so from the Court's very beginning. Consider, for example, a case entitled *Hylton v. United States*,[12] which was decided in 1796 during the term of the Court's first Chief Justice, John Jay. The *Hylton* case involved a tax ranging from $1.00 to $10.00 that had been levied by Congress on carriages. Mr. Hylton, who was in the carriage trade and owned 125 carriages, understandably was unhappy about the tax, and went to court to challenge it. He claimed that the tax violated section 2 of Article I of the Constitution, which provides that direct taxes shall be apportioned among the several states according to their populations. Hylton argued that this tax was a direct one, and therefore unconstitutional because it had not been apportioned among the states by population. This, of course, was years before the enactment of the Sixteenth Amendment in 1913, authorizing a federal income tax. Prior to that, Article I prohibited a federal income tax, but what about a tax on the use or ownership of carriages—was that the sort of "direct" tax that was only permissible under Article I if apportioned among the states by population?

The Supreme Court, with several justices filing separate opinions in the case (which was customary at that time), upheld the tax as constitutional on the ground that it was not direct, and therefore not required to be apportioned. What is most significant about the *Hylton* case is how the Court went about making its decision. As described by Professor David Currie of the University of Chicago Law School, the Court in *Hylton* "paid little heed to the Constitution's words," and "policy considerations dominated all three opinions" filed by the justices.[13] In fact, each of the opinions asserted that apportioning a carriage tax among the states would be unfair, because a person in a state with fewer carriages would have to pay a higher tax. While this may or may not be unfair, the justices pointed to nothing in the Constitution itself or the intent of the framers to support their personal views of fairness. Moreover, one of the justices, Justice Patterson, went so far in his opinion as to assert that the constitutional requirement of apportioning direct taxes was "radically wrong," and therefore should not be extended to this case. In other words, he based his decision, at least in part, upon his antipathy to a constitutional provision.

While Justice Patterson went too far in that respect, he and his colleagues on the Court could hardly have made a decision in the case by looking to the text of the Constitution or the intent of the framers. The language of the document simply does not provide an answer to the constitutional issue raised by the situation in *Hylton*. The text of the document merely refers to "direct" taxes and provides no definition of what is meant by a direct tax. Furthermore, as Professor Currie points out, the records of the debates at the Constitutional Convention show that "the Framers had no clear idea of what they meant by direct taxes."[14] Thus, to fulfill their responsibility to decide the case and interpret the law, the justices found it necessary to create meaning for the Constitution.

Creating meaning

Indeed, it is often necessary for the Supreme Court to create meaning for the Constitution. This is so because the Constitution, being a document designed (in the words of John Marshall) to "endure for ages,"[15] is rife with general and abstract language. Those two great sources of liberty in the Constitution, the due process and equal protection clauses, are obviously examples of abstract constitutional language that must be invested with meaning. The Fourth Amendment uses extremely general language in prohibiting "unreasonable" searches and seizures, and the Eighth Amendment is similarly general in disallowing "cruel and unusual" punishment.

Even many of the more specific provisions of the Constitution need to be supplied with meaning that simply cannot be found within the four corners of the document. The First Amendment, for instance, states that Congress shall not abridge freedom of speech—but does that mean that the government may not regulate obscene, slanderous, or deceptive speech? The First Amendment also says that Congress shall not abridge the free exercise of religion—does that mean that the government may not prohibit polygamy or child labor when dictated by religious belief? These questions—which, by the way, all arose in actual cases—and, in fact, the vast majority of constitutional questions presented to the Supreme Court, cannot be resolved by mere linguistic analysis of the Constitution. In reality there is no choice but to look beyond the text of the document to provide meaning for the Constitution.

There are those, such as Attorney General Meese, who would hope to find meaning for the Constitution from its authors, the beloved and hallowed framers of the sacred text. By reputation, these fellows are considered saints and geniuses; in actuality, they were politicians motivated significantly by self-interest.

Theoretical drawbacks

But even if the framers do deserve the awe that they inspire, reliance on their intentions to find meaning for the Constitution still has serious theoretical drawbacks. In the first place, why should we be concerned only with the intentions of the 55 individuals who drafted the Constitution and not the intentions of the people throughout the nation who ratified it, not to mention the intentions of the succeeding generations who retain the Constitution? After all, even when finally framed, the Constitution remained a legal nullity until ratified by the people, and would be a legal nullity again if revoked by the people. The framers wrote the Constitution, but it is the people who enacted and retain the Constitution; so if anything, it is the people's intent about the document that would seem to be the relevant inquiry.

Moreover, there are considerable difficulties in discerning what in fact the framers intended. The *Journal of the Constitutional Convention*, which is the primary record of the framers' intent, is neither complete nor entirely accurate. The notes for the *Journal* were carelessly kept, and have been shown to contain several mistakes.[16]

Even when the record cannot be faulted, it is not always possible to ascertain the framers' intent. As might be expected, the framers did not express an intention about every constitutional issue that would arise after the document was drafted and adopted. No group of people, regardless of its members' ability, enjoys that sort of prescience. When the framers did address particular problems, often only a few of them spoke out. What frequently is taken to be the intent of the framers as a group turns out to be the intent of merely a few or even only one of the framers.

There are also constitutional issues about which the framers expressed conflicting intentions. A collective body of 55 individuals, the framers embraced a widely diverse and frequently inconsistent set of views. The two principal architects of the Constitution, James Madison and Alexander Hamilton, for instance, had extremely divergent political views. Madison also on occasion differed with George Washington over the meaning of the Constitution. When Washington, who had presided over the Constitutional Convention, became president, he claimed that the underlying intent of the Constitution gave him the sole authority as

president to proclaim neutrality and to withhold treaty papers from Congress. Madison, who had been a leader at the Constitutional Convention, disagreed vehemently. And so, the man who would come to be known as the father of this nation and the man who would come to be known as the father of the Constitution had opposing views of what the framers intended.[17]

These examples demonstrate that it simply makes no sense to suppose that a multi-member group of human beings such as the framers shared a unitary intent about the kind of controversial political issues addressed in our Constitution. We can see, then, that, at best, the so-called framers' intent is inadequately documented, ambiguous, and inconclusive; at worst, it is nonexistent, an illusion.

Even if these insurmountable obstacles could be surmounted, there are other serious problems with trying to follow the path laid down by the framers. The framers formed their intentions in the context of a past reality and in accordance with past attitudes, both of which have changed considerably since the days when the Constitution was drafted. To transfer those intentions, fashioned as they were under past conditions and views, to contemporary situations may produce sorry consequences that even the framers would have abhorred had they been able to foresee them. Blindly following intentions formulated in response to past conditions and attitudes is not likely to be an effective means of dealing with the needs of contemporary society.

Locked to the past

Some scholars take this line of reasoning one step further by maintaining that the framers' intent is inextricably locked to the past and has no meaning at all for the present.[18] In other words, because the framers formed their intentions with reference to a reality and attitudes that no longer exist, their intentions cannot be transplanted to the present day. What the framers intended for their time is not what they may have intended for ours. Life constantly changes, and the reality and ideas that surrounded the framers are long since gone.

The futility of looking to the framers' intent to resolve modern constitutional issues can be illustrated by several cases that have arisen under the Fourth and Fifth Amendments. The Fourth Amendment prohibits unreasonable searches and seizures, and further requires that no search warrants be issued unless there is probable cause that a crime has been committed.

Are bugging and other electronic surveillance devices "unreasonable searches?" May they be used by the police without a warrant based on probable cause? What about the current practice of some law enforcement agencies of using airplanes to fly over a suspect's property to take pictures with a telescopic camera—is that an "unreasonable search?" The Fifth Amendment states that no person shall be compelled to be a witness against himself. What about forcing a suspect to take a breathalyzer test, or a blood test, or to have his or her stomach pumped—do those procedures amount to self-incrimination that violates the Fifth Amendment?

Whatever you may think should be the answers to these questions, you cannot find the answers by looking to the framers' intent. The framers had no intent at all about electronic surveillance, airplanes, telescopic cameras, breathalyzer tests, or stomach pumping, for the simple reason that none of those things existed until well after the days of the framers. Not even Benjamin Franklin, for all his inventiveness, was able to foresee that in the 20th century constables would zip around in flying machines taking snapshots of criminal suspects through a telescopic lens.

Many of the difficulties in attempting to resolve constitutional issues by turning to the framers are illustrated by the school prayer cases.[19] The religious beliefs of the framers ranged from theism to atheism, and among even the more devout framers there was a wide diversity of opinion concerning the proper relationship between church and state. Moreover, as often happens when human beings ponder complex issues, the views of individual framers about church and state did not remain the same over time. As a member of Congress, James Madison, for example, once voted to approve a chaplain for the House of Representatives, but later decided that the appointment of the chaplain had been unconstitutional.[20] Insofar as school prayer specifically was concerned, the framers expressed virtually no opinion on the matter, for the simple reason that at the time public schools were extremely rare. Thus, the framers had no intention, either pro or con, about prayer in public schools.

Given the theoretical deficiencies of trying to decide constitutional questions by looking to the framers' intent, it should come as no surprise that this approach has been a failure when attempted by the Supreme Court. Scholars who have closely studied the Court's use of this approach commonly agree that it has not been a satisfactory method of constitutional decision making, because the Court ends up manipulating, revising, or even creating history under the guise of following the framers' intent.[21] The fact of the matter is that neither the framers' intent nor the words of the document are capable of providing much constitutional meaning.

Bare bones

What we are left with, then, are the bare bones of a Constitution, the meaning of which must be augmented by the justices of the Supreme Court. And that is exactly what the justices have been doing since the Court was first established. The overwhelming evidence of history shows that the meaning of the Constitution has undergone constant change and evolution at the hands of the Supreme Court. Through the continual interpretation and reinterpretation of the text of the document, the Court perpetually creates new meaning for the document. Although it is formally correct that we, unlike the citizens of Great Britain, have a written Constitution, its words have been defined and redefined to the extent that for the most part we, like the citizens of Great Britain, have an unwritten Constitution, the meaning of which originates with the Supreme Court.

Strict constructionists argue that it is undemocratic for Supreme Court justices—unelected officials who are unaccountable to the populace—to create meaning for the Constitution. Of course, using the framers' intent to interpret the Constitution also is undemocratic; following the will of the 55 persons who supposedly framed the Constitution or the smaller group of them who actually participated in the framing is hardly an exercise in democracy.

When strict constructionists cry that the Court is undemocratic, they are ignoring that our government is not (and was not intended by the framers) to be a pure democracy. Rather, it is a limited or constitutional democracy. What this means is that there are constitutional limits to what the majority may do. The majority may not, for example, engage in racial discrimination, even if it votes to do so in overwhelming numbers. The majority may not abridge freedom of speech or the free exercise of religion or other constitutional rights guaranteed to every individual.

Article III of the Constitution states that there shall be a Supreme Court, and, in combination with Article II, decrees the Court's independence from the electorate. By its very terms, the Constitution establishes a counter-majoritarian branch of government, the Supreme Court, in juxtaposition to the more democratic executive and legislative branches. This scheme reflects one of the guiding principles that underlies the Constitution—the principle of separate powers that check and balance one another. The Supreme Court's constitutionally mandated independence functions as a check and balance upon the more majoritarian branches of federal and state governments. It thereby provides a means of maintaining constitutional boundaries on majoritarian rule.

The role of the Supreme Court is to enforce constitutional requirements upon the majoritarian branches of government, which otherwise would be completely unbridled. As dictated by the Constitution, majority control should be the predominant feature of our government, but subject to constitutional limits.

Moreover, the Supreme Court is not quite as undemocratic as the strict constructionists sometimes like to portray it to be. While it is true that the justices who sit on the Court are appointed rather than elected and that they may be removed from office only for improper behavior, it is also true that they are appointed by a popularly elected president, and their appointments must be confirmed by a popularly elected Senate. Turnover of the Court's personnel, which sometimes occurs frequently, enhances popular control of the Court. Additionally, the Court's constitutional rulings may be overruled by the people through constitutional amendment, which, though a difficult procedure, has been accomplished on four occasions.[22] Thus, while the Court is not directly answerable to the public, it is not entirely immune from popular control.

The ultimate authority

The people also have the ultimate authority to abolish the Supreme Court. That they have not done so during our two centuries of experience indicates popular acceptance of the Court's role. Admittedly, there are particular decisions rendered by the Court that have aroused considerable public outcry, but given the many controversial issues that the Court must decide, this is inevitable. More telling about the public attitude toward the Court is that the people have taken no action to curtail the Court's authority to interpret the Constitution. Indeed, the public has shown little, if any, inclination toward abolishing the Court or even restricting its powers. Despite Franklin Delano Roose-velt's overwhelming popularity, his "court-packing plan" was a dismal failure;[23] the proposal to establish a "Court of the Union" composed of state court justices which would have the power to overrule the Supreme Court evoked such widespread public disapproval that it was quickly abandoned;[24] the campaigns to impeach Justices Earl Warren and William O. Douglas never got off the ground;[25] and although various members of Congress often propose bills threatening to restrict the Court's jurisdiction, the full Congress always rebuffs those threats.[26] These experiences suggest that even in the face of controversial constitutional decisions, there has been abiding public consent to the role of the Supreme Court in our scheme of government.

The Court's role, when all is said and done, is to create meaning for a Constitution that otherwise would be a hollow document. It is perfectly appropriate for anyone to disagree with Supreme Court decisions, and to criticize the Court on that basis. But it is not appropriate to attack the court's decisions as illegitimate on the ground that they do not follow the framers' intent. Pretending to use the framers' intent to impugn the legitimacy of the Supreme Court is a spurious enterprise. The Court's legitimate function is, and always has been, to provide meaning for the Constitution.

Notes

This article originally appeared in Volume 71, Number 2, August–September 1987, pages 80, 84–87, 122.

1. Address by Attorney General Edwin Meese, III, before the American Bar Association, Washington, D.C. (July 9, 1985); "Q and A with the Attorney General," *A.B.A. J.* 81 (July 1985), 44.
2. Brest, "The Misconceived Quest for the Original Understanding," *B.U. L. Rev.* 60 (1980), 204.
3. Ely, "Constitutional Interpretation: Its Allure and Impossibility," *Ind. L. J.* 53 (1978), 399.
4. Nowak, "Realism, Nihilism, and the Supreme Court: Do the Emperors Have Nothing but Robes?" *Washburn L. J.* 22 (1983), 246, 257.
5. 410 U.S. 113 (1973).
6. *Reynolds v. Sims*, 377 U.S. 533 (1964).
7. *Engle v. Vitale*, 370 U.S. 421 (1962); *Abington School Dist. v. Schempp*, 374 U.S. 203 (1963).
8. 347 U.S. 483 (1954).
9. *See, e.g.*, Boudin, *Government by Judiciary* (New York: W. Goodwin, 1932), 433–434; Haines, *The American Doctrine of Supreme Court, 1789–1888* (Chicago: University of Chicago Press, 1985), 34.

10. Ford (ed.), *Writings of Thomas Jefferson,* vol. 9 (1902), 275–276.

11. Grey, "Origins of the Unwritten Constitution: Fundamental Law in American Revolutionary Thought," *Stan. L. Rev.* 30 (1978), 843, 844.

12. 3 U.S. (3 Dall.) 171 (1796).

13. Currie, *The Constitution in the Supreme Court 1789–1888* (Chicago: University of Chicago Press, 1985), 34.

14. Ibid. at 36.

15. *McCulloch v. Maryland,* 17 U.S. (4 Wheat.) 316, 414 (1819).

16. *See* Rohde & Spaeth, *Supreme Court Decision Making* (1976), 41; 1 *The Records of the Federal Convention of 1787,* Farrand ed. (San Francisco: W. H. Freeman, 1937), xii–xiv.

17. Burns, *The Vineyard of Liberty* (New York: Knopf, 1982), 101–104.

18. Wofford, "The Blinding Light: The Uses of History in Constitutional Interpretation," *U. Chi. L. Rev.* 21 (1964), 502.

19. *Supra* n. 7.

20. Stokes & Pfeffer, *Church and State in the United States* (Colorado Springs: Shepard's, 1975), 481–482.

21. *See, e.g.,* tenBrock, "Uses by the United States Supreme Court of Extrinsic Aids in Constitutional Construction," *Calif. L. Rev.* 27 (1939), 399, 404; Kelly, "Clio and the Court: An Illicit Love Affair," *Sup. Ct. Rev.* (1965) 119, 122–125; Alfange, "On Judicial Policymaking and Constitutional Change: Another Look at the 'Original Intent' Theory of Constitutional Interpretation," *Hastings Const. L. Q.* 5 (1978), 603, 617.

22. The Eleventh Amendment overruled the holding of *Chisholm v. Georgia,* 2 U.S. (2 Dall.) 419 (1793); the Four-teenth Amendment nullified, in part, the decision in *Dred Scott v. Sandford,* 60 U.S. (19 How.) 393 (1857); the Sixteenth Amendment nullified the holding of *Pollock v. Farmers' Loan and Trust Co.,* 157 U.S. 429 (1895); the Twenty-sixth Amendment neutralized *Oregon v. Mitchell,* 400 U.S. 112 (1970).

23. "Not all the influence of a master politician in the prime of his popularity was quite enough to carry a program that would impair judicial review," McCloskey, *The American Supreme Court* (Chicago: University of Chicago Press, 1960), 177. The plan was rejected vehemently by the Senate Judiciary Committee. See *Senate Comm. on the Judiciary, Reorganization of the Fed. Judiciary, Adverse Report,* S. Rep. No. 711, 75th Cong., 1st Sess. 23 (1937).

24. Pfeffer, *This Honorable Court* (Boston: Beacon Press, 1965), 424–25.

25. Those who campaigned for Chief Justice Warren's impeachment were unable to have impeachment proceedings initiated against him. While impeachment proceedings were instituted against Justice Douglas, they never got beyond the subcommittee stage and were eventually forsaken. See *Special Subcomm. on H. Res. 920 of the House Comm. on the Judiciary,* 91 Cong., 2d Sess., Final Report, Associate Justice William O. Douglas (Comm. Print 1970).

26. "In the fifteen years between 1953 and 1968, over sixty bills were introduced in Congress to eliminate the jurisdiction of the federal courts over a variety of specific subjects; none of these became law." Bator, Mishkin, Shapiro & Wechsler, *Hart & Wechsler's The Federal Courts and the Federal System,* 2d ed. (Mineola, N.Y.: Foundation Press, 1973), 360.

Actors in the Judicial Process

Judges: Judicial Selection Systems and Their Consequences

Among all of the actors in the U.S. judicial process it is the judge who often emerges as the focal point, the participant at the heart of the courtroom who controls and directs an unfolding legal drama and often decides its outcome. The subject of judicial selection—how judges obtain their positions—has frequently engaged analysts. Many think that the nature of selection processes has critical implications for the kinds of people chosen and, ultimately, for judicial decision making.

There are many kinds of judicial selection systems in the United States, including presidential appointment and senatorial confirmation for the three levels of the federal bench and elective, appointive, and hybrid selection systems (which can incorporate elements of election, appointment, or merit processes) throughout the states. Making matters even more complex, in some states there are fundamentally different selection procedures for choosing judges for different levels of the judiciary. Indeed, given the reality of fifty distinct state judiciaries and a three-tiered federal judicial system, the possibilities for important nuances of difference among judicial selection procedures is staggering. The articles in this section attempt to come to grips with understanding the workings of alternative approaches to judicial selection while unraveling some of their possible consequences.

At the outset, Larry Berkson, in "Judicial selection in the United States," surveys the history and rationales for the alternative approaches to choosing judges in this country. Berkson underlines that "the combination of schemes used to select judges is almost endless. Almost no two states are alike, and few employ the same method for choosing judges at all levels of the judiciary."

One thing made clear in Berkson's accounting is that some form of the electoral process for choosing judges, whether partisan, nonpartisan, or retention, is utilized in the vast majority of the states for some level of judgeships and for the selection of most state judges. In a thorough and provocative article, "Interest groups and state court elections: a new era and its challenges," Clive Thomas, Michael Boyer, and Ronald Hrebenar provide a sobering account of the challenges in the dramatically changed judicial electoral settings that have emerged since the late 1970s. Primary among them is the difficulty of maintaining judicial independence in an increasingly competitive, costly, and highly politicized campaign context in which interest groups often hold the upper hand, even over the candidates themselves. In the authors' view, today's judicial elections are characterized by "an inherent contradiction in the states between the twin democratic desires for an independent judiciary on the one hand and subjecting judges to popular election or reconfirmation on the other." The authors portray a selection system that has run amuck on many dimensions. The reality is that incumbency is a tremendous advantage in judicial campaigns, quality information for the electorate is low, and voter interest is equally muted. Interest groups with financial resources and few campaign constraints can target specific judicial elections and literally control the nature of campaigns if not necessarily their ultimate outcomes, as seen in the 2000 Ohio Supreme Court election profiled in this study.

Thomas, Boyer, and Hrebenar suggest several possible reform initiatives that, they argue, could better inform the voting public, constrain the role of money in judicial elections, and offer candidates a stronger hand in orchestrating judicial campaigns in their competition with interest groups. They suggest that these reforms may have even greater impact in the wake of a 2002 Supreme Court decision, *Republican Party of Minnesota v. White*, in which some legislative constraints placed on the campaign "speech" of judicial candidates in Minnesota were determined to be a violation of their First Amendment rights. Readers may differ over the likely impact of the reforms suggested here; however, it would be difficult to dispute the authors' contention that if the spiral of politicized judicial elections is not abated and placed under some control, "both the quality of those seeking judicial office and the independence of state judiciaries may be seriously undermined."

While not immune to the problematic trends described by Thomas, Boyer, and Hrebenar, retention elections associated with "merit selection" systems illustrate the great advantages of incumbency and the inherent difficulties of defeating "somebody" with "nobody" in elections in which voters are simply deciding on a judge's continuance in office. In "Trends in judicial retention elections, 1964–1998" Larry Aspin documents that more voters are participating these days in what remain, for the most part, generally low visibility and low interest affairs. Targeted judges can be defeated in their retention bids, but the data demonstrate that, in the aggregate, fewer judges have been defeated in retention elections in recent years and the mean affirmative vote in retention elections actually has been on the rise. One might readily conclude that in the highly politicized atmosphere portrayed by Thomas, Boyer, and Hrebenar and the more somnolent retention election setting detailed by Aspin there are a number of reasons to question whether judicial elections of any stripe are serving the role that they were designed to play as democratically based processes for selecting judges.

When we turn to selection processes for federal judges we are met by a dramatically different system marked by presidential nomination of judges and justices to lifetime appointments confirmed with the advice and consent of the U.S. Senate. Utilization of a different approach, however, has by no means solved the problems documented in state electoral systems. In "A historical perspective on federal judicial selection," Elliot Slotnick argues that while tension between the president and the Senate in nominating and confirming judges has always existed, the seemingly unprecedented acrimony that has characterized the presidential tenures of Bill Clinton and George W. Bush has its roots in contemporary alterations of the selection process. Slotnick argues that it is perhaps ironic that Jimmy Carter's pursuit of affirmative action in judicial selection, sought largely through his use and encouragement of nominating commissions, coupled with his policy preference for nominees who had "demonstrated a commitment to equal justice" opened the door to greater politicizing of the process. This was witnessed most pointedly in the centralized and ideologically driven selection approach taken during the Reagan administration. As contemporary federal judicial selection battles amply demonstrate, "once this genie of avowedly open policy consideration in judicial selection had been let out of the bottle, and once an increase in the White House's political role in judicial selection, as distinct from the Justice Department's role in assessing the credentials of candidates increased . . . it would be very difficult to return to old ways."

Slotnick largely credits the actions of contemporary presidents with raising the temperature of advice and consent relationships, but it must also be noted that, in recent years, members of the Senate have been more than willing to enter the fray by taking positions on and opposing judgeship nominees, even lower federal court judgeship candidates serving far from a senator's home state. Indeed, during George W. Bush's administration, the Senate's Democratic minority has even gone so far as to block several nominees for courts of appeals through the use of filibusters that, at the time of this writing, have not been broken by the slim Republican Senate majority. The reasons for senatorial willingness to actively oppose what, historically, have been routine lower court confirmations are explored at length by Nancy Scherer in "The judicial confirmation process: mobilizing elites, mobilizing masses." Scherer's analysis details the rise of interest group concern about lower court judgeships, which corresponded with the Reagan administration's ideologically oriented appointments. Whereas lower court selection is a relative non-issue for the mass public, it can be a highly salient one for political elites who can convince senators of the electoral consequences of not supporting a group's position on a judicial nominee by utilizing the muscle of the interest groups they lead. As Scherer puts it, " 'Inside the Beltway' activists play a crucial role in getting senators re-elected. When they demand that senators fight against objectionable judicial nominees, senators must respond." Scherer's analysis, based largely on interviews with key players in judicial selection politics, offers a useful perspective through which to better understand the unusually contentious lower court confirmation battles witnessed in recent years.

The last two articles in this section focus on appointment politics during the presidency of George W. Bush, as well as a preliminary analysis of the judicial behavior of the district court judges the president has seated. In both instances, the analytical focus is not exclusively on the Bush judges but rather is extended back in time to draw comparisons with the most recent presidential administrations. "W. Bush remaking the judiciary: like father like son?" represents the most recent in a series of articles published in *Judicature* that dates back to the Carter administration. Sheldon Goldman and his colleagues utilize multiple data sources, including interviews with key participants in and observers of the nomination and confirmation processes, nominee questionnaires submitted to the Senate Judiciary Committee, home state newspaper accounts, voter registration lists, secondary source materials, and direct inquiries to nominees, to draw a detailed portrait of an administration's selection processes and their outcomes. In the present study, Goldman's team reveals a process in which staffing the federal bench was a prime component of the president's domestic policy agenda. The most important activities in judicial selection centered in the White House, specifically in its Office of Legal Counsel. The article vividly depicts the confrontational tone that dominated confirmation politics from the perspective of several key participants in the process. Despite prominent public controversy over a number of highly publicized nominees, at the end of the 107th Congress and midway through the president's term, eighty-three Bush nominees to the district courts and sixteen nominees to courts of appeals were confirmed. A statistical portrait of these nominees is presented, with comparisons drawn to the appointees of Presidents Bill Clinton, George H. W. Bush, Ronald Reagan, and Jimmy Carter. The authors characterize George W. Bush's cohort as one of "high competence and professionalism" yet, they add, "ever more so than the father's, the son's administration is clearly coordinated and is expending resources to place on the bench appointees who share the President's judicial philosophy. How successful has the administration been thus far in achieving that objective? . . . Only a detailed examination of the appointees' performance on the bench will be able to answer [that question]."

Such a detailed analysis, albeit one based on relatively limited data because of the short time they have served as judges, is the responsibility of Robert Carp, Kenneth Manning, and Ronald Stidham's study, "The decision-making behavior of George W. Bush's judicial appointees: far right, conservative or moderate?" The authors address the charge that Bush's appointees have been ultra-conservatives. They do this by first assessing the nature and scope of the opportunity that Bush has had to shape the bench in his political image and, secondly, through an empirical examination of Bush's district court nominees' voting behavior. Across all of the cases examined, George W. Bush's judges decided in a liberal direction only 36.1 percent of the time. Only Ronald Reagan's appointees (35.8 percent liberal) were more conservative. And this dating back to Lyndon Johnson's presidency, the starting point for the analysis.

In a key area of ideological divide in this country, civil rights and liberties, the liberalism score of George W. Bush's judges (27.9 percent) is clearly the most conservative metric among all of the presidential cohorts. While not characterizing the Bush judges as "extremists" since, in fact, their behavior does resemble that of the judges of the first George Bush and Reagan's and Nixon's judges before them, the authors conclude, "President Bush's judges are among the most conservative on record for modern administrations." More generally, it is instructive to note that the data suggest that modern Republican presidents have been a good deal more successful in seating conservative jurists than Democratic presidents have been in appointing liberals.

Judicial selection in the United States: a special report

Larry C. Berkson

Historically there has been considerable controversy about how American judges should be chosen. During the colonial era, they were selected by the king, but his intolerably wide powers over them was one of the abuses that the colonists attacked in the Declaration of Independence. After the Revolution, the states continued to select judges by appointment, but the new processes prevented the chief executive from controlling the judiciary.[1]

Gradually, however, states began to adopt popular election as a means of choosing judges. For example, as early as 1812 Georgia amended its constitution to provide that judges of inferior courts be popularly elected. In 1816, Indiana entered the Union with a constitution that provided for the election of associate judges of the circuit court. Sixteen years later, Mississippi became the first state in which all judges were popularly elected. Michigan held elections for trial judges in 1836.

By that time the appointive system had come under serious attack. People resented the fact that property owners controlled the judiciary.[2] They were determined to end this privilege of the upper class and to ensure the popular sovereignty we describe as Jacksonian Democracy.

During the next decade, there was little opposition to those who advocated popular elections. For example, in the New York Constitutional Convention of 1846 there was not even a lengthy discussion of the subject. As one writer has stated:

> The debates on an elective judiciary were brief; there was apparently little need to discuss the abuses of the appointive system, or its failures, or why election would be better. A few delegates argued cogently for the retention of the old system, and indeed forecast the possible evils if the judiciary fell under political domination . . . . But the spirit of reform carried the day.[3]

New York's adoption of an electoral system signaled the beginning of this trend. By the time of the Civil War, 24 of 34 states had established an elected judiciary with seven states adopting the system in 1850 alone.[4] As new states were admitted to the Union, all of them adopted popular election of some or all judges until the admission of Alaska in 1959.

No panacea

Within a short time, however, it became apparent that this new system was no panacea, and the need for reform again was recognized. For example, as early as 1853 delegates to the Massachusetts Constitutional Convention viewed the popular election of judges in New York as a failure and refused to adopt the system. One delegate claimed that it had "fallen hopelessly into the great cistern" and quoted an article in the *Evening Post* that illustrated that judges had become enmeshed in the "political mill." [5] By 1867, the subject was a matter of great debate in New York, and in 1873 a proposed amendment to return to the appointive system gained strong support at the general election.[6]

One of the main concerns during this period was that judges were almost invariably selected by political machines and controlled by them. Judges were often perceived as corrupt and incompetent. The notion of a judiciary uncontrolled by special interests had simply not been realized. It was in this context that the concept of nonpartisan elections began to emerge.

The idea of judicial candidates appearing on the ballot without party label was used as early as 1873 in Cook County [Chicago], Illinois. Interestingly, it was the judges themselves who decided to run on a nonpartisan ballot rather than doing so pursuant to a statute or some other authority. Elections in 1885 and 1893 were also nonpartisan (Cook County subsequently returned to partisan elections). By the turn of the century the idea of nonpartisan judicial elections had gained strength, and several states had adopted the idea. By 1927, 12 states employed the nonpartisan idea.[7]

Once again, criticism of nonpartisan elections arose almost as soon as such elections began. As early as 1908 members of the South Dakota Bar Association indicated dissatisfaction with how the idea was working in their state. By 1927, Iowa, Kansas, and Pennsylvania had already tried the plan and abandoned it.[8] The major objection was that there was still no real public

Judicature Volume 64, Number 4, pp. 176–193

choice. New candidates for judgeships were regularly selected by party leaders and thrust upon an unknowledgeable electorate, which, without the guidance of party labels, was not able to make reasoned choices.

The rise of commission plans

While others attacked nonpartisan elections, a number of well-known scholars, judges and concerned citizens began assailing all elective systems as failures. One of the most outspoken critics, Roscoe Pound, delivered a now classic address to the American Bar Association in 1906 on "The Causes of Popular Dissatisfaction with the Administration of Justice." He claimed that "putting courts into politics, and compelling judges to become politicians in many jurisdictions ... [had] almost destroyed the traditional respect for the bench." [9]

Several years later in a speech before the Cincinnati Bar Association, William Howard Taft claimed that it was "disgraceful" to see men campaigning for the state supreme court on the ground that their decisions would have a particular class flavor. It was "so shocking, and so out of keeping with the fixedness of moral principles," he said, that it ought to be "condemned." [10]

Reformers claimed that the worst features of partisan politics could be eliminated through what they called a "merit plan" for selecting judges. The plan would expand the pool of candidates to include persons other than friends of politicians. Selectors would not consider inappropriate partisan factors such as an individual's party affiliation, party service, or friendship with an appointing executive so the most distinguished members of the bar, regardless of party, could be elevated to the bench.[11]

Origins of the plan are usually traced to Albert M. Kales, one of the founders of the American Judicature Society. Versions of his proposal were introduced in state legislatures throughout the 1930s. The American Bar Association endorsed a merit plan in 1937, and in 1940 Missouri became the first state to put one into effect. Today it is variously known as the Kales plan, Missouri plan, merit plan, or commission plan.

Almost none of the state plans is identical, but they do share common features. Most include a permanent, nonpartisan commission composed of lawyers and nonlawyers (appointed by a variety of public and private officials) who actively recruit and screen prospective candidates. The commission then forwards a list of three to five qualified individuals to the executive, who must make an appointment from the list.

Usually the judge serves a one- or two-year probationary period, after which he must run unopposed on a retention ballot. The sole question on which the electorate votes is: "Shall Judge ____ be retained in office?" A judge must win a majority of the vote in order to serve a full term.

Judicial selection today

Today the combination of schemes used to select judges is almost endless. Almost no two states are alike, and many states employ different methods of selection depending upon the different levels of the judiciary, creating "hybrid" systems of selection. It is possible, however, to classify selection methods in the states. The most frequently used classification differentiates between states that appoint their judges and states that elect their judges. The two groups turn out to be fairly equal in number.

Appointment

Thirty two states and the District of Columbia use nominating commissions to help the governor select state judges. Twenty-three states and the District of Columbia use the commission plan to make initial appointments to most or all of their courts and nine others use panels only for interim appointments.

Six states use gubernatorial or legislative appointment without the aid of a nominating commission. In four (California, Maine, New Jersey, and New Hampshire), the governor appoints judges (subject to senatorial confirmation in Maine and New Jersey, confirmation by a 3-member commission on judicial appointments in California, and approval by an elected council in New Hampshire). In Virginia and South Carolina, the legislature appoints judges (in South Carolina, the legislature does so with the aid of a 10-member judicial merit selection commission that screens candidates and reports to legislators). In Hawaii, judges themselves appoint their colleagues to preside over limited jurisdiction courts.

Elections

Seven states elect all of their judges in partisan elections, and four states use partisan elections to elect some of their judges. Thirteen states use nonpartisan elections to select all of their judges. An additional eight states use nonpartisan elections to select some of their judges. In total, 31 states choose some, most, or all of their judges using some form of popular election.

Given the "hybrid" systems that appear in many states, it is also helpful to examine how states choose their judges at each level of the judicial system. Again, the states are fairly evenly divided between those that elect and those that appoint their judges.

Supreme courts

Twenty-one states hold elections for judges serving on courts of last resort: 8 use partisan elections, 13 use nonpartisan elections. In 23 states and the District of Columbia, judges are appointed to the highest court by the governor with the assistance of a judicial nominating commission. In California, Maine, New Jersey, and New Hampshire, the governor appoints these judges without the aid of a nominating commission. In South Carolina and Virginia, Supreme Court judges are chosen by the legislature.

Appellate courts

Of the forty-one states that have intermediate appellate courts, 17 elect appellate judges: 6 states use partisan elections and 11 states use nonpartisan elections. Four states use appointment without a nominating commission (2 allow the governor to appoint judges and 2 allow the legislature to select judges). Twenty states use a judicial nominating commission to help the governor appoint judges to intermediate appellate courts.

Trial courts

Eight states use partisan elections to select all judges for their general jurisdiction courts and 19 states use nonpartisan elections to do so. Fifteen states and the District of Columbia use a judicial nominating commission to help the governor appoint all judges for these courts. Maine, New Hampshire, and New Jersey allow the governor to appoint without the aid of a judicial nominating commission and South Carolina and Virginia rely on the legislature to appoint these judges. Three states (Indiana, Kansas, and Missouri) use multiple methods to select judges for general jurisdiction trial courts. In Indiana, the method of selection for

superior court or circuit court judges varies by county. In Kansas, it varies by judicial district (17 districts select district court judges using a nominating commission, while 14 use partisan elections). In Missouri, most circuit court judges are elected in partisan contests, but four counties have adopted the commission plan.

Notes

This article originally appeared in Volume 64, Number 4, October 1980, pages 176–193, and was updated in August 2004. It is condensed from a larger study, *Judicial Selection in the United States: A Compendium of Provisions* (Chicago: American Judicature Society, 1980).

1. Eight of the original 13 states vested the appointment power in one or both houses of legislature. Two allowed appointment by the governor and his council, and three vested appointment authority in the governor but required him to obtain consent of the council. Escovitz, *Judicial Selection and Tenure* (Chicago: American Judicature Society, 1975), 4.

2. Niles, "The Popular Election of Judges in Historical Perspective," *The Record of the Association of the Bar of the City of New York* (November 1966), 523.

3. Ibid. at 526.

4. Escovitz, *supra* n. 1, at 6.

5. Niles, *supra* n. 2, at 528.

6. Ibid. at 535, n. 46.

7. Aumann, "Selection, Tenure, Retirement and Compensation of Judges in Ohio," *U. Cin. L. Rev.* 5 (1931), 412, n. 11 .

8. Ibid.

9. Pound, "The Causes of Popular Dissatisfaction With the Administration of Justice," *J. Am. Jud. Soc'y* 20 (February 1937), 178 .

10. Taft, "The Selection and Tenure of Judges," *A.B.A. Rep.* 38 (1913), 418 .

11. Kales, *Unpopular Government in the United States* (Chicago: University of Chicago Press, 1914), chap. 17. *See also* Harley, "Taking Judges Out of Politics," in *Public Administration and Politics* (Philadelphia: The American Academy of Political and Social Science, 1916); and Winters, "Judicial Selection and Tenure," in Winters (ed.), *Selected Readings: Judicial Selection and Tenure* (Chicago: American Judicature Society, 1973).

Interest groups and state court elections: a new era and its challenges

Clive S. Thomas, Michael L. Boyer, and Ronald J. Hrebenar

If the increasing politicization of judicial campaigns of the past 20 years is not addressed, both the quality of those seeking judicial office and the independence of state judiciaries may be seriously undermined.

The greatest challenge facing state supreme courts in the coming century will be the maintenance of judicial independence in an era of increasing politicization of the judicial office . . . it is a problem for every citizen devoted to the rule of law and its preservation.[1]

The origins of the major challenge encapsulated in the quote above can be traced to the dramatic changes in state judicial elections that began in the late 1970s. By 1980, judicial races in several states were high-profile, highly politicized events, a trend that is fast becoming the norm. These changes were largely a result of interest groups entering judicial campaigns with tactics and a level of funding more akin to legislative and executive elections. To be sure, organized groups have long sought to influence policy through state courts by sponsoring litigation and filing amicus briefs, but the recent intensified focus on state judicial elections is both a new element in interest group activity and a new dimension in judicial selection.

According to one observer, this increased interest group influence in state court elections over the past 20 years has ushered in a new era in judicial politics.[2] In particular, this new era ushered in a trend of increasing politicization of judicial elections and produced a major disparity in campaign tactics and funding in favor of interest groups. If this trend is not contained and if this campaign disparity is not addressed, both the quality of those seeking judicial office and the independence of state judiciaries may be seriously undermined.

While definitions of an interest group vary, it may be broadly defined as: "an association of individuals or organizations . . . which on the basis of one or more shared concerns, attempts to influence public policy."[3] Interest groups are indispensable to a liberal democracy as they are a major means by which the views of citizens are represented to government. Among other important functions, groups are a major source of information on issues for policy makers and the public alike; plus, they often play an important role in educating the public during elections and help candidates get elected through financial and other assistance. The role of interest groups is implicitly protected by the First Amendment to the U.S. Constitution and similar provisions in many state constitutions. However, the potential and actual abuses of interest groups have often given them an unsavory image with the public.

James A. Thurber posits that five basic ethical dilemmas accompany interest group activity in politics: (1) groups inject huge sums of money into the process; (2) they make wide use of issue advertising; (3) they contribute to what has been termed the permanent political campaign; (4) conflicts of interest abound when groups fund candidate campaigns; and (5) a norm of reciprocity exists between those in government and those supporting their campaigns.[4] These are certainly concerns involving elected legislative and executive branch officials in the states, but they are particularly troublesome in regard to the role of judges—especially as they affect the election of those to serve on the bench.

The power of interest groups to help elect or defeat a candidate for a state legislature or executive office can be formidable. In such cases, however, there are few legal restrictions on candidates to counter the activities of interest groups. In contrast, judges seeking election, reelection, or reconfirmation are subject to codes of conduct that restrict what they can say in campaigns, but there are few restrictions on interest groups. Add to this the huge sums of money that interest groups can pour into campaigns, compared to judicial candidates, to buy ads to shape the attitude of voters who usually have a very low interest in elections, and the disparity between groups and judges in the election process becomes even wider.

And for a candidate that an interest group supports with major promotional campaigns, the question of conflict of interest may arise as to the payoff that the group will receive once that candidate is on the bench. Furthermore, the threat of a challenge to their reelection or reconfirmation by a well-financed and formidable interest group may make some judges cautious to support unpopular, mainly minority causes.

The central argument in this article is a simple one—that the ideal is to achieve a situation where judges are able to make decisions as free from outside influence and bias as possible. In practice this is not possible to completely achieve in the vast majority of states because, unlike the federal judiciary where there is no reelection or reconfirmation, there is an inherent contradiction in the states between the twin democratic desires for a independent judiciary on the one hand and subjecting judges to popular election or reconfirmation on the other.

However, it is possible to reduce interest group influence on state judicial elections by taking steps to depoliticize these elections or by mitigating the disparities between interest groups and judicial candidates that have increased in recent years. The final section of this article suggests some possible ways that this might be achieved. The article begins by tracing the development of interest group involvement in judicial elections and then places the contemporary influence of interest groups in perspective. The bulk of the article is devoted to exploring the elements of contemporary and likely future problems arising from this increased interest group involvement and why reforms are urgently needed.

Evolution of involvement

The vast majority (87 percent) of state court judges in the United States owe their positions to some form of popular election.[5] Fueled by notions of Jacksonian democracy of the 1830s and 1840s and the populism of the 1870s, 1880s and 1890s, with few exceptions, states entering the Union after 1846 provided for the popular election of some or all of their judiciary, a legacy that remains today.[6] Early opponents of judicial elections feared a politicization of state courts, but the popular election of state judges failed to radically alter the composition of the judiciary because "most sitting judges who ran again won again."[7] Nineteenth century judicial elections were generally quiet events where incumbents won and partisan politics played little part. But there were notable exceptions.

In the early history of state court elections, several high-profile races saw a prominent judge removed

from the bench. These races involved not only partisan politics but also high levels of interest group participation. For instance, in 1873 the defeat of Illinois Chief Justice Charles B. Lawrence came at the hands of the Grangers, an interest group described as a "herd of angry farmers."[8] Similarly, in 1885 Michigan's most "illustrious Supreme Court Justice," Thomas M. Cooley, was removed by labor interests and farmers opposed to his close ties with railroads.[9] Although unusual at the time, the Lawrence and Cooley races demonstrated the power that organized interests could exert and were harbingers signaling the direction of statewide court elections 100 years later.

In the late 1970s and early 1980s, interest groups began to focus on state court elections and dramatically changed the tenor of state judicial politics. This trend has steadily increased so that today extensive interest group participation has become a prominent factor in many statewide judicial elections.[10] A business group leader offered one explanation for this recent development: "in state after state business groups focused on judicial elections after seeing legislative gains undermined by unsympathetic courts."[11]

After the 1986 Ohio Supreme Court election, one of the most publicized multimillion dollar judicial elections of the 1980s, the president of the state bar association explained the impetus for increased interest group involvement more bluntly: "[t]he people with money to spend who are affected by court decisions have reached the conclusion that it's a lot cheaper to buy a judge than a governor or an entire legislature and he can probably do a lot more for you."[12]

Along with increased interest group involvement have come rapidly rising campaign costs and major changes in campaigning techniques. In the early and mid-1980s, judicial elections in Texas, Ohio, and California were among the first multi-million dollar state judicial campaigns complete with television and radio advertisements. One observer encapsulated the dramatic shift in the character of judicial election campaigning as follows:

> Forty-four years ago, I participated in a judicial campaign in Dallas. We put up a few billboards, pasted fliers on telephone poles, and passed out small handbills. Our successful campaign cost a few thousand dollars. There were no contributions of any size. . . . All that has changed dramatically in the last two decades [1980–2000] . . . the amount of money being spent on statewide judicial campaigns has increased exponen-

tially. Judicial campaign expenditures have been doubling every biennium in several states.[13]

Interestingly, those pouring money into these campaigns are not just business groups or conservative interests bent on restricting the rights of various minorities, such as gays. State bar associations and associations of specialty lawyers, particularly trial lawyers, are among the most consistently powerful interests across the states, regardless of whether a state uses the election, merit, or appointment system for judges.[14] These legal lobbies have increased in prominence and effectiveness during the new era of judicial politics. Although state bar associations may have some general public interest in mind in their political activities, narrowly focused professional groups, such as trial lawyers and corporate attorneys, are as much special interests, bent on promoting their own professional benefit, as any business or other special interest group. Thus, ironically, judges up for election may need protection from their former colleagues and current "friends."

To be sure, states have developed varying rules regarding judicial elections (though the core provisions in virtually every state are based on The Model Code of Judicial Conduct promulgated by the American Bar Association). However, existing rules of conduct were developed in an older, tamer era of judicial politics. Consequently, such codes fail to address the role of interest groups in judicial elections and are becoming increasingly outmoded as interest group activity increases.

In perspective

Interest groups participating in judicial elections face barriers that do not exist in legislative or executive races. While there are cases in which state supreme court justices have been removed from office, features of state judicial elections and judicial politics generally serve to insulate incumbents. Thus incumbents still retain major advantages even in the face of increased interest group involvement. In the 2000 judicial elections, for example, the vast majority of incumbents survived well-funded attacks against them by interest groups.

The protections afforded by incumbency serve to illuminate two common features of judicial elections in the states. The foremost feature—even in the new era of judicial politics—is that, once on the bench, a judge is still a relatively permanent fixture. In most states, judges face re-election in some manner, but

"[o]nce on the bench, judges can generally anticipate successful reelection," and even more secure are those up for retention: "in only about 1 percent of . . . retention elections is a judge defeated." [15]

This permanence is likely due, in large part, to one or a combination of two factors. First, competing interest groups may have canceled out each other's efforts to alter the composition of the courts. The second major feature is low voter interest in judicial elections. While low interest can work to the advantage of an interest group, voter indifference has likely worked against interest groups opposing incumbents in judicial elections, causing voters to perfunctorily check the box for incumbents. Despite multi-million dollar campaign efforts, the subtleties of judicial elections are often lost on the average voter.

For example, one Ohio poll during the 2000 judicial race, the "hottest supreme court race in decades," revealed only half of those polled had even "tuned in to the race," and 69 percent of those polled said the incumbent's name sounded familiar while only 45 percent had heard of the challenger.[16] In Michigan, despite record spending, "30 percent of voters were expected to skip choosing judges." [17] In many judicial elections it is unlikely that a majority of voters are familiar with the candidates and even less likely that most voters understand the policy implications of electing judges with different judicial philosophies.

The factors of the permanence of incumbents and voter indifference, which provide shelter from interest group influence, not only protect judges who owe their office to election but also those placed on the bench by merit selection or appointment. Yet selection through a merit plan or gubernatorial appointment does not remove interest groups or lobbying from either the selection or confirmation process.[18] In almost every state that uses the gubernatorial or merit selection method, judges must stand for retention election. And so interest groups may enter the picture and mount challenges to appointees at a later date.[19] Sometimes groups are active in the initial appointment process. Thus, appointment and merit selection, rather than eliminating interest group influence and lobbying, may only delay or place group activity in a different forum.

Even though interest groups—from outside or within the legal profession—may change the composition of a state bench in only a very few instances, the general atmosphere that is being created by this injection of power politics into judicial elections is highly detrimental to the day-to-day work of judges. If one judge can be targeted then all are potential targets. Thus, in the words of Thurber, a "permanent election campaign" could be introduced into judicial selection where judges will have to be careful of their every decision for fear of provoking some interest—conservative or liberal—to oppose them for reelection or reconfirmation. And at election times, the contests have the potential to become as acrimonious and unsavory as many legislative and executive races. A deep-rooted politicization, dirty politics, even gutter politics may well come to judicial elections, as the following case study illustrates.

The 2000 Ohio Supreme Court race. In the fall of 2000, interest groups spent close to $8 million on commercials in their efforts to either retain or replace Ohio Supreme Court Justice Alice Robie Resnick. Ohio trial lawyers, teachers, and unions formed a political action committee (PAC), Citizens for an Independent Court, to support Justice Resnick. Another group, Citizens for a Strong Ohio, was formed by business interests to support the challenger, Terence O'Donnell. And a third group, Ohioans for Fair and Independent Judges, was formed by the insurance industry just to oppose Resnick.[20] A journalist summed up the impact of widespread interest group involvement in this race:

> In a powerful illustration of how special interests can dominate an election and skirt ethics rules, [interest groups from] the two sides ... spen[t] ... millions more than either Justice Resnick, a Toledo Democrat, or Republican challenger Terence O'Donnell, a Cuyahoga County appeals court judge.... The dominance of special interest groups in the election means that voters will see a harsher, more spirited campaign than if candidates alone paid for the advertising. Under Ohio ... rules judicial candidates may not make any promise or attacks on opponents that hint at how they would decide a case ... None of the special interest groups have to follow those rules. In their ads they are free to say what they want.[21]

When interest groups can "say what they want" and a candidate cannot, a disparity of campaign tactics and content develops. In addition, this race was a perfect example of interest groups having far greater resources than the candidates. A feature of the Ohio Code of Judicial Conduct actually sets dollar limits on campaign contributions and expenditures.[22] Despite a federal court ruling such expenditure limits unconsti-

tutional, both candidates vowed to stay within them. Therefore, a financial disparity, albeit self-imposed, existed in the Ohio race. Interest groups wishing to exceed the spending limits and avoid the restrictions on negative campaigning have simply opted to run their own campaigns rather than contribute to candidates.

A 2002 federal court decision has legitimized this interest group tactic used in Ohio and elsewhere. The United States Court of Appeals for the Fifth Circuit, in *Chamber of Commerce of the U.S.A. v. Moore,* ruled that the U.S. Chamber was not subject to state disclosure requirements despite its barrage of ads in the 2000 Mississippi Supreme Court race. These, and similar issue ads, do not advocate specific electoral action and thus escape state disclosure laws. This factor compounds the advantage of interest groups because unsavory but powerful ads will not be linked to the particular group responsible. This lack of accountability further exacerbates the discrepancy between proactive, often aggressive and brazen interest groups and cautious and prudent judicial candidates.

Financially and tactically, the 2000 Ohio Supreme Court election was dominated by interest groups. The U.S. Chamber of Commerce and a group aligned with the Ohio Chamber of Commerce spent an estimated $5 million on advertisements to get out the message that Justice Resnick based her judicial decisions on who had donated to her campaign. Yet both candidates combined could only spend $1 million. So just two related interest groups outspent both candidates five times over. More important, the content of ads bought by interest groups was hard hitting, very direct, and largely unconstrained, which enabled them to get more rhetorical force from their expenditures, a factor exacerbating the spending disparity.

The lack of constraints on interest group campaign content allowed these groups to dictate the tone of campaign dialogue through unsavory attack ads. One anti-Resnick advertisement showed her weighing campaign contributions and stated that she reversed a judicial decision for a contributor. Although Justice Resnick won the election, the upshot was "the nastiest and most expensive Ohio Supreme Court race ever." [23] Even Resnick's opponent, Judge O'Donnell, who stood to benefit from the negative ads sponsored by anti-Resnick interest groups, called them "reprehensible."

The Ohio case illustrates two related and major problems with interest group involvement in judicial campaigns, problems common across the 50 states. One is that the increasing amounts of money poured into these campaigns by interest groups may well threaten judicial independence in the way that major increases in campaign expenditures by interest groups have affected many legislators and executive branch officials. The second is that judges are being increasingly placed at a distinct disadvantage in elections when interest groups get involved and employ tactics hitherto reserved for legislative and executive races. However, a recent U.S. Supreme Court ruling on judicial campaign speech may work to alleviate some of the disparities between interest groups and candidates.

The *White* decision

In *Republican Party of Minnesota v. White* (2002), the U.S. Supreme Court ruled unconstitutional a provision of Minnesota's judicial code of conduct restricting candidates from announcing their views on legal or political issues. By a narrow majority (5–4), the Court found that Minnesota's rule ran afoul of the First Amendment to the U.S. Constitution by infringing upon a candidate's freedom of speech. This decision expanded the protection for judicial campaign speech considerably. Although the Court left intact Minnesota's prohibition on promises or pledges (to decide cases a certain way if elected), as a result of *White,* restrictions prohibiting judicial candidates from announcing their positions on a legal or political issue are unconstitutional.

In addition to expanding the parameters of judicial campaign speech, the Supreme Court's split opinion revealed two fundamentally different views of the judicial branch of state government. The four dissenting justices argued that judicial office is different from executive and legislative office and that judicial campaigns are unique and should be protected to ensure the impartiality of candidates. "Judges . . . are not political actors," wrote Justice Ginsberg. However, the majority of the Court disagreed and argued that the difference between judicial and legislative races is greatly overstated. The majority refused to insulate state court judges "from the enterprise of representative government."

The entire Supreme Court did agree, however, that Minnesota's constitution put judicial officers at the mercy of the electorate, considerably weakening the state's argument for continuing the restriction. Minnesota insisted that prohibiting what judicial candidates can say was necessary in order to protect the integrity of the judicial branch. The Supreme Court disagreed because Minnesota, like many other states, had created the threat to its own judicial branch by mandating that judges be elected. Both the dissent and majority agreed that there was an inherent contradiction in Minnesota law: judicial elections were required yet candidates were prohibited from discussing what the elections were about. The Court's decision tacitly acknowledged the new era of judicial politics and elevated the free speech rights of candidates above states' interest in preserving the impartiality of the judiciary. Using a common First Amendment refrain, the majority felt the solution to threatened impartiality is more speech—not less.

Implicitly, what the majority of the Court was saying in White was that, in the modern era of judicial politics, it is impossible to depoliticize state court elections. Their approach was to accept politicization but to try and even up the balance in campaigns which may, in fact, ratchet up, or even accelerate the trend in politicization of court elections. In contrast, we can conjecture that the minority on the Court have not given up the possibility that state court elections can be considerably depoliticized.

Campaign financing

The key determinants of success in judicial elections are party affiliation, incumbency, and campaign contributions. Campaign contributions are becoming the most decisive factor in determining the outcome of judicial elections in some states. A recent study of judicial elections in Texas from 1980 to 1998 revealed "that in 24 of 28 contested, two party races since 1980, the candidate with the largest contributions total has won." [24] The financing of judicial elections has enormous impacts on public confidence in the judiciary. Today, 75 percent of the public believes that campaign contributions influence judicial decisions.[25]

Two recent in-depth studies have explored judicial campaign financing in individual states. Examining Pennsylvania Supreme Court campaign financing from 1979 to 1997, James Eisenstein identifies patterns of contributions and raises questions about the effects of this private funding on judicial integrity.[26] Kyle Cheek and Anthony Champagne studied Texas Supreme Court races from 1980 to 1998 and found campaign contributions alone may determine outcomes. These studies clearly demonstrate that campaign contributions have the potential to determine the composition of state courts as well as undermine the independence of the state judiciary by creating conflicts of interest.

Campaign contributions are a major, and in many states the major, component of interest group participation in judicial elections. Some PACs are formed solely to influence judicial elections. This is the case, for example, with M-Law in Michigan, "a pro-business organization that spends money for advertising and other public outreach in an effort to influence Michigan judicial elections."[27] Expenditures reported across the states for the 2000 races indicate major interest group involvement. In the Ohio race, considered above, independent interest group campaigning accounted for $8.5 million of the total $10 million spent in the chief justice race.[28] In Michigan, interest group expenditures in the supreme court race reached the $15 million mark.[29]

A glance at funding sources in several states reveals similar patterns as well as areas of concern. Predictably, interest groups that tend to favor candidates from one party for executive or legislative office also tend to favor judicial candidates from the same party. In the 2000 Michigan Supreme Court race, labor unions and trial lawyers spent $2 million on three different Democratic court nominees; business groups and auto makers gave even more to the Republican candidates; and not to be left out, the Democratic and Republican parties pledged to spend more than $2 million each on their respective candidates.

In Alabama, plaintiff law firms were large contributors to court candidates running as Democrats. Nine law firms gave a total of almost $2 million to the State Democratic Executive Committee, which passed on half of it to judicial candidates for appellate and supreme court positions.[30] Insurance and business interests poured similar amounts into Republican campaigns for the same races. In fact, Alabama's 2000 supreme court race was the costliest in the nation, with candidates raising an average of $1.2 million. Alabama is known for its high verdicts in tort cases, and this likely contributed to the level of contributions as business and insurance groups tried to capture the state judiciary and reign in these large awards.

As indicated earlier, one aspect of judicial campaign financing that has proven problematic is the participation by the legal community. In the Eisenstein study, the legal community in Pennsylvania accounted for over half of all contributions and business interests accounted for most of the remaining half.[31] As a general rule, lawyers may contribute to a judicial candidate's campaign as long as the contribution is not intended to influence that candidate's judicial decisions or directly benefit the lawyer or firm. However, some states prohibit contributions from attorneys with cases pending in the candidate's court.[32] Despite potential conflicts of interest, lawyers and groups of lawyers with allied interests are often the most frequent contributors to judicial campaigns, a fact raising questions and concerns.

In North Carolina, for example, attorneys for the plaintiffs in a dispute involving the largest attorney fee award in state history ($64 million) asked their clients, 200,000 retirees in a class action suit, to contribute to the re-election campaign of the chief justice of the state supreme court.[33] Perhaps in response, North Carolina has now ushered in a public funding scheme for judicial elections.

Compelling arguments exist both for and against lawyer contributions to judicial campaigns. Lawyers, it is argued, have the best vantage point from which to consider the suitability of candidates for judicial office. In contrast, the average voter is not knowledgeable enough to determine the competency and performance of a jurist. Ethics opinions (rules that guide the conduct of lawyers) in some states actually encourage lawyer contributions for these reasons.[34]

Even so, the merits of lawyer donations must be weighed against the potential conflicts of interest and diminished perceptions of impartiality. When advocates offer support to a decision maker, the potential for a conflict of interest arises. Lawyers and judges owe a duty of impartiality and fairness to the public, and campaign contributions could potentially compromise that duty. For lawyers, there is a temptation to support judicial candidates with inclinations that benefit their position, client, or client group. For judges, there is a temptation to tread lightly so as not to alienate supporters or potential supporters. Several states have mitigated these temptations by controlling the amount a lawyer or law firm can donate to candidates. The fact that members of the legal community are major campaign donors points to an irony of judicial campaign financing: Those charged with upholding the integrity of the legal system may be partly responsible for its growing problems.

In the new era of judicial politics, campaign expenditures by interest groups, whether to candidates' campaign funds or through independent expenditures, will continue to be a major determinant in contested judicial races and raise increasing concerns among the public about the effects of such donations on the integrity of the judiciary. According to recent surveys by Justice at Stake, a nonpartisan consortium of groups focused on judicial reforms, eight out of ten state court judges and nine out of ten voters are concerned that special interests are using courts to further their own policy goals. That perception is driven by a system that increasingly seats judicial candidates based on their fundraising abilities and interest group support rather than their competency as jurists. The following case study illustrates this clearly.

A single interest group tips the balance—the U.S. Chamber of Commerce in Mississippi's 2000 judicial elections. In 2000, Mississippi saw a hotly contested, high-profile, expensive state supreme court campaign. This was largely due to a U.S. Chamber of Commerce strategy to cast a $10 million net over state supreme court races in Ohio, Alabama, Illinois, Michigan, and Mississippi in order to gain a more business-friendly judiciary in these states.[35] These expenditures contributed to these states being the top five in total judicial campaign fund-raising that year.

Of the five states targeted by the U.S. Chamber, Mississippi was perhaps most impacted by the influx of cash. Almost one-third of the total money raised by the nine Mississippi supreme court candidates came from the Chamber. The result was an informative lesson in interest group influence in state court elections: that the support of a single, powerful interest group in an arena that lacks significant countervailing interest groups can make a difference in the outcomes of judicial elections.

Consider the case of incumbent Mississippi Chief Justice Lenore Prather. She was initially backed by the U.S. Chamber, but later asked them to withdraw their support for her campaign and pull advertisements on her behalf. She was defeated in a very surprising upset by a municipal judge. Two other candidates supported by the Chamber won their seats. The impact of interest group activity in Mississippi revealed that the support of a single powerful group may influence outcomes.

Campaign information

The Ohio and Mississippi case studies clearly show that the level of information in a campaign plays an important role in voter behavior and is critical to understanding the outcome of statewide judicial elections. In contrast to most of the twentieth century's low-profile races, the new era of judicial politics has brought high-profile, multi-million dollar campaigns providing masses of information to voters through television, radio, and newspaper ads as well as mass mailings. Whether the dramatic increase in election information over the past 20 years has actually influenced voter

behavior is an open question. This is because, in contrast to races for legislative and executive office, the impacts of increasing information about candidates and issues in judicial elections must be understood in light of the constraints resulting from judicial office and the information cues available to the public.

In this regard, a study by Hojnacki and Baum is particularly enlightening. They studied voter behavior after the high-profile Ohio Supreme Court races of 1986 and 1988, two races that, at the time, were considered exceptional because of the high expenditures of the candidates and the number of mass media advertisements in the campaign. According to Hojnacki and Baum the effect of increased information on judicial elections depends not only on the quantity of information but also on the quality of that information. They theorized that "changes in the judicial elections have the potential to produce changes in voter behavior" because "provided with greater and more meaningful information about the candidates, voters might be able to make substantial use of high information cues." [36]

According to this theory, if voters were given "high information" cues about a candidate, such as his or her ideology, or a candidate's issue position, the voter could use this to discern between candidates. High information cues are contrasted with "low" and "moderate" information cues. Low information cues include personal characteristics of a candidate or a general impression of candidates and are often determined "from [the] candidates' names alone." [37] Moderate information cues include a candidate's job performance, character, or association with other individuals.

The results of the Hojnacki and Baum study indicated most Ohio voters cited moderate or low information rationales for their choices in the 1986 and 1988 judicial elections. While the increased spending in the 1986 and 1988 elections led to more advertisements and a greater quantity of campaign information, there was no significant increase in the quality of information upon which voters made their decisions. Similarly, the dramatic increases in the amount of information in judicial campaigns over the past 20 years has not led to an increase in the quality of judicial election information.

This trend will continue largely because of several unique features of judicial office that influence the quality of information available to voters in judicial campaigns. Specifically, rules regarding judicial campaign speech have impeded past attempts to inject high information cues, such as policy issues and a candidate's position, into campaigns. However, the Supreme Court's decision in *Republican Party of Minnesota v. White* has, in theory, substantially expanded what a candidate for judicial office may say.

Information post *White*

While *White* gives judges added leeway in announcing their positions, judicial candidates will continue to be far more cautious in terms of the information they present in their campaigns than executive or legislative candidates. This is because most state codes of judicial conduct continue to contain prohibitions against pledges and promises as well as a prohibition on misrepresentations of fact, qualification, or position. In addition, a vague but powerful prohibition in many states requires that judicial candidates "maintain the dignity appropriate to judicial office." The tradition and culture of judicial politics as well as the remaining legal constraints mean that, in practice, judicial candidates are still far from unfettered in devising their campaign message and tactics and will remain at a disadvantage to the interest groups that dominate campaign discourse.

Republican Party of Minnesota v. White is also unlikely to lead to highly informative judicial campaigns in the near future because high information cues are simply more difficult to inject into judicial campaigns than legislative and executive races. The nature of judicial office entails concealing individual ideology and preferences in order to ensure impartiality. This makes it more difficult for voters to determine how a vote for one candidate or another will impact the voter's daily life. But differences in judicial philosophy among candidates do exist, and these can lead to significant policy implications. Indeed, interest groups have flocked to judicial campaigns over the past 20 years to exploit subtle differences in perspective. However, these differences among candidates are very difficult to convey to voters in modern campaigns.

For example, trying to explain one judicial candidate's reverence for legal precedence or that another is a strict constructionist of the constitution is a message both lost on the average voter and unsuitable for a 30-second commercial. In addition, attempts to center a judicial campaign on judicial ideology or past decisions (high information cues) require a preliminary lesson in civics and the common law to bring the general public up to speed. Such a campaign would be expensive to fund, not to mention dull. A highly informative judicial campaign could even backfire and

lead to a public debate about the value of an independent judiciary.

While the major issues and subtle differences in judicial elections often translate poorly into campaigns, interest groups have found other moderate or low information methods to convey their messages. Attack ads and sound bytes now serve as a common default method for conveying low to moderate information cues and avoiding the complexities involved in a high information judicial campaign. Interest group ads are much more likely to be attack ads than are those sponsored by candidates or political parties. A recent report found that of 4,459 television ad airings sponsored by interest groups in the 2000 judicial elections, 3,575 (80.3 percent) were attack ads, but only 18.4 percent of ads sponsored by candidates and only 27 percent of those sponsored by parties were attack ads.[38]

The reason negative campaigning, attack ads, and sound bytes are so popular is because little information is required for a voter to base his or her vote on a candidate's inadequacies. It is much easier to develop an ad portraying a candidate as a scoundrel than to explain why the group opposes the candidate. Moreover, the average voter is more apt to grasp a moderate or low information cue that seeks to create a negative impression than a high information cue about judicial ideology.

Consider Chief Justice Resnick in our Ohio case study. Business groups took issue with an opinion regarding corporate liability authored by Resnick. The television advertisement that followed spoke little about corporate liability, ideology, or the merits of the case. Instead "the ad shows Lady Justice peeking out of her blindfold as an unidentified person dumps money onto her scales," and the voice in the background states, "Resnick became the only justice to reverse herself in the case—Alice Resnick, is justice for sale?"[39] But it is not only a candidate's character that is under fire in the new era of judicial politics; unpopular causes are also at a high risk of losing ground.

Collateral damage

An observable consequence of the increased involvement of certain interest groups in judicial elections is the negative effect on unpopular causes. As state courts become arenas for interest group policy battles, a number of politically charged issues have taken on a new dimension. State judges are now more vulnerable than ever with respect to certain cases and subjects that come before them. Most notably, a judge who preserves the legal rights of a criminal defendant in a death penalty case (particularly if the defendant committed a shocking crime) could give powerful ammunition to his opposition in the next election. For example, a common attack ad format provides the inflammatory details of a grisly murder followed by a statement that the incumbent did not think the death penalty was appropriate.

Interest groups have successfully painted numerous judicial candidates as soft on crime and reluctant to impose the death penalty. This approach has led to the removal of state supreme court justices, but additional side effects may be linked to this tactic. The tendency of interest groups to attack judges on their death penalty records could be linked to increases in the rates at which death penalty judgments are affirmed by state supreme courts. Gerald Uelman notes that from 1985 to 1995 supreme courts in six states increased the rates in which they affirm death penalty judgments from 63 percent in 1985 to 90 percent in 1995. This period of dramatic increase corresponds with the rise in interest group influence in state courts and high-profile judicial elections.

Other politically charged issues that produce campaign fodder include abortion, term limits, the environment, and gay rights. Paradoxically, the judicial branch was established, in part, to protect the legal rights of unpopular constituencies by upholding the values of equal protection, due process, fairness, and privacy. Yet the threat of well-funded attacks by interest groups may have eroded not only judicial autonomy, but also the rights of politically unpopular groups and causes that only an independent judiciary can protect. No matter which candidate wins in a judicial election, the real losers in the new era of judicial politics are often the unpopular groups that the judiciary was partly designed to protect.

Reform possibilities

Changes in judicial elections have far outpaced measures for reform over the past 20 years. Lawyers, judges, and political scientists have suggested several reforms that range from minor adjustments in existing judicial election rules to the most extreme recommendation of completely doing away with such elections.

Although there is certainly human bias in federal judges and often intense battles over their confirmation, the federal judiciary is largely insulated from politics and is likely no more politicized today than it was during the New Deal, perhaps less so. To have

maintained the tenure of state court judges along similar lines, as in the early state constitutions, would likely mean that today state courts would not be facing the problems of politicization. But a return to the federal system is very unlikely to occur in any state in the foreseeable future. Thus other reforms, that are in the realm of political possibility, both formal (legal) and informal (political), must be made if the trend toward politicization and the unevenness of the electoral contest between judicial candidates and interest groups is to be alleviated and possibly reversed.

Set out below are several possible reforms. Some will advance depoliticization while others will even up the balance between interest groups and judges in elections.

Public funding of state judicial elections. Reforms aimed at public funding for state appellate and supreme court races are among the most effective means of countering interest group influence in state court elections. Full public funding immediately mitigates the conflicts of interest present when interest groups fund judicial candidates' campaigns. Also, public funding schemes that entail spending caps also put all candidates on an equal footing regardless of interest group support.

In October of 2002, North Carolina became the first state to pass such a law. Similar bills have been introduced in Texas and Illinois, and coalitions of reform groups have organized efforts to publicly fund judicial elections in Idaho, Georgia, and Ohio. Wisconsin has partially funded supreme court elections since the 1970s, but the system currently provides insufficient funds to candidates. However, a bill to restore Wisconsin's public funding of judicial elections to meaningful levels recently passed the state senate.

Disqualification. Forbidding judges to hear cases in which campaign contributors are also litigants could be a first step in reform; a per se rule has yet to be put into practice. As long as judicial elections are privately funded, disqualification rules will remain problematic. However, disqualification rules could be used to blunt the effect of interest groups that circumvent campaign disclosure and spending rules. For example, a judge could be disqualified from a case involving an organization that made undisclosed campaign expenditures in excess of statutory limits. The disqualification could apply to any organization that made campaign expenditures designed to influence the outcome of the judicial election in which the judge was retained or elected to office.[40]

Campaign finance limits. States should adopt the August 24, 1999 American Bar Association amendments to the Model Code of Judicial Conduct that deal with judicial election contribution limits and require judges to disqualify themselves if parties or their lawyers have contributed in excess of these limits. Only a minority of states have adopted these reforms.

Public education. States should institute programs to educate the public regarding the judicial branch of government and judicial elections. This is particularly needed in the nation's high schools, where civics classes rarely cover the role of the judiciary and the special circumstances associated with judicial office. Topics could include: the merits of judicial independence; what judges do and how their opinions affect citizens; and the problems popular elections pose to the goals of an independent judiciary. Educational efforts could also explain the sources of ads at election time, including who funds them and how judges may be limited in their response.

Reform-minded public interest groups. From a political perspective, an effective antidote to undue interest group influence is often countervailing interest groups. In the 1980s and early 1990s, there was a noticeable lack of countervailing organizations advocating for judicial independence. Recently, however, a growing number of interest groups have taken up judicial election reform. These include: the Courts Initiative (formerly Citizens for Independent Courts), the National Center for the Influence of Money on State Politics, the Center for Responsive Politics, the Justice at Stake Campaign, the Institute on Money in State Politics, the Brennan Center for Justice, Public Citizen, and the Center for Public Integrity at the national level; and in individual states, Kansans for an Independent Judiciary, the Illinois Campaign for Political Reform, Texans for Public Justice, the North Carolina Center for Voter Education, and Wisconsin Citizen Action. These reform groups can help restore the balance to judicial campaigns by countering the messages of much more narrowly based interests. The U.S. Supreme Court, in *Republican Party of Minnesota v. White,* has agreed with this reform in principle by hinting that the answer to threats from increasingly political judicial elections is more speech, not less.

As indicated above, *White* may well increase the politicization of state court elections rather than depoliticize them, while the goal of most of these reform groups is to depoliticize the courts and judicial elections and promote judicial independence. However, given the limits to which state judiciaries and judicial elections can be depoliticized in the new era of judicial politics, this countervailing role of reform groups is probably their major contribution to the judicial election process at the moment.

Improved voter guides. In many states these guides inform voters about judicial candidates. Until now they have provided moderate information cues about candidates and filled the information void resulting from a barrage of low information media ads. Because judicial campaign speech rules are now expanded, voter guides have the potential to become a source of high information cues about candidates that could counteract sound bytes and attack ads sponsored by interest groups.

Further clarification of judicial campaign speech limits. White has opened the door for state court candidates to announce their positions on legal and political issues but leaves several unresolved issues regarding judicial campaign speech. For example, the line between announcing a position and pledging to decide cases in a certain way is not well defined. Also, many state codes of judicial conduct include broad language requiring that judicial candidates maintain the dignity appropriate to judicial office and act in a manner consistent with an independent judiciary.[41] This vague prohibition has been used to limit the political activity of candidates in the past, and it remains to be seen how this prohibition will square with the Court's decision in White that permits candidates to be more open in their campaigns.

Required public renunciations. A required public renunciation (RPR) could be incorporated into a state's code of judicial conduct. It could require that all judicial candidates publicly and in a timely manner renounce any advertisement or public statement by an individual or group on behalf of or relating to candidates if the ad or statement would violate the code had it been made by a judicial candidate. The goal would be to counter unregulated attacks and negative issue ads while not infringing on free speech rights.

An RPR could be as simple as a press release or a repeated radio or television public announcement.

Guidance as to the content of RPRs could come through model RPR statements drafted by committees of judges, lawyers, and the public. The statements would be unemotional and neutral, and would state that the candidate is neither the source of the advertisement nor does the candidate condone the advertisement. While not for advocacy purposes, the RPRs could serve to educate the public regarding the funding sources of attack ads, the aggressive tactics of some interest groups, and the nature of judicial office in the state.

While not expressly adopting the required public renunciation, the Mississippi Supreme Court has planned to create a rapid response team to combat third-party attack ads. The rapid response team would assess an ad's veracity, then hold a press conference to state its findings.[42] While different in name, the two concepts both entail countering an interest group attack ad in a public forum.

The above reforms are designed to either depoliticize judicial elections or to allow judicial candidates to meet interest groups with equal rhetorical force in the campaign while also seeking to promote civil and informative campaign discourse that balances judicial independence with political accountability. The reforms reflect a new model of judicial politics that takes into account the dramatic changes over the past 20 years in state judicial elections. In designing their models of reform, states should focus on guiding the statements candidates can make and activities that should be appropriate in light of the realities of the twenty-first century judicial campaign.

Notes

This article originally appeared in Volume 87, Number 3, November–December 2003, pages 135–144, 149.

1. Uelmen, "Crocodiles in the Bathtub: Maintaining the Independence of State Supreme Courts in an Era of Judicial Politicization," *Notre Dame L. Rev.* 72 (1997), 1133–1153.

2. Champagne, "Interest Groups and Judicial Elections," *Loy. L.A. L. Rev.* 34 (2001), 1391–1408.

3. Thomas and Hrebenar, "Interest Groups in the States," in Gray and Hanson, eds., *Politics in the American States: A Comparative Analysis,* 8th ed., chap. 4 (Washington, D.C.: CQ Press, 2003).

4. Thurber, "Interest Groups: From Campaigning to Lobbying," in Nelson, Dulio and Medvic, eds., *Shades of Gray: Perspectives on Campaign Ethics* (Washington, D.C.: Brookings Institution, 2002).

5. Maute, "Selecting Justices in State Courts: The Ballot Box or the Backroom," *S. Tex. L. Rev.* 41 (2000), 1197–1245.

6. Friedman, *A History of American Law,* 2nd ed. (New York: Simon & Schuster, 1985), 371–372.

7. Ibid.

8. Ibid.

9. Ibid.

10. Champagne, *supra* n. 2. *See also* Hrebenar, Thomas, and Boyer, "Interest Group Politics in State Courts," a paper presented at the annual meeting of the Western Political Science Association, Las Vegas, Nev., March 15–17, 2001.

11. Danos, "The Sizzle of Judicial Election Reform: Implications for Judicial Leadership," www.ncsc.dni.us/KMO/Projects/Trends/99-00/Articles/JudclElecReform.htm, citing Mathesian, "Bench Press: Its Legislative Gains Undone by Unsympathetic State Supreme Courts, the Business Lobby Bringing Its Political Resources to Bear on Judicial Elections," www.governing.com.

12. Kaplan, "Justice For Sale," *Common Cause Mag,* May–June 1987, 29–30.

13. Carrington, "Big Money in Texas Judicial Elections: The Sickness and Its Remedies," *SMU L. Rev.* 53 (2000), 263.

14. Thomas and Hrebenar, *supra* n. 3.

15. Stumpf and Culver, *Politics of State Courts* (New York: Longman, 1992).

16. Brown, "Ohio Voters Cool to Red-Hot Contests for Supreme Court," *Cleveland Plain Dealer,* Oct. 23, 2000.

17. Shepardson, "Stakes Rise in Court Race," *The Detroit News,* Oct. 31, 2000.

18. *See, e.g.,* Maute, *supra* n. 5.

19. Stumpf and Culver, *supra* n. 15: Massachusetts, Rhode Island, and New Hampshire are the exceptions which give state judges life tenure.

20. Hunt, "Special Interests Dominate Ohio Supreme Court Race," *The Cincinnati Enquirer,* Oct. 2, 2000.

21. Ibid.

22. Ohio Code of Judicial Conduct, Canon 7(C)(6)(a)(i)&(ii).

23. Brown, *supra* n. 16.

24. Cheek and Champagne, "Money in Texas Supreme Court elections: 1980–1998," *Judicature* 84 (2000), 20–25.

25. Mauro, "Judges Shouldn't Have to Please Voters," *USA Today,* Oct. 18, 2000.

26. Eisenstein," Financing Pennsylvania's Supreme Court candidates," *Judicature* 84 (2000), 10.

27. Champagne, *supra* n. 2.

28. Provance, "Ohio Supreme Court Elections May Cost 10 Million," *Toledo Blade,* October 31, 2000.

29. Shepardson, "Stakes Rise in Court Race," *Detroit News,* Oct. 31, 2000.

30. Bailey, "Bench Hopefuls Get Lawyers' Donations," *Birmingham News,* Oct. 6, 2000.

31. Eisenstein, *supra* n. 26.

32. *See, e.g.,* N.Y. State Bar Ass'n Comm. on Prof. Ethics, Op. 289 (1973).

33. Rice, "Donations to Justices Questioned," *Winston-Salem Journal,* Oct. 21, 2000.

34. *See, e.g.,* Ky. Bar Ass'n Ethics Comm., Op. E-277 (1984); Fla. Sup. Ct. Comm. on Standards of Conduct Governing Judges, Op. 80-9 (1980); N.Y. State Bar Ass'n Comm. on Prof. Ethics, Op. 289 (1973).

35. Stone, "Jousting over Judges," *The National Journal,* June 24, 2000.

36. *See* Hojnacki and Baum, "Choosing judicial candidates: How voters explain their decisions," *Judicature* 75 (1992), 300.

37. Ibid. at 51.

38. Goldberg, Holman and Sanchez, "The New Politics of Judicial Elections," a report prepared February 2002 for Justice at Stake Campaign, Brennan Center for Justice, and The Institute on Money in State Politics.

39. National Public Radio, Morning Edition, Peter Overby, Nov. 3, 2000.

40. See generally, Carrington, *supra.* n. 13.

41. *See, e.g.,* ABA Model Code of Judicial Conduct (1990), Canon 5: A Judge or Judicial Candidate shall refrain from inappropriate political activity.

42. Darden, "Irving Supports Electing Judges," Greenwood (Mississippi) *Commonwealth,* Nov. 16, 2001.

Trends in judicial retention elections, 1964–1998

Larry Aspin

*Fewer judges are being defeated, their affirmative vote is increasing,
and more voters than ever are participating in retention elections.*

"Is it true that the affirmative vote in judicial retention elections continues to decline?" "Are judges increasingly being voted out of office?" Such fundamental concerns are addressed by the Judicial Retention Project,[1] which now contains judicial retention election results from the 1960s, when several states adopted the merit-retention system, to 1998. The basic electoral patterns were first reported through 1984,[2] these findings were later updated through 1994,[3] and now the 1996 and 1998 elections can also be reported. The purpose here is to describe the general trends in four significant areas: the affirmative vote, defeated judges, voter differentiation, and rolloff.

Affirmative vote

Figure 1 and Table 1 report the variability in the national mean affirmative vote across time. The national average dropped 9 points from 1968 to 1974, whereupon it remained relatively stable until 1990. Then the affirmative vote suffered a 7-point drop in a single election cycle, declining from 76.7 percent in 1988 to 69.4 percent in 1990. The average then again drifted upward until the sharp increase in the 1998 election brought it back to the level of the 1980s.

Part of this temporal variability in the affirmative vote can be attributed to changes in political trust. The volatile trust index is more sensitive to trust in national institutions/officials than to trust in state and local officials, yet parallel trends in the political trust index and the affirmative vote are clearly evident in Figure 1. The correlation coefficient between the trust index and affirmative vote is .89 for the years 1964 through 1998.

In addition to the yearly variation, the affirmative vote continues to vary from state to state and from district to district within states (see Table 1). However, even though the Alaska and Wyoming means are 10 points apart in 1998, all the state means are well above the thresholds required for retention. Thus, the vast majority of judges have been retained; only occasionally have voters removed them from the bench.

Defeated judges

In only 52 of 4,588 judicial retention elections were judges not retained. The type of court is of no relevance to whether a judge is defeated, but the required threshold is important. Of the 4,588 elections, 86.2 percent were major trial court elections and, similarly, 92 percent of the defeated judges were trial court judges. In contrast, while 32.7 percent of all elections were in Illinois, which alone requires a 60 percent affirmative vote for retention, 53.8 percent of the defeated judges were in that state. Interestingly, of the 28 defeated Illinois judges only 1 had an affirmative vote below 50 percent.

As seen in Table 2, after the 1990 peak, when 10 Illinois judges were defeated, the number of defeated judges has steadily declined. This decline culminated in 1998 when, for the first time since 1970, no judge was defeated. While this recent downward trend is an interesting development, we must be careful in interpreting patterns. One reason for caution is that the most significant factors in a typical retention election may be very different than those in elections where judges are not retained. In the typical retention election, non-judge-specific factors (e.g., political trust) play large roles, whereas judge-specific variables (e.g., a judge's controversial act) play large roles when judges are defeated. Thus, we should not assume a simple direct relationship between the national affirmative vote and the number of judges defeated.[4] Judges are not defeated simply because of a general decline in the affirmative vote.

Voter differentiation

The defeat of 52 judges demonstrates that voters can and do single out some judges for special attention. However, in most elections voters have increasingly painted all judges with the same brush.

One way to express the typical lack of voter differentiation among judges is with a judge's absolute deviation from the district-year mean. This district-year mean, which controls for inter-state and inter-district variation

Figure 1. Affirmative retention vote, rolloff, and political trust

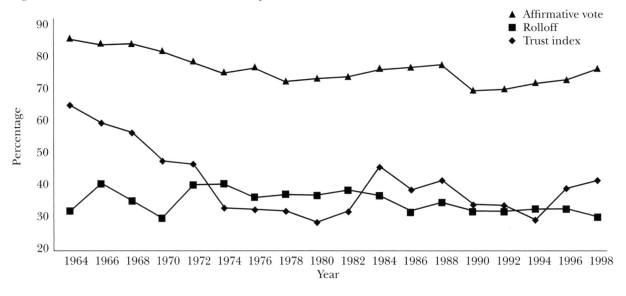

Table 1. Mean percentage vote for retention by state and year

Year	Alaska	Arizona	Colorado	Illinois	Indiana	Iowa	Kansas	Missouri	Nebraska	Wyoming	Yearly average	Number of elections
1964	71.7	—	—	85.5	—	—	71.6	82.0	87.2	—	84.7%	(127)
1966	72.9	—	—	87.2	—	—	—	80.3	84.8	—	83.8%	(56)
1968	74.6	—	—	86.4	—	—	78.8	80.6	85.8	—	83.6%	(47)
1970	76.6	—	75.7	84.5	—	—	73.2	78.3	83.4	—	81.2%	(172)
1972	74.9	—	74.0	79.5	68.1	84.4	78.8	79.0	82.6	—	78.0%	(246)
1974	71.5	—	75.9	73.7	67.4	84.1	77.8	76.5	80.9	66.1	74.6%	(143)
1976	69.0	77.2	73.9	76.7	66.0	80.5	80.9	76.9	77.6	80.5	76.6%	(215)
1978	67.2	73.4	70.6	72.7	64.7	78.5	80.0	73.2	77.9	79.5	73.7%	(310)
1980	63.9	81.6	71.7	73.4	66.9	78.2	77.1	71.1	77.2	76.0	74.2%	(271)
1982	60.2	80.0	72.1	74.3	65.9	78.2	81.7	69.5	79.2	75.2	74.7%	(326)
1984	68.4	81.0	74.2	77.2	71.2	77.4	82.6	72.8	73.6	75.6	76.4%	(324)
1986	71.1	79.8	71.7	75.5	63.0	80.2	84.1	71.0	74.7	73.8	76.2%	(310)
1988	68.9	78.7	75.0	76.7	66.1	79.1	79.5	69.5	78.7	78.2	76.7%	(320)
1990	68.2	69.2	67.4	69.7	63.4	76.5	73.4	58.5	75.2	74.3	69.4%	(370)
1992	64.4	66.8	68.8	72.8	63.3	74.2	72.1	63.0	70.3	58.2	69.6%	(329)
1994	66.3	72.7	67.3	75.3	62.1	73.7	70.7	64.6	72.5	76.6	71.6%	(351)
1996	68.9	72.1	66.5	75.0	68.8	74.1	76.0	67.6	67.1	77.5	72.0%	(340)
1998	68.4	75.8	73.2	78.6	71.5	77.0	75.4	68.7	75.8	78.4	75.8%	(331)

in the affirmative vote, is the average affirmative vote for all judges on the same ballot—when there are at least four judges on the ballot. The absolute difference between a judge's affirmative vote and the district-year mean indicates the degree to which the judge has been treated differently—for whatever reason—than his or her fellow judges in the same judicial district.

For the 2,485 elections where four or more judges were on the ballot, the average absolute deviation was 2.1 percent. Thus, while the affirmative vote varies con-

Table 2. Defeated judges: number and mean percentage vote for retention by year and retention threshold

	1964	1972	1974	1976	1978	1980	1982	1984	1986	1988	1990	1992	1994	1996	1998	Total
50 percent required																
mean	46.7	39.2	44.2	0	42.7	25.3	42.7	34.6	36.5	48.8	0	42.3	43.5	40.6	0	41.2%
number	1	1	1	0	5	1	3	2	1	1	0	4	2	2	0	24
60 percent required																
mean	0	0	59.8	58.8	57.0	52.1	56.3	0	56.4	55.4	55.3	55.3	57.8	0	0	55.8%
number	0	0	1	1	4	3	1	0	3	1	10	2	2	0	0	28
Total																
mean	46.7	39.2	52.0	58.8	49.0	45.4	46.1	34.6	51.4	52.1	55.3	46.6	50.6	40.6	0	49.1%
number	1	1	2	1	9	4	4	2	4	2	10	6	4	2	0	52

Illinois requires a 60 percent affirmative vote for retention; all other states require a 50 percent affirmative vote.

Figure 2. Average absolute difference from the district-year mean affirmative vote

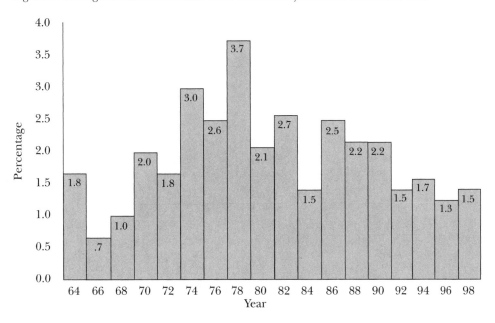

siderably from state to state and district to district, within a district the typical judge's affirmative vote differs very little from that of the other judges in the district.

As reported in Figure 2, the mean absolute difference from the district-year mean peaked in 1978 at a high of 3.7 percent. From 1980 to 1990 the average absolute difference was 2.2 percent; it then declined to 1.5 percent for the elections from 1992 though 1998. Voters apparently are differentiating less among judges in the 1990s then they were in the previous two decades.

Rolloff

While voters may be differentiating less among judges, they are increasing their rate of participation in judicial retention elections. Rolloff is the percentage of balloting voters who do not vote in the retention election. As illustrated in Figure 1, rolloff has declined across the decades and now stands at an all-time low. The average rolloff was 36.0 percent between 1976 and 1984, 32.4 percent between 1986 and 1996, and 29.5 percent in 1998.

****

The last decade has been one of evolutionary change for the four reported elements of judicial retention elections. The affirmative vote has recovered from its 1990 plunge, but remains below the highs of the 1960s. The number of judges being defeated peaked in 1990 and then slowly declined to no losses in 1998. More voters are participating in judicial retention elections than ever before, but they are differentiating less than ever among the judges on the ballot.

Notes

This article originally appeared in Volume 83, Number 2, September–October 1999, pages 79–81.

1. The 4,588 retention elections in the data set are all major trial court, appellate court, and supreme court retention elections held in Alaska, Arizona, Colorado, Illinois, Indiana, Iowa, Kansas, Missouri, Nebraska, and Wyoming from 1964 through 1998. These 10 states use pure retention elections for the major trial court and all higher courts, hold the elections during fall general elections in even-numbered years (i.e., 1978, 1980, etc.), and began using retention elections at least by 1976.

2. Hall and Aspin, "What twenty years of judicial retention elections have told us," *Judicature* 70 (1987), 340.

3. Aspin, Hall, Bax, and Montoya, "Thirty years of judicial retention elections: an update," *Soc. Sci. J.* 37 (2000).

4. Note that the sharp 1990 decline in the affirmative vote occurred in 9 of 10 states, but the only judges defeated in 1990 were in Illinois. Conversely, the defeat of 10 judges in 1990 was not the reason for the decline in the national affirmative vote that year. There are so few defeated judges that removing them from the data produces no effect on the national average affirmative vote.

A historical perspective on federal judicial selection

Elliot E. Slotnick

Although the tension between the executive and legislative branches over judicial selection is not new, today we are at a crossroads in determining how the process will work in the future.

Federal judicial selection, at least for the lower courts, has been a relatively invisible focal point for public interest until recent years. This has been so despite the fact that judicial selection processes represent that very rare interface in American politics where, as is the case in some largely ceremonial occasions such as a State of the Union Address, all three branches of government come into play at the same time and enter the public stage at the same time.

The contemporary tensions between the executive and legislative branches that we witnessed during the Clinton administration between a Democratic president and a Republican Senate and that we clearly are seeing between a Republican president and what is now a Democratic Senate during the first year and a half of the Bush administration are not completely new phenomena.

Indeed, debate at the Constitution's founding demonstrates that the relative roles of the executive and the legislative branches in this arena were a bone of contention among the framers. The Virginia Plan called for congressional selection of judges, while the New Jersey Plan lodged the power in the executive. Ultimately a compromise was reached, and the new constitutional language for "advice and consent" grew out of the language of the Special Committee on Postponed Matters, the Convention Committee whose workload included some of the most contentious and important matters in our country's founding.

Historically, and for the most part, choosing lower federal court judges, as distinct from Supreme Court justices, has been a relatively routine activity of American presidents. While, clearly, presidents have accentuated patronage historically, they did not necessarily accentuate policy in their appointment behavior. This has been particularly the case when those choices were initially suggested by, or at minimum received a clearance from, the senators from the president's party if there were any from the state in which a vacancy existed.

This clearance would be obtained through two mechanisms: across institutions, through senatorial courtesy exercised by the White House in conferring with the home state senators of the president's party; and within the Senate itself through the Judiciary Committee's blue slip. The blue slip has worked to ensure that home state senators of both parties, whether or not they are of the president's party, have some say when judges are being nominated from their state.

This isn't to say that policy motivations never entered into the president's choices. One can look, for example, to the Roosevelt administration and its efforts to support the New Deal through lower court appointments for some clear-cut evidence of these kinds of considerations. For example, in late 1936, William Denman, who was a Ninth Circuit Roosevelt appointee, wrote bluntly to the president, "The New Deal needs more federal judges." [1] In January 1937, three weeks before the unveiling of the court packing plan by the president, Roosevelt asked his appointment secretary about the potential candidacy of Sidney Mize for a district court judgeship:

"I want more information on this man as to whether he is a liberal or a reactionary. What sort of fellow is he?" [2]

Roosevelt received assurance from his assistant attorney general that he had, "looked carefully into the matter. I am convinced that Mr. Mize is a man of liberal views and would measure up in all respects to the expectations of the president."

Still, however, prior to the Nixon administration, policy considerations and/or ideological ones didn't often take primacy in lower court selection processes, both in the president's nomination behavior and in the Senate's exercise of advice and consent. Timely confirmation of virtually all presidential nominees was, in essence, routine and somewhat pro forma. Obviously, a good deal has changed in recent years, which of course brings us here today. I would like to explore some of those changes.

How it changed

For its part, the Nixon administration recognized the potential that judicial appointments, even those in the lower courts, perhaps especially those in the lower courts, could play in its policy agenda—in this instance, an agenda that stressed "law and order" and "strict construction of the Constitution" to quote the words of the administration.

Perhaps the most historically interesting "smoking gun" of the policy implications of judicial selection can be found in a seven-page memo written by a then young Nixon aide by the name of Tom Charles Huston, a memo that Nixon himself endorsed. Huston wrote, and I quote, "Perhaps the least considered aspect of presidential power is the authority to make appointments to the federal bench, not merely the Supreme Court, but to the district and circuit court benches as well. Through his judicial appointments a president has the opportunity to influence the course of national affairs for a quarter of a century after he leaves office." Huston concluded that if the president "establishes his criteria and establishes machinery for ensuring that those criteria are met, the appointments he makes will be his in fact as well as in theory." [3]

After this memo was read by H. R. Haldeman and John Ehrlichman, it was sent directly to the president who in turn forwarded it to his Deputy Assistant Attorney General, Richard Kleindeist, who handled judicial nominations. There was a handwritten presidential notation on the memo, "RN agrees. Have this analysis in mind when making judicial nominations."

I think despite this memo it is a bit too easy to point to the Nixon administration as the historical point in time where the most significant changes took place in the nature of federal judicial selection. For one thing, I think the apparatus that was sought by Huston and the policy implications of judicial selection of which he spoke were not fully realized until the centralization of the judicial selection process that took place during the Reagan years in the White House.

For my part—and I think this is where my analysis gets off the track a little from the standard stories of this—I think the modern era of contentious politicized judicial selection politics can be traced to, perhaps surprisingly, the Carter administration. The reasons are many.

Selection under Carter

Framing judicial selection in the Carter administration, the Omnibus Judgeship Act of 1978 created 152 federal judgeships. This was the most ever handed at one time to a sitting president. Thirty-five of these seats were at the appeals court level. This unprecedented expansion of the judiciary did not go unnoticed by interested parties of every political stripe who recognized the policy role that these new judges would play well into the future.

Second, Jimmy Carter took actions that really struck at the heart of "business as usual" in judicial selection by establishing the United States Circuit Judge Nominating Commission. This was a set of 13 panels, one in each judicial circuit, with members appointed by the president who would prepare a confidential report for the president for each vacancy recommending the five persons best qualified to fill the judgeship.

While the identification of appeals court appointments has always been tied more directly to the president than to specific identifiable senators because, of course, judicial circuits cross state boundaries, it remains the case that there have been traditions of state seats on the circuit courts. And historically, overwhelmingly, the majority of replacement appointments for appeals court vacancies have, indeed, gone to judges from the state in which the vacancy arose. So, senators often did have a personal stake in circuit appointments, and to many senators Carter's actions were seen as an unwarranted inroad on senatorial prerogatives of fairly long standing.

Making matters worse, from this kind of conflictual perspective, President Carter attempted to intervene in district court appointments as well—clearly, processes which were even much more closely tied to the choices of home state senators from the president's party. Indeed, he wrote a personal longhand letter to every Democratic senator urging them to establish similar nominating commissions in their home states for the selection of district court judge nominees. It was to this suggestion that Senator Lloyd Bentsen is alleged to have responded, "I am the merit commission for the State of Texas."

Policy motivations

I think in the Carter administration there was a "stirring of the pot" of judicial selection processes that raised critical tensions in the balance between executive and legislative roles, tensions that continue with us today. Further, and I think as important as Carter's reforms and processes were, the president's strong personal interest in judicial selection was tied to some very strong policy motivations and substantive concerns regarding issues of affirmative action and the representativeness of the federal bench along racial and gender lines.

Not until the presidency of Franklin Roosevelt was the first woman appointed to a lifetime position on the federal bench. Harry Truman appointed the first African American to a lifetime appointment. Eisenhower did not name a single woman or black to a lifetime judgeship during his eight years in office. Some increases in judicial diversity occurred during the Kennedy, Johnson, and Nixon years, but they were by no means dramatic.

It was in this context that Carter's concerns about this issue were articulated in two ways, both of which ended up being controversial. First, in an Executive Order addressed to his Circuit Judge Nominating Commission, the president stated that, "Each panel is encouraged to make special efforts to seek out and identify well-qualified women and members of minority groups as potential nominees."

This strong and, frankly, previously unheard of push for meaningful affirmative action in judicial selection and the concern for diversity and representativeness among the president's nominees were not taken to kindly by many senators. Once again, the president wrote to each Democratic senator urging that they recruit women and minorities for the new judgeships and other vacancies. Indeed, sometimes, when names weren't forthcoming, the attorney general would literally send back the names and ask them to reopen the search.

In addition to a call for affirmative action, the president also ordained in another Executive Order that nominating commissions ensure that the candidate, and here was the kicker, "Possesses and has demonstrated a commitment to equal justice under the law." This was seen by many conservative senators as a euphemism for liberal judicial activism. As one senator on the Judiciary Committee told me in an interview at the time, "Fairminded? Equal justice? Maybe I am not picking up on the secret code, but I don't think I like what that means."

Interestingly and ironically, the president's open avowal of a substantive preference in his nominees even created tensions with people we would think were his "nominal friends." For example, Ted Kennedy, who you may recall chaired the Judiciary Committee in those days and was also a potential rival to Carter for the 1980 Democratic presidential nomination, authorized a Judiciary Committee questionnaire in which nominees were asked, "In what specific ways have you demonstrated a commitment to equal justice during your career?" Carter was, in effect, being criticized from the right for his substantive commitment in appointments, while, from the left, his feet were being held to the fire to make sure that his nominees actually met those very commitments.

Importantly, though, I think it should be noted that the Carter reform efforts did bear fruit. When Jimmy Carter took office, six women had been appointed to lifetime federal judgeships in our nation's history—Carter appointed 40 in four years. Similarly, while 33 ethnic minorities—blacks, Hispanics, and Asians—had been appointed prior to the Carter administration in the nation's history, 55 were seated during Jimmy Carter's four-year tenure.

Letting out the genie

Once this genie of avowedly open policy considerations in judicial selection had been let out of the bottle, and once an increase in the White House's political role in judicial selection, as distinct from the Justice Department's role in assessing the credentials of candidates increased, as it did during the Carter years, it would be very difficult to return to old ways.

In the wake of the Carter years, we were met by the two-term presidency of Ronald Reagan in which the policy agenda of the president and centralized White House control of judicial selection was clearly a major facet of the selection processes. Indeed, the Republican platform of 1980 pledged to award judgeships to those sharing conservative values. In the words of the platform:

> We pledge the appointment of women and men whose judicial philosophy is consistent with the belief in the decentralization of the federal system and efforts to return decision-making power to state and local elected officials. We will work for the appointment of judges at all levels of the judiciary who respect traditional family values and the sanctity of innocent human life.

More recently, in the Clinton years, we witnessed the added tensions in executive/legislative relationships that divided government can bring about as Clinton's nominees met with unprecedented delay in the Republican-controlled Senate with, again, an unprecedented number of nominees not even being given a Judiciary Committee hearing or a subsequent floor vote.

The Clinton experience, however, presents us with a bit of an ironic twist. First, several articles in the symposium issue of *Judicature* on judicial selection in the Clinton years (March–April 2001) clearly documented that the president's nominees were all too often treated as if they were ideological zealots, while their behavior on the bench has demonstrated that they were quite moderate, actually the most conservative appointees of any Democratic president sitting on the bench today.

Indeed, I think it is fair to say that many of the Democratic party's natural constituents were somewhat frustrated with the decidedly nonideological nature of the Clinton appointees and the processes that produced them. Nevertheless, President Clinton experienced unprecedented difficulties in getting his nominees confirmed because of ongoing tensions with the Senate majority about the appropriate balance of power in the appointment process. Again, this is a particular irony, since there is little evidence, unlike in the Reagan years, of the presidents seizing on judicial appointments as a major component of his policy agenda.

At a crossroads

So, it is this crisis in lower federal court judicial selection, and I think it is fair to label it a crisis, that brings us here today. We are, I think, at a crossroads in lower federal court judicial selection processes. Here, approximately a year and one half into one very atypical year and one half in the Bush administration, the shoe is now on the other foot—a Republican president and a Democratically controlled Senate. Appointment relationships are still in the process of being resolved, I think, and large questions are still being addressed about what the appropriate and relative roles of the president and the Senate, and in particular its Judiciary Committee, will be in these appointment processes.

It is in the continuing and emerging answers to these questions that I think we will find out whether the Clinton years were simply an anomaly in executive/legislative relations in this critical domain, or whether an era of unprecedented contentiousness and gridlock will be the newly institutionalized model that selection processes will follow. It seems to me that there are two alternative paths that could define the road ahead. One is premised on the lessons that we teach in our very first political science classes or that we learned in our first political science classes—what goes around comes around. The other is something I think we learned from our mothers—two wrongs don't make a right.

Despite a good deal of rhetoric from every political stripe over the past months, I am not sure we know quite yet which path is about to be followed because, at bottom, President Bush's first year and one half in office was so very, very different. There were some predictable givens at the beginning. Thus, for example, the process inherited the legacy of the mistreatment of Clinton's nominees. There was the reality of John Ashcroft, a lightening rod for partisan bickering, heading up the Justice Department. There was the legacy of Bush versus Gore and what some would argue was a tainted electoral victory. Of course, there was at first the specter of an evenly divided Senate.

In a situation that seemed like it could not get any worse for the president, it very clearly did. First, the Democrats took control of the Senate, and all legislative work stopped as the struggle for organizing the body proceeded to center stage. Then the tragedy of 9/11 struck, and judicial selection matters took a back seat at the Judiciary Committee to those dealing with national security and terrorism. The presence of anthrax closed down a Senate office building.

In this context, it seems to me, the actual record of judicial confirmations in President Bush's first year and one half is really somewhat difficult to characterize. For some it has been a glass that is half empty, and for others it is half full. Clearly, there remains much to be said and much to be written about where we are today and where we are heading.

Notes

This article originally appeared in Volume 86, Number 1, July–August 2002, pages 13–16. It is an edited version of an address presented on May 17, 2002 at the AJS symposium, "Selecting Federal Court of Appeals and District Court Judges: The Role and Responsibilities of the Executive and Legislative Branches."

1. Goldman, *Picking Federal Judges: Lower Court Selection from Roosevelt Through Reagan* 32 (New Haven: Yale University Press, 1997).
2. Ibid. at 19–20.
3. Ibid. at 205–207.

The judicial confirmation process: mobilizing elites, mobilizing masses

Nancy Scherer

"Inside the Beltway" activists play a crucial role in getting senators re-elected. When they demand that senators fight against objectionable judicial nominees, senators must respond

Given the amount of attention devoted by the Senate in recent years to lower federal court appointments, the political science literature would suggest that this issue must be highly salient with the American public; certainly, that is the view when it comes to Supreme Court nominations.[1] In contrast, battling with the president over the appointment of the first black jurist to the Fourth Circuit Court of Appeals, former senator Jesse Helms (R-NC) once quipped, "You go out on the streets of Raleigh . . . and ask 100 people: 'Do you give a damn who is on the 4th Circuit Court of Appeals?' They'll say: 'What's that?' . . . [Judicial appointments] matter only to politicians and newspaper editors." [2] Public opinion polls would seem to confirm Helms' view. For example, an oft-cited *Washington Post* poll reported that more people could identify Judge Wapner, then host of the television program *The People's Court,* than could identify Chief Justice of the United States William H. Rehnquist.[3]

Considering that the American electorate knows little about the Supreme Court, it would seem problematic to suggest that they are following the Senate's battles over lower federal court judgeships. Why, then, do senators invest so much political capital in the lower federal court confirmation process if their constituents are not paying attention?

Marrying the literatures of voter mobilization and congressional activity, I proffer an explanation of this recent, and important, development in American politics: "elite mobilization." The empirical support for my new explanation comes from in-depth interviews with the leading conservative and liberal political elites engaged in the politics of lower court judgeships. Drawing on these interviews, I demonstrate that, unlike regular voters, there are political activists located on the far-left and far-right of the ideological spectrum who actually care—and care quite deeply—about who sits on the lower federal courts because they

see federal court litigation as key to achieving their political objectives.

The interviews also suggest that these Washington elites are acutely aware of the crucial role they play in getting senators re-elected, and how they exploit their mobilization power to influence the judicial confirmation process. In short, the more closely divided the American electorate remains in any given election, the more power these activists wield because they are critical in getting the party base to vote. And so, when these political activists demand that senators stand up and fight against objectionable judicial nominees— demands made even when the activists concede that a nominee is sure to be confirmed—senators must respond; to do otherwise is to risk serious political repercussions at the polls.

Elite mobilization

Elite mobilization rests on two well established principles. First, in order to get re-elected, congressmen strategically target those paying the closest attention to the most salient issues—political elites; they, in turn, mobilize the masses. As Rosenstone and Hansen explain in their work *Mobilization, Participation and Democracy in America:*

> Locked into struggles for political advantage, political leaders mobilize public involvement strategically. They target and time their efforts for maximum effect. They target their efforts on people they know, people who are well positioned in social networks, people who are influential in politics, and people who are likely to participate. They organize their efforts around salient issues, time them to avoid other distractions, calibrate them to impending decisions, and escalate them when outcomes hang in the balance.[4]

Accordingly, the theory begins with the grasstop elites in Washington who represent interest groups dealing with some of the nation's most salient issues—*e.g.*, crime, race, and abortion—and who also believe that positive outcomes in federal court litigation are the best way for them to achieve their desired policy goals. For these activists, then, judicial confirmation votes in the Senate are the most important legislative actions affecting their interests.

Also critical to the theory is the fact that these Washington elites have access to tens of thousands of grass-roots members nationwide. Not only are these grass-roots activists most likely to vote, but more importantly, they are the constituents who will be responsible for mobilizing the party's base to get out and vote. Thus, in an age when the electorate is so closely divided, these grass-roots activists are often the key to winning elections. Elites, then, do an effective job at conveying constituency preferences to senators.[5]

The second principle on which elite mobilization rests comes from Mayhew's classic book *Congress: The Electoral Connection*.[6] He argued that congressmen are singularly focused on getting re-elected, and engage in three activities to further this end: position taking, credit claiming, and advertising. Though their efforts to shape the federal judiciary go largely unnoticed by the American public writ large, senators are nonetheless still engaging in important strategic mobilization efforts when they oppose an objectionable judicial candidate. In short, this is simply one of Mayhew's three classic legislative activities designed to mobilize votes—*i.e.*, position taking. Mayhew describes position taking as:

> the public enunciation of a judgmental statement on anything likely to be of interest to political actors. The statement may take the form of a roll call vote. The most important classes of judgmental statements are those prescribing American governmental ends. . . . The congressman as position taker is a speaker rather than a doer. The electoral requirement is not that he make pleasing things happen but that he make pleasing judgmental statements. The position itself is the political commodity.[7]

Though position taking often involves speaking on issues of high salience, senators are nonetheless still engaging in position taking when speaking to a select audience of political elites, as they are regarding the judicial confirmation process. Indeed, as Mayhew recognized, "the most alert watchers are doubtless representatives of attentive interest groups."[8]

In sum, in today's political environment, senators strategically use the lower court confirmation process to mobilize elites who believe that the federal judiciary holds the key to achieving their policy goals. For a senator to defy the demands of these interest groups to block a judicial nominee is to risk having his political base stay home come election day, thus jeopardizing his chance for re-election.

The interviews

Interviews were conducted with individuals located on both the right and left of the ideological spectrum, and who play the most active roles in the politics of judicial nominations.[9] On the left, the following interest group leaders were interviewed: Nan Aron, president of the Alliance for Justice (the "Alliance"); Kim Gandy, president of the National Organization for Women ("NOW"); Elizabeth Cavendish, Legal Director of the National Abortion Rights and Reproductive Action League ("NARAL"); and Ralph Neas, former Executive Director of the Leadership Conference on Civil Rights and current Director of People for the American Way ("PFW"). These groups represent different types of interest groups. PFW and NOW are multi-issue civil rights organizations. NARAL is a single issue organization dealing with a woman's right to choose. And the Alliance is an organization that represents other interest groups, and specifically monitors the federal judiciary on those groups' behalf (sometimes referred to as an "umbrella" organization).

On the right, the following individuals were interviewed: Thomas Jipping, former director of the Free Congress Foundation's Judicial Selection Monitoring Project ("JSMP") and current Senior Fellow in Legal Studies at Concerned Women for America ("Concerned Women"); Roger Pilon, director of the Cato Institute's Center for Constitutional Studies ("Cato"); Eugene B. Meyer, President of the Federalist Society; and a senior fellow for a conservative coalition of interest groups that asked not to be named. For clarity's sake, I will refer to the unnamed source as "Conservative Judicial Watchdog." Like the liberals interviewed, the conservatives represent groups with much variation. JSMP is an umbrella organization monitoring the federal judiciary; it represents hundreds of conservative interest groups. Concerned Women is a multi-issue family values interest group. And Cato and the Federalist Society are policy think tanks that comment on the judicial selection process.

These interest groups and think tanks were chosen because they represent the organizations most often cited in the press commenting on the judicial confirmation process, on specific nominees and/or on the process in general.[10] To identify these groups, I conducted a series of comprehensive searches in the Lexis/Nexis database of four newspapers, two "liberal" (the *New York Times* and the *Washington Post*) and two "conservative" (the *Washington Times* and the *Wall Street Journal*). The searches were intended to find newspaper reports, op-ed pieces, and editorials mentioning an interest group or policy group in connection with the judicial confirmation process, and published between January 1, 1993 and May 31, 2002. This time frame was chosen so as to capture all confirmation fights during the Bill Clinton and George W. Bush presidencies that had occurred prior to the interviews. The interviews were conducted between June 2002 and August 2002, and all interviews were tape recorded and later transcribed. Each interview lasted between ½ hour and 2 hours.

The activists who care

In the 1950s and 1960s, liberal political activists began turning to the federal courts, rather than federal and state legislatures, to achieve policy goals through interest group litigation.[11] This strategy made good sense to these groups, given the liberal bent of the Supreme Court during this period under the leadership of Chief Justice Earl Warren (1954–1969) and a firmly held belief that the elected branches of government, particularly in the South, were not accessible to disadvantaged groups. This prompted Alexander M. Bickel to observe that "all too many federal judges have been induced to view themselves as holding roving commissions as problem solvers, and as charged with a duty to act when majoritarian institutions do not."[12] As the president of Alliance aptly noted, the federal courts became a safe haven for the "discreet and insular minorities" to which the Supreme Court referred in its now famous "footnote four" in *United States v. Carolene Products* (1938) (Aron interview).

By the mid-1970s, perceiving that these liberal activists had successfully bypassed the legislative process and achieved the policy goals they sought through federal court litigation during the Warren Court era, and then later in their landmark abortion victory in *Roe v. Wade* (1973), conservative interest groups were up in arms. As Cato's constitutional scholar explained:

The clearest example [of liberals' use of the courts] is the abortion case.... That is a right to be decided under the general police power that belongs to the states. There is no federal police power. States in the early 1970s were already moving to change their abortion laws.... But apparently, they were not moving fast enough, and so feminist organizations went to the Supreme Court to try to obtain there what they were unable to obtain through state legislatures. And the Court gave them what they were looking for by finding a right that was dubiously among our enumerated rights (Pilon interview).

Accordingly, by the 1980s, conservative activists began to co-opt the liberal's litigation strategy—*i.e.*, to use the federal courts to *undo* the substantial gains made by the liberal activists in the previous 20 years, most notably in the areas of abortion rights and affirmative action.[13]

Some liberal activists believe that the litigation strategy of conservative activists in the 1980s was actually driven by the same frustration with the legislative process that the liberal groups had experienced 20-30 years previously. In other words, according to PFW's director, Neas, unable to win conservative victories in the U.S. Congress during the early years of the Reagan administration, conservatives started seeing the federal courts as the key to accomplishing the policy goals they could not achieve through the legislative process, particularly given Reagan's willingness to "pack" the lower court with conservative judges:

Going into 1981, the Republican right thought that, "wow, we have the presidency, we have the Senate, and we're really going to change things." And I think they were astonished, for example, during the [fight over] extension of the Voting Rights Act. Here was the heart and soul of the civil rights laws, and I'm convinced they thought it was a slam dunk to get either the so-called simple extension, or no Voting Rights Act extension at all. And by simple extension I mean just enacting the current language at that time without addressing a 1980 Supreme Court case [*City of Mobile v. Bolden*] that had dramatically weakened the Voting Rights Act. And what happened is that the Leadership Conference on Civil Rights led a national legislative campaign with strong bipartisan support that rejected the Reagan-Ed Meese-William Bradford Reynolds-William French Smith position, [the vote going] 85–8 in the Senate, and 389–24 in the House. And all of a sudden that commenced a string of victories [for the left] that lasted 12 years (Neas interview).

And, the president of NOW contends that the conservatives' desire to bypass the legislative process continues today: "they want us essentially to get down to one branch of government where basically the judicial branch does everything and it doesn't matter what Congress does because these right wing judges, if they don't like them [congressional statutes], they throw them out and that's the end of that" (Gandy interview).

Activists shift focus

Beginning with Reagan's re-election in 1984, interest groups began to focus more on the politics of lower court judgeships.[14] When asked why, the interest group leaders cited four different reasons. First, there are so few opportunities to affect Supreme Court appointments in the modern political era. Consider that there has not been a single Supreme Court vacancy in nine years. In contrast, a president names hundreds of judges to the lower federal courts in each four-year term.

Second, with the Rehnquist Court hearing about half the number of cases that the Burger Court did, activists began to recognize that, as a practical matter, the lower federal courts today serve as the final arbiter of more than 99 percent of all federal court litigation; in other words, important policy is being made every day in the lower federal courts. According to Elizabeth Cavendish, Legal Director of NARAL, today it is the *lower* federal courts where all important legal issues in the pro-choice/pro-life debate are being decided:

> There's a real recognition that lower court judges hold vast power over women's reproductive lives and right now the composition of the Supreme Court is stable, and so there isn't an immediate threat to overturn *Roe [v. Wade]*, but what is an underappreciated phenomenon, is how much chipping away there has been at . . . a woman's right to choose. *Casey [v. Planned Parenthood]*, in 1992, . . . empowered lower court judges because it established an undue burden standard. So it took the courts' focus away from strict scrutiny—which has been called fatal in fact to abortion restrictions—to an undue burden standard, which is obviously a mushier standard, and more fact dependent and subject to the interpretations of district and court of appeals judges (Cavendish interview).

Third, in an apparent attempt to reduce uncertainty about the way Supreme Court nominees are likely to vote once becoming a justice, presidents have increasingly turned to the courts of appeals in searching for Supreme Court candidates. Indeed, seven of the nine current justices were elevated from the federal appellate courts. Gandy, Aron, and Neas all specifically referred to the courts of appeals as the "farm team" for the Supreme Court. And so, for these litigation-oriented liberal interest groups—and those conservative groups that oppose them—having the "right" kind of judges seated on the appellate courts ensures the "right" kind of judges on the Supreme Court.

Fourth, according to liberal activists, presidents, starting with Ronald Reagan, began a trend of appointing lower federal court judges, who enjoy life tenure, at much younger ages. While less than 3 percent of Eisenhower, Kennedy, Johnson, and Carter appellate judges appointed were under age 40, 10 percent of Reagan's court of appeals appointments were in their 30s.[15] As Gandy, president of NOW, explained of the pre-Reagan era: "back [then] . . . the idea was not that you appointed somebody at 35. . . . Ford and Carter were appointing people who were in their late 50s. A [judicial appointment] was to cap your career." In short, because presidents are appointing younger federal court judges, that means less turnover occurs when there is a change of party in the White House, and consequently, fewer appointments for the new administration.

And so, during Reagan's presidency, liberal interest groups began to target nominees to the lower federal courts. Then, with a change of party in the White House, conservative interest groups began to challenge lower court nominees; however, there was a marked increase in the number of nominees challenged by conservative interest groups during Clinton's eight years in office compared to the number challenged by liberal interest groups in eight years of the Reagan-H. Bush presidencies. While liberal interest groups launched public confirmation fights against five Reagan-H. Bush nominees to the courts of appeals, conservative interest groups launched 16 public nomination fights against Clinton nominees to the courts of appeals.[16] And, with another change of party in the White House has come an escalation of lower court challenges. In only two years of the W. Bush presidency, liberal interest groups launched 12 public confirmation fights against court of appeals nominees.[17]

Targeting nominees

As an initial matter, I asked the interest group and think tank leaders what activities they engage in when a president they support is in the White House, and is presumably nominating judicial candidates they support. In other words, what do conservative groups do now while W. Bush is president, and what did liberal groups do when Clinton was president?

Conservative think tank leaders all stressed that they do not take positions on individual nominees during Democratic administrations or Republican administrations (Pilon, Meyer interviews). Thus, a change of administration, they claim, has little to no impact on their activities concerning judicial appointments. This is true even of the Federalist Society, which was reportedly going to assume the American Bar Association's traditional role of rating all judicial nominees early in W. Bush's presidency:[18]

> [Before W. Bush was elected] We had been trying to present information and facts about the ABA. And then the ABA was going to be taken out of the process by this administration. I suppose that, because we had been writing about this function, and in Washington everyone wants to be involved in things like selecting judges, [people thought we were taking over the ABA's role]. We're not a position-taking organization. It's a totally different thing than the sort of things that we do and it's not something we aspired to (Meyer interview).

In contrast, interest groups on the left and right go through drastic role reversals when there is a change of party in the White House. During the Clinton administration, conservatives were on the attack—seeking to defeat Democratic judicial nominees—while liberal groups played defense—defending the records of Clinton nominees under siege and keeping "score" in terms of how many minority and female judges Clinton had appointed (Aron, Gandy interviews). With few exceptions,[19] Clinton nominees were deemed acceptable to liberal interest groups (Aron, Cavendish interviews). Some liberals did, however, express disappointment that Clinton chose mostly moderates for the bench, rather than trying to balance 12 years of conservative Republican appointments with truly liberal judges (Aron, Gandy interviews).

Once W. Bush was elected, conservatives moved into the defensive position, while liberals went on the offensive (Jipping interview). As the Conservative Judicial Watchdog explained:

> In the Clinton administration we would have [sent information to senators] more often. . . . What we are doing now [is] . . . trying to press for what our side

would say is fair treatment for someone like Priscilla Owen getting the floor vote. Saying, "Senator Biden, you are on record as saying the Constitution requires the Senate, the full Senate and not the Judiciary Committee, to advise and consent." Trying to raise these points. How effective that is—that's another story.

In short, if there is to be a confirmation battle, it is the out-of-power interest groups who put the nominee in play, and the in-power groups then respond. The in-power groups do not, however, engage in activity on behalf of a nominee who is not being targeted by opposing groups (Aron, Gandy, Jipping interviews).

How do the out-of-power groups ultimately make a decision about whom to target? Not surprisingly, with hundreds of judicial vacancies on the lower federal courts in each presidential term, those interviewed concede that they lack the resources to try to defeat every lower court nominee named by a president of the opposing party (Jipping, Gandy, Aron, Cavendish interviews). Instead, there is unanimous agreement that they must choose their battles carefully.

In order to make that decision, groups must first conduct research on the nominees' backgrounds. While some groups conduct research on each and every nominee in trying to reach a decision, including district court nominees—NOW, for example —most of the liberal groups initiate research only on court of appeals nominees and those district court nominees who are brought to their attention as being particularly troublesome candidates.

Similarly, grassroots members of these organizations might bring information to the attention of the grasstop activist in Washington (Gandy interview). In fact, Gandy stated that grassroots members of NOW have even gone so far as to telephone in "anonymous" tips on where important information might be found to use against nominees who oppose NOW's civil rights agenda (Gandy interview). As a practical matter, then, confirmation battles are fought almost exclusively on court of appeals nominees; district court nominees will be investigated and targeted only in extreme cases (Aron, Gandy interview).

Conservative groups did not appear to be quite as systematic about their research efforts. Jipping, when he was with the leading conservative umbrella group, JSMP, claimed to initiate investigations of Clinton nominees only when a problematic candidate was brought to his attention—a more passive strategy than that practiced by the liberal interest groups:

How those nominees were brought to our attention [happens] in a variety of ways. Sometimes . . . Senate staffers . . . would call and say [check out] so and so. Sometimes it would be a grassroots activist in a state where there was an active discussion [about] a prominent lawyer being considered for a judgeship, and [the grassroots activist] had a lot of information (Jipping interview).

Initiating a campaign

Once having done the research on a nominee, the organizations must decide whether to initiate a campaign against that judicial candidate. That decision, on both the left and the right, seems to turn on several factors. First and foremost are considerations about the nominee's political ideology or judicial philosophy. Whether the group focuses on judicial philosophy as opposed to political ideology seems to turn on whether the organization is an umbrella organization or think tank—*e.g.,* JSMP, the Alliance, Cato, and the Federalist Society—or is an issue- oriented membership group— *e.g.,* NARAL, PFW, NOW, and Concerned Women. Another way to look at it is this: is judicial selection all that this activist must be concerned with—certainly the case at JSMP and the Alliance—or is there a greater cause beyond judicial selection with which the political elite must be concerned —*e.g.,* the right to choose at NARAL, or the right to life at Concerned Women?

For conservative elites at umbrella groups or think tanks, they want to focus the judicial selection debate on a nominee's philosophical view of the role of the judiciary in American government. Specifically, this involves a debate about "judicial activism" versus "judicial restraint"—a debate begun in the early 1980s by the founders of the Federalist Society, and then taken up by several high-ranking officials in the Reagan administration, including former Attorney General Edwin Meese (Cavendish interview). Jipping, who led an umbrella organization while at JSMP, explained the debate as follows:

An activist judge is one who believes he has the authority to change or make the law. . . . A restrained judge takes the law, either a statute or constitutional provision, as he finds it with the meaning it already has. Meaning is given to law by the lawmaker, not by judges (Jipping interview).

To conservatives, an "activist" judge is one that not only recognizes rights allegedly not contained in the Constitution, but also, one that "finds power by refus-

ing to hold the federal government to its enumerated powers" (Pilon interview). In other words, these conservatives want neither the federal courts to find rights that they believe are not found in the Constitution, nor Congress to find power not found in the Constitution (Pilon interview).

The director of the Federalist Society would frame the debate somewhat differently. Fearing that the term "activist" can—and indeed has been—used by the left to attack the Rehnquist Court's penchant for overturning congressional legislation deemed to violate principles of federalism, Meyer frames the debate about judicial philosophy as whether or not a judge will employ a "textualist" interpretation of the Constitution—*i.e.,* seeking only to interpret the meaning of the actual text of the document as written:

The proper question to ask in our view is not "is this judicial activism," because that is vague. The proper question would be, "is the Court interpreting the text and meaning of the Constitution." If it is, and they're doing the best they can do . . . [even if] their judgment might be off, [then] there's not a structural problem. If the Court is saying, "gee, we don't like the direction policy is going in this country" [or] "we want to change the direction of policy" . . . that's not a proper role for the courts.

On the left, Aron's umbrella group, the Alliance, also tries to steer the debate away from specific political issues; when asked about what makes a nominee objectionable to her organization, she tries to focus the issue on whether the president is nominating candidates who will be "open minded" once taking the bench, and who view the courts as accessible to all groups:

We want fair judges with an open mind. . . . We don't expect that they'll agree with us every time. We do expect that judges will at least listen to the evidence presented to them with an open mind and give an aggrieved plaintiff, a group of discriminated women, or people of color, the same opportunity that they will the corporations. . . . We want judges who will bring experience from having done pro bono work, not your corporate [lawyer] type. Lawyers who know what it's like to be poor or represent someone who is poor and who has a difficult time getting to the court. . . . [T]he most important question to be asked of a nominee is: what is the nominee's view of the role the courts play in American society today? Is it a view of the courts that they should be open and accessible to unrepresented people (Aron interview)?

However, *all* of the political elites who focus on judicial philosophy readily concede that their approach to judicial selection is at odds with the issue-oriented focus advocated by leaders of membership organizations, such as NARAL and Concerned Women—indeed, these two groups are almost singularly interested in whether a judge supports or opposes *Roe*—as well as the membership organizations' grassroots activists at the local level:

> The basic principle which I articulate [about judicial activism], nonetheless is not the common way of understanding and talking about judicial appointments out there in grassroots land. Unfortunately, even on the conservative side, the way that [appointments are discussed] most often is in terms of issues. Are they pro-gun? Are they anti-this? Are they pro-that? ... What that means is some constituency groups that are focused on certain issues where that issue agenda is impacted by the judiciary, say the abortion issue or the gun issue ... they'll be very interested in [a judicial nomination], but they'll be interested in it from that issue kind of perspective. ... So we get questions like, "well, what's his position on guns?" If [the nominee] didn't have a position on their issue, then they weren't interested in being involved. It's a bedeviling problem (Jipping interview).

It is impossible, however, for the umbrella groups to ignore the issue-oriented approach advocated by the grassroots organizations. That is because, in order for their message to have any real impact in influencing the appointment process, it is not enough for elites "inside the Beltway" to voice objections to nominees—by posting information on their web sites, publishing op-ed pieces in leading conservative or liberal media outlets, or lobbying politicians directly. Rather, as everyone interviewed readily conceded, it is absolutely critical that they also get *grassroots activists* involved in the process—by writing letters, sending e-mails and telephoning their senators; in some extreme cases, even organizing rallies against specific lower court nominees (Jipping, Cavendish, Aron, and Gandy interviews).

These grassroots activities are critical because, taken together, they send a message to senators that *thousands* of the *most mobilized constituents* in their party object to a particular nominee, and that their critical support of that politician in the next election may turn on the senator's public stance on that nominee. For example, on the conservative side, Jipping stated:

> We don't do a lot of direct lobbying from us to the senators [in order to get them to vote against a particular nominee]. It wouldn't be effective. ... I long ago disabused myself of the notion that because Republican senators articulate the right principles that there would be spontaneous combustion. That they'd do what they said they would do. It just doesn't work. It's too much of an insider game to just work [at defeating a nominee from] ... inside the Beltway. You have to get your constituents involved. ... The structure we were building [at JSMP] was a grassroots [structure]. That's the approach JSMP took from the beginning (Jipping interview).

In fact, discussing his move from JSMP—an umbrella group affiliated with a network of conservative grass-roots organizations—to Concerned Women, a membership group with its own grassroots activists dedicated to conservative family values, Jipping highlighted the enormous benefits to working more directly with people at the grassroots level because of the electoral power they wield over senators:

> [Concerned Women] is a membership organization, as opposed to just a think tank like [JSMP]. You don't want to do things just hoping people will use them. Here [at Concerned Women], you can do things and put them directly to your members. For example, we had ... our members participating in rallies supporting Miguel Estrada's nomination [to the District of Columbia Circuit]. We can go directly to our state leaders, give them some information, and in a couple of days, they can get rallied. ... The impact that grass roots citizens can have on the political process, whether that be through lobbying or elections, is more direct than any organization (Jipping interview).

Similarly, on the Democratic side, Gandy explained that, "there are only so many pressure points you have with members of Congress and it mostly boils down to the people who can vote for them or who can give them money" (Gandy interview). Cavendish of NARAL concurs:

> I think ... NARAL is really powerful because we're a grassroots organization. There are some other groups that [are] very well-respected ... like the National Law Center ... and their research is considered really solid

and a lot of senators listen to them a lot. But I think NARAL brings the grassroots component to the table and when we're [involved there is] the threat of grass-roots backlash, the positive carrot of possible grassroots contributors.... Just the political oomph. Because they [senators] know we mobilize people at election time (Cavendish interview).

How, then, are these two very different approaches to framing the judicial selection debate ultimately reconciled? Grass-top elites advocating a philosophical approach must walk a fine line; their rhetoric cannot be solely focused on lofty ideals about judicial philosophy or they will risk alienating grass-roots activists—so critical to the process. Accordingly, the Washington elites' public pronouncements on specific nominees almost always reference judicial candidates' political ideologies and the way these nominees can be expected to vote in controversial cases before them. In other words, Jipping would label a Clinton nominee an "activist" based on specific decisions the nominee had made on hot-button issues such as crime or race.

For example, in objecting to Rosemary Barkett, nominated by Clinton to the Eleventh Circuit, Jipping stated: "Judge Barkett's record reveals views far outside the mainstream as well as aggressive judicial activism.... Judge Barkett's empathy for convicted killers often leads her to vote to keep them from receiving the just punishment for their crimes." [20] Such approach allows him to stay true to his philosophical standards for judicial selection, and at the same time signal conservative activists that a nominee has taken issue positions hostile to their conservative policy preferences.

There is, however, a risk at basing a confirmation fight on specific issue positions. In fact, this is exactly why some "inside the Beltway" elites would prefer to keep the debate about judicial nominees on the philosophical level, so as not to alienate potential votes in the Senate. For example, Jipping very much wants to avoid turning all judicial confirmation debates on W. Bush nominees into one about abortion so as not to lose pro-choice Republican senators' votes in close confirmation battles:

Let's say that you have a Supreme Court nominee, and all the pro-life groups are demanding that he be a pro-life person and commit to overruling *Roe v. Wade,* and the left is saying exactly the opposite. So that the only thing that's being talked about is abortion. And let's say you know from all kinds of evidence that he will vote to overturn *Roe v. Wade,* so he is somebody that the right

would really like. Can you tell me how you get to 51 votes [for confirmation] if the only issue being talked about is abortion. You don't get any Democrats. You don't get half a dozen Republicans. Tell me how you win if you're not giving even all the Republican senators something else to talk about. Is the left going to talk only about abortion. Of course, that's all they care about. But, I'd like to frame the issue in a way that gives the Kay Bailey Hutchinsons of the world, for example, who care about issues beyond abortion, but on the issue of abortion is pro-choice, something to ... hang their decision on.... If you go to the Senate and you want to get the 51 votes on somebody who the conservatives believe is very, very good, you have to frame it [the issue] ... from a crass, political, how do you win scenario ... you've got to broaden your message. You've got to have other things to talk about (Jipping interview).

For activists on the left, the dichotomy between the right's stated focus in the judicial selection debate—*i.e.,* judicial activism—and what they believe to be the right's true agenda—turning back the clock on abortion and civil rights—is particularly frustrating:

There's a real divide between the way Republicans play with ideology and the way Democrats do. Republicans talk about how they want judges who interpret the law not make the law. And there should be no ideological litmus tests. They use that term [as one] of aspersion. When you watch their feet and look at their documents, like their own Justice Department documents from the '80s where they are trying to chart where the Court should go, they want the judicial nominees to be very well aware of where all the division points are in the law, and how the law could go in so many different ways ... and why judicial nominees should be so sensitive to this, and why judicial nominees matter. They [Republicans] really care [about issues] (Cavendish interview).

In the final analysis, whether the focus is on judicial philosophy or policy preferences, presumably, all of Clinton's nominees were unacceptable to groups on the right, and all of W. Bush's nominees are unacceptable to groups on the left. So, interest groups must consider additional factors in making a decision to challenge or not challenge, given their limited resources.

Another variable that interest groups say they consider when deciding whether to fight or not is the existence of a written record. Do the interest groups have sufficient evidence on which they can base their case?

As one of the liberal activists put it, "Interest groups with limited resources need to try and find those battles where there are enough persuadables that you can actually win" (Cavendish interview). On the conservative side, Jipping explained the decision process to oppose a Clinton nominee as follows:

We had to be able to articulate the case. To actually be able to put it on paper. To give real examples. Explain it, not just go on intuition or what someone said. Even if it was a widespread perception, if we couldn't make the case, particularly in written form, then we wouldn't be credible in coming to that conclusion. . . . Basically, it [the decision to fight] had to be not just on the basis of one [prior lower court] decision. Not one single activist decision. It had to be a pattern. We had to be able to make the case about their judicial philosophy or anticipated judicial philosophy if they were not already a judge (Jipping interview).

A third consideration in choosing whom to fight, at least for liberal groups, is how recently were they successful at winning another confirmation fight. That is because they firmly believe that Democratic senators on the Judiciary Committee will only vote against so many judicial nominees in deference to the president. How many no votes each senator has is a huge question mark for these groups. Accordingly, for liberals, yesterday's confirmation fight directly impacts today's confirmation fight and tomorrow's confirmation fight. Liberal activists do not expect to win two high profile battles in a row. And so, they must carefully time when they will fight and when they will remain silent:

I think it's an obstacle that senators think and know these [W. Bush nominees] are bad but won't vote against them because there's no political price to be paid for it. And our polling shows [that] people support a strong role for the Senate. They don't want their senators to be potted plants. . . . They say that senators are elected as checks on the president. They think that senators should vote no if it's going to roll back rights. It's sort of weird that senators haven't assimilated that thinking into their own role. And they feel very deferential to presidential nominees (Cavendish interview).

Some groups also pay close attention to the ideological balance on a given circuit court of appeals or the ideology of the states in those circuits when trying to reach a decision on whether or not to fight a nominee. For NARAL, the question is how many judges on a circuit currently oppose choice and how many states in that circuit are controlled by anti-choice legislatures:

You'd say, "how bad is this person's record and how much of a difference does it make." Like the Fifth Circuit is swinging [to the] right now—from being a circuit that was the real protector of rights, knock[ing] down many of the Jim Crow barriers and [being] a hugely progressive force. . . . And, you look at the composition of the states. Are the states going to be spewing up anti-choice legislation for those judges to rule on. In politics you're always thinking about persuadables. Where you can make a difference. What's in play? What's swinging? The Fifth Circuit is swinging, and it has Louisiana down there, they've tried to ban abortion since *Roe v. Wade* in 1990 or 1991. Mississippi is absolutely calamitous for choice and [so is] the vast basis of Texas (Cavendish interview).

Other groups, like NOW, say they will not engage in such strategic considerations when they believe that none of a president's judicial nominees are acceptable. Instead, they have, in varying degrees, objected to all of W. Bush's nominees (Gandy interview).

Finally, though my interviews were conducted before control of the Senate changed parties in January 2003, it appears that liberal groups are now taking into consideration process-related objections when choosing whom to target. For example, regarding the Estrada nomination, Aron stated in a recent debate before the Federalist Society that the Senate was justified in blocking his confirmation given his reticence to turn over memoranda he wrote while working for the Solicitor General's Office during the Clinton administration.[21]

In sum, having chosen a judicial nominee to target; having educated their grass roots activists on those views; and having had the grass roots activists make their views known to their senators; it now becomes incumbent for senators "to take a position" (using Mayhew's term) and respond to their elite constituents.

Senators "take a position"

The next critical step in the elite mobilization process is for senators to capitalize on the fact that critical constituents on the left and right, unlike the general electorate, find the composition of the lower federal courts to be an extremely salient issue. In short, Republican senators do this by sending cues to conservative activists who support the Republican Party, and Democratic senators do this by sending cues to liberal activists who support the Democratic Party. The cues ultimately tell the activists: expressly, I stand with you in opposition to a specific nominee, and implicitly, I consider that nominee's political views to be unacceptable.

What form do these cues take? Senators have a number of options. Most optimal from the interest groups' perspective is to defeat a nominee at the Judiciary Committee level (Gandy, Jipping interviews). Thus, interest groups on the left spend most of their efforts trying to persuade Democratic Judiciary Committee members to vote against objectionable nominees, and groups on the right try to persuade Republican members of the Committee to vote against judicial candidates to which they object. Groups do not try to persuade senators of the opposite party at the committee level. Accordingly, the clearest cues are no votes by Judiciary Committee members.

When the Judiciary Chairman does not have the votes to defeat a candidate at the committee level, despite being in the majority party, another way for a senator to send a cue indicating support for the activists' position is to delay a committee vote. Most often, such delays are initiated by the chairman and thus are only likely to happen when there is divided government. And, in fact, studies confirm that delays are much more likely to take place during a regime of divided government.[22] This tactic was used successfully by Orrin Hatch (R-Ut) when he chaired the Judiciary Committee during the Clinton administration and by Patrick Leahy (D-Vt) when he chaired the Committee during the W. Bush administration. Ironically, each side complains that their chairman allowed too many nominations to go through (Gandy, Aron, Conservative Judicial Watchdog, Jipping interviews).

There is another cue available to home state senators. They have the option of pleasing sympathetic interest groups by not returning their blue slips, a Senate tradition which allows them to kill effectively a nomination. This tactic has been used quite successfully by both Republican and Democratic senators from Michigan regarding Sixth Circuit Court of Appeals nominations. During the Clinton presidency, former senator Spencer Abraham (R-Mi) refused to return his blue slip on two Clinton nominees: Kathleen McCree Lewis and Helene White. Accordingly, neither candidate received a hearing, and their nominations died with the inauguration of W. Bush. However, having defeated Abraham in the 2000 Michigan Senate election, current senator Debbie Stabenow (D-Mi)—along with fellow Democratic senator Carl Levin

(D-Mi)—has retaliated. At one time, they were holding up all Sixth Circuit nominees—those from Michigan, as well as other states in the Sixth Circuit. They have since moderated their position slightly, declining to return their blue slips on all Michigan nominees to the Sixth Circuit. Before the November 2002 elections, four W. Bush nominees to the Sixth Circuit from Michigan awaited Judiciary Committee hearings.

Assuming that the activists fail in defeating a nomination at the committee level, or in persuading senators to stall the nomination, there still remains another way for senators to send favorable signals to their political activists. All of the activists interviewed made it clear that, even when the outcome of a confirmation battle is virtually certain—*i.e.,* there are more than 50 votes to confirm the nominee—they nevertheless still push for the nomination to go to the floor of the Senate for a full floor debate and roll call vote. This forces the senators to stand up and make their views known, and allows the activists to be certain where these politicians stand. This is critical information that they can use against a politician when he or she is up for re-election. Moreover, it sends a "signal" to senators on the opposite side of the aisle that future candidates will also be facing tough confirmation battles. In other words, there will no longer be a free ride for anyone seeking a lifetime appointment to the lower federal courts.

For example, during the Clinton administration, Jipping did not often agree with the Republican Senate Majority leadership's decisions simply not to hold hearings or roll call votes on many Clinton nominees:

> I did not support the decision to put them [Clinton nominees] on the shelf and hope they die. I wanted them [the Republican leadership] to hold votes. I wanted them to have debates. When Frederica Massiah Jackson [a nominee to the Eastern District of Pennsylvania] came up and there was a vote scheduled for the floor, we were outraged that Trent Lott canceled the vote to allow the president to withdraw the nomination. We wanted that vote to take place. We wanted the hearings to be held. We wanted the debates to be on C-Span (Jipping interview).

The leader of another conservative organization also believes that role call votes are a way to get Republican senators to take the judicial selection issue more seriously:

> One of the biggest things we changed in Clinton's administration was emphasizing that nominees should

not be rubber-stamped. What I mean is that you should have a roll call vote on them instead of unanimous consent. It shows you are taking this seriously. I don't think there is anything wrong with putting it to a roll call vote good or bad. It puts everybody on the record and shows that it is a considered decision rather than "no objection, so ordered." We got Republicans to begin taking this more seriously, particularly when they looked at some of the Clinton judges and how they were ruling on particular issues and what it showed about their judicial philosophies. I think that might have raised an awareness (Conservative Judicial Watchdog).

Liberal activists also like this tactic. For example, conceding that a full vote by the Senate was likely to result in the confirmation of D. Brooks Smith to the Third Circuit—a candidate that liberal groups forcefully opposed—Aron, Gandy, and Cavendish all concurred that a vote should take place nonetheless because they "want to know where every senator stands" (Aron interview). Gandy echoed this sentiment regarding the Smith vote:

We have many [senators] who are going to ask for floor time, which is a major thing. . . . We have people asking for floor time because we want to make it public, we want to make it a fight, we want to say that if you screw women, you're going to have to deal with this, and you better not do it again because we're going to make it so painful that you did it. . . . [Even if we're going to lose] it's totally important because it sends a message that the people [Democrats] on the committee who voted to send this nomination to the floor were not supported by their own party (Gandy interview).

Interest group demands for roll call votes would seem to explain why, in the 1990s, we began to see so many lower court nominees confirmed not by voice vote—the traditional method used with lower court nominees for 200 years—but by roll call vote after a full floor debate.[23]

Threatening consequences

Notwithstanding strong opposition from key women's interest groups, three Democrats ultimately voted to confirm D. B. Smith, including two who are viewed as possible candidates for the Democratic presidential nomination in 2004: Joseph Biden and John Edwards (Herbert Kohl of Wisconsin was the third). This confirmation battle—which was ongoing at the time of the interviews—provided good insight as to how step three

of elite mobilization unfolds. In other words, how do interest groups react when senators send the "wrong" message?

Because the fight over D. B. Smith turned on charges of sex discrimination, most vocal over Biden's and Edwards' refusal to go along with the liberal interest groups was NOW. Immediately after the Committee vote was held, Olga Vives, NOW's vice-president of grass-roots activism, issued a press release. The message was unequivocal: "the field of Democratic presidential candidates narrowed significantly today." [24]

To indicate just how seriously senators fear the political repercussions of dissatisfied interest groups, consider Edwards' efforts to engage in damage control following the Smith vote. According to Gandy, NOW's president, almost immediately following his vote in favor of Smith, a member of Edwards' staff called Gandy to explain what happened:

I said [to Edwards' aide], "Oh, I guess you've seen our press release." And he [the staff member] said, "Oh god. It was faxed to us from all over the country." That's a direct quote. . . . He was very clear. He said, "Look. This nomination was gone. Biden had already made up his mind." His story was that Edwards wanted to be able to ride to the rescue, I'm paraphrasing, on bad nominations, but being from North Carolina, as he is, there are only so many [nominees] he can vote against. And that he [Edwards] was perfectly willing to vote no on this nominee, but that once Biden had voted yes, and it was clear that it was sailing away, then there was no point in using up a no vote (Gandy interview).

Gandy was particularly shocked, though, that Biden, previously thought to be a champion of women's rights, voted for Smith:

We had tried [to meet] with Biden in particular because we felt that he was the key [to defeating Smith]. The [Smith] letter promising to resign [from the all-male Spruce Creek Rod and Gun Club] had been written to Biden because Biden was chair of the committee back in 1988 when he [Smith] got the district court nomination. I thought, "he's [Biden] been dissed." He took this man's word. Plus, [Smith came out publicly against] the Violence Against Women Act, just to add insult to injury, which was Biden's baby. . . . And he was a sitting judge at the time that he was opining on the constitutionality of the Violence Against Women Act, which [legal issue] actually could have come to him [for a decision]. It was at a time when it [the issue] was percolating.

When asked what NOW would have done had they been forewarned that Biden would vote for Smith, Gandy immediately threatened electoral consequences:

> [W]e would've had every Delaware donor of Joe Biden on an airplane, and they would've been standing in his office if we had known in advance that Joe Biden was going to vote yes [on Smith]. . . . [W]e could've gone that far, and we would have. . . . We'd get on the phone with our allies saying, "we just heard Joe Biden is about to vote yes on this nomination. He's going to carry Edwards and Kohl with him because they don't want to use up their limited [no votes]" (Gandy interview).

In sum, once senators, and sometimes even political candidates, send cues to the activists—either favorable or unfavorable—activists kick into action. If satisfied with the politicians' response, activists will likely gather their resources and mobilize the party base to turn out and vote for that senator on election day. If unsatisfied with a senator's response, activists will either do nothing to mobilize the party base, or may go one step further and mobilize the party base against that candidate. At the very least, they will threaten senators to take such action.

Conclusion

Through in-depth interviews with the liberal and conservative interest groups and policy elites most actively involved in the judicial confirmation process, we are able to glean important new insights into the relationship between interest groups and senators. Most importantly, we learned why senators expend so much political capital on lower court judicial confirmation votes even though the issue is not in the least bit salient with voters. In short, senators are engaging in one of the three primary mobilization activities—position taking—and are strategically aiming those efforts at a very specific target: political elites on the far left and far right who believe that federal court litigation is the key to achieving favorable policy objectives. Absent the "right" signals from senators opposing objectionable nominees, the activists will take action—by mobilizing the party base against that senator or, equally troublesome to a senator, by not taking any action to mobilize the party's base on the senator's behalf. And, as the activists are keenly aware, without their mobilization efforts, senators may well have an uphill battle winning re-election, given the fact that the country is now so closely divided along partisan lines; whichever party

does a better job at mobilizing voters will likely determine the outcome of an election.

It should also be stated that not only senators engage in elite mobilization through the politics of lower court judgeships. The president, as well as presidential candidates, also employ this strategy. Rather than signaling over a confirmation fight, presidents and presidential candidates signal party and issue activists over whom they will *nominate* to the courts. For example, Carter and Clinton used this tactic effectively through their efforts to diversify the racial and gender make-up of the federal bench, satisfying women and civil rights activists; Reagan and George H. Bush made much of their nomination of pro-life judges to the lower federal courts, thereby satisfying "family values" activists.

Notes

The author wishes to thank the participants in the University of Miami, Department of Political Science, workshop for their insightful comments and suggestions to an earlier version of this article, particularly Jonathan West. In addition, the author would like to thank Elliot Slotnick, Sheldon Goldman, and Gregory Caldeira for their encouragement with this project in general, and their comments and suggestions on this particular piece. Finally, the author thanks Amy Steigerwalt for her assistance in scheduling and conducting the interviews that went into this piece.

This article originally appeared in Volume 86, Number 5, March–April 2003, pages 240–250.

1. Carp and Stidham, *The Federal Courts,* 3rd ed. (Washington, D.C.: C.Q. Press, 1998); Perry, *A Representative Supreme Court? The Impact of Race, Religion and Gender on Appointments* (New York: Greenwood, 1991).

2. Savage, "Clinton Losing Fight for Black Judge," *L A Times,* July 7, 2000, at A1.

3. Caldeira, "Courts and Public Opinion," in Gates and Johnson (eds.) *The American Courts* (Washington, D.C.: C.Q. Press, 1991).

4. Rosenstone and Hansen, *Mobilization, Participation and Democracy in America* (New York: MacMillan, 1993), 6–7.

5. Caldeira and Wright "Lobbying for Justice: Organized Interests, Supreme Court Nominations and the United States Senate," *Am. J. Pol. Sci.* 42 (1998), 499–523.

6. Mayhew, *Congress: The Electoral Connection* (New Haven: Yale University Press, 1974).

7. Ibid. at 61–62.

8. Ibid. at 115.

9. Several interviews were conducted jointly with Amy Steigerwalt, a graduate student at the University of Cali-

fornia, Berkeley: NOW, NARAL and the Alliance. In addition, due to scheduling difficulties, Ms. Steigerwalt conducted the interviews of PFW and the Conservative Judicial Watchdog by herself and asked questions on my behalf.

10. The only interest group contacted which did not respond to requests for an interview was the National Association for the Advancement of Colored People. However, as the NAACP's interests are directly aligned with those of PFW, also a civil rights organization, I do not believe this omission will bias my sample.

11. Pacelle, *The Role of The Supreme Court in American Politics* (Boulder, Colo.: Westview Press, 2002); Silverstein, *Judicious Choices: The New Politics of Supreme Court Confirmations* (New York: W. W. Norton & Co., 1996).

12. Bickel, *The Supreme Court and the Idea of Progress* (New York: Harper and Row, 1970), 134.

13. Epstein, *Conservatives in Court* (Knoxville: University of Tennessee Press, 1985).

14. Silverstein, *supra* n. 11; *see also* Goldman, *Picking Federal Court Judges* (New Haven: Yale University Press, 1997).

15. Schwartz, *Packing the Courts: The Conservative Campaign to Rewrite the Constitution* (New York: Charles Scribners' Sons, 1988), 60.

16. Caldeira, Hojnacki & Wright, "The Lobbying Activities of Organized Interests in Federal Judicial Nominations," *J. Pol.* 62 (2000), 51, 60; Scherer and Steigerwalt (2003). "Tracking Trouble: What Makes a Court of Appeals Nominee Objectionable to Interest Groups?" unpublished

paper presented at the 2003 Annual Midwest Political Science Association Conference.

17. Scherer and Steigerwalt, *supra* n. 16.

18. Lewis and Johnston, "Bush Would Sever Law Group's Role in Screening Judges," *New York Times,* March 17, 2001, at A1.

19. The exceptions were those instances when Clinton would nominate a candidate favored by a conservative senator as part of a deal to secure confirmation of a nominee favored by Clinton who had been held up at the committee level. These "log roll" nominees include Barbara Durham, nominated to the Ninth Circuit to satisfy Senator Slade Gorton (R-Wa) in exchange for confirmation of William Fletcher to the Ninth Circuit, and Ted Stewart, nominated to the District Court in Utah to satisfy Senator Orrin Hatch (R-Ut) in exchange for confirmation of Richard Paez and Marsha Berzon to the Ninth Circuit.

20. Jipping and Lombardi, "The Judicial Activism of Rosemary Barkett," Washington Times, Mar 17, 1994, at A19.

21. Comments by Nan Aron, February 21, 2003, broadcast live on C-Span.

22. Martinek, Kemper and Van Winkel, "To Advise and Consent: The Senate and Lower Federal Court Nominations, 1977–1998," *J. Pol.* 64 (2002), 337–361.

23. Cohen, "Missing in action: Interest groups and federal judicial appointments," *Judicature* 82 (1998), 119–120.

24. McFeatters, "Senate Panel Recommends Confirmation for Smith," *Pittsburgh Post-Gazette,* May 24, 2002, at A1.

W. Bush remaking the judiciary: like father like son?

Sheldon Goldman, Elliot Slotnick, Gerard Gryski, Gary Zuk, and Sara Schiavoni

George W. Bush's judicial appointees so far are comparable to his father's. Even more so than his father's, his administration is clearly coordinated and is expending the resources to place on the bench those who share the President's judicial philosophy.

Turbulent is as good a description as any of American political life over the last decade. Turbulence was certainly at the forefront of the birth of the George W. Bush presidency in the context of a popular vote loss and a contested electoral college victory facilitated by an unprecedented and controversial Supreme Court decision. The first two years of the Bush presidency were marked by political turbulence over his bold and divisive domestic policy initiatives and the virtually even split in party control of the United States Senate. With the defection of Vermont Senator Jim Jeffords from the Republican Party, control of the Senate shifted from the Republicans to the Democrats barely five months after Bush's inauguration. And then the horrific events of September 11, 2001, thrust the country into a war against terrorism both at home and abroad.

Within the context of these momentous events, the administration of George W. Bush nominated judges to the lower federal courts. Some of the nominations themselves added to the political turbulence. This article explores the first two years of the Bush administration's efforts to staff the federal bench, the politics of confirmation in the United States Senate, and the demographic and attribute profile of the Bush nominees who were confirmed to lifetime positions to lower courts of general jurisdiction by the 107th Congress. Like previous articles in this series, which began a quarter of a century ago with the Carter administration,[1] reliance is placed on interviews with key participants in and observers of the nomination and confirmation processes as well as data drawn from the questionnaires submitted by the nominees to the Senate Judiciary Committee. In addition, data were collected from the newspapers of nominees' home states, registrars of voters or boards of election, standard biographical sources,[2] and in some instances directly from the Bush appointees themselves.

The selection process

Any assessment of the processes used for selecting judges during the first two years of the Bush presidency must start with the recognition that staffing the judiciary was a central component of the President's domestic policy agenda. As stated by Assistant Attorney General Viet Dinh:

> The legal legacy that the president leaves [is as] important as anything else we do in terms of legislative policy. . . . We want to ensure that the highest quality judges, the highest quality intellects, men and women with the highest integrity, populate the federal bench. And let's be clear about it, we want to ensure that the President's mandate to us that the men and women who are nominated by him to be on the bench have his vision of the proper role of the judiciary. That is, a judiciary that will follow the law, not make the law, a judiciary that will interpret the Constitution, not legislate from the bench.[3]

Associate White House Counsel Brett Kavanaugh added that the President

> is very interested in this and thinks it is one of his most important responsibilities on the domestic side. Obviously, he has a lot of things going on, but he has devoted more attention to the issue of judges than any other president.[4]

Such a characterization stands, for some, in sharp contrast to the place of judicial selection in the presidential priorities of the Clinton White House where, according to Nan Aron, Executive President of the Alliance for Justice, the administration could be accused of "not making judgeships a priority. . . ."[5] In the Bush administration, however, "it was very clear from the outset that judges were going to be such a visible part of the President's program. Judgeships were both symbolically and actually symbols of presidential power."

For its part, of course, the Bush administration would characterize its judicial vision in terms of the way in which nominees view the scope of judicial power and not through an orientation towards reaching particular results. Indeed, as Viet Dinh noted,

Judicature Volume 86, Number 6, pp. 282–309

We are extremely clear in following the President's mandate that we should not, and do not, and can not employ any litmus test on any one particular issue, because in doing so we would be guilty of politicizing the judiciary and that is as detrimental as if we were unable to identify men and women who would follow the law rather than legislate from the bench.

Structurally, at the most basic level, the processes used by the Bush administration for designating judicial nominees are not dramatically different than recent presidencies in their reliance upon senior personnel from the White House, primarily the Office of the White House Counsel, where both Alberto Gonzalez, White House Counsel, and Brett Kavanaugh, Associate White House Counsel, are deeply involved in judicial selection matters, and the Department of Justice, primarily through the Office of Legal Policy (OLP), a division headed during the period covered by this article by Assistant Attorney General Viet Dinh. The OLP replaced the Office of Policy Development (OPD) from the Clinton and Bush Sr. years, a change that has been seen as symbolically significant by some.

The Office of Legal Policy was the name given to the new Justice Department division created by the Reagan administration. By returning to the original name of the office, this perhaps signalled that this President Bush's judicial selection behavior would be more like that of President Reagan, known for his aggressive pursuit of a conservative agenda through judicial appointments, than that of his two successors. C. Boyden Gray, who served as the White House Counsel during the first Bush's tenure, did not see any such motivation in the change, noting that "Every Justice Department is slightly different. I think it's just a question of personal style." [6] Viet Dinh opined that the change underscored that it was

important to us to get back to the history of the establishment of the office. The day I was sworn into office, the Attorney General signed the order renaming the office, the Office of Legal Policy. That's the name [that] . . . reflects the fact that what we do is not simply development policy, but also evaluating, implementing and generating policy.

At the heart of the Bush administration's judicial selection processes is the Judicial Selection Committee, a joint enterprise between White House personnel and OLP, chaired by Alberto Gonzalez. In our interviews with Viet Dinh and Brett Kavanaugh, we attempted to ascertain the precise membership of this group but, beyond confirming their own participation and that of Gonzalez, we were unable to identify the other participants. This stance was taken, Dinh explained, "in order to preserve the deliberative process for the President. But suffice it to say that the primary participants are from the White House Counsel's Office and the Department of Justice comprising both this office and the Attorney General when appropriate." Kavanaugh explained that not identifying names was "part of a larger principle that we don't usually discuss who is involved in the deliberative process and who is making what recommendations to the President." However, their counterparts in the Reagan, Bush Sr., and Clinton administrations were more forthcoming in this matter and helped to flesh out the historical record by indicating committee participants.

When we noted that our research during the Clinton administration revealed that representatives from the First Lady's office, the Vice-President's office, legislative affairs, and the President's Chief of Staff, among others, were present at meetings of the Judicial Selection Committee during the Clinton years, Dinh added that "the people who would have an interest in this process are represented" but did not offer further elaboration.

The Judicial Selection Committee, according to Kavanaugh, "gets together and discusses just where we stand on both the nominations side and the confirmation side." At the outset of the selection process, the Committee oversees the development of names to take to the President for his initial approval, what Dinh labeled "the presidential check-off." Characterizing the level of presidential involvement at this relatively early stage of judicial selection, Dinh noted "I do know that he has [exercised] direct, personal and specific decision-making authority on each and every candidate. So when I say it is a presidential check-off, I mean it is [literally] a presidential check-off." As in past administrations, the names of potential district court nominees are initially submitted, according to Dinh, "from the [home state] senators, or whomever the relevant player is. . . ." For the circuit courts the names tend to be generated more by the administration.

Once the President approves to move forward, the Department of Justice oversees a two-pronged background investigation of the potential nominee, including an internal vetting process conducted by OLP staff as well as a field investigation conducted by the FBI, which is characterized by Dinh as "your normal background investigation for presidential personnel" but specifically targeted toward judicial nominees, going into issues of temperament and impartiality in addition to the normal background check. In describing the OLP investigation, Dinh noted that it "is quite similar, actually, to the activities of interest groups such as the American Bar Association where we contact members of the bench and bar in the affected community and do a staff vetting report." The American Bar Association's own vetting of candidates, however, historically done prior to their nomination by the president, has been removed from the Bush selection processes, a matter that will be explored further below.

Dinh reported that the meetings of the Judicial Selection Committee are held "as necessary and once a week unless there is no business," a luxury rarely if ever enjoyed during the first two years of the Bush administration when large numbers of nominees were processed to be sent to the Senate. All interviews of potential nominees were conducted at the White House, although both Viet Dinh and Brett Kavanaugh characterized the Judicial Selection Committee as completely collaborative in its operation, with no distinct role played by White House as distinct from Justice Department participants. According to Dinh,

> We do not think of ourselves as separate offices serving different functions. We do have primary responsibilities, we do have specific expertise, but when we introduce ourselves to the candidates or other people we may introduce ourselves as being from the Department of Justice or we may not. We do not think of our participation as part of the White House Counsel's Office or part of the Department of Justice. I think it is just a concerted effort to serve the President the best way we can.

Kavanaugh concurred, describing the process as "really collaborative, we work together, [and] try to be a seamless whole."

Significantly, under Clinton the political facets of judicial selection were openly avowed to be the province of White House personnel while the more professional facets of the evaluation of candidate credentials were handled by the Justice Department. Under Bush, it appears, no such distinctions are recognized. As assessed by Dinh,

It's just a matter of we're all sitting here contributing to the decision-making process. There's not a separate Department of Justice interview and then a White House interview. There's a joint interview, with joint input, with joint assessment that is not divided between politics and qualifications.

Dinh did concede, however, that there was one important facet of the process where some distinction of function could be found:

> The outreach to senators, the liaisons for senators, are done by the White House Counsel's Office, and that may be more in regard to what you mean by politics, whether it [the nomination] is going to fly or not. The White House Counsel's Office handles the contact and consultations to all home state senators, even on circuit courts, and even if the person is from the opposite party.

And it is in the performance of this consultative role that one finds the greatest divide between the characterization of the process by the administration and its supporters, and the perception of Senate Democrats and the administration's critics. Viet Dinh put it quite succinctly, "We recognize home state senators' prerogatives; that's why we consult." Brett Kavanaugh concurred, noting, "We consult with the home state senators on both district court and courts of appeals and run by them, before an FBI background check, names of people who are under consideration to get their reactions ahead of time, and that helps avoid problems down the road." Kavanaugh added, "We maintain consultation logs, and I think there's been extensive consultation."

Consultation does not, in any sense, convey, however, that senators have a veto power over the administration's choices, whether the senators are Democrats or Republicans. According to Kavanaugh:

> Consultation doesn't mean, obviously, that the home state senator picks . . . the judge, but it does mean that we consult in the sense of discussing potential names with them and hear what they have to say. If someone says . . . "I wish you would pick my person," and that's an overstatement just to give you a flavor, that's different from a home state senator [saying] "Gee, that person has real problems, let me tell you about the problems." That kind of thing we take very seriously. Sometimes home state senators have specific information that may not have come to us.

Sharing this view of extensive White House consultation with home state senators was Judiciary Committee Republican Chief Counsel Makan Delrahim, a senior staff assistant serving Senator Orrin Hatch: "I don't think we have to worry about this White House. They've been just incredible, the amount of consultation they've had with the home state senators. . . ." [7]

As noted, however, the area of consultation is one about which there is considerable disagreement concerning the performance of the President's judicial selection team. According to Elliot Mincberg, Vice President, General Counsel, and Legal and Education Director of People for the American Way, for example,

> What you saw was almost a complete abandonment of Clinton's efforts to put the advice back into advice and consent. Unfortunately, what we've been seeing from the president is confrontation rather than consultation and cooperation.[8]

Marcia Kuntz, of the Alliance for Justice, linked the issue of consultation with broader concerns:

> The administration's penchant for secrecy is very much evident in its conduct of the judicial selection process, both in cutting out the ABA and not circulating these names ahead of time, and in its failure to consult with the Senate before nomination. The names just don't get out there in the same way. There's no public discussion, there's no vetting outside the administration.[9]

Democratic staff members in the Senate who were involved in discussions of potential nominees in consultative processes raised similar themes. One noted:

> There is no interest or evidence that there will be balance or moderation coming from the White House. They don't want a check and balance on this, they want a blank check. Their view of consultation, negotiation, building relationships, is a very narrow view. It remains a unilateralist view of how to create a relationship. There were times, fairly early in the process, where suggestions were being made, arrangements could have been made, nobody was trying to rub anybody's face in anything, where we thought accommodations on all sides could have been worked out. But there was no interest in doing that. There was a lot of the "permanent campaign" going on.

If, indeed, the fundamental approach to the nature of consultative processes has been altered from the Clinton years, and we must note that none of the parties interviewed and quoted here are disinterested, there are important consequences that can follow. A Democratic staffer observed:

The President has every right to nominate . . . but all we're asking is, "Don't send us the worst guys." Hatch used to call up Clinton and say, "Don't send me that guy. I don't think I can get him through." Or, "I'm not going to be able to support him." And they'd listen. Now I've had a federal judge tell me "You know what? I give the Republicans their due. They play hardball. That's why they are going to win." Clinton certainly didn't [play hardball]. And we don't. We believe in this institution too much. There was a check and balance . . . that is pretty much going to go away. What we're going to be left with is when you can get 51 guys to vote against a judicial nominee or 41 people to filibuster a judicial nominee, that's the only time they're in trouble.

When the administration's vetting of a potential nominee, through its Judicial Selection Committee, is completed, and there is satisfaction that appropriate consultations have been held and the candidate passes muster, the name will be forwarded to the President for his signing off on the formal nomination. At this stage, according to Brett Kavanaugh, the President

> is very involved in the process. Obviously, you don't discuss things with a president, this president or any president, until you have everything refined and the recommendation and options tied up in a way that's appropriate for his time, particularly now since there are a number of issues on his plate, since September 11th.

Departures from status quo

There remain two areas of judicial selection processes under Bush that warrant additional exploration because they represent potentially significant departures from the status quo characterizing the approach of past administrations. First, at the outset of his administration, President Bush ended the formal role played by the American Bar Association in the rating of candidates before final decisions on nominations were made by the President. More recently, on October 30, 2002, the President offered a timetable proposal suggesting the parameters for the flow of all phases of the judicial selection process, from notification requirements suggested for sitting judges regarding their plans for stepping down from the bench through the time taken to conduct various facets of the confirmation process.

From the administration's perspective, the swirl of controversy that surrounded the removal of the ABA's formal participation in the presidential stages of judicial selection could be characterized as much ado about very little. Viet Dinh noted that the administration recognized that the ABA,

> through the Senate Judiciary Committee and through individual senators, had a role in this process. It was very clear when I took office that Senator Leahy, then Chairman of the Senate Judiciary Committee, would not clear any person for a hearing unless and until that person had received a rating from the ABA. So the ABA was an integral part of the Senate Judiciary Committee's consideration of the candidacy and we did everything in our power to cooperate in that process.

Towards that end, Dinh established a procedure whereby when a nomination was sent to the Senate for confirmation consideration, the name was concurrently sent to the ABA so that it could start its review processes.

Brett Kavanaugh further elaborated on the administration's position on ABA involvement in judicial selection, a position he felt was

> widely mischaracterized. The President felt it was unfair and unwise to give one outside group preferential access to the process, particularly when there are a number of bar associations that we hear from and the ABA had this preferred role, which seemed unwise. It was not a suggestion that the ABA shouldn't be rating judges. In fact, the President has touted on numerous occasions the fact that the ABA has rated people like Justice Owen well qualified, unanimously. So it wasn't commentary on whether it was appropriate for the ABA to rate judges. It was commentary on the fact that no one outside group should really be part of the nomination process, and it goes, in some ways, to a broader issue of presidential prerogatives and what's appropriate. It was obviously interpreted by some as a way of kicking the ABA out. And, obviously, the ABA would rather be involved in the front end rather than the confirmation side, the back end. But we felt, the President certainly felt, that the appropriate thing was for the ABA and every other group that was to rate the President's nominees to have the same shot. I think there was a sense by some Democrats at the beginning that this means that the President is going to be turning to people who are not qualified because he's scared or afraid of the rating process. Nothing could be further from the truth. We welcome an examination of the qualifications of his nominees. So I think it was mischaracterized by some, as things often are when deci-

sions are made by a president, that there was a lot of politics going on. But it was really a principled decision about what the appropriate role for the ABA was and not a decision about what kind of nominees there would be nor a decision about whether the ABA appropriately could rate the judges as other groups could.

Boyden Gray succinctly summarized the view that little has really changed. "The ABA, I think, is just as honored now as it was when I was here. The only thing is that they don't get the upfront knowledge about it, but they're full players. They're getting everything they've always had." A similar assessment was offered by Makan Delrahim from his perspective as Republican Chief Counsel of the Judiciary Committee which, when first chaired by Orrin Hatch during the Clinton years, had ended the ABA Committee's "most favored" status in the process, a change lasting until the Democrats regained control of the Senate chamber and Patrick Leahy assumed the Judiciary Committee chairmanship.

> Senator Hatch looked at it as a matter of equity. Should the Hispanic Bar Association do a vetting before the Committee acts on it or the president sends it down? What about the Minority Law Students Association? Any association could provide useful advice and they should. And the ABA is just one of them. . . . They've provided their service and it has been valuable.

Since the advent of the 108th Congress, with the ABA removed from the presidential facets of judicial selection, the Republicans back in control of the Senate, and Senator Orrin Hatch again chairing the Judiciary Committee, the question of what status the ABA's post-hoc ratings will play in the confirmation process looms both larger and on somewhat more tenuous footing. Indeed, as Delrahim underscored,

> The ABA can do its work, but we're not going to allow the ABA to delay our consideration of judicial nominees. I mean there's no constitutional reason . . . to allow any outside group to delay the advice and consent process of the Senate.

Critics of the administration's posture towards the ABA see the implications of its removal from the front end of the selection process in a much more negative light, with unhappy consequences. Nan Aron, for example, argues that,

> one difference between now and years before is the chilling effect that excluding the ABA has had on the

desire and ability of lawyers to be upfront, to share their views of the nominees. It's staggering. I remember from the '80s lawyers would call and say, "Just got word from the ABA that so and so had been nominated. You guys ought to take a look."

Now, as Marcia Kuntz added, "there is a lot of pressure on people not to be candid. Once somebody is nominated, there is an inevitability to confirmation, so why would they stick their necks out and say anything negative?"

In Aron's view, this reality is consistent with a broader administration motivation for altering the ABA's role in the process in the first place:

I am convinced, I am absolutely convinced, that the reason the administration removed the ABA, I don't care what they say, is not because they are afraid of the rating, because we all know that ratings were uniformly high. It wasn't the ratings that caused them to take them out. It was their desire for total and complete secrecy, and that's another thing that's a huge departure. It's a major change. It's shrouding the entire judicial selection process in secrecy.

The second major departure of the Bush approach to judicial selection, the nascent effort to regulate the time parameters of the process, was not unveiled until October 30, 2002, just one week before the 2002 congressional elections. The President's proposal, stemming, in part, from his view that the Senate had displayed a poor record in confirming his nominees, contained four central recommendations, collectively targeted at filling vacancies expeditiously as seats on the federal bench became open. To succeed, the President's proposal would require behavioral changes not only in the administration's own behavior, in some instances, but in the institutional behavior of the Senate and the judiciary as well:

1. Federal judges should give a year's notice of their intention to take retirement or senior status.

2. The president should nominate a replacement judge within 180 days of receiving such notice.

3. The Senate Judiciary Committee should hold hearings within 90 days of receiving a nomination.

4. The full Senate should hold a floor vote within 180 days of the initial receipt of the nomination.

Adding to its luster was the notion that the proposal was targeted at the process irrespective of the occupant of the White House. Viet Dinh emphasized this point. "I think it's a perfectly sensible plan. It operates irrespective of who is in power, either in the administration or in the Senate." Recognizing that the plan required considerable cooperation from participants in the process outside of White House control, Dinh noted the administration's flexibility in how meeting the guidelines might be accomplished:

We would support a Senate rule change to codify this, but we would support anything short of a rule change. A Judiciary Committee rule change, a bipartisan gentlemen's agreement, Judicial Conference resolutions, whatever it is in order to get as close to the ideal that there should be an orderly process of at least giving a person a full day hearing and an up or down vote.

In a similar vein, Associate White House Counsel Brett Kavanaugh noted that "things rarely happen overnight, but he has set out a marker. The President ultimately would like to see the Senate come around to the view that it would make sense to have a standard process that applies to every judicial nominee." In Kavanaugh's view, such a standardized process would enable the judicial selection process to emerge from the tit-for-tat obstructionism that has characterized both the Clinton and Bush administration's selection efforts. Kavanaugh added:

Have a process where people know the rules in advance, the rules of the road. We're going to have hearings; we're going to have votes. And if you think someone is out of the mainstream, it is incumbent upon you to make that case, whether you are a Republican objecting to a Clinton nominee or a Democrat objecting to a Bush nominee. And, ultimately, you have to convince your colleagues that is the case and not bottle up a nominee. That's not fair to the nominee, it's unfair to the president, it hurts the courts, [and] breaks down the whole process. It deters good people from getting involved.

While committed, in the long run, to the necessity of a Senate rule change as an ultimate goal, Kavanaugh admitted,

That takes time. A lot of times, ideas like this, you keep plugging, you keep plugging and, ultimately, it may come to fruition. And that's what we plan to do with this. The President said the goal is to have a new judge ready to take office the day the old judge retires. That's the seamless transition we're seeking. That's a process.

Diversity on the bench

Bench diversification in the first two years of the Bush administration, as seen in Table 1, slowed from the rather frenetic pace of the Clinton era. When all three court levels are combined, the percentage of nontraditional judges in active service increased 6.7 percent (as compared to 36.2 percent in Clinton's first two years). There were modest gains for women, African Americans, and Hispanics. The number of Asian Americans remained the same, and with the resignation of Judge Billy Michael Burrage from the Eastern District of Oklahoma in March 2001 the federal judiciary lost its only jurist with a Native American heritage.

Table 1. Proportion of nontraditional lifetime judges in active service on courts of general jurisdiction— January 1, 2001, through January 1, 2003

	2001		2003		
	%	(N)	%	(N)	% increase
U.S. district courts					
Women	19.9*	(130)	21.1*	(140)	7.7
African American	10.7	(71)	11.3	(75)	5.6
Hispanic	4.8	(32)	5.3	(35)	9.4
Asian	0.8	(5)	0.8	(5)	—
Native American	0.2	(1)	0.0	—	—
U.S. courts of appeals					
Women	21.0**	(35)	21.6**	(36)	2.9
African American	7.1#	(12)	7.8	(13)	8.3
Hispanic	6.0	(10)	6.0	(10)	—
Asian	0.6	(1)	0.6	(1)	—
U.S. Supreme Court					
Women	22.2***	(2)	22.2***	(2)	—
African American	11.1	(1)	11.1	(1)	—
All three court levels					
Women	19.9	(167)	21.2	(178)	6.6
African American	10.1	(84)	10.6	(89)	6.0
Hispanic	5.0	(42)	5.4	(45)	7.1
Asian	0.7	(6)	0.7	(6)	—
Native American	0.1	(1)	0.0	—	—
Total nontraditional****	32.1	(270)	34.3	(288)	6.7

  * Out of 664 authorized lifetime positions on the U.S. district courts.
 ** Out of 167 authorized lifetime positions on the numbered circuits and the U.S. Court of Appeals for the District of Columbia Circuit, all courts of general jurisdiction.
*** Out of nine authorized positions on the U.S. Supreme Court.
**** The total does not double count those who were classified in more than one category.
  # Includes Roger Gregory, who was given a recess appointment on December 27, 2000. Note that Gregory is not included as a Clinton appointee for purposes of Table 4 in the main text, which is confined to confirmed lifetime appointees. President George W. Bush nominated Gregory, who was confirmed and is thus included in the 2003 figures for this table and statistics for the W. Bush appointees in tables 6 and 7 in the main text.

The only net gains on the courts of appeals were one additional female and one African American. Currently, each appeals court has at least one female judge in active service. The Ninth Circuit is highest in absolute numbers with six women in active service. Only the First and Tenth Circuits are without African American judges; in fact an African American has yet to serve on those two courts.

Table 2. Diversity on the district courts, January 1, 2003: active judges aggregated by circuit

Circuit	% Female, district courts	% African American, general population	% African American, district courts	% Hispanic, general population	% Hispanic, district courts
First	17.2	5.2	3.5	31.5	27.6
First*		4.1	4.5	5.6	4.5
Second	25.9	14.5	8.6	13.9	1.7
Third	21.1	11.7	15.8	7.2	3.5
Fourth	14.6	22.3	14.6	4.0	0.0
Fifth	16.5	17.4	8.6	24.2	11.1
Sixth	23.2	12.7	12.3	2.3	0.0
Seventh	22.7	11.3	11.4	8.1	6.8
Eighth	24.4	7.1	14.3	2.8	0.0
Ninth	29.0	5.3	14.0	25.0	5.0
Tenth	23.7	4.2	7.7	14.0	7.7
Eleventh	23.0	20.4	11.3	11.2	4.8
D.C.	26.7	60.0	28.6	7.9	7.1

* Excluding Puerto Rico

The Sixth, Eighth, and D.C. courts have two African American judges, and the remaining seven courts have one. Historically, the court that has had the most African Americans serving (five) is the Sixth Circuit. Hispanic judges—both currently and historically—have yet to serve on the Fourth, Sixth, Seventh, Eighth, and D.C. Circuits. Three courts (Second, Fifth, Ninth) have two Hispanic judges and the First, Third, Tenth, and Eleventh Circuits each have one. Ninth Circuit Judge Atsushi Tashima is the only Asian American to be in active service on the courts of appeals.

The biggest increase in nontraditional representation was on the district bench. Women, African Americans, and Latinos advanced significantly. Ten nontraditional judges left the bench during the 107th Congress; five of those vacancies are unfilled. Parenthetically, in the other five cases a nontraditional judge was replaced by a white male. The district benches in eight states (Alaska, Idaho, Maine, Montana, New Hampshire, North Dakota, Vermont, and Wyoming) have never had a nontraditional judge. Of course, none of the states in question has either a large judge complement or sizable minority population. Ten states have never had a female district judge, 15 an African American, 36 a Hispanic, and 47 an Asian American. As mentioned

above, the only jurist with a significant Native American heritage in the history of the district courts was from Oklahoma.

Table 2 aggregates the district courts by circuit, and lists the percent of female judges in each jurisdiction. Also, the percent of African Americans and Hispanics is compared to the percentage of each group in the general population.* The percentage of women is highest on the district courts of the Ninth Circuit, and falls below 20 percent on the First, Fourth, and Fifth. A fairly close match exists for the percent of African American judges and percent in general population for the First, Sixth, and Seventh Circuits, with the largest disparities present in the Fifth, Eighth, Ninth, Eleventh, and District of Columbia. The discrepancies for Hispanics are considerably wider; in fact, two circuits (Fourth and Eighth) have no Hispanic judges in active service. The fit is closest in the First, Seventh, and District of Columbia Circuits.

—Gerard Gryski and Gary Zuk

* Asian Americans and Native Americans are excluded because the number of relevant judges is either too small or nonexistent. Calculations for the First Circuit are done with and without Puerto Rico to get a firmer view of the match between the Hispanic population in the states of the First Circuit and the proportion of Hispanics on the district courts.

Perfection will probably never be achieved in every case. But improving the process significantly, we think, can be achieved with these kinds of timetables.

In analyzing the President's mandate, it is important to underscore the critical "end game" of the proposed process-floor action on a nomination. According to Viet Dinh,

> This process is not meant as a way to override . . . prerogatives of home state senators. To the extent that we can accommodate those interests and also succeed in expeditious resolution, great! With respect to holds, a hold is nothing but an intention to filibuster. And its only force is the prerogative to filibuster on the floor. We have absolutely no intention of disturbing [the] century old tradition of Senators to filibuster on the floor. . . . [T]he call for a vote on the floor within 180 days is nothing but a statement, "Hey, let's get it out in the open." It's not necessarily a call that you have to have passed cloture within 180 days. If you want to exercise the floor prerogative of denying cloture, fine, just do it. Do it within 180 days, according to normal rules of floor debate, including filibuster, but do it out in the open.

Some skepticism about the President's proposal can be seen among the administration's supporters. Boyden Gray, for example, noted

> I think they'll try and hold to it. Maybe they'll be able to. But I, myself, am a little bit skeptical of finite timetables that you have to get so and so out. It's just not quite susceptible to such precision.

In addition to such practical concerns about the plan's operation, substantive criticisms of the proposal were also offered, in this instance, from the Democratic side of the Senate aisle. One aide noted that

> the proposal doesn't take into account when a president stacks nominations, numerous nominees at the beginning. There is no regard to how controversial they may be, how time consuming the records may be. They are just supposed to get a hearing pretty quickly.

Another Senate aide offered,

> Portraying it as a situation that has gotten worse is just playing into their argument. Their argument has now gotten to the point where the President is seriously committed to the proposal that he made right before the election. "Okay, let's just take politics out of this; I'll just take all the marbles. Forget about blue slips, forget about hearings, forget about everybody. We'll just have this arbitrary time clock that says within 180 days I get an up or down vote." A Democratic president's moderate nominees were not allowed to go forth, but now we're supposed to flip the switch.

While not opposed, in principle, to a "neutral" proposal instituted under a veil of ignorance at some future time when nobody could know the identity of the president or the partisan balance of the Senate, he continued,

> We should say we will start this with the next president. This is an interesting set of concepts. Let's start it with the next set of guys so that none of us really benefit. Well, I can assure you that will never be offered.

Synthesizing the multiple concerns raised about the President's proposal Elliot Mincberg of People for the American Way asserted that, "aspirational goals may not be a bad idea to suggest in the abstract, but it's important to always consider individual circumstances." Citing complaints that some of the earliest Bush nominees were still waiting to have their hearings, Mincberg continued:

> Well, from the perspective of the administration of the courts, there is a very good reason for that. If you process nominees first in, first out, you're going to have a huge number of vacancies because if the first ones are the most controversial ones, and you take the most time to review, then the result is that the ones who are less controversial don't get reviewed. So I think it's important, frankly, from my perspective, to add some things of a more qualitative nature. I think that the more moderate, less controversial nominees should get priority in processing and they always have, and they should, because it makes perfect sense from the perspective of helping the courts do their job. And that's something that's hard to write in the rules, but is something that has to be considered. And it's a bit counterintuitive to the notion that every nominee should follow a particular schedule. It is certainly true that there is a need to try and make the process work better, but again, I think where that starts, is not with attempted timetables, but with attempts to try and lower the temperature of the process a little.

In the final analysis, Mincberg noted, there was a certain irony in the President's proposal.

> It really isn't appropriate for a president on the one hand to say, at least quietly, I'm going to put a strong

ideological stamp on the judiciary but, on the other hand, I want these guys processed in an assembly line process. It doesn't make sense. It's not consistent with the whole division of authority in advice and consent.

Confirmation politics

The confirmation vote on federal judgeship nominees is the final stage in a contextual process in which, historically, the drama has been played out before a nominee is actually brought to the Senate floor. Indeed, only under the rarest of circumstances, representing the worst case scenario of a breakdown in "normal" judicial confirmation processes, will a candidate be reported out of Committee and then be defeated on the Senate floor. This was the case, however, with former President Clinton's attempt to appoint Ronnie White to a district court vacancy in Missouri. In this instance a strict party-line vote resulted in White's defeat on the Senate floor. While the first two years of the Bush presidency did not witness a floor defeat for any of his nominees, two of his candidates (Priscilla Owen and Charles Pickering) received almost equally rare negative votes from the Democratic-controlled Senate Judiciary Committee, while the nominations of 28 other district and circuit court candidates expired at the end of the 107th Congress and were returned to the President without any action being taken on them by the Committee.

The context for the playing out of the confirmation process in the first two years of the Bush presidency serves as ample prelude to an understanding of the Bush confirmation record. At the outset, there was the legacy of Bush v. Gore and a very tenuous electoral victory for the President that could not be seen, in any sense, as a rousing mandate in the judicial selection arena. There was the legacy of the acrimonious judicial selection politics of the Clinton years and what many would characterize as unprecedented mistreatment of Clinton's nominees, particularly during his second term in office.[10] There was the reality and the irony of the lightning rod of John Ashcroft, a key participant in judicial selection battles during the Clinton years (and the central player in the aforementioned defeat of Ronnie White) now serving as the head of the Justice Department, the very part of the executive branch that would play a lead role in vetting potential judicial nominees. And, of course, there was, at first, the specter of an evenly divided Senate.

Adding to these potential problems for judicial selection inherited by the President were new ones that emerged once he was in office. First, the Democrats regained control of the Senate when Jim Jeffords left the Republican Party caucus and all legislative work came to a halt for several weeks as struggles to reorganize the body proceeded at center stage. Then the tragedy of September 11 struck and judicial selection matters vied for attention at the Judiciary Committee with pressing legislative issues of anti-terrorism and national security. The presence of anthrax in mail sent to Senator Leahy even shut down the then Judiciary Committee Chair's office. In such a setting, the politics of judicial confirmation would inevitably be problematic and, it is fair to say, the nomination behavior of the administration only served to fan the flames of potential confirmation controversy in the eyes of the President's critics.[11] The relationship between the confirmation environment faced by President Bush and the context that preceded it was well tapped by Elliot Mincberg of People for the American Way:

> You kind of have to talk about the last two years in the context of the six and a half years or so that occurred before that. President Clinton, some would argue to his credit and some would argue to the detriment of various interests, really made an effort with respect to all judicial nominations from the Supreme Court down, to depolarize the issue, to genuinely put some advice back into advice and consent in terms of soliciting views from senators from both sides of the aisle. Unfortunately, the reward for that, in large measure, was not moving people along but some unprecedented stonewalling. And I think all of that really set a very bad tone, frankly, for what happened in the past two years.

That "tone" was only exacerbated, according to one Democratic Senate staff member, by the approach that the administration took coming out of the starting gate. In his view, the Bush team was

> very skillful in making arguments to editorial writers and others which sounded neutral and fair but would have had the result of being unfair in the historical context in which we found ourselves, in a context where they had held all nominees to the 6th Circuit for four years and all the nominees to the D.C. Circuit for four years. For them to then insist on rushing a bunch of guys through who were not as close to the center line as the Clinton nominees had been seemed, to some, to be overreaching.

More broadly, the aide added,

> What they're willing to do, better than any other group I know, is simply be a-historical [and say], "That was then," or just ignore it and say, "This is now."

This point was seconded by Marcia Kuntz of the Alliance for Justice, who asserted that nominations were made

> with absolutely no recognition of the obstructionism during the Clinton years. These were the Administration's choices and then to say they were held up is also completely unfair because Leahy did move people— certainly much more quickly than we would have liked.

History, of course, is a two-edged sword, and any suggestion that Democratic efforts to obstruct and delay Bush's nominees were simply "payback" for the treatment received by Clinton's nominees was rejected outright by C. Boyden Gray:

> What changed two years ago was doing slowdown the first year of a president's term, and that was new. The Democrats will argue, though, that it's just tit for tat for what happened during the Clinton years. But it isn't really, because you're measuring last year versus first year and, of course, if the first year figures carry through, then the appellate nominees will really be decimated.

Conceding that slowing down confirmation processes occurs routinely when a presidential election draws near, Gray emphasized, "What has not been tradition is doing it to appellate nominees in the first two years. That was new."

It was into this contentious environment that the President, on May 9, 2001, formally announced his first 11 judicial nominees. Associate White House Counsel Brett Kavanaugh noted of this group that they exemplified what the President

> was looking for. A group of nominees, in terms of their excellence, which they all shared, and their integrity, which they all shared, and support, which is huge, which they all shared. It was a diverse group, a well qualified group, a bipartisan group. It was an incredibly credentialed group.

There was no denying that the group was symbolically diverse and significantly experienced. Seven were sitting judges and four had extensive experience as advocates before the Supreme Court. Six of the 11 were women or minorities. These included Roger Gregory, Barrington Parker, and Miguel Estrada. Gregory, first nominated by Bill Clinton, had failed to gain confirmation to the Fourth Circuit Court of Appeals, ultimately being seated on that court as a recess appointment. By virtue of that appointment, he became the

first African American to sit on the Fourth Circuit, yet his term would automatically expire if he were not renominated and confirmed. Parker, also an African American, was a sitting district court judge first appointed by President Clinton. Estrada was the first Hispanic nominated to the D.C. Circuit Court of Appeals, arguably second only to the Supreme Court as the most important court in the country.

Yet several of the nominees raised red flags for many Democrats, largely because of their prominent conservative credentials which, in some instances, were paired with close associations with the Federalist Society. The purported conservatives included Estrada as well as Dennis Shedd, former aide to Strom Thurmond, Texas Supreme Court Justice Priscilla Owen, Ohio Supreme Court Justice Deborah Cook, Jeffrey Sutton, an Ohio litigator with strong "state's rights" credentials associated with cases testing the reach of the Americans with Disabilities Act, conservative legal scholar and law professor Michael McConnell, District Court Judge Terrence Boyle, a former aide to Jesse Helms, and a nominee, John Roberts, Jr., whose nomination nine years earlier during the administration of the President's father, George H.W. Bush, languished in the Senate and went unconfirmed.

Elliot Mincberg gave the President some credit for some of the designees:

> I think Bush took one very small step in a positive direction by renominating Gregory for the Fourth Circuit. That was a nominee who was supported pretty firmly by both the Republican senators who had pledged before the election to support him but, nonetheless, I think there is no question he deserves credit for that. But with that exception, and possibly Parker from the Second Circuit as well, I think it is very clear that nominations, with respect to the Courts of Appeals in particular, have been very centrally and somewhat secretively controlled at the White House level. And in a way that is very clearly designed to go one step further beyond the Reagan/Bush strategy in the '80s and early '90s to really put a very strong ideological stamp on the federal courts.

Responding to a question about whether Gregory and Parker could be considered an "olive branch" from the administration, a Democratic Senate aide replied:

> As far as I know, Judge Parker was President Bush's choice from day one. Roger Gregory was included because John Warner and, to a lesser extent, George

Allen, were committed to that nomination, and followed through on it. It was all done within the Republican family. It was the right thing to do.

Nan Aron of the Alliance for Justice took note that the President

had a very public press conference, invited his nominees, and proudly showed them off to the world and talked about the kind of judges he wanted. And that was a departure, certainly, from the way in which the Clinton administration picked judges. For one thing, it was very clear from the outset that judges were going to be such a visible part of the President's program.

This bold nomination strategy was characterized by one Senate aide as, perhaps, flowing from the need to act quickly with both a slim Republican majority in the Senate and the precarious health of Senators Thurmond and Helms. Such nomination behavior could also be seen as a "payoff" of sorts to the most conservative elements of President Bush's electoral coalition. Whatever the reason for the approach, it did not play well among Democrats. As one Democratic aide put it:

It certainly seemed to us that there was an effort at really packing the courts, at really skewing the courts and changing the balance on a number of circuits. I think their intention was to ram them through, to work very quickly to get these judges confirmed while the Republican majority held. It was heavily front-loaded and they were going to be very aggressive.

Critics of the administration's choices, such as Nan Aron, felt that there were alternatives to the President's approach, such as turning to some of the unconfirmed nominees of the Clinton administration, that could have gotten the confirmation process off on a better footing.

If they had really meant to put up an olive branch, they would have gone back to the circuits where there was real obstructionism. They would have put up nominees who had Republican support. Kent Marcus had support from DeWine and Voinovich. . . . They've had ample opportunity to do that and, in fact, every time Carl Levin has tried to sit down with the White House to talk to them about the Sixth Circuit they've shunned him and, finally, they said, "Oh, we'll put a Democrat on the district court."

Interestingly, the administration expected that judicial selection and the initial announcement of nomi-

nees would be a catalyst for controversy. As noted by Associate White House Counsel Brett Kavanaugh:

We recognized, even then, and that was before Senator Jeffords switched parties, that there was a lot of focus on the judicial selection issue. That was clear from day one. And that two things were already clearly in play. Number one, the potential payback for frustration by some Senate Democrats over what they perceived to have happened to some of President Clinton's nominees and, second, a different vision of the judiciary, a result oriented vision of the judiciary that some interest groups have. . . . [P]eople who have that view are not going to be very happy with people who don't. And that's a short answer to a much more complex issue but, in shorthand, that summarized what was going on. So we knew there was going to be controversy.

Clearly, however, it is unlikely that the administration would have predicted that two years after the President's 11 initial nominations to the courts of appeals, over one-fourth (Boyle, Estrada, Owen) would remain unconfirmed.

Confirmation difficulties for these nominees as well as other prominent candidates, such as Brooks Smith (Third Circuit), Charles Pickering (Fifth Circuit), and Carolyn Kuhl (Ninth Circuit), and, in particular, the negative votes in the Judiciary Committee on Charles Pickering and Priscilla Owen which, effectively, killed their candidacies during the 107th Congress coalesced to make federal judicial selection to the lower courts an election issue of some, perhaps unprecedented magnitude in the midterm congressional elections of 2002.[12] As Elliot Mincberg noted, "The issue of nominations has been one for a long time that both the secular and religious right had been very concerned about, and Bush gave them everything they could have wanted."

Nan Aron amplified on this theme:

Bush's speech a couple of days before the election about judges was clearly designed to draw out the . . . base of Republican voters. . . . It was a demonstration of, again, the ability of the Republicans to talk about the issue of the courts in a way that will pump up, placate, a part of their base. Not all of their base, but enough of their base to draw them out to voting.

Brett Kavanaugh did not dispute the electoral implications of the issue:

It is what it is, and the President made it a campaign issue. Not THE central one but A central one. [It was]

Partisan makeup of the bench

Despite having appointed the largest cohort of district judges of any president and the second largest complement of appellate judges (after Reagan), Bill Clinton was unable to overcome the Republican gains made by his two predecessors. At the start of the 107th Congress 51 percent of the judges sitting on the lower federal bench were appointed by Republican presidents. Ironically, at the end of that Congress, as shown in Table 3, the partisan scales had tilted the other way, with 50.6 percent of active judges appointed by Democratic presidents.

This rather odd result stems from two factors. First, 54 of the 71 (76.1 percent) judges who left the bench during George W. Bush's first two years in office were appointed by Republican presidents. This fits the historical pattern in which accelerated departures—especially retirements—from the bench accompany changes in partisan control of the White House.[1] In fact, of the 62 judges who either took senior status (56) or resigned (6), fully 76 percent were appointed by Republican presidents. The figures for the district and appeals bench are 81 percent and 60 percent, respectively.

Second, the consequences of the bitter partisan politics of the first half of 2001 that were followed by the fractious politics of divided government for the remainder of the term were in no way on more prominent display than in the area of judicial selection. To be sure, George W. Bush benefitted from the extraordinary number of vacancies he inherited (82), courtesy of the same brand of partisan stalemate he also would witness. Had he been able to fill

Table 3. Makeup of federal bench by appointing president, January 1, 2003 (lifetime positions on lower courts of general jurisdiction)

	District courts				Courts of appeals			
	Active		Senior		Active		Senior	
	%	(N)	%	(N)	%	(N)	%	(N)
W. Bush	12.4	(83)	—	—	9.6	(16)	—	—
Clinton	44.0	(292)	—	—	34.1	(57)	1.0	(1)
Bush	17.8	(118)	4.1	(14)	16.2	(27)	7.1	(7)
Reagan	14.5	(96)	32.1	(109)	18.0	(30)	35.7	(35)
Carter	4.2	(28)	28.2	(96)	6.0	(10)	24.5	(24)
Ford	0.5	(3)	6.2	(21)	0.6	(1)	6.1	(6)
Nixon	0.6	(4)	17.9	(61)	0.6	(1)	14.3	(14)
Johnson	0.2	(1)	7.9	(27)	—	—	10.2	(10)
Kennedy	—	—	2.4	(8)	—	—	1.0	(1)
Eisenhower	—	—	1.2	(4)	—	—	—	—
Vacancies	5.9	(39)	—	—	15.0	(25)	—	—
Totals	100.0	(664)	100.0	(340)	100.0	(167)	100.0	(98)

* Percentages rounded to 100%

kind of astonishing in the Coleman-Mondale debate the day before the election they were talking about Judge Pickering. [During] the Senate debate in Minnesota they were talking specifics about a Mississippi Court of Appeals nominee which is somewhat extraordinary, which shows, I think, how the president had made the issue national.

As to whether the President's activity altered electoral outcomes, Kavanaugh opined:

there's no way for anyone to know that but, certainly, the President thought it was an issue that people should consider when they were voting for Senate candidates, and he said that in Georgia and Minnesota, Missouri, Iowa, all over the place. In Texas, certainly, before the election he talked about Justice Owen. I don't think anyone can ever determine exactly what motivated people but, certainly, the President thought it was important and should be factored into the voters' decisions.

even a fraction of the 64 vacancies extant at the start of the 108th Congress, Republican appointees easily would comprise a majority of the federal judiciary.

In 2001 the Judicial Conference of the United States, the administrative arm of the federal judiciary, recommended to Congress that 10 and 44 new judgeships be authorized for the appellate and district courts, respectively (along with the permanent authorization of 7 temporary district judgeships). The congressional response in the climate of divided government was no appellate bench expansion, 8 new, and 7 temporary seats on the district courts, and permanent authorization of 4 temporary positions.[2]

Nonetheless, 12 of Bush's 83 (14.5 percent) appointment opportunities for the district courts were to fill new positions. Bill Clinton had been awarded a rather modest bench expansion of 19 seats on these courts, only 7 of which he was able to fill before his term expired.[3] The lion's share of district court appointment opportunities were occasioned by retirements (61 or 73.5 percent), with a relative handful from elevations (4), resignations (4), and deaths (2). Of the 16 appointment opportunities at the appellate level, 14 came from judges taking senior status, 1 from a new position,[4] and 1 from resignation.

Partisan control of the courts of appeals is in the hands of the Republicans who have appointed 52.8 percent of all active judges, and this control is likely to be solidified by the 2004 presidential election. The levels of partisan rancor over appointments to the appellate bench soared in the 107th Congress, triggered by especially confrontational politics over nominations to the Fifth, Sixth, and District of Columbia Circuits. Sixteen Bush nominees were confirmed, a modest figure but one that nonetheless puts him on track to surpass Clinton and perhaps even exceed the record 78 appeals courts judges appointed by Ronald Reagan. Clearly, partisan control of the lower federal bench will be among the issues hinging on the outcome of the 2004 presidential election.

Factoring senior status judges into the equation redounds to the Republican advantage. Combining both court levels, 53.9 percent of all seats are occupied by Republican-appointed judges. The Republican edge is more evident at the appellate level, where Republicans enjoy a 57.1 percent majority, compared to 53.2 percent for the district courts. When senior status judges are added to those in active service, the bench size of these two Article III courts grows to 1,205. Add to that the number of vacancies, and the figure swells to 1,269.

—Gerard Gryski and Gary Zuk

---

1. See Barrow, Zuk, and Gryski, *The Federal Judiciary and Institutional Change* (Ann Arbor: University of Michigan Press, 1996).

2. Act of November 2, 2002; 116 STAT. 1786.

3. The politics of divided government reared its head in Clinton's case as well. The recommendations of the Judicial Conference were for 6 permanent and 4 temporary positions on the courts of appeals, and 30 permanent and 23 temporary new seats on the district courts. The number of judgeships given by Congress to Clinton and thus far to Bush are—excepting the short-lived Ford administration—the smallest since the omnibus format took hold during FDR's presidency.

4. Although this Fourth Circuit seat was authorized in 1990, it was not filled for 10 years because "holds" were put on the nominations. In 2000, Clinton made the first judicial recess appointment since 1980 when he placed Roger Gregory, an African American, on that court. In 2001 Bush nominated Gregory for a regular appointment and he was confirmed by the Senate.

Like most electoral issues, judicial selection may have cut both ways. Thus, as Nan Aron noted,

Mary Landrieu voted against Dennis Shedd, which was something that she thought was probably pretty risky at the time. And what has interested a lot of people is that when Bush came to her state [Louisiana] the weekend before the election, Bush did not bring up her vote on Dennis Shedd, which says to a lot of people that the Republicans could be afraid that publicizing some of these votes on some very distasteful nominees might actually be harmful.

While the Republicans would regain control of the Senate by a slim margin in the 2002 election, it is difficult to gauge, overall, what role the politics of advice and consent played in the election's national outcome. Further, during the first six months of the 108th Congress, it remains equally clear that the Republican majority has remained frustrated in its efforts to confirm some of the administration's highest priority nominees. In part, that may be explained by the actions the President took on the opening day of the legislative session of the 108th Congress on January 7, 2003, when he renominated all of the judgeship candidates whose names had been returned to him, unconfirmed, at the end of the legislative session of the 107th Congress less than two months earlier. These included those of Priscilla Owen and Charles Pickering, who had been voted down in Committee. Our interviews for this article were conducted both the day before and the day after these judges were renominated and, consequently, were quite revealing in both the prognostications that were made and the reactions engendered.

The process, as described by Assistant Attorney General Viet Dinh, for deciding which nominees among those unconfirmed by the 107th Congress would be resubmitted was a fairly straightforward one:

> Those nominees were sent letters requesting them to update their files and make sure that their Senate questionnaires were current. Those whose nominations went unconfirmed for more than a year and a half were asked to go through an updated FBI background check and a truncated re-interview. The requests included wording that, by design, preserves the maximum option for the president: Your nomination has been returned to us. We are now evaluating candidates to recommend to the President for renomination and we proceed on the assumption that you would like to be considered for renomination. Please call me if you have a second thought about that renomination.
>
> Nobody, up to this point, I think I can say this without breaking confidences, has notified me that they would like not to be considered. Of course, the President's decision whether to nominate or renominate a person is his [alone].

Brett Kavanaugh stressed the underlying principle guiding the administration, "which the President made clear, that every judicial nominee deserves an up or down floor vote. And that stands for those people who were nominated in May, 2001 who still haven't gotten an up or down floor vote and those people who were nominated just a few months ago." The critical implication of this baseline principle is that there is no distinction whatsoever in the decision to renominate a Charles Pickering or a Priscilla Owen, defeated in a Judiciary Committee vote, from the decision to renominate any of the nominees whose nominations expired

at the end of the 107th Congress without having received a Committee hearing or vote.

> There is no logical difference between someone who never gets a Committee hearing or a Committee vote and someone who does, but gets a negative vote in Committee in our judgment. In both cases you've been prevented from getting to the floor of the Senate for your up and down Senate floor vote to which we think the Constitution entitles you and which Senate rules indicate as the final Senate action on any nominee vote. Justice Owen and Judge Pickering—their nominations were not returned to the President as they would have been had they been voted down on the floor of the Senate. It's a formality but it's indicative of a broader principle, and the broader principle is the one the President has articulated.

This position, strongly held by Kavanaugh and the administration, flows from the premise that the Senate's advice and consent role does not lie with the Judiciary Committee but, rather, with the entire chamber.

Within hours of our interview with Brett Kavanaugh, all of the failed nominations from the 107th Congress, including those of Pickering and Owen, were renominated. Makan Delrahim, Judiciary Committee Counsel, noted of the White House, "I don't know what goes into their thinking about their nominees or how they did it, but they looked at the batch; they were qualified nominees; [and they] sent them down and, I think, did the right thing."

Others, however, had different expectations for the President's renomination behavior and/or different reactions to it. One voice from the Democratic side of the Senate aisle predicted that Owen would be renominated, perhaps not right away, but that Pickering would not in the wake of the controversy surrounding the difficulties and ultimate removal from the majority leadership position of Trent Lott, Pickering's primary Senate sponsor.

> I believe that Senate Republicans and the White House feel vindicated [by the congressional elections of 2002] and that they have received a mandate to continue down this path. . . . They feel even more strongly [than in 2001] that their being strident will be more desirable to their constituencies and acceptable to the American people.
>
> And I also believe that the outcome of this election will have very serious consequences because of the pow-

ers of the majority. . . . I think it will be the most successful court packing we have ever seen. . . . I begin
[this year] with a great sense of foreboding and a sense
that much of what the most extreme elements in the
White House want to achieve will be achieved within
the next two years.

With the benefit of knowing that all the nominees
were resubmitted to the Senate,[13] Elliot Mincberg
observed the following day:

> I am a little surprised that it was quite so in your face. It
> is clear that they want to push the envelope. [The
> Administration's strategy is] we are going to go for the
> max and we realize we may not get it. But that will get
> us more in the end. And from a political hardball per-
> spective, one could understand it. From the perspec-
> tive of the federal courts and the future of the nomina-
> tions process, I think it's not the way to run a railroad.

Indeed, as confirmation politics proceeds into
the 108th Congress, it is clear that the President's
approach to renomination (and new nominations) has
focused attention on two procedural phenomena in
the Senate that could have profound implications for
the ongoing pace of advice and consent processes.
Clearly, it is incumbent to include discussion of the
Senate's blue slip process as well as any senator's prerogative to engage in unlimited debate, to mount a
filibuster against a judicial nominee, as two mechanisms through which the President's judicial appointment goals can be seriously hampered and, in some
instances, defeated.

The blue slip system is an internal Senate norm
operating through the Judiciary Committee aimed at
protecting the interests of home-state senators when
district and appeals court vacancies are being filled by
residents of their states.[14] Under the custom of senatorial courtesy, presidents will routinely consult with
home-state senators of their own party when filling
such vacancies. In effect, the senatorially developed
blue slip system serves to protect the interests of all
home-state senators, regardless of whether or not they
are from the president's party. Operationally, whenever a lower federal court nomination is received by
the Judiciary Committee, blue slips are sent out by the
chair soliciting comments from the two home-state
senators. Historically, absent the return of the blue slip
by both home-state senators, a hearing on the nominee
would not be scheduled, thereby giving all home-state

senators a meaningful potential to delay or obstruct a
nomination while serving, at the same time, to induce
the president to consult on nominations, even across
party lines.

The "normal" flow of blue slip processes, as outlined
above, has met with a few "wrinkles" over the course of
the past three decades. First, when Senator Edward
Kennedy chaired the Judiciary Committee during the
Carter administration, perhaps fearful of some southern senators using their blue slip prerogative to block
the appointment of progressive and/or minority judges,
he announced that a blue slip hold would not be honored in instances where the Committee's judgment was
to move forward with a hearing, thereby allowing the
Senate to work its will. Later, when Joseph Biden
chaired the Committee starting in 1987 and into the
early 1990s, a variant of the Kennedy rule was instituted.
It remains unclear, however, whether the rule was ever
actually put into play to hold a hearing absent a
returned blue slip (blue slip logs were not public at that
time though they are at present and can be found on
the Justice Department's web site).

What is clear is that, during the Clinton administration, numerous nominees went without Senate hearings when the Republicans had a majority and Senator
Orrin Hatch chaired the Committee. Presumably, this
was because a home-state senator had withheld a blue
slip or, in some instances, totally outside of the blue slip
process, an "anonymous hold" had been placed on a
nomination utilizing norms in the Senate regarding
the scheduling of legislative matters that were never
meant to have such significant and definitive reach.
Through the use of the blue slip system and/or such
holds, it appears that virtually any Republican senator
could stall a nomination and keep it from going forward. In a similar vein, during the first half of the Bush
administration, corresponding to the 107th Congress,
the blue slip would now become a mechanism which
the chamber controlling Democrats could honor to
delay or obstruct some of the President's nominees.
During this period, however, the withholding of blue
slips became a public matter and anonymous holds on
nominees did not appear to be standard fare. After the
midterm congressional elections, with the Republicans
back in the majority and Orrin Hatch returning to the
Committee's center chair, the issue of what role the
blue slip would play in assuring Democrats some say
regarding the processing of Bush's nominees has
assumed new urgency.

From the perspective of Makan Delrahim, nothing has or will change under Hatch's stewardship, which he describes as proceeding along the same lines as previous Judiciary Committee chairs. He characterizes the blue slip process as a

> Senate versus President, not a Democrat/Republican issue. It was to protect ourselves from embarrassing political appointments by a president. It's a way to cut against the White House prerogative and constitutional role of appointing judges. There are not going to be any changes. We will take the home-state senators' views. They'll be given weight. They will not be dispositive if there has been consultation by the White House. So we don't anticipate any policy changes there.

Viet Dinh characterized the administration's expectations regarding the blue slip system in similar terms, also tracing Hatch's approach to historical precedent:

> It continues Senator Biden's blue slip policy which basically says that if the senator had been consulted prior to nomination then the blue slip will be advisory and the views of the senator will bear weight. [On the other hand] if there had been no consultation, the blue slip will be dispositive. That's a mechanism for the Senate to enforce its own prerogatives in getting some sort of advance warning, to know that there is consultation.

As noted above, however, the Biden precedent may be less clear cut than characterized by the Senate majority and the administration, something akin to simply "advance warning" and, again, we are met by alternative takes on history. Indeed, as one Democratic staff aide predicted:

> What they'll say is, nothing has changed. And what he'll attempt to do, given his room to do it, will be to totally abandon the practice he followed as Chairman when the Republican senators were exercising their blue slips against a Democratic president's nominees and will instead have seen the light and decide that it is an abhorrent practice. . . . The blue slip for Democrats is not something they relish using in a negative way. Rather, it's supposed to set up a system where it is never used.
>
> I mean the whole point of it is to encourage meaningful consultations in advance of the nomination. There are a number of Democratic senators who don't feel they received meaningful consultation in advance of the nominations over the last two years. In such

instances, where meaningful consultation has not occurred in the eyes of the home state senators, and blue slip holds are not seen as dispositive by the Chair because there has been advance warning, we have reached a juncture in the confirmation process where the prospect of mounting a filibuster against such a lower court nominee becomes not only real, despite its unprecedented nature, but may even be seen by some as a necessity.

For his part, Makan Delrahim advised against resort to a filibuster on judicial nominees because

> it's a way to debate, it's not a way to write into the Constitution [that] a super majority of the Senate needs to advise and consent on a president's nominees. If the majority of the Senate would like to [vote to confirm] it's the height of politicization to employ filibusters.

Viet Dinh also lamented the potential for utilization of a filibuster, while allowing it to serve as documentation of the degree to which advice and consent processes had deteriorated:

> I've seen everything in the last two years that I did not think I would see and hoped, for our Constitution's sake, that we would never see. So, do I anticipate it? Probably not. Do I look forward to it? Absolutely not. Do I hope that it doesn't happen? Yes, simply because that would be unprecedented and it would just move us further down into the cesspool of partisan politics over nominations. Is [the] filibuster the next ground? We keep seeming to break new ground with each Congress starting with the last one. How bad can we make it? How painful can we make it for the nominees? How bad can we obstruct this process?

Regardless of how destructive a filibuster would be to the process, Dinh asserted that, nevertheless, the administration would not alter its nominating approach or behavior.

> We are putting our work product on the line. We're putting the President's credibility on the line when we send a nominee up. . . . We are confident that each and every single one of our candidates would make a great federal judge.

That the utilization of a filibuster was a possibility at the outset of the 108th Congress was noted by Elliot Mincberg, whose position was that "all tools should be on the table in light of the kind of aggressive attitude we've seen." Tactical decisions will have to be made that "will depend on particular circumstances. I think Pickering and Owen, precisely because they were rejected already by the Senate, may be considered better candidates for that than others may be."

Nan Aron agreed, noting in the case of Owen:

I think they have to filibuster Priscilla Owen, not that they want to filibuster but simply because there are ten of them on record who voted against her. And so it seems to me not to engage in a filibuster where you have your ten Democrats opposed would, I think, lead people to believe that they don't even care that much.

An overall assessment of the administration's judicial selection success during the first two years of the Bush presidency depends, in some respects, on the eyes of the beholder. Boyden Gray highlighted a point made by all those sympathetic to the administration's selection strategy and frustrated with the fruits of two years of nomination and appointment outcomes.

The Constitution says nothing about appellate versus district, but the fact remains that the senators basically control the district nominees. So to say you've put out a lot of district court nominees doesn't really meet the issue. The issue is over appellate nominees. That's where the fights always have been, are now, and will be in the future.

Associate White House Counsel Brett Kavanaugh offered, perhaps, an even stronger indictment.

District Courts have moved along. Courts of Appeals have been completely unsatisfactory. The President used the word 'lousy,' and I'll stay with his word. The pace at the Court of Appeals level is really unsatisfactory, and the President stated so quite often. And it was. There's no other way to describe it, compared to the first two years of past administrations.

Accentuating the positive, Viet Dinh noted that

the good part is that we have nominated at a record pace.... [J]udicial nominations [should not be thought of] as something apart from and secondary to [the] policy agenda but as an integral part of it. ... And because of that strong pace, we had one hundred judges confirmed.

Dinh was quick to add, however, "We would have liked to have had even more confirmed."

Others offered evaluations that were considerably less despondent about the administration's success rate and, correspondingly, less critical of the confirmation processes that created the record. As Elliot Mincberg put it:

When you combine the fact that you had a White House that was clearly, at the appellate court level, moving in a very strong ideological direction with the fact that they were not consulting, from a procedural perspective, the result of that is that there is inevitable conflict, and that is what we saw in the last two years. And I think it is very clear, from the basis of the historical record, that the number of people processed is quite good by comparison to the six and a half years preceding it.

The beneficial consequences of confirming so many judges in the congressional session, as portrayed by one Senate aide, were that, "the vacancies numbers are down, down, down. It isn't as if the crisis were growing." Another Senate aide, also from the Democratic side of the aisle, downplayed the rhetoric of "crisis" and, instead, attempted to highlight the palpable progress that had been made:

Those who say "oh it's a crisis, oh it's a crisis, oh it's a continuing crisis, oh the crisis is getting worse, things are deteriorating" are wrong. Because, practically, we actually made progress in the last year and a half in what should have been the worst and most adversarial setting of them all. Not only were one hundred nominations voted on and confirmed, some unanimously, some with a bunch of negative votes, but twenty judgeships were authorized in one way or another, in the DOJ authorization bill, which is more than the Republicans authorized in six years. So, portraying it as a situation that has gotten worse is just playing into their argument.

Regardless of the nomenclature utilized to describe the current advice and consent setting, it remains clear that neither side is very happy. The administration and its supporters do not feel that they are getting their fair share of judges through the confirmation maze; for its part, the Democratic opposition does not feel that it is receiving appropriate consultation from the White House nor sufficient respect, within the Senate, for long time institutional norms and traditions. Instead, they feel, crass power politics has become the name of the game.

Predicting the future of federal judicial selection and advice and consent processes is, of course, a risky business. Few, for example, would have predicted when the Bush administration first came into office that filibusters would become a part of the confirmation landscape for lower federal court judgeships and, perhaps, an increasingly utilized one in the days ahead. If there is a formula for overcoming the present acrimonious atmosphere and doing "better" in this arena, according to Elliot Mincberg,

> there needs to be, from the top, from the President on down a commitment to lowering the temperature. What it will probably take is a very strong commitment by folks who are respected by both parties to call for bilateral disarmament, if you will, rather than unilateral disarmament.

Mincberg was not, however, very optimistic that such "disarming" was likely to occur in the foreseeable future. "I don't think the prognosis, for ratcheting down the controversy is very high." In a similar vein, a Democratic staff member acknowledged that:

> There are vacancies ... that have been around too long. But with no cooperation, a lot of progress was made. With a modicum of cooperation and moderation, there wouldn't be a problem. . . . [But] I think, barring some unforeseen development, or real willingness to take this on by some stalwart members of the Democratic caucus, they are going to win.

At the end of the 107th Congress, when all was said and done, 83 Bush nominees to the district courts were confirmed as were 16 nominees to the appeals courts of general jurisdiction.[15] Fifteen district court and 15 appeals court nominees were not acted upon by the 107th Congress. The statistical portrait of those confirmed follows.

District court appointees

President George W. Bush's commitment to racial and gender diversity in his administration was extended to his district court appointments. Almost one-third were nontraditional appointees, the best record of any Republican administration, and a record surpassed only by Bill Clinton and that is within one percentage point of Jimmy Carter's. Table 4 looks at the demographic and attribute profile of Bush's 26 nontraditional appointees as compared to his 57 traditional (white male) appointees.

Table 4 shows that a significantly larger proportion of the nontraditional candidates were serving in a judicial capacity (either on the state courts or as federal magistrates or bankruptcy judges) than were the traditional appointees. It is possible that the administration was more comfortable going with nontraditional candidates who had a judicial track record compatible with the President's judicial philosophy. This is particularly significant, as the proportion of nontraditional appointees who were Republicans was lower than that of the traditional appointees and in terms of past party activism was significantly lower than that for the traditional appointees. There was a lower proportion of nontraditional than traditional appointees who had neither judicial nor prosecutorial experience, suggesting that on the whole the nontraditional appointees may have been even better qualified and more experienced than the traditional appointees.

The nontraditional and traditional appointees had relatively small differences in educational background and were approximately equal in the proportion receiving the highest ABA rating. They also had a similar net worth. A majority of both groups were millionaires. However, the nontraditional appointees were on average a full three years younger than the traditional appointees.

Table 5 examines the composite portrait of the W. Bush appointees compared to the appointees of the four previous administrations. The proportion of the W. Bush appointees who were serving in the judiciary at the time of their nomination was tied with the Clinton appointees' proportion as the highest of all five administrations.

The trend of a career judiciary has continued with the W. Bush appointees. Over the past 40-plus years, the proportion of appointees who were already serving as federal magistrates or U.S. bankruptcy judges has climbed from almost none to 8 percent of the Ford, 5 percent of both the Carter and Reagan, 11 percent of Bush Sr., 12 percent of Clinton, and a record 16 percent of all W. Bush district court appointees. W. Bush named 11 U.S. magistrates and 2 U.S. bankruptcy court judges to the federal district bench and 6 of the 13 were nontraditional. About three-quarters of the Clinton district court appointees who were serving as magistrates or bankruptcy judges were nontraditional but before Clinton most such appointees were white males. Clearly, service on the state and federal judiciaries is the most favored route to a federal district judgeship, and this is especially true for women and minorities.

Table 4. Bush's nontraditional appointees compared to his traditional appointees to the federal district courts, 2001–2002

Occupation	Nontraditional appointees		Traditional appointees	
	%	(N)	%	(N)
Politics/government	7.7	(2)	8.8	(5)
Judiciary	61.5	(16)	42.1	(24)
Large law firm				
100+ members	11.5	(3)	8.8	(5)
50–99	—	—	8.8	(5)
25–49	3.9	(1)	10.5	(6)
Medium size firm				
10–24 members	3.9	(1)	5.3	(3)
5–9	3.9	(1)	5.3	(3)
Small firm				
2–4	—	—	3.5	(2)
solo	—	—	3.5	(2)
Professor of law	3.9	(1)	1.8	(1)
Other	3.9	(1)	1.8	(1)
Experience				
Judicial	61.5	(16)	49.1	(28)
Prosecutorial	53.8	(14)	49.1	(28)
Neither	15.4	(4)	26.3	(15)
Undergraduate education				
Public	34.6	(9)	45.6	(26)
Private	57.7	(15)	49.1	(28)
Ivy League	7.7	(2)	5.3	(3)
Law School Education				
Public	57.7	(15)	50.9	(29)
Private	34.6	(9)	42.1	(24)
Ivy League	7.7	(2)	7.0	(4)
Gender				
Male	34.6	(9)	100.0	(57)
Female	65.4	(17)	—	—
Ethnicity/race				
White	53.9	(14)	100.0	(57)
African American	23.1	(6)	—	—
Hispanic	23.1	(6)	—	—
ABA rating				
Well Qualified	73.1	(19)	68.4	(39)
Qualified	26.9	(7)	29.8	(17)
Not Qualified	—	—	1.8	(1)
Political identification				
Democrat	11.5	(3)	5.3	(3)
Republican	69.2	(18)	89.5	(51)
None	19.2	(5)	5.3	(3)
Past party activism	38.5	(10)	64.9	(37)
Net worth				
Under $200,000	3.9	(1)	5.3	(3)
$200–499,999	26.9	(7)	19.3	(11)
$500–999,999	15.4	(4)	17.5	(10)
$1+ million	53.8	(14)	57.9	(33)
Average age at nomination	48.2		51.2	
Total number of appointees	26		57	

Like his father's appointees, approximately 10 percent of the appointees were members of extremely large law firms, proportions significantly higher than those for the other three administrations. Likewise the proportions of those practicing in small firms was lower for the two Bush administrations than for the other three.

In terms of professional experience, the W. Bush appointees had the lowest proportion of all five administrations with neither judicial nor prosecutorial experience. More than half the appointees had both judicial and prosecutorial experience—the only administration of all five with such a record. Unlike his father's record, with the highest proportion of those with neither judicial nor prosecutorial experience, the son's record thus far is the lowest proportion of all five administrations. Like the previous four administrations, there was a larger proportion with judicial experience than with prosecutorial experience. This underscores the trend toward a career judiciary.

In terms of undergraduate and law school education, the proportion of W. Bush appointees receiving an Ivy League school education was the lowest of all five administrations. With law school education, if we add to the Ivy League law schools such prestigious law schools as Berkeley, Duke, Georgetown, Stanford, Texas, Vanderbilt, and Virginia, the proportion of W. Bush appointees with a prestige legal education is about 19 percent. In contrast, the Clinton appointees with a prestige legal education was about 38 percent and for the Bush Sr. appointees 34 percent.

The proportion of W. Bush's women appointees was second only to the Clinton record but within a percentage point of Bush Sr.'s record. Approximately one-fifth of both father and son's appointees were women—approximately one third higher than the breakthrough Carter appointments and about two and a half times larger than the Reagan record. The proportion of Hispanic appointments was the highest for all five administrations but the proportion of African-American appointees was well below the record for Democrats Clinton and Carter but higher than the Reagan record and approximately the same as Bush Sr.'s record. The impact of the Bush appointees on racial and gender diversity on the district courts is suggested in "Diversity on the bench," page 92.

In light of the administration's decision to remove the Standing Committee on Federal Judiciary of the American Bar Association from the pre-nomination stage, it is of interest to find that the proportion of

Table 5. U.S. district court appointees compared by administration

	W. Bush		Clinton		Bush		Reagan		Carter	
Occupation	%	(N)	%	(N)	%	(N)	%	(N)	%	(N)
Politics/government	8.4	(7)	11.5	(35)	10.8	(16)	13.4	(39)	5.0	(10)
Judiciary	48.2	(40)	48.2	(147)	41.9	(62)	36.9	(107)	44.6	(90)
Large law firm										
100+ members	9.6	(8)	6.6	(20)	10.8	(16)	6.2	(18)	2.0	(4)
50–99	6.0	(5)	5.2	(16)	7.4	(11)	4.8	(14)	6.0	(12)
25–49	8.4	(7)	4.3	(13)	7.4	(11)	6.9	(20)	6.0	(12)
Medium size firm										
10–24 members	4.8	(4)	7.2	(22)	8.8	(13)	10.0	(29)	9.4	(19)
5–9	4.8	(4)	6.2	(19)	6.1	(9)	9.0	(26)	9.9	(20)
Small firm										
2–4	2.4	(2)	4.6	(14)	3.4	(5)	7.2	(21)	11.4	(23)
solo	2.4	(2)	3.6	(11)	1.4	(2)	2.8	(8)	2.5	(5)
Professor of law	2.4	(2)	1.6	(5)	0.7	(1)	2.1	(6)	3.0	(6)
Other	2.4	(2)	1.0	(3)	1.4	(2)	0.7	(2)	0.5	(1)
Experience										
Judicial	53.0	(44)	52.1	(159)	46.6	(69)	46.2	(134)	54.0	(109)
Prosecutorial	50.6	(42)	41.3	(126)	39.2	(58)	44.1	(128)	38.1	(77)
Neither	22.9	(19)	28.9	(88)	31.8	(47)	28.6	(83)	31.2	(63)
Undergraduate education										
Public	42.2	(35)	44.3	(135)	46.0	(68)	37.9	(110)	55.9	(113)
Private	51.8	(43)	42.0	(128)	39.9	(59)	48.6	(141)	34.2	(69)
Ivy League	6.0	(5)	13.8	(42)	14.2	(21)	13.4	(39)	9.9	(20)
Law school education										
Public	53.0	(44)	39.7	(121)	52.7	(78)	44.8	(130)	52.0	(105)
Private	39.8	(33)	40.7	(124)	33.1	(49)	43.4	(126)	31.2	(63)
Ivy League	7.2	(6)	19.7	(60)	14.2	(21)	11.7	(34)	16.8	(34)
Gender										
Male	79.5	(66)	71.5	(218)	80.4	(119)	91.7	(266)	85.6	(173)
Female	20.5	(17)	28.5	(87)	19.6	(29)	8.3	(24)	14.4	(29)
Ethnicity/race										
White	85.5	(71)	75.1	(229)	89.2	(132)	92.4	(268)	78.7	(159)
African American	7.2	(6)	17.4	(53)	6.8	(10)	2.1	(6)	13.9	(28)
Hispanic	7.2	(6)	5.9	(18)	4.0	(6)	4.8	(14)	6.9	(14)
Asian	—	—	1.3	(4)	—	—	0.7	(2)	0.5	(1)
Native American	—	—	0.3	(1)	—	—	—	—	—	—
Percentage white male	68.7	(57)	52.4	(160)	73.0	(108)	84.8	(246)	67.8	(137)
ABA rating										
EWQ/WQ	69.9	(58)	59.0	(180)	57.4	(85)	53.5	(155)	51.0	(103)
Qualified	28.9	(24)	40.0	(122)	42.6	(63)	46.6	(135)	47.5	(96)
Not Qualified	1.2	(1)	1.0	(3)	—	—	—	—	1.5	(3)
Political identification										
Democrat	7.2	(6)	87.5	(267)	6.1	(9)	4.8	(14)	91.1	(184)
Republican	83.1	(69)	6.2	(19)	88.5	(131)	91.7	(266)	4.5	(9)
Other	—	—	0.3	(1)	—	—	—	—	—	—
None	9.6	(8)	5.9	(18)	5.4	(8)	3.4	(10)	4.5	(9)
Past party activism	56.6	(47)	50.2	(153)	64.2	(95)	60.3	(175)	61.4	(124)
Net worth										
Under $200,000	4.8	(4)	13.4	(41)	10.1	(15)	17.9	(52)	35.8*	(53)
$200–499,999	21.7	(18)	21.6	(66)	31.1	(46)	37.6	(109)	41.2	(61)
$500–999,999	16.9	(14)	26.9	(82)	26.4	(39)	21.7	(63)	18.9	(28)
$1+ million	56.6	(47)	38.0	(116)	32.4	(48)	22.8	(66)	4.0	(6)
Average age at nomination	50.3		49.5		48.2		48.6		49.6	
Total number of appointees	83		305		148		290		202	

* These figures are for appointees confirmed by the 96th Congress for all but six Carter district court appointees (for whom no data were available).

W. Bush appointees with the highest ABA rating was the largest of all five administrations. By ABA standards, the W. Bush appointees are the most qualified appointees since the ABA began rating appointees in the administration of Dwight D. Eisenhower. About 7 out of 10 appointees received the highest rating. It is possible that eliminating the ABA from the pre-nomination stage has meant that once a nomination has been announced those surveyed in the nominees' legal community would be reluctant to voice negative evaluations of individuals whose appointments are a virtual fait accompli. But it is also possible that the administration's screening process has been able to identify extremely accomplished and well-thought-of persons for appointment.

The proportion of the W. Bush appointees who were Republicans was lower than that of his father's appointees. The proportion of Democrats and Independents was higher than his father's. About 1 in 10 had no party affiliation—a record high. The proportion with a record of past political activity was higher than the proportion for the Clinton appointees but lower than that of the three other administrations' appointees.

The net worth figures show that for the first time, well over half the appointees were worth in excess of $1 million. Only about one in four had a net worth under $500,000, the lowest proportion of all five administrations. Given the relatively low pay for federal district judges, it would seem that only the relatively well-off could afford to go on the bench. The problem of low judicial salaries is an ongoing one and one that has been voiced by Chief Justice Rehnquist in his annual reports on the state of the judiciary.[16]

Interestingly the average age of the W. Bush appointees was the highest of all five administrations. Bush Sr.'s appointees were on average more than two years younger than his son's appointees. Both Bush administrations as well as the Reagan administration were known as concerned with reshaping the judiciary in the president's image and surely one of the most effective ways to do this is by appointing younger judges. However, the record for W. Bush will only be complete when his tenure is over and only at that time will the finished portrait of his appointees emerge.

Appeals court appointees

Sixteen persons were confirmed to lifetime positions to courts of general jurisdiction on the U.S. Courts of Appeals. Fifteen nominations were not acted upon.

Six, or slightly more than one-third of those confirmed, were nontraditional. Because the numbers are small, comparisons between groups must be made with extreme caution. Table 6 compares the nontraditional to the traditional appeals court appointees.

Despite the small numbers involved, there are some findings that stand out as significant. All but one of the nontraditional appointees were serving on the bench at the time of their nominations (more than 80 percent), while only 3 out of the 10 traditional appointees (30 percent) were in active judicial service. The one non-judge among the nontraditional judges was serving in a governmental position but had previous judicial experience. Equally striking is that 4 (or 40 percent) of the traditional appointees had neither judicial nor prosecutorial experience.

In terms of undergraduate and law school education, both groups were similar. The same was true for their ABA ratings—about two-thirds of each group received the highest rating. As for political party identification, there was a dramatic difference between the groups. Every one of the traditional appointees was a Republican and 9 of the 10 (90 percent) had a background of political activity. In contrast, only half the nontraditional appointees were Republican and only half had a background of political activity. In terms of net worth, about half the nontraditional candidates were worth more than $1 million as compared to 70 percent of the traditional appointees.

Although both groups were closer in age than their district court counterparts, the average age of the nontraditional appointees was lower than that for the traditional appointees.

Table 7 aggregates all of W. Bush's appeals court appointees and compares them to the previous four administrations. Because the total number of appeals court appointees confirmed during the 107th Congress is relatively small compared to the appointees of the previous administrations, percentage differences must be interpreted with caution.

Half the W. Bush appointees were sitting as judges at the time of their nominations, the second lowest proportion of all five administrations but not by much. On the other hand his appointees had the largest proportion with judicial experience. All five administrations had proportions of their appointees with judicial experience well above the 50 percent level, reinforcing what we found for the district courts—that the trend toward the professionalization of the judiciary continues.

Table 6. Bush's nontraditional appointees compared to his traditional appointees to the federal appeals courts, 2001–2002

Occupation	Nontraditional appointees		Traditional appointees	
	%	(N)	%	(N)
Politics/government	16.7	(1)	—	—
Judiciary	83.3	(5)	30.0	(3)
Large law firm				
100+ members	—	—	—	—
50–99	—	—	10.0	(1)
Moderate size firm				
10–24 members	—	—	20.0	(2)
Small firm				
2–4	—	—	10.0	(1)
Professor of law	—	—	20.0	(2)
Other	—	—	10.0	(1)
Experience				
Judicial	100	(6)	50.0	(5)
Prosecutorial	16.7	(1)	30.0	(3)
Neither	0.0	(0)	40.0	(4)
Undergraduate education				
Public	50.0	(3)	40.0	(4)
Private	33.3	(2)	40.0	(4)
Ivy League	16.7	(1)	20.0	(2)
Law school education				
Public	50.0	(3)	50.0	(5)
Private	16.7	(1)	30.0	(3)
Ivy League	33.3	(2)	20.0	(2)
Gender				
Male	50.0	(3)	100	(10)
Female	50.0	(3)	—	—
Ethnicity/race				
White	50.0	(3)	100	(10)
African American	50.0	(3)	—	—
Hispanic	—	—	—	—
ABA rating				
Well Qualified	66.7	(4)	70.0	(7)
Qualified	33.3	(2)	30.0	(3)
Political identification				
Democrat	33.3	(2)	—	—
Republican	50.0	(3)	100	(10)
None	16.7	(1)	—	—
Past party activism	50.0	(3)	90.0	(9)
Net worth				
Under $200,000	16.7	(1)	—	—
$200–499,999	—	—	20.0	(2)
$500–999,999	33.3	(2)	10.0	(1)
$1+ million	50.0	(3)	70.0	(7)
Average age at nomination	49.8		51.0	
Total number of appointees	6		10	

The W. Bush appointees had the smallest proportion of appointees with neither judicial nor prosecutorial experience, suggesting that on the whole their professional credentials were as impressive, if not more so, than appointees of previous administrations.

The proportion of those who were in large law firms at the time of appointment was the lowest of all five administrations.

In terms of undergraduate and law school education, the statistical profile was similar to the Clinton appointees. One in four had an Ivy League law school education. If we add to these law schools such prestigious law schools as Chicago, Georgetown, Michigan, and Virginia, about 56 percent had the highest quality legal education, which is about the same proportion as that of the Clinton appointees (57 percent). This compares to 45 percent of each of the Reagan and Bush Sr. cohorts with such a prestigious legal education.

In terms of gender and ethnicity, the proportion of women was about the same as Bush Sr.'s proportion and considerably lower than Clinton's historic record. Proportionately, however, the W. Bush African-American appointees set a new record, exceeding the Clinton administration proportion. However, two of the three appointees were Democrats nominated as part of the compromise package of first appeals court appointees unveiled on May 9, 2001, and it is doubtful that this proportion will be sustained. There were no Hispanic appointees although the administration sought to place Miguel Estrada on the D.C. Circuit. But even had the administration been successful, the proportion of latinos would have been considerably lower than Clinton's historic record. Overall, the proportion of nontraditional appointees was approximately the same as Carter's but did not match Clinton's unprecedented proportion of a majority of appeals court appointments going to women and minorities.

The proportion of W. Bush appointees with the highest ABA ratings was the highest of all three Republican administrations but lower than the Carter and Clinton records. Nevertheless, the close to 70 percent receiving the highest rating, taken in conjunction with judicial and prosecutorial experience, buttresses the conclusion that the appointees tended to meet high standards of professional competency.

Because the compromise package of May 9, 2001, included two Democrats, the proportion of opposition party appointees was the highest of all five administrations. Since then, as far as we can determine, no Democrat has been nominated to the appeals courts, and thus this proportion most assuredly will not be sustained.

The proportion with a background of past political activity was an impressive three out of four. This is close to the proportions of three previous administrations,

Table 7. U.S. appeals court appointees compared by administration

Occupation	W. Bush %	W. Bush (N)	Clinton %	Clinton (N)	Bush %	Bush (N)	Reagan %	Reagan (N)	Carter %	Carter (N)
Politics/government	6.2	(1)	6.6	(4)	10.8	(4)	6.4	(5)	5.4	(3)
Judiciary	50.0	(8)	52.5	(32)	59.5	(22)	55.1	(43)	46.4	(26)
Large law firm										
100+ members	—	—	11.5	(7)	8.1	(3)	5.1	(4)	1.8	(1)
50–99	6.2	(1)	3.3	(2)	8.1	(3)	2.6	(2)	5.4	(3)
25–49	—	—	3.3	(2)	—	—	6.4	(5)	3.6	(2)
Medium size firm										
10–24 members	12.5	(2)	9.8	(6)	8.1	(3)	3.9	(3)	14.3	(8)
5–9	—	—	3.3	(2)	2.7	(1)	5.1	(4)	1.8	(1)
Small firm										
2–4	—	—	1.6	(1)	—	—	1.3	(1)	3.6	(2)
solo	6.2	(1)	—	—	—	—	—	—	1.8	(1)
Professor	12.5	(2)	8.2	(5)	2.7	(1)	12.8	(10)	14.3	(8)
Other	6.2	(1)	—	—	—	—	1.3	(1)	1.8	(1)
Experience										
Judicial	68.8	(11)	59.0	(36)	62.2	(23)	60.3	(47)	53.6	(30)
Prosecutorial	25.0	(4)	37.7	(23)	29.7	(11)	28.2	(22)	30.4	(17)
Neither	25.0	(4)	29.5	(18)	32.4	(12)	34.6	(27)	39.3	(22)
Undergraduate education										
Public	43.8	(7)	44.3	(27)	29.7	(11)	24.4	(19)	30.4	(17)
Private	37.5	(6)	34.4	(21)	59.5	(22)	51.3	(40)	51.8	(29)
Ivy League	18.8	(3)	21.3	(13)	10.8	(4)	24.4	(19)	17.9	(10)
Law school education										
Public	50.0	(8)	39.3	(24)	32.4	(12)	41.0	(32)	39.3	(22)
Private	25.0	(4)	31.1	(19)	37.8	(14)	35.9	(28)	19.6	(11)
Ivy League	25.0	(4)	29.5	(18)	29.7	(11)	23.1	(18)	41.1	(23)
Gender										
Male	81.2	(13)	67.2	(41)	81.1	(30)	94.9	(74)	80.4	(45)
Female	18.8	(3)	32.8	(20)	18.9	(7)	5.1	(4)	19.6	(11)
Ethnicity/race										
White	81.2	(13)	73.8	(45)	89.2	(33)	97.4	(76)	78.6	(44)
African American	18.8	(3)	13.1	(8)	5.4	(2)	1.3	(1)	16.1	(9)
Hispanic	—	—	11.5	(7)	5.4	(2)	1.3	(1)	3.6	(2)
Asian	—	—	1.6	(1)	—	—	—	—	1.8	(1)
Percentage white male	62.5	(10)	49.2	(30)	70.3	(26)	92.3	(72)	60.7	(34)
ABA rating										
EWQ/WQ	68.8	(11)	78.7	(48)	64.9	(24)	59.0	(46)	75.0	(42)
Qualified	31.2	(5)	21.3	(13)	35.1	(13)	41.0	(32)	25.0	(14)
Political identification										
Democrat	12.5	(2)	85.2	(52)	2.7	(1)	—	—	82.1	(46)
Republican	81.2	(13)	6.6	(4)	89.2	(33)	96.2	(75)	7.1	(4)
Other	—	—	—	—	—	—	1.3	(1)	—	—
None	6.2	(1)	8.2	(5)	8.1	(3)	26.2	(3)	10.7	(6)
Past party activism	75.0	(12)	54.1	(33)	70.3	(26)	66.7	(52)	73.2	(41)
Net worth										
Under $200,000	6.2	(1)	4.9	(3)	5.4	(2)	15.6*	(12)	33.3**	(13)
$200–499,999	12.5	(2)	14.8	(9)	29.7	(11)	32.5	(25)	38.5	(15)
$500–999,999	18.8	(3)	29.5	(18)	21.6	(8)	35.1	(27)	17.9	(7)
$1+ million	62.5	(10)	50.8	(31)	43.2	(16)	16.9	(13)	10.3	(4)
Total number of appointees	16		61		37		78		56	
Average age of nomination	50.6		51.2		48.7		50.0		51.8	

* Net worth was unavailable for one appointee.

** Net worth only for Carter appointees confirmed by the 96th Congress, with the exception of five appointees for whom net worth was unavailable.

but not Clinton's, whose proportion was the lowest of all five presidencies.

In terms of net worth, the table shows a steady increase in the proportion of those with a net worth in excess of $1 million. Close to two-thirds of the W. Bush appointees were millionaires. Like the findings for the district courts, these findings provide additional support for the Chief Justice's plea for higher judicial salaries to enable more of the less well-to-do to be able to afford going and remaining on the bench.

The average age of the W. Bush appointees was 50.6, almost two years older than the Bush Sr. appointees' average age. However, that may well change given the younger ages of most of those renominated and newly nominated during the 108th Congress.

What lies ahead

The results of the congressional election of 2002 placed the Senate back in Republican hands. But Democrats made it clear that they would oppose nominees to the appeals courts who they believed were too extreme. Democrats mounted a filibuster against Miguel Estrada and Priscilla Owen. As of this writing, Democrats appeared prepared to filibuster some other nominees as well. The message Democrats seem to be sending to the White House is that any future nominee to the Supreme Court and nominees to the appeals courts would have to be considerably more moderate ideologically and philosophically in the eyes of the Democrats in order to win confirmation.

Republicans have argued that by preventing a vote by the Senate because of filibustering, which can only be stopped by a cloture vote of 60 senators, the Democrats are changing the Constitution from a majority vote needed to confirm to a supermajority vote of at least 60 to confirm court nominees. Democrats have countered that it is fairer and more democratic to have opposition to nominees out in the open and fully debated than for the nominations to languish in the Senate Judiciary Committee without hearings as had happened to numerous Clinton nominees. However, it is questionable whether the Democrats will be able to mount filibusters against more than a token number of Bush nominees. The filibuster is clearly a weapon that can only be used sparingly. Although this is not a problem with unified government, the problem of obstruction and delay at the committee level, when there is divided government, is not likely to go away unless both parties agree on a set of ground rules that would hold from Congress to Congress, whichever party controlled Congress or the presidency.

The record thus far is one of contentiousness. Yet despite this, the 107th Congress confirmed 83 district court judges and 16 appeals court judges to courts of general jurisdiction. As of June 15, 2003 the 108th Congress, notwithstanding the filibusters, has confirmed 22 district court and 9 appeals court judges. Because Republicans control the Senate, all nominees are or will be having hearings and votes in the Senate Judiciary Committee with the nominations sent to the Senate floor. This is hardly the crisis that the administration and Republican senators have proclaimed.

To be sure, all lower court or only appeals court nominations coming to a standstill would, of course, constitute a crisis. Arguably it would also be a crisis if Chief Justice William Rehnquist's replacement was the subject of a filibuster. However, a filibuster over a nominee to fill an associate justiceship might not reach the level of a judicial branch crisis no matter how undesirable it would be for the Supreme Court to operate at less than full strength. The solution, of course, is for President George W. Bush to do what President Bill Clinton did when filling two vacancies on the Supreme Court and indeed when filling vacancies on the circuit courts—nominate people who will win broad support among senators of both parties.

Aiming for consensus rather than confrontation is surely the prudent course of action. But on the basis of our interviews with key participants in the selection and confirmation process as well as close observers of it, we fear that such a conservative strategy is not in the offing. What this means is that we can expect all but the most high profile judicial nominations, particularly to the Supreme Court but also a select few at the lower court level, to be confirmed—which means the vast majority of nominees will get through. But the fight over those few nominees actively opposed and obstructed by the Democrats will reinforce and even enhance the bitterness and ideological warfare in the Senate. How this will play with the electorate will be seen in the elections of 2004.

When it comes to an assessment of the 99 Bush appointees confirmed by the 107th Congress, the statistical portrait is one of high competence and professionalism. The cohort is generally comparable to the Bush Sr. appointees, appointees also confirmed by a Senate controlled by the Democrats. Even more so than the father's, the son's administration is clearly coordinated and is expending the resources to place on the bench appointees who share the President's judicial philosophy. How successful has the administration been thus far in achieving that objective? Have his appointees provided fair and impartial justice? Only a detailed examination of the appointees' performance on the bench will be able to answer those questions.

Notes

This article originally appeared in Volume 86, Number 6, May–June 2003, pages 282–309.

Sheldon Goldman, Gerard Gryski, and Gary Zuk wish to thank the Law and Social Science program of the National Science Foundation (NSF grants SBR-9810838 and SBR-9800000), which helped support the gathering of some of the data for this article. The NSF bears no responsibility for the conclusions drawn herein. Sheldon Goldman is grateful to Commonwealth College of the University of Massachusetts at Amherst for providing research assistance and to Michael Conlow, Russell F. Ferri, and Nathaniel R. Beaudoin for their assistance. The authors appreciate the help of the dedicated staffs of Senators Patrick J. Leahy and Orrin G. Hatch at the Senate Judiciary Committee and the staffs of other senators who serve on the committee. In addition, members of the Bush administration, and several people outside government, gave generously of their time and offered valuable help. We are especially thankful to Nan Aron, Viet Dinh, C. Boyden Gray, Brett Kavanaugh, Marcia Kuntz, Sheila Joy, and Elliot Mincberg. The authors are also appreciative of the several Bush appointees who graciously supplied missing biographical information. Errors of fact and interpretation are solely the responsibility of the authors.

1. See Goldman, "A profile of Carter's judicial nominees," *Judicature* 62 (1978), 246 and "Carter's judicial appointments: a lasting legacy," *Judicature* 64 (1981), 344. Other articles in this series are: Goldman, "Reagan's judicial appointments at mid-term: shaping the bench in his own image," *Judicature* 66 (1983), 334; Goldman, "Reaganizing the judiciary: the first term appointments," *Judicature* 68 (1985), 313; Goldman, "Reagan's second term judicial appointments: the battle at midway," *Judicature* 70 (1987), 324; Goldman, "Reagan's judicial legacy: completing the puzzle and summing up," *Judicature* 72 (1989), 318; Goldman, "The Bush imprint on the judiciary: carrying on a tradition," *Judicature* 74 (1991), 294; Goldman, "Bush's judicial legacy: the final imprint," *Judicature* 76 (1993), 282; Goldman, "Judicial selection under Clinton: a midterm examination," *Judicature* 78 (1995), 276; Goldman and Slotnick, "Clinton's first term judiciary: many bridges to cross," *Judicature* 80 (1997), 254; Goldman and Slotnick, "Clinton's second term judiciary: picking judges under fire," *Judicature* 82 (1999), 264; and Goldman, Slotnick, Gryski, and Zuk, "Clinton's judges: summing up the legacy," *Judicature* 84 (2001), 228.

2. See *The American Bench*, 13th ed., *Who's Who* (national and regional editions), *Martindale-Hubbell Law Directory*, and *The Judicial Staff Directory*.

3. Interview with Viet Dinh on January 6, 2003. Other quotes from Assistant Attorney General Dinh are drawn from this interview.

4. Interview with Brett Kavanaugh on January 7, 2003. Other quotes from Associate White House Counsel Kavanaugh are drawn from this interview.

5. Interview with Nan Aron, President of the Alliance for Justice, on January 6, 2003. Other quotes from Ms. Aron are drawn from this interview.

6. Interview with C. Boyden Gray, former White House Counsel to the first President Bush, on January 7, 2003. Other quotes from Mr. Gray are drawn from this interview.

7. Interview with Makan Delrahim, Republican Chief Counsel and Staff Director, on January 8, 2003. Other quotes from Mr. Delrahim are drawn from this interview.

8. Interview with Elliot Mincberg, Vice President, General Counsel, and Legal and Education Director of People for the American Way, on January 8, 2003. Other quotes from Mr. Mincberg are drawn from this interview.

9. Interview with Marcia Kuntz, Alliance for Justice, on January 6, 2003. Other quotes from Ms. Kuntz are drawn from this interview.

10. In general, see the data and findings in Goldman, "Assessing the Senate judicial confirmation process: The Index of Obstruction and Delay," *Judicature* 86 (2003), 251. Also see, Hartley and Holmes, "The Increasing Senate Scrutiny of Lower Federal Court Nominees," *Pol. Sci. Q.* 117 (2002), 259; Binder and Maltzman, "Senatorial Delay in Confirming Federal Judges, 1947–1998," *Am. J. of Pol. Sci.* 46 (2002), 190; Martinek, Kemper, and Van Winkle, "To Advise and Consent: The Senate and Lower Federal Court Nominations, 1977–1998," *J. of Pol.* 64 (2002), 337.

11. In general, see Holmes and Savchak, "Judicial appointment politics in the 107th Congress," *Judicature* 86 (2003), 232.

12. For an analysis of the Pickering nomination and its fate in the 107th Congress, see Goldman, "Unpicking Pickering in 2002: Some Thoughts on the Politics of Lower Federal Court Selection and Confirmation," *U.C. Davis L. Rev.* 36 (2003), 695 .

13. During the 107th Congress, William H. Steele had been nominated for a position on the U.S. Court of Appeals for the Eleventh Circuit. At the start of the 108th Congress he was nominated for a position on the federal district bench in Alabama (southern district). Thus, technically, that was not a renomination but a new nomination.

14. *See, generally,* Denning, "The judicial confirmation process and the blue slip," *Judicature* 85 (2002), 218.

15. One nominee to the United States Court of Appeals for the Federal Circuit, Sharon Prost, was confirmed but is not included in our statistics, which are confined to lifetime appointments to the federal courts of general jurisdiction.

16. *See, e.g.,* the most recent report in *The Third Branch* 35 (January 2003), 1 at 2.

The decision-making behavior of George W. Bush's judicial appointees: far-right, conservative, or moderate?

Robert A. Carp, Kenneth L. Manning, and Ronald Stidham

An analysis of overall voting patterns indicates that President Bush's judges are among the most conservative on record.

What is the ideological direction of the judges whom President George W. Bush has appointed to the bench during his first term? Until now we have had no quantitative, empirical data to respond to this query. Critics of the President, often liberal Democrats, have suggested that Bush's judicial appointees are ultra-conservatives who are hostile to the interests of racial minorities, women, the environment, personal privacy, and so on. "Right-wing extremists" is often the catch word of those who have opposed the President's judicial appointments, as echoed in this high ranking Democratic staff member's appraisal of the 2002 elections on the future content of the federal judiciary:

> I . . . believe that the outcome of this election will have very serious consequences because of the powers of the majority. . . . I think it will be the most successful court packing we have ever seen. . . . I begin[this year] with a great sense of foreboding and a sense that much of what the most extreme elements in the White House want to achieve will be achieved within the next two years.[1]

President Bush and his supporters clearly have a very different view of the men and women whom he is selecting for federal judicial posts. Former Assistant Attorney General Viet Dinh conceded that the administration was eschewing candidates who might appear to be "judicial activists," but he asserted that

> We are extremely clear in following the President's mandate that we should not, and do not and can not employ any [political-ideological] litmus test on any one particular issue, because in doing so we would be guilty of politicizing the judiciary and that is as detrimental as if we were unable to identify men and women who would follow the law rather than legislate from the bench.[2]

This article seeks to shed some light on whether or not the President is making ideologically based appointments and whether his judicial cohort is decid-ing cases in the manner anticipated by most court observers. It is organized around two basic questions: What might we expect of the Bush administration's potential to have an ideological impact on the federal courts? What do the empirical data tell us so far about the way that the Bush cohort has been deciding cases during the four years of his presidency?

A sympathetic judiciary

Judicial scholars have identified four general factors that determine whether chief executives can obtain a judiciary that is sympathetic to their political values and attitudes:[3] the degree of the president's commitment to making ideologically based appointments; the number of vacancies to be filled; the level of the chief executive's political clout; and the ideological climate into which the new judicial appointees enter.

Presidential support for ideologically based appointments

One key aspect of the success of chief executives in appointing a federal judiciary that mirrors their own political beliefs is the depth of their commitment to do so. Some presidents may be content merely to fill the federal bench with party loyalists and pay little attention to their nominees' specific ideologies. Some may consider ideological factors when appointing Supreme Court justices but may not regard them as important for trial and appellate judges. Other presidents may discount ideologically grounded appointments because they themselves tend to be non-ideological. Still others may place factors such as past political loyalty ahead of ideology in selecting judges.

For example, Harry Truman had strong political views, but when selecting judges he placed loyalty to himself ahead of the candidate's overall political orientation. On the other hand, Presidents Ronald Reagan and Lyndon Johnson are examples of presidents who had strong ideological beliefs on many issues and

Judicature Volume 88, Number 1, pp. 20–28

who took great pains to select judges who shared these beliefs.

What do we know about whether or not President George W. Bush is committed to making ideologically based judicial appointments? The evidence suggests that the President is indeed using ideology as a basis for his judicial nominations. Recall, for example, that just prior to the election of 2000 George W. Bush publicly expressed admiration for Justice Antonin Scalia, who is one of the most conservative members of the Supreme Court.[4] Justice Scalia usually interprets the Constitution as restraining congressional power to regulate commerce and seeks to limit the expansion of many Bill of Rights freedoms (generally conservative positions).

In May of 2001, after sending forth his first batch of judicial nominees, President Bush made it clear that his judges will adhere to his conservative judicial philosophy. "Every judge I appoint will be a person who clearly understands the role of a judge is to interpret the law, not to legislate from the bench," he said.[5] And early in 2003, Bush's assistant attorney general said in an interview that "we want to ensure that the President's mandate to us that the men and women who are nominated by him to be on the bench have his vision of the proper role of the judiciary. That is, a judiciary that will follow the law, not make the law. . . ."[6]

Still, there is no solid evidence that Bush's nominees are being screened for their ideological purity to the same degree that judicial candidates were during Ronald Reagan's administration. Furthermore, diluting the ideological commitment to a slight degree is the fact that Bush may have some interest in increasing the number of women and minorities on the bench. The record indicates that W. Bush has so far appointed a larger percentage of women and minorities to the bench than did either his father or Ronald Reagan, although still fewer than did Clinton. Still, the evidence suggests that conservative ideology rather than "affirmative action" is the predominant motivating force behind the Bush judicial appointments.

The number of vacancies to be filled

A second element affecting the capacity of chief executives to establish a policy link between themselves and the judiciary is the number of appointments available to them. The more judges a president can select, the greater the potential of the White House to put its stamp on the judicial branch. For example, George Washington's influence on the Supreme Court was significant because he was able to nominate 10 individuals to the High Court. Jimmy Carter's was nil because no vacancies occurred during his term as president.

The number of appointment opportunities depends on several factors: how many judicial vacancies are inherited from the previous administration (Clinton, for example, was left with a whopping 100 district and trial court vacancies—14 percent of the total—by former president Bush), how many judges and justices die or resign during the president's term, how long the president serves, and whether Congress passes legislation that significantly increases the number of judgeships.

Historically, the last factor seems to have been the most important in influencing the number of judgeships available, and politics in its most basic form permeates this process. A study of proposals for new-judges bills in 13 Congresses tested the following two hypotheses: (1) "proposals to add new federal judges are more likely to pass if the party controls the Presidency and Congress than if different parties are in power," and (2) "proposals to add new federal judges are more likely to pass during the first two years of the president's term than during the second two years." The author concluded that his "data support both hypotheses—proposals to add new judges are about five times more likely to pass if the same party controls the presidency and Congress than if different parties control, and about four times more likely to pass during the first two years of the President's term than during the second two years." He then noted that these findings serve "to remind us that not only is judicial selection a political process, but so is the creation of judicial posts."[7]

When George W. Bush assumed the presidency he inherited 82 vacancies, which was quite a sizable number by historic standards.[8] This was largely due to the bitter partisan politics that had occurred during the Clinton administration, causing many of his judicial nominees to go without Senate confirmation. A second factor in this equation is that the number of judges who die or who retire while on the bench is occurring at about the same rate under the Bush administration as it has for previous chief executives: during Bush's first two years in office 71 judges left the trial and appellate court bench. If this rate continues throughout a full first term, it would mean that President Bush would appoint about 17 percent of active federal judges just through the normal process of attrition.

What about the possibility of Congress passing a new omnibus judges bill that would give the President the opportunity to pack the judiciary with men and women of like-minded values, a phenomenon that greatly enhanced President Kennedy's and Carter's ideological impact on the judiciary? Unfortunately for President Bush, he has had no such luck. It is true that in 2001 the Judicial Conference of the United States recommended to Congress that it create 54 new district and appellate judgeships. It also called for "permanent authorization" of seven temporary district judgeships that had been previously established. However, the politically divided Congress was not too obliging. Congress refused to create any new appellate judgeships; it established only eight new district court judgeships; and it granted permanent authorization to only four temporary positions.[9]

So what is one to conclude about this second predictor of whether President Bush will potentially have a substantial impact on the ideological direction of the federal judiciary—the number of vacancies he can fill? The data suggest that in terms of pure numbers the President is having about an average set of opportunities to make an ideological impact on the federal bench. The real question seems to be whether he will be re-elected in 2004. If he is, then approximately a third or more of all active federal judges will bear the W. Bush stamp, and that will be a substantial impact. If his re-election bid is not successful, then the effect of the Bush judges will be much more modest.

The president's political clout

Another factor is the scope and proficiency of presidential skill in overcoming political obstacles. One such stumbling block is the U.S. Senate. If the Senate is controlled by the president's party, the White House will find it much easier to secure confirmation. Sometimes when the opposition is in power in the Senate, presidents are forced into a sort of political horse-trading to get their nominees approved. For example, in the summer of 1999 President Clinton was obliged to make a deal with the conservative chairman of the Senate Judiciary Committee, Orrin Hatch. To obtain smooth sailing for at least 10 of Clinton's judicial nominations that were blocked in the Senate, the President agreed to nominate for a federal judgeship a conservative Utah Republican, Ted Stewart, who was vigorously opposed by liberals and environmental groups.

The Senate Judiciary Committee is another roadblock preventing presidents who have the requisite will from placing their chosen men and women on the federal bench. Some presidents have been more adept than others at easing their candidates through the jagged rocks of the Judiciary Committee rapids. Both Presidents Kennedy and Johnson, for example, had to deal with the formidable committee chairman James Eastland of Mississippi, but only Johnson seems to have had the political adroitness to get most of his liberal nominees approved. Kennedy lacked this skill. Clinton, despite the President's considerable political acumen, was never able to parlay those skills into much clout with the conservative and often hostile Senate Judiciary Committee.

Finally, the president's personal popularity is another element in the political power formula. Chief executives who are well liked by the public and command the respect of opinion makers in the news media, the rank-and-file of their political party, and the leaders of the nation's major interest groups are much more likely to prevail over any forces that seek to thwart their judicial nominees.

In light of this "political clout" variable, how would we assess President Bush's capacity to make an ideological impact on the composition of the federal judiciary? Immediately after the 2000 election, the Senate was evenly divided between the two political parties, but with Vice President Dick Cheney available to break any tie vote the Republicans were in control of this chamber. In principle this would enhance President Bush's potential to obtain confirmation for judicial nominees of like-minded values.

But soon after the election a series of events occurred that greatly clouded this scenario. First, the Democrats regained control of the Senate when Vermont Senator Jim Jeffords unexpectedly left the Republican Party caucus. All legislative action came to a halt for several weeks as the struggle to reorganize the Senate became the major focus of attention. Equally important after Jeffords' defection, control of the Judiciary Committee went to the Democrats. The new committee chair, Senator Patrick Leahy, was in no frame of mind to become a rubber stamp for President Bush's judicial nominees. Then came the terrorist attacks on September 11, and public and legislative attention became riveted on matters of anti-terrorism legislation and national security.

At the end of President Bush's first two years in office, his scorecard indicated mixed results. On the down side, two of his nominees (Priscilla Owen and Charles Pickering) received negative votes from the

Judiciary Committee, and the names of 28 other district and appellate court candidates were returned to the President without any action being taken by the committee. But the news was by no means all bad for the President. None of his judicial nominees was defeated on the floor of the Senate, and 99 individuals, presumably all staunch conservatives, were approved by the Judiciary Committee and the Senate.

More recently, two series of events have produced countervailing effects on the President's political clout in the Senate. On the positive side for President Bush, the Republicans regained control of the Senate in the midterm elections of 2002, and along with it control of the Judiciary Committee, now headed by Bush-friendly Senator Hatch. But on the negative side, his approval ratings by the voters have been slipping steadily. This is attributed to the public's perception that the nation may have been grossly misled on the reasons for going to war in Iraq and also the belief by many Americans that the rebuilding of Iraq is becoming much too costly both in terms of dollars and military casualties. Furthermore, the American economy has continued to be troubled with soaring deficits and relatively high unemployment. Indeed, by the summer of 2004 some opinion polls were suggesting that the President was running behind John Kerry in his bid for a second term.[10]

Although the decline in the President's popular support has not translated into any marked decline in the rate at which his judicial nominees are being approved, neither is there any evidence that the Judiciary Committee and the Senate are rushing to do the President's bidding. As of May 1, 2004, there were 48 vacancies on the district and appellate courts[11]—not evidence that the President's judicial nominations are at a standstill, but neither does it suggest that the Senate and its Judiciary Committee are giving President Bush rapid action on his judicial nominations.

In the most recent session of Congress, Senate Democrats were successful in blocking a number of the President's appellate court nominations by the use of the filibuster. The Republicans, while having a bare majority in the Senate, did not have the votes necessary to cut off debate and end the filibusters. President Bush retaliated by the use of recess appointments on two occasions—actions that infuriated Democrats. In May of this year a deal of sorts was cut between the White House and the Senate. Under this agreement, the President agreed to no more recess appointments during the remainder of his current term ending January 20, 2005. "In return, Democrats, who had been holding up action on all of Bush's judicial choices since March to protest the recess appointments, agreed to allow votes on 25 mostly noncontroversial nominations to district and appeals posts over the next several weeks." [12]

The judicial climate the new judges enter

A final matter affects the capacity of chief executives to secure a federal judiciary that reflects their own political values: the current philosophical orientations of the sitting district and appellate court judges with whom the new appointees would interact. Because federal judges serve lifetime appointments during good behavior, presidents must accept the composition and value structure of the judiciary as it exists when they first take office.

If the existing judiciary already reflects the president's political and legal orientation, the impact of new judicial appointees will be immediate and substantial. However, if new chief executives face a trial and appellate judiciary whose values are radically different from their own, the impact of their subsequent judicial appointments will be weaker and slower to materialize. New judges must respect the controlling legal precedents and the constitutional interpretations that prevail in the judiciary at the time they enter it, or they risk being overturned by a higher court. Such a reality may limit the capacity of a new set of judges to do their own thing—at least in the short run.

President Reagan's impact on the judicial branch continues to be substantial. By the end of his second term he had appointed an unprecedented 368 federal judges, 50 percent of those on the bench. When he entered the White House, the Supreme Court was already teetering to the right because of Richard Nixon's and Gerald R. Ford's conservative appointments. Although Carter's liberal appointees still had places on the trial and appellate court benches, Reagan found a good many conservative Nixon and Ford judges on the bench when he took office. Thus he has had a major role in shaping the entire federal judiciary in his own conservative image for some time to come. The Bush judges had a much easier time making their impact felt because they entered a judicial realm wherein well over half the judges already professed conservative Republican values.

However, President Clinton's impact on the judiciary has been slower to manifest itself because his judicial nominees entered an arena in which more than 75 percent of the trial and appellate court seats were held by judges appointed by GOP presidents with very conservative orientations. When George W. Bush entered the White House, 51 percent of the federal judges had been appointed by Democratic presidents.

How does this affect President Bush's potential for leaving his ideological mark on the composition of the judiciary? When the President first took office, the partisan backgrounds of the judges were balanced with almost mathematical precision: 51 percent of the judges on the lower federal bench were appointed by Republican presidents; 49 percent by Democrats. In such a situation, even a slight tilt in one direction can give one party a controlling edge in the judicial decision-making process, and perhaps more importantly, in the composition of the policy-making appeals court panels.

Evidence for this phenomenon is already evident at the end of President Bush's three-and-a-half years in office. By the summer of 2004, Republican appointees control a solid majority of the 13 circuit courts in the country. Assuming a normal attrition rate for judges leaving the bench, it is likely that by the end of his first term in office all of the 13 circuits will have a majority of Republican judges. This will greatly enhance President Bush's potential for leaving a significant ideological mark on the composition of the federal judiciary.

In sum, the overall evidence suggests that President Bush should be able to continue to move the federal judiciary in a more conservative direction. He has indicated a clear desire to appoint more conservative jurists. He is filling an average number of new vacancies, although his clout in getting his nominees through a highly divided Senate, coupled with the President's declining popularity, is a negative factor. Finally, given the narrow balance of the judiciary at the beginning of the President's term between Republicans and Democrats, President Bush continues to be in a critical position to tilt the ideological balance in a decidedly more conservative vein.

Sources and definitions

Before we examine the data we have collected, we need to say a word about its source, and offer some working definitions of the terms "conservative" and "liberal." The data on trial court decisions were taken from a database consisting of more than 70,000 opinions published in the Federal Supplement by more than 1,700 judges from 1933 through the spring of 2004. We coded 410 decisions handed down by judges appointed by President George W. Bush.[13] Only those cases that fit

easily into one of 27 case types and contained a clear underlying liberal-conservative dimension were used. This included cases such as state and federal habeas corpus pleas, labor-management disputes, questions involving the right to privacy, and environmental protection cases, among others. Excluded were cases involving patents, admiralty disputes, and land condemnation hearings. The number of cases not selected was about the same as the number included.

In the realm of civil rights and civil liberties, "liberal" judges would generally take a broadening position; that is, they would seek in their rulings to extend these freedoms. "Conservative" jurists, by contrast, would prefer to limit such rights. For example, in a case in which a government agency wanted to prevent a controversial person from speaking in a public park or at a state university, a liberal judge would be more inclined than a conservative to uphold the right of the would-be speech giver. Or in a case concerning affirmative action in public higher education, a liberal judge would be more likely to take the side of favoring special admissions for minority petitioners.

In the area of government regulation of the economy, liberal judges would probably uphold legislation that benefited working people or the economic underdog. Thus, if the secretary of labor sought an injunction against an employer for paying less than the minimum wage, a liberal judge would be more disposed to endorse the labor secretary's arguments, whereas a conservative judge would tend to side with business, especially big business.

Another broad category of cases often studied by judicial scholars is criminal justice. Liberal judges are, in general, more sympathetic to the motions made by criminal defendants. For instance, in a case in which the accused claimed to have been coerced by the government to make an illegal confession, liberal judges would be more likely than their conservative counterparts to agree that the government had acted improperly.

What the data reveal

Figure 1 compares the total liberalism scores of the judicial cohorts appointed by eight of the most recent presidents, three Democrats and five Republicans. The data indicate that 36 percent of the decisions of the George W. Bush jurists have been decided in a liberal direction. These numbers are certainly more conservative than the liberal scores of Presidents Johnson, Carter, and Clinton, which were respectively 52, 52, and 45. Still, they can hardly be termed "extreme" since they are quite in

Figure 1. Percentage of liberal decisions by judges appointed by the eight most recent presidents.

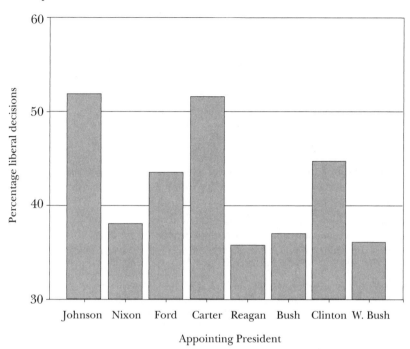

line with the numbers of his GOP predecessors Nixon, Reagan, and Bush, Sr., which were respectively 38, 36, and 37. George W. Bush's appointees are very conservative, but at least in the aggregate they are no more conservative than recent Republican appointees.[14]

Let us turn up our examining microscope a notch and compare the voting patterns of Bush's jurists with that of other modern presidents on the three composite variables of civil rights and liberties, criminal justice, and labor and economic regulation. The first column in Table 1 focuses on the dimension of civil rights and liberties; that is, it examines judges' voting behavior on issues such as abortion, freedom of speech, the right to privacy, charges of racial minorities, and so on. It is here that we find the best evidence for some meaningful ideological screening by President Bush's judicial appointment staff. Only 28 percent of the Bush cohort voted on the liberal side of issues pertaining to Bill of Rights and civil rights matters, thus giving the President the lowest score of any modern chief executive. With this score President Bush's trial judges are some 14 points more conservative than the appointees of President Clinton, but they are also more right of center than the judges appointed by Presidents Nixon, Ford, Reagan, and Bush, Sr.

Table 1. Percentage of liberal decisions in three case types

Appointing president	Civil rights & liberties	Criminal justice	Labor & economic regulation	All cases
Johnson	58.1	36.4	63.1	51.9
Nixon	37.9	26.9	48.5	38.1
Ford	40.3	34.9	52.5	43.5
Carter	51.3	38.4	61.3	51.6
Reagan	32.3	25.3	48.7	35.8
Bush	32.2	29.9	50.6	37.0
Clinton	42.1	39.0	54.3	44.7
W. Bush	27.9	33.3	52.5	36.1

This should come as little surprise since the major controversies surrounding President Bush's judicial nominees have focused on their stances on issues such as affirmative action, gay rights, abortion, establishment of religion, and the right to privacy (all of which are included in our civil rights and liberties composite variable). Furthermore, the President's electoral base has clearly centered on these same issues, and there is considerable evidence to suggest that the President has sought to please and strengthen this base through his judicial appointments.

Few observers, friend or foe, have commented on Bush's nominees in terms of their possible effect on judicial issues pertaining to labor-management disputes, the power of the bureaucracy, or major curtailments in the rights of routine criminal defendants.

In sum, the very areas in which we would expect meaningful ideological screening of judicial nominees, namely on civil rights and liberties issues, is the same realm in which that screening is manifesting itself in the decision making of the Bush cohort.

The second column in Table 1 provides data on judges' voting on criminal justice issues, such as habeas corpus pleas, motions made before and during a criminal trial, and forfeiture of property in a criminal case. In this realm the voting record of the Bush team seems somewhat more liberal than one might anticipate. Some 33 percent of his cohort's published decisions have favored the criminal defendant. This is certainly less than the number of 39 percent for President Clinton's judicial cohort, but it is noticeably higher than the averages for previous modern Republican presidents. (Only 25 percent of Reagan-cohort decisions favored the criminal defendant, and only 30 percent of Bush Sr.'s judges' decisions were liberal in this realm.)

The comparatively high liberalism score for Bush's judges is something of an anomaly to us, and we can offer a possible explanation. Our numbers in this area are still rather small, which makes generalizations more tentative, but as more and more conservative Bush judges are appointed, the overall numbers may move in a more conservative direction. Indeed, as our "n" has been increasing over the past several months, the liberalism score of the Bush judges on criminal justice issues has been declining. This may indicate that the initial batch of Bush appointees were somewhat more moderate in this realm but that phenomenon is being mollified as more "typical" conservative Bush appointees come on line.

Table 1's third column contains data on the judges' voting pattern in the realm of labor and economic regulation. (A typical case might be that of a labor union versus a company, a worker alleging a violation of the Fair Labor Standards Act, or a petitioner challenging the right of a government regulator to circumscribe his activity.) On this composite variable 53 percent of the decisions of the Bush appointees have been on the liberal side. This puts the Bush team only one percentage point behind the score of 54 percent for Clinton's judges and some 4 and 2 points more liberal than the

decisions of Presidents Reagan and Bush, Sr., respectively. What are we to make of these findings?

First, there should be little surprise that the Bush cohort is not as dramatically conservative in the realm of labor and economic regulation as it is in the area of civil rights and liberties. In his campaign for the presidency, George Bush made no serious calls for cutting back the power of organized labor unions or for a drastic curtailing of the power of the federal government and its regulators. During his presidency, there have been no major initiatives against organized labor, and furthermore the size of the federal government and its deficits have soared. Thus there would be little reason to predict that the Bush administration has been screening its judicial nominees for particularly conservative values when it comes to labor and economic issues.

Second, what is notable about the labor and economic regulation scores of all appointees in the past quarter century is how comparatively similar they are. This is part of a larger political-judicial phenomenon that we have discussed elsewhere: since the end of the New Deal, and particularly since the 1950s, the major political battles between the presidential candidates, in Congress, and within the Supreme Court have been over Bill of Rights and 14th Amendment issues, not over matters of labor and economic regulation.[15]

Moreover, in recent decades Congress has legislated, often with precision, in the areas of economic regulation and labor relations, and this has further restricted the discretion of judges in these fields.[16] In sum, the serious political and judicial battles of recent decades have not been fought in the labor and economic arenas, and relatively clear guidelines provided by Congress and the courts have eroded whatever wiggle room there might have been for Republicans to be inordinately conservative and Democrats to be correspondingly liberal. As a result, the moderate Bush-judges scores in Table 1 is just a manifestation of this overall phenomenon.

Traditional v. non-traditional

One final subject of interest is to compare the decision-making patterns of Bush's traditional (that is, white male) appointees with that of his non-traditional jurists (women and minorities). Such comparisons are increasingly meaningful because, as noted earlier, President Bush has appointed the largest number of women and minorities to the federal bench of any Republican president (as did Clinton for the Demo-

Table 2. Percentage of liberal decisions by traditional and non-traditional judges appointed by George W. Bush*

	% liberal decisions (n)	% conservative decisions (n)
Traditional	34.7% (83)	65.3% (156)
Non-traditional	38.0% (65)	62.0% (106)
Odds ratio (a) = .868; Chi square = .466 (p = .281)		

*"Non-traditional" judges are women and/or members of an ethnic minority group. "Traditional" jurists are white males.

crats). Conventional wisdom often suggests that women and minorities might be somewhat more liberal in their voting patterns than their white male counterparts (although evidence for this tends to be inconclusive).[17] This is because historically they have often been subjected to racial and gender discrimination by law and also in the workplace in terms of equal pay for equal work and promotions to managerial positions.

Table 2 provides some modest evidence for the above assertion: 35 percent of the overall decisions of Bush's "traditional" judges have been in a liberal direction, whereas 38 percent of the rulings handed down by his female and minority jurists have been liberal. However, we are cautious in our conclusions here because the differences are substantively not very great nor are they at levels of statistical significance that would allow us to have more confidence in the findings. We must await the accumulation of a larger number of decisions in our database before we can offer any conclusions about this phenomenon with greater certainty.

The final imprint?

This article has explored the ideological impact that President George W. Bush has had so far in the decision-making patterns of the trial court judiciary. To perform this task, we sought to determine the degree to which he and his appointment team have possessed a strong commitment to make ideologically based appointments, the number of vacancies to be filled, the extent of the president's political clout, and the ideological climate into which his judicial cohort is entering.

Our estimation was that President Bush should be having a moderately strong impact on the ideological orientation of the federal judiciary, particularly in the realm of civil rights and liberties, since it is Bill of Rights and equality issues that have defined much of the President's domestic political and judicial agenda and it is in that same area that judges still have maximum room for honest differences (as opposed to the more settled area of labor and economic regulation). The quantitative data from our investigation lend support to these hypotheses.

First, in terms of overall voting patterns, President Bush's judges are among the most conservative on record for all modern administrations, being on a par with Ronald Reagan's judicial team. Furthermore, in the realm of civil rights and liberties the Bush jurists are clearly the most conservative on record, being a full 4 points more conservative than even the trial judges appointed by Presidents Reagan or Bush, Sr. Finally, in accordance with "conventional wisdom," President Bush's non-traditional jurists are deciding cases in a somewhat more liberal manner than the white males who have been selected for judicial service.

The record of the past four years suggests that, should George W. Bush win reelection to a second term, the final imprint that he may leave upon the judiciary after eight years would consist of a sharp turn to the right. On the other hand, should Senator John Kerry win in November, it is likely that his administration would pursue a different ideological direction, and the effect that George W. Bush may ultimately have could be limited. There is little question, therefore, that the election in November will have a significant impact upon the ideological direction of the federal judiciary for years to come.

Notes

This article originally appeared in Volume 88, Number 1, July–August 2004, pages 20–28.

1. As quoted in Sheldon Goldman, Elliot Slotnick, Gerard Gryski, Gary Zuk, and Sara Schiavoni, "W. Bush remaking the judiciary: Like father like son?" *Judicature* 86 (2003), 282, 300.
2. Ibid. at 284.
3. For a summary of this literature, see Robert A. Carp, Ronald Stidham, and Kenneth L. Manning, *Judicial Process in America*, 6th ed., chap. 7 (Washington, D.C.: CQ Press, 2004).
4. Stuart Taylor Jr., "The Supreme Question," *Newsweek*, July 10, 2000, at 20.

5. Bennett Roth, "Bush Submits 11 Names for Federal Bench," *Houston Chronicle*, May 10, 2001, at A1.

6. *Supra* n. 1, at 284.

7. Jon R. Bond, "The Politics of Court Structure: The Addition of New Federal Judges," *Law and Pol. Q.* (1980), 182, 183, 187.

8. However, many court observers argue that Bush's appointment opportunities in this realm may be more apparent than real. That is, many vacancies exist because President Clinton was stymied in his efforts to fill them toward the end of his term, and it may now be "pay back time" for the Democrats. For example, Michigan's Democratic senators have so far been successful in blocking the appointment of Republican judges for the Sixth Circuit Court of Appeals, despite the presence of nominees for these open positions.

9. Act of November 2, 2002; 116 Stat.1786.

10. "Poll: Bush Losing Ground on Iraq," *Houston Chronicle*, June 22, 2004, at A4.

11. "Judicial Boxscore," *The Third Branch* (2004), 8.

12. Helen Dewar, "President, Senate Reach Pact on Judicial Nominations," *Washington Post*, May 19, 2004, at A21.

13. These rulings were handed down in three key issue areas: Civil liberties & rights n = 208; Criminal justice n = 84; Labor and economic regulation n = 118. Though we only coded district court rulings, prior research suggests that the behavior by jurists at this level of the judiciary is comparable to the behavior of judges appointed by the same president to the courts of appeals. See Ronald Stidham, Robert A. Carp, and Donald R. Songer, "The voting behavior of President Clinton's judicial appointees," *Judicature* 80 (1996), 16–20; and Robert A. Carp, Donald Songer, C. K. Rowland, Ronald Stidham, and Lisa Richey-Tracy, "The voting behavior of judges appointed by President Bush," *Judicature* 76 (1993), 298–302.

14. It might be argued that the relationship between appointing president and the voting patterns of his appointees would be comparatively weak for district judges because of the phenomenon of "senatorial courtesy," which in principle acts to restrict the president's appointing power. On the other hand one might argue that the appointment effects would be greater for circuit court appointments for which "senatorial courtesy" do not apply. However, the reality is that studies over the years have demonstrated that presidential effects at the district court level have been quite robust. For example, see Carp et al., *supra* n. 3, at 157–168 and 289–294.

15. See ibid. at 314–317.

16. Ibid. at 314.

17. See Robert A. Carp, Kenneth L. Manning, and Ronald Stidham, "President Clinton's district judges: 'Extreme liberals' or just plain moderates?" *Judicature* 84 (2001), 284–288; and Carp et al., supra n. 3, at 106–107.

Actors in the Judicial Process

Magistrates, Clerks, and Judicial Support Staff

While a great deal has been written about judges and their role in judicial politics, such is not the case regarding other functionaries such as U.S. magistrate judges, law clerks, and other judicial support personnel. U.S. magistrate judges are critically important yet largely invisible actors in the federal judiciary. In "From U.S. magistrates to U.S. magistrate judges: developments affecting the federal district courts' lower tier of judicial officers," Christopher Smith traces the history of the U.S. magistrate and documents the expansion in tasks taken on by U.S. magistrate judges from the time that the position was established in 1968 through formal recognition of the broadened scope of the office's authority signaled by the position's name change in 1990. With the exception of trying and sentencing felony cases, U.S. magistrate judges can now do pretty much what federal district judges do. Still, the magistrate judge's job can vary a good deal depending upon the district in which he or she serves. Smith provides a typology that underscores that the U.S. magistrate judge may be characterized primarily as an additional judge in the district, a team player, or a specialist. As Smith notes, "the specific mix of tasks assigned to magistrate judges within each district depends upon a variety of factors, including district judges' views on magistrate judges' proper judicial role and the nature of the caseload pressures."

In "Law clerks: their roles and relationships with their judges," David Crump explores the benefits and liabilities of the clerking system in the judicial process. While most often utilized as preliminary drafters of opinions, Crump underlines the considerable diversity in what clerks do and examines their potential influence in judicial decision making. The author's analysis pays heed to arguments that suggest clerks wield too much power and to those that suggest clerks play a positive role in the fostering of change and innovation in judicial decision making.

Magistrate judges and law clerks are relatively invisible actors who play critical roles in judicial processes and their outcomes. However, it is also important to recognize that one can delve even more deeply into the judicial system to locate other levels of even less publicly prominent players. These include centralized research staff, whose role in providing support for judges undergoes little scrutiny yet may hold great importance and, at times, controversy. Such centralized staff may be used in some courts to screen cases, provide research, and make recommendations, tasks that have become necessary because of overwhelming caseloads. The justification for utilizing these individuals is, of course, that they can help alleviate delay while facilitating judicial efficiency. The concern raised by their utilization, however, is that judges are no longer the central decision makers per se but are instead the validators of decisions that have been made elsewhere.

Although functionaries, such as the centralized support staff just described, are relatively unseen internal support for judges, other court personnel may play a more visible role in rendering service to the public, particularly to litigants. In the final article in this section, "Legal information vs. legal advice: developments during the last five years," John Greacen explores some concerns related to staff who provide such service. In an era when courts deal with a significant proportion of litigants who represent themselves, there is a fine line between court staff supplying legal information, a purely instructional task, and rendering legal advice that may cross lines of propriety. This line is not only difficult to draw but is, perhaps, not always desired. As Greacen notes, "The significant and as-yet unanswered question is whether self-represented litigants' rights obligate the state to take affirmative steps to provide them with some form of 'adequate' legal assistance." In this provocative article that raises many questions about the appropriate public role for court personnel, Greacen conservatively concludes that, "It is neither necessary nor realistic to expect the courts to serve not only as dispute resolvers but also as counselors and advocates for both sides."

From U.S. magistrates to U.S. magistrate judges: developments affecting the federal district courts' lower tier of judicial officers

Christopher E. Smith

With their new title and increased opportunities to educate the bar about the breadth of their judicial authority, magistrate judges are poised to fulfill the potential their supporters have envisioned for broad, flexible contributions to case-processing responsibilities.

Congress created the office of U.S. magistrate in 1968 to provide additional case-processing resources for the federal district courts. In December 1990, the title for the office was changed to "U.S. magistrate judge" as part of the Judicial Improvements Act.[1] Full-time magistrate judges are appointed by district court judges for renewable eight-year terms and part-timers are appointed for renewable four-year terms.[2] Because they do not possess the attributes of Article III judges (i.e., presidential appointment, senate confirmation, and protected tenure), magistrate judges are considered "adjuncts" of the federal courts who perform tasks delegated by the district judges.

Initially, the magistrates' authority was primarily confined to the limited tasks performed by the old U.S. commissioners, lay judicial officers who handled warrants, arraignments, and petty offenses from 1793 until they were replaced by the newly-created magistrates after 1968.[3] Congress subsequently amended the Magistrates Act in 1976 and 1979 to authorize magistrates to assist district judges with a broad spectrum of tasks, including the supervision of complete civil trials with the consent of litigants.[4] After the 1979 Act, magistrates could perform virtually any task undertaken by district judges except for trying and sentencing felony defendants.[5] By June 1990, the 323 full-time and 153 part-time magistrates were such an integral component of the federal district courts that they were responsible for completing 450,565 tasks, including 4,220 civil and criminal evidentiary hearings, 45,201 civil pretrial conferences, and 1,008 complete civil trials.[6] Article III judges acknowledged that magistrates "contribute significantly to the administration of justice in the United States and are an integral part of the Federal judicial system"[7] by including the magistrates' interests in arguments presented to Congress concerning the need for higher salaries for judicial officers.[8]

Because these subordinate judicial officers were intended to be utilized flexibly according to the needs of each district court, the precise judicial roles performed by magistrate judges vary from district to district. For example, one 1985 study of magistrates' roles found that they could be classified as performing three model roles: "Additional Judge," supervising complete civil cases and otherwise sharing caseload responsibilities with district judges; "Team Player," handling motion hearings, conferences, and other tasks to prepare cases for trial before district judges; and "Specialist," primarily processing Social Security disability appeals and prisoner petitions for the district judges.[9] The specific mix of tasks assigned to magistrate judges within each district depends upon a variety of factors, including district judges' views on magistrate judges' proper judicial role and the nature of the caseload pressures.[10] Because the tasks performed by magistrate judges vary, their roles within each district court are susceptible to change as court reforms, changing caseload compositions, and other factors affect the demands on federal courts and the district courts' case-processing capabilities. This article will discuss how recent developments affecting the federal courts are likely to shape the tasks and roles performed by the district courts' lower tier of judicial officers.

A new title and enhanced status

The magistrate judges' original title, "magistrate," was a source of unhappiness for many of the lower-tier judicial officers. District courts throughout the country received authorization to appoint magistrates in the early 1970s. Because neither district judges nor practicing attorneys knew how these new judicial officers, with their vaguely defined authority, ought to be regarded, many judges simply used magistrates as if they were merely permanent law clerks. Practicing attorneys followed suit by failing to treat magistrates with the deference and respect they would normally accord to a recognized judicial officer.[11] As a result, many magistrates believed their effectiveness was hampered because lawyers did not understand that they were indeed authoritative judicial officers. For example, a lawyer interviewed for one study said that "when a [district] judge tells you to do something, you jump. But when a magistrate tells you to do something, well, you do it, but it's not the same." [12]

"Magistrate" is a respected title in the British legal system, but in the United States it is merely a generic term for judicial officer. Because many state court systems employ the title "magistrate" for low-level lay officials, practicing attorneys often confused the authoritative federal judicial officers with the relatively inconsequential lay "justices of the peace" who bear the title "magistrate" in many states. The potential confusion that the title could cause was recognized when the new federal judicial office was created and the Judicial Conference of the United States subsequently discussed the issue in a report to Congress:

> Those who would prefer a change in title state that the term "magistrate" has traditionally referred to a low-level local official who performs a narrow range of functions in criminal cases, i.e., a justice of the peace. They point out that this traditional association of the term is inaccurate when applied to the full-time United States magistrates. They also note that many state magistrates are not well regarded and some have been prosecuted for wrongdoing.[13]

The title "magistrate" contributed to many practical problems when lawyers did not accord the subordinate judicial officers with appropriate deference and respect. If lawyers do not "jump" when instructed to take a specific action by a magistrate, then magistrates must waste time in the aftermath of motion hearings and discovery conferences trying to ensure that attorneys comply with the magistrates' orders. District judges could always force compliance by reiterating the magistrates' orders, but such redundant actions diminish the advantages for saving the judicial system's resources that Congress sought to attain by making magistrates authoritative judicial officers.[14] In addition, because magistrates' authority to preside over civil trials depends upon the consent of litigants,[15] the failure of attorneys to recognize magistrates' status and authority as judicial officers can reduce the likelihood

that litigants will consent to magistrates' jurisdiction and thereby hinder the implementation of this mechanism to reduce district judges' civil caseload burdens. The magistrates' title may be an important component of attorneys' willingness to recommend the consent trial option to their clients:

> Some magistrates view the title "judge" not only as an entitlement [for themselves as authoritative federal judicial officers], but as a functional necessity if they are to perform effectively when presiding over trials.... Many litigants may automatically prefer to have their cases heard by someone bearing the title of "judge." As a result, magistrates lose opportunities to gain visibility and build their reputations as judicial officers, and the potential flexibility and judicial economy of the magistrate system are diminished.[16]

In order to combat the confusion over magistrates' title, district judges in some districts addressed the magistrates as "judge" and instructed attorneys to do the same. This action reinforced the magistrates' status as judicial officers in those districts, but it exacerbated morale problems among magistrates in other districts who desired similar recognition but were forbidden by their supervising district judges from using the title "judge." [17]

As a result of the title change contained in the Judicial Improvements Act, the magistrate judges can expect to be more readily addressed as "judge." The new title and form of address will help educate attorneys and litigants about the magistrate judges' status as authoritative judicial officers within the federal courts. This should enhance the magistrate judges' contributions to effective case processing within the district courts by encouraging full cooperation and compliance from attorneys and by increasing the visibility and credibility of the litigants' option to consent to have civil cases tried before magistrate judges.

In 1979, when Congress considered the legislation that authorized magistrates to oversee consent trials, two members of Congress complained that "[f]rom the standpoint of appearance, procedure, and function, an impartial observer will not be able to tell the difference between a magistrate and an Article III judge." [18] In the context in which they raised this concern as part of the debate about the proper authority of non-Article III judicial officers, this was a significant issue to consider. But is this question as compelling today? Now that Congress has explicitly endorsed magistrate judges as "federal judicial officers," [19] federal appellate court decisions have accepted the constitutionality of magistrates' authority,[20] and magistrates have supervised civil trials for more than a decade, does it matter whether an outsider observer, be it a litigant or an attorney, knows the precise difference between a magistrate judge and an Article III district judge?

There may be legitimate, principled reasons to reopen the debate about the appropriate scope of non-Article III judges' authority.[21] However, because legislative and judicial policy makers have endorsed broad authority for magistrate judges, there is strong reason to give magistrate judges the title and status necessary for maximizing their contributions to the work of the district courts. Magistrate judges are different than Article III district judges in regard to their scope of authority and the delegation of tasks.[22] The title change contained in the Judicial Improvements Act merely indicates that when magistrate judges serve as the presiding judicial officers for matters pending before the district courts, the litigants and attorneys should be made well aware that the magistrate judges are indeed authoritative judicial decision makers who are to be accorded appropriate deference and respect.

Consent trial authority

Recent court reform initiatives threatened the magistrates' status and authority within the federal courts. One of the recommendations made in 1989 by the Brookings Institution's task force on civil justice reform[23] was aimed directly at the broad exercise of authority by magistrates: "Procedural Recommendation 11: Ensure in each district's plan that magistrates do not perform tasks best performed by the judiciary." The phrase "tasks best performed by the judiciary" seemed to imply that district judges rather than magistrates should preside over civil trials.

The task force report served as the basis for legislative proposals by Senator Joseph Biden, the chairman of the Senate Judiciary Committee. Biden's court reform bill, entitled "The Civil Justice Reform Act," contained, among other things, provisions requiring mandatory discovery/case management conferences and monitoring conferences for complex litigation that would both be "presided over by a judge and not a magistrate." [24] Such mandatory conferences would be designed to force district judges to become involved in case management for each civil case and would consequently reduce the likelihood that entire civil cases would be referred to magistrates by the consent of the litigants. In

proposing his court reform legislation, Senator Biden made it quite clear that he did not think that magistrates could manage civil litigation effectively.[25]

Ultimately, Biden's "Civil Justice Reform" bill was scrapped in favor of "The Judicial Improvements Act of 1990," which was developed through negotiations between the Senate Judiciary Committee and the Judicial Conference of the United States.[26] In regard to authority of magistrates,[27] the legislation enacted by Congress followed the recommendation of the Federal Courts Study Committee's 1990 report to encourage more consent trials before magistrates. The Federal Courts Study Committee urged that "Congress . . . allow district judges and magistrates to remind the parties [in civil litigation] of the possibilities of consent to civil trials before magistrates." [28] The statutory change affecting magistrates' consent trial authority suited the interests of both district judges and magistrates by, respectively, maintaining district judges' discretion and autonomy with regard to case management[29] and encouraging the referral of more complete civil trials to the newly retitled magistrate judges.

The Judicial Improvements Act encourages civil consent trials by now permitting district judges and magistrate judges to inform litigants directly about their option of consenting to a trial before a magistrate judge: "[E]ither the district court judge or the magistrate may again advise the parties of the availability of the magistrate, but in so doing, shall also advise the parties that they are free to withhold consent without adverse substantive consequences." [30] The involvement of judicial officers in informing litigants about the consent option represents a significant change from previous statutory language that made clerks of court exclusively responsible for communications about the consent option and precluded any involvement by judges or magistrates.[31] When Congress officially authorized magistrates to preside over complete civil trials with the consent of litigants in 1979,[32] the statute precluded involvement by judicial officers and emphasized the voluntariness of litigants' consent in order to avoid the possibility that judicial officers might pressure litigants to consent.[33]

Magistrate judges in many districts should enjoy increased opportunities to oversee complete civil cases as a result of the statutory change. Some districts had failed to implement regular procedures for educating litigants and their attorneys about the consent option through notices from the clerk of court. Litigants often remained uninformed about their options because the court personnel with whom they came into the most frequent, direct contact through pretrial conferences and hearings, namely the district judges and magistrates, were forbidden from discussing the magistrates' consent authority.[34] Now judicial officers will be able to remind parties about the consent option throughout the stages of civil litigation. Under the previous system, some districts that had routinized the notice process informed litigants about the consent option only at the outset of litigation.[35] If litigants did not understand the scope of magistrates' authority, they would be reluctant to consider immediately consenting to an unfamiliar process under the authority of an unfamiliar judicial officer.[36] Because the parties may not recognize the desirability of consenting to a magistrate judge's jurisdiction for a firm and expedited trial date until after the initiation of discovery and pretrial conferences, the new procedure will provide the opportunity for useful reminders to litigants when judicial officers perceive that such a referral might be beneficial.

Pressure to consent

Although the new procedure will increase the flexible utilization of magistrate judges and increase their status and authority in some districts, the involvement of judicial officers in informing litigants about the consent option also entails risks. The original statutory provision concerning notice to parties precluded the participation of judicial officers because they might coerce litigants into consenting. Congress was aware of the possibility, for example, that district judges might be "tempted to force disfavored cases into disposition before magistrates by intimations of lengthy delays manufactured in district court if the parties exercise their right to stay in that court." [37] Subsequent research revealed that this was a genuine risk that, in fact, came to fruition in some districts despite the statutory prohibition on communications from judicial officers to litigants concerning consent. A Federal Judicial Center study found that:

> There was a clear consensus among the [California lawyers] interviewed that when a judge raises the question of consent to a magistrate—for whatever reason—lawyers feel that they have little choice but to go along with the suggestion. Attorneys consistently reported feeling some pressure to consent, particularly in a "smaller" case; when interviewees were asked to describe the reasons for consent, the overriding one given was that the judge had suggested it.[38]

Another study found examples of district judges engaging in precisely the behavior that Congress feared, namely pressuring litigants to consent to the referral of disfavored cases to magistrates.[39]

Because the statutory revisions from the Judicial Improvements Act now invite judicial officers to communicate with litigants about the consent option, there are even greater risks that parties will be or will feel pressured to waive their right to have their case heard before an Article III judge. Such actions by judges are not likely to be challenged by attorneys: "Lawyers are not likely to admit publicly that they were weak in the face of improper conduct. They also [may] think twice about directly challenging the ethical conduct of a judge sitting in a court that provides a basis for their legal practice and livelihood." [40] Moreover, even if the issue of coercion is raised, it would be difficult to prove to an appellate court that a district judge had improper motives or undertook improper actions. Judges' coercive actions identified in one study "were essentially immune from external scrutiny because scheduling trial dates and refusing to grant continuances (two of the most frequently-manipulated mechanisms to pressure litigants) are part of a judge's prerogatives. Thus, the coercive actions were cloaked in the impenetrable discretionary authority of judges." [41] Because the new notice provision invites the participation of judicial officers, district judges and magistrate judges must become much more self-conscious about their own motives and the possible coercive consequences of their communications with litigants concerning the consent option.

Task assignments

Current developments affecting the federal courts are certain to affect magistrate judges' task assignments, although it is uncertain precisely how those assignments will be affected. Although the changes affecting the subordinate judicial officers' title and consent trial authority should encourage increased references of complete civil cases to the magistrate judges, other factors may impede an increase in trials before magistrate judges.

The Judicial Improvements Act requires each district court to develop and implement a "civil justice expense and delay reduction plan." [42] In the course of examining mechanisms for effective case management and cost-effective discovery, districts may create new procedures that actually limit the exercise of magistrate judges' authority. For example, expense and delay reduction plans may make magistrate judges exclusively responsible for oversight of discovery, pretrial conferences, and other preliminary matters. Thus formalizing the subordinate judicial officers' roles as "trial preparers" rather than as "autonomous judges" presiding over civil consent trials.[43] Because district judges exert significant control over the magistrates' roles through their authority to appoint and reappoint the subordinate judicial officers and through their power over the delegation of tasks,[44] Article III judges will continue to have substantial influence over the definition of magistrate judges' roles within each district court. If the judges within a district believe that magistrate judges should exercise limited authority, the expense and delay reduction plans are likely to reflect that preference.

The precise tasks assigned to magistrate judges within a district depend not only upon the district judges' conceptualizations of the proper role for their judicial subordinates, but also upon the caseload composition within the district.[45] If magistrate judges work within a district containing large prisons, they may become "specialists" in prisoner petitions. Similarly, in districts that receive especially large numbers of Social Security disability appeals, the magistrate judges' working lives may be absorbed by the process of reviewing administrative law judges' findings in such cases. Although some districts utilize alternative mechanisms (e.g., staff attorneys, pro se law clerks, district judges' law clerks) for processing prisoner and Social Security cases, these two particular categories of cases have a significant impact upon workloads of magistrate judges in many districts.[46]

How are the federal courts currently being affected by these categories of cases? In regard to Social Security disability appeals, the federal district courts have experienced a steady decline in such cases. Disability cases peaked in 1984 at 24,215[47] in the aftermath of the Reagan administration's attempt to remove summarily 336,000 beneficiaries from that Social Security program.[48] By contrast, in 1990 there were only 5,212 of such cases filed in the federal district courts.[49] Thus, unless a magistrate judge serves a district that is especially affected by disability cases, these Social Security cases are becoming less burdensome and therefore are having fewer limiting effects upon magistrate judges' availability for other tasks, such as consent trials.

In regard to prisoners' petitions, the burden upon the federal courts has continued to grow. There were only 29,303 prisoners' petitions filed in the district courts in 1982[50] but that number grew to 42,630 in 1990.[51] After handling only 11,578 prisoner matters in 1980, the magistrate judges' burden peaked at 27,002 in 1987 and then dropped back to a consistent plateau just below 21,000 in 1989 and 1990.[52] Because prisoners' filings in the federal courts have shown steady annual increases throughout the 1980s, the recent reduction in the magistrate judges' burden must indicate that district judges are employing alternative mechanisms for processing such cases, such as pro se clerks[53] or their own law clerks. Although the burden upon the magistrate judges generally has, for the moment, stabilized, the tremendous increases in the number of people imprisoned throughout the United States make it likely that the number of prisoners' petitions will increase as well. There were only 329,821 people in prison in 1980, but that number leaped to 771,243 in 1990 as the result of aggressive prosecutions and stiffer sentences for narcotics and other offenses.[54]

Although rising prison populations make it appear likely that magistrate judges will continue to have some portion of their working lives absorbed by prisoners' petitions, other developments may reduce the number of such petitions in the federal courts. The Supreme Court has taken the initiative to create new rules for habeas corpus petitions that have the effect of precluding multiple petitions, enforcing procedural bars, and otherwise limiting prisoners' access to the federal courts.[55] Other potential exclusionary mechanisms have been discussed in justices' opinions[56] and may be on the horizon for implementation in future decisions. In addition, President Bush and Congress are working on legislative proposals that would, if passed, place additional limitations upon prisoners' opportunities to file habeas corpus petitions in the federal courts.[57] Although habeas corpus petitions typically constitute only 25 to 30 percent of the prisoners' petitions filed in federal court, they have constituted 40 percent of the magistrate judges' prisoner tasks in recent years.[58] The current developments aimed at reducing the number of habeas corpus petitions may reduce the magistrate judges' burden or, alternatively, district judges may simply assign their judicial subordinates more prisoner civil rights cases, which typically comprise more than 60 percent of the prisoner filings.[59]

Effect of felony prosecutions

Magistrate judges' workload is being affected by the increase in federal felony prosecutions, especially for narcotics offenses. Increases in felony prosecutions tie up the district judges because "speedy trial" require-ments make criminal cases move to the head of the docket queue. Because magistrate judges cannot con-duct trials and sentence offenders in felony cases, an increase in felony prosecutions should make litigants more inclined to consent to civil trials before magis-trate judges, as district judges' time becomes increas-ingly absorbed by felony cases. By consenting to a trial before a magistrate judge, litigants in civil cases can obtain an early and firm trial date. They may also be able to choose which magistrate judge will preside over the trial if the district court's case-processing proce-dures utilize references to multiple available magis-trate judges. Although the increases in felony prosecu-tions may lead to more civil case responsibilities for magistrate judges, the subordinate judicial officers also have their time absorbed in assisting the felony work of district judges: "Magistrates handled 313 percent more detention hearings in 1990 than in 1985, 111 percent more search warrants, 45 percent more preliminary examinations, 44 percent more arrest warrants, and 38 percent more arraignments." [60]

As with other developments affecting the federal courts, the magistrate judges' task assignments are affected by increases in criminal prosecutions, but it is not clear that such changes will necessarily lead to broader, more flexible utilization of the subordinate judicial officers. For example, although the magistrate judges' responsibilities for preliminary criminal mat-ters increased in conjunction with the increasing crim-inal caseload in the district courts, the number of civil consent cases for magistrate judges was virtually the same in 1990 as it was in 1986 (4,958 to 4,960).[61] Although the increase in felony cases during the late 1980s did not consistently escalate the number of civil consent cases for magistrate judges, the new statutory notice provisions permitting judicial officers to inform and remind litigants about the consent option may generate such an increase in the future. The number of civil consent trials before magistrate judges is most likely to rise if district judges continue to be preoccu-pied with felony cases and if those judges evince a con-comitant willingness to refer complete civil cases to their judicial subordinates.

Conclusion

Recent and ongoing developments in the federal courts will shape the status, authority, and workload of the U.S. magistrate judges. With their new title and increased opportunities to educate the bar about the

breadth of their judicial authority, especially their abil-ity to supervise civil consent trials, magistrate judges are poised to fulfill the potential that their supporters have envisioned for broad, flexible contributions to the case-processing responsibilities within each district court.

Although the subordinate judicial officers received a vote of confidence from Congress in the passage of the supportive Judicial Improvements Act instead of Sena-tor Biden's limiting Civil Justice Reform bill, it remains to be seen whether the magistrate judges will be able to exercise the full range of judicial tasks authorized by statute and desired by many of the incumbent judi-cial officers themselves.[62] Because the precise tasks assigned to magistrate judges are still significantly influ-enced by the preferences of the district judges with whom they work and by the nature of their individual districts' caseloads, the recent efforts to enhance mag-istrate judges' status, authority, and usefulness within the federal courts may, in fact, have little effect upon the subordinate judicial officers' contributions to the court system. The Judicial Improvements Act and con-tinuing docket pressures have set the stage for broader, more innovative use of magistrate judges, but the actual implementation of reforms is dependent on the district judges' willingness to delegate important responsibili-ties to their judicial subordinates.

Notes

This article originally appeared in Volume 75, Number 4, December–January 1992, pages 210–215.

1. References to the lower-tier judicial officers con-cerning their status and authority prior to December 1990 will use the previous title "magistrate" rather than the new title "magistrate judge."

2. *See* Smith, "Who are the U.S. magistrates?" *Judicature* 71 (1987), 143; Smith, "Merit Selection Committees and the Politics of Appointing United States Magistrates," *Just. Sys. J.* 12 (1987), 210.

3. *See* Spaniol, "The Federal Magistrates Act: History and Development," *Ariz. L. Rev.* (1974), 566; Peterson, "The Federal Magistrates Act: A New Dimension in the Implementation of Justice," *Iowa L. Rev.* 62 (1970), 56.

4. *See* McCabe, "The Federal Magistrates Act of 1979," *Harv. J. Legis.* 16 (1979), 343.

5. *See, e.g., Gomez v. United States,* 109 S. Ct. 2237 (1989) (magistrates not authorized to supervise the selection of jurors in felony criminal cases).

6. Administrative Office of the U.S. Courts, *Annual Report of the Director of the Administrative Office of the U.S. Courts* 25 (1990). Because these figures are drawn from

individual magistrate judges' reports concerning their own activities and the categories of activities are not precisely defined (e.g. different activities may be classified as separate "civil pretrial conferences" by different magistrate judges), case-processing statistics provide only a rough picture of magistrate judges' responsibilities. Although the statistics from the Administrative Office cannot provide precise information on the magistrate judges' accomplishments, the figures demonstrate substantial contributions to the work of the district courts by the lower tier of judicial officers.

7. Committee on the Judicial Branch of the Judicial Conference of the United States, *Simple Fairness: the Case for Equitable Compensation of the Nation's Judges* (1988), 81–82.

8. *See*, Smith, "Federal Judicial Salaries: A Critical Appraisal," *Temple L. Rev.* 62 (1988), 849.

9. *See* Seron, *The Roles of Magistrates: Nine Case Studies* (Washington, D.C.: Federal Judicial Center, 1985); Seron, "Magistrates and the work of the federal courts: a new division of labor," *Judicature* 69 (1986), 353.

10. *See* Smith, *United States Magistrates in the Federal Courts: Subordinate Judges* (New York: Praeger, 1990) 115–146.

11. Smith, "The Development of a Judicial Office: United States Magistrates and the Struggle for Status," *J. Legal Prof.* 14 (1989), 175, 184–185.

12. Smith, *supra* n. 10, at 135.

13. *The Federal Magistrates System: Report to the Congress by the Judicial Conference of the United States* 62 (1981).

14. Many magistrates can cite examples of incidents in which the judicial officers wasted time reinforcing to attorneys the idea that magistrates are indeed authoritative federal judicial officers: "In some instances, it is very obvious to the magistrate that the attorney regards the magistrate as being of lesser importance. The magistrate may be forced to marshal resources in order to maintain his or her desired judicial role. For example, in a . . . case in which an attorney attempted to go over the magistrate's head to the judge in order to get a conference rescheduled, it was clear that the attorney never would have attempted such a maneuver if the district judge were presiding over the conference. After an attorney approached a judge about rescheduling, there would be nothing that the attorney could do but comply with the judge's orders. [In this] example, the magistrate hurried to contact the judge to ensure that the judge upheld the magistrate's decision. Thus the magistrate, because of the relatively new judicial office and uncertainty about [the] appropriate status and role for the magistrate position, must often actively seek to maintain proper behavior and respect on the part of attorneys." Smith, *supra* n. 10, at 135.

15. "Upon the consent of the parties, a full-time United States magistrate or a part-time United States magistrate who serves as a full-time judicial officer may conduct any or all proceedings in a jury or nonjury civil matter and order entry of judgment in the case, when specially designated to exercise such jurisdiction by the district court or courts he serves." 28 U.S.C. sec. 636(c)(1).

16. Smith, *supra* n. 11, at 181–182.

17. Ibid. at 180-184.

18. *H.R. Rep. No. 1364,* 95th Cong., 2d Sess. (1978) at 37 (statement of Reps. Drinan and Kindness).

19. The "definition" section of the Judicial Improvements Act clearly endorsed the magistrate judges' status as judicial officers: "As used in this chapter, the term 'judicial officer' means a United States district court judge *or a United States magistrate*" (emphasis supplied). 28 U.S.C. sec. 482 (1990).

20. *See, e.g., Pacemaker Diagnostic Clinic of America, Inc. v. Instromedix, Inc.,* 725 F.2d 537 (9th Cir. 1984) (*en banc*), *cert. denied,* 469 U.S. 824 (1984).

21. *See* Resnik, "The Mythic Meaning of Article III Courts," *U. Colo. L. Rev.* 56 (1985), 581.

22. For example, district judges control the delegation of tasks to magistrate judges and, unless the parties have consented to a magistrate judge's authority, magistrate judges merely make recommendations to district judges concerning dispositive motions.

23. *See* Litan, "Speeding up civil justice," *Judicature* 73 (1989), 162.

24. The relevant provisions proposed: "A requirement that . . . a mandatory discovery/case management conference, presided over by a judge and not a magistrate, be held in all cases within 45 days following the first responsive pleading" (S. 2027, 101st Cong., 2d Sess. sec. 471(b)(3) (1990)); and "[F]or cases assigned to the track designated for complex litigation, calendar a series of monitoring conferences, presided over by a judge and not a magistrate, for the purpose of extending stipulations, refining the formulation of issues and focusing and pacing discovery" (Ibid. at sec. 471(b)(3)(I)).

25. Biden's statement introducing his court reform legislation expressed doubts about the magistrates' effectiveness: "The [pretrial] conference may lose some of its significance in the minds of the attorneys if presided over by a magistrate, since the unfortunate fact is that many attorneys seem to be far more willing to take frivolous positions before a magistrate. . . . [M]agistrates may themselves be more reluctant than judges to frame the contours of litigation, limit discovery, establish a date-certain briefing schedule and address the full panoply of discovery/case management conference issues." 136 Cong. Rec. S414 (daily ed. Jan. 25, 1990) (statement of Sen. Biden).

26. Some aspects of the negotiation process between the judiciary and Congress apparently angered members of the Senate Judiciary Committee: "The [Senate Judiciary] [C]ommittee complied with the request of the Judi-

cial Conference to work with one body [i.e., a four-judge task force appointed by Chief Justice William Rehnquist], only to have the [Judicial] Conference seemingly defer to another body [i.e., the Conference's Committee on Judicial Improvements which rejected the negotiated legislative proposal]—which had no role whatsoever in the discussions and negotiations—at the point of decision. Such actions only serve to undermine the cooperative relationship between Congress and the judicial branch that our citizens rightly expect and deserve." S. 416, 101st. Cong., 2d Sess. (1990) at 5.

27. To counteract Senator Biden's perception that magistrates are ineffective because lawyers do not respect their authority, district judges argued that magistrates can be very capable and authoritative, especially in districts in which judges permit them to perform a broad range of tasks: "[Magistrates] have informed me that it is a rare occasion indeed, that any attorney ever takes a frivolous position when appearing before them. If that should occur in some districts, I suspect that it is more of a reflection of how the magistrates are perceived by the Article III judges, and what duties or powers those judges have permitted the magistrates to perform. If that suspicion is true, one way to address the concerns of the [Brookings Institution's] Task Force is to leave the matter of who presides at the conference to the discretion of the district court adopting its plan." Enslen, "Prepared Statement of the Hon. Richard Enslen, U.S. District Court for the Western District of Michigan, Presented in Testimony Before the Senate Judiciary Committee During Consideration of S.2027, The Civil Justice Reform Act of 1990" (Mar. 6, 1990) at 45.

28. *Report of the Federal Courts Study Committee* 79 (Apr. 2, 1990).

29. The district judges had argued to Congress that "the proposed diminution of the role of magistrates would hamper the proposed legislation's underlying purpose of improving case-processing efficiency." Robinson, "Prepared Statement of the Hon. Aubrey E. Robinson, Jr., Chief Judge, U.S. District Court for the District of Columbia, Presented in Testimony Before the Senate Judiciary Committee During Consideration of S. 2027, The Civil Justice Reform Act of 1990" (Mar. 6, 1990) at 4.

30. 28 U.S.C. sec. 636(c)(2) (1991).

31. "[T]he clerk of court shall, at the time the action is filed, notify the parties of their right to consent to the exercise of such jurisdiction. The decision of the parties shall be communicated to the clerk of court. Thereafter, neither the district judge nor the magistrate shall attempt to persuade or induce any party to consent to reference of any civil matter to a magistrate." 28 U.S.C. sec. 626(c)(2) (1982).

32. At least 36 district courts referred civil cases to magistrates for trial before Congress explicitly endorsed this practice with the 1979 Act. *H.R. Rep. No. 1364, supra* n. 18, at 4.

33. *See* Smith, "Assessing the Consequences of Judicial Innovation: U.S. Magistrates' Trials and Related Tribulations," *Wake Forest L. Rev.* 23 (1988), 455, 474–476.

34. *See* Smith, *supra* n. 10, at 85–87.

35. One former magistrate described the old statutory notice provision as "unworkable on its face" because the notice was frequently attached to the summons and "such boilerplate is commonly ignored." Sinclair, *Practice Before Federal Magistrates* sec. 2303 (New York: Matthew Bender, 1987).

36. In the districts in which magistrates were used as "Additional Judges," the practicing bar became familiar with the individual magistrates and knowledgeable about their authority. Thus there was greater willingness to consent. *See* Seron, *The Roles of Magistrates, supra* n. 9, at 38–39.

37. *H.R. Rep. No. 1364, supra* n. 18, at 14.

38. Seron, *The Roles of Magistrates, supra* n. 9, at 61–62.

39. Smith, *supra* n. 10, at 103–104.

40. Ibid. at 180.

41. Ibid.

42. 28 U.S.C. sec. 471 (1991).

43. For a detailed typology of eight possible model roles for magistrates, *see* Smith, *supra* n. 10, at 127–132.

44. Ibid. at 115–119; *see* Seron, "The Professional Project of Parajudges: The Case of the U.S. Magistrates," *Law & Soc'y Rev.* 22 (1988), 557.

45. Smith, *supra* n. 10, at 140–141.

46. *See* Seron, *The Roles of Magistrates, supra* n. 9, at 83–92.

47. Administrative Office of the U.S. Courts, *Annual Report of the Director of the Administrative Office of the U.S. Courts* (1986), 180.

48. *See* Mezey, *No Longer Disabled: The Federal Courts and the Politics of Social Security Disability* (New York: Greenwood, 1988).

49. Administrative Office, *supra* n. 6, at 138.

50. Administrative Office, *supra* n. 47, at 179.

51. Administrative Office, *supra* n. 6, at 138.

52. Ibid.

53. *See* Zeigler & Hermann, "The Invisible Litigant: An Inside View of Pro Se Actions in the Federal Courts," *N.Y.U. L. Rev.* 47 (1972), 157.

54. Cohen, "Prisoners in 1990," *Bureau of Justice Statistics Bulletin* 1 (May 1991). Increases in prisoner filings are not purely a function of increases in prison populations. *See* Thomas, Keeler & Harris, "Issues and Misconceptions in Prisoner Litigation: A Critical View," *Criminology* 24 (1986), 775.

55. *See, e.g., McCleskey v. Zant,* 111 S.Ct. 2841 (1991) (failure to raise claim in initial habeas corpus petition in federal courts barred subsequent petition concerning claim); *Coleman v. Thompson,* 111 S.Ct. 2546 (1991) (procedural default under state court rules barred raising claim in subsequent federal court habeas corpus petition).

56. In a concurring opinion in *Duckworth v. Eagan*, 109 S.Ct. 2875 (1989), Justice O'Connor argued that the Supreme Court should emulate its decision in *Stone v. Powell*, 428 U.S. 465 (1976), which precludes federal court consideration of habeas corpus "exclusionary rule" claims that have been previously raised in state courts, by similarly precluding federal court review of *Miranda* claims.

57. *See* Diemer, "Blood for blood: Senate focuses upon fighting crime," *Cleveland Plain Dealer,* June 30, 1991, at 15-A.

58. Administrative Office, *supra* n. 6, at 25, 140.

59. Ibid.

60. Ibid. at 24.

61. Ibid. at 25.

62. *See* Smith, *supra* n. 10, at 69–75, 182–187.

Law clerks: their roles and relationships with their judges

David Crump

Although nearly everyone agrees that law clerks are necessary,
there is considerable disagreement as to what their role should be.

To some people, law clerks are part of a long and noble tradition. To a few others, they are 25-year-old Svengalis influencing the judicial process toward views inculcated into them by a phalanx of activist law professors.

In any event, nearly everyone views law clerks as necessary. Justice John Paul Stevens has said that the Supreme Court is "too busy to decide whether there [is] anything we could do about the problem of being too busy." [1] And United States District Court Judge Norman Black, whose docket is roughly double the national average and who has managed, through hard work, only to hold down the amount of its annual increase, says simply: "I couldn't function without them." [2]

For the law clerk, the experience is likely to be a high point in his or her legal career. "It was wonderful," says Sal Levatino, a former law clerk to a federal district judge in Austin, Texas. "It really ought to be at the end of your career, rather than at the beginning." [3] In fact, law clerks speak of "law clerk letdown" when they begin practicing law. The clerkship represented a "pure" experience with the law, constantly exciting—and without the risk of failure. [4]

In contrast, the practice of law itself involves clients with unrealistic expectations, cases or transactions that don't turn very fast, and work that is more often tedious than exciting. To the law clerk's surprise, the possibilities of missing time deadlines, failing to get evidence admitted, or making any one of a variety of similar mistakes aren't something that happens to lesser practitioners. They are very real dangers for the inexperienced—such as a lawyer fresh from a judicial clerkship.

The clerk's duties

The functions of law clerks vary tremendously. A few judges use them as research assistants only. For other judges they may perform a screening function: summarizing the contents of papers filed by the parties in the manner of an honest broker. Still others—and these are clearly the majority—use law clerks as preliminary drafters of opinions or orders. The amount of direction supplied to a clerk drafting an opinion varies enormously from judge to judge.

In a trial court, as Judge Black points out, more than 90 percent of cases are typically settled. [5] A federal district judge may well find that he can use his clerks most effectively in motion practice, because prompt, simple rulings on motions make the cases settle faster, more cheaply, and more fairly. A typical district judge may assign each of his clerks half the docket by odd and even numbers, having them coordinate with the district clerk's office to study each motion as soon as possible after its submission date. [6]

Screening of each motion for complexity and for the need for a hearing is the typical first step. As the judge considers each motion, informal discussion with the law clerk—or a memorandum prepared by the clerk, probably with a recommendation—highlights the issues (the practice varies). The judge may then orally outline the chosen disposition and discuss the general content of the order or memorandum the clerk is to prepare. If the motion does require a hearing or a conference, the assigned law clerk is likely to be made responsible for coordinating with the district clerk's office to see that it is properly scheduled. At trial, a law clerk's functions may range from assistance in charge preparation to on-the-spot research on evidence questions. And if an opinion results, the first draft will probably be written by the law clerk.

In appellate courts, law clerks' time is often largely occupied in preparing pre-argument memoranda and writing initial drafts of opinions. In courts of last resort with discretionary review, clerks often have significant (some would say, excessive) functions in deciding which cases will be heard.

The influence of clerks

There is no question among former law clerks now practicing law that the decision of their own cases can be influenced or even determined by the judgments of law clerks. Should a lawyer use different tactics if he is trying a case before a trial judge with a full complement of clerks? Former Supreme Court clerk John O'Neill says that if the judge relies heavily on his clerks, "It's important to appeal to *their* imagination." [7] In that endeavor, says O'Neill, "You'd make more academic and policy arguments." [8] Before a judge without clerks, the lawyer might do well to put more emphasis on explaining the case law. Former state appellate law clerk Rob Johnson says, "You'd play to the sympathies of the person who's really" going to report on the case.[9] Following his law school training, the law clerk may be more likely than the judge to see the case as controlled by social policy.

But Mike Kuhn,[10] a former Fifth Circuit clerk, disagrees. "There are too many variables," he says. "I don't think I'd stress public policy just because the judge has law clerks; the clerk himself might be more interested in *stare decisis*." Besides, he points out, it's risky to "play to the clerks" when the judge is still the one who makes the final decision.[11]

But whether the law clerk performs a research function, a screening or "filtering" function, or a drafting or recommending function, the judgment factor is there. And even though the judge "is the judge," and remains so, the judgment of the law clerk is frequently an ingredient in the decision.

To some observers, this "leavening effect" is a positive thing. "In our ideal form," writes John B. Oakley, a former law clerk to a judge of the Supreme Court of California, "the law clerk is meant to fiddle with the law, to advocate innovation, to introduce to its inner sanctums the views of those outside." [12] Oakley's work, *Law Clerks and the Judicial Process* (co-authored with Robert S. Thompson), is the most comprehensive recent work on the subject. The law clerk "gives the law needed capacity for change," [13] Oakley and Thompson write. "[T]he fabric of the law has been woven from the warp of the judiciary and the woof of their law clerks." [14] This metaphor depicts the judge as the lengthwise thread (or warp) in the weave of the law and the clerk as its crosswise thread (or woof). If there are to be "passing variations in texture and elasticity," says Oakley and Thompson, "they must be woven into the fabric by means of the woof." [15] And in what they correctly acknowledge is a very bad pun, Oakley and Thompson argue that the law clerk should be "a fiddler in the woof." [16]

In a written opinion, the Fifth Circuit has provided some support for this model. "The association with law clerks is also valuable to the judge; in addition to relieving him of many clerical and administrative chores, law clerks may serve as sounding boards for new ideas, often affording a different perspective. . . .," said the court in *Fredonia Broadcasting Corporation v. RCA Corporation*.[17] Judge Frank M. Coffin, in his book *The Ways of a Judge,* adds that law clerks "bring to chambers their recent exposure to excellent professors in demanding schools of law from all parts of the country. They are questioning, articulate, idealistic." As a result, they "provide the judge with a continuing seminar that cannot fail to keep his mind open and his mental juices flowing." [18]

Oakley and Thompson point out that the historical ideal of the law clerk fits the warp-and-woof metaphor too.[19] Felix Frankfurter was given to lengthy substantive discussions with his law clerks, in which "[a]nger, scorn, [and] humor buttressed straightforward argument." [20] The law clerk was placed "on an equal footing" with the judge in the "ecstasy of combat." [21]

Oakley and Thompson recognize that the judge must make the final decisions. But this result, they argue, will flow from "the judge's natural resistance to the influence of a young and fleeting law clerk." [22] In fact, Oakley and Thompson conclude, a greater problem may be that the judge's thinking wins out merely because of his position and tenure. For that reason, they say, the law clerk will have a proper incentive to "fight the judge for every inch of fair ground." [23]

A different view

But to others, this "ideal" is not so attractive. They point out that the law clerk is not appointed by the president, is not confirmed by the Senate, and has not been qualified under the Constitution to perform judicial functions.

Oakley and Thompson's statement that law clerks are innovators who fiddle with the law and provide it with capacity for change is hotly disputed by most former law clerks interviewed for this article. "That's naive," says O'Neill.[24] He points out that most activist judges do not need the intervention of law clerks to make them into innovators. "What about Mr. Justice Douglas?" he asks. "The function of the law clerk ought to be to find what the law is," he says. "And a lawyer who's practiced a long time [*i.e.,* the judge] ought to make the policy decisions." [25]

Rob Johnson, who was the single clerk for a state appellate court with three judges back in the days when "I'm not sure we even had an electric typewriter," is more blunt. "I don't like the idea of wild-eyed 24- and 25-year-olds, who come right out of law school, tinkering with the law in a way that might affect my life," he says.[26] And Judge Black (who teaches in law school himself) disagrees with the notion that a judge's chambers are "an ivory tower" that needs a recently graduated lawyer to provide "a pipeline to reality." [27] Judge Black has a simple answer to the model of the law clerk as "innovator:" "I've seen the argument made," he says. "I've never seen it put into effect." [28]

In addition to the law clerk's lack of constitutional authority, there are at least two other reasons for opposing a decision-making role. One is the effect of the law clerk's education. Harvard law student Alexander Troy describes his first year torts class (which, it is to be hoped, was atypical) as "a desultory survey of economics, epistemology and social psychology, but the professor also found time to address the issue of the limits of a court's power in a democratic society." [29] That issue, according to Troy, was resolved by the professor's conclusion that "[j]udicial decisions are substantively indistinguishable from legislative ones." Thus the "inference left for students to draw is that there is little a court cannot do." [30] Many judges may feel a need to counteract the pronouncements of some of Troy's professors who, he says, were critical of judicial restraint as a general principle.[31]

The merit of this view is not really the issue; the point is that, for the judge himself, presidential appointment and Senate hearings—or election, in a state system—provide an acceptable filtering process as well as a reminder of the separation of powers. But as Rob Johnson says: "A law clerk, all he's done is get good grades in law school." [32]

The second reason against the law clerk as decision-maker is experience, both in law and in life. Law clerks are less likely to have had mortgages—or children whom they must decide to send to either public or private school. "They don't see the tugs and pulls; they don't see the results down at the end of the line," says Johnson.[33] He points out that "school cases just look different when you haven't got school-age kids and neither do any of your close friends. So does freedom of speech when you don't have a home that might have an x-rated movie across from it." [34] What is more, a 25-year-old may not realize that such experiences are likely to mature his outlook. The "fiddler in the woof" viewpoint might regard this inexperience as a net plus, characterizing it as a fresh approach; a less positive view would see the lack of self-knowledge as a negative factor.

And in the law itself, lack of experience is likely to reflect itself in harmful naivete. The difficulty of pre-

serving error for appeal, of maintaining a trial schedule, and even of presenting the bodies of one's witnesses physically at the trial may be unknown to law clerks. The proposition that an error-free criminal trial is unusual may be differently perceived by those who have seen trials firsthand and those who have seen them only in law school casebooks, through what Mr. Justice Fortas once called the "remote knothole" of appellate decisions.[35]

As Levatino puts it, even the law clerk's job itself is "somewhat deceptive." [36] As a law clerk, one might draft an opinion in a case presented by attorneys, "And you say, 'hey, this is easy.' " But "it's harder to have clients come into your office and dump something on your desk and ask if there's something you can do, when you can't even tell if it's a securities case, or a labor matter, or what." As a result, says Levatino, "If I went back now, 13 years later, I'd have a whole lot more empathy for the attorneys." [37]

The difference between the "fiddler and innovator" argument, and the opposing view (as expressed by Johnson) that the law clerk's job "is to do what he's told to," can easily be exaggerated.[38] Most law clerks acknowledge that delegation by judges to clerks of the task of writing a first draft of an opinion is common. If the judge handles the delegation properly, and deals adequately with the result, the judge remains the decisionmaker.

And former Fifth Circuit law clerk Michael Kuhn, although not himself in favor of judicial activism, defends the law clerk's prerogative. "A law clerk has a right and a duty to express his views," he says. "If you think your judge has missed a point, if he's off base, it's your job to say, 'Judge, you're deciding this case as though it were a rule-of-reason case and it's not; it's a per se violation.' " [39] Other law clerks give examples of occasions, in fact, in which law clerks have restrained judicial activism (or even prevented unfortunate displays of anger by judges with hair-trigger tempers).

The other side of the coin, says Kuhn, is that the law clerk "shouldn't be offended if his recommendation isn't adopted." If the judge replies, "I don't care; I think the rule of reason is the better way to decide this case," Kuhn concludes that the law clerk ought to draft a good, sound opinion—"using the rule of reason, as the judge said." [40]

Using law clerks well

Since law clerks are here to stay, the real question concerns the way a judge ought to go about using them.

Lawyers and law clerks have a variety of opinions on the subject.

The number of law clerks. Each United States Supreme Court justice presides over a law firm of four clerks. Each federal court of appeals judge has three, and California's chief justice has an astounding 14 (although many of their duties are performed for the court as a whole or for other justices).

The suspicion arises that a plethora of law clerks dilutes the judge's ability to make the important decisions. Former district court clerk Tom Houghton thinks even a lawyer who is a good manager "can't personally supervise more than three or four associates." [41] And if he is not a good manager, he may supervise one law clerk poorly. With numbers like 14, intermediate managers are required, says Houghton. In such a situation, asks Johnson, "Does the judge write any opinions at all? It sounds as though they wouldn't have time. They'd be reading reams of paper from their law clerks." [42]

But busy judges without adequate assistance from clerks draw criticism too. As Levatino says, a conscientious judge working alone in a complex case "may not even have time to read all of the briefs." [43]

Length of opinions. One consequence of the number of law clerks is an opinion explosion. United States Supreme Court Reports have gone from 2133 pages in the 1960 October term to 4269 in the 1983 term, not so much because of workload as because of the length of individual opinions. "When the opinions start looking like law review articles, you know you're in trouble," says one former law clerk.

The result is an increase in complexity—a proliferation of conflicting opinions—all without the benefit of the consistency and certainty that are the apparent aim. While it is desirable that judges express the reasons for their decisions as a means of encouraging rational decision making, there is little utility in a district court summary judgment opinion that contains a treatise on Rule 56. Former trial court clerk Levatino says flatly, "most trial level cases don't require opinions." [44] Findings and conclusions would be preferable from a functional standpoint. And Houghton points out that the great appellate judges of the past—Hand, Cardozo and Holmes—wrote long opinions when it was necessary, "but most of their opinions are a page and a half in the reporter system." [45]

The types of opinions law clerks may produce is also a matter of concern. Dan Peterson, a former law clerk on the Iowa Supreme Court, suspects that law clerks left to their own devices might draft "opinions that are full of global statements that you don't need to support the holding and don't apply as globally as they're written." These statements "muddle things in the next case and have to be distinguished." [46] A judge's experience, Peterson thinks, would help him avoid that sort of writing and eliminate it from a law clerk's preliminary draft.

Discretionary review. In courts of last resort or other courts with discretionary review, there is heavy reliance on law clerks in the selection of cases for decision. For example, it is an open secret (reported in the newspapers) that at least six Supreme Court justices rely on one designated law clerk to summarize each certiorari petition. "I do not even look at the papers in over 80 percent of the cases that are filed," Justice Stevens has publicly stated. [47]

Former Supreme Court clerk O'Neill points out that when law clerks perform such a task, "they may reflect values learned in law school, not over a career." Hence the problems they may find significant are "the ones they've been taught about, not the great practical ones that you'd identify over 10 years of practice." [48] Issues that O'Neill calls "interstitial"—crucial issues in energy, finance, or similar areas that determine the fate of the nation just as surely as do constitutional questions—may not commend themselves to a law clerk's imagination simply because they are not the subject of any law school course. [49]

It is probably inevitable that discretionary review will prompt heavy reliance on clerks, because the task is tedious. The supreme courts of Texas and California also rely heavily upon law clerk involvement. Anonymously poring over reams of dross to discover one case for review is obviously less satisfying than crafting a signed opinion, and a judge may not regard it as the most productive use of his time.

But because they are more experienced lawyers, with longer memories for recurring issues, judges can provide a corrective to the syndrome of selection by law school course content. The judge can do so by express direction to his clerk, by discussions exposing "law clerk's bias" to the law clerk himself, or by a final review in which the judge consciously tries to counteract the fact that he is, to a degree, the prisoner of his law clerk's education.

Guidance, supervision, and orientation. A good many law clerks learn about office policies of the judge through trial and error. A few judges have had success in the use of office manuals or memoranda explaining the job to new arrivals. Given the planned turnover of clerks, such a practice might be a good management tool. In a district court, identification of various procedures (different kinds of motions, jury charge preparation, etc.) and the approach the judge uses on each would shorten the learning curve—and not incidentally, would help the judge to promulgate his own decisions. In appellate courts, a written explanation of standards for the court's summary docket, methodology in handling motions, and like matters would be just as helpful.

There is, in fact, a "Law Clerk Handbook," published by the Federal Judicial Center; certain states have published similar aids. Ranging from the general to the specific, the Handbook covers such topics as the history of law clerks (the tradition was begun at the Supreme Court by Justice Horace Gray in 1882 and continued by his successor, Oliver Wendell Holmes) to telephone etiquette ("If the judge is . . . unavailable, you should inquire, 'May I take a message?' ").[50] Its coverage of procedure, drafting tips, and organization appears quite useful. It is necessarily general, and its usefulness would be enhanced if individual judges rewrote it to reflect their own practices (having their law clerks, of course, do the drafting!).

There are early limits to the usefulness of this idea; many practices in a court are "not suitable for a memorandum," as former district court clerk Tom Houghton puts it.[51] "What it takes is treatment of the clerk the way a senior lawyer uses an associate," with individual day-to-day attention recognizing that the law clerk needs supervision.[52]

Another suggestion is that law schools might provide courses in their curricula for future law clerks. For example, a one-hour course based upon the "Law Clerk Handbook" (and other materials) is under active consideration at the South Texas College of Law, which in 1985 supplied more clerks to the Texas Supreme Court than any other school. There is some question, however, whether it is feasible thus to prepare clerks for such diverse environments as federal trial courts and state appellate courts—and for an infinite variety of individual judges' preferences. Furthermore, some academics doubt that a law school's resources should be expended in a way that will guide so few students for such a brief period in their careers. Still, the proposal is worth trying because of its possible public benefits.

An alternative suggestion of a national orientation program, perhaps conducted by the Federal Judicial Center, might offer some benefits, but they are not likely to justify the costs.

Management styles. Many former clerks are skeptical of proposals for periodic staff meetings, believing them to be ineffective in a small office handling highly individualized problems. But if the office handles a large volume of matters—a district court with a large backlog, for example, or a court of last resort that has a considerable discretionary docket—staff meetings in which the status of each case is reviewed may make dispositions more efficient. Similarly, if the judge has more than three or four law clerks, staff meetings may be necessary to reinforce the policies the judge wants followed.

Both judges and clerks seem to regard a one-on-one relationship as preferable. A "committee" or "intermediate manager" approach may be necessary in a larger office, however, and the trial of a larger case may require the services of more than one clerk. In normal operations, most judges and clerks view direct supervision of the clerk by the judge as more efficient. It also seems clear that this management style is best for reasons unrelated to efficiency: it maximizes control of actual decision making by the judge, and it avoids the dilution of his personal responsibility for each case.

Confidentiality and the appearance of propriety. Most law clerks probably recognize that public identification of the law clerk as a decisionmaker is undesirable. Most probably come to the task with an appreciation that what they see and hear is privileged. "I'm their client," says Judge Black. "They're my lawyers."[53] The "Law Clerk Handbook" is explicit and eloquent on the subject: "If judges wish to publish their jurisprudential, economic or social views, they know how to do so."[54]

But unfortunately, the available evidence indicates that understanding of these concepts is neither innate nor universal among law clerks. Furthermore, says Houghton, "the judge needs to emphasize that the need for circumspection goes on after the clerkship is over." "*The Brethren*[55] is inexcusable," he says.[56] Such disclosures come about because law clerks "sometimes come out of clerkships with bloated heads" and with a need to expand upon their roles in major decisions.[57] (It might be added that if one has doubt that the maturity of law clerks is a real concern, one might consider *The Brethren*—and the hemorrhage of confidential disclosures it reflects—a strong piece of evidence to that effect.)

One trial lawyer tells a related story that is equally disconcerting. While interviewing a prospective new associate, he mentioned a case he had recently tried. "Oh," said the interviewee, "That was John Smith's case." John Smith (a fictitious name) was the judge's law clerk; he had drafted the opinion. The interviewee, a former clerk himself, was apparently unaware that such disclosures do not serve the judge who trusted his circumspection. To the trial lawyer (who, of course, thought it was *his* case), it meant a more jaundiced view of the court. This was especially so since John Smith hadn't been in the courtroom when the case was orally argued, leaving the lawyer to conclude that, if the case was indeed "John Smith's," his arguments were not heard.

The subject is difficult, because courts are a part of the government. And a blanket prohibition upon law clerks talking to reporters would be inappropriate, for the same reason that it would be inappropriate to impose a gag upon personnel in other governmental offices. The important issue is one of confidentiality and deference to the judge.

A personal relationship

There is another side to the law clerk issue. Judges benefit personally from relationships with their law clerks, and not just because they need clerks' research skills. The job of a judge, strictly defined, is solitary and remote. If we are to attract good judges, perhaps we must consider the need that lawyers and judges have in common with most of the human race: the need for a collegial atmosphere, in which one's work is shared with other people.

For the best of the profession—the sort of lawyers we would like to attract to the judiciary—the job doesn't pay well in comparison to private practice. And as Judge Black points out, "Making decisions is hard work." [58] For that reason, Judge Black points out, emotional and mental maturity in a law clerk applicant is a primary qualification; there's "nothing to assure you," as he puts it, "that a person with a 98.5 grade average will be a good law clerk." [59]

The old adage holds that a federal judge is just a lawyer who knows a senator. But as far as almost every law clerk is concerned, *his* judge is extraordinary. Talking to Judge Black, one senses immediately that the affection is usually mutual—and that relationships with law clerks can sometimes go a long way toward fill-

ing the compensation gap. As Judge Coffin puts it, "[T]he pleasure of their company is one of a judge's most refreshing fringe benefits." [60]

Notes

This article originally appeared in Volume 69, Number 4, December–January 1986, pages 236–240.

1. Middleton, "High Court's Case Load too Heavy: Three Justices," *A.B.A. J.* 68 (October 1982), 1201.
2. Interview with Judge Norman Black, United States District Court, in Houston, Texas (December 1, 1982).
3. Telephone interview with Sal Levatino, former law clerk (October 21, 1982).
4. Ibid.
5. Interview Black, *supra* n. 2.
6. Ibid.
7. Interview with John O'Neill, former law clerk, in Houston, Texas (October 21, 1982).
8. Ibid.
9. Interview with Rob Johnson, former law clerk, in Houston, Texas (October 21, 1982).
10. Interview with Mike Kuhn, former law clerk, in Houston, Texas (October 21, 1982).
11. Ibid.
12. Oakley and Thompson, *Law Clerks and the Judicial Process* (Berkeley: University of California Press, 1980), 138.
13. Ibid.
14. Ibid.
15. Ibid.
16. Ibid.
17. *Fredonia Broadcasting Corp. v. RCA Corp.*, 569 F.2d 251, 255–256 (5th Cir. 1978).
18. Coffin, *The Ways of a Judge* (Boston: Houghton Mifflin Co., 1980), 72.
19. Oakley and Thompson, *supra* n. 12, at 138.
20. Sacks, "Felix Frankfurter," in 3 *The Justices of the United States Supreme Court 1789–1969* (New York: Chelsea House in association with Bowker Company, 1969), 2403–2404.
21. Ibid.
22. Oakley and Thompson, *supra* n. 12, at 38.
23. Ibid.
24. Interview O'Neill, *supra* n. 7.
25. Ibid.
26. Interview Johnson, *supra* n. 9.
27. Interview Black, *supra* n. 2.
28. Ibid.
29. Troy, "Learning the Law at Harvard," *Wall St. J.*, August 6, 1982, at 14 col. 2.
30. Ibid.
31. Ibid. at col. 3.
32. Interview Johnson, *supra* n. 9.

33. Ibid.

34. Ibid.

35. *Time Inc. v. Hill,* 385 U.S. 374 (1967).

36. Interview Levatino, *supra* n. 3.

37. Ibid.

38. Interview Johnson, *supra* n. 9.

39. Interview Kuhn, *supra* n. 10.

40. Ibid.

41. Interview with Tom Houghton, former law clerk, in Houston, Texas (October 27, 1982)

42. Interview Johnson, *supra* n. 9.

43. Interview Levatino, *supra* n. 3.

44. Ibid.

45. Interview Houghton, *supra* n. 41.

46. Interview with Dan Peterson, former law clerk, in Houston, Texas (October 21, 1982).

47. Middleton, *supra* n. 1, at 1201.

48. Interview O'Neill, *supra* n. 7.

49. Ibid.

50. Dileo and Rubin, *Law Clerk Handbook: A Handbook for Federal District and Appellate Court Law Clerks* (Washington, D.C.: Federal Judicial Center, 1977).

51. Interview Houghton, *supra* n. 41.

52. Ibid.

53. Interview Black, *supra* n. 2.

54. Dileo and Rubin, *supra* n. 50.

55. Woodward and Armstrong, *The Brethren: Inside the Supreme Court* (New York: Simon and Schuster, 1979).

56. Interview Houghton, *supra* n. 41.

57. Ibid.

58. Interview Black, *supra* n. 2.

59. Ibid.

60. Coffin, *supra* n. 18, at 71.

Legal information vs. legal advice: developments during the last five years

John M. Greacen

The increase in self-represented litigants nationwide heightens the need for assistance from courts and their staff.

In 1995 my article "No Legal Advice From Court Personnel What Does That Mean?"[1] was the first published attempt to examine critically the standard court instruction to staff not to give legal advice. It explored legal and practical definitions of the term "legal advice" and suggested guidelines a court could give staff members on what answers they can and cannot provide. This article reviews that article's discussion and recommendations, as well as developments during the past five years.

"No Legal Advice" argued that the phrase "legal advice" had no inherent meaning to the courts or to court staff who were required to interpret it. The use of a vague term has negative consequences for the courts and the public; it causes staff to limit unnecessarily the flow of information to the public about court operations and it creates opportunities for discrimination among different categories of court users. The article addressed the concerns that cause courts to prohibit their staffs from providing information about court processes to the public—concerns about their "practicing law," about their giving incorrect information, and about their binding the judge by such incorrect information. It articulated five general principles that court staff should keep in mind in answering questions:

1. Court staff have an obligation to explain court processes and procedures to litigants, the media, and other interested citizens.

2. Court staff have an obligation to inform litigants, and potential litigants, how to bring their problems before the court for resolution.

3. Court staff cannot advise litigants whether to bring their problems before the court, or what remedies to seek.

4. Court staff must always remember the absolute duty of impartiality. They must never give advice or information for the purpose of giving one party an advantage over another. They must never give advice or information to one party that they would not give to an opponent.

5. Court staff should be mindful of the basic principle that neither parties nor their attorneys may communicate with the judge *ex parte*. Court staff should not let themselves be used to circumvent that principle by conveying information to a judge on behalf of a litigant, or fail to respect it in acting on matters delegated to them for decision.

Finally, the article suggested 11 guidelines for staff to use in responding to questions. The first six are positive statements. All staff are expected to perform the following tasks:

1. Provide information contained in docket reports, case files, indexes and other reports.

2. Answer questions concerning court rules, procedures, and ordinary practices. Such questions often contain the words "Can I?" or "How do I?"

3. Provide examples of forms or pleadings for the guidance of litigants.

4. Answer questions about the completion of forms.

5. Explain the meaning of terms and documents used in the court process.

6. Answer questions concerning deadlines or due dates.

The last five are negative statements. In providing information, staff will not:

1. Give information when you are unsure of the correct answer. Transfer such questions to supervisors.

2. Advise litigants whether to take a particular course of action. Do not answer questions that contain

Judicature Volume 84, Number 4, pp. 198–204

the words "Should I?" Suggest that questioners refer such issues to a lawyer.

3. Take sides in a case or proceeding pending before the court.

4. Provide information to one party that you would be unwilling or unable to provide to all other parties.

5. Disclose the outcome of a matter submitted to a judge for decision until the outcome is part of the public record, or until the judge directs disclosure of the matter.

Responses to the article

Many judges and court managers used the article and its recommendations in creating policies and training for court staff. And a court manager from Canada reported that it is the standard reference point for the courts of Canada as well. I have conducted training sessions for court administrators and court staff based on the principles set forth in the article in both federal and state courts throughout the country. The guidelines have been included in the curriculum of the "Litigant Without Lawyers" seminars presented by the Maricopa County Superior Court and in educational sessions at conferences of the National Association for Court Management and its Mid Atlantic Association for Court Management.

The Michigan Court Support Training Consortium, under a grant from the Michigan Judicial Institute, developed an interactive training program using compact disk interactive technology, called the Legal Advice CD-i program, based on the principles set forth in the article. That training program has been widely used by courts in other states and received the Justice Achievement Award from the National Association for Court Management in 1998.

Several states have adopted their own guidelines derived from those suggested in the article.

- In 1997, the Michigan Judicial Institute prepared and distributed a booklet entitled, *Legal Advice v. Access to the Courts: Do YOU Know the Difference?* The booklet provides general guidelines, together with specific applications of those guidelines through the use of questions and answers. The booklet was endorsed by the Michigan Supreme Court as a model for providing information to the public and access to the Michigan court system.

- In June 1998, the New Mexico Supreme Court adopted a standard notice entitled "Information Available from the Clerk's Office." It requires all courts to post that notice "in lieu of any other notices pertaining to the topic of information or advice that court staff may or may not provide." The notice sets forth the information that court staff can and cannot provide and includes information on how to find a lawyer; New Jersey has created a similar notice.

- In November, 1998, the Ventura County Superior Court adopted guidelines for its employees staffing its Self Help Legal Access Center.

- The Supreme Court of Florida, with one dissent, has adopted a rule of court, Florida Family Law Rule 12.750, entitled "Family Self Help Programs," that sets forth the services that court "self help" staff can and cannot provide.

- A Customer Service Advisory Committee for the Judicial Branch, created by order of the Iowa Supreme Court, has developed *Guidelines for Clerks Who Assist Pro Se Litigants in Iowa's Courts.* The Iowa Supreme Court recently approved the guidelines. The Advisory Committee also developed a guidebook for clerks containing 25 pages of model responses to frequently asked questions.

- A Task Force on Unrepresented Litigants of the Boston Bar Association conducted a comprehensive study of the needs of self-represented litigants in all levels of courts in Massachusetts. Its August 1998 *Report on Pro Se Litigation* is one of the most thorough treatments of the topic, including extensive recommendations to the courts and the bar for improving their programs. Exhibit F of that report is a set of "Sample Staff Guidelines" for Massachusetts courts.

- Finally, in 2000, the Utah Judicial Council adopted guidelines for all court staff in that state.

Critiques

Jona Goldschmidt and his colleagues have criticized the suggested guidelines on two grounds. First, they believe that the article does not go far enough in its analysis of the court's obligation to provide information to the public. The United States Constitution, through the privileges and immunities clause, the First Amendment, or the due process or equal protection clauses of the Fourteenth Amendment, may create a fundamental right of access to the courts for persons representing themselves.[2]

The closest that any U.S. Supreme Court opinion has come in articulating such a broad right of access is Justice Brennan's concurring opinion in *Boddie v. Connecticut* (1971), finding that Connecticut's mandatory filing fee for divorce cases violated an indigent person's right to due process. Justice Brennan objected to language in the majority opinion limiting the reach of the decision to divorce proceedings—"the exclusive precondition to the adjustment of a fundamental human relationship." Justice Brennan wrote:

> I cannot join the Court's opinion insofar as today's holding is made to depend upon the factor that only the State can grant a divorce and that an indigent would be locked into a marriage if unable to pay the fees required to obtain a divorce. A State has an ultimate monopoly of all judicial process and attendant enforcement machinery. As a practical matter, if disputes cannot be successfully settled between the parties, the court system is usually 'the only forum effectively empowered to settle their disputes. Resort to the judicial process by these plaintiffs is no more voluntary in a realistic sense than that of the defendant called upon to defend his interests in court.' . . . I see no constitutional distinction between appellants' attempts to enforce this statutory right and an attempt to vindicate any other right arising under federal or state law. . . . The right to be heard in some way at some time extends to all proceedings entertained by courts.

If there is such a right of access to the courts, then, argues Goldschmidt and colleagues, the courts must provide information sufficient to enable self-represented persons to exercise that right.

The significant and as-yet-unanswered question is whether self-represented litigants' rights obligate the state to take affirmative steps to provide them with some form of "adequate" legal assistance. Until a definitive ruling on this question is made, courts should—if only for efficiency reasons—begin (or continue) to develop creative means of guiding the increasing number of self-represented litigants through the legal process.[3]

Second, Goldschmidt and colleagues argue that the guidelines are too general in nature. They believe that court staff need explicit direction on the answers to be given to specific questions, not just general direction differentiating legal information from legal advice. All

courts owe their staff the support of an operating manual, describing basic court operations and instructing them how to handle routine matters. These materials, in turn, serve as a reference for staff in answering questions from the public. The most extensive manual of this sort that I have seen is the *Clerk's Practice and Procedure Guide* developed by the United States Bankruptcy Court for the District of New Mexico. The judges of the court instructed the clerk to develop the manual in order to give lawyers who did not specialize in bankruptcy law the basic information they would need to practice before the court. With the help of a committee of the local bankruptcy bar, the court prepared a manual detailing the court's procedures with respect to all parts of the bankruptcy process. The manual is available to the public. It also serves as a resource for court staff in answering questions posed by the public.

A knowledgeable staff

My experience in providing training on this topic all over the country has convinced me that lack of staff knowledge of procedures is not a significant impediment to the ability of court staff to provide information to the public. In training sessions I ask participants to write down the questions they have the most difficulty answering and use them as the basis for the discussion. I ask for volunteers to answer the questions, following my suggested guidelines. Experience has shown that court staff are extraordinarily knowledgeable about court procedures, requirements, and practices. With one exception, some participant in every seminar has been able to provide the procedural or substantive information needed to answer a question. The exception was in Delaware, where all participants agreed there was no answer to a particular question—their case management information system did not provide the requested information.

My experience suggests, therefore, that court staff throughout this country *know the correct answers* to the questions they are asked by the public. Consequently, courts should not delay authorizing their staff to provide procedural information until they develop detailed guidebooks or reference materials.

As additional courts develop rules and guidelines, they are becoming more detailed. See, for instance, the elaboration provided by the Florida rule of court and the draft Iowa guidelines. In addition, the drafters of the Iowa guidelines have included a substantial number of standard answers to frequently asked questions.

Suggested answers to recurring questions

Here are some of the most common questions presented by participants in seminars on this topic, and suggested answers:

Do I need a lawyer?

You are not required to have a lawyer to file papers or to participate in a case in court. You have the right to represent yourself. Whether to hire a lawyer must be your personal decision. You may want to consider how important the outcome of this case is to you in making that decision. A lawyer may not cost as much as you think. I have information on the Lawyer Referral Service if you want help in finding a lawyer who specializes in your kind of case. [Lawyers participating in the Albuquerque Bar Association lawyer referral service offer one half hour of consultation for $25 plus tax.]

Should I hire a lawyer?

Same as above.

Can you give me the name of a good lawyer?

The court cannot recommend a particular lawyer. I have information on the Lawyer Referral Service if you want help in finding a lawyer who specializes in your kind of case.

Should I plead guilty?

You need to decide that for yourself.

What sentence will I get if I plead guilty [or do not plead guilty]?

The judge will decide what sentence to impose based on the facts and the law that apply to your case. I cannot predict what the judge will do.

What will happen in court?

Suggested answer to a plaintiff in a small claims case: The judge will call on you to present your evidence first. Then [he][she] will call on the other side to present its evidence. The judge will ask questions if [he][she] needs clarification. When the judge has heard all the evidence, [he][she] will announce [his][her] decision.

What should I say in court?

You must tell the truth.

How do I get the money that the judge said I am entitled to?

You are responsible for taking the steps necessary to enforce a judgment (or an award of child support). Here is a pamphlet that describes the procedural options available to you. When you decide what option to pursue, I can provide you with the appropriate forms. [It may be appropriate to refer a litigant to an agency for help, e.g, with child support enforcement.]

What should I put in this section of the form?

You should write down what happened in your own words.

What should I put down here where it says "remedy sought"?

You should write in your own words what you want the court to do.

Would you look over this form and tell me if I did it right?

You have provided all of the required information. I cannot tell you whether the information you have provided is correct or complete; only you know whether it is correct and complete.

I am not able to read or write. Would you fill out the form for me?

In that case, I am able to fill out the form for you, but you have to tell me what information to put down. I will write down whatever you say and read it back to you to make sure what I have written is correct.

What do I do next?

Describe the next step in the court process.

I want to see the judge. Where is his office?

The judge talks with both parties to a case at the same time. You would not want the judge to be talking to the [police officer][landlord] about this case if you were not present. Your case is scheduled for hearing on _____ at _____. That is when you should speak with the judge.

The judge heard my case today but did not make a decision. When will he decide?

There is no way for me to know when the judge will issue a decision in your case. In general, judges try to reach a decision within [60] days of taking a case under advisement. But there is no guarantee that the judge will decide your case within that time.

Some such standard answers, based on the most common questions that recur in training sessions on this subject, appear on page 141.

A just outcome

Russell Engler, Professor of Law and Director of Clinical Programs at the New England School of Law, has written a thought-provoking article arguing that judges, mediators, and court staff *should* provide legal advice to self-represented litigants.[4] Engler argues that most persons representing themselves in court do so because they cannot afford to retain counsel. Without competent advice concerning available options and their advantages and disadvantages, litigants cannot obtain a just outcome. He argues that principles underlying the concept of the court's impartiality must be reconsidered. Instead of giving no advice to either side, Engler believes that the court must give whatever help is needed to *both* sides, giving more help to one side than to the other where needed. He argues that true impartiality exists when both parties are fully informed of their rights, their procedural options, and the benefits and detriments arising from exercising them.

The most obvious instance in which the court has an obligation to provide different levels of help to one side than to the other is when one side is represented by counsel and the other is not. In order for the courts to do justice, Engler argues, the courts must be prepared to provide whatever assistance is needed to both sides in order for them to understand their rights and remedies and make a reasoned, informed judgment of their best interests. Current restrictions on court staff, mediators, and judges inhibit their ability to ensure justice. He poses the problem of the mediator who is prohibited from informing one party that his proposed settlement terms are foregoing a remedy to which he is clearly entitled by law. His article goes on to argue that the type of advice needed, and who should provide it, depends on the context—the nature of the legal proceeding and the type of dispute.

Professor Engler's analysis is thought-provoking. He forcefully points out the injustices that can result from imbalances in the power and knowledge of self-represented parties. However, his view that a dispute cannot be resolved justly without fully informing both parties of every substantive and procedure right and option available is not one to which I am willing to subscribe. It is neither necessary nor realistic to expect the courts to serve not only as dispute resolvers but also as counselors and advocates for both sides.

Unauthorized practice of law

Much of the concern about court staff providing information arises from apprehension they will be practicing law without a license. In my view, laws or court rules prohibiting the unauthorized practice of law do not apply to court staff performing tasks at the direction of the court. Preoccupation with the topic of unauthorized practice of law focuses attention on the wrong issues and provides either too much or too little guidance to the courts on what information their staff should and should not provide.

First, as a matter of law, when court clerks are providing information that the courts direct them to provide, they cannot be engaged in the *unauthorized* practice of law. The courts have authorized them to do what they are doing. When the authorization comes from the state court of last resort, which is the body responsible for deciding what constitutes the practice of law, there can be no doubt that court staff are insulated from any statute or rule prohibiting the unauthorized practice of law. The Supreme Court of Florida recognized this principle in its family court rule on self-help programs. Section (e) of Rule 12.750 reads:

> **(e) Unauthorized Practice of Law.** The services listed in subdivision (c), when performed by nonlawyer personnel in a self-help program, shall not be the unauthorized practice of law.

A committee of the Washington State Bar Association has reached the same conclusion. The Committee to Define the Practice of Law worked for almost a year and a half to develop a comprehensive definition of the practice of law for the State Bar Association to recommend to the state supreme court for adoption. Section (b)(2) of its Definition of the Practice of Law excludes "serving as a court house facilitator pursuant to court rule". . . "whether or not [it] constitute[s] the practice of law."

The attorney general of Vermont has applied this reasoning to court staff activities authorized by the trial court, not the court of last resort. In Vermont, the unauthorized practice of law is prohibited by rule of the state supreme court. An attorney wrote to the Vermont attorney general asking that it commence a criminal contempt proceeding to enforce that rule, complaining about an advertised job description that included the following duties of a court case manager: "assist litigants to complete court documents and to understand the judicial process" and ensure "that all persons involved in child support actions understand the court process, their rights under the law and all documents that they are asked to file or agree to." The complaint also questioned the court's production and distribution of various booklets that define legal terms and discuss the divorce process. While expressing his opinion that the activities set forth in the job description did not constitute the practice of law, Chief Assistant Attorney General William Griffin noted that "[e]ven if they did, since the activities are authorized by the Court and performed on its behalf, the Attorney General would be hard pressed to argue that they are unauthorized." [5]

Analyzing this issue in terms of the unauthorized practice of law focuses attention on what lawyers do, not on what courts must, and must not, do. First, courts must provide self-represented litigants with the information they need to bring their cases before the court. Whether or not there is a constitutional right to access to the courts, there are overwhelming policy reasons for the courts to provide effective access. That is what courts are for—to serve as the forum for resolving disputes. For the courts to enjoy the public trust and confidence of the people, they must make their services practically, as well as theoretically, available to the public. So, the focus of the courts must be on providing the information that citizens need in order to avail themselves of the courts' dispute-resolving services.

The limitations on the court staff in answering questions from the public arise not from what lawyers do, but from the principle of impartiality central to public trust and confidence in the courts. Court staff should not advise a person accused of crime whether to plead guilty—not because lawyers give such advice, but because that advice causes the court staff, and hence the court itself, to be taking sides in the outcome of the case.

An example where courts are misled by looking to unauthorized practice of law principles, rather than to the needs of the courts, is with respect to court forms. Some courts consider the choice of the appropriate form for a litigant to use to be a function that lawyers perform for their clients and therefore restrict the role that staff can play in pointing out the correct form to a litigant requesting assistance. See, for instance, the discussion of this issue by Goldschmidt and colleagues.[6]

As a practical matter, court staff are fully competent to direct litigants to the correct form. This service constitutes an essential part of the information a litigant needs in order to be able to present his or her case to the court. And, because the court provides equal services to all litigants—e.g., to petitioners as well as respondents—the court does not depart from its impartial role in providing forms and directing litigants to their proper use.[7]

By focusing on the issue of the unauthorized practice of law, courts may not go far enough in limiting the role that staff can play. For instance, does the fact that a particular court staff member is a lawyer free the court from concerns arising from the court's need to remain impartial? Or, in Arizona, where there is no unauthorized practice of law statute, can the courts decide that there are no limitations on the role that their staff should play in assisting litigants?

Finally, the ethical opinions analyzing the functions that clerks can and cannot perform from the standpoint of the unauthorized practice of law draw the same line in the same place as does my analysis based on the principle of maintaining the court's impartiality. The Massachusetts Advisory Committee on Ethical Opinions for Clerks of the Court reviewed five scenarios that regularly occur, approving clerk conduct in three and disapproving it in the remaining two. In summarizing its opinion, it stated:

> [P]roviding assistance with filling out forms and offering procedural advice clearly do not run afoul of the prohibition on the practice of law. Drafting documents, taking over a case and becoming an advocate on behalf of a litigant would clearly violate the prohibition.

***

The increase in numbers of self-represented litigants throughout the nation heightens the need to provide them with information. Court staff are the first people litigants come into contact with, and there are many ways they can assist. Recognizing this, courts are developing guidelines and providing the staff training necessary to ensure access to justice for all.

Notes

This article originally appeared in Volume 84, Number 4, January–February 2001, pages 198–204.

1. 34 *The Judges Journal* 10 (Winter 1995). A slightly different version appeared contemporaneously in "Clerks, Office Staff Cannot Give Legal Advice: What Does That Mean?" *Court Manager* 10 (Winter 1995) 35–40.

2. See the discussion on pages 19 to 24 in Goldschmidt, Mahoney, Solomon and Green, *Meeting the Challenge of Pro Se Litigation: A Report and Guidebook for Judges and Court Managers* (American Judicature Society, 1998).

3. Ibid. at 24.

4. Engler, "And Justice for All—Including the Unrepresented Poor: Revisiting the Roles of the Judges, Mediators and Clerks," 67 *Fordham L. Rev.* 1987 (1999).

5. Letter from William Griffin, Assistant Attorney General, to Jan Rickless Paul, Esq., dated August 8, 1994.

6. *Meeting the Challenge, supra n.* 2, at 43.

7. It is clear that the New Mexico Supreme Court, the state in which an ethics opinion questioned the propriety of a judge's providing litigants with forms he drafted, finds it acceptable for court staff to provide approved court forms to litigants. *See* the New Mexico legal information form.

Actors in the Judicial Process
Lawyers and Legal Practices

The role of lawyers in the American judicial process has been romanticized and glamorized through accounts, both real and fictional, of the exploits of the Daniel Websters, Clarence Darrows, and Perry Masons of courtrooms past and present. At this writing, several television series that focus on aspects of legal processes, including *Boston Legal, Judging Amy, Kevin Hill,* and *Law and Order,* are among the most highly rated shows on the air. Not surprisingly, actual legal professionals must fulfill many tasks, roles, and job responsibilities that would be quite foreign to our folklore's most famous litigators. Indeed, a great many lawyers never try a case and many never see the inside of a courtroom. The articles in this section address several facets of the legal profession and the diverse practices it may entail.

The section begins with Arlin Adams's broad brush-stroke essay, "The legal profession: a critical evaluation." This critique of the contemporary practice of law is an important one that raises fundamental questions about the profession's commitment to pursuing its mission in the wake of the great "professional metamorphosis" of the past several decades. Adams documents important changes in the law as well as fundamental changes in lawyering that have caused both problems for the judicial process and "the disappearance of the individual legal personality." He feels that professionalism has given way to commercialism and that the civic values that lawyers historically possessed while serving as the nation's "security ministry" have eroded. The sobering account ends with a call for lawyers to reassert the values of service to the community, legal craftsmanship, and professional devotion that Adams associates with earlier generations of his colleagues.

Nathan Posner focuses on finer details when he raises the question, "Truth, justice and the client's interest: can the lawyer serve all three?" He explores many ethical dilemmas faced by advocates whose clients' personal interests may conflict with the ideals of truth and justice that the lawyer must also serve. Posner is "convinced that our adversary system in its present form endorses various techniques that at best avoid the truth and at worst make a mockery of 'justice.' "

Whereas Posner's essay focuses, in some sense, on the "justice" function of the legal practitioner, Herbert Kritzer's empirical analysis of "Contingency fee lawyers as gatekeepers in the civil justice system" takes one broad area of the law and explores the systemic realities that are the consequences of attorneys' decisions to take or not to take cases in the first place. Through a survey of practitioners in Wisconsin, Kritzer documents how the conventional wisdom of ambulance chasing civil litigators is belied by the day-to-day reality of attorneys turning down at least as many potential plaintiff cases as they accept. Most often, the decision to not take on a client flows from the weak basis for a viable case. Kritzer argues that, "In a sense, the lawyer is making decisions about which cases to include in his or her portfolio of risks." At the same time, however, such "rational" decision making by attorneys serves the system's interest in avoiding immobilizing case overload.

The legal profession: a critical evaluation

Arlin M. Adams

The legal profession and the practice of law have undergone a drastic transformation in recent years, and the changes have not been for the better. Members of the profession must regain a sense of their individual legal personality and faith in the ultimate mission of their calling.

All professions, especially one as central to American life as the legal profession, should undergo a continuing process of examination and self-evaluation. Any group that does not engage in such an exercise loses much that makes it a profession: a shared set of principles and customs that transcend self-interest and speak to the essential nature of the particular calling or trade.

There are greater reasons beyond periodic examination, however, that make this topic most compelling. In recent years, the legal profession has undergone fundamental changes that threaten to sever it from its traditional moorings. A qualitative revolution has occurred within the legal community to the extent that the practice which existed 40 years ago is hardly recognizable today.

No calling has occupied a more important and undeviating role in the emergence and development of American society. The practice of law, almost by definition, should establish and promote the common good and bring forth the advancement and betterment of society. As a profession, however, we have departed from the practice as it has been envisioned from the early days of the Republic. This dramatic change has strong overtones for the future. Although many authors have chronicled the recent transition of the legal profession, few are willing to argue that these developments have evolved for the betterment of society.

The sources causing the changes in the legal profession are both external and internal. The external pressures arise from great movements in the body of substantive law and in the types of services that lawyers are now required to perform. The changes in what constitute the practice of law, in turn, have transformed who constitutes the practitioners of law. From an internal standpoint, the profession has undergone as drastic a transformation as the substantive law that governs us. I shall attempt to address these two antecedents of professional metamorphosis.

Changes in the law

Just a few decades ago the rules governing society were almost entirely of the common law variety. Under the common law system, the recognized doctrines of law originated from historic precedent and were gradually forged by lawyers and judges as society advanced and matured. In recent years, however, the proliferation of statutory and regulatory law has relegated the common law to a far less prominent position.

The common law system was designed to adjudicate disputes between two relatively equal parties according to well-established principles. The former common law practitioner drew on diverse and traditional doctrines regarding the relationship between government and property, whereas the modern day practice consists primarily of various statutory, regulatory, and administrative specialties. A great share of litigation today entails large and complicated breach of contract suits, complex real estate transactions, intricate corporate matters, and financial maneuvering in the international capital markets. The substance and function of the types of matters the law addresses has shifted from the small scale of the common law to the large scope of a practice dominated by extensive financial concerns.

The second source of change in the law is the burgeoning areas of practice relating to government. The rise of the administrative state—the so-called headless fourth branch of government—has been sweeping. The establishment of quasi-judicial authorities and agencies, such as the Federal Communications Commission, the Occupational Safety and Health Administration, and the Environmental Protection Agency, has accelerated continuously since World War II, and shows little sign of abating. The number of federal agencies alone has increased from 20 to well over 70, many with narrow, sometimes overlapping purposes.

Furthermore, in the coming months additional federal bodies governing the closing of industrial facilities and merger-and-acquisition transactions undoubtedly

Judicature Volume 74, Number 2, pp. 77–83

will be established. The proliferation of federal administrative agencies has been matched by a parallel expansion of state and local bodies. As expected, a government of greater size and scope has necessarily increased the share of legal work devoted to relatively novel, specialized administrative areas.

A third and perhaps most significant development in the law in the past few decades is the emergence of several new forms of legal actions. The number of class action suits and other types of multiparty litigation has grown substantially. This phenomenon has led to the introduction of "public" issues into the private litigation setting. Public issues are generally defined as those involving societal concerns and numerous parties, and are thus arguably more appropriate for legislative consideration. In contrast, private controversies are those amenable to judicial resolution between two discrete parties.

The distinction between public and private issues serves as a point of comparison between the past and the present era. Matters that once were clearly within the realm of public affairs now routinely appear before courts. There has been a clear departure in the perceived role of the judiciary. Litigation encompassing environmental and public health issues, products liability, industrial and nuclear safety, civil rights, and other litigation involving nontraditional plaintiffs is a relatively new development, which reflects this departure.

Much of the expansion in public interest litigation can be attributed to the characteristics of our latter-day economy. Mass producers of consumer goods, environmental polluters, and other large industrial aggregations now possess the ability to affect or injure large classes of citizens. Whether the radical innovations in the conduct of judicial affairs are a reflection of a change in the prevailing notions of the law or of greater economic forces, however, is not the issue at hand. The question whether law is a product of economic determinism or whether law shapes the path of economic change is a subject worthy of its own discrete forum.

In either event, the effect of these innovations on the profession is undeniable. The characteristic of gradualism—the belief that law originated from natural truths and was fashioned, through time, to accommodate newly developing human relationships—was the foundation of our common law history. Around this basic orientation, ethical norms and mores developed that fostered the evolution of the common law.

Taken as a whole these practices emerged into a philosophy of legal professionalism. This concept of gradual change through reasoned treatment, however, is subjugated, or at least strained, in a legal climate of rapid and drastic transformation.

Changes in lawyering

The decline in professionalism as it relates to the law has occurred, at least in part, because of a diminution in the defining element of gradualism. Change in the law necessarily causes change in the profession. The great emphasis in today's practice on large transactional matters at the expense of individual client service particularly tends to undermine the values that define professionalism. The results of this transformation are readily apparent in how the typical law practice has changed.

A few years ago, single practitioners and small groups of lawyers dominated the practice. A firm with 20 attorneys was considered large. Today, firms with over 200 lawyers are not unusual, and a partnership of 20 is generally limited to handling small matters. In 1975, there were only four firms with over 200 lawyers in the United States, and they were viewed with great skepticism. In contrast, a recent survey reported well over 150 firms with more than 200 attorneys and there is far less reservation about the wisdom of the large firm as a legal institution. Indeed, last year, one of these firms celebrated the hiring of its 1,000th lawyer.

The advent of megafirms has substantially altered law practice. It is not unusual now to have firms with offices throughout the nation and even in major cities abroad. Moreover, a firm in Philadelphia attempting to hire students from Harvard, Yale, or Stanford will likely have to bid against firms from New York, Los Angeles, Chicago, and Denver. Thus, the marketplace for legal services and the marketplace for attorneys has grown national, sometimes international, in scope.

The small-town practitioner with intimate ties only to his local community is becoming a vanishing figure. Industry analysts predict that the growth in firm size will continue and will lead to a shakeout where the giant conglomerates will be the principal survivors. Indeed, proposals have been made in many state bars that would allow non-lawyers to own and control law firms so that they may operate more like business corporations. If this trend continues, there may be no place left for the individual practitioner or the small group of practitioners.

The expansion in the large, institutionalized practice has been made possible, I believe, by three developments in the way lawyers are trained and work. Taken as a whole, these elements—the new labor economies of the practice—constitute the changing internal climate of the profession.

The first development is the proliferation of law schools and lawyers. The number of lawyers in the United States has doubled since 1970 and is now well over 700,000, far and away the most lawyers for any nation in the world. The students fueling this expanding army are being trained at a growing number of law schools and in larger entering classes. The elite schools such as Harvard, Yale, and Pennsylvania have attempted to maintain the same number of students. Other law schools, however, especially state university law schools, have greatly expanded their enrollments.

A second factor allowing the progression of larger and larger firms is the fees for services that these firms now charge. This development is especially pertinent to the transactional nature of the practice. Forty years ago, the cost and time spent on legal services were a negligible part of business decisions. Today, the consideration of legal fees is a major factor in many of these transactions.

The rise of large legal fees has had other significant effects. Many have read about the $75,000 starting salaries and $10,000 bonuses given to graduating students, but even these numbers do not reflect the magnitude of the factor of money in large firm practice. *The American Lawyer,* a publication devoted to glamorizing big firms, now publishes annual financial data on such firms. Recent figures show firms realizing over $1,000,000 per year in revenues per lawyer; $1,000,000 in profit per partner; and one New York firm approaching $300,000,000 in total revenues.[1] Under headlines that blare: "Generating Revenue: The Key to The Bottom Line,"[2] the editors assure that faltering local economies will not affect business,[3] and warn that excessive pro bono work may lower a firm's profitability.[4]

Concentration on profit-maximization provides less and less time for lawyers to spend on public and professional activities. Obligations to the community and to the profession are subordinated when constant attention must be given to monetary aspects. Consequently, these vital elements undergirding the ideal of the principled, public-minded practitioner of old are victims of the recent preoccupation with fees, firm profits, and inordinate salaries.

The third element permitting the growth of large institutional firms is the level of specialization now required in the legal profession. At one time a lawyer may have dealt with a number of different types of matters in any particular period. Today's young attorneys, however, are required to specialize almost immediately. Sizable firms generally are organized into departments practicing one type of law. Differentiation of the legal labor force is essential to sustain these large organizations. The necessity to develop "instant expertise" is particularly troublesome, I believe, as it is inconsistent with the traditional vision of legal practice as a diverse and liberal endeavor. Excessive specialization inevitably detracts from the rich and full legacy of the profession.

The strained judicial process

With a clearer understanding of what the changing legal environment encompasses, we can now focus on its implications for the historic mission of the practitioner in our society. It is appropriate to ask what effect the confluence of these pressures has had on the judicial system that attempts to adjust to them. The structure of our system of courts and judges was shaped, essentially, for the common law practice of yesteryear. Consequently, just like any other infrastructure designed to accommodate traffic, be it an interstate highway or a shopping mall, the addition of greater and greater amounts of traffic creates a strain and hinders the ability of the system to function efficiently.

The exponential growth in litigation in recent years has imposed such a tension on our legal infrastructure. The number of lawsuits filed in both state and federal courts is unprecedented. Heavier caseloads and the growing percentage of complex multiparty actions create a burden that courts are not institutionally equipped to handle. As a result, the level of procedural excess and abuse of pretrial procedures has risen as well. That our judicial system, which is charged in large part with the development of substantive law and the efficient administration of justice, must now endure a constant state of procedural impasse is without precedent and is a poor reflection on the state of the profession. A pivotal role of an advocate in our adversarial system is the public duty to advance the edification of the courts and to assist in their efficient administration. Abuse of the discovery process and dilatory tactics abridge this duty and diminish yet another public aspect of the profession.

The political response to the judicial crisis caused by the changing legal atmosphere has been primarily to add more judges to an already overburdened system. Thus, in 1945 there were 100 federal judges; today there are more than 700. To a lesser extent, the response has been to hire court administrators and to install high-tech equipment. The emergence of court administrators, whose jobs are primarily to facilitate the operation of the courts, is illustrative of the continuing need simply to keep traffic moving. The question then arises as to what effect a constant preoccupation with the quantity of judicial output has on the qualitative aspects of that product.

The destruction and replacement of historic doctrines of the law, I believe, is at least a partial result. The introduction of public issues into a judicial setting and increased use of class action methodologies are directly attributable to and symptomatic of justice dispensed in wholesale fashion. In a larger sense, the role of judges in this type of environment has changed. The gradualism and intellectual spirit of the common law, where the judge performed the passive roles of preserving legal doctrine and pursuing thoughtful objectivity, are often lost in today's courtrooms.

In recent years, there has been a robust debate within the legal community as to whether judges should follow a path of judicial activism or restraint. In many ways, this debate embraces a non-issue. The distinction between active and passive interpretation is, I believe, tenuous and better given to philosophical consideration. It is significant, however, that such a debate even exists. Whether a judge should engage in aggressive intervention in disputes departs from the ideal of the neutral and objective arbitrator. Nonetheless, many judges are now known for their predisposition to engage in activism by creating new causes of action rather than the traditional qualities of consistent thoughtful deliberation. This new emphasis in the judicial process is a direct function of what is perceived as the changing legal profession.

Disappearance of legal personality

A second, more noteworthy, consequence of the shift in the profession is the disappearance of what may be characterized as the individual legal personality. Just as increased traffic flow means that one is unlikely to be acquainted with the person driving the automobile next to yours, the increased traffic within the profession creates its own type of anonymity. Legal relationships, whether lawyer-client or among lawyers, have become far less personal in the past few decades. Practice in a large law firm has a tendency to mechanize the relationship between counsel.

At one time, admission into the bar meant passage into a sort of egalitarian fraternity. The large law firm of today, however, imposes both explicit and implicit hierarchical arrangements among its attorneys. Under these circumstances, professional alienation can flourish. A lawyer who is required, even before graduation, to focus on a specialty can easily view himself more as a technician and less as a servant of the profession itself and its role in the larger community. Since practice in a sizable firm necessarily involves large, institutionalized clients, the real sense of inclusion and obligation to the broader community is often lost.

The idea that a lawyer's day-to-day experience can be so divorced from actual contact or knowledge of his or her clients was virtually unknown just a few short years ago. Yet an attorney working for a substantial institutional client can have very little, if any, relationship with his client on a personal basis. Deprived of this type of gratifying professional satisfaction, more and more attorneys must find an external reason, whether individual enjoyment or money, to gain a sense of purpose.

Although there are numerous and diverse opportunities for an attorney to obtain satisfaction through public interest or pro bono work, those relationships too have taken on a distinct institutional flavor. Large organized programs are now required to provide pro bono services. It is most unfortunate that a graduating law student, because of the demands of time and money, has so little opportunity to secure a personal sense of reward by using his or her skills to assist an indigent individual.

Perhaps even more significant than the mechanism of lawyer-client relations is the loss of personal community among lawyers themselves. It is not unusual, in fact it is quite likely, that lawyers in a typical firm are practically strangers. This fact alone is not startling because any large organization, be it a university, a hospital, or a bank, must be operated on an impersonal, organizational level. The case of the large, urban law firm is particularly disturbing, however, because of what must be subordinated to organizational structure.

The collegiality and democratic spirit that once governed relations within a firm have been replaced by bureaucratic forms of control and frequently a somewhat oppressive "up-or-out" mentality. The sense of individual legal personality is sacrificed to the concept of firm identity. Moreover, the sense of professionalism and professional identity among lawyers is often replaced by the commercial exigencies of large firm competition.

Lawyers have historically provided a wellspring of governmental and political leadership to the nation. The common law was an incomparable incubator for developing the qualities and dedication that we ascribe to sound, progressive, and energetic civil leadership. Scholarship, broad vision, and equanimity—elements that marked a successful common law practitioner—also defined the hallmarks of a dedicated public servant.

The disappearance of the individual legal personality threatens to disrupt the profession's important role in preparing public servants. I question whether apprenticeship in a large firm today can be a measure of the training that the common law practice provided. Can the specialized, institutional experience of a large firm become the equivalent of development through individual common law practice in the selection of our next generation of governors, judges, mayors, and other officials? These questions should be quite high in the pantheon of considerations for the continuing mission of our profession as large legal entities capture the most promising legal talent available.

Regrettably, the answers to these questions appear to be in the negative. The large firms of today are simply not producing this type of leadership. Last year, of the nearly 11,000 students graduating from the top law schools, only 243 chose to begin their careers in some type of public interest work.[5] Plucked directly from school and dropped into well-paying positions that demand enormous commitments of time and energy, it is not surprising that these young attorneys might view public service as secondary and unrewarding.

The law firms themselves, however, must also share responsibility for not contributing to the leadership of their communities. As a young attorney, I was encouraged to enter public life by the senior partner of my firm as an opportunity to serve the public. Today, the structural and financial necessities of maintaining a large firm create pressures that, in turn, deter young lawyers from entering public service. Within the business mindset of large firms, it simply is not profitable to lend talent to the community at large.

Commercialization of law and practice

The third, and perhaps most pervasive, manifestation of the change in the legal climate is the decline of professionalism and its replacement with commercialism. If one general theme could encompass the many changes in our legal environment, it would be the adoption of the mores and manners of the marketplace at the expense of expressions of professional affiliation. One might legitimately ask: "What is wrong with this?" After all, lawyering is like any other calling; young people still choose to go into law primarily for monetary reasons and, more often than not, are rewarded for that choice. I suppose that one would be hard-pressed to persuade the general public, whether on a street corner in New York City or Davenport, Iowa, that what the practice of law is all about is not money. But the real danger lies when those within the profession are convinced that what it is all about is material success.

The profession occupies a key role in a democratically organized society. Americans tend to divide the dimensions of public life into two general spheres. One half is the business or economic realm. An economy based on capitalism and the institution of private property is the source of this culture. Economic freedom, efficiency, and material reward are its basic values. The other half of what constitutes our public affairs is the political or civil culture. The highest virtues here are political freedom, equality, and justice. Its institutional foundations are the free-functioning political process and the unbiased administration of justice.

Each culture or set of values must be allowed to flourish; that is what, to a considerable extent, constitutes the genius of the American polity. Furthermore, it is important that neither should grow to dominate the other. A correct balance between the influences of our civil government and the business marketplace is the perpetual challenge of democracy. Given this challenge, it is the proper role of the lawyer to stabilize the social equilibrium of the forces and counterforces of a dynamic society. The law is an affirmation or expression of the structure of our government and our consensual beliefs. Lawyers must operate as its vigilant defenders. Just as the true entrepreneur may be viewed as the paradigm of the business culture, each lawyer should represent the epitome of the values and virtues of the civic culture.

When the legal profession adopts too many of the commercial aspects of business, the civic values that lawyers should represent are in danger of being eroded. It is for this reason that mourning the decline in professionalism is not merely an exercise in sentimentality. We must not permit the practice of law to become just another white-collar industry. Nor must we permit lawyers to be viewed as economic units of production and their work product to be seen as "widgets." Such a mercantilistic vision would be tantamount to an admission that our civic heritage is quantifiable and can be exchanged, and that what was once self-evident and inalienable is no longer so.

Yet, evidence of this development can be found in several respects. The one that is perhaps most representative, and coincidentally the one I personally find quite troubling, although probably necessary, is the timesheets that lawyers are required to have nearby throughout the working day. Aside from being a continuous distraction, these instruments are a repeated reminder that everything a lawyer does can and should be quantified for payment. In large cities, some firms have begun billing based on one-twelfth of an hour. That means that every action that a lawyer performs, whether opening mail or answering a short telephone call, will be recorded and billed to the client.

The commercialization of the profession, however, runs far deeper than timesheets or expense accounts. The decline in professionalism has deprived an entire generation of practitioners of suitable role models. At the risk of sounding nostalgic, I believe that the profession has lost its grasp of the big picture and of the aspects and aspirations of the higher calling of this secular ministry.

Lawyers that are perceived as most successful today, or at least the ones gaining the most remuneration, are those who specialize in merger and acquisition work. This development is particularly illustrative of the overall commercialization of practice, in that elaborate takeover schemes in large part involve the reorganization of interests while adding little value to society. Seldom in these complex, money-changing arrangements is there room for consideration of the public interest or societal consequences. The ideal of the lawyer as vindicator of the rights vested in our civic culture is lost. Just as the inventor of the hula hoop or bikini once gained the greatest reward in the business culture, the lawyer specializing in junk bonds is the new example of success in the legal firmament.

Nor is commercialization of the civic culture lost on the general public. One astute social observer remarked recently that members of our society are no longer referred to as "citizens" but instead are simply grouped into the class known as "consumers." When the philosophy of every free person possessing an equal franchise in our democratic society is lost, and citizens are best

recognized for their position in the macroeconomy, our civic heritage has been seriously compromised.

Just as we might despair over the loss of the true entrepreneur in society, the decline of professionalism in legal practice should invite equal consternation. The public perception of the profession is now gained more through avenues such as *The People's Court, L.A. Law,* or television and telephone book ads for attorneys, rather than from the practice of the profession. What could be more discouraging than a generation of individuals receiving their understanding of their civic rights and obligations through these vistas?

Equally distressing is the prospect of members of the profession *affirmatively accepting* this commercialized vision of themselves. Law schools, which should be the bulwark of the loftiest ideals of the profession, are frequently more hospitable to various hucksters or personalities of law rather than to the great role models of yesteryear. It is a melancholy commentary that the inventor of a heart valve frequently will labor in obscurity while the promoter of some new patent medicine, whether a baldness cure or weight loss miracle, will gain immediate attention and riches. But the decline in the professionalism of the legal practice and the rise of the poor substitute of commercial manners, is an equally regrettable indictment of our society. When the giants of legal history are relegated to the back of the classroom or the rear of a bar association meeting, it is important to consider who is moving to the front.

Conclusion

We must be on guard to assure that my assessment of the state of our profession is not merely the product of an affection for days past. In this regard, I am reminded that in 1905, Louis Brandeis, later a Supreme Court Justice, remarked that the profession at that time caused him much concern. He was alarmed at the progressive encroachment of material influences on the great and beloved principles of the law. A year later, Roscoe Pound, soon to be Dean of Harvard Law School, in a seminal address entitled "Causes of Popular Dissatisfaction with the Administration of Justice," criticized the prevailing legal institutions as not being able to serve a nation on the verge of realizing its destiny. Pound noted the absence of any encompassing "Philosophy of the Law" that would allow the profession to guide the nation through the challenges of the new century.

Even if what I have said thus far can be attributed to generational politics, and I concede that the thrust of my comments parallels to some extent those of

Brandeis and Pound, there still remains the constant necessity to reexamine the ideals and premises of the profession. Even if we are not in the last days of the principled practice of law, the current developments, as I have sought to describe them, deserve careful attention. The quest for Pound's "Philosophy of the Law" must continue if our profession is to lead society once again into the potentials of a new century that soon will be upon us.

Assuming that the state of the practice deserves the scrutiny of both the legal and non-legal communities, it is customary for the commentator to point out the obvious but unchosen answer. If there exists such an answer or path to be pursued, however, it will not be found in these remarks. The most compelling reason for this is simply that I am not in possession of any such remedy.

If there is an answer to the renewal of the professional ethic in the legal community, I do not believe it will come from any technical adjustment in the rules. The dramatic forces at work in the profession, both internally and externally, will not recede through administrative tinkering. That type of technocratic answer does not exist and, even if we could discover it, it recalls a solution more representative of the business culture. There simply is no quick antidote to materialism.

Rather, if a reassertion of professional faith is to occur, it must arise from a reaffirmation of our civic heritage. Members of the profession, the lawyers and the judges, must again possess a sense of their individual legal personality and faith in the ultimate mission of their calling. Additional bar programs or law school requirements may help, but by themselves they will not recapture the passion and dedication of elapsed faith. The role of the lawyer has not changed. The members of the profession must be willing to reassume it, and to do so with necessary vigor.

On the occasion of the 200th anniversary of our Constitution, I outlined the aspects of what I view as the unchanged role of the practitioner.[6] These basic qualities, I submit, merit reiteration. The first is service to the community. Lawyers must again recognize that they have been entrusted with a great privilege, and that obligations to the community go with that privilege. Attorneys have occupied a singular role in service to our society from the framing of our Constitution to the Civil Rights Movement. Members of the profession must once again accept the responsibility of formulating theories and rules to allow the various elements of

the public to expand the ability of a nation to serve its citizens. Any enduring philosophy regarding legal practice must be rooted in the belief that lawyers receive their license and are empowered by the greater society, and must therefore labor to insure its progress. The idea of the practice of law as a completely private exercise of private ends is contrary to this conviction.

A second characteristic is dedication to what Justice Holmes called the "craftsmanship" of lawyering. There must be a renewed sense of pride in the work that lawyers do, not merely for its value in the marketplace, but for its historic function of vindicating the rights of citizens.

The third characteristic is devotion to the profession itself. The changing face of the law demands that lawyers reassert their professional ties and responsibilities. Members of the bar have traditionally recognized the importance of supporting their bar associations and continuing an active role in legal education. Profit must not become our dominant ethic. Nor must profit become the primary engine for professional change. A renewal in the faith of professionalism must originate from within and reverse our troubling path. Only when such a new direction is pursued will good sense and professional virtue prevail.

Despite the sobering tone of my remarks, I am not completely discouraged. Although many of us have halting doubts about recent developments in the profession, I believe it can still fulfill what is highest in the yearnings of the human spirit. Our history has been replete with inspiring figures: John Marshall, Oliver Wendell Holmes, Benjamin Cardozo, and Learned Hand, to name a few. Each can serve as a beacon.

As Judge Hand eloquently put it in addressing the conflict that is normal in a pluralistic society:

> For it is always dawn. Day breaks forever, and above the eastern horizon the sun is now about to peep. Full light of day? No, perhaps not ever. But yet it grows lighter, and the paths that were frequently so blind will, if one watches sharply enough, become hourly plainer. We shall learn to walk straighter. Yes, it is always dawn.[7]

Notes

This article originally appeared in Volume 74, Number 2, August–September 1990, pages 77–83. It was adapted from *Dickinson Law Review* Vol. 93, No. 4, Summer 1989, copyright 1989 by Dickinson School of Law and was originally delivered as the Tresolini Lecture at Lehigh University on November 10, 1988.

1. "The Am Law 100 Report," *The American Lawyer,* July/August, 1988.

2. Ibid. at 34

3. Ibid. at 58.

4. Ibid. at 20.

5. Kaplan, "Out of 11,000, 243 Went into Public Interest," *Nat'l. L. J.,* Aug. 8, 1988, at 1, col. 1.

6. Adams, Remarks at the "We the People 200" Convocation with the Supreme Court Justices at the Arch Street Friends Society (Oct. 2, 1987).

7. Hand, *The Spirit of Liberty: Papers and Addresses of Learned Hand,* 3d ed. (I. Dillard, 1974), 101.

Truth, justice, and the client's interest: can the lawyer serve all three?

Nathan L. Posner

Our changing society confronts the lawyer with a serious problem: can there be a truly rational administration of justice unless *all* relevant facts are accurately determined? The lawyer usually satisfies himself with the belief that the adversary system is the proper and best means for dispensing justice. I would like to adopt such a philosophy, but I am convinced that our adversary system in its present form endorses various techniques that at best avoid the truth and at worst make a mockery of "justice." Adversary procedures must be amended and altered if we seek a better determination of where the truth lies in any issue.

A lawyer's traditional obligation is to seek justice and truth. This duty must be invulnerable to attack, because the lawyer is an officer of the court and a pillar of the system of the administration of justice. A lawyer has a professional obligation to seek the truth in every instance.

The adversary system reveals one of its major weaknesses when a skillful, well-prepared lawyer opposes an incompetent or unprepared lawyer. It is questionable whether the system enhances the cause of justice in such a case, and whether the verdict is a dispensation of justice or merely the product of competence versus incompetence. On occasion, the effect of incompetence is minimized because of the safeguards provided by the judge and jury in their respective functions of determining the law and finding the facts. Therefore, some may argue, after proper instructions from the court concerning the weight of the evidence and its credibility, the verdict rendered must be fair and proper. Nevertheless, the administration of justice in such instances has been hampered, and the adversary system has impeded rather than aided our democratic approach to the administration of justice.

Much has been written concerning lawyers' ethics in the adversary system. Some suggest that the lawyer's devotion to the success of the client's cause regardless of means and expedience overrules the requirement of decency and the search for truth. Such zealous advocates hold that the lawyer, because of his confidential relationship with the client, may not disclose the truth, and, even when the lawyer has learned the truth from sources other than the client, may not bring it to the knowledge of the authorities because it might adversely affect the client.

More to the point, despite expressly contrary prohibitions contained in the Code of Professional Responsibility,[1] some theorists argue that when the client or a witness commits perjury in the offering of testimony, the lawyer may not protest, withdraw from the case, or in any other fashion divulge the fact that perjury has been committed. I cannot agree that zealous advocacy embraces the ignoring of obvious perjury. Such behavior is equivalent to subornation.

No one would suggest that, in a case in which the life or personal liberty of one accused of a crime is at stake, there should be any diminution of the many safeguards provided by the Constitution and Rules of Criminal Procedure. The constitutional rights of a defendant charged with crime must be resistant to all attacks, and it is the duty of the lawyer to protect those rights. It is because of this principle of law that all those who advocate the lawyer's obligation to effect the cause of the client, regardless of truth and justice, feel justified in maintaining their obligation as paramount.

But let us for the moment dismiss from our minds the criminal law and the constitutional privileges of criminal defendants and view the matter of ethics and the adversary system in the context of the civil courts. There, weighty considerations of constitutional rights, which concern the members of the criminal bar who champion the client's cause above all else, are less important. In the civil courts it is largely monetary benefits and property rights that are at stake.

Even in the criminal adversary system, there has been recognition of the principle of full disclosure; the prosecutor's primary duty is to seek justice rather than simply to win cases and achieve convictions. Accordingly, he or she should attempt[2] during the course of his investigation to ferret out *all* relevant evidence even if it detracts from his case or tends to exonerate the defendant; and, at trial, should disclose *all* relevant evidence, again without regard to which side evidence

Judicature Volume 60, Number 3, pp. 111–113

favors. It is also presently recognized that the lawyer representing the government in a civil adversary proceeding should seek justice by developing a full and fair record, and should not use the power of the government and the procedural rules to harass opposing parties.[3]

Why should this responsibility not be extended to all lawyers engaged in the trial of civil cases? Such a duty would complement the existing admonition to all lawyers in all types of cases[4] to disclose to the tribunal all law applicable to the litigation, including the existence of precedents or statutes adverse to the legal positions of their clients. Once the facts and the law have been presented in this manner, the lawyers are free to zealously advocate the inferences and conclusions to be drawn from them in a light most favorable to their clients, and may challenge the applicability or the soundness of any unfavorable law. The likelihood of a truly just result is much greater under this system than under a system of trial by concealment, half-truth and subterfuge.

No one is prepared to venture an opinion concerning what perjury or subornation is committed in a typical civil case. However, it is sure that exaggerations and half-truths abound. A few examples should serve to highlight the problem.

- The adversary system is stultified when a lawyer suggests that a witness avoid certain statements because they might influence a jury against the cause of the client. I consider a lawyer in violation of his oath when he dares suggest to a witness prior to trial: "If the facts in this case are what I have been led to believe, then the proper answer to this question should be . . . ."

- I question the ethics of a lawyer who, during the preparation of a tort case, reads to the client various decisions of the appellate courts dealing with distances and car lengths, emphasizing that the appellate courts affirmed a finding of contributory negligence where the distance between the two cars was less than the certain quoted number of yards, and that therefore recovery was denied. He then asks the client, "And how many yards away were you when you first saw the other car?" Conceding that the lawyer may be properly disturbed with certain arbitrary rules that would preclude recovery to the client, has he the right to make suggestions that will give the right of recovery to his

client based on "induced" testimony? Is he seeking justice and truth, or is he seeking to win the case for his client no matter what?

- Then there is a theory known as "selective ignorance." This refers to the lawyer who tells the client during their first meeting, "Don't say anything that will hurt your case." Not having been told, the lawyer can proceed with the case as he sees it on the information supplied to him after the warning. This lawyer does not recognize his responsibility to society, and does not serve the cause for which he became a lawyer. He is merely trying to justify his conduct by his rationalization of "service to the client," which unfortunately, in most instances, involves substantial fees.

- Similar problems arise with respect to documentary evidence. A letter or memorandum that was never received by one party and which purports to confirm an oral agreement made by him, which in fact was never made, will appear as evidence in his opponent's case. Conversely, some clients have heeded the "message" conveyed by their lawyer when he suggests at the outset that "all those old accounting records, which you are not legally required to keep and which would be helpful evidence to your adversary, must take up a lot of filing space. Many businesses like yours dispose of their outdated records so that they can use their filing space for more current material."

- Finally, I do not believe it is ethical for a lawyer to seek delay in a matter because of the client's inability to make payment on a judgment that will be secured unless a defense is interposed.[5] There have been instances where rules have been used against parties, and technicalities raised in pleadings, in order that more time could be accorded the defendant before the inevitable judgment would be entered against him. When a lawyer is aware that there is no defense to an action, and that his sole obligation to the client's cause is to "buy" time, he is breaching the Code of Professional Responsibility. The "justice" that he seeks is one-sided and brings prejudice to others involved.

Other areas of the civil practice removed from the trial of cases have readily adopted and followed the suggested higher standards of full disclosure. For example, a lawyer representing a corporation that desires to sell its securities to the public must be certain that all relevant facts are fully and accurately represented in the documents filed with the Securities and Exchange Commission, including the prospectus that is to be distributed to the investing public in connection with the offer and sale of the securities.

Such a lawyer may not merely accept the client's description of the facts but must make his own independent investigation, using due diligence to assure himself that the client's records support the factual representations being made, that the various assets of the client are fully and accurately described in the documents, and that all financial information is correct and not misleading. If the lawyer finds a mistake, an omission of a fact, or an adverse fact, he must insist that the client make the appropriate disclosure.

These same principles are applicable to the lawyer retained to prepare the periodic reports required to be filed by public companies. Some even contend that such a lawyer, should he fail to convince the client to make the necessary full disclosure, has the obligation to report the client's failure to the appropriate regula-

tory agency. In the practice of decedents' estates and trusts as well, the lawyer's responsibility to disclose all assets subject to tax has long been recognized and unquestioned. Should the civil litigation system settle for lower standards?

A true lawyer must realize that he is an administrator of justice as well as an advocate on behalf of his client. Each lawyer must know and seek to inform those who are training to become lawyers of the positive responsibility on the part of every member of the profession to nurture and encourage justice and truth. The accomplishment of that goal transcends the obligation of advocacy.

Notes

This article originally appeared in Vol. 60, No. 3, October 1976, pages 111–113.

1. DR 7–102. *See also* EC 7–6 and EC 7–26.
2. EC 7–13.
3. EC 7–14.
4. EC 7–23.
5. *See* EC 7–4, EC 7–9, and DR 7–102 A(1) and (2).

Contingency fee lawyers as gatekeepers in the civil justice system

Herbert M. Kritzer

A recent study indicates contingency fee lawyers generally turn down at least as many cases as they accept, most often because potential clients do not have a basis for their case.

Lawyers, particularly contingency fee lawyers, are gatekeepers who control the flow of civil cases into the courts. Although they can exercise this gatekeeping role in ways that either encourage or discourage potential litigants, the popular image of lawyers is that they stir up trouble. In *A Nation Under Lawyers,* Mary Ann Glendon argues that this should not be the case; she quotes an observation attributed to Elihu Root: "About half of the practice of the decent lawyer consists in telling would-be clients that they are damned fools and should stop." [1] Glendon implies that today lawyers are more interested in encouraging clients to sue than in being the "decent lawyers" of yesteryear.

This image is particularly associated with contingency fee lawyers. This is not surprising because of the apparent logic of the contingency fee: the lawyers get a cut of whatever they recover, and without cases there is no cut to get. Various interests—physicians, accountants, auto executives, chemical companies—blame contingency fee lawyers for much of what they view as crises arising from the liability system. Undoubtedly, there are lawyers who push the edge of the liability frontier, or who engage in practices pejoratively referred to as ambulance chasing. However, the day-to-day reality of most contingency fee legal practices is very different. While virtually every contingency fee practitioner wants to find highly lucrative cases, such cases are relatively rare. Many cases presented to lawyers are not winnable, or they do not offer a prospect of even a moderately acceptable fee. The contingency fee practitioner seeks cases that offer a high probability of providing at least an acceptable return, hoping to find some fraction of cases that present the opportunity to generate a significant fee.

Thus, while lawyers may encourage or seek out cases, the contingency logic suggests that contingency fee lawyers should reject a large number of potential cases. Lawyers evaluate cases in terms of the risks involved and the potential returns associated with those risks. An attorney will reject cases that do not satisfy some risk/return criteria. Thus, contingency fee lawyers resemble portfolio managers, choosing to "invest" (their time) in risky cases hoping to obtain adequate or better returns.

Most of the above is speculative, and there is little published information that provides systematic insights into case-screening practices. Occasional articles in the legal press describe case-screening practices of top-end law firms [2] and prescriptive articles in periodicals targeted to the legal profession discuss what should be considered in screening cases. [3] However, there is only one, 25-year-old published study, and it focuses solely on medical malpractice. [4]

A recent survey of contingency fee practitioners in Wisconsin provides the first systematic data on case-screening patterns and practices. A total of 511 Wisconsin attorneys whose practices involve contingency fee work responded (about 48 percent). The survey covered a variety of aspects of contingency fee work, with one section focusing on the screening of potential cases. This survey is part of a larger project (see "The Wisconsin contingency fee study," page 159).

Screening cases

As shown in Table 1, among the 455 survey respondents who provided usable data, the number of potential clients contacting the respondents or their firms ranged from 1 to 5,000. (The number of clients accepted ranged from 0 to 600.) Seven respondents reported more than 1,000 contacts; an average of about 20 contacts (or more) a week, or four per day. At the other extreme, almost half reported about two or fewer contacts per month (25 or less over the year).

One problem with the figures is that some lawyers (about 10 percent of the 455 respondents) work in firms where case screening is handled on a firm-wide basis while other lawyers handle screening on an indi-

Table 1. Case volume

Number of contacts	All respondents				Individual screeners			
	Number of respondents		Total number of contacts		Number of respondents		Total number of contacts	
	%	n	%	n	%	n	%	n
1–10	23	106	1	683	21	87	1	571
11–25	24	109	3	2,058	25	99	5	1,874
26–75	24	111	8	5,195	26	103	12	4,815
76–200	18	80	18	11,207	18	72	23	9,477
201–1,000	9	42	30	19,131	9	37	39	15,781
over 1,000	2	7	40	25,300	1	4	20	8,000
All	100	455	100	53,584	100	402	100	40,518

vidual basis either in a firm or as solo practitioners. Preliminary analyses indicated that the general pattern in the results is the same regardless of whether the "firm-level" screeners are included or excluded. Consequently, because the analysis considers individual characteristics as control variables, much of the following discussion focuses only on those lawyers in firms where individual lawyers are responsible for screening cases. Looking only at those respondents, the range of contacts is from 1 to 2,500; aggregating across all of these respondents, there were 40,518 contacts.

Selectivity

Overall, lawyers reported accepting cases from a mean of 46 percent (median 45 percent) of the potential clients who contacted them. Aggregating across the 455 lawyers, the lawyers accepted 16,519 (of 53,584) cases for an acceptance rate of 31 percent. Eliminating the seven respondents reporting 1,000 or more contacts, the mean acceptance rate is 47 percent (median 48 percent). These firms had contacts from 36,884 potential clients; they accepted 15,224 (41 percent).

As shown in Table 2, there appears to be a fairly clear link between volume and selectivity. For those lawyers or firms receiving about 1½ or fewer contacts per week, the acceptance rate tends to be on the order of 50 percent; for those with more than 1½ and up to about 20 contacts per week (1,000 cases per year), the acceptance rate is a little under 40 percent; for the very high volume practices with more than 20 contacts per

Table 2. Acceptance rates by case volume

Number of contacts	Number of respondents	Mean percent accepted	Total number of contacts	Total number of cases accepted	Percent of total cases accepted
All respondents					
1–10	106	47	683	319	47
11–25	109	50	2,058	1,008	49
26–75	111	52	5,195	2,674	51
76–200	80	39	11,207	4,199	37
201–1,000	42	37	19,131	7,116	38
over 1,000	7	10	25,300	1,295	8
All	455	46	53,584	16,519	31
Individual screeners					
1–10	87	48	571	265	46
11–25	99	50	1,874	921	49
26–75	103	51	4,815	2,440	51
76–200	72	38	9,477	3,804	40
201–1,000	37	36	15,781	5,991	38
over 1,000	4	12	8,000	855	11
All	402	46	40,518	14,276	35

week, the acceptance rate drops off sharply to less than 10 percent. Table 2 also eliminates those respondents who work in firms that screen at the firm level. Other than reducing the number of higher volume respondents, the general pattern is essentially the same.

There are many variables that might influence acceptance rates: gender, experience, specialized nature of practice or firm, and size of community. Because these might be correlated with contact volume, which the analysis above shows is clearly related to acceptance rate, volume was controlled for using two categories: low (75 or fewer contacts over the year) and medium (76 to 1,000 contacts). Eliminating the respondents in firms where screening is a firm-level function (which is necessary to look at any types of attorney characteristics), there are only four high volume (over 1,000 cases per year) respondents; the characteristics of those four respondents is reported in the right column of Table 3.

Table 3 shows acceptance rates controlling for 10 different variables one might expect to be related to how selective lawyers are in accepting cases. Of the 20 comparisons in the table (10 comparisons done separately for low and medium volume practices), only six achieve statistical significance. Five are for the low volume lawyers:

- Women lawyers are more selective than men.

- Lawyers with more than 20 years experience are less selective than those with 20 or fewer years of experience.

- Lawyers describing their practice as primarily personal injury plaintiffs or general practice are less selective than are those who do primarily personal injury defense or other types of litigation.

- Lawyers whose contingency fee caseload is predominantly (50 percent or more) personal injury are less selective than those whose contingency fee caseloads are not dominated by personal injury cases.

- Selectivity decreases as the lawyer's dependence (in terms of income) on contingency fee work goes up.

The only statistically significant difference among the medium volume lawyers is that those whose caseloads involve 10 percent or more medical malpractice work are more selective than are those with little or no medical malpractice work. The absence of statistically significant patterns for medium volume respondents

The Wisconsin contingency fee study

To remedy the lack of good contemporary data on screening of potential clients, and the more general dearth of systematic information on contingency fee legal practice, I undertook a multi-faceted study of contingency fee practice focusing on lawyers in Wisconsin. This study, funded by the National Science Foundation, involved three separate data collection components.

The first was a mail survey of Wisconsin contingency fee practitioners based on the State Bar of Wisconsin's Litigation Section mailing list. A total of 511 useable questionnaires were returned; a 48 percent response rate. Most of the information in this article draws upon the survey data.

The second aspect of the data collection involved full time observation of lawyers at work. I spent approximately one month in each of three different contingent fee practices. In each practice, my formal status was that of a paralegal, and in each practice I provided some assistance with research and other activities. The practices were chosen to reflect different types of settings: Two specialized in contingency fee cases, one relatively high volume and one low volume; the third was a mixed trial or court practice in which contingency fee work constituted about 20 percent of the lawyer's work. The specific practices were chosen based on a combination of personal contacts and suggestions by persons knowledgeable about local practitioners.

The third part of the data collection consisted of semi-structured interviews with approximately 50 contingency fee practitioners, insurance defense counsel, and current or retired insurance adjusters. The plaintiffs' lawyers were chosen by selecting from directories and yellow page listings. Defense counsel or firms were identified by the plaintiffs' lawyers, and insurance adjusters were identified by defense counsel.

—*Herbert Kritzer*

Table 3. Acceptance rates by practice and lawyer factors

	Low contact volume			Medium contact volume			High contact volume
	Mean percent	Overall percent	n	Mean percent	Overall percent	n	
Gender							
Male	*50%*	50%	245	40%	39%	89	all male
Female	*42*	40	35	34	36	18	
Type of practice							
Personal injury plaintiffs	*55*	54	52	41	39	79	all personal injury plaintiffs
Personal injury defense	*45*	42	63	—	—	3	
Other litigation	*45*	48	88	35	46	13	
General practice	*54*	52	78	32	30	9	
% of income from contingency fees							
0–19%	*44*	42	116	—	—	(4)	all 90–100%
20–49%	*52*	49	94	34	43	12	
50–89%	*54*	55	58	40	38	34	
90–100%	*60*	55	20	43	39	57	
Firm specializes in plaintiffs work?							
Yes	53	54	54	40	40	64	all in plaintiff specialist firms
No	49	48	213	40	36	36	
Medical malpractice cases							
10% or more	47	50	29	*28*	27	25	all less than 10%
less than 10%	50	50	260	*42*	42	84	
Products cases							
10% or more	51	47	36	45	48	26	all less than 10%
less than 10%	49	50	253	37	36	83	
Nonpersonal injury contingency fee work							
50% or more	*41*	46	50	31	50	7	all 10% or less
11–49%	*51*	51	60	44	45	17	
10% or less	*50*	51	136	37	36	69	
Position in firm							
Solo	50	50	49	45	41	18	
Partner/owner	50	50	183	40	41	73	
Nonpartner	46	47	50	30	27	16	
City size							
Milwaukee	50	49	86	35	34	35	all Milwaukee
100,000 & up	45	48	54	33	36	22	
50,000–99,999	49	49	62	42	39	27	
under 50,000	53	53	79	44	43	22	
Years of experience							
10 or less	*45*	43	73	42	37	26	2, 10 or less
11 or 20	*47*	46	117	36	35	46	2, 11–20
21 or more	*56*	59	96	41	42	36	

Note: Bold italics indicate differences statistically significant at .05 level or better.

probably reflects the smaller number of such respondents compared to the low volume respondents; the directional patterns for some of the variables mentioned above were similar for medium volume lawyers even though the differences did not achieve statistical significance.

The only discernible pattern in Table 3 is what appears to be an inverse relationship between selectivity and dependence on contingency fee (particularly personal injury) work: selectivity decreases as dependence on contingency fee cases increases. That is, lawyers who have substantial work that is not contingency fee based are able to be more selective in the cases that they accept. For these lawyers, the question is why take contingency fee cases that will be less lucrative than hourly fee work? One lawyer put it bluntly when he said, "I'm in contingency fee cases to beat my hourly rate."

What the table does not show is that at least some of those who are most dependent upon such work are among the most selective in which cases they take. At the extreme is the lawyer who reported that his/her firm had 5,000 contacts per year but accepted only 200 cases (an acceptance rate of 4 percent). However, most lawyers with substantial dependence upon contingency fee cases are not able to be as selective as either those lawyers or firms who "cherry pick" among potential cases or those who combine contingency fee work with hourly fee work.[5]

The most striking aspects of Table 3 are the relative lack of variation (taking into account the volume variable) and the absence of any identifiable group that accepts "most" of the cases that are screened. In fact, almost no categories accept substantially more than 50 percent of the cases screened, and the highest acceptance rate is only 60 percent. Simply stated, contingency fee lawyers generally turn down at least as many cases as they accept, and often turn down considerably more than they accept.

Declining cases

Typically, the first contact between lawyer and client comes in a phone call. This first call is extremely important because, on average, lawyers declined about half of all eventually declined cases based on this initial contact (see Table 4). Looking at aggregate numbers of cases declined (i.e., adding up all of the cases declined), the rate of decline based on initial telephone contacts increases as call volume goes up (see Table 4), with the low volume lawyers declining 53 percent of the total declined after the first phone conversation, medium volume 60 percent, and high volume 83 percent. Lawyers drop about 5 percent of the declined cases after a potential client fails to keep a first appointment. Most of the rest of the cases declined were declined after the first in-person meeting. Thus, lawyers make relatively quick decisions on most potential contingency fee cases.

Respondents were asked whether there was a minimum damage figure for each of three types of cases: auto accidents, medical malpractice, and products liability. Most (94 percent) provided a response for auto accidents, but only 43 percent stated that there was a minimum for such cases (the median minimum was $5,000). Substantially fewer responded regarding medical malpractice (61 percent) or products liability (69 percent), reflecting that many lawyers did not handle these kinds of cases. Of those who did respond, a higher

Table 4. When cases are declined

	All cases	All cases without high volume	Low volume	Medium volume	High volume
	Mean percentages				
After first phone call	51%			49%	55%
Client did not appear for first appointment	7			7	5
After first appointment	30			33	21
After additional investigation	15			15	13
	Aggregate percentages				
After first phone call	65%	59%	53%	60%	83%
Client did not appear for first appointment	5	5	7	5	5
After first appointment	18	22	29	21	6
After additional investigation	11	13	14	13	6

Other forms of gatekeeping

In addition to lawyers, there are other potential gatekeeping mechanisms. One would be to ban the contingency fee and require that potential litigants be prepared to bear the cost of seeking recompense for injury or other losses. This shifts the risk from the lawyer to the potential litigant. In some countries where contingency fees are prohibited, systems of legal insurance shift the risk.[1] Such a system would disadvantage those at the bottom of the economic ladder because "legal expense insurance" would probably be one of those "extras" that would be the first item to be cut from a tight budget.

Another way of gatekeeping, which also focuses on the incentive structure/risk preferences of the potential litigant, is fee shifting, where the loser of a lawsuit is required to pay the winner's costs. This system serves to disadvantage the middle class, which has to choose between foregoing compensation or putting at risk other resources (e.g., savings); those at the bottom of the economic ladder are essentially "judgment proof" and have nothing to lose through fee shifting.[2]

Interestingly, in 1995 England, which had both a ban on contingency fees and a fee shifting regime, relaxed the former by permitting a variant the government preferred to call "conditional fees."[3] At that same time the Law Society (the professional organization of solicitors) came forth with an insurance scheme to ameliorate the problems created by fee shifting (i.e., the client can be insured against the risks of the fee shifting rule). The result is gatekeeping may be shifting from incentives focused on the potential litigant to incentives focused on the solicitor. It is too early to know what impact this has had, or will have, on the English court system.

—*Herbert M. Kritzer*

1. This is perhaps most developed in Germany; see Blankenburg, "Changes in Political Regimes and Continuity of the Rule of Law in Germany," in Jacob, Blankenburg, Kritzer, Provine, and Sanders, *Courts, Law & Politics in Comparative Perspective* (New Haven: Yale University Press, 1996), 298.

2. See the recent study of fee shifting in Alaska (the one state that has a blanket fee-shifting rule, although limited), Di Pietro, "The English Rule at Work in Alaska," *Judicature* 80 (1996), 88. A similar pattern was reported when Florida briefly imposed a fee shifting rule in medical malpractice cases; see Snyder and Hughes, "The English Rule for Allocating Legal Costs: Evidence Confronts Theory," *J. L. Econ. and Organization* 6 (1990), 345 at 356.

3. The American contingency fee is a commission system that takes on the contingency element through the fact that 33 percent of nothing is nothing. The English conditional fee system allows the solicitor to add a bonus to his or her usual fee (of up to 100 percent), but this fee is not a direct function of the amount recovered; see Kritzer, "Courts, Justice, and Politics in England," in Jacob et al., *supra* n. 1, at 136.

percentage reported a minimum damage figure: 61 percent for medical malpractice (median $100,000) and 60 percent for products liability (median $75,000).

Lawyers were also asked what percentage of cases declined were due to lack of liability, low damages or inadequate fee potential, both lack of liability and low damages, falling outside the area of the lawyer's practice, and other reasons. Not surprisingly, lack of liability and inadequate damages (singly or together) are the dominant reasons for declining cases, accounting for about 80 percent of the declined cases. Table 5 shows the aggregated figures for all lawyers, for all lawyers omitting the four high case volume lawyers, low volume lawyers, and medium volume lawyers. Lack of liability alone accounts for the largest proportion of cases declined, particularly for those lawyers with a higher volume of contacts from potential clients. Excluding the high volume lawyers (who are not shown as a separate column in Table 5 because there are only four such respondents),[6] only about a quarter of the declined cases were due solely to low damages.

The right cases?

One question this analysis cannot answer is whether lawyers turn away too many or too few cases, or whether they turn away the right cases. Many have lamented the supposed growth in "litigiousness" among the American population, but it is not necessarily self-evident that Americans are too eager to seek compensation when under our law compensation is due. We might return to Elihu Root's injunction, "about half of the practice of the decent lawyer consists in telling would-be clients that they are damned fools and should stop," as one possible measure. If we take "half of the prac-

Table 5. Reasons for declining cases

	All cases	All cases without high volume	Low volume	Medium volume
	Aggregate percentages			
Lack of liability	48%	40%	35%	41%
Inadequate damages	18	23	24	23
Both lack of liability and inadequate damages	13	17	21	16
Outside lawyer's area of practice	11	10	11	10
Other reasons	10	10	10	11
	Mean percentages			
Lack of liability	36%	35%	33%	41%
Inadequate damages	20	21	20	22
Both lack of liability and inadequate damages	20	20	22	16
Outside lawyer's area of practice	9	9	9	9
Other reasons	11	11	11	11

tice," to refer to the proportion of potential cases accepted, then most contingency fee lawyers achieve this measure of decency.

While the survey data do show variations among lawyers in selectiveness, they do not provide direct information on variations among types of cases. Observations, however, make it clear that lawyers are more selective in some types of cases than in others. To some degree this reflects the simple fact that injury victims are more knowledgeable about whether they are entitled to compensation for some types of injuries (auto accidents) than for others (slip and falls, medical malpractice, etc.). During a month observing in a law office in the middle of a Wisconsin winter, there were several significant snow falls and a number of calls from persons who had slipped on snow or ice. Most of these cases were turned away simply because Wisconsin law allows property owners time to remove snow or ice from sidewalks before they become liable for injuries from falls.

Medical malpractice is one of the areas most talked about as needing reform to provide relief to medical providers from increasing law suits. During three months of observation in three different law practices, lawyers dealt with contacts from 14 potential medical malpractice clients; only one of which resulted in a retainer being signed, and it did not involve the potential malpractice aspects of the case. Lawyers are extremely cautious in accepting medical malpractice cases, and the lawyers observed spent a lot of time explaining to potential clients why their negative med-

ical outcome did not constitute malpractice, or the difficulty in establishing that it did arise from malpractice, or that even if it was malpractice, the ultimate medical outcome was probably not affected by the error (and the interim consequences did not give rise to damages that made pursuing the matter financially attractive).

For example, one potential client had a surgical procedure to correct a swallowing problem that involved insertion of an instrument down his esophagus. During the procedure the esophagus was injured necessitating surgery through the chest. The potential client was upset because he had been in substantial pain in the recovery room and there was a delay in realizing the problem with the esophagus, and the recovery from the more major surgery was several months longer than it would have been from the simpler procedure.

As it turned out, a torn esophagus was a known risk of the simpler procedure (and the client had been warned of that risk as indicated by a signed informed consent). Furthermore, there was a significant chance that a more invasive procedure (through the chest) would have been needed even without the injury to the esophagus because the simpler procedure was substantially less than 100 percent effective. In this case, the lawyer explained to the potential client that the physician who conducted the original procedure probably had not committed medical malpractice (even if the recovery room staff had been slow to realize that there was a problem), and that there would be questions about damages because the final result was very good (i.e., the original problem had been corrected) and there were no residual problems from the chest surgery.

One of the standard laments of proponents of change is that lawyers pursue too many cases that prove to be unfounded, particularly medical malpractice cases. Is this the result of poor screening decisions, or is there another explanation? Michael Saks has nicely laid out the dilemma that arises in assessing case selection in medical malpractice litigation.[7] Injuries during medical treatment are common, but only a very small fraction of those injuries is attributable to negligence. The injured persons are not very good at determining whether their injuries are due to negligence, and so large numbers of persons whose injuries are not due to negligence are likely to seek legal counsel. Let us assume the following:

- 100,000 persons experience injuries during medical treatment;

- 1,000 (1 percent) of these were injured due to negligence and the injuries of the other 99,000 were not due to negligence;

- 500 (half) of those injured due to negligence seek legal counsel as do 10 percent (9,900) of whose injuries were not a result of negligence;

- the lawyers make the correct decision in 90 percent of the cases;

- this means that 450 (90 percent of 500) of the cases accepted did involve negligence and 990 (10 percent of 990) did not.

The bottom line is that even though those who actually experienced medical negligence are much more likely to seek legal counsel than those who were not so injured (50 percent versus 10 percent), and lawyers make the correct decision 90 percent of the time, more than two-thirds of the cases pursued did not involve negligence. By these figures, around 1 percent of injuries not arising from medical negligence leads to legal claims, a percentage which is about the same as the rate of negligence among medical injuries.[8]

*****

This research makes it clear that contingency fee lawyers do operate as gatekeepers: they turn away substantial numbers of potential clients, most often because those potential clients simply do not have a basis for pursuing the case. The contingency fee structure means that lawyers carry out this function in large part as an exercise in economic self-interest. That is, lawyers try to choose cases they believe will yield fees at least equal to what they could earn from either nonhourly fee cases or from other contingency fee cases. In a sense, the lawyer is making decisions about which cases to include in his or her portfolio of risks. The lawyer knows that some cases will fail to yield a fee sufficient to compensate for expenses while other cases will yield a profit that will at least offset the "unsuccessful" cases,[9] and hopefully yield a profit across the entire portfolio. Some lawyers explicitly include in their portfolios a mix of hourly and contingency fee cases on the expectation that the former will cover the overhead and the latter will produce the profits; others have a mix of cases simply because that is the nature of the clientele they are able to attract.

Notes

This article originally appeared in Volume 81, Number 1, July–August 1997, pages 22–29.

The original version of this paper was prepared for presentation at 1996 Annual Meeting of the American Political Science Association, San Francisco, California. A short version of the analysis presented here appeared as "Holding Back the Floodtide: The Role of Contingent Fee Lawyers," *Wisconsin Lawyer* 70, 10. The research reported here is supported by National Science Foundation Grant No. SBR-9510976. Research assistance was provided by J. Mitchell Pickerill.

1. Glendon, *A Nation Under Lawyers: How the Crisis in the Legal Profession Is Transforming American Society* (Cambridge: Harvard University Press, 1994), 37, 75.

2. Crane, "Lawyers Don't Take Every Case," *National Law Journal* (January 25, 1988), at 1, 34.

3. *See, for example,* Trine and Luvera, "Pros and Cons of Accepting a Case," *Trial* 16 (May 1994), 16.

4. Dietz, Baird, and Berul, "The Medical Malpractice Legal System," in *Appendix: Report of the Secretary's Commission on Medical Malpractice* (Washington, D.C.: Department of Health, Education and Welfare, 1973 [DHEW Publication No. (OS) 73-89]), 95–101. This study found that, overall, attorneys accepted only about one in eight potential medical malpractice clients who contacted them.

5. One minor pattern is the difference between male and female attorneys, with females accepting a lower percentage of cases. Additional analyses indicated that this was probably not simply a result of women working in practice settings where the percent of cases accepted was lower. Why women tend to accept a lower percentage of cases than do men is not clear.

6. These four lawyers report declining a total of 7,145 cases, 68 percent solely on liability grounds, 7 percent due to low damages, 5 percent due to a combination of low

damages and lack of liability, 12 percent because they were outside the lawyers' areas of practice, and 8 percent for other reasons.

7. Saks, "Do We Really Know Anything About the Behavior of the Tort Litigation System—and Why Not?," *U. Pa. L. Rev.* 140 (1992), 1147 at 1193–1196; the numbers used here differ somewhat from those used by Saks, but the pattern is the same (although the numbers Saks uses produce an even more extreme result).

8. Ibid. at 1196, n. 150.

9. A case may be unsuccessful if no recovery is obtained, if an unexpectedly small recovery is obtained, or if the costs of obtaining the recovery (i.e., the amount of lawyer time) are much higher than expected. For more on these various risks see Kritzer, "Rhetoric and Reality . . . Uses and Abuses . . . Contingencies and Certainties: The American Contingent Fee in Operation," DPRP Working Paper, Institute for Legal Studies, University of Wisconsin, 1996.

Actors in the Judicial Process

Interest Groups

Unlike the legislative process, in which a governmental institution may address a problem simply as a matter of choice, courts are responsive bodies and can deal only with cases brought before them by actual litigants. On the surface, litigation often appears to be an effort to redress individual concerns. It is important to recognize, however, that litigation can have significant policy consequences for society that extend far beyond the importance of a case for individual litigants. The judicial process can be the most efficient means by which interest groups pursue their preferred policy ends, either through the filing of an amicus curiae brief or by making the larger commitment of sponsoring a "test case." While not a great deal of systematic knowledge is available about individual litigants (except, perhaps, for our knowledge of criminal defendants brought to court by the government against their will), we continue to learn much about the role of interest groups in the judicial process. This section of readings examines several facets of group participation in the American judiciary.

In "Civil rights litigation by organizations: constraints and choices," Stephen Wasby examines the real-world operation of planned litigation in which a group attempts to pursue societal change through the courts. Wasby's specific focus is the NAACP's efforts in the civil rights arena, and he demonstrates convincingly that in litigation much group behavior that seeks social change "is often reflexive and far from completely planned, with many constraints ... many detours along the road to organizational goals, and much flexibility of action by both the litigating organizations and individual staff attorneys."

One of the most graphic examples of interest group participation in Supreme Court litigation occurred in *Webster v. Reproductive Health Services* (1989), a case that dealt with state legislation regulating abortions. It was perceived by many analysts as the instrument through which the Court might overturn *Roe v. Wade* (1973), the seminal precedent enhancing freedom of choice. Two selections in this section focus on the *Webster* case. Susan Behuniak's article, "Friendly fire: amici curiae and *Webster v. Reproductive Health Services*," offers a detailed study of group participation in the case. Behuniak's analysis examines who filed amicus briefs and what arguments were raised. It also explores the impact of these briefs on the diverse opinions of the justices

and the possible reasons for differences in behavior between groups on the anti-abortion and pro-choice sides of the case.

In a related article with a somewhat different focus, Jack Rossotti, Laura Natelson, and Raymond Tatalovich utilize content analysis to explore "Nonlegal advice: the amicus briefs in *Webster v. Reproductive Health Services*." Their study documents that the amicus briefs used in this case rely on many sources of arguments beyond legal ones. Perhaps not surprisingly, when the justices cited amici in their opinions, the briefs they utilized were not those that focused primarily on legal issues per se. As the authors note, "It makes perfect sense that a justice would look to his or her own knowledge of case law or rely upon clerks to research legal precedents. ... But to do an extensive search of cognate disciplines as wide-ranging as medicine, theology, history, and psychology is beyond the capacity of any judge, and it was this need for substantive knowledge and third-party representation that gave rise to the use of amicus briefs." It is in this sense that interest groups and the briefs they author can be credited with broadening the scope of litigation before the Court and, in the process, the public policy focus of judicial decisions.

Without question, the most frequent interest before the Court, both as a litigator and as a filer of amicus briefs, is the U.S. government acting through the Office of the Solicitor General on behalf of the executive branch. The government is a party to a suit or files an amicus brief in the vast majority of Supreme Court cases. In "The solicitor general as amicus, 1953–2000: how influential?" Rebecca Deen, Joseph Ignagni, and James Meernik offer a detailed portrait of the government's amicus participation through a half century of Supreme Court litigation. The study traces a long-term trend towards increased amicus participation by the government, significant variance among presidential administrations in the nature of their amicus activity, and a decline in the relative success of the government's amicus filings that is traceable back to the Reagan administration. The authors raise the possibility that this decreased success rate reflects the politicization of the solicitor general's office by presidential administrations aggressively pursuing their agenda cases to the Supreme Court with an eye more towards policy preferences than the state of the law.

Civil rights litigation by organizations: constraints and choices

Stephen L. Wasby

Litigation for social change is far from completely planned. Numerous external and internal factors affect both the planning and execution of a campaign.

Organized groups have long made use of the courts in their efforts to produce—or retard—social change. Despite claims that "social policy" litigation, which courts are said to lack the capacity to handle,[1] is new, such litigation has long taken place. In the 1930s, for example, conservative groups went to court to challenge New Deal legislation. In terms of litigation systematically brought by interest groups—a litigation "campaign" or "planned" litigation—the efforts to overturn school segregation, resulting in *Brown v. Board of Education*,[2] are most likely to come to mind. These efforts by the NAACP Legal Defense Fund (LDF) have become the model for planned litigation, followed both by those seeking civil rights for other segments of society, for example, women, and those litigating outside the civil rights field, such as environmental groups like the Sierra Club and the Natural Resources Defense Council.[3] The growth of public interest law firms, both liberal and conservative, indicates the use of the model across the political spectrum.[4]

Not all litigation aimed at producing social change is "planned" litigation or takes the form of litigation campaigns. Nor are all test cases instances of planned litigation. For example, it was only recently that the American Civil Liberties Union (ACLU), which we associate with test case litigation, began to undertake systematic litigation in particular areas of the law through "projects" staffed by particular attorneys, instead of litigating primarily against "targets of opportunity." [5]

Mounting a litigation campaign is no easy task. It requires attention not only to strategy in particular cases but also to larger strategy, including choosing areas of law in which to litigate, choosing cases within those areas of law, and developing the resources necessary to undertake the litigation.

Planning any individual case, such as a large antitrust case, a class action toxic injury case or a drug case like the DES litigation, poses many problems for the lawyers involved. Yet when an organization, such as a civil rights group like LDF, contemplates undertaking a litigation "campaign" in a particular area of the law,[6]

matters become even more difficult: the organization must worry not simply about individual cases but about a number of them.

In an effort to cast more light on "planned" litigation, particularly in the area of civil rights, this article explores some aspects of civil rights litigation undertaken by interest groups and the lawyers associated with them, emphasizing cases on school desegregation, employment discrimination (primarily cases under Title VII of the Civil Rights Act of 1964), and housing discrimination. After a look at some possible effects of litigation campaigns on the work of courts, we turn our attention to lawyers' perspectives on the role of interest groups in planned litigation, with particular attention to organizations' choices of areas of law in which to litigate and of cases to pursue, and to the internal dynamics of those cases. Then we will examine relations between staff attorneys and "cooperating" attorneys and interorganizational relationships affecting litigation.

Primary attention is paid to the work of the National Association for the Advancement of Colored People (NAACP) and the NAACP Legal Defense and Educational Fund, Inc. (LDF) from the late 1960s through the early 1980s. This period was chosen because it was an "age of complexity" for race relations interest group litigators. The environment in which the litigators functioned became increasingly complex; in addition to having to attend to judicial rulings, they had to focus on statutes and implementing regulations as well. Moreover, pubic opinion concerning civil rights became more conservative than it had been in the early and mid-1960s. Congress also became less supportive of civil rights, as did the executive branch, in the transitions both from the Johnson to Nixon presidencies and later, from the Carter to Reagan administrations.

Litigation itself became more complex; school cases were no longer a matter of attacking segregation statutes but required considerable resources both to prove violations and then to develop and implement remedies or involved challenges to "second-generation" discrimination within schools. In employment discrimination, the most blatant forms of discrimination had been replaced by more subtle forms, varying from industry to industry, which also required considerable resources to demonstrate.

This article is based primarily on interviews with more than 40 attorneys who are or were associated with the NAACP, the LDF, or other active organizational participants in race relations litigation (e.g., the Lawyers Committee for Civil Rights Under Law, the National Committee Against Discrimination in Housing, the Center for National Policy Review, and the Center for Law and Education). Among those interviewed were the senior attorneys for these organizations; several lawyers closely involved in organizations' litigation planning, although they did not serve as staff attorneys; and many "cooperating attorneys" in major race relations cases. The cooperating attorneys include some who were expert in a particular type of litigation such as school desegregation, some who tried cases across the country, and others involved in cases in their own states and communities.

The interviews, based primarily on open-ended questions, were structured but allowed respondents to discuss matters they thought especially salient. Among matters covered were organizations' choices of areas of law in which to litigate, choices of particular cases, organizations' use of cooperating attorneys, relations between litigating organizations, and the effect and importance of factors that might affect the litigation in which the respondents or their organization had been involved. Aspects of the particular cases in which the cooperating attorneys had been involved were explored in interviews with these individuals.

Litigation campaigns and the courts

Although interest groups attempt to use the courts to achieve social change, such litigation does not *necessarily* add significantly to the courts' work. Particularly when precedent is an organization's goal, a litigation campaign may involve bringing a number of cases so that the organization has several appropriate cases reach the appellate courts in the appropriate sequence, with allowance being made for some cases being settled and some "washing out" for other reasons. Nonetheless, the number of cases may be no greater than if individual plaintiffs asserted their rights in separate cases. Whether or not a litigation campaign was under way to achieve school desegregation, suits would have had to be filed against many school districts, and many Title

VII lawsuits would have been necessary to resolve complaints of employment discrimination even if the LDF had not decided to proceed systematically.[7]

Without the efforts of the NAACP and the LDF, fewer school desegregation or employment discrimination cases would have been brought, but that is primarily because those organizations provided resources—staff attorneys, cooperating attorneys, and expenses—not otherwise available to many prospective plaintiffs. It is thus the interest groups' efforts and injection of resources, not that these efforts took the form of planned litigation, that may have produced more cases for the courts, just as governmental actions with respect to schools, or action by private entities concerning employment, often prompted the litigation.

Litigation campaigns may in a way have *reduced* the number of cases with which the courts had to contend because class action suits combining many claims were major vehicles in the LDF Title VII campaign. Without the class action suits, there might have been more individual plaintiffs' suits. As it was, there were many of those, brought by attorneys using materials made available by organizational litigators. The class action suits, however, were more complex and thus took more time to litigate, just as northern school desegregation suits involved significant problems of proof. Civil rights litigation often took the form of "public law" cases—polycentric controversies involving multiple parties and entailing detailed and continuing relief, and thus requiring prolonged involvement by the judge hearing the case[8]—or "structural lawsuits" with "an array of competing interests and perspectives organized around a number of issues and a single decisional agency, the judge." [9]

The growing complexity of cases can affect case outcomes in a number of ways. Litigators' needs for substantial resources may mean that they may not be able to pursue some complaints or that some complaints once commenced must be abandoned. Principal civil rights litigating organizations concentrating only on the "big," potentially precedent-setting cases have fewer resources to devote to "small," individual-plaintiff cases, which must be pursued, if at all, by local counsel. Judicial standards, requiring proof of intent to discriminate, not merely of disparate effects,[10] not only require civil rights lawyers to put on a more elaborate case but also make it less likely that civil rights plaintiffs will prevail.

The courts have themselves contributed to the complexity of civil rights litigation—and thus to their own workload. One way is through the just-noted requirement of proof of intent to discriminate. Courts also affect litigation in other ways, for example, by their receptivity to certain arguments and, because of groups' need for financial resources for civil rights litigation, their willingness to grant attorneys fees under the Civil Rights Attorneys Fees Awards Act of 1976. The Supreme Court's willingness to grant review to cases in certain areas of the law and its disinclination to hear cases in other areas affect litigators' pursuit of cases to that level. For example, the Court's not having previously granted certiorari in restrictive covenant cases made the NAACP pay particular attention to framing cases so that the Court would grant review[11] and the Court's unwillingness to hear claims of discrimination in public housing and urban renewal cases "depressed the market" for such cases.[12]

The Court's procedural rulings, such as those on the standing of parties to sue, have important effects as well: *Warth v. Seldin*[13] is said to have had a devastating effect on the campaign against exclusionary zoning. And of course the Court's substantive rulings are crucial. An example is the decision in *San Antonio School District v. Rodriguez,*[14] which shut off federal court challenges to the property tax basis for financing public education. That case led civil rights lawyers to redirect their efforts to state courts, an indication of the effect of judicial decisions on litigators' choice of federal or state forum. The abortive campaign to reform the welfare system through litigation provides another example.[15] Although the Court issued favorable rulings in benefit termination cases on due process grounds,[16] when it handed down adverse rulings on benefit levels[17] the campaign came to an end.

Planned litigation

To write about litigators' perspectives on "planned litigation" is to assume that such litigation exists.[18] We must, however, be careful not to assume that all litigation to which some attach the label "planned" is thoroughly or fully planned, with litigators in control of the areas of law in which they focus their efforts, of particular cases, or of sequence of cases. To use the term is to say, at the least, that some make efforts at planned litigation; it is not to say how thorough or successful those efforts are.

If the conventional wisdom is that civil rights litigation of the 1940s and early 1950s consisted of planned, organized campaigns to produce social change, the picture presented here of the more recent period is quite different. Even in the litigation leading to *Brown v. Board of Education,* we get a picture rather different from Kluger's portrayal in *Simple Justice,* which Mark Tushnet has properly criticized as being one of "essentially unproblematic success." [19] Instead, there was "a tremendous amount of matter extraneous to policy which determined whether a case was brought in one state rather than another or one place rather than another," and policy was made primarily "around Thurgood Marshall's desk," with a "lot of improvisation." [20]

Recent civil rights litigation certainly contains elements of planning, and much of the litigation is undertaken systematically. However, much about that litigation is problematic, in part because it is quite complex and much is unplanned, so that to a considerable degree even principal civil rights lawyers do not fully control it. Particularly in point is the observation by a major civil rights litigator, "The vagaries of litigation are such that if you bring a case solely to go the Supreme Court, there are 100 ways not to get there, and if you try to play cute in order to stay away, you end up there."

Nor do all those who have participated in "planned litigation" share a view of the activity as derived from a blueprint. Litigation, said one lawyer, is a "responsive posture" inhibiting one from doing anything. Litigation provided "some room for maneuver," but was "not a strategic tool." Civil rights lawyers—lawyers with definite goals, working for organizations which have clear statements of purpose—frequently volunteered comments about the unplanned nature of their enterprise and unhesitatingly stressed the difficulties of keeping litigation strategy under control. In particular, one must keep in mind one litigator's acerbic comment, "Retrospective analyses that discern grand (and not so grand) strategies are often piffle. Many initiatives are impromptu." Furthermore, in general "the nature of the business prevents it from being a grand design: Whatever gets done, gets done, rather than by design."

Control of litigation

At the heart of planned litigation is *control*.[21] This includes the ability to "influence the development and sequence of cases," so that lawyers can "produce cases which presented the issues they wanted decided, where and when they wanted them," [22] something "far from automatic and not subject to tight control." [23] Among the many matters not subject to control are, in the words of one LDF lawyer, "the chance occurrences of any lawsuit, the defection of the plaintiffs or capitulation of defendants, disagreement among counsel, unanticipated precedents, and the effect of public sentiment and political currents on adjudication." [24] Litigators might be able to exercise control at the level of the individual case and might also be able to choose areas of law in which to litigate and to establish priorities among those areas. Within any area of law, however, there is a less tidy picture; lawyers' ability to control the flow of cases and thus to choose cases decreases because there are more problems "whenever you clutter the landscape with litigation." Many decisions are made *inductively* (or responsively), a result of pressure, circumstance, and the flow of cases to litigators, rather than *deductively*, following logically from certain established criteria.

That an organization does more than respond idiosyncratically to cases cannot be taken for granted. Even when organizations bring test cases—the quintessence of planned litigation—they may not have done so as a result of broad litigation planning. Instead they may have responded to "fortuitous events." Even where an organization has undertaken a planned litigation campaign, such as LDF's Title VII litigation, some cases have been taken reflexively, in response to client and membership pressure. Thus even when an organization does attempt to plan litigation, its activities may not result from strategy. Although an organization may be capable of developing "offensive" strategies, "circumstances control." Thus it has been difficult for the NAACP "to control priorities and time expenditures," making it "reflective and responsive to events and developments." If at times it seemed "as if there was a grand strategy applied from New York, the opposite was true:" matters "arose in the countryside" and then moved to the national level. Moreover, when there is a plan, flexibility—essential to success—will result in departures from it. The speed with which cases arise may also make it difficult for litigators to control litigation.

Strategy sessions can be an important element of "planning" in planned litigation.[25] However, observers believe that efforts to get lawyers together to plan strategy have seldom produced "grand strategizing;" they produce "petty strategizing if anything." When six people were brought together in a hotel room to plan, "not much came out of any of that type of activity," because what results from "sitting around" is "too abstract" for use in actual situations. Even where strategy has been planned, the presence of a larger number of litigators increases the likelihood that "another actor will enter the fray and set matters back several

years." Indeed, "too many people are doing too many things for planned litigation to be more than a myth. If you are going to bring up cases A, B, C, and D, before you can, 12 others bring it up." That forces you to "move when you can where you can," with litigation more like "secret warfare."

Choosing areas of law

If planning involves choice, what do we find about interest group litigators' choices?[26] The choice of particular areas of law in which to focus litigation activities is a crucial part of planned litigation. Certain areas in which organizations litigate, for example, Title VII and capital punishment by LDF, are chosen with some care, with constraints imposed mostly by limited resources. School desegregation, the "most programmatically developed" area of NAACP litigation, has been that organization's primary litigation focus, taking up "90 percent of the conscious effort" in litigation. The NAACP has also been active in the fight against employment discrimination, but that area of law did not receive the same attention by the group's legal department. Indeed, as a result of a request from the NAACP's labor director, highly involved for many years in battling job discrimination, the LDF did the "biggest piece" of the NAACP cases; the lack of NAACP resources meant the organization had to "funnel" many Title VII cases to the LDF, with "the strategy [being] LDF strategy."

Litigation in some other areas of the law evolves because many cases on a topic come to an organization, such as the sit-in and demonstration cases of the early 1960s.[27] Other areas are said "simply [to] arise naturally." To the extent staff attorneys can "freewheel" and pursue cases that fall outside the organization's basic litigation agenda, its litigation focus will become more diffuse.

Among the elements entering into the choice of areas of law for attention is an organizational one; the NAACP "had to consider that other organizations were considering some issues." The branches' "significant input" is an important intra-organizational fact, with the size and strength of a branch a relevant factor. Resolutions by the board of directors are also relevant, but board votes don't translate directly into litigation campaigns because of the "interplay" between board votes and the views of the general counsel, who has considerable autonomy to pursue his own interests, subject to his having to deal with the organization's own "bureaucratic" problems and having to serve as NAACP's house counsel. Staff lawyers play an important role, "orchestrating, certainly in tactical matters," and their views predominate, particularly when NAACP branches do not have lawyers among their officers. As with any litigating organization, resources are a crucial matter, indeed a "primary consideration" in NAACP's choice of areas of law.

The mid-1960s enactment of new civil rights statutes provided a "natural dividing line" in LDF's litigation efforts. Its focused litigation campaign, the most significant of private efforts to enforce Title VII, came about in part because job discrimination was an issue with substantial, immediate, and visible economic ramifications for minorities. This indicates that pressures on a nonmembership "public interest law firm" like LDF may be similar to those on the membership-based NAACP. Pressure may not be felt directly by LDF, but it is felt through clients coming to cooperating attorneys, from whom LDF gets most of its cases. Indeed, although neither the LDF nor the NAACP preferred having "ad hoc" cases, both had some. "Given the nature of the [NAACP] organization," that is, its membership base, the NAACP did "have to have some ad hoc cases" and has had more than has LDF.

Funding—particularly foundation funding—has been said to particularly influence the areas in which LDF has litigated. LDF has also been thought quite persuasive in getting foundations to support what LDF wanted to do. In short, LDF "solicits for specific issues," and "to the extent the funds are earmarked, [LDF staff] play a part in the earmarking."

Choosing cases

Once cases are channeled to an organization, decisions must be made as to which ones to pursue. Choosing areas of law and choosing cases are closely related. Decisions about the former help channel certain types of cases to the litigators. At least equally important, and reinforcement for the "inductive" or responsive view of "planned" litigation, is that decisions about areas of law in which to concentrate are influenced by the flow of cases to an organization. This makes how cases come to a litigating organization quite important. With cooperating attorneys the primary source of cases, organizational control of litigation planning may be reduced unless cooperating attorneys' choices are influenced by national organizational criteria. Nor do litigating organizations enter all cases from the beginning, which would facilitate control; they may become involved in some cases already initiated by others—sometimes

defensively to prevent "bad" precedent or avoid rulings not in line with organizational strategy. This is a clear indication of the limits on organizations' ability to plan their litigation and control implementation of their strategy.

Lawyers associated with civil rights groups identify a variety of criteria used to select cases, but there is no clear consensus on the criteria used; moreover, constraints and organizational politics affect attempts to apply the criteria. NAACP decisions to take cases were based on several factors, including the significance of the case (those with broad impact were preferred) and the importance of the branch that initiated a case.

The NAACP took some cases because people in a particular community "had started to do the right thing" and one "had to help them." The NAACP also took cases because governments took actions that were "affronts [that] had to be challenged," giving the organization "no choice" but to get involved even if the cases did not fit with litigation strategy. However, the NAACP preferred not to fund a case unless the organization and its lawyers controlled the case and the case was "consistent with organizational policy." Particularly when a case had already been started, the NAACP would enter it only if it could "exercise significant direction" over the case. The view is "that general counsel and the New York staff will control litigation in which the organization is involved." Thus "if a branch went off with inconsistent litigation, or hadn't precleared the case, there would be hell to pay."

A number of observers felt, however, that case selection did not function according to prescribed procedures or on the basis of criteria related to litigation strategy. Indeed, the process by which cases came to NAACP has been called "helter-skelter," with the NAACP having "no sense of direction" and "jumping into cases without an idea of the factors or what the costs will be." At times the NAACP got involved in cases because its attorneys focused on the particular case rather than on the "larger picture." Some staff lawyers did not consider themselves "social engineers" and thus were not firm believers in planned litigation for social change. Not able to "tell what the effects of precedent will be," they focused on racial problems in individual cases. And because the organization was "relatively flexible internally as to lawyers' choices," at times it was up to the individual lawyer to decide whether to take a case.

The received tradition about LDF's planned litigation would lead one to expect case selection to be governed by a highly developed set of regularly applied criteria. Instead, LDF was criticized by lawyers associated with it for not having done more to "institutionalize" its process for deciding which cases to take and for not developing criteria for the purpose. Moreover, the process for choosing cases was "not organized, it's organic." "Greater organizational sophistication," a result of experience and organizational growth, did mean, however, "an ability to deal with the brush fires" with which the organization had to contend.

Once brought to LDF's attention, a case was evaluated to determine its "strength" in terms of cost, the quality of the cooperating attorney, "other cases doing the same thing," the state of the law, and "the likelihood of winning." LDF's criteria seemed better developed in Title VII litigation, perhaps because of the focused litigation campaign within that area of the law, leading to special attention in choosing the industries and geographical areas in which to focus litigation. In general, however, lawyers' views were that at LDF "you assess cases as they come to you," with a focus on "how to get the job done in the case."

Thus "LDF didn't make policy in the abstract; it made it through cases." The situation was "not the National Security Council with a weekly sitting-down." Instead, "by sitting in the doctor's office, you get a view of the world." There was attention to issues, "but on a day-to-day basis, you pick the best cases." One reason was that the importance of a case was not always clear when the case was initiated. More than one case had to be picked because "cases drop out for any number of reasons," including settlements offered "which you can't refuse"—although in addition to recommending taking the settlement, the lawyer "might also point out that we took the case to develop the law." In short, there was no "unified legal theory in the civil tradition" from which LDF operated; LDF took "individual cases, from which legal theory was deduced."

LDF made an "enormous commitment to initiating cases" but, while "we prefer to be in from the beginning," LDF entered other cases, particularly if it could play no other role or a cooperating attorney had handled the case, because it was "good at putting cases on the record." LDF would also enter a case after its initiation if the case was seen to have a potentially significant precedential effect. Although there are "obvious problems if you'd not had a part in planning and developing a case," some of these cases were actually viewed favorably because developments in the case provided more information than LDF would otherwise have at

the case-selection stage, giving the organization a clearer picture of what it might be facing.

Case dynamics

The internal dynamics of cases also affect—and can frustrate—attempts to plan litigation. Day-to-day litigation matters often get in the way of litigation planning; lawyers "don't plan that far ahead; they deal with immediate issues." For example, lawyers are "concerned with the violation" in school cases and are "not planning ahead to the remedy stage." [28] Decisions from the Supreme Court coming in mid-litigation—likely because of the extended nature of planned civil rights litigation—can undermine the theory at the heart of a litigant's case. The effects of the Supreme Court's ruling on the welfare litigation campaign were noted previously, as were the effects of the Court's adverse ruling on standing to challenge exclusionary zoning. [29]

Although, to be successful, litigators must be responsive to changes in judicial doctrine, momentum or inertia, the *absence* of dynamics also limits planning in litigation by hindering groups from responding to changes in their environment. For example, Derrick Bell has argued that lawyers have persisted in seeking racially balanced schools despite changes in judicial outlook, "reverses in the school desegregation campaign," and "membership demands for more attention to quality education." [30] Continuing success in litigation, like the Warren Court's expansion of civil rights, is quite likely to kindle a spirit propelling a group to continue litigation and thus to limit shifts in litigation strategy. Apart from success, however, many lawyers believe in the "myth of rights," the idea that litigation can produce positive statements of rights as well as the implementation of those rights. The hold of this myth helps explain why lawyers continued to turn to the courts in pursuit of their clients' rights, even when earlier "ground-breaking" rulings had not been implemented. [31]

Closely related is the fact that victorious litigants do not wish to give up, or be seen as giving up, what they had pressed hard to achieve; altering legal theories in mid-litigation may be thought to be particularly inappropriate. Success thus reinforces what has been called lawyers' general conservatism in planned litigation. "People tend to repeat lessons from the past; lawyers trying to win a case will use what's worked." Moreover, the pace of litigation makes litigation "not a process giving one time to think," further limiting one's ability to respond to changes in one's legal environment.

The presence of other litigators, who may get to the appellate courts first—and "on a worse record"—also serves to press litigators to continue to take cases to those appellate courts even when favorable rulings are not expected. (There are, of course, other reasons, such as the belief that perhaps a limited victory might be obtained or "damage control" achieved.) This helps explain why the talk by civil rights and civil liberties lawyers of avoiding the Burger Court was not matched by a significant decrease in "going to the High Court." After all, said one lawyer, "It's the only Supreme Court we've got." Moreover, in cases where lower court rulings have favored civil rights claims, a conservative high tribunal will be more likely to accept appeals from defeated defendants—extremely evident in recent criminal procedure cases—thus removing from the hands of civil rights litigators the choice not to pursue the case further.

Cooperating attorneys

The prescribed method by which an organization obtains cases may indicate a relatively highly centralized relationship between the organization and cooperating attorneys;[32] this is particularly the case if one looks at the formal process by which cases are supposed to come to the NAACP. However, use of cooperating attorneys means decentralization of the organization's work. An important aspect of that decentralization is whether and to what extent an organization's local units and their goals, as well as the goals of cooperating attorneys, are guided by the goals of the organization at the national level.[33]

One way to assure that cooperating attorneys act within the scope of national policy is to transmit that policy to the local level; providing assistance to the cooperating attorneys also helps achieve this goal.[34] Otherwise, decentralization can cut against a group's national strategy and local membership pressure can dominate determination of the cases to which cooperating attorneys give greatest attention. This is particularly likely when local affiliates initiate cases[35] or when lawyers act independently.[36] At times, national staff attorneys may be "lead counsel" only nominally, with local lawyers handling much of the case and planning much of the strategy and tactics. Lawyers who share a national organization's "world view" may be allowed to "fine-tune or even make major changes in litigation," and may be allowed to run the case instead of being given marching orders. However, with cases becoming more complex, local attorneys are more likely to need assistance, thus binding them more closely to the national organization.

Attorneys' roles

The processes by which cases come to national litigating organizations, and the ways in which the organizations involve cooperating attorneys in their work, serve to define cooperating attorneys' varying roles. In some situations, national staff attorneys handle all trial work, with the cooperating attorney playing a clearly "subordinate role," gathering information and filing papers, serving as required local counsel, and acting principally as liaison between national staff lawyers and the local community. In short, cooperating attorneys may seem like little more than "water carriers" for the staff attorneys, although such a role may be assumed without complaint, particularly when local counsel have their own practices to attend to and realize they can't "carry" a major case.

In another role relationship, an organization's national staff lawyers develop new theories of litigation, with cooperating attorneys applying those theories. In still other situations, cooperating attorneys, who may have generated the cases themselves, serve as "lead counsel." Having greater familiarity with state court rules, local attorneys may be used for state cases, with staff attorneys handling federal litigation.

Roles are also affected by the *availability* of cooperating attorneys to pursue cases. Here race enters the picture. The use of white counsel rather than black counsel in cases brought by the NAACP or LDF is a question of long standing, although black lawyers have long handled civil rights cases. In cases originated locally, especially in the South, one occasionally found an especially courageous white lawyer or a local black lawyer who needed even more courage. The question of who was preferred by the national organizations was complicated when local black attorneys took the initiative in bringing test cases and adopted a position the national NAACP would have preferred not be pursued.[37] In the South, NAACP branch cases were often undertaken by white attorneys, who also "bore the principal burden of the national office's legal activity." White attorneys also handled many Northern cases because the law practices of many Northern black attorneys were not focused on civil rights and constitutional law, making "their usefulness to the . . . NAACP . . . limited."[38]

One thus found the predominant use of prestigious—and often conservative—white lawyers until the

1930s, which marked "a decisive turning point" toward greater use of black attorneys as a result of "pressure . . . from a small but growing elite of brilliant young Negroes educated in ivy league law schools" in the mid-1920s[39] and the National Bar Association's criticism of civil rights organizations for not using black attorneys. However, even when lawyers like Charles Houston and William Hastie were brought into NAACP cases,[40] there was not an adequate pool of black attorneys—nor of cooperating attorneys of any race—to handle Southern cases. This led to programs to prepare civil rights lawyers. The LDF's intern program is the best known and has been a notable success: Julius Chambers, the newly-named director-counsel of LDF, was one of LDF's first two interns, and other Southern attorneys who are "graduates" of that program are now judges. The number of available cooperating attorneys, both in solo practice and in large prestigious law firms, "recruited" by the Lawyers Committee for Civil Rights Under Law (LCCRUL), also increased because of the possibility of attorneys' fees, which provide an incentive for large law firms to handle civil rights cases.

Attorneys' views

How does the staff attorney–cooperating attorney relationship look to the attorneys? Lawyers associated with LDF suggest that there has been little change in recent years in LDF's use of cooperating attorneys, although the intern program "expanded the base" of those with whom the organization could work. The organization found itself, because of its work in poverty law and the campaign against the death penalty, in contact with attorneys with whom it had not been previously involved, altering the "relatively small and ethnically homogeneous group" with which LDF had worked. Those changes affected LDF staff attorneys' relations with cooperating attorneys.

Overall relations between staff and cooperating attorneys are "remarkably cooperative and supportive," with "remarkably little competition" between the two sets of lawyers. They work well together in part because they have a "recognized common enemy" and a common purpose. The skills of each are recognized by the other, with relationships adjusted to be appropriate to attorneys' backgrounds and case issues. When a cooperating attorney is experienced, staff might be able to help simply by providing briefs developed for other cases, which the cooperating attorney would know how to use; indeed, the staff attorneys prefer to work with those who do much work but only "need support and help."

Staff attorneys don't appreciate it when a cooperating attorney "tries to dump all the work on the staff." Indeed, they try to "keep to a minimum" cases handled solely by staff, although in some categories (e.g., Title VII for LDF), and particularly in new areas of the law, staff attorneys may do "virtually all the work." It should also be remembered that they wish to leave their own mark on a case, which can lead to a situation in which cooperating attorneys feel they are not being allowed to do very much.

Staff attorneys acknowledge the value of having cooperating attorneys who know the community from which a case comes; the cooperating attorneys "tend to know local people and problems better, and are not regarded as outsiders;" they understand the judges and the local courthouse. They may well provide a balance to the idealism and naivete of the young staff lawyers. They can also help those lawyers from New York City obtain the trust of local clients, and can provide a buffer between the organization and its clients so that client contact does not eat up a great deal of staff attorney time.

One should note that there are differences between organizations in the relations between staff and cooperating attorneys. NAACP's posture toward local attorneys seems more directive than is true at LDF, which may not need to exert pressure because cooperating attorneys who have been through the LDF internship program are well socialized in LDF values and procedures. NAACP does not appear to hesitate to assign lead counsel from outside the community, justifying this practice as being done to "protect local lawyers from pressure." The NAACP may also remove local counsel from a case if there is disagreement on how the case should be handled. NAACP staff attorneys shrug off "negative publicity" from such intervention, but there is some criticism of NAACP's willingness to engage in such "strong-arm" tactics.

Interorganizational relations

Litigation is affected by the number of litigating groups. In recent years, more groups have been litigating, and, as a result, intergroup relations have become more confused. Prior to *Brown v. Board of Education*, there really was only one national civil rights litigating entity: the NAACP and LDF were functionally one organization, but now the two are fully separate and indeed have been involved in litigation against each other. There are also many other civil rights litigating units in crucial, if less central, roles. Proliferation of litigators has led to a loss of control by any single litigator and thus has decreased the ability to pursue a concerted strategy.[41] Further dispersion has been produced by the feeling of some that instead of "total coordination," a "decentralized, multi-faceted approach" was preferable.

Dispersion and competition *and* convergence and cooperation characterize intergroup relations affecting litigation. Cooperation between groups is most likely to take the form of information exchange, which is important for control of cases as well as for more efficient resource allocation; such cooperation is likely to continue despite friction between organizations. At times more than information exchange occurs. Sessions are held among litigating groups, organizational representatives, and other attorneys to discuss issues and plan litigation,[42] and there are efforts to enlist other groups as companion plaintiffs or as amicus curiae participants in litigation.

In the latter situation, groups do make efforts to coordinate their briefs. Despite difficulties, civil rights lawyers on the whole felt—perhaps because of their frequent interactions—that coordination was not particularly difficult and that they were successful in achieving it. An attorney for a group contemplating filing an amicus brief in another group's case might "feed arguments" to the sponsoring group's attorney for those briefs; indeed, potential amici may help regular counsel develop their principal arguments. Likewise, attorneys for the parties would indicate to attorneys for groups contemplating filing an amicus brief "the general direction of their briefs." This would not, however, be a matter of "orchestrating" the other organization's amicus participation; a staff lawyer simply "would try to make them assist his case." Such attempts at coordination were not always appreciated, however, and there was a "problem of having to send a brief around" to everyone. As one lawyer put it, "writing briefs by committee doesn't work very well," leading the organization to allow others to join its brief but without attempting to coordinate with other groups.

In general, groups did not want to be associated with another organization through amicus participation unless they had input into the brief. This effort to "try to have some substantive input" was fairly general. That didn't mean civil rights litigators were always stand-offish about amicus participation even when concerned about protecting their own reputation: "It's to one's advantage to work with" some groups, said one lawyer, because "there are first-rate lawyers" working

with those groups. Nonetheless, "ecumenical amicus briefs" (where everyone signed on) were generally to be avoided and a number of lawyers quoted former federal judge Marvin Frankel: "If you want to file a petition, go to Congress."

Although "some civil rights lawyers are . . . ideologically opposed to national coordination," as can be seen from the looseness of the "campaign" against exclusionary zoning,[43] a partial convergence of perspectives develops among lawyers in the generally small and relatively cohesive "civil rights bar." This convergence leads members of this "civil rights bar" to assist each other regardless of their organizations' formal positions. The civil rights bar is thus part of the "glue" that serves to hold the pieces of civil rights litigation together at both the national and local levels. Cooperation here is also more likely than in litigation that has a "commercialized purpose" because the civil rights lawyers "shared a real enemy" and "shared a conception of that enemy." This allows them to work together even when their organizational superiors are at odds, an instance of captains doing more talking to each other than the commanders-in-chief.

We also find dispersion and competition. That groups interested in a particular area of the law have similar views does not necessarily mean that they will participate conjointly in activity; instead they may decide to go separate ways as long as one of their number is stating their basic position on a particular case. This differentiation—or "comparative advantage"— allows each group to focus its efforts most effectively; some groups will concentrate on certain subjects or activities while others focus their efforts elsewhere *because* of the former's efforts. For example, at the national level, LDF did not initially direct its resources to the campaign against exclusionary zoning because other national groups already were investing their efforts there.[44] The local level also provides instances of division of labor. For example, in Mississippi, the LDF handled school desegregation cases while the Lawyers Committee for Civil Rights Under Law undertook criminal defense work, and the Lawyers Constitutional Defense Committee dealt with both criminal defense work and police and prison brutality matters.[45]

Division of labor is less likely to be the result of explicit agreement than to be implicit, to be more a matter of "we saw what they were doing" and of groups "trying to stay out of each other's way" than of explicitly "carving up the territory." This can be seen in a number of areas of race relations law. One is school desegregation, where the LDF focused on the South and the NAACP dealt with the North—in part because they used divergent theories on which to base their cases, and in part because LDF made a "tactical choice as to where to get mileage" and felt it could do so in Southern and border states rather than in Northern cases which others, particularly the NAACP, were litigating.

Examination of these instances suggests that the litigation pie is not neatly and completely divided as a result of intergroup interaction. However, clear patterns develop, thus decreasing the considerable "potential for legal chaos" possible when a number of groups are litigating issues in a major area of the law; the picture is *not* one of "fragmentation." Because of the LDF's litigating predominance, NAACP's major involvement, and the regular presence of specialized litigating entities, there is some "order and stability" with respect to the areas of law in which litigation is carried out.[46]

Conclusion

Perhaps the most important generalization to be drawn from recent interest group civil rights litigation is that much of it is responsive and reflexive, and not subject to organizational control. Thus organizational litigators definitely do not dominate the domain in which they seek to operate.

Litigators make clear that each of the major civil rights litigation organizations have intentionally focused their energies in certain areas of the law, and each also has other designated interests, such as welfare for LDF a decade ago and voting rights for both NAACP and LDF more recently; criminal justice concerns have come to occupy a major place in race relations litigation as a result of LDF and NAACP efforts. NAACP and LDF have differed in the degree to which they focused their efforts and mounted resources for concentrated litigation "campaigns." However, not even for LDF, whose work is the "model" for "planned litigation for social change," were all areas of law in which the organization became involved subjects of litigation campaigns.

Among principal factors affecting organizational attention to specific areas of law have been resources, including the availability of foundation money, and the views of staff lawyers, also a major element in determining which cases to pursue. The goal of eliminating discrimination and concern for the well-being of minorities help explain why both the membership-based NAACP and the nonmembership LDF focus on employment discrimination and, more recently, on the

administration of criminal justice. In addition to such overlap, there also has been an implicit division of labor, leading the two groups to emphasize differing subjects or different geographical areas within a subject. This serves to spread overall litigation resources further than if the choices of the two organizations converged fully and thus duplicated each other.

Litigators' perspectives on organizations' choices of cases indicate rather clearly that the process of choosing cases has been far more diffuse than the term "planned litigation" might suggest, with case-selection decisions inductive and much affected by the flow of cases, rather than being deduced from a firm application of previously selected criteria. Litigating organizations' legal staffs, which operate in a flexible and "noninstitutionalized" way, seem to play a larger role in choice of cases than do organizational processes on "the books."

Some selection criteria are noted by most litigators, and seem likely to be taken into account in many cases. However, identification of other criteria seems largely a post hoc process. There is also agreement that criteria are not applied systematically or uniformly, in part because events require that certain cases be pursued, with civil rights litigators entering cases even when control, identified as crucial to planned litigation for social change, is not likely. Cooperating attorneys serve as the principal source of cases for litigators, with organizations taking the experience, credibility and competence of cooperating attorneys into account in choosing cases. LDF's socialization of cooperating attorneys has facilitated organizational control of cases, and has meant that LDF's case selection is not as likely as NAACP's to be diffuse.

Not surprisingly, we have found some differences in perspectives about civil rights litigation. The world looks somewhat different from a staff position at an organization's national headquarters than it does to a cooperating attorney in the field. However, there is probably more diversity of perspectives *among* cooperating attorneys than *between* them on the one hand and staff attorneys on the other. This is largely the result of the varying roles played by cooperating attorneys. Some of the divergence of perspectives noted here is organizationally-based; NAACP lawyers and LDF attorneys tend to see the world of race relations somewhat differently. However, in the larger view of things, differences in perspectives among principal litigating organizations and other lawyers laboring in the civil rights vineyard are limited. There are also similarities in perspectives stemming from litigating experience and the cohesiveness resulting from the presence of a "civil rights bar" sharing commitment to a particular goal. Litigation for social change, then, is often reflexive and far from completely planned, with many constraints on the planning of litigation campaigns, many detours along the road to organizational goals, and much flexibility of action by both the litigating organizations and individual staff attorneys.

Notes

This article originally appeared in Volume 68, Numbers 9–10, April–May 1985, pages 337–352. A more complete treatment is found in Stephen L. Wasby, *Race Relations Litigation in an Age of Complexity* (University Press of Virginia, 1995).

I wish to express particular appreciation to Dr. Hubert Locke, Director, William O. Douglas Institute, for prompting the study from which this article is taken. For research support I am indebted to the Institute, the Johnson Research Fund of American Philosophical Society, and the Office of Research and the Graduate School of Public Affairs, State University of New York at Albany. I also wish to thank colleagues who have contributed useful comments at various stages of this process and two anonymous reviewers for this journal and David Richert, its editor, for their observations.

This article is dedicated to the memory of the late Clement Vose, who died in January, 1985. His presence and work stimulated the study of interest group litigation.

1. Horowitz, *The Courts and Social Policy* (Washington, D.C.: The Brookings Institution, 1977). *But see* Wasby, "Arrogation of power or accountability: 'judicial imperialism' revisited," *Judicature* 65 (1981), 209.

2. 347 U.S. 483 (1954); Kluger, *Simple Justice: The History of* Brown v. Board of Education *and Black America's Struggle for Equality* (New York: Alfred Knopf, 1976). *See also* Vose, *Caucasians Only: The Supreme Court, the NAACP and the Restrictive Covenant Cases* (Berkeley: University of California Press, 1959).

3. O'Connor, *Women's Organizations' Use of the Courts* (Lexington, Mass.: Lexington Books, 1980); Melnick, *Regulation and the Courts: The Case of the Clean Air Act* (Washington, D.C.: The Brookings Institution, 1983).

4. *See* Weisbrod et al., *Public Interest Law: An Economic and Institutional Analysis* (Berkeley: University of California Press, 1978); O'Connor and Epstein, "The Rise of Conservative Interest Group Litigation," *J. of Pol.* 45 (1983), 479.

5. Scheingold, *The Politics of Rights: Lawyers, Public Policy, and Political Change* (New Haven: Yale University Press, 1974), 5. *See also* Rabin, "Lawyers for Social Change: Per-

spectives on Public Interest Law," *Stan. L. Rev.* 28 (1976), 207, at 221.

6. Belton, "A Comparative Review of Public and Private Enforcement of Title VII and the Civil Rights Act of 1964," *Vand. L. Rev.* 31 (1978), 905; Meltsner, *Cruel and Unusual: The Supreme Court and Capital Punishment* (New York: Random House, 1973).

7. Belton, *supra* n. 6.

8. Chayes, "The Role of the Judge in Public Law Litigation," *Harv. L. Rev.* 89 (1976), 1281, at 1284.

9. Fiss, "The Social and Political Foundations of Adjudication," *Law and Hum. Behav.* 6 (1982), 121 at 123; *see also* Fiss, "Foreword: The Forms of Justice," *Harv. L. Rev.* 93 (1979), 1.

10. *See City of Mobile v. Bolden,* 446 U.S. 55 (1980) (Sec. 2 of Voting Rights Act); *Washington v. Davis,* 426 U.S. 299 (1976) (employment cases under 14th Amendment).

11. Vose, *supra* n. 2, at 155–158.

12. Wasby, D'Amato, and Metrailer, *Desegregation From Brown to Alexander: An Exploration of Supreme Court Strategies* (Carbondale: Southern Illinois University Press, 1977), 228–235; Ulmer, "The Longitudinal Behavior of Hugo L. Black: Parabolic Support for Civil Liberties, 1937–1971," *Fla. St. U. L. Rev.* 1 (1973), 131, at 149.

13. 422 U.S. 490 (1975).

14. 411 U.S. 1 (1973).

15. *See* Greenberg, "Litigation for Social Change: Methods, Limits and Role in Democracy" (Cardozo Lecture), Association of the Bar of the City of New York (1973).

16. *Goldberg v. Kelly,* 397 U.S. 254 (1970) and *Wheeler v. Montgomery,* 397 U.S. 280 (1970).

17. For example, *Dandridge v. Williams,* 397 U.S. 471 (1970).

18. This and the following sections are based on Wasby, "How Planned is "Planned Litigation?" *A. B. F. Res. J.* (1984), 83.

19. Tushnet, "Organizational Structure and Legal Strategy: The NAACP's Campaign Against Segregated Education, 1929–1950," unpublished ms. (1980), at I-1 to I-2.

20. Material which appears in quotation marks without attribution is drawn from interviews conducted by the author.

21. *See* O'Connor, *supra* n. 3, at 87–88, 144–145.

22. Greenberg, *supra* n. 15, at 20.

23. Ibid.

24. Belton, *supra* n. 6, at 943.

25. *See* Sorauf, *The Wall of Separation: The Constitutional Politics of Church and State* (Princeton: Princeton University Press, 1976), 84; Vose, *supra* n. 2, at 58, 151; and Meltsner, *supra* n. 6, at 114, 238–239.

26. This section draws on Wasby, "The Multi-Faceted Elephant: Litigator Perspectives on Planned Litigation for Social Change," paper presented to Law & Society Association, Denver, Colorado, June 1983.

27. Grossman, "A Model for Judicial Policy Analysis: The Supreme Court and the Sit-In Cases," in Grossman and Tanenhaus, eds., *Frontiers of Judicial Research* (New York: John Wiley, 1969).

28. Leubsdorf, "Completing the Desegregation Remedy," *B.U.L. Rev.* 57 (1977), 34, at 94.

29. *See* Danielson, *The Politics of Exclusion* (New York: Columbia University Press, 1976), 168.

30. Bell, "Serving Two Masters: Integration Ideals and Client Interests in School Desegregation Litigation," *Yale L. J.* 85 (1976), 470, at 428, 487, 492.

31. Scheingold, *supra* n. 5, at 5, 95, 151, 197.

32. This section and the next two draw on Wasby, "Some Horizontal and Vertical Dynamics of Civil Rights Litigation: Litigator Perspectives," paper presented to Southern Political Science Association, Birmingham, Alabama, November 1983.

33. *See* Vose, *Constitutoinal Change: Amendment Politics and Supreme Court Litigation Since 1900* (Lexington, Mass.: Lexington Books, 1972), 321.

34. Casper, *Lawyers Before the Warren Court: Civil Liberties and Civil Rights, 1957–66,* (Urbana: University of Illinois Press, 1972), 142–143.

35. Orfield, *Must We Bus? Segregated Schools and National Policy* (Washington, D.C.: The Brookings Institution, 1978), 371; Rabin, *supra* (1976) n. 5, at 212–213.

36. For examples, see Vose, *supra* n. 2, at 157; Vose, *supra* n. 33, at 315.

37. See Vose, *supra* n. 33, at 315.

38. Meier and Rudwick, "Attorneys Black and White: A Case Study of Race Relations Within the NAACP," *J. of Am. Hist.* 62 (1976), 913, 915–916.

39. Ibid. at 930, 933.

40. Note that "the first case in which the NAACP had employed exclusively black counsel before the U.S. Supreme Court" was *Hillins v. Oklahoma*, 295 U.S. 394 (1935), in which an Oklahoma black man had been sentenced to death for rape. McNeil, *Groundwork: Charles Hamilton Houston and the Struggle for Civil Rights* (Philadelphia: University of Pennsylvania Press, 1983), 121–122.

41. O'Connor, *supra* n. 3, at 145.

42. *See supra* n. 25.

43. Orfield, *supra* n. 34, at 372; Shields and Spector, "Opening Up the Suburbs: Notes on a Movement for Social Change," *Yale Rev. of L. and Social Order* 2 (1972), 300.

44. Shields and Spector, *supra* n. 43.

45. *See* Heck and Stewart, "Ensuring Access to Justice: the Role of Interest Group Lawyers in the 60s Campaign for Civil Rights," *Judicature* 66 (1982), 84; Stewart and Heck, "The Day-to-Day Activities of Interest Group Lawyers," *Soc. Sci. Q.* 64 (1983), 173.

46. For intergroup relations in church-state litigation, see Sorauf, *supra* n. 25, at 81.

Friendly fire: amici curiae and Webster v. Reproductive Health Services

Susan M. Behuniak

With Roe v. Wade *in the balance, the unprecedented 78 amicus briefs filed in* Webster *played an important role in helping to inform and shape the Court's debate over abortion.*

The unprecedented number of amicus curiae briefs filed in *Webster v. Reproductive Health Services*[1] signaled not only the intensity of the abortion battle, but also the extent of interest group politics before the United States Supreme Court. If the response of 57 amicus briefs to *Regents of the University of California v. Bakke*[2] was unusual, the response to Webster was extraordinary. A total of 78 amicus briefs were filed; 46 on behalf of the appellants and 32 on behalf of the appellees. With over 400 organizations signing on as cosponsors, and thousands of individuals joining as signatories, *Webster,* though not a typical case, demonstrates the importance of interest group politics before the Court.

With the 1988 appointment of Justice Anthony Kennedy to fill the vacancy left by Justice Lewis Powell, a reversal of *Roe v. Wade*[3] was possible. Court watchers tallied a 4–1–4 line-up. Expected to support *Roe* were Justices Harry Blackmun, William Brennan, Thurgood Marshall and John Paul Stevens. The original dissenters in *Roe,* Justices William Rehnquist and Byron White were expected to be joined by Justices Antonin Scalia and Kennedy. With Justice Sandra Day O'Connor viewed as the swing vote, *Roe* was now subject to a 5–4 reversal. When the Court agreed to hear *Webster* during its 1988 term, the time was ripe for a major abortion decision. Such anticipation led to the unprecedented number of amicus briefs.

At issue in *Webster* was a Missouri statute which contained: (1) a preamble stating that "the life of each human being begins at conception,"[4] (2) sections restricting public facilities and employees from performing or assisting in an abortion (except to save the mother's life), (3) sections prohibiting the use of public funds, employees or hospitals from encouraging or counseling a woman to have an abortion (again, with the maternal life preservation exception), and (4) sections requiring that when a physician believes a woman to be 20 or more weeks pregnant, viability will be tested by performance of "such medical examinations and

tests as are necessary to make a finding of the gestational age, weight, and lung maturity of the unborn child."[5]

Because of the number of briefs filed and the fact that all the briefs were spawned by the same constitutional issue, the *Webster* amicus briefs offer a unique opportunity to study this particular form of interest group litigation and to examine how the public debate over abortion is carried out in a legal arena. In focusing on these amicus briefs, several questions will frame the study: who submitted the briefs, what was argued in the briefs, and what impact did the briefs have on the outcome of the case? These questions are asked with two goals in mind. First, what do the amicus briefs demonstrate regarding this type of interest group activity? Second, what do the amicus briefs reveal concerning the nature of the two movements involved in the struggle over abortion rights?[6]

Who filed?

Table 1 provides a list of the names of the first group or individual listed as a sponsor hereinafter called "first sponsors" for each of the amicus briefs filed on behalf of the appellants, and Table 2 lists the first sponsors of those filed on behalf of the appellees.[7] When there are two organizations jointly filing a brief, both names are listed. When there are more than two organizations, only the first sponsor is named followed by "et al." (indicating that there are other filers), followed by a number enclosed in parentheses to indicate how many. If the individuals who signed a brief were not united under an organizational title (either permanent or ad hoc), the abbreviation "ind." also appears within the parentheses. At the right of both tables is the total number of organizational sponsors for each brief.

Coalition building. Tables 1 and 2 show that 85 organizations filed on behalf of appellants, while 335 filed on behalf of appellees. The percentage of briefs with a sin-

Table 1. 46 briefs in support of appellants

First sponsors of amicus briefs	Total sponsors
1. Agudeth Israel of America	1
2. Alabama Lawyers for Unborn Children, Inc.	1
3. Edward Allen	1
4. American Academy of Medical Ethics	1
5. American Assoc. of Pro-Life Obst. and Gynecol. and The American Assoc. of Pro-Life Pediatricians	2
6. American Collegians for Life, Inc. and Catholic League for Religious & Civil Rights	2
7. American Family Association, Inc.	1
8. American Life League, Inc.	1
9. Association for Public Justice and The Value of Life Committee, Inc.	2
10. Attorneys General of Louisiana, Arizona, Idaho, Pennsylvania, and Wisconsin	1
11. Birthright, Inc.	1
12. Catholic Health Association of the US	1
13. Catholic Lawyers Guild of the Archdiocese of Boston, Inc.	1
14. Catholics United for Life, et al. (10)	11
15. Center for Judicial Studies and Certain Members of Congress (56)	2
16. Certain American State Legislators (over 250)	1
17. Certain Members of the General Assembly of PA (69)	1
18. Christian Advocates Serving Evangelism	1
19. Covenant House and Good Counsel, Inc.	2
20. Doctors for Life, et al. (4)	5
21. Feminists for Life of America, et al. (4)	5
22. Focus on Family and Family Research Council of America	2
23. Free Speech Advocates	1
24. Holy Orthodox Church	1
25. Human Life International	1
26. International Right to Life Federation	1
27. Larry Joyce	1
28. Knights of Columbus	1
29. Lutheran Church-Missouri Synod, et al. (2)	3
30. James Joseph Lynch, Jr.	1
31. Paul Marx	1
32. 127 Members of the Missouri General Assembly	1
33. Missouri Catholic Conference	1
34. Bernard Nathanson, M.D.	1
35. National Legal Foundation	1
36. National Right to Life Committee	1
37. New England Christian Action Council, Inc.	1
38. Right to Life Advocates, Inc.	1
39. Right to Life League of Southern California, Inc.	1
40. Rutherford Institute, et al. (18)	19
41. Hon. Christopher H. Smith, et al. (9 Senators, 44 Representatives)	1
42. Southern Center for Law and Ethics	1
43. Southwest Life and Law Center, Inc.	1
44. United States	1
45. US Catholic Conference	1
46. Austin Vaughn and Crusade for Life, Inc.	1
Totals: 85 organizations + 5 single individuals =	90

gle sponsor was 76 percent for the appellants and 44 percent for the appellees. The number of appellants' sponsors per brief ranged from 1 to 19 (the high being the 19 branches of the Rutherford Institute), while the number of the appellees' filers per brief ranged from 1 to 115 (the high being the brief submitted by the National Council of Negro Women and 114 others). Using rough averages, appellants had 2 sponsors per brief, while appellees had 10 sponsors per brief. What these numbers suggest is that the two sides differed concerning the value of coalition building.

Clearly, the appellees acted as if the number of sponsors was more important than the number of briefs filed, while the appellants favored the strategy of filing the most briefs (46 to 32). This raises the question of which is a more effective strategy, to file as many individual briefs as possible or to gather a larger total number of cosponsoring organizations? Caldeira and Wright have observed that there "is a general absence of large coalitions of groups on individual briefs," and that this implies that those who make the decision about filing the amicus believe "it is the number of briefs, not the number of organizations listed on each brief, that impresses the justices."[8]

So why did the appellees appear to reject this general belief? There are several possible explanations: (1) the desire to save money, (2) the belief that the justices are susceptible to the democratic principle that the majority should rule, (3) the fact that only a finite number of arguments can be made, (4) a difference between multi-issue interest groups and single-issue interest groups concerning the need to file independently, and (5) adoption of a strategy that valued impact of the collection over the number of briefs filed.

First, while the amicus brief offers groups that are limited in time and resources the access to influence litigation without assuming the financial and time burdens required of a full-fledged party,[9] there is no question that even the filing of an amicus makes demands upon the organization. In Caldeira and Wright's study of the amicus briefs filed during the Court's 1982 term, the cost of preparing and filing a brief ranged from $500 to $50,000 with a mean slightly above $8,000.[10] For some groups, the cost of filing an amicus is prohibitive. Caldeira and Wright note, "The litigation budgets of most organizations are quite modest, and most do not have sufficient in-house manpower and legal expertise to prepare briefs on their own."[11] Many of the appellees' cosponsoring groups would appear to fit this profile. For them, cosponsorship allowed par-

Table 2. 32 briefs in support of appellees

First sponsors of amicus briefs	Total sponsors
1. American Civil Liberties Union, et al. (5)	6
2. 281 American Historians	1
3. American Jewish Congress, et al. (35)	36
4. American Library Assoc. and Freedom to Read Foundation	2
5. American Medical Assoc., et al. (7)	8
6. American Nurses Assoc. and The Nurses' Assoc. of the Amer. College of Obstet. and Gynec.	2
7. American Public Health Assoc., et al. (8 & inds.)	9
8. American Psychological Assoc.	1
9. Americans for Democratic Action, et al. (4)	5
10. Americans United for Separation of Church and State	1
11. Assoc. of Reproductive Health Professionals, et al. (7 & inds.)	8
12. Attorneys General of California, Colorado, Massachusetts, New York, Texas, and Vermont	1
13. Bioethicists for Privacy	1
14. California National Org. for Women, et al. (2 & inds.)	3
15. Canadian Women's Orgs. (4)	4
16. Catholics for a Free Choice, et al. (3 & inds.)	4
17. Center for Population Options, et al. (3)	4
18. Certain Members of the Congress of the US (25 Senators, 115 Representatives)	1
19. Committees on Civil Rights, Medicine & Law, Sex & Law of the Assoc. of the Bar of the City of New York, et al. (6)	7
20. 167 Distinguished Scientists and Physicians Including 11 Nobel Laureates	1
21. Group of American Law Professors	1
22. International Women's Health Organizations (22)	22
23. National Assoc. of Public Hospitals	1
24. National Assoc. of Women Lawyers and National Conference of Women's Bar Associates	2
25. National Coalition Against Domestic Violence	1
26. National Council of Negro Women, Inc., et al. (114 & inds.)	115
27. National Family Planning and Reproductive Health Assoc.	1
28. National Organization for Women	1
29. 77 Organizations Committed to Women's Equality	77
30. Population-Environmental Balance, et al. (6)	7
31. 608 State Legislators from 32 States	1
32. Women Who Have Had Abortions (2887) and Friends (627)	1
Totals:	335

ticipation in the *Webster* case without the financial hardship involved in preparing an individual brief.

Second, the appellees seemed to act on the democratic belief that the justices would be swayed by the numbers associated with the abortion rights position. Indeed, several of their briefs resembled petitions as they included lists of individuals as signatories.[12] Collectively, the appellees' briefs signaled to the Court that their position has the support of the majority of the population and that a reversal of *Roe* would place the Court in the uncomfortable position of fighting against the mainstream. However, reliance on the democratic argument also poses risks. Justices may take offense at being pressured to defer to majority rule.[13] Another risk of assembling petition briefs is that coalition building may work to limit the number of arguments presented to the Court by decreasing the number of amicus briefs.

The appellees, however, seemed to minimize both risks. While the democratic argument was implicit in the number of sponsors and signatories, this claim was not explicitly made by the appellees. Instead, appellees let the numbers speak for themselves, thereby avoiding reliance on the democratic argument while at the same time signaling to the Court in a not-so-subtle way where the majority of the population stood on the issue. The second risk was overcome by the filing of a significant number of briefs. While 14 less than the number submitted by the appellants, 32 briefs is by any measure a considerable number. Therefore, the appellees' coalitions did not come at the price of sacrificing the number of arguments presented. In sum, the appellees' strategy of garnering the support of several hundred cosponsors was intended to add weight to the already numerous briefs.

A third explanation of the appellees' coalition building is that since there is a finite number of legal arguments to be made on any issue, too many briefs lead to repetition and perhaps even work to irritate the justices. In light of charges that amicus briefs are a waste of time, "repetitious at best and emotional explosions at worst,"[14] and that a large number would increase the already heavy burden on the justices, the appellees may have opted to limit the number of briefs even though they knew that the appellants would file more.

Fourth, an examination of multi-issue interest groups versus single-issue interest groups may explain the different values appellants and appellees attributed to coalition building. Appellees' base of support was largely multi-issue interest groups while single-issue

Table 3. First sponsors categorized

	Appellants*	Totals	Appellees**	Totals
Individual	3, 27, 30, 31, 34	5		0
Citizen groups	1, 6, 7, 8, 9, 11, 14, 21, 22, 24, 25, 1, 3, 7, 9, 10, 14, 15, 16, 17, 22, 26, 26, 28, 29, 33, 36, 37, 38, 39, 45, 46 28, 29, 30, 32	21 15		
Professional	2, 4, 5, 13, 20	5	2, 5, 6, 8, 11, 13, 19, 20, 21, 24	10
Public interest law	15, 18, 23, 35, 40, 42, 43	7		0
Government	10, 16, 17, 32, 41, 44	6	12, 18, 31	3
Peak organizations	12	1	4, 23, 25, 27	4
Other		19 46	1	0 32

* Numbers refer to sponsors in Table 1.
** Numbers refer to sponsors in Table 2.

interest groups were more prevalent among the amici of the appellants. [This fact will be discussed in greater detail below.] Multi-issue interest groups enjoy more of a choice in determining whether or not to file an amicus brief than do single-issue interest groups. "The broader a group's political interests, the less intense its attachment to a particular interest . . . . Focus is crucial to intensity." [15] Single-issue interest groups must react when there is a direct threat to their membership's interests. Within this context, the appellants' pro-life organizations were compelled to file independent briefs. In contrast, the multi-issue interest groups of the appellees could meet internal demands through coalitional activity rather than as independent sponsors.

Finally, the appellees' amici were organized according to a strategy that favored impact over the number of briefs. Kathryn Kolbert, who worked on behalf of the American Civil Liberties Union and Planned Parenthood Federation to coordinate all of the amicus briefs, attempted to discourage duplication among the briefs and to encourage coalition building among amici with similar interests.[16] It was believed that overlapping arguments would work to "dilute the overall impact of the collection," [17] so groups who shared interests were encouraged to form a coalition. Coalitions were organized so that each argued points most appropriate to their interests and expertise. This contrasted with appellants who appeared to strive for a large number of briefs at the expense of repetition. For example, attorney Robert L. Sassone filed six separate

briefs on behalf of clients with very similar interests rather than one brief with six sponsors.[18]

Diversity. An attempt was also made to look closer at the groups who filed in order to determine the level of diversity among the first sponsors of the 78 briefs. Seven of the 14 membership categories developed by Caldeira and Wright were used to distinguish the groups: individuals, citizen-based interest groups, professional organizations (where members share the same occupation), public interest law firms or research groups, government sponsors, peak organizations (an organization consisting of groups), and other.[19] Table 3 lists the seven categories and refers to each first sponsor according to the number assigned to it in Tables 1 and 2. Table 4 compares the percentage of briefs filed by groups of each of the seven categories.

Study of Table 4 reveals that both appellants and appellees drew the most support from briefs filed by citizen-based groups, 45.7 percent and 46.8 percent, respectively. Of all seven categories employed, the citizen-based groups category contains the most diversity in ideology, membership numbers, prestige, goals, and resources. For instance, The American Civil Liberties Union, Population-Environmental Balance, American Life League, and Agudeth Israel of America are all classified as citizen-based groups.

Next in order of frequency for the appellants were briefs filed by: public interest law firms (15.2 percent), government sponsors (13 percent), professional

Table 4. First sponsors percentages

	Appellants	Appellees	Totals
Individual	5 (10.9%)	0 (0%)	6.4%
Citizen groups	21 (45.7%)	15 (46.9%)	46.2
Professional	5 (10.9%)	10 (31.3%)	19.2
Public interest law	7 (15.2%)	0 (0%)	9
Government	6 (13.0%)	3 (9.4%)	11.5
Peak organizations	1 (2.2%)	4 (12.5%)	6.4
Other	1 (2.2%)	0 (0%)	1.3
	46 (100.1%)*	32 (100.1%)*	78 (100.0%)

* Figure over 100% due to rounding.

groups and individuals (both with 10.9 percent), then peak organizations, and other (both with 2.2 percent). Appellees had no briefs filed by individuals, public interest law firms or other. After the citizen-based groups, the order of frequency were briefs filed by: professional groups (31.3 percent), peak organizations (12.5 percent), and government sponsors (9.4 percent).

One drawback of the seven divisions is that they hide three types of groups relevant to the abortion controversy—the religious groups associated with the pro-life position, the feminist groups aligned with the pro-choice cause, and the single-issue interest groups present in both movements.[20] To remedy this problem, Table 5 was constructed to identify these three types of groups. While these three categories are not mutually exclusive, they reveal some interesting trends concerning the nature of the groups who participated as amici on both sides of *Webster.*

Table 5 confirms some expectations concerning the role feminist and religious groups play in each movement. The appellants drew great support from religiously oriented groups (16 sponsors), but also drew support from one feminist sponsor (Feminists for Life).

There were nine feminist sponsors for the appellee side, but also two from religious groups. Altogether, these 28 religious and feminist sponsors account for only about 36 percent of the amicus briefs filed. Clearly, the abortion issue was of great concern to organizations whose memberships did not fit either description.

Indeed, as Table 5 reveals, single-issue interest groups played an important role in this case. In order to study the abortion issue here, a single-issue interest group is defined as an organization that is formed to advocate a position on the abortion rights question. While it is admittedly arguable whether a pro-life group has an agenda that is broader than the abortion issue, or whether NOW is more a single-issue than a multi-issue interest group, an initial appraisal of the groups indicates that about 70 percent of the first sponsors on behalf of the appellants were single-issue interest groups, while about 40 percent of the appellees' first sponsors were single-issue interest groups. When these single-issue interest groups are compared, it becomes evident that there was a difference in the nature of the permanency of the groups. Appellants drew support from permanent single-issue organizations, while appellees' single-issue organiza-

Table 5. Special interests of first sponsors

	Appellants*	Totals	Appellees**	Totals
Feminist	21	1/46	14, 15, 22, 24, 25, 26, 28, 29, 32	9/32
Religious	1, 6, 7, 9, 12, 13, 14, 18, 22, 24, 28, 29, 33, 37, 45, 46	16/46	3, 16	2/32
Single-issue	2, 3, 4, 5, 6, 7, 8, 9, 10, 11, 14, 16, 17, 20, 21, 22, 23, 25, 26, 27, 30, 31, 32, 34, 36, 37, 38, 39, 40, 41, 43, 46	32/46	2, 12, 13, 15, 16, 18, 20, 21, 22, 27, 29, 31, 32	13/32

* Numbers refer to sponsors in Table 1.
** Numbers refer to sponsors in Table 2.

tions tended to be ad hoc groups of professional individuals or peak organizations.

Some tentative conclusions can be drawn from this information concerning the nature of the two movements. Overall, the appellants' amici appear to be more singular in purpose. The public interest law firms, the individuals, the governmental coalitions, and even the professional groups were united in that most were specifically formed either to oppose abortion rights or already had religious tenets supportive of such a political posture. With the exception of the government coalitions, these were permanent groups. In contrast, the appellees relied heavily on the support of professional groups with multiple interests, five of which were ad hoc organizations formed in order to file a brief. These observations suggest that the appellants had a more single-mindedly committed and more permanent group of amici, while the appellees relied on the support of amici who joined together temporarily and who distributed their resources over a range of issues. The question of whether diversity or homogeneity translated into unity will be examined below.

In sum, the question of who filed these 78 briefs has revealed differences in coalition building and a diversity of interests among the sponsoring groups. It is expected that these organizations employed an assortment of strategies as well as provided the Court with a variety of information. The next question to be examined, therefore, is what was argued in the briefs. Did the diversity among the sponsors translate into a richness of resources for the Court?

What was argued?

Both Webster and the Reproductive Health Services had to launch an offensive campaign while maintaining a defensive posture. The appellants had to defend the Missouri statute while attacking the legal doctrines set down in *Roe*. The appellees guarded *Roe* as precedent while they took aim at the restrictive law. The strategies of the sides and the roles left to the amicus briefs are best informed by an examination of the party briefs. The party briefs carry the burden of presenting the legal arguments for the litigants and, therefore, form a good basis for comparison of the two sides as well as the 78 amicus briefs.

The appellants' brief first summarized the case and then opened its argument by attacking *Roe*, criticizing the "viability" dividing point as arbitrary and calling for the Court to overrule *Roe*. This offensive took only four

pages. The rest of the party brief, approximately 28 pages, was a point-by-point defense of the Missouri law. In contrast, the appellees' brief, which omitted a reconstruction of the case, began by defending *Roe* as a fundamental constitutional right and supporting the viability concept as both legally and medically sound. This defense occupied 17 pages. The next 32 pages challenged the Missouri law section by section. For both sides, then, *Roe* was of primary concern. It was only once this precedent was either challenged or defended that a discussion of the state law could begin.

Arguments. Turning to the amicus briefs and referring to the "List of amici arguments," pages 186–187, it can be seen that when the major arguments for the amici are compared, a point and counterpoint pattern emerges. There were six main points of contention concerning *Roe:* (1) fetal vs. women's rights, (2) if a constitutional basis for a right to abortion exists, (3) whether the trimester scheme is of utility, (4) how abortion fits within the context of American history and tradition, (5) the applicability of the doctrine of *stare decisis,* and (6) the consequences of overturning or following *Roe* as precedent. There were also six main disputes regarding the Missouri statute: (1) whether the state had the power to restrict abortion through its democratic process, or whether the Court must act to prevent the violation of constitutional rights, (2) the rational basis test vs. strict scrutiny as the appropriate standard of review, (3) if the statute's preamble was prefatory or of substance, (4) the constitutionality (or mootness) of the ban on funding abortion counseling, (5) the constitutionality of the ban on abortions in public facilities, and (6) the constitutionality of the viability tests requirement.

Amid the noise of these debated issues, silence is also instructive. Some of the arguments presented by the amici were not present in the party briefs. Referring again to the "List of arguments," a "*" sign indicates those arguments that were employed by both the party brief and at least one amicus. Therefore, absent from the appellants' party brief were arguments that: fetuses are constitutionally protected persons; abortion has harmful effects on women and on society; the law would not involve criminal prosecutions; and the states are better suited than the courts to decide such a politically charged issue. On the appellee side, there was a greater overlap between the party and amicus briefs. Only two major points made by amici were not present in the party brief: the freedom of religion argument and an examination of the consequences of a *Roe* reversal. The latter, nonlegal point constituted an important focus for many of the appellee amicus briefs.

Strategies. The differences between party and amicus argumentation suggest that appellants and appellees adopted different strategies. Once again the 4–1–4 Court configuration must be appreciated. Litigants had to hold together their four-person coalition while vying for O'Connor's vote. The two sides divided the workload in different ways. O'Connor appears to be the main target of the appellants' party brief while appellees seem to make a bid for her vote through the filing of amicus briefs which focus on her central concerns.

The appellants' party brief is striking in its avoidance of any "pro-life" rhetoric or argumentation. It carefully sidesteps any discussion of the rights of the "preborn," the sacredness of human life, or the uncertain basis for the right to privacy (discussing it in terms of a liberty interest instead). The party brief challenges *Roe* in terms that would most appeal to O'Connor. It questions the textual, historical, and doctrinal basis of *Roe* and challenges the trimester approach by citing O'Connor's dissent in *Akron v. Akron Center for Reproductive Health.*[21] The brief also argues that should the Court uphold *Roe,* then it should apply the "undue burden" test (favored by O'Connor) to uphold the Missouri regulations. This moderate approach, then, appears to be crafted for O'Connor. However, this strategy was not universally applied as some of the amici did include language and claims from the pro-life movement.[22] The more controversial arguments on behalf of fetal rights and a ban on abortion were voiced not by the parties but by the amici. It was the amici who urged Rehnquist, White, Scalia, and Kennedy to go further than the party brief suggested and to make abortions illegal by recognizing constitutionally protected fetal rights.

The division of labor helps to explain why the appellant briefs, sponsored by organizations more homogeneous than those of the appellees, had more conflicts, inconsistencies, and contradictions. One trouble undoubtedly arose from the fact that the party brief appeared willing to "give" on two important points within the abortion debate. First, it did not call for a total ban on abortion, instead arguing that should the Court overturn *Roe,* the law should once again allow the states to determine abortion policy (presumably either way). Second, it did not assert that a fetus is a constitutionally protected person. Since these were concessions

that not all the 46 amici could accept, why would the parties risk such conflict? Again, the answer seems to be the effort to capture O'Connor's vote while hoping that the arguments presented by the amici might persuade all five justices to recognize fetal rights.

In contrast, the appellees appeared to assign the amici the task of capturing O'Connor's vote. There were at least two routes to her. One was to challenge O'Connor to use her test of whether the abortion restrictions in question posed an "undue burden" on women exercising their constitutional right.[23] The amicus briefs presented her with technical information regarding the dire impact of a *Roe* reversal. In fact, the brief from the National Council of Negro Women, citing the disproportionate impact on women of color, the poor, and the young, was crafted especially for O'Connor and her test.[24] A second strategy was to challenge her statement in *Akron* that *Roe* is "on a collision course with itself."[25] O'Connor had used scientific sources to conclude that the point of "viability" would shift forward as medical technology improved. The Brief by 167 Scientists and Physicians not only refuted her argument, but included the signatures of some of the authors on whom she had relied in *Akron.*[26]

What may seem surprising is that the more diverse appellee side produced the more internally consistent argument. This can be explained in two ways. First, the parties and all the amici were aware of how the Court had already chipped away at the right to abortion. All understood that there was no room for concessions without jeopardizing the right itself. Second, this consistency was yet another payoff of organization and coalition building. Kathryn Kolbert, the coordinator of the briefs, helped groups identify what was at issue in *Webster* and how they could best contribute to the case.[27] What emerged was a collection of evidence startling in its singularity of purpose.

Roles. While it is difficult to accurately assess the roles adopted by each interest group, the amici do appear to serve three general purposes.[28] First, there are the endorsement briefs that either repeat the party's position or offer a variation. These briefs may recount all the party's arguments or may center and expand on one point alone. Second are the technical briefs that offer the Court specialized knowledge that is predominantly nonlegalistic in nature. Third are the risk takers. These briefs range from those who undertake an unconventional legal argument to those who shun the legal ele-

List of amici arguments

Roe: offense and defense

Issue 1: Rights

Appellants: The preborn are constitutionally protected persons under the 14th Amendment. This fact is supported by scientific data which shows that life begins at conception. The Court has erred before in denying personhood to blacks and American Indians.

*Appellees: Medical evidence is not clear when life begins. Constitutional rights are only bestowed upon live birth. Therefore, there is no comparison between the history of slaves and Indians, and the rights of fetuses. To rule otherwise will threaten not only abortion, but birth control methods as well.

Issue 2: The Constitution

Appellants: *Roe* lacks a sound constitutional basis. The right to privacy is a judicial construct, and there is no constitutional right to abortion.

*Appellees: The constitutional right to privacy is fundamental and includes the right to abortion. This right is supported by the 14th's liberty guarantee as well as the concept of equality.

Issue 3: The Trimester Scheme

*Appellants: *Roe's* trimester scheme is arbitrary, incoherent, and unworkable. Due to medical technology, the viability point shifts and is too uncertain to serve as a marker for dividing the second from the third trimester.

*Appellees: Viability is a reliable cutoff point between the second and third trimesters. Medical technology has not caused the point to shift.

Issue 4: History

*Appellants: A right must be supported by the nation's history and tradition. Abortion conflicts with the American tradition in that it was restricted by the states throughout most of American history.

*Appellees: American history demonstrates an acceptance of abortion until the 1820s. Then, restrictions were for the sake of the mother's health, not to protect the fetus.

Issue 5: Stare Decisis

*Appellants: Because *Roe* is a Court created error, *stare decisis* should not stand in the Court's way in overruling this precedent.

*Appellees: *Stare decisis* requires adherence to the *Roe* precedent.

Issue 6: Consequences

Appellants: Overturning *Roe* will not lead to criminal prosecutions. It will, however, end the exploitation of women at the hands of abortionists and will prevent women from the harmful physical and emotional effects of having had an abortion.

Appellees: Overturning *Roe* will have dire consequences for women's rights, with a disproportionate impact on the lives of the poor, teenagers, and women of color. Ending abortion rights would be a violation of the 13th Amendment's prohibition on servitude. Legalized abortion is safe, and there is no evidence of harmful psychological impact. Illegal abortions will force women to obtain abortions from backalley butchers. A reversal of *Roe* has international consequences for population control.

ments of the case in favor of an emotional appeal. Among the *Webster* briefs, all three types of briefs were present on each side. Some examples illustrate the different roles and strategies that amici can assume.

The endorsement briefs allow interest groups to throw their prestige behind a party. While these briefs are often repetitive, Barker argues that "this very repetition reflects the 'group combat' flavor of the briefs." [29] This was true with the briefs on behalf of appellants filed by the United States, National Right to Life Associ-

ation, and the Center for Judicial Studies and on behalf of appellees filed by Members of Congress, NOW, and 77 Organizations Committed to Women's Equality. These briefs presented legal arguments already present in the party briefs, although they usually focused on one element and expanded on it.

The technical briefs concentrated on providing information concerning history and medical science. Many focused on the questions of whether abortion is a part of the American social tradition, how the medical

The Missouri Statute: offense and defense

Issue 1: States' Rights vs. Constitutional Rights

*Appellants: The states are the appropriate forum for resolving political issues. The majority should rule in these issues, not the undemocratic Court. The states retain powers under the 9th and 10th Amendments to protect their citizens from harm.

*Appellees: When rights are violated, the Court has a duty to step in and void the offending state law. Rights are not subject to majority rule. The state of Missouri's law violates the constitutionally protected rights of privacy, speech [and religion—amici only].

Issue 2: Standard of Review

*Appellants: The Court should use the rational basis test in evaluating the Missouri law. This level of scrutiny is appropriate since no fundamental right is at stake and in order to protect the state's rights.

*Appellees: Strict scrutiny is required in evaluating this statute since it threatens fundamental rights. Rights cannot be balanced, they must be protected.

Issue 3: The Preamble

*Appellants: The preamble should be allowed to stand since it is a prefatory statement without legal effect.

*Appellees: The preamble should be struck down since it contradicts *Roe*, violates the Missouri Constitution, and will be used as a guide to interpreting the statute.

Issue 4: Ban on Funding Abortion Counseling

*Appellants: This section does not obstruct privacy rights. Neither is it vague nor a violation of the 1st Amendment. There is no obligation to subsidize constitutional rights.

*Appellees: There is no longer a case or controversy regarding the public funds provision. The state has not contested the District Court's ruling declaring these restrictions unconstitutional. If there is a case or controversy, then the provision is unconstitutional.

Issue 5: Ban on Abortions in Public Facilities

*Appellants: This restriction does not constitute an undue burden on the woman in obtaining an abortion. The Court held in *Poelker v. Doe* (1977) that a public hospital is not obliged to provide abortion services.

*Appellees: This provision goes beyond the restrictions upheld in *Poelker* as it bans the performance of abortions in public hospitals even when no public funds or public employees are involved. It therefore unconstitutionally interferes with wholly private medical treatment.

Issue 6: Viability Testing

*Appellants: The state has a compelling interest in determining viability in order to exert its power to protect fetal life. The *Colautti v. Franklin* (1979) precedent does not apply here since not one but three factors are used to determine viability. The law does not require that all three tests be performed, but that the physician performs such tests as are necessary to make the viability determination.

*Appellees: Under any standard of review, the viability testing is unconstitutional. The required tests are expensive and dangerous and of little use in determining viability until the 28th week. The law should be read to indicate that the three tests are required in order to make specific findings regarding viability.

and social sciences contribute to our understanding of fetal life, and what impact legal versus illegal abortion has on women. For the appellants, the Association for Public Justice and Certain American State Legislators argued against abortion being an acceptable part of American society. Briefs filed by the American Association of Pro-life Obstetricians and Gynecologists, Doctors for Life, Paul Marx, and Bernard Nathanson argued that the "preborn" are persons. For the appellees, refutations of these arguments were offered by 281 American Historians, the American Medical Association, 167 Distinguished Scientists, and the Association of Reproductive Health Professionals. The National Council of Negro Women (with 114 other groups) offered both statistical and anecdotal information illustrating the disproportionately severe impact that a reversal of *Roe* would have on poor women and women of color.

The risk takers offered the most unusual arguments. On the appellants' side, the Free Speech Advocates took a confrontational approach, arguing that the abortion cases were "shams" and that the Court "has grown to accept fawning over all its errors." [30] James Joseph Lynch, Jr. contradicted the party brief's assurance that preambles are without legal effect by asserting that the fetus is protected by the reference to "posterity" made in the United States Constitution's preamble. Agudeth Israel also challenged the party line by insisting that the Missouri preamble be struck down as a violation of religious freedom. American Collegians adopted an argument sometimes used by abortion rights advocates that the Ninth and Tenth Amendments are substantive in that they reserve rights that are not listed in the Constitution's text to the states and citizens. Birthright admitted that its brief contained "very little legal precedent," and instead relied on "logic, common sense, reasoning, intelligence, and conclusions in accord with what is best for all the people of this nation." [31]

The risk takers on behalf of the appellees argued that there was a right to be free from government imposed harm to health (American Public Health Association), that a denial of abortion rights would violate the equal protection clause (National Coalition against Domestic Violence), and that religious freedom demanded that women be free to choose (Catholics for a Free Choice). An emotional appeal made by Women Who Have Had Abortions took the form of a petition-like brief containing letters of testimony.

This survey of the three types of amici suggests that certain types of groups tend to gravitate to a specific amicus role. The most obvious connection is that between professional organizations and technical briefs. A professional organization has the knowledge and expertise necessary to provide the Court with information outside of the legal realm. There also seems to be a relationship between single-issue interest groups and the role of risk taker. Since these groups enjoy a unified constituency that is devoted to promoting a particular issue, these groups may have more freedom in speaking from a perspective outside the mainstream. They can assume a challenging voice without losing their constituents. The endorsement briefs are sponsored by a variety of groups, but tend to gain the support of multi-issue interest groups. These groups tend to have less of a stake in the interest at issue, and they have to hold together a diversified constituency. Multi-issue interest groups can satisfy organizational demands by merely endorsing the party brief.

This analysis would explain why the appellants had more amici act as risk takers while the appellees had

more amici submit technical briefs. Since single-issue interest groups were more prevalent among appellants' amici, it could be expected that appellants would have more amici who assumed the role of risk taker. In contrast, since professional organizations were three-to-one behind the appellees, it was predictable that this side would submit more technical briefs.

Together these three types of briefs offered the Court not only an abundance of information concerning abortion, but a sense of the urgency and complexity of this political issue as well. The Court saw briefs which toed the party line, others which offered specialized information, and still others that challenged the Court to break new legal ground. While many perspectives were present, the next question is how many were heard?

What impact?

While the main purpose of an amicus brief is to persuade the Court to rule on behalf of a particular litigant, the impact of amici is not limited to this result alone. Interest groups may also claim success if the Court adopts the language or perspective of the brief, or if the litigant's argument is strengthened by the endorsement of the amicus.[32] In filing an amicus, an interest group may gain publicity, an opportunity to refine and articulate its position, and experience in the judicial system.[33] Such third-party involvement also allows groups to feel as though they have participated in the decisional process.[34] Some of the impact of amici may not be apparent until future cases emerge which reflect the information, argument, or concerns of the earlier amici.

Impact is of course most readily identifiable in terms of the winners and losers of a case. However, such an approach is obviously limited for a case like *Webster* where the Court lineup was 4–1–4 from the start. With this in mind, the discussion here will also include a content analysis of which briefs were cited by the justices in the decision, and a study of how some of the arguments made by the amici seemed to sway certain justices.

In a 5–4 vote with two concurrences and two dissenting opinions, the *Webster* decision upheld the sections restricting public employees and facilities from performing or assisting in abortions, and the sections requiring viability testing. While the Court did not rule on the constitutionality of the statute's preamble, it declared the counseling section moot. In the course of deciding these issues, the Court also began to disman-

Table 6. Briefs cited by the justices

	Majority			Minority		
	Rehnquist	O'Connor	Scalia	Blackmun	Stevens	Total
Appellants' brief	4	—	—	—	2	6
Agudeth Israel	—	—	—	—	1	1
American Assoc. of Pro-Life Obstetricians	—	3	—	—	—	3
Holy Orthodox Church	—	—	—	—	2	2
Lutheran Church	—	—	—	—	2	2
Missouri Catholic Conference	—	—	—	—	1	1
United States	1	—	—	2	—	3
subtotals	5	3	—	2	8	18
Appellees' brief	5	3	—	—	—	8
American Medical Association	—	2	—	2	—	4
Americans United for Separation of Church & State	—	—	—	—	2	2
Association of Reproductive Health Professionals	—	1	—	1	4	6
Catholics for a Free Choice	—	—	—	—	2	2
Group of American Law Profs.	—	—	—	1	—	1
National Association of Public Hospitals	—	1	—	1	—	2
subtotals	5	7	—	5	8	25
total amici alone	1	7	—	7	14	29
total briefs	10	10	—	7	16	43

tle the principles of *Roe,* the trimester scheme in particular. Chief Justice William Rehnquist, with Justices Byron White and Anthony Kennedy, attacked the "rigid trimester analysis" as inconsistent with the Constitution.[35] He argued, "We do not see why the State's interest in protecting human life should come into existence only at the point of viability...."[36] Justice Antonin Scalia concurred stating that Rehnquist's argument would effectively overrule *Roe,* but that he would do so more explicitly.[37] Justice Sandra Day O'Connor agreed with the constitutionality of the Missouri statute, but not with the need to unravel *Roe.* She relied instead on *Roe* and its progeny to uphold the Missouri law.[38] The four dissenting justices, Harry Blackmun, William Brennan, Thurgood Marshall, and John Paul Stevens, would have used *Roe* to void the Missouri statute.

Therefore, when speaking strictly in terms of win versus lose, the appellants emerged as the victors in this case. The Missouri law was upheld, the Court signaled its willingness to uphold restrictive state abortion policies, and four justices indicated a willingness to overturn *Roe.* Within these terms, appellees could claim only that *Roe* survived—for now. Yet, measuring impact in this way assumes that the win is due to arguments set forth by amici. It also ignores the fact that amici on the losing side have impact as well. Therefore, it is important to consider as well two other indicators:

the amici cited by the Court, and evidence that the Court accepted arguments advanced only by the amici.

The counting of citations demonstrates that the justices considered the arguments set forth by the amici.[39] This is not to say, of course, that the only briefs which had impact were the ones cited, but the data is useful as a "blunt indicator" of how the Court used the briefs.[40] Table 6 presents the results of counting each direct reference to a brief made by one of the five justices who wrote an opinion in the *Webster* case. References to the appellants' party briefs totaled six while the appellees' party briefs were cited eight times. Excluding party briefs, amicus briefs were cited 29 times. Twelve different amicus briefs, six from each side, were cited at least once. Appellants' amici were cited 12 times while appellees' amici were cited 17 times. The amicus briefs cited tended to be those that contained either religious arguments or which provided technical information on medicine or on the law. Besides the direct references to the amicus briefs, Justices Blackmun and Stevens together cited seven different published articles: three which were largely scientific, two commenting on religious issues, one on the impact of illegal abortions, and one on the law.

Rehnquist, writing for the majority, cited the appellants' brief four times and the appellees' brief five times. The only amicus to which he referred was that of the United States. In O'Connor's concurring opinion, she cited the appellees' brief three times, and referred to the four amicus briefs containing medical and scientific information, again indicating her struggle with the viability issue. Scalia's concurrence made no direct references to briefs or outside sources. The dissents of Justices Blackmun and Stevens did not cite the party briefs of either side. These justices referred instead to the amicus briefs for a total of 29 citations. As with O'Connor, most of Blackmun's references came from the technical medical briefs. In contrast, Stevens cited mostly the religiously oriented briefs.

Yet, briefs can be cited and then rejected. Did the briefs have any real influence on the justices in constructing their decision? It is suggested that the answer is yes. Consider again the role of the amici. The appellants' amici seemed to urge their coalition of four justices to overturn *Roe*. The appellees' amici appeared to focus on convincing O'Connor to cast the fifth vote to protect *Roe*. The amici on both sides enjoyed some success.

The victory enjoyed by the appellants was not of the parties' making alone. The Court went further than the parties had urged, surging ahead on the path marked by the appellants' amici. When the Court accepts an argument that was advanced only by an amicus brief, it is an indication of influence.[41] Again, the party brief had devoted only four pages to challenging *Roe* and the viability point. It was instead the amici who supplied both the technical and legal information which subverted the *Roe* trimester scheme.

There are signs that the appellees' amici had influence as well. Again, their target was O'Connor and the two routes to her were to have her apply her "undue burden" test to strike down the Missouri statute, and to have her retreat from her criticism of *Roe*'s trimester scheme. While the amici were unsuccessful concerning the first point, there are signs that they made some progress concerning the second.

It is not what O'Connor's *Webster* opinion says but what it does not say that is important.[42] Considering her *Akron* dissent in which she argued that the trimester approach was "completely unworkable"[43] and on a "collision course with itself,"[44] and that she adhered to this position three years later in *Thornburgh v. American College of Obstetricians and Gynecologists*,[45] it is curious that in *Webster*—a case that brings the viability issue to the forefront and causes four other justices to voice concerns that the trimester framework is indeed unworkable—O'Connor remarks only that she continues

to regard the trimester approach as "problematic."[46] She cites her *Akron* dissent not to repudiate the trimester scheme, but to illustrate how to apply the "undue burden" test. If indeed O'Connor is retreating from her *Akron* critique, the appellees' amici may be responsible for planting the seed of doubt in her mind.

Conclusion

The 78 *Webster* amici produced an uncomparable collection of information on the abortion rights issue. While *Webster* is certainly not a typical case, nor was the response of interest groups usual, it does serve to magnify the amicus curiae role. Interest groups can lobby the Court concerning an issue even as politicized as abortion if they enter the Court through the open door extended to amici. In working to present their arguments before the Court, the pro-life and pro-choice movements also revealed something about themselves. The briefs reflected the composition of their constituencies, their legal strategies, and their core values. The study of amici, then, is not only instructive for court watching but for monitoring interest group politics as well.

The writing and organization of 78 briefs was a monumental undertaking, but it was not a wasted effort. It appears that the amici on both sides made inroads with the Court. The briefs were not only read; they also had impact. Their arguments and information helped to shape the terms of the Court debate. Whether the justices refuted the briefs, modified an argument because of them, or accepted and integrated their points, the amici mattered. Through the presentation of the briefs, the battle over abortion rights was waged before the Court. It is no surprise, then, that in the midst of this friendly fire, some of the justices were struck.

Notes

This article originally appeared in Volume 74, Number 5, February–March 1991, pages 261–270.

I would like to thank Lee Epstein and Gregory Caldeira for sharing their research and ideas, and the anonymous reviewer who provided a list of insightful comments. Special thanks to Catherine Bell Fleming of the National Abortion Rights Action League for providing me with all the appellees' amicus briefs.

An earlier version of this article was presented at the Annual Meeting of the Northeastern Political Science Association, Philadelphia, Penn., November 9–11, 1989.

1. 492 U.S. __; 109 S.Ct. 3040 (1989).
2. 438 U.S. 265 (1978).

3. 410 U.S. 113 (1973).

4. 109 S.Ct. 3040, 3041 (1989).

5. Ibid. at 3047.

6. While I have framed the controversy in terms of abortion rights, throughout this article I refer to the two movements as "pro-life" and "pro-choice." While these labels cloud the actual legal issue, they represent not only how the popular media refer to the movements but also how the movements refer to themselves.

7. While focusing on the first sponsor may not accurately reflect the organization that assumed the bulk of the legal work, it usually illustrates the character and role of the brief. For example, although the Center for Constitutional Rights constructed the brief for which the National Council of Negro Women appears as the first sponsor, the NCNW is representative of the nature of the brief since it speaks of the impact that restrictive abortion policy will have on women of color.

8. Caldeira and Wright, "Amici Curiae Before the Supreme Court: Who Participates, When and How Much?" *J. Pol.* 18 (1990).

9. O'Connor and Epstein, "Amicus Curiae Participation in U.S. Supreme Court Litigation: An Appraisal of Hakman's 'Folklore'," *Law & Soc'y Rev.* 16 (1981–1982), 313.

10. Caldeira and Wright, "Why Organized Interests Participate as Amici Curiae in the U.S. Supreme Court," paper presented at the 1989 Annual Meeting of the American Political Science Association, Atlanta, Georgia, page 11.

11. Ibid.

12. *See,* Brief for Women Who Have Had Abortions (2887 signatures and 627 signatures of friends); Brief for 608 State Legislators from 32 States; Brief for Group of American Law Professors (885 signatures); 281 American Historians; Brief for 167 Distinguished Scientists and Physicians; Brief for Certain Members of the Congress of the United States; Brief for Catholics for a Free Choice; Brief for Bioethicists for Privacy.

13. In fact, Justice Scalia's *Webster* opinion did object to the belief of interest groups that unelected and life-tenured justices should weigh popular opinion. *See,* Scalia's dissent at 3065–3066.

14. Harper and Etherington, "Lobbyists Before the Court," *U. Pa L. Rev.* 101 (1953), 1172.

15. Kobylka, "A Court-Created Contest for Group Litigation: Libertarian Groups and Obscenity," *J. Pol.* 49 (1987), 1073.

16. Telephone interview with Kathryn Kolbert, attorney-consultant to the ACLU Reproductive Freedom Project, November 30, 1990; Kolbert, "Webster v. Reproductive Health Services: Reproductive Freedom Hanging by a Thread," *Women's Rights L. Rep.* 11 (1989), 153, 156.

17. Kolbert, *supra* n. 16, at 157.

18. Brief for Edward Allen, Brief for Human Life International, Brief for Paul Marx, Brief for Bernard Nathan-

son, Brief for Right to Life League of Southern California, and Brief for Austin Vaughn and Crusade for Life, Inc.

19. Caldeira and Wright, *supra* n. 5.

20. Alternative typologies were considered and rejected. Dividing the groups according to their purpose (governmental, religious, advocate, and multi-interest) did not provide enough detail to gain a sense of the diversity among the groups. More substantive divisions, such as religious, medical, feminist, and academic, did not provide mutually exclusive categories. An ideological divide of liberal versus conservative would essentially divide the amici into the already existing appellant versus appellee lineup. *See,* O'Connor and Epstein, "The Rise of Conservative Interest Group Litigation," *J. Pol.* 45 (1983), 479–489. O'Neill's typology of oligarchic, democratic, and managerial groups was designed more to study the structures of the groups themselves than the nature of Court politics. *See* O'Neill, *Bakke and the Politics of Equality: Friends and Foes in the Classroom of Litigation* (Middletown, Conn.: Wesleyan University Press, 1985). Bradley and Gardner's underdog versus upperdog distinction provides only two divisions and appears to be designed for studying diverse cases over a period of time. *See,* Bradley and Gardner, "Underdogs, Upperdogs and the Use of the Amicus Brief: Trends and Explanations," *Just. Sys. J.* 10 (1985), 78–96.

21. 462 U.S. 416, 452 (1983).

22. *See,* Brief for Alabama Lawyers for Unborn Children, Inc.; Brief for Edward Allen; Brief for Attorneys General from Five States; Brief for Catholics United for Life; Brief for Alan Ernest; Brief for Free Speech Advocates; Brief for The Holy Orthodox Church; Brief for Human Life International; Brief for International Right to Life Federation; Brief for Larry Joyce; Brief for the Knights of Columbus; Brief for James Joseph Lynch, Jr.; Brief for Paul Marx; Brief for Bernard Nathanson; Brief for the Right to Life League of Southern California; Brief for the Southwest Life and Law Center, Inc.; Brief for Austin Vaughn and Crusade for Life, Inc.

23. *See,* Akron, *supra* n. 21, at 453.

24. Kolbert, *supra* n. 16.

25. Akron, *supra* n. 21, at 458.

26. Kolbert, *supra* n. 16.

27. Ibid.

28. Krislov, "The Amicus Brief: From Friendship to Advocacy," *Yale L. J.* 72 (1963), 694–721.

29. Barker, "Third Parties in Litigation: A Systemic View of the Judicial Function," *J. Pol.* 29 (1967), 62.

30. Brief for Free Speech Advocates, at 6, 23.

31. Brief for Birthright, at 17.

32. O'Connor, *Women's Organizations' Use of the Courts* (Lexington, Mass.: Lexington Books, 1980), 146.

33. Ibid.

34. Krislov, *supra* n. 28, at 721.

35. Webster, *supra* n. 1, at 3056.

36. Ibid. at 3057.

37. Ibid. at 3064.

38. Ibid. at 3060.

39. Angell, "The Amicus Curiae: American Development of English Institutions," *Int'l & Comp. L. Q.* 16 (1967), 1036–1044.

40. O'Connor and Epstein, "Court Rules and Workload: A Case Study of Rules Governing Amicus Curiae Participation," *Jus. Sys. J.* 8 (1983), 43.

41. Angell, *supra* n. 39, at 1036.

42. This point was brought to my attention by Kathryn Kolbert; interview, *supra* n. 16.

43. Akron, *supra* n. 21, at 454.

44. Ibid. at 458.

45. 476 U.S. 747, at 814 (1986).

46. Webster, *supra* n. 1, at 3063.

Nonlegal advice: the amicus briefs in Webster v. Reproductive Health Services

Jack E. Rossotti, Laura Natelson, and Raymond Tatalovich

Although justices rely on their own knowledge of case law and legal precedent, they are likely to accept and incorporate the views of amici on nonlegal issues.

During the past decade the study of group litigation has increased substantially, but researchers "have not fully explored the kinds of tactics groups use to influence judicial decisions once they decide to sponsor a case or participate as amicus curiae." [1]

What is needed are answers to questions such as:

- Do amici seek to influence judicial decision-making through the use of one-sided nonlegal information?

- Do amici rely more heavily on nonlegal than legal information?

- Is the information supplied by amici most one-sided when it is from nonlegal sources?

- Do amici manipulate legal precedent to strategically promote their ideological agenda?

- Are Supreme Court justices more likely to accept and incorporate the views of amici on nonlegal rather than legal sources?

Previous research on amicus activity has focused on the *legal* strategies by interest groups at various stages and levels of the judicial process, the frequency of group litigation and the coalition-building process among interests, and the issues that encourage groups to file amicus briefs. But quantitative methods have not been applied to studying how amici utilize *nonlegal* information to influence judicial decision making. For example, previous scholarship on the briefs filed in *Webster v. Reproductive Health Services* relied on textual or qualitative examination,[2] not content analysis.

Webster, decided in 1989, provides a particularly useful case study of amici activity since it prompted the largest number of amicus briefs ever submitted in a single case before the Supreme Court.[3] Unlike the prior record in *Regents of the University of California v. Bakke,*[4] the 1978 case involving affirmative action, the range of interests in *Webster* was much larger.[5] *Webster* also was a defining

moment for pro-choice groups as the prospects of an adverse Supreme Court decision prompted an outpouring of amici among women's advocacy organizations. *Webster* was widely perceived in lay and legal publications[6] as having the potential to reverse or fundamentally redirect *Roe v. Wade,* the 1973 case that established the precedent of a woman's constitutional right to an abortion during the pre-viability stage of a pregnancy. The outcome of *Webster,* moreover, was uniformly judged by feminist legal scholars as opening the door to further state regulations and undercutting a woman's right to abortion.[7]

Methodology

All sources to legal and nonlegal authorities and the frequency of citations to those sources in the 78 amicus curiae briefs filed in *Webster* were grouped into four broad categories—legal, medical, religious, and other (such as historical). This permitted drawing conclusions about the use of legal and nonlegal sources by the amici.

In addition, the three most important abortion decisions prior to *Webster*—*Roe, City of Akron v. Akron Center for Reproductive Health, Inc.* (1983), and *Thornburgh v. American College of Obstetricians and Gynecologists* (1986)—were used to illustrate how the amici offered one-sided interpretations of those precedents to influence the Court. Citations to *Roe, Akron,* or *Thornburgh* were classified as to whether they referenced the majority, concurring, or dissenting opinions and then, for each citation, its ideological direction: pro-regulation, anti-regulation, or neutral (meaning the source was used for informational purposes or indicated no ideological position). Finally, to examine whether the arguments of amici influenced any of the five written opinions in *Webster,* all direct references to the amicus briefs were categorized based on whether the justice agreed with, modified, or rejected the argument put forth by the amici.

Judicature Volume 81, Number 3, pp. 118–121

Table 1. Sources cited in the *Webster* amicus briefs (Total number of citations in parenthesis)

	By pro-life only	By pro-choice only	By both sides
Legal cases	535 (782)	528 (587)	184 (2,664)
Legal statutes	223 (322)	98 (236)	18 (344)
Other legal	232 (606)	131 (178)	12 (144)
Medical sources	224 (293)	397 (776)	22 (172)
Religious sources	50 (68)	31 (47)	2 (5)
Other sources	231 (366)	216 (254)	9 (79)
Totals	1,495 (2,473)	1,401 (2,078)	247 (3,408)

Sources cited

Nearly all (92 percent) of the sources cited by the 78 amici in *Webster* were used only by pro-life or pro-choice advocates, not both, meaning that they were selectively chosen to defend a particular viewpoint. (See Table 1.) The remaining 8 percent of sources were used by both sides. However, these two-sided references accounted for 43 percent of the total citations. The 247 sources used by both parties were cited an average of 14 times each. For three categories of legal references (cases, statutes, other), barely more (11 percent) two-sided references were used. But 97 percent of non-legal references (medical, religious, other) were one-sided.

The distribution of nonlegal citations is even more skewed. Only 1 percent of the cites to nonlegal authorities were made by both pro-life and pro-choice amici. Activists who lobby the Supreme Court are more likely to make distinct arguments based on nonlegal evidence than where legal sources are involved. These patterns showing one-sided use of information, especially for nonlegal sources, indicate that amici do seek to influence judicial decision making through the use of one-sided nonlegal information and that the information is most one-sided with respect to nonlegal sources.

While each side almost never used the same references to nonlegal research to bolster its argument, one-sided sources to legal cases equaled 43 percent for pro-life amici and 42 percent for pro-choice amici, while the 15 percent of legal cases referenced by both sides accounted for 66 percent of all citations to case law. But *Roe, Akron,* and *Thornburgh* together accounted for 25 percent of all cites to legal cases and 37 percent of two-sided citations to case law. Thus one must differentiate between abortion case law and other kinds of cases. Of 17 abortion cases from 1973 through 1988 only eight were referenced by the 78 amici, but all eight were two-sided references by pro-life and pro-

choice amici. If all citations to those eight cases are tabulated, they would represent 47 percent (or 1,243) of the total 2,664 two-sided citations to legal cases.

In sum, there were six times as many one-sided references to non-abortion cases by pro-life (535) and pro-choice (528) amici as there were two-sided references to non-abortion case law. Thus, one-sided references to non-abortion case law were idiosyncratic insofar as those cases did not draw upon abortion precedents but rather were used to establish a link between some medical, scientific, or religious knowledge and other constitutional issues relevant to the abortion controversy (such as church-state separation).

Medical and religious arguments held particular sway, as indicated in the number of sources involving those topics. Only 22 (3 percent) of the medical sources were referred to by both sides, and there was even less overlap on religious sources (2 percent).

Since nearly one-half of the two-sided citations to case law involved abortion cases, we need to unravel how those precedents were manipulated by the amici to promote their unique arguments. Composite statistics were derived to show how often the pro-life and pro-choice amici referred to the majority and concurring opinions in *Roe, Akron,* and *Thornburgh* or the dissenting opinions that took issue with that jurisprudence. The patterns for the amici confirm suspicions that the antagonists did not rely upon the precedents from the majority opinions to argue the same legal position in *Webster.*

To a degree the competing amici chose selectively because 26 percent of the pro-life citations were to the dissenting opinions in the three abortion cases whereas pro-choice amici would hardly look for support from those justices who opposed *Roe, Akron,* and *Thornburgh.* Thus only 9 percent of the pro-choice citations were to the dissents. But what was not anticipated is that amici who oppose each other would rely heavily on the majority opinions in *Roe, Akron,* and *Thornburgh.* Pro-life amici cited the majority opinions 488 times (72 percent of the total), and pro-choice amici cited the majority opinions 266 times (85 percent of the total). This pattern suggests that precedent may mean something less than stare decisis for those who are opposed to *Roe.*

None of the pro-choice citations to the majority opinions in *Roe, Akron,* or *Thornburgh* were used to argue that states can promulgate regulations on abortion, and there were very few "neutral" usages of precedent by pro-choice amici. A total of 95 percent of the pro-choice cites to those abortion cases affirmed their precedents as disallowing any state regulations on a woman's right to an abortion. Similarly, none of the pro-life citations to *Roe, Akron,* or *Thornburgh* made an argument against state regulation of abortion and, again, their briefs had very few neutral references to those cases. As a whole, 98 percent of the pro-life cites were used to justify controls by state government on abortions. Clearly, amici do manipulate legal precedent to strategically promote their ideological agenda.

How influential?

The fifth research question posed at the outset asked to what degree sources referenced by the amici were influential with the justices in writing their opinions. The opinions by Rehnquist, O'Connor, Blackmun, and Stevens contained 29 citations to amicus briefs, and Scalia cited no amicus briefs in his concurring opinion. The content of the amicus brief was compared with the argument made in the opinion to determine if that justice accepted, modified, or rejected the amicus view. The analysis found that justices usually cite amici for nonlegal information and that those cites are often incorporated into their opinions.

Of the 29 citations to amicus briefs, only two referenced legal issues, 18 cited medical arguments, and nine were citations to religious sources. Overall 16 of the references were accepted by the justices. The information in eight were modified by the opinions, and five arguments referenced in the written opinions were rejected outright.

Of the 10 references to pro-life briefs, Rehnquist rejected the legal argument advanced by the United States as amicus, and Blackmun offered a modified interpretation of another point in the same brief. O'Connor accepted the medical arguments made by three other pro-life amici, and Stevens modified three

religious claims and rejected two religious arguments by pro-life amici. Thus Blackmun and Stevens, who dissented in *Webster,* never incorporated the arguments of pro-life amici in their opinions, whereas O'Connor's concurrence accepted pro-life arguments in three instances.

There were 19 references by mainly liberal justices to pro-choice briefs. However, O'Connor twice rejected the medical arguments of pro-choice amici and modified the interpretation of two other pro-choice medical briefs. Blackmun agreed with all six of his references to pro-choice medical briefs as did Stevens in five instances. Stevens also modified the religious arguments from two pro-choice amici.

Implications

It makes perfect sense that a justice would look to his or her own knowledge of case law or rely upon clerks to research legal precedents. This analysis shows that the ideological bent of each justice extends to his or her manipulation of precedent when writing opinions. But to do an extensive search of cognate disciplines as wide-ranging as medicine, theology, history, and psychology is beyond the capacity of any judge, and it was this need for substantive knowledge and third-party representation that gave rise to the use of amicus briefs.

All five of the research questions posed at the outset can be answered in the affirmative. First, the amici did supply one-sided nonlegal information, and the pro-life and pro-choice amici generally did not use the same nonlegal sources. Second, amici relied more heavily on nonlegal sources and non-abortion cases as compared to purely abortion case law, which illustrates how both sides pick and choose to support their own viewpoint. Third, nonlegal information was much more one-sided than were the legal sources simply because both sides had to give some attention to the precedential cases on abortion. Fourth, even though both sides may have referenced the same abortion precedents, each side tried to manipulate those precedents by selectively citing arguments that bolstered only the pro-life or the pro-choice position. Fifth, while there were only 29 direct references to the amicus briefs in the five *Webster* opinions, all but two referenced nonlegal sources rather than the case law, and the arguments in 16 were wholly accepted by the justices.

It was obvious that pro-choice amici would accept nothing less than a reaffirmation of the validity of *Roe, Akron,* and *Thornburgh.* There was some tendency for justices in the majority in *Webster* to cite pro-life briefs in crafting their opinions and for dissenting justices to cite pro-choice briefs. The much more important finding is that precedent was binding only on pro-choice amici, who defended the right of abortion, while every cite to precedent in *Roe, Akron,* and *Thornburgh* by pro-life amici were efforts to discredit stare decisis. Thus what at first glance appeared to be a situation where precedent might constrain judicial decision making ultimately was shown to be a technique by the amici to advance their policy goals. It was also apparent that the justices in *Webster* made the most direct use of amicus briefs primarily for the nonlegal information they provided, but the nonlegal sources were shown to be far more one-sided than the legal authorities.

It is alleged that judges are unlike other kinds of political actors because their actions are constrained by the force of precedent and stare decisis. Adherence to the settled law is one of the canons of jurisprudence, but analysts have begun to evaluate the legal model against a behavioral (ideological) model as predictors of judicial decisions.[8] A recent critique of legal precedent hypothesized that "liberal Courts should overrule conservative precedents, and conservative Courts those that are liberal." [9] They do, and this research explains how interest groups fashion their use of amicus briefs to achieve those kind of ideological results. Amici are not interested in compromise or a balanced presentation of the facts. As partisans in a political battle to influence the Court, the amici manipulate the use of nonlegal sources as well as references to legal precedent to achieve a victory.

Notes

This article originally appeared in Volume 81, Number 3, November–December 1997, pages 118–121.

1. Epstein, "Courts and Interest Groups," in Gates and Johnson, eds., *The American Courts: A Critical Assessment* (Washington, D.C.: CQ Press, 1991), 336–337, 349.

2. "The *Webster Amicus Curiae* Briefs: Perspectives on the Abortion Controversy and the Role of the Supreme Court," *Am. J. L. & Med.* 15 (1989), 153–243; Woliver, "Lobbying the Supreme Court: Coalitions of Abortion Interests and the Webster Decision," Paper Delivered, Annual Meeting, Southern Political Science Association (1991); Colker, "Feminist Litigation: An Oxymoron?—A Study of the Briefs Filed in William L. Webster v. Reproductive Health Services," *Harv. L. J.* 13 (1990), 137.

3. Behuniak-Long, "Friendly Fire: Amici Curiae and *Webster v. Reproductive Health Services,*" *Judicature* 74 (1991), 261–270.

4. O'Neill, *Bakke and the Politics of Equality: Friends and Foes in the Classroom of Litigation* (Middletown, Conn.: Wesleyan University Press, 1985).

5. Tatalovich and Daynes, "The Lowi Paradigm, Moral Conflict, and Coalition-Building: Pro-Choice versus Pro-Life," *Women & Pol.* 13 (1993) 39–66.

6. *See, e.g.,* "Abortion on the Ropes," *Time,* December 5, 1988, at 58; Reidinger, "Will *Roe v. Wade* be Overruled?" *ABA J.* 66 (1988), 66, 68–70.

7. Mezey, *In Pursuit of Equality: Women, Public Policy, and the Federal Courts* (New York: St. Martin's Press, 1992), 262; Baer, "What We Know As Women: A New Look at *Roe v. Wade,*" *NWSA J.* 2 (1990), 558–582; Binion, "*Webster v. Reproductive Health Services*: Devaluing the Right to Choose," *Women & Pol.* 11 (1991), 41–59.

8. George and Epstein, "On the Nature of Supreme Court Decision Making," *Am. Pol. Sci. Rev.* 86 (1992), 323–337.

9. Brenner and Spaeth, *Stare Indecisis: The Alteration of Precedent on the Supreme Court, 1946–1992* (New York: Cambridge University Press, 1995), 110–111.

The solicitor general as amicus, 1953–2000: how influential?

Rebecca E. Deen, Joseph Ignagni, and James Meernik

Although solicitors general are filing more amicus briefs before the Supreme Court,
their success rate is declining.

The United States' political system is built on the premise that power is both separated and shared. In fact, the history and evolution of our government is continually marked by the shifting balance of power among the three branches. Understandably, scholars have examined the interaction among them, and there is an ever-increasing amount of literature on inter-institutional relations involving Congress and the Supreme Court[1] and Congress and the president.[2]

Research on the relationship between the executive and judicial branches, however, is less voluminous. Although certainly classic studies[3] and more recent articles[4] can be found, there has not been nearly the amount of systematic inquiry we have seen in other inter-institutional relationships. This is important because rather significant political and theoretical questions of institutional power are at stake, such as: When do these institutions act independently from one another? When do they exhibit deference? To what extent can each branch influence the other's decision making?

This article examines this relationship through an exploration of cases in which the solicitor general's office filed amicus briefs before the U.S. Supreme Court. First, it describes the unique position of the solicitor general as the representative of the executive branch before the Court. Then, it provides evidence of the changes in this relationship over time. The number of briefs filed has increased and the nature of these briefs has changed. Most striking, the executive branch's use of these briefs in an attempt to influence the Court has met with varying degrees of success. The article concludes with a brief discussion of what might have affected these trends.

The solicitor general

Though the solicitor general reports to the attorney general, in many ways this office holds a special position, both within the executive branch and as the representative of the executive branch before the Supreme Court. The president appoints the solicitor general and "can remove solicitors who do not live up to expecta-tions."[5] The president and solicitor general "maintain frequent contacts about the issues currently or potentially before the United States Supreme Court."[6]

By using amicus briefs, Puro writes, ". . . the Solicitor General attempts to explain executive policy to the Supreme Court." The solicitor general almost exclusively represents the executive branch and federal government before the Supreme Court. He is also generally responsible for advancing the president's agenda in the legal system.[7]

It has thus been long-accepted wisdom that the solicitor general enjoys special advantages before the Court. O'Connor claims that the solicitor general has "extraordinary influence" and that his amicus briefs "have a substantial effect on public policy."[8] Other commentators have dubbed the solicitor general the Court's "nine-and-a-half" member or the "tenth justice."[9] Additionally, the federal government appears more frequently (as a litigant or amicus) than any other party or group. In recent years, such cases have constituted in excess of 50 percent of the Court's workload (Baum notes, for example, that during the 1998 term the government "played an official role in 84 percent of the cases in which the Court heard arguments").[10]

The solicitor general also plays a significant role in deciding the cases the federal government appeals to the Supreme Court. Only a few federal agencies have the authority to appeal a case to the Court without the solicitor general's approval. When appealing cases, the solicitor general has had great success in obtaining certiorari.[11] In terms of actually winning cases on the merits, previous research indicates that the U.S. government has won an average of 63 percent of all cases between 1953 and 1991.[12] The solicitor general does even better when participating as an amicus than when the government is a direct party to a case.[13] In fact, from 1952 to 1990, no presidential administration won less than 65 percent of its cases as an amicus, while others won more than 80 percent.[14]

There is evidence, however, to suggest that the perception of the relationship between the office of the solicitor general and the Court has changed over time. In his provocative book, *The Tenth Justice*, Lincoln Caplan concludes by asserting that the office under the Reagan administration had lost its reputation for political independence. While Reagan's first solicitor general, Rex Lee, was significantly more ideological than his predecessors,[15] it was his successor, Charles Fried, who drew the most criticism for politicizing the office.

Caplan asserts that Fried, especially in the early years of his tenure, used the office as a tool to advocate Reagan's political positions. While this assertion was controversial and contested at the time of the book's publication,[16] others in the legal news community also pointed to the office's politicization. They highlighted unusually high numbers of departures of career lawyers working for the office and unnamed sources who expressed concern over the perception of Fried's use of politics.[17]

Additionally, other research complements Caplan's findings that Reagan did begin the process of publicly advancing "agenda cases," specifically in the area of individual-rights cases. However, the point has also been made that Reagan was not the first president to use his solicitor general to advance his administration's agenda. Rather, his use of the office was simply more widely known.[18]

Whether these assessments of the politicization of the office are completely accurate, clearly the percep-

tion of the office being used as part of the partisan agenda of the administration has been more pronounced since the Reagan administration. Each solicitor general following Fried has had to address the issue of his perspective on politics and the office.[19] Previous presidents were more likely afforded the perception that their solicitor general was independent from political machinations.

Trends over time

Participation rates. As the previous discussion indicates, there is some evidence to suggest that the office of the solicitor general has changed over time in terms of behavior and of the perception of it by the legal community. Additionally, we know from important earlier studies[20] that the office historically has filed amicus briefs regularly in an attempt to influence the Court. As additional years of information about this relationship are now available, it is instructive to reexamine the behavior of the solicitor general to see if this pattern remains.

Figure 1 represents all 834 cases where the solicitor general filed an amicus brief in cases the Supreme Court decided from 1953 through 2000.[21] From it we can see that although there is substantial variation in filings over time, there is also a clear trend toward more filings. In particular, we note the dramatic upsurges in solicitor general activity during the Kennedy and Rea-

Figure 1. Amicus brief filing rates over time

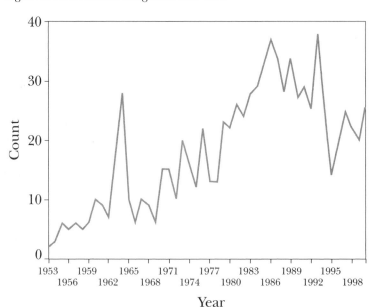

Year

Figure 2. Average number of briefs filed per year across presidential administration

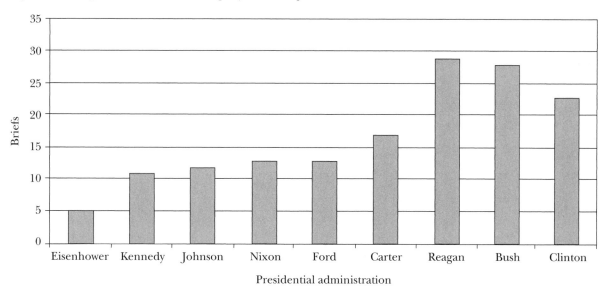

gan administrations. Both presidents came into office with a broader, more activist agenda that heavily involved the Justice Department in litigation (e.g., civil rights and social issues). We explore this subject in more detail later.

If we examine the frequency of amicus filings by presidential administration, a similar picture emerges. From Figure 2 we see that the average number of briefs filed per year in a given administration has increased substantially with the Reagan, Bush, and Clinton administrations. Not only did the total number of briefs filed increase, but more briefs were also filed, on average, per year. In fact, there is an approximate 500 percent increase in the rate of filings from Eisenhower to Reagan.

These data may also be compared across Courts (see Table 1). Again, we see the clear pattern of increased filings over time. In fact, the average number has almost doubled from the Warren to Rehnquist Courts.

Interestingly, these trends exist concurrent with the decrease in the number of cases decided by the Supreme Court. During the period 1953 to 2000, there were 8,412 cases decided by the Supreme Court[22]—an average of 179 per year. This average has fluctuated dramatically, from 113 cases during the Eisenhower administration, to the high average of 255 cases during the Reagan administration, to the low average of 108 cases (during the Clinton administration). Thus, when one examines the proportion of cases decided by the

Table 1. Amicus brief filing rate across Courts

Court	# of cases filed	Average per year
Warren	143	13
Burger	332	20
Rehnquist	353	25

Court on which the solicitor general's office files an amicus brief, the pattern is striking (see Figure 3).

While the Court was becoming increasingly more discriminating in the number of cases to which it granted certiorari, the solicitor general actually increased the number of amicus briefs it filed. Consequently, the solicitor general's office filed briefs in proportionally more cases heard before the Court over time. Comparing the Eisenhower administration to Clinton's, there is more than a three-fold increase. In other words, most recently, amicus briefs were filed by the solicitors general in more than one-fifth of the cases on the Supreme Court's docket.

These data suggest that solicitors general, across time, have believed filing amicus briefs is important. In fact, it appears that this belief has only increased with time. One would assume this filing rate is at least at the acquiescence, if not the beckoning, of the sitting president. This trend also leads to the conclusion that

Figure 3. Proportion of cases heard on which the solicitor general filed an amicus brief.

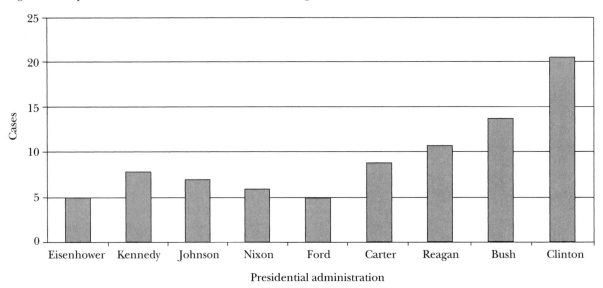

either the solicitors general, the presidents themselves, or both believe that filing these briefs is an appropriate use of an administration's resources. It appears that the executive branch views these briefs as either being effective in influencing Supreme Court decision making, or as tools in satisfying political pressure groups.

This is congruent with others who have found that there has been an increase in general in the number of amicus briefs filed by all groups.[23] In the early 1950s, approximately 15 percent of all cases had one or more amicus briefs. By the middle 1990s, this had increased to more than 80 percent; for example, in the 1998 term "such briefs were submitted in more than 90 percent of the cases decided on the merits." [24] The federal government, thus, is not alone in its propensity to file amicus briefs in an attempt to influence the Supreme Court.

Participation rates across issue area. There is an important substantive variation in the cases in which the solicitors general file amicus briefs (see Table 2).

Examined across all years, most briefs were filed in civil rights cases. Other areas of high amicus filing activity included economic activity, criminal procedure, and federalism. When this pattern is compared with the Court's docket over this time period, one can see that in three of these four areas the solicitor general's office filed disproportionately more briefs (civil rights, economic activity, federalism).

Conversely, there were areas in which the office did not file as large a proportion of briefs as would be sug-

Table 2. Amicus brief filing rates across issue area

Issue area	# of cases filed	% of all cases filed	% of Court's docket
Civil rights	223	27.0	17.3
Economic activity	194	23.5	15.4
Criminal procedure	133	16.1	27.1
Federalism	94	11.4	3.6
Judicial power	61	7.4	13.9
First Amendment	37	4.5	8.7
Unions	30	3.6	3.6
Due process	29	3.5	3.5
Attorneys	15	1.8	1.2
Privacy	7	0.8	1.1
Interstate relations	1	0.1	0.8
Federal taxation	1	0.1	3.0

gested by the Court's docket. For example, though 16 percent of all briefs were on criminal procedure cases, the Court's docket consisted of 27 percent criminal procedure cases. Similarly, slightly more than 7 percent of amicus briefs were filed on judicial power cases, while that issue constituted almost 14 percent of the cases on the Court's docket.

It appears that the executive branch and the Supreme Court do not always see eye to eye in terms of which issue areas are most important. These data suggest that each institution may feel differently about

Table 3. Filing rates by issue area, across presidential administrations

	DDE	JFK	LBJ	Nixon	Ford	Carter	Reagan	Bush	Clinton	Total
Civil rights	6 (14%)	14 (42.4%)	27 (43.5%)	32 (42.7%)	8 (30.8%)	25 (37.3%)	50 (21.8%)	19 (17.0%)	42 (23.6%)	223 (26.9%)
Economic activity	13 (30.2%)	8 (24.2%)	10 (15.9%)	12 (16%)	7 (26.9%)	16 (23.9%)	54 (23.6%)	28 (25%)	46 (25.8%)	194 (23.4%)
Judicial power	3 (7.0%)		6 (9.7%)	6 (8%)	3 (11.5%)	4 (6.0%)	12 (5.2%)	11 (9.8%)	16 (9.0%)	61 (7.4%)
Federalism	13 (30.2%)	9 (27.3%)	9 (14.5%)	8 (10.7%)	1 (3.8%)	6 (9.0%)	22 (9.6%)	7 (6.3%)	19 (10.7%)	94 (11.4%)
Unions	5 (11.6%)	1 (3.0%)	5 (8.1%)	1 (1.3%)	1 (3.8%)		8 (3.5%)	6 (5.4%)	3 (1.7%)	30 (3.6%)
Attorneys		1 (3.0%)		1 (1.3%)		4 (6.0%)	6 (2.6%)	3 (2.7%)		15 (1.8%)
Criminal procedure			3 (4.8%)	9 (12%)	2 (7.7%)	7 (10.4%)	51 (22.3%)	30 (26.8%)	31 (17.4%)	133 (16.1%)
First Amendment	1 (2.3%)		2 (3.2%)	6 (8%)	2 (7.7%)	1 (1.5%)	14 (6.1%)	4 (3.6%)	7 (3.9%)	37 (4.5%)
Due process	2 (4.7%)				2 (7.7%)	3 (4.5%)	10 (4.7%)	4 (3.6%)	8 (4.5%)	29 (3.5%)
Privacy							1 (0.4%)		6 (3.4%)	7 (0.8%)
Federal taxation							1 (0.4%)			1 (0.1%)
Interstate relations						1 (1.5%)				1 (0.1%)
Total	43 (100%)	33 (99.9%)	62 (99.7%)	75 (100%)	26 (99.9%)	67 (100.1%)	229* (100.2%)	112 (100.2%)	178+ (100%)	825 (99.6%)

* The issue variable was undeterminable for 2 briefs.
+ The issue variable was undeterminable for 1 brief.

how to distribute resources across the political agenda. However, one must take care in examining of these figures because they do not take into account cases in which the U.S. is directly involved as a party to the case.

For example, in criminal procedure, the percentage of amicus filings may be lower than the docket percentage because some of the cases involve federal crimes. Therefore, the solicitor general does not file amicus briefs, not because the executive branch is uninterested, but because the U.S. is a party to those cases.

This relationship between issue area and pattern of filing amicus briefs becomes more clear when trends across presidential administrations are examined. Table 3 shows the filing rates by issue area, across presidential administrations. The clearest pattern that emerges is the constancy of civil rights, economic activity, judicial power, and unions as areas in which presidential admin-istrations' solicitors general file briefs. By contrast, criminal procedure cases only became predominant in the Reagan, Bush, and Clinton administrations. Similarly, no due process cases received amicus briefs from the solicitors general of Kennedy, Johnson, or Nixon. Other issues, such as privacy, federal taxation, and interstate relations were important cases in which to file briefs for only a few administrations.

Table 3 also allows us to focus on the differences within a single issue across presidents. Take, for example, civil rights. Eisenhower's solicitors general filed amicus briefs in only six cases, constituting 14 percent of the briefs filed in that administration. However, in the very next administration, Kennedy's solicitor general filed briefs at a much higher rate, 42.4 percent. As is well known, the Kennedy administration took a more active interest in civil rights policy.

Table 4. The three most frequent areas of amicus filing, across presidential administrations

Issue	% cases	(N)	% Court's docket	(N)
Eisenhower				
Economic activity	30.2	(13)	27.9	(252)
Federalism	30.2	(13)	4.5	(41)
Civil rights	14.0	(6)	10.3	(93)
Kennedy				
Civil rights	42.4	(14)	14.5	(62)
Federalism	27.3	(9)	4.2	(18)
Economic activity	24.2	(8)	21.3	(91)
Johnson				
Civil rights	43.5	(27)	17.1	(150)
Economic activity	15.9	(10)	17.2	(151)
Federalism	14.5	(9)	3.4	(30)
Nixon				
Civil rights	42.7	(32)	20.7	(253)
Economic activity	16.0	(12)	12.4	(152)
Criminal procedure	12.0	(9)	25.9	(316)
Ford				
Civil rights	30.8	(8)	16.2	(81)
Economic activity	26.9	(7)	13.8	(69)
Judicial power	11.5	(3)	16.4	(82)
Carter				
Civil rights	37.3	(25)	18.8	(148)
Economic activity	23.9	(16)	15.8	(124)
Criminal procedure	10.4	(7)	28.3	(223)
Reagan				
Economic activity	23.6	(54)	11.3	(230)
Criminal procedure	22.3	(51)	32.5	(661)
Civil rights	21.8	(50)	17.5	(356)
Bush				
Criminal procedure	26.8	(30)	32.8	(257)
Economic activity	25.0	(28)	12.5	(98)
Civil rights	17.0	(19)	18.4	(144)
Clinton				
Economic activity	25.8	(46)	15.1	(132)
Civil rights	23.6	(42)	19.1	(167)
Criminal procedure	17.4	(31)	26.3	(230)

To simplify the information provided in Table 3, let us examine the three issue areas, across each administration, in which the solicitor general files most often. Not surprisingly, Table 4 shows that there is also variation across administrations as to the areas in which most of the briefs were filed.

These data show that certain issue areas (economic activity, civil rights, and criminal procedure) are ones in which solicitors general file friend of the court briefs most often. However, what is striking about this is the fact that this propensity to file briefs in these areas is not a function of the Court's docket. For example, during the Eisenhower administration, only 4.5 percent of the cases on the Court's docket were on federalism. Yet, of all the amicus briefs his solicitors general filed, more than 30 percent were on federalism cases. In fact, in all of the administrations that prioritized federalism (Eisenhower, Kennedy, Johnson, and Carter), the filing rate was higher than is suggested by the distribution across issue area of the Court's docket.

The pattern across civil rights cases is extremely interesting. All of the administrations, except President Bush's, filed briefs at rates higher than would be suggested by the Supreme Court's docket. However, in the administrations of Kennedy, Johnson, Nixon, Ford, and Carter, the disparity between the solicitors' general filings and the Court's docket is on the order of 20 to 30 percentage points. Whether these administrations chose to make civil rights a priority or were simply responding to an increasing number of challenges to civil rights laws, this issue dominated the solicitors' general agenda. By contrast, in the administrations of Eisenhower, Reagan, and Clinton, the disparity is more modest (3.7, 3, and 4.5 percent, respectively).

When examining these figures we should note two important considerations. First, there might be an ideological disparity between the Supreme Court and the preferences of the president. For example, recall that the Clinton administration filed briefs in civil rights cases at a rate only slightly higher than the Supreme Court's docket would suggest. This might be because Clinton's solicitors general believed that their arguments would not be well received by the Rehnquist Court, which is generally seen as being more conservative than that administration. A second and related point is that these data do not provide any information about the policy goals of the administration.

So, while both the Nixon and Johnson administrations filed briefs at a high rate, the briefs filed by these two administrations likely vary significantly in their substance, the former arguing a more conservative position than the latter. Similarly, the high rates of participation in civil rights cases during the Johnson administration likely reflect the federal government's role in the enforcement of civil rights laws. In contrast, the Reagan administration was likely more interested in restricting these laws.

Ultimately, what is most interesting is that there is such continuity in the issue areas argued by the solicitors general. This is not surprising—rarely do we see the kinds of factors necessary to move the national agenda away from the status quo. The most contentious and important issues confronting society, and thus the solicitors general, are relatively constant across time.

Variation in success rates

The previous discussion outlines the clear variation in filing patterns over time, by administration, across courts, and within issue areas. While this is interesting and important, a greater challenge to conventional wisdom about the solicitors' general office emerges from an analysis of the success of these amicus briefs in attempting to influence the Court. Conventional wisdom tells us that the solicitor general is very successful in exerting influence as a friend of the Court. The Court's decision is congruent with the positions argued by the office of the solicitor general almost 75 percent of the time (or 13 wins per year).

However, when that rate is examined over time, a somewhat different picture comes into focus. On a yearly basis, the success rate is, in fact, variable. The win rate has fluctuated over the years a great deal. When one examines this information within presidential administrations, it becomes clear that while the solicitor general may be successful in influencing the Court, each president does not enjoy the same level of success (see Table 5).

It is also clear that, except for Bush's administration, there has been an overall downward trend in the success rate of this office. The solicitors general under

Table 6. Amicus brief success rates across Courts

Court	Total # of cases won	% of cases won
Warren	121	84.6
Burger	240	72.3
Rehnquist	258	73.1

Eisenhower, Kennedy, and Johnson enjoyed higher than average success rates. However, among the last six presidents, only Bush's solicitors general were victorious at a rate above the historical average.[25]

Likewise, the conventional wisdom of the constancy of solicitor general influence is challenged when one examines success across Courts (see Table 6). While the number of cases won in each Court has risen over time, this is largely a function of the increase in the number of cases the Court hears. More instructive is to examine the trend over time in the winning percentage that solicitors general enjoy. During the Warren Court, solicitors general won at a rate higher than the historical average (whereas in both the Burger and Rehnquist Courts, the solicitors general success rate fell below this average).

Table 7 further illustrates the variability in the success of the solicitors general. It shows the win rates within issue areas, across presidential administrations. So, for example, as Table 3 cites that while Eisenhower's solicitors general filed only six cases in civil rights, Table 7 indicates a 100 percent success rate. In contrast, President Carter's solicitor general filed 27 cases in civil rights but had a losing record, winning only 44 percent of the time.

The first trend evident in Table 7 is that there is a great deal of variability in solicitor general success as amicus. Simply put, this office does not win consistently, across every administration, and within every issue area. In fact, for some presidential administrations, there are areas in which the solicitor general is just as likely to lose as to win.

President Ford's administration provides an example. In three issue areas (economic activity, federalism, and criminal procedure), Ford's solicitor general had a 50/50 shot or worse at being successful in having his argument prevail. This comports with expectations about the Ford administration, given the historical events of that administration (i.e., an unhealthy economy, political and constitutional crises). Similarly, as discussed previously, President Carter, known for the

Table 5. Success rates across presidential administrations

President	% of cases won
Eisenhower	79.1
Kennedy	84.8
Johnson	88.7
Nixon	73.3
Ford	69.2
Carter	65.7
Reagan	70.3
Bush	80.4
Clinton	69.0

Table 7. Win rates of solicitors general within issue area, across presidential administration

	DDE	JFK	LBJ	Nixon	Ford	Carter	Reagan	Bush	Clinton	Total
Civil rights	100%	100%	85.2%	75%	87.5%	44%	66%	68.4%	61.9%	76.4%
Economic activity	84.6%	62.5%	100%	75%	42.9%	81.3%	70.4%	75%	73.9%	74%
Judicial power	66.7%		83.3%	83.3%	66.7%	50%	50%	90.9%	75%	70.7%
Federalism	69.2%	77.8%	88.9%	50%	0%	83.3%	72.7%	100%	89.5%	70.2%
Unions	100%	100%	100%	100%	100%		62.5%	83.3%	66.7%	89.1%
Attorneys		100%		100%		100%	66.7%	100%		93.3%
Criminal procedure			100%	77.8%	50%	57.1%	86.3%	83.3%	74.7%	75.6%
First Amendment	0%	50%	66.7%	100%	100%	100%	57.1%	50%	100%	65.5%
Due process	50%				100%	100%	90%	100%	50%	81.7%
Privacy							0%		83.3%	41.7%
Federal taxation							0%			0%
Interstate relations						100%				100%

value he placed on diversity and race relations, had a losing record when his solicitor general filed amicus briefs in civil rights. These findings are a striking departure from the conventional wisdom of unparalleled and unwavering solicitor general success.

The other clear trend is that solicitors general are the least successful in the areas in which they file the most briefs. For example, during the Kennedy administration, though economic activity was an area in which many briefs were filed (24.2 percent), it was the area in which his solicitor general had the worst success rate (62.5 percent). In the two areas of the most filing activity during the Nixon administration (civil rights and economic activity), the office of the solicitor general was successful 75 percent of the time.

The pattern is very clear during the Ford administration. His success rate in economic activity (the area of second most activity) was less than half (42.9 percent). Again, with Carter's administration, the area in which the most briefs were filed was the area in which he was the least successful (civil rights). During the Bush administration, we see the same trend. The areas in which his solicitor general filed the most briefs (criminal procedure, economic activity, and civil rights) are areas in which his office was not as successful as others. Finally, during the Clinton administration, the success rate was less than or at the average rate across time in each of the most active issue areas (economic activity, civil rights, and criminal procedure).

One possible interpretation of this finding is that solicitors general are filing more amicus briefs in issue areas where the chief executive is more engaged. Presidents' own policy preferences, or the need to address the concerns of important constituencies, may be influencing these filings. While many of these amicus briefs may advocate worthy causes, others may be filed more because of political pressure than the merits of the case. As well, we find that several of these issue areas where solicitors general are filing many briefs and losing are also issues that appear less frequently in the Supreme Court's docket, as compared to the solicitors' general agenda. Perhaps these presidents and their solicitors general are simply out of step with the policy preferences of the High Court. They are simply advocating more cases that are less meritorious and more at odds with the Supreme Court's issue agenda.

Ideology

The last piece of the puzzle we believe can fill in this picture of declining solicitor general success on amicus briefs over time is ideology. To what extent does the solicitor general's ideological preferences conflict with the ideological make up of the Supreme Court? To investigate this issue we ascertained whether or not the solicitor general sought a liberal or conservative outcome at the High Court. Table 8 examines the success rate of presidential administrations in obtaining liberal and conservative outcomes on issues in which the solicitors general were most active.[26]

First, the most noticeable trend arises in civil rights cases, long one of the most contentious issues in judicial politics. President Carter lost a majority of the civil rights cases when his solicitor general advocated a liberal position. While President Clinton's solicitor general won on cases where he argued a liberal position more than he won on conservative stances, for both categories the win rate was well below the overall average success rate of 75 percent. More interestingly, President Reagan fared even worse when his solicitor general advocated a conservative position rather than a liberal

Table 8. Win rates of solicitors general by ideology, within issue area, across presidential administration

	Eisenhower		Kennedy		Johnson	
Civil rights	CON	LIB	CON	LIB	CON	LIB
	Lose 0	0	Lose 0	0	Lose 1 (100%)	3 (11.5%)
	Win 0	6 (100%)	Win 0	14 (100%)	Win 0	23 (88.5%)
Economic activity	CON	LIB	CON	LIB	CON	LIB
	Lose 1 (20%)	1 (12.5%)	Lose 0	3 (50%)	Lose 0	0
	Win 4 (80%)	7 (87.5%)	Win 2 (100%)	3 (50%)	Win 2 (100%)	8 (100%)
Federalism	CON	LIB	CON	LIB	CON	LIB
	Lose 4 (100%)	0	Lose 0	2 (33.3%)	Lose 1 (33.3%)	0
	Win 0	9 (100%)	Win 3 (100%)	4 (66.7%)	Win 2 (66.7%)	6 (100%)
Unions	CON	LIB				
	Lose 0	0				
	Win 0	5 (100%)				

	Nixon		Ford		Carter	
Civil rights	CON	LIB	CON	LIB	CON	LIB
	Lose 5 (45.5%)	3 (14.3%)	Lose 0	1 (16.7%)	Lose 2 (33.3%)	12 (63.2%)
	Win 6 (54.5%)	18 (85.7%)	Win 2 (100%)	5 (83.3%)	Win 4 (66.7%)	7 (36.8%)
Economic activity	CON	LIB	CON	LIB	CON	LIB
	Lose 0	3 (30%)	Lose 0	4 (57.1%)	Lose 1 (20%)	2 (18.2%)
	Win 2 (100%)	7 (70%)	Win 0	3 (42.9%)	Win 4 (80%)	9 (81.8%)
Judicial power			CON	LIB		
			Lose 0	1 (50%)		
			Win 1 (100%)	1 (50%)		
Federalism					CON	LIB
					Lose 0	1 (25%)
					Win 2 (100%)	3 (75%)
Criminal procedure	CON	LIB			CON	LIB
	Lose 2 (25%)	0			Lose 2 (33.3%)	1 (100%)
	Win 6 (75%)	1 (100%)			Win 4 (66.7%)	0

	Reagan		Bush		Clinton	
Civil rights	CON	LIB	CON	LIB	CON	LIB
	Lose 11 (42.3%)	6 (25%)	Lose 2 (25%)	4 (36.4%)	Lose 3 (42.9%)	13 (37.1%)
	Win 15 (57.7%)	18 (75%)	Win 6 (75%)	7 (63.6%)	Win 4 (57.1%)	22 (62.9%)
Economic activity	CON	LIB	CON	LIB	CON	LIB
	Lose 7 (25.9%)	9 (33.3%)	Lose 4 (26.7%)	3 (23.1%)	Lose 5 (21.7%)	7 (30.4%)
	Win 20 (74.1%)	18 (66.7%)	Win 11 (73.3%)	10 (76.9%)	Win 18 (78.3%)	16 (69.6%)
Criminal procedure	CON	LIB	CON	LIB	CON	LIB
	Lose 7 (13.7%)	0	Lose 5 (17.2%)	0	Lose 7 (24.1%)	1 (50%)
	Win 44 (86.3%)	0	Win 24 (82.8%)	1 (100%)	Win 22 (75.9%)	1 (50%)

CON = Conservative
LIB = Liberal

one (57.7 percent versus 75 percent). Nixon's solicitors general also lost more civil rights cases when they advocated a conservative preference, but they also argued fewer such cases. President Bush's solicitor general took comparatively fewer positions on civil rights cases than Reagan's or Clinton's Justice Department, but tended to win more often when arguing a conservative position.

While there are interesting trends across presidential administrations in the relationships among ideology, success, and issue area, civil rights stands out. In this area, Presidents Carter and Reagan fared the worst, while Presidents Nixon and Carter did worse than the other presidents. Thus, we are confronted with two interesting questions. First, why does solicitor general success fluctuate substantially in the civil rights arena? Second, why do the aforementioned presidents' solicitors general fare poorly in the Supreme Court in comparison with other administrations?

Success may vary more in civil rights cases both because of the growing conservative majority on the Court and because of the contentious and changing nature of the issue itself. While some of the core issues in civil rights cases remain stable, the particular form discrimination takes, the remedies to overcome discrimination, and the sector of society in which cases arise have changed. For example, in education, civil rights cases have evolved from desegregation, to busing, to affirmative action. As the specific issue evolves, increasingly the Supreme Court has proven more reluctant to set far-reaching precedents and has increasingly sided against minority rights. This fluctuation in the substance of civil rights cases may make success more variable than constant.

While we do not have any substantial basis on which to reach conclusions for the varying success of particular administrations on civil rights cases, it may be that some presidents are more susceptible to political pressure on this issue from powerful interest groups. The Nixon and Reagan administrations may have come to the defense of conservative groups, states, and corporations that wished to challenge civil rights precedents. Perhaps because they came into office after periods of Democratic control, these administrations sought to placate conservative groups that had been on the "outs" in Washington by seeking to modify judicial doctrine on civil rights. Presidents Carter and Clinton, who entered office after lengthy periods of Republican control, may have taken up the torch for the civil rights community upon whom their electoral fortunes heavily depended.

The pressure on both sets of administrations to promote the judicial preferences of key constituents may have led their solicitors general to select less meritorious cases or advocate positions at odds with current Supreme Court doctrine. It is interesting that the one exception to this trend in recent years was the Bush administration that assumed office after eight years of Republican control. Certainly future research should examine the civil rights cases in more depth—both because they are so contentious and revealing of important trends, and also because they are one of the few issues that reappear on the Supreme Court docket with such frequency.

A change in view?

This study examined the interaction between the solicitor general and Supreme Court by looking at cases where an amicus brief was filed by the solicitor general's office from 1953 through 2000. This large data set and time period allows us to spot trends that were not as evident earlier and which, to some degree, changes our view of this relationship.

First, we find that there is a clear trend of an increased use of such briefs by solicitors general. There is an approximately five-fold increase in the rate of filings over this time period. When one considers that during these years the number of potential cases in which to file decreased, one sees that there is a greater proportion of Court cases in which the solicitor general is filing amicus briefs.

Second, one might suspect that the number of amicus briefs has increased because the success rate of such briefs has increased over time. If the president finds that these briefs provide an effective vehicle for conveying arguments that the Court finds persuasive, he might be tempted to invest more resources in this area. We find, however, the opposite to be true. While solicitors general have certainly remained successful, their overall winning percentage has dropped from 85 percent during the Warren Court years to 73 percent under Rehnquist. Therefore, there appear to be incentives in filing briefs in addition to attempting to influence the Supreme Court's decision. It is possible that the executive branch is hoping to receive political benefits or credit from others including the Congress, interest groups, or the general public, even if its arguments do not prevail.

It is also important to note that the conventional wisdom concerning the solicitor general usually does not take into account the issue area being considered. It is generally assumed that the solicitor general simply wins almost every time and in every setting. As was just discussed, with the passing of time solicitors general have not fared as well. When one also takes into account the issue being decided, there is great variance in success. In certain areas, solicitors general lose more cases than they win. Success rates certainly depend upon what presidential administration the solicitor general represents, who is sitting on the Supreme Court, and what type of case is being considered. Therefore, the conventional wisdom needs some adjustment.

Why has there been this decrease in the solicitor general's ability to win cases before the Court? As mentioned above, there could be a correlation with the politicization or perceived politicization of the solicitor general's office. Some of this may be due to the solicitors general advocating issues and ideological positions at variance with those of the Supreme Court, resulting in the Court putting less faith or trust in the arguments. However, if this is true, then it begins earlier than has been reported. It appears to start during the Nixon administration, not during Reagan's tenure.

It is also possible that since there has been such an increase in the number of amicus filings that the quality or impact has been diluted. They are taken less seriously since they have become so commonplace. Finally, it is also quite possible that the quality or repeat player status of legal adversaries has improved.[27] This change in the lawyers or law firms the solicitor general faces could have evened the playing field to some degree.

There is certainly more work to be done in this area. One could attempt to delve into and uncover the incentive structure that determines whether to file a brief or not. What strategies have been used by various administrations? It is certainly important to consider further the ideological direction of briefs and their congruency with the ideology of the Supreme Court and how that correlates with success. Additional work should also be done on the degree to which individual justices support solicitors general, and where the U.S. is party to a case and not an amicus.

Notes

This article originally appeared in Volume 87, Number 2, September–October 2003, pages 60–71.

We wish to give special thanks to Professor Thomas Marshall for his counsel and support. In addition, we wish to thank the following people for their assistance at various points in this project: Tamara Benson, Michele Budz, Danielle Gonzales, Heather Helton, Alice Holland, Kris Kriofske, H. Jessica Mayraz, Teresa Mazzello, David McClelland, Janet Payne, John Rousey, Heather Scott, Rogelio Valdez, Katherine Wachowiak, Bill Ward, and Nancy Whitted.

1. *See, for example,* Clark and McGuire, "Congress, the Supreme Court and the Flag," *Pol. Res. Q.* 49 (1996), 771–781; Eskridge, "Overriding Supreme Court Statutory Interpretation Decisions," *Yale L. J.* 101 (1991), 331–455; Eskridge, "Reneging on History? Playing the Court/Congress/President Civil Rights Game," *Cal. L. Rev.* 79 (1991), 613–684; Henschen, "Statutory Interpretations of the Supreme Court," *Am. Pol. Q.* 11 (1983), 441–458; Ignagni and Meernik, "Explaining Congressional Attempts to Reverse Supreme Court Decisions," *Pol. Res. Q.* 47 (1994), 353–371; Keynes and Miller, *The Court vs. Congress: Prayer, Busing, and Abortion* (Durham, N.C.: Duke University Press, 1989).

2. *See, for example,* Bond and Fleisher, "Presidential Popularity and Congressional Voting: A Re-examination of Public Opinion as a Source of Influence in Congress," *W. Pol. Q.* 37 (1984), 291–306; Bond and Fleisher, *The President in the Legislative Arena* (Chicago: University of Chicago Press, 1990); Collier and Sullivan, "New Evidence Undercutting the Linkage of Approval with Presidential Support and Influence," *J. Pol.* 57 (1995), 197–209; Covington, Wrighton, and Kinney, "A 'Presidency-Augmented' Model of Presidential Success on House Roll Call Votes," *Am. J. Pol. Sci.* 39 (1995), 1001–1024; Edwards, *At the Margins* (New Haven, Conn.: Yale University Press, 1989); Edwards, "Presidential Influence in Congress: If We Ask the Wrong Questions, We Get the Wrong Answers," *Am. J. Pol. Sci.* 35 (1991), 724–737. Neustadt, *Presidential Power: The Politics of Leadership from FDR to Carter* (New York: John Wiley & Sons, 1980).

3. Abraham, *Justices and Presidents* (New York: Penguin Books, Inc., 1974); Rossiter *The Supreme Court and the Commander in Chief* (Ithaca, N.Y.: Cornell University Press, 1976); Scigliano, *The Supreme Court and the Presidency* (New York: The Free Press, 1971).

4. McGuire, "Repeat Players in the Supreme Court: The Role of Experienced Lawyers in Litigation Success," *J. Pol.* 57 (1995), 187; McGuire. "Explaining Executive Success in the U.S. Supreme Court," *Pol. Res. Q.* 51 (1998), 505–526; Segal, "Amicus Curiae Briefs by the Solicitor General During the Warren and Burger Courts," *W. Pol. Q.* 41 (1988), 135–144; Segal, "Supreme Court Support for the Solicitor General: The Effect of Presidential Appointments," *W. Pol. Q.* 43 (1990), 137–152; Segal, "Courts, Executives and Legislatures," in Gates and Johnson, eds., *American Courts: A Critical Assessment* (Washington, D.C.: CQ Press, 1991); Segal and Reedy, "The Supreme Court and Sex Discrimination: The Role of the Solicitor General," *W. Pol. Q.* 41 (1988), 553–568; Yates and Whitford,

"Presidential Power and the United States Supreme Court," *Pol. Res. Q.* 51 (1998), 539–550; Deen, Ignagni, and Meernik, "Executive Influence on the U.S. Supreme Court: Solicitor General Amicus Cases, 1953–1997," *Am. Rev. Pol.* 22 (2001): 3–26.

5. Segal, "Amicus Curiae Briefs," *supra* n. 4, at 136.

6. Puro, "The United States as Amicus Curiae," in Ulmer, ed., *Courts, Law and the Judicial Process* (New York: Free Press, 1981) 222.

7. *See, for example,* Baum, *The Supreme Court,* 7th ed. (Washington, D.C.: CQ Press, 2001); Meinhold and Shull, "Policy Congruence Between the President and the Solicitor General," *Pol. Res. Q.* 51 (1998), 527–537; Salokar, *The Solicitor General: The Politics of Law* (Philadelphia: Temple University Press, 1992); Scigliano, *supra* n. 3; Segal, "Amicus Curiae Briefs," *supra* n. 4.

8. O'Connor, "The amicus curiae role of the U.S. solicitor general in Supreme Court litigation," *Judicature* 66 (1983), 256–264; Segal, "Amicus Curiae Briefs," *supra* n. 4.

9. Caplan, *The Tenth Justice: The Solicitor General and the Rule of Law* (New York: Alfred A. Knopf, 1987); Scigliano, *supra* n. 3; Werdegar, "The Solicitor General and Administrative Due Process," *G.W. L. Rev.* 36 (1967), 481–514.

10. Abraham, *The Judicial Process,* 7th ed. (New York: Oxford University Press, 1998); Baum, *supra* n. 7, at 99.

11. *See, for example,* Caldeira and Wright, "Organized Interests and Agenda Setting in the Supreme Court," *Am. Pol. Sci. Rev.* 82 (1988), 1109–1127; Provine, *Case Selection in the United States Supreme Court* (Chicago: University of Chicago Press, 1980); Tanenhaus, Schick, Muraskin, and Rosen, "The Supreme Court's Certiorari Jurisdiction: Cue Theory," in Schubert, ed., *Judicial Decision-Making* (New York: The Free Press, 1963).

12. Epstein, Segal, Spaeth, and Walker, *The Supreme Court Compendium* (Washington, D.C.: CQ Press, 1996), 569.

13. *See, for example,* O'Connor, *supra* n. 8; Puro, *supra* n. 6; Segal, "Amicus Curiae Briefs," *supra* n. 4; Segal and Reedy, *supra* n. 4.

14. Epstein et al., *supra* n. 12, at 551.

15. Lauber, "An Exchange of Views: Has the Solicitor's Office Become Politicized?" *Legal Times,* November 2, 1987.

16. Neuborne, "In Lukewarm Defense of the Solicitor General: Charles Fried's 'Bum Rap,' " *Manhattan Lawyer,* October 20–October 26, 1987; Groner, "Marshall, Powell Deny Criticizing SG," *Legal Times,* November 2, 1987.

17. Lauter, "A New Polarization for the High Court," *National Law Journal,* August 11, 1986.

18. Salokar, *supra* n. 7.

19. Watson, "Fried's Legacy Shadows Starr," *Legal Times,* May 8, 1989; Moore, "Middle Man," *National Journal,* April 9, 1994 at 825–828; Gest and Caplan, "Bill Clinton's Man to See," *U.S. News and World Report,* October 14, 1996 at 48–49.

20. *See, for example,* Segal, "Amicus Curiae Briefs," *supra* n. 4; Segal and Reedy, *supra* n. 4.

21. Our dependent variable consists of all Supreme Court cases from 1953 through 2000 on which the solicitor general filed an amicus brief and where it was clearly indicated which position he was advocating. To make these determinations we used a team of coders to examine every Supreme Court decision found in the U.S. Reports from 1953 through 2000. In all of the cases, multiple coders recorded the presence and direction of solicitor general amicus involvement, as indicated by the U.S. Reports. In 50 instances, the U.S. Reports were unclear about the position taken by the solicitor general and thus these cases were excluded from our analysis. Data on other factors such as issue and direction of Supreme Court opinion come from Spaeth's Supreme Court Judicial Database.

22. U.S. Supreme Court Database, Harold Spaeth, principal investigator. These include full decisions, per curium, and memoranda decisions.

23. *See, for example,* Bradley and Gardner, "Underdogs, Upperdogs and the Use of the Amicus Brief: Trends and Explanations," *Just. Sys. J.* 10 (1985), 78–95; Caldeira and Wright, *supra* n. 11; Caldeira and Wright, "Amici Curiae before the Supreme Court: Who Participates, When, and How Much?" *J. Pol.* 52 (1990), 782–806; O'Connor and Epstein, "Amicus Curiae Participation in U.S. Supreme Court Litigation: An Appraisal of Hakman's Folklore," *Law & Soc'y. Rev.* 16 (1981–1982), 311–320; Songer and Sheehan, "Interest Group Success in the Courts: Amicus Participation in the Supreme Court," *Pol. Res. Q.* 36 (1993), 339–354.

24. Baum, *supra* n. 7, at 92; McGuire, *Understanding the U.S. Supreme Court: Cases and Controversies* (New York: McGraw-Hill, 2002), 151.

25. It should be noted, however, that because most presidents had more than one solicitor general serve during their time in office, there were individual solicitors general with success rates higher than the historical average. For example, although Nixon's average success rate was 74%, his first solicitor general, Erwin Griswold, averaged 67% and his second, Robert Bork, averaged 87%.

26. To determine the solicitor general's ideological preferences, we used the Spaeth U.S. Supreme Court Database to determine the direction of the Supreme Court opinion (liberal or conservative). Using our data on solicitor general wins and losses before the Court, we deduced that when the outcome was liberal/conservative and the solicitor general won, the outcome desired was liberal/conservative. When the solicitor general lost, we assumed the reverse.

27. McGuire, "Lawyers and the U.S. Supreme Court: The Washington Community and Legal Elites," *Am. J. Pol. Sci.* (1993), 365–390.

Actors in the Judicial Process

Juries

Juries are at once the most romanticized and most vilified actors in the American judicial process. They are at times credited with being the public's guarantor of fairness and equity in court, but they are also sometimes heavily criticized for reaching arbitrary decisions that do not reflect the dictates of the law. Both extreme characterizations probably accurately capture the behavior of some juries some of the time. It is also important to note, however, that jury trials are relatively rare. Most legal problems are resolved by settlement prior to trial or by a bench trial in which a judge, acting alone, renders the verdict. Nevertheless, dramatic jury trials remain the mythical view of judicial processes held by most Americans, and their potential use in most trial settings does render them important and warranting of our consideration. Unfortunately, scholarly attention to juries has been limited somewhat by lack of direct access to jury deliberations and by the inherent difficulties of conducting jury research based on simulation and post-hoc interviewing techniques.

Peter Sperlich's article ". . . And then there were six: the decline of the American jury" portrays the decline in the use of juries and the changes in their nature brought about by a series of Supreme Court rulings during the 1970s. These rulings allowed for reductions in jury size and less than unanimous jury verdicts. Sperlich argues that the Court's rulings were ill considered and endanger the very rights that juries were fashioned to protect. While the cases discussed by Sperlich are more than three decades old, the framework they established for defining "constitutional" jury procedures still largely defines the state of jury law.

In "Jury Summit 2001," Robert Boatright and Elissa Krauss report on a national meeting of judges, court administrators, attorneys, academicians, and members of the lay public that focused on the state of our nation's jury systems. Dominant among the concerns discussed were representation and communication as they relate to jury makeup and performance. Discussion of jury representation must, of course, include consideration of the pools from which juries are chosen and how they are created, as well as consideration of the representativeness of the actual juries that emerge from these pools. The concept of jury communication, as treated by the conference discussions, was broadly conceived to include consideration of how one can facilitate juror education, comprehension, and participation. Boatright and Krauss conclude by examining several states in which jury reforms aimed at fostering jury representation and communication have been implemented and the impact of these efforts.

One of the topical issues discussed in "Jury Summit 2001" highlights the inherent difficulties faced by juries when they are asked to decide cases with complex and highly technical components. This issue is confronted head on by Robert Myers, Ronald Reinstein, and Gordon Griller in "Complex scientific evidence and the jury," with specific reference to the implications of major research breakthroughs in human genetics on the operation of courts and the role of juries. As the authors note, "critics have questioned whether a jury of untrained and inexperienced people can be a competent fact finder and decision maker in lengthy trials that require comprehension of substantial quantities of complex scientific, technical, or statistical evidence, and resolving the testimony of duplicative expert witnesses whose opinions conflict."

The authors reject the view that juries are incapable of performing well in such settings, arguing that, "courts can and must seek new ways to help jurors cope more effectively." From their assessment of existing research they conclude "that the trial process itself may be as much an impediment to jury comprehension and understanding as the complexity of the legal concepts and evidence, or the competencies of jurors." They add that the fix for this situation lies in courtrooms becoming classrooms for their jurors. Many reforms, as evidenced in Arizona and elsewhere, facilitate juror performance by making them active participants in trial processes through such actions as allowing note taking, submission of written questions to a judge, and participation in pre-deliberation discussion of evidence. According to Myers, Reinstein, and Griller, "It is intellectually arrogant for those in the legal system to assume that lay jurors are incapable of processing complex information."

When the focus turns directly to concerns about jury behavior, some research has suggested that the demographic characteristics of jurors may be related to the decisions that they reach. If identifiable juror characteristics are related to specific juror dispositions, it then becomes possible and desirable for attorneys to try to structure juries to produce favorable results. The state of the art regarding this possibility is explored by Shari Seidman Diamond in "Scientific jury selection: what social scientists know and do not know." Diamond's argument is a sobering one for critics who contend that with enough money and social science know-how congenial outcomes from jury trials can be assured. She cautions that anyone considering the use of a consultant to help develop a desired juror profile "needs to be a vigilant and critical consumer of the services that are offered."

Two selections in this section focus on two special kinds of jury settings. As noted previously, in the absence of access to direct observation of juror behavior, post-hoc interviews of jurors has emerged as a method for gaining an empirical handle on the decision-making processes of juries. Such an approach is utilized by William Bowers in "The capital jury: is it tilted toward death?" Bowers's disturbing documentation of the deliberative process in death penalty cases suggests that jurors often have their minds made up about the punishment to be meted out in the sentencing stage of a trial while they are still engaged in an initial determination of a defendant's guilt or innocence.

He goes on to note that capital jurors tend to misunderstand the sentencing guidelines that they have been given and, more often than not, fail to take personal responsibility for the designation of a defendant's punishment. Indeed, "8 of 10 jurors assign foremost responsibility to the defendant or to the law."

The final selection in this section, written by Susan Brenner, asks the question, "Is the grand jury worth keeping?" Brenner offers the reader a detailed accounting of the intended purpose of grand juries and ultimately concludes that significant reforms are needed to ensure that such purposes are met. She is particularly concerned (as were many analysts of Kenneth Starr's central role in investigating the Clinton presidency, for example) that there is too much prosecutorial dominance and discretion in contemporary grand jury proceedings. To combat this tendency, the author suggests that grand juries be given their own attorneys to represent their unique interests. According to Brenner, "the counsel would act as a buffer between the grand juries and prosecutors and between the jurors and the targets of their inquiries." Such an approach, already operative in some state settings, would help to ensure that grand jury processes are perceived to be "fair" in their operations and in the decisions that they reach.

... And then there were six: the decline of the American jury

Peter W. Sperlich

In the last 10 years, the Supreme Court has allowed states to reduce the jury's size and abolish the unanimous verdict. But the Court generally ignored social science evidence that shows the importance of both these factors to the jury in performing its traditional role.

The 1970s may well be remembered as the decade in which we almost lost the jury. The institution of *trial by jury* came to this continent as part of the general transfer of the English legal system to the colonies. For nearly 400 years, Americans have regarded the common law trial jury as one of the bulwarks of their liberty, and for nearly 400 years, there was no essential disagreement that trial by jury meant a body of 12 deciding unanimously.

No institution is without critics, of course. In recent years, a number of judges adopted the position that the jury was no longer needed, that judges could be entrusted with the liberties of the people, and that, in any case, the jury was an inefficient and expensive instrument of dispute resolution, one that no longer could be afforded.[1] Nevertheless, the American jury seemed secure, particularly because the U.S. Supreme Court always was one of the common law jury's strong supporters. As late as 1968, the Court extended the Sixth Amendment right to trial by jury to defendants accused of serious crimes in state courts.[2]

But then came *Williams v. Florida*[3] in 1970. *Williams* was the first act in what turned out to be a major reorientation of the Court's approach to the trial jury. The *Williams* ruling, permitting state criminal juries of six, came unexpected and sent a shock through the legal and scholarly community. Given the open-ended nature of the ruling (six was not necessarily to be the lower limit), the very survival of the jury seemed in doubt. Had the Court begun to side with the abolitionist minority? Was this the beginning of the end of lay participation in the American judicial process? Hans Zeisel, an observer not given to panic, expressed these concerns in the very title of his *Williams* review: ". . . And Then There Were None." [4]

The title of this article is somewhat less despairing, reflecting two recent decisions (*Ballew* and *Burch*, *infra*), which indicate that the American jury will survive the 1970s. But the jury that has survived is not the jury of 10 years ago. Except for some state experimen-

tations, the American criminal and civil trial jury at that time was the jury at common law, 12 persons deciding unanimously. As the decade ends, juries of 12 are no longer required in federal civil trials or in state criminal trials. Majority verdicts have been held to be constitutionally adequate in state criminal trials. Majority verdicts in federal criminal trials have been averted (so far) by the vote of a single justice.

What the future will bring we cannot know. But it is clear that what remains of the American jury at the end of the decade is less than firmly planted. It is possible that American developments will replicate English legal history, leading to an almost complete abrogation of trial by jury.[5] It is also possible that the worst is over. The vigorous defense of the jury that followed *Williams* and the other jury-diminishing decisions may have persuaded the Court of the error of the *Williams* approach.

I. The revolution in jury law

The U.S. Supreme Court changed the American trial jury in a sequence of six cases, spanning the full decade from 1970 to 1979. The first four served to diminish the jury: *Williams v. Florida, Johnson v. Louisiana,*[6] *Apodaca v. Oregon,*[7] and *Colgrove v. Battin.*[8] The last two indicate the current limits of jury diminution: *Ballew v. Georgia*[9] and *Burch v. Louisiana.*[10]

In *Williams,* the Supreme Court ruled that the U.S. Constitution does not require a jury of 12, and that a state may use a jury of six in criminal trials even when the sentence is as severe as life imprisonment. The decision applied only to state criminal juries, but the opinion of Justice White clearly signaled what was to come: "In sweeping language, the Court removed the constitutional obstacles to decreasing the size of federal and state juries in both civil and criminal cases." [11]

Federal judges quickly took the hint. In 1972, a year before *Colgrove,* a majority of the federal district courts already had adopted six-person civil juries. *Colgrove* legitimated this change. The Court formally ruled that the U.S. Constitution does not require 12-person civil juries, and that six-person federal civil juries are constitutionally adequate. *Johnson* and *Apodaca,* finally, produced the ruling that majority verdicts are constitutionally permissible in state criminal trials.[12]

The four cases amounted to no less than a revolution in American jury law.[13] But not only was this revolution unexpected, it also was uncompelled. There were no irresistible forces of legal or societal development to which the justices were forced to pay homage. Indeed, to achieve the goal of smaller and nonunanimous juries, the Court had to do considerable violence to legal history and empirical evidence. Not surprisingly, it reaped sharp criticism in the scholarly community.[14] Support for the decisions came largely from the same judges who had advocated jury slicing all along.[15]

The casualties of *Williams*

Williams signaled the transformation of the American trial jury and established the pattern of judicial reasoning in support of the change. The reasoning, as noted, left much to be desired, and three specific areas were short-changed: history, the American constitutional tradition, and empirical evidence.

History suffered the first blow. For nearly seven centuries, the common law jury of England and, thus, of the United States, had been a body of 12. It is not known how that size became standardized at 12 in 14th-century England; perhaps the number could equally well have been 11 or 13. It is not likely that the number could just as well have been five, or six, or seven.

The Court, however, took the position that unless it could discover a rational justification in history for the number 12, then that number could be regarded as an accident. As could have been predicted, no such justification was to be found. The Court concluded that the number 12 "appears to have been a historical accident, unrelated to the great purposes which gave rise to the jury in the first place."[16]

At least three objections must be raised to the Court's historical scholarship. The first is epistemological: the failure to discover a reason is not proof of its nonexistence. The second regards the conversion of quantitative into qualitative changes: as noted, the choice between 12 and 11 may not be of much consequence, but a change from 12 to six involves fundamental differences. The third objection involves objectivity of analysis and validity of inference: the Court only looked for reasons *for* removing the requirement of 12; it did not look for reasons *against* such a removal.[17]

The second blow was struck against an American constitutional tradition. While the Court had not explicitly ruled that the American trial jury was a body of 12 deciding unanimously, all the Court's statements and dicta had supported this position.[18] Firm tradition and invariate interpretations, however, had little power to protect the jury. The Court decided to treat the issue of jury size as open and unresolved, asking in leading language whether "this accidental feature of the jury has been immutably codified into our Constitution."[19] The answer, of course, was *no.* The Court revealed that all its prior interpretations were in error because they had assumed "that if a given feature existed in a jury at common law in 1789, then it was necessarily preserved in the Constitution."[20]

The third casualty of *Williams* was empirical evidence. The Court took the position that the six-person criminal jury would satisfy the requirements of the Sixth Amendment of "trial by an impartial jury" if it could be shown to be *functionally equivalent* to a 12-person jury: "The relevant inquiry, as we see it, must be the function that the particular feature [size] performs and its relations to the purposes of the jury trial."[21] The purpose of the jury trial "is to prevent oppression by the Government," and its essential feature is the "interposition between the accused and his accuser of the common-sense judgment of a group of laymen, and . . . the community participation and shared responsibility that results from that group's determination of guilt or innocence."[22] The Court examined the evidence and came to the conclusion that "[t]he performance of this role is not a function of the particular number of the body that makes up the jury. . . . And, certainly the reliability of the jury as a factfinder hardly seems likely to be a function of its size."[23] As will be seen, the facts do *not* support these conclusions.

Other jury-size cases

Colgrove v. Battin is the second jury-size case, legitimating the six-person civil jury in the federal courts. In substance and style, *Colgrove* was pure *Williams.* Historical, constitutional, and empirical reasoning was flawed. *Colgrove* was particularly difficult to justify on constitutional grounds since the Seventh Amendment (in contrast to the Sixth Amendment in *Williams*) explicitly refers to the common law.

The Court overcame this obstacle by announcing that the size of the common law jury was not part of the real "substance" of the common law right of trial by jury, but was a "mere matter of form or procedure." [24] What remained, as in *Williams*, was the question of functional equivalence, "whether jury performance is a function of jury size." [25] The Court inspected the evidence and ruled that performance is not a function of size. Unfortunately, once again the facts fail to support the conclusion, as we will see later.

Ballew v. Georgia,[26] the third jury-size case, was a decision of the greatest importance. It was the first indication that the diminution of the jury had come to a halt. The Court decided that Georgia's criminal trial jury of five was constitutionally inadequate, that state criminal juries must consist of at least six. *Ballew* also was the first indication that the vigorous scholarly defense of the jury, mounted in the post-*Williams* years, had met with some success.

As will be seen below, the success was far from complete. The Court still did not refrain from using empirical evidence in questionable ways. But there were signs of a new spirit. The Court concluded "that the purpose and functioning of the jury in a criminal trial is seriously impaired, and to a constitutional degree, by a reduction in size below six members." [27] And Justice Blackmun was explicit that the empirical studies play a major role in the development of this conclusion:

> But the assembled data raise substantial doubt about the reliability and appropriate representation of panels smaller than six. Because of the fundamental importance of the jury trial to the American system of criminal justice, any further reduction that promotes inaccurate and possibly biased decisionmaking, that causes untoward differences in verdicts, and that prevents juries from truly representing their communities, attains constitutional significance.[28]

The decision-rule cases

Johnson v. Louisiana and *Apodaca v. Oregon* were decided on the same day, May 22, 1972; both belong to the set of four cases that diminished the American trial jury.[29] *Johnson* permitted a 9/12 and *Apodaca* a 10/12 majority verdict in state criminal trials. *Johnson* and *Apodaca* moved along similar tracks as *Williams* and *Colgrove*. Once more, the keystone was the assertion of functional equivalence:

> Our inquiry must focus upon the function served by the jury . . . As we said in *Duncan,* the purpose of trial by jury is to prevent oppression by the Government . . . In terms of this function we perceive no difference

between juries required to act unanimously and those permitted to convict or acquit by votes of 10 to two or 11 to one.[30]

For this claim the Court offered no evidence at all.[31] Instead, it was satisfied to rely upon its "longstanding perceptions about jury behavior." [32] The Court did not reveal how these "perceptions" were gathered, or what kind of systematic comparisons were made between unanimous and majority-verdict juries. Nor did the Court dispute the fact that jury deliberations are secret and not easily perceived. It is unlikely that the "longstanding perceptions" are more than an exercise of judicial creativity, throwing a cloak over the uncomfortable sight of an empirical issue having been decided without reference to empirical evidence.[33]

After *Johnson* and *Apodaca* joined *Williams* and *Colgrove*, a deep and widespread concern developed for the jury's future. No end was in sight to reductions in size (*Ballew* was not decided until 1978). And combinations of smaller size and majority rule could be expected to be legitimated next. *Burch v. Louisiana,* as *Ballew,* halted the diminution of the jury this year. The Court decided in *Burch* that "conviction by a nonunanimous six-member jury in a state criminal trial for a nonpetty offense deprives the accused of his constitutional right to trial by jury." [34]

It remains to be seen, of course, whether such combinations as 6/7 or 5/8 will be found constitutionally inadequate. At least the worst fears have been set aside by *Burch*. In the foreseeable future the American trial jury will not be a body of three, deciding with a majority of two. As in the other decision-rule cases, it should be noted, the Court offered no empirical evidence for its ruling on the functional equivalence issue in *Burch*.

II. 'Functional equivalence' of juries

The major issue that emerges from the six jury decisions is the functional equivalence or nonequivalence of juries of different size and decision rules. The issue is closely related to the general question of the use of scientific evidence in the legal process. (See Sperlich, "Social science evidence in the courts: reaching beyond the adversary process," 63 *Judicature* 280 [1980]). Of course, important questions also can be raised about the Court's treatment of legal history and constitutional law. However, since the Court decides what the Constitution requires and what has been "immutably codified into our Constitution," little is to be gained by disputing with the Court about such matters as "the intent of the framers."

The U.S. Supreme Court, however, is not the highest authority on matters of fact. The case facts (adjudicative facts) must be determined by the trier of the facts, the trial judge or the trial jury. Wisely, the appellate courts have adopted a bearing of great restraint regarding case facts and generally refuse to second-guess the trier of the facts. Such well-placed restraint, unfortunately, has been less common in respect to the social facts relevant to the case in question.[35]

There is a tendency to rely on common sense and personal experience, and to take "judicial notice" of "common knowledge" rather than to obtain the required information from the appropriate expert sources, the relevant scientific disciplines. Untrained in scientific methods and isolated from the world of scientific investigations, judges seem to come quite easily to the view that judicial horse-sense is a more dependable guide to valid knowledge than scientific expertise.

Common knowledge and judicial intuition are notoriously unreliable paths to empirical fact. More often than not they lead into blind alleys and embarrassing retreats. Just as theological wisdom and common observation could not, in the long run, prevail against the expertise of scientific astronomers, so judicial wisdom and common sense could not prevail against scientific expertise in ballistics.[36] The Court reasonably can maintain its interpretation of the Constitution against the views of other constitutional experts. The Court cannot maintain its own view of social facts and scientific principles against the testimony of the experts from the relevant sciences—at least it cannot do so without being seen as willful and incompetent.[37]

In the jury decisions of the 1970s it was indeed appropriate for the justices to determine upon which principle the rulings should be based, i.e., functional equivalence. It was not appropriate, however, for the justices to assume the role of competent determiners of the facts of equivalence or nonequivalence. It is disturbing when justices decide issues of social fact by relying upon their "longstanding perceptions about jury behavior." Nor will it do for justices to complain about "reliance on numerology,"[38] when after years of erroneous determination of the facts, reliable scientific investigations finally are being used.[39]

At this time in history, of course, and perhaps for a long time to come, there are many questions to which the sciences, particularly the social sciences, cannot give unequivocal answers. Not all details have been filled out in the studies of jury behavior.[40] There is much that is not known about just how different juries differ. This much, however, is well-established: Juries of different sizes and decision rules are *not* functionally equivalent. The protections offered by smaller and majority-rule juries are not the same as those offered by the traditional common law jury—12 persons deciding unanimously.

As noted earlier, *Johnson, Apodaca,* and *Burch* decided on the equivalence/nonequivalence of different decision rules *without any reference* to empirical evidence, relying instead on mysterious "longstanding judicial perceptions." *Williams, Colgrove,* and *Ballew,* the jury size cases, do refer to empirical evidence. The relevance and validity of that evidence, thus, can be examined.

Relevance and validity of evidence

Given the path-setting nature of the *Williams* decision and the continuing dominance of the *Williams* doctrine (6=12), it is of considerable interest to see how the claim of functional equivalence was established. The Court cited six "experiments" to support its contentions.[41] This was the substance of the evidence: (1) an unsupported claim that "it could be argued that there would be no differences"; (2) the unsupported statement of a judge that he found five-person juries quite satisfactory; (3) an unsupported report that one court clerk and three attorneys had said that they could not detect any difference in the verdicts of 12- and six-person juries as these had been used on an experimental basis in a Massachusetts court; (4) another report of the same opinions as recounted in the previous item; (5) a notice, without any evaluation, that a court has experimented with a six-person jury in a civil negligence case; (6) a judge's thoughts on the economic advantages of smaller juries.[42]

Williams' notion of "empirical evidence" was of embarrassing incompetence,[43] and the reviews did not spare the Court. Zeisel concluded that the six items were "scant evidence by any standards," and pointed out how and where better evidence could have been obtained.[44] Saks noted that the scholarship displayed in *Williams* would not win a passing grade in high school.[45] Walbert chided the Court for its errors of interpretation and for its failure to make use of available competent evidence.[46] And Wick charged that "[t]he willingness of the Court to be persuaded by such flimsy evidence lays bare its lack of concern for the institution of jury trial."[47] *Williams* did not demonstrate that juries of six and of 12 are functionally equivalent. By its own chosen standard, the Court had rendered a constitutionally invalid decision.[48] The error still awaits correction.

It may appear difficult to do worse than *Williams*. Yet *Colgrove*, the next jury-size decision, in some ways did worse indeed. The Court showed itself supremely scornful of the scholarly criticisms and suggestions that had followed *Williams*. Not only did the Court not change its general approach to empirical evidence, it even returned for support to some of the *Williams* items, the inadequacy of which had clearly been demonstrated.[49]

The Court refused to show doubt regarding *Williams*. To the contrary, it practically taunted its critics. There was the bold restatement of the false claim that the *Williams* decision rested on actual jury "studies." And there was the pointed comment that the critical literature generated by *Williams* was "nonpersuasive." Said the *Colgrove* court:

> We had no difficulty reaching the conclusion in *Williams* that a jury of six would guarantee an accused the trial by jury secured by Art. III and the Sixth Amendment. Significantly, our determination that there was 'no discernible difference between the results reached by the two different-sized juries' . . . drew largely upon the results of studies of the operations of juries of six in civil cases. Since then, much has been written about the six-member jury, but nothing that persuades us to depart from the conclusion reached in *Williams*.[50]

The flaws in *Colgrove*

In addition to resurrecting the deficient items of *Williams*, *Colgrove* sought to present new support for the functional equivalence assertion, reporting that "four very recent studies have provided convincing empirical evidence of the correctness of the *Williams* conclusion."[51] Far from providing "convincing empirical evidence," however, the new items were entirely incapable to support the Court's contentions. The flaws can be stated briefly:[52]

- One situation permitted attorneys to choose a jury of 12 rather than six. The choices of the larger jury did not occur at random but reflected the nature and complexity of the case.

- The second new item also reported a procedure in which the litigants had a choice between six- and 12-person juries. The choices, again, were not random.

- The next study used a before-and-after design to take advantage of a recent change from 12- to six-person juries. Other changes, however, occurred at the same time (mediation board, discovery of insurance). None of these three items permitted valid comparisons of the behavior and verdicts of larger and smaller juries.

- The final study used videotaped mock trials with student subjects. The study contained serious errors, such as a wholly one-sided case presentation and faulty computations.[53]

Again, there were many critical reviews. Zeisel and Diamond wrote that *Colgrove*'s handling of evidence presented a "disconcerting picture,"[54] and suggested that it was one of the cases where the intent of references to empirical evidence is not to shed light on the facts, but "merely to ornament an already determined result."[55] Regarding the functional equivalence assertions, Zeisel wrote elsewhere that "[w]ith all due respect to the judges who composed the majority of the Court in these cases—on this point they were simply wrong. The Court's so-called evidence proved nothing of the sort."[56] Referring to *Colgrove*'s "convincing empirical evidence," Wick wrote that "[t]he only conviction which emerges from examination of these four studies is that the majority of the Court was predisposed to be convinced."[57]

The *Williams-Johnson-Apodaca-Colgrove* sequence of opinions furnishes one of the more depressing sets of readings to emerge from the pens of U.S. Supreme Court justices. One aspect is technical: the uncritical and incompetent treatment of empirical evidence. The other is substantive: the continuous slicing away at the traditional common law jury and, thus, the continuing reduction in the protective function of trial by jury. The second was worrisome all the more because of strong signs that the Court would legitimate trial juries even smaller than six,[58] and majorities even smaller than *Johnson*'s nine-to-three division.[59] Indeed, there was reason to be concerned that the two methods of jury reduction would be legitimated in a combined format.[60]

Partial remedies

Eight years after *Williams* and five years after *Colgrove* the Court decided *Ballew v. Georgia* and at least partially remedied the inadequacies of the earlier cases. As *Williams* is the milestone marking the beginning of the decline of the American jury, so *Ballew* may well be the milestone marking the onset of recovery.[61] The *Ballew* Court ruled[62] that Georgia's criminal jury of five was constitutionally inadequate because it did not meet the Court's test of functional equivalence.

For the first time in the jury decisions of the 1970s, the Court correctly used empirical evidence to establish a social fact: deliberative bodies of five and of 12 are *not* equivalent. Criminal juries of five do not offer the same protection to the accused as those of 12. The irony of *Ballew* is that the evidence used to deny five just as much condemns six. The scientific investigations cited in *Ballew* were designed to test the *Williams* doctrine of 6=12. The findings exposed the error of that doctrine. Yet *Ballew* includes an explicit affirmation of *Williams*.[63] *Ballew*, thus, is only a partial redress for the Court's past failings.

Justice Blackmun noted many functional inequalities between larger and smaller juries. He arranged them in five major groups:

(1) **Effectiveness of group deliberation.** The quality of group performance and group productivity is higher in larger groups.[64] Reduction in the size of the group leads to impaired fact-finding and common-sense application. Members of smaller groups are less likely to contribute to the solution of the problem, and (collectively) are less likely to overcome the biases of their members.[65]

(2) **Accuracy, consistency, and reliability of deliberation results.** Smaller panels produce a larger proportion of conviction errors, i.e., convicting innocent persons. (Increases in panel size increase the opposite error: not convicting guilty persons.)[66] Smaller panels show more verdict inconsistency and produce less reliable decisions.[67]

(3) **Detriment to the defense.** The functional difference between smaller and larger panels is not neutral in criminal trials. Smaller panels are detrimental to the defense. The number of hung juries is substantially reduced with smaller panels, largely because of less support for the juror holding the minority viewpoint.[68]

(4) **Community participation and representativeness.** Smaller panels reduce the representativeness of the jury and allow less participation of the minority groups in the community.[69]

(5) **Substantial effects of small differences.** Some studies have found that larger and smaller juries would produce different verdicts in only a relatively small proportion of the cases, e.g., 14 percent. These small percentages, however, mask a very large number of cases. Furthermore, it is precisely in those cases of disagreement, when the evidence is not clear-cut, that the jury system is of greatest value. A similar point applies to the small percentage differences often found between jury verdicts and judge verdicts. Aggregate comparisons mask the true extent of differences. Case-by-case comparisons show higher rates of disagreement.[70]

Having noted all these differences, Justice Blackmun wrote that these studies "lead us to conclude that the purpose and functioning of the jury in a criminal trial is seriously impaired, and to a constitutional degree, by a reduction in size to below six members."[71]

It is ironic that one of the best listings of evidence to refute the *Williams* doctrine should be found in a decision that explicitly affirms that doctrine.[72] The assembly of empirical evidence in *Ballew* is particularly impressive[73] when it is recognized that the litigants brought to the attention of the Court only a small part.[74] Additional literature, however, could have been drawn upon.

Saari, for example, has pointed out that from some perspectives six is not even one-half of 12. One of the crucial issues in the jury-size controversy is the interaction of the jurors. The evidence is that both quality and quantity differ. Saari points to the interesting fact that juries of 12 have 261,624 potential relational patterns, but juries of six only have 301 (about 1/10 of 1 percent).[75] Missing from *Ballew* are references to the extensive work of Gelfand and Solomon,[76] Grofman,[77] Buckhout,[78] and Snortum et al.,[79] as well as to the partially unpublished but well-known study of Padawer-Singer and Barton.[80] A recent review of the jury literature by Davis et al. also would have been a useful addition.[81] It is important to emphasize, however, that the inclusion of these items would not have changed any of the findings of *Ballew* regarding the functional non-equivalence of five- and 12-person juries, though, again, the real message was the non-equivalence of six and 12.

A halt to jury reduction

Burch v. Louisiana is the final case in this decade's sequence of jury decisions. *Burch* stands in the same relationship to *Johnson* and *Apodaca* as *Ballew* to *Williams* and *Colgrove*. *Burch* ruled that conviction by a nonunanimous six-person jury for a nonpetty offense violates the right to trial by jury as guaranteed by the Sixth and Fourteenth Amendments.[82] While *Burch* resembled *Ballew* in putting a halt to the further diminution of the American trial jury, it greatly differs from *Ballew* in its treatment of evidence.

Burch makes no reference to empirical evidence,[83] except for an allusion to the "reasons that led us in *Ballew* to decide that use of a five-member jury threatened the fairness of the proceeding and the proper role of the jury." [84] Justice Rehnquist, the author of the *Burch* opinion, had associated himself with the Powell complaint about *Ballew*'s "reliance on numerology" (*cf* note 38 *supra*), seemingly having less use for science as a source of social facts than Justice Blackmun.

In addition to references to *Ballew* (but no analysis of the *Ballew* evidence for its relevance to *Burch*), Justice Rehnquist sought to support the *Burch* decision by taking note of current practice:

> We are buttressed in this view by the current jury practices of the several States. It appears that of those States that utilize six-member juries in trials of nonpetty offenses, only two, including Louisiana, also allow nonunanimous verdicts. We think that this near uniform judgment of the Nation provides a useful guide in delimiting the line between those jury practices that are constitutionally permissible and those that are not.[85]

Justice Rehnquist also found it profitable to resurrect and reaffirm once more the functional equivalence error of the *Williams* court "that a jury of 12 was neither more reliable as a factfinder, more advantageous to the defendant, nor more representative of the variety of viewpoints in the community than a jury of six." [86]

What Justice Rehnquist failed to do was to examine relevant and competent evidence. The Court's self-chosen test in all of the jury cases is that of the functional equivalence of different juries. The question of functional equivalence is an empirical question. It can be answered only by the examination of empirical evidence. It cannot be answered by an audit of current court practices. Nor can the question of the functional equivalence of different decision rules be answered by referring to the Court's reasoning in the jury-size cases, particularly given the less than competent treatment of evidence in these cases.

The reasoning of *Burch* is sorely deficient. Nevertheless, the decision is welcome to those who have an interest in preserving trial by jury in the courts of this nation. As *Ballew* before it, *Burch* creates an important obstacle against the additional diminution of the jury.

III. Hidden agendas?

It has been argued that the Court's use of empirical evidence is "real," if occasionally faulty. But the view that the Court also refers to empirical evidence to ornament and to camouflage has considerable prevalence.[87] Short of judicial disclosure, there seems to be no clear way to verify such propositions, and judicial denial may not convince everyone.

The matter must be approached with care. We do not need another conspiracy theory. Yet, the problem cannot be ignored.[88] The conclusion that the Court ornaments and camouflages is almost inescapable when confronted with "evidence" of the nature and quality used in *Williams* to justify a jury of six.[89] The jury cases and their context suggest the possible existence of four hidden agendas: jury cost, court delay, judicial power, and law and order.

Jury cost

Five of the six jury cases are silent on the issue of jury cost, and *Ballew* rejects Georgia's argument of an overriding state interest in "savings in court time and in financial costs." [90] Yet the jury reduction literature[91] of recent decades has placed such strong emphasis on the savings to be realized by smaller juries that it is difficult to dismiss the thought altogether that the Court may have wanted to reduce the cost of justice as well as to permit jury diversity in deciding these cases. The thought is particularly hard to dismiss because *Williams* justified the six-person jury by relying, *inter alia*, on Judge Phillips' article, which is a purely economic argument for reduction,[92] and because of Chief Justice Burger's remarkable media and lecture circuit activism in the cause of court reform, more than once linking economic considerations and jury size.[93]

The jury reform/reduction literature almost without exception presents expected financial savings as a justification for reducing the size of the jury. The savings are said to occur for several reasons, including the claims that: (a) fewer panelists are required for the jury venire,[94] (b) less time is needed for the voir dire of the prospective jurors,[95] (c) less time is required for courtroom proceedings,[96] (d) jury deliberation time is shorter,[97] (e) juror fees and expenses are reduced.[98] Some of the assertions, especially (a) and (e) are quite plausible; the others are more questionable.[99] There actually appears to be rather little saving in voir dire time and trial proceedings, and, thus, in judicial time and court cost.[100]

Juror fees probably are the item in which the largest savings can be achieved by reducing the size of the trial jury. Since juror fees are notoriously low,[101] however, and since juror fees consitute a miniscule part of a court's budget,[102] the actual amount is not all that large. Even the figures presented by proponents are not particularly impressive. Bogue and Fritz write:

> Minnehaha County [spent] $27,164.50 for juror fees in 1971. There are an estimated 95,000 people living in Minnehaha County. Divide $27,164.50 into 95,000 people and it will be ascertained that it cost [sic] each person in Minnehaha County about 35¢ plus for the cost of trial by jury.[103]

This, it should be noted, is an argument *for* reducing the jury to six members. If the six-person jury saves about half the amount, it means that each resident of Minnehaha County could enjoy the full benefits and protections of the common law jury for about 18¢ extra per year.

Judge Devitt offers a nationwide figure:

> The saving in jury expenses if the six-man rule were in effect nation-wide is impressive. In fiscal year 1970, 3,371 civil jury trials were conducted in the federal court system. These cases took 10,701 trial days and, with twelve-person juries, a total of 128,512 juror days. If this figure is cut in half and multiplied by $25, the approximate saving effected by employing a jury of six, rather than twelve, could exceed $1,600,000.[104]

Assuming even a cost of $2 million, given a population of about 200 million, the saving per person per year is about *one cent*. Zeisel and Diamond have estimated a saving of $4 million annually if all federal juries consisted of six rather than 12 persons (as the civil juries now largely do). This still works out to only two cents of savings per person per year.[105]

Savings of $4 million must also be seen in the context of other expenditures, such as annual outlays of $631 million for golf equipment.[106] While, of course, no one argues in favor of waste in the judicial system, the cost of the traditional common law jury seems bearable.[107] But if savings must be achieved, there are other

court reforms we can undertake, such as the elimination of the continuous presence of a newspaper-reading bailiff in all non-jury civil and in many non-jury criminal trials, and a more efficient administration of the jury system itself.[108]

Delay

This is not a topic in any of the six jury cases either. Yet there are some grounds for suspecting that this issue may also have been on the Court's mind. The chief justice has frequently spoken about the need to eliminate delay and has clearly linked the use of the jury to the existence of trial delay.[109] And the jury-reduction literature is just as emphatic that delay can be cured by jury reform,[110] as it is on the point that much money can be saved. Particularly the civil jury is seen as cause of delay. Judge Devitt, for example, writes:

> I think it is fair to say that the backlog of cases in the federal courts, particularly in the metropolitan centers, is caused largely by the number of civil jury trials required by the Seventh Amendment.[111]

This type of analysis tends to be based more on wishful thinking than on fact. Inferences often are drawn from judge/jury comparisons, without full recognition of the differences in the types of cases that are submitted to bench and to jury trials. Courts without juries, it should be noted, also experience substantial delay. "The New York Court of Claims, dealing with cases against the State of New York, is almost two years behind on its calendar, yet does not use the jury system."[112]

It has been pointed out that delay is caused by some administrative practices of the courts, and that much of the delay can be cured by the addition of rather small increments in judicial work-time or judicial position.[113] While delay in court can damage the cause of justice and should indeed be cured, smaller juries, majority juries, and reduced use of jury trials do not seem to be the cure. What little *systematic* analysis exists does not identify trial by jury as the cause of delay.[114]

Judicial power

The jury reduction literature contains some interesting hints about the desirability of increasing the power of the judges. American legal history can be read as a struggle between judge and jury, between the professional and the lay element. It is evident that professional judges are in ascendance. The power of the jury to decide on the law has largely been taken away, at least as a matter of right.[115] In effect, juries still have the power to set aside laws that are perceived to be unjust (in general or in application to the case at hand). But when they exercise this power, they are regarded as "runaway" or "lawless." [116]

The argument for smaller juries sometimes is stated in the terms that this will make the court more "businesslike." [117] Often the language is stronger. Gleisser, for example, argues that the trial judge should be the "master of his own courtroom," and that he should be "free to comment in any way he wishes on the evidence," including "which witnesses are to be believed." [118] In jurisdictions where this is not currently permissible, what can this mean but a greater judicial influence on the fact decision of the jury?[119] It should be noted, however, that studies show that the majority of trial judges favors trial by jury, even in civil trials.[120] It cannot be guessed, of course, whether the Court saw increased judicial power as one of the benefits of smaller juries and resulting reductions in the use of juries.[121]

Law-and-order

The smaller criminal jury works to the disadvantage of the defendant.[122] This fact, not acknowledged by the Court until *Ballew,* and even then applied only to the five-person issue, underlies the speculation that an increase in the rate of criminal convictions was one of the hidden agendas of the jury cases.

The 1960s saw a strong public concern with law-and-order. It was a strong factor in the election of President Nixon, and, as political pundits say, the Court follows the election returns. More importantly, the Nixon appointees to the Court were selected to at least some degree because of their position on the law-and-order issue.[123] While presidents tend to have little luck in appointing justices who will carry forward the judicial philosophy that made them attractive, it cannot be denied that the Burger Court has produced some fairly "Nixonian" rulings in respect to such matters as freedom of the press, search and seizure, admission of evidence, self-incrimination, and right to counsel.[124] Some of these decisions point in the same direction as the smaller and the majority jury: an increase in the rate of criminal convictions, reflecting a general climate of punitiveness. Zeisel has raised the issue in this way:

One wonders what is behind this new zeal for cutting into the jury. The ostensible argument is reducing costs and delay. . . . There is obviously more to this concerted drive at this point in time.

Unconsciously, perhaps, the motives are likely to be similar to those that went into the rewriting of the military code of procedure; not only more efficiency, but also less tolerance toward a dissenting minority.[125]

And again Zeisel:

One must see the reduction of the jury size in civil cases in the federal courts as but one move in a major attack on the jury system that began in the 'law-and-order days,' when it was thought that the jury, as we have known it since the founding of the Republic, might stand in the way of law enforcement.[126]

Speculating about hidden agendas, unstated reasons, and concealed motivations is to skate on thin ice. While some inferences may be plausible, little can be proven, yet the matter cannot be avoided. The true reasons and motivations producing the Court's decisions are among the most important facts of judicial policy analysis, constitutional law, and the planning of litigation. When, as in the jury cases, the Court's cited evidence does not support the decisions, and when the Court persists in affirming demonstrably false doctrines, speculation about hidden agendas inescapably will emerge.

IV. A role for ordinary citizens

The Declaration of Independence (1776) set forth a series of complaints against the King to justify the revolution. One of the key complaints was "For depriving us in many cases, of the benefits of Trial by jury." It can be argued that the Court's jury decisions of this decade have caused a similar deprivation. In the Virginia Ratification Convention the Wythe Committee declared that "the ancient trial by jury is one of the greatest securities to the rights of the people, and is to remain sacred and inviolable." [127] And until *Williams,* essentially, it did. It does no longer. The evidence is clear: six does not equal 12, and 75 percent does not equal 100 percent.

How will the Court decide future jury cases? *Ballew* and *Burch* indicate that the worst may be over. Yet majority verdicts for the federal criminal jury were avoided by only a single vote, and it remains undetermined what type of majority rule for less-than-12-person state criminal juries will be legitimated. *Ballew* and *Burch* are no cause for leaving the ramparts. Trial by jury is likely to survive only through vigorous efforts on its behalf.

It is unclear what combination of reasons and motivations produced *Williams* and the subsequent decisions. To the degree that empirical evidence played an important role—however mistakenly used—extraordinary scholarly efforts will be required to provide the Court with social facts, to educate the Court in the use of scientific findings, and to help the legal profession in developing new institutions and processes by which the flow of scientific evidence to the Court can be improved, while preserving principles of procedural fairness.[128]

To the degree that hidden agendas were instrumental in the decisions, scholarly and political efforts will be required. The Court needs more information about just how much (how little) time and money will be saved by smaller juries and non-unanimous decisions. In addition, however, the political process will have to carry the message to the Court that the jury shall not be destroyed to save pennies or to increase the rate of criminal convictions, and that the people will not trust the professional judges with their liberties,[129] but that ordinary citizens shall retain their role in the American judicial process.

The task of preventing any further decline of trial by jury does not appear hopeless. Indeed, over time it may even be possible to persuade the Court to acknowledge the error of the functional equivalence doctrine and to reverse itself. Stare decisis is not the only principle in law. There is no *final word*, even from the U.S. Supreme Court.

Notes

This article originally appeared in Volume 63, Number 6, December–January 1980, pages 262–279.

I am indebted to William Zinn for criticism of the first draft, to Karin Carmin and Coronet Galloway for finding some of the economic data, and to the Institute of Governmental Studies of the University of California for various forms of assistance and typing of the manuscript.

1. "When the Declaration of Independence was adopted and the Constitution drafted, we had every reason to be concerned about citizen-juror protection from King George's judges. But King George is long gone, and so are his judges. We have our own now, and they are competent, experienced, fair, and well qualified to decide law and fact issues in civil cases." Devitt, "Federal Civil Jury Trials Should be Abolished," *A.B.A. J.* 60 (1974), 570, 572.

For a sampling of judicial criticism of the jury, from the mid-1950s to the mid-1970s, *see:* Augelli, "Six-Member Juries in Civil Actions in the Federal Judicial System," *Seton Hall L. Rev.* 3 (1972), 281; Lumbard, "Let the Jury Be—But Modified," *Trial* 7 (Nov.–Dec. 1971), 17; Tamm, "A Proposal for Five-Member Civil Juries in the Federal Courts," *A.B.A. J.* 50 (1964), 162; Thompson, "Six Will Do," *Trial* 10 (Nov.–Dec. 1974), 12; and Wiehl, "The Six Man Jury," *Gonzaga L. Rev.* 4 (1968), 35.

Summaries of criticisms can be found in: Comment, "With Love in Their Hearts but Reform on Their Minds: How Trial Judges View the Civil Jury," *Colum. J. L. Soc. Probl.* 4 (1968), 178; James, *Crisis in the Courts,* rev. ed. (New York: David McKay, 1971) 193–199; and Powell, "Reducing the Size of Juries," *U. Mich. J. L. Ref.* 5 (1971), 87. The most comprehensive attack on the jury system still is Frank, *Courts on Trial* (Princeton: Princeton University Press, 1949).

Views supportive of the traditional common law jury can be found in: Avakian, "Trial by Jury: Is It Worth the Ordeal?" *Litigation* 2 (Winter 1976), 8; Baum, "The Six-Man Jury—The Cross Section Aborted," *Judge's J.* 12 (1973), 12; Hogan, "Some Thoughts on Juries in Civil Cases," *A.B.A. J.* 50 (1964), 752; Kalven, "The Dignity of the Civil Jury," *Va. L. Rev.* 50 (1964), 1055; Nunnelly, "When a Trial by Jury?," in Winters, *The Jury* (Chicago: American Judicature Society, 1971), 25; Summers, "Some Merits of Civil Jury Trials," *Tul. L. Rev.* 39 (1964), 3; and Zeisel, "The Jury and Court Delay," *Annals* 328 (March 1960), 46.

2. *Duncan v. Louisiana,* 391 U.S. 145 (1968). The Court extended the Sixth Amendment right of trial by jury in criminal cases to the states by way of the Fourteenth Amendment.

3. 399 U.S. 78 (1970).

4. Zeisel, ". . . And Then There Were None: The Diminution of the Federal Jury," *U. Chi. L. Rev.* 38 (1971), 710.

5. Trial by jury has fared better in the U.S. than in the home country. Beginning in 1854, England reduced the use of the civil jury in a series of steps from complete usage (in non-equity cases) to about 2 percent of current cases. The use of the criminal jury also has been greatly reduced (employed in less than 10 percent of current cases). The grand jury (an endangered American institution not discussed in this essay) was abolished in England in 1933.

For discussions of English jury abolition and diminution *see:* Abraham, *The Judicial Process,* 3rd ed. (New York: Oxford University Press, 1975), 245; Clark, *The Grand Jury* (New York: Quadrangle, 1972), 104; Devlin, *Trial by Jury* (London: Stevens and Sons, 1966), 129–133; Ehrmann, *Comparative Legal Cultures* (Englewood Cliffs, N.J.: Prentice Hall, 1976), 97–100; and Zander, "The Jury in England: Decline and Fall?" in Annual Chief Justice Earl Warren Conference on Advocacy in the United States, *The American Jury System* (Cambridge, Mass.: American Trial Lawyers Foundation, 1977), 29–34.

6. 406 U.S. 356 (1972).

7. 406 U.S. 404 (1972).

8. 413 U.S. 149 (1973).

9. 435 U.S. 223 (1978).

10. 47 L.W. 4393 (1979).

11. Zeisel, *supra* n. 4, at 712.

12. The legitimation of majority verdicts in federal criminal trials was averted by a single vote. Justice Powell interpreted the Sixth Amendment to require unanimous jury verdicts. He was unwilling, however, to extend this requirement to the states through the Fourteenth Amendment.

13. The discussion of the cases must be brief. For a more detailed treatment, *see:* Sperlich, "Trial by Jury: It May Have a Future," *Supreme Court Review* (1979), 191, 195–209, 218–222.

14. For some of the major criticisms, *see,* for *Williams*: Beiser and Varrin, "Six-Member Juries in the Federal Court," *Judicature* 58 (1975), 424; Stevens, "Defendant's Right to a Jury Trial: Is Six Enough?," *Ky. L. J.* 59 (1971), 996; Walbert, "The Effect of Jury Size on the Probability of Conviction," *Case W. Res. L. Rev.* 22 (1971), 529; Zeisel, "The Waning of the American Jury," *A.B.A. J.* 58 (1972), 367; and Zeisel, *supra* n. 4.

For *Colgrove*: Diamond, "A Jury Experiment Reanalyzed," *U. Mich. J. L. Ref.* 7 (1973), 520, and Zeisel and Diamond, "Convincing Empirical Evidence on the Six Member Jury," *U. Chi. L. Rev.* 41 (1974), 281.

For *Williams* and *Colgrove*: Lempert, "Uncovering 'Nondiscernible' Differences: Empirical Research and the Jury-Size Cases," *Mich. L. Rev.* 73 (1975), 643; Saks, "Ignorance of Science Is No Excuse," *Trial* 10 (Nov.–Dec. 1974), 18; and Wick, "The Half-Filled Jury Box: Is Half Loaf Better Than None?" *Litigation* 2 (Winter 1976), 11.

For *Johnson* and *Apodaca*: Buckhout, "Unanimous vs. Majority Verdicts in Jury Deliberations," *Soc. Action and the L.* 4 (Sept. 1977), 15.

For *Williams, Johnson,* and *Apodaca*: Padawer-Singer, "Justice or Judgments?" in Annual Chief Justice Earl Warren Conference on Advocacy in the United States, *The American Jury System, supra* n. 5, at 45; Padawer-Singer and Barton, "Interim Report: Experimental Study of Decision-Making in the 12- Versus 6-Man Jury Under Unanimous Versus Non-Unanimous Decisions," Columbia University, Bureau of Applied Social Research (1975); and Saks, *Jury Verdicts: The Role of Group Size and Social Decision Rule* (New York: Lexington, 1977).

For all four cases: Buckhout et al., *Jury Verdicts: Comparison of Six vs. 12 Person Juries and Unanimous vs. Majority Decision Rule in a Murder Trial*, Report No. CR-12 (New York: Center for Responsive Psychology, 1977).

15. *Cf. supra* n. 1.

16. 399 U.S. at 89–90.

17. *Cf.* Stevens, *supra* n. 14, at 1000–1001, and Zeisel, *supra* n. 4, at 712.

18. The leading statements are found in *Thompson v. Utah,* 170 U.S. 343 (1898), *Maxwell v. Dow,* 176 U.S. 581

(1900), *Rasmussen v. United States,* 197 U.S. 516 (1905), *Patton v. United States,* 281 U.S. 276 (1930), and *Capital Traction Co. v. Hof,* 174 U.S. 1 (1899), a civil action.

19. 399 U.S. at 90.

20. Ibid. at 92–93.

21. Ibid. at 99–100.

22. Ibid. at 100.

23. Ibid. at 100–101.

24. 413 U.S. at 156.

25. Ibid. at 157.

26. The facts of *Ballew* can be stated briefly. (A more detailed discussion is found in Sperlich, *supra* n. 13, at 191–193.) The petitioner, Claude Davis Ballew, manager of a movie theatre, was convicted by a jury of five on a two-count misdemeanor charge for knowingly exhibiting obscene materials. In various motions and appeals, Ballew raised a number of issues regarding the constitutionality of his trial and conviction. The U.S. Supreme Court decided the case entirely on the issue of the constitutional adequacy of a state criminal jury of five. The other issues were not reached.

27. 435 U.S. at 239.

28. Ibid.

29. It may seem at first glance that a change in decision rule does not as such constitute a case of jury diminution. But a 12-person ten-to-two jury is equivalent to a ten-person jury. "The important element to observe is that the abandonment of the unanimity rule is but another way of reducing the size of the jury. But it is reduction with a vengeance, for a majority verdict is far more effective in nullifying the potency of minority viewpoints than is the out-right reduction of a jury to a size equivalent to the majority that is allowed to agree on a verdict." Zeisel, *supra* n. 4, at 772.

30. 406 U.S. at 410–411.

31. Justice White, nevertheless, did not shrink from complaining that the petitioner (Johnson) did not provide empirical evidence to support the claim that jury deliberations are not the same under unanimity and majority rule. The matter is particularly astonishing since by this complaint Justice White shifts the burden of proof from the State of Louisiana, seeking to change a constitutional tradition, to the petitioner, pleading for his customary rights. *Cf.* 406 U.S. at 362.

32. Ibid.

33. Some, of course, would argue that empirical evidence had rather little to do with the decision on the functional equivalency issue in the four cases that diminished the trial jury. The notion is prevalent that the Court used empirical evidence not so much to reach decisions, but to dress them up after they have been made. *Cf.* Zeisel and Diamond speaking of decisions "merely ornamented by the 'facts'," *supra* n. 14, at 281.

34. 47 L.W. at 4394.

35. Legal scholars and judges have not yet agreed on a standard terminology to refer to various types of facts and evidence. "Legislative facts," "social facts," "situation sense," and other terms are used in a variety of meanings. *Cf.* Davis, *Administrative Law Treatise* 2 (St. Paul, Minn.: West, 1958), 353, and Louisell and Mueller, 1 *Federal Evidence* (San Francisco: Bancroft-Whitney, 1977), 395, as well as Horowitz, *The Courts and Social Policy* (Washington, D.C.: Brookings Institute, 1977), 274–284; Marvell, *Appellate Courts and Lawyers* (Westport, Mass.: Greenwood Press, 1978), 149–153; and Rosen, *The Supreme Court and Social Science* (Urbana: University of Illinois Press, 1972), 53–54.

In this essay, *case fact* refers to the question: did this apple fall from the defendant's tree and hit the plaintiff on the head? *Social fact* is used to refer to relevant scientific principles, i.e., the law of gravity: do apples normally move up, down, or sideways when breaking off the stem?

36. Even a "hard" science, such as ballistics, has not been immune from judicial know-it-all. In *People v. Berkman*, 307 Ill. 492, 501, 139 N.E. 91, 94 (1923), "the court characterized offered testimony concerning ballistics as 'preposterous,' a denunciation tacitly withdrawn only seven years later in *People v. Fisher*, 340 Ill. 216, 172 N.E. 743 (1930)." Strong, "Questions Affecting the Admissibility of Scientific Evidence," 1970 *U. Ill. L. Forum* (1970), 1, 10, n. 31.

37. Courts, of course, are put into a most difficult position when experts disagree. The problematic nature of psychiatric testimony readily comes to mind. Disagreement among competent scientific studies was not, however, the cause of the Court's inept handling of social fact issues in the jury decisions.

38 435 U.S. at 246. Opinion of Justice Powell, joined by Justices Burger and Rehnquist.

39. Nor is it particularly gracious to refer to the investigations of the academic experts on jury behavior as "merely . . . [the] findings of persons interested in the jury system." Ibid.

40. To a large extent, the lack of knowledge about jurors and juries is due to the non-cooperation of the courts. To a smaller degree it is due to congressional opposition. *Cf.* Sperlich, *supra* n. 13, at 201, note 38.

41. 399 U.S. at 101, note 48.

42. For a detailed review of the six items, *see* Zeisel, *supra* n. 4, at 714–715.

43. The Court not only relied on incompetent items, but misinterpreted the evidence presented in competent studies. Zeisel was forced to complain that "[i]n *Williams* the Court cites the studies conducted in connection with *The American Jury* to support its proposition that 'jurors in the minority on the first ballot are likely to be influenced by the proportional size of the majority aligned against them.' It is only fair to point out that the findings were quite different." Ibid. at 719.

44. Ibid. at 715. In the circumstance, "scant evidence" is a mild rebuke. As Lempert has pointed out: "Zeisel is gentle with the Court; he never emphasizes the majority's extreme disingenuousness in citing these reports as experiments and in relying on them as evidence . . ." Lempert, *supra* n. 14, at 645.

45. Saks, "Ignorance . . . ," *supra* n. 14, at 18.

46. Walbert, *supra* n. 14, at 535.

47. Wick, *supra* n. 14, at 14.

48. "The test laid down in *Williams* indicates that the reduced jury is unconstitutional if the smaller size impairs its performance. Consequently, a correct application of the Court's test would hold that a jury of six persons is unconstitutional." Walbert, *supra* n. 14, at 554.

49. In his review of *Williams*, Zeisel noted the spurious nature of the first of the six items, the Court's reference to Judge Wiehl's comments on the six-person jury: "Judge Wiehl approvingly cites Joiner's *Civil Justice and the Jury*, in which Joiner somewhat disingenuously states that 'it could easily be argued that a six-man jury would deliberate equally as well as one of twelve.' Since Joiner had no evidence for his conclusion, Judge Wiehl also does not have any." (*Supra* n. 4, at 714) The *Colgrove* Court was well aware of Zeisel's criticism. (413 U.S. at 159, n. 15) Nevertheless, Joiner's opinion is included in the list of items offered by *Colgrove* in support of the functional equivalence assertion. (Ibid.)

50. 413 U.S. at 158–159.

51. Ibid. at 159, n. 15.

52. For detailed discussions, *see* Zeisel and Diamond, *supra* n. 14, at 282–290, and Diamond, *supra* n. 14.

53. It must be acknowledged that some of the flaws contained in the four studies were not immediately obvious and required a certain amount of methodological understanding for their detection. This, however, does not permit the inference that the justices were victimized by inadequate science. First, the Court has consistently failed to take notice of deficiencies in the evidence that were well within the competence of the justices to discover (e.g., that an unsupported opinion that there would be no differences cannot validate a claim that there are none).

Second, the degree of methological expertise required to spot the inadequacies of the *Williams* and *Colgrove* items actually was very modest (*Cf.* Saks, "Ignorance . . . ," *supra* n. 14, at 20, and Zeisel and Diamond, *supra* n. 14, at 292).

Third, the Court had the ability to call for advice on specific technical questions, without having to return the case to the trial courts. Fourth, reading the Court's opinions raises substantial doubt that the "empirical evidence" actually decided these cases. The suspicion is not easily dismissed that the empirical references served "merely to ornament an already determined result" (Zeisel and Diamond, *supra* n. 14, at 281).

54. Zeisel and Diamond, *supra* n. 14, at 290.

55. Ibid. at 281.

56. Zeisel, "Twelve is Just," *Trial* 10 (Nov.–Dec. 1974), 13.

57. Wick, *supra* n. 14, at 14.

58. *Williams* included this sentence: "We have no occasion in this case to determine what minimum number can still constitute a 'jury,' but we do not doubt that six is above the minimum." (399 U.S. at 91, note 28) As the State of Georgia would correctly but unsuccessfully argue in *Ballew,* if six is above the minimum, five cannot be below it, given that juries cannot consist of five and one-half persons.

59. This possibility was considered by Justice Blackmun in his concurring opinion to *Johnson,* writing that "a system employing a 7–5 standard, rather than a 9–3 or 75 percent minimum, would afford me great difficulty." (406 U.S. at 366).

60. Reducing the proportion of jurors required to convict decreases the effective size of the jury. Indeed, it may be a more severe reduction in jury size than a direct decrease in the number of jurors. *Cf.* Zeisel, *supra* n. 29.

61. If not signaling recovery, *Ballew* (and *Burch*) indicate at least that there is a limit to the Court's favorable view of state experimentation with the trial jury.

62. It is of interest to note that *Ballew* does not have a majority opinion. Justice Blackmun's opinion for the Court was joined by Justice Stevens. Justices Blackmun, Powell, Rehnquist, Stevens, White, and the chief justice concurred in the judgment. Justices Brennan, Marshall, and Stewart concurred in the holding, but disagreed that the petitioner should be subjected to a new trial.

63. 435 U.S. at 239.

64. The relationships reported here do not have infinite linear extensions, of course. The quality of performance is not likely to be greater in a group of 2,000 than in a group of six. The smaller/larger comparisons in this context refer only to the 6/12 or 5/12 contrast.

65. 435 U.S. at 232–234. The findings were secured by references to Kelley and Thibaut, "Group Problem Solving" in 4 Lindsey and Aronson, *Handbook of Social Psychology,* 2d ed. (Reading, Mass.: Addison-Wesley, 1969), 29; Lempert, *supra* n. 14; Saks, *Jury Verdicts, supra* n. 14; and, by way of Lempert, Barnlund, "A Comparative Study of Individual, Majority, and Group Judgment," *J. Ab. & Soc. Psych.* 58 (1959), 55; Faust, "Group versus Individual Problem-Solving," *J. Ab. & Soc. Psych.* 59 (1959), 68; and Thomas and Fink, "Effects of Group Size," *Psych. Bull.* 60 (1963), 371.

66. Justice Blackmun's analysis of the empirical materials, *as it regards the five person issue,* stands in marked contrast to the treatment of "evidence" in the earlier decisions. The specific items are fair selections from the relevant literature, though a number of items could usefully have been added (*Cf. infra*).

The treatment of the selected items is competent, if not without weaknesses. The most important error occurs in the treatment of Nagel and Neef's modeling effort, which seems to have been regarded as an inductive-empirical study, without adequate attention to the dependence of the conclusions on the highly speculative assumptions made by the model. The justice relied on Nagel and Neef for the inference that the optimal jury size was between six and eight. (435 U.S. at 234) It can equally well be concluded from the model that the ideal jury size is 23. *See* Sperlich, *supra* n. 13, at 216, n. 107.

67. 435 U.S. at 234–235. The findings were secured by references to Friedman, "Trial by Jury," *Am. Stat.* 27 (1972), 21; Lempert, *supra* n. 14; Nagel and Neef, "Deductive Modeling to Determine an Optimum of Jury Size and Fraction Required to Convict," *Wash. U.L.Q.* 1975 (1975), 933; Saks, *Jury Verdicts, supra* n. 14; Walbert (Note), *supra* n. 14; and, by way of Nagel and Neef, Kalven, and Zeisel, *The American Jury* (Boston: Little, Brown, 1966).

68. 435 U.S. at 236. The findings were secured by reference to Lempert, *supra* n. 14; Zeisel, *supra* n. 4; and, by way of Lempert, Asch, "Effects of Group Pressure upon the Modification and Distortion of Judgments," in Cartwright and Zander, *Group Dynamics,* 2d ed. (New York: Row, Peterson, 1960), 189.

69. 435 U.S. at 236–237. The findings were secured by references to Lempert, *supra* n. 14; and Saks, *Jury Verdicts, supra* n. 14.

70. 435 U.S. at 237–239. The findings were secured by references to Diamond, *supra* n. 14; Kalven and Zeisel, *supra* n. 67; Lempert, *supra* n. 14; Nagel and Neef, *supra* n. 67; Saks, "Ignorance . . . ," *supra* n. 14; Saks, *Jury Verdicts, supra* n. 14; Walbert (Note), *supra* n. 14; and Zeisel and Diamond, *supra* n. 14.

71. 435 U.S. at 239.

72. Justice Blackmun's opinion becomes tortured when it affirms that six equals 12, while denying that five equals 12, all of this based on evidence that does not even consider the issue five, but clearly demonstrates the falsity of 6 = 12. It is inconceivable that the justice was oblivious to the situation. One might speculate that the explanation lies in the political realities of Supreme Court decision making, i.e., that the votes to strike down *five* were available only at the price of affirming *six.*

73. In addition to the items referred to in the preceding paragraph, Justice Blackmun took note of a number of other studies. *See* 435 U.S. at 231, n. 10.

74. The State of Georgia was satisfied to dig out one of Judge Tamm's articles of questionable relevance: "The Five-Man Civil Jury: A Proposed Constitutional Amendment," *Geo. L.J.* 51 (1962), 120. The attorneys for the petitioner utilized a total of six items. *Cf.* Sperlich, *supra* n. 13, at 217, n. 111.

75. Saari, "The Criminal Jury Faces Future Shock," *Judicature* 57 (June–July 1973), 12, 14.

76. For example, Gelfand, "A Statistical Case for the 12-Member Jury," *Trial* 13 (Feb. 1977), 41, and Gelfand and Solomon, "Analyzing the Decision-Making Process of the American Jury," *J. Am. Stat. Assoc.* 70 (1975), 305.

77. For example, Grofman, "Jury Decision-Making Models," in Nagel, *Modeling the Criminal Justice System* (Beverly Hills, Calif.: Sage, 1977), 191.

78. For example, Buckhout, "The U.S. Supreme Court vs. Social Science: The Jury" (unpublished manuscript, 1977), as well as the many items published in *Social Action and The Law*.

79. Snortum et al., "The Impact of an Aggressive Juror in Six-and Twelve-Member Juries," *Crim. Justice & Behav.* 3 (1976), 255.

80. Padawer-Singer and Barton, "Interim Report," *supra* n. 14.

81. Davis et al., "The Empirical Study of Decision Processes in Juries: A Critical Review," in Tapp and Levine, *Law, Justice, and the Individual in Society* (New York: Holt, Rinehart and Winston, 1977), 255.

82. 47 L.W. at 4393.

83. Many of the items cited in *Ballew,* as well as almost all of those suggested as additions in the preceding paragraph, offer evidence on the decision-rule issue. For purposes of *Burch,* it would also have been useful to direct attention to the work of Nemeth; for example, "Interactions Between Jurors as a Function of Majority vs. Unanimity Decision Rules," *J. Appl. Soc. Psych.* 7 (1977), 38.

The various decision-rule studies lead to the same conclusion: different decision rules are not functionally equivalent. They also show quite clearly that unanimity differs not only from *Burch*'s 5/6 majority rule, but also from the fractions of *Johnson* and *Apodaca.* Not critically reviewing empirical evidence, Justice Rehnquist, of course, had no opportunity to doubt the wisdom of the earlier two decisions.

84. 47 L.W. at 4395.

85. Ibid.

86. Ibid. at 4394, n. 7.

87. *Cf. supra* n. 33. *See also* Horowitz, *supra* n. 35, at 279, Lempert, personal communication, as quote by Grofman, *supra* n. 77, at 6, Lochner, "Some Limits on the Application of Social Science Research in the Legal Process," *L. & Soc. Order* 197 (1973), 815, 835–836, and Rosenblum, "A Place for Social Science Along the Judiciary's Constitutional Law Frontier," *NW. U.L. Rev.* 66 (1971), 459. The notion also has adherents that judicial camouflaging extends far beyond the use of references to empirical evidence. "The judicial process is overwhelmingly a means of rationalizing preferred ends." Levy, *Against the Law* (New York: Harper and Row, 1974), 36.

88. False information has consequences. If the real basis of a decision is not known, parties cannot effectively respond to it, which undermines the adversary process.

Camouflage also is likely to mislead constitutional scholarship, lead counsel into faulty argument, and create erroneous expectations among litigants.

89. *Cf.* 240–241 *supra.*

90. 435 U.S. at 243.

91. *Cf. supra* n. 1.

92. Phillips, "A Jury of Six in All Cases," *Conn. Bar J.* 30 (1956), 354.

93. As examples, *see* Burger, "Report on the State of the Federal Judiciary," *Suffolk U.L. Rev.* 6 (1972), 776, 781, and "Interview with Chief Justice Warren E. Burger," *U.S. News & World Report* 69 (Dec. 14, 1970), 32, 39.

94. Augelli, *supra* n. 1, at 292; Tamm, *supra* n. 74, at 134; Thompson, *supra* n. 1, at 14; Wiehl, *supra* n. 1, at 292; and Institute of Judicial Administration, *A Comparison of Six- and Twelve-Member Civil Juries in the New Jersey Superior and County Courts* 19 (New York: 1972).

95. Augelli, *supra* n. 1, at 291–292; Comment, "With Love...,"*supra* n. 1, at 192; Institute of Judicial Administration, *supra* n. 94, at 27–28, 33–34; Phillips, *supra* n. 92, at 356; Powell, *supra* n. 1, at 96–97; Tamm, *supra* n. 74, at 131–132; Thompson, *supra* n. 1, at 14; and Wiehl, *supra* n. 1, at 40.

96. Augelli, *supra* n. 1, at 292; Institute of Judicial Administration, *supra* n. 94, at 24–26; Phillips, *supra* n. 92, at 356–357; Powell, *supra* n. 1, at 97; Tamm, *supra* n. 74, at 132; Thompson, *supra* n. 1, at 14; Wiehgl, *supra* n. 1, at 40; Bogue and Fritz, "The Six-Man Jury," *S.D. L. Rev.* 17 (1972), 285, 288; and Devitt, "The Six-Man Jury in the Federal Courts," *F.R.D.* 53 (1971), 273, 275.

97. Augelli, *supra* n. 1, at 292; Comment, "With Love...," *supra* n. 1, at 192; Devitt, *supra* n. 96, at 276; Institute for Judicial Administration, *supra* n. 94, at 28–32; Phillips, *supra* n. 92, at 357; Powell, *supra* n. 1, at 97, 101; Tamm, *supra* n. 74, at 132; Thompson, *supra* n. 1, at 14; and Wiehl, *supra* n. 1, at 40.

98. Augelli, *supra* n. 1, at 291; Bogue and Fritz, *supra* n. 96, at 288–289; Devitt, *supra* n. 96, at 276–277; Phillips, *supra* n. 92, at 357–358; Powell, *supra* n. 1, at 98; Tamm, *supra* n. 74, at 133; Thompson, *supra* n. 1, at 14; and Zimmerman, "Evaluating the Six Member Jury," *Soc. Science* 36 (1961), 45, 46.

99. Some of the claims are amusing, showing a rather desperate desire to justify smaller juries by appealing to thrift and fiscal responsibility. One learns, for example, that fewer jurors can move in and out of the jury box in a shorter time than a larger number. Devitt, *supra* n. 96, at 275, and Phillips, *supra* n. 92, at 357. One also learns that smaller juries can do with smaller jury boxes and smaller jury rooms. Thompson, *supra* n. 1, at 14.

It is astonishing to see that judges are capable of arguing that in deciding the fate of the jury we should take into account the few seconds saved in the movement of the jurors, and the few square feet of courtroom space saved by a smaller jury box. Besides, most American courtrooms serve a variety of trials, some of which will still require juries of 12, so that the larger jury box has to be preserved. Furthermore, most existing jury rooms are so small to begin with, that cutting them in half to create two smaller rooms would have juries deliberate in spaces resembling cells or closets.

100. For studies and discussions, *see* Baum, *supra* n. 1, at 128; Padawer-Singer, *supra* n. 14, at 50; Zeisel, *supra* n. 4, at 771–772; Zeisel, *supra* n. 56, at 13–15; Zeisel and Diamond, *supra* n. 14, at 294; Bloomstein, *Verdict: The Jury System* (New York: Dodd, Mead, 1972), 128; Broeder, "The University of Chicago Jury Project," *Nebraska L. Rev.* 38 (1959), 744, 747; Pabst, "Statistical Studies of the Costs of Six-Man Versus Twelve-Man Juries," *William and Mary L. Rev.* 14 (1972), 326; and Pabst, "What Do Six-Member Juries Really Save?," *Judicature* 57 (1973), 6.

101. Daily juror fees range from zero to about $20, and some courts pay a fee only when a juror actually serves on a jury, not when he waits to be chosen. For an overview of fees paid, *see* Pabst and Munsterman, "The Economic Hardship of Jury Duty," *Judicature* 58 (1975), 495.

102. For example, the total 1975–1976 budget of New York City was $12.3 billion, of which $200 million, or 1.6 percent, was allocated to the city's courts. Juror fees can be estimated to have been $2 million, that is, less than one-tenth of one percent of the total city budget, one percent of the budget of the city courts, and approximately 25¢ per resident, per year. Looking at a state, juror fees constituted one-tenth of one percent of the Connecticut budget for 1976–1977. Annual Chief Justice Earl Warren Conference on Advocacy, *The American Jury System, supra* n. 5, at 8–9.

103. Bogue and Fritz, *supra* n. 96, at 289.

104. Devitt, "Six-Member Civil Juries Gain Backing," *A.B.A. J.* 57 (1971), 1111, 1112.

105. Zeisel and Diamond, *supra* n. 14, at 294.

106. Multi-million dollar savings become less impressive when it is remembered that this country spends millions of dollars each year on such products as pet rocks, animal jewelry, and white walls for tires, as well as about $156 million for nail polish, $500 million for recreational outboard motors, $2 billion for movie tickets, $17 billion for tobacco products, and uncounted billions for alcoholic beverages, drugs and gambling.

107. With the "Spirit of Proposition 13" in the country, it is particularly important to examine the relative cost of the jury system, and the actual savings that could be realized by reducing or even abolishing the trial jury. A candidate, looking for issues, might even run for president by opposing "the waste of the jury system."

108. Substantial savings, for example, can be gained by eliminating the wasteful practice of calling much larger numbers of jurors than needed to court each day. *See* Pabst, "An End to Juror Waiting," *Judicature* 55 (1972), 277, and

Note, "D.C. Court Achieves Jury Economies," *Judicature* 43 (1960), 171.

109. *See, for example, "Burger, Report. . . ,"* supra n. 93, at 781.

110. Comment, "With Love. . . ," *supra* n. 1, at 180, 189; Lumbard, *supra* n. 1, at 17; Phillips, *supra* n. 92, at 354 *et seq.;* Tamm, *supra* n. 74, at 120 *et seq.;* Thompson, *supra* n. 1, at 12; Wiehl, *supra* n. 1, at 35 *et seq.;* Bullivant, "Abolition of Jury Trial in Civil Cases," *Oregon L. Rev.* 5 (1926), 185, 192; Gleisser, *Juries and Justice* (New York: Barnes, 1968), 203, 205; Kaufman, "Harbingers of Jury Reform," *A.B.A. J.* 58 (1972), 695; *see also* three articles reprinted in Winters, *The Jury: Selected Readings* (Chicago: American Judicature Society, 1971): Desmond, "Juries in Civil Cases—Yes or No?," 17–19; Kronzer and O'Quinn, "Let's Return to Majority Rule in Civil Jury Cases," 71–73, and Landis, "Jury Trials and the Delay of Justice," 20–21.

111. Devitt, *supra* n. 1, at 570.

112. Bloomstein, *supra* n. 100, at 128. Appellate courts function without juries, it should further be noted, but experience delay.

113. *See* Zeisel, Kalven, and Buchholz, *Delay in Court* (Boston: Little, Brown, 1959), 83–86; Kalven, *supra* n. 1, at 1058–1061; Zeisel, *supra* n. 4, at 711; Pabst, "Statistical Studies. . . ," *supra* n. 100, at 330; and Flynn, "Public Preference for the Jury," *N.Y. State Bar Bull.* 32 (1960), 103, 108–109.

114. In a recent study of urban criminal courts, Levin found that delay has a variety of sources, including the *benefit* of delay to some of the parties: One of the "most striking counterintuitive findings is that, in the five criminal courts analyzed, delay did not seem to be an external phenomenon thrust upon unwilling participants. Rather, it was primarily associated with the voluntary behavior of the judges, defense attorneys, and prosecutors as they pursued their own interests. This differs from the conventional causal explanations that stress the delays caused by large caseloads thrust upon mismanaged, inefficient courts," Levin, *Urban Politics and the Criminal Courts* (Chicago: University of Chicago Press, 1977), 3.

115. "In American legal theory, jury power was enormous and subject to few controls. There was a maxim of law that the jury was judge both of law and of fact in criminal cases. This idea was particularly strong in the first, Revolutionary generation, when memories of royal injustice were fresh. . . . But the rule came under savage attack from some judges and other authorities," Friedman, *A History of American Law* (New York: Simon and Schuster, 1973), 251. Broeder speaks of the process of the "judicial emasculation" of the jury. "The Functions of the Jury: Facts or Fictions?" *U. Chi. L. Rev.* 21 (1954), 386, 403.

116. For discussions of current jury practice regarding law decisions, *see* Jacobsohn, "The Right to Disagree: Judges, Juries and the Administration of Criminal Justice in Maryland," *Wash. U.L.Q.* 1974 (1976), 571; Jacobsohn,

"Citizen Participation in Policy-Making: The Role of the Jury," *J. of Politics* 39 (1977), 73; Kadish and Kadish, *Discretion to Disobey: A Study of Lawful Departures from Legal Rules* (Stanford: Stanford University Press, 1973): especially 46–66; and Scheflin, "Jury Nullification: The Right to Say No," *So. Cal. L. Rev.* 45 (1972), 168.

117. Phillips, *supra* n. 92, at 357.

118. Gleisser, *supra* n. 110, at 309–310. Gleisser also believes that "the judges themselves would be performing a valued service to their courts if they would encourage the waiving of juries altogether. . ." Ibid. at 310.

119. Judge Lumbard, for one, wants to speed up trials, reduce the use of the jury, and give the trial judge greater control. Regarding voir dire, he advocates that all examinations of the jurors should be conducted by the judge, and writes in a singularly revealing phrase: "It should be enough that counsel be *permitted to suggest* questions to the judge." Lumbard, *supra* n. 1, at 17; emphasis added.

120. The majority of attorneys seems to favor the larger jury. The public, particularly former jurors, strongly favors trial by jury. For data regarding the views of the various groups, *see* Association of Trial Lawyers of America, "Judges and the Jury: A Distillation of a Survey," in Annual Chief Justice Earl Warren Conference on Advocacy in the United States; *The American Jury System, supra* n. 5, at 97–99;

Comment, "With Love. . . ," *supra* n. 1, at 183–194; Flynn, *supra* n. 113, at 103–104; Institute of Judicial Administration, *supra* n. 94, at 5, 9–14 *et seq.;* Kalven, *supra* n. 1, at 1072–1074; and Joiner, *Civil Justice and the Jury* (Englewood Cliffs, N.J.: Prentice-Hall, 1962), 201–205.

121. As Zeisel has pointed out: "If the jury size is reduced from twelve to six, [the lawyer's perception] of the approximate balance between jury and bench trial will be disturbed. Henceforth, the 'gamble' with a jury will be significantly greater than the 'gamble' with a judge and, as a result, more lawyers might waive their right to a jury, perhaps a consequence not unexpected by those who initiated the reform." Zeisel, *supra* n. 1, at 719.

122. *Cf.* p. 273 *supra.*

123. Levy, *supra* n. 87, at 12–36, 43–60.

124. Ibid., especially Chapters 2–4.

125. Zeisel, *supra* n. 14, at 370.

126. Zeisel, *supra* n. 56, at 15.

127. Berger, *Government by Judiciary* (Cambridge, Mass.: Harvard University Press, 1977), 399.

128. See, "Social science evidence in the courts: reaching beyond the adversary process," *Judicature* 63 (Dec/Jan 1980), 280 for a systematic examination of these matters.

129. *Cf. supra* n. 1.

Jury Summit 2001

Robert Boatright and Elissa Krauss

A report on the first national meeting of the ever-growing community concerned with improving the jury system.

In January 2001, more than 400 judges, court administrators, interested citizens, attorneys, and academics met in a nationwide Jury Summit in New York. It was the first national meeting of the ever-growing community concerned with improving the jury system. The Summit addressed efforts by courts throughout the nation to improve the quality of jury trials, to ensure representative jury pools, and to improve the overall satisfaction of jurors and litigants with the jury system through plenaries and panels organized around two main themes: representativeness and communication.[1]

The *jury representativeness* panels addressed means by which courts can ensure that jury lists are accurate and inclusive, ways of ensuring truly random summoning of jurors, efforts to ensure that all summons recipients are willing and able to serve, and voir dire techniques and procedures that do not discriminate against any groups within society.

The *jury communication issues* panels addressed juror education, comprehension, and participation; communication between judges and jurors; media communication with jurors; and juror privacy, trial procedures, and jury instructions. A third set of panels considered ongoing reform efforts and challenges facing jury systems. The over-riding theme of all discussions was that jurors are key players in our justice system whose needs and concerns should be respected.

This article highlights some of the ideas discussed at the Jury Summit and concludes with a look at how representatives from seven states and the District of Columbia have implemented various jury system improvements in their courts.

Representativeness

The summoning and qualification process is at the heart of a jury that is representative of the community. Many panels looked at ways to improve representativeness, including multiple source lists, efforts to increase public response to juror qualification questionnaires, and reforms that increase public satisfaction with jury service.

Source lists. For much of this century, courts relied exclusively on lists of registered voters. Today, 34 states provide for use of other lists in addition to or instead of voter registration lists to ensure inclusiveness.[2] Driver's license lists are the most common supplement, but many states have gone further. For example, New Jersey and New York use tax lists. New York added lists of welfare and unemployment insurance recipients.

Use of multiple lists, however, can create a duplication problem. While social security numbers or dates of birth can be used to match name listings, inconsistencies in data entry can lead to duplications. To minimize errors, New York and Connecticut use the National Change of Address Service to catch duplicates. Connecticut also uses official state lists to eliminate from the rolls individuals who have died.

Carnegie Mellon statistics professor Joseph Kadane discussed an easy, low-tech way to eliminate duplicates: merely send questionnaires to a random sample from, for instance, a list of registered voters and a list of licensed drivers, ask the drivers whether they are registered, and if so, discard these as duplicates.

Use of multiple source lists cannot guarantee representativeness, as other factors can still come into play. One solution to continuing unrepresentativeness is stratified selection from source lists. Stratified sampling is used in Connecticut to ensure that individual towns are represented in the jury pool commensurate with each town's percentage of the jurisdiction's population. Georgia has adopted a supreme court rule requiring summoning stratified by race and sex. Where statutes require random selection, stratified sampling is not an option.

Summons nonresponse rates. Failure to respond to juror questionnaires or jury summonses affects representativeness. In some jurisdictions, as many as 50 percent or more potential jurors do not respond to mail questionnaires. Summit participants noted that shorter terms of service and higher jury pay are important keys to reducing nonresponse rates and encouraging citizen participation in the jury system.

Boatright, in his study of nonrespondents, found that patterns of willful nonresponse reflect attitudes as well as socioeconomic factors.[3] Thus, economic factors such as lost wages and the need for child care are not the only reasons given by less wealthy individuals for not responding to juror qualification questionnaires. These potential jurors also report that they hesitate to respond due to fears that they will not be treated fairly and respectfully. By contrast, individuals of higher socioeconomic status report that they fail to respond due to fears that their time will be wasted.

Summons enforcement practices. A variety of methods have been developed to minimize failure to respond to questionnaires and summonses. Massachusetts Jury Commissioner Frank Davis and New York County Jury Division Chief Clerk Vincent Homenick both reported that vigorous enforcement procedures reduced the overall nonresponse rate, but acknowledged that there are substantial costs in persistent follow-up. Second, third, and sometimes fourth notices are sent by registered mail or sometimes personally delivered by a sheriff.

Maricopa County, Arizona, Jury Commissioner Gordon Griller noted that in the absence of resources to pursue nonrespondents another effective approach to reducing nonresponse rates is to simplify procedures for deferral. According to Anthony Manisero, New York State Coordinator of Jury Services, when jurors are given the opportunity to take one automatic postponement and to select a new appearance date, more than 70 percent appear on the date scheduled.

Juror compensation. Increased juror pay can also encourage participation. Alabama, Colorado, Connecticut, the District of Columbia, Massachusetts, New Jersey, and New York require employers to pay jurors' salaries for part of their jury service. New York and Massachusetts have been most successful in raising juror pay—both requiring employers to pay the jury fee for the first three days. After three days New York State pays jurors $40 a day, Massachusetts pays $50 a day. In the same vein, California has conducted campaigns to encourage employers to pay employees while they are on jury service.

Juror hardship can be minimized in other ways. For example, the District of Columbia provides on-site child care for jurors. Colorado, Connecticut, and Massachusetts provide child care reimbursements to unemployed jurors who must pay for child care as a result of being called to serve. Minnesota pays for child care for all jurors who require child care in order to serve (in addition to the $30 fee plus mileage).

Other approaches to streamlining jury systems were discussed, including: processing and compensating jurors more quickly, conducting part of the qualification or orientation process on-line; and other measures to reduce time spent at the courthouse. Barcoding is also widely used in automated systems to provide jurors with proof of service or compensation checks immediately upon completing their jury service. Such practices enhance efficiency while making jurors feel more appreciated.

Accessibility. The Americans with Disabilities Act requires courts to ensure that jury service is accessible to citizens with disabilities. New York County's Homenick noted that in many older courthouses, acoustics can be a problem for jurors who do not even realize that they have hearing difficulties. He commented that sometimes costs prevent adjusting staircases to accommodate wheelchairs, but noted that where staircases or elevators cannot be changed, reasonable accommodation can involve simply having a clerk or court officer available to assist jurors entering and exiting the courthouse. Jurors can also be reassigned to courthouses that are more accessible.

Attorney Oral Miller of the American Blind Lawyers' Association demonstrated Braille writing devices that enable jurors to fill out questionnaires and take notes. Participants also recommended the American Judicature Society publication on procedures for making jury service accessible, including assisted listening devices, sign language interpreters, or real-time transcription to accommodate deaf and hard-of-hearing jurors.[4]

Voir dire and selection. Once representative jury pools are created, the next step is voir dire and jury selection. The Summit opened with a plenary session moderated by Harvard Professor Charles Ogletree. A panel of judges, former jurors, members of the bar, and jury administrators discussed ways to maximize jury representativeness and to enable jurors to be active and knowledgeable participants in the jury system. In a wide-ranging discussion that covered everything from the comfort and cleanliness of jury assembly facilities to juror comprehension of complex trial information, some panelists called for the elimination or reduction of peremptory challenges suggesting that they are arbi-

Jury Reform: A Work in Progress

Our democracy depends on a strong court system, and a strong court system in turn depends on public trust and confidence. If we want the public to have confidence in our courts, we can take nothing for granted—especially the jury system, the place where citizens most often come face-to-face with the courts.

We must be concerned with both the reality and the appearance of fairness in the jury system—from summoning to verdict—so that decisions will not be second-guessed. We must examine the substance of the process and ask if we are doing everything we can to ensure that juries render informed verdicts. And we must be concerned with the quality of the jury experience for each person summoned to serve. We want jurors to experience a court system that works well, respects their time and their lives, and values their performance of this most vital civic duty.

Publication of this report on the 2001 Jury Summit by no means signals the completion of jury reform. Rather, it is a reminder of a continuing commitment to our prized, time-honored jury system—and that jury reform remains a work in progress.

—Judith S. Kaye

diction would grant a challenge for cause. The exercise, based on a research project under way in several jurisdictions, highlighted the importance of judges' practices with regard to the granting of cause challenges in the debate about reducing or eliminating peremptory challenges.

Communication

The second major theme of the conference addressed communication between courts and jurors before, during, and after the trial. These sessions concerned public education, juror privacy and media issues, and jury reforms and innovations that affect jurors' comprehension and involvement in the jury system.

Many state programs highlight **public and juror education** as a key component of effective jury management. Annette Kirby of California's Statewide Taskforce on Jury Improvements noted that civic education programs are most effective if directed at children and young people. She said that California courts focus on reaching out to elementary and high school students. Zelda DeBoyes of Colorado agreed and said that her state is focusing on young "future jurors."

James McFadden, a Washington, D.C., school teacher who works with the Council for Court Excellence, suggested that school-based programs can "demystify" jury service by addressing the actual experience of being in court and serving as a juror. Emil Zulio of the New York State Bar Association noted that presentations to students can help make courts appear more accessible and friendly to students, their parents, and their communities.

Los Angeles County Jury Commissioner Gloria Gomez noted that civic education programs play a role in reducing nonresponse rates. She noted that citizens from countries without a jury system may not understand that jury service is a requirement and suggested that targeted education programs can increase jury participation. One suggestion was to include education about jury service as part of naturalization or immigration procedures in order to reach new citizens. New York Judge Shirley Troutman, who headed an Erie County commission that reviewed juror summoning practices, recommended community-based mini-jury summits to demystify the criminal justice process.

Multi-media information sources are widely used to enhance juror comprehension. For example, Orlando, Florida, provides films and court information through the Internet. One Florida film concerns logistics, while

trary and biased, weeding out jurors who are eager to serve. Others noted that peremptory challenges can be a vital tool for removing jurors who may bring biases into the jury room.

The latter view was echoed in a voir dire demonstration moderated by Hon. Rosalyn Richter of the New York Supreme Court. Jurors role-played by New York State judges were questioned by attorneys in a hypothetical criminal case involving a number of potentially prejudicial issues. The judges noted that even though they were "acting" in assigned roles, the exercise taught them a great deal about what it's like to be a juror in voir dire.

In another Summit session, Northwestern University Professor Shari Seidman Diamond presented participants with trial scenarios and then asked each one to vote on whether or not a typical judge in their juris-

another educates jurors on the procedures of the court, explains the one day/one trial system, and presents some basics of different types of cases.

New York shows jurors a film when they arrive in court, but before they are called to a courtroom. Narrated by New York-based television personalities Ed Bradley of *60 Minutes* and Diane Sawyer of *Prime Time,* the film dramatizes the history and benefits of the jury system. Chief Judge Judith Kaye tells viewers that she, like them, has been summoned for jury service. The film is available to schools or other interested parties.[5]

Many jurisdictions, including California and New York, sponsor Juror Appreciation Days, inviting celebrities who have served as jurors to join judges in a media spotlight aimed at increasing public interest in the jury. In Philadelphia, Pennsylvanians for Modern Courts, a private organization, organizes juror appreciation events with the assistance of the mayor.

One element of a juror-friendly court system is to gather information about jurors' experiences and concerns in an effort to make responsive changes as appropriate. Judge Michael Dann, formerly of Arizona, noted that a wealth of information can be obtained from post-trial de-briefings with jurors. Many courts distribute exit questionnaires to measure jurors' participation in the system and elicit their reactions to jury service. New York City has gone one step further with a Citizens Jury Project operated by the privately funded Fund for Modern Courts. At all major New York City courthouses, Citizens Jury Project volunteers answer questions and provide practical information to jurors while collecting information from jurors about their experiences and concerns.

Two sessions of the Summit addressed **jury trial innovations**. Named for the book of the same name edited by Tom Munsterman and Paula Hannaford of the National Center for State Courts, and Marc Whitehead of the Jury Initiatives Task Force, ABA Section on Litigation, these "innovations" refer to procedures that increase juror involvement and participation in the trial process.[6] The book discusses more than 60 measures ranging from jury representativeness, administration, and management to jury selection, trial management, trial procedures, jury instructions, and post-verdict considerations. The conference panels focused primarily on innovative trial procedures; that is, changes in the ways in which jurors participate in the trial process itself.

Courts across the nation have experimented with and adopted procedures that increase juror involvement in the trial process, including: encouraging attor-

neys to give mini-opening statements to the entire panel before voir dire; allowing jurors to take notes and to submit written questions to witnesses; allowing structured discussion of evidence by jurors during the trial; allowing attorneys to make interim statements to the jury; providing jurors with notebooks containing key evidence and information about witnesses; and providing jurors with written copies of the jury charge or suggestions for deliberations.

One session heard reports of jury trial innovations pilot projects from Judge Jacqueline Conner of the Los Angeles Superior Court and Judge Peter Lauriat of Massachusetts. For six months, 11 Los Angeles judges tested preliminary opening statements to the jury panel (before voir dire), preliminary instructions to the jury (before trial), use of juror notebooks, permitting jurors to ask questions during trial, giving written instructions to jurors during deliberations, and use of juror numbers rather than names.[7] In Massachusetts, 24 trial judges experimented with 16 different jury trial innovations over a two-year period.[8] Judge Michael Dann, well known for his leadership in the Arizona jury trial procedures reforms, added his experience to the mix.[9]

Discussion focused on allowing attorneys to give brief opening statements before voir dire questioning, allowing jurors to submit written questions to witnesses, and giving the jury written copies of the charge during deliberation. Judge Connor highlighted the benefits of **pre-voir dire statements**, noting that without judge-imposed time limits each attorney usually takes between five and eight minutes to describe the major issues. She concluded that these statements lead to more complete and candid juror responses in voir dire, increased interest in serving, and greater understanding among those excused about why it might not be appropriate for them to sit on a particular case.

Many different approaches to **allowing jurors to question witnesses** were discussed. All involved use of written and not oral questions. In most jurisdictions that permit the practice, it is explained to jurors along with admonitions that the questions must be written, addressed to a particular witness, may include questions for clarification, and may not be answered because in some circumstances evidence rules preclude response. Judge Connor simply asks her bailiff to show the written questions to counsel and they decide whether or not to answer them. In Massachusetts, written questions are discussed with counsel out of the presence of the jurors. Sometimes a question is addressed by the judge. In other instances, counsel asks the question. In some jurisdictions a question is not asked if either party objects. Judge Lauriat noted that even improper questions, though not asked of a witness, can provide valuable insights about jurors' comprehension and concerns. The Supreme Judicial Court of Massachusetts has held that there is no reason why jurors should not be allowed to ask questions, and notes that case law in 26 states permits the practice while only five states prohibit it.[10]

In Arizona, juror note taking and question asking were adopted as statewide court rules following pilot programs in Pima and Maricopa Counties. After implementing these rules, the Arizona Supreme Court embarked on another pilot program permitting jurors to discuss evidence during civil trials, but only when all of the jurors were present.[11]

Judge Lauriat also described his use of **interim summaries by lawyers**, noting that they add continuity to the case and give jurors an indication of how the evidence fits together. He allows each lawyer 30 minutes for interim commentary, to be allotted as counsel chooses.

Participants agreed that giving **trial notebooks** to jurors is no longer controversial in most jurisdictions. Nevertheless, practical considerations arise. Panelists discussed how materials are chosen for the notebooks; for example, should mutually agreed upon "key" exhibits be included or only those that are actually discussed by witnesses? They also discussed how to provide the materials to the jurors. Judge Lauriat mentioned that where exhibits are so extensive that individual notebooks are impractical, two sets of exhibits can be left in the jury room for jurors to review during breaks and over lunch.

Jury instructions and deliberation assistance. Jury instructions are frequently a major source of confusion for jurors. Loyola Marymount University Law Professor Peter Tiersma described several techniques for ensuring clarity in jury instructions and provided several examples of complex instructions that could be simplified relatively easily. Judges can sometimes eliminate unnecessary complexity in jury instructions by simple changes in language.

Both Judge Dann and Judge Lauriat lauded the value of giving jurors written instructions during deliberations, agreeing that the practice virtually eliminates questions about the jury charge. Judge Dann noted that there has been a wealth of experience with these practices and extensive research confirming their use-

fulness to the jury and the trial process. *Behind Closed Doors,* a guidebook produced by the American Judicature Society for deliberating jurors, gives jurors some guidance about actions to take when instructions are not easily understood.[12]

Juror privacy and media contact. Some jurors relish the opportunity to discuss their decisions with the media when the case is over. Others fear reprisals or invasions of privacy for having done a job they did not seek.

Juror privacy concerns begin during voir dire. Some judges and courts have used numbers instead of jurors' names, although anonymous juries have generally been limited to individual high profile cases. Participants noted that selective use of numbers instead of names may send a signal to jurors that there is reason to fear reprisals, which are virtually unknown in real-life experience. The public may, however, have a fear of reprisal because of perceptions gained from Hollywood or the media.

Sociologist Mary Rose of the American Bar Foundation noted that courts collect a substantial amount of information from jurors. Personal questions are asked on the qualification questionnaire and during voir dire. Some citizens wonder what happens to this information when the trial is over. Rose was joined by Paula Hannaford of the National Center for State Courts in suggesting that courts carefully consider what information is truly necessary and what is the most tactful method to collect the information. Acknowledging and protecting juror privacy concerns can mean maximizing the use of written questionnaires, conducting voir dire on sensitive issues in chambers, and being vigilant about requiring attorneys to demonstrate the need for particular questions.[13]

Some jurors are also concerned about post-trial media contact. *New York Times* General Counsel George Freeman noted that, whether fictional or true, stories of post-trial media "hounding" of jurors abound. He noted that courts and media representatives agree that intrusions into juror privacy should be avoided. Lucy Quinn Livan of the *St. Paul Pioneer Press* emphasized that trial judges can provide media access to jurors while giving the jurors a choice about whether to talk.

Mark Curriden of the *Dallas Morning News,* whose series on jury service included a study of judge and juror attitudes and experiences, reported that in his experience "most jurors want to talk."[14] The nature of the case and the nature of the story may play a role in this decision, as can official court acknowledgment of the reporter. Curriden also noted that a judicial instruction *not* to talk to reporters can hide trial defects or contribute to distorted public perceptions of the verdict, as he argued was the case in the McDonald's spilled coffee suit. As Curriden explained, high profile cases will be covered whether or not the media has access to the jurors, and jurors have a crucial role to play in setting the story straight.

Jury Trial Innovations notes that jurors often want—even need—to discuss their deliberations. There may even be a therapeutic element to these discussions. Post-verdict discussions may be most salient in high profile cases, but attorneys have always been interested in learning how the jurors perceived their arguments and academics may want to engage in discussions with jurors to pursue research goals. Post-verdict discussions between judge and jury can provide a venue for interested jurors to participate in discussions without feeling unduly put upon by their interviewers. Rules concerning other post-verdict contact with jurors vary widely by jurisdiction.

Unusual trial situations. Recently, courts and court researchers have wondered whether **hung juries** present a problem to the administration of justice. University of Delaware psychologist Valerie Hans noted that historically federal hung jury rates have been about 4 percent, while hung jury rates in state courts for which there is information available average less than 6 percent.[15] Professor Hans and Paula Hannaford recently completed a study of hung juries in Washington, D.C.; Los Angeles; Bronx, New York; and Phoenix, Arizona. They found that juries hung on all counts in only 7.5 percent of the 382 cases studied, and there was considerable variation in the hung jury rate by jurisdiction. The most common reason given for failing to reach unanimous decisions is the perception that the evidence was weak.[16]

In some cases, juror management or deliberation assistance may be far more important than in others. Judge Hiller Zobel, who presided over the trial of Louise Woodward, popularly known as the "nanny trial," led a panel on **jury issues in notorious cases**. He noted that in trials that are expected to be particularly long, seating a jury may be difficult and the jury may not truly represent the population. The judge must be sensitive to jurors' scheduling requests—allowing for doctor's appointments, important family events, and juror scheduling needs.

Scheduling should also maximize use of the jurors' time. Thus, depositions, Daubert hearings, evidentiary arguments, and so forth may be scheduled in the evenings or at times when the jury is told in advance it is not needed. Admonitions to avoid media exposure are particularly important in high-profile trials; in some cases, sequestration may even be considered. Judge Zobel discussed the lengths to which the court went to avoid sequestering jurors in the Timothy McVeigh case. As a creative alternative to the disruptions of sequestration, the jurors met at a different restaurant each morning for breakfast, and were bussed to the trial.

Death penalty cases also demand more juror management. Here, many of the same issues apply as in the high profile cases—jury selection is usually more complex and lengthy. Because of the likelihood of appeals, instructions and other aspects of the trial also become more important.

Perhaps most important, however, from the point of view of the jury, is what takes place after the trial. Death penalty cases can put a tremendous strain upon jurors. Judge Dana Levitz of Maryland was one of several judges who suggested that it should be a standard procedure to have psychologists speak with jurors after the verdict in death cases.

The special role of the American jury system as a beacon of democracy was highlighted in a panel on **jury systems in other countries** moderated by Professor Neil Vidmar of Duke University. Richard Lempert, professor of law and sociology at the University of Michigan, noted that juries "rise with democracy and sink with authoritarian rule."

Lessons from the states

A final conference panel addressed experiences implementing jury reforms. New York has been in the forefront of reforms addressing representativeness, inclusiveness, and improving the experience of jury service. Arizona took the early lead in adopting jury trial innovations that enhance juror participation. The success in both states can be attributed in large measure to key leadership roles played by each state's highest court. After a description of efforts in these two states, we will quickly review approaches to these issues in other states with an eye toward providing readers with tools for implementing reform in their own states.

New York. New York's reform efforts were implemented under the leadership of Chief Judge Judith Kaye, who has become a national spokesperson for jury system reform. In the 1990s, New York State revamped its jury system: eliminating all exemptions, increasing juror pay, reducing jurors' term of service, implementing use of five source lists from which to select potential jurors, and centralizing juror summoning through a combination of leadership from the highest court, broad-based involvement, and effective legislative lobbying. The reform effort included improving conditions in jury assembly rooms and developing a juror handbook and an orientation film.

New York's Chief Administrative Judge Jonathan Lippman explained at the Summit that New York's success relied on participation by former jurors, administrators, academics, attorneys, and community groups. The project was propelled by the consensus by the late 1980s that New York "had a system that can only go up." Judge Lippman pointed out that "not being defensive about that really worked very well for us." He emphasized that diverse membership in the New York Jury Project was influential in persuading the legislature to make necessary legislative change. The state raised pay from $15 to $40 per day over a period of years, thus limiting the budgetary impact and spreading it out. The Jury Project also worked closely with attorneys' organizations to achieve agreement on the changes in juror eligibility and in jury selection.

Arizona. Arizona, by contrast, used its courts as a laboratory for proposed reforms, starting its jury innovation efforts with pilot projects in the state's two largest counties—Pima and Maricopa. In addition to limiting the term of jury service, Arizona was an early leader in implementing other innovations, including: use of pre-voir dire mini-opening statements; allowing jurors to ask questions and take notes during the trial; encouraging juror questions during deliberation; and allowing jurors to discuss evidence during civil trials.

Judge Dann, chair of the Arizona Committee on More Effective Use of Jurors, explained that some of the Arizona policy changes faced resistance but that pilot studies designed to assess the effects of different in-court techniques helped reduce resistance. In addition, the task force broadcast training programs and sent newsletters to judges and attended presiding judges' meetings.

California. In California pivotal events like the O. J. Simpson trial and the trial of police officers accused of assaulting Rodney King, among other high profile cases, focused public attention on the jury. In October 1995, on the heels of the Simpson acquittal, California's

Judicial Council called for establishment of the California Blue Ribbon Commission on Jury System Improvements. Appointed in January 1996 under the leadership of State Supreme Court Chief Justice Ronald George, the commission made recommendations later that year.

State legislators initially balked at proposals to raise juror pay in California, which, at the time of the commission's report, was the lowest in the nation. While there has been movement statewide to a one-day/one-trial system, the large number of trials and nonrespondents has made it more difficult to move to that system in Los Angeles (as it has been in New York City, where most jurors serve for three days or one trial).

Judge Dallas Holmes, chair of California's implementation task force, agreed that judicial education is a key element to ensuring that judges are following through on rule changes. He added that the implementation task force was working to provide new orientation films, redesign the California jury summons, expand free transportation for jurors, and develop more aggressive follow-up procedures for nonrespondents.

Colorado. Colorado created a standing committee on jury improvements in 1994 that issued recommendations in 1996 and 1997. The Colorado task force paid particular attention to balancing its standing committee by including former jurors, attorneys, judges, and legislators, and by maintaining geographic balance to reflect Colorado's urban and rural areas. Cathlin Donnell, a member of Colorado's task force, noted that there has been disagreement within the standing committee about whether to allow juror questions and discussions. The state is conducting pilot studies and working to improve its juror debriefing programs. Donnell singled out the ability of the standing committee to enlist the efforts of a number of particularly well-spoken former jurors as one of its strengths.

District of Columbia. District of Columbia Judge Gregory Mize highlighted the public/private partnership in the Washington, D.C., reform effort. The District of Columbia Jury Project coordinated by the Council for Court Excellence, a private organization, included both the federal court and the superior court along with participants from the public and private bar, former jurors, and academic researchers concerned with improvements in the jury system. Its report and recommendations, *Juries for the Year 2000 and Beyond,* was issued in 1998. Since then, the District of Columbia has expanded source lists and adopted many in-court innovations.

Outreach and education, particularly to students, has been a major part of the reform effort in Washington. The council sponsored a series of town hall meetings titled "Jurors Talk—Judges Listen," which were broadcast on public radio and open to all.

Legislator involvement in jury reform has particular importance in the District, where legislative changes are made in Congress. Judge Mize noted that former United States Senator Patrick Moynihan served as an advocate for the D.C. reforms in the Senate.

Massachusetts. Massachusetts has received far less media attention as a jury innovator than other states. Massachusetts was an early state to implement a one-day/one-trial system and is among the few states that require employer compensation for jurors for the first few days of their jury service—a change that was passed by the legislature along with the introduction of the one-day/one-trial system.

For innovative jury trial procedures, Massachusetts has used public-private partnerships wherever possible to expand judicial education programs, research, and outreach efforts. Instead of being mandated by legislation or court rule, trial innovations have been adopted by individual judges and encouraged in state law schools. Massachusetts approached the issue of jury trial innovations by inviting the National Center for State Courts to study the state's courts and work with a group of judges interested in experimenting with change. The two-year pilot study by 24 Massachusetts judges led to publication of *Jury Trial Innovations in Massachusetts,* a bench book for Massachusetts judges. Trial procedure innovation is encouraged through presentations at law schools and a mentoring program for new judges.

Other states. Michael Garrahan of the New Jersey Administrative Office of the Courts reported on pending legislation to reduce the number of peremptory challenges and standardize voir dire practices. A Pennsylvania commmission is investigating race and gender bias in jury summoning and jury selection. The Ohio State Bar Association has begun to convene conferences on reform issues. Attendees from Connecticut, Delaware, Florida, Indiana, Maryland, the Dakotas, Washington, and Wisconsin reported on individual counties or judges experimenting with jury innova-

---

The Georgia Jury Summit

Georgia's representatives to the national Jury Summit in New York were so excited by the program that they ran a summit of their own. In May 2002, Georgia's Institute for Continuing Judicial Education hosted a local jury summit modeled on the national summit. The two-day program, funded by the Georgia Council of Superior Court Judges, was attended by 120 Georgia court administrators and judges, and a handful of attorneys. Nearly 50 panelist participants from the national summit made presentations in Georgia. Two new panels addressed local concerns: Georgia's system of stratified sampling to ensure representative jury pools, and approaches to providing assistance to jurors who serve on emotionally charged cases. Participants were gratified to learn that across the state individual judges and court administrators were experimenting with many of the jury innovations highlighted by the summit. Like the national meeting, the Georgia Summit gave all participants a chance to share ideas and to learn about new approaches to old problems.

— Elissa Krauss

---

tions and task forces that have issued preliminary recommendations.

An American Judicature Society publication titled *Enhancing the Jury System,*[17] published in 1999, cataloged reform proposals in each of the states, but the variety of efforts discussed at the Jury Summit provided evidence that any such catalog will quickly fall out of date. In the AJS study, several recommendations were made for establishing statewide jury reform efforts. These included finding a strong sponsor or spokesperson, ensuring that the reform commission is representative of the different constituencies that will be affected, and devising an implementation strategy.

****

At the Summit's closing session, New York's Chief Judge Judith Kaye encouraged participants to note and celebrate the diversity of perspectives that were presented at the Jury Summit, and to celebrate as well the diversity within the jury pools of each state. To this exhortation one might add, of course, that the jury itself is a celebration of the diversity of the community from which it is drawn. The American jury provides a unique opportunity in contemporary society for Americans to speak to each other across the barriers of race, class, age, occupation, or education level.

Jury Summit participants took away with them a renewed desire to raise the consciousness of the American public about the importance of the jury and to work together to ensure that jury systems continue to adapt to the changing needs of American society and the American justice system.

Notes

This article originally appeared in Volume 86, Number 3, November–December 2002, pages 144–151, 165.

1. The Summit was hosted by the New York State Unified Court System and the National Center for State Courts and co-sponsored by the Conference of Chief Judges, Conference of State Court Administrators, American Judges Association, and the National Conference of Court Management. Funding was provided, in part, by the State Justice Institute, the Bureau of Justice Assistance, and the American Bar Association Section on Litigation. Forty-four states, the District of Columbia, Puerto Rico, and Japan were represented. Judges accounted for 30 percent of participants; attorneys were 20 percent. Another 20 percent was made up of court administrators and jury commissioners. The remainder included members of the media, former jurors, and representatives of public interest groups and court-related organizations.

2. For a state-by-state listing of the statutory qualifications and source lists for juror service, including statutory authority, minimum age, residency requirements, literacy and language qualifications, and other provisions, visit www.ojp. usdoj.gov/bjs/pub/pdf/sco9806.pdf.

3. Boatright, "Why citizens don't respond to jury summonses," *Judicature* 82 (1999), 156.

4. Fallahay, *The Right to a Full Hearing: Improving Access to the Courts for People Who Are Deaf or Hard of Hearing* (American Judicature Society, 2000).

5. Readers interested in obtaining a copy of the film can contact Anthony Manisero, New York State Coordinator of Jury Services, (212) 428-2990 or amanisero@courts. state.ny.us.

6. The book is available from the National Center for State Courts (www.ncsconline.org).

7. Connor, "Los Angeles County Trial Courts Test Jury Innovations and Find They Are Effective," *Defense Counsel J.* 67 (2000), 186.

8. *See* Lauriat, ed., *Jury Trial Innovations in Massachusetts* (The Flaschner Institute, 2000). This bench book describes the state's jury innovations project and provides detailed instructions and supporting data and case law concerning when, how, and why to use the tested innovations.

9. Dann, " 'Learning Lessons' and 'Speaking Rights:' Creating Educated and Democratic Juries," *Ind. L. J.* 68 (1993), 1229.

10. *Commonwealth v. Britto*, 433 Mass 596 (2001).

11. Diamond and Vidmar, *Civil Juror Discussions During Trial: A Study of Arizona's Rule 39(f) from Videotaped Discussions and Deliberation*, A Report Prepared for the Pima County, Arizona, Superior Court and the Supreme Court of Arizona and the State Justice Institute (2002). Available at: www.law.northwestern.edu/diamond/papers/arizona_civil_discussions.pdf and www.law.duke.edu/curriculum/courseHomepages/460_02/ArizonaCivilDiscussions.pdf.

12. Available from the American Judicature Society at www.ajs.org.

The 2001 Civil Litigation Manual for Federal Judges prepared and distributed by the Judicial Conference of the United States recommends that jurors be permitted to take notes and ask questions and that they be instructed both before and after closing argument.

13. For more on juror privacy, *see* Rose, "Expectations of privacy? Jurors' views of voir dire questions," 86 *Judicature* 10 (2001), and Hannaford, "Safeguarding juror privacy: A new framework for court policies and procedures," *Judicature* 86 (2001), 18.

14. His study led to a law review special issue: "The American Jury: A Study in Self-Governing and Dispute Resolution," *SMU L. Rev.* (Winter 2002).

15. Hannaford, Hans, and Munsterman, "How much justice hangs in the balance? A new look at hung jury rates," *Judicature* 83 (1999), 59.

16. Hannaford-Agor, Hans, Mott, and Munsterman, *Are Hung Juries a Problem?* (September 30, 2002). Available at www.ncsconline.org/wc/publications/res_juries_hungjuriespub.pdf.

17. Available from the American Judicature Society at www.ajs.org.

Complex scientific evidence and the jury

Robert D. Myers, Ronald S. Reinstein, and Gordon M. Griller

*Increasingly complex scientific issues, such as genetics, will further tax the jury system.
Courts can and must seek new ways to help jurors cope more effectively*

DNA—deoxyribonucleic acid, the chemical molecule inside cells which carries biological information. DNA is a double stranded molecule held together by weak hydrogen bonds between complementary base pairs of nucleotides (Adenine and Thymine; Guanine and Cytosine). This molecule carries genetic information from parent to offspring.

Genome—one copy of all the DNA found in each cell of an organism. The human genome is composed of three billion base pairs of DNA packaged as 23 chromosomes. There are two copies of each [chromosome] in a cell, one copy from each of your parents. The genome contains the organism's genes, the instructions for building that life form.

These definitions of DNA and genome, two scientific concepts at the heart of this issue of *Judicature,* seem rather straightforward and simple. One may think that even without scientific background and learning, these concepts can be readily understood, perhaps with a few additional definitions, or a little more explanation from someone knowledgeable. But as the twentieth century draws to a close, the U.S. Human Genome Project moves closer to its goal: determining and mapping the complete sequence of DNA in the human genome by the year 2003. The implications of the Project's work for courts and the entire legal system are enormous:

The HGP's ultimate goal is to discover all of the more than 80,000 human genes and render them accessible for further biological study. . . . Information obtained as part of the HGP will dramatically change almost all biological and medical research and dwarf the catalog of current genetic knowledge. Both the methods and data developed through the project are likely to benefit investigations of many other genomes, including a large number of commercially important plants and animals. In a related project to sequence the genomes of environmentally and industrially interesting microbes, in 1994 DOE initiated the Microbial Genome Program. For this reason, in addition to the DOE and NIH pro-

grams, genome research is being carried out at agencies such as the U.S. Department of Agriculture . . . and the private sector. In a departure from most scientific programs, research also is being funded on the ethical, legal, and social implications (ELSI) of HGP data.[1]

Potential government and private sector applications of this knowledge—gene therapies, gene transfers, genetic screening, and new biotechnologies—ultimately will give rise to a myriad of disputes that will make their way into the courts for resolution. The legal issues involved in these controversies, and the evidence that underlies them, will be far more complex than the two brief definitions of DNA and genome at the outset of this article. As judges and lawyers ready themselves for this growing level of scientific evidence, one principal justice system decision maker is largely unprepared . . . the trial juror.

Already, the most familiar form of genomic evidence, DNA "fingerprinting" (or "profiling," or "typing") in criminal cases, is widely admissible in state and federal courts, by court decision or legislation. The possible uses of genomic evidence, however, are not limited to criminal matters. Some states have already enacted legislation regulating health insurers' use of genetic testing data. Disputes involving insurance coverage, medical malpractice, product liability, toxic torts, employment discrimination, paternity, privacy, and intellectual property will become increasingly complex as the knowledge of not only human, but plant and animal genetics, and the practical applications of that knowledge, become more widespread. As one commentator has said, it is "not whether genetic evidence will ever be admitted into court, but when and under what kinds of circumstances." [2]

Against this backdrop, the ability of juries to adequately understand genomic evidence, distinguish between and resolve contradicting opinions of expert witnesses, and properly apply the law to the evidence is being called into question. Some court watchers believe juries are not competent to resolve scientific

Judicature Volume 83, Number 3, pp. 150–156

evidence issues, and matters of complex scientific evidence should be removed from them. Others argue that the societal values represented by both criminal and civil juries are too important to forego, and that the common sense approach jurors bring to disputes equip them in a unique, capable manner to comprehend novel and complex scientific evidence. In reality, the truth likely lies somewhere in between. Yet, there is little doubt that increasingly complex scientific issues have the potential to further tax the jury system, and that courts must seek new ways to help jurors deal with scientific evidence. To do so, courts will have to promote an active learning environment within the courtroom—in effect, turn courtrooms into classrooms.

This new approach to jury trials is under way in some states today, pioneered by Arizona in its far-reaching 1995 jury rule changes including permitting jurors to ask questions, take notes, and in civil cases allowing jurors to discuss the evidence during the trial.[3] Arizona's objective: improve the experience and decision making of jurors by redefining their role from passive observers to active participants, using applied, proven adult learning methods, and permitting information to unfold during the trial in more meaningful and understandable ways—in other words, to increase the potential of the "search for the truth."

As research on Arizona's jury reform experience progresses, there is growing evidence that the courtroom, turned juror-friendly classroom, is more conducive to juror comprehension and promotes ease in understanding complex concepts and data. If such is the case, must others wait for statewide system changes? The simple answer: no. Courts and lawyers already possess the means and discretion to enable juries to better carry out their vital roles. Judges and lawyers can independently recognize their roles as educators by embracing ground breaking jury reforms and introducing them in their own courts. These reforms will become increasingly important as genomic evidence appears ever more routinely in America's courtrooms.

Juries and complex cases

Over the past 30 to 40 years, the perceived performance of juries has been criticized, both in high-profile criminal cases and in complex civil litigation in antitrust, securities, intellectual property, and product liability cases. Critics have questioned whether a jury of untrained and inexperienced people can be a competent fact finder and decision maker in lengthy trials that require comprehension of substantial quantities of complex scientific, technical, or statistical evidence, and resolving the testimony of duplicative expert witnesses whose opinions conflict.

Moreover, it is alleged, juries in complex trials will have greater difficulty understanding and remembering the court's instructions, and properly applying the law to the facts. Faced with such a burden, say critics, jurors who are untrained in science and technology are ill-equipped for sound fact finding. As a result, critics allege, jurors will base their decisions less on the evidence and a careful consideration of the reliability of expert testimony, than on external cues, such as the perceived relative expertise and status of the expert witnesses, and will be more susceptible to "junk science" and emotional appeals.[4]

Intuitively then, we would expect juries to have enormous difficulties with the complex legal issues and scientific evidence that will confront the courts as disputes involving the strange, new world of human genetics and statistical probabilities become more commonplace. We would expect, as well, new proposals for replacing juries with such expert bodies as science courts and expert or "blue ribbon" panels. At the same time, however, a growing body of research on juries and their performance in both "simple" and complex cases is giving us a different picture.[5] This research, based on case studies and "lab" or experimental studies, shows that jurors, rather than giving up in the face of voluminous evidence and conflicting expert opinions, take their fact-finding and decision-making responsibilities seriously.

The research shows that while certain elements of complex trials do tax jurors' comprehension and understanding, there is no firm evidence that their judgments have therefore been wrong. Jurors are in fact capable of resolving highly complex cases. These studies have also shown that factors such as length of trial, and evidentiary complexity in itself, are not necessarily the critical factors in jury performance in complex matters. The problem presented by conflicting testimony of experts hired by the respective parties, for example, is present in simple as well as complex cases. Finally, the research shows that jurors, rather than being passive participants in the trial process, are active decision makers and want to understand. Jurors actively process evidence, make inferences, use their common sense, have individual and common experiences that inform their decision making, and form opinions as a trial proceeds.[6]

What the research shows then, along with the experiments and experiences of active and concerned judges in complex cases, is that the trial process itself may be as much an impediment to jury comprehension and understanding as the complexity of the legal concepts and evidence, or the competencies of jurors.[7] Many factors, including failure to follow instructions, confusing instructions, non-sequential presentation of evidence, "dueling" expert witnesses, evidentiary admissibility rulings, and attorney strategic errors, affect the jury's ability to follow and comprehend complex evidence. Researchers, and increasingly many progressive courts, suggest that reforming and improving the "decision making environment"[8] can improve not only jury comprehension and performance, but juror satisfaction with their trial experience.

Challenging the current model

The Arizona Supreme Court's Committee on More Effective Use of Juries recognized these issues when it made 55 recommendations to reform the jury system, many of which resulted in the officially adopted comprehensive jury reform rules in 1995. In the introduction to *Jurors: The Power of 12,* its report to the supreme court, the Committee cited "unacceptably low levels of juror comprehension of the evidence" as one of the motivating factors in urging the Supreme Court to adopt its proposed jury reform rules.[9] Arizona's reforms, designed to make jurors active participants during the trial, include juror note taking, pre-deliberation discussions of evidence during civil trials, and the right of jurors to ask written questions. The Arizona reforms also permit judges greater latitude in exercising their inherent powers to provide to each juror preliminary and final written jury instructions, as well as to open up a dialogue between the jurors, the judge, and the lawyers when a jury believes it is deadlocked or needs assistance. The result has been increased satisfaction with the judicial process by judges, lawyers, jurors, and litigants.

For years, jury reforms such as note taking and question asking were opposed on the assumption that jurors would miss crucial pieces of evidence or assume the role of advocate rather than neutral fact-finder. The empirical evidence collected thus far, however, overwhelmingly indicates that such opportunities do not adversely affect the pace or outcome of trials.

It is intellectually arrogant for those in the legal system to assume that lay jurors are incapable of processing complex information. We have all been thrust into a technologically advanced world, and lawyers and judges are hardly better prepared for the task of sifting through scientific evidence than the jury. But common sense suggests that jury reform measures will aid understanding, and jurors themselves support reforms such as those described above.[10] We should recognize that it makes little sense to oppose practices that make jurors more comfortable with complex scientific information. To drive the point home, we have often made the observation that it is difficult to imagine an academic setting in which taking notes and asking questions would not be permitted.

Fortunately, the tides are beginning to shift in the debate over jury reform. Already a number of states are adopting new rules; Arizona, Colorado, and California are just a few.[11] In New York, much of the reform debate has centered on the selection, administration, and management of the jury, but substantive changes are not far behind. Reforms such as increased jury fees and security, and a juror hotline to report problems have been quite successful. However, the trend in these states and others is to expand beyond administrative concerns and attempt to improve jury deliberations and performance. These grassroots efforts led the American Bar Association in 1998 to adopt a number of jury reform ideals drafted by a Section of Litigation task force as part of its *Civil Trial Practice Standards.* In adopting these standards, the ABA recognized the need to provide juries, lawyers, and judges with the tools to increase jury comprehension in this era of increasingly complex evidentiary issues.

However, a complete overhaul of state and local jurisdictional rules is not necessary. These reforms can often be implemented, consistent with existing rules, at the discretion of the trial judge. Of course, when local rules conflict, those rules control, but most judges possess the inherent power to implement reforms in complex cases. For example, Rule 611 of the Federal (and Arizona) Rules of Evidence permit the judge to control the mode and order of questioning witnesses and presenting evidence. With the number of complex cases dramatically on the rise, judges and lawyers need to collaborate to help the jury become better fact-finders.

A practical guide

Many lawyers and judges seem to have forgotten the proper role of juries. Alexis de Tocqueville, the renowned historian, once said:

[t]he jury ... may be regarded as a gratuitous public school, ever open, in which every juror learns his rights, ... and becomes practically acquainted with the laws, which are brought within the reach of his capacity by the efforts of the bar, the advice of the judge, and even the passions of the parties ... I look upon the [the jury] as one of the most efficacious means for the education of the people which society can employ.[12]

It is this idea of educating the jury, of treating the courtroom as a classroom, that judges and lawyers alike need to recapture. We urge all members of the legal profession to implement, on their own initiative, the appropriate reforms when cases require an understanding of complex scientific evidence.

Before we discuss individual reforms in more detail, it is important to note the role of judges in rigorously applying the rules of evidence. The judge plays a very important role in improving jury comprehension by appropriately screening evidence and admitting only that which meets the appropriate standards. The judge must scrupulously protect the jury from unreliable scientific evidence.[13]

Jury selection. Lawyers are often criticized for using their peremptory challenges to "dumb down" the jury. In complex cases, however, it is in the best interest of all concerned to select educated jurors and not strike persons based on the extent of their education. While there is little empirical evidence to demonstrate that more educated jurors are struck more often than less educated jurors, there does seem to be an unwritten rule of practice that professionals should be struck when possible. The authors themselves plead guilty to using that approach as trial lawyers.

Perhaps lawyers fear that highly educated individuals will dominate in the jury room and be able to persuade the jury to their side during deliberations. However, preliminary data suggest, and we believe, that jurors take their job seriously and will not be easily persuaded to a position with which they do not agree.[14] Those lawyers who believe in "dumbing down" juries should adjust their views accordingly, and recognize the important role of jurors as fact finders and decision makers. Of course, both lawyers and judges must still attempt to detect jurors with prejudices or preconceived ideas, but they should also seek to empanel the best jurors available from the pool.

Juror note taking and notebooks. Of all the reforms discussed, allowing the jury to take notes during the trial must be the most common-sense and least controversial. Nevertheless many jurisdictions just don't get it. Research indicates that note taking does not distract jurors, nor does it create an undue influence on those jurors who choose not to take notes. Judges in Arizona instruct jurors that they are not obligated to take notes, and they tell the jury to pay attention to all aspects of the trial including witness demeanor and the documentary and testimonial evidence.

The vast majority of courts recognize that it is within the sound discretion of the trial judge to permit jurors to take notes. Judges need to thoughtfully exercise their discretion and allow juror note taking in complex cases, and lawyers must urge judges to do so. Jurors need to be encouraged to take an active role in the trial. Allowing the jury to keep track of parties, witnesses, testimony, and evidence by taking notes will empower juries to improve their recall and understanding of all issues, simple and complex.

Jurors in complex cases should also be given a comprehensive notebook containing items such as simplified jury instructions, layouts of the courtroom with the names and locations of lawyers and parties, and glossaries of scientific terms or helpful scientific diagrams, photographs, charts, and background data of all types.

Better jury instructions. Judges historically instruct juries at the end of the trial. There are few rules or cases, however, that prohibit judges from instructing juries earlier. Judges in Arizona provide juries with pretrial instructions that, for example, define the elements of the alleged crime or define terms such as "negligence" and "fault." This permits the jury to understand the basic legal standards early in the case, refer to them during the trial, and then concentrate on the presentation of the evidence.

Jury instructions should be written in plain English. When drafting jury instructions, both judges and lawyers should avoid unnecessary legal jargon. In Arizona, the state bar's Civil Jury Instruction Committee even includes a linguistics professor from a local university. Jury instructions must also be tailored to the case at trial. Instead of using only pattern jury instructions, judges should work with counsel to draft case-specific instructions that include party names and actual facts in the case, without commenting on the evidence. Instructions should be given early in the case both orally and in writing for maximum comprehension and memory retention. The written instructions should be included in the jury notebook. Jurors need to understand the legal context of the evidence presented, and early instruction facilitates a better understanding of its legal relevance.

Finally, jurors should each be given a written copy of the final instructions and they should be allowed to have the instructions in the deliberation room. Arizona's rules require judges to provide each juror with a copy of all the jury instructions. After all, why should jurors have to pass a single copy when a few dollars can provide copies all around? And where is it written that jury instructions must only be oral?

Permitting the jury to ask written questions. When it comes to issues of scientific evidence, lawyers and judges collaborate to understand and narrow the issues before the court. They ask each other questions to clarify misunderstandings prior to trial, and will confer even during the trial. Yet, once the trial begins, jurors traditionally are not permitted to ask questions. It is time to end this nonsensical practice.

Jury questions should be written and given to court personnel before the witness leaves the courtroom. Counsel should be given the opportunity to object in a sidebar, or outside the hearing of the jury, and the jury should be instructed about the limitations on questions that can be asked. In Arizona, there have been no reports of problems with this type of procedure after thousands of trials over the last four years. A study reported in the March-April 1996 issue of *Judicature* found that jury questions helped jurors understand the facts and issues, that jurors did not ask inappropriate questions, and that jurors did not draw inappropriate inferences when their questions, due to counsel's objection, for example, were not asked.[15]

As the comments to the *ABA Standards* noted, state and federal courts have overwhelmingly recognized that it is within the sound discretion of the trial judge to allow juror questioning of witnesses. We encourage judges and lawyers to experiment with jury questions in complex cases. The empirical evidence, and our own experience, reveals that the fears and concerns about jury questions are unfounded. As two Arizona attorneys recently wrote, "Our experience [with juror questions] reinforces for us the effectiveness of juror questions in keeping the jury engaged and in improving the quality of our own trial presentations. The jurors' questions

revealed areas of confusion or concern, enabling us to adjust our presentation accordingly."[16]

Juror discussion during civil trials. Perhaps one of the most controversial Arizona reforms at the time of its adoption, and still controversial today, is allowing jurors in civil cases to discuss the evidence prior to final deliberation. In Arizona, jurors are carefully instructed by the trial judge that they may discuss the case, so long as all members of the jury are present and they reserve judgment until final deliberations. The general consensus of the Arizona bench and bar is that this reform has been a success. In fact, the Committee on the More Effective Use of Jurors, in its second report to the Arizona Supreme Court (in June, 1998), recommended that the rules be expanded to allow pre-deliberation discussions during criminal trials. As of this writing, however, the supreme court has not adopted that recommendation.

Traditionally, the view has been that permitting jurors to discuss the evidence early in the trial will lead them to make up their minds before hearing both sides. Recent studies suggest that this is not true.[17] In fact, some studies have gone so far as to say that requiring jurors to refrain from discussing evidence actually hinders their ability to process information.[18] Pre-deliberation discussion can help improve juror comprehension, improve memory recall, and relieve the tension created by a forced atmosphere of silence with regard to the evidence presented at trial.[19]

Social scientists report that jurors naturally tend to actively process information as it is received. Therefore, it is not surprising to find that studies show that anywhere from 11 to 44 percent of jurors discuss the evidence among themselves during the trial despite judicial admonitions to avoid such discussion.[20] Explicitly allowing pre-deliberation discussions, then, is really an acknowledgment of what often occurs naturally.

Perhaps surprising to some, Arizona's experience has shown that when one individual juror makes a preliminary judgment during pre-deliberation discussions, that judgment is often tested or challenged by the entire group.[21] In *United States v. Wexler* (1987) Judge Ditter aptly explained that "jurors are concerned, responsible, conscientious citizens who take most seriously the job at hand." Like Judge Ditter, we believe the jurors are more interested in doing justice than in justifying their own loosely based preliminary conclusions, which are frequently subject to modification as a result of group discussions.

A recent study of jury discussions during Arizona trials found that jurors overwhelmingly support this reform and report that it has positive effects.[22] Specifically, jurors said that discussions improved comprehension of evidence, that all jurors' views were considered, and evidence was remembered accurately. Additionally, only a very low percentage of participants in the study said that trial discussions encouraged jurors to make up their minds early on. The study also found that, among judges, lawyers, and jurors, support for this reform increases with experience.

Permitting pre-deliberation discussion, more than any other reform, challenges the legal profession's traditional notions of jury behavior, but it is time to recognize the need for juries to have better tools in dealing with complex evidentiary issues.

Independent court appointed or stipulated experts. Unlike fingerprint or ballistic evidence, where it is easier to understand the samples juries are asked to compare, genetic evidence requires juries to sit through conflicting scientific interpretations from expert witnesses presented by the opposing parties. Early presentation of independent experts, either court appointed or stipulated, can help solve many of the problems presented by genetic evidence. Recent surveys suggest that judges favor appointing independent experts in complex cases. However, statistics show that the actual use of court appointed experts is relatively low.[23] This situation is unfortunate because there are many advantages to be realized by the use of independent experts. For example, a case involving the admissibility of DNA evidence using a particular type of analysis was recently before the Arizona Superior Court. Both parties agreed to the appointment of a neutral court expert to testify about the procedures used in this analytical method. Substantial saving, in time and money, were realized by the appointment of the court expert. Judicial economy and fairness demand the use of innovative techniques in dealing with admittedly complex scientific issues.

In most jurisdictions trial judges have inherent authority to appoint experts as technical advisors to assist the court. In fact, judges may appoint expert witnesses for testimonial purposes under Rule 706 of the Federal Rules of Evidence and similar provisions in force in most states. However, the use of court appointed experts to serve as a jury tutor on the basics of, for example, DNA evidence, is an under-utilized tool.[24] Pre-recorded video "lectures" may be another avenue to explore when considering how to educate jurors on issues of "common" scientific knowledge. The basic building blocks of DNA and the basic methods of DNA testing could be simplified and presented to the jury in such a fashion as to make it much less intimidating.[25]

Many lawyers may argue that "dueling experts" is the model courts should adhere to, based on the adversarial nature of our justice system. However, a recent study found that jurors do not rely on cross-examination of expert witnesses designed to point out flawed scientific methodology.[26] The authors suggest that this is because jurors do not believe lawyers are sincere in their attempts to educate jurors, but rather see cross-examination as the lawyer's attempt to undermine the expert through any means possible.

Independent experts present an opportunity to not only improve juror comprehension and performance, but also decrease the substantial costs of expert witnesses, and increase judicial economy. The adversarial nature of the trial may be diminished, but that is actually a benefit, not a cost, according to independent experts considering jury reactions to lawyer cross-examination of opposing party witnesses. It is the judge's responsibility to be proactive in ensuring that the trial is a search for the truth, and that it is not about lawyers setting up roadblocks to that search.

Allow a dialogue between jurors, lawyers, and the judge during deliberations. In place of the traditional "pep talk" judges often give to deadlocked juries, Arizona explicitly provides for an opportunity for further instruction by the judge and argument by the parties. Why should the opportunity to educate jurors further stop once deliberations begin? Allowing additional evidence, argument by counsel, or providing further instruction is not problematic, legally or pragmatically. Of course, judges must be careful not to influence jurors and need to limit further inquiries only to those issues that confuse or divide the jury. Once again, there are many cases approving the judge's inherent authority to reopen a case for additional evidence or argument where the jury needs further admissible evidence to reach a verdict, or to determine if a deadlock is unavoidable.[27]

Opening the courtroom to more creative learning. Increasingly, the Human Genome Project's Ethical, Legal and Social Implications Program is sensitizing the judicial and legal community about the changing rule of the law in light of new genetic discoveries and testing methods. Primers reviewing DNA and genome science have been written, memorable cartoon drawings simplify sophisticated concepts,[28] and video background resources explaining genetics in meaningful non-scientific ways are growing in number.

Further, difficult concepts can be reduced to plain English and conveyed to juries through innovative technologies, including live, videotaped, or interactive Internet-based testimony. These approaches can easily be presented while simultaneously ensuring that complex scientific evidence is afforded the utmost of seriousness.

Educating the jury early in the trial, by using court appointed experts, better written jury instructions, jury notebooks, and basic adult education techniques, will provide a foundation for later testimony of experts presented by the lawyers. Jurors who have been tutored early about complex scientific issues will be in a better position to judge both the content and character of dueling experts.

Who benefits?

Two central participants in the courtroom are the ultimate beneficiaries of reform-oriented jury approaches when heavy doses of scientific evidence are the subject of an unfolding courtroom drama: jurors, and more importantly, litigants. Contemporary behavioral research, and Arizona's jury reform experience, substantiate that comprehension and understanding are significantly enhanced when information is actively processed. Most courts already possess the tools to implement the educational techniques discussed above. Whether through system-wide jury reform or the efforts of individual trial judges and trial lawyers, a more jury-centered trial will not only allow jurors to actively and intelligently participate in the fact-finding and decision-making process, but also give the litigants a better truth-finding forum.

Notes

This article originally appeared in Volume 83, Number 3, November–December 1999, pages 150–156.

The authors wish to thank Timothy D. Keller, a law researcher for Judge Robert D. Myers, and Richard Teenstra, assistant director of the Maricopa County Superior Court Law Library, for their assistance.

1. Department of Energy, Office of Biological and Environmental Research, Life Sciences Division, *Human Genome Research: An Introduction* (visited Sept. 2, 1999) (www.er.doe.gov/production/ober/hug_top.html).

2. Denno, "Legal Implications of Genetics and Crime Research, in Bock and Goode, eds., *Genetics of Criminal and Antisocial Behaviour* (Chichester, N.Y.: Wiley, 1996), 235.

3. *See* Arizona Supreme Court Orders, Nos. R-94-0031, R-92-004 (1995).

4. *See* Adler, *The Jury: Trial and Error in the American Courtroom* (New York: Times Books, 1994); *Jury Comprehension in Complex Cases: Report of a Special Committee of the ABA Litgation Section* (Chicago: American Bar Association, 1989).

5. For a review of criticisms of civil jury competencies and the jury research literature, *see* Lempert, "Civil Juries and Complex Cases: Taking Stock after Twelve Years," in Litan, ed., *Verdict: Assessing the Civil Jury System* (Washington, D.C.: Brookings Institution, 1993), 181–247; Vidmar, "The Performance of the American Civil Jury: An Empirical Perspective," *Ariz. L. Rev.* 40 (1998), 849; Cecil, Hans and Wiggins, "Citizen Comprehension of Difficult Issues: Lessons from Civil Jury Trials," *Am. U. L. Rev.* 40 (1991), 727.

6. Hans, Hannaford, and Munsterman, "The Arizona Jury Reform Permitting Civil Jury Trial Discussions: The Views of Trial Participants, Judges, and Jurors," *U. Mich. J.L. Reform* 32 (1999), 349.

7. *See* Dann, " 'Learning Lessons' and 'Speaking Rights': Creating Educated and Democratic Juries," *Ind. L.J.* 68 (1993), 1229.

8. Cecil, Hans, and Wiggins, *supra* n. 5, at 765.

9. *Jurors: The Power of 12*, Report of the Arizona Supreme Court Committee On More Effective Use of Juries (November 1994).

10. Hans, Hannaford, and Munsterman, *supra* n. 6, at 371–372.

11. For a review of state jury reform efforts, *see* Munsterman, "A brief history of state jury reform efforts," *Judicature* 79 (1996), 216; Murphy et al, *Managing Notorious Trials* (Williamsburg, Va.: National Center for State Courts, 1998); *Enhancing the Jury System: A Guidebook for Jury Reform* (Chicago: American Judicature Society, 1999).

12. de Tocqueville, *Democracy in America* (Vintage ed. 1945), 295–296.

13. *Daubert v. Merrell Dow Pharm. Inc.,* 509 U.S. 579 (1993).

14. Hans, Hannaford, and Munsterman, *supra* n. 6.

15. Heuer and Penrod, "Increasing juror participation in trials through note taking and question asking," *Judicature* 79 (1996), 256, 260–261.

16. Cabot and Coleman, "Arizona's 1995 Jury Reform Can be Deemed a Success," *Arizona Journal,* July 12, 1999, at 6.

17. *See* Hans, Hannaford, and Munsterman, *supra* n. 6; Hannaford, Hans, and Munsterman, "Permitting Jury Discussions During Trial: Impact of the Arizona Reform" 9 (1998) (unpublished manuscript, on file with the authors).

18. Chilton and Henley, "Improving the Jury System, Jury Instructions: Helping Jurors Understand the Evi-

dence and the Law," §II, *PLRI Reports* (Spring 1996) (www. uchastings.edu/plri/spr96tex/juryinst.html).

19. Hans, Hannaford, and Munsterman, *supra* n. 6; Hannaford, Hans, and Munsterman, *supra* n. 17; Chilton and Henley, *supra* n. 18.

20. Chilton and Henley, *supra* n. 18.

21. Myers and Griller, "Educating Jurors Means Better Trials: Jury Reform in Arizona," *Judges J.* 36 (Fall 1997), 13–17, 51.

22. Hans, Hannaford, and Munsterman, *supra* n. 6.

23. Sanders, "Scientifically Complex Cases, Trial by Jury, and the Erosion of Adversarial Processes," *DePaul L. Rev.* 48 (1998), 355, 378–379.

24. *The Evaluation of Forensic DNA Evidence* (Washington, D.C.: National Research Council, 1996), 169–171.

25. For examples of excellent illustrations and explanations, *see* Hoagland and Dotson, *The Way Life Works* (New York: Time Books, 1995).

26. Kovera, McAuliff, and Hebert, "Reasoning About Scientific Evidence: Effects of Juror Gender and Evidence Quality on Juror Decisions in a Hostile Work Environment Case," *J. of Applied Psychology* 84 (1999), 362, 372–373.

27. Myers and Griller, *supra* n. 21, at 16–17.

28. *See* Hoagland and Dotson, *supra* n. 25.

Scientific jury selection: what social scientists know and do not know

Shari Seidman Diamond

The effects of scientific jury selection are modest at best. Social science consultants offer the most valuable aid when they help attorneys develop trial presentations that are clear and convincing.

A jury is rarely unanimous when it takes its first vote,[1] but its final verdict is generally the decision initially favored by a majority of the jurors.[2] If the voir dire in a close case replaces only a few jurors who would favor one side with jurors who will favor the opposing side, jury selection can be critical. A voir dire that shifts the distribution of jurors to create a new majority can dramatically affect the probability of a favorable verdict.

The evidence presented at trial cannot account for initial disagreements among jurors: all jurors are exposed to the same evidence. The differences in juror reaction must stem from pre-existing differences among the jurors that affect juror responses to the evidence.[3] If "scientific jury selection" (SJS) can help identify attributes of unfriendly jurors in advance, the attorney can exercise peremptory challenges to remove those jurors during voir dire. The prospect is enticing: what litigator faced with the uncertainties of trial would not appreciate a little assistance?

Before 1970, attorneys had to rely solely on their personal and trial experience with people and on their knowledge of their cases to develop voir dire questions and weed out unsympathetic jurors. The expert advice available from various trial specialists offered conflicting guidance.[4] A survey of litigators showed similarly inconsistent philosophies in jury selection.[5] Against this background of inconsistency, social scientists have offered their assistance, claiming a scientific basis for the advice they offer.

SJS began when the Berrigan brothers, two anti-war activist priests, were put on trial for conspiring to kidnap then Secretary of State Henry Kissinger. Sociologist Jay Schulman and his colleagues assisted the defense in selecting the jury that hung 10 to 2 for acquittal. In the early days of SJS, the method was used largely in political criminal cases that involved substantial publicity. Prospective jurors in those cases often had strong preconceived notions about the defendants or the alleged offense. More recently, an active consulting industry has applied SJS to a wide variety of criminal and civil actions.

Methods of SJS

A primary research method used in SJS is a telephone survey in which members of the public who would be eligible to serve as jurors are asked three sets of questions. One set asks for the respondent's background characteristics (age, sex, occupation, prior jury service, prior experience as an accident victim if the case involves personal injury, etc.). The attorneys will be able to obtain this same information on each prospective juror during the voir dire.

The second set of questions on the survey may or may not be asked during voir dire. This set measures beliefs and attitudes that are likely to be associated with a favorable or unfavorable trial verdict (a dislike of oil companies or of the particular oil company which is the defendant; for a malpractice case, the belief that doctors generally do what is best for their patients).

The third set of questions directly attempts to assess which side the respondent would favor in the trial. A brief description of the case is read and the respondent is asked to vote as if on a jury deciding the case.

The jury consultant then analyzes the responses to the survey to determine which juror characteristics correlate with favorable attitudes and verdict preferences, and which attitudes and beliefs correlate with verdict preferences. This information is used to create juror profiles to guide jury selection.

Researchers may also develop selection profiles by testing respondents at research facilities. Respondents are shown opening statements or full mock trials. When they are brought into a testing facility respondents can be exposed to a better approximation of what the trial will actually involve and can be questioned more extensively than when they are tested in a telephone survey. To the extent that the simulation accurately portrays the crucial elements of the trial as it will

Judicature Volume 73, Number 4, pp. 178–183

unfold, the verdict preferences in the simulation will more accurately reflect juror reactions to the trial than the preferences expressed in the telephone survey.

The disadvantage of tests in a research facility is that a telephone survey can test a much larger and more representative sample at a much lower cost per respondent. One large jury consulting firm uses a facility for mock trials in a north suburb of Chicago. Respondents cannot easily get to the location without a car and, not surprisingly, inner city residents who appear on the jury rolls do not appear at this facility. While facilities for mock trials can be more carefully chosen, representativeness is easier to obtain in a telephone survey because more potential respondents are willing to answer a few questions over the phone than attend a testing facility. Because each method has disadvantages, SJS often relies on a combination of telephone surveys and mock trials.

The primary test of any jury selection technique is whether it can predict, based on information available before challenges must be exercised, how jurors will react to the evidence presented at trial. For SJS there is an additional test: assuming that SJS does have some predictive power, under what conditions does the 'scientific' method outperform the more intuitive method of jury selection traditionally used by the trial attorney?

There is significant disagreement in the legal and scientific communities about the answers to both of these questions. In this article, I analyze the evidence for and against the claims made for SJS. After concluding that the approach can have a modest effect at best and that it can *decrease* as well as *increase* the probability of a favorable verdict, I outline some methods the trial attorney can use to test the value of the advice a consultant offers in a particular case. Finally, I suggest that the emphasis on SJS as the key social science tool in trial preparation is misplaced. The primary determinant of the jury's outcome is the evidence, and social science consultants offer the most valuable aid when they help the attorney to develop a trial presentation that is clear and convincing.

Effect of SJS

The consultants who offer selection advice are quick to point to cases in which the winning side used SJS techniques. While such victories are not unusual, no one has yet produced convincing evidence that advice on jury selection made the difference. The demands of the courtroom preclude a full controlled test of the

technique in the courtroom setting. In the ideal test of SJS, a series of cases would be tried before multiple juries, some 'scientifically' selected and others traditionally chosen. A comparison of the verdicts rendered by the two types of juries would test the value of the method.[6] This direct test of SJS has not yet been done.

The early pioneers in SJS conducted some indirect tests. Schulman and his colleagues[7] interviewed jurors who were excused during voir dire or jury eligible community members who did not go through jury selection at all. They compared the verdict preferences of these potential jurors with those given by the jury that decided the case, that is, a jury selected with the help of SJS. The flaw in such tests is that only the real jurors have sat through the case and heard all of the evidence—those excused or never called have not. As nearly every study of jury decisionmaking indicates, the evidence presented at trial is the primary determinant of a jury verdict.[8] Accordingly, verdicts of the actual jury and the excused or never called jurors may differ, not because of the selection strategy, but because they are responses to different evidence.

In an interesting attempt to conduct a controlled test of the effects of SJS, Horowitz trained law students in either SJS or the traditional clinical approach to jury selection.[9] The law students then used the assigned technique to conduct a voir dire. Those trained to use SJS were given data from a survey of prospective jurors to guide their jury selection.

All of the prospective jurors, whether chosen or rejected, listened to the case and indicated their preferred verdicts. Horowitz then evaluated how well each method performed by examining the verdict preferences of the jurors selected by each method. On two of the four cases, the law students who used SJS made more accurate choices than those who used the traditional approach; on one case the students using the traditional approach were more accurate and on the remaining case there was no difference.

These results suggest that superior performance by SJS occurs in some, but not all, cases. The results, however, may not generalize beyond law student-attorneys. It is not clear whether the SJS method used in these cases fully replicated the range of questions used by other SJS practitioners; it is certainly clear that the law students lacked the training and experience of many trial attorneys.

SJS uses juror characteristics to predict verdict preferences and thus inform selection choices. Accordingly, a test of the foundations of SJS is the extent to which juror characteristics which predict juror verdicts can be identified. In one such study, Saks measured 461 Ohio jurors on 27 attitudes and background characteristics.[10] His respondents then watched a videotaped burglary trial and deliberated to a verdict. The best predictor of juror verdict preferences was whether a juror believed that crime was mainly the product of "bad people" or "bad social condition."[11] That question accounted for a modest 9 percent of the variance in verdict preferences.[12] Only three other predictors improved the prediction—and together the four predictors accounted for less than 13 percent of the variance in juror verdict preferences.

Penrod tested 367 Massachusetts jurors on 21 attitude and background characteristics and then had them indicate verdict preferences in three criminal cases and one civil case.[13] One predictor accounted for 7 percent of the variance in verdict preferences on the rape case: jurors who favored conviction were more likely to agree that there should be evidence of physical resistance before a defendant is convicted of rape. The best predictors were able to account for about 14 percent of the variance on the murder case, 16 percent on the rape, under 10 percent on the negligence case and under 5 percent on the robbery. Juror verdict preferences on one case did not predict verdict preferences on any of the other three cases and the best predictors of verdict were not the same across the four cases.

Hastie et al. showed 828 jurors the videotaped reenactment of a real murder trial.[14] Four of the 12 background characteristics of the jurors were significant predictors of verdict preferences; they accounted for 3.2 percent of the variance in verdicts. A sub-sample of 269 jurors was tested on a number of additional background characteristics and attitudes. With these additional predictors, Hastie et al. were able to explain 11 percent of the variance in juror verdicts.

In an effort to predict juror verdicts in real trials, Moran and Comfort mailed questionnaires to jurors who just completed jury service.[15] They obtained responses from 319 jurors who reported what their verdict preferences had been when they began deliberating as jurors, answered questions on 11 background characteristics and filled out 13 opinion/personality scales. Two of the personality measures explained 11 percent of the variation in verdict preferences for female jurors; no other variable increased the accuracy of the prediction. For males, only one measure was

a significant predictor of verdict preference and it explained 6 percent.

Other studies have shown similar or lower correlations between predictors and verdict preferences.[16] While each of the studies reviewed here suffers from some limitations, the pattern of results is consistent. The most important implication of this research is that claims for predicting juror responses to trial evidence should be modest indeed. The studies reviewed here report an ability to account for up to 15 percent of the variation in juror verdict preferences.

It is, of course, possible that more powerful attitudinal measures can be developed, but there is good reason to be skeptical about the potential of SJS to improve selection decisions substantially. Assuming that more powerful attitudinal measures are available or can be developed, the measures will be valuable for jury selection only if they can be administered in court. The courtroom version of an attitude scale is a crude cousin to the sensitive measure that shows predictive power in the preparatory research. A reliable measure of attitude is generally composed of a set of questions which each respondent answers independently. In the courtroom, judges will not ask or permit attorneys to ask each potential juror the 17 questions that form the measure of empathy.[17] Even if jurors are questioned individually, they are exposed to the responses of other jurors to those same questions and their answers may be affected by those earlier responses. Moreover, courts do not permit voir dire questions unless they appear logically relevant to the case. For example, while juror support for the death penalty is consistently associated with a greater willingness to convict,[18] the question can only be asked in capital cases. Attorneys who use the results of SJS in the courtroom must thus decide which jurors to excuse based on abbreviated tests of attitudes distorted by the public arena in which they are expressed.

The national trend is toward a limited voir dire, often conducted almost entirely by the judge.[19] Under these conditions, the predictors from SJS that will be available to the attorney during jury selection will be confined to background characteristics that appear to offer limited predictive power. Even if the judge agrees to ask some of the additional questions proposed by the attorneys, the judge may change the wording so that they lose all predictive power.[20]

A second implication of the research on jury selection is that there is no profile of the good defense (or prosecution or plaintiff) juror that can be used across cases. Characteristics that emerge as predictors on one case do not show the same pattern on another case. Jurors who are most favorable to the defense in one trial will not necessarily make the best defense jurors in another trial. This is not particularly surprising. Psychologists have spent years trying to predict behavior and the results have revealed only modest levels of consistency across situations.[21] The jury consultant who provides a profile of the good defense juror suitable for all cases and applicable to all communities is offering the most blatant voodoo voir dire advice.

Finally, research on jury selection indicates that the survey efforts of SJS will not improve the accuracy of jury selection in every case. In some cases, a jury consultant may even be less accurate than the trial attorney operating without consultant advice. Statistical prediction is usually, but not always, more accurate than clinical prediction.[22] The trial attorney knows the evidence in the case, both on the client's and on the opposition's side, better than does the consultant. In addition, the attorney operating in a familiar court may be able to use the incidental information that emerges during voir dire (e.g., the strike at a local business where a prospective juror is employed). The attorney can eliminate some hostile jurors without expert advice.[23] Accordingly, the attorney should accept advice from a survey formula for jury selection only when provided with hard evidence that the advice offers the genuine prospect of improved prediction.

Testing the consultant's advice

Consultants using SJS typically test the predictive power of a large battery of juror beliefs, attitudes and background characteristics that the consultants, the parties, and the attorneys think may be related to verdict preferences: publications read, frequency of watching the news, age, gender, number of children, occupation, marital status, income, prior jury service, attitudes toward big corporations, etc. Each of these possible predictors is compared with the juror's preferred verdict.[24] The juror characteristics that are statistically significant predictors of preferred verdicts are then included in the juror profile that will be used during jury selection.

As an example, a jury survey done in preparation for a personal injury case includes 40 potential predictors. The consultant analyzes the results of the survey and reports that males are significantly more likely to favor a verdict for the plaintiff than females; respondents who think that people generally get what they deserve are significantly more likely to favor the defense. Both relationships are significant at the traditional .05 probability level.[25] No other characteristics are significant predictors.

Any use of these results in selecting a jury would be like basing predictions on patterns in a roulette wheel. A relationship is statistically significant at the traditional .05 level if there is one chance in 20 that the result would occur in the absence of any relationship between the predictor and the verdict preference. Thus, if all 40 predictors were totally unrelated to verdict preferences, 1 in 20 or 2 of those predictors would show a significant relationship to verdict preference.[26]

Such explorations for relationships are often referred to as "fishing." They may disclose unexpected relationships between juror characteristics and verdict preferences; they may also turn up "relationships" that are simply due to chance and which will not exist when they are applied to the next set of jurors—the ones at trial. Fortunately, there are several ways to test before trial how likely it is that a relationship revealed in the survey is due to chance.[27]

First, if the number of significant predictors exceeds the number expected by chance, then the most powerful of these are likely to reflect reliable relationships.[28] Thus, if gender, age, and attitude toward oil companies are the three predictors out of 40 that are significant, it is likely that only one of the three is a dependable predictor. A consultant can easily produce the probability levels and effect sizes associated with each predictor to assess which predictor deserves attention.

Second, reliable prediction models should be reproducible on new samples. A consultant should be prepared to demonstrate that the prediction model produced from one half of the respondents in a survey can explain responses by the remaining respondents to the survey, or a new set of respondents if more than one survey is conducted. A statistical model that is based on the vagaries of sample selection or other chance elements will not produce robust results that explain the behavior or a new set of respondents. In one test of the reliability of a selection model, Baker[29] tested 18 potential predictors to produce a model with four predictors that explained 11 percent of the variance on a measure of conviction. When tested on a new sample of respondents, respondents that the model predicted would be pro-conviction did not have higher conviction scores than those the model predicted would be anti-conviction. The model was a complete failure.

Finally, when mock juries or focus groups are held after the survey results are in, it is possible to test the consultant's model prospectively and compare it with the attorney's prediction.[30] A mock trial exposes simulated jurors to opening statements or abbreviated trial enactments. The jurors answer background questions before the mock trial takes place. They also fill out questionnaires during and after the evidence is presented. After the fact, it often seems obvious why particular jurors turned out to be pro-plaintiff or pro-defendant; the key is whether those predictions can be made before the juror's verdict preference is known. The attorney who plans to use the advice of a consultant can arrange a test in which both attorney and consultant make predictions about the likely responses of prospective jurors. If attorney and consultant use the juror background questionnaires to predict juror verdicts and the survey results do not guide the consultant to more favorable jurors, the attorney should seriously question the value of the consultant's advice in jury selection.[31]

The other role for social science

Some jury consultants are well aware of the weakness of much of their selection advice. Yet prospective clients are often eager to believe that consultants can reduce the uncertain prospect of a hostile jury and consultants are naturally reluctant to reject a friendly marketing opportunity. The result is that the client gets selection advice. In addition, however, the consultant may in the process provide other services that substantially enhance the client's position at trial. These include support for a motion for change of venue or expansive voir dire, and assistance in identifying arguments jurors will and will not find persuasive.

Change of venue. When, because of pretrial publicity or the identity of one of the parties, prospective jurors in the community may have strong preconceived notions about the facts of the case or deeply held biases towards one of the parties, a party may seek a change of venue. Evidence in the form of a community survey is one standard way to demonstrate the extent of community knowledge about the case and the prospects of a biased jury pool. It is crucial that the consultant used to conduct such a survey be able to testify competently that appropriate random sampling techniques were used to identify respondents for the survey, and that the responses were verified according to the usual survey standards.[32]

Even if the court denies a motion for a change of venue, evidence of potential prejudice may persuade the court to expand the questioning of prospective jurors during the voir dire, may convince the court that individual as opposed to group questioning is appropriate and may increase the willingness of the court to grant challenges for cause when a juror gives some sign of predisposition in the case.

Clarity and persuasiveness of the evidence. The focus on SJS neglects the key determinant of trial outcomes: the evidence. In studies that have measured the contributions of juror characteristics and trial testimony to jury verdicts, the trial testimony dominates. For example, Visher[33] studied the judgments of defendant guilt by 340 jurors in actual trials for sexual assault. She was able to explain nearly half the variation in the juror's judgments: evidence factors accounted for 34 percent of the variance, victim and defendant characteristics accounted for an additional 8 percent, and jurors' characteristics and attitudes accounted for only 2 percent.[34]

The litigator has limited control over the potential evidence in a case, but litigation can involve massive amounts of potential evidence. No jury can absorb every piece of evidence that could be, or even is, presented at trial. The litigator must decide how to distill the mass of information and organize it in a framework that will be maximally intelligible and convincing. The structure provided in opening statements helps the jury organize the evidence and guides the jury's thinking during the trial.[35]

Experienced trial attorneys are skilled communicators, but they cannot see the themes of the dispute through the eyes of the juror. A pretrial test of juror reactions to the facts of the case and arguments that both sides are expected to make can provide a crucial warning that the message is unclear, that the theme initially selected is not plausible, that jurors will be bothered or unconvinced by parts of the message or that jurors are troubled by missing information that could be supplied.

By comparing the reactions of jurors to various versions of the opening statement, the consultant can help the attorney to construct the clearest and most persuasive statement of the client's position. For example, damages in the form of a firm's lost profits may be computed by showing past earnings and extrapolating into the future or by providing data on the profits of another comparable firm. A trial simulation compares jurors' reactions to the two damage models in order to determine which damage model should be emphasized at trial, and whether the presentation of both models undermines or increases the credibility of the damage estimate. Similar questions about issues like the ordering of witnesses and the best way to present statistical data can be explored before trial.

The consultant provides this feedback by selecting lay respondents representative of those who will serve as jurors in the trial, running the focus groups or trial simulations and designing appropriate questions and questionnaires to measure juror reactions. The consultant may also help prepare opening statements and trial presentation materials, ensuring in particular that the opposition's case is powerfully presented. The attorneys can watch the simulated juries as they deliberate or the focus groups as they are questioned, or they may get transcripts or videos of the juror's discussions and reports on their questionnaire responses.[36] Whether formal or informal, these "dry runs" are nearly always instructive for the attorneys. After all, aside from verdicts and an occasional question to the jurors after a verdict comes in, few attorneys have had the opportunity to get direct feedback on their courtroom attempts to persuade.

Conclusions

Attorneys are professional critics of evidence. Why then are they willing to accept the advice of consultants on jury selection so uncritically? For most attorneys, the jury is the unknown element in the trial process. The jury trial takes place precisely because the parties do not agree what the jury's verdict will be. And, unlike the judge, a jury has no reputation before the trial begins and has made no previous rulings in the case. Silent throughout the trial, the jury has the last word.[37]

The attorney preparing to select a jury at the beginning of a trial thus confronts an uncertain outcome. The active attorney, attempting to achieve control, culls his or her store of knowledge for useful counsel, some of it based on experience and logic, and some of it based on folklore, superstition, and magic.[38] Scientific magic in the form of SJS may reduce dysfunctional stress or simply appease a client who wants to be assured that every available tool has been used to prepare for trial. Significant harm is unlikely and there may be some improvement in the use of challenges if the attorney does not simply turn the decisionmaking responsibility over to the consultant or forget that evidence, far more than jury selection, determines trial outcomes.

If the effects of SJS are generally modest at best, what promise does the method offer for jury selection, apart from its value as a placebo to build litigant and attorney confidence? It is likely that SJS can in some cases affect the proportion of jurors who favor a particular verdict, just as in some cases the peremptory challenges exercised by attorneys can make a difference.[39] The difficulty is that we currently have no reliable way to identify which cases will be amenable to SJS, so that at this point we cannot be sure when the effort will justify the expense.[40] When enormous sums of money are at risk so that even a small increase in the probability of one more favorable juror represents a major achievement, a cost-benefit analysis may justify the investment in SJS despite the uncertainty. In most other cases, the uncertainty suggests a challenge for jury consultants: to demonstrate when and how their techniques are predictive. Until such documentation is provided, the attorney who considers hiring such a consultant needs to be a vigilant and critical consumer of the services that are offered.

Notes

This article originally appeared in Volume 73, Number 4, December–January 1990, pages 178–183.

I am indebted to many people, for I have watched the development and practice of scientific jury selection as an academic psychologist, practicing attorney, and consultant. Among those who shared their views with me along the way (but are in no way responsible for mine) are Geraldine M. Alexis, Philip J. Crihfield, Reid Hastie, Richard Lempert, Henry L. Mason III, Thomas Munsterman, Arthur Patterson, Zick Rubin, and Sarah Tanford. I am grateful for their insights and suggestions.

1. Kalven and Zeisel, *The American Jury* (Boston: Little Brown, 1966).

2. Ibid.; Zeisel and Diamond, "The Effect of Peremptory Challenges on Jury and Verdict: An Experiment in a Federal District Court," *Stan. L. Rev.* 491 (1978), 30; *also see* Davis, "Group Decision and Procedural Justice" in Fishbein (ed.) *Progress In Social Psychology,* Vol. 1 (Hillsdale, N.J.: Erlbaum, 1980); Penrod and Hastie, "Models of Jury Decision Making: A Critical Review," *Psy. Bull.* 86 (1979), 462.

3. Diamond and Zeisel, "Jury Behavior" in *Encyclopedia Of Crime And Justice* (New York: Macmillan, 1983).

4. *E.g.,* Darrow ("Attorney for the Defense," *Esquire,* May 1936) counseled defense attorneys to avoid women jurors, while Katz ("The Twelve Man Jury," *Trial* 42 [1969–1970], 39) considered women to be favorable defense jurors unless the defendant was a woman.

5. Kallen, "Peremptory Challenges Based upon Juror Background—A Rational Use?" *Trial Lawyer's Guide* 13 (1969), 37.

6. This research design was approximated in a test of the accuracy of traditional attorney jury selection (Diamond and Zeisel, "A Courtroom Experiment on Jury Selection and Decision-Making," *Personality and Soc. Psy. Bull.* 1 (1974), 276; Zeisel and Diamond, *supra* n. 2). In that study, the jurors excused by either side were retained to form a separate jury that stayed through the case and deliberated to a verdict. The results indicated that, using traditional selection methods, defense attorneys in some cases increased their odds of winning as a result of their choices during voir dire.

7. Schulman et al., "Recipe for a Jury," *Psychology Today* 37 (June 1973); Kairys et al., *The Jury System: New Methods For Reducing Jury Prejudice* (Philadelphia: National Jury Project, 1975).

8. *E.g.,* Lafree et al., "Jurors' Responses to Victims' Behavior and Legal Issues in Sexual Assault Trials," *Soc. Prob.* 32 (1985), 389.

9. Horowitz, "Juror Selection: A Comparison of Two Methods in Several Criminal Cases," *J. App. Psy.* 10 (1980), 86.

10. Saks, *Jury Verdicts: The Role of Group Size and Social Decision Rule* (Lexington, Mass.: Lexington, 1977).

11. Interestingly, people who believed that crime was primarily the product of bad social conditions were *more* likely to regard the defendant as guilty.

12. When jurors differ in their verdict preferences, the measure of that variability is referred to as 'variance'. If a juror characteristic or belief can help to predict jurors' verdict preferences, it is said to explain part of the variance. The more powerful the predictor or set of predictors, the higher the proportion of the variance explained and the more accurate the prediction. Explained variation in principle can be as low as 0 or as high as 100 percent.

13. Penrod, "Study of Attorney and 'Scientific' Jury Selection Models." Unpublished Doctoral Dissertation, Harvard University (1980).

14. Hastie et al., *Inside the Jury* (Cambridge: Harvard University Press, 1983).

15. Moran and Comfort, "Scientific Juror Selection: Sex as a Moderator of Demographic and Personality Predictors of Impaneled Felony Juror Behavior," *J. Pers. Soc. Psy.* 43 (1982), 1052.

16. *E.g.,* Simon, *The Jury and the Defense of Insanity* (Boston: Little Brown, 1967); Berg and Vidmar, "Authoritarianism and Recall of Evidence about Criminal Behavior," *J. of Research in Personality* 9 (1975), 147; Buckhout et al., "Discretion in Jury Selection" in Abt and Stuart (eds.), *Social Psychology and Discretionary Law* (New York: Van Nostrand Reinhold, 1979); Bridgeman and Marlowe, "Jury Decisionmaking: An Empirical Study Based on Actual Felony Trial," *J. of Applied Psy.* 64 (1979), 91; Mills and Bohannon, "Juror characteristics: to what extent are they related to jury verdict?," *Judicature* 64 (1980), 23.

17. Moran and Comfort, *supra* n. 15.

18. *See, e.g.,* Cowan et al., "The Effects of Death Qualification on Jurors' Predisposition to Convict and on the Quality of Deliberation," *Law & Hum. Behav.* 8 (1984), 53.

19. Berman and Shapard, "The Voir Dire Examination: Juror Challenges and Adversary Advocacy in Sales (ed.), *Perspectives in law and Psychology, Vol. 2: The Trial Process* (New York: Plenum, 1981); Van Dyke, *Jury Selection Procedures* (Cambridge, Mass.: Ballinger, 1977). Some evidence indicates that jurors are less candid about their attitudes when a judge conducts the voir dire than when the attorneys conduct the voir dire (Jones, "Judge-Versus Attorney-Conducted Voir Dire: An Empirical Investigation of Juror Candor," *Law & Hum. Behav.* 11 [1987]), 131. As a result, the trend toward judge-conducted voir dire should reduce the reliable information available to counsel during jury selection.

20. Some courts permit the parties to submit questions that the jurors answer in writing before selection begins. This procedure of course standardizes the questions and permits parallel analysis of the survey and the responses to the court questionnaire.

21. Mischel, *Personality and Assessment* (New York: Wiley, 1968).

22. Meehl, "When Shall We Use Our Heads Instead of the Formula?" *J. of Counseling Psy.* 4 (1957), 268; Kleinmuntz, "Why We Still Use Our Heads Instead of Formulas: Toward an Integrative Approach," *Psychological Bulletin.* Human judges make systematic errors when they gather and combine information to make prediction (Dawes, "A Case Study of Graduate Admissions: Application of Three Principles of Human Decision Making," *Am. Psychologist* 26 [1971], 180; Dawes, "The Robust Beauty of Improper Linear Models in Decision Making," *Am. Psychologist* 34 [1979], 571), but even this imperfect decisionmaking can be superior to a computer model if the model omits predictors that the human decisionmaker can use.

23. Diamond and Zeisel, *supra* n. 6; Zeisel and Diamond, *supra* n. 2.

24. A proxy for the verdict preferences may be a factor score that summarizes a series of responses to questions that are expected to indicate which side the juror is likely to favor.

25. Scientific research generally accepts a difference between two groups on some measure (e.g., the verdict preferences of males versus females) as real if a difference as big as that shown in the research would occur less than five chances in a hundred if there was no real difference between the two groups on that measure.

26. The same problem arises when multiple predictors are simultaneously tested in a multiple regression analysis

and no adjustment is made in the explained variance or R2. The probability of 'discovering' relationships due to chance is even greater when AID (automatic interaction detector) is used to test combinations of predictors (Berk et al., "The Vagaries and Vulgarities of Scientific Jury Selection: A Methodological Evaluation," *Evaluation Q.* 1 [1977], 143). Moreover, unless sample sizes far exceed the usual 300–500 respondents typically tested in jury selection surveys, predictions about the behavior of jurors based on combinations of characteristics (e.g., female physicians) will be highly unreliable.

27. One of the reviewers suggested that no consultant would agree to cooperate with the tests proposed in this section. Markets and clients, however, determine what suppliers are willing to provide.

28. Berk et al., *supra* n. 26.

29. Baker, "Conviction Proneness as a Predictor of Sworn Jury Decisions." Unpublished Doctoral Dissertation, C.U.N.Y. (1984).

30. To adequately conduct such a test it is necessary to have a sufficient number of jurors participate in the mock trial. Even when SJS assists in selection, it only improves the odds. As a result, SJS may not appear to cause any increment in predictability in a test with a small sample, while in a large sample a genuine improvement could be detected.

31. It may be desirable to conduct a simulated voir dire before the trial simulation, but such an elaborate approach is costly in both attorney and juror time.

32. *See* National Jury Project, *Jurywork: Systematic Techniques* (New York: Clark Boardman, 1986), chap. 7, for a good discussion of motions for change of venue.

33. Visher, "Juror Decision Making: The Importance of Evidence," *Law & Hum. Behav.* 11 (1987), 1.

34. *See* Saks and Hastie, *Social Psychology in Court* (New York: Van Nostrand Reinhold, 1978), chap. 3, for a review of research that demonstrates the dominant effect of evidence on jury verdicts.

35. Wrightsman and his colleagues have studied the way that the timing and content of opening statements can affect verdict preferences (Pyszczynski and Wrightman, "The Effects of Opening Statements on Mock Jurors' Verdicts in a Simulated Criminal Trial," *J. of Applied Soc. Psy.* 301 [1981], 11; Wells, Wrightsman & Miene, "The Timing of the Defense Opening Statement: Don't Wait Until the Evidence is in," *J. of Applied Soc. Psy.* 15 [1985], 758). They suggest that an opening statement sets up a thematic framework that guides jurors in their processing and interpretation of subsequent testimony and evidence.

36. With little or no assistance from a consultant, an attorney can also obtain a low cost, informal reading on prospective juror reaction. Consultants generally sub-contract to field services in the city where the trial is to take place. The field service obtains respondents who are eligible for jury service according to the specifications of the consultant. Attorneys who, for example, want to try out an opening statement before a jury-eligible audience can use these same field services to obtain respondents. It may, however, be useful to use the services of a consultant to probe juror reactions.

37. The exception is that rare case in which the jury's verdict is so inconsistent with the evidence that the court sets it aside.

38. Saks, "Blaming the Jury," *Geo. L. J.* 75 (1986), 693.

39. Diamond and Zeisel, *supra* n. 6; Zeisel and Diamond, *supra* n. 2.

40. Two requirements appear to be an opportunity for extensive voir dire and subject matter about which prospective jurors have substantial experience or strong opinions.

The capital jury: is it tilted toward death?

William J. Bowers

Preliminary findings from the Capital Jury Project indicate that jurors make life and death punishment decisions early in the trial, misunderstand sentencing guidelines, and often deny their responsibility for the punishment given to a defendant.

How the capital jury should make the grave life or death sentencing decision has been the subject of two decades of capital jurisprudence. The U.S. Supreme Court's dissatisfaction with what the plurality found to be the "arbitrary," "capricious," and "standardless" manner in which the decision to impose the death penalty was being made, as articulated in *Furman v. Georgia*,[1] brought the use of capital punishment to a halt in 1972. And it was the efforts of states to reform the capital sentencing process by guiding jurors' exercise of sentencing discretion that revived the death penalty and has become the focus of vastly expanding capital jurisprudence since *Furman*.

Whether the capital sentencing process has been sufficiently purged of arbitrariness by these reforms is a nagging constitutional question.[2] The chief challenge has been that the imposition of the death penalty remains arbitrary in one very specific respect: racial bias. Evidence of racial disparities, especially race-of-victim bias, was brought to the Court in *McCleskey v. Kemp*.[3]

The Court, in *McCleskey*, acknowledged the presence of victim based racial disparities in sentencing outcomes, but it held 5–4 that these statistical disparities did not, in themselves, impeach the sentencing of capital jurors. Disparate sentencing outcomes were no substitute, the Court said, for knowing how individual jurors focus their collective judgment in particular cases. The Court implied that it would be necessary to look inside the "black box" of jury decision making to address the issue of arbitrariness—that knowing what comes out of the black box is no substitute for knowing what goes on inside the box.

This is what the Capital Jury Project (CJP) is doing—looking inside the black box of capital sentencing. It has taken the Court's view in *McCleskey* of what would be needed to demonstrate arbitrariness as a guide, finding out what real jurors do in actual cases to decide whether defendants should live or die. In each of 14 participating states,[4] Capital Jury Project investigators attempt to interview four randomly selected jurors from each of 20–30 full capital trials that had both guilt and sentencing phases. The trials are chosen to provide equal numbers with life and death verdicts; preference is generally given to more recent trials.

In 3–4 hour interviews, CJP investigators ask a common core of questions in all states, and additional questions tailored to the particular concerns of investigators in their own states. In the development and pretesting of the interview instrument, it was found that jurors often provided rich, detailed narrative accounts of their decision making, in addition to their briefer responses to structured questions. To capture this richness and detail, with jurors' permission (granted by four out of five), the interviews are tape recorded. Some of the findings of the Capital Jury Project to date are reported below.[5]

Premature decision making

What jurors tell researchers about their thinking and deliberations during the guilt stage of the trial indicates that many began taking a stand on what the defendant's punishment should be well before they were exposed to the statutory guidelines for making this decision. In response to the question "After the jury found [defendant's name] guilty of capital murder but before you heard any evidence or testimony about what the punishment should be, did you then think [defendant's name] should be given . . . a death sentence, a life sentence, [or were you] undecided?" virtually half of the jurors said that they thought they knew what the punishment should be before the sentencing stage of the trial began, and those for death outnumbered those for life by 3–2. A follow-up question to the jurors who thought they knew what the punishment should be at this point asked, "How strongly did you think so?" Of all jurors, more than 3 out of 10 said they were "absolutely convinced" of what the punishment should be and nearly 2 in 10 were at least "pretty sure."

Judicature Volume 79, Number 5, pp. 220–223

Why are so many jurors absolutely convinced or at least pretty sure what the punishment should be even before the sentencing stage? One possibility is that they talk about what the punishment should be when they are supposed to be deliberating on guilt. When asked, *"How much did the discussion among the jurors [during guilt deliberations] focus on . . . jurors' feelings about the right punishment?"* half of the jurors said "a great deal" and almost two thirds said at least "a fair amount."

On the assumption that discussion of the "right punishment," might not necessarily mean that considerations of punishment actually figured in the guilt decision, jurors were asked a more pointed question specifically about the death penalty as a consideration in the jury's guilt decision. It read, *"In deciding guilt, did jurors talk about whether or not the defendant would, or should, get the death penalty?"* Four out of 10 jurors conceded that in deciding guilt the jury explicitly discussed whether the defendant would or should be sentenced to death.

Thus, some who said the jury discussed the "right punishment" a great deal during guilt deliberations did not mean to say that they talked specifically about the death penalty or that such discussion actually figured in their guilt decision. But more notable is the fact that so many jurors claimed that in deciding guilt they talked about whether the death penalty would or should be the defendant's punishment.

Misunderstanding guidelines

CJP investigators for North and South Carolina have found that jurors misunderstand how the capital sentencing decision should be made; which factors can and cannot be considered, what level of proof is needed, and what degree of concurrence is required for aggravating and mitigating factors. And, they do so in a way that leads them to improperly accept aggravating and improperly reject mitigating considerations. The bias is especially pronounced for mitigating factors.[6] The North Carolina investigators also examined how jurors understood the procedure for weighing aggravating against mitigating factors and for deciding what the punishment should be. "[I]t is disturbing that roughly one-fourth of the jurors felt that death was mandatory when it was not and approximately one-half of the jurors failed to appreciate those situations which mandated life."[7]

More fundamental to capital sentencing than which factors can be considered, what level of proof is needed,

whether unanimity is required, or how the weighing of factors must be conducted and interpreted, is the prohibition against having a "mandatory" death sentence; that is, requiring jurors to impose a death sentence without considering mitigation.[8] Hence, no state "requires" the death penalty simply or solely upon the finding of a particular aggravating factor.[9]

To test jurors' understanding of this basic principle, they were asked, "After hearing the judge's [sentencing] instructions, did you believe that the law required you to impose a death sentence if the evidence proved" that the defendant's "conduct was heinous, vile or depraved," or if it proved that the defendant "would be dangerous in the future?" Four out of 10 capital jurors wrongly believed that they were "required" to impose the death penalty if they found that the crime was heinous, vile, or depraved, and nearly as many mistakenly thought the death penalty was "required" if they found that the defendant would be dangerous in the future.

In every aspect of sentencing guidelines CJP investigators have so far examined, then, there is a "tilt toward death" in jurors' understanding. Some of this may be a "carryover" of the rules for decision making from the guilt to the sentencing phase of the trial. But some of it may reflect a tendency among jurors to hear sentencing instructions in a way that justifies or reinforces decisions that many have already made. One question bears on this latter point, *"Would you say the judge's sentencing instructions to the jury . . . simply provided a framework for the decision most jurors had already made?"* Three out of four jurors said "yes."

Alternative punishment

The most common question jurors ask judges during sentencing deliberations, according to an analysis of Georgia capital trial transcripts, is how long would the defendant actually spend in prison if not given the death penalty.[10] Judges usually respond that the law prohibits them from answering this question; soon thereafter, the jurors typically return a death sentence.[11]

With the data now available from more than 800 jurors in 11 states the CJP has further documented jurors' considerable ignorance and consistent underestimation of the death penalty alternative, and the connection between their erroneous perceptions of the alternative and their decisions to impose the death penalty. When asked, "How long did you think someone not given the death penalty for a capital murder in this state usually spends in prison?" in only 2 of 11 states are most estimates within a 10-year interval, and in all seven states where interviewing is now complete a majority of the jurors who give an estimate believe such offenders usually get out of prison even before the law makes them eligible for parole. What is more, jurors most mistaken about the death penalty alternative are the ones most apt to vote for the death penalty in all seven states where the CJP data collection has been completed.

The evidence from juror interviews thus indicates that it is not simply whether or not, but *how soon,* jurors think the defendant will get out of prison that influences their final punishment decision. Since life without parole is the alternative to the death penalty in only a small fraction of cases, to inform jurors only when it is the alternative, as provided by *Simmons v. South Carolina,* does relatively little to remedy the arbitrariness introduced by the widespread ignorance and consistent underestimation of the alternative punishment.[12]

What about the other limitation in *Simmons,* namely, that future dangerousness be advanced as a reason for the death penalty before the defendant may have the jurors know what the alternative punishment really is? This issue was addressed by examining whether jurors' perceptions of the alternative punishment are associated with their sentencing decisions only when the defendant's possible dangerousness is an issue, or, as well, when dangerousness is not a factor.

As expected, jurors' perceptions of the alternative punishment are a strong predictor of a final vote for the death penalty when the prosecutor argues that the defendant would be dangerous in the future, when jurors believe the evidence proves this to be true, and when jurors are concerned in their sentencing deliberations about the possibility that the defendant will return to society someday. But, there is also a statistically reliable association between jurors' perceptions of the alternative punishment and their likelihood of voting for the death penalty, when these respective indications of dangerousness are not present. That is to say, the decision to impose the death penalty is definitely a function of what the alternative punishment is thought to be even when dangerousness is not an issue. Hence, the application of *Simmons* only to cases of alleged dangerousness, like its application only when the alternative is life without parole, makes it a very minor corrective to a major problem in the exercise of capital discretion.

Further analysis reveals that: (1) it is early in sentencing deliberations (at the first vote on punishment) that

underestimating the alternative is most strongly associated with favoring death as punishment; and (2) it is among those who were undecided about what the punishment should be before sentencing deliberations began that underestimating the alternative is especially apt to yield a vote for death on the first jury ballot. The data thus indicate that it is primarily at the point when jurors sit down to deliberate about what the punishment should be that their typically mistaken underestimates of the death penalty alternative come into play.

Denying responsibility

It is an "intolerable danger" for jurors to believe that "the responsibility for any ultimate determination of death will rest with others," the Supreme Court said in *Caldwell v. Mississippi.*[13] Yet, as Robert Weisberg has argued,[14] sentencing guidelines, by appearing to provide jurors with an authoritative formula that yields the "correct" or "required" punishment, may actually diminish their sense of responsibility for the awful punishment they may be called upon to impose.

To see where capital jurors place foremost responsibility for the defendant's punishment, jurors were asked to rank five options from "most" through "least" responsible for the defendant's punishment. The five options, together with the percent saying each option was "most responsible," are:[15]

47.2 the defendant because his/her conduct is what actually determined the punishment
34.0 the law that states what punishment applies
9.1 the jury that votes for the sentence
6.0 the individual juror since the jury's decision depends on the vote of each juror
3.8 the judge who imposes the sentence

Eight of 10 jurors assign foremost responsibility to the defendant or to the law. While the defendant is more often seen as "most responsible," for the punishment, the law more consistently outranks the defendant in responsibility for the punishment.[16] By contrast, jurors overwhelmingly deny that they individually or as a group are primarily responsible for the defendant's punishment. Altogether, only 3 in 20 said that the jurors as a group or individually were the most responsible. The jury ranked third, the individual juror fourth, and the judge fifth in punishment responsibility.[17]

The *Caldwell* Court speculated that when jurors minimize the importance of their role, "[O]ne can easily imagine that in a case in which the jury is divided on the proper sentence, the presence of appellate review could effectively be used as an argument for why those jurors who are reluctant to invoke the death sentence should nevertheless give in."[18] One question bears on this issue. It asked jurors whether during their sentencing deliberations they thought responsibility for deciding what the defendant's punishment should be was shared with trial or appellate judges or was strictly the jury's. Two of three jurors think of themselves as sharing responsibility with trial or appellate judges in states where the jury's decision is binding on the trial judge, and nearly all do so in states where the trial judge can override the jury's sentencing decision.

The data also show that jurors who see the punishment decision as shared with judicial authorities were more likely to vote for death than those who take sole responsibility for the decision. Moreover, this greater readiness to vote for death among those who see the decision as shared comes at or near the end of sentencing deliberations, as the *Caldwell* Court surmised. Thus, it is between their first and final vote on the defendant's punishment that jurors who feel the decision is shared or passed on to judicial authorities as compared to those who accept sole responsibility for the decision were especially likely to cross over from life to death, especially unlikely to cross over from death to life, and far more likely than others to move from undecided to death than to life. In other words, as jurors move closer to the final life or death decision, those who deny full or strict responsibility for the defendant's punishment are more apt to impose the death penalty, indeed are more apt to move from being for life or undecided to a death vote.

Most capital jurors disclaim primary or sole responsibility for the awesome life or death decision they must make. They want the cover of law for their decision, although they often make their decision before learning what the law says they should consider, often misunderstand what the law requires of them after being told by the judge, and often do not know what the alternative punishment actually is because the law prohibits the judge from telling them. Yet, most jurors still want to see the law as more responsible than they themselves for the defendant's punishment. Significantly, this tendency to deny full responsibility for the defendant's punishment appears to make it easier for jurors to vote for death.[19] Joseph Hoffmann's examination of Indiana jurors' narrative accounts of their sentencing decisions documents the importance to jurors of "higher authority" for guidance in the momentous life or death decision, not infrequently including "divine

guidance"—hardly what the Supreme Court had in mind as "guided discretion."[20]

*****

The findings at this still early stage of research present a picture of capital sentencing afflicted with a "tilt toward death." It will take longer to learn just how decisions are being made, what dynamics are at work, and what model or models of decision making best fit the way jurors think and act in making their life or death decisions. As the work proceeds, it should become clearer in what ways and to what extent the operation of modern capital statutes do and do not conform to constitutional requirements. The inevitable questions will be, just how arbitrary can the system be and still remain constitutionally acceptable, and how much impropriety of what kinds by how many jurors can the Constitution tolerate—especially in light of the constitutionally mandated higher standard of care and reliability for capital cases?[21]

Notes

This article originally appeared in Volume 79, Number 5, March–April 1996, pages 220–223.

This research has been supported by grant NSF SES-9013252. The author thanks the members of the Capital Jury Project who helped bring together this partial overview of the work to date, and expresses appreciation to Patricia Igo for her able assistance.

1. 408 U.S. 238 (1972) (per curiam).
2. *See* Justice Harry Blackmun's dissent in the denial of cert. in *Callins v. Collins,* 114 S.Ct 1127 (1994).
3. 481 U.S. 279 (1987). The empirical evidence on which the *McCleskey* challenge was based is reported in Baldus et al., *Equal Justice and the Death Penalty: A Legal and Empirical Analysis* (Boston: Northeastern University Press, 1990).
4. States have been chosen to represent the principal forms of guided discretion capital statutes, and to ensure regional diversification of the sample. *See* Bowers, "The Capital Jury Project: Rationale, Design, and Preview of Early Findings," *Ind. L.J.* 70 (1995), 1043 for a discussion of the state sample selection criteria and a listing of the participating states.
5. Previously published CJP research appears in the *Indiana Law Journal* 1995 CJP symposium issue, and other sources including: Bienen, "Helping Jurors Out: Post-Verdict Debriefing for Jurors in Emotionally Disturbing Trials," *Ind. L.J.* 68 (1993), 1333; Bowers, "Capital Punishment and Contemporary Values: People's Misgivings and the Court's Misperceptions," *Law & Soc'y Rev.* 27 (1993), 157; Eisenberg and Wells, "Deadly Confusion: Juror

Instructions in Capital Cases," *Cornell L.J.* 79 (1993), 1, 4; and Hoffmann, "How American Juries Decide Death Penalty Cases: The Capital Jury Project" in Bedau, ed., *The Death Penalty in America: Current Controversies* (forthcoming, 1997).

6. Luginbuhl and Howe, "Discretion in Capital Sentencing Instructions: Guided or Misguided?," *Ind. L.J.* 70 (1995), 1161, 1170.

7. Ibid. at 1173.

8. *Woodson v. North Carolina,* 428 U.S. 280 (1976).

9. Oregon and Texas make the defendant's possible future dangerousness a prominent aggravating factor in the punishment decision, though not to the exclusion of mitigating considerations, see *Penry v. Lynaugh,* 492 U.S. 302 (1989).

10. Lane, "Is There Life Without Parole?: A Capital Defendant's Right to a Meaningful Alternative Sentence," *Loy. L.A. L. Rev.* 26 (1993), 327; *also see,* Paduano and Stafford-Smith, "Deathly Errors: Juror Misperceptions Concerning Parole in the Imposition of the Death Penalty," *Colum. Hum. Rts. L. Rev.* 18 (1987), 211.

11. Lane, ibid. at 338ff.

12. In *Simmons v. South Carolina,* 114 S.Ct. 2187, 2193 (1994) the Supreme Court ruled that a capital defendant was entitled to have the jury know what the alternative to the death penalty would actually be under two conditions: (1) when the alternative was a life sentence with no chance of parole, and (2) when the prosecution argued that the defendant's possible danger to society was a reason for imposing the death penalty.

13. 472 U.S. 320 (1985) at 333.

14. "Deregulating Death, 1983" *Sup. Ct. Rev.* 305, at 343. Weisberg posits that sentencing instructions give no real guidance, but have the appearance of legal rules. He argues that these pseudo-instructions dilute the jury's sense of responsibility, rather than guide discretion.

15. The following percentages are based on the responses of the 729 jurors who ranked all five options, so that the ranks sum to 15. The percentages add to 100.1 percent because of rounding error.

16. *See* Bowers, *supra* n. 4, Table 10 for the full distribution of jurors' responsibility rankings of these five agents in 7 of the 11 states examined here.

17. In three states (Alabama, Florida, and Indiana) that permit the judge to override the jury's sentencing decision, the judge ranks third, the jury fourth, and individual jurors fifth in responsibility for the defendant's punishment. *See* Bowers, *supra* n. 4, at note 233 and accompanying text.

18. *Supra* n. 13.

19. Weisberg, *supra* n. 14, at 391, draws a parallel between capital jurors and Stanley Milgram's experimental subjects who were willing to impose painful shocks so long as they could remain convinced that it was the experimenter not they themselves who were responsible for the suffering. *See* Milgram, *Obedience to Authority: An Experimental View* (New York: Harper & Row, 1974), 132–134.

20. Hoffman, "Where's the Buck?—Juror Misperception of Sentencing Responsibility in Death Penalty Cases," *Ind. L.J.* 70 (1995), 1137.

21. Woodson, *supra* n. 8, at 305.

Is the grand jury worth keeping?

Susan W. Brenner

The grand jury plays a critical role in law enforcement, but reforms are needed to restore its intended purposes.

Independent Counsel Kenneth Starr's investigation of alleged crimes surrounding President Clinton's relationship with a White House intern has focused a great deal of popular attention on the grand jury as an institution. Unlike the petit, or trial, jury, the grand jury operates in secret and ignores principles such as the Fourth Amendment's exclusionary rule, *Miranda* rights, and the Federal Rules of Evidence.

To the grand jury's proponents, these are essential characteristics of an institution that plays a critical role in law enforcement. To its critics, these and other aspects of the grand jury make it an instrument of oppression, a modern-day Star Chamber. Defenders of the status quo are correct in maintaining that grand juries cannot, and should not, be bound by many of the strictures imposed on courts and law enforcement officers. However, prosecutors do have too much control over grand jury proceedings.

What can be done to reduce the prosecutor's dominance and restore the grand jury to its intended purposes? A review of the functions of a grand jury and the relationship between a grand jury, a court, and a prosecutor is helpful to provide some answers.

An inquisitorial body

In some states grand juries handle civil matters, but for the most part they concentrate on criminal activity. The federal system and most of the states use them to bring charges for serious crimes, the felonies for which one can be incarcerated a year or more. Grand juries do this by hearing evidence presented by prosecutors and then reviewing a set of charges—an indictment—a prosecutor drafts and submits to them. The prosecutor asks the grand jurors to vote for the indictment. To do so, the jurors have to find that the evidence they heard establishes probable cause to believe the charges in the indictment are true. If a majority of the jurors find there is probable cause and vote for an indictment, it is "returned" and a criminal case is initiated against those named as defendants. If a majority does not vote for an indictment, no case results.

As part of this process, grand juries investigate. The investigations can be wide-ranging, because a grand jury (according to the Supreme Court in a 1950 case, *U.S. v. Morton Salt Co.*) "can investigate merely on suspicion that the law is being violated, or even just because it wants assurance that it is not." In approving the breadth of these inquiries, the Supreme Court in a 1919 case, *Blair v. U.S.*, described the grand jury as "a grand inquest, a body with powers of investigation and inquisition, the scope of whose inquiries is not . . . limited . . . by questions of propriety or forecasts of the probable result of the investigation, or by doubts whether any particular individual will be found properly subject to an accusation of crime." Practically speaking, therefore, a grand jury can investigate whomever and whatever it will, and those from whom a grand jury seeks information will almost certainly be unable to resist its demands.

These demands take the form of subpoenas that require the recipient either to testify before a grand jury or to provide the grand jury with documents or other evidence. Prosecutors obtain blank subpoenas from the court clerk's office and issue them to anyone who may have evidence relevant to an investigation. The recipient of such a subpoena may not want to comply with its demands, but if she ignores it she will be held in contempt of court and jailed, because the subpoena is an order from the court.

Consider one infamous example involving President Clinton's former business partner Susan McDougal. When she was subpoenaed by a Whitewater grand jury in 1996 and refused to testify, she was incarcerated for civil contempt and held for almost two years, until the grand jury's term was about to expire, which meant it would be dissolved and prosecutors would have had to start over with a new grand jury. Prosecutors could then have subpoenaed her before a new grand jury. If she still refused to testify, she would have been held in contempt and incarcerated until she spoke or until that grand jury's term ended. (Instead, they chose to indict her for criminal contempt and for obstruction of justice, both charges being based on her refusal to testify.) Since federal grand juries sit for up to three years, this is an unnerving prospect, one that usually convinces recalcitrant witnesses to cooperate with the grand jury. There are no records showing how many grand jury witnesses are serving sentences for contempt or how long recalcitrant witnesses generally serve, but in one state case a witness spent more than seven years in jail for refusing to testify after being subpoenaed.

Relevance-related objections to trial subpoenas are not usually successful in the grand jury context. In a 1991 case, *U.S. v. R. Enterprises, Inc.,* the Supreme Court held that the trial standard of relevance does not apply to grand jury subpoenas because, unlike trials, grand jury investigations do not focus on a set of issues defined by an indictment or by the complaint in a civil case. The Court explained that since grand juries investigate to ascertain whether charges should be brought, it is impossible to put limits on the scope of their inquiries. The justices held that grand jury subpoenas are presumed to seek relevant information and that when a subpoena recipient raises a relevance challenge, the challenge must be denied unless the court finds there "is no reasonable possibility that the category of material the Government seeks will produce information relevant to the general subject of the grand jury's investigation."

This can give rise to the appearance of unfairness, especially when a subpoena for documents is involved. For instance, a few years ago a modest midwestern trucking company received a subpoena that ordered the company to provide the grand jury with all records it had generated or received during the preceding 15 years. When company officials began the process of complying with the subpoena, they realized doing so would require them to locate, collate, and transport more than a million pages of documents that would have to be copied if the company were to retain a set of these essential records.

Like many who have found themselves in this position, the officials were appalled when they realized that the effort and expense of complying with the subpoena would cripple their ability to operate the business. They moved to quash the subpoena, arguing that it must seek irrelevant information because it was inconceivable the entire universe of documents sought could pertain to an inquiry within the grand jury's purview. Since the motion was filed after the Supreme Court decided *R. Enterprises*, the trucking company

lost. The Court found the company had not shown there was "no reasonable possibility" that the records sought by the subpoena would "produce information relevant to the general subject of the grand jury's investigation."

It may seem odd, and even unfair, that grand juries are given such latitude, but this is at once necessary and reasonable. Those who criticize the *R. Enterprises* decision tend to misunderstand the nature of a grand jury, to think of it as a court. It is not a court; it is an investigative body whose inquiries are more analogous to those of the police than they are to those of the judiciary. When the police investigate a crime, they operate according to broad notions of relevance, in that they seek information that can be used to identify the precise contours of the crime and those who perpetrated it.

Like a grand jury, the police want to solve a crime and charge the perpetrators. Often, when the police or a grand jury begin an investigation, they believe a crime may have been committed but know very little about the specifics of the offense; they must be able to explore any avenue that can produce evidence about the crime which originally came to their attention and about any satellite offenses of which they may originally have been unaware. It would be as difficult, and as unreasonable, to limit the scope of a grand jury's inquiry as it would be to enforce relevance limitations on police investigations.

Privilege

However, grand juries are not perfect analogues of the police. Grand juries defer to the notion of privilege, while police do not. Privilege usually arises at trial; trial witnesses can claim evidentiary privileges to avoid testifying. While grand juries generally ignore the rules of evidence, they honor privileges. The federal system and most states implement the privileges that arose at common law. These include the attorney-client privilege, the marital privileges, the doctor-patient privilege, and the clergy-penitent privilege. Many jurisdictions add a reporter's privilege and executive privilege, and a few recognize a parent-child privilege. If someone subpoenaed to testify before a grand jury invokes a privilege recognized by the jurisdiction in which the grand jury sits, the grand jury must respect the privilege and cannot require the witness to answer questions on any issue it protects.

The availability of these privileges gives grand jury witnesses an advantage over police suspects, but they are disadvantaged in another respect. To understand why, it is necessary to begin with the different categories into which grand jury witnesses fall. Since grand juries investigate to ascertain whether criminal charges should be brought, those subpoenaed can occupy an uneasy state, somewhere between witness and suspect. Many of them are summoned simply as sources of information, as "fact witnesses." If they are forthcoming with the grand jury and do not perjure themselves or try to conceal evidence of criminal activity, their testimony will end their involvement with the investigation. But others who receive subpoenas are "subjects" or "targets" of the investigation. "Targets" are analogous to police suspects; the grand jury believes they committed crimes and is trying to gather the evidence it needs to charge them. "Subjects" exist in a gray area between witness and target—the grand jury believes they may have been involved in the crimes being investigated, but has not yet focused its energies on trying to charge them.

Suspects brought to a police station for interrogation are protected by *Miranda*. The police must warn a suspect that *Miranda* gives him the right to remain silent and the right to an attorney. Unlike suspects, grand jury witnesses are not protected by *Miranda*, not even when they are a subject or target of the investigation. In a 1976 case, *U.S. v. Mandujano,* the Supreme Court held that *Miranda* is limited to police interrogations because the rights it defined were designed to prevent the police from using physical intimidation to elicit confessions. The Court explained that since neither grand jurors nor the prosecutors with whom they work are likely to use physical violence against a witness, there is no need to apply *Miranda* to grand jury inquiries.

Before *Miranda* was decided, suspects cited the Fifth Amendment's privilege against self-incrimination as their reason for not cooperating with police interrogators. Grand juries honor this privilege, but it is harder to claim the privilege than it is to invoke *Miranda*, and the privilege offers less protection. A suspect can invoke *Miranda* rights at will. If a suspect invokes the right to silence, the police cannot ask him any questions. If a suspect invokes the right to counsel, the police must give him an attorney and cannot ask him any questions unless his attorney agrees and is present.

A grand jury witness, on the other hand, cannot claim the privilege against self-incrimination unless she shows that the grand jury wants (1) to compel her (2) to give testimony (3) that can be used to convict her of a crime. If a witness tries to claim the privilege, the prosecutor can challenge her claim, asking the court supervising the grand jury to decide if she has met all three requirements. The subpoena acts as compulsion, since she must do what it requires or be incarcerated for contempt, but the other requirements can be problematic. A witness cannot, for instance, claim the privilege and refuse to give samples of her handwriting or blood because both are physical evidence, not testimony, and physical evidence is not protected. And a witness cannot claim the privilege because testifying would embarrass her or would incriminate someone she cares for. She can only claim it if testifying would yield information that can be used to convict her of a crime.

If the court finds the witness cannot claim the privilege, it will order her to testify or be held in contempt. If she agrees to testify, she will enter the grand jury room alone, unaccompanied by an attorney. In most jurisdictions, a witness's attorney (if she has one) stays outside the grand jury room, and the witness is given a "reasonable opportunity" to go outside and confer with him during questioning. In practice, this opportunity is very limited.

Unlike suspects, witnesses are in a perilous situation. Suspects can cut off questioning whenever they want by invoking their rights to silence or to an attorney. But for witnesses, even a valid claim of privilege does not stop prosecutors from asking questions, and a skilled prosecutor can use ostensibly innocuous questions in an effort to trick a witness into inadvertently making incriminating statements. Once she does so, she has waived the privilege on that issue, and the prosecutor can explore the topic with further questions.

While this may seem unfair, it is consistent with the constitutional rules that govern police interrogations. *Miranda* is not one of them. According to the *Mandujano* Court, *Miranda* did not reflect constitutional requirements; it merely established prophylactic rules designed to deter specific police tactics. Consequently, the only constitutional standards governing interrogations are the Sixth Amendment's right to counsel, the due process voluntariness test, and the Fifth Amendment privilege.

The Sixth Amendment only applies when someone has been indicted. Since grand jury investigations precede indictments, they generally do not implicate this right to counsel. The due process test bars the government from using physical violence or extreme psychological ploys to extort a confession, but it lets interrogators trick people into confessing. Neither grand jurors nor the prosecutors assisting them use violence or psychological ploys to break down witnesses. If a prosecutor tricks a witness into making incriminating statements by asking seemingly innocuous questions, that does not violate the due process voluntariness standard. And since grand juries enforce the Fifth Amendment privilege, their treatment of witnesses is constitutionally unimpeachable.

Immunity

Aside from tricking witnesses into waiving the privilege, prosecutors can deprive them of it. If a witness shows she can claim the Fifth Amendment privilege, a prosecutor can prevent her from doing so by giving her immunity, the government's promise to a witness that it will not use what she says before the grand jury, or any evidence it finds as a result of what she says, to prosecute her for a crime. The Supreme Court has held that this kind of immunity is constitutional because it puts the witness in the same position she would have been in had she not testified. A witness can also try to persuade the prosecutor to give her another kind of immunity, one in which the government promises not to prosecute her if she testifies before the grand jury. This kind of immunity is also constitutional, since it puts the witness in an even better position than she would have been in had she not testified.

Immunity can be a bargain for some witnesses. Often, though, witnesses do not want immunity and try desperately to avoid it; some even go so far as to persist in claiming the privilege after they have been immunized and can no longer do so. Witnesses resist immunity for various reasons, one being the fear of retaliation. Someone who was involved, say, in organized drug activity may be told that if he accepts immunity and testifies against the leaders of that organization, his family will be killed. On hearing this, the witness will try to avoid immunity. He may petition the court for relief, reporting the threats. This will not prevent his being forced to cooperate; courts have held that the possibility of retaliation cannot interfere with an immunized witness' duty to testify, as any other result would simply encourage witness intimidation.

As this overview illustrates, grand juries exercise an extraordinary amount of power in a context that is seldom held up to public scrutiny. Why are grand juries given such power, and what can be done to prevent abuse of power?

A constitutional fixture

The grand jury is often characterized as a sword and a shield: As the Sixth Circuit ruled in a 1977 case, *U.S. v. Doss,* the grand jury "wields the sword of accusation against persons who the grand jurors have probable cause to believe are involved in criminal activity, and shields the innocent against oppressive prosecution." This characterization implies that the grand jury somehow stands apart from other branches of government, and that implication was the focus of a recent Supreme Court opinion.

For centuries, grand juries were considered part of the court system, presumably because of the close working relationship between courts and grand juries. While grand juries were regarded as an arm of the courts, federal judges readily exercised a measure of control over grand jury proceedings, citing their inherent supervisory power over the administration of federal criminal justice as the basis for doing so.

In 1992, the Supreme Court repudiated this view in *U.S. v. Williams.* The issue was whether federal courts could use their supervisory power to require prosecutors to present to the grand jury evidence pointing against indictment. The Court held that they cannot, that federal courts do not possess broad supervisory authority over grand jury proceedings because the grand jury "is an institution separate from the courts, over whose functioning the courts do not preside." The Court pointed out that while the grand jury is mentioned in the Fifth Amendment, it was not included in the "body of the Constitution" and, therefore, "has not been textually assigned . . . to any of the branches described in the first three Articles." It explained that "the whole theory of [the grand jury's] function is that it belongs to no branch of the institutional Government, serving as a kind of buffer or referee between the Government and the people."

The *Williams* holding was a departure from earlier decisions in which the Court (for instance in 1959's *Brown v. U.S.*) had described the grand jury as "an appendage of the court." Despite what the Court ruled in *Williams,* an excellent case can be made that the grand jury is part of the judicial branch, if only because of its dependence on the courts. A court decides when a grand jury should be convened and issues an order to that effect. Upon receiving this order, the clerk's office uses the same procedure it employs for petit jurors to summon a panel of prospective grand jurors from whom the members of the new grand jury are chosen. The court swears in the grand jurors and charges them, and they meet in a room located in the courthouse and guarded by courthouse security personnel. As discussed earlier, the grand jury relies on the court's subpoena power to obtain testimony and other evidence. And, of course, without the court, the grand jury could not exist. Outside the common law movement, grand juries do not convene themselves, just as petit juries do not convene themselves.

Most states regard the grand jury as a component of the judicial branch. *Williams* creates an anomaly in which the federal grand jury is in effect a fourth branch of government, while in most (if not all) states it is part of the court system. *Williams*'s characterization of the grand jury also produces another anomaly: The federal system includes two juries—the petit jury and the grand jury. In most (if not all) states, both are considered part of the court system, just as both were traditionally considered part of the federal court system. Under *Williams,* the federal grand jury becomes an institution unto itself, while the petit jury presumably remains part of the judicial system. Unlike the grand jury, which is not referred to in the body of the Constitution, the petit jury is mentioned in Article III, which requires that all criminal charges be tried by jury. Since Article III established the federal judiciary, it seems to follow that the petit jury is part of the federal court system.

Anomalies aside, why does it matter whether the grand jury is considered part of the judicial branch or an independent entity? The answer is that the grand jury's status is very important insofar as it determines whether any outside agency can exert a measure of control over a grand jury's activities. The grand jury is a powerful institution. As such, it has the potential to wreak a fair amount of havoc, especially when it acts as a "sword." For example, as Richard Younger explained in his 1963 book, *The People's Panel: The Grand Jury in the United States 1634–1941,* early in this nation's history a grand jury overreacted and indicted a congressman for criticizing the federal government. Recently, a California county grand jury nearly brought local government to a halt when it returned "rogue indictments" against eight top county officials, and a Texas county grand jury's investigation of a former mayor seriously damaged his reputation even though it turned up no evidence of wrongdoing.

Under *Williams,* courts cannot head off these misguided enthusiasms. The Supreme Court ruled that because the grand jury is a separate institution, courts cannot intervene unless a grand jury is violating a specific statute or rule of law. Since grand juries operate relatively unimpeded by statutes or other rules of law, this leaves the courts relatively powerless.

Prosecutorial dominance

On one level, the courts' powerlessness is probably of little moment given prosecutors' ascendance over grand jurors. For the most part, grand juries operate under the de facto control of a prosecutor who initiates and directs an investigation. One source of a prosecutor's control is the relationship he or she cultivates with a grand jury. Prosecutors try to develop a rapport with grand jurors, which is usually easy because prosecutors are the only people the jurors see consistently. Once established, this rapport becomes an informal control mechanism that ensures the jurors will accede to a prosecutor's wishes. In this sense, grand jurors become the prosecutor's cheering section. Or, as former New York Court of Appeals Judge Sol Wachtler famously put it, a good prosecutor can get a grand jury to "indict a ham sandwich." This dominance is exacerbated by the prosecutor's legal expertise. Grand jurors rely on prosecutors to interpret the law and put the facts they uncover into a legal context. Even if grand jurors for some reason do not identify with the prosecutor, their ignorance of the law makes it very difficult to challenge a prosecutor's conduct of an investigation or wish to indict.

The extent to which prosecutors dominate grand jury proceedings is both good and bad. Prosecutorial control is good in that it channels the grand jury's awesome power into areas of legitimate law enforcement concern and minimizes, if it does not eliminate, the possibility that a grand jury will begin inquiring into matters that should be out of bounds for legal or policy reasons. The expansive, capricious inquiries of common law grand juries that suited the small, rural communities from which they emerged would introduce an unpredictable and disruptive element into modern law enforcement.

To understand why this is true, one needs only to consider the Clinton-Lewinsky investigation to imagine the specter of a runaway federal grand jury that, infatuated with its own publicity, pursues ever more outrageous inquiries to its own detriment and to the ruin of many of those on whom it focuses its attentions. Of course, while prosecutors' influence may keep grand juries in line, it does nothing to keep prosecutors themselves from exploiting the grand jury, which many are accusing Independent Counsel Starr of doing. In several post-*Williams* decisions, federal judges lament their inability to stop prosecutors from engaging in conduct that, while it may not explicitly violate federal law, is clearly abusive.

Unfortunately, prosecutorial control effectively nullifies the role grand jurors are supposed to play in the investigating and indicting processes. Having grand jurors become a prosecutor's cheering section may not interfere with their ability to act as the sword of justice, but it certainly does not encourage them to shield individuals from unwarranted investigations and accusations. A grand jury should second-guess the prosecutor's decisions. The whole purpose of the grand jury is to have the jurors act as the voice of the community, injecting a lay perspective, a ration of common sense, into the law enforcement process.

In the 1930s, for instance, a New York grand jury did something that would be improbable in the 1990s. It rejected the efforts of Tammany Hall prosecutors who wanted to limit its inquiries into racketeering and corruption. The grand jurors barred the prosecutors from appearing before them and embarked on their own investigation, which resulted in the indictment and convictions of 73 racketeers. It is highly unlikely this could happen today: One attorney interviewed for a recent *Chicago Tribune* article described the modern grand jury as "23 people in a room taking up oxygen and having lunch," and it is not uncommon for witnesses to report having seen grand jurors sleeping or reading newspapers during their testimony. The relationship prosecutors develop with grand jurors and the complexity of the law combine to overwhelm the jurors and mute the voice of the community.

A proposal

"The principal value of a grand jury . . . consists in the independence of the jurors." That was the conclusion reached by the judge in a federal court case, *U.S. v. Watkins,* in 1829. What can be done to restore that independence recognized as necessary so long ago?

A number of possibilities have been suggested, but one offers the best hope of restoring the grand jury to what it once was, and was intended to be. The greatest threat to a grand jury's ability to exercise independent judgment comes from the influence prosecutors exert

over the grand jurors. It follows that reducing a prosecutor's influence over grand jurors should enhance a grand jury's independence. The obvious way to do this is to bar prosecutors from grand jury proceedings, leaving the jurors to act on their own, but this brings it own risks.

The solution is to give grand juries their own attorney. In 1978, Hawaii began providing grand juries with their own counsel. The purpose was to increase the independence of grand juries by minimizing a prosecutor's influence over grand jurors. Grand jury counsel, appointed by the state's chief justice, serve one year terms and are available to provide legal advice throughout a grand jury's proceedings. Grand jury counsel serve along with prosecutors, who bring matters warranting investigation to a grand jury's attention, provide it with evidence, and submit proposed indictments for its review.

Other jurisdictions would do well to follow Hawaii's lead. The court impaneling a grand jury could appoint its grand jury's counsel when it swears the jurors in. To avoid biases resulting from serving an extended tenure as grand jury counsel, each counsel should be appointed to serve for a limited period. This period could be linked to the grand jury's term or set generically, such as Hawaii's one-year term. Giving each grand jury its own counsel would produce a close working relationship between the two without creating the unhealthy dependence that currently results from prosecutor-grand jury relationships. Unlike a prosecutor, who serves as both advocate and legal adviser, the grand jury counsel would act solely as a legal adviser, one with no stake in the outcome.

The counsel would act as a buffer between the grand jurors and prosecutors and between the jurors and the targets of their inquiries. He or she could advise the jurors on the advisability of hearing exculpatory evidence or of subpoenaing additional evidence beyond that presented by the prosecutor. Since the counsel is impartial, he or she would be more likely to recommend that the jurors take these steps. This would let them hear a more balanced presentation, which would itself increase the objectivity of their decision making.

Grand jury counsel could also facilitate the jurors' consideration of illegally obtained evidence. The Fourth Amendment's exclusionary rule does not apply to grand jury proceedings, the Supreme Court having held that the prohibition on illegal search and seizure is adequately protected by preventing illegally obtained evidence from being used at trial. A grand jury's counsel could advise them on the ramifications of basing their decision to indict on evidence that was seized in violation of the Fourth Amendment. The jurors could weigh this information in deciding whether such charges are warranted. Aside from enhancing the accuracy and objectivity of the jurors' decision making, this step reduces the perception that grand juries implicitly approve lawless police behavior by basing their decisions on the fruits of such conduct.

Along with enhancing a grand jury's independence, the grand jury counsel could intervene to prevent grand jurors from abusing their authority. Grand jury counsel cannot be given the power to veto grand juror decisions. This would substitute his or her opinions for those of the grand jury and effectively transform the "voice of the community" into a one-person grand jury. Counsel would have to exert control informally, in the same way prosecutors currently control grand jury proceedings. That is, counsel would develop a close relationship with grand jurors, one in which the jurors relied on their counsel and accepted his or her advice. Once this relationship was established, it should help the counsel persuade grand jurors not to embark on unfounded, ill-advised inquiries.

Conversely, counsel could assist a grand jury that wants to initiate a legitimate investigation of matters that have not been presented to it by a prosecutor. In many states, grand juries are statutorily authorized to initiate investigations based on their own knowledge of community affairs, without waiting for a prosecutor to request such an investigation. Counsel would help grand jurors decide when such an inquiry was, and was not, appropriate. This would revive the independence found in the racket-busting New York grand jury while avoiding the abuses of unfettered grand jury discretion.

Giving the grand jury its own counsel does not run afoul of the Supreme Court's characterization of the grand jury's unique institutional status. Prosecutors play two roles before a grand jury—advocate and legal adviser. By creating the position of grand jury counsel, a jurisdiction simply divides the prosecutor's responsibilities among two people, thus freeing the prosecutor from the inherent conflict of interest involved in wearing two hats, that of advocate and that of disinterested legal adviser. Unlike federal courts' pre-*Williams* efforts to use their supervisory powers to shape the course of grand jury proceedings, this simply reallocates the performance of duties that have been an integral part of the grand jury since it emerged in 12th-century England.

Note

This article originally appeared in Volume 81, Number 5, March–April 1998, pages 190–199.

The American Judiciary and the Politics of Representation

Unlike legislatures, courts are not generally thought of as representative institutions. Nevertheless, most judges do have jurisdiction over well-defined geographical constituencies and, in state court systems, many are elected to serve such constituencies. To the degree that judges in a given judicial system carry unequal workloads, or service different numbers of people, we may even legitimately raise a concern about judicial malapportionment. The issue of representation and the judiciary is a multifaceted and nuanced one, and the articles in this section explore this issue in its diversity.

The section starts with a provocative selection that focuses on some normative and policy concerns about representation and the judiciary. Sheldon Goldman's "Should there be affirmative action for the judiciary?" is an advocacy piece written during a time when considerable controversy existed over the Carter administration's efforts to increase the number of women, blacks, and other minorities on the federal bench. Goldman considers the litany of criticism leveled at affirmative action in judicial recruitment and offers his arguments for why none of these is a compelling indictment. In so many respects, the concerns over affirmative action and judicial representation highlighted in Goldman's thoughtful essay remain with us today.

A much more empirically focused view of representation and the judiciary is contained in Mark Hurwitz and Drew Lanier's data driven study, "Women and minorities on state and federal appellate benches, 1985 and 1999." The comparisons drawn here are important on two levels. First, they document temporal trends regarding diversity on the bench in judicial snapshots taken fifteen years apart. Second, they portray the nature of judicial representation in two distinct judicial locales, state and federal, each of which harbors a multitude of possible judicial selection systems. Writ large, Hurwitz and Lanier find that appellate courts have become considerably more diverse between 1985 and 1999, literally doubling the proportion of women and minorities holding seats on state appellate courts while increasing their numbers proportionally by over 60 percent on the federal appeals courts.

These gains, however, have largely been associated with greater gender, not minority representation. The proportion of African American males on state and federal appellate benches actually decreased slightly between 1985 and 1999, and approximately three out of four judgeships in the United States continue to be occupied by white males. Also of considerable interest, the authors find that diversification of the bench does not appear to be related to the system used to choose judges. It has been argued by some that merit selection systems and the attainment of diversity were mutually exclusive goals; however, Hurwitz and Lanier conclude that, "it appears that efforts to produce normatively good courts do not necessarily conflict with a more representative judiciary."

Hurwitz and Lanier present the big picture of judicial representation in the United States. In "Clinton and diversification of the federal judiciary," Rorie Spill and Kathleen Bratton work with the much smaller palette of the Clinton administration to offer compelling evidence of how a strong commitment to affirmative action by a president can bear dramatic results in enhancing diversity in a relatively short time, at least at the federal level. Going beyond the raw numbers, Spill and Bratton demonstrate that increasing diversity requires strategic choices on a number of different fronts. Thus, "Clinton appointed more women and minorities to the federal branch than any of his predecessors. He did this by maintaining existing diversity, by using newly created seats, and by replacing white or male judges with minority or female judges."

To this point, this examination of representation and diversity on the bench has focused primarily on their symbolic aspects, with an eye towards the degree to which our courts look like the public that they serve. Clearly, symbolic representation can be important in its own right, with a representative judiciary fostering the view that the courts are fair and impartial. And women and minority judges certainly may have important parts to play in American society as highly valued role models. Yet the notion of representation must be viewed from a substantive as well as a symbolic perspective. Does it make a difference what kinds of people sit on the courts when we view the decisions that judges actually make?

Considerable research has explored the question of whether women and minority judges decide cases differently than white males, yet the results of these studies can best be characterized as mixed and suggestive. One such example, "Voting behavior and gender on the U.S. courts of appeals," by Sue Davis, Susan Haire, and Donald Songer is offered here. The study focuses on the dictates of feminist legal theory and, in particular, the work of Carol Gilligan, to frame the question, "How might the alleged different perspective of women manifest itself in judging?" In two of the three legal areas examined, gender-based differences are, indeed, found in case outcomes. Women were more likely than men to favor claimants in employment discrimination cases and defendants in search and seizure cases. No significant gender-based differences were found, however, in decisions regarding obscenity. Given their mixed results, the authors are appropriately cautious in drawing interpretations from their findings.

Another approach to examining the relationship between judicial decisions and representation was taken by Thomas Marshall in his study, "The Supreme Court and the grass roots: whom does the Court represent best?" Marshall's analysis attempts to link public opinion data to 110 actual Supreme Court decisions during the Warren, Burger, and Rehnquist courts in an effort to assess which of four competing representational models the Court's work output most closely resembles. That is, does judicial decision making reflect the will of numerical majorities, unpopular minorities, politically and economically advantaged elites, or the attitudes of those in the polity who share the justices' partisan leanings? Readers may be surprised to learn that Marshall's analysis leads to the conclusion that, "The modern Supreme Court has been relatively evenhanded in representing different social and demographic group attitudes." The article attempts to both explain this finding and explore its implications and consequences.

Should there be affirmative action for the judiciary?

Sheldon Goldman

*Special efforts to find qualified women and minorities for the federal bench
are not incompatible with merit selection because they ensure that we choose
the "best" judges from among all possible candidates.*

The Carter administration jolted the legal community with its outspoken and widely publicized affirmative action policy of placing women and ethnic minorities on the federal bench. Many of the arguments raised against the implementation of affirmative action programs elsewhere are now being heard with regard to the judiciary along with arguments attuned to the special status of the federal bench. But after considering the nature of the administration's efforts and successes in implementing judicial affirmative action, I have concluded that the legal profession ought to applaud President Carter and Attorney General Bell.

As I see it, six major objections can be raised against an affirmative action approach to federal judicial selection. Each, I believe, can be persuasively answered. I would like to discuss these objections briefly and the rejoinders I find convincing.

1. The dangers of classifying people. Affirmative action inevitably leads government agencies to define race, critics argue, and it leads government officials to make judgments about racial characteristics. Is an individual with one black grandparent or great-grandparent (say, Homer Plessy) to be classified as black? What about someone with one black parent who was raised by white foster parents? Is an American-born individual with an American father and Mexican mother Hispanic? The argument, essentially, is that it is dangerous for government to make any racial classifications. Such activities stir memories of the racial laws of Nazi Germany and run counter to the value Americans have traditionally placed on treating individuals on the basis of their personal qualities and not their racial attributes.

Response: While many (including myself) are uncomfortable with government concern with race/ethnicity, I believe there is a crucial and fundamental distinction between America's official racial consciousness for purposes of affirmative action and the racial classifications of totalitarian regimes. America's purpose is to aid definable classes of persons who have historically suffered from official discrimination. Racial classifications in Nazi Germany were, of course, for ghastly purposes, and in more contemporary totalitarian societies ethnic designations on identity cards and other records form the basis for official discrimination.

The federal judiciary has been and still is an overwhelmingly white, male institution, for many reasons. America's long-standing racism and sexism, for example, have historically limited opportunities in the judiciary for women, blacks, and Hispanics. It does not seem unreasonable to make special efforts to recruit from these groupings of Americans for federal judgeships. Deliberate considerations of race and sex should not be given negative connotations so long as the government demonstrates positive, anti-racist, anti-sexist motives and purposes.

2. The threat of reverse discrimination. The real result of affirmative action, opponents argue, is reverse discrimination. Government selects a group or groups of persons for favored treatment, thereby putting all others at a disadvantage. This is reminiscent of George Orwell's *Animal Farm* where all animals are equal but some are more equal than others. On an individual basis this produces reverse discrimination; individuals are ruled out of consideration *because* they are the "wrong" race or sex. Furthermore, when it comes to judicial selection, those women, blacks, and Hispanics who are favored for judgeships are frequently from the same social class and similar backgrounds as competing white males, and their careers have not necessarily suffered from discrimination. Why then should they have an advantage?

Response: I cannot be persuaded that affirmative action is reverse discrimination—at least when the objective is *not* to give minorities a majority hold. I have not seen evidence that any affirmative action program of any kind in the United States has seriously threat-

Judicature Volume 62, Number 10, pp. 488–494

ened the majority status of white males in government, industry, the professions, or academia. Certainly the type of affirmative action that the Carter Administration is promoting for the judiciary in no way threatens the overwhelming majority status of white males.

Although the administration's efforts thus far to place women, blacks, and Hispanics on the federal bench have been spectacular when compared with the record of previous administrations, taken alone the results of the Carter administration's affirmative action policy are actually very modest. About 12 percent of the Carter nominees have been black, and about the same proportion have been women.[1] In terms of the entire federal bench, the proportions of blacks and women are exceedingly small and for Hispanics almost non-existent.

At the individual level, the charge of reverse discrimination potentially can be more troublesome, as it was in the *Bakke* case. But we do not have to be concerned with this since judicial selection traditionally has involved numerous variables. The addition of racial/ethnic and sexual considerations is in no way inconsistent with the host of other considerations that have been involved in judicial selection, including geography, party affiliation, party activity, sponsorship by senators and other key politicians, professional connections, ideological or policy outlook, and so on. Race/ethnicity and sex are today politically relevant variables and they have been added to other political type variables in a selection process that historically has been political.

3. The error of focusing on group affiliation. No matter how worthy an objective it may be, critics say, affirmative action is inconsistent with the professional goal of merit selection, which many judicial reformers and the Carter administration itself espouse. How can one accept the principle that only the best qualified should be given judgeships and then decree that women, blacks, and Hispanics are to be given special preference? Merit selection emphasizes individual qualities; affirmative action stresses group affiliation.

Response: It does a disservice to women, blacks, and Hispanics to suggest that they do not ordinarily possess as strong a set of professional credentials as white males do, but I will not dwell on this obvious rejoinder. What I find persuasive is the fact that, based on my own extensive research and that of others,[2] we never had,

we do not now have, and we probably never will have a judicial selection method based solely on professional merits. The professional credentials of candidates do play a part in judicial selection, but rarely have they been the determining factor. Of course, it is important to have qualified persons sitting on the bench, and there is no question in my mind that Attorney General Bell, under affirmative action, is recommending to the president only persons with the professional credentials essential to perform the job.

Ironically, affirmative action may provide a more potent push towards merit selection than anything else that has ever been done. By searching for well qualified women, blacks, and Hispanics, the administration and Democratic senators are downplaying party activity and political connections. This breaks with the past judges-as-patronage syndrome that historically characterized much of judicial selection.

Let me add for the record that the administration's so-called merit selection of appeals judges is not merit selection in fact. As recent issues of *Judicature* have shown,[3] mostly Democrats (including large numbers of Carter loyalists) have chosen mostly other Democrats for placement on the lists given the president. Other Democrats then lobby the Democratic president as to which Democrats to choose.

However, the selection process has become more open in large part due to institution of merit commissions and the affirmative action push. It is highly unrealistic to expect a civil service type merit approach to judicial selection ever to be established. Even assuming that an effective merit selection process could be instituted, I would have to be persuaded that the sorts of people chosen were better suited for the bench than the sorts of people chosen through our traditional political processes.

4. The need for government neutrality, not favoritism. Affirmative action is a remedy to right a proven constitutional wrong, critics emphasize. Even if it could be proven that racism and sexism served to exclude blacks, women, and Hispanics from the judiciary, that would not justify affirmative action in choosing the highest officials of the federal government. It would only justify efforts to ensure that these groups were no longer deliberately excluded.

Blacks prevented from voting were eventually protected by federal legislation and action to enable them to exercise the franchise, but they were not given the right to elect so many black congressmen or black state representatives. Women given the right to vote in 1920 were not given the right to have a specific number of women in high elective or appointive office. Isn't it sufficient that the judicial selection process be non-discriminatory? Isn't affirmative action inappropriate here?

Remedy: The racial and sexual make-up of the judiciary, past and present, speaks for itself. It is clear that all-pervasive societal attitudes toward women, blacks, Hispanics, and indeed other groups such as Asian-Americans and American Indians severely limited their opportunities in the law and that they were, in fact, routinely and systematically excluded from federal judgeships. Justice Department officials and senators were not necessarily themselves racist or sexist. It is simply that within the framework of political reality and racist and sexist belief systems in the larger society, appointments of women, blacks, and some other ethnic groups were impossible.

But leaving aside the difficult questions of proof, and, indeed, whether constitutional wrongs were committed in the past, it can be argued that government can serve as a teacher by setting a good example and structuring situations in which learning and personal growth can occur. Clearly, the widespread racist and sexist attitudes of the past and the discrimination so widely practiced were moral, if not constitutional, wrongs. We should seize this opportunity to correct them.

By seeking out and appointing to federal judgeships a visible number of qualified women and minorities, government is teaching the nation that racial and sexual stereotypes are invalid. Government is also teaching young women, young blacks, and young Hispanics that it no longer recognizes as political reality the racial and sexual biases of the past, and that individual accomplishment and achievement are more important than race and sex.

Yes, it is ironic that affirmative action that recognizes race and sex is necessary in order to hasten the time when race and sex will be irrelevant, and when racism and sexism are virtually non-existent. Perhaps most importantly, by voluntarily undertaking affirmative action, the government is practicing what it preaches (although, make no mistake about it, the Carter administration is responding to its own political needs and commitments). We ought to welcome any diminution of government hypocrisy.

5. The problem of quotas. Affirmative action in practice results in a quota system, opponents contend, and quotas are dysfunctional for the workings of American institutions. Quotas based on group affiliation and not individual merit can work grave hardship on well-qualified individuals who are in excess of their group's quota, and, in general, quotas tend to promote mediocrity. Quotas can exclude superior qualified persons who have the wrong sex, race, religion, or ethnic affiliation; they can include not only the marginally qualified, but even unqualified persons. Affirmative action is the first step on the road to the balkanization of America, and the courts—our prized palladiums of justice—should be the last place where this concept is imposed.

Response: Affirmative action programs have existed for close to a decade, and I am not persuaded that the parade of horrors suggested above has even begun to come about. I see no movement within the United States for each ethnic or religious grouping to claim a quota of public or private jobs. Most Americans accept individual merit as the proper basis for school admissions and employment opportunities.

Although the distinction may be fuzzy, I do see a difference between affirmative action and a quota system. Affirmative action does not have a rigid numerical goal; it retains flexibility yet is a good faith effort to widen the recruitment net, indeed to vigorously recruit, and pay particular attention to women and disadvantaged racial/ethnic groups. Affirmative action also means selecting the individual from the previously discriminated-against group when all else is approximately equal.

I have not heard or read the word "quota" in connection with the Carter administration's affirmative action objectives for judicial selection. I would oppose the use of a quota system as unnecessarily rigid and singularly inappropriate for the judiciary, but this is not at issue. The Carter administration itself, as I understand it, is making strenuous efforts to recruit, or have selection commissions and senators recruit, qualified women, blacks, and Hispanic candidates. The administration, as I also understand it, is quite concerned with the qualifications of minority and women candidates.

If the politics of federal judicial selection today makes it unlikely that incompetent white males will go on the bench, the politics of affirmative action requires that only competent minorities and women be appointed. The surest way to sabotage affirmative action is to link it with incompetency. The Carter Administration's record of minority and women appointments thus far has been excellent and there is every reason to believe that the concern with credentials of minority and women candidates will continue to yield well-qualified judges.

6. An inappropriate program for the judiciary. No matter what the merits of affirmative action may be for other spheres of American life, critics insist, it is highly inappropriate for the judicial branch. Even though merit may not actually be the sole criterion for judicial selection, it is recognized as ideally the basis for choosing judges, and leading professional groups have been working to make progress towards that goal. But if a criterion other than individual merit gains legitimacy, it becomes all the more difficult to assign to oblivion the "extraneous" political considerations that have traditionally "polluted" the process. And it becomes more difficult to win support for a partisan-free merit selection process.

Part of the justification for merit selection is that a federal judge must be highly skilled since the federal courts are the fastest legal tracks in town. We need the best people for the job; would we select a surgeon to perform a highly complex and delicate operation on any basis other than the best person available? Why should we do less with the judiciary? We need the best people on the bench regardless of race, sex or national origin. In the words of the president, "Why not the best?"

Response: This is a slippery argument to counter. To be sure, there must be highly competent judges to service the trial and appellate courts of the nation. Official recognition of race and sex does appear at first blush to detract from the goal of a non-discriminatory process for obtaining the best qualified persons to serve. But a closer look at the job of federal judges should make it clear that our judges have always been involved in the major political controversies of the day. As Tocqueville so perceptively observed over 140 years ago, "Scarcely any political question arises in the United States that is not resolved, sooner or later, into a judicial question." [4]

Today, racial and sexual discrimination are major legal issues before the courts. A judge who is a member of a racial minority or a woman cannot help but bring to the bench a certain sensitivity—indeed, certain qualities of the heart and mind—that may be particularly helpful in dealing with these issues. This is not to say that white judges are necessarily insensitive to issues of racial discrimination or that male judges cannot cope with issues of sexual discrimination. But the presence on the bench in visible numbers of well qualified judges drawn from the minorities and women cannot help but add a new dimension of justice to our courts in most instances.

These judges cannot help but educate their colleagues by the example they set, by the creation of precedents, and by informal as well as formal interchange. They are likely the "best" people to fill certain of the vacancies and new judgeships.

Yes, we ought to aspire to obtaining the "best" people for our judiciary—but the "best" bench may be one composed of persons of all races and both sexes with diverse backgrounds and experiences and not necessarily only those who were editors of the Harvard and Yale law reviews. It is difficult to define—much less find—the "best." Despite occasional mistakes, the current selection process with its political sensitivity has served the nation well. But affirmative action of the sort advocated and being practiced by the Carter Administration should strengthen the federal bench. And perhaps most significantly, it may be that by searching for the best possible women and minority candidates, a precedent will be established for emphasizing the individual professional merits of all candidates for judgeships, regardless of race and sex.

Notes

This article originally appeared in Volume 62, Number 10, May 1979, pages 488–494.

1. Goldman, "A profile of Carter's judicial nominees," *Judicature* 62 (November 1978), 246.
2. *See* the text and citations in Goldman and Jahnige, *The Federal Courts as a Political System*, 2nd ed. (New York: Harper & Row, 1976), 47–78.
3. Carbon, "The U.S. Circuit Judge Nominating Commission: a comparison of two of its panels," *Judicature* 62 (November 1978), 233 at 236; Slotnick, "What panelists are saying about the circuit judge nominating commission," *Judicature* 62 (February 1979), 320.
4. de Tocqueville, *Democracy in America*, vol. 1 (New York: Random House, Vintage Books edition, 1945), 290.

Women and minorities on state and federal appellate benches, 1985 and 1999

Mark S. Hurwitz and Drew Noble Lanier

Appellate courts are becoming more diverse—and selection method no longer seems to be associated with the characteristics of those selected for the bench.

The presence of political minorities in the U.S. judiciary provides enormous symbolic, and perhaps political, import to a vital branch of government. Indeed, over the last 25 years there has been a myriad of efforts to increase the number and proportion of female and minority judges on both the state and federal courts. At the same time, there also has been a movement in the state courts toward greater use of merit systems for judicial appointment, as opposed to lifetime tenure or elections in which the influence of money is increasingly emphasized.[1] The literature in these areas is extensive—both in terms of examining the manner in which selection system may affect diversity on the state benches and how different presidential administrations have approached the nomination process in the federal courts.[2]

Research on these issues remains compelling today, in part because the goals of judicial diversity and merit reforms may conflict, and because ideological partisanship may impede efforts to increase diversity in the federal courts. Political minorities may thus face greater and perhaps qualitatively different obstacles in attaining office than other candidates.[3] Moreover, while the differences in the decision making of women and minority judges are not profound, there are some notable deviations.[4] Inclusion of these groups is vital in maintaining and even increasing the legitimacy of the nation's judicial tribunals.

However, many of the prior studies on these issues were idiosyncratic to an individual setting or context, such as a single court, subgroup, or selection method, or to a limited number of states. Moreover, most concerned only the state courts, and few compared the federal and state systems or the intermediate courts of appeals and courts of last resort.[5] With this in mind, Slotnick has urged scholars to engage in comparative studies of judges on both state and federal benches to build a deeper understanding of "the strengths, weaknesses, capabilities, and unique roles of judiciaries operative at diverse governmental levels." [6] We thus seek to further this body of research by comparing the real and relative gains that women and minorities recently have made on both state and federal appellate courts.

To do so, we gathered data on the racial and gender composition of all judges on the courts of last resort and intermediate appellate courts for each of the 50 states and the District of Columbia for two cross-sections of time, 1985 and 1999. We obtained the state data from courts' Web Sites, if one existed, and by telephoning the clerks of each court. This information was supplemented and cross-checked for validity and comprehensiveness by reference to various sources.[7] We also compiled data on federal appellate court judges for the same time periods, relying on the database constructed by Zuk, Barrow, and Gryski[8] for the 1985 cross-section and official information from the Federal Judicial Center for the 1999 cross-section.[9] The 1999 federal data were supplemented and cross-checked for validity by reference to various sources, such as court clerks and Web Sites. By comparing the number and proportion of women and minorities who have become appellate judges across disparate courts over time, we are able to obtain a more comprehensive picture of political minorities on appellate benches and the changes over the final years of the 20th century.[10]

Methods of attainment

State appellate judges may reach the bench in several ways—by election, either partisan or nonpartisan; gubernatorial appointment; legislative appointment; or merit selection.[11] By contrast, all judges in the federal court system are appointed by the President and confirmed by the Senate. While these represent the formal mechanisms for appointment, state judges also can be selected by informal methods, which usually dominate the process when certain vacancies are filled, such as interim appointments. In fact, Graham demonstrated that a significant number of judges in formal elective systems actually achieved their seats on the bench by informal methods, usually appointment of some kind.[12] Yet Glick and Emmert found that "the informal method of selection within the elective states makes no important differences in the characteristics of judges." [13] This study follows up on Glick and Emmert's findings, focusing only on formal methods of judicial selection, in part because informal methods likely affect the makeup of judges in elective systems more so than in the other formal methods.[14]

Researchers have debated whether the method of selection has any substantive influence on women and minorities attaining judicial commissions. Those interested in cultivating judicial diversity have argued that appointive systems in general, and merit systems in particular, tend to favor the status quo by perpetuating the dominance of elites in the judiciary, thus decreasing judicial opportunities for political minorities who may not have conventional legal backgrounds or experience. In support of this argument, some scholars have found that the method of selection does influence the diversity of the bench, although these studies are not entirely consistent.[15]

Others have argued that the evidence implies that selection systems are not systematically associated one way or another with minority representation in the courts. For instance, a number of studies have determined that the merit system has no substantial influence on women and minorities becoming state judges.[16] Esterling and Andersen's recent study found that merit selection systems may actually enhance minority representation.[17] And in the federal system, one scholar found that President Carter's nominating commission produced somewhat more diversity of judicial nominees than had previously been generated.[18] Consequently, scholars have suggested that other factors may influence diversity on the bench—including region, the applicable pool of potential judges, and the prestige of the court.[19] Of course, most of these studies did not consider informal methods in their analyses. Thus, while the collective evidence intimates that selection systems do not minimize judicial diversity or otherwise affect representation on the courts, the issue remains an open one.

Selection systems

Between 1985 and 1999, states have made changes in the types of formal selection processes they employ.

Table 1. Type of initial selection system in state appellate courts: 1985, 1999

	Number and percentage of courts	
	1985	1999
Judicial election (partisan or nonpartisan)	42 47.2%	42 45.2%
Legislative election	5 5.6%	5 5.4%
Gubernatorial appointment	7 7.9%	7 7.5%
Nomination by commission	35 39.3%	39 41.9%
Total	89 100%	93 100%

(See Table 1.)[20] Interestingly, the aggregate number of appellate courts employing either judicial elections, legislative elections, or gubernatorial appointment seems to have remained stable over time. In fact, the only increase was observed in states that moved toward a system of nomination by commission, the first element of a merit selection system; even there, however, the change was very slight, from 35 to 39 courts.[21] Nevertheless, while the virtues of a merit system of appointment continue to be exhorted by its many advocates, presently more appellate courts utilize some sort of formal electoral process to fill positions than a version of a merit system.[22]

Table 2 provides a more detailed view of the information in Table 1. In particular, there were a number of changes in the types of selection systems in state appellate courts, even though these variations washed out in the aggregate. For instance, of the 26 courts that utilized nonpartisan elections in 1985, 23 continued to do so in 1999, while two moved to a partisan electoral system and one shifted to nomination by commission. Two newly established courts employed this system in 1999, along with one other court that previously had used partisan elections; thus, the aggregate number remained at 26.

Similar exchanges occurred among the other selection systems. Nomination by commission gained courts that changed from all of the other selection systems, including one each from nonpartisan and partisan

Table 2. Change in type of initial selection system in state appellate courts: 1985, 1999

		1999 initial selection system					
		Nonpartisan election	Partisan election	Legislative election	Gubernatorial appointment	Nomination by commission	1985 Total
1985 initial selection system	Nonpartisan election	23	2	0	0	1	26
	Partisan election	1	14	0	0	1	16
	Legislative election	0	0	3	0	2	5
	Gubernatorial appointment	0	0	0	5	2	7
	Nomination by commission	0	0	2	2	31	35
	Court established after 1985	2	0	0	0	2	4
	1999 Total	26	16	5	7	39	93

Note: Numbers refer to the number of state appellate courts matching the intersection of both categories.

Table 3. Merit system of appointment in state appellate courts: 1985, 1999

		1999 merit selection system?		
		Yes	No	1985 Total
1985 merit selection system?	Yes	25	0	25
	No	6	62	68
	1999 Total	31	62	93

Note: Numbers refer to the number of state appellate courts matching the intersection of both categories (*See* n. 21, which explains why some systems that utilize judicial nominating commissions are not considered merit selection systems).

elections, two each from legislative election and gubernatorial appointment, and two from new courts. Concurrently, two courts that had employed nomination by commission in 1985 switched to legislative selection, and two others substituted gubernatorial appointment. As a consequence, Table 2 demonstrates that the changes in the use of various selection systems from 1985 to 1999 were more complex than four appellate courts accepting the perceived benefits of a merit system, which might otherwise have been implied from the results reported in Table 1.

Table 3 illustrates that 25 of these courts had a merit plan in place in 1985, none of which shifted to a non-merit system by 1999. Sixty-two courts did not use a merit system in 1985; six of these had adopted the merit procedure by 1999. Thus, the merit system of appointment did not lose any courts in the aggregate but rather made modest gains during the final 15 years of the 20th century.

Diversity levels

There have been intriguing changes in the proportion of women and minorities in both the state and federal appellate courts since 1985. This information is displayed in Tables 4 and 5, which report distinctions between the racial and gender makeup of the state and federal appellate courts in 1985 and 1999. Judges are categorized according to certain representative characteristics, including an aggregate measure of women and minorities (all non-white males on the bench), minorities (whether male or female), women of any race, minority females, African-American males, African-American females, Hispanic males, Hispanic females, Asian/Pacific Island males, and Asian/Pacific Island females.[23]

An immediate impression of the changes that have occurred since 1985 is that women and minorities have made great strides in terms of their representation as appellate court judges. As indicated by the aggregate classification of women and minorities in Table 4, the rate of the category of non-white males (hereafter, "NWMs") on the state appellate courts doubled, from roughly 13 to 27 percent. In terms of real numbers, this increase proved to be even greater: there were 140 NWM judges in 1985 and 341 in 1999.

Table 5 additionally illustrates the proliferation of NWMs in the federal courts from 1985 to 1999, who increased their representation from approximately 17 to 28 percent, with the number of these federal judges growing from 27 to 47. Thus, it appears that diversity on the appellate benches in the United States clearly has been augmented during the period of study.[24] Nevertheless, while these changes may be somewhat encouraging to those who support increasing diversity

Table 4. Representation of women and minorities in the state appellate courts: 1985, 1999

	Total	Merit system	No merit system	Judicial election	Appt by governor	Court of last resort	Intermediate appellate court	At-large district (statewide)	District sub-division
Women and minorities (non-white males)									
1985	13.23 (140)	10.73* (28)	14.05* (112)	10.04* (55)	20.13* (31)	12.39 (43)	13.64 (97)	14.69 (88)	11.33 (52)
1999	27.11 (341)	24.86 (92)	28.04 (249)	26.83 (187)	28.18 (51)	30.77* (108)	25.69 (233)	29.10 (190)	24.96 (151)
Minorities (males and females)									
1985	6.52 (69)	4.21* (11)	7.28 (58)	4.93 (27)	8.44* (13)	5.76 (20)	6.89 (49)	7.18 (43)	5.66 (26)
1999	7.31 (92)	5.68* (21)	8.00 (71)	7.17 (50)	8.29 (15)	7.12 (25)	7.39 (67)	7.20 (47)	7.44 (45)
Women (any race)									
1985	6.81 (72)	6.51 (17)	6.90 (55)	5.29 (29)	10.39* (16)	7.20 (25)	6.61 (47)	7.85 (47)	5.45 (25)
1999	21.14 (266)	19.46 (72)	21.85 (194)	21.66 (151)	20.44 (37)	24.79* (87)	19.74 (179)	22.82 (149)	19.34 (117)
Minority females									
1985	0.47 (5)	0*	0.63 (5)	0.18 (1)	1.30* (2)	0.58 (2)	0.42 (3)	0.33 (2)	0.65 (3)
1999	1.35 (17)	0.27* (1)	1.80 (16)	2.01* (14)	0.55* (1)	1.14 (4)	1.43 (13)	0.92 (6)	1.82 (11)
African-American males									
1985	4.06 (43)	3.45 (9)	4.27 (34)	3.10 (17)	4.55 (7)	3.17 (11)	4.50 (32)	4.01 (24)	4.14 (19)
1999	3.66 (46)	2.43* (9)	4.17 (37)	3.87 (27)	2.76 (5)	3.99 (14)	3.53 (32)	4.13 (27)	3.14 (19)
African-American females									
1985	0.47 (5)	0*	0.63 (5)	0.18 (1)	1.30* (2)	0.58 (2)	0.42 (3)	0.33 (2)	0.65 (3)
1999	0.79 (10)	0*	1.13 (10)	1.43* (10)	0*	0.57 (2)	0.88 (8)	0.46 (3)	1.16* (7)
Hispanic males									
1985	1.23 (13)	0.77 (2)	1.38 (11)	1.64 (9)	1.30 (2)	0.86 (3)	1.41 (10)	1.84 (11)	0.44* (2)
1999	1.67 (21)	2.43* (9)	1.35 (12)	1.29 (9)	3.87* (7)	0.85* (3)	1.98 (18)	1.07 (7)	2.31 (14)
Hispanic females									
1985	0	0	0	0	0	0	0	0	0
1999	0.40 (5)	0*	0.56 (5)	0.57 (4)	0*	0*	0.55 (5)	0.15 (1)	0.66* (4)
Asian/Pacific Island males									
1985	0.76 (8)	0*	1.00 (8)	0*	1.30* (2)	1.15 (4)	0.56 (4)	1.00 (6)	0.44 (2)
1999	0.64 (8)	0.54 (2)	0.68 (6)	0*	1.10* (2)	1.14* (4)	0.44 (4)	1.07 (7)	0.17* (1)
Asian/Pacific Island females									
1985	0	0	0	0	0	0	0	0	0
1999	0.16 (2)	0.27 (1)	0.11 (1)	0	0.55* (1)	0.57* (2)	0	0.31 (2)	0

* Significant at the .05 level or better (p = .05; 2-tailed test). The first number in each cell for each year represents the percentage within that category as compared to the appropriate total, while the number in parentheses is the actual number of minority and/or female judges. Judges of Asian and Pacific Island descent are aggregated together based upon aggregation in the source of information.

Table 5. Representation of women and minorities in the federal appeals courts: 1985, 1999

		Total	1st Circuit	2nd Circuit	3rd Circuit	4th Circuit	5th Circuit	6th Circuit	7th Circuit	8th Circuit	9th Circuit	10th Circuit	11th Circuit	DC Circuit
Women and minorities (non-white males)	1985	17.31 (27)	16.67 (1)	15.38 (2)	25.00* (3)	0*	12.50 (2)	20.00 (3)	0*	10.00* (1)	25.00* (7)	20.00 (2)	16.67 (2)	33.33* (4)
	1999	28.14 (47)	33.33 (2)	30.77 (4)	42.86* (6)	13.33* (2)	29.41 (5)	31.25 (5)	27.27 (3)	18.18* (2)	25.00 (7)	33.33 (4)	33.33 (4)	25.00 (3)
Minorities (males and females)	1985	8.33 (13)	16.67 (1)	15.38* (2)	8.33 (1)	0*	0*	13.33* (2)	0*	10.00 (1)	10.71 (3)	0*	8.33 (1)	16.67* (2)
	1999	11.38 (19)	16.67 (1)	23.08* (3)	7.14 (1)	0*	17.65* (3)	12.50* (2)	9.09 (1)	9.09 (1)	10.71 (3)	8.33 (1)	8.33 (1)	16.67 (2)
Women (any race)	1985	9.62 (15)	0*	7.69* (1)	16.67* (2)	0*	12.50 (2)	6.67 (1)	0*	0*	14.29 (4)	20.00* (2)	8.33 (1)	16.67* (2)
	1999	19.76 (33)	16.67 (1)	23.08 (3)	35.71* (5)	13.33 (2)	11.76* (2)	18.75 (3)	27.27* (3)	9.09* (1)	17.86 (5)	25.00 (3)	25.00 (3)	16.67 (2)
Minority women	1985	.64 (1)	0	7.69 (1)	0	0	0	0	0	0	0	0	0	0
	1999	2.99 (5)	0	15.38* (2)	0*	0*	0*	0*	9.09* (1)	0*	3.57 (1)	0*	0*	8.33* (1)
African-American males	1985	6.41 (10)	0*	7.69 (1)	8.33 (1)	0*	0*	13.33* (2)	0*	10.00 (1)	7.14 (2)	0*	8.33 (1)	16.67* (2)
	1999	4.19 (7)	0	0*	7.14 (1)	0*	5.88 (1)	12.50* (2)	0*	9.09* (1)	0*	0*	8.33* (1)	8.33* (1)
African-American females	1985	.64 (1)	0	7.69* (1)	0	0	0	0	0	0	0	0	0	0
	1999	1.80 (3)	0	7.69* (1)	0	0	0	0	9.09* (1)	0	0	0	0	8.33* (1)
Hispanic males	1985	1.28 (2)	16.67* (1)	0	0	0	0	0	0	0	3.57* (1)	0	0	0
	1999	3.59 (6)	16.67* (1)	7.69* (1)	0*	0*	11.76* (2)	0*	0*	0*	3.57 (1)	8.33* (1)	0*	0*
Hispanic females	1985	0	0	0	0	0	0	0	0	0	0	0	0	0
	1999	1.20 (2)	0	7.69* (1)	0	0	0	0	0	0	3.57* (1)	0	0	0
Asian males	1985	0	0	0	0	0	0	0	0	0	0	0	0	0
	1999	0.60 (1)	0	0	0	0	0	0	0	0	3.57* (1)	0	0	0
Asian females	1985	0	0	0	0	0	0	0	0	0	0	0	0	0
	1999	0	0	0	0	0	0	0	0	0	0	0	0	0

* Significant at the .05 level or better (p = .05; 2-tailed test). The first number in each cell for each year represents the percentage within that category as compared to the total, while the number in parentheses is the actual number of minority and/or women judges.

in the judiciary, these figures also demonstrate that roughly three-quarters of current United States appellate judges are white males, with women and minorities comprising the remaining judicial positions.

Furthermore, Tables 4 and 5 reveal that the proliferation of NWM judges was not uniform among all political minority groups. Indeed, the vast majority of the increase of NWMs stemmed from gains by women, not minorities. In the state courts, the increase in minority judges was less than 1 percent, which in real numbers represented an increase of only about one-third; in fact, there were proportionally fewer African-American male judges in the state appellate courts in 1999 than there were in 1985. On the other hand, the rate of women judges in the state courts increased from less than 7 percent in 1985 to more than 21 percent in 1999; in real numbers, there were three-and-one-half times more women judges by the end of this time period.

Although not as dramatic, the results for the federal courts were similar to those for the state courts. In particular, minority federal judges increased from about 8 to 11 percent, while the figure for women judges rose from less than 10 to nearly 20 percent. But, there were fewer African-American male judges in the federal circuits in 1999, both in terms of percentage and real numbers, than in 1985. These represent considerable increases for women judges, especially when compared to the relatively negligible advances that African Americans made during this same time. Consequently, even though the systems of judicial appointment are very different in the state and federal courts, it appears as if somewhat analogous forces may be acting to magnify the proportion of women judges relative to minorities.

Diversity and selection systems

While there were differences in diversity rates according to the type of formal selection system in state appellate courts in 1985, most of these disparities had decreased, if not entirely disappeared, by 1999. For instance, as Table 4 illustrates, in 1985 less than 11 percent of NWM judges had attained their positions through a merit system, while more than 14 percent of NWMs reached the bench outside of a merit system, a difference that was statistically significant for both selection methods. Thus, in 1985 it appears that NWMs were at a greater advantage in non-merit systems than when a merit system was in place. However, by 1999 not only had the percentage of NWMs increased to about 25 and 28 percent for merit and non-merit systems,

respectively, neither difference was significantly different from the prevailing norm. So, while NWMs fared better in 1985 in non-merit systems, by 1999 there was no tangible difference in the ability of NWMs to attain a position in the judiciary via either merit or non-merit systems.

Nevertheless, we must reiterate that this lack of disparity was much more apparent for women than it was for minorities, the latter of whom did not fare nearly as well in merit systems. On the other hand, while the numbers are small, Hispanic males fared better under merit systems than otherwise. Finally, in both 1985 and 1999, far fewer judges attained their seats through merit systems (261 and 370, respectively) than through non-merit procedures (797 and 888). However, there was a greater proportion, by nearly 10 percent, of merit-based judges in 1999 than there was in 1985. The trend toward greater numbers of judges attaining their judicial commissions via merit systems appears to be confirmed by these results, although this inclination may have stabilized somewhat in recent years.

Similarly, the distinctions associated with formal judicial elections and gubernatorial nomination abated over time. In 1985, nearly every category of NWM was more successful in attaining a commission on an appellate bench when nominated by the state executive than when selected in a formal electoral system. These apparent distinctions, however, were inconsequential by 1999. In the more recent cross-section, in fact, African American and other minority women actually attained higher rates of representation in judicial election systems than they did through gubernatorial nomination. We cannot state definitively that these results are due to informal gubernatorial appointments in formal elective systems, or whether authentic changes in the nature of minority success in judicial elections have been achieved. Nevertheless, representation of NWMs on state appellate benches has substantially appreciated over time, irrespective of differences in formal selection systems.[25]

Various scholars have asserted that NWMs are more likely to attain their judicial commissions in less prestigious courts, such as intermediate appellate courts as opposed to courts of last resort, or on courts with a district subdivision rather than a statewide, at-large division. These expectations, however, were not realized in either cross-section examined. As Table 4 displays, in 1985 there were trivial differences in the ability of every category of NWM judge to attain a seat on a court of last resort or an intermediate appellate court. Yet, by 1999 NWMs were more likely to become judges on a court of last resort than they were on an intermediate appellate court. Similarly, there were no observed differences in the rates of these political minorities on courts that employed district subdivisions as opposed to statewide partitions. Based on these results, we suggest that prestige theory, which asserts that NWMs are less likely to reach the bench on courts of higher distinction, does not appear to be supported.

Federal courts

The numbers of federal appellate court judges are much smaller than those for states: there was a total of 156 and 167 of these judicial positions authorized in 1985 and 1999, respectively, compared to well more than 1,000 state appellate judges. Thus, it is difficult to ascertain levels of statistical significance of comparisons across circuit courts, considering that an addition or subtraction of only one or two NWM federal appellate judges would make a substantial difference. Accordingly, the reader may wish to exercise some caution when interpreting the federal appellate court notations in Table 5.

Notwithstanding, there are some generalizations that may be gleaned from the data on federal judges, the first of which is that the overall proportions and trends of diverse representation were fairly similar to those for the state courts. Moreover, there were distinctions among the various circuits. In 1985, the courts with the greatest proportion of NWMs were the Third, Ninth, and D.C. Circuits. The Fourth, Seventh, and Eighth Circuits had the lowest percentages of these judges in 1985; in fact, the Fourth and Seventh Circuits had no NWMs at all. Yet, by 1999 every federal circuit save one remained the same or increased its magnitude of NWM judges. The Fourth and Seventh Circuits, which previously had no NWMs, added at least two NWM judges by the latter time period. Only the D.C. Circuit dropped below its prior level, with one fewer NWM in 1999 than in 1985.

Interestingly, by 1999 every circuit had at least one woman. The Fourth Circuit had no minorities, however, and six of the 12 circuits retained only one minority judge. As was observed in the states, the overall increase in political minorities on the federal bench for the most part stemmed from increasing numbers and percentages of women. Still, while there was only one minority woman in 1985, there were five in 1999, three of whom were African American (Second, Seventh, and D.C. Circuits) and two of whom were Hispanic (Second and Ninth Circuits). While there were

no Asian circuit court judges in 1985, there was one in 1999 (Ninth Circuit).

In terms of real numbers, by 1999 the Third and Ninth Circuits had the greatest number of minorities (six and five, respectively); yet only the Fourth and Eighth Circuits had a lower percentage of minority judges than the Ninth (with 28 appellate judges, the latter is the largest federal circuit by far). While the Second, Sixth, Ninth, and D.C. Circuits had more than one African-American judge on their panels in 1985, this was true only for the Sixth and D.C. Circuits in 1999. And the Fifth Circuit in 1985 was the only federal appeals court to have more than one Hispanic on its panel in either cross-section.

A final comparison, which concerns President Clinton's judicial appointments and those of his predecessors, demonstrates that much of the increase in diversity in the federal courts can be attributed to the 42nd President. Overall, NWMs comprised about 28 percent of the federal appellate bench in 1999 (see Table 5). A majority of the Clinton appointees—52 percent—were NWMs, whereas the comparable figure for the non-Clinton judges who were active on the federal bench in 1999 was significantly lower, at 22 percent. Stark differences are found for the non-aggregate categories as well.[26] These results exhibit what appears to be a clear motivation on the part of the Clinton administration to diversify the federal judiciary, even though the aggregate increase of NWMs in the federal courts was similar to that which took place in the state courts during this time period.[27]

Substantial progress

This study has endeavored to discover particularized differences in the relative rates of success that various political minorities have recently experienced on the judiciary in the United States. The data examine women and several minority groups on both state and federal courts across two cross-sections of time; furthermore, the state data view both courts of last resort and intermediate appellate courts. Consequently, the breadth of the data permits drawing a number of inferences regarding the changing nature of the use of particular judicial selection systems and the number of judges who are political minorities.

One of the findings implies that the advocates of merit selection may face a difficult task in convincing states to utilize this process in the future. Glick and Emmert reported that four state supreme courts utilized a merit system in 1960, a number that had increased to 14 by the late 1970s.[28] While the number of state supreme courts employing a merit selection system had increased to 20 by 1985, only one additional state supreme court has adopted this system since that time. It thus appears that the trend toward adoption of merit systems in the state courts has leveled off, with a great deal of unrealized potential for additional courts to adopt the merit system of selection.

Another important finding is that political minorities have made substantive progress in attaining the bench over the past 15 years, although clearly there remains room for improvement. For nearly every category observed, both the number and percentage of NWMs increased since 1985. Nevertheless, while the presence of political minorities in the judiciary has become somewhat more representative over time, most appellate judges in the United States are still white males. Moreover, women realized far greater improvements in their ability to become judges than did other political minorities, particularly African Americans. In fact, the levels of African-American judges remained somewhat stable over the period of study; African Americans did not achieve anywhere near the gains that women or Hispanics realized. While these results are tempered somewhat by the fact that women comprise a greater percentage of the overall population and represent a larger available pool of judicial candidates, clearly the gains realized by African Americans in particular were negligible at best, particularly in relation to other political minorities.

Scholars must explore why African Americans have failed to increase their representation on the courts relative to women. Has a tacit, societal quota been met—is there, in other words, a perception that the courts are of sufficient color, with no need for any additional fortification in this regard? Are other factors, such as the applicable pools of potential women and African-American judges, driving these results? While beyond the scope of this study, further scholarship that seeks a systematic explanation of the dissimilar success rates of women and African Americans is necessary. Moreover, the forces influencing the rates of NWMs on the courts seem to be qualitatively different for various political minorities. This study demonstrates that data on this topic should be disaggregated into separate women and minority categories in order to draw valid conclusions and generalizations regarding each type of political minority.

A final implication from this study concerns the lack of association merit systems seem to have with the abil-

ity of political minorities to attain seats in the judiciary. The 1985 results demonstrate that there were differences, however slight—yet any disparity was no longer observed by 1999. Similar deductions regarding diversity can be articulated from the most recent cross-section for the other institutional distinctions examined. The analogous findings between the state and federal courts are additional evidence that selection method does not seem to be associated with the diversity characteristics of those selected for the bench.

While previously it may have been accurate to assert that merit systems and judicial diversity were mutually exclusive concepts, this study suggests that this claim was no longer the case at the end of the 20th century. As a consequence, it appears that efforts to produce normatively good courts do not necessarily conflict with a more representative judiciary.

Notes

The article originally appeared in Volume 85, Number 2, September–October 2001, pages 84–92.

Research for this article was made possible in part by DSR Grant No. 11-80-933-00 from the Office of Sponsored Research at the University of Central Florida. The authors thank Jennifer Robinson and Raylene Strickler at UCF and Diane Oyler at UB for their research assistance. The authors are listed alphabetically, as each contributed equally to this article.

1. Glaberson, "Fierce Campaigns Signal a New Era for State Courts," *New York Times,* June 5, 2000, at A-1.
2. For the impact of selection systems on diversity, *see, e.g.,* Canon, "The Impact of Formal Selection Processes on the Characteristics of Judges—Reconsidered," *Law & Soc'y Rev.* 6 (1972), 575–593; Slotnick," Judicial Selection Systems and Nomination Outcomes: Does the Process Make a Difference?," *Am. Pol. Q.* 12 (1984), 225–240; Glick and Emmert, "Selection systems and judicial characteristics: The recruitment of state supreme court justices," *Judicature* 70 (1987), 228–235; Graham, "Do Judicial Selection Systems Matter? A Study of Black Representation on State Courts," *Am. Pol. Q.* 18 (1990), 316–336; Esterling and Andersen, "Diversity and the Judicial Merit Selection Process: A Statistical Report," in *Research on Judicial Selection 1999* (Chicago: American Judicature Society, 1999), 1–32. For presidential administrations' nomination approaches, *see, e.g.,* Slotnick, "Federal Appellate Judge Selection During the Carter Administration: Recruitment Changes and Unanswered Questions," *Just. Sys. J.* 6 (1981), 283–304; Martin, "Gender and judicial selection: A comparison of the Reagan and Carter administrations," *Judicature* 71 (1987), 136–142; Goldman, "Bush's judicial legacy," *Judicature* 67 (1993), 165–173; and Goldman, "Judicial selec-

tion under Clinton: A midterm examination," *Judicature* 78 (1995), 278–291.

3. Alozie, "Selection Methods and the Recruitment of Women to State Courts of Last Resort," *Soc. Sci. Q.* 77 (1996), 110–126.

4. Songer, Davis, and Haire, "A Reappraisal of Diversification in the Federal Courts: Gender Effects in the Courts of Appeals," *J. Pol.* 56 (1994), 425–439; Songer and Crews-Meyer, "Does Gender Matter? Decision Making in State Supreme Courts," *Soc. Sci. Q.* 81 (2000), 750–762; Glick and Emmert, *supra* n. 2.

5. *See* Lyon, *The Proportions of Black Judges to Black Population in Supreme and Appellate Jurisdictions: Elective vs. Appointive Systems of Judicial Selection* (Chicago: Committee on Courts and Justice, 1981) for an exception to this generalization.

6. Slotnick, "Review Essay on Judicial Recruitment and Selection," *Just. Sys. J.* 13 (1988), 109, 122.

7. These included Henry et al., *The Success of Women and Minorities in Achieving Judicial Office: The Selection Process* (New York: Fund for Modern Courts, 1985); *The Book of the States, 1984–85* (Lexington, Ky.: The Council of State Governments, 1984); *The Book of the States, 1998–99* (Lexington, Ky.: The Council of State Governments, 1998); Gallas, Rottman, and Roper, *State Court Organization 1987* (Williamsburg, Va.: National Center for State Courts, 1988); Warrick, *Judicial Selection in the United States: A Compendium of Provisions*, 2nd ed. (Chicago: American Judicature Society, 1993); Flango and Rottman, *Appellate Court Procedures* (Williamsburg, Va.: National Center for State Courts, 1998).

8. Zuk, Barrow, and Gryski, *A Multi-User Database on the Attributes of U.S. Appeals Court Judges, 1801–1994* (Ann Arbor, Mich.: Inter-university Consortium for Political and Social Research, 1997).

9. *See* www.fjc.gov for the Federal Judicial Center Web site.

10. Our examination focuses solely on appellate rather than trial courts. The selection process in the latter may differ entirely, due to their divergent functions and places within the judicial hierarchy.

11. Warrick, *supra* n. 7. Merit selection is defined here as a process in which a nonpartisan or bipartisan commission nominates a few individuals for a judicial position, for appointment (usually) by the executive based on the commission's recommended names, with subsequent tenure on the bench dependent upon a retention election at specific intervals. *See* Esterling and Andersen, *supra* n. 2.

12. Graham, *supra* n. 2.

13. Glick and Emmert, *supra* n. 2, at 231.

14. While distinctions may arise between the structural effects of formal selection systems due to informal interim appointments, our study concerns the two-fold issues of the gains made over time by judges who are political

minorities and the variance observed regarding these political minorities across seemingly disparate judicial contexts. Accordingly, the reader should exercise caution with respect to reported differences in selection methods, particularly those concerning elective systems. *See* Graham, *supra* n. 2; Glick and Emmert, *supra* n. 2.

15. Warden, Schlesinger, and Kearney, *Women, Blacks, and Merit Selection of Judges* (Chicago: Committee on Courts and Justice, 1979); Lyon, *supra* n. 5; Henry et al., *supra* n. 7; Glick, "The Promise and Performance of the Missouri Plan," *U. Miami L. Rev.* 32 (1978), 509–541; and Graham, *supra* n. 2.

16. Flango and Ducat, *supra* n. 2; Glick and Emmert, *supra* n. 2; Alozie, *supra* n. 2; Dubois, *supra* n. 2.

17. Esterling and Andersen, *supra* n. 2.

18. Slotnick, *supra* n. 2, at 229. For a more thorough review of the characteristics of federal appellate court judges, *see* Gryski, Zuk, and Barrow, "A Bench that Looks Like America? Representation of African Americans and Latinos on the Federal Courts," *J. Pol.* 56 (1994), 1076–1086; and Goldman, *Picking Federal Judges: Lower Court Selection from Roosevelt through Reagan* (New Haven: Yale University Press, 1997).

19. Glick and Emmert, *supra* n. 2; Welch, "Recruitment of Women to Public Office: A Discriminant Analysis," *West Pol. Q.* 31 (1978), 372; Martin, *supra* n. 2; and Alozie, *supra* n. 3.

20. Since the federal system is based on executive appointment, our analysis here relates solely to state courts. Categorizing the variants of selection systems necessarily entails some subjectivity; hence, our classifications may differ slightly from those of other studies.

21. A system employing nomination by commission technically differs from a merit system in that in the former an advisory committee aids the governor or legislature in making selections, while in the latter the selected judge is also required to stand in a subsequent retention election. Hence, nomination by commission is a necessary, but not sufficient, condition of a merit plan.

22. *But see* Graham, *supra* n. 2.

23. Our data sources for federal judges identify only African Americans, Hispanics, Asians, and Whites; accordingly, there is no identifying information for judges of Pacific Island descent in Table 5.

24. Interestingly, with two women and one minority as current members of the United States Supreme Court, the proportion of women and minorities on the nation's highest judicial tribunal seems to comport with the results for the appellate courts in this study.

25. We also collected data on regional differences of minority judges. We do not report this information because region and formal selection system tend to correlate with each other, and because factors such as the applicable pool of judicial candidates might influence such distinc-

tions. These data may be obtained from the authors upon request.

26. Clinton judges were 35 percent women, 13 percent African American, and 10 percent Hispanic, while non–Clinton judges were 17 percent women, 3 percent African American, and 3 percent Hispanic.

27. President Clinton's record of judicial appointments was made in the presence of a hostile Republican majority in the Senate for most of his tenure in office. *See* Goldman and Slotnick, "Clinton's second term judiciary: Picking judges under fire," *Judicature* 82 (1999), 264–284. While it is unclear whether this political reality influenced the diversity of his appointments, we speculate that it may have been responsible, in part, for the increased number of vacancies in federal appellate courts in 1999 (24) compared to 1985 (17).

28. Glick and Emmert, *supra* n. 2.

Clinton and diversification of the federal judiciary

Rorie L. Spill and Kathleen A. Bratton

In his eight years in office, Clinton went beyond maintaining to increasing diversity on the federal bench.

As the era of William J. Clinton closed, it was clear that one of the legacies of his presidency will be the increased diversity of the federal bench. Like Jimmy Carter many years before him, Clinton valued diversity and worked to create a federal bench more reflective of society. The increased numbers of nontraditional nominees have been well documented by scholars, as have their backgrounds and qualifications.[1] This article moves beyond the aggregate level and examines the pattern of appointments in the Clinton presidency across both the courts of appeals and the district courts. It investigates whether the increase in diversity came about through the exercise of a color- and sex-blind strategy, or whether Clinton was more likely to create diversity under certain conditions.

The appointment of women and minorities to the federal bench is still a relatively new phenomenon. It is only as more women and minorities are available and qualified to fill these lofty positions that we can assess whether presidents consider existing diversity when filling vacancies.[2] On the surface, presidents may express concern about or prioritize diversity; however, their actual appointments may serve to provide a token level of diversity across courts rather than simply appointing qualified minorities and women without concern for an overall pattern of representation.

Anecdotal evidence at the federal level suggests that the appointment process is not race- or sex-blind; presidents do take existing diversity into account in the appointment process. The classic example is President George Bush's appointment of Clarence Thomas to fill Thurgood Marshall's seat on the Supreme Court—an appointment that only sustained a token level of minority representation on the High Court. On the other hand, with the appointment of Ruth Bader Ginsburg, Clinton moved gender diversity on the Supreme Court beyond the token level. While this appointment provides some insight into Clinton's appointment strategy, it is by no means concrete evidence that he disregarded current court composition in most instances.

At the state level, there is much debate regarding the effect of the selection system on the appointment of women and minorities to the bench. Prior evidence has been mixed regarding the actual differences between merit/appointment and election systems,[3] but more recent evidence suggests that women are somewhat advantaged by merit/appointment systems after accounting for the existing gender diversity.[4] However, the general advantage that may be granted women in the merit selection process may disappear when the selectors (governors and merit commissions) are cognizant of the current composition of the bench, and this knowledge reduces the likelihood of additional female appointees.[5] In electoral systems, where voters are generally ignorant of current levels of diversity when making their decision, the likelihood of additional female appointees is unaffected by the selection method.[6]

The federal selection system closely mirrors the gubernatorial selection system in this respect: like governors and state merit commissions, the decision makers in the federal selection system—the Justice Department and, for President Clinton's administration, the White House Counsel's Office[7]—are well aware of the current composition of each district and circuit court before filling any vacancies. Therefore it is reasonable to expect that existing diversity plays a role in the selection process, and that selection to the federal bench is neither race- nor sex-blind. Is there any pattern in Clinton's appointment of nontraditional judges? This question is best answered by an investigation of the lower federal courts.

The data used for this analysis were collected from the Federal Judicial Center.[8] This source provides information on all of President Clinton's Article III judicial appointments. For each district and circuit court, we identified the race and gender of all judges sitting before Clinton took office in January 1993, and the race and gender of each of Clinton's appointees. This information permits assessment of the overall

Table 1. Composition of the courts of appeals before and after Clinton

	All male	All white	No African Americans	No Latinos	No Asians
Before Clinton	2	4	6	10	11
Currently	0	2	4	8	12

level of diversity of each court before and after Clinton's appointments and the overall diversity of Clinton's appointees. We are also able to identify all predecessors of Clinton's appointees to discern any overall pattern in the appointment or replacement of nontraditional judges.

Clinton appointed a total of 370 judges to the two levels of the judiciary under study, 65 to the courts of appeals, including the U.S. Court of Appeals for the Federal Circuit, and 305 to the district courts. He appointed 108 women (including one to the U.S. Supreme Court); 61 African Americans; 25 Latinos; 5 Asian-Americans, and 1 Native American.

Courts of appeals

When Clinton took office, the courts of appeals displayed a modicum of diversity. Only two circuits were all male, although four were all white. (See Table 1) Eight circuits had more than one woman. This level of diversity is not totally surprising. There are only 13 circuit courts, counting the Federal circuit, and the size of these courts is fairly large. While the First Circuit only has six judges serving, all others have at least 11. Prior research at the state level indicates that larger courts are more likely to be gender diverse.[9]

Relative to their previous numbers, Latino judges made the greatest gain; in 1992 only three were serving

on the courts of appeals, whereas by the end of Clinton's second term 10 were serving. Clinton was also effective in appointing women and increasing gender diversity on the courts of appeals. In total, 5 women left the appeals bench and 20 were appointed. In absolute numbers, when Clinton arrived 24 women were serving on the courts of appeals and when he departed 36 were serving.[10]

Increases in representation of African-American and Asian-American judges were less marked. The number of African-American judges increased from 9 to 11 while the number of Asian-American judges stayed constant at one. In part because of replacement patterns, and in part because of the creation of new seats, the number of white judges stayed fairly constant; 52 white judges left the bench and 49 were appointed to vacancies or new seats.

In eight courts, Clinton increased gender diversity and reduced it in only one. Currently, there are no all-male circuit courts, and two are all-white.[11] Only four circuits have no African-American representation; eight have no Latino representation and only the Ninth Circuit has an Asian-American judge serving on the bench. Indeed, Clinton increased minority representation in five circuits. In six circuits he appointed more than one woman to serve on the same court; he appointed multiple minority members to three circuit courts. He appointed more than one African-American judge to the Sixth Circuit and more than one Latino judge to the Second and Ninth Circuits over the course of his administrations.

Clinton was relatively likely to replace African Americans with African Americans. Table 2 shows that only 6 percent (3 of 52) of white judges who left the bench were replaced with African Americans, whereas two-thirds of the African Americans (4 of 6) who left the bench and were replaced, had their seats filled by

Table 2. Racial breakdown of Clinton's courts of appeals appointees and their predecessors

Appointee	Predecessor*					
	White	African American	Latino	Asian	New seat	Total
White	44	1	0	1	3	49
African American	3	4	0	0	1	8
Latino	5	1	0	0	1	7
Asian	0	0	1	0	0	1
Total	52	6	1	1	5	65

* These numbers reflect those judges who left the bench *and* were replaced by Clinton.

Table 3. Gender breakdown of Clinton's courts of appeals appointees and their predecessors

Appointee	Predecessor*			
	Male	Female	New seat	Total
Male	38	4	3	45
Female	17	1	2	20
Total	55	5	5	65

* These numbers reflect those judges who left the bench *and* were replaced by Clinton.

African Americans (and one was replaced by a Latino judge). The process seems much more gender-blind than race-blind; out of the five women who left the bench during Clinton's terms, only one was replaced by a woman. As Table 3 shows, approximately 31 percent of men (17 of 55) who left the bench were replaced by a woman.

District courts

The total number of judges leaving each circuit on the courts of appeals during Clinton's two administrations was relatively small. Additionally, the relatively low levels of minority and female appointments made by Clinton's predecessors ensured that he would not be replacing many nontraditional circuit judges during his tenure. The higher turnover rate on the district courts provides more opportunity for a president to shape the composition of the courts. This level of the judiciary is thus likely to provide more substantial evidence for any pattern in appointments.[12]

Surprisingly, when Clinton arrived in the White House the district courts were not nearly as diversified as the courts of appeals. Fifty-two of the 91 district courts included in this analysis were all male and all white. Over the course of his two terms, Clinton successfully appointed 305 district court judges. Through these appointments he was able to reduce the number of all white and all male courts to 36 and 40 respectively.[13] Only 26 of these courts are still all white and all male. (See Table 4.)

Relative to their previous numbers, women and African Americans made substantial gains on the district courts. Over the course of his eight years, Clinton appointed at least one woman to 45 different district courts and at least one African American to 40 different courts. He appointed multiple women to 22 courts and multiple African Americans to nine courts. He also increased the presence of Latinos and Asians, although

Table 4. All white male district courts at the end of the Clinton administration

1. Southern Alabama*
2. Alaska*
3. Western Arkansas[1]
4. Southern Georgia*
5. Idaho*
6. Southern Illinois*
7. Northern Iowa*
8. Southern Iowa*
9. Maine*
10. Western Michigan[2]
11. Northern Mississippi*
12. Montana*
13. Nebraska*
14. Nevada[3]
15. New Hampshire*
16. Northern New York[4]
17. Western New York*
18. Eastern North Carolina*
19. Western North Carolina*
20. North Dakota*
21. Eastern Texas*
22. Vermont*
23. Western Virginia*
24. Eastern Washington[5]
25. Southern West Virginia[6]
26. Wyoming*

This list represents the current composition of these courts; it does not include nontraditional judges on senior status. An asterisk indicates that no woman or minority has ever served on this court.

1. Two women and one African American have served on this court. Elisjane Roy served from 1977 to 1989. She left active service in 1989 and remains on senior status in the Eastern District of Arkansas. Susan Wright replaced her in 1989, but was moved to the Eastern District in 1990. George Howard received his commission in 1980 and served until 1990; he was then moved to the Eastern District.

2. One African American has served on this court. Benjamin Gibson received his commission in 1979. He assumed senior status in 1996 and retired in 1999.

3. One African-American woman has served on this court. Johnnie Rawlinson received her commission in 1998. She was elevated to the Court of Appeals for the Ninth Circuit in 2000.

4. One woman has served on this court. Rosemary Pooler received her commission in 1994. She was elevated to the Court of Appeals for the Second Circuit in 1998.

5. One African American has served on this court. Jack Tanner received his commission in 1978 and in that same year he was moved to the Western District of Washington. He assumed senior status in 1991.

6. One woman has served on this court. Elizabeth Hallanan received her commission in 1983 and assumed senior status in 1996. She still serves in this capacity.

not as substantially. Additionally, Clinton appointed one Native American to serve, thus creating a court in Oklahoma with both judges of Native American heritage. (See Table 5.)

Again, some pattern emerges regarding the appointment of minorities to replace judges who left the bench. Out of 19 African-American judges who left the

Table 5. Clinton's impact on diversity in the district courts*

Increased gender diversity	40
Decreased gender diversity	2
No change in gender diversity	39
Increased racial diversity	29
Decreased racial diversity	3**
No change in racial diversity	50
No opportunity to appoint	10

* This count reflects the final composition of the district courts at the end of the second Clinton administration.
** Includes the District of Western Michigan where the number of judges was reduced by statute and this caused a decline in racial diversity.

district courts and were replaced, six (or about 30 percent) of the seats were filled by other African-American judges, and one by a Latino judge. Conversely, out of the 233 whites who left the bench, 39 (or about 17 percent) were replaced by African Americans. Out of 15 Latino judges who left the courts, almost half (7) were replaced by Latino judges;[14] only six of the 233 whites who left the bench were replaced by Latinos. Of the three Asian Americans who left the bench, one was replaced by an Asian American; the other Asian American appointed to the bench replaced a white judge. (See Table 6.)

As with the circuit courts, the pattern is much more race-specific than gender-specific: Out of 245 men who left the bench, 71 (approximately 29 percent) were replaced by a female judge, whereas about 36 percent (9 of 25) of the women who left the bench were replaced by other women. (See Table 7.)

Did Clinton use the creation of new seats to increase diversity? We find some moderate evidence that he used this strategy with respect to racial diversity (see Tables 2, 3, 6 and 7). Of the five new seats on the circuit courts, two (40 percent) were filled by minorities (compared to about 23 percent of the existing open seats). Of the 35 new seats on the district courts, about one-third (12 of 35) were filled by minority judges; less than a quarter (65) of the 270 other open seats were filled by minority judges.

Less evidence exists regarding a pattern with respect to gender. On the circuit courts, 40 percent of the new seats were filled by women, compared to 30 percent of the vacancies. On the other hand, on the district courts about 23 percent of the new seats were filled by women, whereas 30 percent of the vacancies were filled by women.

Was Clinton more likely to appoint women and minorities to larger courts? (See Table 8.) Not surprisingly, the courts without either racial or gender diver-

Table 6. Racial breakdown of Clinton's district court appointees and their predecessors

		Predecessor*				
Appointee	White	African American	Latino	Asian	New seat	Total
White	186	12	7	1	23	229
African American	39	6	1	0	7	53
Latino	6	1	7	1	3	18
Asian	1	0	0	1	2	4
Native American	1	0	0	0	0	1
Total	233	19	15	3	35	305

* These numbers reflect those judges who left the bench *and* were replaced by Clinton.

Table 7. Gender breakdown of Clinton's district court appointees and their predecessors

		Predecessor*		
Appointee	Male	Female	New seat	Total
Male	174	16	27	217
Female	71	9	8	88
Total	245	25	35	305

* These numbers reflect those judges who left the bench *and* were replaced by Clinton.

Table 8. Number of nontraditional appointments by size of court

	Number Men	Number Women	Number African Americans	Number Latinos	Number Asian-Americans	Number Native Americans	Number White	Current all male	Current all white	No appoint-ments
1–4 judges	45 (87%)	7 (22%)	8 (15%)	0	1 (2%)	2 (4%)	41 (79%)	28	26	7
5–9 judges	66 (75%)	22 (25%)	13 (15%)	6 (7%)	1 (1%)	1 (1%)	67 (76%)	10	11	3
10–14 judges	41 (67%)	20 (33%)	12 (20%)	3 (5%)	0	0	46 (75%)	1	0	0
15–19 judges	35 (65%)	19 (35%)	11 (20%)	3 (6%)	0	0	40 (74%)	0	0	0
20 + judges	33 (60%)	22 (40%)	9 (16%)	6 (11%)	2 (4%)	0	38 (69%)	0	0	0

sity do indeed tend to be the smaller courts. There are many fewer larger courts, and each of these has a higher number of retirements. More interesting is the finding that the percentage of vacancies that were filled by women on the larger courts is much higher than the percentage of vacancies that were filled by women on the smaller courts. Clinton had the opportunity to fill 52 seats on the smallest courts: only seven of those vacancies were filled by women. He had roughly the same opportunity to fill vacancies on the largest courts (55 appointments); however, 22 of those were filled by women. This does not appear to be the result of a desire to avoid creating homogeneous courts; were that the case, smaller courts would be the target of a diversifying strategy. More research should be done to examine the political factors that might lead to this pattern, particularly senatorial recommendations to the president.

Beyond maintaining diversity

William Jefferson Clinton appointed more women and minorities to the federal bench than any of his predecessors. He did this by maintaining existing diversity, by using newly created seats, and by replacing white or male judges with minority or female judges. We find that minority judges are relatively likely to be replaced by minority judges; gender-specific patterns were much less evident. In a prior study of state supreme courts,[15] we found that women were most likely to be appointed to otherwise all-male courts; that is, pressures definitely exist to diversify to at least a token level. This may also account for the apparent race-specific pattern; Clinton may have replaced minority judges with other minority judges in order to avoid creating a homogeneous court. Less pressure may have existed to

replace female judges with other women because additional women were already serving on the court. Clinton also used new seats to increase diversity. These two strategies allowed him to increase diversity while leaving the numbers of white and male judges relatively constant.

Finally, Clinton went beyond maintaining diversity to increasing diversity by replacing white and male judges with minorities and women. More research should be done to investigate the conditions under which this was most likely. Indeed, Clinton passed up an opportunity to increase gender diversity on 39 district courts and racial diversity on 50. He also occasionally appointed white men to non-diverse courts. Further research is needed to investigate the role that political factors, such as the composition of Senate delegations, pressure from interest groups, and a supply of suitable candidates, play in such a decision.

Notes

This article originally appeared in Volume 84, Number 5, March–April 2001, pages 256–261.

This paper was prepared for presentation at the annual meetings of the Law and Society Association and Research Committee on Sociology of Law (ISA) in Budapest, Hungary, July 4–7, 2001. The authors wish to acknowledge the adept research assistance provided by Laura Stockel of the University of Northern Iowa.

1. For example, *see* Goldman and Slotnick, "Clinton's First Term Judiciary: Many Bridges to Cross," *Judicature* 80 (1997), 254; Segal, "The decision making of Clinton's nontraditional judicial appointees," *Judicature* 80 (1997), 279; Segal, "Representative Decision Making on the Federal Bench: Clinton's District Court Appointees," *Pol. Res. Q.* 53 (2000), 137; Stidham et al., "The voting behavior

of President Clinton's judicial appointees," *Judicature* 80 (1997), 16.

2. While it has been suggested that delays by the Senate stalled Clinton's minority and female nominees, and such a trend could affect our analysis, Hartley shows that while Clinton's nominees were slowed, the pattern is similar to other presidents dealing with a Senate controlled by the opposition. *See* Hartley, "Senate Delay Of Minority Judicial Nominees: A Look at Race, Gender, and Experience," *Judicature* 84 (2001), 190.

3. Esterling and Andersen, "Diversity and the Judicial Merit Selection Process: A Statistical Report, in *Research on Judicial Selection 1999* (Chicago: American Judicature Society, 1999); Githins, "Getting Appointed to State Court: The Gender Dimension," *Women and Pol.* 15 (1995), 1; Goldman, *Picking Federal Judges: Lower Court Selection from Roosevelt through Reagan* (New Haven, Conn.: Yale University Press, 1997); Fund for Modern Courts, *The Success of Women and Minorities in Achieving Judicial Office* (New York, N.Y.: Fund for Modern Courts, Inc., 1985); Alozie, "Selection Methods and Recruitment of Women to State Courts of Last Resort," *Soc. Sci. Q.* 77 (1996), 110; Graham, "Judicial Recruitment and Racial Diversity on State Courts: An Overview," *Judicature* 74 (1990), 28.

4. Bratton and Spill, "Moving Beyond Tokenism: The Effect of Existing Diversity on the Selection of Women to State Supreme Courts," n.d. In this piece, we take the more sophisticated studies of Alozie and others one step further by examining selection in light of current court composition in all 50 states. This additional control leads us to a slightly different conclusion regarding the effect of the different selection systems, however, we also find that the effects are attenuating over time.

5. Bratton and Spill, *supra* n. 4; Esterling and Andersen, *supra* n. 3, hypothesize that governors will select more women and minorities when these categories are presented by a merit commission and find that there is a great deal of variation in gubernatorial tendencies to select women or minorities in merit and appointment systems. However, they did not account for existing diversity when examining the rate of appointment.

6. Baum, *American Courts: Process and Policy,* (Boston: Houghton Mifflin, 1998); Hojnacki and Baum, "Choosing Judicial Candidates: How Voters Explain Their Decisions," *Judicature* 75 (1992), 300.

7. Goldman and Slotnick, *supra* n. 1

8. www.fjc.gov

9. Alozie, *supra* n. 3

10. Our numbers reflect the composition of the courts of appeals on the day Clinton took office—January 20, 1993, and the inclusion of the Federal Circuit. Goldman et al. in this issue use November 3, 1992—the day Clinton was elected—as their start date and they do not include the Federal Circuit, and so our numbers are slightly different. Over Clinton's two terms, eight women left the courts of appeals and only 5 were replaced. Clinton appointed 20 women to the courts of appeals.

11. Clinton's effort to appoint a minority to the Fourth Circuit before leaving office was blocked by Senator Jesse Helms. Eventually, in the final days of his administration, Clinton appointed Roger Gregory of Virginia as a recess appointment to the Fourth Circuit. His appointment was withdrawn by George W. Bush on March 19, 2001. For this reason, we do not include Gregory in our analyses. For a more detailed account, see Eggen, "Clinton Names Black Judge to Appeals Court: Recess Choice for Richmond Circuit is Challenge to GOP," *Washington Post,* December 28, 2000, and Goldman et al., "Clinton's Judges: Summing Up the Legacy," *Judicature* 84 (2001), 228.

12. These numbers include the judges from 91 of the federal district courts. The district courts of Guam, Mariana Islands, and Virgin Islands are not included in the analysis; these judges are not Article III judges, therefore they are not included in the Federal Judicial Center's database.

13. In instances where one individual is appointed to serve on more than one court, the appointment counts for each court. For example, Jennifer Coffman serves on both the Eastern and Western Districts of Kentucky. With one appointment, Clinton increased the gender diversity on both of these courts and he appointed a female to two 5-judge courts. She is not, however, included twice in tables 6 or 7 since she only replaced one white male (Eugene Siler).

14. These numbers should be considered in light of the inclusion of the District Court of Puerto Rico in the dataset. This court is the only all Latino court and all members leaving this court were replaced with other Latinos.

15. Bratton and Spill, *supra* n. 4

Voting behavior and gender on the U.S. courts of appeals

Sue Davis, Susan Haire, and Donald R. Songer

The votes of women circuit court judges in employment discrimination
and search and seizure cases differ from those of their male counterparts.

Not long ago, women judges were too scarce to study in any meaningful way. Only two women had served on the federal appellate bench when President Jimmy Carter reformed the judicial selection process in 1977.[1] Subsequently, 11 women were appointed to the U.S. courts of appeals during Carter's term. Ronald Reagan appointed four women to the intermediate appellate judiciary, and George Bush appointed seven. Thus, a minimally sufficient number of women of various political persuasions now hold positions on the courts of appeals to make it feasible to study their decision making. This analysis of voting behavior on the U.S. courts of appeals attempts to reveal whether voting patterns of women judges differ from those of their male colleagues.

Although feminist scholarship encompasses a variety of perspectives,[2] much of feminist legal theory argues that the presence of significant numbers of women as professionals in the legal system will have a profound impact on the law. Some feminist scholars argue that women lawyers and judges will bring a different perspective to the law, employ a different set of methods, and seek different results from prevailing legal tradition.

The work of psychologist Carol Gilligan[3] provides a source of feminist legal theory as well as empirical support for its claims. Gilligan discovered differences in the ways men and women understand themselves and their environment and the way they resolve moral problems. She found that men tend to define themselves through separation, measure themselves against an abstract ideal of perfection, equate adulthood with autonomy and individual achievement, and conceive morality in ladder-like hierarchical terms. In contrast, women often define themselves through connection with others and activities of care, and they perceive morality in terms of an interconnected web. While women tend to perceive moral conflicts as a problem of care and responsibility in relationships, men tend to emphasize rights and rules.

Gilligan by no means claimed to make generalizations about men and women. Rather, she argued that since the traditional theory of human psychological development was based on studies of male subjects only, that theory invariably found that women failed to develop on measurement scales. Gilligan showed how an alternative perspective emerged when researchers included women in their studies and when they discarded frameworks constructed with only men in mind. Her "different voice" refers not to a voice that differs from men, but one that differs from traditional theory. Gilligan also pointed out that most people in her studies (an average of 65 percent across six studies) represented both voices in defining moral problems. Still, there was a strong tendency to focus on one voice or the other. About 70 percent of those who used both orientations focused on one. Only 3 men from a total of 60 demonstrated a focus on care. Among the women, about 60 percent focused on care.[4]

Gilligan's findings parallel the assertion of many feminist legal scholars that because the law has been so thoroughly infused with the male perspective, an approach to legal decision making that is based on separation, rights, and abstract rules has come to represent the "correct" legal method. Any departure is viewed as illegitimate and is judged to fall outside the framework of law. Thus, the female perspective is excluded. As one writer explained, "It takes no sophistication . . . to recognize that American law is predominantly a system of the ladder, by the ladder, and for the ladder." [5] Gilligan's work combined with much of feminist jurisprudence provide the foundation for a theory that the presence of women judges has tremendous potential for significantly changing the law.

Gender difference and judging

How might the alleged different perspective of women manifest itself in judging? Generally, the traditional legal approach could be expected to focus on individual rights, freedom from interference, procedural fairness, and concern for correctly applying appropriate legal rules. In contrast, the "different voice" would speak about connection, care, response, substantive fairness, communitarian values, and context.

Drawing on Gilligan's work, Suzanna Sherry identified characteristics of a feminine jurisprudence—one that emphasizes connection (in contrast to autonomy), context (as opposed to fixed rules), and responsibility (in contrast to rights).[6] Sherry analyzed the decision making of Justice Sandra Day O'Connor and concluded that it did, in fact, manifest such concerns. Her analysis of O'Connor's opinions in cases where the rights in question belonged to individuals as members of communities rather than as autonomous units revealed a different perspective from her male colleagues. Sherry argued that O'Connor has not been as willing as the other conservative justices to permit violations of the right to full membership in the community. Likewise, Sherry found that O'Connor has tended to support individual rights only when they involve community membership. Sherry also discovered a contextual approach in O'Connor's decision making and a tendency to reject rigid rules.

Social scientists have begun to explore the behavior of women decision makers. Their work, however, has produced mixed results. For example, an examination of interest group ratings of members of Congress suggested that women were more liberal than men, particularly in the areas of social welfare and defense spending.[7] In contrast, studies of the views of political party elites[8] and civil servants[9] failed to reveal significant differences based on the sex of the decision maker. Another study found that women state legislators in California were no more liberal than their male counterparts,[10] while another found women legislators in 12 other states to be only slightly more likely than men to give higher priority to women's issues than to business and commerce.[11]

Similarly, studies of judicial behavior have provided some support for the contention that women will bring a different perspective and decision-making pattern to the bench. For example, an examination of the votes of judges on four state supreme courts found that four of the five women voted on women's issues in a way that placed them at the liberal extreme of their courts.[12] Analyzing the behavior of federal district judges, another study revealed that in cases involving criminal procedure and women's policy issues, there were no significant differences between men and women judges.

But for personal liberties and minority policy issues, the differences between male and female judges were statistically significant: male judges were 1.5 times more likely than female judges to support the liberal position. These results also indicated that female judges were significantly more likely than their male counterparts to defer to positions taken by government.[13] On the other hand, recent research on the voting behavior of women judges on the federal appellate courts has revealed only slight differences between men and women.[14]

Methods

The federal intermediate appellate judiciary was chosen as the subject of this study for several reasons. The U.S. courts of appeals play a vital role in interpreting federal law, enforcing norms, and creating public policy.[15] Because the Supreme Court can review only a limited number of cases from the lower federal courts, the decisions of the courts of appeals are final in an overwhelming majority of cases.[16] Studies also have shown that the appellate courts have substantial decision-making discretion.[17]

Voting behavior was analyzed in three areas: employment discrimination, criminal procedural rights (search and seizure), and obscenity. Gilligan's studies and feminist legal theory would suggest that women judges can be expected to vote differently from their male colleagues in ways that reflect a tendency to emphasize interdependent rights—the right to full membership in a community—rather than rights against the community. When communitarian values and individual rights conflict, women judges would be expected to support the former.

The votes of all judges on the U.S. courts of appeals, including those on senior status, from the District of Columbia Circuit and the 11 numbered circuits from 1981 to 1990 were analyzed.[18] Table 1 lists all women who have served on these courts. The analysis of obscenity cases was based on all opinions published in the *Federal Reporter* during this period. Those opinions contained 239 votes suitable for analysis. Since there were more than 3,000 published opinions for both search and seizure and employment discrimination cases, samples of each of these case types were drawn.[19] The samples contained 1,283 votes in search and seizure cases and 519 votes from the employment discrimination cases. The samples included the votes of 9 female and 122 male judges in obscenity cases, 15 females and 237 males in search and seizure cases, and

Table 1. The women on the U.S. courts of appeals, 1979–1992

Name	Circuit	Appointing president	Date of appointment
Amalya Kearse	12	Carter	6/21/79
Carol Los Mansmann	13	Reagan	4/4/85
*Jane Roth	13	Bush	6/27/91
Dolores Sloviter	13	Carter	6/21/79
*Karen J. Williams	14	Bush	2/27/92
Edith Jones	15	Reagan	4/4/85
Carolyn Dineen King	15	Carter	7/13/79
*Alice M. Batchelder	16	Bush	11/27/91
Cornelia Kennedy	16	Carter	9/26/79
*Ilana D. Rovner	17	Bush	8/12/92
Betty Fletcher	19	Carter	9/27/79
Cynthia Holcolm Hall	19	Reagan	10/4/84
Dorothy Nelson	19	Carter	12/20/79
*Pamela Ann Rymer	19	Bush	5/22/89
Mary Schroeder	19	Carter	9/26/79
Stephanie Seymour	10	Carter	11/2/79
Deanell Reece Tacha	10	Reagan	12/16/85
Phyllis Kravitch	11	Carter	3/23/79
*Susan H. Black	11	Bush	8/11/92
Ruth Bader Ginsburg	D.C.	Carter	6/18/80
*Karen LeCraft Henderson	D.C.	Bush	7/11/90
Patricia Wald	D.C.	Carter	7/26/79

* Excluded from the analysis.
Sources: Want's *Federal-State Court Directory*, 1992 ed. (Washington, D.C.: Want Publishing Co., 1991); Wildman, *Federal Judges and Justices: A Current Listing of Nominations, Confirmations, Elevations, Resignations, Retirements*, 102nd Congress, rev. September 1992 (Littleton, Co.: Fred B. Rothman and Company, 1992).

16 females and 188 males in employment discrimination cases. No judge cast more than 2.4 percent of the votes in any one area.

For employment discrimination cases, votes were categorized as follows: (1) "conservative," supporting either the defendant's position or, in cases where a male challenged an affirmative action plan, the plaintiff's position; and (2) "liberal," supporting the plaintiff's charge of discrimination in all other cases. For search and seizure decisions, votes holding that a challenged search was unreasonable or that challenged evidence could not be used were classified liberal, and votes upholding a search or allowing the use of challenged evidence were classified conservative. For obscenity cases, votes were categorized as either supporting or opposing a restriction on the use and dissemination of the materials in question. A simple cross-tabulation of votes by the sex of the judge for each of the three types of cases was conducted. Cross-tabulations for each type of case controlling for party of appointing president and region were also performed. These variables have been found to be associated with voting patterns.[20]

Results

The analysis revealed statistically significant differences between men and women judges in two of the three areas examined. The employment discrimination cases revealed that women, more often than their male colleagues, supported claimants (Table 2). More than 63 percent of the votes cast by women judges supported the plaintiff's claim of discrimination. In contrast, male judges supported the plaintiff 46 percent of the time.[21] For search and seizure cases, women judges were more likely than their male colleagues to support the claims of criminal defendants (Table 3). In the

Table 2. Gender differences in judges' voting in employment discrimination cases

Gender	Liberal	Conservative	% for plaintiff
Female	140	123	63.5
Male	210	246	46.1

n = 519, chi square = 6.74, P <.01

Table 3. Gender differences in judges' voting in search and seizure cases

Gender	Liberal	Conservative	% liberal
Female	122	1,102	17.7
Male	126	1,033	10.9

n = 1283, chi square = 5.18, P <.05

Table 4. Gender differences in judges' voting in obscenity cases

Gender	For suppression	Against suppression	% against suppression
Female	119	14	30.8
Male	156	70	30.9

n = 239, chi square = 0.01, P >.10

Table 5. Gender differences in Democratic and Republican judges' voting in employment discrimination cases

	Democratic		
Gender	Liberal	Conservative	% for plaintiff
Female	134	16	68.0
Male	107	90	54.3

n = 247, chi square = 3.05, P <.08

	Republican		
Gender	Liberal	Conservative	% for plaintiff
Female	116	117	46.2
Male	103	156	39.8

n = 272, chi square = 0.21, P >.10

obscenity cases, there were no significant differences in the behavior of male and female judges (Table 4).

Addition of a control for party of appointing president produced the following results (Table 5). Differences persisted in employment discrimination cases as women judges appointed by a Democratic president (all by Jimmy Carter) supported the plaintiff's claim at a level of 68 percent, whereas the men appointed by Democrats (including but not limited to Carter) supported the plaintiff's claim at a level of 54.3 percent. The analysis revealed no statistically significant differences in votes of judges appointed by Republican presidents in employment discrimination cases.

Table 6. Gender differences in Southern and non-Southern judges' voting in employment discrimination cases

	Southern		
Gender	Liberal	Conservative	% for plaintiff
Female	130	110	75.0
Male	122	158	43.6

n = 320, chi square = 13.86, P <.001

	Non-Southern		
Gender	Liberal	Conservative	% for plaintiff
Female	19	10	47.4
Male	85	77	52.4

n = 181, chi square = 0.18, P >.10

In search and seizure cases, once the control for the appointing president's party was added, there were no statistically significant differences in the votes of male and female judges. In obscenity cases, the addition of this control supported the initial finding that there were no significant differences.

With the addition of the control for region, statistically significant differences remained in the voting behavior of women and men judges in employment discrimination cases (Table 6).

In search and seizure cases, the analysis revealed no significant differences in the voting behavior of male and female judges in the South and elsewhere. In obscenity cases, the controls for region did not alter the results—there were no statistically significant differences in the votes of males and females.

To further explore the gender differences in employment discrimination cases, a cross-tabulation with controls for both party and region was conducted. Table 7 displays the results of a comparison of votes by Southern males and Southern females appointed by a Democratic president, suggesting that the differences are attributable to the sex of the judge rather than region or party of appointing president.

Table 7. Gender differences in Southern Democratic judges' voting in employment discrimination cases

Gender	Liberal	Conservative	% liberal
Female	27	16	81.8
Male	58	53	52.2

n = 144, chi square = 9.19, P <.002

Discussion

Overall, the results of this analysis provide some support for the thesis that women judges bring a different perspective to the bench. Employment discrimination may be viewed as a problem of exclusion, as members of certain groups are precluded from participating as full members of the community. Thus, women judges' support for plaintiffs may reflect a concern for the right to such membership. The rights of criminal defendants may be conceived as involving claims against the community, but such a generalization may not hold for all cases. Support of some claims could result in harm to innocent people and to the community, while support of other claims may recognize the need to preserve relationships. If concerns of connection and community underlie women's votes, those votes would vary depending on the facts of each case. Consequently, they would manifest no pattern distinguishable from their male colleagues. In the context of obscenity, explicit sexual materials may be viewed not only as a source of the oppression of women but also as detrimental to the moral quality of the community. The analysis, however, failed to produce any evidence that such concerns provide the basis for women's votes in obscenity cases.

Although the results in two of the three areas examined are consistent with the proposition that women judges bring a different perspective to their decision making, drawing conclusions is problematic. Women may support plaintiffs in employment discrimination cases because they identify with members of subordinate groups rather than because of a particular concern for relationships or the right to full membership in a community. Also, the absence of difference between women's and men's votes in search and seizure cases may not reflect women judges' support for community and relationships. Instead, it may simply be a manifestation of a method of resolving claims involving individual rights that does not differ from that of their male counterparts.

The analysis of employment discrimination cases is consistent with the thesis that women judges are more concerned than their male colleagues with relationships and inclusion than with personal autonomy and individual rights. Yet the analysis revealed no such difference in decisions involving obscenity—an area that commonly raises concerns associated with the community's moral health. How might these results be explained?

First, it is possible that the psychological and legal theories of difference are simply wrong—that women's purported tendency to approach and resolve moral and legal problems differently from men does not exist.[22] As noted, women may tend to support the claimant in employment discrimination cases simply because they are likely to have experienced such discrimination directly, or have encountered gender-related obstacles in their professional lives, or feel a close affinity with those who have.

Second, while it is possible that a different voice exists, it might not reveal itself readily in analyses of voting behavior. Additional research is needed before any conclusions can be drawn regarding the extent to which, if at all, women judges differ from their male colleagues. Although Sherry[23] found that Justice O'Connor's opinions differed from the male conservatives on the Supreme Court, a recent analysis of opinions of judges on the U.S. Court of Appeals for the Ninth Circuit concluded that while women judges sometimes spoke in a different voice, men judges did as well.[24]

Third, it is possible that differences between men and women judges are neutralized by the very nature of law and legal processes. For example, to succeed in law school and subsequently in the legal profession, an individual—male or female—must master the tools of legal reasoning and adopt the norms of the profession. In Gilligan's framework, those tools are distinguished by their male character: legal reasoning is rule-based and abstract, and American law is thoroughly grounded in a political theory of individualism. Thus, any propensity to emphasize context, caring, and community would be discouraged and subverted by the constraints imposed by legal education, the legal profession, and the process of judicial socialization. Moreover, because they are still relatively new and constitute a small minority on the federal bench, women judges are likely to be particularly conscious of the importance of maintaining their reputations as neutral decision makers—that is, "good judges." In short, the constraints of the judicial process may well overcome differences based on the sex of the judge.

Fourth, a generational phenomenon may mask any possible gender differences. Women currently serving on the federal courts attended law school and pursued careers in an environment thoroughly controlled by men, in which any hint of a different approach would most likely have been considered evidence of women's lack of capacity to acquire legal skills and understand the law. Therefore, women judges who have been socialized into and have succeeded in the male world are unlikely to manifest the differences attributed to women by feminist theory.

Finally, it is possible that differences between men and women in judicial decision making are obscured by a selection process designed to produce judges—male or female—whose views are compatible with those of their appointing president. The Reagan administration took great care to fill vacancies on the federal bench with individuals who clearly endorsed the president's political agenda.[25] And while Carter clearly gave his nominating commissions an affirmative action mandate, he was also careful to nominate only women who shared his basic values and approach to judging. Virtually all the women on the courts of appeals have been selected by presidents who were extraordinarily successful in selecting judges whose policy preferences were compatible with their own.

The findings presented here certainly do not preclude the possibility that women will transform the law in ways that many feminist legal scholars predict. It is unlikely, however, that any evidence of women's unique voice will emerge until women are trained and socialized in an environment that welcomes diversity in values and approaches to decision making.

Feminist jurisprudence and women judges are both new to the legal process, and the study of women judges has barely begun. Only future research examining the career patterns and socialization of women judges, as well as their voting behavior and opinions, will make it possible to assess the nature and extent of women's impact on the legal system.

Notes

This article originally appeared in Volume 77, Number 3, November–December 1993, pages 129–133.

1. *See* Berkson and Carbon, *The United States Circuit Judge Nominating Commission: Its Members, Procedures and Candidates* (Chicago: American Judicature Society, 1980); Martin, "Women on the federal bench: a comparative profile," *Judicature* 65 (1982), 307–313; and "Gender and judicial selection: a comparison of the Reagan and Carter administrations," *Judicature* 71 (1987), 136–142; Cook, "Women as Judges," in *Women in the Judicial Process* (Washington, D.C.: The American Political Science Association, 1988).

2. *See, e.g.,* Goldstein, "Can This Marriage Be Saved? Feminist Public Policy and Feminist Jurisprudence," in Goldstein, ed., *Feminist Jurisprudence: The Difference Debate* (Savage, Md.: Rowman and Littlefield, 1992); Sunstein, "Feminism and Legal Theory," *Harv. L. Rev.* 101 (1988), 826–848.

3. Gilligan, *In a Different Voice: Psychological Theory and Women's Development* (Cambridge: Harvard University Press, 1982).

4. Marcus, Spiegelman, DuBois, Dunlap, Gilligan, MacKinnon, and Menkel-Meadow, "The 1984 James McCormick Mitchell Lecture. Feminist Discourse, Moral Values and the Law—A Conversation," *Buffalo L. Rev.* 34 (1985), 47–49.

5. Karst, "Woman's Constitution," *Duke L. J.* 1984 (1984), 463.

6. Sherry, "Civic Virtue and the Feminine Voice in Constitutional Adjudication," *Va. L. Rev.* 72 (1986), 543–615.

7. Leader, "The Policy Impact of Elected Women Officials," in Cooper and Maisels, eds., *The Impact of the Electoral Process* (Beverly Hills: Sage Publications, 1977). A factor analysis of congressional voting from 1961 to 1975 led Kathleen Frankovic to similar conclusions. "Sex and Voting in the U.S. House of Representatives," *Am. Pol. Q.* 72 (1977), 315–331. Additionally, Freida Gehlen found more support among female members of Congress for both the Civil Rights Act of 1964 and the Equal Rights Amendment. "Women Members of Congress: A Distinctive Role" in Githens and Prestage, eds., *A Portrait of Marginality* (New York: McKay, 1977). Susan Welch, who analyzed conservative coalition scores, found that women were more likely than men to cast liberal votes, but that the differences had decreased over time. "Are Women More Liberal Than Men in the U.S. Congress?" *Leg. Studies Q.* 10 (1985), 125–134.

8. Constantini and Craik, "Women as Politicians: The Social Background, Personality and Careers of Female Party Leaders," *J. Soc. Issues* 28 (1972), 217–236.

9. Thompson, "Civil Servants and the Deprived: Sociopolitical and Occupational Explanations of Attitudes Towards Minority Hiring," *Am. J. Pol. Sci.* 22 (1978), 325–347.

10. Thomas, "The Effects of Race and Gender on Constituency Service." Presented at the Annual Meeting of the American Political Science Association, August 1987.

11. Thomas and Welch, "Women Legislators: Legislative Styles and Policy Priorities," *W. Pol. Q.* 44 (1991), 445–456.

12. Allen and Wall, "The Behavior of Women State Supreme Court Justices: An Update." Unpublished manuscript, 1990; "The Behavior of Women State Supreme Court Justices: Are They Tokens or Outsiders?," *Just. Sys. J.* 12 (1987), 232–244. In contrast, two studies of the sentencing patterns of urban trial court judges revealed no significant differences between males and females. Kritzer and Uhlman, "Sisterhood in the Courtroom: Sex of Judge and Defendant in Criminal Case Disposition," *Soc. Sci. Q.,* 14 (1977), 77–88; Gruhl, Spohn, and Welch, "Women as Policy Makers: The Case of Trial Judges," *Am. J. Pol. Sci.* 25 (1981), 308–322.

13. Walker and Barrow, "The Diversification of the Federal Bench: Policy and Process Ramifications." *J. Pol.* 47 (1985), 596–617. In still another study, Gerald S. Gryski, Eleanor C. Main, and William Dixon found only a weak and statistically insignificant relationship between the presence of a female judge and state high court decision making in sex discrimination cases. "Models of State High Court Decision Making in Sex Discrimination Cases," *J. Pol.* 48 (1986), 143–155.

14. *See, e.g.,* Davis, "The Impact of President Carter's Judicial Selection Reforms: A Voting Analysis of the United States Courts of Appeals," *Am. Pol. Q.* 14 (1986), 320–344; Gottschall, "Carter's Judicial Appointments: The Influence of Affirmative Action and Merit Selection in Voting on the U.S. Courts of Appeals," *Judicature* 67 (1983), 165–173.

15. *See* Howard, *Courts of Appeals in the Federal Judicial System: A Study of the Second, Fifth, and District of Columbia Circuits* (Princeton: Princeton University Press, 1981); Songer, "The Circuit Courts of Appeals," in Gates and Johnson, *The American Courts: A Critical Assessment* (Washington, D.C.: CQ Press, 1991), 35–59.

16. *See* Davis and Songer, "The Changing Role of the United States Courts of Appeals: The Flow of Litigation Revisited," *Just. Sys. J.* 13 (1988–1989), 323–340.

17. See the work cited by Songer, *supra* n. 15, at 41–46.

18. The number of female judges remains so low that in cases in which they participate, the panel usually consists of two males and one female. In the sample, there was never more than one female judge in an obscenity case, there were four search and seizure cases with two women on the panel, and five panels in employment discrimination cases with two female judges.

19. The Westlaw electronic data base identified the universe of cases in which decisions were published in the *Federal Reporter.* A random sample of 200 decisions was selected for each case type. This sample was supplemented to guarantee that there would be a sufficient number of votes by women by identifying the universe of cases in which each woman judge participated and randomly selecting three additional cases from the universe of participations of each woman.

20. *See, e.g.,* Tate, "Personal Attribute Models of Voting Behavior of U.S. Supreme Court Justices: Liberalism in Civil Liberties and Economics Decisions, 1946–1978," *Am. Pol. Sci. Rev.* 75 (1981), 355–367; Goldman, "Voting Behavior on the United States Courts of Appeals Revisited," *Am. Pol. Sci. Rev.* 69 (1975), 491–506; Songer and Davis, "The Impact of Party and Region on Voting Decisions in the United States Courts of Appeals, 195–1986," *W. Pol. Q.* 43 (1990), 317.

21. In a preliminary report of the present study, based on incomplete data (a paper presented at the 1991 meeting of the Midwest Political Science Association), no significant differences were found based on gender in the analysis of employment discrimination cases which controlled for case facts and partisan effects in a logistic regression model. When that logit model on the complete sample was re-run, however, the differences were significant and of approximately the same magnitude as those reported here.

22. *See, e.g.,* Epstein, *Deceptive Distinctions: Sex, Gender, and the Social Order* (New Haven: Yale University Press and New York: Russell Sage Foundation, 1988) reviewing criticisms of Gilligan's work.

23. *Supra* n. 6.

24. Davis, "Do Women Judges Speak in 'A Different Voice'? Carol Gilligan, Feminist Legal Theory and the Ninth Circuit," *Wisc. Women's L. J.* (December 1993).

25. *See, e.g.,* Goldman, "Reagan's judicial legacy: completing the puzzle and summing up," *Judicature* 72 (1989), 318–330; Schwartz, *Packing the Courts: The Conservative Campaign to Rewrite the Constitution* (New York: Charles Scribner's Sons, 1988).

The Supreme Court and the grass roots: whom does the Court represent best?

Thomas R. Marshall

Evidence from nationwide polls during the Warren, Burger, and Rehnquist Courts suggests that the modern Supreme Court's rulings have represented the attitudes of major demographic and social groups at similar rates. This evenhanded pattern of representation contributes to the Court's reputation as a neutral arbiter.

Whether the U.S. Supreme Court represents some groups better than others has long been a question of interest to judicial scholars, journalists, and litigants. Typically, the Court's representation of social or demographic groups has been measured in one of two ways. First, researchers may examine the justices' rulings, dicta, or voting patterns for evidence of sympathy toward group claims. Second, some researchers have computed which interest group litigants have the best win-loss records before the Court, and whether interest group litigants fare better, or worse, over time.[1]

Analyzing the Court's voting patterns and doctrines or counting interest group litigants' successes and failures, however, does not directly indicate how well the Court's rulings represent grass-roots group attitudes. A recent example may help demonstrate the differences among Court doctrine, interest group claims, and grass-roots group attitudes.

In *Johnson v. Transportation Agency of Santa Clara* (1987), a divided Court held, 6–3, that employers could take sex and race into account in promotion decisions and give an advantage to women or racial minorities in promotions to "traditionally segregated job categories." [2] The *Johnson* ruling was widely cited as a victory for women and minority employees; several women's and civil rights interest groups had submitted amicus curiae briefs in support of the Court's eventual ruling.[3] A nationwide Gallup Poll, however, reported that while a 57 percent to 35 percent majority of nonwhites favored the ruling, a 59 percent to 32 percent majority of women opposed it. Many other such examples can be found of apparent conflicts between interest group amicus positions, oral argument, or Court dicta versus grass-roots group poll attitudes.[4]

As *Johnson* illustrates, an alternative approach to answering the question—whom does the Supreme Court represent best?—is to rely on actual attitudes of social or demographic groups, as measured by scientific, nationwide public opinion polls. Here, a "grassroots" demographic or social group does not refer to dues-paying members of organized interest groups. Instead, it refers to the reported attitudes of poll samples of specific demographic groups, such as men, women, Catholics, Protestants, upper-, middle-, or lower-income groups, and so forth.

Pollsters frequently write poll items to tap issues in Supreme Court disputes. Major nationwide polls also routinely report, or at least archive, poll results not only nationwide, but also for major demographic groups. As a result, it is often possible to determine which groups' attitudes a Supreme Court ruling actually represents—according to available public opinion poll results.[5]

Representing groups' claims

In a legal or electoral sense, the Supreme Court does not clearly "represent" social or demographic groups at all. The justices sit for life terms (with good behavior), without any popular election. Few Supreme Court seats are any longer informally "reserved" for a member of a religious, regional, social, or demographic group. The "black" seat of Justices Thurgood Marshall and Clarence Thomas and the "woman's" seat occupied by Justice Sandra Day O'Connor, now remain the clearest concessions to group representation. Several justices currently supervise federal circuits from which they geographically hailed,[6] although the practice of geographically balancing appointments according to circuits apparently died out well before the Warren Court.

Although most Supreme Court justices may not legally, informally, or electorally "represent" specific social or demographic groups, the Court may nonetheless agree with some groups' attitudes more frequently than it agrees with others. For example, in the *Johnson* ruling the Supreme Court agreed with (thus, represented) a majority of nonwhites, but disagreed with a majority of 21 other group attitudes reported in a Gallup Poll. In this sense, the Supreme Court "represents" a group when the Court's ruling agrees with a majority (or at least a plurality) of a group's reported attitudes as measured in a scientific, nationwide poll. The Supreme Court fails to represent a group if it disagrees with a majority (or plurality) of a group's attitudes.

Four widely cited theories exist in the judicial literature, each suggesting that the Supreme Court will represent the attitudes of some demographic or socioeconomic groups better than others. These theories are reviewed briefly below, then tested with available poll data.

As the available poll data since the early 1950s indicates, none of the four theories of Supreme Court representation is completely correct. In part, each errs because modern American public opinion only occasionally has been deeply polarized. In part, each theory also errs because even where group attitudes have been polarized, the modern Supreme Court has been relatively evenhanded in its rulings.

Four theories

The first and perhaps oldest theory suggests the Supreme Court will best represent numerically large, economically and politically dominant majorities. Robert Dahl's much-debated 1957 essay popularized the argument that the Supreme Court is essentially a majoritarian institution, which best represents prevailing political majorities.[7] Except during brief political realignment periods, Supreme Court rulings will typically represent the views of national and legislative majorities. Deaths, retirements, and new appointments ensure that the Supreme Court is seldom long out-of-line with a public opinion majority.

To be sure, majoritarian theories of judicial representation seldom examine actual poll results, largely because scientific public opinion polls were not available until the 1930s, and poll items tapping Court rulings were seldom written until the 1950s.[8] Majoritarian theories of Supreme Court representation, however, might predict that the Supreme Court would best represent groups that comprise numerical majorities and that have also been socially, economically, and politically dominant—for example, Protestants, whites, men, middle-aged or older Americans, and middle- or upper-income Americans.[9]

By contrast, a second theory holds that the Court is—or at least should be—especially responsive to small,

unpopular, or politically impotent minorities who have little other effective access to the political arena. Several accounts have criticized the majoritarian theory and have argued that both the Warren and Burger Courts were often sympathetic to minority claims on civil rights, civil liberties, and political dissent.[10] This countermajoritarian theory of representation also has been argued frequently as a normative theory on behalf of blacks and other racial minorities, women, small religious sects, prisoners, gays and lesbians, children of unwed parents, aliens, and the poor.[11]

Testing this second theory poses several methodological problems. Many minority groups—for example, the Amish or Jehovah's Witnesses—are so few in number that nationwide poll samples of 1,000 or 1,500 cannot reliably measure group members' attitudes. In other instances pollsters do not separately identify minorities—for example, homosexuals or noncitizens. Modern polling techniques usually undercount some minorities—such as the poor, transients, prisoners, or non-English speakers. Even for relatively numerous minority groups—such as blacks, Hispanics, or Jews—measurement errors may be relatively high.[12] Further, only a handful of Supreme Court rulings each term addresses issues of special interest to unpopular or numerically small minorities, and some of these disputes are not of sufficiently general interest to elicit a nationwide poll item.

These methodological problems notwithstanding, major nationwide polls routinely identify several different minority groups' attitudes on poll items. The countermajoritarian theory might predict that the Supreme Court would best represent the attitudes of racial minorities (blacks), religious minorities (Catholics), politically impotent groups (the young, or low income, or less-well-educated Americans), or women—at least on issues of key interest to these groups. These groups are typically underrepresented in top public or private leadership positions,[13] and all (except women) comprise clear numerical minorities in American society.

A third theory also predicts that the Supreme Court will best represent the attitudes of numerically small groups—but in this case, politically and economically advantaged elites. Supreme Court justices, like other policy makers, may respond to the best organized, best financed, most often elected, and most articulate interests in American society.[14] High-status elites may also be more successful in elective politics, and the norm of judicial deference may lead the Court to uphold elite-inspired laws and policies enacted elsewhere. In addition, Supreme Court justices themselves typically come from relatively advantaged backgrounds and enjoy high levels of education and high incomes. As a result, the justices may sense and share elite values.[15] Elite theories predict that the Supreme Court will best represent upper-income and well-educated Americans.[16]

The fourth and final theory argues that the justices best reflect attitudes of their own political party identifiers. A considerable literature documents that federal judges, including Supreme Court justices, sometimes differ significantly in their voting patterns according to their political party ties.[17] This literature does not tie the judges' voting patterns directly into grass-roots Republican and Democrat identifiers' attitudes. Yet one might hypothesize that the justices would best represent their own party identifiers' preferences. As a result, when the Court has a majority of Republican justices, the Court will best represent Republican identifiers' preferences. Conversely, when the Court has a majority of Democratic justices, the Court will best represent Democratic identifiers' preferences.

Data and methodology

Each of these four theories of representation yields different predictions about which group attitudes the Supreme Court will best represent. At present there is no research that indicates which theory is most accurate. These theories, however, can be tested by using breakdowns from available nationwide public opinion polls. Major polling organizations such as Gallup, Harris, the Times-Mirror, CBS/*New York Times,* or the *Los Angeles Times* polls frequently include poll items to measure attitudes toward pending, or recently announced, Supreme Court rulings, at least on prominent controversies. During the Warren, Burger, and Rehnquist Courts (1953–1954 through 1990–1991 terms) some 110 major nationwide poll items could be matched closely with the substantive issues raised in a Supreme Court ruling.[18]

Nationwide polls do not simply report the poll results for the entire nationwide sample. Pollsters also routinely report (or at least archive) results broken down by standard demographic categories. As a result, for poll items that address these 110 Supreme Court rulings, it is also possible to examine the attitudes of 22 social or demographic groups: by sex (male, female); education (college, high school, less than high school); region (East, Midwest, South, West); income (high, medium, low); religion (Protestant, Catholic); age (under 30, 30 to 64, 65 and older); race (black, white); and party identification (Republican, Democrat, Independent).[19]

When a poll item could be closely matched, in substance, with a Supreme Court ruling, that ruling was classified as either "consistent," "inconsistent," or "unclear"—both for nationwide public opinion and also for each of the 22 social and demographic groups described above. This procedure permits an empirical test of how often the modern Court has agreed with major American social groups, and which groups' grass-roots attitudes the Court best represents.

Three simple examples may help clarify this classification. A Supreme Court ruling was classified as "consistent" if it agreed with a public opinion majority or plurality, either nationwide or for a reported group. In *South Dakota v. Dole* (1987), for example, a 64 percent to 23 percent nationwide poll majority favored withholding federal highway funds from states that did not raise their drinking age to 21—a view consistent with the Supreme Court's ruling. Further, majorities of all 22 groups agreed with the Supreme Court's ruling, with majorities in favor ranging from 55 percent (among Independents) to 72 percent (among Republicans).[20]

By contrast, a 63 percent to 29 percent nationwide poll majority disagreed with the "inconsistent" *Johnson v. Transportation Agency of Santa Clara County* (1987) ruling to allow the promotion of women or minorities over men or whites to achieve better balance in the workforce. Majorities of all 22 groups disapproved of the Court's ruling—with the sole exception of blacks, among whom a 56 percent to 34 percent majority approved of the Court ruling.[21]

Public opinion was divided more closely on a few "unclear" decisions where the polls were divided closely within the .05-level margin of error, or where contradictory poll results appeared. In *Kassel v. Consolidated Freightways Corp.* (1981), for example, 45 percent favored and 43 percent opposed a state law prohibiting tandem trailers on interstate highways. Because the close poll margin fell within the 95 percent confidence level margin of error, the Kassel ruling was classified as "unclear." In this instance the Kassel ruling was classified as consistent with 4 groups, inconsistent with 11 groups, and unclear for the remaining 7 groups.[22]

Results

Table 1 reports the percentage of Warren, Burger, and Rehnquist Court rulings that were consistent with nationwide polls, and also the percentage of these rulings that were consistent with attitudes of the 22 social and demographic groups reported here. Tables 1 through 5 exclude the few instances of "unclear" poll-

Table 1. Percentage of Supreme Court decisions that represent group attitudes, 1953/1954–1990/1991 terms

	Percent consistent	Percent consistent, reweighted
Nationwide public opinion	59	58
By education:		
College	59	61
High school	59	58
Less than high school	54	54
By race:		
Black	63	63
White	58	57
By region:		
East	60	62
South	53	51
Midwest	64	62
West	58	58
By income:		
High	59	60
Medium	59	57
Low	57	56
By religion:		
Protestant	59	57
Catholic	57	58
By sex:		
Male	62	61
Female	55	56
By age:		
Young	63	64
Middle-aged	58	58
Older	52	52
By party identification:		
Republican	57	55
Democrat	63	61
Independent	61	63

Note: Table 1 excludes instances of evenly divided or contradictory poll results. None of the results in Tables 1 through 5 are statistically significant except as noted: *(.05 level), **(.01 level). To obtain the percentage of inconsistent decisions, subtract the percent consistent from 100 percent.

to-ruling matches, where poll results were evenly divided or where contradictory poll results appeared.

Overall, 53 percent of the 110 decisions were classified as consistent with nationwide polls, another 37 percent were inconsistent, and 10 percent were unclear. If the unclear decisions are excluded, as in Table 1, then 59 percent of the remaining rulings were consistent with nationwide public opinion polls, and the remaining 41 percent were inconsistent.

Of greater interest here are the results for each of the 22 social or demographic groups. Table 1 reports the percentage of consistent decisions in two ways. The first column reports the overall results; the second col-

umn reports results for a reweighted sample to correct for sampling biases over time and across caseload.[23]

Results in Table 1 indicate that the modern Supreme Court has represented all 22 groups' attitudes about equally often. For each of the 22, about three-fifths of the Court's rulings were consistent with group attitudes. The range between the best- and least-well-represented group was only about 11 percent (for the unweighted sample) to 13 percent (for the reweighted sample).

Given the relatively small number of Court rulings that could be matched with identifiable polls, these results should be interpreted cautiously. Table 1 results, however, indicate that there is no strong evidence that the modern Court has significantly better represented some groups than others during this period. Overall, the results in Table 1 offer little support for any of the first three theories of Supreme Court representation reviewed above.

Table 2 breaks down the results for party affiliation for two time periods—first, for Court terms when there was a majority of Republican justices on the Court, and second, for Court terms when there was a majority of Democratic justices on the Court.[24] Table 2 offers little support for the theory of partisan representation, since the Court's representation of party identifiers did not significantly differ depending on the partisan makeup of the Court itself. Grass-roots Democrats were marginally better represented by the Court than were grass-roots Republicans, regardless of whether there were a majority of Democratic or Republican justices on the Court, but the differences were not large.

Why has the modern Supreme Court represented all 22 groups' attitudes nearly equally often? A large part of the answer lies in the structure of modern American public opinion. As the examples in Table 3 indicate, only rarely do majorities of comparison groups (e.g., blacks versus whites) hold opposing views on Supreme Court

Table 2. Representation of grass-roots Republicans and Democrats, by partisan makeup of the Supreme Court

Partisan majority on the Court were:	Percent of rulings consistent with:	
	Grass-roots Republicans	Grass-roots Democrats
Majority Republican	63	66
Majority Democrat	49	58

Note: Percentages indicate the majority of Court rulings that agreed with the indicated group's attitudes during each time period. For neither time period were the reported differences statistically significant at the .1-level.

Table 3. Percentage of Supreme Court decisions in which comparison groups disagree and Supreme Court representation in these decisions

Groups compared	% of decisions in which groups disagree	Supreme Court decision favors (group) where groups disagree
Whites versus blacks	17	Whites (47%); blacks (53%)
East versus South	14*	East (77%); South (23%)
College versus less than high school	14	College (62%); less than high school (38%)
Young versus old	14*	Young (77%); old (23%)
High versus low income	13	High (67%); low income (33%)
Protestant versus Catholic	8	Protestant (43%); Catholic (57%)
Male versus female	7*	Male (86%); Female (14%)
Republican versus Democrat	5	Republican (20%); Democrat (80%)
Republican versus Independent	6	Republican (33%); Independent (67%)
Democrat versus Independent	4	Independent (50%); Democrat (50%)

Note: None of the comparison groups omitted from Table 3 produced statistically significant differences.

controversies.[25] In the extreme instance, majorities (or pluralities) of blacks disagreed with majorities (or pluralities) of whites in 17 percent of the 110 rulings examined here. Yet in the remaining 83 percent of these 110 rulings, majorities (or pluralities) of both blacks and whites held similar attitudes, and the Supreme Court's rulings simultaneously represented both groups' attitudes equally well.

As Table 3 further indicates, most groups disagreed with their comparison group less often than did blacks and whites. Majorities (or pluralities) of men and women disagreed very rarely—in only 8 (7 percent) of the 110 rulings examined here. Majorities (or pluralities) of Democrats and Republicans disagreed in only 6 (5 percent) of the 110 rulings. In short, the typical Supreme Court case has not been one in which group attitudes were sharply polarized.

Further, in most Supreme Court decisions, public opinion is also relatively one-sided. In two-thirds (67 percent) of the 110 rulings examined here, the overall margin between poll item responses was greater than 20 percent.[26] In few instances—only 16 (15 percent) of the 110 rulings—was nationwide public opinion closely divided, with a poll margin between responses of less than 10 percent.[27] Where nationwide public opinion is very one-sided—as is so frequently the case for Supreme Court controversies—few instances of conflicting majorities between comparison groups will occur.

The modern Supreme Court's relatively even-handed pattern of representation may also result, in part, from characteristics of the Court itself—particularly the shifting nature of majority coalitions and lack of clear ideological direction that has characterized the modern Supreme Court during much of this time

period.[28] Ad hoc doctrinal decisions, shifting majorities, and the lack of an overreaching philosophy during much of the Burger and early Rehnquist Courts, coupled with a large number of nonunanimous, closely divided votes, may contribute to the Court's pattern of representing different social and demographic groups at roughly similar rates.

Table 3 also reports which group attitudes the Supreme Court represented for those rulings in which comparison groups (e.g., blacks versus whites) disagreed. These results may offer a good test of Court representation because they consider only the instances where there was actually a disagreement in group attitudes. Here, the Court's ruling would represent one group, but not the comparison group.[29] In these instances, the majoritarian theory would predict that the Court's ruling would represent the more numerous and influential group, but the countermajoritarian theory would predict that the Court's ruling would represent the smaller or politically impotent group.

Polarized group attitudes most often occurred on racial, sex and gender, and crime and punishment issues. Other issues, such as economic issues, seldom led to polarized group attitudes. For example, blacks and whites disagreed on 19 rulings—among them, 7 racial issues, 6 crime and punishment issues, and 3 sex and gender-related issues. Easterners and Southerners disagreed on 15 rulings—among them, 8 racial issues, 1 crime and punishment issue, and 3 sex and gender-related issues. Young and old Americans disagreed on 15 rulings—among them, 4 racial issues, 5 crime and punishment issues, and 3 sex and gender-related issues.

In most instances, the Court remained relatively evenhanded in its decision making. In rulings where

Table 4. Supreme Court representation of group attitudes for selected groups and issues

Issue and number of decisions	Supreme Court agreement with group attitudes in these cases:
Racial (19)	Whites (63%); blacks (89%)
Religious (5)	Protestants (40%); Catholics (40%)
Privacy, gender (19)	Men (53%); Women (44%)
Business, economic (18)	High Income (61%); medium (47%); low (50%)
Free speech, dissent (11)	College-educated (56%); high school (40%); less than high school (40%)
Party-related (55)	Republicans (61%); Democrats (61%); Independents (60%)

majorities (or pluralities) of blacks and whites disagreed, the Supreme Court's rulings agreed with black attitudes in 9 of 17 instances, but agreed with white attitudes in 8 of 17 instances. In only three instances did the modern Court significantly more often prefer one group to its comparison group. The Court more often represented Eastern (versus Southern) attitudes, younger (versus older) attitudes, and male (versus female) attitudes. These mixed and seldom significant results provide little support for any of the four theories of representation reviewed earlier.

Table 4 reexamines the data differently, by reporting only a subset of decisions involving specific issues of special importance to comparison groups. For example, 19 of the 110 rulings involve racial issues. In 17 (89 percent) of these 19 rulings the Court agreed with black majorities (or pluralities), while in 12 (63 percent) of these 19 rulings the Court agreed with white majorities (or pluralities).

These results again provide little support for any of the theories of representation reviewed earlier. The modern Court has sometimes more often (blacks), but sometimes less often (women, low income groups) represented attitudes of less influential groups. On other instances (as for grass-roots Republicans or Democrats) there was no clear pattern.[30] Overall, the evidence as to which groups the Court best represents is mixed and inconclusive; none of the results reported in Table 4 reach statistical significance.

Finally, Table 5 examines the modern Court's pattern of representation of group attitudes by two frequently arising issues: fundamental freedoms and economic decisions. Fundamental freedoms rulings include all disputes over Bill of Rights or Fourteenth Amendment claims, while economic rulings involve employment, taxation, or business regulation disputes.

The differences reported in Table 5 are slight and do not achieve statistical significance. Again they provide little consistent support for any of the four theories. Upper-status group elites (high education, high income) are marginally better represented, especially on economic issues, and males are marginally better represented than females. But some low-status or politically impotent groups (the young, blacks) are also marginally better represented than their comparison groups. Overall, these slight and statistically insignificant results provide little consistent support for any of the four theories of representation.

Table 5 also examines the Court's representation of group attitudes over time. Two time periods are reported. The first comprises the Warren Court and early Burger Court from the 1953–1954 term through the 1975–1976 term—until with Justice Stevens's appointment, the five Nixon-Ford appointees formed a Court majority. The second period spans the remaining Burger and Rehnquist Courts, from the 1976–1977 through the 1988–1989 terms. Again, the evidence fails to support any of the theories. In neither the earlier nor the later periods did the Court statistically significantly better represent a group than its comparison group. Even the over-time decline in support for black attitudes does not achieve statistical significance.

Discussion

The modern Supreme Court has been relatively even-handed in representing different social and demographic group attitudes. Since the early 1950s the Court has not significantly better represented domi-

Table 5. Supreme Court representation of groups, by Court term and type of issue involved

	By issue		By term	
	Fundamental freedoms	Economic decisions	1953/1954–1975/1976	1976/1977–1988/1989
Nationwide:	57%	54%	58%	59%
By education:				
College	57	60	63	56
High school	56	53	56	62
Less than high school	53	47	50	62
By race:				
Black	61	64	68	55
White	57	50	54	62
By region:				
East	61	64	64	57
South	51	44	43	63
Midwest	63	57	60	65
West	57	53	59	58
By income:				
High	58	61	60	60
Medium	57	47	55	62
Low	54	50	52	62
By religion:				
Protestant	58	50	52	64
Catholic	57	50	59	58
By sex:				
Male	60	60	58	64
Female	54	44	56	56
By age:				
Young	60	67	66	59
Middle-aged	56	56	57	60
Older	52	40	50	55
By party:				
Republican	56	53	50	63
Democrat	63	50	59	66
Independent	60	60	64	60

nant majorities, nor unpopular and politically impotent minorities, nor elite groups from which most of the justices themselves come, nor grass-roots Republican or Democratic Party identifiers. Very little support appeared for any of four theories of representation frequently found in the judicial literature.

Why has the modern Supreme Court represented different group attitudes and values in such an evenhanded manner? Two explanations stand out. First, in most Supreme Court controversies, group attitudes are not sharply polarized. As a result, few rulings require the Court to "referee" disputes that pit demographic or social groups against one another.

Even when group attitudes do differ, the modern Court has been relatively evenhanded in deciding between group attitudes. This may result largely from a second reason. The closely balanced ideological coalitions on the modern Court, coupled with ad hoc and shifting doctrinal values during much of this time period, may help create a pattern in which, over time, the Court's rulings have not consistently represented some group's attitudes at the expense of others.

This pattern of evenhanded representation of group attitudes over time may also help explain why the modern Court has enjoyed relatively favorable approval ratings, compared with Congress or the executive branch. Over the last one-third century the Court has "satisfied" American public opinion majorities or pluralities in about three-fifths of its rulings where a clear poll majority actually existed. Further, the Court's rulings have represented most social, economic, and demographic groups at very similar rates.

A Court that satisfies most groups in most rulings and that also satisfies different and sometimes competing groups at roughly similar rates may well come to enjoy an image of a neutral arbitrator, above the routine political fray. In this sense the modern Court's even-handed representation of group attitudes may in part contribute to one element of "mythic" beliefs—that the Court is a fair, neutral, and evenhanded arbiter of social conflict.[31]

Notes

This article originally appeared in Volume 76, Number 1, June–July 1992, pages 22–28.

1. For recent examples of this approach, *see* Epstein and Hadley, "On the Treatment of Political Parties in the U.S. Supreme Court, 1900–1986," *J. of Pol.* 72 (1990), 413; Wheeler, et. al., "Do the 'Haves' Come Out Ahead?," *Law & Soc'y Rev.* 21 (1987), 403; and George and Epstein, "Women's rights litigation in the 1980s: more of the same?," *Judicature* 74 (1991), 314.

2. *Johnson v. Transportation Agency of Santa Clara County,* 480 U.S. 616 (1987), at 626–640.

3. *See, e.g.,* "Supreme Court, 6–3, Extends Preferences In Employment for Women and Minorities," *New York Times,* March 26, 1987, at 1. The NOW Legal Defense and Education Fund, the Lawyers' Committee for Civil Rights Under Law, and the Equal Opportunity Advisory Council, among others, submitted amici briefs in support of the Court majority's position.

4. "The U.S. Supreme Court recently ruled that employers may sometimes favor women and members of minorities over better qualified men and whites in hiring and promoting to achieve better balance in their work forces. Do you approve or disapprove of this decision?" (Gallup, April 10–13, 1987, and June 24–26, 1988).

At least 17 instances appeared among these 110 cases where inconsistencies could be identified between grass-roots group attitudes and the legal positions of organized interest groups or public officials that might be thought to represent these groups. These 17 instances included religious, labor, women, black, state attorney generals, and U.S. solicitor general positions. A complete list of these apparent inconsistencies between grass-roots attitudes and interest group or public official positions is available, upon request, from the author.

5. Random sampling polling replaced quota sampling methods by the 1950s. The poll items here are not a random sample of all Supreme Court cases, and inferential statistics reported herein should be interpreted cautiously. However, reweighting cases for sampling biases over time or between types of cases did not significantly affect the results reported below; see results in Table 1. A listing of cases may be found in Marshall, *Public Opinion and the Supreme Court* (Boston: Unwin Hyman, 1989), 194–201,

and "Public opinion and the Rehnquist Court," *Judicature* 74 (1991), 232. The poll items here overwhelmingly relied on dichotomous, forced-choice responses (e.g., "agree" versus "disagree"); only four poll items used a filter question. If rulings were omitted for poll items where only a poll plurality existed, the conclusions reported below would not change.

6. During the 1991–1992 term, for example, Justices Souter, Stevens, Blackmun, O'Connor, and White supervised circuits from which they had geographically come to the Court.

7. Dahl, "Decisionmaking in a Democracy: The Supreme Court as National Policymaker," *J. of Pub. L.* 6 (1957), 279. For criticisms of Dahl's essay, *see infra,* nn. 10 and 14.

8. For exceptions, see Barnum, "The Supreme Court and Public Opinion: Judicial Decision Making in the post-New Deal Period," *J. of Pol.* 47 (1985), 652; Marshall, *supra* n. 5; and Casper, *The Politics of Civil Liberties* (New York: Harper and Row, 1972).

9. The majoritarian theory may also frequently be found in normative arguments that the Court should defer to political majorities to prevent noncompliance or defiance of Court rulings; *see, e.g.,* Cox, *The Role of the Supreme Court in American Government* (New York: Oxford University Press, 1979); and Kurland, *Politics, the Constitution, and the Warren Court* (Chicago: University of Chicago Press, 1970). Other authors argue that the Court should defer to popular majorities to heighten the people's sense of political responsibility; *see, e.g.,* Thayer, "The Origin and Scope of the American Doctrine of Constitutional Law," *Harv. L. Rev.* 7 (1893), 129; and Bickel, *The Least Dangerous Branch: The Supreme Court at the Bar of Politics* (New Haven: Yale University Press, 1986). Others argue that deference to popular majorities will avoid sanctions against the Court itself; *see* Choper, *Judicial Review and the National Political Process* (Chicago: University of Chicago Press, 1980), 139–162.

In fact, men do not actually comprise a majority of adult Americans, but they have typically so dominated public and private offices that they are usually considered as a dominant majority.

10. *See, e.g.,* Abraham, *Freedom and the Court: Civil Rights and Liberties in the United States* (New York: Oxford University Press, 1982); Cox, *supra* n. 9; Choper, *supra* n. 9; and "The Burger Court: Misperceptions Regarding Judicial Restraint and Insensitivity to Individual Rights," *Syracuse L. Rev.* 30 (1979), 767; Cortner, *The Supreme Court and the Second Bill of Rights* (Madison: University of Wisconsin Press, 1981); Casper, "The Supreme Court and National Policy Making," *Am. Pol. Sci. Rev.* 70 (1976), 50; and Shapiro, "The Supreme Court from Warren to Burger," in King, ed., *The New American Political System* (Washington, D.C.: American Enterprise Institute, 1979).

11. Ely, *Democracy and Distrust: A Theory of Judicial Review* (Cambridge: Harvard University Press, 1980); and Richards, "Sexual Autonomy and the Constitutional Right to Privacy," *Hastings L. J.* 30 (1979), 122; Choper, *supra* n. 9, at 79–122.

12. Bradburn and Sudman, *Polls and Surveys* (San Francisco: Jossey-Bass, 1988), 111, 132; and Thornberry and Massey, "Trends in U.S. Telephone Coverage Across Time and Subgroups," in Groves et al., eds., *Telephone Survey Methodology* (New York: John Wiley & Sons, 1988), 27–36.

13. Ornstein, *Vital Statistics on Congress, 1984–85* (Washington, D.C.: American Enterprise Institute, 1984).

14. Devine, *The Attentive Public: Polyarchial Democracy* (Chicago: Rand-McNally, 1970); and Domhoff, *Who Rules America?* (Englewood Cliffs, N.J.: Prentice-Hall, 1967).

15. Spaeth, *Supreme Court Policy Making* (San Francisco: W. H. Freeman, 1979), 109–118; Abraham, *Justices and Presidents: A Political History of Appointments to the Supreme Court* (New York: Oxford, 1985); Friedman and Israel, *The Justices of the United States Supreme Court, 1789–1969* (New York: Chelsea, 1969); and Schmidhauser, *The Supreme Court* (New York: Holt, Rinehart, and Winston, 1960).

16. Elite theories have more often been applied historically to earlier Court periods, especially the late 1800s and early 1900s, and to individual justice's biographies; *see, e.g.,* Abraham, *supra* n. 7 at 291–293. *See also* Schmidhauser, "The Judges of the Supreme Court: A Collective Portrait," *Midwest J. of Pol. Sci.* 3 (1959), 1.

17. The literature on the impact of political parties on judicial behavior is extensive; *see, e.g.,* Goldman, "Voting Behavior on the United States Courts of Appeals Revisited," *Am. Pol. Sci. Rev.* 69 (1975), 491; and Tate, "Personal Attribute Models of the Voting Behavior of the U.S. Supreme Court Justices," *Am. Pol. Sci. Rev.* 75 (1981), 355.

18. For a listing of the issues and poll matches, see *supra* n. 5.

19. The Gallup Poll routinely reports nationwide results broken down by major social and demographic groups. Breakdowns by groups for the Harris Poll may be obtained from the University of North Carolina, Chapel Hill, NC, and for other network and newspaper polls, from the Roper Center, University of Connecticut, Storrs, Ct. The .05-level error margins were applied to nationwide poll results to classify rulings as consistent, inconsistent, or unclear. When applied to smaller numerical groups, such as blacks or Catholics, this may lead to .1-level error margins.

20. "In 1984 a law was passed requiring all states to raise their legal drinking age to 21 or face reductions in Federal highway funds. At present, nine states and the District of Columbia permit legal drinking under age 21. Would you favor or oppose having the Federal government start withholding funds from these states if they fail to raise their drinking age to 21 by October first?" (Gallup, June 9–16, 1987).

21. *Supra* n. 4.

22. "Would you favor or oppose a law in this state that would prohibit tandem truck rigs—that is, large trucks with two trailers attached—on major interstate highways?" (Gallup, April 29–May 2, 1983).

23. Cases were reweighted to the figures reported in O'Brien, *Storm Center* (New York: W. W. Norton, 1986), 205. The 110 rulings were also tested to see if different levels of representation occurred, depending on whether the poll items were taken before, versus after the ruling was announced. However, pre- versus post-ruling differences results were not significant at the .05 level.

24. Terms during which there were five (or more) Democrat justices include 1953/1954–1956/1957 and 1962/1963–1974/1975. Terms for which there were five (or more) Republican justices include 1975/1976–1990/1991. The 1957/1958–1961/1962 terms were excluded from this analysis since the justices were evenly divided between the two parties, with one self-described Independent justice (Frankfurter).

25. For evidence that these patterns occur frequently, *see* Erikson et al., *American Public Opinion* (New York: MacMillan, 1988), 169–207.

26. Examples of one-sided poll results include *South Dakota v. Dole* (1987) and *Johnson v. Transportation Agency of Santa Clara County* (1987), at *supra* n. 4, 20, and 21.

27. An example of a more narrowly-divided poll result includes *Kassel v. Consolidated Freightways Corp.* (1981), *supra* n. 22.

28. *See, e.g.,* Shapiro, *supra* n. 10; Blasi, *The Burger Court: The Counterrevolution That Wasn't* (New Haven: Yale University Press, 1983), 217; and O'Brien, *supra* n. 23, at 262–275.

29. For the argument that representation is best measured by situations in which conflict occurs, see Dahl, "The Concept of Power," *Behavioral Sci.* 2 (1957), 201, and *A Preface to Democratic Theory* (Chicago: University of Chicago Press, 1956), 63–67.

30. In Table 4, the "partisan" category includes issues where differences between Republicans and Democrats were most often found since the early 1950s. These include racial, foreign policy, business and labor, social welfare, and lifestyle issues. *See* Sorauf and Beck, *Party Politics in America* (Glenview, Ill.: Scott, Foresman, 1988), 141–158; and Gitelson, Conway, and Fiegert, *American Political Parties: Stability and Change* (Boston: Houghton Mifflin, 1984), 138–144.

31. Casey, "The Supreme Court and Myth: An Empirical Investigation," *Law & Soc'y Rev.* 8 (1974), 385; Bass, "The Constitution as Symbol," *Am. Pol. Q.* 8 (1980), 237; and Frank, *Law and the Modern Mind* (New York: Brentano, 1930).

Trial Courts: Civil and Criminal Justice Processes

Trial courts are tribunals of first instance in the American judiciary, the forum in which civil and criminal justice matters are initially heard. Often, the trial court is also the arena in which legal matters are definitively resolved either through pretrial negotiated settlements or actual trial proceedings. The articles in this section consider several aspects of the operation of American trial courts.

Alissa Worden's study, "Policy making by prosecutors: the uses of discretion in regulating plea bargaining," starts with the recognition that different prosecutors have different policies when pursuing plea bargaining agreements and goes on to explore a number of variables that are putatively related to the decisions that prosecutors make. Based on a survey of twenty-seven prosecuting attorneys in the state of Georgia, Worden documents empirically that their values and motives are both complex and varied. Thus, prosecutorial decisions regarding plea bargaining flow from a brew that includes the personal values of the prosecutor, the resource and caseload constraints under which the prosecutor is laboring, the constraints imposed by the courthouse environment in which the prosecutor is just one actor among many, and the local community's needs and expectations. Prosecutors, Worden concludes, "as politicians and administrators must reconcile their policy choices with organizational and political constraints and obligations."

Michael Tonry's essay, "Twenty years of sentencing reform: steps forward, steps backward," explores the enormous changes that have occurred in sentencing policies in the United States since 1970 and the ambiguous consequences such changes have wrought on the American system of justice. Clearly, the biggest alterations in sentencing policies during the past three decades center on efforts to promulgate sentencing guidelines and mandatory sentences in lieu of indeterminate sentencing. While such policies may have reduced racial and gender biases in sentencing, they raise the alternative concern of "unacceptable risks of injustice because they make it impossible to take account of important differences among defendants." Tonry's discussion makes a distinction between the imposition of federal sentencing reform and the changes that have occurred in the states, where the implementation of new policies has been more successful.

A major exception to this generalization was brought to light by the 2004 Supreme Court ruling in *Blakely v. Washington*. The Court found Washington State's sentencing system to be unconstitutional because it allowed judges to exercise discretion in considering aggravating factors that could result in more stringent sentences than the maximum established by the state's guidelines. The Court's ruling indicated that only juries, not judges, could make such a judgment. Because of the similarity of Washington State's approach to that utilized in the federal judiciary, the decision has placed the constitutionality of the federal sentencing guidelines into question and disarray. Indeed, at the time of this writing, the Court has agreed to hear two cases focused on federal sentencing policy. A whole new landscape may soon be in place in this controversial domain.

In " 'Three strikes and you're out': are repeat offender laws having their anticipated effects?" John Clark, James Austin, and D. Alan Henry explore one of the most popular sentencing reforms implemented in many jurisdictions in recent years. As the authors note, "The purpose of these laws is simple: offenders convicted repeatedly of serious offenses should be removed from society for long periods of time, in many cases for life." The Washington State and California models of such "three strikes" policies are examined closely, as are the variations of these two prototypes that exist in other states. The difficulty of assessing the impact of these laws is underscored in the analysis because, as the authors note, " 'Three strikes and you're out' can mean dramatically different things in different states. A review of the provisions of all the states that have enacted this type of legislation reveals differences in how a 'strike' is defined, how many strikes are required to be 'out,' and what it means to be 'out.' " In the final analysis, Clark, Austin, and Henry conclude that most of the publicly prominent three strikes laws will actually have minimal effects in their respective states. Most are targeted toward violent criminals, and as these individuals often are already imprisoned and serving lengthy sentences, the laws will have little impact.

It is difficult to discuss such issues as incarceration, prosecutorial discretion, sentencing policies, and three strikes laws without attention turning at some point to the relationship between race and outcomes in the criminal justice system. Norval Morris's piece, "Race and crime: what evidence is there that race influences results in the criminal justice system?" brings considerable data to bear on the problems he addresses. Morris's data support the argument that the criminal justice system discriminates against blacks at multiple stages in the process, including arrest, conviction, and punishment. The author considers remedies for the problems he highlights and concludes, "The whole law and order movement that we have heard so much about is, in operation though not in intent, anti-black and anti-underclass—not in plan, not in design, not in intent, but in operation."

Hugo Bedau's contribution on "Causes and consequences of wrongful convictions: an essay-review" offers several complementary perspectives to Morris's analysis. Here, the focus is on erroneous convictions, particularly those that occur in capital cases involving the potential of the death penalty for the convicted. Documenting the scope of this problem, Bedau points out that in 2002 the one hundredth wrongly convicted capital defendant since the death penalty was reinstituted in the United States during the 1970s was released on the grounds of innocence. In the face of such evidence, Bedau opines, "what is truly amazing is the extent to which advocates of America's current death penalty system have disregarded or otherwise downplayed the significance of these irrevocable errors—as though they were relics of a distant past."

Bedau notes that all but six of America's death penalty jurisdictions have had at least one incidence of a wrongful capital conviction, with the discovery of error and rectification more often than not coming from sources outside of the formal criminal justice system. Linking the problematic history of capital punishment with Morris's focus on race, Bedau notes that, "just as the paradigm lynchings in American history were carried out by white mobs on helpless black men as a populist method of ruthless social control, so the death penalty is to a troubling extent a socially approved practice of white-on-black violence, especially where the crimes involved are black-on-white." In Bedau's view there are "many disturbing parallels between the lynching practices of a century ago and the death penalty practices of our own day."

This essay includes consideration of several potential reforms that could improve the death penalty system in the United States, including the utilization of DNA evidence whenever possible and the exemption of the mentally retarded from receipt of a death sen-

tence, a reform accomplished by the Supreme Court's ruling in *Atkins v. Virginia* (2002). For the most part, however, Bedau feels that, looking forward, "everything turns on the willingness of legislatures to enact statutes that incorporate reforms," yet he also observes that reforms themselves may be problematic since, "astute observers of the system [argue that it is] impossible to design reforms that would be effective in bringing greater fairness into the death penalty system and still serve rational goals of deterrence, incapacitation, and retribution." In such a setting, what is certain is that, "the struggle over the nation's soul will continue for some time to come."

Edmund Ludwig, who has served on both the state and federal benches, rounds out this section of readings by exploring "The changing role of the trial judge." The changes that Ludwig examines at the federal level stem primarily from dramatic increases in caseloads coupled with both absolute and proportionate decreases in trials as a mechanism to resolve cases. The numbers presented by Ludwig for the thirty-year period between 1970 and 2000 are truly remarkable. For one, 340 authorized federal district court judgeships in 1970 rose by nearly 100 percent to 655 in 2000. While the district courts disposed of 116,000 cases in 1970, dispositions nearly tripled to 335,000 by 2000. It is understandable in this burgeoning caseload context that time-intense and costly trials, which accounted for about 12 percent of the dispositions in 1970, only accounted for approximately 3 percent of the dispositions in 2000. Even more noteworthy, however, is the precipitous drop in the absolute number of trials from 13,600 in 1970 to fewer than 10,000 in 2000, despite the doubling of authorized judgeships and the three-fold increase in cases.

What Ludwig seeks to account for is the "seemingly topsy-turvy statistics" that underscore that federal judges are disposing of considerably more cases per year in 2000 (510) than they were in 1970 (340), while dramatically decreasing the actual trial proceedings they preside over. The explanation for this seeming anomaly is that "changes have occurred in the nature of the adversarial process and in dispute resolution generally, and in the processing of cases." These changes, however, by no means diminish the role of the judges who "can and should think of themselves as functioning within a changing jurisprudence of dispute resolution and should adapt their role accordingly." With such adaptation, "the judge will continue to be the centerpiece and dominant force in dispute resolution."

In the altered legal world depicted by Ludwig, the judge is more active in pretrial processes, serving as "the schoolmaster who encourages and often presses lawyers to do their homework and prepare for trial, instead of the neutral arbiter who lets the lawyers, for better or worse, try their own case." The judge essentially becomes more heavily embroiled in case man-agement and attempts to "bring about a much more efficient and effective dispositional performance record than in the past." At bottom, in an era in which trials have become a "societal luxury . . . the role of the trial judge has taken on new and larger dimensions that are essential to our society's welfare. . . . The courts, as well as numerous other agencies, have put substantial resources into what has become the bur-geoning field of how to settle cases and avoid trials."

Policy making by prosecutors: the uses of discretion in regulating plea bargaining

Alissa Worden

The values and motives of prosecutors are complex and varied. As administrators and politicians, they must reconcile their policy choices with organizational and political constraints and obligations.

Although court observers agree that the prosecutor plays an important role in shaping local legal culture, most research on prosecutors has examined only legal and strategic considerations in charging and other case-processing decisions,[1] and has largely overlooked chief prosecutors' administrative and political uses of discretion in making policies that structure their assistants' day-to-day decisions. Office policies are an important means of standardizing staff behavior and of developing an institutional role within the courthouse community; and there are few formal constraints on prosecutors' discretion in setting policy. Therefore, policy decisions may offer clues to prosecutors' efforts to dominate or adapt to their courthouse colleagues and their political environments.

This article examines prosecutors in their roles as policymakers, focusing on office policies concerning one important feature of criminal adjudication, plea bargaining. The findings offer some support for political and organizational explanations of policy choices: prosecutors' plea bargaining policies represent responsiveness to community crime problems as well as adaptations to the level of workgroup cooperation and conflict in their courthouses. However, plea policies are also associated with prosecutors' personal beliefs about the conflicting values of due process and crime control. These findings are significant because they offer insight into a complex set of motivations behind prosecutors' administrative and political decisions, and thereby illustrate the importance of more systematic study of prosecutors' policy choices.

The uses of discretion

Studies of prosecutors' policies have been more illustrative than definitive. Many examine only one or a small number of jurisdictions, so they are primarily useful for generating, but not for testing, hypotheses about the causes and consequences of policies.[2] Most research on criminal courts has been conducted in urban areas, and therefore variation on theoretically interesting characteristics, such as organizational size, cannot be observed or measured.[3] Moreover, many researchers have focused on practices or patterns of decisions rather than on formal or even informal policies.[4] Finally, research on prosecutors has been handicapped by overly simplified conceptions of prosecutorial motivations, such as the assumption that all prosecutors strive to maximize convictions or to impose maximally harsh sentences, despite the fact that interviews and observation have revealed considerable variation in prosecutors' values and beliefs, incentives, and role orientations.[5] In sum, there have been few systematic attempts to account for how and why prosecutors fashion the rules that govern their staffs' behavior.

One of the most important processes that chief prosecutors can regulate is plea bargaining. All court actors have incentives to negotiate dispositions rather than take cases to trial. Trials are slow and unpredictable, they require prodigious investment of resources for preparation, and they produce one winner and one loser, with no room for compromise. From the point of view of a prosecutor, negotiated guilty pleas offer certain (and virtually irreversible) convictions in return for a commodity, leniency, of which prosecutors have a potentially unlimited supply. It is reasonable to assume that chief prosecutors who attempt to restrict plea bargaining do so in order to counteract these pervasive incentives to negotiate dispositions.

But why do some prosecutors attempt to regulate plea bargaining through formal and informal policies, while others do not? The most common explanation is that restrictive plea bargaining policies represent efforts to crack down on crime by refusing to offer lenient sentences. For example, in one of the jurisdictions he studied, Roy Flemming found that restrictive policies were part of a package of internal office reforms aimed at stiffening sentences and establishing a stronger anti-crime image in the courthouse and the community.[6] But this is only one of several plausible explanations. Plea bargaining policies might be shaped by the personal values of prosecutors, and by organizational opportunities and limitations, as well as by environmental constraints.

Attitudes

Although some theoretical work on prosecutorial decision making has been premised on the assumption that prosecutors uniformly pursue the objectives of maximizing convictions and maximizing sentence severity,[7] the empirical observations of other court researchers challenge this assumption. David Neubauer, for example, studied one Midwestern prosecutor who insulated his staff from community and law enforcement pressures in order to establish policies and practices consistent with his own view of the proper role of the prosecutor in the criminal justice system.[8] Prosecutors' beliefs, Neubauer suggested, lead them to become either crime fighters, deploying resources to maximize the number of wrongdoers convicted, or officers of the court, responsible for ensuring due process even as they argue the state's case. Likewise, Lief Carter observed that prosecutors in a California office varied not only in how much satisfaction they sought (and derived) from the interpersonal aspects of their jobs, but also in whether they placed stronger emphasis on controlling crime or on maintaining high standards of due process.[9]

As Herbert Packer observed more than 20 years ago, although controlling crime and protecting defendants' rights are not theoretically incompatible values, in practice they often conflict.[10] For the purpose of understanding prosecutors' policy choices, this tradeoff may be particularly important. While some critics claim that plea bargaining results in overly lenient sentences, many court actors and observers recognize that plea bargaining is not only a means of conserving scarce resources, but also a way of ensuring conviction and punishment in cases involving evidentiary problems or reluctant witnesses. Critics on the other side of the plea bargaining debate agree with this observation, but object for precisely that reason: plea bargaining is a means of ensuring (perhaps through coercion) the self-conviction of defendants while avoiding the rigorous standards of due process and proof imposed during trials.

It is reasonable to hypothesize that the policy choices of court actors, like those of other politicians, are influenced by personal beliefs, and that the "essential policy choices for judges and prosecutors entail an accommodation of crime control and due process values." [11] Thus, prosecutors who emphasize the court's crime-control mission may be more willing to tolerate practices that compromise due process standards in order to increase convictions, and to implicitly encourage plea bargaining by placing no restrictions on negotiated dispositions. Prosecutors who balance their commitment to crime control with concern about due process may be more likely to restrict or regulate plea bargaining.

Resources and caseload constraints

As administrators, prosecutors must find ways of managing caseloads by efficiently processing cases within the constraints of staff and resources. If, as some have argued, growing caseloads and the increasing costs of trial are responsible for the pervasiveness of plea bargaining,[12] then one might infer that courts with the heaviest caseloads (or, more accurately, the largest ratio of cases to resources) must resort to plea bargaining most frequently.[13]

Of course, case pressure may be felt differently in different sectors of a courthouse. That a jurisdiction has too few judges, courtrooms, or public defenders to keep up with dockets need not imply that the prosecutor's staff feels equally burdened (indeed, such a differential burden might work to the prosecutor's advantage). Therefore, an examination of the effects of caseload on prosecutors' plea bargaining policies must focus on prosecutorial rather than courthouse resources and caseloads.[14] It is hypothesized that where prosecutors operate under conditions of scarce resources, they can ill afford to adopt restrictive policies that may prolong negotiations or, worse yet, encourage defendants to take their chances on trial. Slack resources may be a necessary (albeit not sufficient) condition for the adoption of restrictive plea bargaining practices.

Courthouse constraints

Restrictive plea bargaining policies may also represent pragmatic adaptations to the degree of cooperation and competition evidenced by other actors involved in the sentencing process. One of a prosecutor's most important advantages in plea negotiations is control over sentencing. While prosecutors can implicitly constrain the range of sentence severity through their charging decisions, of even greater value is the opportunity to recommend specific sentences following pleas and convictions. In many courts the sentence recommendation is the means by which a prosecutor communicates the terms of a plea agreement to a judge, so prosecutors who enjoy the cooperation of judges in sentencing have greater credibility and flexibility in plea negotiations.

Judges vary, however, in the extent to which they delegate their sentencing discretion to prosecutors, and not all passively acquiesce to prosecutors' recommendations. In many jurisdictions probation officers conduct pre-sentence investigations (PSIs) for all convicted defendants, and the reports submitted to judges typically include specific sentence recommendations. While these recommendations are not binding, they comprise an important cue for some judges. Unlike judges, defense lawyers, and law enforcement officials, probation officers have little incentive to develop reciprocity relationships with prosecutors, and therefore little incentive to incorporate prosecutorial preferences into their recommendations.[15] Judicial deference to PSI recommendations reduces prosecutors' ability to negotiate with confidence, a point not lost upon defense attorneys and their clients. Where judges are attentive to PSI recommendations, prosecutors' credibility in sentence bargaining is diminished.

Prosecutors' influence over sentencing varies directly, therefore, with the level of judicial receptivity to prosecutors' recommendations, and inversely with the level of judicial receptivity to probation office recommendations. Neither factor is within the control of prosecutors; rather, the degree of judicial cooperation and the presence of competition from probation officers are environmental constraints to which prosecutors must adapt. Prosecutors who find that judges routinely disregard their staffs' recommendations or frequently acquiesce to PSI recommendations may decide that there is little to lose, and perhaps something to gain, by a no-plea policy.

These circumstances appeared to explain the no-plea policy maintained by the district attorney in one of the jurisdictions included in this study. Interviews with a judge, several assistant prosecutors, and the public defender, supplemented by courtroom observations, revealed that although the prosecutor's staff routinely recommended stiff sentences upon entries of guilty pleas, judges routinely disregarded those recommendations in favor of those included in PSI reports. The assistant prosecutors explained that their chief's extremely restrictive plea bargaining policy was the result rather than the cause of judges' apparent indifference to their recommendations. Having learned early in his career that local judges saw the probation office as the legitimate source of sentencing advice, and frustrated in his efforts to establish credibility with the defense bar, the district attorney made the most of his predicament by realizing the political benefits of a widely publicized no-plea policy. This anecdotal evidence suggests a pair of hypotheses: where prosecutors' recommendations are seldom heeded by judges, and where PSI reports are routinely incorporated into sentencing decisions, chief prosecutors are more likely to impose restrictions on plea bargaining.

Community needs and expectations

Prosecutors' policies may be influenced not only by characteristics of the immediate courthouse environment, but by the perceived needs and expectations of the community as well. To an even greater extent than judges, prosecutors are local politicians. Their elections are more likely to be contested, and contested over matters of job performance, than are those of judges; and the job of a prosecutor, in the eyes of the public, is fighting crime. One way of demonstrating determination to "crack down" on crime is to refuse to negotiate with defendants, a policy that may be adopted for its symbolic value (as was the case with the district attorney discussed above), or for its expected impact on sentencing. However, because restrictive policies entail costs, in terms of efficiency and perhaps goodwill among court actors, such policies are worth implementing only when prosecutors feel they are badly needed or that the public will observe and appreciate them. These conditions are most likely to prevail in communities with serious crime problems, communities whose citizens (and media) may be particularly attentive to officials' efforts to combat crime.

Of course, there are other ways of conceiving of prosecutorial responsiveness to the public. Many observers have noted the importance of conviction rate as a measure of individual and collective performance.[16] Conviction rates constitute simplistic but easily advertised indicators of success since they appear to measure prosecutors' ability to win cases. Guilty pleas are the easiest kind of conviction to obtain, of course, so a strong emphasis on maintaining a high conviction rate may be inversely related to policies that restrict or regulate plea bargaining; prosecutors concerned about maintaining high conviction rates may be less inclined to adopt policies that restrict their staff's ability to secure convictions.

Data and analysis

Data were gathered from several sources in the Georgia Superior Courts, the courts of original jurisdiction for felony prosecutions. Georgia is an appropriate site for this study for several reasons. Georgia's court system is representative of many states' systems in that its judges have stable assignments and considerable discretion in sentencing, and its prosecutors are elected to office for four-year terms and operate under few statutory restrictions on their discretion, including discretion to make plea bargains. Moreover, Georgia is economically, culturally, and politically diverse.[17]

Data for constructing the dependent and independent variables were drawn from surveys of all district attorneys, assistant district attorneys, and judges in the superior courts in the summer of 1986. The survey included items on court staffing and organization, perceptions of local adjudication practices and policies, and attitudes toward crime and criminal justice policy. The response rates on the surveys for judges, district attorneys, and assistant district attorneys were 69 percent, 60 percent, and 61 percent, respectively.[18] Data on circuit crime rates and caseload were compiled from archival sources. Complete data were available for 27 of the 45 circuits.

The dependent variable measures the presence of policies restricting plea bargaining. Jurisdictions in which district attorneys formally or informally restricted their assistants' discretion in plea bargaining were identified through prosecutors' responses to a question about the presence of formal or informal policies restricting or prohibiting plea bargaining. Despite the general nature of the question, there was complete agreement among prosecutors and their assistants within every circuit about whether or not such restrictions existed, suggesting that even informal policies are clearly communicated to office personnel.[19] These responses were used to create a dichotomous variable that distinguishes between circuits with no plea bargaining restrictions, and those with some form of restrictive policies. In 14 of the 27 jurisdictions district attorneys impose some limits on plea bargaining discretion.

A simple measure of district attorneys' attitudes about the function of the courts was derived from responses to an item that asked them to indicate, on a six-point scale anchored by the values of crime control (1) and due process (6), their placement of the proper function of the criminal courts. As one might expect, district attorneys as a group clustered closer to the

Table 1. Discriminant analysis of prosecutors' plea bargaining policies

Eigenvalue	.697*
Canonical correlation	.641
Group centroids:	
Restrictive plea policies	.834
Absence of restrictive policies	−.774
Function coefficients:	
Ratio of cases to staff	.165
Judges' receptivity to prosecutors' recommendations	−.459
Judges' receptivity to probation recommendations	.372
Crime rate	.637
Concern with maintaining high conviction rate	.560
Attitude toward crime control/due process tradeoff	.778

n=27
* significant at the .07 level

crime-control end of the scale than did defense lawyers, judges, or assistant prosecutors. However, district attorneys are by no means unanimously committed to a crime-control orientation at the expense of due process concerns; the mean score was 2.8, and scores ranged from 1 to 6.

Measures of judges' receptivity to prosecutors' sentence recommendations, and of receptivity to the recommendations of probation officers,[20] as well as measures of the importance of high conviction rates within prosecutors' offices,[21] were derived from responses to survey items.[22] A measure of office caseload was constructed from the ratio of felony court filings to the number of attorneys working in the office. The magnitude of a circuit's crime problem was measured as the per capita rate of serious personal and property crimes reported during the year preceding the survey.

Table 1 presents the results of a discriminant analysis of plea bargaining policy. Discriminant analysis estimates the effects of independent variables on a nominal or categorical dependent variable by deriving from the independent variables a function or set of functions that maximize discrimination among the groups defined by the dependent variable. The functions are generated such that separation between the groups is maximized, and discriminant scores for cases within each group are similar; group centroids are the points in multidimensional space that represent the mean values on the independent variables for cases within each of the categories defined by the dependent variable.

The variables in the model discriminate moderately well between the two categories of the dependent variable, correctly classifying 81 percent of the cases, an improvement of 29 percent over the percentage that would be correctly classified by chance.

The functions can be interpreted through examination of the discriminant function coefficients (weights attached to the independent variables that describe their contributions to the function); interpretation of these coefficients is analogous to interpretation of the coefficients produced by ordinary least squares regression. Hence, variables that are positively associated with the function are positively associated with restrictive plea policies, and variables that are negatively associated with the function are negatively associated with restrictive plea policies. The magnitude of the coefficients indicates the relative strength of their contributions to the function.[23]

This analysis suggests that preferences between the conflicting values of crime control and due process, and the seriousness of crime problems, have important effects on the way prosecutors run their offices. Contrary to conventional wisdom that restrictive plea policies are manifestations of strong crime-control attitudes, the relationship between prosecutors' attitudes and plea bargaining policy indicates the opposite: greater emphasis on due process protections is strongly and positively associated with the restrictive rules. However, the relationship between plea policy and actual crime rate supports the hypothesis that restrictive rules are associated with serious crime problems.[24]

Of course, plea bargain restrictions may represent sincere efforts to battle serious crime problems, or symbolic reassurance to fearful citizens that such battles are being fought (or both). The data permit only a tentative exploration of these competing interpretations. The survey included two items regarding perceptions of crime: first, a question that asked chief prosecutors to evaluate the seriousness of their circuits' crime problems, compared with that of other areas in the state (less serious than average, about average, more serious than average, very serious); and second, a question that asked how they thought residents of their circuits perceived the local crime problem (same response set). The bivariate correlations among these variables, actual crime rate, and plea bargaining restrictions are presented in Figure 1. These relationships suggest that prosecutors do not believe that citizens accurately gauge the relative seriousness of their communities' crime problems, nor do they allow citizens' perceptions

Figure 1. Crime rate, prosecutors perceptions, public perceptions, and policy

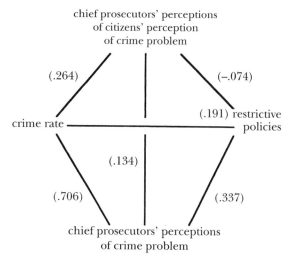

Note: entries are bivariate correlations.

to affect their policy decisions; however, their own perceptions *are* relatively accurate, and they are correlated with policy choices. This offers some support for the interpretation that restrictive plea policies are reactions to actual crime problems, rather than symbolic responses to high levels of public fear. This interpretation is consistent with other research that suggests that the relationships between crime levels, fear of victimization, and decision patterns are weak.[25]

Prosecutors who emphasize the importance of maintaining high conviction rates are more, rather than less, likely to impose restrictions on plea bargaining, contrary to the hypothesized relationship. One possible explanation for this finding is that the observed relationship is spurious, in that plea bargaining restrictions and monitoring of conviction rates might both be manifestations of a close supervisory style, one that tightly constrains assistant prosecutors' professional discretion. However, the data offer no evidence for this explanation. Survey items on closeness of supervision, percent of district attorney's time spent in administrative tasks (rather than on litigation or public relations), and task technology (horizontal or vertical prosecution) were related to each other in predictable ways, but were related neither to emphasis on conviction rate nor to plea policies.[26]

However, these findings offer some support for an explanation of restrictive policies as adaptations to courthouse environments. As predicted, restrictive plea policies are associated with low levels of judicial receptivity to prosecutors' sentence recommendations, and they are associated with high levels of judicial receptivity to PSI recommendations. Finally, case pressure appears to have almost no effect on plea bargaining policies. This suggests that district attorneys do not relax the degree of discretion granted to assistants as a means of coping with heavy caseloads. It also highlights the importance of controlling for other factors when estimating the effects of resource constraints on policy decisions.

Discussion and conclusions

This analysis reinforces the observations of others that the values and motivations of prosecutors are not uniformly oriented toward controlling crime, and that furthermore, these values are reflected in the policies that govern prosecutors' offices.[27] The findings also indicate that high crime rates prompt restrictive policies, and suggest that prosecutors react to genuine crime problems, rather than to constituency perceptions. Furthermore, restrictive policies are associated with courthouse environments that give prosecutors few opportunities to gain the upper hand in plea negotiations through control of sentencing decisions; and while these observed associations are not strong, they are substantively significant. However, when the effects of potentially confounding factors are statistically controlled, caseload appears to have a negligible effect on plea bargaining policy. This does not mean, of course, that case pressure has no effect on plea bargaining rates; but these data offer no evidence that prosecutors' *policies* are constrained by resource limitations.

Of course, these findings must be interpreted carefully. The analysis is based on only 27 prosecutors from a single state. While the research design adopted here permits more systematic examination of hypotheses than can be achieved through case studies, the empirical results are more suggestive than conclusive. All the same, the findings are sufficiently provocative to justify recommendations for further study of prosecutorial policy making; they offer support for some predictions generated by previous research, but cast doubt upon others. More generally, these findings have implications for theoretical models of criminal adjudication, for our understanding of the values and role conceptions of prosecutors, and for future research on the structure and organization of prosecutors' offices.

Empirical work on criminal adjudication, departing from traditional judge-centered models of decision making, has increasingly stressed the importance of understanding personal relationships among court actors,[28] as well as formal and informal constraints imposed by actors' sponsoring organizations.[29] The results of this study offer further support for a growing consensus that courts should be studied as networks of interdependent organizations and actors, characterized by varying rather than uniform levels of cooperation and conflict.[30] The analysis presented here exploits this theoretical framework, examining chief prosecutors who, as administrators and politicians, must reconcile their policy choices with organizational and political constraints and obligations. These findings illustrate the significance of judicial cooperation, and suggest that by refusing to passively acquiesce to plea-bargained sentences (and perhaps by taking cues for sentencing decisions from an independent organization, the probation office), judges can potentially destabilize the system of bargained justice that characterizes prosecutor-dominated courthouses.

This analysis also offers some insight into the relationships between prosecutors' beliefs and behavior. Prosecutors, like law enforcement officials, are frequently stereotyped as punitive individuals motivated to maximize the number of criminals caught, convicted, and punished; but this unidimensional portrait does not square with empirical research that portrays the values and motives of prosecutors, like those of law enforcement officers, as complex and varied.[31] The strong relationship between appreciation for due process and restrictive plea bargaining policies suggests that, contrary to conventional wisdom, regulation of plea practices stems from a preference for adjudication processes that are not compromised by the temptation and coercion inherent in plea bargaining.

This apparently counter-intuitive relationship makes more sense, of course, if one remembers that an appreciation for due process protections does not preclude a preference for severe sentencing (indeed, a preference for harsh punishments is logically consistent with a desire to take every precaution to ensure that innocent defendants are not convicted)—or in other words, willingness to sacrifice due process protections in order to gain convictions may be accompanied by willingness to tolerate more lenient punishments if more offenders can thereby be punished. A strong crime-control orientation may manifest itself in practical efforts to maximize convictions, efforts which include permitting plea bargaining. This finding invites further research into the seldom-examined dimensions of prosecutors' value systems, and into prosecutors' uses of discretion in achieving desired policy objectives.

Finally, this study departs from most research on prosecutors by focusing on an important but often overlooked subject, policy decisions, and by modeling these decisions as expressions of fundamentally political choices. This analysis suggests that we should not only study prosecutors as lawyers, engaged in a series of individual case decisions, but we should also examine them as politicians, obliged to develop decision rules for their staff to follow. There are few formal constraints on prosecutors' discretion in making management decisions about recruitment and retention of personnel, resource allocation, division of labor, and case-processing practices, and therefore these decisions are open to the influence of courthouse and community politics, as well as personal values. This study only begins to explore the factors that influence these choices.

Notes

This article originally appeared in Volume 73, Number 6, April–May 1990, pages 335–340.

The author gratefully acknowledges the research support of the American Judicature Society, the Earhart Foundation, and the Graduate School of the University of North Carolina; the assistance of Theresa Lynn Humphrey; and the advice of Robert E. Worden. The opinions and conclusions expressed in this paper are, of course, the sole responsibility of the author.

1. Albonetti, "Prosecutorial discretion: the effects of uncertainty," *Law & Soc'y Rev.* 21 (1987), 291; Gilboy, "Prosecutors' Discretionary Use of the Grand Jury to Initiate or to Reinitiate Prosecution," *Am. B. Found. Res. J.* 9 (1984), 1; Adams, "The effects of evidentiary factors on charge reduction," *J. of Crim. Just.* 11 (1983), 525; Mellon et al., "The Prosecutor Constrained by His Environment: a New Look at Discretionary Justice in the United States," *J. of Crim. L. and Criminology* 72 (1981), 52. Most of this research has concluded that screening and charging decisions are determined primarily by legally relevant and tactical considerations, such as strength of evidence and likelihood of conviction. However, other findings suggest that extra-legal factors, such as race and victim characteristics, influence these decisions. *See* Radelet and Pierce, "Race and Prosecutorial Discretion in Homicide Cases," *Law & Soc'y Rev.* 10 (1985), 587; Pruitt and Wilson, "A Longitudinal Study of the Effect of Race on Sentencing," *Law & Soc'y Rev.* 17 (1983), 613; Stanko, "The Impact Of Victim Assessment On Prosecutors' Screening Decisions: The Case of the New York County District Attorney's Office,"

Law & Soc'y Rev. 16 (1981–1982), 225; Myers and Hagan, "Private and Public Trouble: Prosecutors and the Allocation of Court Resources," *Soc. Prob.* 26 (1979), 439.

2. Cole, "The Decision to Prosecute," *Law & Soc'y Rev.* 4 (1970), 331; Carter, *The Limits of Order* (Lexington, Mass.: Lexington Books, 1974); Neubauer, "After the Arrest: The Charging Decision in Prairie City," *Law & Soc'y Rev.* 8 (1974), 495.

3. Church, "Examining Local Legal Culture," *Am. B. Found. Res. J.* 10 (1985), 449; Eisenstein and Jacob, *Felony Justice: An Organizational Analysis of Criminal Courts* (Boston: Little Brown, 1977).

4. Scheingold and Gressett, "Policy, Politics, and the Criminal Courts," *Am. B. Found. Res. J.* 12 (1987), 461; Glick and Pruet, "Crime, Public Opinion, and Trial Courts: An Analysis of Sentencing Policy," *Just. Q.* 2 (1985), 319; Jones, "Prosecutors and the Disposition of Criminal Cases: An Analysis of Plea Bargaining Rates," *J. of Crim. L. and Criminology* 69 (1978), 402.

5. Carter, *supra* n. 2; Neubauer, *supra* n. 2; Mellon et al., *supra* n. 1; Flemming, "The Political Styles and Organizational Strategies of American Prosecutors: Examples from Nine Courthouse Communities," paper presented at the annual meeting of the Midwest Political Science Association, Chicago (1989).

6. Fleming, ibid.

7. Landes, "An Economic Analysis of the Courts," *J. of L. and Econ.* 14 (1971), 61; Weimer, "Vertical Prosecution and Career Criminal Bureaus; How Many and Who?," *J. of Crim. Just.* 8 (1980), 369; Reinganum, "Plea Bargaining and Prosecutorial Discretion," *Am. Econ. Rev.* 78 (1988), 713.

8. Neubauer, *supra* n. 2.

9. Carter, *supra* n. 2.

10. Packer, *The Limits of the Criminal Sanction* (Stanford: Stanford University Press, 1988).

11. Scheingold and Gressett, *supra* n. 4, at 466.

12. Alschuler, "Plea Bargaining and its History," *Law & Soc'y Rev.* 13 (1979), 211; Friedman, "Plea Bargaining in Historical Perspective," *Law & Soc'y Rev.* 13 (1979), 247.

13. Feeley, "The Effects of Heavy Caseloads," in Goldman and Sarat, editors, *American Court Systems* (San Francisco: W. H. Freeman, 1978).

14. It is also important to distinguish between plea bargaining policies and plea practices. One would expect to find that case pressure is more strongly associated with plea bargaining rates than with plea bargaining policies.

15. Kingnorth and Rizzo, "Decision Making in the Criminal Courts: Continuities and Discontinuities," *Criminology* 17 (1979), 3.

16. Alschuler, "The Prosecutor's Role in Plea Bargaining," *U. Chi. L. Rev.* 26 (1968), 50; Eisenstein and Jacob, *supra* n. 3; Myers and Hagan, *supra* n. 1.

17. Many of the most populous circuits in Georgia sharply contradict the stereotype of the rural, poverty-

ridden, populist, and racially tense state. The metropolitan area of Atlanta alone comprises seven of the state's judicial circuits, several of which are solidly white, Republican, and economically but not socially conservative. Evidence of the state's political diversity can be found in the wide range of candidates who have successfully run for national office, a list that includes Newt Gingrich, Wyche Fowler, Sam Nunn, and Jimmy Carter. Moreover, the popular image of local politics in the South, which includes closely knit networks of long-time residents, holds only in some of the state's jurisdictions; 40 percent of the state's district attorneys, and 60 percent of the assistant district attorneys, were not born in Georgia.

18. This response rate compares favorably with those achieved by other scholars employing mail surveys; *see* Vetri, "Guilty Plea Bargaining; Compromise by Prosecutors to Secure Guilty Pleas," *U. Penn. L. Rev.* 112 (1964), 865; Jones, *supra* n. 4; Flango et al., "The Concept of Judicial Role: A Methodological Note," *Am. J. of Pol. Sci.* 19 (1978), 277; Ryan and Alfini, "Trial Judges' Participation in Plea Bargaining: An Empirical Perspective," *Law & Soc'y Rev.* 13 (1979), 479; Meeker et al., "Perceptions about the Poor, their Legal Needs, and Legal Services," *Law & Pol.* 9 (1987), 143; Scheb, "State Appellate Judges' Attitudes toward Judicial Merit Selection and Retention: Results of a National Survey," *Judicature* 72 (1988), 170; Hagan et al., "Class Structure and Legal Practice: Inequality and Mobility among Toronto Lawyers," *Law & Soc'y Rev.* 22 (1988), 9. The survey was sent to 127 judges, 45 prosecutors, and 124 assistant prosecutors, all identified through legal directories and court publications.

19. The validity of this measure is further established by the responses of defense attorneys to a similar survey question: lawyers in all circuits fully corroborate the reports of prosecutors.

20. Judges' receptivity to prosecutors' sentence recommendations is the product of responses to two items (and of judges' mean responses in multijudge circuits). The first question asked judges how often prosecutors in their courts made sentence recommendations and the second asked judges how often they accepted sentence recommendations when they were made. Both variables were coded as follows: 1=less than half the time; 2=about half the time; 3=most of the time; 4=always. Neither of these items would be a valid measure by itself, since the frequency with which prosecutors offer recommendations may be depressed in circuits where judges routinely disregard them. Judges' receptivity to probation officer recommendations was coded in a similar fashion.

21. All prosecutors were asked how important maintaining a high conviction rate was in their offices—not very important (=1), somewhat important (=2), or very important (=3). Prosecutors and their assistants tended to be in agreement on this item, and the variable for impor-

tance of office conviction rate is the mean value of DAs' and ADAs' intracircuit responses on this item.

22. While the operationalizations rely on perceptions of actors to measure practices and customs, actors' perceptions are sometimes the most reliable source of information not available in case files or through direct observation; *see, for example,* Nardulli et al., *the Tenor of Justice: Criminal Courts and the Guilty Plea Process* (Urbana: University of Illinois Press, 1988); Church, *Examining Local Legal Culture: Practitioner Attitudes in Four Criminal Courts* (Washington, D.C.: National Institute of Justice, 1982). Moreover, by averaging the responses of actors with potentially different customs (for the judicial receptivity variables), one gains a closer approximation of the situation confronted by the several prosecutors whose circuits contained more than one judgeship.

23. *See* Klecka, *Discriminant Analysis* (Beverly Hills: Sage, 1980).

24. Furthermore, it is important to note that prosecutors' values on the crime control-due process scale are not associated with crime rates; the correlation between these variables is neither statistically nor substantively significant. The absence of a relationship between these two variables suggests (although certainly does not establish) that prosecutors' attitudes about the court's function are not shaped by the objective conditions in which they find themselves.

25. *See* Glick and Pruet, *supra* n. 4; Blumstein and Cohen, "Sentencing of Convicted Offenders: An Analysis of the Public's View," *Law & Soc'y Rev.* 14 (1980), 223. In this analysis, when the prosecutors' perception variable is substituted for crime rate in the discriminant analysis, the coefficients for all variables remain unchanged; the perception variable has a slightly larger coefficient than does crime rate, and the eigenvalue is slightly larger (1.06). The overall explanatory power of the model is not significantly increased.

26. An index measure of supervisory style was constructed from these related measures and was originally included in the analysis. This measure had no substantively significant effect on plea bargain policy, and its presence did not affect the coefficients for other variables included in the model. Since the index was not hypothesized to be *causally* related to plea bargaining policy, and because it had no effect when included as a control variable, it was dropped from the analysis presented here.

27. Flemming, *supra* n. 5; Scheingold and Gressett, *supra* n. 4; Neubauer, *supra* n. 2; Carter, *supra* n. 2.

28. Maynard, "The Structure of Discourse in Misdemeanor Plea Bargaining," *Law & Soc'y Rev.* 18 (1984), 75; Nardulli et al., "Criminal Courts and Bureaucratic Justice: Concessions and Consensus in the Guilty Plea Process," *J. of Crim. L. and Criminology* 76 (1985), 1103.

29. Eisenstein et al., *The Contours of Justice: Communities and their Courts* (Boston: Little Brown, 1987); Myers and

Talario, *The Social Contexts of Criminal Sentencing* (New York: Springer-Erlag, 1987); Church, *supra* n. 3; Feeley and Lazerson, "Policy-Prosecutor Relationships: An Interorganizational Perspective," in Boyum and Mather, editors, *Empirical Theories About Courts* (New York: Longman, 1983).

30. For additional documentation of the persistence of an adversarial culture under conditions that are typically thought to foster cooperation and compromise, *see* McIntyre, *The Public Defender: The Practice of Law in the Shadows of Repute* (Chicago: University of Chicago Press, 1987).

31. Carter, *supra* n. 2; Neubauer, *supra* n. 2; *see also* Brown, *Working the Street: Police Discretion and the Dilemmas of Reform* (New York: Russell Sage Foundation, 1981); Muir, *Police: Streetcorner Politicians* (Chicago: University of Chicago Press, 1977).

Twenty years of sentencing reform: steps forward, steps backward

Michael Tonry

If a time machine were to transport a group of state and federal judges from 1970 to a national conference on sentencing in 1995, most would be astonished by a quarter century's changes. Many, perhaps all, would be disapproving.

Their astonishment would result from the number and enormity of the changes they would learn about. Sentencing, as they knew it, had not changed significantly for many years.[1] In 1970, every American state and the federal government had indeterminate sentencing systems, in which lawmakers enacted and amended the criminal code and set maximum penalties. A few jurisdictions had minimum penalties, which many judges disliked. These penalties generally required one- or two-year minimums except for murder, which carried a mandatory life sentence in some jurisdictions.

Subject only to statutory maximums and the occasional minimums, judges had the authority to sentence convicted defendants either to probation (and under what conditions) or to prison (and for what maximum term). Parole boards decided when prisoners were released. Usually, prisoners became eligible for release after serving a third of the maximum sentence, but they could be held until the maximum term expired. Prison managers typically were allowed to reduce sentences by awarding time off for good behavior.

In 1995, the time-traveling judges would learn that since the mid-1970s, the federal system and many states had rejected indeterminate sentencing and repealed much of its apparatus, often on tough-on-crime political grounds. More than 20 jurisdictions had adopted sentencing guidelines to limit judicial discretion, more than 15 had eliminated parole release, 20 had adopted parole guidelines, most had narrowed time off for good behavior, and all had enacted mandatory minimum sentence legislation, which often included 10-, 20-, or 30-year minimum terms and life without possibility of parole.[2] Most recently, the judges would learn, Congress in 1994 authorized billions of federal dollars to states that abolish parole release, establish guidelines to constrain judicial sentencing discretion, and require abolition or narrowing of time off for good behavior.

There can be little doubt that the time-traveling judges would disapprove much of what they would find. Partly this can be attributed to parochialism. Human beings tend to prefer the familiar over the new and what we know over what we don't. Because the broad outlines of indeterminate sentencing had been the same everywhere since 1930, few judges at work in 1970 would have had experience working in any other system.

Some of their objections would, however, concern matters of principle and conceptions of justice that transcend parochialism. Rigid sentencing laws, including mandatory penalties, they would insist, create unacceptable risks of injustice because they make it impossible to take account of important differences among defendants. Laws that specify penalties for particular cases are unwise, they would argue, because legislators are far likelier than judges to be influenced by short-term emotions and concern for political advantage. Limits on judicial discretion are unsound, they would urge, because they shift discretion into the hands of prosecutors who will exercise it less judiciously than judges.

We can predict that these arguments would be made because many judges from the early 1970s to today have opposed sentencing reforms in these terms, and many judges (and nonjudges) still do. There is, however, one 1970s argument that is seldom heard today—that there is no need for substantial changes in sentencing because there is no convincing evidence that indeterminate sentencing was afflicted by unwarranted sentencing disparities or racial and gender bias. These arguments are seldom heard because the weight of the research evidence has become clear. Unwarranted disparities, explicable more in terms of the judge's personality, beliefs, and background than the offender's crime or criminal history, have repeatedly been demonstrated.[3] So has substantial gender disparity in indeterminate sentencing—in favor of women.[4]

Judicature Volume 78, Number 4, pp. 169–172

The evidence is unclear on the causes of racial disparities, but their existence is well-documented.[5]

State versus federal reforms

The overall impression the time-traveling judges would take back with them would probably be shaped by whether they learn first about federal or state sentencing reforms. If they were to study the changes brought about by the federal Sentencing Reform Act of 1984, they would return to 1970 determined to fight the first signs of the sentencing reform movement. But if they were to study the experiences of states like Delaware, Minnesota, Pennsylvania, Oregon, and Washington, they would be likely to go back apprehensive but with an understanding that meliorable injustices did exist under indeterminate sentencing that can be mitigated without creating larger injustices in their place.

For the time-traveling judges to be able to understand contemporary sentencing issues, they would need a briefing on developments since 1970. Here is what they would learn: Sentencing became a focus of criminal justice reform efforts in the mid-1970s, influenced by several contemporaneous developments. First, civil rights activists, concerned by what they perceived to be racial bias in sentencing and correctional administration, called for controls on the discretion of judges and other officials.[6] Second, research reviews by social scientists reported that little systematic empirical evidence showed that corrections programs successfully reduced recidivism, which undermined the rehabilitative foundation on which indeterminate sentencing stood.[7] Third, proceduralists throughout the legal system— who had been working to make legal processes fairer and decision makers more accountable—argued that sentencing too should be subject to rules and review procedures.[8] And finally, political conservatives, concerned about a specter of "lenient judges," supported sentencing reforms as a way to set and enforce harsher sentencing standards.[9]

Most of these influences shaped an influential book, *Criminal Sentences: Law without Order*, by then-U.S. district judge Marvin Frankel.[10] On fairness grounds, he decried the absence of standards for the sentences federal judges set and the related absence of meaningful opportunities for sentence appeals. As a solution, Judge Frankel proposed creation of a specialized administrative agency, called a sentencing commission, that would develop guidelines for judges to use in making sentencing decisions. The guidelines would be presumptively applicable, and their application would be subject to appeal by aggrieved parties.

Judge Frankel's proposals were based partly on the concerns that influenced sentencing reform generally, but they were also shaped by appreciation of the institutional properties of administrative agencies and legislatures. Over time, agencies such as Judge Frankel's proposed commission develop specialized expertise that legislatures cannot match. Moreover, because commissioners are typically appointed for fixed terms and are ordinarily outside day-to-day political battles, such agencies can be somewhat insulated from emotionalism and short-term political pressures.

Judge Frankel's sentencing commission proposal became the most widely adopted vehicle for sentencing reform. In the 1970s, several states—most notably Minnesota and Pennsylvania—created sentencing commissions. Several others—including California, Illinois, and Indiana—replaced indeterminate sentencing with statutory determinate sentencing schemes, in which criminal codes specified specific prison terms for particular crimes.

The comparative merits of sentencing commissions soon became clear. Evaluations in Minnesota and Pennsylvania (and later in Oregon and Washington) showed that use of sentencing guidelines reduced disparities generally and lessened racial and gender disparities in particular. (Since the effect was to increase sentences for women, some might see this as a mixed blessing.)[11] In addition, many judges in those states came to favor guidelines for two reasons—guidelines provided a starting point for considering sentences, and judges recognized that guidelines reduced disparities. By contrast, the statutory determinate sentencing systems were shown to have had no significant effects on sentencing processes or outcomes.[12]

More importantly, experience confirmed Judge Frankel's ideas about administrative agencies. For instance, Minnesota's commission tied sentencing policy to available prison resources and managed to hold the prison population within capacity throughout the 1980s, while most states experienced record increases. Commissions in Oregon and Kansas and, for a time, Washington also helped insulate sentencing policy from political pressure. But in states like California, where fine-grained sentencing policies were left in legislative hands, statutory sentencing provisions were amended upwards nearly every year, and the prison population increased by 400 percent between 1980 and 1994.[13]

Success and disaster

By 1995, the success of Judge Frankel's innovation was clear. Twenty-two states have created commissions, guidelines are in effect in 17 of these states, and new commissions are at work in the other five.[14] No state adopted a statutory determinate sentencing scheme after the mid-1980s, and some that had, like Colorado, diluted its effects by reintroducing parole release.[15]

Because the federal commission had the prior experiences of the states to draw on, ample resources, and the capacity to recruit staff from throughout the country, all of the auguries would have predicted that the U.S. Sentencing Commission would build on the state experiences and produce the most successful guidelines system to date.

The Sentencing Reform Act of 1984 abolished parole release prospectively and directed the newly created sentencing commission to develop guidelines for federal sentencing. Few outside the federal commission would disagree that the federal guidelines have been a disaster. The highly detailed guidelines divide crimes into 43 different categories, and the rules governing their application are highly mechanistic. The commission has forbidden judges to take account in sentencing of many factors—such as the effect of the sentence on the defendant or his family, or the defendant's mental health or drug or alcohol dependence, or a severely deprived background or victimization by sexual abuse—that many judges believe to be ethically relevant to sentencing. The guidelines are based not on the offense of which the defendant was convicted, but his "actual offense behavior" including alleged crimes of which he was acquitted or never charged. The guidelines allow virtually no role for non-imprisonment sentences.[16]

For all these reasons, the federal guidelines are deeply disliked by most federal judges and lawyers who practice in federal courts, and they are widely circumvented.[17] In addition, a majority of federal judges surveyed in 1991 said they believe sentencing disparities were as bad or worse under the guidelines as before their adoption.[18] Even commission-sponsored research demonstrates that prosecutors and judges disingenuously circumvent the guidelines in a third of cases,[19] while the true rate is probably higher.

Staff of newly created state commissions report that negative stereotypes created by the federal guidelines have been a major obstacle to their work. Commissions in Texas, Ohio, and North Carolina recently adopted resolutions repudiating the federal guidelines

as a model for any policies they might later develop. Both the North Carolina commission and the American Bar Association's sentencing standards project (which proposed that states create sentencing commissions) avoided use of the word "guidelines" because of the negative connotations associated with the federal guidelines.[20]

No one factor can explain why the federal guidelines have been so much less successful than state guidelines. Some judges use words like arrogant and hostile to describe the commission's attitude to the federal judiciary. Some observers argue that the failure was in management: With all of its resources, a better-managed commission that consulted more widely and made efforts to learn from the state experiences could have done better. Others note that only two of the initial commissioners had ever imposed a sentence (one of them 30 years earlier), and three were full-time academics. Still others point out that a number of the initial commissioners were long known to be aspirants for higher judicial office and suggest that the guidelines were an effort to show that the commission's policies were consonant with the views of influential congressional conservatives.

No doubt there is truth in all these explanations. The primary explanation, however, is a structural one: The federal sentencing commission legislation was formulated and agreed on in one political era, in which Judge Frankel's ideas and goals were widely shared. However, they were implemented in a different political era, in which Judge Frankel's ideas had little weight.

The first commission legislation, introduced in Congress in 1974, was a direct outgrowth of a Yale Law School seminar that attempted to convert Judge Frankel's general proposal into proposed legislation.[21] After reintroduction in successive Congresses as a stand-alone bill, the proposal was folded into then-pending federal criminal code bills. By 1979, Senators Edward Kennedy and Strom Thurmond, the ranking Democratic and Republican members of the Senate Judiciary Committee (who succeeded one another as chairs), agreed to support the legislation, which the Senate went on to approve overwhelmingly. Although the House of Representatives did not act that year, the Senate agreement held. The bill including the sentencing commission sections repeatedly thereafter passed both the Senate Judiciary Committee and the full Senate by wide margins.

Eventually, the proposed criminal code was abandoned as unpassable, but the less controversial commission sections became part of an omnibus crime bill enacted in 1984. Unfortunately, when this good-government, rationalistic proposal, initially intended to make sentencing fairer and to distance sentencing policy from politics, took effect, the government in power did not hold those goals.[22]

The crime-control policies of the Reagan administration in 1985, when the commissioners were appointed, were oriented more toward toughness than fairness. It should not therefore be a surprise that many of the commissioners who were appointed did not share Judge Frankel's belief that sentencing policy should be, to the extent possible, insulated from partisan politics. Instead, influential commissioners demonstrated that they too were tough on crime and had little sympathy for "lenient" judges.[23] (This stereotype of judges is odd, since a large percentage of federal district judges by 1987, when the guidelines took effect, were Reagan appointees—as today are a large percentage of the guidelines' fiercest critics).

Mixed results

So the picture the time-traveling judges would see is mixed—federal guidelines that at least match their worst preconceptions of what would happen if indeterminate sentencing were abandoned, and state guidelines that turned out much better than they would have predicted.

This issue of *Judicature* could serve as a briefing document for the judges from 1970. It demonstrates there is merit in most of their concerns and that some good has been achieved in the shift from indeterminate to determinate sentencing. Richard Frase's article summarizes developments in the states and provides information on guidelines activities in more than 20 jurisdictions. Marc Miller's article demonstrates that the eight-year-old federal sentencing guidelines remain deeply disliked and offers suggestions for reform.

An article by Kevin and Curtis Reitz describes the American Bar Association's effort in its sentencing standards project to learn from the combined state and federal experiences and to offer guidance to states that have not yet overhauled their sentencing laws. David Boerner's article traces the evolution of policy and practice concerning prosecutorial powers under guidelines, and concludes, with Frase, that there have been both gains and losses. Saul Pilchen discusses the effects of the "organizational guidelines," a version of the federal guidelines that applies to sentences for corporations and other collective entities. Finally, a tran-

script of an American Judicature Society panel discussion offers the insights of state and federal judges and academics regarding sentencing guidelines.

The conclusion the time-traveling judges would most likely take back is that the judiciary itself must listen to complaints about sentencing and work to address them. Otherwise, other agencies of government will, with results ranging from tolerable to awful.

Notes

This article originally appeared in Volume 78, Number 4, January–February 1995, pages 169–172.

This article is drawn from the author's book, *Sentencing Matters,* to be published by Oxford University Press later this year.

1. Blumstein, Cohen, Martin, and Tonry, eds., *Research on Sentencing: The Search for Reform,* 2 vols. (Washington, D.C.: National Academy Press, 1983), chap. 3.

2. Tonry, "Sentencing Commissions and Their Guidelines," in Tonry, ed., *Crime and Justice: A Review of Research,* vol. 17 (Chicago: University of Chicago Press, 1993).

3. *Supra* n. 1, at chap. 2.

4. Knapp, *The Impact of the Minnesota Sentencing Guidelines: Three Year Evaluation* (St. Paul: Minnesota Sentencing Guidelines Commission, 1984).

5. Tonry, *Malign Neglect: Race, Crime, and Punishment in America* (New York: Oxford University Press, 1995).

6. American Friends Service Committee, *Struggle for Justice: A Report on Crime and Punishment in America* (New York: Hill & Wang, 1971).

7. Lipton, Martinson, and Wilks. *The Effectiveness of Correctional Treatment: A Survey of Treatment Evaluation Studies* (New York: Praeger, 1975).

8. Davis, *Discretionary Justice: A Preliminary Inquiry* (Baton Rouge: Louisiana State University Press, 1969).

9. Messinger and Johnson, "California's Determinate Sentencing Laws," in *Determinate Sentencing: Reform or Regression* (Washington, D.C.: U.S. Government Printing Office, 1978).

10. Frankel, *Criminal Sentences: Law Without Order* (New York: Hill & Wang, 1972).

11. *Supra* n. 2.

12. *Supra* n. 1.

13. Zimring and Hawkins, *Incapacitation: Penal Confinement and the Restraint of Crime* (New York: Oxford University Press, 1995).

14. *See* Frase, "Sentencing guidelines in the states: still going strong," *Judicature* 78 (1995), 173.

15. Wesson, "Sentencing Reform in Colorado: Many Changes, Little Progress," *Overcrowded Times* 4 (1993), 14–17, 20.

16. U.S. Sentencing Commission, *Sentencing Commission Guidelines Manual* (St. Paul, Minn.: West Publishing, 1994).

17. U.S. Sentencing Commission, *The Federal Sentencing Guidelines: A Report on the Operation of the Guidelines System and Short-Term Impacts on Disparity in Sentencing, Use of Incarceration, and Prosecutorial Discretion and Plea Bargaining* (Washington, D.C.: U.S. Sentencing Commission, 1991).

18. Ibid.

19. Nagel and Schulhofer, "A Tale of Three Cities: An Empirical Study of Charging and Bargaining Practices under the Federal Sentencing Guidelines," *S. Cal. L. Rev.* 66 (1992), 501–566.

20. Orland and Reitz, "Epilogue: A Gathering of State Sentencing Commissions," *Col. L. Rev.* 64 (1993), 837–845; Reitz and Reitz, "Building a Sentencing Reform Agenda: The ABA's New Sentencing Standards," *Judicature* 78 (1995), 189.

21. O'Donnell, Curtis, and Churgin, *Toward a Just and Effective Sentencing System* (New York: Praeger, 1977).

22. Stith and Koh, "The Politics of Sentencing Reform: The Legislative History of the Federal Sentencing Guidelines," *Wake Forest L. Rev.* 28 (1993), 223–290.

23. Ibid.

"Three strikes and you're out": are repeat offender laws having their anticipated effects?

John Clark, James Austin, and D. Alan Henry

In recent years, a great deal of legislation has been passed at both the state and federal levels increasing penalties for criminal offenses, particularly violent crimes. These actions have come in response to public concerns about crime, and the belief that many serious offenders are released from prison too soon. Many such laws have come under the general label of "three strikes and you're out." The purpose of these laws is simple: offenders convicted repeatedly of serious offenses should be removed from society for long periods of time, in many cases for life.

For many years, most states have had provisions in their laws for enhanced sentencing for repeat offenders. Yet between 1993 and 1995, 24 states and the federal government enacted new laws using the "three strikes" moniker, with similarly labeled bills introduced in a number of other states.

Washington and California were the first states during this period to implement three-strikes laws. (South Dakota, which has had similar legislation since 1877, is one of several states that have had such laws on the books for many years.) As the proposals in Washington and California were being debated, concerns were raised about how they would affect the criminal justice system. It was argued that defendants facing very lengthy mandatory sentences would be more likely to demand trials, slowing down the processing of cases and adding to the problems of court delay and jail crowding—in effect creating an unfunded mandate for counties and cities. A longer-term concern was that as more and more offenders began serving more lengthy terms of incarceration, prison overcrowding, already at crisis levels in many states, would also grow worse.

Have any of these concerns materialized?

Two models

Differing provisions. Even though the Washington and California laws were enacted within months of one another using the same "three strikes and you're out" rallying cry and include many of the same offenses as strikes, they are very different. The Washington law, which took effect in December 1993 through a voter initiative that passed by a 3-1 margin, requires a life term in prison without the possibility of parole for a person convicted for the third time of any of a number of statutorily-listed "most serious offenses."

The California law, signed by the governor in March 1994 and later ratified by voters in a state referendum, differs from Washington's law in three important ways. First, in Washington, all three strikes must be for felonies specifically listed in the legislation. Under the California law, only the first two convictions need be from the state's list of "strikeable" offenses—any subsequent felony can count as the third strike. Second, the California law contains a two-strike feature in which people convicted of any felony who have one prior conviction for a strikeable offense are to be sentenced to twice the term they would otherwise receive. Third, the sanctions for a third strike differ. Unlike in Washington, a "third striker" has at least the possibility of eventually being released in California, albeit after serving a minimum imprisonment of 25 years. (The Washington law does contain a provision retaining the governor's authority to grant a pardon or clemency, but it also recommends that no person sentenced under this law to life in prison without parole be granted clemency until the offender has reached 60 years of age and is judged to be no longer a threat to society.)

Impact on local courts and jails. Because of these differences, when the three-strike laws were initially implemented in Washington and California, it was projected there would be a much greater impact on the local criminal justice system in California than in Washington, due to the much broader scope of the California law. It was predicted that California courts would become overwhelmed as defendants facing enhanced penalties would demand jury trials. The added time to process cases through trial, and the reluctance to release before trial defendants who were facing long prison terms, would cause jail populations to explode as the number of admissions and length of stay in jail would grow.

Early evidence from California indicated these predictions were proving correct. For example, a 1995 review of 12,600 two- and three-strike cases from Los Angeles showed that two-strike cases remained pending in court 16 percent longer and three-strike cases 41 percent longer than nonstrike cases. In addition, the Countywide Criminal Justice Coordination Committee found that strike cases were three times more likely to go to trial than nonstrike felonies, and four times more likely than the same type of case before the law took effect. This led to a 25 percent increase in jury trials and a rise in the proportion of the jail population held in pretrial status from 59 percent before the law was enacted to 70 percent. Furthermore, a report published in 1995 by the State Sheriffs' Association showed the pretrial detainee population to be growing statewide, from 51 percent of the average daily population before three strikes to 61 percent by January 1995.

However, at least some counties in the state are learning to absorb the increases brought about by the law. A Center for Urban Analysis survey of eight counties with populations of more than 1 million identified several counties that have been successful in disposing of two- and three-strike cases early in the process. Also, under a new pilot delay reduction program in one of Los Angeles County's Superior Court districts, implemented as a result of the added burdens the three-strikes law imposed on the court, the pending caseload of criminal cases has been reduced by nearly half.

In addition, the most recent data from the Los Angeles sheriff's department suggests that the pace of strike cases coming into that system may be slowing. The number of two-strike cases filed by the Los Angeles district attorney from 1995 to 1996 declined by 15 percent. Likewise, there was a 28 percent decline between the two periods in the number of third-strike cases filed. However, the sheriff's department reports that it is too early to say whether these findings indicate a trend, and if there is any possible cause.

Impact on state prison systems. The impact of these laws on state corrections has not been as severe as projected in either Washington or California. Planners in Washington had expected that each year between 40 and 75 people would fall under three-strike provisions. Even this low projection has not been met. In a 3½ year period after the law took effect in December 1993, only 85 offenders—as compared to the 120–225 that had been projected—had been admitted to the Washing-

ton prison system under its three-strikes law, according to the state Department of Corrections.

A similar overestimate has been made on the California law's impact on its prison system. As of December 31, 1996, 26,000 offenders had been admitted to the California Department of Corrections for either a two- or three-strikes sentence. Of this number, nearly 90 percent were sentenced under the two-strikes provision. Although the sheer number of cases affected by the law is significantly higher than for any other state, the numbers are not as great as originally projected. Consequently, the department recently lowered its 5-year projection by nearly 40,000 inmates, principally because there have not been as many two-strikes admissions as expected and because judges have modified their sentencing practices for the two-strikes cases. The Department of Corrections had incorrectly estimated that judges would choose longer sentences within the ranges provided by the law.

One recent development that might further reduce inmate projections is a 1996 California Supreme Court ruling, *People v. Superior Court (Romero),* that allows judicial discretion in applying the law. This ruling may further limit the use of the statute and create a major logjam of appeals for the now nearly 20,000 inmates sentenced under the law who may be eligible for resentencing.

Variations among states

"Three strikes and you're out" can mean dramatically different things in different states. A review of the provisions of all the states that have enacted this type of legislation reveals differences in how a "strike" is defined, how many strikes are required to be "out," and what it means to be "out."

"Strike zone" defined. In keeping with the baseball analogy, the strike zone—what constitutes a strike and under what conditions—varies from state to state. There are some constants—violent felonies such as murder, rape, robbery, arson, aggravated assault, and carjacking are typically included as strike offenses in such legislation. But states have included other charges, such as:

- In Indiana—the sale of drugs.

- In Louisiana—any drug offense punishable by imprisonment for more than five years.

- In California—the sale of drugs to minors.

- In Florida—escape.
- In Washington—treason.
- In South Carolina—embezzlement and bribery.

At least two states define strikeable offenses based on the prior charge and the sentence imposed. Maryland and Tennessee both require that a sentence of incarceration must have been imposed in order for listed offenses to qualify as strikes.

Some states have even defined different levels of strikeable offenses. For example, in Georgia, a second conviction for a defined violent felony mandates a sentence of life without parole, while a fourth felony conviction of any kind requires that the maximum sentence allowable for the charge be imposed.

Number of strikes for an "out." There are also variations in the number of strikes needed to be "out." In South Carolina, a person convicted a second time for any of a list of "most serious offenses" is sentenced to life without parole. There is no third strike.

Three strikes are required to be "out" in 20 states, but seven of them—Arkansas, California, Connecticut, Kansas, Pennsylvania, Montana, and Tennessee—also have enhanced sentences for two strikes in their laws, depending on the offense.

What it means to be "out." Finally, states differ as to what sanction will be imposed when sufficient strikes have accumulated. A mandatory life sentence with no possibility of parole is imposed when "out" in Georgia, Indiana, Louisiana, Maryland, Montana, New Jersey, North Carolina, South Carolina, Tennessee, Virginia, Washington, and Wisconsin. In three states, parole is possible after an offender is out, but only after a significant period of incarceration. In New Mexico, such offenders are not eligible for parole until after serving 30 years, while those in Colorado must serve 40 years before parole can be considered. In California, a minimum of 25 years must be served before parole eligibility.

Most three-strikes laws involve minimum mandatory sentences. Four states—Connecticut, Kansas, Arkansas, and Nevada—have recently enacted laws enhancing the possible penalties for multiple convictions for specified serious felonies, leaving the actual sentence to the discretion of the court.

In Connecticut, judges can sentence an offender to life in prison for the third conviction for any of a group of serious felonies, and to 40 years in prison for the sec-

ond such conviction. In Kansas, legislatively enacted sentencing guidelines provide a range based on the offense and the offender's prior record from which the judge is to choose in sentencing. A recent amendment allows judges to double the sentences on the guidelines for offenders convicted for the second and third time for certain listed violent felonies.

In Arkansas, a judge may choose either a mandatory sentence short of life imprisonment for a second or third strikeable offense, or a life sentence. Similar provisions exist in the Nevada law, which gives the judge the option on a third strike conviction of imposing a life sentence without parole, a life sentence with parole possible after 10 years, or a 25-year sentence with parole possible after 10 years.

Five states—Florida, North Dakota, Pennsylvania, Utah, and Vermont—provide ranges of sentences for repeat offenders that can extend up to life when certain violent offenses are involved.

Pre-existing provisions

To accurately describe the impact of three strike-type laws on a state's justice and corrections systems, one must first consider how each state was equipped to respond to repeat violent offenders *prior to* the enactment of three strikes. Did the new legislation successfully close a loophole in the state's criminal sanctioning authority as hoped, or was the new law in effect targeting a population already covered by existing laws?

As it turns out, all but one of the 24 three-strikes states provided for enhanced penalties for repeat offenders before the passage of the latest three-strike legislation. (Kansas is the only exception.) In Louisiana, Maryland, South Carolina, and Tennessee, the mandatory penalty for a person found to be a repeat violent offender—life in prison without the possibility of parole—already existed and remained unchanged, but the definition of such an offender was expanded under the new legislation.

Preexisting law in Louisiana mandated life in prison without parole for the third conviction for certain violent and drug felonies. It also required life imprisonment with no parole for any fourth or subsequent felony conviction if at least two of the felonies were among the listed violent or drug offenses. The three-strikes provisions were not changed, but the four-strikes provisions now require a sentence of life without parole if any of the four felonies are on the list of violent or drug felonies.

South Carolina, which since 1976 had a law mandating life imprisonment without parole upon the third conviction for a violent felony, simply reduced the number of such convictions needed to two.

Tennessee likewise had a preexisting three-strikes law with a penalty of life imprisonment without parole. Amendments to this law in 1994 and 1995 expanded the number of charges that qualify for a three-strikes sentence and added a new two-strikes category for the most serious violent offenses.

Maryland added carjacking and armed carjacking to a preexisting law that mandates a term of life in prison without parole on the fourth conviction for a listed crime of violence, if separate prison terms have been served for the first three such convictions.

The definition of a repeat offender was expanded in Vermont and North Dakota, with the penalties remaining the same. In Vermont, which had allowed a court to sentence an offender convicted for the fourth time for *any* felony to up to life in prison, a new law allows for a life sentence upon the third conviction for a listed violent offense while retaining the fourth conviction provision for any felony. Under pre-existing law, an offender in North Dakota would receive an enhanced sentence upon the second conviction for Class A or B offenses. The new law expands that statute to include Class C offenders.

In at least one state the definition of a repeat violent offender remained essentially the same (third conviction for a violent offense), but the punishment was enhanced. Virginia moved from providing no parole eligibility for those convicted of three separate violent felonies, regardless of the sentence, to mandating life sentences with no parole eligibility for this group.

Several states supplemented existing habitual offender laws that targeted repeat offenses for *any* felony with new laws that focused on violent felonies. For instance, preexisting Colorado law requires a tripling of the presumptive sentence for people convicted for the third time within a 10-year period of any Class 1, 2, 3, 4, or 5 felony. The new three-strikes law, which mandates a life sentence with no parole eligibility for 40 years for a third conviction for a violent offense, does not contain the 10-year time period of the preexisting law.

In some states, the changes involved both expanding the definitions of repeat violent offenders and enhancing the sentences. For instance, preexisting Pennsylvania law mandated an extended prison term of five years for the second or subsequent conviction for certain specified crimes of violence. The new law expanded the list of violent offenses and amended the extended mandatory minimum prison term from five to 10 years.

Other states had had habitual offender laws that allowed for enhanced sentences, but such sentences were not mandatory. For instance, previous Florida law allowed the court to sentence habitual violent felony offenders to extended prison terms, including up to life in certain instances. The recent law created a new category of "violent career criminal," which establishes mandatory sentences ranging from 10 to 15 years for a third-degree felony, 30 to 40 years for a second-degree felony, and life imprisonment for a first-degree felony. And until New Jersey enacted a law in 1995 mandating life in prison without parole for a third conviction for certain violent offenses, it was left to the discretion of the sentencing judge to determine if the third conviction for a first-, second-, or third-degree felony merited an extended term of imprisonment.

Since many of the new strikes laws target offenders who already would have received lengthy prison terms under existing repeat offender statutes, it is not likely that these laws will have a significant impact on the courts, jails, or prison systems in those states. However, even though the actual number of cases in these states is expected to be small, it is too early to determine more specifically the impact because the laws have not been in place very long, and serious cases, by their nature, take longer to reach disposition.

Conclusion

"Three strikes and you're out" as a typology for criminal justice sanctioning is not easily defined. No common definitions exist for the terms "three," "strike," or "out" across the states. However, certain factors are associated with all of the three-strikes laws passed in the 24 states. The first is the authorization—or in some instances, mandate—for longer periods of incarceration for those convicted of violent crimes. Other similarities include the following:

- Except for Kansas, all of the states that enacted strikes laws had preexisting statutes that targeted repeat violent offenders; the breadth of those earlier statutes will largely determine the effect of the new laws in each state.

- All of the statutes either increase the period of incarceration for violent crime, expand the number of crimes that are included in the violent crime category, or both. In some instances the period of incarceration has simply been changed from a range available to the sentencing judge for a particular crime to a fixed, mandated number of years.

- In the majority of states, the new legislation has reduced judicial sentencing discretion. This appears to continue the recent trend of legislatures imposing more discrete limitations on judges' decisions, as evidenced by the expansion of mandatory minimum sentence legislation and sentencing guidelines.

The rapid expansion of three-strikes laws, regardless of how they are defined, reflects the perception that existing laws did not adequately protect public safety in their application or outcome, that exceptional incidents had occurred that the new laws would address, or that the intent of current laws was being frustrated by other factors, such as prison crowding. It is unclear whether these perceptions were accurate and what impact the new laws will have.

Early evidence, however, suggests that most of these laws will have minimal effects on their respective state prison systems. States have drafted these laws so that they would be applied to only the most violent repeat offenders. In most states, these offenders were already receiving lengthy prison terms under existing statutes. Only broadly defined two-strikes provisions such as California's have the potential to radically alter existing sentencing practices. Even in that state, judicial interpretations of the law—recently supported by a state supreme court decision—as well as prosecutorial discretion in how the law is applied may blunt the anticipated increases.

Follow-up research will continue to track in detail the effect of three-strikes laws on each stage of the criminal justice process (including bail setting, detention, time to trial, type of trial, plea negotiations, and the jail and prison population levels), as well as the budget ramifications of any changes that have taken place. The following questions need to be addressed to learn more about this sentencing reform effort and its impact:

- Is there a measurable effect on crime in any of the states where such a law was passed? Do these trends differ from states that have not adopted such laws?

- What factors differentiate states that have not adopted three-strikes legislation from those that have?

- To what extent are the laws modified by practice or new legislation?

- To what extent are there variations in the application of the laws, both between and within the courts and counties?

- To what extent does the differential application of the law affect inmate behavior within the prison and jail systems?

- What features of two- and three-strikes laws are associated with compliance (or lack of compliance) with the laws' provisions by prosecutors and judges?

- What impact have these sentencing reforms had on public perceptions of the criminal justice system and its ability to incapacitate dangerous offenders?

- Based on the early experiences of California and Washington state, what lessons can be learned about projecting the effect of sentencing reforms on the courts, corrections, and crime?

Note

This article originally appeared in Volume 81, Number 4, January–February 1998, pages 144–149.

This article is adapted from Clark, Austin, and Henry, *Three Strikes and You're Out: A Review of State Legislation, NIJ Research in Brief,* September 1997. The project was supported by contract 95-IJ-CX-0026 awarded to the National Council on Crime and Delinquency by the National Institute of Justice. Findings and conclusions are those of the authors and do not represent the official position or policies of the U.S. Department of Justice.

Race and crime: what evidence is there that race influences results in the criminal justice system?

Norval Morris

I would like to talk about a topic that I find important, yet not much talked about. There is a problem in discussing this topic, and indeed many topics; nowadays, you can't finish framing the question before someone is giving you the answer. That disease is particularly prevalent among my colleagues who study economics and law combined, but I find it increasingly infects lawyers generally and even those people who are referred to as intelligent laymen. As a result, I have turned to fiction. The advantage of fiction is that you can be transported from contemporary society with its knee-jerk reactions to every serious problem; in fiction, you can at least have some hope of framing the question before you get the answer.

Come with me and escape the necessity to avoid talking seriously and quietly about blacks and crime in America. With a teletransporter, we can go to another country and another time to see what conclusions we can draw about that country; what facts we know and what conclusions we might be able to draw from those facts. I've done a lot of work over the years in trying to gather those facts about that country. So let me tell you about that country—not the United States—though it bears a striking resemblance to it. So, "Beam us up, Scottie."

In proportion to the distribution of blacks and whites in that society, let me give you five facts: First, for every one white male in prison, more than seven blacks are in prison. That discrepancy has grown larger, not smaller, over the last 30 years. In 1933, blacks made up less than a quarter of the prison population; now they are nearly a half. Second, although on this "fact" there is some slight doubt, of every 12 black males in their 20s, 1 in every 12 is in prison or jail. That's a fantastic figure. (The Bureau of Justice Statistics says it's not quite that bad, that it's 1 in 15, but I think they are wrong.) The third fact: Of all black babies born in that distant society today, 1 in 30 will die a victim of intentional or non-negligent homicide. Among black males and females, ages 15 to 44, the leading cause of death is homicide.

Let me give you the fourth fact—a little more encouraging about race and crime and a bit more complicated—a fact that has not been publicized much; blacks are not more likely than whites to be persistent offenders. The return to prison rates differ very little, if at all, between blacks and whites of those in prison, first time, second time, etc. The differential in prison populations between blacks and whites is accounted for by the patterns of first-time criminality within each racial group, rather than by any difference in the patterns of continuing criminality. So the great difference is the function of the percentage of those who commit first-time crimes, not of any unique persistence in crime. That is not an unimportant point.

There is a current belief among people in my trade, interested in sentencing reform, that sentencing should be based in part on incapacitation, on taking high-rate offenders out of circulation, and that we should prolong and adjust sentences according to the threat that the individual prisoner presents. We are good at increasing sentences, but not so good at the reduction. Because blacks are not disproportionately likely to be persistent criminals, sentencing policies that target persistent offenders will not further disadvantage them.

The final, fifth fact about this strange country that I ask you to survey today is that in recent years an increasing number of blacks have moved into the middle class from the underclass, leaving the destroyed inner-city neighborhoods with their astronomical crime rates to those left behind. The crime and delinquency rates of incarceration, and rates of arrest and of victimization of those who move away from these slums, are indistinguishable from whites of the same social class. So much for genetic explanations! That doesn't mean that all human behavior doesn't have a genetic trace, it's all a question of degrees of influence, but that the genes of the blacks play a large part in crime is balderdash.

Professional vs. citizen obligations

So, crime in this country we are visiting, just as in the United States, comes from intense pockets of criminality to be found in the destroyed neighborhoods of the inner-city. Street crime is overwhelmingly intra-racial; it is not inter-racial. On average, the profiles of the criminals and the victim are very similar. In Chicago in the 1970s, for example, 98 percent of black homicides were committed by other blacks with their ages and social circumstances tending to match. For black males, that mystical country to which we've transported ourselves may not be the land of the free, but it is certainly the home of the brave!

The overwhelming question is this: "Are these racial skewings, in that country, in large part a product of social prejudice, discrimination conscious or unconscious, among the police, the prosecutors, the courts and the correctional agencies of that country, or are they a product of other forces over which those agents of the criminal justice system have little professional control? It's not an unimportant question. Max Weber made the nice distinction between one's obligation professionally and one's obligation as a citizen. If there is substantial racial discriminatory skewing within our system, then the obligations on us as lawyers to do something about it is a very obvious professional duty. If the criminal justice system is less to blame, being merely a barometer of a serious social problem, there may be citizen obligations of high order but they don't happen to be professional obligations.

It's no good going to the legal scholars of this country to answer this question—they don't deal with it, they don't write about it, and they don't discuss it publicly. The first serious legal work on this question seems to me to have been published very recently—on May 19, 1988. The *Harvard Law Review* published a 200-hundred page developments in the law piece in that issue which, if this topic interests you, you really should read. It's a very well done piece, looking at race in the criminal process. They actually reach rather more extreme conclusions than I will be offering.

Crime reports

So far I have been looking at prison rates in that far country; the ultimate question of discrimination, of course, is whether blacks are imprisoned unfairly in relation to the amount of crime they commit. If you look at the uniform crime reports and the national crime surveys, but particularly the uniform crime reports concerning crimes that are divided into index crimes and other crimes (index crimes are the more serious felonies including homicide, robbery, rape and aggravated assault; others are less serious crimes); the arrest ratio of blacks to whites for index crimes is about

3.6 to 1; for other crimes the ratio is about 2 to 1. But, of course, the prison differential is about 7 to 1. I tried to break those data down into particular crimes and I tried to find a crime in which whites outnumbered blacks proportionately. I thought embezzlement would be right, but it isn't so; I'm afraid the blacks are 2.3 times as frequently arrested as the whites for embezzlement. I couldn't understand that and then I thought about what embezzlement was—it's often a very small purloining of money by a person in a relatively low position of economic trust. The only crime where there was a clear crime report differential adverse to whites was drunk driving, where whites are 1.46 times as likely to be involved in drunk driving as blacks.

There are undoubtedly crimes that whites commit more than blacks, such as insider trading, security fraud, and environmental pollution, but arrest rates don't tell us very much at all about those overwhelmingly white crimes. Many crimes aren't reported to the police and most of those that are reported don't result in arrest. In the inner city, where crimes are highest, a much lower proportion of street crime is reported to the police than is reported in more privileged areas. What we need to know in answer to the question we are addressing is whether there is racial discrimination within the justice system in the differential rates of black and white involvement in crime, as distinct from arrest for crime.

National crime surveys give us some insight into this. There is in every instance some increment of black adversity in the processes that follow commission and arrest for crimes, but nothing like the 7 to 1 differential that is to be found in prison. The starkest prejudice in our system is to be found in the death penalty. Forty-two percent of the occupants of death row are black and the evidence that racial stereotypes influence the death penalty is powerful. The frequency of exercise of prosecutorial discretion in Georgia adverse to blacks is extraordinary. In matched cases, the prosecutors sought the death penalty in 70 percent of the cases where there was a black killer and a white victim. The same prosecutor sought it in 15 percent of the cases when there was a white killer and a black victim, holding constant the gravity of the crime and 200 other matching factors.

To my astonishment, the Supreme Court managed to look at that differential of between 70 percent and 15 percent and concluded that it does not rise to the level of being constitutionally objectionable—the

McCleskey case is simply a miscarriage of justice, irreconcilable with the rest of the jurisprudence of racial discrimination. It's a scandal and will be seen as such, I'm convinced.

Prejudice in the system

What is one left with? One is left with a situation where some areas seem clear of prejudice within our system and others where the prejudice does not seem to be easily measured, but there is some.

Let me pose four questions arising from this overview of the data and give brief answers to them. Does the criminal justice system discriminate unfairly against blacks at arrest, convictions, and at punishment? Is the death penalty applied unfairly to black killers and yet insufficiently to protect black victims? Do the police disproportionately use deadly force against suspected black felons? If there is injustice in all this, what are the remedies? Justice Harry Blackmun put the point beautifully, and it's an important point: "In order to get beyond racism, we must first take account of race, there is no other way. In order to treat some persons equally, we must treat them differently." Nobody can look responsibly at these data and not agree with that approach.

Well, does the criminal justice system discriminate against blacks in arrest, conviction, and at punishment? The *Harvard Law Review* suggests quite strongly that it does. What I would conclude is that there is a fairly strong case of more vulnerability of the black in relation to the police and prosecution and in plea bargaining, and at the punishment stage. The studies of Dean Alfred Blumstein of Carnegie-Mellon and of Joan Petersilia of the RAND Corporation conclude that about 80 percent of the black over-representation in prison can be explained by differential involvement in crime and about 20 percent by subsequent racially discriminatory processes.

That's probably fair. I think it is as much knowledge as we have. So the answer to the first question is: there appears to be measurable skewing on account of race in the criminal justice system but that skewing is not nearly as dramatic as the figures of differential imprisonment would suggest. That is not at all to say that racial discrimination within the criminal justice system is unimportant; it certainly is important. What is suggested is only that it is relatively less important than other discriminatory pressures.

Now, the second question: is the death penalty applied unfairly to blacks who kill? I won't re-hash the cases and studies on this since I do not think that there is much doubt that the answer to that question is "yes." Why is that important?—after all, capital punishment is largely symbolic. It has no effect on the crime rate generally and it seems to be reasonably well established that it doesn't have much effect on any rates of homicide or attempted homicide, so, why worry? Because it is a centrally important symbol.

Now suppose I am wrong about the death penalty, suppose it is an effective deterrent. Suppose that, as some proponents of that punishment implausibly argue, for every one execution seven or eight lives of potential victims are saved. If that is so, then the *McCleskey* case exhibits something worse than what I've said. If you believe in capital punishment then you must conclude that we are failing to protect black victims—you must, there is no way out of it. So, whatever you believe about capital punishment, whether you approve of it or reject it, the discriminatory effect is profound.

So to question three: Do the police disproportionately use deadly force against black felons? This is an important question because it leads to racial tensions and sometimes to racial riots. Police shoot at about 3,600 people in this country each year. Of these 3,600, about 600 are killed, about 1,200 are wounded and about 1,800 are missed entirely. (Anyone who knows anything about handguns knows that is fairly accurate shooting; the handgun, except at close quarters, is a very inaccurate weapon.)

Police officers in New Orleans are 10 times more likely to kill criminal suspects than police officers in Newark. New Orleans and Newark are both high crime rate areas. The general pattern is typical; Chicago is also fairly typical—70 percent of the civilians struck by police bullets in the five years that we collected data were black. An additional 20 percent were white and 10 percent Hispanic. Philadelphia, Los Angeles, New York have similar figures. The general pattern in most cities where these things have been studied is that minorities being shot by the police are approximately proportional to rates of minorities in street crime, but like earlier figures there is a slight added increment and all you can conclude is the data support what common observation and folk tales make very clear—there is an element of racial prejudice in police shooting at minorities. The *Harvard Law Review* goes much farther than that, but I am content to assert the lesser proposition.

Remedies

Now to the final question. If what I have said about that country we are visiting is true, what are the remedies? First, police can do a lot more to protect the rights of potential victims in a non-discriminatory manner. Some police forces are beginning to do so. The key is to break from the tyranny of the 911-reporting system which disrupts the proper allocation of police resources. Police resources are allocated in the United States by the telephone. There has to be a movement to community-based policing. Black communities have to be mobilized to collaborate with the police. The police have to stop seeing the city's high crime areas as if they were hostile territories. There are people in those areas greatly in need of protection. They can be mobilized and they can be helped. Mini-police stations can be created in inner-city ghettos. It's been demonstrated, it does work. It gives those who have to live there a sense of diminution of fear if not of a diminution of crime.

We need more resourceful police leadership. This hasn't happened much but is happening in a small way. There is a core of younger able administrators coming forward in the police, but there remains a lack of effective leadership in the city police forces. Cities focus on the number of officers in the field and on the budgets, but both are largely irrelevant. They overlook inefficiency and the poor mobilization of resources. There are very many police officers in jobs that could be better done by civilians. We have to change the structure of policing to better protect minorities. There is nothing new in what I've said but the political effort of achieving change when there are no votes in it is challenging.

We have to do better to weed out discrimination in prosecution, plea bargaining and sentencing. The sentencing guideline system has as its greatest virtue the promise of a vehicle which can reduce the current demonstrable adversity to blacks in sentencing.

Changes in the criminal justice system won't do much about the problem of blacks in crime in America. The criminal justice system is a necessary, but lim-

ited, system. We've rarely been able to demonstrate any changes in crime rates by making marginal or even relatively substantial changes in policing or in correctional practice. We have got to make these changes because it is the proper thing to do; it's proper to try to diminish unjustified discrimination. But it's not going to make a big difference to the overall crime problem.

Thoughtful scholars now argue that black crime is the symptom, not the disease. The disease, says University of Chicago sociologist William Julius Wilson, the most thoughtful person writing in this field on this problem, is the increasing social isolation of an increasingly concentrated black underclass. University of Chicago political scientist Gary Orfield's study of the schools in Chicago indicates that the problems of the black underclass in the school system of Chicago has grown worse. In family situations today in America, 20 percent of all children are born to unwed mothers. Unwed mothers account for 15 percent of all white births, 60 percent of black births. In Illinois, 64 of each 100 births of black mothers are out of wedlock. I'm not making moralistic propositions, I am speaking of the problems of people being locked in, unable to escape from an inner city underclass. All I've done is underscore an excruciatingly difficult and worsening situation.

To try to sum up, if you look as closely as you can at these data, the bottom line conclusion is: Yes, there is measurable racial discrimination in our police practices, in our prosecutorial practices, in our plea bargaining practices, and in our sentencing, but the bulk of discrimination generating crime lies elsewhere.

I had written a conclusion but a couple of critics I shared these ideas with tell me that I shouldn't say it, since it might be offensive to some. So I have decided not to say it. But, just for your information, the rejected conclusion was: The whole law-and-order movement that we have heard so much about is, in operation though not in intent, anti-black and anti-underclass—not in plan, not in desire, not in intent, but in operation.

Note

This article originally appeared in Volume 72, Number 2, August–September 1988, pages 111–113.

Causes and consequences of wrongful convictions: an essay-review

Hugo Adam Bedau

While erroneous convictions are found throughout the criminal justice system, the consequences of these errors are especially serious in capital cases. The history of capital punishment—in this country and elsewhere, in the distant past as well as today—is a history of erroneous convictions and executions. The range and variety of irreversible errors in the death penalty system is sobering:

- The defendant was convicted of a murder, rape, or other capital crime that never occurred.

- A capital crime was committed, but the wrong person was tried, convicted, sentenced, and executed.

- The defendant did kill the victim but was insane, mentally retarded, or otherwise not fully responsible.

- The defendant did kill the victim but the killing was in self-defense.

- The defendant did kill the victim but the killing was accidental.

- The defendant did kill the victim but because of incompetent trial counsel or other error he was wrongly convicted of first-degree (capital) murder instead of another type of criminal homicide.

- It is not known whether the defendant was guilty because his guilt and punishment were settled by a lynch mob, not by trial in court.

Every jurisdiction in the United States that has used capital punishment has imposed it on one or more defendants in one or more of these erroneous ways. What is truly amazing is the extent to which advocates of America's current death penalty system have disregarded or otherwise downplayed the significance of these irrevocable errors—as though they were relics of a distant past. Recent events suggest that this tolerance and complacency is wearing thin, however, as legislatures, governors, trial and appellate judges—state and federal—are reeling from the impact of a wide variety of research and scholarly studies identifying wrongful convictions in capital cases.

Without a doubt the most remarkable response to this research so far is also the most recent: the decision this past July by Manhattan federal district court judge Jed S. Rakoff in *United States v. Alan Quinones*. Judge Rakoff ruled that the 1994 federal death penalty statute is unconstitutional because enforcing it poses "an undue risk of executing innocent people." On July 2, 2002, the *New York Times* quoted Harvard's constitutional-law scholar Laurence H. Tribe as saying: "I've been thinking about this issue in a serious way for at least 20 years, and this is the first fresh, new and convincing argument that I've seen." In that same issue, the *Times* editorial page observed that while the decision might be reversed on appeal, "it offers a cogent, powerful argument that all members of Congress—indeed, all Americans—should contemplate."

Scope of the problem

The issue of wrongful convictions, sentences, and executions in the United States has its terminus ad quem for the present in the release in April 2002 of Arizona death row prisoner Ray Milton Krone, the 100th capital defendant to be released on grounds of innocence in the past 30 years, that is, since the death penalty was re-introduced in the mid-1970s. The terminus a quo for research on this grim subject was the study "Miscarriages of Justice in Potentially Capital Cases" by Michael L. Radelet and me, published in the *Stanford Law Review* in November 1987. That article was the first extensive and documented report on the subject—expanded (with co-author Constance E. Putnam) in our book *In Spite of Innocence* (1992)—covering the entire nation for most of the 20th century.

We co-authors were most impressed with several findings that no prior research had uncovered:

- All but six of America's death penalty jurisdictions had at least one case of wrongful conviction in a capital case.

Judicature Volume 86, Number 2, pp. 115–119

- The most frequent cause of error was perjury by prosecution witnesses.

- The discovery of error and its rectification was usually not achieved by official participants in the system of criminal justice but by others, in spite of the system.

- In some two dozen cases, reprieve or other form of clemency leading to eventual vindication came just days or even hours before the scheduled execution.

- In all but three dozen of the 350 cases reported in the initial research, the innocence of the convicted defendant was recognized by pardon, indemnity, acquittal on retrial, or some other official action.

Critics typically have ignored these findings and refused to acknowledge the scope of the problem revealed by this research. Instead, they have concentrated on disputing the finding that among the wrongful convictions were two dozen innocent men who had been executed. The critics were quick to respond with various objections, including these three: First, all but one of the innocent-executed cases were pre-*Furman* and thus could be dismissed as ancient history, with no relevance to post-*Furman* statutory safeguards. Second, re-examination of several of the cases tended to confirm rather than disconfirm the trial court's verdict of guilty. Third, no government official in the years under study had ever gone on record admitting that he had been (an innocent) party to, or even knew of, a wrongful conviction that ended in the execution of an innocent defendant.

Perhaps the critics will reconsider their confidence that no innocent persons have been executed when they examine the findings in the recent re-investigation by James Acker and his associates of the eight New York cases in our list (one-third of the two dozen at issue). Acker et al. endorse our judgment that all eight were innocent. (See Acker et al., "No Appeal From the Grave: Innocence, Capital Punishment, and the Lessons of History," in Westervelt and Humphrey, *Wrongly Convicted: Perspectives on Failed Justice* 154–173 [2001]).

New research

Since the work of Radelet, Bedau, and Putnam in 1992, important additional research has been undertaken by several different sets of authors, all of whom have published their results within the past three years. Heading the list by a wide margin is the well named study, *A Broken System: Error Rates in Capital Cases, 1973–1995,* by James S. Liebman, professor of law at Columbia University, and his associates. Part I of the Liebman report appeared in the summer of 2000; Part II became available in February 2002. Because Professor Liebman discusses his research in an article elsewhere in this issue, I need no more than mention it here. The same consideration applies to the second study, the report and recommendations (of April 2002) to Illinois Governor George Ryan by the special commission he created in March 2000; the co-chair of that Commission, Thomas P. Sullivan, discusses the report elsewhere in this issue.

At about the time the Illinois Commission tendered its report, Harvard Law School was host to a conference on "Wrongful Convictions: A Call to Action." The full-day conference was co-sponsored by the Boston law firm of Testa, Hurwitz, and Thibault, and by the New England Innocence Project (an affiliate of the Innocence Project created at Cardozo Law School by Barry Scheck and Peter Neufeld). Although not presenting new research as such and not confined to wrongful convictions in capital cases, the conference proceedings (available on tape from the Criminal Justice Institute, Harvard Law School) amplified printed materials distributed to the participants in a volume of nearly 800 pages, reprinting 56 articles, documents, memoranda, and reports—a virtual omnium gatherum on all aspects of the topic.

Among the many books on the death penalty published in recent years (I discussed nine of them in my essay-review in *Boston Review* for April/May 2002), only two have much to offer by way of original research that bears on the problem before us, and neither is confined to death penalty cases. One is *Wrongly Convicted: Perspectives on Failed Justice,* edited by Saundra D. Westervelt and John A. Humphrey (2001). The 14 chapters, each by a different author or authors, are grouped into four parts: the causes of wrongful convictions, the social characteristics of wrongfully convicted prisoners, illustrative case studies, and prospects for the future. The other book is *Actual Innocence: Five Days to Execution, and Other Dispatches from the Wrongly Convicted* (2000, revised 2001), by attorneys Barry Scheck and Peter Neufeld and journalist Jim Dwyer. *Actual Innocence* is largely devoted to narratives of cases where DNA testing came to the rescue, including what the authors seem to believe was the first such case a decade ago (1992) in New York.

These books are particularly interesting due to their broadened scope. Since capital cases represent a small percentage of all criminal convictions, a reasonable inference can be drawn that large numbers of wrongful convictions occur in non-capital cases. Cases involving biological evidence, whether capital or not, are also a small percentage of all criminal cases, so the DNA exonerations examined in *Actual Innocence,* for example, may indicate a similar conclusion. That is, wrongful convictions likely occur in cases without evidence that can be tested as reliably as can biological evidence with DNA technology.

Use of DNA

No doubt the salient factor in the public's interest in the problem of convicting the innocent is the discovery that DNA could be put to forensic uses and provide virtually unassailable evidence for or against the guilt of an accused—at least in those cases (as in rape or felony-murder-rape) where traces of DNA are available and relevant. Evidence of this sort was not available in 1987, but it was by 1994; the case of Kirk Bloodsworth (wrongly convicted of rape-murder in 1983 and released from Maryland's death row a decade later) pioneered the use of DNA results to free a prisoner on death row.

Forensic evidence from DNA testing has also had a powerful impact on courts and legislatures, and it is perhaps the dominant reform in the entire system of criminal justice currently sought by those who appreciate the impact such testing can have on the question of the guilt of the accused. As Scheck and Neufeld observed in their article in the Westerveld and Humphrey book, "Nothing comparable has ever happened in the history of American jurisprudence; indeed, nothing like it has happened to any judicial system anywhere."

A cottage industry

Recounting stories by or about innocent men released from death row verges on becoming a cottage industry. Two among the many recent additions, not surprisingly, are accounts of Illinois cases. Thomas Frisbie and Randy Garrett, in *Victims of Justice* (1998), tell the story of Alejandro Hernandez and Rolando Cruz, who spent 11 years on death row. David Protess and Rob Warden, in *A Promise of Justice* (1998), tell the story of Dennis Williams (12 years in prison) and Verneal Jimerson (18 years on death row). These cases are discussed further by Lawrence Marshall in his article in this issue.

In 1987, Bedau and Radelet reported that the most frequent causes of wrongful convictions in capital cases, in descending order of frequency, were: perjury by prosecution witnesses; mistaken eyewitness identification; coerced or otherwise false confession; inadequate consideration of alibi evidence; and suppression by the police or prosecution of exculpatory evidence. The two cases involving the four Illinois defendants mentioned above fall into this pattern. Jimerson was a victim of perjured testimony suborned by the prosecution. Williams's alibi testimony proved unpersuasive to the jury, and his attorney was incompetent by any reasonable standard. Cruz and his co-defendant were above all victims of perjury by prosecution witnesses, as well as of excessive prosecutorial zeal, erroneous expert testimony, and misleading physical evidence. In short, the causes of error in these cases were the usual ones.

Also in 1987, Bedau and Radelet reported what their data showed to be the most frequent scenarios of vindication, again in descending order of frequency: The defense attorney persists in post-trial efforts to establish his client's innocence; the real culprit confesses; a new witness comes forward; a journalist or other writer exposes the error; a private citizen discovers the error. Cruz and his co-defendant were rescued by the confession of the real murderer, the dogged efforts of a cadre of defense lawyers, and DNA evidence. Verneal Jimerson and his co-defendants were rescued by the detective work of Protess's journalism class at Northwestern University—a perfect illustration of the principle that vindication comes not because of but in spite of the system.

"Legal lynching"

Thanks to the work of capital defense lawyers—several of whom (Stephen Bright, David Bruck, Bryan Stevenson, Ronald Tabak, Frank Zimring, and especially Anthony Amsterdam) are well known through their lectures and writings—other lawyers and the law-review reading public have been thoroughly educated in the woefully unsatisfactory practices by the defense, the prosecution, and the judiciary in their handling of capital cases at trial and on appeal. This mismanagement, plus the overwhelming evidence that the part of the nation where a death penalty culture is most entrenched is in the southern states of the Old Confederacy, has sparked interest in the connection between yesterday's unlawful lynchings and today's lawful executions. So far, however, to the best of my knowledge, the only serious attempt to connect lynching and the death penalty was in passing references by James W. Marquart, Sheldon Ekland-Olson, and Jonathan R. Sorenson, in their monograph, *The Rope, the Chair, and the Needle: Capital Punishment in Texas, 1923–1990* (1994). Nowhere is the connection more provocatively brought to public attention than in the title of the recent book, *Legal Lynching* (2001), by Jesse Jackson, his son, Jesse, Jr., and journalist Bruce Shapiro.

Taken strictly, of course, "legal lynching" is an oxymoron, and it is tempting to dismiss the whole idea out of hand as a distorting exaggeration. But to do so would be a grave mistake. First, the mentality that once tolerated—indeed, demanded—lynching a century ago can be seen today in the mentality that tolerates—indeed, demands—continuation of our badly flawed death penalty system. Second, the states that historically were the sites of the most frequent lawless executions—lynchings—are also the states with the greatest frequency of lawful executions today. Third, the complete disregard for due process of law and the rule of law manifest in a lynching survives in the indifference and disrespect for law as the instrument of justice to be found in many (most?) capital cases. Fourth, just as the paradigm lynchings in American history were carried out by white mobs on helpless black men as a populist method of ruthless social control, so the death penalty is to a troubling extent a socially approved practice of white-on-black violence, especially where the crimes involved are black-on-white. Fifth, many of those who opposed lynching in the South relied on the argument that the death penalty could do under color of law what lynching did lawlessly—and the record of abandonment in capital cases of any but the thinnest pretence of due process proved the point. Sixth, in cases where a posse was formed to hunt down an accused with the intention of killing him on the spot, rather than merely taking him into custody, it is virtually impossible to tell whether the killing should be judged murder by a mob or a quasi-legal summary execution.

Finally, just as the defense of lynching a century ago was predicated on states' rights and vigorous resistance to federal interference with local self-government, the attack on federal habeas corpus for state capital defendants takes refuge today, to some extent, in the same hostility to judicial intervention from Washington D.C. (This is obscured by the Supreme Court's own inconsistent attempts to regulate the nation's death penalty system, which often puts judicial restraint, respect for federalism, and deference to the legislatures ahead of substantive justice under the Bill of Rights.) One way to view the current moratorium movement, insofar as it is supported by those who seek to defend the death penalty, is to see it as the latest nationwide effort to erase the many disturbing parallels between the lynching practices of a century ago and the death penalty practices of our own day.

Reforms

This naturally leads us to inquire about the proposed reforms aimed at reducing the likelihood of convicting the innocent. The subject is too large to address in this essay-review, nor do any of the books and articles under discussion have a monopoly on recommended reforms. Furthermore, the various voices being heard are too many to summarize and evaluate here. Frequently if not unanimously recommended are two reforms: Obtain DNA evidence wherever possible, and exempt the mentally retarded from liability to a death sentence. This latter recommendation in fact became law under the Supreme Court's ruling this past June in *Atkins v. Virginia.*

Liebman and his associates in *A Broken System* confined their 10 reform recommendations to death penalty jurisprudence. Although one of them—abolishing judicial override of the jury's sentencing decision—has become law, thanks to the Supreme Court's ruling this past June in *Ring v. Arizona,* some of their other recommendations may have a longer and rougher road to adoption. These include: Requiring proof of guilt "beyond *any* doubt" in a capital case; insulating sentencing and appellate judges who deal with capital cases from "political pressure;" and increasing compensation for capital defense lawyers to provide incentives for "well-qualified lawyers" to do the work.

Mandatory Justice: Eighteen Reforms to the Death Penalty, was released last year by The Constitution Project, part of Georgetown University's Public Policy Institute. Among its recommendations are these four: Adopt a better standard for incompetence of defense counsel than is provided by *Strickland v. Washington;* enact LWOP (life in prison without possibility of parole) as the alternative to the death sentence; conduct proportionality review of all capital convictions and sentences; and treat the jury's "lingering doubt" over the defendant's guilt as a mitigating circumstance in the sentencing phase.

Scheck, Neufeld, and Dwyer offer a list of 40 proposed reforms. Seven of them would restrict the admissibility of eyewitness testimony. Fourteen others are devoted to controlling the evidence tendered by jailhouse snitches. Another 14 would constrain forensic laboratories and the use of their findings. Two of their proposed reforms would be relatively easy to implement: Use sequential rather than simultaneous presentation of suspects in police lineups, and videotape all interrogations.

Governor Ryan's Commission on Capital Punishment has produced by far the greatest number of recommendations—no fewer than 85. Nineteen are addressed to police and pretrial practices; the Commission also joins with Scheck et al. in endorsing videotaping of interrogations and in favoring a sequential lineup. Seven of their recommendations address the role of forensic evidence, and of course they urge wider use of DNA testing. Prosecutorial selection of which homicide cases will be tried as capital cases— one of the most troubling and unregulated areas in capital punishment jurisprudence—is the subject of three proposed reforms.

Ten of the recommendations are aimed at overhauling pretrial proceedings, including use by the prosecution of testimony by informants in custody ("jailhouse snitches"). They would not bar such testimony; instead, the Commission would require that the defense be fully informed of the prosecution's intention to use such testimony, and that the "uncorroborated testimony" of such a witness "may not be the sole basis for imposition of a death penalty." The Commission agrees with Liebman et al. in favoring "adequate compensation" for trial counsel (although their Recommendation 80 is unfortunately unclear about comparable compensation for defense counsel in postconviction litigation).

What are we to make of these 150 recommendations (some of which overlap with each other)? Could we imagine a conference devoted to achieving a consensus on reform in which, say, 15 or 20 of these proposals received unanimous endorsement? Could the Supreme Court be persuaded to adopt some if not all of these reforms, just as it has adopted two new rules in *Ring* and *Atkins* this past spring? Or could state legislatures take it upon themselves to introduce some of these reforms, without waiting for the Supreme Court to act? We should have answers to these questions within the next few years.

The struggle continues

The Illinois Commission has done its work well and left us with a comprehensive set of model reforms. Taken together with the reforms proposed by Scheck and Liebman and their associates, lawyers, legislators, and the general public have a set of proposals that—if put into practice—would appreciably improve the system in both capital and non-capital cases. Moratorium study commissions in other states could provide reinforcement on several proposed reforms as well. Yet everything turns on the willingness of legislatures to enact statutes that incorporate reforms. Friends of the death penalty can hardly complain if these reforms narrow the range of death-eligible defendants and increase the economic costs of the entire system, any more than its critics can complain if good-faith adoption of these reforms breathes new life into our current "broken" and deregulated death penalty system.

If the past three decades of struggle over the future of capital punishment in this country have taught us anything, it is this: The appellants in *Gregg v. Georgia* (1976) were right, and the Supreme Court was wrong. The reforms that emerged in the wake of *Furman* (1972) inspired by the Supreme Court's ruling have turned out, to a disturbing extent, to be merely "cosmetic." Astute observers of the system argued even then that it was impossible to design reforms that would be effective in bringing greater fairness into the death penalty system and still serve rational goals of deterrence, incapacitation, and retribution. Whether the death penalty system in this country that would be created if these reforms are enacted will prove to be otherwise cannot be foretold. What can be predicted is that pressure for complete abolition will not vanish or even subside. The struggle over the nation's soul will continue for some time to come.

Note

This essay originally appeared in Volume 86, Number 2, September–October 2002, pages 115–119.

The changing role of the trial judge

Edmund V. Ludwig

Trials, to an increasing extent, have become a luxury. Correspondingly, the role of the trial judge has taken on new and larger dimensions.

In 1970, there were 340 authorized federal district court judgeships and total dispositions amounted to nearly 116,000 cases. Of these, some 13,600, or about 12 percent, were by trials—15.5 percent criminal, 10 percent civil. Total trial dispositions per authorized judge were 40 per year or only somewhat fewer than one a week.[1]

By 2000, authorized federal district judgeships had risen to 655, having almost doubled in 30 years, and total dispositions had just about tripled, climbing to nearly 335,000. Yet total trial dispositions had declined to less than 10,000, or to 5.6 percent criminal and 2.2 percent civil. In other words, while the number of federal judgeships since 1970 multiplied roughly by two and case dispositions by three, the absolute number of trials had actually fallen by a third and the proportionate percentages by two-thirds or more. Trial dispositions per authorized judge had dropped to 15—or not many more than one a month. Trials of civil cases had been reduced by more than 75 percent.[2]

Still, the very same figures reflect that in 2000 the disposition rate per federal trial judgeship exceeded 510 per year as compared to 340 in 1970, a tremendous increase. If the 1970 disposition rate were projected onto the caseload in 2000, many more judges would have been necessary, together with law clerks, administrative staff, jurors, and courthouse space.

Query: What accounts for these seemingly topsy-turvy statistics, which show that district court judges are spending much less time conducting trials while their marginal productivity in disposing of cases has virtually sky-rocketed?

Profound changes

The dramatic decrease in the number of trials, in inverse ratio to the threefold increase in cases, is just one aspect of the profound changes in our justice system in the past 30 years. Changes have occurred in the nature of the adversarial process and in dispute resolution generally, in the administration of our courts, and in the processing of cases. Moreover, what has taken place in the justice system is in turn a reflection or part of a greater wave of changes that have transformed our society. This phenomenon of the latter part of the 20th century can be attributed to the problems involved in the delivery of services to large and growing concentrations of population—whether it is in providing health care, housing, mass transportation, education, or just collecting trash off the streets, or in the instance of the courts, the resolving of disputes. At the same time, some disputes have become inordinately complex and convoluted as our society has become a huge and multi-layered configuration.

Many of these developments have been driven by the expanding of human capacity enabled by technology, on the one hand, and the constraints of limited economic growth, on the other (a kind of Malthusian geometric versus arithmetical progression). And over the years this tension has been aggravated by the competing objectives of quality versus efficiency/cost considerations. The decrease in trials may be thought of as an expression by our society that on many levels trials may not be the best mechanism for resolving disputes. Instead, like radical, high-tech surgery, they have frequently become an extremely expensive and unpredictable last resort.

The self-evident reasons for the attrition in the incidence of trials are primarily economic—both in terms of individual cases and as relates to the entire justice system. Trials have become less and less affordable, and the persistent demands for containment of private and public litigation costs will continue to discourage their use as the disposition of choice—as will the perceptible rise in litigant dissatisfaction.

In an effort to deal with these issues, Congress enacted the Civil Justice Reform Act of 1991, aimed at cost and delay reduction, and, more recently, the Alternative Dispute Resolution Act of 1998, to foster court-sponsored mediation programs and other settlement strategies. But by the late 1980s, a majority of judicial districts had already implemented these loose-fitting legislative requirements; consequently, the laws them-

Judicature Volume 85, Number 5, pp. 216–217, 253

selves have had little effect on case management or court administration. The federal courts had already recognized the need to find less costly and more expeditious ways to deal with the enormous explosion in litigation other than the traditional trial.

A changing jurisprudence

What are *trials*—and what are the future, long-term implications of the almost dinosaur-like dwindling in their number? Litigation represents a breakdown in communication, which consists in the civil area of the inability of the parties to work out a problem themselves and, in the criminal area, of ineffectively inculcating society's rules and the consequences for violating them. Trials are the method we have ultimately used to deal with those breakdowns. However, the goal of our system is not to try cases. Rather, it is to achieve a fair, just, economical, and expeditious result by trial *or* otherwise, where communication has previously failed.

For some trial judges, the greatest day in the sun is in the bright lights of the hotly contested trial. They bitterly resent the trend that has dimmed the theatre of the courtroom and are concerned that the future of the judicial profession, if not their image as judges, is at stake. But judges can and should think of themselves as functioning within a changing jurisprudence of dispute resolution and should adapt their role accordingly. In other words, the decline in trials should not be looked upon as a belittling commentary on the significance of the trial judge but instead from an overall, societal perspective.

Specifically, as regards the importance of the judge's role, the judge will continue to be the centerpiece and dominant force in dispute resolution, a service that has never been more important to society than it is today. Judge Patrick Higginbotham, of the Court of Appeals for the Fifth Circuit, has said, "Trials are not a disease, to be avoided like the plague." While that is true and should not be lost sight of, trials are also not a fitness exercise that is necessary to maintain the system's vitality.

Although some judges have resisted change, many others have demonstrated a remarkable flexibility in devising methods to enhance their own efficiency and their court's capacity to dispose of cases. This has encompassed both procedural and substantive approaches and modifications. The changes in the adversarial process can be seen most graphically in class actions, the asbestos cases and other mass torts, and the multifaceted role of the multi-district litigation transferee judge. When cases are handled in a package or group instead of one at a time, it is hard, if not impossible, for the lawyers or the judge to maintain time-honored concepts of due process and the adversary system. One alternative has been to deal with these voluminous cases administratively as a matter of practicality, but in some instances mass settlements have been stricken down on appeal as violative of an individual's rights and inconsistent with adjudicative principles.

There have been a myriad of other federal court developments that have also had a substantial and cumulative effect: *Daubert* and the judge as evidentiary gatekeeper; *Celotex* and summary judgment; Rule 11 and sanctions for serious civil pleading infractions; Rule 16 and judicial case management; and the detailed discovery rules and self-executing disclosure. These, in varying degrees, have affected the nature of the process and the judge's role by injecting the judge into the pretrial phases of a case. In a sense, the judge has become the schoolmaster who encourages and often presses lawyers to do their homework and prepare for trial, instead of the neutral arbiter who lets the lawyers, for better or worse, try their own case.

So, too, on the criminal side: There has been a surge in pretrial motions, the outcome of which may often determine whether there will be a non-adversarial disposition of the case—*i.e.*, a guilty plea. Also, the Sentencing Guidelines have forced lawyers to make careful calculations about the chances of success in a trial and to prepare themselves for sentencing to an extent not known before. These changes in pretrial proceedings and the judge's pretrial and sentencing roles have also produced a proliferation in judicial work and time involvement far beyond presiding over trials. But the result has been to equip the trial judge with a variety of case management tools and to bring about a much more efficient and effective dispositional performance record than in the past.

Keeping pace

Just as it may be economically infeasible to take a particular case to trial, there is no reason to believe our judicial structure and capacity will be sufficiently enlarged to keep pace with the growth in litigation or its complexities. Although the number of Article III judgeships is almost twice what it was 30 years ago, criminal and civil cases have escalated at a much faster rate. Even without the considerable impact of additional pretrial proceedings, it would now be completely impracticable to try the one out of six-and-a-half criminal cases or the nearly one out of 10 civil cases that were tried in 1970. In 2000, that would have meant 41,000 total trial dispositions, as against the 10,000 that occurred. The cost of the necessarily gargantuan complement of more judges, logistical support, and courtrooms would be an intriguing figure to quantify—and contemplate in the distant mist of a political/economic mirage.

And while court administration since 1970 has become a mighty industry, judges continue to maintain a great deal of control over administrative matters and their own work. The judiciary is fortunate to have survived post-World War II bureaucratization much more intact than some of its institutional counterparts—for example, in health care, where the physicians no longer operate the hospitals, or in academia, where faculty no longer run the universities. In these instances, because of resource availability issues, a new breed of business managers has been empowered to control the delivery of human and social services. While the judiciary's annual budget has become a cumbersome and drawn-out process of negotiation, judges still manage their own assembly lines of cases and sign off on their budgetary applications.

Our cultural views of the law and the problematical nature of trials have also been a factor. Aside from the economic cost, litigants shrink from the uncertainties, the time investment, the lack of finality, the aggravation and stress, as well as the impaired opportunity for more productive activity. Other densely populated countries have found, no doubt impelled by similar considerations of expedience, that consensus and agreement through conciliation and mediation may be a more positive, and less destructive, approach to dispute resolution than an adversarial trial. In England, for example, the rule that the loser in civil cases pays costs, including attorney's fees, means that trials can come at a high price, even though the amounts requested may be reduced by a "costs judge" in a given case. The influence of that type of thinking has also made inroads in our country in the form of fee- and costs-shifting statutes.

Trials, to an increasing extent, have become a societal luxury. Correspondingly, the role of the trial judge has taken on new and larger dimensions that are essential to our society's welfare. Specialized training is available to assist judges in learning to facilitate early settlements and how best to be authoritative neutrals or, as case managers, to recommend the most auspicious referral for a non-trial resolution. The courts, as well as numerous other agencies, have put substantial resources into what has become the burgeoning field of how to settle cases and avoid trials. Some judges have experimented with ways to abbreviate trials, such as mini-trials, summary trials, and resolution hearings, and in many state courts and a few federal districts, there is compulsory arbitration of smaller claims, which is subject to *de novo* appeal.

While trials in some form will remain with us, it is predictable that their number will decline further, and that the role of the trial judge will continue to become more managerial, as the objectives of relatively inexpensive and prompt dispute resolution gain further ascendancy. Judges, characteristically, are conscientious and hard-working professionals, and their evolving role is more demanding of their time and energy, and of their capabilities, than the routinistic obligations of the garden variety trial.

Notes

This article originally appeared in Volume 85, Number 5, March–April 2002, pages 216–217, 253.

1. "Trial dispositions" include all cases attached for trial whether or not they go to verdict. "Authorized judgeships" refers to positions for judges in active service—some of which, when vacated, remain unfilled for several years or more. In the 1990s, the judicial vacancy rate averaged about 9 percent. The shortage was offset by senior judges—those who retire from active service, but who retain reduced or, in some instances, full caseloads.

2. State courts reflect somewhat greater trial percentages, but a similar trend.

Appellate Court Processes

Access and Docketing Decisions

Lawyers who advise their clients that, "We will fight this case all the way up to the Supreme Court," are usually guilty of overstatement. For one thing, cases ultimately heard by the Supreme Court must implicate a question of federal law. More to the point, as a practical matter, only a handful of the cases initiated in the American judicial system ultimately seek Supreme Court review. Further, the Court exercises virtually complete discretion in composing its appellate docket. An overwhelming majority, well more than 90 percent of the cases seeking Supreme Court review, are denied that appellate opportunity.

It is exceedingly unlikely that any one case will be heard by the Supreme Court. At the same time, however, the litigious nature of American society dictates that even if the percentage of cases seeking Supreme Court review is small, and the proportion granted such review smaller still, the numbers remain great enough to raise the possibility of a workload crisis of substantial magnitude. Petitions for review by the Supreme Court (certiorari petitions) have increased geometrically for more than half of a century. Consequently, concerns about the Court's workload and what to do about it have become primary issues in the American judicial system.

This section of readings broadly examines how the Supreme Court determines its docket as well as some suggested reforms for dealing with the Court's workload. It is important to keep in mind that the Court's role as a policymaker is largely a reflection of the types of cases it hears. As a result, reforms that touch upon the accessibility of the Court to cases seeking review may have substantial implications for its policymaking role.

In "Deciding what to decide: how the Supreme Court sets its agenda," D. Marie Provine utilizes a valuable data source, Justice Harold Burton's docket books, to explore how the Supreme Court exercises its discretionary docketing jurisdiction. Unlike earlier work, which focused on the collective institutional outcomes of certiorari voting, Provine's data allow her to focus on the behavior of individual justices as each votes for and against the granting of certiorari. Her work suggests that the justices' conceptions of the Court's proper role have great implications for their case-selection votes. During the time period under study, a broad consensus existed on the Court's role; therefore, the expression of the policy preferences and political attitudes of individ-

ual justices was not widespread in certiorari voting. Other issues in other times, however, such as the cases that sought review of the constitutionality of the Vietnam War in the 1960s and 1970s, exposed greater divisiveness over the Court's role. For this reason, we would expect considerably more contentious certiorari voting than Provine actually found. Her article remains quite instructive in highlighting the wide variety of concerns that may enter into certiorari decision making.

Justice John Paul Stevens's offering of "Some thoughts on judicial restraint" was first delivered as an address to the American Judicature Society. In it, he proposes the establishment of a new federal court with the authority to exercise the Supreme Court's certiorari function and to decide which cases the Supreme Court would decide on their merits, or those in which only the intrinsic rights and wrongs of the arguments would be considered.

Such a court, in Stevens's view, would alleviate the Supreme Court's caseload crisis, which he feels has been responsible for the unwise proliferation of per curiam opinions and the increased dismissal of writs of certiorari as improvidently granted. While it is now widely known that most Supreme Court justices rely heavily on their clerks in the certiorari process and that they participate in a certiorari "pool" with their colleagues, Stevens's 1982 public admission that, "I do not even look at the papers in over 80 per cent of the cases that are filed" was quite startling.

Justice William Brennan's address, "Some thoughts on the Supreme Court's workload," takes issue with Justice Stevens's call for a new tier in the federal judiciary. Brennan asserts that such a tribunal would violate the Constitution's provision calling for "one Supreme Court," and that it could only be established by amending the Constitution. Justice Brennan rejects Stevens's basic premise that the pressures of an inflated docket have compromised the Supreme Court's decisions on the merits.

To reduce the Court's workload, Brennan recommends the exercise of greater care in identifying certworthy cases, coupled with congressional removal of virtually all of the Court's mandatory appellate jurisdiction, a reform that has since largely taken place. He also alludes to various reforms in lower court processes that could alleviate some Supreme Court problems.

Brennan argues that the Court's case screening function gets easier for a justice the more it is done, and he directly confronts Stevens's confession of delegation. ". . . [M]y view that the screening function is second to none in importance is reflected in my practice of performing the screening function myself." Admittedly, however, no justice on the Court today would likely make that statement.

In "Caseload, conflicts, and decisional capacity: does the Supreme Court need help?" Arthur Hellman takes the issues discussed by Justices Stevens and Brennan to a more empirical plane and closely examines one particular reform proposal, the creation of an Intercircuit Tribunal of the United States Courts of Appeals. Such a tribunal, unlike the reform focused on by Stevens and Brennan, would decide cases referred to it by the Supreme Court. Hellman opposes such a plan, finding it both unnecessary to reduce the Court's workload and unlikely that such a court would achieve its stated goal of fostering uniformity in the law.

The article also highlights the disagreement that exists even among the justices themselves over the Court's workload problem, its nature, and appropriate solutions. Hellman offers a thoughtful analysis that suggests that the workload problem may be a more complex one than first meets the eye. He concludes, "There is simply not enough evidence that the Supreme Court's limited capacity for authoritative decision making has significantly frustrated society's need for uniformity and predictability in the law. Moreover, too little attention has been paid to the possible adverse consequences of creating a new court."

David O'Brien's study of "The Rehnquist Court's shrinking plenary docket" examines the expansion and contraction of the Supreme Court's output through the Burger and Rehnquist Court eras. O'Brien agrees that both external factors (such as a diminishing number of litigation-inducing statutes and the expansion of the Court's discretionary jurisdiction) and internal factors (such as personnel changes) have played a role in the contemporary Court's reduced propensity to hear cases. He asserts, however, that the major cause of the smaller workload has clearly been the replacement of grant-prone justices (or those justices who are liberal in supporting the granting of certiorari) by those with a more constrained vision of the judicial role.

Judge Roger Miner's assertion that "Federal court reform should start at the top" takes a bit of an alternative tack in considering the issue of judicial overload. In his view, it is the federal judiciary writ large and not the Supreme Court that is overburdened. And the reasons for this dilemma lie at the doorstep of both Congress and the Supreme Court. For his part, Miner would like to see Congress pull back from the proliferation of statutes, particularly in the criminal domain, that expand the range of potential federal courses of action. He calls for the Court's acceptance of a greater number of cases in which there is interpretive conflict among the circuits, and he issues a plea for newfound clarity in the development of case law. Interestingly, Judge Miner's essay raises the prospect of a reduced workload in the federal judiciary that is brought about, in part, by an increased caseload for the Supreme Court.

In this section's final selection, "Deciding what to decide: the Judge's Bill at 75," Edward Hartnett offers a very provocative contrarian view of the implications of the Judiciary Act of 1925, in which the Court's ability to control its own docket was assured through critical alterations in the certiorari process. While tracing the history of congressional reform of the Court's docketing processes, Hartnett reminds us that "in the years before the Judge's Bill, the Court decided far more cases than . . . we have somehow convinced ourselves [that] the modern Supreme Court—aided by multiple law clerks and computers—can possibly be expected to decide."

In Hartnett's view, the Court's docketing discretion and the manner in which it has been utilized constitute far more than a diminishing numbers game, since in making access choices it becomes difficult to characterize the Court as exercising "merely" judgment and not will. "If asked, 'Why did you exercise the awesome power to declare an act of Congress unconstitutional?' the justices of the Supreme Court can no longer say 'Because we had to.' Instead, they must say, 'Because we chose to.' " To the extent that the classical justifications for judicial power lie in the eschewing of force and will in favor of judgment, as Alexander Hamilton put it in the *Federalist* No. 78, that justification is called into serious question. Further, as long as the contemporary Court focuses on deciding questions presented by cases more so than on deciding cases, per se, Hartnett concludes that, "it may be that the most significant impact of Supreme Court decisions is to increase the political salience of the issues decided—regardless of which way it decides the issues." Clearly, the issues addressed in this article and in the broader selection of readings in this section are controversial and complex ones that will continue to be subject to considerable debate and calls for reform for the foreseeable future.

Deciding what to decide: how the Supreme Court sets its agenda

D. Marie Provine

Justices generally agree about what cases to review largely because they share a concept of the proper business of the Court.

Since the passage of the 1925 Judiciary Act, the U.S. Supreme Court has enjoyed broad discretion to decide which cases it will resolve on their merits. As dockets have grown more crowded in recent decades, this discretion has become an increasingly significant feature of the Court's institutional power. Currently, for example, the justices refuse review to more than 90 percent of the cases which come before them, which amounts to approximately 3,500 cases denied review per term.[1] Clearly the criteria the justices use to set their agenda should be of considerable interest to students of the Supreme Court.

Research on the Court, however, remains fixed almost exclusively upon the cases to which the justices have granted review.[2] One explanation for the paucity of research on case selection is lack of data. The Court issues no opinions and releases no votes in denying or granting review. Traditionally, the only exceptions to complete secrecy in case selection have been occasional published dissents from denials of review, sporadic citations of reasons for granting review in opinions on the merits, general statements by justices and their law clerks on the case selection process, and the broadly-stated criteria of the Supreme Court Rules.[3]

Scholars interested in analyzing case selection criteria with statistical tools had only the bare facts of grants and denials to work with until 1965, when the papers of Justice Harold H. Burton became available. Burton's papers, on file at the Library of Congress, include complete docket books recording the case selection votes of each justice for the 13 terms that Burton sat on the Court (1945–1957). These are the only complete records of case selection votes that are currently available for any period since the advent of discretionary review.

The Burton data make it possible to analyze case selection and its relationship to the more familiar work of the Supreme Court on the merits. Such an analysis suggests that the justices' conceptions of the proper role of the Court have a major impact on their votes to select cases for review. Consensus about the Court's role appears to have channeled and limited the expression of individual policy preferences and political attitudes in review decisions during the Burton period. Even when the justices disagreed in assessing review worthiness, role perceptions seemed to be significant to their decisions. The only case selection records currently available thus suggest that, in agenda setting, judicial sensitivity to the appropriate business of the Court is crucial.

I. Theories of case selection

The case selection process, because of its secrecy, provides the justices with a special opportunity for favoring certain litigants or side-stepping volatile cases, possibilities that have been noted by scholars.[4] Alexander Bickel, for example, suggested that Supreme Court justices should assess the political implications of the merits of cases and use case selection to limit "the occasions of the Court's interventions" in the political process.[5]

Schubert's certiorari game

Theories of how case selection actually proceeds may also take account of the opportunities for politically motivated behavior that the secrecy of the process provides. In the earliest and most provocative analysis, Glendon Schubert used game theory to explore the possibility that in Federal Employers' Liability Act (FELA) cases, a subgroup of justices manipulated others on the Court to gain the outcomes it preferred on the merits.[6] Such manipulation could occur because, by tradition, only four affirmative votes are needed to review, while five are ordinarily necessary to win on the merits. A minority could thus force a reluctant majority to consider minority-selected cases on the merits.

Schubert postulated that the "certiorari bloc," which varied in size and membership over the years, consistently attempted to maximize the number of Supreme Court judgments favorable to worker claims. The object of the bloc was to encourage the lower courts to look more favorably upon worker petitions. To achieve this objective, the bloc would vote against review in all cases brought by railroads, because in those cases the injured worker had been successful below. For worker petitions, the bloc's strategy was to vote for review only when a majority of the whole Court could be expected to reverse on the merits.

Black and Douglas were long-standing members of the "certiorari bloc." Murphy, Rutledge, Clark, Warren, and Brennan were also members during all or almost all of their shorter terms of office. Frankfurter represented an opposing player in the certiorari game. Others on the Court were uncommitted "pawns" to be "coopted" in the conflict between the two sides.

Schubert found that the "certiorari bloc" was not always successful in implementing its goal of achieving a judicial gloss on the FELA most favorable to workers. Its failures to win reversals in as many worker petitions as it might have stemmed in part from its failure to follow what Schubert conceived to be its optimal or "pure" strategy: to vote for review only when the worker won at trial and lost for the first time on appeal.

Schubert's theory is not seriously damaged by the failure of the "certiorari bloc" to adhere to its optimal strategy. Whether or not the justices behaved rationally at all times, the implications of the hypothesis are profound: the behavior of at least some members of the Court in certain cases can be understood in the language of power politics. Schubert's argument, in other words, was that certain members of the Court, desiring to control the Court's decision making to effectuate preferred policies, made use of the opportunity for subgroup manipulation of the majority afforded by the so-called Rule of Four.

Schubert's analysis cannot be dismissed as a theory of Supreme Court decision making simply because of the limited subject matter it considers. Though the Court received, on the average, fewer than 10 worker-brought FELA cases per term in the period Schubert studied (1942–1960), these cases appear to have been a source of sharp disagreement among the justices. Opinions on the merits in FELA cases reveal deep divisions among the justices about the propriety of plenary, or on-the-merits, review. FELA litigation was, in fact, the most likely locus for outcome-oriented case selection voting on the Supreme Court of that era.

Testing Schubert's theory

The theory of voting behavior Schubert offers is open to criticism, however, on grounds that it does not fit actual voting patterns in FELA cases. Schubert based his research on the pattern of grants and denials in these cases, the only information available when he wrote. The Burton docket books make it possible to check the accuracy of Schubert's suppositions about case selection voting against actual votes.

Burton's records indicate that the "certiorari bloc" Schubert identified did not always vote in the pro-worker direction Schubert hypothesized. Members of the "certiorari bloc," for example, occasionally voted *against* the worker in favor of hearing railroad petitioners. Although no member of the Court did this often, alleged bloc members cast four of the seven pro-railroad votes in the period. The "certiorari bloc" also varied considerably in its support of worker cases; Brennan, for example, voted for only one-third of the cases he should have supported unequivocally. Furthermore, in five cases, the negative vote of one bloc member prevented the review on the merits that the rest of the bloc desired, and in five other cases that did gain review on the merits, the votes of non-bloc members neutralized a negative vote from a bloc member.[7]

Most importantly, the overall voting pattern in worker-brought cases does not match the pattern a theory of power-oriented voting would predict. Schubert's hypothesis implies that certiorari votes in FELA cases should tend to clump around zero and four votes for review. Only during the three-term period when the "certiorari bloc" had a fifth member should five vote grants be common. A consistent pattern of five or more votes would indicate that the bloc had more members than Schubert hypothesized, and frequent instances of fewer than four votes would indicate that conscious manipulation of case selection was absent.[8]

When the worker cases are subdivided by the number of votes they received, however, it is clear that a tight-knit power bloc was not operating during the Burton period. Table 1 indicates the actual pattern in these cases. As this table shows, there were 52 instances in which one, two, three, five, or six votes were cast for review in FELA cases, far too many to suggest the operation of a "certiorari bloc." Table 1 also shows that some justices almost invariably opposed review in FELA cases. Their on-the-merits opinions indicate that Justices Frankfurter, Harlan, and Burton were the members of the Court who consistently opposed review.

Table 1. The distribution of votes for review in worker-brought FELA cases and overall, 1945–1957

Number of votes for review	FELA	Overall (appell. dkt.)
1	7 (10%)	762 (24%)
2	12 (17%)	635 (20%)
3	9 (13%)	381 (12%)
4	16 (23%)	317 (10%)
5	16 (23%)	190 (6%)
6	8 (11%)	159 (5%)
7	1 (1%)	159 (5%)
8	0 —	127 (4%)
9	1 (1%)	417 (14%)
	Total = 70	Total = 3,147

Cue theory

Other theories of case selection decision making conceptualize judicial motivation much differently than Schubert did. In an often-cited article, Tanenhaus, Schick, Muraskin, and Rosen hypothesized that Supreme Court justices are concerned with reducing their workload, rather than with competing to get their policy preferences incorporated into decisions on the merits, as Schubert presumed.[9] The authors theorized that the justices cut down case-processing time by summarily eliminating much of the caseload from careful consideration. According to this hypothesis, they use a set of agreed-upon cues to differentiate cases that might be worthy of review from those they know they did not want to hear.

Like Schubert, Tanenhaus and his colleagues wrote before the release of the Burton papers, so they had only the pattern of grants and denials with which to work. Nevertheless, they established an ingenious test of their hypothesis that the Court uses cues to reduce its workload. Relying on the statements of Chief Justice Hughes and others that between 40 percent and 60 percent of the petitions filed were clearly without merit, the authors hypothesized that this percentage of the cases contained no cues and was not examined beyond the initial search for cues. The rest of the petitions, which did contain one or more cues, constituted the pool from which cases were selected. Because only 5 percent to 17 percent of the docket as a whole was reviewed on the merits in the period under analysis, the authors concluded that the grant rate for the pool of cases containing cues must be between 25 percent and 43 percent.

The authors named three cues the Court used to select cases for careful scrutiny, and to eliminate summarily the remaining (cueless) 40 percent to 60 percent of the caseload:

- the presence of the United States as petitioner;

- the existence of a civil liberties issue;

- disagreement among the lower courts.

Testing cue theory

The accuracy of cue theory can be assessed by examining the fate of cue-containing cases during the Burton period, which matches almost exactly the 1947–1958 period Tanenhaus examined. Burton's papers permit a test of cue theory because his records reveal that a significant proportion of cases were eliminated with only cursory analysis, while the remainder were given more careful attention. The separation was accomplished by special listing, an administrative convenience devised by Chief Justice Hughes before Burton joined the Court.

The practice while Burton sat on the Court was for the chief justice and his staff to prepare a special list, or dead list, of cases deemed unworthy of conference time. The list circulated among the justices each week, and unless one of them put a special-listed case up for conference consideration, it was denied review automatically. Burton filed each week's special lists, and he kept a record of any changes justices requested. These records show that such alterations were rare.

Table 2 indicates the percentage of cue-containing cases that were put on the special list, and the number of votes attracted by those cases with and without cues that survived special listing. As this table shows, cases with cues were significantly more likely to get case selection votes than others on the Appellate Docket. Clearly the cues, especially the U.S. as petitioner, are related to the concerns the justices have in selecting cases for review on the merits. This is not surprising, since Tanenhaus settled upon the cues by examining the statements of Supreme Court justices and others about the types of cases of particular interest to the Court.[10]

Were the authors simply suggesting that some types of cases have a better chance of getting votes for review than others, the Burton data would tend to substantiate the hypothesis. Cue theory, however, purports to explain how the justices reduce the mass of petitions they receive to a more manageable number without actually considering the argument each petitioner

Table 2. Disposition of cases containing Tanenhaus cues, 1947–1957

| Disposition of petitions | Tanenhaus cues | | | |
	U.S. petn'r.	Dissen. below	Civ. libs. issue	All other appellate cases
Special listed	1%	27%	16%	45%
In conference:				
Denied unan.	8%	23%	22%	21%
Denied nonu.	25%	25%	26%	18%
Gr'ntd nonu.	41%	16%	21%	12%
Gr'ntd unan.	25%	9%	15%	5%
Total cases:	554	131*	629	6,323

* Includes data only for 1947 Term.

makes for review on the merits. As the authors describe the process:

> The presence of any one of these cues would warn a justice that a petition deserved scrutiny. If no cue were present, on the other hand, a justice could safely discard a petition without further expenditure of time and energy.[11]

If the cues actually served this short-circuiting purpose, cases containing cues should not appear on the special lists. Yet as Table 2 shows, in all three categories, some cue-containing cases are special listed.

Not a mechanical process

This pattern of voting suggests that the case characteristics that Tanenhaus deemed cues may be significant to the justices in case selection decisions, but that the decision-making process is not as mechanical as the authors suggest. Of course, something differentiates special-listed cases from those discussed in conference. The memos Burton's clerks wrote for him on each case and the case selection voting patterns suggest that cases with jurisdictional defects, inadequate records, and no clearly presented issues were the most likely to be special listed.[12]

No easily identifiable case characteristics are invariably associated with special listing, however. This suggests that neither the justices nor the clerks rely on a fixed set of cues to separate cases into those worthy of scrutiny and those to be discarded summarily. With the assistance law clerks provide in digesting cases and writing memos, there is little reason to expect Supreme Court justices need such an abbreviated preliminary screening procedure.

It is more likely that the justices reduce the time they spend in evaluating petitions by relying on the clerks' memos. The justices may then reach a decision by engaging in a weighing process in which a few characteristics of cases—including probably the Tanenhaus cues—encourage at least some of the justices to vote for review, while many other characteristics act like demerits, preventing review in the absence of strong reasons in favor. The special-listed cases are those which contain one or more demerits and no countervailing considerations in favor of review.

The pattern of voting in U.S.-brought cases supports this interpretation. Because of the solicitor general's careful screening,[13] these cases seldom contain characteristics strongly discouraging review, so the Court seldom puts them on the special lists. In fact, as Table 2 indicates, U.S. cases are sufficiently impressive that in the Burton period they usually received at least one justice's vote for review. The evidence does not suggest, however, that the justices initially separate U.S. cases from the rest in an attempt to save reading time.

The attitudinal hypothesis

Another approach for understanding how the Court selects cases for plenary review emphasizes judicial predispositions towards litigants and policies. Sidney Ulmer has actively promoted this perspective, using the Burton papers to test his attitudinal conception of the case selection process.[14]

One of Ulmer's principal findings has been that a justice's votes to review and his later votes on the merits are strongly related to each other.[15] Ulmer was able to show, for example, that for eight of the 11 justices whose votes he examined, a justice's vote to review helped to predict his vote on the merits.[16] Votes to review were associated with votes to reverse on the merits, a pattern which Ulmer explained in terms of judicial attitudes:

> Theories of cognitive dissonance and attitudinal stability would lead one to expect some consistency in decisional direction if the factors underlying both decisions are identical or similar. Moreover, if the judge is conditioned to respond in a particular way to the stimulus (S) presented by a case on the first trial (t1), the conditioned relationship may be reinforced by the mere act of response.[17]

Similarly, in a study limited to cases brought by state and federal prisoners, Ulmer hypothesized that a justice's underlying attitude towards institutional authority explained consistency at both stages of decision.[18]

Recently Ulmer has gone further, arguing that the justices sometimes try to disguise the extent to which they are influenced by their attitudes towards litigants in case selection. According to this hypothesis, when a justice suspects he cannot win review on the merits, he suppresses his ever present desire to vote for the underdog or the upperdog. In so doing, the justices defer to, but do not assimilate, the norm of impartiality in judicial decision making.[19]

Ulmer's emphasis on judicial attitudes in his analysis of case selection raises a question familiar to students of judicial behavior: are broad, pre-existing attitudes toward litigants and the policy issues in which they are entangled the sole or primary determinant of the votes of judges? Or do judges internalize norms that significantly limit the expression of personal preferences in their decisions? This much-debated question is, of course, central to traditional justifications for judicial power in a democracy. It is especially relevant in the context of case selection where, because of the secrecy of the process, external restraints on judicial judgment are absent.[20]

Cross pressures in case selection

While case selection is insulated from the public scrutiny that characterizes decisions on the merits, it is, of course, subject to strictures the justices place on themselves. The Court has consistently articulated one such self-imposed rule: that the justices decide whether a case should be reviewed not on the basis of their agreement or disagreement with the outcome between the parties in the lower court, but on the basis of their assessment of the intrinsic importance of the issues in controversy. A denial of review, therefore, does not mean that the Court agrees with the outcome of the case in the lower court, and a denial carries no significance as a legal precedent. As Frankfurter explained:

> It simply means that fewer than four members of the Court deemed it desirable to review a decision of the lower court as a matter "of sound judicial discretion." [21]

The procedure the Court uses to select cases for plenary review, however, ensures that each justice will be well-acquainted with the arguments for relief from the lower court judgment when he decides whether to vote for review. The parties incorporate their views of the proper resolution of the case into their briefs for and against review.[22]

The Burton papers suggest that law clerks respond to these arguments and may even feel competent to pass on the merits at this stage in the proceedings. Burton's clerks typically suggested what they believed to be the correct outcome of the underlying dispute in their memos to the justice. The case selection process thus provides the justices with an easy opportunity to vote for review on the basis of their agreement or disagreement with the lower court result.

Ulmer's finding that votes to review and votes to reverse were correlated suggests that the justices *do* let their assessment of the merits of cases influence their review decisions. This finding does not necessarily mean, however, that the justices simply vote according to their attitudes towards certain types of litigants or policies at each stage of decision. The justices could just as well be responding to litigants in case selection, and later in votes on the merits, in light of general principles that determine the availability of judicial relief.

Ulmer's finding thus suggests two questions for further analysis: whether case selection and voting on the merits are, as a practical matter, indistinguishable; and, to the extent that they are, whether motivation can be persuasively explained in attitudinal terms.

II. An overview of voting patterns

If case selection is functionally equivalent to decision making on the merits, most case selection decisions should be nonunanimous, as most decisions on the merits are. Also, individual decisions to grant review should correlate highly with votes to reverse the lower court on the merits, and votes to reverse should be rare when a justice did not vote for review. Finally, the frequency with which a justice votes for review should be directly related to the level of his overall dissatisfaction with lower court results.

If attitudes towards litigants explain why individual case selection votes correspond with votes in fully considered cases, then the justices generally presumed to be the most politically liberal and the most conservative should seldom vote to review the same case. On the Court as a whole, disagreement among the justices should be parallel at both stages of decision, and this pattern should be consistent with the liberal-conservative spectrum we see in on-the-merits voting.

With the Burton records, we can determine whether or not these patterns existed during a significant portion of the modern Court's history. Analysis of case selection votes can thus contribute to our understanding of the relative significance of role constraints and attitude in judicial decision making.

Unanimity in case selection

Contrary to what one would expect if judicial views of the merits alone determined review decisions, the prevailing pattern in case selection is unanimity. During the Burton period, 82 percent of case selection decisions were unanimous: 79 percent were unanimous denials of review and 3 percent were unanimous grants.[23] Available evidence indicates that the level of unanimity in case selection has remained high since the Burton era.[24] This numerical evidence alone suggests that case selection decisions are not functionally equivalent to decisions on the merits, and that some norm or norms guide the justices in deciding whether to vote for review.

Analysis of the types of cases decided unanimously during the Burton period suggests that the justices shared a conception of the work appropriate to the Court that overshadowed policy preferences and sympathies for certain litigants. Evidence of this is that the types of cases usually presumed to tap judicial attitudes most directly were the very types most often denied review unanimously: the petitions of prisoners and suits by business interests seeking relief from government regulation.

This pattern of unanimity in presumably ideologically charged cases cannot be attributed to an unusual period of ideological uniformity on the Supreme Court. The Court's membership in this period included civil libertarians like Black and Douglas as well as nonlibertarians like Reed and Vinson. Yet all of them

Table 3. Unanimity in favor of review by case type, 1947–1957

Case type	N	% granted review unanimously
U.S. petitioner	554	25%
Civil rights/liberties claims	630	14%
Labor claims	593	15%
Federalism issues	578	11%
All criminal petitioners	8,572	0%
All other cases not noted above	4,311	2%

were in agreement that most of these cases should not be reviewed. In other words, all of the justices seem to have been convinced that certain types of cases were not important enough to review, even if they touched the private sympathies of individual justices.

A review of memos written by Justice Burton's law clerks suggests that this consensus has both procedural and subject-matter aspects. As noted earlier, cases with defective records from below or other weaknesses unrelated to the substance of their claims tended to be denied review unanimously, usually by special listing. Likewise, certain subject matters almost never got votes for review. Contract disputes, common law issues, and real property litigation were prime candidates for unanimous exclusion. Sixty percent of these cases were special listed.[25]

Unanimity in favor of review

The types of cases in which the justices were most often unanimous in favor of review also suggest the importance of shared views about the proper business of the Court. During the Burton period, as Table 3 indicates, the justices tended to be unanimous in four types of cases which are related to basic areas of responsibility for the court of last resort in a federal system.

- U.S. petitions and labor claims which are similar in frequently raising issues concerning the proper scope of federal law-making authority.

- Civil rights and liberties petitions which usually claimed federal constitutional rights against asserted state and local authority.

- Federalism cases, which require the Court to adjust competing jurisdictional claims among governmental and quasi-governmental authorities and

Table 4. The relationship between votes to review and votes to reverse, 1947–1957

| | (Nonunanimous cases) | | |
Justice	Percent of votes to reverse in cases he voted to review*	Percent of votes to reverse in cases he voted against**	Difference between the two columns
Whittaker	93	43	50
Rutledge	85	37	48
Black	80	36	44
Minton	64	25	39
Warren	76	42	34
Vinson	61	31	29
Douglas	75	46	29
Jackson	62	34	28
Frankfurter	67	39	27
Brennan	79	52	27
Reed	58	31	27
Clark	62	35	27
Harlan	62	41	21
Murphy	74	57	17
Burton	56	39	17

* N = 100 or more for all except Whittaker (27 votes to reverse in 29 cases favoring review).
** N = 100 or more for all except Murphy, Rutledge, Brennan, and Whittaker where instances range from 20 to 50.

which are clearly a central function for the court of last resort in a federal system.

Differences among the justices

When the justices of the Burton era disagreed in case selection, they differed considerably in the extent to which their votes to review paralleled their final votes on the merits, and they differed dramatically in the frequency with which they voted to review. These two measures of differences among the justices appear to be independent of each other.

The association between voting to review and to reverse already noted by Ulmer is evident in Table 4, which ranks the justices according to their tendency to vote for review and then vote to reverse on the merits. As the table shows, although the justices differed in the extent to which considerations favoring review and reversal paralleled each other, all of the justices were more likely to vote to reverse a case they voted to review than one they did not vote to review.

Were the justices considering simply the desired outcome of the dispute in case selection, however, the differences between the two columns in Table 4 would be much closer to 100 percent. Nor can the failure of these differences to approximate 100 percent plausibly be attributed to the effect of mistaken assessments of the merits at the case selection stage. The inadequacy of

transposing the plenary decision to the case selection stage is particularly evident for the justices at the bottom of the table, for whom the relationship between case selection votes and votes for reversal is weakest.

It seems more likely that judicial beliefs concerning the proper work of the Supreme Court explain the imperfect correlations between votes to review and votes to reverse. A justice's failure to vote for reversal in every case he voted to review can be attributed to his belief that the subject was too important to pass over for reasons unrelated to the correctness of the outcome below. Likewise, a justice's vote to reverse a case he voted against reviewing can be attributed to the view that the case was wrongly decided below, but not important enough to review.

Considered in this light, departures from merits-consciousness in nonunanimous votes are consistent with the preponderance of unanimity in case selection: both depend on judicial conceptions of the proper role of the Court which limit the expression of individual sympathies and preferences in case selection votes.

Frequency of votes for review

The significance of role perceptions in case selection decisions is also evident when the Burton period justices are compared according to the frequency with which they voted for review. As Table 5 shows, the jus-

Table 5. Differences in the propensity to vote for review, 1947–1957

Justice	1947–1948	1949–1952	1953–1954	1955	1956	1957	Overall	Rank
Murphy	59	—	—	—	—	—	59	1
Douglas	53	61	61	55	59	54	58	2
Black	43	56	54	57	58	54	53	3
Rutledge	49	—	—	—	—	—	49	3
Brennan	—	—	—	—	42	44	43	5
Warren	—	—	31	43	54	38	40	6
Reed	28	38	31	30	—	—	33	7
Harlan	—	—	—	31	36	31	32	8
Jackson	22	30	31	—	—	—	27	9
Burton	22	33	23	29	30	23	27	10
Frankfurter	23	29	26	24	33	28	27	11
Clark	—	25	26	28	32	25	26	12
Vinson	—	21	—	—	—	—	25	13
Whittaker	—	—	—	—	—	21	21	14
Minton	—	10	10	18	—	—	13	15

Note: Each justice's votes for review/total opportunities to vote for review in pool of cases receiving at least one favorable vote; expressed as percentages.

tices differed greatly in the frequency with which they voted for review. (This table segments the Burton period into natural courts defined by periodic shifts in the membership of the Court.)

Certain justices during the Burton period consistently voted more often for review than their colleagues. The justices often divided into groups on this issue, with 20 percentage points or more separating them in some natural courts. Black and Douglas were the long-standing members of the review-prone group, while Frankfurter and Burton were mainstays of the review-conservative group.

The remaining justices who voted in more than one segment of time also showed consistency in their propensity to vote for review. Generally, when a justice's percentage of votes for review did drop or rise from one natural court to the next, other carryover justices changed in the same direction. The rank order of the justices thus remained fairly constant over the entire period.

Changes in the membership of the Court also did not disrupt voting propensities, even when they affected how a majority of the Court could be expected to vote on the merits. This suggests that those who voted often for review did so with little regard for probable outcome on the merits, and even without regard to marshalling enough votes to gain review. The review-prone justices, in other words, appear to have been unconcerned with the impact of their case selection votes in specific cases.

This pattern raises the question of whether the review-prone justices voted most often for review because they were more dissatisfied with lower court outcomes than the rest of the Court. Such an explanation must assume that, for the more review-prone justices at least, votes to review are motivated primarily by disagreement with lower court outcomes.

Yet the ranking of the justices in Table 4, which estimates the relative tendency to vote to review in order to reverse, does not correlate with the ranking of the justices in their tendency to vote for review (Table 5). The two justices who voted most often for review, for example, were not especially likely to equate case selection and plenary decision making, while the two least review-prone justices were among the most likely to vote the merits in case selection.

In short, the tendency to vote often for review appears to be independent of the tendency to make disagreement with the lower court outcome the primary criterion of review-worthiness. Thus, while disagreement with lower court outcomes almost certainly influences the justices to vote for review, this variable can not by itself account for differences in the tendency to vote for review.

Propensity to vote for review

It seems likely that differences in the frequency with which individual justices voted for review are related to differences in the disposition of the justices to exercise Supreme Court power. Clearly the structure of case

Table 6. Justices' propensities to vote for review by case type, 1947–1957

Justices ranked by overall tendency to vote to review	Criminal rights claims	Civil rights & liberties claims	U.S. claims	Federalism cases
Murphy	77	78	76	61
Douglas	73	76	42	50
Black	67	75	47	39
Rutledge	67	63	60	42
Brennan	68	56	62	56
Warren	42	44	57	34
Reed	23	21	69	27
Harlan	32	38	62	49
Jackson	27	29	33	48
Burton	21	22	54	43
Frankfurter	43	36	21	41
Clark	30	20	53	34
Vinson	12	14	52	47
Whittaker	19	28	23	48
Minton	9	7	35	20
Range:	68	71	41	41
Standard deviations:	26.1	22.9	15.6	10.3

Note: Each justice's votes for review/total opportunities to vote for review in pool of cases receiving at least one favorable vote; in percentages.

selection requires the justices to consider the proper scope of Supreme Court activity in voting for or against review. The identity of the most review-prone and the most review-conservative justices during the Burton period also suggests the relevance of such a concern.

Pritchett's discussion of differences among the justices in plenary decision making is particularly useful in showing this connection. Even though Pritchett restricted his analysis to civil rights and liberties cases, his explanation for voting differences is broad, and it seems applicable to Supreme Court decision making generally.

Those men whom Pritchett labeled "libertarian activists" in *Civil Liberties and the Vinson Court* were the most review-prone justices who sat during the entire Burton period.[26] Pritchett's "less libertarians" are among the least review-prone justices. Frankfurter, Pritchett's lone example of libertarian restraint, is somewhere near the middle in case selection, as he is in Pritchett's typology.

Pritchett described the libertarian activist as the judge whose sympathies are aroused by the underdogs in our society and for whom "the result is the test of a decision."[27] A believer in libertarian restraint, on the other hand, emphasizes the process of judicial decision making and the nondemocratic basis of judicial power. For Pritchett, a justice's activism or restraint is a function of the interaction of two variables: his sympathies towards underdogs and "the conception which the justice holds of his judicial role and the obligations imposed on him by his judicial function."[28]

Information about the frequency with which the justices vote for review is consistent with this two-dimensional interpretation of judicial motivation. Sympathy for underdogs and an expansive interpretation of the availability of Court-fashioned relief seemed to play a part in explaining voting frequency.

As Table 6 shows, review-prone justices tended to be willing to go further than their brethren in voting to hear criminal and civil rights and liberties claims. These were the types of cases that raised new arguments for rights not yet established in precedent or legislation, and they occasioned the greatest disagreement among the justices over review-worthiness. In more established areas of litigation, represented here by U.S.-brought and federalism cases, the review-prone justices were relatively less likely to favor review, although, overall, they still tended to be more likely to vote for review than their colleagues.

The Court's proper workload

Differing convictions among the justices about the workload appropriate to the Court, a question central

Table 7. A comparison of the voting propensities of the four justices who sat together on the Court, 1947–1957

	Number of justices voting with justice in left column						
	0	1	2	3	4	5	6 or 7
Burton	47	78	88	95	94	220	
Frankfurter	27	92	109	103	83	81	219
Douglas	243	353	237	186	139	117	216
Black	221	326	198	187	128	107	195

Note: In numbers of votes for review, nonunanimous cases.

to the role it should perform, also appear to have been crucial. This is particularly evident when differences in voting frequencies are examined in detail. Table 7 provides such a close-up view of the voting history of the four justices who sat together throughout the Burton period: Douglas, Black, Frankfurter, and, of course, Burton. Douglas and Black, as Table 5 showed, were review prone, while Burton and Frankfurter were not.

Table 7 shows that, had two other justices consistently voted with them, Black and Douglas would have engaged the Court in several times as many cases as either Frankfurter or Burton. The willingness of Black and Douglas to involve the Court in this number of plenary decisions suggests that they placed little value on time-consuming methods of decision making. These men exhibited in their case selection behavior a willingness to reach decisions quickly and to justify them without ado, characteristics that are also evident in their behavior on the merits.

Table 7 also shows that Black and Douglas participated in many more four-, five-, and six-vote grants than either Burton or Frankfurter. Only when seven or eight votes were cast were Burton and Frankfurter slightly more likely to have voted for review than Black or Douglas. This pattern indicates that Black and Douglas must have voted for review in many cases without paying much attention to the ideological similarities and differences with their colleagues that were usually in evidence in published decisions. Black and Douglas thus appear to differ from Burton and Frankfurter less in the types of cases they voted to hear than in the numbers they felt competent to decide on the merits.

In the weekly case selection conferences, the contrast between the two approaches must have been continually apparent and frequently irritating. To review-conservative justices like Frankfurter, the more review-prone justices must have seemed insensitive

about the workload they were willing to impose on the Court. To the review-prone justices, those who seldom voted for review must sometimes have seemed callous about the plights of petitioners and the development of legal rights.

Conclusion

This analysis suggests that Supreme Court justices during the Burton period shared a powerful conception of the role of their institution, which appears to have sharply limited the level of disagreement that could otherwise have been anticipated in case selection voting. Consensus on the norms of judicial behavior also appears to have discouraged these justices either from combining forces to achieve the results they preferred on the merits or from voting individually in a way that would indicate routine calculation of probable outcomes in the case selection process.

The voting patterns examined here thus suggest that role conceptions serve both a limiting and a liberating function. Judicial conceptions of appropriate behavior help to limit the expression of judicial predispositions towards litigants in voting. Yet role conceptions also operate to free the justices from ideological isolation, permitting them to vote routinely with ideologically dissimilar justices.

The evidence here also suggests that role conceptions can also be a source of disagreement in case selection. The considerable differences among the Burton-period justices in their willingness to vote for review appear to be at least partly attributable to variation in conceptions of the Court's role.

The self-imposed limits of role conceptions, it is important to note, are essentially the only limits upon judicial discretion in case selection. Because of the secrecy of the process, case selection exceeds even plenary decision making in the scope it provides for the exercise of unfettered judicial judgment. The Taft-period justices campaigned hard for this broad authority, and until recently, Supreme Court justices were unanimous in their efforts to maximize their agenda-setting power.[29]

Disagreement among the current justices has finally made Court-controlled case selection a public issue, however.[30] The question for policymakers is whether the Court should be permitted to maintain complete control in setting its agenda, limited only by the conceptions the justices hold of the proper way to perform this function.

For students of judicial decision making, the significance of role conceptions in case selection has additional implications. The explanatory power of the concept in this context suggests that role perceptions deserve more attention in analyses of Supreme Court decision making on the merits. Differences in role conceptions have, of course, been the focus of some research,[31] but the phenomenon of consensus among justices has received too little attention.

Preoccupation with voting differences among the justices gives a misleading impression of judicial motivation. Differences in judicial attitudes and role conceptions tend to receive lopsided attention, while the influence of shared norms derived from legal and professional socialization tends to be ignored. This makes it difficult to determine the extent to which judicial decision making parallels political decision making in other contexts. A more accurate picture will emerge only when political scientists acknowledge that the work of Supreme Court justices includes more than nonunanimous decisions on the merits.

Notes

This article originally appeared in Volume 64, Number 7, February 1981, pages 320–333. It was adapted from the author's book, *Case Selection in the United States Supreme Court* (Chicago: University of Chicago Press, 1980).

1. See *Annual Report, Director of the Administrative Office of U.S. Courts.* For a brief review of caseload growth, *see* the Federal Judicial Center, *Report of the Study Group of the Caseload of the Supreme Court* (Washington, D.C.: Administrative Office of U.S. Courts, 1972).

2. Ulmer, "Selecting Cases for Supreme Court Review: An Underdog Model," *Am. Pol. Sci. Rev.* 72 (1978), 902.

3. The high degree of secrecy the Court has sought to maintain about all its work prior to the release of final decisions was made evident recently by the flurry of interest which greeted *The Brethren,* a journalistic exposé of

decision making on the Burger Court. Woodward and Armstrong, *The Brethren: Inside the Supreme Court* (New York: Simon and Schuster, 1979).

4. Earp, "Sovereign Immunity in the Supreme Court," *Am. J. of Int'l. L.* 16 (1976), 903; and Hanus, "Denial of Certiorari and Supreme Court Policy-Making," *Am. U. L. Rev.* 17 (1967).

5. Bickel, *The Least Dangerous Branch* (Indianapolis: Bobbs-Merrill, 1962), 128.

6. Schubert, *Quantitative Analysis of Judicial Behavior* (New York: Free Press, 1959); and Schubert, "Policy Without Law: An Extension of the Certiorari Game," *Stan. L. Rev.* 14 (1962), 284.

7. Provine, *Case Selection in the United States Supreme Court* (Chicago: University of Chicago Press, 1980), 168–169.

8. Bloc members intent upon persuading the uncommitted members of the Court to vote for workers on the merits would be ill-advised to throw away votes on losing cases because such behavior would expose the true extent of their pro-worker bias. Of course, occasional instances of three votes would be understandable as mistakes, but even these should be rare.

9. Tanenhaus, Schick, Muraskin, and Rosen, "The Supreme Court's Certiorari Jurisdiction: Cue Theory," in Schubert (ed.), *Judicial Decision-Making* (New York: Free Press, 1963).

10. Ibid. at 122–125.

11. Ibid. at 118.

12. These were some of the considerations Tanenhaus hypothesized to control the review decision *after* the initial search for cues has occurred. Ibid. at 118.

13. Brigman, "The Office of the Solicitor General of the United States," doctoral dissertation, University of North Carolina, 1966.

14. Ulmer was the first, and for a considerable time, the only scholar to mine the Burton papers for evidence of what Supreme Court justices consider in case selection.

15. Ulmer, "The Decision to Grant Certiorari as an Indicator to Decision 'On the Merits,' " *Polity* 4 (1972), 429; and Ulmer, "Supreme Court Justices as Strict and Not-So-Strict Constructionists: Some Implications," *Law & Soc'y Rev.* 8 (1973), 13.

16. Ulmer, "The Decision . . . ," *supra* n. 15.

17. Ibid.

18. Ulmer, "Supreme Court Justices . . . ," *supra* n. 15.

19. Ulmer, *supra* n. 2.

20. Of course, assessments of the relative significance of role perceptions are necessarily tentative because available evidence is indirect, and the concepts of role and attitude are too amorphous to operationalize very satisfactorily. *See* Howard, "Role Perceptions and Behavior in Three U.S. Courts of Appeals," *J. of Pol.* 39 (1977), 916; and Gibson, "Judges' Role Orientations, Attitudes, and Decisions," *Am. Pol. Sci. Rev.* 72 (1978), 911.

21. Frankfurter, opinion explaining denial of review in *State v. Baltimore Radio Show,* 338 U.S. 912 (1950).

22. Prettyman, "Opposing Certiorari in the U.S. Supreme Court," *Va. L. Rev.* 61 (1975), 197.

23. Provine, *supra* n. 7, at 32

24. Brennan, "Justice Brennan Calls National Court of Appeals Proposal 'Fundamentally Unnecessary and Ill-Advised,' " *A.B.A. J.* 59 (1973), 835.

25. Provine, *supra* n. 7.

26. Pritchett, *Civil Liberties and the Vinson Court* (Chicago: University of Chicago Press, 1954).

27. Ibid. at 198.

28. Ibid. at 191.

29. Provine, *supra* n. 7, at 10–12 and 72–73.

30. Commission on Revision of the Federal Court Appellate System, *Structure and Internal Procedures: Recommendations for Change* (Washington, D.C.: U.S. Government Printing Office, 1975); and *Report of the Study Group on the Caseload of the Supreme Court* (Washington, D.C.: Administrative Office of U.S. Courts, 1972).

31. For other research on differences in role conceptions, *see* Pritchett, *supra* n. 26; Grossman, "Role-Playing and the Analysis of Judicial Behavior: The Case of Mr. Justice Frankfurter," *J. of Pub. L.* 11 (1962), 285; and "Dissenting Blocs on the Warren Court: A Study in Judicial Role Behavior," *J. of Pol.* 30 (1968), 1068; Howard, "Role Perceptions and Behavior in Three U.S. Courts of Appeals," *J. of Pol.* 39 (1977), 916; and Gibson, *supra* n. 20.

Some thoughts on judicial restraint

John Paul Stevens

As delivered to the annual meeting and banquet of the American Judicature Society, August 6, 1982.[1]

During my exceptionally long tenure as the junior justice on the Supreme Court of the United States, I was frequently asked to compare the work on that Court with the work on the Court of Appeals for the Seventh Circuit on which I sat for five years. My answer to that question always made the point that I was much more conscious of the similarities between the two courts than of their differences.

During my brief tenure as one of the eight senior justices on the Court, I have frequently been asked to compare the work on an integrated court with the work on a segregated court. My answer to that question has usually made the point that although every retirement and every new appointment produces a different Court than its predecessor, the similarities between the Court on which Justice Stewart sat, and the Court on which Justice O'Connor sits, far outweigh their differences.

My belief that the common characteristics of the work of judges in a free society are far more significant than their differences has persuaded me that it may be worthwhile to share with you some of my concerns about the way the Supreme Court is presently discharging one of its judicial responsibilities. A frank discussion of our problems may identify some pitfalls that all of us should try to avoid and may uncover some possible solutions that merit further study.

The Supreme Court is now processing more litigation than ever before. The Court is granting more petitions for certiorari; litigants whose petitions are granted next fall may have to wait a full year before their cases are argued.[2] The Court is issuing more pages of written material; opinions for the Court are longer and more numerous, and separate opinions are becoming the norm instead of the exception. The Court is deciding more cases on the merits without the benefit of full briefing and argument, using the currently fashionable technique of explaining its reasons in a "per curiam" opinion—a document generally written for the Court by an anonymous member of its ever increasing administrative staff.[3]

More and more frequently, after a case has been fully argued, the Court finds it appropriate to dismiss the writ of certiorari without making any decision on the merits because it belatedly learns that certiorari was improvidently granted.[4] As is true in so many courts throughout the country, the heavy flow of litigation is having a more serious impact on the administration of justice than is generally recognized.

Some of the consequences of this increased flow are predictable and have already begun to manifest themselves. The problem of delay—which is not yet serious—in a few years will be a matter of national concern. Of even greater importance, however, is what may happen within the Court itself. For when a court is overworked, the judges inevitably will concentrate their principal attention on the most important business at hand. Matters of secondary importance tend to be put to one side for further study or to be delegated to staff assistants for special consideration. Two examples illustrate this point.

At the beginning of our last term, after the Court had processed the list of certiorari petitions that had been filed during the summer recess—if my memory serves me correctly there were about a thousand cases on that list—we agreed that it was essential that we confront the question whether the Court should either support legislation that would increase the appellate capacity of the federal judicial system or try to develop new internal procedures that would ameliorate the impact of the case volume on our own work. As the term developed, however, and we became more and more deeply involved in the merits of a series of difficult cases, our initial recognition of the overriding importance of evaluating our own workload problems—and the desirability of scheduling conferences devoted exclusively to that subject matter—gradually dissipated and no such conference was ever held. We were too busy to decide whether there was anything we could do about the problem of being too busy.

Reviewing approximately 100 certiorari petitions each week and deciding which to grant and which to deny is important work. But it is less important work than studying and actually deciding the merits of cases that have already been accepted for review and writing opinions explaining those decisions. Because there simply is not enough time available to do the more important work with the care it requires and also to read all the certiorari petitions that are filed, I have found it necessary to delegate a great deal of responsibility in the review of certiorari petitions to my law clerks. They examine them all and select a small minority that they believe I should read myself. As a result, I do not even look at the papers in over 80 percent of the cases that are filed.

I cannot describe the practice of any of my colleagues, but when I compare the quality of their collective efforts at managing the certiorari docket with the high quality of their work on argued cases, I readily conclude that they also must be treating the processing of certiorari petitions as a form of second-class work. My observation of that process during the past seven terms has convinced me that the Court does a poor job of exercising its discretionary power over certiorari petitions. Because we are too busy to give the certiorari docket the attention it deserves, we grant many more cases than we should, thereby making our management problem even more unmanageable.

At this point I should make clear that I am expressing only my own opinion—an opinion that perhaps none of my colleagues may share. Indeed, some of them believe we should be taking many more cases and that our overflow should be decided by a newly created National Court of Appeals.

Under that view, the aggregate lawmaking capacity of the federal judiciary would be enlarged. There would be a significant increase in the number of federal adjudications binding on courts throughout the nation. Moreover, under that view, the management functions performed by the Supreme Court would require a relatively greater portion of the justices' total time. For the justices would not only decide what cases are important enough to justify decision on the merits at a national level, but they would also decide which of the two courts with nationwide jurisdiction should hear those cases. In other words, they would be managing the docket of two courts instead of just one.

The increased national capacity would also make it more difficult for us to resist the temptation to review every case in which we believe the court below has committed an error. Like a new four-lane highway that temporarily relieves traffic congestion, a new national court would also attract greater and greater traffic volumes and create unforeseen traffic problems. In my

opinion, it would be unfortunate if the function of the Supreme Court of the United States should become one of primarily—or even largely—correcting errors committed by other courts. It is far better to allow the state supreme courts and federal courts of appeals to have the final say on almost all litigation than to embark on the hopeless task of attempting to correct every judicial error that can be found.

In my opinion, the Court and the nation would be better served by re-examining the doctrine of judicial restraint and by applying its teachings to the problems that confront us. The doctrine of judicial restraint is often misunderstood. It is not a doctrine that relates to the merits of judicial decisions; it is a doctrine that focuses on the process of making judicial decisions. It is a doctrine that teaches judges to ask themselves whether, and if so when, they should decide the merits of questions that litigants press upon them.

It is not a doctrine that denies the judiciary any lawmaking power—our common law heritage and the repeated need to add new stitches in the open fabric of our statutory and constitutional law foreclose the suggestion that judges never make law. But the doctrine of judicial restraint, as explained for example in Justice Brandeis' separate opinion in *Ashwander v. Tennessee Valley Authority*,[5] teaches judges to avoid *unnecessary* lawmaking. When it is necessary to announce a new proposition of law in order to decide an actual case or controversy between adversary litigants, a court has a duty to exercise its lawmaking power. But when no such necessity is present, in my opinion there is an equally strong duty to avoid unnecessary lawmaking.

The fact that the court is granting a larger number of certiorari petitions than ever before raises the question whether it is engaging in unnecessary lawmaking. The answer to that question is suggested by a few examples of the way the Court has exercised its discretionary jurisdiction in recent years. For both in deciding when to review novel questions and in deciding what questions need review, the Court often exhibits an unfortunate lack of judicial restraint.

Thus, the various opinions in our recent case involving a school library plainly disclose that the Court granted certiorari at an interlocutory stage of a case in which further proceedings in the trial court would either have clarified the constitutional issue or perhaps have mooted the entire case.[6] Similar considerations in the case involving a court clerk's claim of immunity prompted the Court to dismiss the writ as improvidently granted.[7] The Court's *timing* in these cases demonstrates that patience is both a virtue and a characteristic of judgment that judges sometimes forget.

In other cases, the Court has displayed a surprising unwillingness to allow other courts to make the final decision in cases that are binding in only a limited geographical area and in which no conflict exists. Thus, in *Watt v. Alaska,* apart from the possibility that error had been committed, there was no reason for our Court to involve itself in a dispute between the State of Alaska and one of its counties over the division of mineral leasing revenues that could only arise in the Ninth Circuit.[8]

In *Oregon v. Kennedy,* the Court elected to review a misapplication of double jeopardy doctrine by the Oregon Court of Appeals even though the particular facts of the case may never be duplicated in other litigation.[9] The fact that the new double jeopardy doctrine pronounced in the opinion of five of my colleagues was totally unnecessary to decide that case adds emphasis to the lack of necessity for granting certiorari at all. Moreover, despite that pronouncement, the Oregon court remained free to reinstate its prior judgment by unambiguously relying on Oregon, rather than federal, law to support its holding.

In *South Dakota v. Opperman,* the state supreme court followed that precise course, thereby proving that our Court had unnecessarily taken jurisdiction of a case in which deference to the state court's judgments would have been appropriate in the first instance.[10] The decision to review (and to reverse summarily without argument) a novel holding by a California intermediate appellate court concerning the burden of proof in an obscenity trial,[11] or an equally novel holding by the Pennsylvania Supreme Court concerning a police officer's order commanding the driver of a vehicle to get out of his car after a traffic violation,[12] are examples of the many cases in which the Court has been unwilling to allow a state court to provide one of its residents more protection than the federal Constitution requires, even though the state decision affected only a limited territory and did not create a conflict with any other decision on a question of federal law, and even though the state court had the power to reinstate its original judgment by relying on state law.[13] A willingness to allow the decisions of other courts to stand until it is *necessary* to review them is not a characteristic of this Court when it believes that error may have been committed.

The Court's lack of judicial restraint is perhaps best illustrated by the procedure it followed in the *Snepp* case.[14] A former CIA agent filed a petition for certiorari seeking review of a Fourth Circuit decision holding that his publication of a book about Viet Nam violated his secrecy agreement with the CIA;[15] he contended that his contract was unenforceable because it abridged his right to free speech. The government opposed his petition and also filed a conditional cross-petition, praying that *if* the Court should grant Snepp's petition, it should also consider whether the remedy ordered by the lower court was adequate.

The Court denied Snepp's petition, but nevertheless granted the cross-petition and, without hearing arguments on the merits, issued a per curiam opinion ordering a constructive trust to be imposed on all of the book's earnings, even though there was neither a statutory nor contractual basis for that novel remedy. Since the government had not even asked the Court to review the remedy issue unless it granted Snepp's petition, it is undeniable that the Court's exercise of lawmaking power in that case was totally unnecessary.

If you think the *Snepp* case is unique in the revelatory light it casts on the Court's present approach to the doctrine of judicial restraint, I suggest that you read the Court's per curiam opinion in the *McCluskey* case, decided on the last day of this term, in which the Court exercised its majestic power to reinstate the suspension of a high school student who had consumed too much alcohol.[16]

You may think I have wandered away from a discussion of problems created by the mounting tide of litigation that is threatening to engulf our Court. My purpose in discussing the doctrine of judicial restraint, however, is relevant for two quite different reasons. First, it lends support to a possible solution to the problem that I favor; second, it explains why judges who do not share my respect for the doctrine will surely oppose that solution.

Instead of creating a new court to decide more cases on the merits, thereby increasing the aggregate judicial power that the Supreme Court may exercise, I favor the creation of a new court to which the Supreme Court would surrender some of its present power—specifically, the power to decide what cases the Supreme Court should decide on the merits. In essence, this is the proposal that was made by the committee headed by Professor Paul Freund several years ago[17] with one critical difference. I would allow that court to decide— not merely to recommend—that a certiorari petition should be granted or denied. Let me just briefly explain why I believe the creation of a new court with that power would significantly improve the administration of justice.

First, and of greatest importance, I believe an independent tribunal that did not have responsibility for deciding the merits of any case would do a far better job of selecting those relatively few cases that should be decided by the Supreme Court of the United States. As I have already suggested, I think the present Court does a poor job of performing that task. It grants too many cases and far too often we are guilty of voting to grant simply because we believe error has been committed rather than because the question presented is both sufficiently important for decision on a national level and also ripe for decision when action is taken on the certiorari petition. I recognize that a different court might make similar mistakes, but reflection has persuaded me that such a court would be more likely to develop a jurisprudence of its own that properly focused on the factors—other than possible error— that should determine whether or not a certiorari petition should be granted.

Second, if I am correct in my belief that such a court would grant fewer petitions, this Court would be required to decide fewer cases on the merits. Even if that assumption is not correct, if the vast flood of paper and the small army of administrative personnel associated with the processing of our certiorari docket could be entirely removed from the Supreme Court, the time available to the justices for doing their most important work would be dramatically increased.[18] The threat to the quality of that work that is now posed by the flood of certiorari petitions would be entirely removed.

Finally, if the new court were granted the power to control our docket, I believe capable judges would regard membership on that court as worthy of their talent. When the original Freund Committee proposal was made, my initial reaction to it was the same as that of other circuit judges with whom I was serving— it seemed to offer us the opportunity to become law clerks instead of judges. But an important reason for that reaction was the fact that the proposed court was not expected to exercise any real power—it would have done no more than perform a preliminary screening function for the Supreme Court without the actual power of decision.

If the Supreme Court surrendered that power to the new court, the status of that court would indeed be significant. I am firmly convinced that a proper performance of the function of selecting the cases for the Supreme Court's docket would be rewarding judicial work, requiring a scholarly understanding of new developments in the law and of our democratic institutions that only our ablest judges possess.

Those who question the wisdom of allowing the Supreme Court to relinquish control over its own docket, and who favor the creation of a new National Court of Appeals to decide cases that are referred to it by our Court, rely heavily on the perceived need to enlarge our capacity to resolve conflicts among the circuits. Let me therefore say a word about that asserted need. Again the doctrine of judicial restraint sheds light on the problem.

Putting to one side my own view that the number of unresolved conflicts is exaggerated, I would like to suggest, first, that the existence of differing rules of law in different sections of our great country is not always an intolerable evil and, second, that there are decision makers other than judges who could perform the task of resolving conflicts on questions of statutory construction. As Justice O'Connor noted in her eloquent dissent in the *FERC* case,[19] the fact that many rules of law differ from state to state is at times one of the virtues of our federal system. It would be better, of course, if federal law could be applied uniformly in all federal courts, but experience with conflicting interpretations of federal rules may help to illuminate an issue before it is finally resolved and thus may play a constructive role in the law-making process. The doctrine of judicial restraint teaches us that patience in the judicial resolution of conflicts may sometimes produce the most desirable result.

The doctrine of judicial restraint also raises the question whether the conflict resolution task need always be performed by judges. If the conflict is on a question of constitutional law, it must be resolved by the Supreme Court. But if, as is more frequently the case, the conflict is over the meaning of an ambiguous statutory provision, it may be both more efficient and more appropriate to allow Congress to make the necessary choice between the alternative interpretations of the legislative intent.

If the conflicts problem is—or should become—sufficiently important to justify the creation of an entirely new federal appellate court, I would suppose that the problem would also justify the creation of a standing committee of the Congress to identify conflicts that need resolution and to draft bills to resolve them one way or the other. If the source of the conflict is ambiguity resulting from an omission in a statute, it would seem to make good sense to assign Congress the task of performing the necessary corrective law making.[20]

At the outset, I suggested that a discussion of problems I perceive in our Court might be useful to other judges because the similarities among courts outweigh their differences. Before I close, let me therefore explain why I hope my comments may be relevant to the problems that arise in other courts. First, I would urge you to identify your problems and to discuss them openly and frankly. Disagreements with other judges is a characteristic of our profession that implies no disrespect and no lack of faith in the inherent strength of our institution. We must begin to talk about our problems before we can solve them.

Second, when you are considering possible changes in your procedures—as well as when you are deciding particular cases—keep in mind the teachings of the doctrine of judicial restraint. Consider whether, when, and how the special talent of judges—the thoughtful application of impartial judgment—should play a role in the decision-making process. And finally, I must note that although my remarks have indicated that proper management of a docket requires a court to treat some cases as having a greater importance or priority than others, distinctions that are made for administrative reasons are not applicable to the decisional process itself.

With regard to our primary responsibility, I would urge you to heed the advice of a truly great judge. In an interview a few weeks ago Justice Potter Stewart was asked if there was some opinion of which he was particularly proud. This was his answer:

> I worked hard on every opinion. I think they were all satisfactory. I think it's very important for a judge—any judge, anywhere—to remember that every case is the most important case in the world for the people involved in that case, and not to think of a case as a second-class case or a third-class case or an unimportant case. It behooves the judge or justice to apply himself fully to every case and to give it conscientious consideration.

Justice Stewart's example, as well as his written word, is a great teacher.

Notes

This article originally appeared in Volume 66, Number 5, November 1982, pages 177–183.

1. I wrote these remarks while away from my office and library. Thus, a few of my impressions about our docket have not been borne out by further research. Instead of rewriting the text, I have added a few documentary explanatory footnotes.

2. Of course, cases selected for review under the Court's certiorari jurisdiction are not the only source of backlog. This past year the Court exercised its discretion to grant more petitions for certiorari than ever before, but it also was required to note probable jurisdiction in 25 percent more cases than in any prior year.

3. This sentence needs elaboration in two ways. First, as a factual matter, I was mistaken. When I say "per curiam," I have in mind an unsigned opinion that decides a case on the merits without argument and does not merely remand for reconsideration in light of a recently decided case. The number of per curiams has oscillated over the past 20 years, and this past term's total of 20 was not unusually large. I should probably have stressed a more disturbing statistic—the number of divisive per curiams, those from which three or more justices dissent. The past term produced 10 divisive per curiams, whereas six prior terms I have examined (1951–1952, 1961–1962, 1965–1966, 1971–1972, 1976–1977, 1980–1981) have produced at most four.

Second, my choice of the phrase "ever increasing administrative staff" was unfortunate. I intended the term "staff" to include the justices' personal law clerks as well as other court employees.

4. Here my memory of this past term failed me. In fact, our dismissal of only two petitions for certiorari as improvidently granted was less than our annual average. The fact that this is a recurring phenomenon, however, provides added support for my central thesis.

5. 297 U.S. 288, 341–356 (1936).

6. *Board of Education, Island Trees Union Free School Dist. No. 26 v. Pico*, 102 S. Ct. 2799 (1982).

7. *Finley v. Murray*, 102 S. Ct. 1703 (1982).

8. 451 U.S. 259 (1981).

9. 50 U.S.L.W. 4544 (May 24, 1982).

10. 428 U.S. 364 (1976); on remand, 247 N.W.2d 673 (S.D. 1976). See also *Idaho Dep't of Employment v. Smith*, 434 U.S. 100 (1977), on remand, *Smith v. Department of Employment*, 100 Idaho 520, 602 P.2d 18 (1979) (state ct. originally finds that state statute violates federal equal protection clause; after reversal, state ct. construes statute to be inapplicable to facts of the case).

11. *Cooper v. Mitchell Brothers' Santa Ana Theater*, 102 S. Ct. 172 (1981).

12. *Pennsylvania v. Mimms*, 434 U.S. 106 (1977).

13. See also *Washington v. Chrisman*, 50 U.S.L.W. 4133 (Jan. 13, 1982) (state supreme court held that a police officer violated the Fourth Amendment when, after stopping a student, asking for identification, and accompanying the student back to his room, he entered the room

uninvited and without a warrant; U.S. S. Ct. reversed); *Minnesota v. Clover Leaf Creamery Co.*, 449 U.S. 456 (1981) (state supreme court struck down a statute that banned the retail sale of milk in plastic nonreturnable nonrefillable containers, but permitted such sale in other nonreturnable nonrefillable containers such as paperboard cartons; U.S. S. Ct. reversed); *Arkansas v. Sanders,* 442 U.S. 753 (1979) (state supreme court held that police violated the Fourth Amendment by making a warrantless search of luggage located in an automobile they had lawfully stopped; U.S. S. Ct. affirmed); *County Board of Arlington County, Virginia v. Richards,* 434 U.S. 5 (1977) (state supreme court struck down a county zoning ordinance prohibiting automobile commuters from parking in designated residential neighborhoods; U.S. S. Ct. reversed).

14. 444 U.S. 507 (1980).

15. 595 F.2d 926 (4th Cir. 1979).

16. *Board of Education of Rogers, Ark. v. McCluskey,* 50 U.S.L.W. 3998.25 (July 2, 1982).

17. The Freund Committee said: "We recommend creation of a National Court of Appeals which would screen all petitions for review now filed in the Supreme Court. . . .

The great majority, it is to be expected, would be finally denied by that [new] court. Several hundred would be certified annually to the Supreme Court for further screening and choice of cases to be heard and adjudicated there." Federal Judicial Center, *Report of the Study Group of the Caseload of the Supreme Court* (Washington, D.C., 1972), 18.

18. Perhaps "dramatically increased" overstates the significance of saving approximately one day each week for work on argued cases instead of certiorari petitions. The more important saving would, I believe, result from the selection of a smaller number of cases for plenary review.

19. *Federal Energy Regulatory Comm'n v. Mississippi,* 102 S. Ct. 2126, 2145 (1982).

20. In using the word "assign," I do not mean to suggest that the Supreme Court should seek to certify issues of statutory construction to a legislative committee. Rather, I am suggesting that the policymaking branch of the federal government might assign itself that task and an overburdened Court might do well to consider denying certiorari if a case raises only an issue of statutory or regulatory construction—an issue that could be resolved by another branch of the federal government.

Some thoughts on the Supreme Court's workload

William J. Brennan Jr.

As delivered at the Third Circuit Judicial Conference, September 9, 1982, Philadelphia, Pennsylvania

You doubtless have read of the concern expressed at the ABA and AJS meetings in San Francisco by Justices White and Stevens that the Supreme Court confronts a calendar crisis so severe as to threaten the Court's ability effectively to discharge its vital responsibility. Justice Powell also addressed the problem but in the broader context of proposals designed to lessen the burdens of the entire federal court system. I should like in these brief remarks to address the problems of the Supreme Court calendar.

First, what is the problem? Justice White identified it:

> During last term we granted review in 210 cases, which is 26 more than the term before and 56 more than two terms ago (and I may say parenthetically the largest number of grants in one term during my 26 terms on the Court). Apparently there were just too many petitions for certiorari that we could not conscientiously deny. Our docket is now full through February, next term, and will be completely full (only the March and April sessions remain to be filled) by the end of November if grants next term proceed at the same rate as they did last term.

> Of course this means that we shall not be current in our work; cases will be ready for argument and we shall not be ready for them. This is something new and disturbing ... The [problem thus is] not that the Court [is] not hearing all the cases that it [has] the capacity to hear but that it [does] not have the capacity to review all those cases that the system contemplated would be reviewed at the Supreme Court level.

Justice White asked, "Can or does the Court hear all the cases that must be reviewed and authoritatively decided if the federal law is to survive in the form contemplated by the Constitution?" For now, I think I'd say yes, it does.

It is true, as Justice White said, "that there is a finite limit on the number of cases that the Court can hear and decide with opinion in any one term." For more than 15 of my 26 terms, starting in 1956, the Court averaged about 100 opinions per term plus a few per curiams in argued cases. But since the 1970 term that number has inexorably crept up, first to the high 120, then to the 130s, and last term to 141 signed plus nine per curiam.

That didn't set any record—the 1975 term produced 151 opinions, 138 signed, and 13 per curiam. And since we schedule 160 hours of argument from October through April, it is clear that 150 is the maximum. Of course we could add another month of arguments and theoretically turn out 20 more opinions. But I suggest that the Court, as Justice White says, "should not be expected to produce more than 150 opinions per term in argued cases, including per curiam opinions in such case." There is a limit to human endurance, and with the ever increasing complexity of many of the cases that the Court is reviewing in this modern day, the number 150 taxes that endurance to its limits.

I suppose the solution to the question whether the number of grants can be kept under control and the calendar made manageable without rejection of cases that should be heard and decided depends (a) on what the Court can do for itself to avoid granting cases that should not be granted and (b) on what the Congress and the courts of appeals can do to minimize the necessity for granting review of some cases.

What can we do for ourselves? I must admit frankly that we too often take cases that present no necessity for announcement of a new proposition of law but where we believe only that the court below has committed error. But ever since the Congress enacted the Judges Bill of 1925, the Supreme Court has not been expected to take on the function of primarily—or even largely—correcting errors committed by other courts. As Justice White reminded us, in 1925 Congress was presented with the proposition that after decision in a trial court and after at least one review in federal or state appellate court, further appeal to the Supreme Court should be permitted only where issues of federal law important to the country were involved, or where further review was essential to resolve conflicts between lower courts on questions of federal constitutional or statutory law, which, by definition was to be equally and uniformly applicable in all

Judicature Volume 66, Number 6, pp. 230–235

parts of the country. "Absent these qualifications, one trial and one appellate review were enough."

It was this history that prompted Justice Stevens to remark, "It is far better to allow the state supreme courts and federal courts of appeals to have the final say on almost all litigation than to embark on the hopeless task of attempting to correct every judicial error that can be found."

And, too, we have made mistakes in granting certiorari at an interlocutory stage of a case when allowing the case to proceed to its final disposition below might produce a result that makes it unnecessary to address an important and difficult constitutional question. Last term's school library case is a paradigm example. It presented the question of whether schools boards were in any wise restrained by the First Amendment in the removal of books from a school library. The district judge held not and granted the school board summary judgment. The Second Circuit reversed on the ground that the case presented a genuine issue of fact as to the school board's motivation and therefore the case should be tried. Obviously, further proceedings in the trial court would either have clarified the constitutional issue or perhaps have mooted the entire case. Yet the Court took the case at the interlocutory stage, disposed of it by an affirmance of the remand for trial, and filed eight separate opinions without producing one that commanded the votes of a majority. Surely we should discipline ourselves to be more faithful to the *Ashwander* principle not to address constitutional issues if there is a way properly to avoid doing so.

Congress could afford the Court substantial assistance by repealing to the maximum extent possible the Court's mandatory appellate jurisdiction and shifting those cases to the discretionary certiorari docket. A bill to this end is pending in the Congress and every member of the Court devoutly hopes it will be adopted. Cases on appeal consume a disproportionate amount of the limited time available for oral argument. That's because time and again a justice who would conscientiously deny review of an issue presented on certiorari cannot conscientiously say that when presented on appeal the issue is insubstantial, the test on appeal. Policy considerations that gave rise to the distinction between review by appeal and review by writ of certiorari have long since lost their force, and abandonment of our appellate jurisdiction (leaving a writ of certiorari as the only means of obtaining Supreme Court review) is simply recognition of reality.

Can we perhaps decide more cases on the merits by denying ourselves the benefit of full briefing and oral argument? There is sentiment among some of my colleagues to do so. Because I wholeheartedly agree with Justice Stevens that "oral argument is a vital component of the appellate process," and have too often witnessed colleagues, who favored summary affirmance at the cert stage, change their minds after oral argument— and because I think further that the Court's favorable image in the eyes of both bar and public rests so heavily on oral audience before us—I have continuously protested against summary dispositions, unless at least all of us believe that the judgment below flatly rejects the controlling authority of one of our decisions. If the losing side commands the agreement of a single justice, it seems to me he's entitled to an opportunity orally to persuade others of us.

One of the Court's important functions of course is the resolution of conflicts in statutory construction or constitutional principles decided by the courts of appeals; a major segment of each term's docket is provided by such cases. Both Justice White and Justice Stevens offered some provocative suggestions for reducing the burden of such cases. "If the resolution of conflicting decisions is at the root of the problem," said Justice White,

> there is the option of creating new courts of appeal that would hear appeals from district courts countrywide in certain kinds of cases. For example, the Court of Appeals for the Federal Circuit, created by the merger of the Court of Customs and Patent Appeals and the Court of Claims, will hear all appeals from district courts in cases arising under the patent laws. Another court that hears all appeals from cases arising under specified statutes is the Emergency Court of Appeals. Courts like these, of course, bypass the regular court of appeals, but they eliminate the possibility of conflicts that normally would have to be heard in the Supreme Court.

That surely is a suggestion worth exploring. It does not foreclose Supreme Court review but removes conflict as the reason for review. No constitutional impediment occurs to me, although doubtless policy considerations might be a reason for congressional opposition.

Justice White offered still another and novel idea for reflection: "That is," he said, "to require a court of appeals to go *en banc* before differing with another court of appeals and to make the first *en banc* decision the nationwide rule." I expect that the court of appeals and district court judges here today might want to mull that one over a bit.

Justice Stevens' contribution is equally imaginative and innovative. If, he says, "as is more frequently the case, the conflict is over the meaning of an ambiguous statutory provision it may be more efficient and more appropriate to allow Congress to make the necessary choice between the alternative interpretations of the legislative intent." This could be accomplished, he suggests, by

> the creation of a standing committee of the Congress to identify conflicts that need resolution and to draft bills to resolve them one way or the other. If the source of the conflict is ambiguity resulting from an omission in a statute, it would seem to make good sense to assign Congress the task of performing the necessary corrective law making.

The problem I see with this suggestion is that it overlooks the role of compromise in the legislative process, compromise that often accounts for the studied ambiguity of legislative language, deliberately adopted to let the courts put a gloss on the words that the legislators could not agree upon. If the legislators could not avoid the ambiguity in originally enacting the law it might be no different if they attempted to resolve the conflict.

Justice Stevens also asked whether in any event conflicts of interpretation were necessarily a bad thing. He said,

> the existence of different rules of law in different sections of our great country is not always an intolerable evil . . . it would be better, of course, if federal law could be applied uniformly in all federal courts, but experience with conflicting interpretations of federal law may help to illuminate an issue before it is finally resolved and thus may play a constructive role in the law making process. The doctrine of judicial restraint teaches us that patience in the judicial resolution of conflicts may sometime produce the most desirable result.

I think there is already in place, and has been ever since I joined the Court, a policy of letting tolerable conflicts go unaddressed until more than two courts of appeals have considered a question. Indeed, Justice White has filed opinions in recent terms chiding his colleagues for being too tolerant of conflicts. I confess for myself that I doubt there is much more we can do along those lines.

But suppose, as the Commission on Federal Appellate Revision concluded a few years ago, that these various efforts failed to achieve a manageable calendar and "that at some point the percentage of cases accorded review will have dipped below the minimum necessary for effective monitoring of the nation's courts on issues of federal statutory and constitutional law"—what then? Justice White thought, "There are surely obvious alternatives, particularly if more fundamental structural changes are thought necessary to remedy the problem. Rather than one Supreme Court," he said, "there might be two, one for statutory issues and one for constitutional cases; or one for criminal and one for civil cases." That proposition of course would require a constitutional amendment, but in any event, I cannot see any crisis confronting us that would require so drastic a wrench of our constitutional structure.

Then there is the revival of the proposal originally made a decade ago by the distinguished Freund Commission to create a National Court of Appeals. As Justice White noted, the essence of that proposal was this:

> all certioraris and appeals would come to the Court as they do now. The Court would select cases for its own docket as it does now, but if there were other cases deserving of review that it could not hear, it would have the authority to refer those cases to a so-called national court of appeals . . . that court's decisions would be subject to certiorari review, but it was thought that only rarely would certiorari be granted in those cases. . . .

Justice White acknowledged that a bill is now pending in Congress to create such a court but says, "I see no great flurry of activity around it."

Justice Stevens opposes the suggestion of transferring cases for decision by the proposed national court of appeals, but he also opposes the suggestion that that court assist the Supreme Court in selecting the cases that will be set for oral argument and plenary review. This would be done by that court screening out seveneighths of the cases filed in our Court, leaving us to choose from some 400 to 500 cases the 150 or so that would be heard and decided. Instead of that system, Justice Stevens, in his words,

> favors the creation of a new court to which the Supreme Court would surrender some of its present power, specifically the power to decide what cases the Supreme Court should decide on the merits [Unlike the Freund Committee proposal] I would allow that

court to decide—not merely to recommend—that a certiorari petition should be granted or denied, and that court's decision to deny would not be reviewable.

I completely disagree with my respected and distinguished colleague. I dissented from the form in which the Freund Committee made the proposal and feel even more strongly that adoption of Justice Stevens' proposal would destroy the role of the Supreme Court as the framers envisaged it.

Justice Stevens believes that the screening function "is less important work than studying and actually deciding the merits of cases that have already been accepted for review and writing opinions explaining those decisions." Apart from the fact that the plan would clearly violate the constitutional provision establishing "one Supreme Court," and therefore require a constitutional amendment, I reject Justice Stevens' fundamental premise that consideration given to the cases actually decided on the merits is compromised by the pressures of processing the inflated docket of petitions and appeals.

I don't have time to demonstrate here why that premise is unsupportable. Suffice it for present purposes that my view that the screening function is second to none in importance is reflected in my practice of performing the screening function myself. I make an exception only during the summer recess when the initial screening of petitions is invaluable training for next term's new law clerks.

For my own part, I find that I don't need a great deal of time to perform the screening function—certainly not an amount of time that compromises my ability to attend to decisions of argued cases. I should emphasize that the longer one works at the screening function, the less onerous and time-consuming it becomes. Unquestionably the equalizer is experience, and for experience there can be no substitute, not even a second court.

If the screening function were to be farmed out to another court, some enormous values of the Supreme Court decisional process would be lost. Under the present system, a single justice may set a case for discussion at conference, and in many instances that justice succeeds in persuading three or more of his colleagues that the case is worthy of plenary review. Thus the existing procedure provides a forum in which the particular interests or sensitivities of individual justices may be expressed, and therefore has a flexibility that is essential to the effective functioning not only of the screening process but also of the decisional process which is an inseparable part.

Similarly, the artificial construction of the Supreme Court's docket by others than the members of the Court would seriously undermine the important impact dissents from denials of review frequently have had upon the development of the law. Such dissents often herald the appearance on the horizon of possible re-examination of what may seem to the judges of another court doing the screening work to be an established and unimpeachable principle. Indeed, a series of dissents from denials of review played a crucial role in the Court's reevaluation of the reapportionment question, and the question of the applicability of the Fourth Amendment to electronic searches. This history of the role of such dissents on the right to counsel in criminal cases and the application of the Bill of Rights to the states surely is too fresh in mind to ignore.

Moreover, the assumption that the judges of a national court of appeals could accurately select the "most review-worthy" cases wholly ignores the inherently subjective nature of the screening process. The thousands upon thousands of cases docketed each term simply cannot be placed in a computer that will instantaneously identify those that I or any one of my colleagues would agree are "most review-worthy." A question that is "substantial" for me may be wholly insubstantial to some, perhaps all, of my colleagues. As Chief Justice Warren said:

> The delegation of the screening process to the National Court of Appeals would mean that the certiorari "feel" of the rotating panels of that Court would begin to play a vital role in the ordering of our legal priorities and control of the Supreme Court docket. More than that, this lower court "feel" would be divorced from any intimate understanding of the concerns and interests and philosophies of the Supreme Court Justices; and that "feel" could reflect none of the other intangible actors and trends within the Supreme Court that often play a role in the certiorari process.

I repeat that a fundamental premise of Justice Stevens' proposal is that the screening function plays only a minor and separable part in the exercise of the Court's fundamental responsibilities. I think that premise is clearly, indeed dangerously, wrong. In my experience over more than a quarter century, the screening process has been, and is today, inextricably linked to the fulfillment of the Court's essential duties and is vital to the effective performance of the Court's unique mission "to define the rights guaranteed by the Constitution, to assure the uniformity of federal law, and to maintain the constitutional distribution of powers in our federal union."

The choice of issues for decision largely determines the image that the American people have of their Supreme Court. The Court's calendar mirrors the ever-changing concerns of this society with every more powerful and smothering government. The calendar is therefore the indispensable source for keeping the Court abreast of these concerns. Our Constitution is a living document and the Court often becomes aware of the necessity for reconsideration of its interpretation only because filed cases reveal the need for new and previously unanticipated applications of constitutional principles. To adopt Justice Stevens' proposal to limit the Court's consideration to a mere handful of the cases selected by others would obviously result in isolating the Court from many nuances and trends of legal change throughout the land.

The point is that the evolution of constitutional doctrine is not merely a matter of hearing arguments and writing opinions in cases granted review. The screening function is an inseparable part of the whole responsibility; to turn over that task to a national court of appeals is to rent a seamless web. And how traumatic and difficult must be the screening task of the judges of a court of appeals required to do major Supreme Court work without being afforded even the slightest glimpse of the whole picture of a justice's function.

It is not only that constitutional principles evolve over long periods and that one must know the history of each before he feels competent to grapple with their application in new contexts never envisioned by the framers. It is also that he must acquire an understanding of the extraordinarily complex factors that enter into the distribution of judicial power between state and federal courts and other problems of "Our Federalism." The screening function is an indispensable and inseparable part of the entire process and it cannot be withdrawn from the Court without grave risk of impairing the very core of the Court's unique and extraordinary functions.

You may rightly ask me then, what would you do to bring about the shrinking of the size of the calendar to manageable numbers? First, I would urge greater care by the Court in the selection of cases for review. Second, I would urge repeal by Congress of virtually all the Court's mandatory appeal jurisdiction. Third, I would urge an immediate study of the feasibility of Justice White's suggestion of creating new courts of appeals that would hear appeals from district courts countrywide in certain kinds of cases, thus obviating conflicts. Fourth, I would urge an immediate study of Justice White's other suggestion for minimizing conflicts—to require a court of appeals to go *en banc* before differing with another court of appeals and make the first *en banc* decision the nationwide rule.

But I would most emphatically reject all proposals for the creation of a national court of appeals, or any other court, to which would be assigned the task of doing the Court's work, whether decisional or screening. Adoption of that proposal would sow the seeds of destruction of the Court's standing as we know it. For remember, Justice Brandeis ascribed the great prestige of the Court with the American public to a single factor, "Because we do our own work."

Note

This article originally appeared in Volume 66, Number 6, December–January 1983, pages 230–235.

Caseload, conflicts, and decisional capacity: does the Supreme Court need help?

Arthur D. Hellman

Examining the Court's work, and workload, suggests we should give more thought to the need for—and structure of—the proposed Intercircuit Tribunal.

Congress is now giving serious consideration to legislation that would effect the most far-reaching change in the structure of the federal judicial system since the creation of intermediate appellate courts nearly a century ago. Bills introduced by Senator Dole and Congressman Kastenmeier, with the apparent support of Chief Justice Burger, would create an "Intercircuit Tribunal of the United States Courts of Appeals" that would hear and decide cases referred to it by the Supreme Court. Unless overruled or modified by the Supreme Court, decisions of the Tribunal would constitute binding precedents in all other federal courts and, with respect to federal issues, in state courts as well.[1]

Proponents argue that creation of the new court is necessary for two reasons: "to relieve the dramatically increased workload of the Supreme Court" and to "provide desperately needed additional decisional capacity for the resolution of disputes where nationwide uniformity is needed."[2] Curiously, although the problems perceived by the sponsors originate in conditions that can hardly be expected to disappear as the years go by, the bills now in committee would create only a temporary court composed of circuit judges who would sit on the Intercircuit Tribunal in ad hoc panels while continuing to serve on their own courts.

The premises underlying this proposal raise fundamental questions about the role of the Supreme Court in the American legal system and the extent to which one tribunal of nine justices can fulfill that role. In this article, I shall address those questions. I conclude that notwithstanding its impressive sponsorship, the legislation should not be enacted, at least in its present form. To the extent that it seeks to reduce the workload of the justices, it is unnecessary. To the extent that it seeks to promote uniformity in the law, it rests on assumptions that have not been proved; but even if those assumptions are correct, creation of a temporary tribunal would do little to foster uniformity,

while it would have undesirable consequences for the Supreme Court's performance of the tasks it would not delegate.

One preliminary observation is in order. During the past year, eight of the nine sitting justices have expressed concern about the Court's caseload and the management of its docket. This has led some observers to conclude that the justices agree that the caseload problem has reached crisis proportions and requires immediate legislative reform. However, the more important fact is that the diagnoses offered by the members of the Court are quite different and to some extent contradictory.

Justices White and Rehnquist think that limited decisional capacity is causing the Court to deny review in some cases that require resolution at the national level; Justice Stevens thinks that the Court grants review in more cases than are necessary. Chief Justice Burger finds a plenary docket of 150 cases a term—the current figure—to be so burdensome as to threaten a breakdown of the system; but in the eyes of Justice Rehnquist, it is well within the limits of the tolerable. The chief justice predicts an increase in summary reversals, especially in criminal cases; Justices Brennan, Marshall, and Stevens think that the summary reversal is overused even today. Justices Powell and O'Connor have spoken only in general terms about the Supreme Court's workload; their principal concern has been the proliferation of litigation in the lower federal courts.

This diversity of views provides a poor basis indeed for immediate structural reform. On the contrary, it only emphasizes the need for careful analysis of the Court's functions and practices before any legislation is enacted.

The workload of the justices

In considering whether the justices are overworked, it is necessary to look separately at the two tasks they perform: selecting the cases they will decide, and deciding them. Attention must also be given to the effect of the obligatory jurisdiction on the Court's workload.

Screening cases for plenary review

With the possible exception of Justice Stevens, no member of the present Court has asserted that the process of screening cases for plenary review has become unmanageable.[3] Nor would such an assertion be persuasive. Admittedly, the number of cases to be examined is much greater than it was two decades ago—4,417 in the 1981 term. But a caseload of that size does not impose nearly the burden that it would, for example, at the court of appeals level.

From Taft onward, the justices have emphasized that the function of the Supreme Court is not to correct errors in the lower courts, but to "secur[e] harmony of decision and the appropriate settlement of questions of general importance." [4] Thus, except for the cases that come to the Court on appeal—less than 5 percent of the total—the purpose of screening is not to determine whether there was error, or even probable error, in the court below. Rather, the Court considers whether the case presents an issue of "wide public importance or governmental interest." [5] Making that determination will usually take very little time, compared with assessing the probable correctness of the decision below.

More important, the vast majority of applications clearly do not meet the standard for "certworthiness" that the justices have articulated. A few years ago, Justice Brennan revealed that 70 percent of the cases were so obviously unworthy of review that not even one justice requested that they be discussed at the Court's conference.[6] More recently, Chief Justice Burger— who has been in the forefront of those arguing that the Court is overburdened—has said that two-thirds of the new filings are not only unworthy of review but "utterly frivolous." [7]

Perusal of the case summaries in *United States Law Week* confirms these perceptions. In one case after another, the party seeking review asserts only that the lower court abused its discretion or erred in applying well-established rules to particular facts. And those are the paid cases. Almost half of all applications for review are filed by indigent litigants, nearly all of whom are criminal defendants who have nothing to lose by filing petitions whether or not they present an issue appropriate for the Supreme Court.[8]

Deciding cases and writing opinions

The screening process thus constitutes a relatively small part of the justices' total workload. The more time-consuming task is that of reaching decisions and writing opinions in the 140 to 150 cases that do receive plenary consideration each term. Yet is is far from clear that a calendar of that size truly imposes an intolerable burden on the justices.

Under current conditions, each justice is required to write 15 or 16 majority opinions a term—barely two for each month that the Court is in session. Some of the cases will involve intractable social and political issues warranting extended reflection and research, but not all fit this description. In particular, by the time the Court resolves a statutory issue, the competing arguments should have been thoroughly ventilated in the lower courts and the law reviews, and the justices should be able to reach a decision and write their opinions with a minimum of agonizing.

This is not to deprecate the amount of time and effort required for the process of reaching and justifying decisions in the cases on the plenary docket. After all, the justices not only have their own opinions to write; they should also be giving careful scrutiny to the drafts prepared by their colleagues. And if caseload pressures become too great, review of other justices' opinions is likely to be the first casualty, thus reducing the opportunities for clarifying the language, sharpening the reasoning, or otherwise improving the final product through collegial consultation.

This analysis suggests that whether or not the workload has begun to overwhelm the justices, creation of a new court might still be desirable on a different theory: that the Supreme Court could then reduce the number of cases that receive plenary consideration and thus be able to produce opinions of higher quality— however one might measure that elusive goal. Indeed, that was a major theme of Chief Justice Burger's speech in New Orleans calling for creation of an intercircuit panel similar to the one contemplated by the pending legislation.

It might seem intuitively obvious that the justices would write better opinions if they had more time. Nevertheless, the available evidence indicates that the matter is not that simple. In the middle and late 1950s the Court was hearing fewer cases than at any other time in this century; but that was also the era when eminent scholars filled the law reviews with devastating criticism of the Court's craftsmanship. Not everyone agreed with those criticisms, but the history provides little comfort for those who see a smaller docket as leading to wiser adjudications or more illuminating opinions. More recently, the abortion decisions of 1973 were handed down only after an extended process of research, reflection, and deliberation; yet those opinions too have been subjected to vehement criticism, even by scholars who sympathize with the results.

In any event, before we can reach any conclusions about the burdens imposed by the plenary docket, we must consider the actions of the justices themselves. If the members of the present Court are truly overworked, they are behaving in some very strange ways. Consider:

- Separate expressions of views have proliferated in recent years to an extent never before known. In the 1981 term alone the justices issued more than 175 separate opinions.[9] It is understandable, and indeed desirable, that a justice would write separately when he or she cannot support the result or rationale of the majority opinion. But more than 20 of these separate opinions were written by justices who had already joined the opinion of the majority. In addition, there were half a dozen dissenting opinions by justices who had already joined another dissent. Strangest of all, there was one case in which the author of the majority opinion also wrote a separate opinion reversing the court below on a second ground, and another case in which two opinions were joined by different majorities of justices.[10]

- In recent terms, a major component of the plenary docket has consisted of criminal cases in which the lower courts had upheld the defendant's constitutional claims. In some of the cases, a state court had arguably rested its judgment on adequate and independent nonfederal grounds.[11] Other decisions appeared to involve little more than the application of established rules to a particular set of facts.[12] While a Supreme Court ruling would add something to the body of nationally binding precedents, the contribution would be marginal enough that an overburdened Court could deny review without concern that it would be missing an opportunity to significantly clarify the law.

- In other cases where lower courts have accepted a litigant's federal constitutional claim, the Court has reversed without hearing oral argument. These reversals have been accompanied by per curiam opinions, a few of which approach the length of many signed opinions.[13] Here, too, some of the cases have involved only the application of established rules to particular facts.[14] For the most part, nothing in the per curiam opinions has suggested that the particular situations are recurring ones, or that the decisions below reflect oft-repeated errors or a consistent disregard of the governing law.[15] Thus consideration on the merits could not be justified either from the standpoint of the Court's lawmaking functions or as a necessary exercise of its supervisory power.

- In the current term the Court ordered reargument on an important issue that had neither been litigated in the court below nor raised in the petition for review. As the dissenting justices pointed out, these circumstances make more work for the Court in deciding the case.[16]

Effect of obligatory jurisdiction

Assessment of the "workload problem" also requires attention to the fact that the Court today does not have an entirely free hand in selecting the cases it will decide. When a case comes to it on appeal rather than by certiorari, the Court has no choice but to decide the merits. The Court need not—and usually does not—give the case plenary consideration or write an opinion, but it cannot avoid the duty of determining whether the lower court committed error. In recent terms, about half of the cases decided on the merits have been appeals.

It might be thought that because most of the appeal cases are disposed of by summary orders without opinion, abolition of the obligatory jurisdiction would not significantly lighten the Supreme Court's workload. Study of the Court's practices, however, indicates that the continuing flow of appeal cases imposes at least three kinds of burdens on the justices.

First, the obligation to decide the merits of a case sometimes leads the Court to grant plenary consideration to appeals that would have been denied review if they had come up by certiorari. As the justices have pointed out, "[t]here is no necessary correlation between the difficulty of the legal questions in a case and its public importance." [17] As a result, the Court often feels obliged to call for full briefing and oral argument in appeal cases that are too difficult to decide summarily but not important enough to warrant review by certiorari standards. In the 1981 term, fully one out of every four cases on the plenary docket came to the Court on appeal. While many of the cases were worthy of review by certiorari standards, some—probably 10 or more—were not.[18]

Second, even if the issue presented by an appeal is one that the Supreme Court would ultimately want to decide, the particular case may raise it prematurely or in a setting inappropriate for a definitive resolution. Either circumstance makes the Court's job harder. If the issue has not yet been thoroughly ventilated in the lower courts, the process of reaching a decision and writing an opinion will be more difficult because the Supreme Court will be deprived of the benefits of "percolation." If the case is not an appropriate vehicle, not only will the opinion be harder to write, but the decision may not settle the issues, so that they will come back in somewhat different form and require additional consideration.

Finally, the obligatory jurisdiction adds to the Court's burdens even in the cases that receive summary treatment. Whatever the practice may have been before the Court announced that summary dispositions are decisions on the merits,[19] the Court today must give every appeal a degree of attention and thought that need not be accorded a certiorari petition. After all, if certiorari is denied improvidently, the issue remains open in all other jurisdictions, and if the question is truly worthy of review, it will return in another case. But if the Court improvidently affirms a case on appeal, the effect is to establish a nationally binding precedent and to discourage if not preclude further litigation of the issue.[20] Thus the justices must examine each jurisdictional statement with at least enough care to assure themselves that affirmance will not settle a question that they prefer to leave open.[21]

*****

Two conclusions emerge from this analysis. First, the Court's workload has not yet reached anything resembling crisis proportions. Second, before implementing structural change, Congress should take the uncontroversial and long-overdue step of eliminating the remaining elements of the obligatory jurisdiction.[22] Once that is done, we will have the opportunity to see how the Court manages its docket on a wholly discretionary basis. If, after a few years, the workload is shown to be truly burdensome, there will be no alternative to structural reform; but Congress, the bar, and the public will have had that much more time to consider the merits of various possible solutions.

The problem of disuniformity

To say that the Court's workload does not justify creation of a new tribunal is not to say that the justices could reasonably be expected to increase the number of cases that receive plenary consideration, and indeed no one takes that view. Thus the stronger argument for structural change rests on the assertion that "additional decisional capacity" is needed to secure uniformity and consistency in federal law.

To evaluate this claim, it is necessary to answer four questions. First, to what extent is there disuniformity in the law today as a result of the limited number of cases the Supreme Court can decide on the merits? Second, how has the lack of "appellate capacity" affected those who must conform their conduct to federal precedents—judges deciding cases in the lower courts, lawyers advising clients, and citizens carrying out their everyday activities? Third, how effective would the proposed new court be in reducing the existing uncertainty? Finally, how would the availability of the reference option affect the Supreme Court's performance of the work it would not delegate?

Unresolved intercircuit conflicts

In introducing the bill to create an Intercircuit Tribunal, Senator Dole asserted that the proposed court would "provide desperately needed additional decisional capacity for the resolution of disputes where nationwide uniformity is needed, many of which are now left unresolved because the Supreme Court cannot make room on its docket." In a similar vein, Congressman Kastenmeier stated that hundreds of petitions from the courts of appeals are denied review even though some "identify serious conflicts between circuits." The clear implication is that the Supreme Court is denying review in such a large number of conflict cases, with such a substantial impact on consistency in the law, that the need for additional decisional capacity has reached the point of desperation.

But where is the evidence? Where is a list of 50 cases in which the Supreme Court, during a recent term, has denied review despite the presence of a conflict? Where are 30 unreviewed conflicts? Where are 20? One searches in vain for any such compilation, either in the record of the hearings on similar legislation held in 1981 and 1982 or in the statements submitted on the Senate bill this spring.[23]

Within the Court, the most persistent advocate of the view that intercircuit conflicts remain unresolved because the Court "cannot make room on its docket" has been Justice White. A casual reader of the weekly order lists might get the impression that Justice White has identified a substantial number of cases in which the Court has denied review despite the presence of a conflict. But careful counting reveals that in the 1981 term Justice White published only 12 opinions dissenting from the denial of review on that ground. Two involved the same issue; two others involved issues that are scheduled to be considered in the 1982 term. And study of all unreviewed cases in the 1980 term in which Justice White filed a dissenting notation of any kind yields no more than 15 in which the decision below appeared to conflict with the ruling of another appellate court.[24]

On the basis of the available evidence, then, it cannot be said that the number of conflicts presented to the Supreme Court has, to any substantial degree, outstripped the Court's capacity to resolve them. At first blush, this may seem rather surprising. After all, during the last few decades Congress has substantially added to the body of federal statutes that require interpretation; the number of circuits has been enlarged; and the volume of appellate litigation has grown enormously.

But these developments do not necessarily bring about a proportionate increase in the number of conflicts. For one thing, the courts of appeals generally attempt to avoid intercircuit disagreements if they can conscientiously do so.[25] More important, as new issues arise, old ones become settled (through the accumulation of precedents)[26] or irrelevant (through developments in the law or in the activity being regulated).[27] Finally, as will be discussed more fully below, there are many issues that for one reason or another are just not likely to give rise to conflicting decisions. Thus, even though the United States Code may occupy an ever-larger space on the shelf, the number of questions on which the courts of appeals will actually differ may remain relatively stable.

Potential conflicts

Up to this point I have focused on unresolved intercircuit conflicts as a measure of the adequacy of the national appellate capacity. But the more thoughtful

supporters of the proposed new court argue that the desirability of obtaining a definitive resolution of a particular issue does not depend on the existence of an actual conflict. They point out that for those who must regulate their activities in accordance with federal precedents, the presence or absence of a conflict is almost irrelevant; the crucial question is whether there is an issue that is doubtful enough that the possibility of conflict exists. If conflict is possible, uncertainty is inevitable. And, as Professor Meador has suggested, "uncertainty about the ultimate meaning to be given statutory provisions can make the work of lawyers and administrators difficult and more costly to citizens and to government." [28]

Yet even when these considerations are taken into account, it does not necessarily follow that the focus on unresolved conflicts has been misdirected. At the least, the further we move away from an actual conflict, the less likely it becomes that a given case warrants a decision by the Supreme Court, and the more likely it is that the Court would deny review even apart from caseload pressures. There are two reasons why this is so.

First, the particular explanation for the absence of a conflict may suggest that a decision by the Court is unlikely to make a significant contribution to uniformity in the law. For example, if there are no other cases on point, the reason may be that the precise problem arises very seldom; if so, no other court is likely to confront the issue in the future. If there are several decisions, all reaching the same result, that may be because the answer is obvious, and any reasonable lawyer would confidently predict that future courts will follow in the same path.[29]

Finally, and perhaps most important, if there are multiple decisions that look in somewhat different directions without actually conflicting, the reason may be that the underlying factual contexts are so numerous, and the relevant legal considerations so varied, that no one decision—or six—could be "definitive." In short, a Supreme Court decision is most likely to make a significant contribution to uniformity in the law when the issue it addresses is both discrete and recurring as well as doubtful. Issues of that kind are probably the exception rather than the rule in a common law system.[30]

But even if an issue is discrete and recurring, the justices will often be well advised, from the standpoint of reaching sound decisions, to wait for an actual conflict before addressing it. A contrary voice—whether or not it is ultimately persuasive—can illuminate a problem in a way that a series of generally harmonious opinions will not. Sometimes the nonconforming decision will reveal flaws in the reasoning of the courts that considered the question initially.[31] At other times the unpersuasiveness of the later decision will provide reassurance that the first cases reached the correct result after all.[32] In either situation, the Court benefits from the judicial system's analogue to the adversary process—though with the additional and crucial element that the opposing perspectives come from two or more disinterested courts, each of which must justify its position through reasoning that will have the force of law. Moreover, by looking at the various decisions applying the competing rules, the Court can get a sense of how each works in practice and thus be in a better position to make an informed choice between them.

Some lawyers appear to assume that the desirability of speedy resolution and the probable gain from additional "percolation" are independent values that compete with and must be weighed against one another. But this is not necessarily so. The certainty that is supposed to come from speedy resolution may prove illusory if a premature decision raises more questions than it answers. At best the Court will forthrightly modify the view it took before the additional considerations were brought to its attention. At worst the Court will retain the rule but hedge it about with so many qualifications and subrules that the law is more confused than it was before. It is no accident that justices with widely differing views of the Court's proper role in the American system of government have lauded the values of percolation in both constitutional and statutory cases.[33]

Uncertainty and interstitial lawmaking

Those who argue that an Intercircuit Tribunal is needed to bring about uniformity and consistency in federal law bear the burden of showing that the Supreme Court's limited capacity for decision making has resulted in disuniformity and inconsistency on a large scale. They have not met that burden. But this failure of proof is not necessarily dispositive on the question of whether some sort of auxiliary court should be created. The Supreme Court may be able to resolve all ripe intercircuit conflicts. What it cannot do, to any substantial extent, is engage in interstitial lawmaking—the task of interpreting and elaborating upon its landmark precedents. But the essence of a common law system is that "no case can have a meaning by itself," [34] and that legal rules have meaning only as they are applied in a

series of cases. From that standpoint, advocates of the new court would be quite correct in arguing that one Court of nine justices can do at best an incomplete job of declaring the law.

The difficulty is that the common law process need not take place within a single court. The job of filling in the interstices of the Supreme Court's landmark rulings will be carried on in the federal courts of appeals and state appellate courts in any event. How much difference does it make that the United States Supreme Court can make only a limited contribution to the process?

Even on its own terms, that question may be unanswerable. But it is made even more problematic by the fact that the lack of a squarely controlling Supreme Court precedent is only one of the sources of uncertainty and unpredictability in the law. For example, the legal consequences of a particular transaction may depend on a well-settled rule that gives the factfinder wide discretion to reach different or even inconsistent results that will not be disturbed on appeal.[35] Administrative agencies not only have wide leeway in determining the "facts" upon which legal obligations will be based;[36] they may also modify or even reverse the governing rules without running afoul of appellate courts' willingness to defer to "expertise" or the lessons of experience.[37] Within a single agency or appellate court, different panels may view a given transaction quite differently while applying the same articulated rule of law.[38] Even when the Supreme Court addresses a recurring issue, its opinion may be so ambiguous as to leave the question little more settled than it was before.[39] Finally, life is too varied to accommodate itself to a necessarily finite number of precedents. Inevitably, there will be situations that do not fall within any existing rule; perhaps more commonly, situations will arise that are arguably governed by more than one rule, each of which may point to a different result.

These sources of uncertainty are magnified by the operation of the adversary system. In structuring a transaction or considering litigation, a lawyer must make an informed guess about the probable responses of the other parties. Those responses in turn will depend on such variables as wealth, aversion to risk, transaction costs, and familiarity with the law.

Taking these and other considerations into account, Professor Anthony D'Amato has recently argued that legal certainty actually decreases over time, and that "[r]ules and principles of law become more and more uncertain in content and in application because legal systems are biased in favor of unraveling those rules and principles." [40] One need not accept this extreme position to recognize that there are numerous forces that produce uncertainty in the law, and that these forces will continue to have a powerful effect even if the number of nationally binding decisions is increased from 150 to 200 or even to 300.[41] And as long as it cannot be said that actual intercircuit conflicts are going unresolved to any substantial extent, there is a real question whether a larger number of interstitial decisions by a national tribunal would contribute more than marginally to certainty and predictability in the law. At the least, Congress should wait for more evidence before creating a new structure to issue those decisions.[42]

Uniformity and the proposed court

If the evidence showed that the Supreme Court's limited capacity for definitive adjudication constituted a significant impediment to the achievement of uniformity in federal law, could the proposed Intercircuit Tribunal be expected to solve or mitigate the problem? There is good reason to believe that it could not.

The legislation now under consideration contemplates a court of 27 judges who would hear and decide cases in randomly composed panels of five. This is exactly the system that has led lawyers to complain of inconsistency and unpredictability in the decisions of the large circuits.[43] Nor is this surprising. A court that sits in small panels selected by lot from among a much larger number of judges can hardly develop any kind of institutional approach or recognized set of policies. The lack of continuity in the proposed Intercircuit Tribunal would thus make it difficult if not impossible to achieve the predictability and stability in the law that the design is intended to create.

Recognizing the force of these arguments, several witnesses at the Senate hearings have urged that the new court be composed of a smaller number of judges—seven or nine—who would always sit en banc. That would certainly be an improvement over S. 645 as it now stands, but it would leave untouched the more fundamental flaw in the proposed structure: its reliance on a system of ad hoc case referrals prompted by the need to resolve or perhaps forestall an intercircuit conflict. That approach assumes that cases presenting actual or incipient conflicts typically involve self-contained issues that can be shunted off for resolution by a separate court with little or no effect on the development of the law generally.

But federal law is not a body of distinct rules that operate in isolation from one another. Even a narrow, relatively technical question of statutory construction may depend on the application of doctrines such as the "plain meaning" rule, the weight to be given to an agency's interpretation of the statute it administers, or the significance to be accorded the views of a Congress subsequent to the one that enacted the law. By the same token, lower courts confronted with widely divergent statutory questions will look to the entire corpus of Supreme Court opinions for guidance on these matters.[44] At a simpler level, unclear or ambiguous language in one clause or section often must be interpreted in the light of other provisions of the legislation or with a gloss furnished by the language or law of related statutory schemes.[45] In either situation, the result is to broaden the range of precedents that must be taken into account when any of the various issues are litigated.

If a new tribunal were to issue nationally binding decisions in a selection of cases having nothing in common except the fortuity of an intercircuit conflict, the lower courts would be required to harmonize dual lines of authority in a way that might create more uncertainty rather than less. And the more deeply the new court moves into interstitial lawmaking, the greater the likelihood that its decisions will have arguable relevance for superficially unrelated kinds of litigation.[46] On the other hand, if the new court's docket is confined to square conflicts on narrow issues, the available evidence suggests that there would be very little for the Tribunal to do.

Is there any escape from this dilemma? One possible approach would be to have categorical rather than ad hoc referrals. That is, instead of asking the new court to decide a collection of unrelated cases involving actual or potential conflicts, the Supreme Court would announce in advance, preferably through some kind of rulemaking process, that the new court would be given primary responsibility for overseeing the development of the law in particular areas of federal regulation. Thereafter, all cases in those areas would be referred unless the justices found good reason not to do so. The Intercircuit Tribunal would grant or deny review in accordance with what it perceived the needs of the national law to be.

This arrangement would permit a substantial amount of interstitial lawmaking to be carried on at the national level in those areas of the law that the Supreme Court chose to commit to the new tribunal. And while the Supreme Court would be empowered to review the Tribunal's decisions by writ of certiorari, the assumption must be that review would almost never be granted; otherwise the whole system would be pointless. Thus the new court would provide all of the precedential guidance that otherwise would have to come from the Supreme Court, but in limited areas of the law.

What I have described is, in essence, the approach proposed several years ago by Dean Paul Carrington and other members of the Advisory Council for Appellate Justice.[47] On the surface, at least, it would involve a more radical restructuring than the bills now under consideration. But it would be more consistent with the traditions of the common-law lawmaking process; would minimize (though not avoid entirely) the development of inconsistent lines of authority applicable to the same cases; and would permit the performance of a task that clearly cannot be performed by the Supreme Court alone. Whether this kind of reform is necessary is another question; I am not yet convinced that it is.

Risks for the Supreme Court

In giving qualified support to Chief Justice Burger's proposal for a tribunal very much like the one contemplated by the pending legislation, Professor Daniel Meador suggested that creation of the new court "would involve little expense [and] carry virtually no risk of harm to the system or to anyone's interest." [48] I fear that this view is unduly optimistic.

I do not refer to fiscal costs or to the possible effect on the morale of courts of appeals judges who are not chosen for the new tribunal. What concerns me, rather, is the effect of creating the Intercircuit Tribunal on the Supreme Court's performance of the responsibilities it would not delegate. In particular, I foresee two undesirable consequences. First, the case selection process would become more complex and perhaps more divisive. Second, the Supreme Court would tend to become, even more than it is today, a court of constitutional adjudication—a result that would pose risks both for the decisional process within the Court and for public acceptance of the Court's role.

The case selection process

The current legislation contemplates that the Supreme Court would select the docket of the new court. For reasons I have set forth elsewhere, that is the only acceptable approach.[49] But there is no blinking the fact that it would entail additional work for the justices.

Admittedly, when seven members of the present Court gave their views on the Hruska Commission's

proposal for a National Court of Appeals with reference jurisdiction, none of them—even those who opposed the idea—appeared troubled by the prospect of having to select the new court's docket. But I cannot help wondering whether they fully thought through the implications of this arrangement.

Today, the justices have only three ways of handling the cases that are brought to them for review: they can grant plenary consideration; they can decide the case summarily; or they can deny review altogether. Reference jurisdiction would add a fourth option.[50] It does not take an expert in small-group theory to hypothesize that to expand the number of choices available to a nine-person committee in a large number of decisions would substantially increase the potential for dissension and even deadlock. In particular, the justices are unlikely to share the same view of the appropriate role of the Intercircuit Tribunal in the development of federal law; and even if they do, they will probably differ in the weight that they give to "percolation," both generally and in particular cases.

No doubt the Court could devise procedures or standards that would enable it to handle potentially divisive situations, but it is hard to avoid the conclusion that the availability of an ad hoc reference option would complicate the selection process and thus add to the justices' burdens.[51] A categorical reference system would probably operate more smoothly; to what extent would depend on the nature of the categories used.

Risks of delegating statutory issues

In any event, the more serious cost of creating an Intercircuit Tribunal lies in its effect on the Supreme Court's decisional work. What kinds of cases would the Supreme Court refer to the new court? Surely it would not refer cases involving issues of civil rights or other questions of constitutional law. Almost inevitably, decisions in these cases implicate large questions of social policy or turn on deep-seated ethical judgments about the competing claims of liberty and authority. As a consequence, it is highly unlikely that the justices would be willing to share their jurisdiction with another court, whatever its composition.

Moreover, it is on constitutional issues that differences in language, approach, or emphasis are most likely to convey conflicting messages to litigants and lower courts. For example, Fourth Amendment jurisprudence is confusing enough today with only one Court handing down nationally-binding decisions; to have a separate tribunal participate in the process would invite even greater disarray.[52]

Thus the Court is likely to refer only petitions raising narrow or technical questions of statutory construction. A few such referrals would do no harm, but the temptation would be great to refer all or most cases of this kind. The effect would be to restrict the Court's work largely to great issues of civil rights law, federalism, and the interpretation of statutes such as the Sherman Act or the National Labor Relations Act, which have almost the breadth of a constitutional provision. Indeed, it is quite possible that with a new tribunal to resolve some of the narrow statutory issues that today must be heard by the Supreme Court, the justices would take a larger number of constitutional cases for the purpose of correcting possible error.

For some commentators, a de facto division of the Court's work into constitutional and nonconstitutional issues, with the latter diverted to a new tribunal, would be a welcome solution to the caseload problem. Others will see it as but another step in a process that is already far advanced; in recent terms, only one-third of the Court's plenary decisions have involved pure issues of statutory construction, divorced from constitutional concerns. In my view, however, to move further in that direction would entail grave consequences both for the way in which the Court goes about its work and for the way in which that work is perceived by the citizenry.

Internally, the Court would lose an important source of self-discipline. As Justice Rehnquist has pointed out, "[t]o the extent that the Court must deal with statutory and other nonconstitutional questions, in which the permissible limits of adjudication are narrower, the . . . Court is kept on its toes and pressed to remain a classical court rather than a branch of government largely freed from the necessity for giving closely reasoned explanations for what it does."[53] Statutory cases serve another internal function as well: they remind the justices that the Constitution is not the only source of values and that the decisions of the representative branches of government are entitled to respect.

Routine statutory issues may also play an important role in preserving collegiality within the Court. Voting blocs that persist across a wide range of constitutional issues often tend to break up when less earth-shaking questions of statutory interpretation are presented.[54] The existence of cases in which the Court finds itself unified—or divided along unexpected lines—serves to moderate the tensions that are likely to build up

in cases involving the Bill of Rights, the Fourteenth Amendment, and the division of powers between state and federal governments.[55] Conversely, the loss of routine statutory issues might well serve to intensify and make more bitter the divisions that do exist among the justices.[56]

For the Court to cut itself off from narrow statutory questions would pose even greater dangers for the way in which the Court's work is perceived by legislators and other citizens. In a democratic society, the legitimacy of judicial review depends in no small part on a shared recognition that the Court nullifies decisions by the representative branches of government not because it is empowered to second-guess the wisdom or appropriateness of majoritarian determinations, but only, in Justice Harlan's words, "because [it is] a court of law . . . charged with the responsibility of adjudicating cases or controversies according to the law of the land and because the law applicable to any such dispute necessarily includes the Federal Constitution."[57]

The more the Court devotes itself to constitutional adjudication, and the less attention it gives to statutory questions of a more conventionally "legal" kind, the easier it is to lose sight of the underpinnings of the Court's role, and the more difficult it will be to defend the Court's intervention. And because constitutional decision making necessarily involves a large element of policy choice on matters not addressed by the text or contemplated by the framers, it is all the more important that the public be reminded at frequent intervals that the Court does, after all, decide questions of law.

It is true that a conscientious Supreme Court could minimize these dangers by keeping 30 to 40 relatively routine statutory cases for itself each term. Yet the more the Court attempts to retain a representative sample of statutory issues, the greater the danger that the two courts will develop parallel lines of authority that are arguably applicable to the same cases. Here again, categorical reference would reduce, though perhaps not entirely eliminate, the problem.

Some empirical evidence

Inevitably, debate over the desirability of creating an auxiliary court involves a large degree of speculation. We must first make predictions about how the Supreme Court would manage its docket if it had the option of referring cases to the new tribunal, and then, on the basis of those predictions, gauge the probable effects on the Court and on uniformity in the law. The latter inquiry must be almost entirely hypothetical, but as to the former there is one bit of evidence that may provide some clues.

By examining the Court's published order lists, we can identify those cases that, under the present system, came within one vote of the four required for plenary review. The inference can be drawn—though it is far from compelling—that these are the cases that would have been adjudicated at the national level if the Intercircuit Tribunal had been in existence. That is, if the total national decisional capacity had been enlarged through the availability of the reference option, these are the cases that would most likely have received either four votes for review by the Supreme Court or five votes for reference to the new tribunal.

Study of the order lists in the four terms 1977 through 1980 reveals that there were 119 cases in which three justices voted to grant certiorari or note probable jurisdiction but could not persuade a fourth justice to join them; thus, under the Rule of Four, review was denied.[58] The overwhelming majority were civil rights cases, and the largest portion of these involved issues of criminal law and procedure.[59] Only 27 cases in all four terms dealt with questions of federalism, general federal law, or jurisdiction and procedure outside the context of civil rights.

These findings lend at least some support to the views expressed in the preceding pages. They confirm the justices' strong, indeed overriding, interest in constitutional issues. We already know that the Court cannot expand the number of cases that receive plenary consideration, and that some statutory cases reach the plenary docket only because the Court feels obliged to resolve an intercircuit conflict.[60] Putting these facts together, it is quite plausible to suppose that if the reference option had been available, at least some of the three-vote constitutional cases would have received a fourth vote for consideration within the Court, while an equal number of statutory cases would have been routed to the Intercircuit Tribunal. The effect would have been to bring the Court one step closer to having a purely constitutional docket without necessarily increasing the number of nationally binding precedents on statutory issues, where the need for additional guidance exists if it exists anywhere.

Admittedly, these data are far from definitive. For one thing, there may well be cases in which three justices voted at the Court's conference to grant plenary review, but one or more of them chose not to make their position public. More important, the availability

of the reference option would itself change the justices' voting behavior in ways we cannot fully anticipate. Nevertheless, at the present time we have no better evidence as to what would happen if the national decisional capacity were to be expanded in the manner proposed by the pending legislation. And that evidence is not reassuring.

Nor is reassurance provided by anything the justices have said. On the contrary, statements by one member of the Court tend to confirm the hypothesis advanced here. In his speech to the American Bar Association, Chief Justice Burger predicted that "if there is not prompt action to give relief [to the Supreme Court], there will be a large increase in summary dispositions, particularly in . . . criminal cases when the lower courts have either misread or ignored our controlling holdings." [61] Presumably the Court would not allow these judgments to stand if the new tribunal were created; instead, it would give them plenary consideration. And if the pattern of recent years were to continue, these would be largely cases in which the lower court had accepted the defendant's constitutional claim.[62]

It would be wrong to read too much into the Chief Justice's comments, but they do suggest a line of inquiry that Congress ought to pursue. There would be no point in creating the Intercircuit Tribunal—or any auxiliary court—unless the members of the Supreme Court were in substantial agreement both as to the need for the new structure and on the use to which it would be put. Thus, at some point in the national debate, the justices will have to speak out. Would it not be desirable to ask them to tell us quite specifically how they would use the reference option—perhaps even to identify the cases that would be sent to the new court?

There would be no need for the justices to submit agreed-on case lists to Congress. Rather, they could provide the information in a series of individual or joint opinions dissenting from—or concurring in—the denial of plenary review. Opinions and notations of this kind are already part of the Court's regular practice; the added burden of specifying the cases that particular justices would send to the new court would be minimal. And only on the basis of such a record can Congress and the public make informed judgments about how the reference option would work and what its consequences would be.[63]

Designing a structure

Further research may well show that there are indeed more cases deserving resolution at the national level than one Supreme Court can comfortably handle. The task then will be to design a structure that will enlarge the national decisional capacity without compromising the values that have given the federal judicial system the stature it has today.

I have already argued that a rotating panel system is unlikely to foster uniformity and certainty in the law. Assuming that that problem can be avoided by having a court of seven or nine judges who would always sit en banc, two questions remain to be addressed. First, how should the judges of the new court be selected? Second, should the tribunal be established on a temporary or on a permanent basis?

Selection of the judges

Under the bill now pending in the Senate, the members of the Intercircuit Tribunal would be designated by the circuit councils of the various circuits. There are several difficulties with this approach. To begin with, it is anomalous at best to decentralize the process of selecting judges for a national court. The incongruity is particularly striking in view of the 1980 legislation that gave the circuits wide leeway in deciding how many judges would serve on the councils and how they would be chosen.

More than a lack of symmetry is at stake. Ordinarily, when new judges are selected for a court, the appointing authority considers, among other factors, the composition of the court apart from the positions to be filled. That kind of coordination would be impossible if the members of the Tribunal were chosen in separate proceedings in the various circuits.[64] Indeed, there is surely some irony in creating a court to promote uniformity, but having the judges selected by 13 separate groups of individuals, each employing its own standards and procedures.

Vesting the appointment power in the circuit councils also runs a substantial risk of fostering dissension and politicization among the judges. To avoid those consequences, many if not all of the circuits are likely to adopt some sort of lottery system for choosing the members of the new tribunal. In this they would be following the procedure used by the Ninth Circuit Court of Appeals to select its "limited en banc" panels. But whatever the merits of that system for declaring the law of the circuit, it would introduce a jarring element of arbitrariness, both in appearance and in reality, if a group of judges selected at random were to be given the power to establish the law of the nation.

For all of these reasons, it would be unwise to have the members of the auxiliary court chosen within the various circuits. How, then, might they be selected? Some proposals have vested the appointment power in the Supreme Court as a whole; others, in the chief justice alone. However, neither system is desirable. The former would not only add to the burdens of the justices; it would also provide a fertile ground for tension and dissension within the Supreme Court. The latter would give far too much power to one individual.

It is one thing to authorize the chief justice to designate judges for specialized tribunals such as the Temporary Emergency Court of Appeals or the Judicial Panel on Multidistrict Litigation. It is quite another to allow him to select the individuals who will be establishing nationally-binding precedents on a wide variety of recurring issues, subject only to occasional review by the Supreme Court.

Indeed, a more fundamental point is at stake. Recent events have reminded us of the inherent tension between majoritarian power and an independent judiciary. To allow judges—any judges—to select the members of an important court would upset the delicate balance that has been worked out over the years. By eliminating the role of the Senate and the president at the appointment stage, such an arrangement would severely weaken the majoritarian check that makes it possible for a democratic society to accept the exercise of vast lawmaking powers by judges who, once appointed, are not responsive to the political process.

It is no answer to say that because the new court would be dealing only with statutory issues, Congress could always overrule its decisions. Even if the court has misinterpreted the legislative will, forces such as inertia, deadlock, or the pressure of other business will often make it impossible to amend a statute. Nor is it adequate that the members of the panel, as circuit judges, will have previously been nominated and confirmed through the Article III process. Appointments to the circuit bench are generally treated as regional appointments; often they are the prerogative of a single senator. While the quality of the judges has been very high, the candidates simply do not receive the kind of national scrutiny that could be anticipated for appointments to what would be, in effect, an auxiliary Supreme Court.

I conclude, therefore, that the new tribunal should be constituted in the same way as all existing general-function federal courts: its judges should be appointed by the president with the consent of the Senate. That, indeed, was the recommendation of the Hruska Commission, which reached its conclusion after carefully weighing the alternatives. As already noted, however, the legislation now before Congress takes a different approach: the new court would be composed of sitting circuit judges who would be designated to serve for limited periods of time.

Proponents of this system place great emphasis on how little it would cost. And at a time when both political parties are struggling to reduce government spending, there is an obvious attraction in the prospect of increasing the national decisional capacity without creating any new judgeships. However, in the context of a federal budget that now exceeds $800 billion, the amount of money that would be required for an auxiliary court barely rises above the level of the trivial. In fiscal 1983 the budget for the Supreme Court came to about $15 million—less than was authorized for the maintenance, care, and operation of the House office buildings. If disuniformity is truly rampant in federal law, interfering on a large scale with the efficient planning of transactions and the speedy resolution of disputes, the cost of a new national court, smaller and less prestigious than the Supreme Court, would be a small price to pay to set things right.

In any event, it would be shortsighted to consider only fiscal costs. Even now, Congress is considering a recommendation by the Judicial Conference of the United States that 24 new judgeships be created in the courts of appeals to meet the demands imposed by current caseloads. Those caseloads are not likely to diminish in the years to come. Obviously, judges who are deciding cases at the national level can handle correspondingly fewer cases in their own circuits. Something would have to give: either circuit backlogs would grow, or decisional processes would be further truncated. Whatever the outcome, the system and its users incur costs, albeit not ones that would be reflected in the federal budget.

The preference for the designation approach also rests on the feeling that it would be politically unacceptable to give a single president the opportunity to appoint the entire initial membership of the new court. However, as long as at least one house is controlled by a party other than the president's, it should be possible, at the time of establishing the court, to reach an informal understanding that would require diversity and bipartisanship in the first group of appointments.

Last—and emphatically least—the designation approach may be seen as a way of mollifying the feelings of circuit judges who would otherwise perceive the new tribunal as eroding the prestige of their own courts.

But if the new court is created on the basis of convincing evidence that the present system is not working, it is unlikely that circuit judges would feel more than a twinge of regret at the passing of the old order. In any event, if the lack of national appellate capacity has reached the point of desperation, the judges' sensitivities surely should not be allowed to stand in the way of necessary reform.

Temporary or permanent?

The legislation now before Congress differs from the Hruska Commission's proposal in a second important respect: it would create only a "temporary" tribunal that would automatically go out of existence if Congress did not re-authorize it. The concerns underlying this approach are certainly understandable. The proponents seek to mute the instinctive opposition of the bar and the judiciary to the creation of additional structures within the judicial system. And what could be more reassuring than to provide that unless the new court has proved its worth, it will simply disappear into oblivion? But notwithstanding its surface appeal, I think that a "sunset" provision would be unwise.

To begin with, it is important to remember that Congress can abolish even a "permanent" court. That is precisely what happened with the Commerce Court: three years after it was created, Congress put an end to its existence, and thereafter the judges continued to serve on other Article III courts.

Of course, it must be conceded that the new court is much less likely to suffer this fate if abolition rather than re-authorization requires affirmative action by Congress. And in any event, proponents of the sunset provision will ask, what's wrong with an experiment? What harm can there be in giving the new court a trial run so that advocates and doubters alike can see how it will actually work?

I see three major drawbacks to the "experimental" approach. First, in the words of the Hruska Commission, a new court "would be significantly handicapped . . . if its decisions lacked the authority and credibility of an independent tribunal, the position of which was secured by a permanent charter."[65] Why so? The court would be exercising the power of review over judges who previously had to answer only to the United States Supreme Court. To make matters worse, under a system of reference jurisdiction the panel would be in the anomalous situation of not being able to enforce its precedents without the intervention of another tribunal. If by law the new court were scheduled to go out of existence on a specified day a few years in the future, the authority of its decisions would be rendered even more precarious. In contrast, if the new court were designed to be permanent, both judges and lawyers would have a much stronger motivation to treat it as a fait accompli and respect its judgments.

Second, a sunset provision would make the new court much more vulnerable to the combined effect of various human weaknesses. Making the tribunal only "temporary" reduces the incentive for its creators to build a solid record showing that the present system is inadequate. The weaker the evidence of need, the more likely it is that lower-court judges will resent the new court as an unjustifiable addition to the hierarchy that reduces the authority of their own decisions. And the more widespread that perception, the greater the difficulty the tribunal will have in securing understanding and absorption of its precedents.

Finally, notwithstanding what I have just said, "temporary" structures have a way of becoming permanent. That fate is particularly likely to befall the proposed new court because it will be impossible to know after five or even seven years whether it is achieving its purpose of reducing something as intangible as disuniformity in the law. Thus, unless the tribunal has proved an utter disaster, Congress is likely to extend its life. And given the pressure of other business, there will be neither time nor inclination to rethink any of the particulars. Unfortunately, a structure that is created for the short term is not likely to be satisfactory in the long run, nor is it likely to receive the same degree of care in its design. But that initial structure is the one that is likely to endure.

Thus, if Congress is convinced that the Supreme Court cannot provide all of the nationally-binding precedents that the legal system needs, it should establish a seven-judge court without a termination date.[66] The legislation could provide for a study commission that would come into existence six years after the new court begins operations, and that would be required, three years later, to make recommendations to Congress and the president as to whether the court should be continued. If the evidence shows that the court is not needed or is working badly, Congress would abolish it and designate the judges to sit on the circuit and district courts.

Finally, if political realities compel the inclusion of a sunset provision, the new court should be given an initial lifespan of 10 years rather than five. Without at least that much time, evaluation would be little more

than guesswork. Of greater importance, the limited lifespan need not and should not preclude Congress from providing for appointment of the judges by the president with the consent of the Senate. If, after 10 years, the court is not reestablished, the judges will be able to provide useful service elsewhere in the federal judicial system.

Conclusion

Arguments that the Supreme Court is overworked, or that it cannot resolve all of the issues that deserve resolution at the national level, comport easily with our intuitions. We are a litigious nation of 235 million people, and in an era when the scope and complexity of federal law have expanded far beyond what was contemplated by the framers, it almost strains credulity to suggest that one Court of nine justices does *not* need help in performing the functions assigned to it in our system of government.

Yet all would agree that changes in the structure of the federal judicial system should not be based on intuitions, but on convincing evidence that existing arrangements are not working. Legislation to eliminate the remaining vestiges of the Supreme Court's obligatory jurisdiction meets that test, and should be enacted without further delay. The same cannot be said of proposals to create an auxiliary tribunal to assist the Court in deciding cases. There is simply not enough evidence that the Supreme Court's limited capacity for authoritative decision making has significantly frustrated society's need for uniformity and predictability in the law. Moreover, too little attention has been paid to the possible adverse consequences of creating a new court.

The want of evidence is not less tolerable if the new court is established with a "sunset" provision. Indeed, the saddest aspect of the current drive for a "temporary" tribunal is that the experimental label can all too easily become a substitute for careful analysis of the need for the new court and the structure that would best satisfy it. And if that analysis is not undertaken before the tribunal is first created, it is unlikely ever to be attempted at a time when it can make a difference. Moreover, the shaky empirical foundation would itself increase the difficulty the new court will have in maintaining the authority of its precedents.

In the end, judgments about the need for an Intercircuit Tribunal or something similar to it may depend as much on one's perception of how legal rules operate as on the results of empirical studies. Thus, if it were shown that actual intercircuit conflicts were going unresolved on a large scale, the case for structural reform would be quite strong; but even then there would still be room for "arguments about how essential it is … that … particular question[s] be taken up and authoritatively settled at the highest judicial level." [67] And the more meager the numbers, or the larger the proportion that are no more than "sideswipes," the easier it will be to maintain that inaction by the Supreme Court pales into insignificance in the light of other sources of uncertainty in the law.

Nevertheless, it is a necessary first step to find out what the Supreme Court is not doing and how its limited capacity for decision making actually affects people's ability to plan and litigate efficiently. To forgo this inquiry is to run the risk of pursuing mischievous "solutions" to problems that exist only in the mind of the beholder.

Notes

This article originally appeared in Volume 67, Number 1, June–July 1983, pages 28–48.

1. The Senate bill is S. 645, 98th Cong., 1st Sess. §§601–607 (1983); *see Cong. Rec.* 129 (daily ed. Mar. 1, 1983) (remarks of Sen. Dole), S1947–S1948. The House bill is H.R. 1970, 98th Cong., 1st Sess. (1983); *see Cong. Rec.* 129 (daily ed. Mar. 15, 1983) (remarks of Cong. Kastenmeier), H1 192–193. Congressman Kastenmeier stated that Chief Justice Burger, as an individual, had "expressed support" for his proposal, and indeed the chief justice had endorsed a very similar suggestion in his midyear report to the American Bar Association. *See* Burger, "Annual Report on the State of the Judiciary," *A.B.A. J.* 69 (1983), 442. In this article, I shall focus primarily on the Senate bill, which has already been the subject of hearings.

2. See *Cong. Rec.* 129 (remarks of Sen. Dole), S1947–S1948.

3. Although Justice Stevens has argued that the Court is "too busy to give the certiorari docket the attention it deserves," his real complaint is not that the selection process imposes a great burden, but rather that his colleagues are too free in granting review of cases that he believes need not be heard by the Supreme Court. *See* Stevens, "Some thoughts on judicial restraint," *Judicature* 66 (1982), 177, 179 and *passim*.

4. Address of Chief Justice Hughes at the American Law Institute Meeting, quoted in *A.B.A. J.* 20 (1934), 341, 341. Whether the justices always adhere to this principle is of course another question—one that cannot be pursued here.

5. *Supreme Court Jurisdiction Act of 1978: Hearings on S. 3100 Before the Subcomm. on Improvements in Judicial Machin-*

ery of the Senate Judiciary Comm., 95th Cong., 2d Sess. 40 (1978) (letter signed by all nine sitting justices) [hereinafter cited as *Supreme Court Jurisdiction Hearings*].

6. Brennan, "The National Court of Appeals: Another Dissent," *U. Chi. L. Rev.* 40 (1973), 473, 477–478.

7. "Chief Justice Burger's Challenge to Congress," *U.S. News & World Report*, Feb. 14, 1983, 38, 40 [hereinafter cited as Burger interview].

8. Although the total number of cases on the docket has little significance as a measure of the justices' workload, the figures have been cited so often that two points about them deserve mention here. First, the rate of increase in the overall caseload has declined dramatically from what it was in the 1960s. In the decade preceding the Freund Study Group's report in 1972, the growth rate averaged just under 7 percent a year. Over the past decade the rate has been only about 2 percent. Thus, even in the 1981 term, which brought the largest number of new cases in the Court's history, the total was only 21 percent greater than it was in the 1971 term. In contrast, filings in the federal courts of appeals nearly doubled over the same period. Second, for whatever it is worth, new filings have fallen off in the 1982 term. At this writing it appears that the number of cases docketed will be about 200 under what it was in the 1981 term.

9. This figure does not include concurring and dissenting opinions less than a page in length.

10. See *Logan v. Zimmerman Brush Co.*, 455 U.S. 422 (1982); *Mills v. Habluetzel*, 456 U.S. 91 (1982).

It may be suggested that the proliferation of separate opinions, far from signifying that the justices are not truly overburdened, actually reinforces the conclusion that they are. The premise would be that the pressures of caseload make it impossible for the justices to hammer out consensus opinions, so that the only alternative is the separate expression of views.

But the available evidence does not support this premise. For example, Professor Dennis Hutchinson's study of the Court's decisional practices under Chief Justice Vinson points out that when the Court "was able or willing to debate issues internally at great length, … it frequently produced multiple opinions and judgments with no majority opinion." Hutchinson, "Felix Frankfurter and the Business of the Supreme Court, O.T. 1946-O.T. 1961," *Sup. Ct. Rev.* (1980), 143, 208–209. More recently, former Justice Potter Stewart, when asked shortly after his retirement whether he had any regrets about his tenure on the Court, expressed the wish that he had had more time to write his own dissenting opinions instead of joining dissents that "were written not exactly the way I would have written them." "Interview With Justice Potter Stewart," *Third Branch*, Jan. 1982, at 1, 9.

In short, there can be no doubt that the members of the Court have a strong desire to make known their individual views in the cases before them. The evidence suggests that with a smaller plenary docket the justices would satisfy this desire more often, rather than spend the extra time working with the authoring justice to produce a single opinion that embodied the majority's collective wisdom.

11. See, e.g., *Oregon v. Kennedy*, 102 S. Ct. 2083, 2092 n. 1 (1982) (Stevens, J., concurring in the judgment); *People v. Long*, 413 Mich. 461, __, 320 N.W.2d 866, 870 (1982), cert. granted, 103 S. Ct. 205 (1982).

12. See, e.g., *Marshall v. Lonberger*, 103 S. Ct. 843 (1983); *State v. Bradshaw*, 54 Or. App. 949, 636 P.2d 1011 (1981), cert. granted, 103 S. Ct. 292 (1982).

13. *See, e.g, Harris v. Rivera*, 454 U.S. 339 (1981); *Jago v. Van Curen*, 454 U.S. 14 (1981).

14. *See, e.g., Anderson v. Harless*, 103 S. Ct. 276 (1982); *Board of Educ. v. McCluskey*, 102 S. Ct. 3469 (1982). Justice Stevens believes that most of the recent summary reversals fit this description. See Ibid., 102 S. Ct. at 3473 & n. 4 (Stevens, J., dissenting).

15. Cf. *Bauman v. United States*, 557 F.2d 650 (9th Cir. 1977) (standards for mandamus).

16. *Illinois v. Gates*, 103 S. Ct. 436 (1982) (Stevens, J., dissenting).

17. *Supreme Court Jurisdiction Hearings, supra* n. 5, at 40.

18. See, e.g., *Blum v. Bacon*, 102 S. Ct. 2355 (1982); *Rodriguez v. Popular Democratic Party*, 102 S. Ct. 2194 (1982); *Greene v. Lindsay*, 102 S. Ct. 1874 (1982). In three other appeal cases, the Court unanimously reversed decisions by single district judges holding federal statutes unconstitutional. If the obligatory jurisdiction had been abolished, these cases would have gone to the courts of appeals, which in all likelihood would have upheld the statutes. In that posture it is questionable whether the cases would have merited Supreme Court review.

19. *Hicks v. Miranda*, 422 U.S. 332 (1975). *See* Hellman, "The Business of the Supreme Court Under the Judiciary Act of 1925: The Plenary Docket in the 1970s," *Harv. L. Rev.* 91 (1978), 1709, 1722–1723.

20. *See Sidle v. Majors*, 429 U.S. 945, 949–950 (1976) (Brennan, J., dissenting from denial of certiorari). Here and elsewhere I shall refer to dismissals for want of a substantial federal question as affirmances; certainly they are in effect. *See* Hellman, *supra* n. 19, at 1722 n. 57.

21. The obligatory jurisdiction also imposes another kind of burden: that of determining whether cases have properly been brought as appeals. Particularly in cases from state courts, the scope of the appeal jurisdiction depends on rules that are not always easy to apply. In the 1980 term, 80 state-court appeals were decided summarily on the merits; 47 others were found to have been improperly brought as appeals. Determining which cases fell into each category took time and effort that would not have been necessary if the obligatory jurisdiction had been abolished.

22. I recognize that the legislation would not eliminate every vestige of the obligatory jurisdiction, but the remaining fragments would be of such small moment, from the standpoint of workload, that for the sake of convenience I use the term without qualification.

23. The two most comprehensive empirical studies, both conducted nearly a decade ago, came to very different conclusions. Compare *Commission on Revision of the Federal Court Appellate System, Structure and Internal Procedures: Recommendations for Change* (1975), 93–109 [hereinafter cited as *Hruska Commission Report*], with Casper & Posner, *The Workload of the Supreme Court* (Chicago: American Bar Foundation, 1976), 87–92.

24. There were only five cases in which a dissent by Justice White explicitly adverted to the existence of a conflict. Another dozen or so cases involved recurring issues, and in perhaps half of those there appears to have been a conflict of some sort.

25. See, e.g., *Nygaard v. Peter Pan Seafoods, Inc.*, 701 F.2d 77, 80 (9th Cir. 1983); *Aldens, Inc. v. Miller*, 610 F.2d 538, 541 (8th Cir. 1979), cert. denied, 446 U.S. 919 (1980).

26. See, e.g., *Copper Liquor, Inc. v. Adolph Coors Co.*, 701 F.2d 542 (5th Cir. 1983) (en banc court overrules case that created intercircuit conflict); *United States v. Adamson*, 700 F.2d 953, 956–965 (5th Cir. 1983) (en banc court, overruling prior decisions, adopts rule followed in eight other circuits that had considered the question).

27. See, e.g., *United States v. Gelb*, 700 F.2d 875 (2d Cir. 1983) (circuits divided on scope of 1970 legislation; 1982 law eliminated ambiguity).

28. Meador, "Comment on the Chief Justice's Proposals," *A.B.A. J.* 69 (1983), 448, 449.

29. I put to one side the very serious problems raised by the federal government's practice of relitigating an issue without seeking certiorari even after its position has been rejected in several circuits. In this situation a Supreme Court decision would certainly make a significant contribution to uniformity in the law, but because of the government's litigation policy the Court does not get a chance to address the issue. See, e.g., *May Dep't Stores Co. v. Williamson*, 549 F.2d 1147, 1149–1150 (8th Cir. 1977) (Lay, J., concurring). It is true that the solicitor general, in deciding whether to seek review, probably takes into account the fact that the Court can hear only a limited number of cases; on the other hand, these issues do seem to reach the Court eventually. Compare *Hruska Commission Report, supra* n. 23, at 133–143, with *NLRB v. Enterprise Ass'n of Steam Pipefitters*, 429 U.S. 507 (1977), and *Bayside Enterprises, Inc. v. NLRB*, 429 U.S. 298 (1977). Thus it is not clear whether the problem (apart from government intransigence) is truly one of inadequate decisional capacity or is more a matter of timing.

30. Thus it is somewhat ironic that *United States v. Cartwright*, 411 U.S. 546 (1973), has so often been cited as

exemplifying the kind of question that should be settled at the earliest possible time without necessarily waiting for an intercircuit conflict. Perhaps it is, but the issue presented by that case—whether mutual funds shares in a decedent's estate are to be valued, for federal tax purposes, at the "bid" or the "asked" price—is of a kind that is relatively rare in the law: there are no shades of gray, but only black and white; and once the issue is decided in one case, that ruling will immediately resolve, without further inquiry, all disputes of a similar nature. Compare, e.g., *Florida v. Royer,* 103 S. Ct. 1319, 1329 (1983) (plurality opinion); *Hillsboro Nat'l. Bank v. Commissioner,* 103 S. Ct. 1134, 1144 (1983), discussed *infra* n. 39.

31. See, e.g., *Illinois v. Abbott & Assocs.,* 103 S. Ct. 1356 (1983) (Court unanimously affirms decision that rejected holdings by first two circuits to address issue); *Bayside Enterprises, Inc. v. NLRB,* 429 U.S. 298 (1977) (same); *Otte v. United States,* 419 U.S. 43 (1974) (Court unanimously affirms decision rejecting both of the two alternate positions taken by the circuits that initially addressed the issue).

32. See, e.g., *Coffy v. Republic Steel Corp.,* 447 U.S. 191 (1980) (Court unanimously reverses decision that declined to follow earlier holdings by two other circuits).

33. See, e.g., *Colorado Springs Amusements, Ltd. v. Rizzo,* 428 U.S. 913, 917–918 (1976) (Brennan, J., dissenting from denial of certiorari); *Maryland v. Baltimore Radio Show, Inc.,* 338 U.S. 912, 918 (1950) (opinion of Frankfurter, J., respecting the denial of certiorari); Burger interview, *supra* n. 7, at 39. It is particularly important to note that in the justices' eyes the value of the process is not limited to constitutional cases. See, e.g., *E. I. du Pont de Nemours & Co. v. Train,* 430 U.S. 112, 135 n. 26 (1977): "This litigation exemplifies the wisdom of allowing difficult issues to mature through full consideration by the courts of appeals. By eliminating the many subsidiary, but still troubling, arguments raised by industry, these courts have vastly simplified our task, as well as having underscored the reasonableness of the agency view."

34. Llewellyn, *The Bramble Bush* 48 (Dobbs Ferry, New York: Oceana, 1951).

35. See, e.g., *Pullman-Standard v. Swint,* 102 S. Ct. 1781, 1788–1791 (1982); *Commissioner v. Duberstein,* 363 U.S. 278, 287–291 (1960).

36. See, e.g., *Herman Bros., Inc. v. NLRB,* 658 F.2d 201, 209 (3rd Cir. 1981).

37. See, e.g., *NLRB v. J. Weingarten, Inc.,* 420 U.S. 251, 265–267 (1975); *Permian Basin Area Rate Cases,* 390 –U.S. 747, 784 (1968); *Texaco, Inc. v. NLRB,* 700 F.2d 1039, 1042–1043 (5th Cir. 1983); *Melrose-Wakefield Hospital Ass'n v. NLRB,* 615 F.2d 563, 567 (1st Cir. 1980).

38. *See, e.g.,* Friendly, "Adverting the Flood by Lessening the Flow," *Cornell L. Rev.* 59 (1974), 634, 655.

39. For example, in *Hillsboro Nat'l. Bank v. Commissioner,* 103 S. Ct. (1983), 1134, 1144–1145, the taxpayers and the government proposed competing formulations of the tax benefit rule. The Court rejected both formulations and concluded instead that the rule "must be applied on a case-by-case basis."

40. D'Amato, "Uncertainty," *Calif. L. Rev.* 71 (1983), 1, 1.

41. Chief Justice Burger envisaged a temporary panel that would decide about 50 cases a year. A full-time, seven-judge National Court of Appeals could probably be expected to hand down about 150 decisions annually.

42. Much has been made of the fact that in the 1981 term, for the first time in recent history, the Court granted review in more cases than it could hear in a single term. However, even putting aside the question whether all of the cases truly deserved consideration at the national level, the significance of this development should not be overstated. In the preceding term—1980—the Court had granted review in so few cases that it was unable to fill its argument calendar for the April session. (The figures for the 1977 through 1979 terms were also below the level of the 1971–1976 period.) The justices may well have responded by moving somewhat too far toward the other extreme. In the current term the number of cases granted review has again decreased. In any event, it would be short-sighted to place great reliance on year-to-year fluctuations in the number of cases heard rather than trying to assess the needs of the national law.

43. *See* Hellman, "Legal Problems of Dividing a State Between Federal Judicial Circuits," *Pa. L. Rev.* 122 (1974), 1188, 1208–1209 (citing lawyers' statements).

44. See, e.g., *Mid-Louisiana Gas Co. v. FERC,* 664 F.2d 530, 534–535 (5th Cir. 1981) (in assessing degree of deference due to agency order under Natural Gas Policy Act, court cites cases involving, inter alia, securities regulation, welfare, and truth in lending), cert. granted, 103 S. Ct. 49 (1982); *Montana Wilderness Ass'n v. United States Forest Service,* 655 F.2d 951, 957 (9th Cir. 1981) (in construing Alaska Lands Act, court relies on Supreme Court decision interpreting Freedom of Information Act), cert. denied, 455 U.S. 989 (1982); *Leist v. Simplot,* 638 F.2d 283, 319, 327 (2d Cir. 1980) (majority and dissent differ on implications to be drawn from Supreme Court decision interpreting different statute), aff'd, 102 S. Ct. 1825 (1982).

45. See, e.g., *United States v. Stauffer Chemical Co.,* 684 F.2d 1174, 1187–1188 (6th Cir. 1982) (Clean Air Act and Clean Water Act), cert. granted, 51 U.S.L.W. 3756 (U.S. Apr. 18, 1983).

46. Compare, e.g., *Coffy v. Republic Steel Corp.,* 447 U.S. 191 (1980) (resolving conflict in interpretation of Vietnam Era Veterans' Readjustment Assistance Act; decision has been cited almost exclusively in cases involving veterans' reemployment rights), with *Vermont Yankee Nuclear Power Corp. v. Natural Resources Defense Council, Inc.,* 435 U.S. 519 (1978) (reaffirming and applying precedents on

scope of review of agency action; decision cited in wide variety of administrative law cases).

47. *See* Carrington, Meador, and Rosenberg, *Justice on Appeal* (St. Paul, Minn.: West, 1976), 215–216; Hufstedler, "Courtship and Other Legal Arts," *A.B.A. J.* 60 (1974), 545, 547.

48. Meador, *supra* n. 28, at 449.

49. Hellman, "How Not to Help the Supreme Court," *A.B.A. J.* 69 (1983), 750.

50. In fact, the pending legislation would actually add two new options: referring the case with directions to decide it, or referring the case and giving the new court discretion whether to decide it.

51. Some of the potential complications could be avoided if cases could be referred to the new tribunal only on the affirmative vote of six justices, rather than the five contemplated by the current Senate bill.

52. For this reason, not only disarray but chaos would likely result if the Intercircuit Tribunal (or any other auxiliary court) were given direct jurisdiction to review state-court judgments resting on federal law, as some have suggested. Under a system of reference jurisdiction, the Supreme Court at least has the ability to limit the issues the new court would address; if direct appeals were permitted, the only safeguard against inconsistency would be Supreme Court review of the new court's decisions—an additional burden that would defeat one of the purposes of the enterprise.

53. Rehnquist, "Whither the Courts," *A.B.A. J.* 60 (1974), 787, 790. Dean Terrance Sandalow of the University of Michigan Law School has expressed similar concerns. *See* 2 Commission on Revision of the Federal Court Appellate System, Hearings Second Phase 739–740 (1975).

54. For example, in the 1981 term, Chief Justice Burger and Justice Brennan invariably took opposing positions when the Court divided 5–4 on civil rights issues, but they found themselves on the same side in two cases where matters of general federal law were resolved by 5–4 votes.

55. In the 1981 term, the Court was unanimous in only 25 percent of the civil rights cases decided on the merits, but in the general federal law segment of the docket the figure was 40 percent.

56. I am indebted to Professor David L. Shapiro for bringing this point to my attention.

57. *Mackey v. United States*, 401 U.S. 667, 678 (1971) (Harlan, J., concurring and dissenting).

58. This figure excludes cases in which Justices Brennan, Stewart, and Marshall would have reversed obscenity convictions, along with a few cases in which the dissenting justices would have vacated the judgment below for reconsideration in light of an intervening Supreme Court decision or other development.

Of the 119 cases, 28 came before the Court on appeal, thus the dissents might well have rested on an unwilling-

ness to affirm rulings of dubious correctness, rather than a belief that the cases warranted consideration by the Supreme Court. This interpretation is supported by the fact that in 15 of the appeal cases, one of the three votes for plenary consideration came from Justice Stevens, who takes a very narrow view of the Court's certiorari function and never notes his dissent from the denial of discretionary review.

59. In two-thirds of the cases in which the lower court had rejected a civil rights claim, Justices Brennan and Marshall provided two of the three votes for review. In two-thirds of the cases upholding the claim, Chief Justice Burger and Justice Rehnquist were among the three dissenters.

60. See *Hruska Commission Report, supra* n. 23, at 182 (letter from Justice White).

61. Burger, *supra* n. 1, at 455.

62. See also *Massachusetts v. Podgurski*, 103 S. Ct. 1167 (1983) (Burger, C. J., dissenting from denial of certiorari): "In my view, only the finite limitations of the Court's time preclude our granting review of this case. I would grant certiorari and summarily reverse the judgment of the Supreme Judicial Court of Massachusetts [upholding the defendant's Fourth Amendment claim]." *See also* Stevens, *supra* n. 3, at 179–180.

63. The need for this information is underscored by consideration of the differing views expressed by Chief Justice Burger and Justice Rehnquist. Both have endorsed the idea of an intercircuit tribunal, and both envision sending 35 to 50 cases a year to the new court. However, the chief justice would use the reference option to reduce the Supreme Court's own docket to about 100 cases a year, while Justice Rehnquist would retain the present level of 150. Since a plenary docket of 100 cases would be just about filled by the civil rights and federalism caseloads of recent years, the chief justice's approach would almost certainly bring about the results hypothesized in the text: a Supreme Court devoted almost entirely to constitutional litigation, and little if any increase in the number of nationally binding decisions on statutory issues. Justice Rehnquist's approach might or might not have those consequences; that would depend on how many constitutional cases were heard by the Supreme Court in the place of statutory cases sent to the new tribunal. What the full Court would do, we do not know. But of the 55 cases in which Justice Rehnquist dissented from the denial of plenary review in the 1977–1980 terms, 41 involved constitutional issues.

64. For example, as Professor A. Leo Levin pointed out in his statement to a Senate subcommittee, it would probably be a good idea to have some senior judges on the new court, but it would not be desirable if all of the members of the court had senior status. Under the system contemplated by the pending legislation it would be impossible to assure an appropriate balance.

65. *Hruska Commission Report, supra* n. 23, at 31.

66. Seven is preferable to nine because it distinguishes the new tribunal from the Supreme Court, and because a smaller number of judges can work together more easily. Certainly no showing has been made that the volume of work destined for the court would require more than seven full-time judges.

67. *National Court of Appeals Act: Hearings Before the Subcomm. on Improvements in Judicial Machinery of the Senate Comm. on the Judiciary,* 94th Cong., 2d Sess. (1976), 190–191 (statement of Prof. Rosenberg).

The Rehnquist Court's shrinking plenary docket

David M. O'Brien

Changes in the Supreme Court's composition and case selection process help explain why only about 1 percent of the cases on the docket now receive plenary consideration.

The "incredibly shrinking" plenary docket of the Supreme Court has drawn considerable attention. In the 1995 and 1996 terms, the Court heard only 75 hours of oral arguments and decided just 90 cases by written opinions each term, half the number of a decade ago. Moreover, the total docket has grown rather steadily, reaching more than 8,000 cases in the 1994 term before falling slightly to 7,602 cases in the 1996 term. Yet, since William H. Rehnquist became chief justice in 1986, fewer and fewer cases have been granted annually. Barely 1 percent of the cases now on the docket receive plenary consideration.

Even some justices are "amazed" [1] by the trend. Prior to arriving at the Court in 1990, Justice David H. Souter noticed the number had "come down significantly from the historical highs," which reached 184 decisions in the 1981 and 1983 terms. On the high bench, he found there had not been a conscious decision to reduce the number. "It had in fact just happened."

Justice Souter also considered possible explanations. All were factors external to the Court. Presidential vetoes of legislation by Ronald Reagan and George Bush, according to Justice Souter, may have resulted in "a diminishing supply of new statutes . . . that cried out for some immediate and speedy" interpretation. As for the rights of the accused, he observed that the Fourth Amendment's "basic standards . . . are products of the 60s and the 70s and the 80s." Finally, he speculated that, after 12 years of Republican judicial appointments, the Rehnquist Court had found less disagreement with the lower federal courts because of "a diminished level of philosophical division within the federal courts from which so much of the conflicting opinions tend to arise."

Other external factors may also have played a part. Notably, the Court's discretionary jurisdiction was expanded with the 1988 Act to Improve the Administration of Justice. Virtually all non-discretionary appellate jurisdiction was eliminated. Afterwards the plenary docket did decline. But, as Figure 1 shows, the docket started declining before that.[2]

Factors internal to the Court were undoubtedly decisive. Specifically, fluctuations in the plenary docket register changes in the Court's composition and case selection process. The data and analysis presented here shows that certain members of the Burger Court were predisposed to grant cases review, and thereby inflated the plenary docket in the 1970s and early 1980s. The plenary docket jumped in the 1971 term to more than 170 cases, remaining in that range for the rest of the decade. Beginning in the 1981 term, the docket reached its height of more than 180 cases per term. Following the retirements of Chief Justice Warren E. Burger at the end of the 1985 term and Justice Lewis F. Powell Jr. at the end of the 1986 term, however, the plenary docket gradually declined and then fell more sharply following other retirements in the early 1990s.

The increase in the number of granted cases in the 1970s and early 1980s also appears directly related to changes in the Court's operation made early in Chief Justice Burger's tenure. One important change he persuaded the others to make was in the oral argument calendar. Prior to 1970, attorneys in cases granted oral argument were each given one hour to present arguments. In 1970, the time allotted each side was reduced to 30 minutes. Instead of hearing 12 cases during a two week oral argument session, the justices went to hearing 12 cases in three days. Accordingly, the number of orally argued cases rose from 144 to 151 to 177 during the 1969, 1970, and 1971 terms.

Join-3 votes

Besides increasing the space on the oral argument calendar came another change—a change in the justices' voting practice in granting cases. In the early 1970s Chief Justice Burger and some other justices began casting "join-3" votes rather than simply voting to grant or deny petitions for certiorari. Because earlier in this century the Court adopted the informal "Rule of Four"—namely, that at least four justices must agree that a case merits review—a join-3 vote is a vote to pro-

Figure 1. Cases granted plenary review, 1968–1995

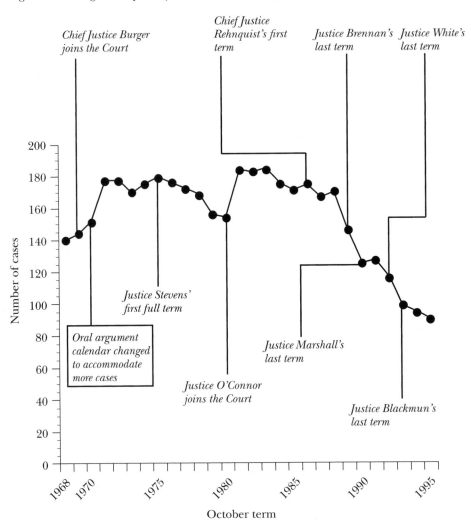

vide a fourth vote if others vote to grant review, but is otherwise considered as voting to deny. The introduction of join-3 votes, arguably, contributed to the Court's taking more cases by lowering the threshold for granting review established by the Rule of Four.

In response to Congress's expansion of the Court's discretionary jurisdiction with the Judiciary Act of 1925, the Rule of Four was adopted in order to ensure important cases would still be granted. At first exceptions were made, but by Earl Warren's chief justiceship (1953–1969), the Rule of Four was firmly in place; his docket books record no join-3 votes.

Although the Rule of Four operates in only a fraction of the cases on the total docket, the percentage of cases granted on that basis is not insignificant. In 1982,

Justice John Paul Stevens concluded that between 20 to 30 percent of the plenary docket was typically granted on only four votes and that those "are significant percentages."[3] He did so after reviewing Justice Harold Burton's docket books and determining that during 1946–1947 about 25 percent of the cases granted had the support of no more than four justices. Based on his docket books, he reported that no more than four votes resulted in granting between 23 and 30 percent of the cases in the 1979–1981 terms. A review of Justice Thurgood Marshall's docket book for the 1990 term reveals, likewise, that 22 percent of the granted cases had only four votes.

In 1982, Justice Stevens thus proposed adopting a "Rule of Five." He did so as an alternative to Chief

Justice Burger's proposal for the creation of a national appellate tribunal as a solution to the Court's workload problems. Abandoning the Rule of Four, Justice Stevens pointed out, would eliminate as much as a quarter of the cases granted review.

In retrospect, Justice Stevens's diagnosis of the Court's workload problem was right on the mark: the justices simply voted to grant too many cases. But at the time, he did not mention that other justices cast join-3 votes. Nonetheless, he had clearly identified the main cause of the Court's workload problem: the Rule of Four no longer imposed the kind of self-restraint it previously had. The propensity of some justices to cast join-3 votes lowered the threshold imposed by the Rule of Four for granting cases, thereby inflating plenary docket.

While the origin of join-3 votes remains unclear, such votes were not recorded prior to Burger's chief justiceship. Justice Harry A. Blackmun, who came aboard in 1970, recalls neither who began the practice nor any "definite discussion about the use of the vote." Neither does Chief Justice Rehnquist have a clear recollection of the origin of such votes. Whatever their origin, join-3 votes were established by the time Justice Stevens joined the Court in 1975. One possible explanation is that in leading conferences Chief Justice Burger began voting to join three, and other justices did the same. Within a few years, join-3 votes became almost routine. After the oral argument calendar was changed, Chief Justice Burger may have felt pressures to fill an expanded plenary docket. In addition, he may have done so because his discussion of cases was often vague and unclear.

Still, two other factors may bear on the casting of join-3 votes. First, following Justice Blackmun's appointment, Justices Powell and Rehnquist joined the Court in 1971. They came aboard with no prior judicial experience, though Rehnquist clerked for Justice Robert H. Jackson in 1952–1953. They arrived after the oral argument calendar was expanded and Chief Justice Burger had already made the rising caseload a major concern. In 1971 he persuaded Harvard Law School professor Paul Freund to head a study group on the Court's workload problems. The increasing size of the total docket and the declining percentage of cases given plenary review caused concerns about the Court's supervisory capacity and may have inclined some justices to vote to grant review.

Second, in response to the "caseload crisis" in 1972, at Justice Powell's suggestion, a majority of the justices agreed to pool their law clerks and to have them write memos on incoming petitions for certiorari and appeals. Traditionally, each justice received the briefs in all cases. However, beginning with Chief Justice William Howard Taft (1921–1930), the justices deferred to the chief justice and his law clerks on which unpaid (in forma pauperis) cases would be discussed at conference. During the chief justiceship of Harlan Fiske Stone (1941–1946), his law clerks' memos on unpaid cases circulated to each justice. That remained the practice until Chief Justice Burger claimed that his chambers could no longer carry that burden. Hence, the creation of the "cert pool."

Noting votes and dissents

The creation of the cert pool provoked controversy within the Court. The four most senior and liberal justices—William O. Douglas, Potter Stewart, William J. Brennan Jr., and Thurgood Marshall—refused to join. Justice Douglas, in particular, adamantly opposed on the grounds that petitions would receive inadequate attention from the justices. During the 1972 term, as senior associate, he began systematically noting his votes to grant petitions and his dissents from denial of review. Notably, his dissents from denial increased almost three-fold from the 1969 term to the 1973 term.[4] Few justices followed his practice. One who did was Justice Byron White, who in 1973 also began noting his votes to grant cases and dissents from denial. As Figure 2 shows, he did so throughout the rest of his career. He also wrote longer dissents from the denial of cases in which he identified a conflict among federal circuit courts or between state supreme court rulings. Not surprisingly, his notations increased as the plenary docket shrank.

What Figure 2 does not reveal is no less important. In the first three terms, 1973 to 1975, in which Justice White noted votes to grant cert, he was joined in 18 out of 24 cases by two other justices. The percentage remained high throughout the decade: during the 1976–1980 terms, 22 percent (183 out of the 818 cases denied) had dissents joined by three justices. Justices Brennan and Marshall often dissented together, but Justices Stewart, White, Powell, and Blackmun tended to join dissents from denial as well.

The practice of noting votes to grant and dissents from denials is strategic, particularly when joined by other justices. In this way, especially by circulating drafts of proposed dissents, justices may persuade others to reconsider votes to grant cases otherwise denied. In short, the practice of noting votes to grant and dis-

Figure 2. Granted and additional cases Justice White would have added, 1968–1995

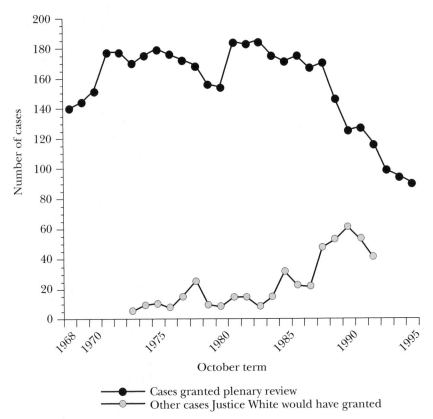

Cases granted plenary review
Other cases Justice White would have granted

senting from the denial of cert encouraged or rein-forced the practice of casting join-3 votes. In other words, Chief Justice Burger and others may have voted to join-3 in anticipation of such notations and dissents from the denial of review.

Regardless of the exact origin of join-3 votes, the practice of casting such votes became accepted. Fur-thermore, as Figure 3 shows, some justices cast an extraordinary share of such votes, whereas others rarely did. In the 1980s, Justice Blackmun led in join-3 votes. By comparison, Justice Stevens never cast such a vote. Other justices fell somewhere between. Figure 3 is based on data from Justice Marshall's bench memos, recording votes on cases granted during the 1979 to 1990 terms.[5] There are 1,556 memos on cases in which oral arguments were heard, and of those, join-3 votes were cast in 408 (26 percent).

More specifically, 192 cases (12 percent) were placed on the plenary docket on the basis of less than four votes to grant plus one or more join-3 votes; some were granted on the basis of only two votes to grant and

two or more join-3 votes. Notably, Justice Blackmun cast join-3 votes in 55 percent of the cases granted on less than four firm votes to grant. Justice Sandra Day O'Connor followed with 21.8 percent, Chief Justice Burger in 12.5 percent, and Justice White in 11.4 per-cent. Justices Powell and Rehnquist each cast 8.8 per-cent. The point is that had these justices not cast join-3 votes and the Rule of Four held, the plenary docket would have been reduced by 12 percent and, possibly, as much as 26 percent.

The shrinking docket

The key to the Rehnquist Court's shrinking docket in the 1990s, therefore, may be found in the Burger Court's responses to its rising caseload. Besides enlarg-ing the plenary docket by changing the oral argument calendar, the Burger Court no longer strictly adhered to the Rule of Four, thereby sacrificing some control over what and how much to decide. After an initial increase in the early 1970s, the number of cases annu-ally decided rose again following the 1981 appoint-

Figure 3. Justices casting join-3 votes, 1979–1990

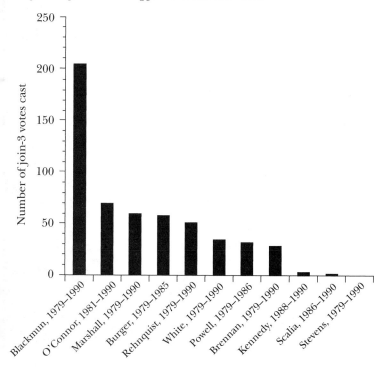

Concerns about the cert pool have grown because, with the exception of Justice Stevens, every justice appointed during the last two decades joined the pool. However, several problems arise with hypothesizing that the increasing number of justices belonging to the pool produces less scrutiny of cert petitions and results in granting fewer cases.

On the one hand, the justices not participating in the cert pool differ in their attention to petitions. Justice Douglas quickly perused them, while Justice Brennan tried to review each but generally relied on his clerks' memos. Justice Stevens relies entirely on his clerks' screening and does "not even look at the papers in over 80 percent of the cases that are filed." In short, there is no evidence that justices not in the cert pool give more attention to petitions than those in the pool. In other words, independent review need not guarantee searching review. So, too, those in the cert pool undoubtedly vary in the amount of time and attention they give to cert memos and petitions. At the beginning of his service, for instance, Justice Scalia found it necessary to read only the memos on cases the justices agreed to carry over for another conference discussion.

On the other hand, the chambers of justices participating in the cert pool might actually give more attention to case selection. Although only one pool memo on each case circulates among the eight chambers, most of the justices in the pool assign at least one of their clerks to review, even draft supplementary memos to, those coming from the cert pool. The cert pool process thus might result in petitions receiving greater attention. If so, ironically, the cert pool could have contributed to increasing the size of the plenary docket in two ways.

First, in the 1970s and early 1980s the justices opposed to the cert pool, and concerned about important cases being overlooked, may have given greater scrutiny to petitions as well as more often voted to grant cases. Justices participating in the cert pool, like Justices Blackmun and Powell, may have been inclined to vote to join 3 in deference to the senior justices not in the pool and due to concerns about the Court's declining supervisory capacity. Second, cert pool memos flag cases alleging intercircuit conflicts. Given concerns about declining

ment of Justice O'Connor, who cast a fair number of join-3 votes, less than Justice Blackmun but more than the others. With several justices casting join-3 votes, by the early 1980s the numbers granted reached their historical highs. Following the retirements of Chief Justice Burger and Justice Powell, the plenary docket began to shrink. Neither Justice Antonin Scalia nor Justice Anthony Kennedy is as inclined as those two former justices to vote to join 3. The decline continued after the retirements of Justices Brennan and Marshall at the end of the 1989 and 1990 terms, respectively, and then fell further after the retirements of Justices White and Blackmun at the end of the 1992 and 1993 terms. In sum, the inflation and contraction in the plenary docket registered changes in the Court's composition and its case selection process.

The cert pool's impact

Yet, some Court-watchers hypothesize that the cert pool remains the primary factor and an independent variable explaining the shrinking plenary docket. For instance, Kenneth W. Starr, a former clerk for Chief Justice Burger, complained that the cert pool exerts too much influence and that important cases are now passed over.[6]

Figure 4. Notations of votes to grant and dissents from denial of review, 1981–1995 terms

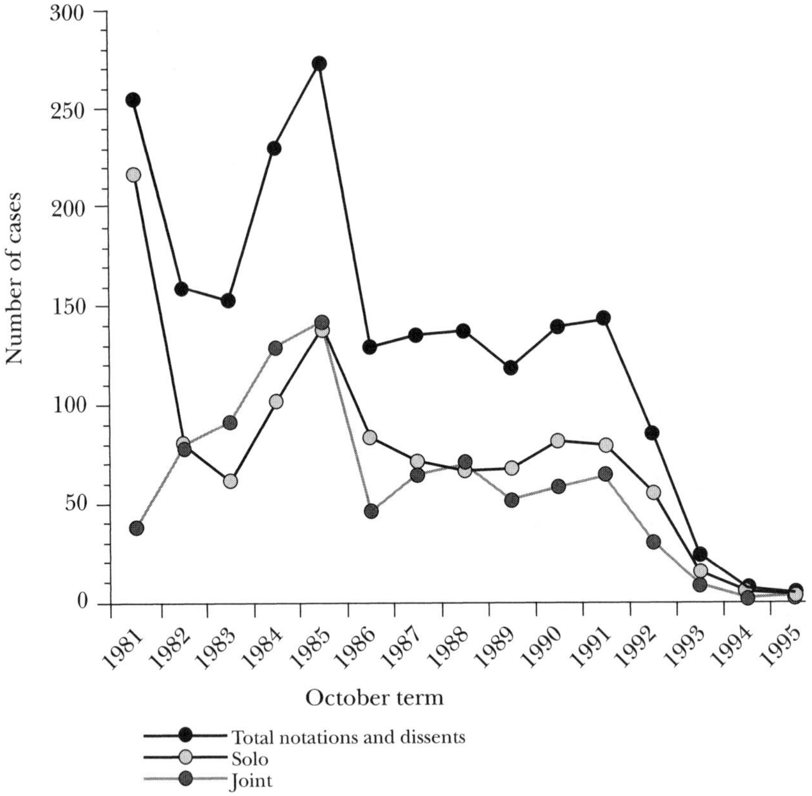

supervisory capacity, pool memos may have inclined some justices, especially Chief Justice Burger and Justice White, to vote to grant those cases, as well as moved the latter to file dissents from denials in them.

Conversely, though, the increase in the size of the cert pool may have contributed to the decline in the plenary docket. With more justices belonging to the cert pool, and assuming greater attention is given to petitions by the justices' chambers, the cert pool process may highlight circuit conflicts, which after further scrutiny are deemed "tolerable" or in need of "percolation." Hence, cases in which particularly Justice White would vote to grant were more frequently denied, resulting in a diminished docket.

In short, it is unclear that the cert pool either determines the amount of scrutiny given petitions or was the underlying factor in increasing, and subsequently decreasing, the size of the plenary docket. Whether in or out of the cert pool, justices differ in their scrutiny of petitions and cert memos. Although measuring the extent of their independent review appears impossible, one indication remains their published notes to grant and dissents from denial. While not an entirely satisfactory gauge, because some justices oppose the practice of publicizing such votes, notations of votes to grant and dissents from denial provide a measure for the theory that the changes in the plenary docket dovetail with those in the Court's composition and voting practices.

Declining notations

As seen in Figure 4,[7] the number of notations of votes to grant and dissents from denial of review tracks the decline in the plenary docket shown in Figure 1. In the 1981 term, when the plenary docket reached its zenith, there were 255 notations of votes to grant additional cases and dissents from denial. Five terms later in 1986, Rehnquist's first as chief justice, the number fell to 129. By the 1994 and 1995 terms there were less than 10 in those combined terms.

As with the diminishing plenary docket, the number of notations of votes to grant and dissents from denial declined in three stages: first, following Chief

Figure 5. Justices' pro-review scores, 1981–1995 terms

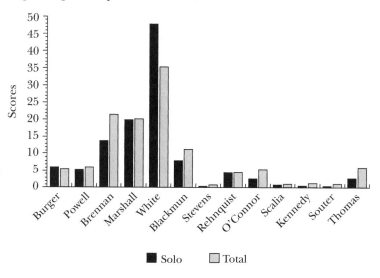

Figure 5 reveals considerable variation among the justices. Justice White filed more solo notations of votes to grant and dissents from denial than any other justice. By contrast, Justice Blackmun, who held the record on join-3 votes, more frequently joined other justices in noting votes to grant or dissents from denials than he did in filing his own.

The pro-review scores further confirm the theory that the inflation in the plenary docket during the Burger Court years and its contraction with the Rehnquist Court reflects changes in the composition of the bench and the justices' voting practices. Given the high pro-review scores of the four justices—Brennan, Marshall, White, and Blackmun—who retired in the early 1990s, the steep decline in the plenary docket should come as no surprise.

Justice Burger's retirement and Rehnquist's elevation to the center chair; second, after Justices Brennan and Marshall retired; and, third, following the retirements of Justices White and Blackmun.

The data underscore that members of the Burger Court were far more disposed to grant cases than those on the Rehnquist Court in the early and mid-1990s. Certain justices were especially inclined to grant review and tried to persuade others to vote to grant by casting join-3 votes as well as by circulating notes of votes to grant review and dissents from denial. The number of notations of votes to grant and dissents from denial provides a measure of the justices' pro-review dispositions, at least in the 1980s; in the 1990s fewer justices issue them and do so in far smaller numbers.

Figure 5 assigns pro-review scores to justices serving during the 1981 to 1995 terms. Two scores are assigned: one for their solo notations and dissents, and another for their total contribution of such issuances, which includes both their solo notes to grant or dissent from denials, as well as those they joined or were joined by one or more other justices. The scores are based on dividing their number of such notations for each term they were on the bench by the total number issued during those periods, and then multiplying by 100. Justice White, for example, served during 12 of those 15 terms. During that time, he issued 532 solo notes to grant and dissents from denial, and there was a total of 1,102 such notations during that period. Thus, he has a 48.2 solo pro-review score for voting to grant cases beyond the number already granted plenary consideration.

*****

It is, perhaps, unremarkable to conclude that the inflation and subsequent contraction of the plenary docket registers changes in the composition of the high bench and the justices' voting practices in case selection. The justices, not their clerks nor external forces, ultimately determine what and how much to decide. Nonetheless, the analysis here confirms the observations of Justices Souter and Stevens. The diminished plenary docket, as Justice Souter put it, "in fact just happened," due specifically to changes in the Court's composition and operation. And as Justice Stevens pointed out, the Court's "workload problem" in the 1970s and 1980s arose precisely because the justices failed to exercise self-restraint in case selection. We are left, then, with an irony of history: While recognized for his interest in judicial administration, Chief Justice Burger failed to appreciate that the Court's "workload problem" was one of its own making.

Notes

This article originally appeared in Volume 81, Number 2, September–October 1997, pages 58–65.

1. Justice David H. Souter, quoted by Shannon Duffy, "Inside the Highest Court: Souter Describes Justices' Relationship, Caseload Trend," *Pennsylvania Law Weekly* (April 17, 1995) at 11. All subsequent quotes from Justice Souter are from this article.

2. The analysis and data presented here is more fully developed by the author in "Join-3 Votes, the Rule of Four, the Cert. Pool, and the Supreme Court's Shrinking Plenary Docket," *J. L. & Pol.* 13 (1997).

3. Justice John Paul Stevens, "The Life Span of a Judge-Made Rule," *N.Y. U. L. Rev.* 58 (1983), 1, 17.

4. *See* Feeney, "Conflicts Involving Federal Law: A Review of Cases Presented to the Supreme Court," in *Structure and Internal Procedures: Recommendations for Change* (Washington, D.C.: Commission on Revision of the Federal Court Appellate System, 1975), 112–113.

5. Thurgood Marshall Papers, Boxes 239, 240, 260, 261, 281, 305, 306, 329, 330, 352, 353, 375, 376, 398, 399, 427, 452, 453, 483, 513, 514 (Manuscripts Room, Library of Congress). Note that some of the bench memos for cases heard during each term were missing, particularly for the 1987 term in which there are memos for only about one third of the cases granted oral argument.

6. Starr, "Supreme Court Needs A Management Revolt," *Wall Street Journal*, Oct. 13, 1993, at A23, and "Trivial Pursuits at the Supreme Court," *Wall Street Journal*, Oct. 6, 1993, at A17.

7. This figure is based on notations of votes to grant review and dissents from the denial of petitions published in the U.S. Reports from the 1981 to 1995 terms. Both notations of votes to either grant or dissents from denial and opinions dissenting from the denial of review were counted. Excluded were opinions concurring in or respecting the denial of review and dissents from denials of requests for stays of execution and other motions. Also excluded are dissents filed by Justices Brennan, Marshall, and Blackmun in death penalty cases unless the dissent provided an explanation for voting to grant other than simply stating their opposition to capital punishment. In the 1980s, Justices Brennan and Marshall had the Court's computer system programmed to print automatically all of their dissents from the denial of certiorari when a capital punishment case was denied review. As a result, each term they filed hundreds of such dissents and including them here would have skewed the data. Justice Blackmun, likewise, adopted their practice in his last term after concluding that the imposition of capital punishment was unconstitutional and announcing his opposition in a dissent from denial of review in *Callins v. Collins*, 114 S.Ct. 1127 (1994).

Federal court reform should start at the top

Roger J. Miner

*An increase in the number of cases decided by the Supreme Court
and changes in its decision-making process would help ease the caseload
of the lower federal courts, an appellate judge suggests.*

There can be little doubt that the federal courts are confronting a caseload crunch of mammoth proportions. How could it be otherwise, with more and more attorneys filing more and more lawsuits as the result of more and more causes of action created by Congress? Let's look at the numbers. In 1981, approximately 180,000 civil cases were filed in the U.S. district courts.[1] In 1991, the number was nearly 208,000.[2] In 1981, approximately 31,000 criminal cases were filed in the district courts, and in 1991 the figure was about 46,000.[3] During the same decade, Congress authorized increases in district judgeships from 516 to 649.[4] The circuit courts of appeals had 132 authorized judgeships and about 26,000 filings in 1981.[5] By 1991, filings had increased by roughly 16,000 cases to 42,000, but there were only 35 more judgeships than there were in 1981.[6]

In the 100 years since the U.S. courts of appeals were formed, authorized judgeships in the Second Circuit have gone from 3 to 13, an increase of 433 percent.[7] During the same period, however, filings in the circuit have gone from 196 to 4,165, an increase of more than 2,000 percent![8] As filings increase, without any corresponding increase in the number of judges, each judge must handle more cases, and the median disposition time for each case necessarily becomes longer.

If the mission of the lower federal courts is to provide for the just, speedy, and inexpensive determination of every dispute brought before them, their present overburdened condition calls into question their ability to perform the mission. There are two options. The first is to continue the present course, with the expectation of incremental increases in the caseload and with expansion of the judiciary continually lagging behind need. The other option is reform, including changes in such areas as court structure, procedural rules, case management techniques, the decisional process, subject matter jurisdiction, and methods of alternate dispute resolution. It seems clear that the time for reform is at hand.[9]

Reforms

Three years ago, the Federal Courts Study Committee, created by Congress to assess the developing crisis and to make appropriate recommendations, rendered its final report. In the report, the committee noted the existence of "mounting public and professional concern with the federal courts' congestion, delay, expense, and expansion."[10] The committee did not recommend any increase in the number of judges, although that would seem to be a logical place to start. A lively debate is now in progress between those who believe that there should be a "cap" on the number of federal judges and those who think expansion is in order, with excellent arguments on both sides.[11] However that question may be resolved, the fact is that in recent years the president and Senate have had a great deal of difficulty in filling current vacancies. At this moment, there are 106 unfilled slots in the district courts and 20 unfilled slots in the courts of appeals.[12]

In 1975, the Hruska Commission proposed the establishment of a National Court of Appeals, a new court to be interposed between the Supreme Court and the regional courts of appeals.[13] It would receive cases on reference from the Supreme Court and by transfer from the regional courts. The study committee rejected the idea of a national intermediate appellate court but did present five structural change possibilities for further inquiry and discussion: A single unified National Court of Appeals operating through regional divisions; a four-tier system, with the first appellate tier consisting of 25 to 30 regional appellate divisions hearing appeals of right from the district courts and the second-tier appellate court taking cases on a discretionary basis from the first; national appeals courts structured according to subject matter, as in the federal circuit; a single, centrally organized court of appeals; and consolidation of existing courts into five jumbo circuits.[14] All these proposals have their unique problems, as the study committee indicated.[15]

Judicature Volume 77, Number 2, pp. 104–108

There are those who see merit in giving the courts of appeals discretion as to what cases they will accept.[16] My chief judge, Jon Newman, has a different approach. He favors a system of discretionary access to federal courts at both the trial and appellate levels in order to reallocate jurisdiction between state and federal courts.[17] Under his proposal, discretion as to access would be vested in the federal courts and would be exercised for individual cases and designated categories.[18] Proposals have been made to modify or severely curtail diversity jurisdiction,[19] to replace with a workers' compensation scheme the statutes allowing injured railroad workers and seamen to sue in federal courts,[20] and to establish a special court to adjudicate claims under the Social Security Act.[21]

Other suggestions for reform have included a small claims procedure for certain federal tort claims,[22] the creation of an Article III appellate division of the United States Tax Court with exclusive jurisdiction over federal income, estate, and gift tax cases,[23] a requirement for exhaustion of state administrative remedies prior to the commencement of prisoners' civil rights suits,[24] and mandatory use of alternative dispute resolution mechanisms.[25]

The federal judiciary, with the assistance of the Federal Judicial Center, long has experimented with case management techniques. The authority of judges to take hold of a case in its earliest stages and to keep the case under close supervision, with established deadlines, has proved to be essential to the achievement of maximum efficiency in court operations. Despite the fact that the lower federal courts are running as fast as they can and have been refining management techniques and administrative procedures over the years, Congress enacted the Civil Justice Reform Act in 1990.[26] The act requires each district court in the nation to create an expense and delay reduction plan. Just what the courts needed at a time when they are understaffed and underfunded: a congressional requirement to micromanage the courts and to reinvent the wheel. What a waste!

Congress's responsibility

It is Congress, of course, that is responsible for all this mess in the first place. Justice Sandra Day O'Connor once referred to the "underdeveloped capacity [of Congress] for self-restraint." [27] Nowhere is the lack of self-restraint more evident than in the federal criminal laws. I have been writing and speaking about the federalization of crimes for more than a decade, but nobody seems to listen. There are about 3,000 separate provisions scattered throughout the U.S. Code criminalizing various forms of conduct. Do you know that it is a federal offense to reproduce the image of Woodsy Owl[28] and Smokey the Bear?[29] To impersonate a 4-H Club member?[30] To transport water hyacinths in interstate commerce?[31] To bring false teeth into a state without the permission of a local dentist?[32]

Every time Congress meets, more state crimes are made federal crimes in response to the problems of the moment. Last year it was car jacking.[33] This year it looks like it will be domestic violence,[34] a quintessential state crime. Is it any wonder that the number of assistant U.S. attorneys has increased two-and-one-half fold since 1980?[35] If the number of Article III judges had increased at that rate, we would have 1,620 judges instead of the 816 we now have.

Criminal statutes have not alone been responsible for the increase in business in the federal courts. Congress continues to create new sources of civil litigation as well. Last year, Congress established a civil cause of action providing for the recovery of damages from any individual who engages in torture or killing under color of the law of any foreign nation.[36] It appears that any victim of state terrorism may sue here if there is no remedy in the place where the conduct occurred.[37] And there is a 10-year statute of limitations.[38] Congress has decided to turn loose on world terrorism the mightiest force it could think of—lawyers pursuing civil litigation. That ought to strike fear into their hearts! In passing that legislation, Congress had no idea how many suits the new statute would spawn or what impact it would have on the federal judicial system.

Such is the way with all congressional legislation. When I was a member of the Judicial Conference Committee on Federal-State Jurisdiction, I participated in the preparation of a checklist for Congress to consider in reviewing proposed legislation.[39] The checklist was designed to identify technical and interpretive problems, duplicative and unnecessary legislation, and the general impact of legislation on the courts. The checklist has, I fear, come to naught.

The Supreme Court's role

One of the major reasons for the inundation of the federal district and circuit courts is the uncertainty of the law. The Scriptures ask this question: "If the trumpet give an uncertain sound, who shall prepare himself to the battle?" [40] My answer is: "Every lawyer worth his salt." If the law is not settled, there is every incentive to litigate.

In our judicial system, only one body can resolve uncertainty—the U.S. Supreme Court. Yet the Court seldom takes the trumpet to its lips, and when it does, the sound often is very weak. I respectfully suggest that, at the Supreme Court level, an increase in the number of cases decided and some changes in the decision-making process itself would go far toward alleviating the caseload problems of the lower federal courts. Federal court reform should start at the top.

The Supreme Court is lumbering into the 21st century at the leisurely pace of the 19th century, seemingly oblivious to the needs of the federal judicial system. The trial and appeals courts are overwhelmed by caseload growth, but the Supreme Court actually is deciding fewer cases each year. This year, 116 cases were decided, 127 the year before, and 125 the year before that.[41] Back in the 1980s, the figure reached as high as 151.[42] The Court certainly is trimming its docket in the face of an explosive growth of cases in the lower courts.

This makes no sense. We need to get the Supreme Court up to speed. The interesting part of it is that the shrinkage has come as the Court has gained more and more control over its docket, culminating in the 1988 legislation that effectively eliminated the Court's mandatory appellate jurisdiction.[43] As most lawyers know, the only way to get there on appeal now is by cert. And the justices are not granting enough cert petitions. For one thing, more cases should be taken in order to settle the law where circuit courts of appeals are in conflict.

Intercircuit conflicts

In the Judicial Improvements Act of 1990, Congress directed the Federal Judicial Center to undertake a study of the problems created by intercircuit conflicts, including economic costs, forum shopping among circuits, unfairness to litigants, and non-acquiescence by federal agencies.[44] The study has not yet been completed, but preliminary reports indicate that the number of conflicts has been greater than originally thought.[45] Justice Byron White, who recently retired, has been in the vanguard of those who believe that the Supreme Court should do more to resolve intercircuit conflicts. He frequently dissented from the denial of cert, pointing out the conflicts and urging his colleagues to resolve them. His dissents include language such as this:

> One of the Court's duties is to do its best to see that the federal law is not being applied differently in the vari-

ous circuits around the country. The Court is surely not doing its best when it denies certiorari in this case, which presents an issue on which the Courts of Appeals are recurringly at odds.[46]

and this:

> I agree with petitioner and the Government that the outcome of a federal criminal prosecution should not depend upon the circuit in which the case is tried.[47]

and this:

> Because a uniform rule should be announced by this Court on this important and recurring issue, I would grant the petition.[48]

Clearly, allowing circuit conflicts to continue generates litigation, because the law remains unsettled, and attorneys take their cases to the forum most favorable. Where the Supreme Court has not spoken on an issue, but some circuits have resolved the question in one way and some in another, litigation is encouraged in those circuits that have not yet spoken. Clients doing business nationally may have their conduct regulated one way in one place and another way in another and continue to challenge unfavorable precedent. Government agencies, charged with the administration of national law in a uniform way, follow policies of non-acquiescence, refusing to accept the views of a circuit that rejects the agency position.

Aside from the fact that fairness is lost and justice is not seen to be done, the lower courts become clogged with cases that would not be brought if the law was clearly stated. The Supreme Court is the only place where the conflicts can be resolved, and the resolution must be accomplished more frequently and in greater numbers of cases. And I think that a greater number of important issues that have not yet festered into inter-circuit conflicts should be identified and decided by the Supreme Court in an effort to head off the inevitable clogging of the pipeline that comes from unsettled questions of law. Included in the issues that need to be resolved are thorny questions of statutory interpretation.

An uncertain trumpet

As a frequent consumer of Supreme Court services, I often am a confused victim of the Supreme Court's uncertain trumpet. For example, in 1990 the Supreme Court decided *Grady v. Corbin*[49] in a 5–4 opinion by Justice William Brennan. The case involved the double jeopardy clause of the Fifth Amendment and changed the rule established in 1932 in *Blockburger v. United States*.[50] According to *Blockburger*, whether you can be prosecuted for the same criminal act under two different criminal statutes requires a determination whether one statute requires proof of a fact that the other does not. *Grady* established a new gloss on the old rule. I was one of a three-member panel of my court to which fell a case requiring an interpretation of *Grady*. Each member of the panel wrote a separate opinion,[51] so disparate were our views of what the Supreme Court had said. It is bad enough to interpret unclear statutes, but it is even worse to interpret some Supreme Court decisions.

In 1992, the Supreme Court modified *Grady* somewhat in *United States v. Felix*,[52] in which it noted our difficulties in deciding the case in the Second Circuit, which it then remanded for consideration in light of *Felix*. We subsequently wrote a new decision in which we all concurred.[53] A little over a month ago, in a case called *United States v. Dixon*,[54] the Supreme Court overruled the *Grady* decision (I think) and returned to the *Blockburger* rule. I say "I think," because five separate opinions were filed in the most recent case. The double jeopardy trumpet continues to emit an uncertain sound.

One author has referred to "the Justices' muddy, footnote-filled expository prose."[55] Far be it from me to accept such a characterization. I do note that the members of the Court have some difficulty agreeing on things. In *Brecht v. Abrahamson*,[56] a habeas corpus case decided this term, the following line-up, not especially unusual, was given: "Rehnquist, C.J., delivered the opinion of the Court, in which Stevens, Scalia, Kennedy, and Thomas, JJ., joined. Stevens, J., filed a concurring opinion. White, J., filed a dissenting opinion, in which Blackmun, J., joined, and in which Souter, J., joined except for the footnote and Part III. Blackmun, O'Connor, and Souter, JJ., filed dissenting opinions."[57]

All those 5–4 and plurality opinions serve only to engender hope among lawyers and a resolve to continue litigating. Maybe there will be a switch in votes. Maybe a new member will join the Court. Maybe some new, persuasive reasoning will be advanced by the bar. Without certainty in the law, litigation proliferates. An attorney would not serve his or her client well if he or she did not litigate issues left open. Forgotten is this admonition of Justice Louis Brandeis: "It is usually more important that a rule of law be settled, than that it be settled right."[58]

Several other cases decided this term do not fully resolve the questions presented. In *TXO Production Corp. v. Alliance Resources Corp.*,[59] the vote was 6–3 to uphold an award of punitive damages, but the reasoning was all over the lot and no one opinion attracted a five-vote majority. The qualifications of expert witnesses were left to the discretion of the district judges in *Daubert v. Merrell Dow Pharmaceuticals*,[60] but little guidance was given as to how that discretion should be exercised. And, despite the strong language about gerrymandering used in *Shaw v. Reno*[61] (another 5–4 decision), acceptable methods of drawing congressional district boundary lines are still very much up in the air.

Thus do cases proliferate in the lower federal courts for failure of the Supreme Court to resolve intercircuit conflicts, to identify and decide important procedural and substantive issues before they ripen into intercircuit conflicts, and to provide clear, crisp, and certain opinions for the guidance of the lower courts, the bar, and the American citizenry. As I see it, a greater volume of cases fully decided at the Supreme Court level as well as more brevity and clarity in the Court's opinions would do much to relieve the congestion in the lower courts.

Proposals for reform

To achieve these ends, I propose consideration of the following possibilities:

- More attention by the individual members of the Court should be paid to cert petitions in an effort to identify the most important conflicts and issues for review. There is some basis for the belief that the present cert pool of law clerks from the various chambers is not the most effective way of handling these matters.[62] More cert petitions should be granted.

- The newest justice has stressed the importance of collegiality, which sometimes includes the need to submerge one's views in unimportant matters for the good of the institution and of the consumers of its products.[63] Let us hope that Justice Ruth Bader Ginsburg is able to persuade her colleagues of the importance of one voice. Too often is heard the cacophony of what appears to be nine separate courts.

- Each Supreme Court opinion need not read as if it were the History of the World, Part I. If brevity is a virtue for judges of other courts and for lawyers, it should also be a virtue for justices of the Supreme Court. The necessary increase in production can also be achieved through per curiam opinions and summary orders. Many an intercircuit conflict could be resolved by a brief opinion adopting the decision of one of the circuits that considered the issue.

- The effort to increase production in the Supreme Court might be assisted by cutting the summer recess from three months to two.[64] That lengthy recess really is a relic of the 18th century, and I know of no justice who must return to the farm at harvest time.

- There is a statutory provision allowing certification of questions of law to the Supreme Court by the courts of appeals.[65] This provision has fallen into disuse, but should be revived, even though the Supreme Court has the right to reject the matter certified.

- The Court should be alert to the availability of its Rule 11, which allows it to grant cert before judgment in the court of appeals. This allows the Court to take up an important case without delay, as it did in *Mistretta v. United States*.[66] In that case, it was important to deal with the constitutionality of the Sentencing Reform Act of 1984[67] quickly, since some district courts throughout the nation were sentencing under the new act, and some were sentencing under the old law.

- Some mandatory appellate jurisdiction might be restored in an effort to increase the Court's production. The erosion of mandatory jurisdiction over the years has been gradual,[68] and the end result seems to be fewer cases decided. Perhaps cases that involve the declaration of unconstitutionality of federal statutes would be a good place to start with mandated appeals.

- The Supreme Court certainly could address more issues if it divided itself into panels to hear cases of a more routine nature. Three panels of three judges each can decide more cases more efficiently and faster than can an en banc panel of nine.[69] Hearings by the full Court could be reserved for cases in which a panel is in disagreement or for important constitutional issues.

- The number of Supreme Court justices is fixed by Congress.[70] Despite the explosion in federal lit-

igation, the number of justices has been fixed at nine since 1869.[71] Before that, the number varied between 5 and 10.[72] There is nothing sacrosanct about the number nine. In light of the potential business that the Court should be addressing, an addition of at least three seems to be warranted. The rejected proposal of Franklin D. Roosevelt to increase the number of justices was known as a Court-packing plan and was highly political in nature. What is called for now is a Court-expanding plan to take care of additional work.

- I suppose there is no way to mandate the issuance of clear and thoughtful opinions in one voice by the Supreme Court. But the observations of one justice on the subject of clarity of opinions is most illuminating. The *New York Times* recently published a photograph of Justice White and, in a caption underneath the picture, noted his retirement after 31 years of service.[73] The caption continued: "He said that he intended to sit on Federal appeals courts during his retirement, and that he hoped that the Supreme Court's opinions would be clear and easy to follow." [74]

I hope that Justice White comes to sit in the Second Circuit as Justice Thurgood Marshall did after his retirement.[75] I hope that I have the opportunity to sit with him and to join him in applying Supreme Court precedent. We will then see if his subtle message to his former colleagues got through. We both can hope, can't we?

Notes

This article originally appeared in Volume 77, Number 2, September–October 1993, pages 104–108.

This article is adapted from Judge Miner's speech at the American Judicature Society-National Conference of Bar Presidents joint luncheon, August 7, 1993, in New York.

1. *Annual Report of the Director of the Administrative Office of the United States Courts* (1991), 86.
2. Ibid.
3. Ibid. at 90.
4. Ibid.
5. Ibid. at 81.
6. Ibid.
7. Miner, "Planning for the Second Century of the Second Circuit Court of Appeals: The Report of the Federal Courts Study Committee," *St. John's L. Rev.* 65 (1991), 673, 677.

8. Ibid.; *United States Courts for the Second Circuit: Second Circuit Report* 1992, at 4.

9. "At times in our system the way in which courts perform their function becomes as important as what they do in the result." *United States v. United Mine Workers of Am.,* 330 U.S. 258, 363 (1947) (Rutledge, J., dissenting).

10. *Report of the Federal Courts Study Committee* (1990), 3.

11. *See, e.g.,* Bermant et al., *Imposing a Moratorium on the Number of Federal Judges: Analysis of Arguments and Implications* (Federal Judicial Center, 1993); Newman, "1,000 Judges—the Limit for an Effective Federal Judiciary," *Judicature* 76 (1993), 187; Williams, "Solutions to Federal Judicial Gridlock," *Judicature* 76 (1993), 185; Sloviter, "The Judiciary Needs Judicious Growth," *Nat'l L.J.,* June 28, 1993, at 17.

12. "Judicial Boxscore," *The Third Branch* (Washington, D.C.: Administrative Office of the United States Courts), July 1993, at 11.

13. *See* Commission on Revision of the Federal Court Appellate System, "Structure and Internal Procedures: Recommendations for Change," reprinted in *F.R.D.* 67 (1975), 195, 236–241; *see also* Wallace, "The Nature and Extent of Intercircuit Conflicts: A Solution Needed for a Mountain or a Molehill?" *Cal. L. Rev.* 71 (1983), 913 (criticizing the Hruska Report).

14. See *Study Committee Report, supra* n. 10, at 117–123.

15. *See* Ibid.

16. *See, e.g.,* Shapiro, "Jurisdiction and Discretion," *N.Y.U. L. Rev.* 60 (1985), 543.

17. *See* Newman, "Restructuring Federal Jurisdiction: Proposals to Preserve the Federal Judicial System," *U. Chi. L. Rev.* 56 (1989), 761, 770–776.

18. Ibid.

19. *See, e.g.,* Sloviter, "Diversity Jurisdiction through the Lens of Federalism," *Judicature* 76 (1992), 90; *Study Committee Report, supra* n. 10, at 38; Miner, *supra* n. 7, at 717 n. 288 (citing sources).

20. See *Study Committee Report, supra* n. 10, at 62–63.

21. *See* Ibid. at 55–59.

22. *See* Ibid. at 81.

23. *See* Ibid. at 69.

24. *See* Ibid. at 48–50.

25. *See* Ibid. at 83–85.

26. Pub. L. No. 101-650, tit. I, 104 Stat. 5089 (1990) (codified at 28 U.S.C. §§471-482 (Supp. 1993)).

27. *Garcia v. San Antonio Metropolitan Transit Auth.,* 469 U.S. 528, 588 (1985) (O'Connor, J., dissenting).

28. *See* 18 U.S.C. §711a (1988).

29. *See* Ibid. §711.

30. *See* Ibid. §916.

31. *See* Ibid. §46.

32. *See* Ibid. §1821.

33. *See* Anti-Car Theft Act of 1992, Pub. L. No. 102-519, §101, 106 Stat. 3384, 3384 (codified at 18 U.S.C. §2119 (Supp. 1993)).

34. *See* H.R. 1133, 103d Cong., 1st Sess. (1993); H.R. 688, 103d Cong., 1st Sess. (1993); S. 11, 103d Cong., 1st Sess. (1993); S. 6, 103d Cong., 1st Sess. (1993).

35. *See* Novack, "How About a Little Restructuring?," *Forbes,* Mar. 15, 1993, at 91.

36. *See* Torture Victim Protection Act of 1991, Pub. L. No. 102-256, 106 Stat. 73 (codified at 28 U.S.C. §1350 (Supp. 1993)).

37. *See* Ibid. §2(b), 106 Stat. at 73.

38. *See* Ibid. §2(c), 106 Stat. at 73.

39. *See* Miner, *supra* n. 7, at 722–723.

40. *I Corinthians* 14:8.

41. These statistics were provided by the Office of the Solicitor General (on file with author).

42. Greenhouse, "Lightening Scales of Justice: High Court Trims Its Docket," *N.Y. Times,* Mar. 7, 1992, at A1; *see* Greenhouse, "Case of the Shrinking Docket: Justices Spurn New Appeals," *N.Y. Times,* Nov. 28, 1989, at A1; *see also* Strauss, "One Hundred Fifty Cases Per Year: Some Implications of the Supreme Court's Limited Resources for Judicial Review of Agency Action," *Colum. L. Rev.* 87 (1987), 1093, 1100 (suggesting that Court's docket cannot accommodate more than 150 cases per term).

43. *See* Act of June 27, 1988, Pub. L. No. 100-352, 102 Stat. 662.

44. *See* Judicial Improvements Act of 1990, Pub. L. No. 101-650, §302, 104 Stat. 5089, 5097.

45. *See* Hellman, *Unresolved Intercircuit Conflicts: The Nature and Scope of the Problem* (Federal Judicial Center, 1991).

46. *Taylor v. United States,* 112 S. Ct. 2982, 2982 (1992) (White, J., dissenting) (circuit split over whether indictments against defendants should be dismissed after state officials technically violate the Interstate Agreement on Detainers).

47. *Tomala v. United States,* 112 S. Ct. 1997, 1998 (1992) (White, J., dissenting) (circuit split regarding "whether the weight of uningestible waste material should be included in calculating the weight of a 'mixture or substance' containing a detectable amount of a controlled substance for purposes of [U.S.S.G.] §2D1.1").

48. *Carroll v. Consolidated Rail Corp.,* 112 S. Ct. 916, 916 (1992) (White, J., dissenting) (circuit split over whether the Federal Employers' Liability Act "creates a cause of action for emotional injury brought about by acts that lack any physical contact or threat of physical contact").

49. 495 U.S. 508 (1990).

50. 284 U.S. 299 (1932).

51. See *United States v. Calderone,* 917 F.2d 717, 718–722 (2d Cir. 1990) (Pratt, J.), *vacated,* 112 S. Ct. 1657 (1992);

id. at 722-726 (Newman, J., concurring); Ibid. at 726–729 (Miner, J., dissenting).

52. 112 S. Ct. 1377 (1992).

53. See *United States v. Calderone,* 982 F.2d 42 (2d Cir. 1992).

54. 61 U.S.L.W. 4835 (U.S. June 28, 1993).

55. Hirsch, "Book Review," *Geo. Wash. L. Rev.* 61 (1993), 858, 859 (reviewing Goldstein, *The Intelligible Constitution: The Supreme Court's Obligation to Maintain the Constitution as Something We the People Can Understand* [1992]).

56. 113 S. Ct. 1710 (1993).

57. Ibid. at 1713.

58. *Di Santo v. Pennsylvania,* 273 U.S. 34, 42 (1927) (Brandeis, J., dissenting).

59. 61 U.S.L.W. 4766 (U.S. June 25, 1993).

60. 61 U.S.L.W. 4805 (U.S. June 28, 1993).

61. 61 U.S.L.W. 4818 (U.S. June 28, 1993).

62. *See* Gest, "The Court: Deciding Less, Writing More," *U.S. News & World Report,* June 28, 1993, at 24, 26.

63. *See* Lewis, "The Supreme Court; Ginsburg Affirms Right of a Woman to Have an Abortion," *N.Y. Times,* July 22, 1993, at A1.

64. See "Promoting Public Understanding of the Supreme Court," *Judicature* 76 (1992), 4.

65. *See* 28 U.S.C. §1254(2) (1988); *see also* Sup. Ct. R. 19 (procedure for certifying a question).

66. 488 U.S. 361 (1989).

67. Pub. L. No. 98-473, 98 Stat. 1988 (codified at 18 U.S.C. §§3551 *et seq.* (1988)).

68. *See* Surrency, *History of the Federal Courts* (1987), 254–255.

69. *See* Stern, "Remedies for Appellate Overloads: The Ultimate Solution," *Judicature* 72 (1988), 103, 106–108.

70. U.S. Const. art. III., §1.

71. *See generally* Frankfurter and Landis, *The Business of the Supreme Court: A Study in the Federal Judicial System* (1927); Surrency, *supra* n. 68.

72. *See* Act of Sept. 24, 1789, ch. 20, §1, 1 Stat. 72, 73 (six justices); Act of Feb. 13, 1801, ch. 4, §3, 2 Stat. 89, 89 (repealed 1802) (five justices); Act of Feb. 24, 1807, ch. 16, §5, 2 Stat. 420, 421 (seven justices); Act of Mar. 3, 1837, ch. 34, §1, 5 Stat. 176, 176 (nine justices); Act of Mar. 3, 1863, ch. 100, §1, 12 Stat. 794, 794 (ten justices); Act of July 23, 1866, ch. 210, §1, 14 Stat. 209, 209 (seven justices); Act of Apr. 10, 1869, ch. 22, §1, 16 Stat. 44, 44 (nine justices).

73. *See* N.Y. Times, June 29, 1993, at A11.

74. Ibid.

75. *N. Y. L. J.,* Jan. 15, 1992, at 1.

Deciding what to decide: the Judges' Bill at 75

Edward A. Hartnett

On the 75th anniversary of the Judges' Bill of 1925, which gave the Supreme Court the power to pick and choose which cases to decide, it is appropriate to reflect upon and question this important feature of our legal and political landscape.

Seventy-five years ago the modern Supreme Court was born. In 1925, Congress gave the justices of the Supreme Court what Chief Justice William Howard Taft had aggressively sought from the moment he took his seat on the Court: a far-ranging power to pick and choose which cases to decide.

Congress was remarkably willing to delegate to the Court the case selection power sought by Taft, even as it resisted for another decade delegating to the Court the power to promulgate rules of civil procedure. Senator Thomas Walsh, a progressive Democrat from Montana whose determined opposition blocked the Rules Enabling Act until his death, attempted a lonely fight against the bill sought by the Court. He described that bill—widely dubbed the Judges' Bill—as exemplifying "that truism, half legal and half political, that a good court always seeks to extend its jurisdiction, and that other maxim, wholly political, so often asserted by Jefferson, that the appetite for power grows as it is gratified." [1] Yet even Senator Walsh ultimately relented.

In the 75 years that have followed, we have grown accustomed to the idea that the Supreme Court sets its own agenda, and tend to take it for granted. In the process, we also seem to have simply forgotten that in the years before the Judges' Bill, the Court decided far more cases than the 150 that we have somehow convinced ourselves is the most that the modern Supreme Court—aided by multiple law clerks and computers—can possibly be expected to decide. Although the decline in recent years to less than 100 decided cases has attracted some attention, most readers are likely surprised that in the hearings concerning the Judges' Bill, the solicitor general estimated that the number of cases of public gravity that the Court could decide on the merits was between 400 and 500.

Certiorari before Taft

For more than 100 years, the Supreme Court had no power to pick and choose which cases to decide.

Instead, just as Congress decided which cases and controversies from the list contained in Article III, Section 2, would be decided by the lower federal courts, so too it decided which of those cases and controversies would be decided by the Supreme Court. As a formal matter, of course, the Constitution itself grants the Supreme Court jurisdiction over all cases and controversies listed in Article III, Section 2, and allocates those cases and controversies between original and appellate jurisdiction. And as the Court famously held in *Marbury v. Madison*, Congress lacks the constitutional power to add to the Supreme Court's original jurisdiction. But the Court's appellate jurisdiction is subject to the important congressional power to make regulations and exceptions, and acts of Congress specifying the Court's jurisdiction have long been understood as exercises of this power, implicitly excepting all cases not specified. In short, so long as Congress did not attempt to expand the Supreme Court's jurisdiction to cases and controversies not listed in Article III or to add to its original jurisdiction, the Supreme Court was required to decide those cases within its congressionally-defined jurisdiction and was prohibited from deciding cases outside that jurisdiction.

The number of cases that the Court was obligated to decide grew dramatically after the Civil War. Congress responded in 1891 by creating the circuit courts of appeals, giving the Supreme Court mandatory appellate jurisdiction over many of their decisions, but declaring others "final." For those cases in which the circuit court of appeals' decision was declared "final," however, the Supreme Court nevertheless was granted appellate jurisdiction if the circuit court of appeals certified to the Supreme Court a question of law or if the Supreme Court granted a writ of certiorari to bring the judgment before it for review.

While early versions of the bill provided for circuit court certification, certiorari made its first appearance in the Senate substitute for the House bill. At the time,

Judicature Volume 84, Number 3, pp. 120–127

however, other differences between the House and Senate bills were viewed as far more important, particularly because under the House bill, Republican President Benjamin Harrison (who had lost the popular vote) would get to appoint 18 new circuit judges. The Senate substitute called for only one new circuit judge per circuit, rather than the two provided for in the House bill. An alternative favored by a minority of the Senate Judiciary Committee (including its chairman) would have avoided the appointment of any new judges by authorizing the Supreme Court to sit in panels of three to hear and decide cases that did not present constitutional questions.

Although there was far-ranging debate in the Senate concerning the merits of the various approaches, there was no debate about certiorari. Instead, from what little appears in the legislative history, it seems certiorari was envisioned as a sort of fallback provision should the circuit courts of appeals prove, on occasion, to be surprisingly careless in deciding cases or issuing certificates.

Certiorari did not spread to review of state court judgments until 1914, nearly 25 years later. From 1789 until 1914, Supreme Court review of state court judgments was governed by one central principle: The Supreme Court was obligated to review a final judgment rendered by a state court system that denied a federal claim or defense, but had no jurisdiction to review a state court judgment that upheld a federal claim or defense. In 1914, the Supreme Court was empowered for the first time to review a state court judgment upholding a federal claim or defense. This new category of cases was made reviewable by the writ of certiorari.[2]

The year 1916 marks the first congressional authorization for the Supreme Court to decline to review a state court judgment denying a federal claim or defense. The 1916 statute was sufficiently ambiguous, however, that it was quite difficult to tell just how large the shift from mandatory to discretionary jurisdiction actually was. Construed one way, mandatory review remained when a state court rejected a federal challenge to state legislative and executive action. Construed differently, however, many such cases were shifted from mandatory to discretionary jurisdiction. Congress did not focus on this ambiguity, but instead on relieving the Court from the obligation to decide cases brought under the Federal Employers' Liability Act (FELA). The Court nonetheless interpreted the 1916 Act to eliminate from its mandatory jurisdiction not only FELA and other similar cases, but also cases raising constitutional objections to state executive action.

Taft's efforts

In 1921, William Howard Taft fulfilled his lifelong ambition and became Chief Justice of the United States. A few years earlier, after losing his 1912 campaign for reelection as President, Taft had called for the Supreme Court's mandatory appellate jurisdiction to be limited to "questions of constitutional construction." In all other cases, argued Taft, litigants should be given an "opportunity" to "apply for a writ of certiorari to bring any case from a lower to the Supreme Court, so that it may exercise absolute and arbitrary discretion with respect to all business but constitutional business."[3] When he became chief justice, he quickly began to work toward increasing the Court's "absolute and arbitrary discretion."

Taft was quite willing to depart from tradition and marshal the Court to draft and actively promote legislation. He lobbied the solicitor general and members of Congress, and drafted supportive passages for inclusion in President Calvin Coolidge's annual state of the union messages. He sent Justices Willis Van Devanter, James McReynolds, and George Sutherland to testify before the Senate Judiciary Committee, reasoning that "McReynolds is a Democrat and knows many of the Senators. Sutherland has been a Senator, and Van Devanter is one of the most forcible of our Court and most learned on questions of jurisdiction."[4]

In urging Congress to enact the Judges' Bill, the justices explained that they read and discussed every petition, granted certiorari not only whenever four (or sometimes three) thought appropriate, but also as a matter of course whenever there was a conflict in the circuit courts of appeals. Moreover, they stated that certiorari in constitutional cases would only be denied when the decision sought to be reviewed was clearly correct, expressing confidence that no constitutional question of any real merit or doubt would be denied review. They assured Congress that they intended to continue these methods and not relax their vigilance as the number of petitions increased, and reminded Congress that the circuit courts of appeals, through their certification power, would share in the control of the Supreme Court's docket.

Taft relied heavily on the support of the American Bar Association. Before securing its support, however, he had to overcome the most recent suggestion from the ABA's Committee on Jurisprudence and Law Reform, a suggestion that the burden on the Supreme Court could be relieved by increasing the number of the justices, allowing it to sit in panels of six, while requiring the agreement of five for a decision. In convincing the ABA to abandon this suggestion and support the Judges' Bill, Chief Justice Taft had the help of someone who was both a member of the committee and a member of the family: his brother Henry Taft. Writing in response to his brother's inquiry about the committee's suggestion, Chief Justice Taft lost no time in expressing vehement opposition and noting, "Consider the danger of setting a precedent to a Demagouge [sic] Democratic Administration." [5] Once the ABA was on board, its strategy was to convince congressmen "that this bill was of such a highly technical order that the Bar Association did not feel itself prepared or qualified to act," and warn them "against exposing a tremendous lot of ignorance." [6]

Taft's hand was also strengthened by the 1924 presidential election in which Robert La Follette ran as a Progressive against incumbent Republican Calvin Coolidge and Democrat John Davis. Republicans, fearful of La Follette draining votes from Coolidge, portrayed La Follette as a dangerous radical, pointing particularly to his proposals for curbing federal judicial power. Taft was kept surprisingly informed about the campaign,[7] including how the Court issue was helping Coolidge with Catholic and other ethnic voters—voters who were pleased by the Court's invalidation of a Nebraska law prohibiting foreign language instruction and anticipated the Court's protection of parochial schools from an Oregon compulsory public education law.[8] In this context, Coolidge's landslide victory weakened any opposition to the Court.[9]

Shortly after the election, Taft renewed his push for the Judges' Bill with members of the lame duck Congress. The House of Representatives took up the bill and passed it on a voice vote "almost without discussion."[10] In the Senate a modest amendment was worked out in consultation with Senator Walsh and the justices to redress a perceived disparity in the way the Judges' Bill treated state courts and circuit courts. Indeed, only Senator Heflin voted against the Judges' Bill, arguing that judges "who may be looking for the least work possible and for longer periods of leisure" should not be empowered to deny humble citizens' right to appeal.[11] When the bill returned to the House, it concurred in the Senate amendment by voice vote with even less deliberation than before.

Taft was pleased with his success. As he explained to his son:

We got our Supreme Court Bill through this week, and we are greatly rejoiced. We mollified Walsh and by a slight concession secured his assistance. We did the thing within two days after we started. I have had to give up three full days this week to it. . . . I had a letter from Congressman Sumners of Texas, saying that he never knew of a case in which such an important bill went through so smoothly and in such a short time. He complimented us by saying that it was due to its origin. . . . We have been three years at work on this and it represents really a great effort.[12]

Give 'em an inch

Soon after the Judges' Bill became law, the Court claimed the authority to issue limited grants of certiorari, that is, to decide to decide only a particular issue in a case, ignoring other issues. It asserted this power even though one of Taft's arguments for the Judges' Bill was that there was a "greater need" for discretion as to cases from the circuit courts of appeals than from state courts because in the former the "power of review extends to the whole case and every question presented in it" rather than only to the federal questions.[13]

Indeed, in the famous Olmstead case in 1928, involving the admissibility of wiretap evidence, Chief Justice Taft's opinion asserted the authority to limit review to constitutional questions, thereby ignoring possible non-constitutional grounds of decision. This practice of limited grants of certiorari has become so uncritically accepted that, under current Supreme Court rules, no writ of certiorari brings before the Court all questions presented by the record. Today, then, all writs of certiorari are limited writs. Put slightly differently, the Supreme Court does not so much grant certiorari to decide particular cases, but rather to decide particular questions. The result can well be the affirmance of judgments that, while correct as to the controversial issue on which certiorari is granted, are nevertheless erroneous because they are based on a simpler error that the Supreme Court declines to consider.

The same year that the Court decided Olmstead and claimed the power to issue limited writs of certiorari, it also promulgated a new rule requiring the filing of a jurisdictional statement in appeals, thus laying the groundwork for extending its discretion to cases within its mandatory jurisdiction—cases where Taft dared not propose certiorari for fear of congressional opposition. As early as 1945, a deputy clerk of the Supreme Court wrote that "[j]urisdictional statements and petitions for certiorari now stand on practically the same footing." [14] Eventually it became commonplace to conclude that "[t]he jurisdiction that is obligatory in form is discretionary in fact." [15] Some commentators were critical of such lawlessness,[16] but Congress, rather than objecting to the Court's noncompliance with the statute, instead amended the statute to conform to the Court's practice.[17]

In the hearings on the Judges' Bill, it was repeatedly noted that the Supreme Court would not alone control its jurisdiction, but that the courts of appeals, by use of certification, would share in that control. Yet just as the Court increased its power to set its own agenda by tending to treat appeals more like petitions for certiorari, so too it largely deprived the lower courts of their promised role in controlling the Supreme Court's docket. This process also began soon after the Judges' Bill was enacted. In the decade from 1927 to 1936, courts of appeals issued 72 certificates, while in the decade from 1937 to 1946, that number had dropped to 20.[18] In the period from 1946 until 1985, the Court accepted only four certificates.[19] At this point, certification is practically a dead letter, and, although it remains on the books,[20] I suspect there are few lawyers (and perhaps few circuit judges) who even know it remains an option.

Questioning certiorari

Although the Supreme Court has achieved the ability to select what cases it will decide, there remain important questions to be asked: How can this power be reconciled with the classic justification for judicial review? How can a court with such power claim to be exercising judgment rather than will, and is such a power consistent with the rule of law? Can this power be justified as a form of administrative rather than judicial power?

As Alexander Bickel recognized almost four decades ago, there is a deep tension between certiorari and the classic justification for judicial review.[21] Pursuant to that classic justification, judicial review is the byproduct of a court's obligation to decide a case. In *Marbury v. Madison*, Chief Justice Marshall did more than simply assert that it is "province and duty of the judicial department to say what the law is." In the next two sentences, he immediately explained why:

> Those who apply the law to particular cases, must of necessity expound and interpret the rule. If two laws conflict with each other, the courts must decide on the operation of each.

Because a court lacks the luxury of simply avoiding decision, it must sometimes choose between following a statute and following the Constitution. This justification of judicial review, then, is the point of Marshall's famous passage from *Cohens v. Virginia* (1821):

> It is most true that this Court will not take jurisdiction if it should not: but it is equally true, that it must take jurisdiction if it should. The judiciary cannot, as the legislature may, avoid a measure because it approaches the confines of the constitution. We cannot pass it by because it is doubtful. With whatever doubts, with whatever difficulties, a case may be attended, we must decide it, if it be brought before us. We have no more right to decline the exercise of jurisdiction which is given, than to usurp that which is not given. The one or the other would be treason to the constitution. Questions may occur which we would gladly avoid; but we cannot avoid them. All we can do is, to exercise our best judgment, and conscientiously to perform our duty.

Alexis de Tocqueville and Abraham Lincoln both made the same point. Tocqueville observed in *Democracy in America,* "But the American judge is dragged in spite of himself onto the political field. He only pronounces on the law because he has to judge a case, and he cannot refuse to decide the case." Lincoln, despite his refusal to accept the authoritativeness of the Supreme Court's interpretation of the Constitution in the Dred Scott opinion, noted that he was not making "any assault upon the court, or the judges. It is a duty, from which they may not shrink, to decide cases properly brought before them. . . ." [22]

The Supreme Court's certiorari practice, however, completely undercuts this rationale.

Strikingly, in advocating the Judges' Bill, the justices never attempted to explain its application in cases presenting even arguable constitutional questions. Instead, the only use envisioned in constitutional cases was as a way of quickly dealing with claims that were either frivolous or plainly governed by precedent. In this way, the justices never had to deal with reconciling certiorari and judicial review. Indeed, perhaps the tension between certiorari and the classic justification for judicial review helps to explain why it was not until 1953 that the Court would definitively hold that a denial of certiorari was not a ruling on the merits of a constitutional challenge.[23]

Alexander Bickel did not attempt a reconciliation either, but instead used certiorari as a lever to argue against the classic conception of judicial review. In contrast to the classic conception, Bickel instead justified judicial review by idolizing the Supreme Court as the institutional representative of "decency and reason," and by asserting that its "constitutional function" is "defin[ing] values and proclaim[ing] principles." [24] Some variant of this view is commonplace (either explicitly or implicitly) among constitutional scholars today, but as John Harrison has correctly observed, "[t]he power to interpret the Constitution . . . comes from the case-deciding power. To suggest that the power to interpret is primary and the case deciding power secondary, is to misinterpret the Constitution and to confuse cause and effect." [25] Such a view unhinges the Supreme Court from other courts—all of which exercise the power of judicial review, both within the classic model and in fact. While there is an enormous literature responding to Bickel's "counter-majoritarian difficulty" and "passive virtues," I am not aware of any work that takes up his challenge to reconcile certiorari with the classic conception of judicial review.

A court that can simply refuse to hear a case can no longer credibly say that it had to decide it. If asked, "Why did you exercise the awesome power to declare an Act of Congress unconstitutional?" the justices of the Supreme Court can no longer say, "Because we had to." Instead, they must say, "Because we chose to."

The inability of the Supreme Court to credibly claim that it has to decide a case highlights another profound tension between certiorari and classic conceptions of judicial power. The judiciary, as Hamilton explained in Federalist No. 78, is the least dangerous branch because it possesses only judgment, not force or will. But although this description continues to be widely repeated, it is hardly an accurate description of a court that has the power to set its own agenda. While the judiciary still lacks its own military force, the Judges' Bill gave the Supreme Court an important tool with which to exercise will: The ability to set one's own agenda is at the heart of exercising will.

Moreover, while the idea of the rule of law insists that judges be meaningfully constrained, there is precious little constraint on judicial action where certiorari is concerned. While Justice Van Devanter assured Congress in the hearings regarding the Judges' Bill that petitions were determined by recognized principles, he changed the subject rather than elaborate what those principles were.[26] From Taft's day forward, the Court has refused to elaborate, either by rule or through case law, constraining legal principles to govern the granting of writs of certiorari. Except for specifying certain types of conflicts—and the Court does not consider itself obligated to grant certiorari whenever a petition reveals such a conflict—the Court has "essentially defined certworthiness tautologically; that is, that which makes a case important enough to be certworthy is a case that we consider important enough to be certworthy." [27]

Perhaps the most graphic illustration of how certiorari frequently operates in the area of will and not law is the common practice of defensive denials. In a defensive denial, a justice votes to deny certiorari not due to the unimportance of the issue involved but due to disapproval of the result the Court is expected to reach on the merits. Remarkably, "[m]ost justices view defensive denials as an acceptable strategy." [28]

One possible response that defenders of current certiorari practice might make is that the only issue being decided on a certiorari petition is which court will have the last word in a case. On this view, the judiciary as a whole must decide the case and, in so doing, exercise judgment in accordance with the rule of law rather than will. So understood, the Supreme Court's power to choose which cases to decide and which to leave for final adjudication by other courts is better viewed as a species of administrative power rather than adjudicative power. The Judges' Bill does share kinship with the Rules Enabling Act, and was born in an era of considerable faith in the notion of neutral expertise in general and neutral expertise regarding the establishment of judicial procedure in particular.

There is a fundamental difficulty with viewing certiorari as administrative power: The Supreme Court has certiorari jurisdiction over both the state courts and the inferior federal courts. Yet, it is difficult to see any basis for the Supreme Court to claim administrative power over state courts. As the Court explained earlier this year, "This Court has supervisory authority over the federal courts," but it "is beyond dispute that we do not hold a supervisory power over the courts of the several States." [29] Put slightly differently, when administering its certiorari jurisdiction over inferior federal courts, the Supreme Court could be understood to be allocating cases among the members of the federal judiciary who together exercise the judicial power of the United States, in a way roughly analogous to the way the judicial panel on multi-district litigation allocates cases for pretrial proceedings to various district courts and judges, or even more roughly, the way a multimember court that does not always sit en banc allocates cases among its judges. When the Supreme Court administers certiorari jurisdiction over state courts, however, it is determining whether the judicial power of the United States shall be called into play at all.

Even as limited to inferior federal courts (or assuming that the objections to the Supreme Court exercising administrative authority over state courts were overcome), there remains another significant difficulty with viewing certiorari as administrative power: Faith in such apolitical management by experts has been deeply shaken, not only in administrative law generally, but in procedural law in particular.[30] Debates over the Federal Rules of Civil Procedure reflect this loss of faith, with the rule making process seen less as something to be left in the hands of neutral experts in the "just, speedy, and inexpensive" decision of cases, than as an arena for battle over the substantive results of cases.[31] It is hardly surprising in this environment that the Supreme Court has not heeded the call for clearer and more detailed standards governing certiorari: Not only would any such standards tend to reduce the Court's agenda-setting power, but also the debate over the content of those standards would itself likely be highly political. In any event, it has become far more difficult to justify judicial control over the judicial agenda on the basis of neutral administrative expertise.

Importance of certiorari

In questioning certiorari, I do not doubt its importance. Indeed, the power to select cases—like other doctrinal devices that reduce the impact of particular decisions, such as non-retroactivity and qualified immunity—makes it easier for the Supreme Court to change its interpretation of the Constitution. It also enables the Court to intervene selectively, without committing itself to policing a new area it brings under its supervision. As a result, then, the procedural license given by certiorari has had a profound role in shaping our substantive constitutional law.

Consider, for example, the incorporation doctrine. The Supreme Court launched the idea that some of the protections of the Bill of Rights were "incorporated" in the Fourteenth Amendment's Due Process Clause in 1925, four months after the Judges' Bill.[32] Perhaps that was purely coincidental. Perhaps the First Amendment right to freedom of speech would have been applied to the states regardless of whether Congress gave the Court discretionary control over the bulk of its docket.

But would the Supreme Court have incorporated the Fourth, Fifth, Sixth, and Eighth Amendments if it were obliged to review every state judgment that upheld a criminal conviction or sentence over a defendant's objection based on one of these amendments? And if it did, is it remotely possible that it would have spun out such elaborate doctrinal requirements if it were required to apply and enforce them in every such case? Reflect for a moment on what that would have required (and require) from the Court: deciding every losing claim that evidence should have been excluded because obtained in violation of the Fourth Amendment,[33] every losing *Miranda*[34] claim, every losing *Massiah*[35] claim, every losing *Strickland*[36] claim, every losing *Lockett*[37] claim—and much, much more.[38]

More generally, the Court's unbridled discretion to control its own docket, choosing not only which cases to decide, but also which "questions presented" to decide, appears to have contributed to a mindset that thinks of the Supreme Court more as sitting to resolve controversial questions than to decide cases. Cases tend to be thought of as "vehicles" for deciding controversial questions, and some distinguished commentators suggest that the role of the Supreme Court is to pronounce the law authoritatively, with the limitation of the judicial power to "cases and controversies" simply a way to limit the occasions for those pronouncements.[39]

Second to none

Justice Brennan once stated that choosing cases is "second to none in importance."[40] Indeed, the Supreme Court's power to set its agenda may be more important than what the Court decides on the merits. Recent scholarship has called into serious doubt the notion that the Supreme Court has been or can be the counter-majoritarian hero of some lawyers' dreams, suggesting instead that the Court lacks both the power and the inclination to deviate very far from prevailing elite opinion.[41] Yet when one considers the impact of cases such as *Prigg v. Pennsylvania*,[42] *Dred Scott v. Sandford*,[43] *Brown v. Board of Education*,[44] *Miranda v. Arizona*,[45] *Furman v. Georgia*,[46] *Roe v. Wade*,[47] *Bowers v. Hardwick*,[48] and *Cruzan v. Missouri*,[49] it may be that the most significant impact of Supreme Court decisions is to increase the political salience of the issues decided—regardless of which way it decides the issues.

For 75 of our more than 200 years under the Constitution, we have had a Supreme Court with a far-ranging power to set its own agenda and thereby shape the nation's political agenda. On the 75th anniversary of the Judges' Bill of 1925, it is appropriate to reflect upon and question this important feature of our legal and political landscape.

Notes

This article originally appeared in Volume 84, Number 3, November–December 2000, pages 120–127. An unabridged version appears in the *Columbia Law Review*, vol. 100, no. 7 (November 2000).

1. 62 Cong. Rec. 8547 (1922) (printing speech delivered by Sen. Walsh of Montana on June 8, 1922).

2. *See* Hartnett, "Why Is the Supreme Court of the United States Protecting State Judges from Popular Democracy?," *Tex. L. Rev.* 75 (1997), 907, 913–956.

3. Taft, "The Attacks on the Courts and Legal Procedure," *Ky. L. J.,* 5 (November 1916), 18, (publishing address delivered on May 23, 1914).

4. Letter from William H. Taft to Thomas W. Shelton (Jan. 31, 1924) (Taft Papers Reel 261).

5. Letter from William H. Taft to Henry W. Taft (Apr. 6, 1922) (Taft Papers Reel 240).

6. Letter from Thomas W. Shelton to William H. Taft (Dec. 19, 1924) (Taft Papers Reel 270).

7. *See, e.g.,* Letter from Gus Karger, *Cincinnati Times Star,* to William H. Taft (Aug. 7, 1924) (Taft Papers Reel 266) (enclosing an advance copy of Coolidge's acceptance speech to be held in confidence until Aug. 14); Letter from Charles D. Hilles, Vice-Chairman, Republican National Committee, to William H. Taft (Aug. 8, 1924) (Taft Papers Reel 266) (inquiring, on Republican National Committee letterhead, about Taft's view whether, if the Electoral College fails to select a President and the election falls to the House of Representatives, a state's delegation that is evenly split can cast a fractional vote).

8. *See* Ross, *A Muted Fury: Populists, Progressives, and Labor Unions Confront the Courts, 1890–1937* (1994), 264–265; *Meyer v. Nebraska,* 262 U.S. 390, 396–403 (1923); *Pierce v. Society of Sisters,* 268 U.S. 510, 529–536 (1925). Note that the district court had invalidated the Oregon law in March of 1924, *Society of Sisters v. Pierce,* 296 F. 928 (D. Or. 1924), and that the Supreme Court's affirmance was not until June of 1925.

9. Ross, Ibid. at 284.

10. Murphy, *Elements of Judicial Strategy* (1964), 145.

11. *Cong. Rec.* 66 (Feb. 3, 1925), 2928.

12. Letter from William H. Taft to Charles P. Taft, II (Feb. 8, 1925) (Taft Papers Reel 271).

13. *Cong. Rec.* 66 (Feb. 3, 1925), 2921 (letter from Taft to Copeland (Dec. 31, 1924)).

14. Wiley, "Jurisdictional Statements on Appeals to U.S. Supreme Court," *A.B.A. J.* 31 (1945), 239, 239.

15. Casper & Posner, *The Workload of the Supreme Court* (1976), 1.

16. *See, e.g.,* Wechsler, "The Appellate Jurisdiction of the Supreme Court: Reflections on the Law and the Logistics of Direct Review," *Wash. & Lee L. Rev.* 34 (1977), 1043, 1061 ("If that was so . . . the Court simply disregarded its statutory duty to decide appealed cases on the merits."); Ibid. ("It is simply inadmissible that the highest court of law should be lawless in relation to its own jurisdiction.").

17. *See* Act of June 27, 1984, Pub. L. 100-352, 102 Stat. 662 (eliminating virtually all of the Supreme Court's mandatory jurisdiction).

18. *See* Moore and Vestal, "Present and Potential Role of Certification in Federal Appellate Procedure," *Va. L. Rev.* 35 (1949), 1, 25–26 n.99.

19. Stern et al., *Supreme Court Practice,* 7th ed. (1993), 450. My research has not located any since 1985.

20. 28 U.S.C. §1254(2).

21. *See* Bickel, *The Least Dangerous Branch: The Surpeme Court at the Bar of Politics* (1962), 127.

22. Abraham Lincoln, First Inaugural Address (March 4, 1861), in *The Collected Works of Abraham Lincoln,* vol. 4, Roy P. Basler ed. (1953), 249, 268.

23. See *Brown v. Allen,* 344 U.S. 443, 489–497 (1953) (opinion for Court by Justice Frankfurter) (holding that "in habeas corpus cases, as in others, denial of certiorari cannot be interpreted as an 'expression of opinion on the merits' ").

24. Bickel, *supra* n. 21, at 68, 133.

25. Harrison, "The Role of the Legislative and Executive Branches in Interpreting the Constitution," *Cornell L. Rev.* 73 (1988), 371, 373.

26. *See* Gibbs, "Certiorari: Its Diagnosis and Cure," *Hastings L. J.* 6 (1955), 131, 138 n.41.

27. Perry, *Deciding to Decide: Agenda Setting in the United States Supreme Court* (1991), 34.

28. Ibid. at 198–207 (discussing defensive denials).

29. *Dickerson v. United States,* 120 S. Ct. 2326 (2000), 2332–2333.

30. *See* Post, "Judicial Management and Judicial Disinterest: The Achievements and Perils of Chief Justice William Howard Taft," *J. Sup. Ct. Hist.* (1998), 50, 61 ("As a good child of the Progressive era, Taft seemingly regarded judicial reform as purely technical and apolitical.").

31. *See, e.g.,* Bone, "The Process of Making Process: Court Rulemaking, Democratic Legitimacy, and Procedural Efficacy," *Geo. L. J.* 87 (1999), 887, 889 (noting that "court rulemaking has moved toward a legislative model and away from the traditional model based on reasoned deliberation and expertise. Because procedure has substantive effects and involves controversial value choices, critics argue, rulemaking is 'political'. . . ."); Burbank, "The Costs of Complexity," *Mich. L. Rev.* 85 (1987), 1463, 1473 (reviewing Marcus and Sherman, *Complex Litigation: Cases and Materials on Advanced Civil Procedure* [1985]) (arguing that "the perception that procedural rules are

not neutral makes it important to try to identify the impact of procedural rules and to be candid in describing [both] that impact. . . . [and] the purposes of procedural rules" and that "consideration should be given to the political legitimacy of the process by which they are formulated or applied and of the actors who are formulating or applying them").

32. Compare the Feb. 13, 1925 passage of the Judges' Bill and the Jun. 8, 1925 announcement of the decision in *Gitlow v. New York,* 268 U.S. 652, 666 (1925) (assuming First Amendment right of free speech incorporated in due process).

33. See *Mapp v. Ohio,* 367 U.S. 643, 660 (1961) (applying exclusionary rule to the states). This would include, for example, every losing challenge to the sufficiency of a warrant, *see, e.g., Illinois v. Gates,* 462 U.S. 213, 225–230 (1983) (establishing totality of circumstances test for validity of warrant) and every losing challenge to a stop and frisk, see, e.g., *Terry v. Ohio,* 392 U.S. 1, 16–20 (1968) (frisk acceptable when stop is justified and frisk "reasonably related to circumstances").

34. See *Miranda v. Arizona,* 384 U.S. 436 (1966) (requiring police to give warnings to those in custody prior to interrogation).

35. See *Massiah v. United States,* 377 U.S. 201 (1964) (forbidding use of post-indictment statement elicited by government agents in the absence of counsel).

36. See *Strickland v. Washington,* 466 U.S. 668 (1984) (setting forth standards for claims of ineffective assistance of counsel).

37. See *Lockett v. Ohio,* 438 U.S. 586 (1978) (forbidding exclusion of virtually any evidence regarding the offense or defendant's character preferred as mitigating by the defendant regarding death penalty).

38. See, e.g., *Batson v. Kentucky,* 476 U.S. 79, 93–98 (1986) (forbidding racebased peremptory challenges by prosecutors); *Brady v. Maryland,* 373 U.S. 83, 87 (1963) (requiring disclosure of material exculpatory information). It is likewise inconceivable that the Court would have decided that due process requires a court to determine whether record evidence is sufficient to support a finding of guilt beyond a reasonable doubt, see *Jackson v. Virginia,* 443 U.S. 307, 321 (1979) (sufficiency of evidence "cognizable in federal habeas corpus proceeding"), if it were the Court that had to review every state criminal case in which a defendant asserted that the state courts wrongly rejected his sufficiency argument.

39. *See, e.g.,* Alexander and Schauer, "On Extrajudicial Constitutional Interpretation," *Harv. L. Rev.* 110 (1997), 1359, 1376–1381 (defending judicial supremacy in constitutional interpretation based on view that role of Supreme Court is to settle authoritatively what is to be done); cf. Schauer, "Giving Reasons," *Stan L. Rev.* 47 (1995), 633, 655 (describing ban on advisory opinions as a good strategic way to cabin the courts and prevent overreaching). But *see* Hartnett, "A Matter of Judgment, Not a Matter of Opinion," *N.Y.U. L. Rev.* 74 (1999), 123 (arguing against judicial supremacy and stressing that the judicial function is to decide cases by issuing judgments).

40. Brennan, "The National Court of Appeals: Another Dissent," *U. Chi. L. Rev.* 40 (1973), 473, 477.

41. *See, e.g.,* Rosenberg, *The Hollow Hope: Can Courts Bring About Social Change?* (1991) (showing that U.S. courts rarely produce significant social reform and at best only second social reforms that originate in other government branches); *see also* Klarman, "Brown, Racial Change, and the Civil Rights Movement," *Va. L. Rev.* 80 (1994), 7 (arguing that the decision in *Brown v. Board of Education* did not directly instigate social change; instead, it precipitated Southern white resistance, and the portrayal of this resistance on television roused Northern whites to demand change).

42. 41 U.S. (16 Pet.) 539 (1842) (holding unconstitutional a state law against the use of self help in recovering those claimed to be fugitive slaves).

43. 60 U.S. (19 How.) 393 (1857) (holding that free blacks whose ancestors were slaves are not citizens of the United States under the Constitution and stating that a black slave who is taken to free territory does not become free, but remains the property of his owner).

44. 347 U.S. 483 (1954) (finding racial segregation in public schools unconstitutional).

45. 384 U.S. 436 (1966) (ruling that a person taken into custody by the police must be informed of various rights).

46. 408 U.S. 238 (1972) (ruling that in some cases the imposition of the death penalty may constitute cruel and unusual punishment).

47. 410 U.S. 113 (1973) (holding that the right to privacy is "broad enough to encompass a woman's decision whether or not to terminate her pregnancy").

48. 478 U.S. 186 (1986) (upholding the constitutionality of a Georgia statute that criminalizes sodomy); *see also Boy Scouts of America v. Dale,* 120 S. Ct. 2446 (2000) (holding that the Boy Scouts have a constitutional right to exclude an avowed homosexual and gay rights activist); Zernike, "Scouts' Successful Ban on Gays is Followed by Loss of Support," *New York Times,* Aug. 29, 2000, at A1 (describing erosion of corporate and governmental support of the Boy Scouts since the *Dale* decision).

49. 497 U.S. 261 (1990) (finding that there is no constitutionally-protected fundamental right to die).

Appellate Court Processes

Internal Court Processes and Decisions on the Merits

Many of the efforts of social scientists studying appellate courts have focused on judicial decision making. These scholars have utilized several theoretical perspectives in an attempt to understand why judges decide cases the way that they do. At times, this academic research has even resulted in the successful prediction of outcomes in pending cases. Among the concerns researchers have focused on are such factors as the social backgrounds of judges, their ideological preferences, their interrelationships in a collegial appellate court setting, their judicial philosophies, their concerns about the judiciary's proper role and, moving beyond factors intrinsic to individual judges, the fact patterns present in cases before the court. Even external factors such as public opinion have been seen as possible influences on judicial decisions.

While this is not an exhaustive list of the variables that can enter into a judge's decisional equation, and while none of them on its own is likely to be the exclusive basis for a judge's decision in a case, social science research has demonstrated clearly that such factors do matter and that judicial decisions do not emanate solely from the law itself. Each of the articles in this section focuses on some facet of the judicial decision-making process or the decisional patterns of appellate courts and sheds some light on how such courts reach decisions in the cases before them.

Stephen Wasby's piece, "The functions and importance of appellate oral argument," utilizes data from interviews with lawyers and judges to explore this under-examined area of the judicial process. While examining oral argument in a specific intermediate appellate court setting, the federal Ninth Circuit, Wasby's observations have clear relevance for all appellate courts, including the U.S. Supreme Court. The article examines two alternative perspectives on the value of oral argument. On one end of the spectrum, some contend that it facilitates the development of information, clarifies issues, and helps focus case proceedings. Face-to-face contact among the actors in the judicial process also provides real and symbolic benefits. It puts a human face on the law while underscoring that both sides to a legal conflict have had their day in court and a chance to be heard. Others hold that oral argument is often unnecessary and exacerbates delay in an already overloaded system.

Wasby finds a degree of truth in both perspectives while acknowledging the inherent tension between them. "On the one hand is the desire to maintain a practice that is not merely an 'amenity' but is also thought to have considerable importance for both appellate judges and appellate lawyers. On the other hand is a feeling of the need to adjust to substantial appellate caseloads by recognizing that different types of cases can be treated differently."

When the Supreme Court reaches a decision, the chief justice, if in the majority, exercises the power of designating the majority opinion writer for the case. Analysts have long noted that this authority gives chief justices considerable ability to structure the reasoning used to justify and explain a case's outcome. Chief justices may, at times, decide to author opinions themselves or assign the case to an ideological ally. In closely divided cases, they may follow a strategy aimed at holding the Court's tenuous majority together, such as choosing an opinion writer in the ideological center of the majority coalition. In the exercise of their authority, chief justices must also be concerned about maintaining equitable workloads among the justices and ensuring both collective and individual satisfaction with the assignments that have been made.

Historically, justices who wished to dissent from the Court's rulings generally did so as an individual act. While one or more of their colleagues may have joined them, the decision to pen a dissent was an exclusively personal one. That such is no longer the case is well documented in Beverly Blair Cook's study of "Justice Brennan and the institutionalization of dissent assignment."

Cook's fascinating analysis begins with a historical discussion of dissent on the Supreme Court and documents how Justice William Brennan fostered an institutional role with significant power potential for the Court's senior associate justice in the minority. Delving into the private papers of justices, Cook illuminates the internal workings of the Supreme Court and highlights an environment in which "minority opinion solidarity [becomes] a strong tool with which to threaten the majority." The author concludes that both the routine reality of dissent assignments and the propensity for solo dissenters to author opinions explaining their stances underscore that the norm of consensus that once characterized the Court has been trumped by the institution's openly competitive environment.

The institutional role and importance of the spirit of dissent is also the focus of the piece by J. Louis Campbell III. Here, dissent is described as analogous to civil disobedience and characterized as "institutional disobedience" that offers protest and seeks systemic change. At bottom, dissents are "sources of energy and cogency in the law." Examples of now-famous dissenting opinions and their impact are offered throughout Campbell's analysis.

Whereas Cook and Campbell focus on evolving norms for dissent behavior on the Supreme Court, Jeffrey Segal and Robert Howard's study, "How Supreme Court justices respond to litigant requests to overturn precedent," examines adherence to stare decisis. This fundamental legal norm dictates that courts should, whenever possible, decide cases by following established precedent. The authors are quite aware of the difficulties of examining the influence of precedent as an empirical question because "influence requires that the precedent lead them to a result that they would not otherwise have reached," a difficult matter to prove. Thus, for example, in the aftermath of *Roe v. Wade*, "Justices Blackmun, Marshall, Brennan, etc., certainly followed *Roe*, in that their decisions were consistent with *Roe*'s commands. But it is difficult to assess whether they were influenced by *Roe*, for they were supportive of the right to abortion to begin with." As a practical matter, Segal and Howard point out that the Court overturns 2–3 prior decisions each year and that, "in any given decade, the Court overturns less than .002 percent of its previous decisions!"

The fact that overturning precedent occurs so infrequently does not mean that it defies analysis. The authors examine the propensity of justices to overturn precedent in cases in which they have been explicitly asked to do so (a relatively rare occurrence) and in the context of their attitudinal preferences. They argue that, "to conclude that a justice generally upholds precedent in the face of a request for overruling, we submit that she must generally defer both when that precedent is in a liberal direction and when the precedent is in a conservative direction." In their interesting analysis, Segal and Howard found that all of the jus-

tices under study between 1985 and 1994 (except for Rehnquist, Scalia, and Thomas) voted to uphold precedent more often than to overturn it.

As importantly, however, only four of the thirteen justices studied (Brennan, Stevens, Kennedy, and Souter) supported precedent a majority of the time across ideological lines—that is, regardless of whether the precedent itself was liberal or conservative. Ultimately, the justices were found to be willing to overturn precedents when they ran against their ideological proclivities. As Segal and Howard conclude, "stare decisis survives at the Supreme Court, but it is conditioned, like so much else, on the attitudes and values of the justices."

In "Justice Frankfurter and Justice Reed: friendship and lobbying on the Court," Bradley Canon, Kimberly Greenfield, and Jason Fleming utilize private correspondence and interview data to take readers behind the Court's closed doors. They offer a detailed case study of how the collegial relationships among justices may include substantial efforts to influence behavior on the bench. In this instance, Justice Frankfurter, who sought to be the Court's intellectual leader, is portrayed in his relentless attempts to sway Justice Reed's votes and the content of his opinions. Interestingly, despite all of the evidence presented of Frankfurter's overbearing pursuit of Reed, considered to be a swing justice on a highly divided court, "Reed possessed sufficient independence to become neither a devotee of Frankfurter nor a victim of too much manipulation." The authors also point out that one should not necessarily view the Frankfurter-Reed relationship as evidence of a judiciary run awry. "The ideal of a collegial court . . . envisions decisions and opinions stemming from discussions among the justices instead of, as Justice John M. Harlan put it, 'a tally of individual votes.' "

The articles discussed so far have, in one fashion or another, made reference to the special roles on the Court that might be occupied by chief justices, senior associate justices in opposition to the chief, and justices who perceive themselves to be intellectual leaders. Conventional wisdom has dictated that the Court's least senior members hold another "special" place on the Court. These individuals are said to succumb to a "freshman effect." According to this line of thought, freshmen jurists generally take a centrist position and do not ally with any existing ideological extremes. In addition, they allegedly carry lighter and less consequential workloads than their colleagues in terms of opinion writing responsibilities.

Empirical analyses of these characteristics of the supposed freshman effect have raised serious questions as to its existence in fact. In "Freshman opinion writing on the U.S. Supreme Court, 1921–1991," Terry Bowen and John Scheb II utilize an extensive data set to demonstrate definitively that freshmen jurists are assigned cases as frequently as their more senior colleagues and that the cases they are assigned are as difficult as those assigned to the rest of the Court. At least as far as the question of opinion writing is concerned, "the freshman effect posited . . . as part of the conventional wisdom regarding the Court simply does not exist." Bowen and Scheb's analysis is quite compelling, utilizing data on all freshman Supreme Court justices since 1921 except Justices Ginsburg and Breyer.

The articles in this section underline the considerable diversity in subject matter and methodology that characterizes social scientific research on internal court processes and decisions on the merits. Indeed, the questions asked—and the manner in which they are answered—are subject only to the limits of the resources and imagination of the analyst. Eclectic and interesting research in the area of judicial decision making promises to remain a staple in future writing on the subject of judicial politics and in the pages of *Judicature.*

The functions and importance of appellate oral argument: some views of lawyers and federal judges

Stephen L. Wasby

Although some critics have proposed curtailing or eliminating oral argument in certain cases, both judges and lawyers believe it plays a vital role in the appellate process, a recent survey shows.

One of the most traditional and important elements of deciding cases on appeal is oral argument, an element of advocacy older than written briefs in this country. Briefs originally were not required in appeals, and oral argument continued without time limits even when briefs were submitted. Eventually briefs did begin to displace argument: the Supreme Court first waived oral argument when written arguments were submitted, then mandated briefs prior to argument, and finally both reserved argument for the most important cases and reduced the time granted each party.[1]

Curtailment of oral argument in other appellate courts, partly the result of caseload pressure, has attracted continued attention. Various sources have warned that eliminating oral argument in all cases would harm the appellate process.[2] Most recently, the Devitt Committee (the Committee to Consider Standards for Admission to Practice in the Federal Courts of the Judicial Conference of the United States) brought further attention to legal advocacy at both trial and appellate levels. The "substantially divided" committee, however, made no recommendations concerning appellate advocacy because it found "the problems presented ... not sufficiently serious to call for the recommending of remedies"[3]—at least by comparison with trial advocacy, to which the committee devoted the bulk of its attention. Despite the Devitt Committee's view, appellate advocacy remains of considerable importance.

Recent literature shows tension between two divergent tendencies: to retain an essential practice, part of the "procedural amenities" through which courts are "seen to be obeying and enforcing the law,"[4] and to curtail its use in some types of cases to facilitate its retention in others, where it is thought more useful.[5] This article looks at the opinions of the two groups most immediately concerned with appellate argument: lawyers and judges. It is based on interviews with circuit and district judges in the Ninth U.S. Circuit Court of Appeals and with attorneys who had argued before that court.[6]

All the circuit judges and most of the district judges, in their careers as lawyers, had argued appellate cases, but only a few had done so extensively. The experience of the surveyed lawyers is disproportionate to that of most lawyers because not many lawyers engage frequently in appellate work and still fewer argue appellate cases. Two of the attorneys had argued more than 200 state and federal appellate cases each, two others had argued more than 100, and two more had argued between 50 and 100. The least experienced attorneys, by contrast, had argued fewer than 20.

Half the circuit judges said their views of oral argument had changed since their days as practicing lawyers, also true of most of the district judges responding; the other half of the circuit judges said their views had not changed. Those whose views had changed used to feel that as lawyers they could help judges or could "guide the judges" with their knowledge and that "there was something I could add."[7] Now, observed one, he had found as a judge that a "strong minority" of cases was so deficient in merit that "if John Davis argued, it wouldn't make a difference." Other judges now realized that the court's caseload prevented oral argument in every case. Moreover, one noted, judges' preparation—consistently high, unlike the situation in some state appellate courts—made argument less useful, as did the short time allowed for it.

Almost two-thirds of the lawyers had changed their views of appellate argument from prior to participating in it; most now saw it as less important. They found that "brilliance" had little effect on the court, that argument was not "the highly persuasive medium for the judges" they had thought it would be, and that the judges asked fewer questions than they had anticipated. Indeed, some said that at times argument seemed superfluous.

This did not, however, stem from any dissatisfaction with the Ninth Circuit. On the whole, the lawyers were satisfied with oral argument in that court—"by and large, an agreeable court to argue to," "prepared," and "open," with the judges asking "intelligent questions."

In the remainder of this article, we examine first whether appellate oral argument is thought more important for judges or for lawyers. Then we turn to discuss ways in which oral argument helps judges and attorneys and the functions oral argument is thought to perform. We follow this by a look at whether judges and lawyers believe oral argument significant or determinative, as well as the types of cases in which oral argument is thought to be most and least helpful. We draw on Ninth Circuit interviews and on comments from other studies, particularly Federal Judicial Center surveys of judges and of attorneys in the Second, Fifth, and Sixth Circuits.[8]

How oral argument helps

"A great many appellate judges . . . strongly believe that the arguments are a major help," Marvell has noted.[9] The chief judges of the U.S. courts of appeals, responding to Judge Myron Bright's queries, generally found oral argument valuable—"sometimes when least expected," according to First Circuit Judge Frank Coffin,[10] but generally "only in some cases." Screening out cases thought not worthy of argument, the practice in most circuits, has made argument valuable more often when it takes place. Some feel, however, that when judges have long thought about a problem, oral argument is not likely to add much to the resolution of a case.

Both circuit and district judges and lawyers in the Ninth Circuit were almost unanimous in finding appellate oral argument helpful. An interesting difference does occur, however, between judges' and lawyers' opinions on whether argument is more important for lawyers or judges or is equally important for both. Roughly half the circuit judges felt oral argument equally important for both groups; the other half was divided between those who thought it more important for judges and those who thought it more important for lawyers.[11] However, *no* lawyers believed oral argument more important for themselves, except perhaps as a way of impressing clients; two-thirds said it was equally important for the two groups, with the remainder finding it more important for the judges. The lawyers' position may be explained by a circuit judge's observation that "at the appellate stage, the case is no longer the lawyer's but the court's."

A retired state supreme court justice has written that the functions of oral argument are, in descending importance:

> (1) to persuade judges, (2) to focus on one important matter only, (3) to reiterate most major points in the brief, (4) to clarify facts, (5) to counter opposition's arguments, (6) to appeal to "justice," "right," and "fairness," (7) to legitimate the legal process by a public confrontation of issues, (8) to urge judges to read (or reread) briefs, (9) to prepare judges for conference deliberations, (10) to force judges to communicate with each other.[12]

Ninth Circuit judges and attorneys differed in the emphasis each group placed on ways that appellate argument helped.[13] Judges found principally that argument helped them clarify matters and focus on important issues, with the opportunity to communicate with lawyers and ask questions only slightly less important. Judges also suggested that oral argument provided information and aided in disposing of cases. Least frequently noted was argument's assistance in increasing the visibility of the court.

For attorneys, clarification and an opportunity for communication with judges were mentioned more than other functions of argument for the judges, with neither function predominant. Attorneys gave far less attention to providing information, assisting in disposition of cases, giving judges an opportunity to ask questions, and helping to save judges' time.

Judges' and lawyers' comments on argument's functions for lawyers also revealed differences. Most frequently mentioned by judges were argument's functions of assisting lawyers in clarifying matters, persuading judges, and generally in communicating with the judges. Least frequently noted were providing information to judges, answering judges' questions, and making the lawyer's case more visible.

Lawyers spoke about the usefulness of argument for themselves in persuading and prodding judges. They also gave considerable weight to argument's help in clarifying issues. Lawyers also found of moderate importance that oral argument helped them learn about judges. Least frequently mentioned as a function of appellate argument for lawyers were the opportunities to answer questions or to help facilitate disposition of cases.

Assisting the judge

Public relations. There is a "public relations" reason for oral argument—so that lawyers and their clients will feel that their cases have been heard. As one judge observed, lawyers need the satisfaction of knowing they have presented their cases well. The other side of this "P.R." coin is that oral argument assists in legitimating the court's judicial function.[14] The Federal Judicial Center's lawyer survey showed that slightly more than half the lawyers in each circuit studied agreed that "when a litigant is denied the right to have his lawyer argue his appeal, the litigant will feel that he has not had his day in court." [15] Submission of briefs is not thought sufficient to assure lawyers and litigants that judges have focused on the case, because one could not be sure the briefs were read.

As Marvell notes, the "public relations function" of contact between attorneys and judges during argument "is especially important when attorneys suspect that not all judges read the briefs or that the court's staff plays a major role in the decision process." [16] An observer of the First Circuit adds that "by demonstrating the openness and the balanced presentation of all material issues in an individual case, the court assures the public that each action is being given their personal and undivided attention in order to reach a reasoned solution." [17] The Hruska Commission echoed this perspective in pointing out that oral argument "assures the litigant that his case has been given consideration by those charged with deciding it." [18]

Communication. Oral argument is valuable for "establish[ing] a human connection between bench and bar" because it is the only face-to-face communication between attorneys and judges during a case's appellate course. As a Ninth Circuit judge noted, argument assists lawyers by "help[ing] the judges to know who the attorneys are" as well as giving lawyers "a notion of the orientation of the court" and the way it is thinking.

The crucial role of the judge-attorney communication has often been stressed. According to the late Third Circuit Judge William Hastie, "The oral argument is the court's one chance to invite counsel to meet head on what seemed to be the strongest opposing contentions." [19] In the Federal Judicial Center survey, there was extremely high agreement among lawyers that "oral argument permits the attorney to address himself to those issues which the judges believe are crucial to the case." [20]

In addition to the above considerations, the process and "mechanics" of conducting argument help Ninth Circuit judges, particularly because argument comes after a judge has read the briefs. The judge thus hears counsel "against the generalized background of the case." Some judges found this particularly so when a lawyer is "a better talker than a writer"—and some judges simply hear better than they read, as one judge commented. (Oral argument also allows judges to criticize an incompetent lawyer without having to reduce the criticism to writing.)

A less-well-noted aspect of oral argument is communication *among* judges. Questions ostensibly directed to an attorney may be intended for a judicial colleague, to sway that judge or at least to warn of the need to face certain issues.[21] As one lawyer noted, judges "may use the attorney's mouth to convince his colleagues." Appellate argument thus provides judges an "opportunity to respond to each other's questions" and to communicate the "key points of a case" to other members of the panel. If this is effective, at argument's conclusion judges "will have an excellent idea of the key points of a case" and of a problem's "soft underbelly" as well as a sense of other judges' views. Concessions may be more important to judges when a lawyer makes them than if they heard the same argument from a colleague during their collective consideration of the case in conference.

Questions. Central to communication during appellate argument are the judges' questions. Ninth Circuit judges emphasized the opportunity that oral argument provides for exploring doubts they had about the record and "items not entirely clear." A lawyer's response may emphasize a point differently from the emphasis conveyed by the briefs. As a result, "Sometimes we can't understand until we ask questions." (Ninety percent of attorneys in the Federal Judicial Center survey agreed that "by asking questions of counsel, the judges are better able to avoid erroneous interpretations of the facts or issues in the case.") [22]

Questions also allow judges to test attorneys' positions, particularly to see whether the lawyer can help the judge "decide the case his way easily." A lawyer unable to answer effectively will not carry the court. In a complex case, an attorney's responses may provide a judge with necessary "reinforcement" for tentatively adopted positions.

Ninth Circuit attorneys found it easier to argue to judges who asked more questions. They disliked "passive judges," "who stare at you or over your head" or "just smile or go to sleep." Indeed, one lawyer said he didn't object to a judge "disposed against him" if the judge asked questions. The lawyers were, however, concerned about the quality as well as about the frequency of questions; judges who merely "interrogated" were not appreciated, but lawyers generally preferred "tough" or "perceptive" questions.

Despite lawyers' general preference for judges who asked (good) questions, some lawyers felt that judges' questioning cut into the time needed to argue their cases. This is like the conflict Marvell found: several attorneys he interviewed "said they liked questions; yet they complained that the questions cut into their allotted time so much that they had to abandon some of the points they had wished to emphasize." [23]

Information, clarification, and focus

Questioning allows judges to obtain information and to clarify elements of a case. Appellate argument brings to their attention matters not evident in the briefs or not available earlier.[24] Finding out about matters the last brief left unresolved is of some importance when much time has elapsed between filing of the last brief and oral argument. Information conveyed to the judges through argument includes factual and procedural items as well as new legal arguments. Argument is particularly likely to provide judges new information when a lawyer " 'lays back' and doesn't put everything in the briefs." Argument also allows judges to "learn where new cases would go if unleashed in this case" as well as to learn about the "practical effect" unique cases might have.

Oral argument "allows the judges . . . to clear up any doubts that the court might have about the case or the lawyer's approach to it," observes Eighth Circuit Judge Myron Bright;[25] many Ninth Circuit judges agreed that clarification was a salient function of appellate argument. Clarification occurs not only when briefs are "ambiguous" or even poor, but also when they are of high quality, especially in extremely complex cases.

Argument can lead to clarification when it prompts judges to return to the record, but a lawyer can also "straighten out" a judge at argument before the judge engages in such research. Clarification involves the correction of errors, but it also includes "cast[ing] new light" on important aspects of cases that are vague in the briefs when the court requires the lawyer to clarify his position through a "good, logical analysis of the briefs" during argument.

Part of clarification is a focus on issues. Several federal judges have testified to argument's importance in this regard.[26] At least a majority of judges surveyed by the Federal Judicial Center favored oral argument in part because it "focuses the court's attention on the issues [and] provides the needed impetus to get the 'tough' thinking done efficiently." [27] The late Judge Frederick Hamley of the Ninth Circuit commented that judges found argument helpful because of its "tendency to narrow and pinpoint the question to be decided and the points of law to be reviewed," with "the exact point of disagreement which must be resolved" emerging during argument.[28] The Ninth Circuit judges interviewed concurred. They noted argument's function of narrowing issues, allowing judges to "determine what counsel thinks most salient," and permitting worthless arguments to be swept away.

Disposition. Both clarification and focus assist with disposition of a case; focus is essential before the court can bring a case to resolution. The argument process assists in this regard by setting some issues aside as peripheral, so that the judges can deal with the key issues more directly and quickly. By sharpening judges' thinking, argument provides an "opportunity to formulate a judgment." Even if argument does not itself speed disposition, judges' preparation for it does so.[29]

Improving assistance to judges. Before appellate argument takes place, judges must engage in some communication, among themselves and with the attorneys who are to present argument, if argument is to be most helpful both to the court and the attorneys. A preargument conference of the judges can serve this purpose; it can result in questions to be asked to help guide argument in ways that will assist the judges without the attorney having to cover ground of little (or less) interest to them.

More helpful would be communication before the argument session, where judges could indicate points from the briefs on which they wished lawyers to concentrate, those they wished developed further, and questions they wanted answered. Of course, judges need not pose all their questions prior to argument. They could, however, provide some guidance while reserving further questions for argument itself. Judges often object to such suggestions either because their heavy caseload makes it difficult to consider briefs or the record in advance or because they feel it interferes with the adversary process. Yet argument would be more useful for the judges even if attorneys received questions—perhaps developed from staff attorneys' bench memoranda—only a couple of days before argument.

A further and more extreme suggestion is to hold argument *after* the judges have written and circulated a tentative opinion. Marvell made such a suggestion because of his concern about "the lack of communication back and forth between counsel and the court to iron out exactly what points interest the court so that the counsel can give information the court needs." [30] A natural objection is that judges' views would tend to become frozen. However, if judges could keep their opinions tentative, such a procedure would certainly communicate to attorneys the issues the judges wanted addressed. To be effective, however, the procedure does require judges to put "a good deal of work into a case early, in time to tell counsel of their concerns and to give counsel a chance to prepare answers." [31]

Assisting the lawyers

Communication. Judges, we have noted, find that appellate argument assists them in establishing communication with lawyers. Lawyers find it similarly helpful in establishing communication with judges. Argument provides a lawyer "the opportunity to discourse with the court, and to argue and discuss with the court, or share ideas," as well as to get "points firmly lodged in the judicial mind." [32] For Ninth Circuit attorneys, appellate argument "allows face-to-face contact between an attorney and the court," thus permitting a lawyer "to grapple with a mind which has already come to grips with the problem" in a case and work through problems bothering the judges.

Appellate argument also allows indirect communication of certain messages. If an attorney tells judges at argument that the attorney's client is present, judges, who appreciate such candor, "understand that some of the things he says are for the benefit of the client, who came to hear them said." An important part of what is communicated at appellate argument is information. This includes "background details," material not covered in briefs, and information about cases decided since the briefs were filed. (Argument may also serve to warn lawyers that they should file supplemental briefs to provide more information on specific points.)

Lawyers also use appellate argument to persuade judges. One senior circuit judge observed that it is the "forcefulness, preparation, and dedication" of particular lawyers that made argument helpful. Part of persuasion for the lawyers was catching the judges' attention or "stimulat[ing] their minds into active thought processes." Another part was to "challenge the judges' concept of a case" and to make them "re-examine their positions."

Clarification and focus. Clarification is a particular significant function of oral argument for attorneys, just as it is for judges. Argument is "enormously beneficial in illuminating . . . precisely what the issues are as counsel sees them." [33] In addition, argument can "cure factual misapprehensions and legal misconceptions," "the two areas than can be met only by oral argument." [34]

Also involved in clarification is the "opportunity to explain seeming contradictions, inconsistencies, or weaknesses in the client's position." When argument allows a lawyer to sense the court's problems with a case, the lawyer can "develop a new theory" to help resolve them. As roughly three-fifths of the attorneys surveyed by the Federal Judicial Center responded, oral argument "allows counsel to gauge the feelings of the judges and to couch his arguments accordingly." [35]

The most crucial element involved in focusing a case at argument is the direct emphasis that can be placed on the most important issues in the case: the lawyer can provide "the crystallized oral statement of the 'gut issue.' " [36] Focusing may entail discarding certain issues as well as stressing others. When flaws in a lawyer's position are revealed at argument, the court does not have to deal with those matters. A lawyer may also use argument to "signal . . . that one or more points in his brief are not well taken"; the judges, realizing that the points were included "to satisfy his client," can then "apply more attention to what he says about his important points" and the lawyer also gains "a little extra credit for his candor."

Oral argument's importance

Relative importance and significance. A large majority of both Ninth Circuit judges and lawyers felt oral argument not of equal importance in all cases. Moreover, no Ninth Circuit appellate judge and only two district judges believed that all cases required the same amount of argument time. Their position is like that of judges surveyed by the Federal Judicial Center, who stressed "varied sets of criteria" for determining appropriate time length for argument and indicated "that a case-by-case method is mandatory with an examination of issue complexity and nature of record and briefs as a starting point." [37]

Ninth Circuit judges felt that complex cases—those with either legal or factual complexity or cases with multiple issues or multiple-defendant criminal cases—required more extended argument. However, they noted only a few specific areas of law in which longer argument was thought necessary, although antitrust, patent, and securities were mentioned by several judges.

Asked to estimate the proportion of cases where appellate argument was "significant," Ninth Circuit judges gave opinions ranging from 5 percent to 85 percent. However, only five judges gave estimates of over 10 percent. Several judges commented specifically that argument was helpful in greater proportions of cases if criminal cases were excluded, because so many of those cases were thought not to raise important issues. Several judges, however, were especially sensitive about eliminating oral argument in criminal appeals; they thought retaining it necessary for the appearance of justice. All the circuit judges and most district judges responding also thought oral argument "determinative" [38] in at least some cases, but, as expected, the proportion of cases in which argument was thought determinative was much smaller than the proportion in which it was considered significant; most estimated the proportion of cases to be "relatively small" or "minimal."

Where most helpful? In what types of cases is appellate argument thought most helpful? In the Federal Judicial Center study, a majority of circuit judges thought oral argument "essential" in "cases that involve matters of great public interest despite the absence of substantial legal issues" and in only one other category—cases involving the constitutionality of a state statute or state action. By contrast, in civil appeals based on sufficiency of the evidence, only 9 percent thought argument essential.[39]

In the present study, Ninth Circuit judges defined helpfulness in terms of both legal subject-matter and case characteristics. All but a couple of the judges stressed that appellate oral argument helped most in government regulation cases, particularly those involving new statutes or new administrative agencies. *No* judge found appellate argument more helpful in criminal appeals. Ninth Circuit lawyers primarily found appellate argument most helpful when cases were complex or novel. They cited "novel or undeveloped legal

issues," "issues of first impression," or "changing fields of law," as well as "sensitive, complicated, political issues" where a lawyer's views tended to differ from prevailing judicial sentiment or where a lawyer was trying to move the law in a new direction.

Lawyers form the Second, Fifth, and Sixth Circuits considered oral argument essential in "cases which involve matters of great public interest (despite the absence of substantial legal issues) [and] cases involving the constitutionality of a state statute or a state action." [40] Half of the Sixth Circuit lawyers and a clear majority of those from the Second Circuit also thought oral argument essential in direct criminal appeals.[41] Generally, lawyers were more likely than judges to find appellate argument essential, although "the essentiality of oral argument varies from case-type to case-type for [both] judges and lawyers, with order of preference almost the same from the perspective of bench and bar." [42]

Where least helpful? Ninth Circuit judges tended to find argument least helpful in cases where the circuit had controlling precedent. Resolution of such cases was "largely mechanical." Otherwise, they found argument least helpful in "frivolous cases" or "factual, run-of-the-mill" cases. Not surprising in view of their other comments, argument commonly was felt least helpful in criminal cases. The lawyers also suggested that argument was least helpful in cases where briefs were short and the issue simple (a simple fact pattern), particularly if the law were "static." However, in a comment counter to the typical views, one attorney found oral argument not helpful "when the lawyer was trying to overturn old legal principles and establish new rules of law." Such matters, he believed, were best argued in the briefs.[43]

Some judges said oral argument was not needed when briefs are adequate and "address the issues and are cogent" or when judges and lawyers agree as to what the principal argument is. Thus, ironically, for these judges, good briefing makes argument of less help. Others thought a lawyer might make his point better orally when briefs were poor, but some colleagues felt poor briefs usually meant poor argument.

Most judges, however, focused on lawyers' deficiencies at argument; lawyers agreed that deficiencies in attorney skills detracted from oral argument. (Some attorneys also suggested that certain characteristics of judges interfere with the effectiveness of argument, for example, when judges were "not inclined to listen" or were "impatient," appearing to "have made up their minds." Only one circuit judge blamed judges—when they preempt argument time—for detracting from argument.)

Judges thought that in a number of cases lawyers' argument was of little help because the lawyers were "not well prepared," not "up to" argument, or were "not good on their feet when asked questions." Lawyers agree that "boring, incompetent presentations" by lawyers can cause damage. Just as important is that lawyers not "take too rigid a position" or adopt a stance they know is not valid—something that will produce a loss of credibility.

Judges noted and lawyers also frequently mentioned as less than helpful situations in which attorneys read their presentations or "simply repeated the briefs." Recitation of facts not woven into the law were also thought not helpful. Lawyers who made speeches, engaged in fancy rhetoric, or made "impassioned jury pleas to an appellate judge" were also thought ineffective. However, comments about the need for a "just result" in a case are thought appropriate if they are related to the law—not made in isolation from the law.

Attorneys may not make most effective use of appellate argument because relatively few of them have tried appellate cases. Still fewer have handled appeals in the federal courts. The skills of a trial lawyer and an appellate attorney can differ markedly, and attorney specialization decreases the likelihood that an individual attorney will possess both. Ability to make an effective jury argument is not the same as being able to focus succinctly on often rapid-fire questions from a "hot" bench of three appellate judges, well-prepared from having read the briefs.

A Federal Judicial Center survey of lawyer competence casts some light on types of lawyers judges think least effective in appellate argument. A majority "believe there is a serious problem among lawyers employed by state or local governments," but less than 10 percent thought such a problem existed among "public or community defenders, Justice Department lawyers other than those in U.S. attorneys' offices and on strike forces, and private practitioners representing corporate clients in civil cases." [44] Age, size of a lawyer's office, previous courtroom experience, and a lawyer's educational background were all found not to be related to judges' ratings.

Curtailing and eliminating oral argument

The Hruska Commission stated in 1975 that "to mandate oral argument in every case would clearly be unwarranted." The Commission also thought it inappropriate to ignore "risks to the process of appellate adjudication inherent in too-ready a denial of the opportunity to present a litigant's case." [45] At about the same time, the Advisory Council on Appellate Justice recommended that "oral argument should be allowed in most cases" but also conceded "it may be curtailed or eliminated in certain instances." [46] The American Bar Association's position was most direct. In 1974, the ABA's House of Delegates opposed "the rules of certain United States courts of appeals which drastically curtail or entirely eliminate oral argument in a substantial proportion of non-frivolous appeals. . . ." [47]

Federal Judicial Center surveys show agreement between judges and lawyers on limiting oral argument but definite disagreement on situations in which it might be eliminated. *All* circuit judges found it acceptable to limit argument to 15–20 minutes per side and over 98 percent of the lawyers agreed. [48] Continuing their agreement, both judges and lawyers were less willing to limit oral argument to 15–20 minutes per side and to deny argument completely when the reason was "avoidance of extreme delay" than they were to do so either when an appeal was close to "frivolous" or where clear issues could be decided by circuit precedent.

Moreover, "approximately 90 percent of the judges recognized occasions when elimination of oral argument is an acceptable procedure." Eighty-eight percent of the circuit judges agreed that denying oral argument was "ever acceptable." However, the percentages of lawyers agreeing with such a proposition ranged from 84 percent (Fifth Circuit) to only 67 percent (Second Circuit). [49]

Roughly 95 percent of judges were willing either to limit or eliminate oral argument in frivolous cases, and similarly high percentages were willing to do so in cases governed by precedent. When the reason was to avoid extreme delay, the proportions declined (86 percent for limiting argument, only 62 percent for denying it). [50] Lawyers showed a similar pattern of differences between cases types, with ranking parallel to the judges'. By comparison with the judges, however, proportionately far more lawyers objected to eliminating argument than were willing to accede to time limitations.

Lawyers' objections to time limits on argument can be seen in the Hruska Commission testimony of Moses Lasky, "dean" of Ninth Circuit appellate attorneys. Lasky argued against any "official limitation on the time for arguments." Arguments, he felt, should take as much time as necessary for the judges "to squeeze all the values out of it that they can get out." Endless argument would not be the result, said Lasky, citing the comment attributed to Abe Lincoln: "When asked how long should a man's legs be, he replied, 'Long enough to reach the ground.' " Some arguments would take no longer than 15 minutes, while some might profitably extend for hours.[51]

A clear majority of judges in the Federal Judicial Center survey saw oral argument as dispensable in two types of cases: prisoner petitions seeking alteration of prison conditions, and collateral attacks on federal and state convictions. Almost half the judges also thought oral argument could be eliminated in sufficiency-of-evidence cases. However, only 7 percent of circuit judges thought that courts could dispense with argument in "cases which involve matters of great public interest despite the absence of substantial legal issues."[52]

Not surprisingly, a greater proportion of judges than attorneys thought oral argument was dispensable for each type of case.[53] In no case category did a majority of attorneys agree that oral argument was dispensable, although the proportion reached 30 percent for challenges to prison conditions and diversity-of-citizenship cases raising only state law questions.[54] Furthermore, faced with limitations on traditional procedures, including argument, lawyers were less willing to accept limitations—"to the extent that they accept [them] at all"—for "administrative reasons" than for "substantive legal reasons."[55]

All Ninth Circuit circuit and district judges interviewed believed that oral argument could be eliminated in some cases. Four of 12 circuit judges thought, however, that eliminating oral argument would not "assist the court in completing its business." Despite the repeated concerns about the need to allow argument in criminal cases for the sake of the appearance of justice, criminal cases were most frequently mentioned as the type where argument could be eliminated. However, some judges distinguished between direct criminal appeals, in which they were reluctant to eliminate argument, and habeas corpus cases, where they would do so, particularly in pro se appeals.

At least some judges found some civil cases—particularly simple ones—to require "no oral argument,"

especially if all members of a panel agreed that all problems were already presented in the briefs. Even if a case contained more than one issue, argument might not be necessary if all issues were simple. Some judges also did not find argument helpful in administrative agency cases, where their task was a limited review of the record. Similarly, argument was not thought to aid the judges in agency cases involving the "abuse of discretion" standard.

Only a bare majority of Ninth Circuit attorneys agreed that the court could dispense with argument in even some cases. Other than an occasional mention of criminal cases and a suggestion of cases involving ineffective counsel or misjoinder of offenses, lawyers seldom mentioned specific subject-matter areas for eliminating oral argument. They instead focused on cases where "it is perfectly obvious how it would go," and noted as well cases that had been dispositively handled by the circuit, particularly if the briefs indicated agreement on the issues.

Oral argument versus written opinion

Reduction or elimination of oral argument is only one way of reducing appellate court workloads. Both judges and lawyers in the Federal Judicial Center surveys were more willing to accept limitations on oral argument than to approve limitations on written opinions. However, judges, faced with a choice between argument and full written opinions, clearly preferred retaining argument and making greater use of memorandum opinions or "reasoned oral disposition" in most categories of cases. A majority of judges also agreed on the importance of issuing at least memoranda, so the courts "do not give the appearance to litigants of acting arbitrarily." However, only one-third of the circuit judges thought that "the absence of a reasoned disposition" would provide "no guidance to . . . district judges or the bar in future cases."[56] Conversely, in terms of the courts' legitimacy, "nearly half the circuit judges agreed that in the absence of a reasoned disposition, members of the bar may infer that the court has acted arbitrarily, yet little more than a quarter of the district judges concurred."[57]

Fifty-six percent of attorneys from the Second Circuit preferred oral argument and memorandum opinions or reasoned oral disposition rather than full opinion and limited or no oral argument, a preference consistent with practice in their circuit. Attorneys from the Fifth and Sixth Circuits had the reverse preference.[58] Ninth Circuit attorneys in the present study were closely divided in their preferences.[59] Among those preferring oral argument, one attorney found "bad results without it" but thought written opinions were "needed for development of the law." The value of a written opinion, said another attorney, was the "proper check" placed on "the court's superficiality and discretion"; an opinion forced the court to express its views in ways "credible to the bar."

Willingness to accept delay in order to obtain certain practices is a measure of support for those practices. A "large proportion" of judges surveyed by the Federal Judicial Center felt that retaining both argument and written opinions was worth waiting longer than the current time to disposition. Judges were, however, "more concerned about avoiding extreme delay" than were attorneys.[60] Lawyers also wanted both argument and written opinions even if more time would be consumed in the process.

Indeed, "the speed with which opinions are rendered is a matter of relatively low priority" for the attorneys; few felt that eliminating argument or limiting opinions is "the most acceptable way to avoid long delays in the court's calendar when the docket becomes crowded." [61] In no category of cases were more than one-fifth of the attorneys willing to give up both oral argument and written opinions to reduce time to disposition. Conversely, slightly over three-fourths would accept longer disposition times to obtain traditional practices.[62]

Conclusion

Although trial advocacy has received more attention than appellate argument in recent years, the latter also is significant and deserves attention. Efforts by both federal and state appellate courts to "streamline" proceedings require an understanding of the functions appellate oral argument is expected to perform. Lawyers need a better grasp of judges' views concerning the types of cases for which reduced oral argument or elimination of argument is considered appropriate and vice versa. The view of Ninth Circuit judges and lawyers and data from Federal Judicial Center surveys should make clear that the range of opinions about appellate argument is wide. It should also be clear that appellate oral argument is expected, by both attorneys and judges, to serve multiple functions.

Beneath all these views runs a recurrent theme of tension between perspectives, a tension that shows little sign of abating. On the one hand is the desire to maintain a practice that is not merely an "amenity" but

is also thought to have considerable importance for both appellate judges and appellate lawyers. On the other hand is a feeling of the need to adjust to substantial appellate caseloads by recognizing that different types of cases can be treated differently. Despite "inroads" some feel have been made in appellate argument, neither element in the tension has ousted the other, and appellate argument is in no danger of being extinguished as a significant part of appellate practice.

Notes

This article originally appeared in Volume 65, Number 7, February 1982, pages 340–353. It is drawn from a more extensive report, Wasby, "Oral Argument in the Ninth Circuit: The View from Bench and Bar," *Golden Gate L. Rev.* 11 (1981), 21. Financial assistance for the research came from the Office of Research and Projects, Southern Illinois University at Carbondale, and from the Penrose Fund of the American Philosophical Society.

1. *See generally* Wasby, D'Amato, and Mertrailer, "The Function of Oral Argument in the U.S. Supreme Court," *Q. J. Speech* 62 (1976), 410, particularly at 412.

2. *See* Commission on Revision of the Federal Court Appellate System, *Structure and Internal Procedures: Recommendations for Change* (1975), 106, 107.

3. Judicial Conference of the United States, Committee to Consider Standards for Admission to Practice in the Federal Courts, Report and Tentative Recommendations (1978), 30–31.

4. Carrington, "Ceremony and Realism: Demise of Appellate Procedure," *A.B.A. J.* 66 (1980), 860.

5. Godbold, "Improvements in Appellate Procedure: Better Use of Available Facilities," *A.B.A. J.* 66 (1980), 863.

6. In the spring of 1977, all but one of 11 active-duty circuit judges and five of the seven senior circuit judges were interviewed as were a dozen district judges, primarily from California and Oregon, chosen from those who had sat frequently on the appellate court "by designation." To provide some comparison with the judges' responses and a different perspective, 13 San Francisco lawyers (all those contacted) were also interviewed, and responses to mail questionnaires were obtained from six Los Angeles lawyers (roughly one-third of those contacted). All the lawyers had argued more than one case before the Ninth Circuit in the previous year. Lawyers and judges were, for the most part, asked parallel questions.

7. Material appearing in quotation marks without attribution is drawn from the author's interviews.

8. Goldman, *Attitudes of United States Judges Toward Limitation of Oral Argument and Opinion-Writing in the United States Courts of Appeals* (Washington, D.C.: Federal Judicial Center, 1975); Drury, Goodman, and Stevenson, *Attorney*

Attitudes Toward Limitation of Oral Argument and Written Opinion in Three U.S. Courts of Appeals (Washington, D.C.: Bureau of Social Science Research, 1974).

9. Marvell, *Appellate Courts and Lawyers: Information Gathering in the Adversary System* (Westport, Conn.: Greenwood Press, 1978), 75.

10. Bright, "The Changing Nature of the Federal Appeals Process in the 1970s: A Challenge to the Bar," *F.R.D.* 65 (1975), 496, 505 n. 8.

11. Both one senior district judge and two lawyers thought argument equally unimportant for both lawyers and judges.

12. Weaver, quoted in Sheldon and Weaver, *Politicians, Judges, and the People: A Study in Citizens' Participation* (Westport, Conn.: Greenwood Press, 1980), 86.

13. In discussing oral argument's functions as viewed from the Ninth Circuit, we draw primarily on judges' comments about why oral argument is helpful to them, and on lawyers' responses as to why they find argument helpful. Although a high proportion of lawyers found oral argument more important for judges than for themselves, they made few specific comments as to how it helped the judges. Perhaps they simply found reasons why oral argument was helpful to judges to be the complement of reasons why it assisted lawyers.

14. *See* Wasby et al., *supra* n. 1, at 418.

15. Drury, *supra* n. 8, at 306 n. 13.

16. Marvell, *supra* n. 9, at 306 n. 13.

17. Corey, "Some Aspects of Oral Argument in the United States Court of Appeals for the First Circuit," *Boston B. J.* 21 (1977), 21, 32.

18. *Structure and Internal Procedures, supra* n. 2, at 106.

19. Quoted in Maris, "In the Matter of Oral Argument," 1 Practical Lawyer (1955), quoted in Commission on Revision of Federal Appellate System, *First Phase: Hearings* (Washington, D.C.: 1973), 67.

20. Drury, *supra* n. 8, at 38 (Table 26).

21. *See* Wasby et al., *supra* n. 1, at 418; Wasby, "Communication Within the Ninth Circuit Court of Appeals," *Golden Gate L. Rev.* 8 (1977), 1, 5.

22. Drury, *supra* n. 8, at 38 (Table 26).

23. Marvell, *supra* n. 9, at 79.

24. However, less than half the attorneys in federal appellate practice surveyed by the Federal Judicial Center felt oral argument the *only* way to inform judges effectively of facts and issues in a case. Drury, *supra* n. 8, at 38 (Table 26).

25. Bright, *supra* n. 10, at 506.

26. See Commission, *Hearings: Second Phase 1974–1975,* 2 (Washington, D.C.: 1975), 408, 826.

27. Sutcliffe, addendum to Goldman, *supra* n. 8, at 2 (1975).

28. Quoted at *First Phase, supra* n. 19, at 777.

29. For examination of judges' preparation for argument, *see* Wasby, "Oral Argument in the Ninth Circuit: The View from Bench and Bar," *Golden Gate L. Rev.* 11 (1981), 21, 74–78.

30. Marvell, *supra* n. 9, at 247.

31. Ibid. at 248.

32. *First Phase, supra* n. 19, at 66, 322.

33. *Second Phase, 1, supra* n. 26, at 350.

34. *First Phase, supra* n. 19, at 804.

35. Drury, *supra* n. 8, at 38 (Table 26).

36. *First Phase, supra* n. 19, at 794.

37. Sutcliffe, *supra* n. 27, at 1.

38. Like "significant," "determinative" was not further defined when the question was asked. When a judge inquired as to its meaning, the interviewer said he was interested in cases in which oral argument made the judge change his mind or made the essential difference in the case.

39. Goldman, *supra* n. 8, at 8 (Table V). The only other categories where substantial proportions of circuit judges found oral argument essential were direct criminal appeals (38 percent) and en banc cases previously heard by a panel (35 percent). For the views of Ninth Circuit judges on the latter, *see* Wasby, *supra* n. 9, at 69–71.

40. Drury, *supra* n. 8, at 22.

41. Intercircuit differences in responses could be explained in part by intercircuit differences in argument practices. Goldman, *supra* n. 8, at 20–21. The Second Circuit had oral argument in every case, but decided a number of cases from the bench without opinion: the Fifth Circuit made "extensive use of truncated procedures," ibid. at 3, with "no oral argument" in a high percentage of cases; and the Sixth Circuit, by contrast, had retained a relatively traditional oral argument arrangement.

42. Ibid. at 8–10.

43. *See also* comments by Hruska Commission Executive Director A. Leo Levin, *First Phase, supra* n. 19, at 503–504.

44. Partridge and Bermant, *The Quality of Advocacy in the Federal Courts* (Washington, D.C.: Federal Judicial Center, 1978), 25.

45. *Structure and Internal Procedure, supra* n. 2, at 107.

46. Advisory Council on Appellate Justice, Recommendations, summarized in *Third Branch* 7 (November 1975).

47. *See A.B.A. J.* 60 (1974), 1214.

48. Goldman, *supra* n. 8, at 13 (Table III).

49. Ibid. at 5; *id.* at 13 (Table III); Drury, *supra* n. 8, at 19 (Table 13).

50. Goldman, *supra* n. 8, at 7a (Table IV).

51. *First Phase, supra* n. 19, at 932.

52. Goldman, *supra* n. 8, at 11 (Table IV).

53. Drury, *supra* n. 8, at 16; Goldman, *supra* n. 8, at 12.

54. Drury, *supra* n. 8, at 24 (Table 16). The difference among the three circuits was less severe for judgments about dispensability of argument than for judgments that

argument was essential. However, "in the Second and Sixth Circuits, where oral argument is generally allowed, the idea that oral argument should always be accorded unless the appeal is frivolous received the greatest support." Ibid. at 47.

55. Ibid. at 19.

56. Goldman, *supra* n. 8, at 12, 17 (Table IX).

57. Ibid. at 20 (Table XII).

58. Drury, *supra* n. 8, at 26 (Table 17).

59. The judges were not asked about their preference between oral argument and full written opinions.

60. Goldman, *supra* n. 8, at 7, 14.

61. Drury, *supra* n. 8, at 32, 34.

62. Ibid. at 33 (Table 22) and 34 (Table 24). *See also ibid.* at 35–36 (Table 25), indicating the median number of months attorneys perceive required to obtain a final disposition and median number of months they are willing to wait to have both oral argument and written opinion.

Justice Brennan and the institutionalization of dissent assignment

Beverly Blair Cook

The formal assignment of dissenting opinions is a recent but now firmly established practice for which Justice William Brennan was largely responsible.

While the practice of assigning U.S. Supreme Court majority opinions dates back to the Marshall Court, the practice of assigning dissenting opinions is a recent development. Textbooks on the Supreme Court make no reference to dissent assignment by the senior justice in the minority. A 1988 article on dissenting opinions indicated that authorship was voluntary, and that "no one formally assigns such opinions." [1] The first published reference to the practice was in 1987, when Chief Justice William Rehnquist explained that the "senior justice among those who disagreed with the result reached by the majority at conference usually undertakes to assign the preparation of the dissenting opinion. . . ." [2]

Institutionalization of the assignment of dissenting opinions required the recognition of dissent as a legitimate option. In early years, public disagreement violated a Court norm, and special opinions were seldom joined. Because justices often dissented or concurred without written explanation, opinion assignment was not an issue. Not until the regular appearance of written opinions joined by a bloc of justices did ad hoc arrangements for dissent writing prove inefficient.

Today, a dissent unaccompanied by reasoning is rare. To the extent that routine behaviors exemplify norms, a Court norm requiring a written opinion to support a dissent now exists: assignment of dissenting opinions is by the senior justice in the minority. Responsibility for the firm establishment of this practice belongs to Justice William Brennan Jr., who stated his duty clearly in a 1979 memo to Justice Lewis Powell: "I am undertaking to apportion the dissents in which I am senior." [3]

Traditional practices

Assignment procedures on the Court have become formal and institutionalized, not on the basis of written rules, but through usage. Other informal "rules" of Supreme Court decision making that have become fixed include the rule of four to grant certiorari, the rule of unanimity to bring closure to any Court matter, and the rule of seniority for leadership. The new practice of dissent assignment imitates the established practice of majority opinion assignment.

Guidelines for Court opinion assignment developed over time include assignment by the senior justice in the majority, distribution of the workload among the justices, circulation of draft opinions to every member of the conference, negotiation of the final product through a series of revised drafts, and public identification of the opinion writer (except for per curiams). Surviving today of early opinion practices are the single Court opinion, the public announcement of per curiam decisions by the chief justice, and control over most assignments by the chief (by suiting his votes to the conference majority).

Dissent assignment was not an issue on the early courts because public disagreement by dissent or concurrence, with or without opinion, was considered deviant behavior. Justices referred to the "misfortune" of bringing their differences over law and policy to public attention, a rhetoric repeated with less sincerity into this century. [4] In the first Marshall period, conflict did arise in minor cases, but beginning in the 1812 term, strong differences were openly expressed. Before the end of the Marshall era, the publication of a few opinions by dissenting blocs signalled the breakdown of the solidarity norm. [5]

There was no need to assign dissents as long as each justice simply noted disagreement or wrote separately. When two or more justices agreed on the reasoning behind the minority preference, they could exercise one or a combination of three options: write a separate opinion, jointly write one opinion, or join another's writing.

Separate opinions were the rule if justices did not circulate drafts in timely fashion to give their colleagues opportunity to join. The notation of dissent was a work-saving but uninformative practice, employed with less frequency over the Court's history. But the increasing workload of Court opinion writing, from more than 100 per term after the Civil War to more than 200 between 1875 and 1925, increased the justices' incentive to avoid individual writing.

The second option, joint writing, was an intermediate step between separate writing and joining an opinion written by a like-minded justice. Joint writing was inefficient but useful to signal the strong commitment of the signers to their result and doctrine.

The third option was efficient and also carried a message of unity but required some method for selecting the writer, informing the bloc members, and circulating the draft. The practical utility of an opinion assignment practice for dissents became evident in the mid-19th century when multiple opinions and open disagreement became common.[6]

In the absence of such a standard operating procedure, justices lacked accurate and timely information on the intentions of colleagues in the conference minority. A justice who is weakly committed to the minority position and unwilling to invest time in writing might drift to the majority. But assured of an opportunity to support another's labor, such justices could delay their final votes until the dissent draft appeared.

Justice William O. Douglas's response to a circulated majority opinion was typical of the attitude of a justice not highly motivated to write a dissent. He joined an opinion by Justice Stanley Reed in the 1942 term with this warning: ". . . I will stay quiet and acquiesce, unless perchance some Brother with lots of time on his hands decides to write."[7] Justice Robert Jackson revealed the same viewpoint in the 1947 term, writing to Justice Hugo Black: "Unless someone writes a dissent I will keep still." Justice John Marshall Harlan's attitude as expressed in a 1957 memo was typical of the justice who did not desire to use his own resources to develop an opinion. He wrote to Douglas: "Do you intend to write something in No. 89? If so, I shall hold up my return on Bill Brennan's opinion, awaiting yours." At the end of the 1971 term, Douglas sent a note to Lewis Powell: ". . . I voted the other way. But I acquiesce in your opinion subject to reexamination if anyone writes in dissent."

Prior to the Burger era, justices who felt obligated to provide some reasoning for their disagreement with the Court would at times urge a like-minded colleague to do the writing. Justice Louis Brandeis persistently

pressed Justice Oliver Wendell Holmes to write for both of them.[8] Following Brandeis's pattern, Justice Felix Frankfurter in the 1950s exchanged memos pressing Justices Douglas, Harold Burton, and Brennan to write dissents.[9] Such behavior was informal and collegial.

The simple but effective practice of giving notice of intent to write a dissent to the assigned majority opinion writer, with copies to the conference members, developed over time. No doubt the earliest mode of communication, in the days of the boardinghouse conferences, was informal and oral. When the justices were scattered on circuit or in separate home studies, and without the technology for producing multiple copies of memos, some would remain unaware of a member's intent to dissent. Moreover, there was no opportunity to join a dissent when the author kept his plan to himself or delayed writing and publication until after the majority opinion appeared in print. By contrast, typical of the modern period are Brennan's terse memos during the 1950s: "Please be advised that I plan to write a dissent in No. 27 . . . " and "I shall, in due course, undertake the writing of a dissent in the above case."

Precursors

When did the senior justice in a dissenting bloc first take responsibility for opinion assignment? It is reasonable to suppose that a chief justice, when in the minority, made the first dissent assignment. Because the chief, when in the majority, routinely chooses Court opinion authors, it would seem natural to adopt the same practice when in dissent. Prompt selection of the dissent author increases efficiency, since in modern times no decision is announced until the conference has ascertained that every special opinion is ready, and every justice is satisfied with the finality of his or her choice.

Chief justices, however, have few opportunities to make dissent assignments because they avoid membership in the minority unless driven by strong principle. Of the cases where any dissent was registered, Chief Justices Marshall and William Howard Taft joined the minority in less than 10 percent of the cases; Roger Taney, Morrison Waite, Edward White, and Charles Evans Hughes did so in less than 15 percent; Melville Fuller, Fred Vinson, and Earl Warren in less than 20 percent; and Salmon Chase, Harlan Fiske Stone, Warren Burger, and William Rehnquist in less than 30 percent of the cases.[10]

A chief seldom in the minority would have little motivation to streamline the assignment process. When in dissent, Vinson evidently made no effort to produce a rationale; he waited until someone else wrote and then joined or simply noted his dissenting vote.[11] Recent chiefs, who have found themselves in dissent more often, have felt more pressure for efficiency. Burger, with his special concern for court management, probably facilitated the new practice.

Dissent assignment practice was not institutionalized before the Burger era. Prior to the 1970s, justices in dissent tried to reduce their workloads through informal consultation and agreement on a writer. On the Stone Court, Black, the senior liberal justice, evidently chose the dissent writer in some cases.[12] On the Vinson Court, there was still no formal assignment process; the dissenters conferred informally to choose a writer or simply wrote separately.[13]

In the Vinson and Warren eras, Frankfurter took steps toward institutionalization by pushing for a single dissent and assigning writers. In the 1950 term, he urged Vinson, Black, and Douglas to find a formula for their minority position and promised to join them. During the 1953 term, Burton drafted a dissent in response to an oral invitation by Frankfurter and Jackson. Frankfurter reported to Reed in the 1955 term that "Harold has been good enough to undertake to write for the dissenters."

The first written memo of assignment was found in papers from the 1956 term; Frankfurter cleared it with the other senior dissenters and then invited newcomer Brennan to write for the bloc: "Harold and John agree with me in asking you to write for us in dissent in *LaBuy*. I hope you will." Brennan responded, "Delighted to! Thanks very much." Most invitations, however, continued to be oral.

The justices followed no standard operating procedure in the 1950s and 1960s. Dissenters often had to wait for a volunteer to write. In the 1956 term, Douglas sent a memo to the author of the Court opinion: ". . . I will acquiesce in it unless someone else writes in dissent. If anyone does write in dissent I will reconsider. . . ."[14] In 1963 Douglas switched his conference vote to the majority side and then revoked it when a dissent draft reached his desk. He wrote to Justice Potter Stewart, ". . . now that the dissent has come around, I have decided to adhere to my original view and to join it."

In the later Warren period, some justices openly admitted their cooperative efforts to conserve individual resources. Brennan explained in 1963 that the "dissenters agree among themselves who shall write the dissenting opinion."[15] This collegial consultation apparently operated sporadically and was a middle stage between voluntarism and senior responsibility for assignment. In the absence of a fair distribution of dissent assignments by a senior, the volunteers or recruits rationed their efforts. The effect of this informal system was to discourage dissents; the effect of the new formal practice has been to encourage the writing of a single dissent.

Indirect evidence

Indirect evidence suggests that the dissent assignment practice developed during the Burger period when the increasing number of close votes made minority opinion solidarity a strong tool with which to threaten the majority. From the Hughes through Rehnquist eras, the number of decisions per term with minimal majorities trended upward: from 5.8 percent in 1933, 12.5 percent in 1943, 10.7 percent in 1953, 12.2 percent in 1963, 21.9 percent in 1973, to 19 percent in 1983.[16] The sudden increase in close decisions in 1973 matches the period when the senior dissenter took responsibility for assignments.

From Hughes through Warren, success in holding a four-member coalition behind a single dissent decreased: from 89 percent under Hughes, 77 percent under Stone, 57 percent under Vinson, to 49 percent under Warren.[17] The trend reversed in the Burger period, with 63 percent of the 5–4 decisions producing an opinion signed by all four dissenters. On the Rehnquist Court (1986–1992 terms), the ratio of successful coalitions to opportunities increased again to 69 percent.

Another measure of minority coalition unity is the change in the ratio of dissenting opinions to dissenting votes. If each justice wrote separately to explain a dissenting vote, the ratio would be 1:1.[18] On the Warren Court, there was a dissenting opinion for every 1.7 dissenting votes, on the Burger Court for every 2.0 votes, and on the Rehnquist Court (1986–1990 terms) for every 2.3 votes. One explanation for these changes is that the new practice of dissent assignment contributed to holding the coalition together.

The abrupt end of the practice of notation (dissenting without opinion) at the beginning of the Burger period was another indicator of change in the assignment practice. On the Hughes Court, the average number of dissents without opinion per term was 10.5, on the Stone Court, 15, and on the Vinson Court, 26. The average dropped to 11.5 on the Warren Court. On the Burger Court, evident from the first (1969) term, the practice almost disappeared with an average per term of only 1.5. On the Rehnquist Court (1986–1990 terms), the average dropped to less than one per term.

One can speculate that under the new assignment practice where an opinion is prepared for every minority, justices acquiesce to dissenting opinions that do not entirely satisfy them, just as earlier they acquiesced to Court opinions. The sharp reduction in dissents by notation signals a new norm requiring an explanation for every vote rejecting the majority disposition.[19]

Additional encouragement for the open expression of dissent was implicit in a change that appeared to be purely administrative. Through the Warren period, a justice could convey an impression of agreement with the majority without going on record, since the official reporter did not list the names of joiners of the opinion. The official reports named the authors of Court opinions (except for per curiams) and special opinions and named the joiners of special opinions but not of Court opinions. The attentive reader of a Supreme Court reporter could thus reconstruct the composition of the majority in the announced decision only by assumption.

Early in the 1971 term, Chief Justice Burger expanded the duties of the court reporter to include the writing of a syllabus specifying each justice's vote in a case. Burger's format for the official reports offered a modest response to the contemporary movement for open meetings, providing explicit information about each justice's final vote without giving access to conference deliberations. For the first time, every justice was publicly accountable for every vote. This change helped press the justices toward the rationalization of dissent writing.

Direct evidence

In the two transitional terms of the Burger Court while Black continued as senior justice, the archives offer no evidence of routine or written dissent assignments. In his first term as senior justice in 1971, Douglas made some written dissent assignments but did not cover all cases. He believed it appropriate to consult first with his senior colleagues in dissent. In the 1972 term, Brennan began to spur his senior to take responsibility for assigning the dissenting opinions. He offered suggestions for dissent assignments after looking at the chief's periodic assignment sheets for Court opinions.

As Douglas's disabilities increased, Brennan employed his diplomatic talents to assist the senior justice in distributing dissents. Throughout the 1973 term, Brennan indicated to Douglas that every dissent was to be assigned. He wrote, ". . . I note that from the very first October Argument List there is one dissent that hasn't been assigned by you. . . ," and "I've been looking at the assignment list with the view to possible dissents." Douglas's law clerks embellished Brennan's lists of unassigned cases, providing the names of justices available to write, adding information on current chambers' work on each case, and attaching the chief's assignment sheet to show who would be writing the Court opinion.

In the 1974 term, Brennan persisted in reminding Douglas of his duty: "I've been going over the assignment sheet anticipating that there will be dissents to be written." But even as he took the initiative to suggest assignments, Brennan took care to leave the authority with his senior. He indicated that he was simply serving as expediter, using phrases such as: "I'll be happy to take that if you want me to"; ". . . I think you can do a better job than either of us"; and "I have taken the liberty of asking Thurgood to take on the dissent."

Despite his disinterest in routine duties, Douglas proposed to Burger in 1972 the reinstatement of an old policy that emphasized the importance of dissenting opinions:

> I have been planning to bring to the attention of the Conference, for discussion, a practice which was in vogue when I took my seat under Hughes and which has been more or less in vogue since that time, although some regimes have not observed it as faithfully as others. Stone, for example, meticulously observed it. Vinson, and to an extent Warren, did not. I refer to the policy that whenever an opinion for the Court is circulated that the dissenters drop everything else and prepare their dissents. It is, I think, a good practice as it enables the case to come to a rather rapid focus.

Burger did not renew the policy Douglas described, but Chief Justice Rehnquist did take such an initiative.

Brennan's role

Brennan's "enormous influence on the Court and the enduring legacy of his opinions" have been noted.[20] His leadership, before and after Douglas's retirement, in the institutionalization of dissent assignment must also be recognized. When senior justice in the minority, Brennan made an opinion assignment in every case, even when unsure that he would remain with the minority. His law clerks kept for him a running record of opinion assignments, circulations, and vote changes. Immediately after conference, he sometimes made an oral request of a justice, particularly one who was not closely aligned with the liberal bloc, and followed up with a written notification. By sending a memo describing his distribution of the dissent workload to each dissenting justice at the end of every oral argument period, Brennan assured colleagues of his fair and complete coverage of the assignments.

Brennan moved expeditiously to make his dissent assignments. In the 1985 term, he made them the day before or on the same day that the chief justice distributed his assignment sheet for the Court opinions. Brennan's timely actions helped hold the minority together. He favored consensus among the dissenters and tried to identify the writer who would preserve the coalition. His purpose was obvious in his 1986 note to Justice Thurgood Marshall: "Please join me in your superb dissent. . . . It is really a great job and ought to change some votes."

The formal assignment of the dissenting opinion, like that of the majority opinion, was simply a stage in the process of resolving the case issues and did not bind the justices. Sometimes no justice wanted to author a dissent until after reading the majority's reasoning. Nor could Brennan promise that all members of the minority would sign the dissent. When Justice John Paul Stevens wrote in 1982 that "I will be delighted to try to spell out the reasons. . . ," Powell wrote that he was not committed to Stevens's approach. Brennan was not always certain of his own posture after a close vote in conference. In the 1979 term, for instance, Brennan wrote, "I must say my vote is a little weak" and invited Blackmun to write.

Brennan did not try to bring together dissenters who offered different reasoning at conference or who were bound into a personal stare decisis. If a justice agreed on disposition but not on doctrine, he did not propose a joint dissent. Brennan's note to Douglas in the 1972 term was typical: "I assume you'll be expressing your own view . . . whereas I dissent there only on the search and seizure question. And as usual with me in Establishment Clause cases, I'll be writing out my own view . . . ."

After a conference during the 1974 term, Brennan recognized that the reasoning of several dissenters differed. He wrote to Douglas: "You and I have different views . . . and I will be writing my own dissent in those

two cases." Even when Brennan wrote separately, however, he wanted to make sure that a dissent was assigned. Justices who decided not to join after reading the proposed bloc opinion were, of course, free to write separately or switch to the majority.

Selecting authors

In selecting authors for the dissents, Brennan kept in mind two important considerations—to make a fair distribution of the workload and to give recognition to a particular justice's interests and precedential writings. In the 1976 term he wrote, "I am at the task again of trying to distribute dissents equitably." If a justice not usually in his camp, such as Powell or Rehnquist, became available, Brennan would select him. Brennan himself took a large share of the work, including some of the most interesting cases.

Brennan was continually aware of the work pressures on his colleagues. A typical letter read: "I have the feeling that you are very badly overloaded and accordingly I hesitate to ask you to take on the dissent." He noted in a close vote: "If Lewis can fit it in an already crowded schedule he'll try his hand at a dissent. . . . The assignment may be subject to further consideration if he's pressed for time."

Familiarity with and commitment to the issues formed the second basis for assignment. A memo to Potter Stewart in the 1977 term explained: "Actually the only reason I thought to ask you to do it was that I expect it would turn on *Florida Power* which you wrote." A similar memo to Stevens in the 1982 term asked: "As author of *Henderson v. Morgan,* John would you be willing to undertake the dissent?" If a justice had already written a draft in the prior term, he was also likely to be selected.

Some voluntarism for dissent writing still occurred but always in relation to the senior justice's lead role. Justices with a special interest in a case could volunteer to the senior. Powell wrote to Brennan in the 1979 term, "As you are the senior in dissent in this case, I write to say that I will be happy to draft a dissent for the four of us if you wish. . . . I merely want you to know of my availability."

The thorough institutionalization of dissent assignment by Brennan was symbolized by changes in the distribution of information on dissent writing. In each case, the senior assigner sent a memo to other justices in the conference minority announcing his choice of writer. The assignee notified the Court opinion author of intent to write (as did the volunteer in the past), and finally the senior informed the entire conference of the assignment. Beginning in the 1983 term, in the notes on his chamber's case circulation sheets, Brennan listed his specific assignment letters, instead of the traditional memos that he would "await the dissent." [21] By the 1980s, every justice had full and timely information on the distribution of both the Court and dissenting opinions.

By the end of his tenure, Burger assumed that the senior justice in dissent would make an assignment. In the 1982 term, he wrote a note to Blackmun emphasizing his responsibility: ". . . the dissent will be up to the 'affirms,' of which group you are 'senior.' " Although he occasionally needed a reminder from Brennan, Burger routinely made the dissent assignments when he was in the minority.

Brennan's contribution was to routinize the assignment of dissenting opinions and to place the authority of delegating assignments firmly in the hands of the senior justice in the minority bloc. Consultation with others was possible but no longer expected, and every justice now had full information on the writing plans of colleagues. The work pattern of the senior's chambers for distributing the dissents imitated the established pattern for distributing the majority opinions.

The post-Brennan era

For justices serving on the Rehnquist Court, dissent assignment has been standard practice. Its routine nature seems evident in the note from O'Connor to Rehnquist in 1990: "My vote at Conference was very tentative. I plan to see what Tony writes and decide whether I can join it. Is it all right with you if we defer assignment of this dissent?" Stevens, appointed in 1975, was the first justice socialized into the new practice from his first term. With Blackmun's retirement in 1994, only Rehnquist has personal experience under the less structured system of dissent writing.

The survival of a new practice depends upon its adoption by those who follow its founder. Brennan's long tenure as senior (1975–1989 terms) and his preference and ability to mediate and produce consensus gave the practice a firm foundation. Marshall assumed Brennan's role of selecting the writer of liberal dissents for one term. In fact, he followed the new practice even earlier on those rare occasions when he disagreed with both Brennan and Rehnquist. Marshall continued the policy of giving Blackmun the opportunity to respond to the conservative majority in abortion cases, and, further reinforcing the new practice, ensured that the

small as well as the large minorities produced joint opinions. For each assignment period of the 1990 term, Marshall's clerks kept track of the cases requiring his dissent assignment and recommended an assignee.

The role of senior on the liberal side devolved on Blackmun in the 1991 term. Blackmun writes that he "tried to follow the Brennan practice." [22] Upon White's retirement in 1993, Blackmun took the senior seat for one term but was replaced by Stevens in the 1994 term. Despite Stevens's record as a maverick with a preference to write lone dissents even when a group dissent was available, it is probable that he is also following the Brennan practice.[23]

With six newcomers on the Rehnquist Court by the 1994 term and with the unfolding of new issues and doctrines, the critical senior in dissent may not be Stevens but O'Connor, the senior member of the centrist bloc. With talents more similar to Brennan's, she would appreciate the utility of maintaining and further institutionalizing the practice. O'Connor's political experiences in Arizona and her preference to negotiate suggest the possibility that she may make good use of Brennan's legacy when she moves into the senior position upon Stevens's retirement.[24]

Survival of the practice also depends on its use by the chief justice in dissent. Rehnquist has indicated that he considers dissent assignment a routine practice. In 1989 Rehnquist proposed to levy a serious penalty on justices who failed to circulate a promised dissenting opinion after the Court opinion had been available for four weeks.[25] Such a policy would reinforce the production of work-saving coalitional dissents.

Court vs. dissent assignments

The practice of assigning dissents is not identical to the practice of assigning the opinion for the Court. One of the expectations associated with opinion assignment is that the assignee automatically and graciously accepts the chief's (or senior's) directive; it is not considered fitting for the associate justice to complain or resist. Only a few excuses are legitimate: disagreement with the reasoning of the largest bloc in the majority coalition, the potentially adverse effect of the author's identity on the Court's image of impartiality, and the undermining of the writer's reputation for consistency.

In the 19th century, justices complained about, rejected, and solicited case assignments.[26] In the late 20th century, however, justices accept without question the senior's authority to distribute Court opinions, except to inform him of an ethical issue, a miscount of conference votes, or a prior promise. The assignment of a Court opinion, signed or per curiam, has become over time a mandate; the assignment sheets circulated by the chief justice constitute, in effect, work orders. By including the assignments made by seniors on the sheets, the chief thereby places his authority behind them. Associate justices accept their writing jobs as the price of the Court's institutional productivity and reputation.

Dissent assignments, however, do not carry the same authority; they are couched in a language of collegiality rather than of hierarchy. Seniors address their juniors with circumspection in making dissent assignments. For example, in the 1973 term Douglas wrote to Stewart: "Would you want to undertake the dissent. . . ?" Brennan's courtesy is evident in his request to Marshall during the 1975 term: "I know how jammed up you are going to be but John is taking on nine dissents after a discussion with me and I've got about twelve. I know you have several but can I add [two more]?"

Justices treat the letter from their senior in dissent as an invitation, not an order, and immediately respond. The assignee may not write the dissent as promptly as the senior hoped but does feel an obligation to complete the work unless he or she intends to switch sides or develop an idiosyncratic argument. If a dissenter does reject the assignment, however, the senior chooses a substitute to ensure that the case is covered.

The coalitional dissenting opinion has at least two important functions—the efficient utilization of justices' writing time and the development of a doctrine to replace the precedent. A well-crafted dissenting opinion also has the potential to force the rethinking and modification of the majority opinion, but this can occur only if the dissenting opinion appears before the opinion of the Court reaches final draft form. The assignment of the dissent by memo at the same time as the assignment for the Court has the virtue of expediting its production and increasing its leverage over the majority. For justices on the fence, the dissenter's reasoning is a resource to press for revisions in the majority opinion.

Moreover, under the new practice, the goal of the assigner is to produce a single dissent. By articulating the arguments of the minority, the opinion gives a legitimacy to its point of view that discourages defection. The strategic purpose of the solidary dissent in a close case is to win a majority. As Harlan wrote to Brennan in the 1956 term, "I hope you won't spare full dress treatment of the problem in writing for the dissenters. . . .

I am hoping that your opinion will be so convincing as to pick up one more vote, and thus carry the day."

A powerful vehicle

Dissent assignment contributes to efficiency and offers a powerful vehicle for a four-justice bloc to present its alternative reasoning to external constituencies. Unity of viewpoint by dissenters in a close case sends a message to potential litigants about their chances of winning in the future and about the line of argument most likely to retain or to expand the coalition supporting their positions.

Politicians involved in the judicial appointment process will also be interested in any opportunity to change the direction of Court doctrine by the substitution of a new justice who shares the large minority's view for a retiring justice in the majority. Although appointment strategies do not necessarily work, the repetitive voice of a unified large minority in a series of cases on the same issue calls attention to Court disequilibrium.

Beyond its putative functions, what meaning does the new practice carry? The routinization of the practice is an indicator of the normalization and acceptance of dissensus. Although Chief Justice Marshall's strong norm of solidarity behind a single opinion for the Court, preferably announced by the chief justice, was not effectively enforced after his own era, the weaker norm encouraging consensus, except on matters of special salience to the individual, did survive at least into the Hughes Court.[27]

The behavior of justices, however, openly belied the existence of any consensual norm after 1940. Judges and commentators who persist in debating the virtue of presenting a facade of Court harmony are discussing a model, not an institutional reality. When minority justices on the Stone and later courts did overlook their disagreements to join a large majority, their motives were more relevant to their personal budgets of time and interest than to any normative philosophy of Court behavior.

Both routine assignment of the writing of a dissenting opinion when two or more justices disagree with the majority at conference and the routine production of an opinion to explain a lone dissent are unobtrusive indicators that the consensual norm has expired. Institutions do not develop standard procedures to accomplish an activity that violates its norms. Instead, the dissent assignment practice, established during the

Burger era and continued into the Rehnquist period, indicates that the Court's normative structure now includes a competitive norm. Justice John Catron claimed that disagreement on the Taney Court was "just as natural as in the Senate, and almost as common." [28] Court practice has caught up with Catron's observation. By institutionalizing the selection of its spokesperson for the minority, the Court has adopted a fundamental feature of other American political institutions.

Notes

This article originally appeared in Volume 79, Number 1, July–August 1995, pages 17–23.

1. Brenner and Spaeth, "Ideological Position as a Variable in the Authoring of Dissenting Opinions on the Warren and Burger Courts," *Am. Pol. Q.* 16 (July 1988), 317–328, at 318, 320.
2. Rehnquist, *The Supreme Court* (New York: William Morrow, 1987), 302.
3. William J. Brennan papers, Box 548, Library of Congress, to Lewis from Bill, 3/5/79. Subsequent quotations from the justice's papers are not cited, but a copy of the article with full documentation is available from the editor or from the author (e-mail: bcook@pinot.callamer.com).
4. White, *The Marshall Court and Cultural Change, 1815–35* (New York: Macmillan, 1988), 187, n. 131. Joseph Story was probably the last justice to internalize the solidarity norm. In 1844 he was the senior justice and the only holdover of the "old Court." "He had to choose between continuous dissent and yielding in the face of his own convictions. Neither alternative seemed tolerable." Swisher, *The Taney Period, 1836–64,* (New York: Macmillan, 1974), 233.
5. Justice Smith Thompson challenged Marshall's solidarity norm by writing separately in constitutional cases. He followed Oliver Ellsworth's seriatim rule for this important set of cases by producing a series of concurrences. Although the senior justices generally followed the chief's lead, justices new to the Court after Thompson arrived in 1823 were not disturbed to reveal their real policy differences in published opinions. White, *supra* n. 4, at 307, 318. Justice William Johnson explained in *Gibbons v. Ogden,* 9 Wheat. 1, 223 (1824), that it was his "duty to the public" to write out his dissent on "questions of great importance and great delicacy." In the Taney era Peter Daniel felt "constrained" to dissent in a large number of cases that stimulated his strong feelings on states' rights. Swisher, *supra* n. 4, at 69.
6. White, *supra* n. 4, at 195.
7. William O. Douglas papers, Box 77, Library of Congress, 11/13/42. *See* n. 3.

8. White, *Justice Oliver Wendell Holmes: Law and the Inner Self* (New York: Oxford University Press, 1993), 322.
9. Harold Burton papers, Box 303, Library of Congress, to Harold from FF, 5/23/57. *See* n. 3.
10. Ulmer, "Exploring the Dissent Patterns of Chief Justices: John Marshall to Warren Burger," in Goldman and Lamb (eds.), *Judicial Conflict and Consensus* (Lexington: The University Press of Kentucky, 1986), 53 Table 2.1. Burger and Rehnquist data from Spaeth, *U.S. Supreme Court Database, 1953–1993* (Ann Arbor, Mich.: ICPSR).
11. Note, "Chief Justice Vinson and His Law Clerks," *Nw. U. L. Rev.* 49 (March–April 1954), 26–35.
12. John P. Frank, who was Black's law clerk in the 1942 term, writes, "I have no doubt but that he assigned the dissenting opinion" but does not recall his modus operandi. Letter to author, April 28, 1995. A Black law clerk from the later 1940s also recalls his assignment of some dissents. Eugene Gressman, Murphy's law clerk from 1943 to 1948, reports that Black assigned his judge to write in *Western Union v. Lenroot* (1945) for the four dissenters. Newman, *Hugo Black, A Biography* (New York: Pantheon Books, 1994), 335 n. *.
13. *Supra* n. 11.
14. Earl Warren papers, Box 350, Library of Congress, to Chief from Bill, 2/18/57. *See* n. 3.
15. Brennan, "Inside View of the High Court," *N.Y. Times Magazine,* Oct. 6, 1963.
16. Easterbrook, "Agreement Among the Justices: An Empirical Note," *1984 Supreme Court Review,* 389–409, extrapolated from appendix tables, 401–409. Note that Easterbrook calculated the rate of "real" disagreement based on his interpretation of the doctrinal issue, see appendix, 397–400.
17. Figures on close cases, and on dissents without opinion, are based on the author's collection of data from the reporters for Hughes through Vinson courts and on the Spaeth data set for Warren through Rehnquist.
18. The ratio is calculated after subtracting the instances of dissent without opinion.
19. Thurgood Marshall papers, Box 536, Library of Congress, to Thurgood from HAB, 5/3/91. *See* n. 3.
20. Irons, *Brennan vs. Rehnquist: the Battle for the Constitution* (New York: Alfred A. Knopf, 1994), 330.
21. Prior to the 1983 term, Brennan's dissent assignments are not recorded on the circulation sheets kept in his chambers. Some are recorded for 1983 and all for 1984 and 1985.
22. Letter to author, May 19, 1995.
23. Sickels, *John Paul Stevens and the Constitution* (The Pennsylvania State University Press, 1988), 159.
24. Cook, "Justice Sandra Day O'Connor: Transition to a Republican Court Agenda," in Lamb and Halpern (eds.), *The Burger Court* (Champaign: University of Illinois Press, 1991), 239, 272.

25. His proposed penalty was to deny new majority opinion assignments until the laggard justice produced the dissent. His memo stated that he would weigh three factors in making majority opinion assignments. Besides the late dissenting opinions, he would take account of any failure to circulate a majority opinion within four weeks after assignment or of any delay in deciding to join circulated opinions. He wrote that "it only makes sense in the assignment of additional work to give some preference to those who are 'current' with respect to past work." "Policy Regarding Assignments." Memorandum to the Conference from William H. Rehnquist, Papers of Thurgood Marshall, Box 492, Folder 7, 11/24/89.

26. Magrath, *Morrison R. Waite: The Triumph of Character* (New York: The Macmillan Company, 1963), 261–263.

27. Haynie, "Leadership and Consensus on the U.S. Supreme Court," *J. Pol.* 54 (November 1992), 1158–1169.

28. Swisher, *supra* n. 4, at 64.

The spirit of dissent

J. Louis Campbell III

*Although there is a bias in the legal community against judicial dissent,
dissenting opinions function analogously to acts of civil disobedience in
bringing about needed legal and political changes.*

Since the advent of collegial courts minority-view judges have used published dissents to register their objections and reservations to majority judgments.[1] This has been particularly true of the U.S. Supreme Court, where, in fact, the first reported opinion of a justice was a dissent, coming as the justices delivered their opinions *seriatim*.[2] Chief Justice Marshall, though highly regarded for his dissent in *Ogden v. Saunders*,[3] fostered a preference against dissents and secured the Court tradition of one majority opinion standing as the last word on the law.

Marshall's leadership and a rather homogeneous tribunal militated against dissents for some time.[4] Then with Marshall's death and the ascendency of Chief Justice Taney (1836), the era of dissent began. The great dissenters in the Court's history have since included some of our most illustrious justices, such as Holmes, Brandeis, and Douglas.

Notwithstanding, there remains a bias in the legal community against dissent. There seems in particular to be some question about its efficacy. Prominent legal philosopher H. L. A. Hart has written that "A supreme tribunal has the last word in saying what the law is, and when it has said it, the statement that the Court was 'wrong' has no consequence within the system: no one's rights are thereby altered."[5]

Nevertheless, statements that the Court was wrong, I propose, do have important consequences apart from direct and immediate alteration of rights and duties, and these consequences may be found within the system. Dissenting opinions function analogously to acts of civil disobedience in offering protest and securing systemic change. "Institutional disobedience" is a good term to characterize dissents and their authors. That is, in writing and publishing dissents, judges are protesting as authorities within institutional roles, analogous to civilians in non-institutional roles who physically enact their protest. Dissent can influence change in both the judicial system and the larger political milieu,

and many legal professionals have provided corroborative evidence for this theory of dissent.

The roots of civil disobedience

First, what is "civil disobedience"? Civil disobedience is an appeal to controlling authorities and to the general public "to alter certain laws or policies that the minority takes to be incompatible with the fundamental principles of morality, principles to which it believes the majority is committed," [6] according to Marshall Cohen. In self-governing communities its essence is:

> . . . propositional, stipulative, suggestive. Discovery, harangue, advocacy are its instruments of corrective persuasion of the beliefs and desires of others . . . . Its central function is not directly to change the law . . . by forcing new policy . . . its function is to *locate* wrong, *inform* the public of such wrong, and *persuade* the electorate to reconsider.[7]

Perception, identification, criticism, persuasion—these are the mechanisms of civil disobedience as a means of social change, influence, and coordination toward a point of view. It is not purposeless, reckless, or anarchistic. On the contrary, the civil disobedient has chosen to participate in democratically sanctioned processes for democratically praiseworthy ends.

A civil disobedient person serves two such democratic ends: First, the reinforcement of the ideal of self-choice, the freedom to arrive at one's own perspective, "a fundamental condition of free government and of all moral judgment;" and second, persuasion of others to join the cause celebre.[8] The cause of the disobedient is:

> concerned with improving the existing legal system. He envisions his role as therapeutic rather than destructive. He believes that the ideal of justice is being violated in some way in the existing laws . . . . He therefore makes of himself a martyr, bearing witness to the truth,

and hoping thereby to educate and enlighten and to move men of good will.[9]

The civilly disobedient person appeals to the democratic ethos:

> [He is] a man who defies that law out of conscience or moral belief .... If he acts out of conscience it is important to remember that he appeals to it as well. ... It is to protest the fact that the majority has violated these principles that the disobedient undertakes his disobedience.[10]

The form of civil disobedience need not, and indeed some would argue that it must not, be violent. It is a "quiet, symbolic act ... aimed at peaceful revision of attitude."[11] Acts that run counter to the majority can be justified as civil disobedience only when they are acts of political speech, appeals, a form of persuasion as opposed to coercion.[12]

Institutional disobedience

It is this nonviolent quality of civil disobedience that has allowed modern democracies to provide *institutional* means of protest to minorities in recognition of their prerogative to oppose majority viewpoints.[13] This type of dissension can "observe, or follow, lines of political 'due process.' "[14] In fact, contemporary scholars suggest that instead of perceiving civil disobedience as essentially contrary to the ideas of authority and obligation, "we might consider building into the very idea of authority and obligation in a democracy a conception of allowable civil disobedience."[15] Dissenting opinions, indeed, may be seen in just this kind of light, as inherent, disparate, due process "acts" allowed to system authorities on behalf of minority viewpoints, or in other words, as institutional disobedience.

Dissents are protestual, propositional, stipulative, and suggestive in appealing to the authority of conscience, with the hope of a future remedy for a present wrong. Thus they militate against monolithic solidarity in the judiciary, reflecting the innate nature and exigence of law in contemporary society as a mosaic. Dissents offer an avenue of representation for perceptions at variance with the dominant vision. They locate wrong in the majority, inform the audience of such wrong, and persuade the audience to reconsider.[16] Thus in this respect dissents function analogously to civil disobedience in our society.

Further, as the world changes so must the law. And the dissenting opinion is "one of the processes that aids that development as the law meets and solves new situations."[17] The dissent initiates and presses change in the system, again analogous to civil disobedience. Without the judicial dissent, "boulders which are fused together with time-defying cement form a wall which could some day obstruct the passage of a needed road to the City of the Realized Hope of Man."[18]

Though there may be various bases for dissent, many dissents are grounded in moral or ethical terms, just as is civil disobedience. These subsets of judicial opinion move beyond the purely legal world "by placing the imprimatur of respectable moral leadership upon controversial social or economic reforms."[19] The appeal is to conscience. Justice Douglas wrote that dissents "may salvage for tomorrow the principle that was sacrificed or forgotten today. Their discussion and propagation of the great principles of our Charter may keep the democratic ideal alive in the days of regressions, uncertainty, despair."[20]

Contesting the imprimatur of infallibility for majority opinions, dissents are foresighted.[21] Chief Justice Hughes pointed to the conscience inherent in minority opinions, regardless of specific rationale, when he wrote, "The dissent is an appeal to the brooding spirit of the law, to the intelligence of a future day. ..."[22] Advocacy is the instrument of this corrective persuasion. Dissents are evidence that the minority view has been heard—the wrong located, the public informed and persuaded. Though the minority view has not triumphed, it has been endowed with a quality of permanence for constant review by sympathetic advocates and system authorities.

The symbolic means of protest is an area of difference between civil and institutional disobedients. Civil disobedients use acts to oppose, such as sit-ins. Judges, on the other hand, use rhetoric. This difference does not make either civil or institutional disobedience inherently more effective. Rather, it reflects a strategic awareness of which symbols, acts or words, can best facilitate protest given the different contexts.

Civil disobedients resort to action because language has failed to effectively oppose. "Mere speech may fail to produce change in many situations because it does not demand a response."[23] To elicit a response, protesters act. In the civil context, this works well as a tool of opposition.

Language and the law

It is fitting that institutionally disobedient persons oppose through rhetoric the majority encroachment of their values. Law and language are inherently related. By stressing conflict resolution through procedure, ceremony, and rhetoric, "legal institutions provide the methods both for symbolically encouraging change while preserving continuity, and for symbolically assuring stability while fostering change." [24] Specifically, it has been argued that "language is the greatest instrument of social control. . . . law is only a division of language." [25] Why is it that language has such power?

In part, the answer lies in the nature of rhetoric. "Words are important as words in that they represent symbolically and artificially an order which exists nowhere in the actual daily lives of persons." [26] Words are able to represent a sense of order because they continuously interact with the human psyche. We naturally experience a need for order, for structure. This need arises out of our normal experience of life, its vastness, complexity, variety. Words organize our thoughts, feelings, responses. They are therefore able to produce a sense of satisfaction, a reduction of the psychological tension arising from our need for order in the face of massive quantities and qualities of stimuli. Language acts as a screen through which our inherent needs, particularly for order, can be filtered. This essential nature of language is of critical significance in law, and makes words appropriate tools of protesting an order imposed by the majority, and designing an alternative order.

A second reason why rhetoric is appropriate deals with its communicative advantage. Laws, as rules and guidelines, must be persuasively communicated to those for whom they will serve as frameworks, and they must be communicated in such a way that the person absorbing them understands that they apply to a variety of situations.[27] The two main devices available for communicating are the example and rhetoric.[28]

H. L. A. Hart argues that examples are imprecise means of communication. While they may be couched in explicit or implicit "do as I do" directives, they still "may leave open ranges of possibilities, and hence of doubt, as to what is intended." [29] Walter Probert agrees that examples are too indeterminant left embedded in concrete with the actor. Others then must speculate on intent, on what will be approved, and on the extent to which one's behavior must trace that of the actor in order to rightly follow the guidelines.[30]

In contrast, language may offer a clearer, more dependable means of communicating standards. The rules are no longer embedded within the confines of a single actor. They are contained in words and language structures about which there is broad agreement as to

meaning. The observer, the respondent, can know what he or she must do in the future and at what time. "He has only to recognize instances of clear verbal terms to 'subsume' particular facts under general classificatory heads and draw a simple syllogistic conclusion." [31]

The power of judicial dissent

This theory of dissent sounds rather romantic, relying on such supporting phrases as "the brooding spirit of the law," "the City of the Realized Hope of Man," and other idealized references. But beyond the romance of dissent are important, substantive, systemic effects. The primary persuasive objective of disobedience is remedy—the remedy of a perceived wrong. And the remedy has been applied successfully in numerous cases. The dissent of a Supreme Court justice avoids the civil disobedient's scorn as "mere speech" that does not demand a response, and it can "heavily influence the allocation of values among relevant competing interests . . . . In broader social terms [it] may modify or enhance the legitimacy that relevant publics in the larger social system accord a decision, a policy, or a law." [32] Three major examples in the area of civil and human rights alone, where dissents eventually became the majority viewpont, add substance to the romance.[33]

In *Plessy v. Ferguson,* [34] the Supreme Court upheld the East Louisiana Railway's right to require Homer Plessy to ride in the "separate but equal Colored" car of the train, contrary to Plessy's wish. Justice John Marshall Harlan dissented, describing "the thin disguise of 'equal' accommodations" for what it really was, a veil of racism. Fifty-six years later, in 1952, the Court began hearing the series of cases known as *Brown v. Board of Education.*[35] And the core premise of Harlan's dissent became law—separate was no longer to be considered equal. Harlan's view of segregation as unconstitutional and a social evil became the majority position.

In 1938 Smith Belts, an unemployed farm worker on relief, was charged with armed robbery and assault. At arraignment, Belts, unable to afford a private counsel, asked Judge Forsythe to appoint an attorney for him. The judge informed him that attorneys were appointed only for indigent defendants charged with murder or rape. Declaring his innocence, Belts saw no possibility of conducting a jury trial himself, so he waived his right to trial by jury. The court found Belts guilty and handed down a prison sentence. From prison Belts sought a writ of habeas corpus, the denial of which he appealed to the Supreme Court. In *Belts v. Brady,*[36] the Court found no violation of due process.

Justice Hugo Black dissented, supported by justices Douglas and Murphy, arguing for the right of counsel for the poor as a safeguard of freedom. Twenty-one years later, in *Gideon v. Wainwright*,[37] analogous circumstances saw Black's dissent become a majority position, and the right to counsel became a cornerstone in American law.

A final example from the many available is Justice Douglas' dissent in *Dennis v. United States*.[38] Here 11 persons were convicted under an extremely broad Smith Act for conspiring to organize a Communist Party and to advocate the forcible overthrow of the U.S. government. The Supreme Court upheld the conviction of the 11 with justices Black and Douglas dissenting. While Black's opinion was brief, revolving around an absolute view of the First Amendment, Douglas wrote a more detailed argument on the clear and present danger test. Six years later, after the close of the McCarthy Era, a similar case reached the Supreme Court. In *Yates v. United States*,[39] however, the Court moved largely within Douglas' preview. Douglas concurred in part and dissented in part. Notwithstanding, the guarantee of freedom of advocacy had been substantially restored.

Courts are not alone in accepting the persuasion of non-majority opinions. Legislatures frequently accept remedial measures advocated therein.[40] Justice Iredell's dissent in *Chisolm v. Georgia*,[41] became part of the Constitution as the Eleventh Amendment.[42] The Dred Scott dissenters' arguments became the foundations for the Thirteenth, Fourteenth, and Fifteenth Amendments to the Constitution.[43] Justice Story's dissent in *Cary v. Curtis*[44] was enacted into law by Congress in 36 days—before the publication of the volume containing his opinion.[45]

Judicial dissents may also influence lawyers. Advocates note not only the majority opinions and the ratio therein, but also the non-controlling, non-majority messages.[46] "Essentially retrospective, [lawyers] search for a comforting precedent, whether it be in a majority or dissenting opinion."[47] Prospectively, lawyers may draw lines of difference among majority and minority opinions and justices, and anticipate future results and alignments under changed facts.[48] Thus, judicial history has shown that non-majority opinions have "exercised a corrective and reforming influence upon the law."[49]

Dissent has potential effects outside the judicial system, as well, in a larger political context. Public allies of the ideology embodied in the dissent find image enhancement in this form of due process disobedience

a positive step in resolving discord. Rehetoric from authorities with status also tends to defuse more violent acts of civil disobedience, and to calm those who must be persuaded.

> Official support of one group's claim acts as a positive statement of the stature of that group's subculture. . . . The use of supportive rhetoric . . . would allow opponents of the functioning ideology to strive for and occasionally gain official support while reducing the overt threat to the governmentally sanctioned value set.[50]

Perceptions of dissent

What the dissenter intends to do by dissenting may be identified in part by what he or she says. But another crucial element in recognizing intent is what members of the legal community believe about the dissents. What are mutual beliefs about the genre of judicial opinion labeled, "dissent"?

The metaphors used when discussing dissents are important clues to perception. More than a literary device, the metaphor represents a way of seeing, a way of believing. It symbolizes inferences the thinker has made through comparison or analogy regarding the subject.

For example, Richard Stephens, writing in the *Florida Law Review,* perceived authors of dissents "acting" as advocates.[51] Here, the metaphor is "acting," and Stephens sees dissenters as engaging in physical behavior, with the implicit comparison to civil disobedients who enact their protest.

Justice Douglas conjured images of civil disobedience when he wrote:

> It is the right of dissent, not the right or duty to conform, which gives dignity, worth, and individuality to man. As Carl Sandburg recently said, 'There always ought to be beatniks in a culture, hollering about the respectables.'[52]

Thus we have judicial dissenters analogyzed to nonconformity, individualistic "beatniks hollering about the respectables." Mr. Douglas' view of dissent must surely have flowed from his view of the Supreme Court's role in our cultural lives. He wrote, "The Court that *raises its hand against the mob* may be temporarily unpopular; but it soon wins the confidence of the nation. The court that fails to *stand before the mob* is not worthy of the great tradition."[53]

Significantly, there are others who share Mr. Douglas' point of view on dissent while avoiding his reputation as a maverick. Benjamin Cardozo used metaphor to characterize judicial dissent:

> The voice of the majority may be that of force triumphant, content with the plaudits of the hour, and recking little of the morrow. The dissenter speaks to the future, and his voice is pitched to a key that will carry through the years. Read some of the great dissents . . . and feel after the cooling time of the better part of a century, the glow and fire of a faith that was content to bide its hour. The prophet and martyr do not see the hooting throng. Their eyes are fixed on the eternities.[54]

Again, the dissenter is painted in colors of civil disobedience.

A final example comes from prominent legal philosopher Karl Llewellyn. Though he prefers the quantity of dissents kept at a minimum, as indicated below, he nevertheless acknowledges the quality of dissent in terms familiar to civil disobedients. He writes, "the dissent, by forcing or suggesting full publicity, rides herd on the majority."[55] Thus, from scholars, attorneys, and dissenters we have seen a mutual belief about dissents. These beliefs seem to confirm the analogy of dissent as civil disobedience.

A second mutual belief that lends support to dissent as civil disobedience concerns the reception of dissents. Dissents do not have to be received as illegitimate to be versions of disobedience. On the contrary, due process is at the core of civil disobedience. And judicial dissent is the institutional due process equivalent to civil disobedience. However, acknowledgment of the disparate nature of the act or opinion, its contraction of the mainstream or authoritative will, would seem necessary to warrant the characterization, "disobedience." There is evidence of such a belief about dissent.

Though dissents have been published since the earliest cases and are common today, they remain eschewed. Justice Douglas alluded to the controversy surrounding dissents when he wrote, "All of us in recent years have heard and read many criticisms of dissenting . . . opinions. Separate opinions have often been deplored. Courts have been criticized for tolerating them."[56] Justice Edward White declared that the only purpose a dissent could serve is to weaken the Court.[57] Chief Justice Hughes deprecated "persistent expressions of opinions that do not command the agreement of the Court."[58] Philosopher Llewellyn prefers dissents to be few in number because they tend to diminish a "single way of seeing."[59]

Conclusion

The importance of judicial dissent has been debated for years. A school of thought represented by H. L. A. Hart has argued that dissents have no system-wide consequences because they do not alter rights in immediate cases. Here, I have disagreed. To the goal of system-wide change is dissent, its effects, and supporting perceptions deployed.

The conclusion that dissents are sources of energy and cogency in law is important in order to understand how and why we carry on the ideals of our system of justice. Knowledge enhances our effectiveness. The makers of dissent need not question the efficacy of their effort, and the audiences of dissent can appreciate the value of the message. They are both engaged in a significant expression of the legal process.

More generally, analysis of any function of that process can offer insight into the process itself, and ease the identification of essential characteristics. The analysis of dissent here points to the conclusion that the law is far more complex than the status of rights in immediate cases. First, law is transcendent—it lives not only within a particular set of facts and determines a particular set of rights, but also rises to a more universal plane of consciousness. It encompasses more than the present in its spread.

Second, and related to the first, law is enduring rather than ephemeral. It lives beyond the cases that animated it; it is progenerative. Its participation in the historical process into which all humans are born gives even aged or overturned law a role in contemporary dynamics. And third, law is infused with humanity, and thus is inherently concerned with symbolizing human yearnings and the persuasion of humans by means of the quintessential human process, the power of language. Dissent calls forth these characteristics of the judicial system, and helps illumine Chief Justice Hughes' perception that the dissent appeals to the "brooding spirit" of the law.

Notes

This article originally appeared in Volume 66, Number 7, February 1983, pages 304–312.

1. Evans, "The Dissenting Opinion—Its Use and Abuse," *Mo. L. Rev.* 3 (1938), 120.
2. McWhinney, "Judicial Concurrences and Dissents: A Comparative View of Opinion-Writing in Final Appellate Tribunals, *Canadian B. Rev.* 31 (1953), 609–610.
3. 12 Wheat 22, 331 (1827).

4. Ganoe, "The Passing of the Old Dissent," *Or. L. Rev.* 21 (1942), 286.

5. *The Concept of Law* (New York: Oxford University Press, 1961), 138.

6. "Civil Disobedience in a Constitutional Democracy," *Philosophic Exchange* (1970), 104. "Morality" here broadly refers to that which is considered "good" or "valuable." Additional discussions may be found in Power, "Civil Disobedience as Functional Opposition," *J. Pol.* 34 (1972), 37; and "On Civil Disobedience in Recent American Democratic Thought," *Am. Pol. Sci. Rev.* 64 (1970), 35; Spitz, "Democracy and the Problem of Civil Disobedience," *Am. Pol. Sci. Rev.* 48 (1954), 386.

7. Black, "The Two Faces of Civil Disobedience," *Soc. Theory & Prac.* 1 (1970), 21.

8. Ibid.at 22.

9. Morano, "Civil Disobedience and Legal Responsibility," *J. Value Inquiry* 5 (1971), 193.

10. Cohen, *supra* n. 6, at 99.

11. Black, *supra* n. 7, at 22.

12. Frazier, "Between Obedience and Revolution," *Phil. & Pub. Aff.* 1 (1972), 316.

13. Endres, "Civil Disobedience and Modern Democracy," *Thought* 43 (1968), 503.

14. Martin, "Civil Disobedience," *Ethics* 80 (1970), 36

15. Ibid.

16. "Persuade" here refers to the process of influencing, not necessarily the result.

17. Simmons, "Use and Abuse of Dissenting Opinions," *La. L. Rev.* 16 (1956), 498.

18. Musmanno, "Dissenting Opinions," *Kan. L. Rev.* 6 (1958), 411.

19. Davis and Reynolds, "Juridical Cripples: Plurality Opinions in the Supreme Court," *Duke L. J.* 1974 (1974), 63.

20. Carter, "Dissenting Opinions," *Hastings L. J.* 4 (1953), 121.

22. Hughes, as quoted in Edwards, "Dissenting Opinions of Mr. Justice Smith," *U. Det. L. J.* 34 (1956), 82.

23. Frazier, *supra* n. 12, at 317.

24. Ingber, "Procedure, Ceremony and Rhetoric: The Minimization of Ideological Conflict in Deviance Control," *B. U. L. Rev.* 56 (1976), 321.

25. Williams, "Language and the Law," *L. Q. Rev.* 62 (1945), 71.

26. Pranger, "An Explanation for Why Final Political Authority is Necessary," *Am. Pol. Sci. Rev.* 60 (1966), 996.

27. Probert, "Law Through the Looking Glass of Language and Communicative Behavior," *J. Legal Educ.* 20 (1968), 51.

28. Hart, *supra* n. 5, at 121.

29. Ibid. at 220.

30. Probert, *supra* n. 27, at 51.

31. Ibid.

32. Ulmer, "Dissent Behavior and the Social Background of Supreme Court Justices," *J. Pol.* 32 (1970), 581.

33. These examples, along with others, are discussed in detail in Barth, *Prophets With Honor: Great Dissents and Great Dissenters in the Supreme Court* (New York: Random House, 1974, 1975). For additional examples *see* Carter, *supra* n. 21; Brown, "A Dissenting Opinion of Mr. Justice Story Enacted as Law Within Thirty-Six Days," *Va. L. Rev.* 26 (1940), 759; Ganoe, *supra* n. 4, at 295; Lashly and Rava, "The Supreme Court Dissents," *Wash. U. L. Q.* 28 (1943), 191; Sanders, "The Role of Dissenting Opinions in Louisiana," *La. L. Rev.* 23 (1963), 676; and McWhinney, *supra* n. 2, at 611.

34. 163 U.S. 537 (1896).

35. 347 U.S. 483 (1954).

36. 316 U.S. 455 (1942).

37. 372 U.S. 335 (1963).

38. 341 U.S. 494 (1951).

39. 354 U.S. 298 (1957).

40. Brown, *supra* n. 33, at 759.

41. 2 U.S. 419 (1793).

42. Carter, *supra* n. 21, at 119.

43. Musmanno, *supra* n. 18, at 140.

44. 3 Howard 236, 252 (1845).

45. Brown, *supra* n. 33, at 760. For additional examples *see* Fuld, "Voices of Dissent," *Col. L. Rev.* 62 (1962), 927.

46. Freedman, "Dissenting Opinions and Justice Musmanno," *Temp. L. Q.* 30 (1957), 253.

47. Sanders, *supra* n. 33, at 675.

48. Jackson, "Dissenting Opinions," *Pittsburgh L. J.* 100 (1952), 3.

49. Carter, *supra* n. 21, at 118.

50. Ingber, *supra* n. 24, at 269.

51. Stephens, "Function of Concurring and Dissenting Opinions in Courts of Last Resort," *U. Fla. L. Rev.* 5 (1952), 404.

52. Douglas, *America Challenged* (Princeton: Princeton University Press, 1960), 4–5.

53. Douglas, *We The Judges* (Garden City, N.Y.: Doubleday, 1956), 443.

54. Cardozo, *Law and Literature and Other Essays and Addresses* (New York: Harcourt, Brace & Co., 1931), 36.

55. Llewellyn, *The Common Law Tradition: Deciding Appeals* (Boston: Little, Brown, 1960), 26.

56. Douglas, *supra* n. 20, at 104.

57. *Pollack v. Farmers Loan and Trust Co.,* 157 U.S. 429, 608.

58. *Federal Trade Comm'n v. Beechnut Co.,* 257 U.S. 441, 456 (1922).

59. Llewellyn, *supra* n. 55, at 463. For a discussion of non-majority opinions as anathema to Continental European jurists, *see* Dumbauld, "Dissenting Opinions in International Adjudication," *U. Pa. L. Rev.* 90 (1943), 929; *see also* Fuld, *supra* n. 45, at 924–925.

How Supreme Court justices respond to litigant requests to overturn precedent

Jeffrey A. Segal and Robert M. Howard

Stare decisis survives at the U.S. Supreme Court, but it is conditioned, like so much else, on the attitudes and values of the justices.

Weathering a century of legal realism, attitudinalism, and critical legal studies, stare decisis remains at the heart of scholarly thinking about law. It resides at or near the core of the thinking of our most prominent legal theorists, continues as the most frequent explanation provided in law reviews for legal decisions, and has even found new homes in endeavors as disparate as the "team" [1] and "constitutive" [2] theories of judicial decision making.

Moreover, social science techniques, which have most predominantly been used to analyze the influence of attitudes and values on judicial decision making,[3] have recently been put to use in the new systematic study of stare decisis. This article brings simple but systematic social-scientific evidence to bear on how justices react to requests that they overturn one of the Court's previous decisions. As compared to the everyday following and distinguishing of precedents, a request to overturn places the greatest stress on this legal doctrine. How do justices react to such requests in general, and is their reaction conditional on the ideological direction of the request?

Systematic studies

Stare decisis has both vertical and horizontal components. Most extensively examined, at least until the last few years, has been the vertical component. The main focus of these studies has been the extent to which lower court judges follow their own preferences compared to the extent that they follow higher court (usually Supreme Court) precedents.

One relatively early systematic analysis of this question examines changes in decision making on the U.S. courts of appeals following doctrinal changes by the Supreme Court in 1936 in substantive due process and during the 1950s and 1960s in First Amendment cases.[4] The study found that circuit court decision making did not get more liberal as Roosevelt made appointments between 1933 and 1936. It was not until

after the Supreme Court switched its position that the circuit courts started doing the same. Similarly, the circuit courts followed Supreme Court trends on the First Amendment, voting conservatively in the 1950s, liberally in the 1960s, and conservatively again in the 1970s. Alternatively, more recent studies have found that after controlling for the facts of the case, lower court judges respond not only to changes in Supreme Court preferences, but to the judges' own preferences as well.[5]

Most recently, scholars have tested more sophisticated strategies that lower courts might follow in an attempt to escape hierarchical review. For example, courts of appeals judges who are ideologically opposed to an agency's decision are more likely to follow the Supreme Court's 1984 *Chevron* decision requiring due deference to agency decisions when the panel contains a whistleblower, one who would prefer to defer to the administrative agency's decision, than when it does not.[6] This result is consistent with the thrust of research conducted by Steven Van Winkle, who has found that as the probability of en banc review decreases, judges who are panel outliers become increasingly likely to follow their own preferences as opposed to those of their circuit.[7]

Systematic evidence as to horizontal stare decisis has been much more difficult to come by. A series of recent studies, however, has begun to add to our knowledge. First, we consider what we call "everyday" stare decisis, the routine use of precedent in judicial decision making. Certainly, this level of stare decisis permeates the decisional process at the Supreme Court. For the briefs on the merits, previous decisions typically outnumber constitutional provisions, statutes, regulations, and all other sources combined in the Table of Authorities.[8] Moreover, justices frequently make appeals to precedent in their private conference discussions.[9] Additionally, justices more frequently cite precedents in their written opinions than any other source of information.[10]

The question of whether this everyday stare decisis actually influences the decisions of the justices or,

Judicature Volume 86, Number 3, pp. 148–157

rather, merely rationalizes their decisions, is a bit more complex. This is because while justices in virtually every case follow one line of precedent or another, it is difficult to determine whether they were *influenced* by that line of precedent. "Influence" requires that the precedent lead them to a result that they would not otherwise have reached. As Judge Jerome Frank stated, "Stare decisis has no bite when it means merely that a court adheres to a precedent that it considers correct. It is significant only when a court feels constrained to stick to a former ruling although the court has come to regard it as unwise or unjust." [11]

Thus, in the progeny of *Roe v. Wade,* Justices Blackmun, Marshall, Brennan, etc. certainly followed *Roe,* in that their decisions were consistent with *Roe*'s commands. But it is difficult to assess whether they were influenced by *Roe,* for they were supportive of the right to abortion to begin with. According to Spaeth and Segal,[12] such assessments can be made about Rehnquist and White in progeny of the *Roe* case, or indeed, the dissenters from any precedential case. In the progeny of such cases, they argue, one can arguably tell if the dissenters from the original decision were influenced by the precedent thus established by seeing how they behaved in future cases.

For example, while Justice Rehnquist dissented in the jury exclusion cases *Batson v. Kentucky* (1986) and *Edmonson v. Leesville Concrete Co.* (1991) he concurred in *Georgia v. McCollum* (1992), providing an explicit and quintessential example of what it means to be constrained by precedent: "I was in dissent in *Edmonson v. Leesville Concrete Co.* and continue to believe that case to have been wrongly decided. But so long as it remains the law, I believe it controls the disposition of this case. . . . I therefore join the opinion of the Court."

Using this type of operational standard for the influence of stare decisis, Spaeth and Segal find little such influence throughout not just modern times, but the history of the Court. They do, however, find some substantively meaningful levels of deference to stare decisis in the least salient of the Court's cases.[13]

Perhaps, though, horizontal stare decisis doesn't constrain justices in their everyday decisions, where fact freedom abounds. Maybe its constraint is only felt in crisis, in the most extreme of circumstances, when justices must confront overruling a previous decision. As Chief Justice Rehnquist recently noted, "While *stare decisis* is not an inexorable command, particularly when we are interpreting the Constitution, even in constitu-

tional cases, the doctrine carries such persuasive force that we have always required a departure from precedent to be supported by some special justification." [14]

Certainly, the Court rather infrequently overrules its prior decisions. According to the leading authority on such overruling, the Supreme Court overturns merely 2.5 cases per year or so.[15] In any given decade, the Court overturns less than .002 percent of its previous decisions![16]

What leads to cases being overturned? A survival analysis by Spriggs and Hansford shows that several factors make it more likely that a Supreme Court precedent will be overturned: the ideological distance between the majority that established the decision and the current Court; the existence in the precedent of a constitutional issue; the existence in the precedent of one or more concurring opinions; the existence in the precedent of a minimum winning coalition; a legally complex case; and negative treatment by the Court of the precedent in recent cases.[17]

One limit to the studies that examine the overturning of precedent, one that we seek to remedy here, is that they do not examine the overruling of precedent as a function of the opportunity to overturn precedent. Overwhelmingly, as we will show, the Court will not consider overruling a precedent unless it is asked to do so. Thus, while Brenner and Spaeth examine the votes of justices for and against overturning precedents, they only do so in cases in which a precedent is overturned. That is, they look at the numerator (cases overturning precedent) only, and not the denominator (measurable opportunities to overturn precedent).

Research strategy

Unlike the everyday stare decisis examined by Spaeth and Segal, where deference to precedent was found only at minimal levels, the gravitational force of stare decisis should be relatively greatest when the doctrine is pushed to its outermost limit, i.e., when justices are asked to overturn previous decisions. Arguably, if justices don't defer to precedent here, they never will.

We test this using the research strategy first used by Harold Spaeth to test for judicial restraint nearly 40 years ago.[18] Spaeth first noted that while justices frequently cast votes that could be classified as "restrained," e.g., supporting state economic regulations or upholding the decisions of federal regulatory commissions, such support was conditional on the ideological direction of the agency decision.

For example, Justice Frankfurter, the purported paragon of judicial restraint, voted to uphold 60 percent of NLRB decisions during the first seven terms of the Warren Court. But breaking the data down by ideological direction of the agency's decision reveals that while Frankfurter upheld 88 percent of the agency's anti-union decisions, he upheld only 29 percent of the agency's pro-union decisions. Thus Spaeth (correctly) concludes that Frankfurter's voting behavior was consistent with economic conservatism, not judicial restraint.

Similarly, to conclude that a justice generally upholds precedent in the face of a request for overruling, we submit that she must generally defer both when that precedent is in a liberal direction and when that precedent is in a conservative direction.

We note as well that given our focus on "crisis" stare decisis, we use a very generous definition of "upholding" a precedent: anything short of overturning. Of course, often the Court can significantly limit, or avoid, an unfavorable precedent without actually overturning that precedent. In such a case we do not code the action as an overturning of precedent. For example, in *Shaw v. Reno* (1993), the court overturned a redistricting plan that created black majority congressional districts. The appellants, five North Carolina residents, argued that the districts were highly arbitrary, and among other things, violated equal protection. However, a 1977 case, *United Jewish Organizations v. Carey*, appeared to uphold such districts if they were created to achieve minority representation. The appellants asked that the court overturn the *United Jewish Organizations (UJO)* precedent, calling it a "dangerous relic of the past that should be overturned."

Justice O'Connor, writing for the majority, did not overturn *UJO*. Instead, she held that "The highly fractured decision in *UJO* does not foreclose the claim recognized here, which is analytically distinct from the vote-dilution claim made there" (in *UJO*).

Justice White in dissent, however, said, "The Court today chooses not to overrule, but rather to sidestep, *UJO*. It does so by glossing over the striking similarities, focusing on surface differences, most notably the . . . shape of the newly created district . . . and imagining an entirely new cause of action." Justice Blackmun, in commenting upon the so called "fractured" decision in *UJO*, stated that he did not join the equal protection portion of White's opinion in *United Jewish Organizations of Williamsburgh, Inc.* because it was not necessary to decide that case. Blackmun argued that the use of race in redistricting does not violate the Equal Protection Clause unless the effect of the redistricting plan is to deny a particular group equal access to the political process or to unduly minimize its voting strength.

Florida Bar v. Went For It, Inc. (1995) provides another example of a potential disposal of a troublesome precedent without actually so doing. The Florida bar prohibited lawyers from sending direct-mail solicitations to victims and their relatives for 30 days following an accident or disaster. A lawyer referral service and a Florida attorney sued to enjoin the rule, and a federal district court granted them summary judgment, citing *Bates v. State Bar of Arizona* (1977). In that case, the Supreme Court struck down a ban on price advertising for legal services. The petitioner Florida Bar Association asked the Court to overturn *Bates*.

The Court, however, continued to uphold *Bates*, while distinguishing the challenged Florida regulation from the prohibited regulation in *Bates*. O'Connor ruled that *Bates* held that lawyer advertising is commercial speech and is accorded only limited First Amendment protection. The Florida restriction is permissible because there was a substantial interest in protecting the privacy of personal injury victims against invasive, unsolicited contact by lawyers and in preventing the erosion of confidence in the profession, and because the ban's scope is reasonably well tailored to its stated objectives.

The dissent, led by Justice Kennedy, argued that the majority endangered the holding of *Bates*. Kennedy stated that the First Amendment protected "Attorneys who communicate their willingness to assist potential clients . . . that principle has been understood since *Bates v. State Bar of Arizona*. The Court today undercuts this guarantee." Kennedy went on to argue "Today's opinion is a serious departure, not only from our prior decisions involving attorney advertising, but also from the principles that govern the transmission of commercial speech."

In both *Shaw* and *Florida Bar* the majority effectively gutted an unfavorable precedent, but in neither case does it meet our standard of overturning precedent.

Data collection

Our data consist of all briefs on the merits filed by petitioners and respondents between the start of the 1985 Term and the end of the 1994 Term.[19] We trained coders to assess whether either the petitioner or respondent asked the Court to overturn a previous

Supreme Court decision. We combined these data with data from Harold Spaeth's U.S. Supreme Court Judicial Data Base.[20]

To test the reliability of the data we double coded 100 cases. We achieved 96 percent agreement with our coders on whether the petitioner requested that the Court overturn precedent (Kappa = .58; p<.001) and 99 percent agreement on whether the respondent requested that the Court overturn precedent (Kappa = .66; p<.001).

As a second check on our data, we determined whether all cases that showed up in Spaeth's dataset as overturning precedent also showed up in our dataset of requests to overturn precedent. Of the 25 cases during the relevant time period that Spaeth had as overturning precedent, 21 turned up in our dataset. Of the remaining four, we miscoded one case as not requesting an overturn. In the other three cases the parties to the case did not ask the Court to overturn a precedent. In two of those cases, various amici requested overturn of the relevant cases. In the third case, the Court acted sua sponte.

Needless to say, many cases show up on our list that do not show up on Spaeth's. The most obvious reason for this is that the Spaeth dataset only notes when the Opinion of the Court actually overturns a precedent. It does not note those instances when the Court is asked to overturn a precedent but does not do so. Moreover, while our data indicate very little in the way of issue creation (overturning cases when not asked to), we do note a fair amount of issue suppression (refusing to reach a decision on overturning a previous decision, despite being asked to).

Data description

The Supreme Court decided 1,297 cases on the merits that were docketed between the 1985 and 1994 Terms. The most obvious finding is that parties are loathe to ask the Court to overturn any of the Court's prior precedents. In only 37 cases (2.9 percent) did the petitioner ask the Court to overturn a precedent, and in only 30 more (2.3 percent) did the respondent ask the same (See "Litigant requests to overturn precedent," pages 435–437). Overwhelmingly, parties to a suit will tell the Court that unhelpful precedents can readily be distinguished from the current case. Thus for example in *United States v. Irvine* (1994) the issue involved the effectiveness of a written disclaimer of an interest in a trust by one Mrs. Irvine. The Internal Revenue Service, relying on the case of *Jewett v. Commissioner* (1982),

denied the transfer and assessed a gift tax of over $7 million. In *Jewett*, the Court construed a Treasury Regulation to provide that the disclaimer of a remainder interest in a trust effects a taxable gift to the beneficiary of the disclaimer unless the disclaimant acts within a reasonable time after learning of the transfer that created the interest being disclaimed. Here Mrs. Irvine waited 48 years to disclaim an interest in the trust.

While the attorneys for her estate asked the Court to overturn *Jewett*, they also argued that *Jewett* did not apply since the only contingency preventing Jewett from taking his fixed 50 percent share of trust principal was the requirement that he survive the life beneficiaries. By contrast, significant contingencies, in addition to survival, were present for Mrs. Irvine until Trust termination "because the number of remainder beneficiaries and the size of her interest changed considerably during the Trust term and were subject to change until Trust termination."

The argument of the Solicitor General in *Shalala v. Schaefer* (1993) provides an even more blunt example of a party distinguishing an unfavorable precedent in addition to asking the Court to overturn that precedent. *Shalala* involved the timeliness of an application for attorney's fees under the Equal Access to Justice Act (EAJA). In an earlier case, *Sullivan v. Hudson* (1989), the Court ruled that fees incurred during administrative proceedings held pursuant to a district court's remand order might be recovered under the EAJA. The Solicitor General argued, "We do not believe that Hudson must be overruled for us to prevail here." The brief went on to argue that the situation in the present case differs from the situation confronted by the *Hudson* court.

Needless to say, such behavior by litigants suggests that the Court itself prefers not to overturn formally its own precedents if it can at all help it,[21] and indeed there are innumerable means for the Court to avoid distasteful rulings.[22]

Occasionally, though, parties have little alternative but to ask the Court to overturn a previous decision. For example, in *Welch v. State Department of Highways, Texas* (1987), the respondent urged, "the *Parden* Court's notion of constructive consent is dead and needs now only be interred." Moreover, some parties will even reach out to ask that a case be overturned. In *Rust v. Sullivan* (1991), the United States simply and unnecessarily declared, "We believe that *Roe* was wrongly decided and should be overruled."

Because asking the Court to overturn a precedent may be a risky strategy, we expect that those who do ask

Litigant requests to overturn precedent

1. *Richard Solorio v. United States of America* 483 U.S. 435 (1987)

    Overturned *O'Callahan v. Parker* 95 U.S. 258 (1969) (respondent)

2. *California v. Cabazon Band of Mission Indians* 480 U.S. 202 (1987)

    Did not overturn *Bryan v. Itasca County* 426 U.S. 373 (1976) (appellant)

3. *Welch v. State Department of Highways, Texas* 483 U.S. 468 (1987)

    Overturned *Parden v. Terminal Railway Company* 377 U.S. 184 (1964) (respondent)

4. *Business Electronics v. Sharp Electronics* 485 U.S. 717 (1988)

    Did not overturn *Dr. Miles Medical Company v. John D. Park & Sons* (respondent)

5. *Greer v. Miller* 483 U.S. 756 (1987)

    Did not overturn *Chapman v. California* 386 U.S. 18 (1967) (petitioner)

6. *Square D. Co. v. Niagara Frontier Tariff Bureau* 476 U.S. 409 (1986)

    Did not overturn *Keogh v. Chicago & Northwestern Railway* 260 U.S. 156 (1922) (petitioner)

7. *Puerto Rico v. Branstad* 483 U.S. 219 (1987)

    Overturned *Kentucky v. Dennison* 65 U.S. (24 How.) 66 (1861) (petitioner)

8. *Griffith v. Kentucky* 479 U.S. 314 (1987)

    Did not overturn *United States v. Johnson* 457 U.S. 537 (1982) (petitioner)

9. *Hobbie v. Unemployment Appeals Commission* 480 U.S. 136 (1987)

    Did not overturn *Sherbet v. Verner* 374 U.S. 398 (1963) (appellee)

10. *Sun Oil Co. v. Wortman* 486 U.S. 717 (1988)

    Did not overturn *McElmoyle v. Cohen* 13 Pet. 312 (1839) (petitioner)

11. *Arizona v. Roberson* 486 U.S. 675 (1988)

    Did not overturn *Edwards v. Arizona* 451 U.S. 477 (1981) (petitioner)

12. *Houston v. Lack* 487 U.S. 266 (1988)

    Did not overturn *Harris Truck Lines, Inc. v. Cherry Meat Packers, Inc.* 371 U.S. 215 (1962) (respondent)

13. *Harte-Hanks Communications v. Connaughton* 491 U.S. 657 (1989)

    Did not overturn *Bose Corp. v. Consumers Union of U.S., Inc.* 466 U.S. 485 (1984) (respondent)

14. *Kaiser Aluminum & Chemical Corp. v. Bonjorno* 494 U.S. 827 (1990)

    Did not overturn *Bradley v. School Board of Richmond* 416 U.S. 696 (1974) (petitioner)

15. *Sisson v. Ruby* 497 U.S. 358 (1990)

    Did not overturn *Richardson v. Harmon* 222 U.S. 96 (1911) (respondent)

16. *Rodriguez De Quijas v. Shearson/Am. Exp.* 490 U.S. 477 (1989)

    Overturned *Wilko v. Swan* 346 U.S. 427 (1953) (respondent)

17. *Jones v. Thomas* 491 U.S. 376 (1989)

    Limited *In Re Bradley* 318 U.S. 50 (1943) (petitioner)

18. *Healy v. The Beer Institute* 491 U.S. 324 (1989)

    Overturned *Joseph E. Seagram & Sons, Inc. v. Hostetter* 384 U.S. 35 (1966) (respondent)

19. *Michigan v. Harvey* 494 U.S. 344 (1990)

    Did not overturn *Massiah v. United States* 377 U.S. 201 (1964) (petitioner)

20. *McKoy v. North Carolina* 494 U.S. 433 (1990)

    Did not overturn *Mills v. Maryland* 486 U.S. 367 (1988) (respondent)

21. *Webster v. Reproductive Health Services* 492 U.S. 490 (1989)

    Did not overturn *Roe v. Wade* 410 U.S. 113 (1973) (petitioner)

22. *Missouri v. Jenkins* 491 U.S. 274 (1989)

    Did not overturn *Hutto v. Finney* 437 U.S. 678 (1978) (petitioner)

    Did not overturn *Hans v. Louisiana* 134 U.S. 1 (1890) (respondent)

23. *Horton v. California* 496 U.S. 128 (1990)

    Did not overturn *Coolidge v. New Hampshire,* 403 U.S. 443 (1971) (respondent)

24. *Rust v. Sullivan* 500 U.S. 173 (1991)

    Did not overturn *Roe v. Wade* 410 U.S. 113 (1973) (respondent)

25. *United States v. Eichman* 496 U.S. 310 (1990)

    Did not overturn *Texas v. Johnson* 491 U.S. 397 (1989) (petitioner)

26. *California v. Acevedo* 500 U.S. 565 (1991)

    Overturned *United States v. Chadwick* 433 U.S. 1 (1977) (petitioner)

(Box continues on next page)

Litigant requests to overturn precedent *(continued)*

27. *Ohio v. Huertas* 498 U.S. 336 (1991)
     Did not overturn *Booth v. Maryland* 482 U.S. 496 (1987) (respondent)

28. *California v. Ferc* 495 U.S. 490 (1990)
     Did not overturn *First Iowa Hydro-Electric Power v. Federal Power Commission* 328 U.S. 152 (1946) (petitioner)

29. *Burnham v. Superior Court of Cal., Marin County* 495 U.S. 604 (1990)
     Did not overturn *Pennoyer v. Neff* 95 U.S. 714 (1877) (petitioner)

30. *Collins v. Youngblood* 497 U.S. 37 (1990)
     Overturned *Thompson v. Utah* 170 U.S. 343 (1898) (petitioner)

31. *Coleman v. Thompson* 501 U.S. 722 (1991)
     Overturned *Fay v. Noia* 372 U.S. 391 (1963) (respondent)

32. *Lee v. Weisman* 505 U.S. 577 (1992)
     Did not overturn *Lemon v. Kurtzman* 403 U.S. 602 (1971) (petitioner)

33. *Keeney v. Tamayo-Reyes* 504 U.S. 1 (1992)
     Overturned *Townsend v. Sain* 372 U.S. 293 (1963) (petitioner)

34. *Litton Financial Printing Div. v. NLRB* 501 U.S. 190 (1991)
     Did not overturn *Nolde Bros., Inc. v. Bakery Workers* 430 U.S. 243 (1977) (petitioner)

35. *Exxon Corp. v. Central Gulf Lines, Inc.* 500 U.S. 603 (1991)
     Overturned *Minturn v. Maynard* 1854 U.S. (17 How.) 476 (1854) (petitioner)

36. *Payne v. Tennessee,* 501 U.S. 808 (1991)
     Overturned *Booth v. Maryland,* 482 U.S. 496 (1987) (respondent)

37. *Hilton v. S.C. Pub. Rys. Comm'n* 502 U.S. 197 (1991)
     Did not overturn *Parden v. Terminal Railway of Alabama Docks Dept.* 377 U.S. 184 (1964) (respondent)

38. *Withrow v. Williams* 507 U.S. 680 (1993)
     Did not overturn *Brown v. Allen* 344 U.S. 443, 458–459 (1953) (petitioner)

39. *United States v. Dixon* 509 U.S. 688 (1993)
     Overturned *Grady v. Corbin* 495 U.S. 508 (1990) (petitioner)

40. *Quill Corp. v. Heitkamp* 504 U.S. 298 (1992)
     Did not overturn *National Bellas Hess, Inc. v. Department of Revenue of Ill.* 386 U.S. 753 (1967) (respondent)

41. *Allied-Signal v. Dir., Div. of Tax'n* 504 U.S. 768 (1992)
     Did not overturn *ASARCO Inc. v. Idaho Tax Comm'n* 458 U.S. 307 (1982)

42. *Fort Gratiot Landfill v. Mich. DNR* 504 U.S. 353 (1992)
     Did not overturn *Philadelphia v. New Jersey* 437 U.S. 617 (1978) (respondent)

43. *Planned Parenthood of Southeastern PA. v. Casey,* 505 U.S. 833 (1992)
     Did not overturn *Roe v. Wade* 410 U.S. 113 (1973) (respondent)

44. *Burlington Northern R. Co. v. Ford,* 504 U.S. 648 (1992)
     Did not overturn *Power Manufacturing Co. v. Saunders* 274 U.S. 490 (1927) (respondent)

45. *Buckley v. Fitzsimmons* 509 U.S. 259 (1993)
     Did not overturn *Imbler v. Pachtman* 424 U.S. 409 (1976) (petitioner)

46. *Harper v. Virginia Dept. of Taxation,* 509 U.S. 86 (1993)
     Overturned *Chevron Oil v. Huson* 404 U.S. 97 (1971) (petitioner)

---

will be repeat players whose interests will transcend a narrow victory in the instant case. Our data generally support this hypothesis. States in criminal cases most frequently asked for an overturn (28 times). Big business was the next most frequent (10 times). Interest groups sponsoring litigation asked seven times, the same number for individual criminal defendants. The federal government requested overturns six times, with the rest individuals, Native American tribes, and local governments.

In addition, we looked at the age of the precedents that the parties sought to overturn. On average, the previous decision was slightly more than 34 years old. However, the average masks the significant variance (a standard deviation of 38.04 years) of the age of these past decisions. Three litigants made requests for the Court to overturn decisions rendered during the last session, while four requests involved 100-year-old precedents. From this, we could discern little chronological pattern to the requests.

We break down the requests to overturn by issue area and the ideological direction of the party requesting the overturn. For both variables, we rely on the

47. *United States v. Irvine*, 511 U.S. 224 (1994)
    Did not overturn *Jewett v. Commissioner* 455 U.S. 305 (1982) (respondent)

48. *City of Ladue v. Gilleo* 512 U.S. 43 (1994)
    Did not overturn *Metromedia, Inc. v. San Diego* 453 U.S. 490 (1981) (petitioner)

49. *Oklahoma Tax Comm'n v. Sac & Fox Nation* 508 U.S. 114 (1993)
    Did not overturn *Oklahoma Tax Comm'n v. Citizen Band of Potawatomi Tribe of Okla.* 498 U.S. 505 (1991) (respondent)

50. *Shalala v. Schaefer* 509 U.S. 292 (1993)
    Did not overturn *Sullivan v. Hudson* 490 U.S. 877 (1989) (petitioner)

51. *Shaw v. Reno* 509 U.S. 630 (1993)
    Did not overturn *United Jewish Organizations of Williamsburgh, Inc. v. Carey,* 430 U.S. 144 (1977) (petitioner)

52. *Landgraf v. USI Film Products* 511 U.S. 244 (1994)
    Did not overturn *Bradley v. Richmond School Bd.* 416 U.S. 696 (1974) (respondent)

53. *Nichols v. United States* 511 U.S. 738 (1994)
    Did not overturn *Scott v. Illinois* 440 U.S. 367 (1979) (petitioner)
    Overturned *Baldasar v. Illinois* 446 U.S. 222 (1980) (respondent)

54. *Victor v. Nebraska* 511 U.S. 1 (1994)
    Did not overturn *Griffith v. Kentucky* 479 U.S. 320 (1987) (respondent)

55. *Rivers v. Roadway Express, Inc.* 511 U.S. 298 (1994)
    Did not overturn *Bradley v. Richmond School Bd.* 416 U.S. 696 (1974) (respondent)

56. *Allied-Bruce Terminix Companies, Inc. v. Dobson* 513 U.S. 265 (1995)
    Did not overturn *Southland Corp. v. Keating* 465 U.S. 1 (1984) (respondent)

57. *Associated Indus. of Missouri v. Lohman* 511 U.S. 641 114 (1994)
    Overturned *General American Tank Car Corp. v. Day* 270 U.S. 367 (1926) (petitioner)

58. *Board of Ed. of Kiryas Joel v. Grumet* 512 U.S. 687 (1994)
    Did not overturn *Lemon v. Kurtzman* 403 U.S. 602 (1971) (petitioner)

59. *United States v. Shabani* 513 U.S. 10 (1994)
    Did not overturn *Nash v. United States* 229 U.S. 373 (1913) (respondent)

60. *Hubbard v. United States* 514 U.S. 695 (1995)
    Overturned *United States v. Bramblett* 348 U.S. 503 (1955) (petitioner)

61. *Florida Bar v. Went For It, Inc.* 515 U.S. 618 (1995)
    Did not overturn *Bates v. State Bar of Arizona* 433 U.S. 350 (1977) (petitioner)

62. *Rosenberger v. University of Virginia* 515 U.S. 819 (1995)
    Did not overturn *Lemon v. Kurtzman* 403 U.S. 602 (1971) (petitioner)

63. *United States v. Gaudin* 515 U.S. 506 (1995)
    Overturned *Sinclair v. United States* 279 U.S. 263 (1929) (respondent)

64. *Ford v. Wainwright* 477 U.S. 399 (1986)
    Did not overturn *Solesbee v. Balkcom* 339 U.S. 9 (1950) (petitioner)

65. *North Star Steel Co. v. Thomas* 515 U.S. 29 (1995)
    Did not overturn *Silliman,* 3 Pet. (28 U.S.) 270 (1830) (petitioner)

---

issue codings established in Spaeth's U.S. Supreme Court Judicial Database. The results appear in Table 1.

Not surprisingly, given the conservative tenor of the Supreme Court during this era, the majority of requests for overrides (42 of 67) came from litigants who can be classified as conservative, e.g., the government in criminal procedure cases, anti-minority parties in civil rights cases, businesses in economics cases, etc. In terms of issue area, we see that while criminal procedure cases made up only 22.2 percent of the Court's overall docket during the terms studied, they make up 35.8 percent of the cases in which a request

was made to overturn a precedent. Alternatively, while civil rights made up 15.5 percent of the Court's docket, it comprised only 10.4 percent of the cases in which a litigant requested that a precedent be overturned.

Ideological reactions

As noted above, we expect some hesitancy by the justices in formally overturning precedents given the other options available to them. Nevertheless, we also expect that justices will react ideologically to requests to overturn precedent. If justices do not show restraint about formally overturning precedent, then they will support

Notes

This article originally appeared in Volume 86, Number 3, November-December 2001, pages 148–157.

The authors thank Melissa Marschall, Richard Foster, and Robert Johnston for research assistance and Howard Gillman and Kevin McGuire for helpful comments. They also thank the National Science Foundation (SBR 9515335) for financial support.

1. Kornhauser, "Adjudication by a Resource-Constrained Team: Hierarchy and Precedent in a Judicial System," *S. Cal. L. Rev.* 68 (1995), 1605.

2. Kahn, "Institutional Norms and Supreme Court Decision-Making: The Rehnquist Court on Privacy and Religion." In Clayton and Gillman (eds.), *Supreme Court Decision-Making* (Chicago: University of Chicago Press, 1999).

3. Beginning with Pritchett, *The Roosevelt Court* (New York: Macmillan, 1948).

4. Songer and Reid, "Policy Change on the U.S. Courts of Appeals: Exploring the Contribution of the Legal and Democratic Subcultures." Paper presented at the annual meeting of the American Political Science Association, 1989.

5. Songer and Haire, "Integrating Alternative Approaches to the Study of Judicial Voting: Obscenity Cases in the U.S. Courts of Appeals," *Am J. Pol. Sci.* 36 (1992), 963–982; and Songer, Segal, and Cameron, "The Hierarchy of Justice: Testing a Principal-Agent Model of Supreme Court-Circuit Court Interactions," *Am. J. Pol. Sci.* 38 (1994), 673–696.

6. Cross and Tiller, "Judicial Partisanship and Obedience to Legal Doctrine: Whistleblowing on the Federal Courts of Appeals," *Yale L. J.* 107 (1998), 2155–2176.

7. Van Winkle, "Governing Justice: Rotating Three-Judge Panels and Strategic Behavior on the United States Courts of Appeals." Ph.D. dissertation. Ohio State University, 1996.

8. Knight and Epstein, "The Norm of Stare Decisis," *Am. J. Pol. Sci.* 40 (1996), 1018–1035.

9. Ibid.

10. Ibid. *See also* Phelps and Gates, "The Myth of Jurisprudence: Interpretive Theory in the Constitutional Opinions of Justices Rehnquist and Brennan," *Santa Clara L. Rev.* 31 (1991), 567–596.

11. *United States ex rel. Fong Foo v. Shaughnessy*, 234 F.2d 715, 719 (1955).

12. Spaeth and Segal, *Majority Rule or Minority Will: Adherence to Precedent on the U.S. Supreme Court* (New York: Cambridge University Press, 1999).

13. Note, alternatively, that when court of appeals judges dissent from *en banc* rulings, they overwhelmingly tend to follow such rulings in future decisions. *See* Kahn, "An Empirical Study of the Effects of *Stare Decisis* on Appellate Court Judges of the Fourth Circuit." Typescript, University of Chicago, 2000.

14. *Dickerson v. United States*, 530 U.S. 428 (2000). Internal cites omitted.

15. Brenner and Spaeth, *Stare Indecisis: The Alteration of Precedent on the U.S. Supreme Court, 1946–92* (New York: Cambridge University Press, 1995).

16. Knight and Epstein, *supra* n. 7.

17. Spriggs and Hansford, "Explaining the Overruling of U.S. Supreme Court Precedent," *J. Pol.* (2001).

18. Spaeth, "The Judicial Restraint of Mr. Justice Frankfurter—Myth or Reality," *Midwest J. Pol. Sci.* 8 (1964), 22–38.

19. Our focus on the briefs filed by direct parties on the merits excludes two additional sources of information. First, we exclude certiorari briefs, not just in cases granted, but in cases denied as well. Arguably, if a party asks the Court to reconsider a precedent in a cert brief but the Court denies cert, a claim could be made that the Court has upheld that precedent. Beyond the fact that this would mean coding over 120,000 briefs, this misrepresents what a denial of cert means. No one, we believe, could seriously claim that a denied cert petition means that a challenged precedent was upheld or that it means anything else as to the merits of the case (see, e.g., *Brown v. Allen*, 344 U.S. 443 (1953), at 451–452). Moreover, a cert brief has a different function than the merits brief. As Chief Justice Vinson declared, "Lawyers might be well-advised, in preparing petitions for certiorari, to spend a little less time discussing the merits of the case and a little more time demonstrating why it is important that the Court should hear them." Cited in Stern, Gressman, and Shapiro, *Supreme Court Practice,* 6th ed. (Washington, D.C.: Bureau of National Affairs, 1986), 373.

Second, we exclude amicus briefs on the merits. We do so because direct parties, much more than amici, have the highest stake in winning the case. Given the Court's hesitancy to overturn precedents, direct parties are, relatively speaking, much less likely to ask the Court to overturn a precedent unless they need to do so in order to win. Amici, alternatively, usually have goals that go well beyond the merits of the case. Thus, a request by an amicus to overturn a precedent does not establish a valid threshold that the Court should even *consider* doing so in the instant case.

20. *See* Spaeth and Segal, "The U.S. Supreme Court Judicial Data Base: Providing New Insights into the Court," *Judicature* 83 (2000), 228–235.

21. *See* Epstein and Knight, *The Choices Justices Make* (Washington, D.C.: CQ Press, 1998), chap. 5.

22. *See, e.g.,* Segal and Spaeth, *The Supreme Court and the Attitudinal Model* (New York: Cambridge University Press, 1993), chap. 2.

23. Epstein and Knight, *supra* n. 20, at 163–175.

24. According to the Spaeth database, he has done so in just 3 of 24 cases.

25. Given the means of getting around precedents and costs of overturning them, the question might naturally arise as to why the Court ever feels the need to overturn a precedent. This, of course, requires a theory of doctrine, which goes beyond the scope of this study. But if we assume that one goal of doctrine is to constrain lower courts, then overturning *Plessy v. Ferguson* limits recalcitrant lower courts in ways that distinguishing it or even limiting it cannot do.

Justice Frankfurter and Justice Reed: friendship and lobbying on the Court

Bradley C. Canon, Kimberly Greenfield, and Jason S. Fleming

Despite their dissimilarities and Frankfurter's often patronizing attempts to influence Reed, the two justices had a collegial relationship not seen on the Supreme Court today.

The question of who influences whom on the Supreme Court has long intrigued scholars and observers. They realize that the Court's opinions reflect collegial interaction among the justices that is designed to modify or even change positions. But learning about such interaction is difficult since the Court deliberately shrouds its inner workings in secrecy. Thus, secondhand accounts, journalists' reports,[1] or mere speculation based upon the justices' personalities and intellect are relied on to figure out who influenced whom, through what tactics, and to what degree.

Scholars most often pierce the veil of secrecy by analyzing the papers of retired or deceased justices.[2] To be valuable in this respect, such papers must include candid correspondence with other justices. If there are enough such letters, it is possible to develop an understanding about influence on the Court. This article, which focuses on the efforts of Justice Felix Frankfurter to influence Justice Stanley F. Reed during their joint service on the Court (1939–1957), is based primarily upon their correspondence and is supplemented by the recollections of Reed's law clerks.[3]

Frankfurter and Reed were not very similar. Frankfurter was a a Jew, born in Vienna in 1882. His parents immigrated to Manhattan's teeming Lower East Side when he was 12. He learned English as an adolescent yet graduated first in his class at Harvard Law School. As an adult before coming to the Court, Frankfurter, an intimate of Justice Louis Brandeis, led an urbane life, one centering on Boston academic circles and the intellectual rigors of Harvard Law School. He wrote widely, including three scholarly books on the Supreme Court,[4] and frequently advised governors, cabinet officers and, most notably, President Franklin D. Roosevelt. In 1939, he became FDR's third appointment to the Court.

By contrast, Stanley Reed, born in 1884, grew up in Maysville, Kentucky, a small town on the Ohio River. He did not complete law school and practiced small-town

law in Maysville for more than 12 years. Reed started his national career in 1929 as an attorney for the Federal Farm Board. Later he became general counsel for the newly established Reconstruction Finance Corp. In 1935 Reed was named solicitor general and defended several major New Deal programs before the Supreme Court. He was Roosevelt's second Supreme Court appointee in January 1938. Reed was as at home in the camaraderie of middle America as Frankfurter was in that of the East Coast liberal establishment.

Despite their dissimilarities, Frankfurter and Reed developed a friendship during Reed's RFC and solicitor general days. It was refreshed by regular correspondence and further blossomed during their years on the Court. The two often visited each other's offices and in good weather walked the mile and a half to and from the Court together.[5] Apparently, only Justices Hugo Black and (in the 1950s) Tom Clark shared the same degree of friendship with Reed as did Frankfurter.[6]

"Lobbying" Reed

Frankfurter was the Court's premier lobbyist during his era and probably rivaled John Marshall in this respect. He had an image of himself as the Court's intellectual leader in the tradition of Holmes and Brandeis.[7] He was forever writing or talking to his colleagues in an effort to win undecided votes, change ones already stated, soften or strengthen opinions, induce or stifle dissents, or otherwise affect the outcome and nature of a Court decision. While personality or ideological conflicts limited his efforts with some justices such as William O. Douglas, Frankfurter directed his efforts at justices such as Harold Burton, Robert Jackson, and Clark, as well as Reed. In the late 1940s, Reed was perceived as the swing vote on an ideologically divided Court, thus making Frankfurter's efforts to woo Reed even more crucial.[8]

Frankfurter wrote Reed 253 letters or notes during their 17 years on the Court.[9] This is almost half (47 per-

Judicature Volume 78, Number 5, pp. 224–231

cent) of the total correspondence Reed received from every justice during this period. This graphically illustrates how often Frankfurter "lobbied" Reed. No other justice even approached Frankfurter's efforts. Chief Justice Harlan F. Stone and Justice Wiley Rutledge each wrote Reed an average of 7 times per term, compared to Frankfurter's 15 times. Some colleagues rarely wrote Reed. Black, for example, did so at a rate of only 1 time per term.[10] However, the flow of correspondence was asymmetrical: only 18 percent of Reed's outgoing correspondence was directed to Frankfurter. In fact, Reed wrote Stone more often per term than he did Frankfurter and wrote Burton only slightly less often. Reed's letters to Frankfurter were less intimate than those he received from him, but they contained occasional regard or humor.

Frankfurter supplemented his written efforts to lobby Reed with frequent visits to his chambers. As one clerk put it:

[Frankfurter] would frequently try to persuade Reed to his point of view. . . . Sometimes we [would] all end up in a three way conversation or discussion or argument . . . in Reed's office with Frankfurter very vigorously espousing his views and sometimes pontificating, always showing his erudition.[11]

A clerk from the late 1940s recalled:

Reed was sort of a centrist on the Court; he was fair game for judges from both sides to try to get him over to their side to make up a majority. And therefore he was importuned frequently by them to join them. Frankfurter did this a lot. Frankfurter loved argument and discussion. . . . He would frequently try to persuade Reed to his point of view.[12]

There are, of course, no records of how often other justices came to Reed's chambers, but interviews with the clerks leave the clear impression that Frankfurter was far and away the most frequent visitor.

In addition to direct persuasion, Frankfurter was, in one clerk's words, "forever trying to seduce Reed's law clerks in the expectation that they would help seduce Stanley Reed. [But] Frankfurter's efforts in that direction were transparent and Reed had a good time in watching them."[13] Another clerk reported,

Justice Frankfurter was quite fond of using Justice Reed's law clerks as an avenue to the justice's opinions. Frankfurter was quite likely to walk into our [the clerks'] chambers and discuss issues with us that he never talked to the Justice about.[14]

Substantive efforts

Opportunities for Frankfurter to try to influence Reed's positions or the substance of his opinions abounded. The Court's non-unanimous decisions rose sharply after 1940, exceeding 50 percent by the 1943 term, and the justices' willingness to write concurring opinions increased to more than 25 percent of the cases by the late 1940s.[15] While there were few fundamental differences between Frankfurter and Reed, their votes diverged about 40 percent of the time in dissensual decisions.[16] Frankfurter, considerably more ideologically and doctrinally oriented than Reed, often tried to persuade or instruct Reed, particularly—in keeping with his image as heir to Holmes and Brandeis—with regard to judicial restraint.

While both Reed and Frankfurter believed generally in judicial restraint and had few ideological differences, they had divergent perspectives in two areas. One was police behavior, particularly search and seizure cases.[17] With amusing insight, Reed once explained his differences with Frankfurter in this area.

Do you know why Felix and I decide these search and seizure cases differently? . . . Well, when Felix was a young Jewish boy growing up in Vienna, there could be a knock at the door in the night. It could be a policeman coming to take him away. When I was a young boy, I grew up in Maysville, Ky. I had a white pony and I used to ride [him] down the main street . . . and as I passed the main intersection, there was a policeman there and he would stop traffic for me. And as I passed, he would pat me on my golden curls. And when Felix thinks of a policeman, he thinks of a knock on the door in the night, and when I think of a policeman, I think of the man stopping traffic for me and patting me on my curls.[18]

The other area was freedom of speech and the press. Reed subscribed to the "preferred position" doctrine elevating these guarantees above others. He did not apply the doctrine anywhere near as broadly as did Hugo Black, William O. Douglas, Wiley Rutledge, and Frank Murphy, and commentators never touted Reed as a champion of First Amendment claims, but Reed was sympathetic to its application in certain situations.[19] Frankfurter adamantly opposed the preferred position argument and favored a "balancing" approach to the First Amendment. In several First Amendment cases Frankfurter urged Reed to give more weight to other factors and in *Ullman v. U.S.* (1956) he lectured Reed directly and forcefully against the preferred position approach, but to no avail.[20]

While Justice Douglas once said that Frankfurter "never missed a chance to line up a vote," [21] the Reed papers show only four instances when Frankfurter sought Reed's vote directly. Two were on the merits and two were strategic, the latter asking that Reed, who was silently subscribing to a liberal bloc majority opinion, write an opinion concurring in the result but withholding approval of the liberal rationale.[22] Reed rejected all the requests.

Nor did Frankfurter try much to shape Reed's opinions through explicit threats of concurrences or dissents if his suggestions were not incorporated. Justices sometimes resort to this tactic, and Frankfurter used it with some of his brethren.[23] But the correspondence shows Frankfurter putting the matter to Reed in such overt terms only three times, with Reed acceding once.[24]

Much more often Frankfurter tried to persuade Reed to make changes in opinions. This persuasion could take several forms. He often made straightforward arguments that the development of Reed's position was illogical and needed substantial rewriting (the outline of which Frankfurter would suggest) or that it was at odds with important precedents or legal doctrines. He often cautioned Reed against obiter dicta, particularly when he feared that the unnecessary writing might well haunt the Court in future cases. An illustrative case is *Regan v. New York* (1955), involving a police officer who as a condition of remaining one had to waive testimonial immunity in a grand jury appearance. Frankfurter advised Reed to excise a discussion of matters such as what constituted a valid waiver and to stick to settling *Regan* on grounds that the guarantee against compelled self-incrimination was not incorporated into the Fourteenth Amendment. He told Reed:

> You have heard my song before and I am afraid you will hear it as long as we are on the Court together, but nothing but mischief comes from talk that a case does not call for, especially when constitutional issues are involved.[25]

Reed, however, kept such discussion in the opinion and Frankfurter concurred separately.

Frankfurter sometimes tried convincing his colleague by invoking the giants of the legal profession in his behalf, most often Holmes and Brandeis. A good example occurred in *U.S. v. Line Material Co.* (1948), an anti-trust case. Frankfurter first tried to dissuade Reed from upholding a broad interpretation of the act.

> All the 'liberals' threw their hats in the air when Brandeis castigated the then majority for assuming to exercise the power of a 'super-legislature'. It would shock Holmes and Brandeis out of their boots to learn that the beauty of the Sherman Law is its vast vagueness, whereby five members of this Court are able to decide what is good or bad for 'the economy' of this country. Yes, I know I am again invoking the names of Holmes and Brandeis. I am unashamed to be reverent to the great.[26]

A few weeks later Frankfurter urged Reed to suppress his *Line Material* opinion.

> Some of the best writings, by far, both of Holmes and Brandeis were circulated but unpublished opinions. . . . I suspect they no more liked committing intellectual infanticide than do you or I. But they did it frequently during their service on the Court, because it advanced the best interests of the Court and of the Law. Reflecting on the examples of Holmes and Brandeis emboldens me to suggest that the circumstances in which we find ourselves in the *Line* case may make it equally wise for you to subject your opinion in that case to intellectual infanticide.[27]

Reed, however, was not dissuaded and never seemed particularly impressed on those occasions when Frankfurter referred to one or both of the memorable duo.

The same was true when other greats were brought to bear. In a disagreement over a question about federal equity power, Frankfurter told Reed, "My understanding of equitable principles was derived from James Barr Ames, who, I suspect, was the deepest student this country ever produced on that subject." [28]

Scholars have remarked upon Frankfurter's frequent use of flattery in persuading his colleagues, and Reed was often an object of this tactic.[29] For example, one effort to get Reed to reduce his reliance on a set of precedents Frankfurter disliked began, ". . . I know enough to appreciate how deft your job. Therefore I am even more unhappy than I am on ordinary occasions to touch your opinion." [30] In another, he said:

> You have done not only a very faithful and careful but so helpful a piece of work . . . that I dislike to bother you further with a suggestion which may merely resolve

itself to a preferential way of putting a thing. And yet words are the very stuff of our business and inextricably determine substance . . . .[31]

Flattery occasionally worked, largely depending upon how much change Frankfurter wanted.

When other tactics seemed inappropriate, Frankfurter might try to get Reed to see the facts differently. These efforts could result in an exchange of several letters. In *McNabb v. U.S.* (1943) where the Court first held that due process required the arraignment of federal prisoners within a few hours of arrest, Frankfurter sent Reed two long letters emphasizing the delay in arraignment and McNabb's meantime interrogation in isolation; he cited the uncontroverted facts in trial record.[32] Reed nonetheless put a different gloss on the case and dissented solo.

Criminal cases were a prime area for factual disputes between the two, but they could occur in other areas too. In *Poulos v. New Hampshire* (1953), a Jehovah's Witness case, Frankfurter in a three-week series of memos to Reed argued that Poulos had not made a First Amendment challenge in the state courts to a city ordinance requiring a permit prior to using a public park for a religious meeting. Reed was unpersuaded: "it seems to me clear from the motions and the facts . . . that Poulos made an attack in New Hampshire and here on the constitutional validity of this ordinance." [33]

Their longest exchange came in *Williams v. North Carolina* (1945), holding that other states could challenge the validity of their own citizens' six weeks Nevada domicile for purposes of obtaining a divorce. Thirteen letters went back and forth in five weeks. The arguments mixed law and fact and eventually Reed reluctantly came around to Frankfurter's viewpoint.[34]

Frankfurter's success

Reed could be quite stubborn, sometimes illogically so. Frankfurter recorded the following conversation with him about a case where Reed sided with Black against Frankfurter.

> After I circulated my concurring opinion . . . Reed, J. phoned and said 'I am very glad you wrote what you did, because you put in words what I tried inadequately to express to Black to indicate my dissatisfaction with his opinion.'
>
> FF: 'But I understand you are going with him.'
> Reed: 'That's right.'

> FF: 'In other words, you are going with Black because he is not expressing your views, and you're not going with me because I *am* [sic] expressing your views.'
> Reed: 'That's a funny but fair way of stating the situation.' [35]

Because Reed dug in his heels at times, the professor sometimes bluntly expressed his frustration. "Either I have written to no point or you have read to no point," he wrote Reed in one case. "I could not believe that . . . you could support Bill's [Douglas] concoction in *Screws [v. U.S.]*, that you could give adherence to something that has not the support of your mind nor the comfort of your conscience," he said in an early civil rights prosecution. "You are incorrigible in your desire to make law like mathematics," he sighed in an administrative law case.[36]

Sometimes Frankfurter gave up before he began. In a case centering on racial discrimination in grand juries, Frankfurter started to write Reed but ended up writing a concurrence. He told Reed that "it would be a hopeless enterprise and an utter waste of your time for me to ask you to, in effect, revamp your opinion along [my suggested] lines." [37]

But sometimes Frankfurter was successful in persuading Reed to alter an opinion substantially. This was especially likely in Reed's early years when he was more hesitant and cautious in writing majority opinions. *Smith v. Allwright* (1944), which struck down Texas's whites only Democratic primary, is an important and illustrative example.[38] Reed relied heavily upon *U.S. v. Classic* (1941), which held that Congress had power under the Fifteenth Amendment to regulate primary elections. His first draft worked around a 1935 case, *Grovey v. Townsend*, that upheld the whites only primary. Frankfurter strongly believed that *Grovey* should be unequivocally overruled. He wrote Reed:

> You are of the opinion that the South can be gently eased into acceptance of our decision in *Allwright* if only we are not too explicit. My own prophecy is precisely the opposite—that no matter with what tissue paper covering the blow [when it] is administered, it will be felt, and by appearing to screen it an added grievance will be aroused. . . . We are absolutely turning an about face [in] that *Allwright* is a square and unmitigatory overruling of *Grovey*, . . . not a thing is before us now that was not before the Court in *Grovey* [and] no intervening event of legal or practical signifi-

cance has happened except a change in the membership of this Court.[39]

Here Reed listened to Frankfurter and decided to risk angering the South. The final opinion had four sentences not contained in the first draft, ending with "*Grovey v. Townsend* is overruled." [40]

Similarly, in *Viex v. Sixth Ward Building and Loan Assn.* (1940) Reed wrote an opinion rejecting a contract clause challenge to a Depression-era statute designed to protect the solvency of a state's savings and loan banks by making withdrawals more difficult. Doing this was problematical because Reed had to distinguish *Viex*'s outcome from two earlier precedents where the Court had applied the contract clause to somewhat analogous situations. Frankfurter told him:

> since [these two] cases are decisions that we really wouldn't decide that way if we had the deciding of them, I think we ought to carry as little of their baggage as possible. And so I have ventured to put to you a softened rephrasing of what you said about [them].[41]

In the published opinion, Reed followed Frankfurter's suggestions almost verbatim. Reed also adopted some Frankfurter themes in rejecting a convicted murderer's double jeopardy claim when Louisiana's electric chair malfunctioned in the first attempt to execute him. Frankfurter wrote back, "Thank you for the changes you have made. I am confident that history will approve of them." [42]

Reed's editor

When Frankfurter could not or had no desire to convince Reed to change the tenor of his opinion, he would nevertheless suggest numerous changes in his colleague's drafts. It did not matter whether Frankfurter was subscribing to Reed's opinion. As he once told Reed, "[T]o some of my brethren I feel free to make suggestions even as to opinions in which I do not join." [43] Frankfurter made similar suggestions to several other colleagues, particularly Harold Burton and Owen Roberts. But Reed, who did not delegate much opinion writing to his clerks, was a slow and sometimes awkward writer and was particularly receptive to Frankfurter's help.[44] It is fair to say that Frankfurter served as the primary editor for many a Reed opinion.

Some Frankfurter suggestions were aimed at strengthening Reed's arguments. For example, when Reed circulated a draft that responded to Douglas's dissenting point by saying, "We see no reason why . . . ,"

Frankfurter told him that it was "no answer to an argument, if there is anything in it, to say there is nothing in it. . . . if you are going to refer to Bill's argument, you ought to say a little something." Frankfurter then wrote a paragraph-long suggestion on how to "properly" answer the argument. When Reed incorporated much of the paragraph, Frankfurter scribbled on Reed's circulation, "Thank you. Yes! —FF" [45]

In *Champlin Refining Co. v. U.S.* (1946), a pipeline regulation statutory question in which Frankfurter was joining Reed in dissent, Frankfurter enclosed a substitute paragraph for Reed's concluding one, explained why it would better answer the majority opinion, and then told his colleague, "So be a nice boy." The very next day Frankfurter suggested to Reed that if "you insist on keeping in the last sentence of the next to last paragraph, it ought to be phrased more clearly in some such way as the following: . . . ." [46] Reed adopted Frankfurter's language almost verbatim.

When Frankfurter wanted something excised, he could edit through sarcasm. A Reed sentence in a draft of *Breard v. City of Alexandria* (1951), upholding the constitutionality of an anti-canvassing law as applied to magazine subscription salesmen, read: "True liberty is indivisible." Frankfurter scrawled back, "Really, really, . . . How about 'true security is indivisible?' " [47] Later in the draft, Reed wrote, "[F]ortunately, subscribers may be secured [in other ways]." Frankfurter again took exception:

> Why 'fortunately'? If you mean that it is fortunate for our country that *Time, Life,* etc., can sweep in subscriptions, then it is a pronouncement that this Court has no business to make. . . . I can assure you that I am not the only one who does not regard *Time* and *Life* as a blessing for the country, but, on the contrary, deems them among the most powerful forces of miseducation and debasement.[48]

Reed eliminated the objectionable phrases.

Another example: In a copyright case Reed wrote, "Sacrificial days devoted to such creative activities deserve rewards commensurate with the services rendered." In big letters in the margin, Frankfurter observed, "Gawd! A ditchdigger also spends sacrificial days." [49]

In fact, Frankfurter was the Supreme Court's "Mr. Language Person" and Reed his main pupil. By his own admission, Frankfurter was a "pernickety" teacher. His letters and marginal comments were studded with spelling, vocabulary, and grammatical corrections, sometimes at considerable length. He wrote two pages to Reed on the correct usage of "cf.," explained the difference between "presupposition" and "preposition" and between "jurisdiction" and "justiciable," and told him when to use ellipses and when to use brackets in an opinion.[50] Even when Frankfurter was willing to tolerate a grammatical slip-up, he let Reed know about it: "OK. Even with the split infinitive!" he said of one Reed draft.[51]

Patronizing friendship

Frankfurter viewed most of his brethren as lesser intellects. He particularly thought Chief Justices Harlan Fiske Stone and Fred Vinson and Justices Owen Roberts, Frank Murphy, Harold Burton, and Sherman Minton were not strong minds.[52] He also included Reed in this class. In candid letters to Judge Learned Hand, he dismissed Reed as "largely vegetable" and the "least judicial as well as the stupidist" justice.[53] Nonetheless, Frankfurter saw Reed as an oft-time ally, a vote or opinion capable of being won over, and maintained his strong friendship with him.

Even so, Frankfurter was often and obviously patronizing toward Reed. He frequently instructed Reed about legal matters in conversations or long letters. A clerk described Frankfurter's behavior during one of his visits to Reed's office: "It really wasn't a conversation so much as a lecture. And Frankfurter literally dressed Reed down. . . . He was treating Justice Reed almost like a student. . . ."[54]

Some Frankfurter letters were mini-lectures (slightly softened by flattery) in the sense that they treated Reed as someone unlearned in an area of law or legal history. Reed received the first such letter only a few months after Frankfurter came to the Court. It involved a tax case and is excerpted here for style and tone:

> Judges depart from wisdom . . . due to a lack of rigorous realization that even the best of judges are poorly equipped to be shapers of tax policies and that too free use of the power of invalidation inevitably is in effect policy-making. Saying yes to a tax measure has not terribly serious consequences, at the very worst. There are always legislative remedies if the thing hurts too much. But saying no is full of potential danger way beyond the immediate exercise of the taxing power under review. I happen to know that this Court came pretty close to throwing out William J. Bryan's notions of bank deposit

guaranty legislation. What a heavy price we would have had to pay if the poor formulation of that idea had been invalidated instead of sustained in *Noble State Bank v. Haskill.* Take, for instance, the whole relatively recent history on "double" taxation. How wise in the retrospect Holmes' attitude of abstention appears, beginning with his dissent in the *Union Refrigerator Case* and culminating in *Blackstone v. Miller.* Compare the contradictory movement culminating in *Farmers Loan and Trust Co v. Minnesota* and then consider the painful and partial return to the original line. . . .[55]

A half dozen or so such letters lectured Reed each term, falling off somewhat during their last years on the Court. Frankfurter would instruct him on such broad legal questions as when to exercise judicial review, the wisdom of judicial restraint, the canons of statutory construction, the nature of concurrent jurisdiction, and on constitutional questions such as the scope of the commerce clause, the "proper" approach to interpreting the freedom of speech and press guaranties, and the need for restraints on the police. In one commerce clause case, Frankfurter referred Reed to his recent book on that clause, and a few days later he asked Reed whether he had read it yet.[56]

Sometimes a frustrated Frankfurter would simply denigrate a Reed draft opinion like a top sergeant might chew out a poorly performing private. He did not pull his punches. The best example is *Higgins v. C.I.R.* (1941), a tax case in which Frankfurter told Reed that were he still a professor, "I would feel obliged to tear [your opinion] to tatters [because it] lacks even the intellectual forthrightness in which judges can safely indulge." He then suggested the removal of some "disfiguring warts" that "I should like to have done to make me as happy as an otherwise miserable opinion could."[57]

Responding to Reed's draft in *Uverges v. Pennsylvania* (1949), a right to counsel case, Frankfurter excoriated him for treating opinions of the Court and dissents with equal weight. He ended by telling Reed, "[This] is merely the froth of my feeling about your *Uverges* opinion. In due course you will have a full blast."[58] Of another Reed draft he said, "If I did not have . . . a cast iron stomach, your attitude toward Congressional legislation would give me ulcers."[59] A note responding to another Reed draft began "Good God! Truly a shoestring opinion!!!"[60] A case's disposition did not necessarily end the matter. Once, after publication of a Reed opinion for the Court, Frankfurter forwarded him an anonymous criticism of it, saying of the writer: "You know him well and respect him greatly." [61]

Despite being patronized and almost openly taken for a dullard, Reed was better able to tolerate Frankfurter's behavior than were most of his colleagues. He did not have a large ego and genuinely respected Frankfurter's legal intellect. He once said of Frankfurter, "[H]e knows so much he antagonizes, but he is good." [62]

Reed was open to persuasion, but he was his own man. Several Reed law clerks relate amusing anecdotes illustrating their justice's patience with Frankfurter. Once when Frankfurter came into Reed's office to discuss a case with him, the clerk recounted:

> Reed just sat there quietly, nodding his head very politely, and [when] Frankfurter was satisfied with himself he wheeled out, going out like a little bird. . . . Reed turned to us and said, 'What a wonderful disquisition. What a marvelous analysis. What a brilliant mind. Don't you envy that capability? If only he had some common sense!' [63]

Another described a Reed reaction thusly:

> Felix would be jumping around like a hummingbird [with] this great smiling . . . benign figure watching [and] listening with a kind of bemused tolerant smile. At the end of which, he would say, 'Thank you very much, Felix. I appreciate your spending time with me.' [64]

Genuine friendship

By all appearances, the two justices kept a warm friendship despite Frankfurter's open patronizing and his limited success in shaping Reed's positions or opinions. One manifestation of this was Frankfurter's willingness to share with Reed his contempt of their colleagues on the Court's liberal wing. Frankfurter's sarcastic references to them ranged from the simple "Black and Co." to "the great civil libertarians" through "those who profess to be [the Bill of Rights'] special guardians and true interpreters" and on to "the guardians of the great writ." [65] He especially zeroed in on Hugo Black and what Frankfurter saw as his stubborn preconceptions. In one case he wrote Reed:

> I put it to you: do you think that any amount of relevant or irrelevant discussion could shake Hugo loose from his conclusion? . . . You might as well ask him to climb a greased telephone-pole as to change his conclusion by [what you are writing]. [66]

In *Adamson v. California* (1947), which featured the famous debate between Black and Frankfurter about whether the Fourteenth Amendment's due process clause incorporated the entire Bill of Rights, Frankfurter advised Reed (who was writing the opinion) against compromise:

> There are statesmen, whom Neville Chamberlain best illustrates, who seem to think that the way to conciliate enemies is to lose friends. That odd notion has not been wholly unreflected even in the work of this Court. No matter what you wrote in rejecting the claim that there was a denial of due process in the *Adamson* case, because of the disregard of immunity from self-crimination, you could not win the support of Black and Co. [67]

Another time Frankfurter told Reed, "[Your] opinion is impregnable to the assault by the projectiles of the Black-Douglas fountain pen! F. F." [68] When a Black draft misquoted the Constitution's religious test clause so that it appeared to bar such tests for state office as well as national ones, Frankfurter remarked sarcastically, "I suppose the printer is to blame for that." [69] Murphy also came in for a swipe or two. "You would no more eat Murphy's tripe today than you would be seen naked at DuPont Circle at high noon tomorrow," Frankfurter told Reed. [70] Reed was not so denigrating of the liberal justices, although he did once tell Frankfurter that Chief Justice Vinson was "just like me only less educated." [71]

Also revealing of their friendship is the degree to which they were teasing or playful in discussing cases. Frankfurter especially enjoyed this. For example, when Reed's draft dissent in *Pennsylvania v. Nelson* (1956), which struck down state anti-subversion laws on grounds of federal preemption, referred approvingly to Reed's majority opinion in *Cloverleaf Butter Co. v. Patterson* (1942), Frankfurter sent him a copy of the relevant part of *Cloverleaf* with a hand-written comment: "Dear dear dear: I thought that as you grew in understanding you had repented of that reprehensible decision; the inalienable right to sell rancid butter to the poor." [72] Once, after several letters about a case did not move Reed, Frankfurter sent the next letter on just a regular sheet of paper. "The upshot of my correspondences with you is that I shall cease the wasteful use of my fine Seribuer-made Cambridge Stationery." [73]

In an Indian claims case, Frankfurter, with Reed's sometime adherence to Justice Stone's famous Footnote Four philosophy in mind, wrote:

Since Indians are not among the disadvantaged as to whom your 'zeal for the underdog weights your judicial judgment,' I can agree with you on an analysis of your opinion and not have to reconsider everything from the beginning.[74]

"It would be a pleasure to expose the difficulties of your views on the merits, but we lack jurisdiction here," Frankfurter responded to a Reed argument.[75] "You will comfort Chiang," he teased when Reed dissented from a Frankfurter ruling against the Nationalist Chinese government.[76] Frankfurter even sent Reed "groaners." When a 1947 Reed dissent relied on Reed's majority opinion in *Miles v. Illinois Central RR* (1942), Frankfurter wrote playfully, "Must you compound *Miles* of error!"[77]

Reed returned his colleague's humor. After receiving several letters of Frankfurter's philosophical analyses of freedom of speech in *Dennis v. U.S.* (1951), which upheld the constitutionality of the Smith Act, Reed responded with the salutation "Dear Plato."[78] Even in their prolonged dispute in *Poulos v. New Hampshire* noted earlier, Reed could be teasing. When Frankfurter gave Reed a draft of a memo to the conference charging Reed with indifference to the case record and asked, "Should I circulate?" Reed replied in the margin, "One more circulation from you and I am bound to win." Frankfurter fired back in the other margin, "Of course, you mean you can't win on the merits."[79]

Indeed, with Frankfurter's devotion to precision and purity of language in mind, Reed went out of his way to find unusual words to insert in his draft opinions just to get a rise out of the former professor. In one case Reed wrote about the "metal of the road" and Frankfurter crossed it out and inserted "middle." But Reed knew what he was about and, citing the *Oxford English Dictionary*, pointed out that metal was an archaic usage for middle. "Metal" remained in the opinion.[80] Another time he sprang the word "autocephalous" on his colleagues with Frankfurter responding, "I'm glad I'm not without the power of anagnorisis with regard to this."[81]

A full relationship

Clearly Frankfurter and Reed were good friends who shared considerable intimacy in their work. But it was not a friendship based on equal regard. Frankfurter saw himself as the teacher, the transmitter of legal logic and tradition, and Reed as the not-too-bright pupil, at best a follower but more likely a stubborn and intermittant ally. Reed's weak ego and his admiration for his colleague's intellect made him potentially receptive to

Frankfurter's suggestions, despite their often patronizing and sarcastic tone. However, although Frankfurter lobbied Reed frequently both in person and in writing, Reed possessed sufficient independence to become neither a devotee of Frankfurter nor a victim of too much manipulation.

Frankfurter's ability to persuade Reed varied by situation. In general, Reed, while bemusedly tolerant, was not likely to heed Frankfurter's urgings on major points and sometimes rejected minor suggestions as well. He never succumbed to Frankfurter's occasional direct request for a change of position and only seldom, despite repeated attempts, was Reed persuaded to make significant substantive changes in his opinions. Reed could be adamant in shaping an opinion to the way he saw the legal issue, although *Smith v. Allwright* shows that at times he could be persuaded to make important changes. He was, however, often open to Frankfurter's suggestions about giving an opinion greater clarity, felicity, or force. In fact, good writing did not come easily to Reed, and he more often than not gratefully accepted his colleague's services as his editor. In this sense, Frankfurter certainly had an influence in shaping Reed's opinions.

What the correspondence does not contain is also noteworthy. There are virtually no instances of Frankfurter threatening Reed with a pointed dissent or concurrence if an opinion was not altered or suppressed. Frankfurter was certainly manipulative, but he did not engage in "hard ball" negotiation with his friend.

From a modern perspective, a striking thing about the Frankfurter-Reed relationship is its fullness. In this day and age when the Court is described by Justice Lewis Powell as "nine small, independent law firms" or composed of justices who in Justice Byron White's words "stay at arm's length" from one another,[82] it is refreshing to recall a relationship between justices that in fact contained real aspects of collegiality. The idea of a collegial court, of course, envisions decisions and opinions stemming from discussions among the justices instead of, as Justice John M. Harlan put it, "a tally of individual votes."[83] Perhaps Frankfurter and Reed's collegiality reflects a more intimate era on the Court, when each justice had just one law clerk and a secretary until 1948. Or perhaps it reflects the right mesh of personalities in Frankfurter and Reed. Or both.

Notes

This article originally appeared in Volume 78, Number 5, March–April 1995, pages 224–231.

An earlier version of this article was presented at the annual meeting of the Western Political Science Association in Albuquerque, N.M., in March 1994. The authors acknowledge the research help of Terri Ann Smith.

1. *See, e.g.,* Woodward and Armstrong, *The Brethren* (New York: Simon and Schuster, 1979).

2. *See, e.g.,* Mason, *Harlan Fiske Stone: Pillar of the Law* (New York: Viking Press, 1956); Howard, "On the Fluidity of Judicial Choice," *Am. Pol. Sci. Rev.* 62 (1968), 43–56; Ulmer, "Earl Warren and the Brown Decision," *J. Pol.* 33 (1971), 689–702.

3. Justice Reed's papers are at the University of Kentucky's King Memorial Library. Justice Frankfurter's papers at the Library of Congress and the Harvard Law School Library were also used, but they contain little correspondence with Reed that is not also in the Reed papers and they do not contain Frankfurter's marginal comments on Reed's opinions or many of Frankfurter's handwritten notes. Consequently, most correspondence citations are to box numbers and case files in the Reed papers. Oral interviews with Justice Reed's law clerks were conducted by the University of Kentucky Library around 1980, and transcripts are available there. All interview citations are to transcript pages.

4. Frankfurter and Landis, *The Business of the Supreme Court: A Study in the Federal Judicial System* (New York: Macmillan, 1927); Frankfurter, *The Commerce Power Under Marshall, Taney and Waite* (Chapel Hill: University of North Carolina Press, 1937); Frankfurter, *Mr. Justice Holmes and the Supreme Court* (Cambridge: Harvard University Press, 1938).

5. F. Aley Allan interview (1946 term), 8, 17; Robert von Mehren interview (1947 term), 11–12; Joseph Barbash interview (1949 term), 16; George D. Mickum interview (1953 term), 14, 24; Roderick Hills interview (1955 term), 37; Arthur L. Rosett interview (immediate post-retirement clerk), 29, 33.

6. Edwin M. Zimmerman interview (1950 term), 7; Hills interview, Ibid. at 28–29; Rosett interview, Ibid. at 33.

7. Hirsch, *The Enigma of Felix Frankfurter* (New York: Basic Books, 1981), 159.

8. Note, "Mr. Justice Reed—Swing Man or Not?" *Stan. L. Rev.* 1 (1949), 714–729. *See also* Pritchett, *Civil Liberties and the Vinson Court* (Chicago: University of Chicago Press, 1954), 17–18. Black, Douglas, Murphy, and Rutledge composed the liberal bloc and Vinson, Frankfurter, Jackson, and Burton the conservative bloc. Despite this perception, statistical analysis of those terms shows Reed voting with the liberal bloc only slightly more often than the other conservatives. *See* Schubert, *The Judicial Mind* (Evanston, Ill.: Northwestern University Press, 1965), 50–52. In 1949 when Clark and Minton came to the Court following the deaths of Murphy and Rutledge, Reed's vote became less pivotal.

9. The counts reflect correspondence housed at the UK Library. We know of a few letters to or from Reed that are not in the UK collection, so the numbers are not absolute. Our count includes all letters, memos, and handwritten notes sent to or by Reed. This includes letters, etc., addressed to more than one but fewer than five justices (18 items). Simple join letters (e.g., "Dear Stanley: I join your opinion in *Allwright*. Sincerely, Wiley"), comments in the margins of a draft opinion, or the very occasional letters unrelated to Supreme Court business were not counted.

10. These figures are skewed to some extent because of different forms of communication among the justices. For instance, Black sometimes wrote long comments in the margins or on the backs of galley opinions while Rutledge wrote brief comments about draft opinions in short but formal letters.

11. Mac Asbill Jr. interview (1948 term) 6.

12. Ibid. *See also* David Schwartz interview (1942 Term), 11; von Mehren interview, 12; and Barbash interview, 22–23, both *supra* n. 5.

13. Zimmerman interview, *supra* n. 6, at 5. O'Brien, *Storm Center,* 3rd ed. (New York: Norton, 1993), 169–170 notes Frankfurter's frequent lobbying of other justices' clerks.

14. Hills interview, *supra* n. 5. *See also* Mickum interview, *supra* n. 5, and Asbill interview, *supra* n. 11.

15. Walker, Epstein, and Dixon, "On the Mysterious Demise of Consensual Norms on the Supreme Court," *J. Pol.* 50 (1988), 361, 363–364.

16. Pritchett, *The Roosevelt Court* (New York: Macmillan, 1948), 38–44, and Pritchett, *supra* n. 8, at ch. 9.

17. Reed voted for criminal defendants about 20 percent of the time while Frankfurter voted for them about 55 percent of the time, and the gap was even wider in search and seizure cases. *See* Schubert, *Quantitative Analysis of Judicial Behavior* (New York: The Free Press, 1959), 87, 347. *See also* Frankfurter's three letters to Reed in *McNabb v. U.S.,* 318 U.S. 332 (1943), Box 74 (Feb. 24, Feb. 26, and Mar. 3, 1942). In this and subsequent notes, all references are to letters from Frankfurter to Reed unless otherwise noted.

18. Bayless Manning interview (1949 term), 14. Apparently Reed was fond of making this point. Zimmerman, *supra* n. 6, at 6, and Barbash, *supra* n. 5, at 18–19, also remember Reed making this comparison.

19. Pritchett, *supra* n. 16, at 131, shows Reed considerably more supportive of freedom of speech and press claims in the early 1940s. Pritchett, *supra* n. 8, at 190, shows Reed more supportive of such claims against state intrusion than Frankfurter, but considerably less supportive against federal intrusion. Certainly Reed was not perceived as a civil libertarian justice, but his majority opinion in *Poulos v. New Hampshire,* 345 U.S. 395 (1953), and his concurring statement in *Ullman v. U.S.* 350 U.S. 422 (1956),

demonstrated support for the "preferred position" approach. O'Brien, *Justice Reed and the First Amendment,* (Washington, D.C.: Georgetown University Press, 1958), chap. 12, argues that Reed was sympathetic to such claims.

20. Ibid., Box 176 (Feb. 7, 1956; SR reply, Mar. 8, 1956).

21. Douglas, *The Court Years* (New York: Random House, 1980), 173. Frankfurter leveled the same accusation against Douglas and Black, calling their maneuvering for votes "crafty." Hirsh, *supra* n. 7, at 182.

22. On the merits: *Jersey Central Power and Light Co. v. FPC,* 319 U.S. 61 (1943), Box 76 (Mar. 10. 1943), and *Bay Ridge Operating Co. v. Aaron,* 334 U.S. 446 (1948), Box 111 (Mar. 24, 1948). Strategic: *Bridges v. California,* 314 U.S. 252 (1941), Box 171 (Dec. 3, 1941), and *U.S. v. Line Materials Co.,* 333 U.S. 287 (1948), Box 106 (Dec. 9, 1947). Frankfurter once wrote Reed, "If by this time you do not know how foreign it is to my purpose to angle for votes, nothing I can say would persuade you of it," regarding *Black Diamond SS. Co. v. Robert Stewart & Sons,* 336 U.S. 386 (1949), Box 173 (Jan. 31, 1949).

Another example of Frankfurter's (successful) maneuvering is *Winters v. New York,* 333 U.S. 507 (1948). Frankfurter and Chief Justice Vinson were dissenting, but he persuaded Vinson to vote with the liberal majority so that Vinson could assign the opinion to Reed who Frankfurter believed (and lobbied) would strike down a law banning books or magazines depicting excessive crime or violence on grounds of vagueness rather than on First Amendment grounds. *See* Lash, *From the Diaries of Felix Frankfurter* (New York: Norton, 1975), 307.

23. *See* Murphy, *Elements of Judicial Strategy* (Chicago: University of Chicago Press, 1964), 54–68 for a description of such tactics. Hirsh, *supra* n. 7, at 179 and 190, discusses Frankfurter's use of such threats.

24. Reed withdrew an objectionable phrase in *Gray v. Powell,* 314 U.S. 402 (1942), Box 68 (Dec. 2, 1941), and remained firm in *Poulos v. New Hampshire, supra* n. 19, Box 151 (Apr. 20, 1953), where Frankfurter then wrote a lengthy concurrence. Frankfurter sent a draft dissent to Reed in *Fleming v. Rhodes,* 331 U.S. 100 (1947), Box 101 (Apr. 26, 1947). Although Reed did not budge, Frankfurter later withdrew it (but did cast a dissenting vote).

25. 349 U.S. 58 (1955), Box 160 (Jan. 24, 1955).

26. *Supra* n. 22, Box 106 (Nov. 25, 1947). Several of the justices resented Frankfurter's "hero worship" of Holmes and Brandeis. *See* Schwartz, *Super Chief: Earl Warren and His Supreme Court* (New York: New York University Press, 1983), 42.

27. Box 106 (Dec. 9, 1947).

28. *S.R.A. Inc. v. Minnesota,* 327 U.S. 558 (1946), Box 92 (Mar. 20, 1946). Ames was dean of the Harvard Law School at the turn of the century.

29. Hirsch, *supra* n. 7, at 142–144 and 160. O'Brien, *supra* n. 13, at 319.

30. *Viex v. Sixth Ward Bldg. and Loan Assn.,* 310 U.S. 32 (1940), Box 61 (Apr. 5, 1940).

31. *Hawk v. Olson,* 326 U.S. 271 (1946), Box 90 (Nov. 9, 1945).

32. *Supra* n. 17 (Feb. 24 and Feb. 26, 1943).

33. Box 151 (SR Memorandum to the Conference, Apr. 9, 1953). Writing for the majority, Reed acknowledged Poulos's First Amendment right to use the park, but upheld his conviction on grounds that the city's refusal to give a permit should have been litigated prior to the Witnesses' use of the park.

34. *Williams v. North Carolina,* 325 U.S. 226 (1945), Box 172 (letters between Mar. 23 and Apr. 30, 1945). This was a 6–3 decision, Frankfurter for the Court. Reed originally planned a short dissent, then shifted to a short concurrence and finally joined Frankfurter.

35. *Tiller v. Atlantic Coast Line RR.,* 318 U.S. 54 (1943), F. F. papers, Harvard Law School (no date).

36. The citations are respectively: *McDonald v. C. I. R.,* 323 U.S. 57 (1945), Box 172 (Nov. 14, 1944); *Screws,* 325 U.S. 91 (1945), Box 85 (no date); and *Gray v. Powell, supra* n. 24, Box 68 (no date). Ironically, *Screws* involved police brutality of the first magnitude and Frankfurter was voting to overturn the sheriff's conviction.

37. *Cassell v. Texas,* 339 U.S. 282 (1950), Box 127 (Dec. 8, 1949).

38. 321 U.S. 649 (1944). Chief Justice Stone had originally assigned the opinion to Frankfurter. When Justice Jackson suggested that it would be better for a southerner to write the opinion, Stone reassigned *Allwright* to Reed. *See* Mason, *supra* n. 2, at 615–616.

39. *Smith v. Allwright, supra* n. 38, Box 80 (Mar. 15, 1944).

40. Ibid. at 665–666. After all this effort, Frankfurter did not subscribe to Reed's opinion but merely concurred in the result.

41. *Supra* n. 30, Box 61 (April 5, 1940).

42. *Louisiana ex rel. Francis v. Resweber,* 329 U.S. 459 (1947), Box 100 (Dec. 12, 1946).

43. *Joint Anti-Fascist Refugee Committee v. McGrath,* 341 U.S. 123 (1951), Box 133 (Apr. 13, 1951).

44. *See* Hirsch, *supra* n. 7, at 184, on suggestions to other justices. Frankfurter once remarked, "The trouble with Stanley is that he doesn't let his clerks do enough of the work. The trouble with Murphy is that he lets his clerks do too much of the work." Allen interview, *supra* n. 5, at 6.

45. *United Public Workers v. Mitchell,* 330 U.S. 75 (1947), Box 98 (Jan. 13 and 16, 1947).

46. 329 U.S. 29 (1947), Box 98 (Nov. 15 and Nov. 16, 1946).

47. *Breard v. City of Alexandria,* 341 U.S. 622 (1951), Box 137 (no date).

48. Ibid., Box 137 (May 26, 1951).

49. *Mazer v. Stein,* 347 U.S. 201 (1954), Box 156 (no date).

50. Respectively: *U.S. v. Line Material Co., supra* n. 22, Box 106 (Mar. 5, 1948); *Angel v. Bullington,* 330 U.S. 183 (1947), Box 99 (no date); *Thompson v. Gaskill,* 315 U.S. 442 (1942), Box 171 (no date); and *Jay v. Boyd,* 351 U.S. 345 (1956), Box 167 (no date).

51. *Higgins v. Smith,* 308 U.S. 473 (1940), Box 60 (no date).

52. Hirsch, *supra* n. 7, at 136, 144, 184, and 188–189. O'Brien, *supra* n. 13, at 302.

53. Hirsch, *supra* n. 7, at 184–185. Frankfurter once described Reed to the latter's law clerk as "a man who crawls from detail to detail." Zimmerman interview, *supra* n. 6, at 6.

54. Allan interview, *supra* n. 5, at 8.

55. *Ford Motor Co. v. Beauchamp,* 308 U.S. 331 (1939), Box 60 (Nov. 30, 1939).

56. Ibid., Hirsch, *supra* n. 7, at 143, reports that Reed seemed startled by this, and Frankfurter later wrote to soothe his feelings. The book is *The Commerce Power . . . , supra* n. 4. In their argument over the "preferred position" approach in *Ullman v. U.S., supra* n. 19, Box 176 (Feb. 7, 1956), Frankfurter called Reed's attention to another of his books, *Mr. Justice Holmes . . . , supra* n. 4.

57. *Higgins v. C. I. R.,* 312 U.S. 212 (1941), Box 65 (Jan. 30, 1941).

58. *Uverges v. Pennsylvania,* 335 U.S. 447 (1949), Box 120 (Dec. 1, 1948). There is no "full blast" in the Reed papers.

59. *Mastro Plastics Corp. v. NLRB,* 350 U.S. 270 (1956), Box 176 (Feb. 14, 1956). Frankfurter wrote Reed several angry letters about *Mastro* even though Reed did not write the opinion. *See* Schwartz, *supra* n. 26, at 197–198.

60. *Memphis Natural Gas Co. v. Stone,* 335 U.S. 80 (1948), Box 110 (no date).

61. *Johnson v. New York, New Haven and Hartford R.R.,* 344 U.S. 48 (1953), Box 148 (Jan. 3, 1953).

62. Zimmerman interview, *supra* n. 6, at 7.

63. Ibid. at 6.

64. Manning interview, *supra* n. 18.

65. Respectively: *Adamson v. California,* 332 U.S. 46 (1947), Box 100 (Feb. 5, 1947); *U.S. v. Line Material Co., supra* n. 22, Box 106 (Dec. 9, 1947); *Winters v. New York, supra* n. 22, Box 106 (Feb. 28, 1948); *Jones v. City of Opelika,* 319 U.S. 103 (1943), Box 76 (Apr. 9, 1943); and *Wade v. Mayo,* 334 U.S. 672 (1948), Box 108 (May 24, 1948). Lash, *supra* n. 22, at 286–287, notes a Reed-Frankfurter conversation about Black's manipulativeness.

66. *Baltimore Contractors v. Bodinger,* 348 U.S. 176 (1955), Box 159 (Dec. 21, 1954).

67. *Supra* n. 69, Box 100 (Feb. 5, 1947).

68. *American Trucking Assn. v. U.S.,* 344 U.S. 298 (1953), Box 146 (Dec. 19, 1952).

69. *In re Summers,* 325 U.S. 561 (1945), Box 87 (May 31, 1945). Illinois refused to admit Summers to the bar because he was a conscientious objector. Black's draft quoted the clause thusly: no religious test shall ever be required as a Qualification to any Office or public Trust *in* the United States. The clause in Article VI actually reads: . . . any Office or public Trust *under* the United States.

70. Dec. 5, 1951. Part III, Reel 3 (F. F. papers, Harv. Law Sch.). Frankfurter was writing about Murphy's majority opinion (which Reed joined) in *Schneiderman v. U.S.,* 320 U.S. 118 (1943), a denaturalization case. He wrote in the context of *Dennis v. U.S.,* 341 U.S. 494 (1951), involving the conviction of Communist Party leaders under the Smith Act.

71. Lash, *supra* n. 22, at 270. This was a pejorative comment. Reed was under no illusions about his own intellectual capacity.

72. Box 165 (no date).

73. *U.S. v. Felin & Co.,* 334 U.S. 624 (1948), Box 108 (no date).

74. *Hynes v. Grimes Packing Co.,* 337 U.S. 86 (1949), Box 119 (Jan. 27, 1949). Two Reed clerks remarked that Reed was notably unsympathetic to Indian claims. Zimmerman, *supra* n. 6, at 8, quotes Reed as saying of Frankfurter, "he'll give this country back to the Indians." *See also* Rossett, *supra* n 5, at 25. Dissenting in *U.S. v. Alcea Band of Tillamooks,* 329 U.S. 40 (1946), at 57–59, Reed referred to the Indians as a vanquished people whose title to land was extinguished by the sword. The footnote 4 reference is to Stone's famous suggestion in *U.S. v. Carolene Products Co.,* 304 U.S. 144 (1938), that the Court might give special consideration to claims from "discrete and insular minorities."

75. *Johnson v. Muelberger,* 340 U.S. 581 (1951), Box 136 (Feb. 17, 1951).

76. *National City Bank v. Republic of China,* 348 U.S. 356 (1955), Box 159 (no date). The reference is to Chiang Kai-shek, the leader of the Nationalist forces on Taiwan.

77. *Koster v. Lumbermans Mutual Casualty Co.,* 330 U.S. 530 (1947), Box 100 (no date).

78. *Dennis v. U.S., supra* n. 70, Box 137 (Feb. 17, 1951).

79. *Supra* n. 19, Box 151 (handwritten notes on an SR memorandum dated Apr. 9, 1953).

80. Hills interview, *supra* n. 5, at 32–34. The case was *NLRB v. Babcock and Wilcox Co.,* 351 U.S. 103 (1956), at 107.

81. *Kedroff v. St. Nicholas Cathedral,* 344 U.S. 94 (1952), Box 141 (no date).

82. Both quotes are from O'Brien, *supra* n. 13, at 164–165.

83. Ibid. at 165.

Freshman opinion writing on the U.S. Supreme Court, 1921–1991

Terry Bowen and John M. Scheb II

New justices have been no less likely than their senior colleagues to author majority opinions or to be assigned difficult decisions, suggesting the nonexistence of a freshman effect.

Part of the conventional wisdom about the U.S. Supreme Court is the presumed existence of a freshman effect, a distinct pattern of behavior associated with newly appointed justices.[1] In his study of the freshman years of Justice Frank Murphy, Howard asserts that "a season of adjustment has been found necessary by virtually every new justice, regardless of era or of prior occupation, before he became a fully effective member of the Court."[2]

Howard attributes freshman behavior on the Supreme Court to three factors. First, the Supreme Court's enormous workload demands great discipline and sacrifice. Second, disputes before the Court tend to be "infinitely more complex than those [freshmen] have encountered before."[3] Third, the Court's internal procedures ensure a freshman effect. Junior justices "speak last and vote first during conferences, and receive relatively light assignments."[4]

Conventional wisdom, however, is not always borne out by empirical examination. Mounting evidence challenges the freshman effect posited by Howard and other scholars.[5] Despite this evidence, questions remain about certain aspects of the freshman effect.

Most empirical analyses of the freshman effect have focused on the hypothesis that freshmen justices are less likely than their senior colleagues to defend an extreme ideological position and, as a consequence, fail to join existing blocs. Generally speaking, these studies have concluded that while the freshman effect may have been prominent from 1921–1952, it has been declining since 1953.[6] Yet in the most comprehensive study to date on the topic, Bowen and Scheb found no relationship between bloc voting and freshman/senior status, even during the 1921–1952 period.[7] The debate over the freshman effect, however, is not limited to bloc voting behavior. As Howard suggested, an equally important component of the freshman experience is the expectation that junior justices will be assigned lighter workloads.

Majority opinion assignments

The manner in which majority opinions are assigned on the Supreme Court is well established. As a matter of institutional practice, the duty of assigning majority opinions falls to the chief justice. If the chief justice does not vote with the majority, the duty falls to the senior justice on the winning side. Several factors are thought to influence opinion assignment.

A number of scholars submit that the opinion assigner seeks to strengthen or maintain existing coalitions by assigning opinions to the justice whose views are thought to be closest to the minority position.[8] Although these studies provide limited empirical support for this proposition, Brenner and Spaeth found no significant relationship between assignment to the marginal justice and the maintenance of coalition strength.[9]

Other researchers speculate that opinion assignments are made in an effort to further the assigner's policy preferences. Testing this proposition for civil liberties decisions by the Warren Court, Rohde found that majority opinions were either self-assigned or were assigned to the justice whose views were nearest the opinion assigner. This pattern of opinion assignment was more pronounced in important cases and as the size of the majority increased.[10]

Interestingly, Rathjen found that Rohde's findings did not hold for the Warren Court's economics cases,[11] yet he did not discount the influence of the opinion assigner's policy preferences in the assignment decision. Instead, Rathjen suggested that Rohde's explanation was relevant among issues the Court considered most important. Less important opinion assignments were made in an attempt to balance the Court's workload. Subsequent studies have provided some evidence for this belief, finding that while Chief Justices William Howard Taft through William Rehnquist disproportionately assigned important cases, they maintained equality across the total range of cases.[12]

Experience is an additional consideration in the assignment of majority opinions. For Chief Justices Charles Evans Hughes and Harlan Fiske Stone, easing the transition of freshmen members apparently was an important consideration in awarding majority opinion assignments.[13] Hughes, for instance, believed that "the community has no more a valuable asset than an experienced judge. It takes a new judge a long time to become a complete master of the material of his Court."[14] Similarly, Stone thought that "a new judge beginning the work of the Court should be put at his ease in taking on the work until he is thoroughly familiar with it."[15] Such a consideration is not inconsequential. Attempts to ease freshmen justices into the Court's work require other justices to produce at a higher level.[16]

Although some justices might attempt to ease the transition of freshmen members by assigning lighter workloads, Slotnick's study of opinion assignments for the years 1921–1973 suggests that freshmen do not generally receive a disproportionate amount of opinion assignments. Rather, Slotnick argues that "there is no minimal assignment apprenticeship . . . ."[17] Using an opinion assignment ratio (OAR) that reflects the number of opinion assignments with the number of times a justice voted in the majority, Slotnick found that the "relatively young and relatively inexperienced justices are also the most prolific."[18]

More recent studies provide conflicting evidence regarding the assignment of majority opinions. Using the OAR, scholars have found that Justices David Souter, Antonin Scalia, and Anthony Kennedy ranked last in the number of opinions assigned to them during their initial terms.[19] Similarly, Scheb and Ailshie found that Justice Sandra Day O'Connor ranked last in the number of opinion assignments she received, at least in absolute terms.[20]

Workload considerations cannot be fully understood without giving some consideration to the difficulty or importance of the decision. As Melone suggests, "[I]t is not enough to know how many opinions a new justice has written," because important and difficult decisions "may require more legal and political skill than writing many routine ones."[21] Thus, "if new justices must craft difficult and important decisions, then it matters little that they write fewer opinions than their senior colleagues."[22] This suggests that the number of important decisions may be negatively correlated to the number of opinions assigned. Using the headlines on the cover of the advance sheets of the *United States Supreme Court Reports—Lawyers' Edition* to identify important decisions,[23] Melone found that Justice Kennedy received a fair share of important decisions, at least by his second term. Rubin and Melone found that Justice Scalia was not as fortunate.[24] Of 14 important decisions during his initial term, Scalia was assigned none. Likewise, during his inaugural term, Justice Souter received none of the Court's important decisions.[25] Generally speaking, these findings are consistent with Slotnick's.[26] Although his methodology differed,[27] Slotnick found that the greatest number of important opinions was written by justices in their second year.

"Difficult" decisions

A possible objection to using only "important" decisions to understand the justices' workloads is that the total range of the opinion-writing experience is diluted; that is, importance cannot necessarily be equated to difficulty. Therefore, it may be useful to develop a different measure of opinion difficulty: the margin of victory that majority opinions represent. Arguably, as the margin of victory declines, crafting a majority opinion becomes more difficult, because the majority opinion writer strives to deal with dissenting arguments. Conversely, as the Court approaches unanimity, the crafting of the majority opinion becomes easier. This is tacitly acknowledged by the Court's tradition "that precludes any qualifying opinion in a decision involving a new justice's first opinion for the Court."[28]

If opinion difficulty correlates to experience on the Court, freshmen should be less likely to author majority opinions as the margin of victory decreases. This would be consistent with the notion that opinion assigners consider a justice's experience in assigning difficult decisions. This proposition, however, has not yet been tested. Any test of this proposition must take into account Slotnick's finding that chief justices tend to retain unanimous opinions for themselves.[29]

Although earlier studies suggest there are no significant differences between freshmen and senior justices in terms of opinion assignments, the most recent evidence suggests that justices receive lighter assignment loads in their initial terms.[30] How can these differences be explained? One possibility is the type of analysis employed. While earlier findings were based on aggregate results that might have masked individual effects, later studies based their conclusions on data from one justice. To further understand this aspect of the freshman effect, a more definitive study is required.

Hypotheses

The literature regarding majority opinion assignments suggests that opinion assigners are guided by two basic considerations. First, opinion assigners consider the ideology and policy preferences of justices they choose to write majority opinions.[31] Second, opinion assigners attempt to maintain equality in the number of opinions assigned to all justices.[32] Given the first consideration, freshmen justices who are less ideologically committed would be expected to receive significantly fewer opinion assignments. Since freshmen justices are not less ideologically committed than their senior colleagues,[33] however, the equality principle should apply to freshmen as well as senior justices.

Hypothesis 1, therefore, is that the number of majority opinions will be distributed evenly between freshmen and senior justices, at least in the aggregate. This does not discount the possibility that individual justices might indeed exhibit a freshman effect. Therefore, this article develops a criterion that can isolate cases in which the freshman effect may be present.

Even if freshmen are not assigned significantly fewer majority opinion assignments than their senior colleagues, it might nevertheless be the case that they are assigned significantly less difficult opinions.[34] Accordingly, Hypothesis 2 is that opinions by freshmen justices are significantly less difficult than those of their senior colleagues.

Methodology

Data for this research were collected using the decisions of the Supreme Court as reported in the *United States Reports*. The data consist of all plenary decisions of the Court rendered during the period beginning with the 1921 term (the first year studied by Slotnick) and ending with the 1991 term.

To test for a freshman effect in the assignment of majority opinions to new justices on the Supreme Court, the behavior of all justices was examined for the 32 terms in which there were freshmen justices on the Court.[35] A justice's freshman period was defined as his or her first term on the Court, assuming the newcomer participated in at least 70 percent of the Court's plenary decisions on the merits rendered with full opinions. In instances where a new justice did not meet this condition, the freshman period was expanded to include all plenary decisions during the Court's following term.[36] For each term, an opinion assignment ratio was determined for each justice. These scores represent the per-

centage of times a justice was assigned an opinion when voting with the majority.

To test for the existence of the freshman effect, freshmen and senior justices were compared in terms of the proportion of opinion assignments they received. Although no theory defining meaningful differences exists, the existence of the freshman effect is identified here in instances where a justice's assignment load is more than one standard deviation below the Court's mean.

To test the proposition that freshman opinion assignments are less difficult than senior ones, the average size of the victory margin of winning coalitions for each justice for each term was calculated. Freshmen and senior justices were then compared in terms of the consensus level, or margin of victory, underlying their majority opinions.[37] If Hypothesis 2 is correct, the consensus level would be significantly higher for majority opinions authored by freshmen justices. To address Slotnick's finding that chief justices retain unanimous opinions for themselves,[38] the analysis was run again, omitting chief justices.

Finally, to test the "decline of the freshman effect" hypothesis suggested in other studies, separate comparisons were run for the periods 1921–1952 and 1953–1991. Table 1 indicates those OAR rankings relevant to this inquiry.

Results and discussion

For the entire period of the study, 1921–1991, only 24 percent of the freshmen on the Court failed to meet the established threshold of opinion assignments. Overall, between 1921 and 1991, no significant difference exists between freshmen justices and their senior colleagues with respect to opinion assignments, as seen in Table 2. Notwithstanding methodological differences, this finding is consistent with Slotnick's findings for the 1921–1973 period.[39]

For the period 1921–1952, which includes the Hughes-Stone era, there was no greater tendency for freshmen to receive lighter opinion loads, as shown in Table 3. Given Hughes's and Stone's affinity for easing freshmen into the Court, it was surprising to find that only Justices Frank Murphy, Wiley Rutledge, and Harold Burton failed to receive workloads similar to the senior members on the Court while these two were chief justice. This does, however, provide empirical support for the argument that both Murphy[40] and Rutledge[41] were treated differently, at least initially, from their senior colleagues with respect to opinion assignments.

Table 1. OAR rankings on the Supreme Court, 1921–1991, by term

1921	1922	1922–23	1924–25	1930	1931–32	1937	1937–38
Holmes	Taft	Taft	Taft	Hughes	**Cardozo**	Roberts	Roberts
Taft	Holmes	Holmes	Holmes	**Roberts**	Stone	Hughes	Stone
Brandeis	**Sutherland**	Sutherland	Brandeis	Stone	Hughes	Stone	Hughes
Clarke	Brandeis	Brandeis	**Stone**	Holmes	Roberts	Butler	**Reed**
McReynolds	McKenna	**Butler**	Butler	Sutherland	Sutherland	Brandeis	McReynolds
McKenna	McReynolds	McKenna	McReynolds	Brandeis	Butler	**Black**	Black*
Day	Van Devanter*	**Sanford**	Sutherland	Butler	Brandeis	McReynolds*	Butler*
Pitney*		McReynolds	Sanford*	McReynolds	McReynolds		
Van Devanter*		Van Devanter*	Van Devanter*	Van Devanter*	Van Devanter*		
(M=11.90)	(M=12.77)	(M=11.63)	(M=11.16)	(M=11.06)	(M=11.65)	(M=11.94)	(M=12.85)
(S=3.99)	(S=4.28)	(S=2.95)	(S=2.71)	(S=4.91)	(S=4.95)	(S=2.46)	(S=1.58)

1938–39	1939–40	1941	1942–43	1945
Douglas	Douglas	Douglas	Black	Black
Stone	Black	Stone	Stone	Douglas
Hughes	Stone	Roberts	Douglas	Stone
Frankfurter	Hughes	Black	Jackson	Rutledge
Roberts	Reed	Frankfurter	Roberts	Murphy
Black	**Murphy***	**Byrnes**	Reed	Reed
Reed*		Murphy	Murphy	Frankfurter
		Jackson	Frankfurter*	**Burton***
		Reed*	**Rutledge**	
(M=12.86)	(M=13.04)	(M=12.48)	(M=12.25)	(M=14.81)
(S=2.02)	(S=2.45)	(S=3.75)	(S=3.24)	(S=7.16)

1946	1949	1953	1954–55	1956	1956–57	1958	1962	1965
Black	Black	Douglas	Warren	Douglas	Douglas	Douglas	Stewart	Stewart
Douglas	Jackson	Black	**Harlan**	Clark	Harlan	Harlan	**White**	Douglas
Murphy	**Minton**	**Warren**	Douglas	Frankfurter	Clark	Brennan	Clark	Black
Jackson	**Clark**	Reed	Frankfurter	Black	Warren	Frankfurter	Harlan	Brennan
Reed	Frankfurter	Jackson	Reed	Burton	Black	Black	**Goldberg**	White
Frankfurter	Vinson	Frankfurter	Black	**Brennan**	Brennan	Warren	Douglas	Clark
Vinson	Burton	Clark	Clark	Harlan	Frankfurter	**Stewart**	Warren	Harlan
Rutledge	Reed*	Minton	Burton*	Warren	**Whittaker***	Whittaker	Brennan*	**Fortas***
Burton*		Burton	Minton*		Burton*	Clark*	Black*	Warren*
(M=13.76)	(M=12.98)	(M=12.14)	(M=12.87)	(M=11.72)	(M=11.55)	(M=12.55)	(M=11.22)	(M=11.42)
(S=6.92)	(S=4.11)	(S=2.97)	(S=1.82)	(S=2.01)	(S=2.93)	(S=1.80)	(S=1.32)	(S=1.92)

1967–68	1969	1970	1971–72	1975–76	1981
Marshall	Douglas	Douglas	**Powell**	Brennan	Rehnquist
Black	Black	Stewart	Brennan	Marshall	White
Harlan	Stewart	Black	**Rehnquist**	Rehnquist	Marshall
Stewart	**Burger**	White	Douglas	**Stevens**	Brennan
Douglas	White	Brennan	Marshall	White	Stevens
White	Marshall	Burger	White	Stewart	Burger
Brennan	Harlan*	Marshall	Stewart	Blackmun	Powell
Warren	Brennan*	**Blackmun***	Burger	Burger	Blackmun
Fortas*		Harlan*	Blackmun*	Powell	**O'Connor***
(M=10.62)	(M=13.57)	(M=12.15)	(M=12.61)	(M=10.33)	(M=11.50)
(S=1.57)	(S=2.40)	(S=3.21)	(S=2.41)	(S=1.16)	(S=1.41)

1986	1987–88	1990	1991
Marshall	Stevens	Stevens	O'Connor
Brennan	Brennan	Marshall	White
O'Connor	Marshall	O'Connor	Stevens
Powell	White	White	Scalia
Stevens	Blackmun	Rehnquist	Blackmun
Rehnquist	Rehnquist	Blackmun	Rehnquist
White	O'Connor	Kennedy	Souter
Blackmun*	**Kennedy**	Scalia	**Thomas**
Scalia*	Scalia*	**Souter***	Kennedy
(M=13.55)	(M=12.59)	(M=12.43)	(M=13.52)
(S=2.07)	(S=2.07)	(S=3.08)	(S=1.58)

Note: Justices are listed in descending order of OAR scores. Freshmen justices are **boldfaced**; M=mean; S=standard deviation; * indicates that justice's OAR is more than one standard deviation below the Court's mean.

Table 2. OAR scores by freshman/senior status

All terms	Freshman	Senior
Mean	11.60	12.38
Std. dev.	2.63	3.28
Number	38	238
	F=1.94	Sig.=.16
1921–1952 terms	**Freshman**	**Senior**
Mean	11.94	12.53
Std. dev.	3.01	4.23
Number	19	106
	F=.35	Sig.=.55
1953–1991 terms	**Freshman**	**Senior**
Mean	11.26	12.26
Std. dev.	2.22	2.26
Number	19	132
	F=3.21	Sig.=.07

Table 3. Freshman OAR thresholds

1921–1952		1953–1991	
No freshman effect	Freshman effect	No freshman effect	Freshman effect
N = 16 84%	N = 3 16%	N = 13 68%	N = 6 32%
Taft	Murphy	Warren	Fortas
Sutherland	Rutledge	Harlan	Blackmun
Butler	Burton	Brennan	O'Connor
Sanford		Stewart	Scalia
Stone		Goldberg	Souter
Roberts		White	
Cardozo		Marshall	
Black		Burger	
Reed		Powell	
Douglas		Rehnquist	
Frankfurter		Stevens	
Byrnes		Kennedy	
Jackson		Thomas	
Vinson			
Clark			
Minton			
Overall N = 29 76%		N = 9 24%	

Likewise, the 1953–1991 period does not differ from the earlier period. Again, there is no evidence of any greater tendency of freshmen to receive fewer opinion assignments. It is noteworthy, however, that during the Warren-Burger-Rehnquist era, 32 percent of freshmen received lighter workloads (twice as many as the earlier period) than their senior colleagues. This trend has been prominent since 1981, as three of the five new appointees (O'Connor, Scalia, and Souter) received lighter workloads. This finding is consistent with more recent studies that have confirmed the existence of the freshman effect in opinion assignments.

Table 4. Consensus level underlying majority opinions by freshman/senior status (all justices)

All terms	Freshman	Senior
Mean	6.16	6.02
Std. dev.	1.23	1.54
Number	38	238
	F=.30	Sig.=.58

1921–1952 terms	Freshman	Senior
Mean	6.81	6.98
Std. dev.	1.17	1.40
Number	19	106
	F=.23	Sig.=.63

1953–1991 terms	Freshman	Senior
Mean	5.52	5.26
Std. dev.	0.92	1.17
Number	19	132
	F=.87	Sig.=.35

Table 5. Consensus level underlying majority opinions by freshman/senior status (associate justices only)

All terms	Freshman	Senior
Mean	6.08	5.96
Std. dev.	1.23	1.56
Number	34	210
	F=.17	Sig.=.68

1921–1952 terms	Freshman	Senior
Mean	6.77	6.93
Std. dev.	1.15	1.45
Number	17	93
	F=.18	Sig.=.68

1953–1991 terms	Freshman	Senior
Mean	5.38	5.19
Std. dev.	0.86	1.18
Number	17	117
	F=.40	Sig.=.53

There is also no evidence for the proposition that the opinions assigned to freshmen justices are any less difficult than those assigned to senior justices, as shown in Table 4. There is no appreciable difference between the level of consensus underlying the majority opinions authored by freshmen versus senior justices. This remains the case when chief justices are removed from the analysis (see Table 5). Therefore, even if freshmen workloads are lighter, it apparently is not related to the difficulty of the decision.

Conclusion

This study of opinion assignments on the Supreme Court during 1921–1991 terms suggests the freshman effect posited by Howard and established as part of the conventional wisdom regarding the Court simply does not exist. Newcomers are no less likely to author majority opinions, nor are they less likely to be assigned difficult opinions. A cautionary note is appropriate here. This examination of the freshman effect has been limited to the phenomenon of opinion assignments and says nothing about the legal impact or scholarly quality of those opinions. It might well be that freshmen on the Supreme Court differ from their senior colleagues in other meaningful ways. Evidently, they do not differ in terms of being assigned majority opinions.

Notes

This article originally appeared in Volume 76, Number 5, February–March 1993, pages 239–243.

1. *See, e.g.,* Brenner, "Another Look at Freshman Indecisiveness on the Supreme Court," *Polity* 16 (1983), 320; Snyder, "The Supreme Court as a Small Group," *Soc. Forces* 32 (1958), 232.

2. Howard, *Mr. Justice Murphy: A Political Biography* (Princeton: Princeton University Press, 1968), 237.

3. Ibid.

4. Ibid.

5. *See* Bowen and Scheb, "Reassessing the 'Freshman Effect': The Voting Bloc Alignment of New Justices on the United States Supreme Court, 1921–90," in *Political Behavior* (1993); Heck, "The Socialization of a Freshman Justice: The Early Years of Justice Brennan," *Pac. L. J.* 10 (1979), 707; Heck and Hall, "Bloc Voting and the Freshman Justice Revisited," *J. Pol.* 43 (1981), 852; Melone, "Revisiting the Freshman Effect Hypothesis: The First Two Terms of Justice Anthony Kennedy," *Judicature* 74 (1990), 6; Rubin and Melone, "Justice Antonin Scalia: A First Year Freshman Effect?," *Judicature* 72 (1988), 98; Scheb and Ailshie, "Justice Sandra Day O'Connor and the 'Freshman Effect'," *Judicature* 69 (1985), 9.

6. *See* Heck, *supra* n. 5; Heck and Hall, *supra* n. 5; Melone, *supra* n. 5; Rubin and Melone, *supra* n. 5; Scheb and Ailshie, *supra* n. 5. *For a competing view, see* Brenner *supra*, n. 1.

7. Bowen and Scheb, *supra* n. 5.

8. *See* Danelski, "The Influence of the Chief Justice in the Decisional Process of the Supreme Court," in Goldman and Sarat, eds., *American Court Systems* (San Francisco: Freeman, 1978); McLauchlan, "Ideology and Conflict in

Supreme Court Opinion Assignments, 1946–1952," *W. Pol. Q.* 25 (1972), 16; Rohde, "Policy Goals, Strategic Choice, and Majority Opinion Assignments in the U.S. Supreme Court," *Am. J. Pol. Sci.* 16 (1972), 652; Ulmer, "The Use of Power in the Supreme Court," *J. Pub. L.* 30 (1970), 49.

9. Brenner and Spaeth, "Majority Opinion Assignments and the Maintenance of the Original Coalition on the Warren Court," *Am. J. Pol. Sci.* 32 (1988), 72.

10. Rohde, *supra* n. 8.

11. Rathjen, "Policy Goals, Strategic Choices, and Majority Opinion Assignments in the U.S. Supreme Court: A Replication," *Am. J. Pol. Sci.* 18 (1974), 713.

12. Davis, "Power on the Court: Chief Justice Rehnquist's Opinion Assignments," *Judicature* 74 (1990), 66; Slotnick, "Who Speaks for the Court? Majority Opinion Assignments from Taft to Burger," *Am. J. Pol. Sci.* 23 (1979), 60; Spaeth, "Distributive Justice: Majority Opinion Assignments in the Burger Court," *Judicature* 67 (1984), 299.

13. Mason, *Harlan Fiske Stone: Pillar of the Law* (New York: Viking Press, 1956); Pusey, *Charles Evans Hughes,* vol. 1 (New York: Macmillan, 1951).

14. Hughes, *The Supreme Court of the United States* (New York: Columbia University Press, 1928), 74–75.

15. Mason, *supra* n. 13, at 602.

16. Mason, *supra* n. 13.

17. Slotnick, "Judicial Career Patterns and Majority Opinion Assignments on the Supreme Court," *J. Pol.* 41 (1979), 640, 645.

18. Ibid. at 648.

19. Johnson and Smith, "David Souter's First Term on the Supreme Court: The Impact of a New Justice," *Judicature* 74 (1992), 238; Melone, *supra* n. 5; Rubin and Melone, *supra* n. 5.

20. Scheb and Ailshie, *supra* n. 5.

21. Melone, *supra* n. 5, at 8.

22. Ibid.

23. For a description of this method *see* Spaeth, *supra* n. 12.

24. Rubin and Melone, *supra* n. 5.

25. Johnson and Smith, *supra* n. 19.

26. Slotnick, *supra* n. 17.

27. Cases were identified as important if they appeared in two leading public law sourceboooks. *See* Slotnick, *supra* n. 17, at 642.

28. Abraham, *The Judicial Process* (New York: Oxford University Press, 1986), 212, n. 1.

29. Slotnick, *supra* n. 12.

30. Davis, *supra* n. 12; Slotnick, *supra* n. 12; Spaeth, *supra* n. 12.

31. Danelski, *supra* n. 8; McLauchlan, *supra* n. 8; Rohde, *supra* n. 8; Ulmer, *supra* n. 8.

32. Davis, *supra* n. 12; Slotnick, *supra* n. 12; Spaeth, *supra* n. 12.

33. Bowen and Scheb, *supra* n. 5.

34. Melone, *supra* n. 5.

35. There were 37 freshmen justices during the period of this study. Chief Justice Charles Evans Hughes was classified as a non-freshman due to his earlier service on the Court.

36. Based on Howard's study of Justice Murphy, see Howard, *supra* n. 2, it might be argued that a longer period should be examined. Assuredly, the time it takes to be assimilated into the work of the Court is an important consideration of the freshman effect. But this represents an entirely different question. Moreover, no theory has been developed that precisely describes what this period should or might be. We are, therefore, more concerned with identifying if justices, at least initially, systematically differ from their senior colleagues. Fundamental to that comparison is that each justice must hear a similar number of cases during their initiation to the Court. The 70 percent criterion employed here serves that purpose well.

37. "Margin of victory" is not to be confused with the concept of "size of winning coalition." For example, in a 6–3 decision, the margin of victory is three whereas the size of the winning coalition is six. Because this analysis includes unanimous decisions, the average margin of victory is higher than would otherwise be expected.

38. Slotnick, *supra* n. 12.

39. Slotnick, *supra* n. 17.

40. Howard, *supra* n. 2.

41. Mason, *supra* n. 13.

The Courts and Their Publics

Public Opinion and the Media

The judiciary is the most invisible branch of government and the branch about which the public knows the least. Consequently, the media have a uniquely important informational role to play in this domain and, indeed, they may be the exclusive source of information about the courts for most Americans. In this section, the focus is on the complex relationships among the courts, the media, and public opinion.

In "Philosopher kings or political actors? How the media portray the Supreme Court," Rorie Spill and Zoe Oxley document the broad parameters of print and broadcast journalism's coverage of the institution, focusing on the differences in coverage across these two media outlets during the Court's 1998 term. The authors' findings, for the most part, mirrored those found in the extensive literature that they reviewed. Major newspapers covered 11 percent of the Court's decisions, while the major television networks reported on 7.6 percent of the cases. Stories were relatively short across both mediums, although newspaper coverage was significantly more extensive. Not surprisingly then, print pieces tended to provide more detailed information than television newscasts.

Important patterns were also revealed in what kinds of cases were covered. Civil rights and criminal justice decisions garnered a disproportionate share of attention relative to their frequency on the docket. Spill and Oxley conclude that the news media provide "a very skewed view of the work of the justices," with the misrepresentation of the Court's work even more marked on television than in the print media. The article ends with speculation about the likely impact on the public of the limited and distorted information that they receive about the Court from the media, particularly for those who rely exclusively on television as their information source.

Spill and Oxley's conclusions are consistent with those of Elliot Slotnick and Jennifer Segal, who conducted a study to determine if " 'the Supreme Court decided today . . . ,' or did it?" The study starts with the premise that network television newscasts are the primary source of information for the public about the Court's activities. If the newscasts get it wrong, public misunderstanding of judicial policies is bound to follow.

Slotnick and Segal analyze the content of limited news coverage in one term of Supreme Court certiorari decisions, that is, the Court's decisions about which cases it will hear or not hear. Remarkably, in three out of four instances in which the Court declined to hear a case, the newscast misreported the Court's non-action and suggested that a decision had been made on the case's merits. Slotnick and Segal explore the implications of such woeful inaccuracy in reporting on the public.

Rounding out the portrait of the problematic nature of the media's presentation of the judiciary, Kimberlianne Podlas asks, "Should we blame Judge Judy? The messages TV courtrooms send viewers." Cameras in America's courtrooms are a more frequent occurrence today than in the past, but the public still gets most of its information about judicial operations through fictionalized television dramas and, more recently, from such syndicated court-like reality shows as *Judge Judy* and *The People's Court*.

Through the utilization of survey analysis, Podlas set out to assess the degree to which such "syndi-court" shows educate the public about legal rules and judicial processes. The survey results for frequent viewers of these popular programs and for non-viewers were both suggestive and disturbing, with negative images dominating the perspective of frequent viewers. The syndicourt experience takes the place of first-hand knowledge, and there is little countering of that message. "Rather, five days a week, episodes reinforce the model of the syndi-court judge: a not-so-neutral arbiter who is aggressive, inquisitive, and often sarcastic; someone who will indicate his or her opinion about the evidence or witnesses obviously and often; and will do so even when silent." Such characterization inevitably leads to a loss of respect for courts "and breeds contempt for the judicial system as a whole." Podlas concludes her analysis with consideration of some strategies through which the justice system might blunt such undesirable consequences.

The focus of these first readings on the portrayal of courts by the media has shown the impact such coverage can have on the public; however, more direct links between public opinion and the judiciary are explored in the next three articles. Thomas Marshall and Joseph

Ignagni examine the relationship between Supreme Court rulings and public opinion in "Supreme Court and public support for rights claims." Marshall and Ignagni link public opinion on a number of rights issues to specific Supreme Court decisions made over a forty-year period. They find that while the Court's orientation once was marginally more sympathetic towards rights claims than the public's, these differences between judicial decisions and public opinion have eroded over time. The authors conclude that their results "are consistent with the theory that justices sense and share widely held public attitudes." Thus, suggestions that the Court is a predominantly countermajoritarian institution appear to be unfounded.

Whereas Marshall and Ignagni discuss the relationship between specific judicial decisions and public opinion, John Scheb II and William Lyons address the more general issue of how the public regards the Court in "Public perception of the Supreme Court in the 1990s." Utilizing survey data from 1994 and 1997, their analysis reveals a good deal of stability in attitudes about the Court and a much more positive evaluation of the High Court than of Congress. Positive assessments of the Court dissipate somewhat, however, when attention is focused on specific decisions. Interestingly, assessments of the Court do not vary much along racial, gender, or partisan lines. Scheb and Lyons conclude that, "the Court appears to be doing a good job of holding the middle ground, where its legitimacy is likely to be maximized."

If any case tested the Supreme Court's relationship with and support by the public surely that case was *Bush v. Gore,* a decision that definitively decided the outcome of the 2000 presidential election. Herbert Kritzer explores "The impact of *Bush v. Gore* on public perceptions and knowledge of the Supreme Court." Kritzer considers two alternative possibilities regarding public reaction to the case. "First, the Court's image may have suffered generally because of a concern that it had embroiled itself in electoral politics when it should have stayed above the fray. Second, the overall approval of the Court may have been unchanged because of cross-cutting shifts, with those approving of the Court's decision increasing their support and those disapproving the decision decreasing their support; in this case, one would observe a shift in the structure of support rather than the level of sup-

port." Through survey analysis, Kritzer found that this second pattern of cross-cutting shifts occurred in the nature of support for the Court. This produced little overall change in the level of support.

Kritzer also found that attention to *Bush v. Gore* served an educational role, albeit a very small one, since public knowledge about the Court did show a slight increase. As is the case with the changes in the dynamics of support for the Court, it is too early to tell whether the effects of the ruling will be long term or merely temporary blips. Assessing his findings, Kritzer notes, "the Supreme Court's action was dramatic, subject to unprecedented media coverage, controversial, and to many very surprising (the decision by the Court to get involved as well as the decision itself). Nonetheless, the effects are modest. One might ask what, if anything, could lead to dramatic effects in how the public views the Court and how much they know about the Court. The only obvious answer, something the Court has strenuously resisted, would be to open the Court proceedings to television coverage. In many ways, the lessons of the impact of *Bush v. Gore* might be seen as justifying the Court's reluctance to open itself to greater coverage. While the public may lack awareness of many aspects of the Court that might be rectified by greater coverage, keeping the doors closed to television may also serve to limit the vehemence of the public reaction to what the Court decides."

The articles in this section underscore the judiciary's institutional invisibility, the insulation of judges from the public they serve; inadequate, and often misguided, media coverage of the courts; and a generally ill-informed public. It is in this context that we close with Kevin Esterling's "Public outreach: the cornerstone of judicial independence." Esterling's provocative and suggestive analysis argues that, "judges' isolation from politics and society is increasingly insufficient to maintain judicial independence. Contrary to the traditional view of judicial independence, in contemporary society the ability of courts to act as independent decision makers depends on their involvement in local communities through various public outreach efforts." This recommendation, of course, points in a different direction than Kritzer's assessment of the wisdom of the Supreme Court's opening of its doors to television coverage, leaving readers to draw their own conclusions.

Philosopher kings or political actors? How the media portray the Supreme Court

Rorie L. Spill and Zoe M. Oxley

Newspapers and legal beat reporters are more likely to cover broadly Court decisions than are their television and non-beat counterparts.

Media coverage of both the presidency and the Congress tends to depict these institutions as inherently political; stories regularly note the ideological divide as well as the personal stances of politicians.[1] Anecdotal evidence from a recent controversial ruling suggests that coverage of the Supreme Court may similarly focus on the politics of the institution. For example, the CBS morning news reported the decision in *Bush v. Gore* (2000) this way: "The apparent death blow to the Gore campaign was delivered in a separate 5-to-4 ruling along conservative-liberal lines."[2] In other words, the coverage highlighted ideological divisions and attitudes rather than the legal statements of the justices.

But it may be that the portrayal of this decision, which was the culmination of a drawn-out and close electoral battle, was an anomaly. This supposition requires attention to the question of how the media currently portray the Supreme Court's decisions, and without such an understanding we cannot state definitively if the political nature of the coverage of salient cases, such as *Bush v. Gore,* is aberrant or not. Are the justices treated as political actors, basing their votes on partisan and/or personal preferences, or philosopher kings, adjudicating on the basis of unbiased interpretations of the Constitution and natural law? To answer this question, we analyzed newspaper and television coverage of all decisions handed down by the Court in one recent term.

Naturally, the breadth and scope of media coverage of the Supreme Court has long interested scholars. The substance, and potential impact, of a major Court ruling is well known to students of the Court. Equally important, though, is how these rulings are disseminated to or filtered for the public, since public perceptions of decisions may affect the reservoir of public support for the Supreme Court.[3] Analyses of media coverage of the Supreme Court have tended not to focus specifically on whether this coverage portrays the Court as political or similar to other governmental institutions.[4] Instead, many previous studies examine the relationship between the actual docket of the Court and which cases are covered by the media.

Scholars have consistently found that coverage does not reflect the full complement of the Court's docket. Compared to their proportion of the Court's caseload, civil rights and First Amendment cases receive more media coverage, while cases regarding economic and business matters receive less. This misrepresentation of the Court's docket is present in newsmagazine, newspaper, and television news stories.[5] Not all three media equally distort the docket, however. Newspaper coverage more accurately portrays the variety of cases decided by the Court, particularly by devoting more attention to economic cases.[6]

Researchers have also analyzed the actual content of Court news stories, with a considerable focus on the quality or accuracy. Ericson concludes that newspaper coverage of the Court's decisions during the 1974 term was not of high quality.[7] The majority of cases received either incomplete or no coverage in the three newspapers he studied (*New York Times, Detroit News,* and *Ann Arbor News*). Beyond reporting the actual decision, most stories provided no information about the impact of the decision or the process of decision making, or failed to place the decision in the context of other cases.

Conversely, examinations of newsmagazine coverage by Tarpley and by Bowles and Bromley present more positive evaluations of the media's treatment of the Court. Both studies find that a majority of newsmagazine stories provide detailed information about the Court's decisions, such as background facts, the majority's reasoning, the relevant statutes or precedents, and the likely impact of the decision.[8] Most recently, Slotnick and Segal investigated several facets of broadcast coverage of the Supreme Court; in the most germane analysis, they examine the scope of coverage over two terms (1989 and 1994). They conclude that the networks can provide adequate coverage of

Judicature Volume 87, Number 1, pp. 22–29

high-profile cases, but the coverage of the entire docket is lacking and diminishing over time.[9] Additionally, television news stories frequently mischaracterize the Court's refusal to hear a case "as if it were a decision on the merits." [10]

Each of these studies provides important information about the breadth and scope of media coverage of the Supreme Court. We seek to expand our understanding of how the media portray the Court by comparing print and broadcast coverage during the current era of "infotainment." How is the Court covered currently and what disparities exist across media? Do the media characterize the Court as non-political by reporting on the justices as mainly interpreters of the Constitution, or do they continually portray the Supreme Court as a political institution by citing ideological and personal justifications for judicial decisions? Are cases portrayed more similarly to legislative votes, with an emphasis on who wins or who is hurt by the decision rather than on the legal approach or erudite justifications of the justices? The answers to these questions are important as the Court relies heavily on a reservoir of public faith to do its work,[11] and the public's perception of the Court and the justices is based largely upon the media's portrayal.[12]

Media diversity

There is great diversity in the news media, of course. The degree to which media coverage portrays the Court and the justices as political might differ across news mediums and journalists. Thus, we explore whether the characterization of Supreme Court decisions differs across newspapers and television and for reporters who regularly cover the Court versus those who do not. Following previous work, we also examine which of the Court's decisions receive coverage to establish whether this facet of media coverage has remained stable over time. Both analyses, of character and completeness, are necessary to describe fully the current media portrayal of the Supreme Court.

It is reasonable to expect coverage differences across these media, given the differing lengths of broadcast versus print stories. Newspapers can allocate more space, allowing for greater breadth and depth of coverage. The commercial goals of these two media also differ, with television stories more likely to be altered or not aired if they lack sufficient entertainment value.[13] The brevity of television stories coupled with this focus on entertainment likely results in presenting the Court's decisions without much attention to relevant legal issues and arguments.

We also expect variation in the content of stories written by "Court reporters" versus reporters who do not cover the Court regularly.[14] The newsbeat of Court reporters is primarily or exclusively the Supreme Court. Thus, they are specialists in both the Court and the law. While there are some "beat" reporters who may cover the Court along with other institutions, such as the Department of Justice, legal issues are the focus of these reporters' stories.

Non-Court reporters, like all generalist reporters, might be more likely to fall back on familiar story lines when covering the Court. Typically, when covering other political institutions, reporters focus on competition akin to reporting on sports; discussions focus on who is ahead or who won versus who lost after a decision is made. Similarly, the strategies and tactics behind decisions of individual political actors characterize news accounts.

In contrast, many Court reporters have legal training and are more likely than other reporters to display deference toward the Court.[15] Therefore, Court reporters might be more likely to cover the content of the Court's decisions, quote liberally from the justices' opinions, and present the Court as a legal rather than political institution. In other words, Court reporters and newspapers may be more likely to paint the justices as philosopher kings—apolitical oracles of the Constitution and the law.

Examining the data

We collected and content analyzed newspaper articles and major television network news stories reporting a Supreme Court decision during the 1998 term. Although our study is temporally more limited than some previous studies of Supreme Court coverage, we are extremely thorough in our analysis of the actual coverage of Supreme Court decisions. First, we do not limit our examination to national newspapers or news magazines. Rather, we cast a broad net and include coverage by local as well as national news media. We expect, as others have found, that major newspapers, in particular the *New York Times*, will stand out in terms of both breadth and scope of coverage. However, it is important to categorize a larger array of newspapers to understand the picture presented of the Court to smaller media outlets. To this end, we coded stories from 46 newspapers and 3 broadcast networks.[16]

Second, we analyzed the full transcripts of news stories from these sources rather than only summaries of the stories. Specifically, each sentence of each story was

Table 1. Examples of coded sentences

Category	Example
Content of decision	"The Court overturned a judgment won last year by a group of white voters. . ."
Vote breakdown	". . . the Supreme Court ruled today with surprising unanimity . . ."
Facts of case	"In its present form, the district represents the North Carolina Legislature's effort to remedy the constitutional violation the Justices found when they struck down the previous version in a 1996 decision, Shaw v. Hunt."
History of issue	"Until 1993, state officials had a free hand to draw electoral boundaries. The fights in state capitals tend to be political free-for-alls. But the high court upset the status quo that year by ruling that redistricting based primarily on race or ethnicity—such as increasing the number of minority law makers—is discriminatory."
Justification (constitutional)	"But, noting that a man's home is his castle, Chief Justice William Rehnquist writes, 'It's a violation of the Fourth Amendment for police to bring members of the media into a home'. . ."
Justification (statutory)	". . . the court said the disabilities law means the mentally disabled should be placed in a community setting where appropriate."
Political implications	"The 9–0 ruling deals another setback to independent counsel Donald C. Smaltz, the Los Angeles lawyer who led an aggressive, four-year, $20-million probe of alleged corruption involving former Agriculture Secretary Mike Espy."
Implications for future	"It takes away one of the most important opportunities that we have to observe police activity firsthand."

analyzed to determine if it contained content relating to one of seven categories. Table 1 provides examples of sentences for each of the categories. Four of these categories refer to basic case information: the general content of the decision (as well as the content of any concurring or dissenting opinions); the votes of the justices or the numerical equivalent; the facts of the case; and the history of the issue (including prior precedents or earlier legislative conflicts).

We also coded any mentions of justifications for the decision cited by the justices and included in the story.[17] To determine if the coverage was portraying the Court as a legal institution, we coded whether any justification was based upon "first principles" (the Constitution, a statute, legal precedent, and legislative history). These four justification categories would clearly reflect a legalist rather than political characterization, as would lengthy descriptions of precedent, or previous Court doctrine. We also coded any included justifications referring to either the justice's ideology or personal viewpoints; these two categories represent political coverage.[18]

We also included two other categories to help us assess whether coverage of the Supreme Court is closer to coverage of other political institutions or represents a different breed of media reporting. We coded any mention of the political implications of the decision in terms of who would be hurt or helped by the decision. This style of "horse race" reporting is, of course, very common in coverage of elections, the presidency, and Congress. Finally, we coded any statement regarding future implications of the decision, such as what actions another governmental body might take in response to the decision or how the decision might influence a local community. These statements were nearly always provided by non-Court actors (elected politicians, legal experts, interest groups, reporters, etc.) and went beyond the content of the Court's opinion. In total, we coded 408 stories.[19] If any sentence fit into more than one category, we "double" coded the sentence; for example, some stories had 18 actual sentences but 20 codable mentions.[20] On average, fewer than two sentences per story were coded into multiple categories.

Finally, we noted which stories were generated by Court reporters, as opposed to general staff or wire reporters. This information is necessary to determine if any differences in media coverage are due to variations in reporter expertise rather than time or space constraints.[21] We defined a Court reporter as one who

Table 2. Court reporters, 1998 term

Reporter	Media organization	Number of stories
Richard Carelli	Associated Press	30
Laurie Asseo	Associated Press	25
Mike Kirkland	United Press International	0
Bob Greenburger	*Wall Street Journal*	0
Scott Ritter	Dow Jones Newswire	0
James Vicini	Reuters	0
Pete Williams	NBC	2
Terry Moran and Ellen Davis	ABC	2
Nina Totenberg	National Public Radio	N/A
Gaylord Shaw	*Newsday*	0
Lyle Denniston	*Baltimore Sun*	4
David Savage	*Los Angeles Times*	25
Linda Greenhouse	*New York Times*	45
Joan Biskupic	*Washington Post*	32
David Pike	*Los Angeles Daily Journal*	0
Jan Greenburg	*Chicago Tribune*	3
Aaron Epstein	Knight-Ridder	4
Frank Murray	*Washington Times*	0
Tony Mauro	*USA Today*	29
Ted Gest	*U.S. News and World Report*	0
Marcia Coyle	*National Law Journal*	N/A
Steve Lash	*Houston Chronicle*	10
Charles Bierbauer	CNN	N/A
Amie Cogan	C-Span	N/A
David Jackson	*Dallas Morning News*	0
Mary Diebel	Scripps Howard	0
Greg Stohr	Bloomberg Business News	0

received a permanent press pass for the October 1998 term.[22] Reporters receiving permanent passes are simply the ones who expect to be at the Court regularly; reporters who cover the Court more intermittently would not require the permanent pass. The Office of Public Information of the Court provided us with a list of reporters with press passes for the 1998 term. (See Table 2.)[23]

Differences by medium

Most, but not all, newspapers cover a larger number of cases than the broadcast media. The average number of cases covered by newspapers was about 8 decisions, while the networks covered 10 decisions. Yet, if we remove the 12 (out of 46) newspapers that only covered one or two cases within the 1998 term, the average number of decisions covered in newspapers increases to about 15 decisions.[24] Considering that the Supreme Court decided a total of 145 cases during the 1998 term, with 131 cases producing opinions from the justices, these newspapers only covered 11 percent of the docket while the major networks only reported on 7.6

percent of the cases. This finding is not unexpected given previous work.

Both outlets shared the same bias in favor of formally decided cases. Almost 98 percent of the stories reported cases decided after oral argument. Per curiam decisions, memoranda, and decrees were not considered newsworthy by newspapers or television.[25] As noted by other scholars, the media do not accurately reflect the work of the justices.

These news stories tended not to be very long. More than one-third contained 10 or fewer sentences, and half of the stories were complete within 16 sentences. Forty-five stories were longer than 30 lines and only 17 were longer than 60 lines. Not surprisingly, though, given space differences across the two media, newspaper stories were significantly longer than television stories. On average, newspaper stories were 18.3 sentences long while television stories only contained 10.3 sentences.

Other differences emerge by medium when we consider the content of the story sentences (see Table 3). The most common type of information reported both

Table 3. Characteristics of news stories by medium and reporter

	Medium		Type of reporter	
	Newspaper	Television	Court reporter	Non-Court reporter
Content of decision	31.2+ (23.4)	43.4+ (35.2)	30.6 (22.2)	33.6 (27.2)
Vote breakdown	11.7*** (12.7)	2.3*** (6.3)	12.6** (13.0)	9.0** (11.8)
Facts of case	14.9*** (15.3)	6.4*** (7.9)	15.2 (14.3)	13.2 (15.8)
History of issue	7.3*** (9.7)	2.7*** (5.6)	8.1* (10.0)	5.8* (8.9)
Justification for decision	12.3+ (16.2)	7.1+ (12.3)	14.3** (17.3)	9.0** (13.8)
Political implications	2.6* (4.9)	7.7* (12.8)	2.3* (4.3)	3.8* (7.3)
Implications for future	14.7 (16.9)	12.7 (14.6)	12.3** (13.6)	17.3** (19.3)
Number of cases	378	30	211	192

Note: Entries are the mean percentages of news stories that contain each type of characteristic with the standard deviation in parentheses. Levels of statistical significance for the difference of means tests are noted as follows: ***p<.001; **p<.01; *p<.05; and +p<.10.

in newspapers and on television is the content of a decision, with 43 percent of television stories devoted to the content of a decision compared to only 31 percent for newspapers. Newspapers were more likely, however, to present other types of basic information about a case—such as the vote breakdown, the case facts, and the history of the legal issue—than television stories were. In contrast, television reporters were more likely to discuss the political implications of a case, although neither medium dedicated much attention to this topic (7.7 percent of television and 2.6 percent of newspaper stories). Finally, newspaper and television stories devoted about equal attention to the future implications of Supreme Court decisions.

Overall, nearly two-thirds of the stories included some of the justices' justifications for their decisions, but these justifications are not mentioned at length (averaging about two sentences per story). The rationales of the justices more commonly appeared in newspaper stories, though, with slightly more than 12 percent including any of the explanations provided within the opinion. Only 7 percent of television stories contained this information.

If a justification was reported, reporters were most likely to include either a reference to the Constitution or a relevant statute. This finding does not vary by medium. In total, only 34 percent of the stories mentioned that the Court relied upon the Constitution and 30 percent mentioned a statute as a justification for the decision. There were few references by reporters to ideology or precedent as a justification for the decision, and each of these mentions appeared in newspapers rather than on television. Thus, the newspapers are not only providing more breadth or context for the decisions, they are also more likely to include alternative rationales provided by the justices for the outcome reported.

Differences by reporter

As their title would suggest, Court reporters are most often filing or broadcasting stories about Supreme Court decisions. Just over 50 percent of the stories from the 1998 term were filed by Court reporters. Court reporters, however, were not necessarily the ones writing lengthy stories. Court reporters wrote 44 percent of the shortest stories (15 sentences or fewer) and 63 percent of the medium stories (16 to 30 sentences); they were only responsible for slightly less than half of the stories that topped 30 sentences. In other words, the difference between story length and type of reporter is not significant. On average, stories written by Court reporters were 18.8 sentences long compared to 16.8 for stories written by others.

This pattern, however, is likely due to the fact that Court reporters report on more decisions overall, providing for a large number of shorter stories in their yearly dossier. Indeed, when examining the correlation between Court reporters and landmark status[26] of a case, the measure of association is not statistically significant. This result suggests that many shorter stories filed by Court reporters inform readers about uncontroversial or less newsworthy stories. While null results are normally dismissed as not worthy of comment, this particular result is indicative of the greater breadth and scope of coverage offered by outlets retaining beat reporters.

Moreover, Court reporters focus more on the background and general case information (specifically, the vote breakdown and the history of the issues involved in the case) and the justifications for each decision (see Table 3). A closer examination of the specific type of justifications mentioned reveals no differences across reporters. When the reporters opted to include a rationale for the justices' decision, both Court and non-Court reporters were most likely to include constitutional (46 percent and 42 percent, respectively, of all justification mentions) and statutory (32 percent and 38 percent, respectively) justifications.

Turning to the final two of our coding categories, non-Court reporters, like television broadcasts, devote more column space to political and future implications. These differences are important, as they reveal a large discrepancy between the information disseminated by these different reporters. Simply put, Court reporters provide readers with a fuller context of the decision and its legal history while non-Court reporters are more likely to describe a decision in terms of its implications.

Coverage by issue area

Previously, scholars found that the media do not cover the full breadth of the Supreme Court's docket. It is possible that the attention provided to certain cases or issues may underscore larger differences between either the medium or the expertise of the reporter, as well as attest to the adequacy or completeness of cov-

erage. Therefore, we also examined the issue areas covered by the media. The docket of the Supreme Court has changed over time, and it is important to address whether media coverage—print or broadcast, Court reporter or not—reflects these changes.

The Supreme Court Judicial Database provides general codes for the issues addressed by each Supreme Court case decided.[27] First, as one might expect from previous studies, the media still showed a bias for cases dealing with either criminal procedure or civil rights; 20 percent of the stories reported a decision in the criminal procedure area and 36 percent reported a civil rights case.

When compared with the actual docket of the Supreme Court for the 1998 term, the chasm between media coverage and the actual docket continues to be wide. During the 1998 term, criminal procedure cases only comprised 17 percent of the docket, and civil rights covered only 26 percent. The overrepresentation of issues also exists for First Amendment and due process cases; however, the differences are not as large. The diversity of cases before the Court is poorly represented by the media coverage of the docket. The media overrepresented these issue areas and grossly underrepresented all others, such as federalism or taxation, thus providing a very skewed view of the work of the justices, particularly given the landmark federalism and commerce clause decisions handed down by the Rehnquist Court in recent terms.

This misrepresentation is even more marked when we compare television and newspaper stories. We already noted that broadcast reports were few and far between, compared to the frequency of newspaper stories. There is also little diversity in which issue areas are reported on television. Forty-five percent of the television stories reported on civil rights, with another 24 percent dealing with criminal procedure cases. Newspapers covered a greater diversity of issue areas, but still focused heavily on the areas of criminal procedure (21 percent) and civil rights (37 percent). Economic activity, interestingly, accounted for 11 percent of the coverage by papers. This is not terribly surprising given that most newspapers have a separate financial section that provides additional space for the coverage of this particular issue area. Finally, the differences between Court and regular reporters remain here as well. Compared to their counterparts, Court reporters tended to give the areas of criminal procedure, due process, and federalism more attention, while providing less coverage of civil rights and economic activity cases.

Impact on the public

Consistent with previous work, this study found that media coverage is a poor reflection of the Supreme Court's docket. The media, especially television and non-Court reporters, certainly continue to place a heavier emphasis on civil rights and other publicly salient areas than the justices do. More importantly, we find that the information contained in news accounts of Court decisions varies across media and types of reporters. The print media provide more information about the legal facts and background of the case, as well as some of the legal justifications the justices include in their opinions. The typical broadcast story, in contrast, summarizes the content of the decision, discusses its future implications, and states whether any person or group will be helped or harmed by the decision.

Similarly to print stories, Court reporters are more likely than generalist reporters to place cases into a broader legal context and report on justifications for the justices' decisions. In contrast, non-Court reporters focus more attention on the future and political implications of a decision, treating the Supreme Court like any other political institution. And, this portrayal of the Court is disseminated to the widest possible audience through television and local newspapers.

While these findings contribute to the extant literature and expand our knowledge of the judiciary and the media, they are also relevant to our understanding of public support for the Supreme Court. Scholars have been intrigued about the high public support the Supreme Court receives, especially from the more attentive sectors of the populace.[28] James Gibson, Gregory Caldeira, and Vanessa Baird suggest that the presentation of the Court's decisions provides cues to bolster support for the High Court: "Simply put, to know courts is to love them, because to know them is to be exposed to a series of legitimizing messages focused on the symbols of justice, judicial objectivity, and impartiality."[29]

In short, Gibson, Caldeira, and Baird argue that those individuals who know of the Court's decisions—the attentive and educated public—have stronger support for the Court because they receive the cues provided by the justices. As an example of these cues, they cite Justice Scalia's writings: "To hold a governmental act to be unconstitutional is not to announce that we forbid it, but that the Constitution forbids it."[30]

This explanation, however, presupposes that these cues reach the attentive public and that the less aware members of the public receive different cues or no information about the Court's decisions. Based upon our findings, it is quite possible that the differing levels of support for the Court between the more and less attentive segments of the public result from the sources of their digested information. The most informed members of the public tend to receive their information from both newspapers and television; the less attentive are usually only exposed to the latter form. Indeed, this group receives relatively poor information about the Court and its activities and, importantly, does not seem to receive the cues the Court disseminates (as our analysis of inclusion of justices' rationales indicates). The newspapers cover more cases and a greater range of issues, and provide greater breadth to that coverage. Additionally, the newspapers and their Court reporters are more likely to cite the justifications provided by the justices.

When television news shows do cover the Court, they do so faster and with less depth than newspapers. If a beat reporter is not on staff at the network or the newspaper, the coverage of the decision takes on the characteristics of a sporting event. Who won and who lost? Who is more disadvantaged or aided by the outcome? What will happen next? These differences may not be shocking; however, the differences do come at a cost. Emphasis is placed on the political implications and speculation for future activities rather than on the legal facts or on the rationale of the justices.

Do these finding then suggest that the reservoir of good faith among the attentive public stems from the cues disseminated by the justices? We think not, particularly in recent times. Newspapers are more likely to provide information about the political nature of the decision—the role that attitudes or ideology play in the final outcome. Such reporting clearly undermines public faith. Given these findings, it is questionable whether we can attribute the differences in diffuse support for the Supreme Court between the attentive and inattentive publics to the cues provided by the Court. These cues are not well disseminated to the public. They are certainly more prominent in the stories by Court reporters filed for newspapers than by non-beat reporters in papers or on television, but so are references to ideological or partisan decision making.

Clearly the next step requires testing the theoretical link between the types and content of stories and the variation in public support for the Supreme Court. It is possible that even a fleeting reference (two or fewer sentences) to a constitutional or statutory justification is sufficient to sustain the legalistic portrayal of the

Supreme Court as apolitical that is well embedded in the American psyche. However, this is an empirical and testable proposition. The effects of the various types of coverage must be delineated.

Notes

This article originally appeared in Volume 87, Number 1, July–August 2003, pages 22–29.

The authors wish to acknowledge the helpful comments of Tom Rice, University of Northern Iowa; Richard Fox, Union College; Elliot Slotnick, Ohio State University; and our anonymous reviewers.

1. Fallows, *Breaking the News: How the Media Undermine American Democracy* (New York: Vintage Books, 1997); Patterson, *Out of Order* (New York: Vintage Books, 1994); Cappella and Jamieson, *Spiral of Cynicism: The Press and the Public Good* (New York: Oxford University Press, 1997); and Bennett, *News: The Politics of Illusion,* 3rd ed. (New York: Longman, 1996).

2. Divided Supreme Court Hands Down Decision: Florida Recount Stops, CBS Morning News, December 13, 2000. Other examples include: "[t]he conservatives in the majority set aside their concern for states' rights. . ." (Greenhouse, "The 43rd President: News Analysis: Another Kind of Bitter Split," *N.Y. Times,* December 14, 2000, at A-1) and "[t]he Supreme Court . . . risking its reputation for staying above politics, appeared to end the disputed presidential election" (Denniston, "Justices Rule for Bush," *Baltimore Sun,* December 13, 2000, at 1A).

3. Caldeira, "Neither the Purse Nor the Sword: Dynamics of Public Confidence in the Supreme Court," *Am. Pol. Sci. Rev.* 80 (1986); Caldeira and Gibson, "The Etiology of Public Support for the Supreme Court," *Am. J. Pol. Sci.* 36 (1992); Franklin and Kosaki, "Republican Schoolmaster: The U.S. Supreme Court, Public Opinion, and Abortion," *Am. Pol. Sci. Rev.* 83 (1989).

4. But *see* Graber, *Mass Media and American Politics* (Washington, D.C.: CQ Press, 1997).

5. Solimine, "Newsmagazine Coverage of the Supreme Court," *Journalism Q.* 57 (1980); Katsh, "The Supreme Court Beat: How Television Covers the U.S. Supreme Court," *Judicature* 67 (1983); Tarpley, "American Newsmagazine Coverage of the Supreme Court, 1978–81," *Journalism Q.* 61 (1984); Davis, "Lifting the Shroud: News Media Portrayal of the U.S. Supreme Court," *Comm. L.* 9 (1987); Bowles and Bromley, "Newsmagazine Coverage of the Supreme Court During the Reagan Administration," *Journalism Q.* 69 (1992); O'Callaghan and Dukes, "Media Coverage of the Supreme Court's Caseload," *Journalism Q.* 69 (1992).

6. O'Callaghan and Dukes, *supra* n. 5.

7. Ericson, "Newspaper Coverage of the Supreme Court: A Case Study," *Journalism Q.* 54 (1977).

8. Tarpley, *supra* n. 5; Bowles and Bromley, *supra* n. 5.

9. Slotnick and Segal, *Television News and the Supreme Court: All the News That's Fit to Air?* (Cambridge: Cambridge University Press, 1998).

10. Slotnick and Segal, " 'The Supreme Court decided today. . . ,' or did it?," *Judicature* 78 (1994), 95.

11. Pacelle, *The Role of the Supreme Court in American Politics: The Least Dangerous Branch?* (Boulder, Colo.: Westview Press, 2002).

12. Slotnick and Segal, *supra* n. 9.

13. Slotnick, "Media coverage of Supreme Court Decision Making: Problems and Prospects," *Judicature* 75 (1991), 128.

14. Our definition of Court reporter, coupled with our operationalization (see pages 464–465 and n. 20), includes those reporters who work at the Court full-time and those who cover the Court only part-time.

15. Slotnick, *supra* n. 13. Davis, *Decisions and Images: The Supreme Court and the Press* (Englewood Cliffs, N.J.: Prentice Hall, 1993).

16. We analyzed all newspaper stories reporting a decision from the 1998 term that were archived in Lexis-Nexis. We also analyzed all stories about a 1998 term decision that aired on the ABC, NBC, and CBS evening news shows.

17. We wish to emphasize that while the opinion authors likely included many justifications, we only code whether the rationale was included in the news story.

18. While these types of justifications most closely resemble legalistic coverage and political coverage, they are not the only types of justifications that appear in media coverage of the Court's decisions. We coded all types of other legal justifications, including founders' intent, literalism, and other legal approaches, that appeared in the news stories. These other types of justifications were much less common than were those that we examine in the following analyses. Reporters included no other justifications, such as state policy actions or changes in society, frequently enough to warrant coding as a separate category.

19. We defined a story as the total report on one decision. For example, a "Supreme Court Round-up" by Linda Greenhouse may cover three decisions in a day. This would be coded as three separate stories to ensure that we can accurately describe the overall coverage of each Supreme Court decision. We also included wire stories. It is true that many smaller newspapers rely on wire services for their Court coverage. However, local editors make significant choices regarding how much of each wire story to include. Thus, we felt that each story should be analyzed individually. Last, there were three groups of cases that were announced on the same day that the media treated as one decision since the cases were also grouped together by the justices. We also treated each group of cases as a single decision.

20. For example, the following sentence was coded in both the vote breakdown and the decision content cate-

gories: "The high court's 5-4 decision allows EEOC to continue its practice of ordering federal agencies to pay compensatory damages in employment discrimination cases when it deems them warranted" (Fletcher, "High Court Says EEOC Can Levy Damages in Federal Bias Cases," *Washington Post,* June 15, 1999, at A-31).

21. Note that the categories of Court, staff, and wire reporter are not mutually exclusive. One can be both a Court and wire reporter, for example. We categorized journalists as either Court or non-Court reporters, with each category containing both staff and wire reporters.

22. This measure includes reporters who work regularly in the Supreme Court building both full- and part-time as opposed to those who never or rarely visit the Court.

23. While at first blush this list seems quite long, in reality only a handful of these reporters make an appearance in the Lexis-Nexis newspaper archive. Thus, we are confident that the use of the permanent press pass list, even with such a broad range of papers included in the dataset, provides a good list of "Court reporters" for the 1998 term.

24. Not surprisingly, with 47, the *New York Times* covered more Supreme Court decisions than any other newspaper.

However, even this outlet only covered 36 percent of the total decisions.

25. These types of decisions accounted for 25 percent of the Court's output during the 1998 term, according to the Supreme Court Judicial Database; Spaeth, United States Supreme Court Judicial Database (East Lansing, Mich.: Michigan State University, Department of Political Science [producer]; East Lansing, Mich.: Program for Law and Judicial Politics, Michigan State University [distributor], 2002).

26. To identify landmark cases, we use Harvard Law Review's end-of-the-year analysis ("Leading Cases," *Harv. L. Rev.* 11 [1999], 200).

27. *supra* n. 25. If the case was coded as addressing two or more issues, we utilized the first issue for our analysis.

28. Caldeira, "Courts and Public Opinion," in Gates and Johnson, eds., *The American Courts: A Critical Assessment* (Washington, D.C.: CQ Press, 1991), 303–334.

29. Gibson, Calderia, and Baird, "On the Legitimacy of National High Courts," *Am. Pol. Sci. Rev.* 92 (1998), 345.

30. *American Trucking Assoc. v. Smith,* 110 Led. 2d 148 (1990).

"The Supreme Court decided today...," or did it?

Elliot E. Slotnick and Jennifer A. Segal

Despite evidence of the news media's ability to present the U.S. Supreme Court's actions accurately, there is a pronounced tendency for network newscasts to mischaracterize docketing decisions as decisions on the merits.

The woeful state of public knowledge about the U.S. Supreme Court and its decisions is well documented. *Lack* of information is just one component of the problematic relationship between the Court and the public. *Mis*information about the Court's actions and their consequences for public policy making is another.

Network television news is the primary source from which most people receive the bulk of their political information. How accurately do television news stories report the Supreme Court's docketing decisions? Data from the 1989–1990 term reveal a pronounced tendency for newscasts to mischaracterize docketing decisions as merits holdings. This phenomenon inevitably fosters public misunderstanding of the Court's public policy-making role.

Research reveals that most adult Americans have limited knowledge about the Supreme Court.[1] More to the point, "many Americans little recognize or little remember the Court's rulings. On open-ended questions that probe for specific likes or dislikes . . . only about half (or fewer) . . . can offer an opinion on even the most prominent Supreme Court decisions."[2] Perhaps the most telling example of public ignorance is a Wisconsin study that tested respondents' recognition of whether the Court had recently rendered a decision in eight controversies, half of which the Court had actually decided and half of which it had not. A majority of the actual decisions and non-decisions were correctly identified by only 15 percent of the respondents. While only 2 percent could correctly identify all eight items, six times as many people (12 percent) got all eight items wrong.[3] More recently, while less than 10 percent of the public could name the chief justice of the United States, more than a quarter of the populace recognized Judge Wapner of "The People's Court."[4]

Docketing vs. merits decisions

Beyond the problem of limited information is the potential for even well-informed citizens to be misinformed about the Court and its activities. For instance, relatively knowledgeable citizens might recall two actions the Court took in October 1992 and paraphrase them as follows: (1) the Court allowed self-insured employers to curtail insurance coverage for expensive maladies such as AIDS and (2) the Court protected freedom of choosing abortion by overturning Guam's restrictive abortion law.

In both instances these characterizations are, at best, half truths. The Court's action in each of the cases was, in fact, to refuse to hear the case seeking a writ of certiorari or a writ of appeal. Yet incorrect labeling of the Court's actions is quite understandable given the manner in which the media covered the Court's certiorari denials. For example, coverage of these two cases by *The Columbus Dispatch* illustrates what a casual citizen might learn about what the Court had done.

In the first case, the headline announced, "Court Refuses to Outlaw Curtailing AIDS Benefit." The article that followed, taken off the AP wire, began,

> The Supreme Court *refused* yesterday to let AIDS sufferers use a federal pension-protecting law to sue when self-insured employers cut health-care benefits for the disease [emphasis added in all quoted material].[5]

Adding to the potential confusion about what the Court had actually done in this matter, the newspaper's editorial page later contained the following view (reprinted from a *Chicago Tribune* editorial):

> The Supreme Court last week made far more difficult the task of those who argue that whatever solution the nation crafts for its health-care mess ought to rely more on markets than mandates. It did so by (*affirming*) a lower court's decision that an employer may slash an employee's health insurance coverage after the worker contracts an expensive illness.
>
> (This *decision*) further erodes the fundamental principles on which the institution of insurance is based.

And it creates more momentum for great but potentially dangerous simplifications like national health insurance.[6]

In the second example from 1992, *The Columbus Dispatch* ran a front-page banner headline, "Court Again Backs Right to Abortion." The article began, "The nation's most restrictive abortion law died yesterday as the U.S. Supreme Court, for the second time in five months, *confirmed* a woman's right to abortion. Justices voted 6–3 to *reject an appeal* that would have continued the territory of Guam's almost complete ban on abortion. Lower courts had struck down the law."

Mischaracterization of Court actions such as these would not be very significant if the media were not the major source of public information about the Court or if certiorari decisions were generally tantamount to definitive decisions on the merits with widespread precedential value. But the media is and the Court's cert decisions may not be.

The dominance of the media in informing people of the Court's work has been well documented. For example, 76 percent of a Florida sample claimed that newspapers are their primary source of news about Court decisions, and 71 percent said that television plays that role.[7] As Marshall notes, "Public awareness of Supreme Court decisions depends heavily on the quality of coverage provided by the mass media."[8] According to Davis,

> [The media's] role is even more salient here than in the relationship between the mass public and other political institutions due to the absence of any alternative methods of direct communication. The justices, unlike elected officials, lack other nonmedia mechanisms for interactions with this constituency such as town meetings, newsletters, and frequent campaigning. Knowledge on the part of the mass public of the activities of the Court comes exclusively from the [news media].[9]

Increasingly, the role of television in informing the public has overcome other media formats. Katsh notes that most people claim to receive all of their news from television.[10] Iyengar and Kinder have argued, "As television has moved to the center of American life, TV news has become Americans' single most important source of information about political affairs."[11]

Denying certiorari

Misreporting of the Court's decisions to deny certiorari as merits holdings is important only if such decisions are generally not equivalent to decisions on the merits. The literature is replete with persuasive arguments on both sides of the question. Technically, all that a cert denial means is that the Supreme Court, using its appellate discretion, has refused to hear a case, thereby leaving a lower court decision and the immediate holding undisturbed. This formal view of certiorari denial suggests that the Court, by not hearing the case, has given no indication of where it stands on the merits of the lower court judgment or the issues involved. Consequently, the lower court decision prevails but carries no broad legal precedential or policy significance.

Many justices and commentators have aggressively insisted that this minimalist perspective on the meaning of certiorari denials is an accurate one. Justice Felix Frankfurter argued the position most frequently and in the greatest detail. At the most general level, Frankfurter noted that ". . . a denial nowise implies" agreement with a lower court decision. Rather, "It simply means that fewer than four members of the Court deemed it desirable to review a decision of the lower court as a matter 'of sound judicial discretion.' "[12]

In a 1950 dissent, Frankfurter expounded on what a denial of review could signify:

> [I]t seemed . . . to at least six members . . . that the issue was either not ripe enough or too moribund for adjudication; that the question had better wait for the perspective of time or that time would bury the question or, for one reason or another, it was desirable to wait and see; or that the constitutional issue was entangled with nonconstitutional issues that raised doubt whether the constitutional issue could be effectively isolated; or for various other reasons not related to the merits.[13]

On another occasion, Frankfurter simply opined that denial

> means only that, for one reason or another, which is seldom disclosed, and not infrequently for conflicting reasons, which may have nothing to do with the merits and certainly may have nothing to do with any view of the merits taken by a majority of the Court, there were not four members of the Court who thought the case should be heard.[14]

In a similar vein, Justice William Rehnquist also emphasized that the decision to not hear a case may occur for many reasons, none of which necessarily implies a substantive decision. "Some members of the

Court may feel that a case is wrongly decided, but lacking in general importance; others may feel that it is of general importance, but rightly decided; for either reason, a vote to deny certiorari is logically dictated." [15] Thus, it appears reasonable to conclude that "[b]ecause denials are usually not explained, there may be no way of knowing how a majority views the merits of particular cases." [16]

Nevertheless, many analysts and jurists continue to dispute this minimalist interpretation of docketing decisions, often taking as their starting point the words of Justice Robert Jackson: "Some say denial means nothing, others say it means nothing much. Realistically, the first position is untenable and the second is unintelligible. . . . The fatal sentence that in real life writes finis to many causes cannot in legal theory be a complete blank." [17] And, as Wasby and others have noted, cases accepted for review are not randomly decided, but are reversed approximately two-thirds of the time.[18] This seemingly implies that denial generally equates with affirmance.

In addition, lawyers and even some justices themselves have been known to cite certiorari denials and to draw inferences from them. As Neubauer notes, "Some infer consideration of the merits when the Court consistently leaves undisturbed lower court decisions seemingly at variance with past Court rulings." [19] According to Chief Justice Earl Warren, "Denials can and do have a significant impact on the ordering of constitutional and legal priorities. Many potential and important developments in the law have been frustrated, at least temporarily, by a denial of certiorari." [20]

Moreover, using logic some might find faulty, Linzer argues, "If a denial of certiorari were a purely discretionary act, largely or totally unconcerned with the merits of a particular case, it would be anomalous for justices to note their dissents." [21] It can be argued, however, that even if denial were substantively meaningless, a justice seeking a substantive decision might dissent from the Court's refusal to hear a case.

Clearly, there is no obvious or absolute answer to the question of what a certiorari denial means substantively. According to Abraham, "No matter which of these . . . contrasting views may be 'correct,' the effect in the eyes of the disappointed petitioner is necessarily the same: at least for the present, he or she has lost." [22] Taking a more balanced view, Goldman and Jahnige state,

At the most, a denial of certiorari may represent an approval of lower court decision-making; at the least, it

is a nondecision, that is, a decision not to do anything. Because they involve the Court neither in new policy departures nor in the overt responsibility for existing policy, such nondecisions are generally perceived as not being politically salient.[23]

Abraham is certainly correct in noting that in the immediate case at hand, the Court's denial of cert means that the petitioner has "lost." This does not, however, suggest a "loss" from a broader judicial policy-making perspective. Returning to the examples from 1992, it would be difficult to characterize the Court's refusal to hear the appeal in the insurance exclusion case as definitive in any fashion. Many of the considerations outlined by Justice Frankfurter and others easily could have been applicable in this case, and the Court is likely to address the issue on its merits in the foreseeable future.

As for the Guam anti-abortion statute, it is difficult to glean any broad substantive implications, however hard the media tried, from the Court's decision to leave undisturbed a lower court's decision to overturn what was acknowledged to be the most restrictive existing anti-abortion regulation in the United States. The lower court holding and the Supreme Court's refusal to hear the appeal offer no clue about how the Court will treat less restrictive state regulatory laws.

Data analysis

Although the ultimate meaning of certiorari denials is unclear, they are clearly not always tantamount to decisions on the merits. As a consequence, the mischaracterization by news stories of denials as substantive decisions is important and deserves scrutiny.

In earlier research conducted by the authors of this article, all network news stories of the Supreme Court during the 1989–1990 term were examined with a primary focus on television's docket-related coverage.[24] The analysis used videotapes of Court-related stories compiled by the Vanderbilt Television News Archive. Several docket-related stories were coded as merits decisions but were subsequently unable to be matched with any decisions actually rendered by the Court during the term. Coding errors in initially viewing the news stories, coupled with a longtime realization of significant misreporting of docketing decisions by television news, led to the genesis of this article.

For this analysis, all 41 network evening news stories from the Supreme Court's 1989–1990 term that were about docketing decisions—whether or not they were characterized as such by the newscast—were isolated.

The stories were coded along a number of variables tapping the technical facets of the news coverage (such as story placement and length) as well as on a number of variables gauging the stories' substantive content. Most importantly for this analysis, the stories were coded according to the Court's actual action in the case, how the network presented the Court's action, and how definitive the Court's action actually was. Viewed most broadly, the data indicate that while the networks did a credible job when they chose to report grants of certiorari, reporting of the Court's denials of certiorari was much more problematic.

Of the 41 stories examined, 13 (31.7 percent) covered the Court's granting of certiorari in seven cases. Nine of these stories (69.2 percent) reported on three cases that involved important issues: discrimination against women of child-bearing age in jobs involving hazardous chemicals, flag burning, and abortion counseling. Each of these cases was covered by all three networks. The remaining four stories focused on four other cases, each reported by only one network. They involved the death penalty (for those in possession of specified amounts of cocaine), search and seizure (the establishment of road blocks to catch drunk drivers), federalism (state control of the deployment of state national guard troops), and trial rights (whether alleged child abusers have the right to face their accusers).

While these cases represent only a small proportion of those that were actually granted certiorari during the 1989–1990 term, such sparse coverage was less problematic than it might seem because a number of other cases that were granted cert subsequently became the subject of news stories when they were in later stages of the decision-making process.[25]

The cases involving certiorari grants received very little air time and relatively low prominence. Ten of the stories were just 30 seconds or less, and 12 were presented after the first commercial break. Only two stories, both about the abortion counseling case, included considerable substantive information about the litigation. Clearly, despite the importance of many of the issues that were the subject of these cases, stories covering their cert grants were not very substantial.

Nevertheless, all 13 of these certiorari grant stories reported accurately the Court's decision to accept review of the case involved. In reporting the stories, language such as the Court agreed to "decide," "take up," "take on," make "a quick ruling," "review," "hear arguments," and "consider" made understanding the Court's decision to grant certiorari quite clear.

The same cannot be said, however, for the stories about the Court's denials of certiorari. More than two-thirds of the 41 stories (28) about the Court's docketing decisions concerned a decision to deny cert.[26] These stories reported on 16 cases categorized broadly by four issue areas: equal protection, privacy, abortion, and the First Amendment. The greatest number of cert denial stories (10, 35.7 percent) concerned four abortion-related cases. (These four cases involved Operation Rescue blockades and demonstrations, the use of racketeering laws to sue anti-abortion groups, and the legitimacy of tax exemptions for the Roman Catholic Church when it has engaged in anti-abortion lobbying.)

Story characteristics

Cases involving the issue of equal protection—including gender discrimination in a Maryland country club, the rights of homosexuals in the armed services, school programs for handicapped children, and an affirmative action suit by Gulf Oil employees—were the focus of six stories. Five stories involved issues of privacy, including two cases about random drug testing, one about seat belt laws, and another about cordless phones. The First Amendment was the subject of two cases covered in three stories, two about school dances in a public high school and the other about the sinking of Greenpeace's *Rainbow Warrior*. Finally, two other cases were the subjects of four stories, three about a case that sought the reevaluation of the trust fund established for the victims of the Dalkon Shield and a case about water rights in Wyoming.

Thus, these 16 instances of certiorari denials generally involved some of the most contentious political issues of the day. This is not surprising, since such issues allow for interesting, dramatic television stories and are likely to be attractive to the most television viewers. Nevertheless, and despite comprising the vast majority of the docketing decisions broadcast by the networks, these 16 certiorari denials constituted a minute proportion (well under 1 percent) of the 4,705 denials the Court made during its 1989–1990 term.

As was the case regarding stories about the granting of certiorari, almost all the stories about the Court's denial of cert were quite short and placed without prominence in the broadcast. Twenty-four (85.7 percent) were 30 seconds or less in length, and 22 (78.6 percent) were shown after the newscast's first commercial break. On the other hand, most stories (25, 89.3 percent) about a denial of certiorari included at least one piece of substantive information about the case.

The vast majority (23, 82.1 percent) included some case facts, and nearly half of the stories (13, 46.4 percent) identified at least one of the litigants. Other substantive information, however, was rarely given. The four stories about the Operation Rescue cases were unique in their presentation of a large amount of substantive information.[27] Overall, coverage of the Court's cert denials was quite thin, thereby compounding the fundamental problem of misreporting examined below.

Coverage of certiorari denials was divided fairly evenly among the three networks. NBC presented the most stories about cert denials (12, 42.9 percent), with CBS and ABC each airing eight. NBC reported the greatest proportion of its stories accurately (4, 33.3 percent), but it also reported the greatest number of stories inaccurately (8). CBS reported only one story accurately and seven in a misleading or incorrect fashion, while ABC reported only two correctly and six with demonstrable error. Admittedly, the numbers are very small, and it is not the intention here to gauge which network did the "best" job of covering the Court's cert denials. In the final analysis, in those rare instances where certiorari denials were reported, none of the networks did a very thorough or accurate job of reporting what the Court had done.

Indeed, inaccuracy in the newscasts' characterization of the Court's action is clearly the most important deficiency of these stories. In contrast to the stories about grants of certiorari, most of the stories about cert denials (21, 75 percent) were coded as fundamentally inaccurate or, at best, misleading, in reporting what the Court had done. In nearly half of the certiorari denial stories (13, 46.4 percent), the Court's actions were misreported as decisions on the merits rather than as denials of certiorari. In eight stories (28.6 percent), the terminology used to report the story was sufficiently ambiguous to cause some difficulty in determining whether a decision had been made or cert had been denied. After further investigation, the cases that were the subject of these ambiguous reports were determined to be cert denials. Only seven of the 28 stories about denials of certiorari (25 percent) were reported accurately.

The actual language in the stories best illustrates the manner in which the Court's actions were characterized by the three networks during their evening news programs. It is quite apparent from a number of stories that the Court's decision to deny cert can, indeed, be reported correctly. For example, Peter Jennings of ABC News was quite clear in his discussion of the Court's docketing decision in the Dalkon Shield case. "In Washington, the Supreme Court today removed the last major roadblock facing a 2½ billion dollar settlement for women injured by the Dalkon Shield. . . . The Court *refused to hear* a challenge to the settlement which sets up a trust fund to be shared by thousands of the victims" (November 6, 1989, emphasis added in all quoted material). Tom Brokaw of NBC News used similar language when he reported the decision to deny certiorari in a case involving mandatory seat belt laws in Iowa: ". . . the Court *refused to hear* [the petitioner's] arguments" (December 11, 1989). In these instances, as well as others, "refused to hear" is exactly what the Court did when it denied certiorari.

There are, however, many more examples of inaccuracy by the networks. As noted above, 21 stories (75 percent) were erroneous in their portrayal of the Court's action, 13 quite obviously, and 8 somewhat more ambiguously. In each instance, the impression that viewers were likely to gain was that the Court had made a decision on the merits rather than denied certiorari.

Ambiguous language

Ambiguous language such as "refused to overturn" was used in a number of stories, including one about the ban on homosexuals in the military. As ABC's Jennings stated, "In Washington, the Supreme Court has *refused to overturn* the regulation that forbids acknowledged homosexuals from being members of the armed forces" (February 26, 1990). Brokaw used similar terminology in NBC's story on the same case.

In a story about the Dalkon Shield settlement, CBS's Dan Rather reported, "The U.S. Supreme Court *turned down* the last major challenge and cleared the way today for a 2.5 billion dollar settlement for women injured by the Dalkon Shield birth control device" (November 6, 1989.) The Court's action in a random drug testing case was also ambiguously reported when Rather stated,

> The U.S. Supreme Court today *gave qualified approval* for random drug testing among government workers in sensitive jobs. The Supreme Court *turned down appeals* from Justice Department employees and civilian army counselors (January 22, 1990).

In this instance, imprecise characterization of the Court's action is linked with a substantive direction in the Court's holding, perhaps compounding the problem.

In reporting the same case, NBC's Brokaw similarly stated, "Mandatory drug laws *got another vote of confidence* today from the Supreme Court. Without comment, the Court *rejected challenges* to two testing programs for Justice Department employees with top security clearance and for the Army's civilian drug counselors" (January 22, 1990).

These examples illustrate some of the language that was conservatively characterized as ambiguous or misleading for this study. While phrases such as "turned down," "refused to overturn," "rejected challenges," and "killed a lawsuit" may appear to trained ears as indirect means of describing certiorari denials, it is more than likely that the typical viewer of the evening's news would interpret this language to mean that the Court had rendered a substantive judgment in these cases. (Indeed, even the authors of this study, as noted previously, initially miscoded the Court's action in several of these stories.) The networks failed to portray clearly and accurately the Court's actions in these stories.

Most importantly, the largest proportion of stories about the Court's denial of certiorari could not be deemed ambiguous at all. Rather, they were clearly wrong. The most frequently used words to characterize the Court's actions in these stories was "upheld" and "ruled." In reporting on the Court's decision to deny cert to the petition challenging a ban on dances in public schools, Brokaw reported, "The U.S. Supreme Court *ruled* today on an issue that most youngsters in this country say is a fundamental right: the school dance. . . . But the Court *upheld* a ban on dances in the public schools of Purdy, Missouri, where many people are Southern Baptists who believe that dancing is sinful and satanic" (April 16, 1990).

On April 30, Brokaw stated in a story on a case of random drug testing that ". . . the Court *upheld* random drug testing of thousands of air traffic controllers and other Transportation Department employees in safety related jobs." Similarly, Bob Schieffer of CBS News reported on a case regarding special education programs in public schools for handicapped children: "In effect, today's *ruling* means that these schools must keep trying to find programs that will help these children" (November 27, 1989). The implication of these and other stories was that the Court made a decision on the merits of the cases rather than denying them certiorari.

Perhaps the most blatant misreporting of cert denials during the 1989–1990 term occurred in the stories about the demonstrations and protest activities of the anti-abortion group Operation Rescue. On May 14, 1990, both ABC and CBS reported on the Court's refusal to hear the group's assertion that blocking access to abortion clinics in Atlanta was protected by the First Amendment's guarantee of free speech. Ted Koppel of ABC introduced the story by reporting that ". . . before the Supreme Court [there was] *a defeat* today for the anti-abortion group Operation Rescue. The Court *said* that a claim of free speech does not give them the right to block access to abortion clinics in Atlanta, Georgia."

Bettina Gregory followed up on this story by stating, "Today the Supreme Court *said* those restrictions on Operation Rescue blockades instituted in Atlanta did not violate freedom of speech because these protestors had a history of unlawful conduct."

CBS's coverage of this case appeared even more misleading. Schieffer reported,

> . . . the Supreme Court split 5–4 today and *upheld* a ban on anti-abortion demonstrators who tried to block entrances to Atlanta abortion clinics. The Court *rejected the demonstrator's arguments* that they were just exercising free speech.

Beyond using the words "upheld" and "rejected . . . arguments," which imply that the Court made a substantive decision, Schieffer's report included the outcome of a vote taken by the justices. Although it appeared that the justices had made a decision on the merits, the vote was actually taken to determine whether Operation Rescue's application for a stay on a lower court's temporary injunction should be granted. By a 5–4 vote, the application was denied.

If this was not confusing enough, a week later (May 21, 1990) each of the three networks aired stories about Operation Rescue's activities in New York. Once again, the presentation of this certiorari denial was problematic. The stories included erroneous references to the earlier Atlanta case, treating it as if a merits decision had been made. For instance, Jennings reported:

> There has been a second *legal defeat* at the Supreme Court for the anti-abortion group Operation Rescue. The justices today *agreed with lower courts* which ruled the Operation Rescue pickets may not block access to abortion clinics in New York. Last week the Court made a similar *ruling* for clinics in Atlanta.

CBS's explanation of the Court's action went even further. The opening visual headline for the evening's entire newscast was, "The Supreme Court *Bans* Abortion Clinic Blockades." Rather introduced the story by reporting,

> The U.S. Supreme Court *approved* new limits today on protests by anti-abortion groups. The justices *upheld* a permanent ban on demonstrators who physically try to block entrances to abortion clinics. Today's *ruling* was on a case from New York. . .

And, in the expansive follow-up report, Rita Braver repeated the problematic reference to the Atlanta case when she stated, "Last week the Court voted 5–4 to allow a temporary ban against Operation Rescue to stand in Atlanta. But today's action is considered even more significant because it involves a permanent ban and can have an impact on similar cases now underway in other states."

Expanding on the implications of the case, Braver opined, "The Supreme Court action is bad news for Operation Rescue. . . . Abortion rights activists call it a victory for them." Confirmatory interviews were then conducted with spokespersons for the Legal Defense Fund of NOW and the Feminist Women's Health Centers.

These stories starkly illustrate the extent to which the network news programs may misreport the activities of the Court. Both cases were denied review, yet the stories about them gave the distinct impression that the Court had made decisions on the merits. This impression was further substantiated for the Atlanta case by the subsequent references in the stories about the New York case. Moreover, in addition to mischaracterizing certiorari denials as merits decisions, these examples also demonstrate that network newscasts may unjustifiably draw broad policy implications from the Court's certiorari action. Anyone viewing these stories, regardless of which newscast they were watching and how knowledgeable they were about the Court, probably would have misperceived the nature of the action the Court had taken and its implications.

Less egregious errors

Despite the frequency of misreporting revealed in the data, it might be argued that for some cases a denial of certiorari is tantamount to a decision on the merits. As noted previously, that is surely the case for the actual litigants involved. More broadly, however, there are likely to be instances where a case's policy issues are definitively resolved by a cert denial. When, for example, the issue before the Court is a very narrow one and

quite fact-intensive, as in the Wyoming water rights dispute mentioned earlier, certiorari denial clearly ends the matter for all intents and purposes and may serve the same function as a merits ruling. In such a setting, misreporting the cert denial as a merits decision seems to be a less egregious media problem.

It was not the intention of this study to add to the scholarly debate regarding the meaning of certiorari denials. Indeed, it is clear that in some instances it makes good sense to talk in terms of the broad substantive implications of certiorari denials, while in other instances it does not. With that in mind, the certiorari denial news stories were coded for whether the Court's docketing action definitively resolved the underlying policy issue raised by the case. In only 4 of the 21 certiorari denial stories deemed inaccurate (19.0 percent) could the Court's refusal to hear a case be characterized as definitive. Three of the 16 certiorari denial cases were the focus of these stories: the Dalkon Shield settlement, the sinking of the *Rainbow Warrior,* and the Wyoming water rights case. In these instances, the networks' misreporting of the Court's action may not have been very consequential, since the denial of certiorari amounted, practically, to the resolution of the issue involved.

This leaves, however, an overwhelming majority (17, 81.0 percent) of inaccurate stories about the 13 other cases for which the Court's cert denial was not definitive in nature. Faulty reporting here is especially problematic since the issues involved in these cases were very controversial and would likely be raised in subsequent litigation.

Reporting such certiorari denials as if the Court had made substantive decisions on the merits was clearly avoidable. As the data amply illustrate, the networks are indeed capable of reporting cert denials accurately. Thus, it appears that there is little excuse for misreporting the Court's docketing decisions. The consequences of such misreporting can best be seen in instances where the Court ultimately makes a merits ruling that is inconsistent with earlier reporting of a cert denial on the issue involved. Most recently, a graphic example of such an occurrence from the data set emerged when the Court resolved the substantive issues in the Operation Rescue cases in favor of the anti-abortion group.[28]

An unsatisfying picture

The picture that emerges of network news coverage of Supreme Court docketing decisions is not a very satisfying one. Most striking in the findings is this fact: of the 28 stories about certiorari denials, only 7 (25 percent) accurately and unambiguously characterized the Court's refusal to hear the case. In the plurality of stories covering cert denials (13, 46.4 percent), the Court's inaction was presented as if it were a decision on the merits. Coupled with the eight stories coded generously as "ambiguous" in their presentation of what the Court had done, a full three-fourths of the certiorari denial stories (21, 75 percent) misrepresented the Court's action. Importantly, in only four (19.0 percent) of these instances could the Court's cert denial be characterized as "definitive" in any sense. Moreover, there were a number of stories in which the network newscast included a projection of broad policy implications from the Court's action.

The data clearly indicate that coverage of the Court's docketing decisions by the network newscasts is cursory, at best. When given, however, coverage can be more accurate. Because there are examples of accurate reporting of the Court's docketing decisions—even certiorari denials—it is puzzling why the newscasts do not present docketing decisions more accurately more of the time. Some may believe that a focus on accuracy inevitably diminishes drama and induces dullness, thereby hampering a broadcast's commercial viability. Reporters, however, must first "get it right." Then they remain free to analyze, speculate about, and draw implications from a docketing decision that has been presented accurately.[29]

Media coverage of the Supreme Court has consequences for the information the citizenry possesses about what the Court has done. The public may often be constrained in its knowledge by faulty presentations or misrepresentations of the Court's behavior. This link between network newscast coverage of the Supreme Court and citizen knowledge of Court actions can be the subject of experimental testing. Using videotapes of newscast coverage, it is possible, in a future phase of this project, to examine what a subject pool learns from accurate and inaccurate newscasts about the Supreme Court's activities.

Notes

This article originally appeared in Volume 78, Number 2, September–October 1994, pages 89–95.

1. Caldeira, "Neither the Purse Nor the Sword: Dynamics of Public Confidence in the Supreme Court," *Am. Pol. Sci. Rev.* 80 (1986), 1211.

2. Marshall, *Public Opinion and the Supreme Court* (Boston: Unwin Hyman, 1989), 143.

3. Dolbeare, "The Public Views of the Supreme Court," in Jacob, ed., *Law, Politics and the Federal Courts* (Boston: Little, Brown, 1967), 194–212.

4. *Washington Post,* June 23, 1989, at A21.

5. "Court Refuses to Outlaw Curtailing AIDS Benefit," *Columbus Dispatch,* Nov. 10, 1992.

6. "Other Viewpoints," *Columbus Dispatch,* Nov. 22, 1992, at 2B.

7. Berkson, *The Supreme Court and Its Publics* (Lexington, Mass.: Lexington Books, D.C. Heath and Co., 1978), 64.

8. *Supra* n. 2, at 142.

9. Davis, "The Supreme Court in the News: Covering a Political Institution," presented at the annual meeting of the Midwest Political Science Association, Chicago, Ill., 1993, p. 2.

10. Katsh, "Law in the Lens: An Interview with Tim O'Brien," *Am. Leg. Stud.* 5 (1980), F. 31.

11. Iyengar and Kinder, *News That Matters* (Chicago: University of Chicago Press, 1987), 112.

12. *State v. Baltimore Radio Show,* 338 U.S. 912 (1950).

13. *Darr v. Buford,* 339 U.S. 200 (1950).

14. *Brown v. Allen,* 344 U.S. 443 (1953). Frankfurter's voice is not an isolated one on this issue. See, for example, the comments of Justices Jackson (*Brown v. Allen* [1953]), Marshall (*U.S. v. Kras,* 409 U.S. 434 [1973]), and Stevens (*Hambasch v. U.S.,* 490 U.S. 1054 [1989]).

15. *Huch v. U.S.,* 439 U.S. 1007 (1978).

16. O'Brien, *Storm Center: The Supreme Court and American Politics,* 2nd ed. (New York: W. W. Norton and Company, Inc., 1990), 238–239.

17. *Brown v. Allen* (1953), Jackson, J. concurring.

18. Wasby, *The Supreme Court in the Federal Judicial System,* 4th ed. (Chicago: Nelson Hall, Inc., 1993), 215–219.

19. Neubauer, *Judicial Process: Law, Courts, and Politics in the United States* (Pacific Grove, Calif.: Brooks Cole Publishing, 1991), 382.

20. "Retired Chief Justice Warren Attacks Freund Study Group's Composition and Proposal," *A.B.A. J.* 59 (July 1973), 728, quoted in Wasby, *supra* n. 18, at 216.

21. Linzer, "The Meaning of Certiorari Denials," *Col. L. Rev.* 79 (1979), 1255.

22. Abraham, *The Judicial Process,* 6th ed. (New York: Oxford University Press, 1993), 179.

23. Goldman and Jahnige, *The Federal Courts as a Political System,* 3rd ed. (New York: Harper and Row Publishers, Inc. 1985), 188.

24. Slotnick and Segal, "Television News and the Supreme Court," presented at the annual meeting of the American Political Science Association, Chicago, Ill., 1992.

25. *See supra* n. 24.

26. Actually, two stories reported on the Court's decision to deny an application for a stay but for purposes

here, given the manner in which the stories were presented, they have been included in the category of certiorari denials. In fact, Justice Kennedy's dissent in this decision to deny the stay suggested that the application was analogous to a certiorari petition. "The lower court's actions require us to treat the stay application as a petition for certiorari. . ." (*U.S. Reports,* p. 493, No. A-752).

27. Actually, the story about the case of disputed water rights in Wyoming was also quite thorough in its presentation of substantive information about the case. This story was anomalous in the data set, however. Focused on a rather narrowly framed case, it was one of the longest stories and only one of two feature/news stories. Because it was broadcast on a Saturday, we suspect that it was probably aired as filler for a light evening's newscast.

28. *Bray, et al. v. Alexandria Women's Health Clinic, et al.,* 113 S.Ct. 753 (1993).

29. The authors are indebted to Steve Wasby for this succinct phrasing of a solution to the problem.

Should we blame Judge Judy?
The messages TV courtrooms send viewers

Kimberlianne Podlas

A recent study suggests that while syndicated television courtrooms do, indeed, teach the public about the justice system, the content of this curriculum leaves much to be desired.

In the last decade, syndicated television courtrooms have crowded the television "docket." Despite their popularity, however, their impact on the viewing public's perceptions of the justice system and judges is unclear: Do these television representations educate citizens about simple legal rules and encourage jury service, or, in light of their trademark verbally aggressive, sarcastic judges, do they misrepresent the proper role of "judge" and reduce respect for the justice system?

To answer this question, a study of 241 individuals reporting for jury duty was conducted. It investigated the correlation between frequent syndi-court viewing and attitudes about the bench. Findings suggest that syndi-court does, indeed, teach the public about the justice system, but that the content of this curriculum leaves much to be desired.

For instance, frequent viewers tend to believe that judges should be active, ask questions during the proceedings, hold opinions regarding the outcome, and make these opinions known. Furthermore, unlike nonviewers, frequent viewers expressed a desire to uncover clues to a judge's opinion and interpreted judicial silence as indicating belief in one of the litigants.

Although the justice system rests on the creation of and adherence to legal rules and principles, its efficacy depends on collective respect generated from public opinion.[1] Positive opinions reinforce the validity of the justice system, its actors and outcomes, while negative ones undermine its credibility. Such opinions are formed in many ways. Sometimes citizens are influenced by personal experiences as litigants or employees of the court system. Other times information is gained through such means as academic coursework. In most instances, however, citizens do not have intimate contacts with the justice system; thus, media portrayals of courts fill the void.[2]

Both legal scholars and behavioral scientists have asserted that televising trials educates the public by providing a frame of reference for what the court system is, its fairness, and who its arbiters of justice are.[3] Similarly, the Supreme Court,[4] the American Bar Association,[5] and New York's chief judge[6] have all presumed an educative effect on behalf of televised law.

Though televised law has traditionally been confined to news coverage of noteworthy trials and obvious dramatizations, the last decade has marked the era of the syndicated courtroom (syndi-court). "Reality" law programs like "Judge Judy" and "The People's Court"[7] now populate the dial. Although individuals within the legal profession may disregard these "syndi-courts" as aberrational or embarrassing, for many citizens they provide the most accessible court information available.

Indeed, syndi-court is accessible to the average person in a way and to a degree that other televised legal proceedings are not. On any weekday anyone with a television can find at least one syndi-court; cable is not a prerequisite. They are also intellectually accessible: The stories are easily digestible, the conflicts clear, and the resolutions swift. And they follow a remarkably similar format: What one sees on Judge Judy is confirmed by what is seen on Judge Mathis, thus creating a unified body of information.

Ratings demonstrate that syndi-courts are actually seen by a significant portion of the public. One year after her 1996 debut, "Judge Judy" boasted the nation's top syndicated ratings,[8] and continues to enjoy significant popularity.[9] As a result, these shows possess a tremendous potential for impacting public opinion about the justice system.

These attributes make syndi-courts strong vehicles for cultivation and social learning. Cultivation theory considers the relationship between watching television and holding particular beliefs about the world.[10] According to this paradigm, watching a great deal of television will be associated with a tendency to hold beliefs consistent with the primary images and values depicted on screen. The closely related concept of social learning theory posits that viewers will look to the symbols and stories on television, and use these as schemata for their own behavior. In other words, media messages will teach and influence by providing explicit, concrete "models" for behavior, attitudes, and feelings.[11]

With regard to syndi-court, what viewers see on syndi-court will teach them how judges act. The intertwining of social learning and cultivation speaks to the effects that the stable, repetitive, and pervasive images and ideologies presented via televised syndi-court have on the non-litigious majority of the viewing public: Televised courtrooms become a primer through which the viewing public will come to know (or believe they know) how the law and judges operate.

One of the most visible symbols of law is the judge. Not only are judges vested with authority to orchestrate legal proceedings, but empirical evidence suggests that a judge can direct a jury to a verdict, even one the jury feels is unjust.[12] The primary focus in syndi-court is also the judge. Most shows are named after the judge, and the judge monopolizes much of the airtime. Even when litigants speak, the camera pans to the judge to capture his or her reaction.

Yet, many viewers do not understand that syndi-court is not a real court and that television brethren are not acting as (or may not even be) real judges. In fact, "the public regularly submits complaints about Judge Judy and other TV judges" to the California Commission on Judicial Performance. Apparently, many viewers do not "understand that Judge Judy and most of her cohorts are not present members of any judiciary."[13] This confusion is not surprising, as the tag-line of many of these shows reminds viewers that they are watching "real people," "real judges," and "real cases." Thus, the line between law and pop-culture blurs.

The study

Despite the intuitive logic that television images of law have some educative effect, neither the overall nor educational impact of televised trials (real or syndicated) on the public's perception of the legal system is known. Thus, this study sought to discover whether those who did and did not regularly watch syndi-court held different opinions regarding judges and their expected behavior.

The study also considered whether prior court-related experience stymied any influence of syndi-court. Prior research suggests that people who lack direct experience with the court system are most influenced by television portrayals,[14] and, therefore likely to use them as substitutions. This might apply to syndi-court viewers:

Experienced individuals who have seen a real judge in action and been instructed regarding the role of the judge, burdens of proof, and appropriate behavior of trial participants might be less inclined to exhibit the characteristics of the frequent viewers.

One criticism of many jury studies is that their findings lack practical value and cannot be generalized to actual jurors. Consequently, this study surveyed individuals reporting for jury duty, i.e., 241 juror-respondents from courthouses in Manhattan, the District of Columbia, and Hackensack, New Jersey.

While queuing up to enter the courthouse (and, in some instances, during breaks), individuals called for jury duty were approached, identified as being on jury duty, and asked to complete a questionnaire. Questionnaires were immediately retrieved as jurors completed them, and, in exchange for their participation, jurors were given elite pens and candy bars. All jurors approached returned questionnaires. Questionnaires that were substantially incomplete, and those collected from individuals unable to communicate with the researcher in English, were excluded from analysis.

To discern whether viewing was associated with certain factors contemplated by the questionnaire, the 225 respondents ultimately analyzed were divided into two groups: frequent viewers [FV] or non-viewers [NV]. A "frequent viewer" watched syndi-court between two to three times and more than five times per week. Non-viewers did not watch syndi-courts or did so, at most, once per week. Of the 225 juror responses analyzed, 149 (66 percent) were FV and 76 (34 percent) NV.

Findings

The questions highlighted in this article focused on negative characteristics that may be associated with syndi-court judges and their potential ramifications. Among the questions posed were:

- Should a judge have an opinion about the outcome/verdict in the case?

- Should a judge make her/his opinion about a case clear or obvious to the jury?

- Will you look for clues or try to figure out what the judge's opinion about the case is?

- Should a judge frequently ask questions?

- Should a judge be aggressive with the litigants OR express her/his displeasure with their testimony or behavior?

Table 1. Summary of findings

	FV	NV
Judicial opinions, activity		
judges should have opinion regarding verdict	75%	48.6%
judge should make opinion "clear"	76.5%	31.58%
jurors will "look for clues" to judge's opinion	74.5%	31.58%
Aggressive, investigatory behaviors		
judge should ask questions during trial	82.5%	38.16%
judges should "be aggressive with litigants or express displeasure with their testimony"	63.76%	26.32%
Interpretation of judicial silence		
judge's silence indicates belief in litigant	73.8%	13%

Table 2. Express negative view of bench

Experience level	FV	NV
Prior court service or experience	23%	19%
No prior court service or experience	77%	80%

As reported in Table 1, though it appeared that some respondents of both groups envisioned an "active" bench, frequent viewers anticipated this to a much greater degree. Indeed, frequent viewing was associated with beliefs that judges should have an opinion regarding the verdict (FV = 75 percent, NV = 49 percent) and make it "clear or obvious" (FV = 77 percent, NV = 32 percent). The import of this intensifies as frequent viewers also stated they would "look for clues" or "try to figure out" the judge's opinion (FV = 75 percent, NV = 32 percent).

Frequent viewers also treated judicial silence differently. One question asked whether the judge's silence meant that she favored the plaintiff, favored the defendant, had no opinion, or it would depend on the evidence. Whereas few (13 percent) of non-viewers attributed any significance to silence, a majority of frequent viewers (74 percent) concluded (incorrectly so) that it meant that the judge strongly favored *either* the plaintiff or defendant.

Differences also emerged regarding the expectation of aggressive and investigatory judicial behavior. Eighty-three percent of frequent viewers (NV=38 percent) believed that judges should ask questions during proceedings and 64 percent (NV=26 percent) believed that a judge should "be aggressive with the litigants or express his/her displeasure with their testimony or behavior."

Finally, there was no evidence that prior court service either mediated the effects of frequent viewing or otherwise explained the differential responses of the

frequent and non-viewers. Instead, prior court service was not shown to be positively or negatively associated with any of the variables assessed, such as opinions regarding judicial activity or its meaning. Additionally, as shown in Table 2, prior court experience was also not predictive of whether jurors held a negative or positive view of the bench.

Implications

The study suggests that the TV experiences provided by syndi-court are either substituted for accurate, first-hand court experience or integrated with existing knowledge of the court system. Moreover, there is little check on this stream of information as few competing models (such as regular transmission of complete trials) to syndi-court's representation exist. Rather, five days a week, episodes reinforce the model of the syndi-court judge: a not-so-neutral arbiter who is aggressive, inquisitive, and often sarcastic; someone who will indicate his or her opinion about the evidence or witnesses obviously and often; and will do so even when silent.

Reducing respect for the bench. The American legal system sets a high bar for the behavior of judges. It envisions a bench that is metered and thoughtful and the pinnacle of propriety. Indeed, this philosophy is reflected in The Model Code of Judicial Conduct. Canon 1 of The Code requires judges, at all times, to conform with the highest behavioral standards "so that the integrity and independence of the judiciary will be preserved." With regard to the appearance of impropriety, it is applied to judges both on and off the bench, in their professional activities as well as their personal lives.

Canon 2 is concerned with the appearance of justice, and recognizes the connection between the public's observation of judges and their perception of the integrity of the judicial system. It requires judges, at all times, to act in a manner that promotes public confidence in the integrity and impartiality of the judiciary: "Public confidence in the judiciary is eroded by irresponsible or improper conduct by judges." Canon 3 provides that a judge shall be patient, dignified, and courteous to litigants, and shall perform duties without bias or prejudice.

Yet, the syndi-court bench seems to operate in opposition to these standards. Syndi-court judges are typically sarcastic, accusatory, and opinionated. When the public is fed the judicial model of syndi-court to the exclusion of accurate judicial representations, it is likely to conclude that these traits are common to real judges. Hence, the syndi-court personality may eclipse or infect the true behavior of judges, reducing respect for the bench and the decisions it must enforce. This diminishes the "brand" of judge—what a judge is supposed to be, supposed to represent—and breeds contempt for the judicial system as a whole.[15]

Moreover, that shows feature judges who continue to or have recently sat on the bench furthers this effect. For example, during the first years of his nationally syndicated television show "Judge Joe Brown" continued to sit in Shelby County, Tennessee. Judge Judy and The People's Court Presiding Justice Gerry Sheindlin both left the bench to pursue television opportunities.

Misinterpreting judicial behaviors and temperament. The law assumes that jurors enter the courtroom as blank slates free of bias. Yet people tend to interpret new information in the light of past experience.[16] The lesson of syndi-court is such a past experience that jurors may bring into the courtroom and apply during trial. Indeed, it sends messages about judge behavior that viewers may later use as interpretive guides in jury service.

Although caselaw establishes that a judge should neither be the focal nor vocal center of attention at trial,[17] syndi-court does not endorse this model of judicial restraint. To the contrary, viewers see precisely the opposite, and, therefore, are taught (as demonstrated by the responses of frequent viewers) that judges should, do, and will disclose opinions regarding the case. This may cause them as jurors to unduly focus on the judge and imbue banal action with profound, yet unintended, meaning. When confronted with uncertainty of whether a doubt qualifies as reasonable or whether evidence quantifies as preponderant, jurors may look for other clues, particularly from a legal expert who has also heard the evidence.

Indeed, the U.S. Supreme Court has recognized that the judge possesses a tremendous potential to influence the jury.[18] Where a jury is given clues to a judge's belief regarding the case or the parties, even a suggestion of opinion might be seized upon by the

jury, "throw the scales [of justice] out of balance," and influence the eventual outcome.[19]

Seeking to limit this effect, the law cautions that the power of the judge must "be exercised sparingly, without partiality, bias, or hostility. . . ." [20]

Courts have reversed criminal convictions where the running commentary of one judge mimicked that of syndi-court[21] or where the judge engaged in prolonged questioning.[22] Such questioning, even without an inappropriate or obviously disparaging tone, suggests to the jury that the court doubts the credibility of that particular witness, and deprives the accused of her constitutional right to a fair trial.

Furthermore, frequent viewers even believe that silence is meaningful, indicating the court's belief in one of the litigants. This is not surprising for, in syndi-court, activity and commentary is the norm. It appears that the only time the judge is silent (and not mugging disdain) is when the testimony or evidence is beyond reproach. Thus, silence is significant, equaling belief in one of the parties. Unfortunately, this inverts and misinterprets the accurate judicial standard of silence and neutrality.

Altering expectations of the legal system. Syndi-court also becomes an Emanuel for the procedure of trials and litigation of disputes. It creates in viewers expectations regarding legal rules and becomes a barometer against which all other judicial action is evaluated. When real courts fail to conform to these television expectations, the public, or at least frequent viewers, may become disillusioned with the justice system or lose respect for it.

For example, in syndi-court, the stories are easily digestible, the conflicts clear, and the resolutions swift. They promise instant legal gratification that real courts cannot. There are never breaks for in limine motions or hearings on admissibility. Thus, "the public is mystified when they see actual court cases taking so long to be decided. [It] wonders why judges and lawyers seem to encumber the process with so many unnecessary technicalities and criticizes them for it." [23] As judges fail to live up to their television personae, disputes drag on for more than 22 minutes, and decisions are not contemporaneous, confidence in the justice system is eroded.[24]

Syndi-court viewers may also reconceive how the law is supposed to function and what it is supposed to do. Syndi-court's themes of humiliation and moral reproach seep in and distort the public's context for personal and social judgments regarding the law. For instance, the president of the California Judges Association stated that sitting judges are reported to the commission or that some litigants are disappointed when they win the case but the judge has not humiliated their opponent.[25]

Syndi-court also idealizes the culmination of disputes. The payment of monetary awards and settling of grievances is quick and efficient. Winners always get their money and never need to embark on the arduous journey of enforcing settlements. Losers always appear, and never need to be brought to court through service of process or suffer default judgments.

Additionally, significant legal nuances are lost, leading to misunderstandings of burdens, presumptions of guilt, and evidentiary issues. The inherent and often contrived "dramatization" of syndi-court contributes to a lay tendency to embrace absolutes and dichotomies—black or white, right or wrong, guilt or innocence—which retards their ability to comprehend subtle analyses. Viewers may conclude that the justice system obfuscates issues, denies justice, and that judges are complicit in this injustice.

A model for litigant behavior. Finally, with repeated viewing, viewers may begin to model their behavior to comport with what they have witnessed on syndi-court. Hence, Judge Judy tutors viewers to present their cases in a real court, be it the trial, mediation, or small claims level. Litigants might, therefore, alter their behavior when appearing in court, attempting to play out what they have repeatedly seen on TV.[26]

Frequent viewers may also be inclined to represent themselves pro se. After all, though they may not be lawyers, they've seen it all on TV. Syndi-court presents average people litigating their own disputes without the aid of a lawyer, almost half of whom win. Thus, viewers may come to believe that either pro se representation is not very difficult or that pro se representation still ensures a 50 percent likelihood of success. It may also cause viewers to believe that judges will assist them, as this is what occurs on television. Indeed, there is evidence suggesting this interaction between frequent viewing of syndi-court and litigant behavior. This, in turn, might contribute to litigiousness, as one impediment to bringing suit is the expense of retaining a lawyer.

Additionally, by bringing a courtroom into the homes of viewers, it might make the real courtroom seem more accessible, and, therefore, litigation a more viable option. Some citizens who have legitimate legal gripes will forgo assertion of their legal rights because they cannot afford an attorney or, where that complaint is appropriate for the no-lawyers-allowed forum of small claims court, or were afraid to represent themselves. Thus, by demonstrating the nature of disputes appropriate for and litigant preparedness of syndi-court, courtroom-shy litigants may increase their comfort level with the small claims court. Though this might produce a benefit of providing access to some who may have otherwise foregone enforcement of their rights, it might produce litigiousness in others. By showcasing all nature of disputes, however menial, as worthy of court action, syndi-court might promote litigiousness in American society.

Proposals

As with other attempts to connect television imagery with viewer behavior, this study cannot identify causation. The results may prove that frequent viewing of syndi-court teaches or cultivates in viewers a particular view of judges, or merely report that people who already hold such views are frequent viewers of such TV fare. Results may also speak to socio-economic status: a particular group of people may seek out these shows or may be the ones who are at home during the day and early evening to watch them.

Nevertheless, causation aside, the study demonstrates that a significant number of jurors walk into the courthouse with syndi-court experience. Indeed, a majority are frequent viewers. Furthermore, these frequent viewers possess a number of beliefs about judges and the justice system that, in many ways, are contrary to reality. And, regardless of how those beliefs were formed, they may improperly impact the delivery of justice and perceptions of the bench. Accordingly, court administrators, advocates, and judges should implement corrective actions to these potential influences. This is particularly warranted, since there is no evidence that prior court experience, such as jury service or being a witness or litigant, immunizes viewers against the effects of syndi-court.

Correcting the misimpressions borne of syndi-court and displacing them with the appropriate manner and etiquette of the courtroom should begin as soon as potential jurors enter the courthouse. Though all vicinages order jury duty differently, all share one thing: at some point, all prospective jurors sit in a room and wait. This is an opportunity to orient prospective jurors to the correct process and gently address the juxtaposition of syndi-court.

One method is a short (5–7 minute) video played on a constant loop in the juror "waiting room." In addition to explaining the basics of jury service, this information should also include reference to syndi-court, explaining that syndi-court's representation of judges is "dramatized" for effect, and that the judges that jurors will encounter in the courtroom will not and should not act like those on TV. It might also include video snippets of real trials with real judges in action—or, rather, inaction—with a voice over noting the differences. Many courthouses already have juror orientation programs in place; adding syndi-court cautions is relatively simple.

Attorneys might address the imagery of syndi-court through either instructive or investigative voir dire much like voir diring prospective jurors on any pertinent issue in the news, bias, or propensity toward police testimony. Counsel might ask the panel neutral questions pertaining to familiarity with, viewing habits of, and preference of judges on syndi-court. She can then shift to a more instructive tone, posing a series of leading questions designed to impart that syndi-court judges are not real, their behavior is uncommon, that judges typically are not to ask questions, that a judge who is quiet is not a judge who agrees, and even that the procedure or burdens (and testimony) will be different.

In conjunction with a voir dire strategy, counsel should request an instruction regarding syndi-court or an enhanced instruction that the jury is not to look to the court for an opinion regarding the outcome of the case. This will be more or less important depending on the personality of the court or whether it has been particularly quiet or talkative in response to certain aspects of the trial.

Regardless of counsel's actions, a court should also take precautions by instructing the jury. For example, when the slate of prospective jurors is first brought into the courtroom, as well as when the preliminary instructions are delivered to the impaneled jury, the court could simply explain to jurors that what they may have seen on syndi-court is incorrect, that judges are not to speak, that the court truly has no opinion, and that jurors are not to assume, look for clues to, or infer the existence of one. It is important to address these perceptions as soon as possible, otherwise a bias borne of syndi-court might take root that will be difficult to later remedy.

A similar instruction should be repeated in the main charge. Although final charges typically instruct that the judge has no opinion, where frequent viewers imbue the inactive behavior of "no opinion" with meaning, such an instruction remains impotent against the syndi-court effect: where juror preconceptions about the law differ from what judges state in their instructions, jurors are more likely to follow the instructions if the judges explicitly address the preconceptions, explaining how the law differs. Consequently, the naked "no bias, no opinion" instruction will likely be an ineffective remedy in contrast to an explicit instruction referring to syndi-court.

***

The law has long been fictionalized on television, but recently the reality programming of syndi-court has gained significant popularity. For many citizens, syndi-court is their only connection with the justice system. Thus, its representations of judges and law become unopposed reality. Unfortunately, the reality of syndi-court often diverges from the reality of the justice system, and imparts in frequent viewers beliefs about judicial behavior and demeanor that are illegitimate and even damaging to the system. This study demonstrates that a majority of prospective jurors are "frequent viewers," and thus the potential for damage is significant. Consequently, the justice system should implement strategies to disabuse jurors of misperceptions borne of syndi-court.

Notes

This article originally appeared in Volume 86, Number 1, July–August 2002, pages 38–43.

1. Selya, "The Confidence Games: Public Perceptions of the Judiciary," *New Eng. L. Rev.* 30 (1996), 909, 909–910. Opinions about the fairness of the justice system reflect its legitimacy: "[A] decision contrary to the public sense of justice . . . diminish[es] respect for the courts and for law itself." *Flood v. Kuhn*, 407 U.S. 258, 293 n.4 (1972) (Marshall dissenting).

2. Selya, *supra* n. 1, at 913; Harris, "The Appearance of Justice: Court TV, Conventional Television, and Public Understanding of the Criminal Justice System," *Ariz. L. Rev.* 35 (1993), 785, 786, 798; Slotnik, "Television news and the Supreme Court: a Case Study," *Judicature* 77 (1993), 21, 22 (majority of public obtains only information about law from television).

3. Selya, *supra* n. 1, at 913–14 (education of public should include media); *cf.* Roberts, "An Empirical and Normative Analysis of the Impact of Televised Courtroom Proceedings," *SMU L. Rev.* 51 (1998), 621, 627 (prohibiting public from viewing trials eliminates educational opportunity).

4. See e.g., *Estes v. Texas*, 381 U.S. 532 (1965) (State asserting First Amendment right to view trial); *Richmond Newspapers, Inc. v. Virginia*, 448 U.S. 555, 575 (1980)

(Burger noting "educative effect" of televised proceedings on the public and right of press and public to attend trial implicit in First Amendment); *Chandler v. Florida,* 449 U.S. 560, 571 (1981) (State has interest, independent of wishes of defendant, to view and televise trial).

5. A recent American Bar Association report suggested "that the media can and does impact some people's knowledge" of the law. As reprinted in, "Symposium: American Bar Association Report on Perceptions of the US Justice System," *Alb. L. Rev.* 62 (1999), 1307, 1315, reprinted report, "Perceptions of the US Justice System," sponsored by the American Bar Association.

6. Kaye, Symposium, "Rethinking Traditional Approaches," *Alb. L. Rev.* 62 (1999), 1491, 1493.

7. There are approximately 10 syndicated courtroom shows presently airing. Belcher, "New Court Shows, Dab of Talk, Games Fill TV Docket," *Tampa Tribune,* Sept. 11, 2000, at 1.

8. Gunther, "The Little Judge Who Kicked Oprah's Butt; Daytime Television's Hottest Property," *Fortune,* May 1999, at 32; Schlosser, "Another Benchmark for 'Judge Judy,' " *Broadcasting & Cable,* Mar. 29, 1999, at 15.

9. "Judge Judy" presently garners 7,061,000 viewers and remains among the top 10 syndicated shows. Keveny, "Syndicated Goldies Are Oldies: New Shows Are No Match," *USA Today,* Nov. 26, 2001, at 4D.

10. Shanahan and Morgan, *Television and Its Viewers, Cultivation Theory and Research* (1999), 172. Cultivation speaks to the implications of stable, repetitive, and pervasive images and ideologies that TV, here, syndi-court, provides.

11. Bandura, *Social Learning Theory* (1977).

12. Olson and Olson, "Judges' Influence On Trial Outcomes and Jurors' Experiences of Justice: Reinscribing Existing Hierarchies Through the Sanctuary Trial," *J. Applied Comm. Res.* 22 (1994), 16.

13. Farrel, "If Judge Judy Could Only Be Judged. . . ," *Broward Daily Business Rev.,* July 7, 2000, at B4.

14. Eschholz, "The Media and Fear of Crime: A Survey of the Research," *U. Fla. J.L. & Pub. Pol'y* 9 (1997), 37, 43

(viewers with no prior criminal justice experiences were more likely than viewers with previous experience to believe that police show portrayals were accurate).

15. The 1999 ABA "Perceptions of the US Justice System" study, *supra* n. 5, reported that only one-third of respondents felt very strong or strong confidence in judges. This did not apply to the Supreme Court, in which 50 percent of respondents reported strong confidence.

16. This is consistent with research demonstrating that non-evidentiary information can sensitize jurors to evidence or testimony elicited at trial. *See* Kovera, Gresham, Borgida, Gray, and Regan, "Does Expert Psychological Testimony Inform or Influence Juror Decision Making? A Social Cognitive Analysis," *J. Applied Psych.* 82 (1997), 178–180.

17. *People v. Jamieson,* 47 N.Y.2d 882, 883–884 (1979).

18. *Turner v. Louisiana,* 379 U.S. 466, 472 (1965) (juries are "extremely likely to be impregnated by the environing atmosphere").

19. *People v. Bell,* 38 N.Y.2d 116, 120 (1975).

20. *People v. Jamieson,* 47 N.Y.2d at 883–884.

21. *People v. De Jesus,* 42 N.Y.2d 519, 520 (1977). There, the trial court responded to the testimony of an alibi witness by saying "It is not good enough . . . and you know better," and commented "Let's not be playing any games," "I don't need any help from you," and "Oh, come on."

22. This can suggest that the court is skeptical of the witness's testimony. *People v. Carter,* 40 N.Y.2d 933, 934 (1976).

23. Editorials, *New Jersey Lawyer,* March 27, 2000, at 6.

24. Sherwin, *When Law Goes Pop, The Vanishing Line Between Law and Pop Culture* (2000), 8.

25. Cox, "Judicial Watchdog Agency Wants to Protect Public From TV 'Judges,' " Fulton County Daily Report, June 9, 2000.

26. An assistant court executive in California related an exchange with one pro se litigant who explained that he and his wife obtained all of their information about the courts from watching Judge Judy. Carter, "Self-Help Speeds Up," *A.B.A. J.* 87 (July 2001), 34.

Supreme Court and public support for rights claims

Thomas R. Marshall and Joseph Ignagni

Until the 1980s, the modern Supreme Court supported rights claims more often than did American public opinion. Today, that difference has narrowed significantly.

Of great concern to litigants, scholars, and civil libertarians alike is the level of support in American society for civil liberties, civil rights, and equality rights claims. Since the mid-20th century, the federal courts, especially the U.S. Supreme Court, have accepted many new rights claims, but rejected others. Many of these claims, which have been made in cases involving issues such as abortion, flag burning, and affirmative action, have been among the most controversial in American politics. Not surprisingly, such controversies have often sparked the interest of pollsters, and numerous public opinion polls have gauged public support for these rights claims. This article examines the question of who supports rights by directly comparing public opinion polls with Supreme Court decisions for a variety of rights claims that have reached the Court since the 1950s.

Perhaps the most memorable study of public support for new rights claims focused on the Cold War era of the 1940s and 1950s, when public opinion remained extremely hostile toward the free speech, free association, and employment protection rights of accused leftists.[1] In the face of this, the Supreme Court seldom supported civil liberties claims by accused leftists. Indeed, as Justices Hugo Black and William O. Douglas complained in one often-cited dissent:

> Public opinion being what it is now, few will protest the conviction of these Communist petitioners. There is hope, however, that in calmer times, when present pressures, passions, and fears subside, this or some later Court will restore the First Amendment liberties to the high preferred place where they belong in a free society.[2]

The "classical tradition" of public opinion has typically assumed that public opinion during most periods is hostile toward individual rights.[3] Other literature suggests that a large share of American public opinion continues to be intolerant toward controversial or dissenting individuals or groups.[4] Taken together, this research suggests that public opinion may seldom be supportive of civil liberties, civil rights, or equality rights claims.

At the same time, several studies suggest that the federal courts have usually been more accepting than the public of rights claims. Jonathan Casper's historical study, for example, reported that the Supreme Court often struck down restrictive state laws, and occasionally even federal laws, that penalized controversial or unpopular claimants.[5] Other accounts suggest that the Warren Court strongly supported civil liberties, civil rights, or equality rights claims, even for controversial individuals or groups who had previously fared poorly in the political process.[6] The Burger Court continued to support rights claims, albeit less predictably.[7] Indeed, even the generally conservative Rehnquist Court was more tolerant toward controversial rights claims in the flag-burning controversy[8] than public opinion and state and federal laws.[9]

In short, past research suggests that while public opinion has often been hostile toward rights claims, especially in highly publicized cases or during times of crisis, the Supreme Court has been, on the whole, more tolerant. Whether these assumptions accurately describe the modern Supreme Court is examined in the remainder of this article.

Examining rights claims

To explore how often American public opinion and the Supreme Court supported new rights claims, public opinion polls were compared with Supreme Court decisions in 88 instances in which a civil liberties, civil rights, or equality claim against a restrictive federal, state, or local law or policy reached the Supreme Court between 1953 and 1992.

These 88 matches average about 2.2 rulings per term, and include every identifiable instance in which a scientific, nationwide poll item closely matched the substantive issue in a Supreme Court decision during the Warren, Burger, and Rehnquist Courts.[10] As a result, it is possible to directly examine public opinion versus Supreme Court support for rights claims across a wide variety of claims.

These 88 poll-to-decision matches tap a wide variety of civil liberties, civil liberties, and equality claims. The central issues involved racial equality,[11] abortion and gender rights,[12] political and religious dissent,[13] gay and lesbian rights,[14] labor,[15] welfare,[16] the death penalty,[17] criminal defendant rights,[18] students,[19] and commercial media claims.[20]

To be sure, these 88 poll-to-decision matches are not a purely random sample of all the Court's rights claims rulings, and they do not necessarily capture how intensely public opinion was focused on each controversy. Rather, they represent a diverse sample of the Court's high-profile decisions involving rights claims—at least in that each of these 88 decisions elicited at least one poll item.[21] As the evidence below indicates, however, reweighting the sample to correct for under- or over-sampling of caseload does not change the results.

Examining the 88 controversies suggests that public opinion support for rights claims ranged from strong support for some to equally strong opposition to others. Three well-known examples illustrate this diversity. At one extreme, an 80-to-12 percent poll majority agreed with the claim in *U.S. v. U.S. District Court* (1972) that citizens should not be "spied on by any kind of electronic surveillance, except with a court order." [22]

In a few instances, available polls were closely divided. Before the *Roe v. Wade* (1973) ruling, the last available pre-decision Gallup Poll reported that 46 percent of Americans favored and 45 percent opposed "a law which would permit a woman to go to the doctor to end pregnancy at any time during the first three months." [23]

At the other extreme, large majorities of the public opposed several rights claims. The controversy over school prayer provides an example.[24] In *Engle v. Vitale* (1962) and *Abington School District v. Schempp* (1963), the Supreme Court held that officially sponsored school prayers or Bible readings violate the Constitution. These rulings disagreed with large public opinion majorities. A Gallup Poll taken shortly after the *Abington* ruling indicated that a 70-to-24 percent majority disapproved of the rulings.[25]

For each of these 88 claims, a "poll margin" was computed, measuring the percentage who favored the claim minus the percentage who opposed it. For example, for *U.S. v. U.S. District Court,* the poll margin was +68 percent (80 percent in favor of the claim, minus 12 percent opposed to the claim). For *Roe v. Wade,* the poll margin was +1 percent, well within the .05-level error margin. For *Engle v. Vitale* and *Abington v. Schempp,* the poll margin was a –46 percent, indicating strong disapproval of that claim.

Public and court support

Overall, public opinion support for rights claims during the Warren, Burger, and Rehnquist Courts has been decidedly mixed. In slightly more than half (53 percent, or 47) of the 88 claims, public opinion opposed the claim in question. In 13 percent (or 11) of them, nationwide polls were evenly divided (within the .05 margin level of error). In the remaining 34 percent (or 30) of the 88 claims, public opinion favored the claim.

Some disputes (such as death penalty or abortion rulings) are polled more often than others.[26] To correct for this bias, the 88 poll-to-decision matches were also reweighted to correct for over- or under-sampling.[27] Results for the reweighted sample were nearly identical to the unweighted sample. For the reweighted sample, public opinion opposed 55 percent of the claims, supported 35 percent, and was evenly divided on 10 percent.

Overall, the modern Supreme Court has been marginally more supportive than public opinion. For all 88 poll-to-decision matches, the Supreme Court supported the rights claim 53 percent of the time (or 47 instances), and opposed the claim 47 percent of the time (41 instances). At first glance, then, the Supreme Court has indeed been more sympathetic to rights claims than the mass public.

The Court's record of supporting rights claims often follows public opinion. When public opinion opposed the claim, so typically did the Supreme Court, supporting less than half (40 percent) of these claims. When public opinion was either evenly divided or supported the claim, however, the Court supported 73 percent and 67 percent of these claims, respectively. Table 1 compares public opinion with Supreme Court support for rights claims.

Another way to examine public attitudes toward rights claims is to examine the poll margin. The average margin for all 88 claims was -9 percent, indicating that slightly more Americans opposed the average claim than favored it.

An average poll margin of –9 percent is quite small compared to public opinion toward earlier Cold War–era claims of accused leftists. For six of these rights claims,[28] the average poll margin was –27 percent, indicating that public opinion was very hostile. By comparison, attitudes toward the 88 rights claims during the Warren, Burger, and Rehnquist Courts were much more closely balanced. For only 22 of the 88 (or 24 percent) were attitudes as negative as for the average Cold War–era leftist dissent claim.

Table 1. Public opinion versus Supreme Court support for rights claims

	Public opinion		
	Opposed	Divided	Favorable
Supreme Court ruling:			
Opposed the claim	60%	27%	33%
Favored the claim	40%	73%	67%
(Number of cases)	(47)	(11)	(30)

Note: Chi-square significant at .05; Mantel-Hanzel significant at .02.

Table 2. Public attitudes toward rights claims during the Warren, Burger, and Rehnquist Courts

Type of claim:	Percent of times public favored the claim	Percent of times Court favored the claim
Overall	34	53
Labor	33	67
Racial	47	82
Death penalty	38	63
Gay and lesbian	25	0
Media	33	67
Gender	29	59
Criminal (non-death)	39	31
Political and religious dissent	33	100
Student	25	25
Welfare	0	40

The poll margins varied widely according to the type of rights claim asserted. Only labor and racial rights claims received, on average, a positive poll margin, +9 percent and +2 percent, respectively. The most negative margins involved student or welfare rights, where the average margin was –24 percent and –53 percent, respectively.

The public opinion poll margin can also be compared with the vote split among the Court's justices by computing the (net) percent of justices who favored or opposed a rights claim. For example, in *Roe v. Wade*, concerning first-trimester abortions, seven justices voted for and two justices voted against the claim, yielding a "vote margin" of +56 percent (7 justices minus 2 justices, or 78 percent minus 22 percent).

In almost all types of cases, the justices gave more support to rights claims than did available public opinion polls. Overall, the poll margin was –9 percent, but the vote margin among the justices was +24 percent. Except for gay and lesbian rights, the vote margin among the justices was always more favorable toward rights claims than the poll margin was.[29]

Public opinion support versus Supreme Court support for rights claims can also be compared for different types of claims. Admittedly, the number of claims per category is small, ranging from 17 for racial and women's rights claims, to only four gay and lesbian rights claims. Table 2 compares public opinion with Supreme Court support for each type of claim.

The first column in Table 2 reports the percentage of times that American public opinion clearly favored each type of rights claim. Again, welfare rights claims were the least popular: not in a single instance did public opinion support a rights claim for welfare recipients. Racial claims were the most often favored, with public opinion supporting nearly one-half of the 17 such claims.

The second column in Table 2 reports the Supreme Court's record of support for different types of claims. For most types of rights claims, the Supreme Court was more likely to support the claim than public opinion was. In only two instances (gay and lesbian rights and non-death-penalty criminal claims) were rights claims less likely to prevail at the Supreme Court than among the American public.

Public attitudes toward rights claims that reach the Supreme Court have changed surprisingly little over time. During the 1950s and 1960s, the public opposed 56 percent of the rights claims examined here, favored 28 percent, and was split on the remaining 17 percent. During the 1970s, the public opposed 49 percent of rights claims, favored 35 percent, and was evenly divided on the remaining 16 percent. During the 1980s and through 1992, the public opposed 54 percent of claims, favored 37 percent, and was split on 9 percent.

The Supreme Court's record of support for rights claims has varied much more dramatically over time, as the Court has become less willing to support rights claims.[30] Among the 88 cases, for example, the Court supported 67 percent of rights claims during the 1950s and 1960s, but only 58 percent of the claims during the 1970s. During the 1980s and 1990s, the Court supported only 37 percent of the rights claims. This pattern is opposite to the trend of American public opinion.[31] Figure 1 depicts the over-time change in support for rights claims, comparing public opinion to the Court.

Taken together, these results suggest that American public opinion has been decidedly mixed, not uni-

Figure 1. Percent of times public opinion or the
Supreme Court supported rights claims, by
decade

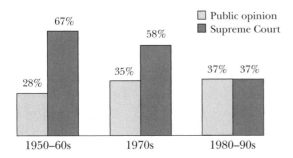

formly hostile, toward civil liberties, civil rights, or
equality claims since the early 1950s. The public in
nationwide polls has more often opposed than supported rights claims, but the differences should not be
exaggerated. The modern Court's support for rights
claims has usually exceeded public opinion support,
although these differences have eroded over time.

Predicting Court support

How important is public opinion compared to other
well-known predictors of Supreme Court decision making? Public opinion appears to be closely related to the
modern Court's support for new rights claims, either
when considered separately or when also considering
other predictors of Supreme Court decision making.

Seven predictors of Supreme Court decision making were tested for the 88 claims, among them two separate measures of American public opinion. The first,
the poll margin for each dispute, was described above.
The poll margin is a ratio-level (percentage) variable
that measures the extent to which the public in nationwide polls favors (or opposes) a specific rights claim
before the Court.

A second, less direct measure of public opinion is the
"national mood," a more general measure of the nation's
prevailing leanings. Two accounts have estimated the
national mood by tracking identically worded poll items
over time.[32] Both studies suggest that the national mood
moved from more liberal to more conservative, and
then back again, from the mid-1950s through the early
1990s.[33] Three separate versions of the national mood
were tested—the current (annual) national mood,
mood with a three-year lag, and mood with a five-year
lag. The national mood is also a ratio-level variable.

Public opinion is not the only predictor of Supreme
Court decision making. The presidential elections and
judicial appointments model has also been widely
used. In this model, Republican-appointed justices less
often support rights claims than do Democrat-
appointed justices.[34] Over time, presidential elections
and judicial appointments significantly impact the
Court's support for rights claims.[35] To test this model,
the number of Republican-appointed justices on the
Court was coded. The number of GOP-appointed justices on the Court during the 1953 through the 1991
terms ranges from a minimum of two to a maximum
of eight.

Another predictor of the Supreme Court's decision
making is the U.S. solicitor general's position. Many
studies have reported that the solicitor general's position has great influence on the Court.[36] This variable
was coded as (+1) to indicate support for the rights
claim, (0) to indicate no federal position, and (–1) to
indicate opposition to the claim.

A fifth predictor is whether the rights claim challenged a restrictive state law or policy. Typically, the
Court gives less deference to state-level laws and policies than to federal laws.[37] This variable was coded as
(1) to indicate the presence of a restrictive state-level
law or policy, otherwise (0).

A sixth predictor measures the decision's visibility.
Research has shown that the Supreme Court may behave differently in highly visible cases than in less visible ones.[38] Here, a simple variable tapped whether the
decision captured news coverage in the *New York Times*
within two days of the decision's announcement. A (2)
indicates one or more post-decision front-page news
stories, (1) indicates inside news coverage only, and (0)
indicates no coverage at all.[39]

Finally, to examine a possible artifact of the poll's timing, a seventh variable examined whether the poll was
taken before or after the Court's decision. Most research
has indicated that the Court has little, if any, ability to
influence public opinion through its announced decisions.[40] If the public opinion poll was taken before the
Court's decision was announced, the decision was coded
(1). Post-decision polls were coded (2).

When all seven variables are combined in a joint
probit model to predict whether the Court will support a rights claim (coded 1), or reject it (coded 0),[41]
only three variables significantly predict the Court's
support for new rights claims.[42] As the number of GOP
justices increases, Court support for rights claims de-

clines. For example, when the Court had its maximum number of Democratic appointees (either 6 or 7), the Court made pro-rights rulings 67 percent of the time. By comparison, when the Court had its minimum number of Democratic appointees (only 1 or 2), the Court ruled in favor of rights claims only 25 percent of the time.[43]

The Court also has more often supported a rights claim either when the solicitor general or public opinion supported the claim. Overall, public opinion was roughly as strong a predictor as the solicitor general's position, and nearly as strong a predictor as the Court's partisan makeup.

These results were also reexamined in a reduced model, eliminating the insignificant predictors. A three-predictor model combined only the solicitor general's position, the Court's partisan makeup, and public opinion. This model predicted decisions as well as did the full, seven-variable model,[44] and all three variables remained significant (at the .05-level).

On grounds of parsimony, however, a two-variable model stood out as the most attractive. This two-variable model included only the public opinion poll margin and the number of GOP-appointed justices.[45] Adding other variables, even the solicitor general's position, did not improve on this model's ability to predict Court decisions correctly.[46] For example, even when the solicitor general's position was added, the number of correctly predicted decisions barely improved (only to 69 percent).

In short, public opinion support for a rights claim is a significant predictor of whether the Supreme Court will accept it. Public opinion remains a strong predictor even when other, more traditional explanations of Supreme Court decision making are considered.[47]

Table 3 reports the probability that the Court will accept a rights claim, based solely on the Court's partisan makeup and public opinion toward that claim. The number of Republican-appointed justices varied between two and eight (as it did during the 1953 to 1991 terms). Public opinion is considered for three examples—when the polls strongly supported the claim (a poll margin of +30 percent), when polls were evenly divided, and when polls strongly opposed the claim (a poll margin of −30 percent).

Overall, the likelihood of a pro-rights claim ruling by the Court changes about as much when the polls change by a large margin as when the Court's partisan makeup changes by one seat. For example, with five

Table 3. Probability of a pro-claim ruling based on public opinion and the Supreme Court's partisan makeup

Number of GOP justices	Poll margin		
	Strongly favorable (+30%)	Evenly divided (0%)	Strongly opposed (−30%)
2	88%	85%	79%
3	81%	75%	69%
4	70%	63%	56%
5	57%	50%	43%
6	44%	37%	30%
7	32%	25%	19%
8	21%	15%	11%

GOP-appointed justices and evenly divided polls, the chance of a pro-claim rights ruling would be exactly 50 percent. Still with five GOP justices, but strongly favorable polls, the probability of a pro-claim ruling is 57 percent. With five GOP justices but strongly negative polls, the probability of a pro-claim ruling is only 43 percent.

Conclusions

This research points to several conclusions. First, since the mid-1950s public opinion has been quite mixed, but not uniformly hostile, toward civil liberties, civil rights, and equality rights claims. Available polls indicate that the American public clearly opposed about one-half, and clearly favored about one-third, of these claims. Public opinion may now slightly more often support rights claims than it did during the 1950s and 1960s.

Second, until the 1980s, the modern Supreme Court more often supported rights claims than did public opinion. Rights claims have usually received wider support from the justices than from the public. The Supreme Court's greater support for rights claims, however, has declined over time, and in more recent times, these differences no longer exist.

Third, public opinion is closely linked to the Supreme Court's own support for rights claims. Recent debates in judicial politics have reconsidered the question of what influences Supreme Court decision making, pointing to the judges' own values, solicitor general positions,[48] or the weight of legal arguments.[49] To those explanations may well be added public opinion. When public opinion either supports a rights claim, or when the polls are closely divided, the Court itself has overwhelmingly supported that claim. Indeed, public opinion remains closely linked to the Court's support for rights claims even when other explanations of Supreme Court decision making are also considered, such as the solicitor general's position or the Court's partisan makeup.

Exactly how this influence works remains somewhat speculative. However, these results are consistent with the theory that justices sense and share widely held public attitudes. As Chief Justice William Rehnquist once wrote:

> . . . I was recently asked . . . whether the justices were able to isolate themselves from the tides of public opinion. My answer was that we are not able to do so, and it would probably be unwise to try. We read newspapers and magazines, we watch news on television, we talk to our friends about current events. No judge worthy of his salt would ever cast his vote in a particular case simply because he thought the majority of the public wanted him to vote that way, but that is quite a different thing from saying that no judge is ever influenced by the great tides of public opinion that run in a country such as ours. Judges are influenced by them. . . .[50]

Even so, this research also suggests that public opinion is only one of several influences on the Court.[51] The Court's unusually unbalanced current partisan makeup strongly influences it against accepting rights claims, regardless of prevailing public opinion.[52] Even if both the solicitor general and the American public favor a rights claim, the probability of the current Supreme Court accepting that claim will remain quite small until the Court's composition itself changes.

Finally, this research also addresses the longstanding debate over judicial review. By far, the most commonly cited argument for this institution is that it helps protect controversial or unpopular minorities' civil liberties and rights.[53] The results here suggest that this argument should be reconsidered. True, the modern Supreme Court has been somewhat more sympathetic to rights claims than has public opinion. The difference, however, should not be overstated, and varies according to the time period considered. In recent years, the Supreme Court has not been more likely to support rights claims than public opinion. Those who advocate judicial review on the grounds that it is, in practice, countermajoritarian—that is, it defends beleaguered minorities against a hostile public opinion—might consider the evidence here.

Notes

This article originally appeared in Volume 78, Number 3, November–December 1994, pages 146–151.

1. Murphy, *The Constitution in Crisis Times* (New York: Harper & Row, 1972); Becker, *Comparative Judicial Politics* (Chicago: Rand McNally, 1970), 229.

2. *Dennis v. U.S.* 341 U.S. 494, at 580 (1951).

3. Marshall, *Public Opinion and the Supreme Court* (Boston: Unwin Hyman, 1989), 2, 9.

4. For a review, *see, e.g.,* Sullivan, Pierson, and Marcus, *Political Tolerance and American Democracy* (Chicago: University of Chicago Press, 1982).

5. Casper, "The Supreme Court and National Policy Making," *Am. Pol. Sci. Rev.* 70 (1976), 50.

6. *See, e.g.,* Murphy, *supra* n. 1, at 310–457; McCloskey, *The Modern Supreme Court* (Cambridge: Harvard University Press, 1972).

7. Shapiro, "The Supreme Court from Warren to Burger," in King, ed., *The New American Political System* (Washington, D.C.: American Enterprise Institute, 1979); Blasi, *The Burger Court: The Counterrevolution that Wasn't* (New Haven: Yale University Press, 1983); Schwartz, ed., *The Burger Years* (New York: Viking, 1987).

8. *Texas v. Johnson,* 491 U.S. 397 (1989); *U.S. v. Eichman,* 496 U.S. 310 (1990).

9. Savage, *Turning Right—The Making of the Rehnquist Supreme Court* (New York: John Wiley & Sons, 1992).

10. The breakdown of poll-to-decision matches, by Court, is 19 Warren Court rulings, 56 Burger Court rulings, and 13 Rehnquist Court rulings (through 1992).

11. Racial rights claims and the issue involved include: *Loving v. Virginia,* 388 U.S. 1 (1967), miscegenation; *Cooper v. Aaron,* 358 U.S. 1 (1958), Little Rock school desegregation; *South Carolina v. Katzenbach,* 383 U.S. 301 (1966), federal voting registrars; *Heart of Atlanta Motel v. U.S.,* 379 U.S. 241 (1964), integration of public accommodations; *Swann v. Charlotte Mecklenburg Board of Education,* 402 U.S. 1 (1971), same-district school busing; *Brown v. Board of Education of Topeka, Kansas,* 354 U.S. 483 (1954), school integration, and 349 U.S. 294 (1955), speed of integration; *Bob Jones University v. U.S.* 461 U.S. 574 (1983), tax exemptions for segregated schools; *Jones v. Mayer,* 392 U.S. 409 (1968), racial discrimination in housing; *Regents of the University of California v. Bakke,* 428 U.S. 265 (1978), fixed racial quotas, and affirmative action without rigid quotas; *Green v. New Kent Co. School Board,* 391 U.S. 430 (1968), federal funds cutoff to segregated schools; *Alexander v. Holmes Co. Board of Education,* 396 U.S. 19 (1969), immediate public school desegregation; *Griggs v. Duke Power Co.,* 401 U.S. 424 (1971), employment discrimination; *Fullilove v. Klutznick,* 448 U.S. 448 (1980), affirmative action programs in industry for minorities; *Milliken v. Bradley,* 418 U.S. 717 (1974), cross district school busing; and *Boynton v. Virginia,* 364 U.S. 454

(1960), segregation in public transportation waiting rooms. Companion cases are not listed here.

12. *Harris v. McRae,* 448 U.S. 297 (1980), federally funded abortions; *Carey v. Population Services International,* 431 U.S. 678 (1977), contraceptives for teenagers; *Eisenstadt, Sheriff, v. Baird,* 405 U.S. 438 (1972), contraceptives for single persons; *Planned Parenthood of Central Missouri v. Danforth,* 428 U.S. 52 (1976), spousal consent for a married woman's abortion; *Roe v. Wade,* 410 U.S. 113 (1973), first, second, and third trimester abortions; *Doe v. Bolton,* 410 U.S. 179 (1973), hospital abortion requirements; *Bowen v. American Hospital Association,* 476 U.S. 610 (1986), Baby Doe case; *Johnson v. Transportation Agency of Santa Clara Co.,* 480 U.S. 616 (1987) affirmative action in hiring and promotions; *Board of Directors of Rotary International v. Rotary Club of Duarte,* 481 U.S. 537 (1987), club discrimination by sex; *Webster v. Reproductive Health Services,* 106 L. Ed. 2d 410 (1989), public hospital restrictions, and fetal viability tests; *Planned Parenthood of Southeastern Pennsylvania v. Casey,* No. 91-744 (1992), husband notification, informed consent, and 24-hour waiting rule; *Rust v. Sullivan* 114 L. Ed.2d 233 (1991), gag rule.

13. *Abington School District v. Schempp,* 374 U.S. 203, and *Engle v. Vitale,* 370 U.S. 421 (1962), school prayers; *New York Times Co. v. U.S.* and *U.S. v. Washington Post,* 403 U.S. 713 (1971), Pentagon Papers; *Albertson v. SACB,* 382 U.S. 70 (1965), registration of Communist Party members; *U.S. v. U.S. District Court,* 407 U.S. 297 (1972), warrantless electronic surveillance; *Edwards v. Aguillard,* 482 U.S. 578 (1987), creation science; *Texas v. Gregory Lee Johnson,* 491 U.S. 397 (1989), flag burning.

14. *Gaylord v. Tacoma School District No. 10,* cert denied, 434 U.S. 879 (1977), school teachers; *Doe v. Commonwealth's Attorney for the City of Richmond,* 425 U.S. 901 (1976), private acts; *Beller v. Lehman,* cert denied, 452 U.S. 905 (1981), military service; *Bowers v. Hardwick,* 478 U.S. 186 (1986), private acts.

15. *Pipefitters Local Union 562 v. U.S.,* 407 U.S. 385 (1972), campaign funds; *PATCO v. U.S.,* cert denied, 454 U.S. 1083 (1981), air traffic controllers' strike; *Rogoff v. Anderson,* 404 U.S. 805 (1971), public employee right to strike; *NLRB v. Bildisco & Bildisco,* 465 U.S. 513 (1984), bankruptcy and labor union contracts; *AFSCME v. City of Muskegon,* cert denied, 375 U.S. 833 (1963), public employees' right to join a labor union; *United Federation of Postal Workers v. Blount,* 404 U.S. 802 (1971), public employees' right to join a labor union.

16. *Shapiro v. Thompson,* 394 U.S. 618 (1969), waiting period for welfare recipients; *Shapiro v. Doe,* 396 U.S. 488 (1970), naming the father of illegitimate children for AFDC payments; *Dandridge v. Williams,* 397 U.S. 471 (1970), maximum welfare grants per family; *Wyman v. Boddie,* 402 U.S. 991 (1971), local cost-of-living AFDC adjustments; *New York State Department of Social Services v. Dublino,* 413 U.S. 405 (1973), work rules.

17. *Coker v. Georgia,* 433 U.S. 584 (1977), death penalty for rape; *Woodson v. North Carolina,* 428 U.S. 280 (1976), mandatory death penalty; *Roberts v. Louisiana,* 428 U.S. 325 (1976) and 431 U.S. 633 (1977), mandatory death penalty for killing a policeman; *Gregg v. Georgia,* 428 U.S. 153 (1976), death penalty for first degree murder; *Moore v. Duckworth, Warden,* 443 U.S. 713 (1979), insanity defense; *Furman v. Georgia,* 408 U.S. 238 (1972), death penalty; *Wilkins v. Missouri,* No. 87-6026 (1989), death penalty for teenagers; *Penry v. Lynaugh,* No. 87-6177 (1989), death penalty for mentally retarded.

18. *Miranda v. Arizona,* 384 U.S. 436 (1966), *Gideon v. Wainwright,* 372 U.S. 355 (1963), and *Escobedo v. Illinois,* 378 U.S. 478 (1964), criminal confessions; *Schmerber v. California,* 384 U.S. 757 (1966), blood tests for drunk driving; *Delaware v. Prouse,* 440 U.S. 648 (1979), random traffic spot checks; *Glaser v. California,* cert denied, 385 U.S. 880 (1966), possession of marijuana; *New York v. Quarles,* 467 U.S. 649 (1984), *Nix v. Williams,* 467 U.S. 431 (1984), and *U.S. v. Leon,* 468 U.S. 897 (1984), exclusionary rule; *Smith v. Maryland,* 442 U.S. 735 (1979), pen registers; *Oatis v. Nelson, Warden,* cert denied, 393 U.S. (1969), warrantless searches; *Skinner v. Railway Labor Executives Assn.,* No. 87-1555 (1989), and *National Treasury Employees Union v. Von Raab,* No. 86-1879 (1989) drug testing in the workplace.

19. *Ingraham v. Wright,* 430 U.S. 651 (1977), corporal punishment; *Stamos v. Spring Branch ISD,* No. 85-1232 (1986), no-pass, no-play; *New Jersey v. T.L.O.,* 469 U.S. 325 (1985), student searches; *Goss v. Lopez,* 419 U.S. 565 (1975), student suspension hearings.

20. *Branzburg v. Hayes,* 407 U.S. 665 (1972), reporters' confidentiality; *New York Times Co. v. U.S.,* and *Washington Post v. U.S.,* 403 U.S. 713 (1971), Pentagon Papers case; *Zurcher v. The Stanford Daily,* 436 U.S. 547 (1978), search warrants for newsroom searches; *Richmond Newspapers, Inc., v. Virginia,* 448 U.S. 555 (1980), attendance at criminal trials; *Nebraska Press Assn. v. Stuart,* 427 U.S. 539 (1976), right to print information about criminal trials; *American Booksellers Assn. v. Hudnut,* No. 85-1090 (1986), pornography restrictions.

21. Further, a large majority of these 88 decisions received front-page coverage in prominent newspapers. Some 72 percent of these cases received front-page post-decision coverage in the *New York Times,* while another 18 percent received coverage on an inside page.

22. Harris Poll, September 5, 1974.

23. Gallup Poll, December 8–11, 1972.

24. Weissberg, *Public Opinion and Popular Government* (Englewood Cliffs, N.J.: Prentice Hall, 1976), 121–126; Sorauf, *The Wall of Separation* (Princeton: Princeton University Press, 1976).

25. Gallup Poll, June 21–26, 1963: "The United States Supreme Court has ruled that no state or local government may require the reading of the Lord's Prayer or

Bible verses in public schools. What are your views on this? (favor or oppose)."

26. Marshall, *supra* n. 3, at 78–79.

27. The 88 cases were reweighted to reported numbers in the Spaeth database for the 1954–1989 period for comparable civil liberties, civil rights, and equality claims.

28. *Trumbo v. U.S.*, 339 U.S. 934 (1950), cert denied; *American Communications Association, C.I.O. v. Doud*, 339 U.S. 382 (1950); *Garner v. Board of Public Works of Los Angeles*, 341 U.S. 716 (1951); *Bailey v. Richardson*, 341 U.S. 918 (1951); *Dennis v. U.S.*, 341 U.S. 494 (1951); and *Weiman v. Updegraff*, 344 U.S. 193 (1952).

29. The largest single difference was for welfare rights claims, where the poll margin was a very negative –53 percent, but among the justices, the vote margin was +23 percent. Gay and lesbian rights claims are the only exception to this pattern, receiving a poll margin of –6 percent, but among the justices, a less favorable vote margin of –22 percent.

30. Sheehan, Mishler, and Songer, "Ideology, Status, and the Differential Success of Direct Parties Before the Supreme Court," *Am. Pol. Sci. Rev.* 86 (1992), 464; Lamb and Halpern, "The Burger Court and Beyond," in Lamb and Halpern, ed., *The Burger Court* (Urbana: University of Illinois Press, 1991).

31. Sheehan, Mishler, and Songer, *supra* n. 30; Segal and Spaeth, *The Supreme Court and the Attitudinal Model* (New York: Cambridge University Press, 1993), 244–251.

32. Stimson, *Public Opinion in America—Moods, Cycles, and Swings* (Boulder, Colo.: Westview, 1992); and Smith, "Liberal and Conservative Trends in the United States Since World War II," *Public Opinion Q.* 54 (1990), 479.

33. The Stimson (1992) data were used here, with updated figures through 1992, courtesy of the author.

34. Epstein and Kobylka, *The Supreme Court and Legal Change* (Chapel Hill: University of North Carolina Press, 1992), 13–21, report that 11 GOP-appointed justices voted for (non-unanimous) civil liberties claims only 41 percent of the time, versus 69 percent of the time for 7 Democrat-appointed justices during this time period.

35. For recent descriptions, see Segal, "Senate Confirmation of Supreme Court Justices," *J. of Pol.* 49 (1987), 998; Overby, Henschen, Walsh, and Strauss, "Courting Constituents? An Analysis of the Senate Confirmation Vote on Justice Clarence Thomas," *Am. Pol. Sci. Rev.* 86 (1992), 997.

36. Segal and Spaeth, *supra* n. 31, at 237–239 and 313–314.

37. Wasby, *The Supreme Court in the Federal Judicial System* (New York: Holt, Rinehart, and Winston, 1984), 228–267; Abraham, *The Judicial Process* (New York: Oxford, 1980), 296–297; Segal and Spaeth, *supra* n. 31, at 310–312, 320; Spaeth, "Burger Court Review of State Court Civil Liberties Decisions," in Spaeth and Brenner, *Studies in U.S. Supreme Court Behavior* (New York: Garland, 1990).

38. Marshall, *supra* n. 3, at 82–83.

39. Whether the decision was one of the three top problems in the Gallup Poll's "most important problem" was not significantly related to pro-rights outcomes; see Smith, "The Polls: America's Most Important Problems," *Public Opinion Q.* 49 (1985), 264, and subsequent Gallup Polls.

40. Page, Shapiro, and Dempsey, "What Moves Public Opinion?," *Am. Pol. Sci. Rev.* 81 (1987), 23; Marshall, *supra* n. 3; Bass and Thomas, "The Supreme Court and Policy Legitimation," *Am. Pol. Q.* 12 (July 1984), 335.

41. A probit equation estimates the probability of a (0,1) dichotomous outcome where the dependent and independent variable may not be related in a linear fashion. For a detailed explanation, see Aldrich and Nelson, *Linear Probability, Logit, and Probit Models* (Beverly Hills: Sage, 1984).

42. The "national mood" was not a significant predictor, either in the year-to-year version or when lagged either three or five years.

43. The differences are statistically significant at the .05 level. As Table 3 indicates, even when public opinion is quite hostile to a rights claim, the Court has a 79 percent probability of supporting that claim if there are seven Democrats on the Court. By contrast, if there are seven Republicans on the Court, the probability of supporting an equally unpopular rights claim falls to only 19 percent.

44. In this model, MLEs, standard errors and MLE/S.E., respectively, were: poll margin (.006, .004, and 1.64*); number of GOP justices (–.273, .138, and –1.97*), and solicitor general position (.394, .242, and 1.63*). The three-variable model correctly predicted 69 percent of the decisions. *Asterisked figures were significant at the .05 level.

45. In this two-predictor model, MLEs, standard errors, and MLE/S.E., respectively, were: poll margin (.007, .004, and 1.72*) and number of GOP justices (–.338, .132, and –2.56**). This model correctly predicted 68 percent of the decisions. *Asterisked figures were significant at the .05 level; ** at the .01 level.

A two-variable model with solicitor general position and the number of GOP justices was somewhat less successful—predicting only 64 percent of the decisions correctly.

46. Solicitor general position failed to significantly improve predictions over the two-variable model, in large part because the number of GOP justices was significantly correlated to solicitor general support for rights claims (r = .27). Public opinion, however, was uncorrelated with either solicitor general position or the Court's partisan makeup.

47. Public opinion is significant at the .05-level when entered alone in a probit equation (MLE = .007; S.E. = .004; MLE/SE = 1.75*; constant = .15 n.s.). *Asterisked figures were significant at the .05 level.

48. Segal and Spaeth, *supra* n. 31.

49. Epstein and Kobylka, *supra* n. 34.

50. Rehnquist, *The Supreme Court* (New York: William Morrow & Co., 1987), 98.

51. For example, the presence of partisan unbalanced courts may counterbalance a one-sided public opinion. When the Court handed down pro-rights rulings despite strongly anti-rights polls, it typically had an above-average number of Democrats; see, e.g., *Abington School District v. Schempp* (1963), *Jones v. Mayer* (1968), or *Albertson v. Sub-versive Activities Control Board* (1965). By contrast, when the Court handed down anti-rights rulings, despite strongly pro-rights polls, it typically had an above-average number of Republicans; see, e.g., *Penry v. Lynaugh* (1989), *NLRB v. Bildisco & Bildisco* (1984), or *Rust v. Sullivan* (1991).

52. *See also* Sheehan, Mishler, and Songer, *supra* n. 30.

53. Rostow, "The Democratic Character of Judicial Review," *Harv. L. Rev.* 66 (1952), 195; Choper, *Judicial Review and the National Political Process* (Chicago: University of Chicago, 1980).

Public perception of the Supreme Court in the 1990s

John M. Scheb II and William Lyons

The results of surveys conducted in 1994 and 1997 indicate the Court is doing a good job of finding and holding the middle ground, where its legitimacy is likely to be maximized.

Although the Supreme Court is ostensibly immune to the ebbs and flows of public opinion, most observers agree that it must enjoy a reasonable measure of public support or risk losing the legitimacy that undergirds its decisions. The question, then, is simple: How do the American people regard the Supreme Court? This question, using data from a national survey conducted during the winter of 1994, was addressed four years ago in *Judicature*.[1] A survey conducted during the fall of 1997 enables us to delve more deeply into the matter to see whether the public's perception of the Court has changed significantly and to explore further the contours of public opinion.[2]

As in 1994, respondents to the 1997 survey provided an overall rating of both the Supreme Court and Congress. Just as they did nearly four years earlier, Americans in late 1997 rendered a relatively positive assessment of the Court (see Table 1). In 1994, 45 percent said the Court's performance was "good" or "excellent." In 1997, 47 percent gave these responses. In 1994, 51 percent rated the Court's performance as "fair" or "poor." In 1997, 49 percent gave these ratings. Thus, attitudes toward the Court appear to be rather stable. If one considers the "excellent" and "good" ratings to be positive assessments of the Court and the "fair" and "poor" ratings to be negative assessments, then public attitudes toward the Court in the 1990s tilt slightly in the negative direction.

But to fairly evaluate the public's view of the Court, we need comparative data, which is why Congress was included in the surveys. Looking at the dismal ratings of Congress in both 1994 and 1997, the Court's ratings appear relatively positive. Clearly, the Court continues to fare much better in public opinion than does Congress.

As in 1994, respondents in 1997 were almost twice as likely to rate the Court's performance as "good" or "excellent" than they were to provide these positive ratings to Congress. By the same token, respondents in both 1994 and 1997 were more than twice as likely to rate Congress' performance as "poor" than they were

to render this most negative assessment of the Court. These data are certainly not unique; virtually all public opinion polls that compare confidence in Congress and the Court find the same phenomenon. The public continues to hold Congress in low esteem while it harbors a relatively positive view of the Court.

Court decision making

When asked about specific areas of Court decision making—civil rights, criminal justice, abortion, and school prayer—the public renders a more negative assessment (see Table 2). Not surprisingly, the percentage of "not sure" responses rises sharply when the questions become more specific and require greater attentiveness to the Court's output. Evidently, respondents who are inattentive to the Court's decisions in particular areas are more favorable to the Court generally. Only in the area of civil rights does the public's assessment of the Court's performance begin to approach its overall evaluation of the Court.

The Court's worst performance rating is on school prayer, where roughly 4 in 10 respondents in 1997 rated the Court "poor." Given the unpopularity of school prayer decisions going all the way back to the early 1960s, this is not surprising. The Court also is perceived poorly on abortion, where it has arguably tried to steer a middle course in recent years and thus has displeased people on both sides of this sharply divisive issue. On criminal justice, where the Court has been most consistently conservative over the last decade, the public's continuing fear of crime probably detracts somewhat from the public's assessment of the Court's work.

Variation in opinions

Conventional wisdom holds that the liberal activism of the Warren Court during the 1960s, especially in the criminal justice area, contributed to a decline in public confidence in the Court. When asked whether they agreed or disagreed with the statement that "The Supreme Court today is doing a better job than it did

Judicature Volume 82, Number 2, pp. 66–69

Table 1. Performance ratings of congress and the Supreme Court

| | Congress | | Supreme Court | |
	1994	1997	1994	1997
Excellent	2%	2%	4%	7%
Good	21	23	41	40
Fair	46	47	40	37
Poor	28	26	11	12
Not sure	3	2	5	4

Table 2. Supreme Court ratings in several areas of decision making, 1997

	Overall	Civil rights	Criminal justice	Abortion	School prayer
Excellent	7%	3%	4%	3%	3%
Good	40	32	28	20	19
Fair	37	36	32	30	30
Poor	12	17	25	35	41
Not sure	4	12	11	12	7

in the 1960s," half the respondents to the 1997 survey agreed, about a quarter disagreed, and about a quarter were not sure (see Table 3). Responses varied somewhat by age, with older respondents being slightly less likely to agree that the Court is doing a better job today. Not surprisingly, respondents who identified themselves as "liberals" were most likely to disagree with this proposition. Still, there appears to be a reasonable degree of consensus that the Court today, which is both more conservative and more given to judicial restraint than the Warren Court, is performing better.

How do opinions vary, if at all, across the lines that often divide Americans politically? In 1994, Democrats, Independents, and Republicans differed slightly in their overall assessments of the Court. In 1997 these differences appeared to be more pronounced, with Democrats seeming to render more favorable judg-

Table 3. "The Supreme Court today (1997) is doing a better job than it did in the 1960s."

	All	18–35	36–55	Over 55
Strongly disagree	4%	3%	3%	7%
Disagree	20	14	22	27
Agree	43	49	44	34
Strongly agree	7	6	8	8
Not sure	26	28	23	24

ments than Republicans and Independents, but given the sample size the differences were not statistically significant (see Table 4). The Supreme Court can ill-afford to have its decisions second-guessed as expressions of partisan politics. One could well argue that given the controversial nature of its work, the Court is about as even-handedly regarded as it could hope to be. There is very little difference between the attitudes of Republicans and Democrats; about half of each group provide "excellent" or "good" ratings.

The results are rather different when ideology is considered. There is evidence in the surveys that the Court enjoys more support among liberals and moderates. In 1994 conservatives were twice as likely as moderates and liberals to render "poor" assessments of the Court. In 1997, the pattern was the same (see Table 5). Although the Court of the 1990s is clearly more conservative than the Warren Court or even the early Burger Court, conservatives probably object to the fact that many of the precedents from a more liberal era remain in effect. In the 1997 survey, conservatives rendered more negative assessments of the Court's work in the criminal justice and civil rights areas, and *much* more negative ratings in the school prayer and abortion areas.

Interestingly, no significant differences by ideology were found in the 1997 survey when support for the basic power of judicial review was measured. It is not that self-identified conservatives harbor some deep-seated populist aversion to the role and function of the Court. Rather, they seem to object to what they perceive to be the ideological tenor of the Court's output over the years.

There is no evidence that the Court is seen through a racially tinted lens. In 1994 nonwhites rendered more negative assessments of the Court, but the differences were not statistically significant. In 1997, there was even less evidence of racial differences in evaluations of the Court (see Table 6). There also does not appear to be a "gender gap" in the public's view of the Court. As in 1994, there were no significant gender differences in assessments of the Court in 1997 (Table 6).

Ideology and decision making

As observed in 1994, traditional views of the judicial role dictate that the ideology of the judge ought not to have an impact on that judge's decisions. Of course, numerous political scientists and legal commentators have argued that ideology is in fact a major determi-

Table 4. Supreme Court performance rating by party affiliation, 1994–1997

	Democrats	Independents	Republicans	Democrats	Independents	Republicans
Excellent	4%	3%	4%	8%	8%	4%
Good	42	42	39	42	39	40
Fair	34	42	40	40	33	39
Poor	14	9	12	7	15	15
Not sure	5	4	5	3	5	2

Table 5. Supreme Court performance rating by ideology

	1994			1997		
	Liberals	Moderates	Conservatives	Liberals	Moderates	Conservatives
Excellent	4%	4%	3%	12%	7%	2%
Good	48	44	33	44	44	35
Fair	34	41	42	33	36	42
Poor	8	9	16	8	9	18
Not sure	6	3	6	3	4	3

Table 6. Supreme Court performance rating by race and gender

	1994				1997			
	Whites	Non whites	Males	Females	Whites	Non whites	Males	Females
Excellent	4%	2%	5%	2%	7%	6%	7%	7%
Good	41	38	40	41	41	37	41	39
Fair	40	37	40	39	36	43	35	40
Poor	10	18	11	12	13	10	14	10
Not sure	5	5	4	7	3	4	3	4

nant of judicial decision making. Most of the people who responded to the survey in 1994 said that the ideologies of the justices should not be a factor in Supreme Court decision making. This was generally true regardless of respondents' ideological orientations. Much the same thing was found in 1997, when 6 out of 10 respondents said that the ideologies of the justices should have no impact on the Court's decisions. Not surprisingly, moderates were more likely to take this position than either liberals or conservatives (see Table 7).

In 1994, respondents were closely divided between those who thought the Supreme Court was too liberal and those who thought it was too conservative (see Table 8). About 40 percent thought that the Court's ideological orientation was "about right." In 1997,

there was a definite shift, with fewer Americans regarding the Court as "too conservative." This change seems to have taken place among those classifying themselves as liberals, 49 percent of whom thought the Court was too conservative in 1994 as opposed to 27 percent in 1997. The Court may be approaching a realistically attainable "preferred position." Those of either ideological persuasion feel the Court leans too far in the other direction, while those in the middle tend to think the Court is where it should be.

*****

Both the 1994 and 1997 surveys demonstrated that the public holds the Supreme Court in substantially higher regard than the Congress, although the public's high regard for the Court appears to break down some-

Table 7. "How much impact should ideology, that is whether the judges are liberals or conservatives, have on the Supreme Court's decisions?"

	1997			
	All	Liberals	Moderates	Conservatives
Not much	61%	53%	66%	57%
Somewhat	29	34	27	29
A lot	8	12	5	12
Not sure	2	1	2	2

Table 8. "Do you think that the current U.S. Supreme Court is too liberal, too conservative, or about right in its decisions?"

	1994				1997			
	All	Liberals	Moderates	Conservatives	All	Liberals	Moderates	Conservatives
Too liberal	26%	11%	20%	48%	28%	12%	21%	51%
About right	41	33	46	40	43	48	46	35
Too conservative	24	49	26	5	16	27	17	8
Not sure	8	8	8	7	13	13	16	6

what in the context of specific, controversial areas of decision making. Moreover, assessments of the Court do not appear to vary substantially across the race, gender, and party lines that often divide Americans. Thus, the Court appears to be doing a good job of finding and holding the middle ground, where its legitimacy is likely to be maximized.

Notes

This article originally appeared in Volume 82, Number 2, September–October 1998, pages 66–69.

1. Lyons and Scheb, "Public holds U.S. Supreme Court in high regard," *Judicature* 77 (March–April 1994), 273.

2. The survey was conducted October 6–16, 1997 by the Social Science Research Institute at the University of Tennessee, Knoxville. 658 randomly selected adults were interviewed by telephone using a computer-assisted telephone interviewing (CATI) system. The margin of error is +/–4 percentage points at the 95 percent confidence level. The response rate, defined as number of completed interviews as a proportion of contacts with eligible subjects, was 50.7 percent.

The impact of Bush v. Gore on public perceptions and knowledge of the Supreme Court

Herbert M. Kritzer

The Court's action in Bush v. Gore *was dramatic, subject to intense media coverage, and controversial, but the effects on public perceptions and knowledge of the Court were modest.*

To those who pay close attention to the United States Supreme Court, its involvement in the 2000 presidential election, through its decisions concerning recounts of the vote in Florida, was an extremely important, perhaps watershed, event in the Court's role in the American political and legal system. The volume and tone of the online and print discussions about the Court's actions among political scientists and law professors has been heated, contentious, and at times strident.[1] A central concern, particularly among critics of the decision, is that the Court may have undermined its own legitimacy, at least among members of the public who had been ardent supporters of Al Gore or ardent opponents of George W. Bush.

What impact *did* the Court's action actually have on the public's view of the Court? There are two types of hypotheses that one might advance. First, the Court's image may have suffered generally because of a concern that it embroiled itself in electoral politics when it should have stayed above the fray. Second, the overall approval of the Court may have been unchanged because of cross-cutting shifts, with those approving of the Court's decision increasing their support and those disapproving the decision decreasing their support; in this case, one would observe a shift in the structure of support rather than the level of support.

While most of the commentary has been on the impact of *Bush v. Gore* on the public's view of the Court, there is another type of effect that may have resulted from the high level of attention focused on the Court and the unprecedented nature of media coverage (that is, the broadcasting of recordings of oral argument immediately upon the conclusion of those arguments). The controversy over the election, including the involvement of the Supreme Court, has been described as a massive civics lesson;[2] did this national civics lesson increase the public's knowledge about the Court?

Most research on the public's knowledge of the Supreme Court concludes that the public knows little about the Court or its workings.[3] A regularly cited example of the public's ignorance is that in 1989, 71 percent could not name a single member of the Court while 54 percent of the same sample could name the judge on the television show "The People's Court."[4] That this survey found such results was not news to political scientists, who have long documented the minimal knowledge most citizens have about the Court.[5] One impact of the Court's involvement in resolving the 2000 election was extensive discussion of the role of discretion on the Court, how the Court operates, and how it is staffed. It might well be that the national civics lesson has increased public knowledge about the Court.

What evidence is there regarding the impact of *Bush v. Gore* on the public's evaluation of and knowledge about the U.S. Supreme Court? Ideally one needs to have comparable before and after data. By good fortune, I happen to have exactly that type of data.

Data

In the spring of 2000 I placed a set of questions about public knowledge of the Supreme Court (and some other aspects of the judicial system) on an ongoing survey conducted by the University of Wisconsin Survey Center (UWSC). (See "Measuring knowledge of the U.S. Supreme Court," page 501).

In addition, the survey routinely includes a general evaluation question regarding the Court:

> On a scale of 1 to 10, where 1 means very poor and 10 means excellent, how would you rate the job the Supreme Court is doing?

Starting December 14, 2001 (*Bush v. Gore* was announced the evening of December 12), I added the following question:[6]

> The United States Supreme Court ruled that the plan for recounting presidential votes in Florida ordered by the Florida Supreme Court violated the U.S. Constitu-

Measuring knowledge of the U.S. Supreme Court

How many members sit on the United States Supreme Court?
____ nine
____ (other number ____)
____ don't know

Please tell me the name of the current chief justice of the United States Supreme Court? (DO NOT READ LIST)
____ William Rehnquist
____ mentions another name
        (_____)
____ don't know

Who appoints justices of the Supreme Court?
____ President
____ Congress
____ other (_____)
____ elected
____ don't know

What is the mandatory retirement age of Supreme Court justices?
____
____ none
____ don't know

Can you tell me whether the Supreme Court uses juries to help it decide cases?
____ yes, uses juries
____ no, does not use juries
____ don't know

Can you tell me whether the Supreme Court decides cases without using juries?
____ yes, without juries
____ no, with juries
____ don't know

Is it correct to say that the U.S. Supreme Court has to decide every case that is appealed to it?
____ yes, correct
____ no, not correct
____ don't know

Is it correct to say that the U.S. Supreme Court can choose which of the cases appealed to it that it wants to decide?
____ yes, correct
____ no, not correct
____ don't know

Questions asked May 23, 2000–March 19, 2001.

tion and thus could not proceed. Would you say you strongly approve of this decision, somewhat approve, somewhat disapprove, or strongly disapprove of the decision?

The survey also has a variety of general questions about political preference, party identification,[7] attention paid to public affairs, interest in politics, education, income, race, and gender.

In a typical week UWSC interviews 20–40 randomly selected respondents from around the United States. Each week's interviews can be treated as an independent random sample, which means that weeks can be aggregated to obtain random samples covering periods of time.

A total of 291 respondents were interviewed after December 12, 2000, and 874 were interviewed through December 12, 2000.[8] Because of the holiday season, relatively few interviews were conducted in the three weeks immediately after the decision (a total of 23), but the weekly totals returned to the 30–40 range starting in January. In order to assure some reasonable minimum number of respondents, the overtime analyses presented below will aggregate into two 1-week (14-day) periods.

Changes in evaluations

Figure 1 shows the biweekly fluctuation in the public's evaluations of the Court; the vertical line demarcates the before and after periods for the Court's decision ending the election controversy. While the figure may show some drop in the average evaluation, that drop is neither clear cut nor particularly sharp. Overall, the average evaluation for the before period is 6.04 compared with 5.81 for the after period, hardly an earth-shattering change; a t-test of the difference of means shows no statistically discernible difference.

Figure 1. Public approval of the U.S. Supreme Court

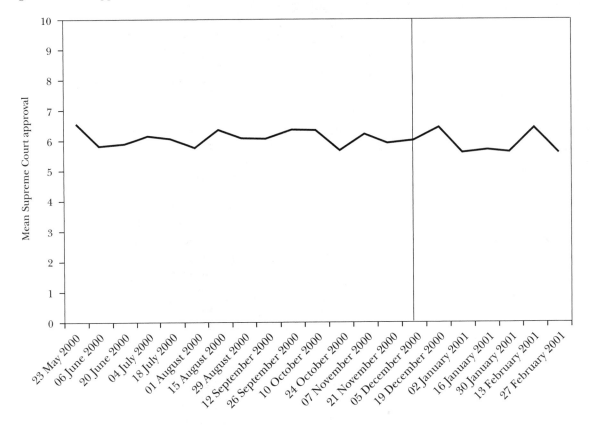

This should not be particularly surprising. Given the fact that the public was evenly divided by the election, and the apparent pattern from public discourse that supporters of George W. Bush approved the Court's decision and supporters of Al Gore disapproved, that might well be cross-cutting changes with Bush supporters (Republicans) increasing their approval of the Court and Gore supporters (Democrats) decreasing their approval.[9]

Breaking the responses into categories (1 to 4 "unfavorable", 5 and 6 "neutral", and 7 to 10 "favorable") results in the pattern for approval of the Court by party

seen in Table 1. There are clear shifts for Democrats (17 percentage points less favorable) and Republicans (about 13 percentage points more favorable), with no appreciable shift for Independents.[10] One might expect that strong partisans would demonstrate greater shifts than weak partisans or leaners. The evidence on this is mixed. Figure 2 shows the shift in favorable response across the full range of the party identification scale. There is no clear relationship between strength of party identification and the magnitude of the shift in percentage favorable to the Court. Among Democrats, strong partisans and independent leaners shift more

Table 1. Approval for the U.S. Supreme Court by party

	Before			After			Shift
	Favorable	Unfavorable	(n)	Favorable	Unfavorable	(n)	
Democrats	51.6%	15.3%	353	34.1%	31.1%	132	−17.5
Republicans	45.8%	19.7%	330	58.9%	11.2%	107	+13.1
Independents	31.5%	35.6%	73	34.5%	34.5%	29	+3.0

Figure 2. Shift in approval by party affiliation

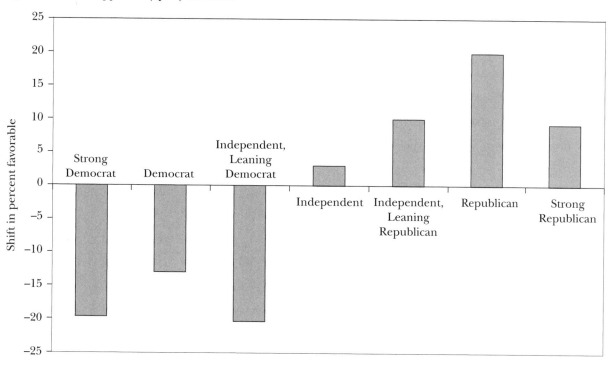

than weak partisans, while among Republicans, it is the weak partisans who show the strongest shift.

I also explored the possibility that stronger shifts might be found using self-reported ideology as the basis of comparison rather than party identification. The survey included the following item measuring the respondent's ideology:

> We hear a lot of talk these days about liberals and conservatives. On a scale of 1 to 10, where 1 is extremely liberal and 10 is extremely conservative, where would you place yourself?

Collapsing this into liberal (1 to 3), moderate (4 to 7), and conservative (8 to 10), shows shifts similar to those based on party identification. The shifts for conservatives are slightly less sharp than for Republicans; the shifts for liberals are about the same vis-à-vis "favorable", but slightly sharper for "unfavorable" (17 percent unfavorable before, 42.5 percent unfavorable after for about a 25 percentage point shift).

Impacts on evaluation

The Supreme Court's *Bush v. Gore* decision ending the recount of the presidential vote in Florida had mea-

surable consequences for the public's view of the Court, *at least in the short term*. Importantly, the net effect on the public's evaluation of the Court was essentially nil; increases in negative evaluations were almost exactly offset by increases in positive evaluations. The more important impact was on the structuring of public evaluations of the Court. Where before the decision on December 12 partisanship was not related to evaluation of the Court, after the election it was, and this relationship was clearly mediated by the specific approval or disapproval of the Court's decision in *Bush v. Gore*. It is clearly too early to tell whether the impacts are temporary, or whether the Court's action will fade from the public consciousness resulting in a return to the situation where evaluation of the Court is unrelated to political partisanship. However, although these changes are measurable (on the order of one third to one half of a standard deviation for Democrats and for Republicans) and significant, their magnitude should not be overstated; the shift in the means for the two groups of partisans was on the order of about one to one and a half points on the 10-point scale used to measure the public's evaluation of the Court. Given the heated discussion and rhetoric during and immediately after the election controversy, those actively

Table 2. Knowledge of the U.S. Supreme Court

	Percent (or mean) correct		
	Total	Before	After
Size of Court***	31.3%	28.7%	39.0%
Mandatory retirement age+	47.9%	46.4%	52.6%
Who appoints justices	68.4%	67.9%	69.8%
Who is chief justice***	19.8%	16.0%	31.0%
Supreme Court's use of juries*	74.6%	73.2%	79.0%
Control of docket	71.9%	70.9%	74.9%
Mean number correct***	3.15	3.04	3.48

+ p<.10, * p<.05, **p<.01, *** p<.001 (before/after difference; two-tailed)

involved in the shouting almost certainly presumed that the impact would have been greater.[11]

Changes in knowledge

If the Court's decision in *Bush v. Gore* was limited in its effect on the public's assessment of the Court, can that also be said of the "national civic's lesson"? Was there a measurable effect on the public's knowledge of the structure and operation of the Court? Recall that the survey included six knowledge questions (see "Measuring knowledge of the U.S. Supreme Court," page 501):

• Size of the Court

• The age at which justices must retire

• Who appoints the justices

• Who the current chief justice is

• Whether the Court uses juries

• Whether the Court must hear all cases brought to it

For purposes of analysis I combined incorrect and "don't know" responses.

Table 2 shows the percentage of correct responses (versus incorrect and "don't know" responses) for each of the six questions, before and after December 12, 2000; in addition, it shows the mean number of correct responses. One striking feature of the data is the relatively high awareness of the public. Two thirds or more respondents gave correct responses on a number of the questions: who chooses justices, the [non]use of juries by the Supreme Court, and the Court's discretion in which cases it will decide. About half the respondents knew that there is no mandatory retirement age for jus-

tices. Relatively few respondents could name the current chief justice—a pattern that has been found again and again in survey research—and only a minority of respondents knew the number of justices who serve on the Court. On average, respondents were able to give correct answers for slightly more than 3 of the questions (3.15, standard deviation 1.74); 64.1 percent knew correct responses to three or more of the items, 46.1 percent four or more, and 24.9 percent five or more.

Comparing before and after figures, for every item the percentage of correct responses was higher after *Bush v. Gore* than before, although for only three is the increase statistically significant. Looking at the mean number of correct responses, this goes from about three (3.04) to about three and a half (3.48). This is a statistically significant change, but it represents only about one quarter of standard deviation; recall that the shift in the scale measuring approval of the Supreme Court was on the order of one third to one half a standard deviation among partisans (down for Democrats and up for Republicans).

In terms of the individual responses, the biggest change was in being able to name the chief justice: only 16 percent of respondents could do this before *Bush v. Gore* compared with 31 percent after; this is all the more interesting given that the chief justice did not play a particularly prominent role in this case (the majority decision was *per curiam* although Justice Rehnquist did file the only concurring decision, advancing additional reasons for stopping the recount).

Clearly, one impact of the massive coverage of the Supreme Court's handling of the ballot controversy in Florida was to increase modestly the public's knowledge about the Court. Whether this increase is a permanent change or simply a temporary "blip" only time will tell.

What the Gallup Poll found

Question: Do you approve or disapprove of the way the Supreme Court is handling its job?

	Aug 29–Sept 5, 2000		Jan 10–14, 2001		Jun 11–17, 2001	
	approve	disapprove	approve	disapprove	approve	disapprove
All	62%	25%	59%	34%	62%	25%
Democrats	70%	18%	42%	50%	54%	32%
Republicans	60%	35%	80%	15%	74%	18%
Independents	57%	34%	54%	38%	59%	26%

Question: Now I am going to read you a list of institutions in American Society. Please tell me how much confidence you, yourself, have in each one—a great deal, quite a lot, some, or very little? First, . . . Next, [Supreme Court included in list of five institutions; the order of the institutions was randomized.]

	June 22–25, 2000		Dec 15–17, 2000		Jun 8–10, 2001	
	Great deal/ quite a lot	Some/ Very little	Great deal/ quite a lot	Some/ Very little	Great deal/ quite a lot	Some/ Very little
All	47%	49%	49%	48%	50%	44%
Democrats	44%	50%	40%	56%	46%	47%
Republicans	48%	50%	67%	32%	62%	36%
Independents	48%	46%	45%	52%	42%	50%

Modest effects

The events in November and December, 2000 were dramatic. Clearly they had measurable impacts on public opinion and public awareness. However, it is easy to overestimate the magnitude of these impacts, and it is too early to determine whether the impacts are lasting or temporary (see "What the Gallup Poll found," above, which shows later results). This analysis shows that the net effect on the public's evaluation is essentially nil. However, this obscures the cross-cutting changes that occurred: Republicans became more supportive and Democrats became less supportive. Not surprisingly, this is directly related to whether they approved or disapproved of the Court's decision (statistical analysis available from the author), which in turn is almost certainly a function of whom individuals voted for.

Political scientists have debated whether approval of specific decisions of the Court, labeled "specific support," affects the public's general evaluation of the Court, labeled "diffuse support."[12] My analysis, albeit based on a very unsophisticated measure of diffuse support, does show a clear linkage in the case of the Court's action in the 2000 election ballot controversy. Still, while the effects on public evaluations are clear, they are, on average, not strikingly large. Given the dramatic nature of the events, an expectation of dramatic shifts in public evaluations of the Court seemed reasonable. Dramatic changes did not materialize.

Similarly, while there were clear increases in the public's knowledge of the Supreme Court, these increases were not dramatic. The largest change was in knowing the name of the chief justice, even though Chief Justice Rehnquist did not play a particularly prominent role during the events of early December. If one were to look at my six measures of knowledge, the one that probably played most prominently during this period was related to who appoints the justices; there was significant commentary about the fact that the justices were determining who would be choosing their new colleagues or their own replacements. Public knowledge on this item was unchanged between the two periods; while the level of knowledge was high, and hence there was less for the public to learn than for many other items, an item with an even higher level of knowledge did show a significant increase—whether the Supreme Court uses juries. With regard to the level of knowledge, it will be interesting to see whether the changes are permanent or only temporary.

The modesty of the overall effects is probably the most interesting part of these findings. The Supreme Court's action was dramatic, subject to unprecedented media coverage, controversial, and to many very surprising (the decision by the Court to get involved as well as the decision itself). Nonetheless, the effects are modest. One might ask what, if anything, could lead to dramatic effects in how the public views the Court and how much they know about the Court. The only obvious answer, something the Court has strenuously resisted, would be to open the Court proceedings to television coverage. In many ways, the lessons of the impact of *Bush v. Gore* might be seen as justifying the Court's reluctance to open itself to greater coverage. While the public may lack awareness of many aspects of the Court that might be rectified by greater coverage, keeping the doors closed to television may also serve to limit the vehemence of the public reaction to what the Court decides.

Notes

This article originally appeared in Volume 85, Number 1, July–August 2001, pages 32–38.

I would like to thank the University of Wisconsin Survey Center, and the University of Wisconsin College of Letters and Science that supports the Center, for making space available on the Center's national survey. Comments may be directed to the author at kritzer@polisci.wisc.edu.

1. *See, for example*, Bork, "Sanctimony Serving Politics: The Florida Fiasco," *The New Criterion*, March, 2001, at 4; Sunstein and Epstein (eds.), *The Vote: Bush, Gore, and the Supreme Court* (Chicago: University of Chicago Press, 2001).

2. A search on the "CURNWS" file on Lexis/Nexis done on April 23, 2001, using the search phrase "civics lesson and election and supreme court w/2 (u.s. or united states)" produced 202 "hits."

3. But see Gibson, Caldeira, and Spence, "Report on Knowledge of the Supreme Court," Washington University, St. Louis, Department of Political Science (http://artsci.wustl.edu/~legit/Courtknowledge.pdf).

4. Morin, "Wapner v. Rehnquist: No Contest: TV Judge Vastly Outpolls Justices in Test of Public Recognition," *Post*, June 23, 1989, at A21. A survey one year later found that 59 percent could not name a single justice, Coyle, "How Americans View High Court," *National Law Journal*, February 26, 1990, at 1.

5. Casey, "The Supreme Court and Myth: An Empirical Investigation," *Law & Soc'y Rev.* 8 (1974), 385; Dolbeare,

"The Public Views the Supreme Court," in Jacob (ed.), *The Public Views the Supreme Court* (Boston: Little, Brown, 1967). One should not overstate the public's ignorance. A 1990 survey found that 80 percent of the public knew that a woman was on the Court, 50 percent knew that an African American was on the Court, and 59 percent knew that justices serve for life, see Coyle, *supra* n. 4.

6. No interviews were conducted on December 13, 2000.

7. For purposes of analysis, party identification is measured along the "standard" seven-point scale: strong Democrats, "weak" Democrats, Independents leaning toward the Democratic Party, Independents, Independents leaning toward the Republican Party, "weak" Republicans, and strong Republicans. All respondents who initially did not self-describe as Democrats or Republicans were asked the follow-up question about which party they were closer to; respondents who named one or the other party were coded as "Independents" leaning toward that party, and those who explicitly stated they did not lean toward either, were coded as "Independents" not leaning toward either party.

8. Because the decision actually came down late during the evening of December 12, I include the interviews conducted on December 12 as before the decision.

9. The presence of a partisan dimension to public evaluations of the Supreme Court has been recognized since at least the 1960s, see Dolbeare and Hammond, "The Political Party Bias of Attitudes Toward the Supreme Court," *Pub. Opinion Q.* 32 (1968), 16.

10. One intriguing element of the results in Table 1 is the high, unfavorable rating by independents, constant over the two periods and higher than even for Democrats after the Court's decision.

11. There is one other point worth noting from the results presented above. While the evaluation of the Court by self-identified Democrats and Independents who leaned toward the Democratic Party shifted clearly in the unfavorable direction, the post-election negativity of these segments of the citizenry only approached the negativity both before and after the election of Independents who did not lean toward one party or the other. This may portend a change in the nature of those who call themselves Independent without *any* preference between the parties. Where historically these individuals were seen as unengaged in politics, today the group may be comprised more of persons who are seriously alienated from government and politics.

12. Calderia and Gibson, "The Etiology of Support for the Supreme Court," *Am. J. Pol. Sci.* 36 (1992), 635; Tanenhaus and Murphy, "Patterns of Public Support for the Supreme Court: A Panel Study," *J. of Pol.* 43 (1981), 24.

Public outreach: the cornerstone of judicial independence

Kevin M. Esterling

The ability of courts to act as independent decision makers depends on maintaining public confidence through involvement in the community.

Judicial independence is an essential component of constitutional government and the separation of powers. A politically independent judiciary serves as an important check and counterweight to the political branches and majority opinion. Courts, in turn, depend on citizen support to perform their constitutional function as independent interpreters of the law. As Alexander Hamilton wrote in *The Federalist* No. 78, courts "have neither Force nor Will, but merely judgement." If the public does not have confidence in courts' judgment, then their legitimacy and influence as democratic institutions are endangered.

The public gets much of its information about courts secondhand, mostly from the mass media and through the political process. And courts can find themselves vulnerable to the representations these outsiders give to the public. A recent American Judicature Society survey of state and federal judges in the Midwest demonstrates the difficulties for courts in relying on third parties to represent their functioning to the public, and that these dilemmas are becoming more pronounced over time. These findings suggest that judges' isolation from politics and society is increasingly insufficient to maintain judicial independence. Contrary to the traditional view of judicial independence, in contemporary society the ability of courts to act as *independent* decision makers depends on their *involvement* in local communities through various public outreach efforts.

The traditional view is that the courts' institutional legitimacy arises from decision-making fairness, a result of political independence and due process. This view was articulated, for example, in a 1986 article in *Justice System Journal,* which stated, "when individual judges render decisions fairly, responsively, and competently, the courts as an institution will presumably enjoy the respect and goodwill of the citizens." This view, however, overlooks the vulnerability of courts to media sensationalism, political campaigns against judges, and issue-oriented attacks on the outcomes of judicial deci-

sions, all of which can impair citizens' willingness to accept judicial decisions.

Criticism of judicial practices is not only a First Amendment right, it also provides judges with important feedback for improving their decision making, at minimum reminding judges that they are public servants. But as legal scholar Stephen Bright notes, irresponsible critics will occasionally frame their message in a way inappropriate to courts' role. Irresponsible critics may focus on the outcome of a decision without regard for the facts or legal reasoning underlying the decision, or single out one among many decisions a judge has made over a career.

Such critical attacks on courts appear to be on the rise. Judges, however, have limited means to respond to public criticism or to clarify the reasoning or a point of law underlying a decision, principally because of ethical restrictions on judicial speech. When a judge is constrained from responding to a public critique or attack on a judicial process or decision, the public often has no countervailing information to evaluate the persuasiveness or veracity of the message. As in any exchange of ideas, the truth of a criticism is exposed only when the audience is able to weigh a response.

Because judges have a difficult time responding publicly to criticism, their isolation from society is increasingly insufficient for maintaining their courts' legitimacy. Organized public outreach efforts instead represent the best institutional response to issue-oriented attacks on judicial decisions, inaccurate or incomplete media reporting, and citizen disenchantment, frustration, or skepticism.

Public outreach programs can benefit courts in several ways. These programs help to educate citizens about courts' role in government, which may help citizens to evaluate criticism of judges as it occurs. In addition, these programs provide a means for courts to remain in touch with, and be more responsive to, the more enduring norms of fairness and justice in the local community, as well as citizens' perceptions of the effectiveness of the local administration of justice.

Conflicting perspectives

This emphasis on public outreach is related to, but often is outside of, most debates over judicial independence. For example, many observers of courts suggest that judges can promote independence by isolating themselves from politics and the community. Several judges' remarks in the AJS survey reflect this view. One judge wrote that the greatest threat to judicial independence is the "politicization of the judiciary," especially due to judicial elections at the state level. According to another judge, the high-visibility interest group campaign in 1996 against former Tennessee Supreme Court Justice Penny White "proves that retention elections are not the sole answer" to judicial independence at the state level.

In response, other commentators voice strong democratic concerns over judicial retreats to isolation since this make judges less responsive. They object to unaccountable judges deciding underlying political or policy issues as constitutional or purely legal matters. This view is reflected in the remarks from several judges in the survey who identified the greatest threat to judicial independence as the judiciary itself. One judge wrote that the greatest threats to courts are

> Judges who exceed their role as interpreters of the law and substitute their own policy views for those of our elected officials. All of the other sources of threats . . . are reactions to perceived judicial excesses and, unfortunately, judges too often give the media and the politicians the excuse they need to attack judges.

Another judge wrote in response to a survey question that the greatest threat to judicial independence is "Judgeitis; arrogance, unaccountability. . . ."

These conflicting perspectives on judicial independence, focusing either on the importance of judicial autonomy or accountability, reflect an inevitable tension for courts in a democratic society. The democratic instinct demands both that government officials be responsive to citizens' preferences, and that the government not infringe on the rights of individuals irrespective of the popular opinion of the day. These two expectations appear in many ways contradictory, and courts often find themselves caught in between.

A middle ground to this debate holds that judicial public outreach programs aimed at maintaining the public's confidence in the courts can promote both independent and responsive judicial decision making. Public outreach programs promote judicial independence when they enable citizens to evaluate critical attacks on judges as they occur. These programs also promote judicial responsiveness to the extent they help judges know local social values and perceptions on the effective administration of justice.

In this vein, a plurality of the judges in the survey state that the problem of the independence of the courts lies in the level of public discourse on courts and the law in contemporary society. One judge wrote,

> We are living in a time in which many people decide major issues (including who to vote for) based upon sound bites: 'soft on crime,' 'anti-teacher,' 'anti-family,' 'pro-traditional values.' Politicians and the media buy into that method of communication with the public. There is little public discussion of the legal process in judicial decision making.

The media, politicians, and interest groups at times serve to elevate public dialogue on courts and the judicial process. Judges' responses to the survey show, however, that the media and political actors do not reliably represent court processes and judicial decision making to the public. Relying exclusively on these third parties is a particular concern for courts since judges have a difficult time responding publicly to criticism. In contrast, reaching out to the public can benefit courts as institutions in many perhaps unforeseen ways.

Responding to the media

Although citizens get much of their information about government from the press and other mass media, Midwest judges take a pretty dim view of how the mass media reports on courts. Ninety-seven percent of respondents to the AJS survey feel that media coverage of courts focuses on sensational or high-visibility cases. Amazingly, none of the respondents strongly disagreed with this statement or had no opinion (see Figure 1). A majority of judges who had an opinion on the matter feel that the national media's coverage of courts is not accurate, while only a bare majority feel that their local media's coverage of courts is relatively accurate.

Nearly all judges in the survey, 91 percent, indicated that they would be comfortable speaking to a reporter about an area of law or judicial process that is commonly misunderstood (exclusive of commenting on active cases) (see Figure 2). As a practical matter, how-

Figure 1. Media coverage of the courts usually focuses only on high-visibility or sensational cases.

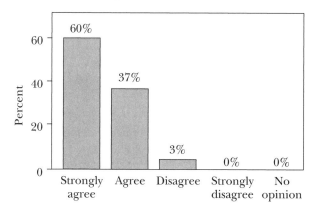

Figure 2. As a judge, I would feel comfortable speaking with a reporter about an area of law or judicial process that is generally misunderstood.

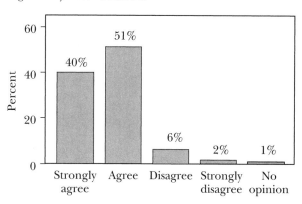

ever, judges are not very effective at communicating with the media. Professor Robert Drechsel, writing in *Judicature*, has shown that judges often do not have an established policy for how to approach the media. And, as Professor Doris Graber wrote in her book *Mass Media and American Politics* "Judges infrequently grant interviews, almost never hold news conferences, and generally do not seek or welcome media attention, primarily because they fear their impartiality might be compromised." This judicial isolation can adversely affect even the most responsible reporting. U.S. Court of Appeals Judge Bruce Selya argues that courts "impede the development of a more responsible press by turning their backs on the media."

Responding to political actors

The political process also produces information for citizens on how courts function, through such activities as election campaigns, legislative debate, and interest group grassroots efforts. The survey results show, however, that judges perceive a considerable amount of political criticism of the judiciary. Seventy-three percent of responding judges report observing what they feel are political attacks on the judiciary in their state or jurisdiction in recent years (see Figure 3). (There is no way to know if the criticisms the respondents are reporting are in fact fair or unfair, since the survey does not explicitly define what counts as an issue-oriented or political "attack" on judges. The reader should bear in mind that some judges may feel that any public statement about their work is an "attack" on their court.) Courts need to be concerned about pub-

lic criticism, irrespective of the nature or relative merits of the message, to the extent judges are unable to respond to or rebut the criticism.

More than half of the judges responding to the survey (52 percent) had themselves been publicly criticized in the past five years. Most of the first-hand criticisms that judges reported were sparked by criminal cases. Other types of cases that prompted public comment involved hot-button issues such as abortion, civil rights, death penalty, domestic violence, adoption, and relations with local Indian tribes. Some judges experienced public criticism as well for governmental process and constitutional issues, such as term limits, legislative and judicial redistricting, and religion in public life. Federal judges mention in particular labor,

Figure 3. Have there been any recent political attacks on state or federal judges in your state . . . by interest groups or politicians?

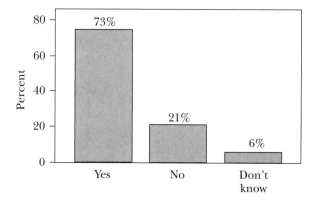

bankruptcy, and organized crime rulings as ones that sparked public criticism.

Ethical as well as some pragmatic concerns, however, will limit the extent to which a judge will be able to respond publicly to unfair or inaccurate criticism, or to some form of issue-oriented public attack. Of the 88 judges in the survey who had been recently and publicly criticized, only 9 percent responded to the criticism in some way. The most common reason judges gave for not responding was concern over violating the Code of Judicial Conduct or a feeling that it is not appropriate for, or is beneath the dignity of, judges to respond to criticism (40 percent mentioned this).

Other judges report that they did not respond to public criticism because they felt that the criticism did not warrant a response, that a response would have no effect, or would prolong the attack (38 percent mentioned one of these reasons). With respect to the media, one judge cautioned: "Don't argue with anyone who buys ink by the barrel"; another mentioned that "the media always gets the last word." On the effectiveness of responding to political actors, one judge wrote that politically-oriented attackers often do not "wish to understand the opinion and simply do not agree with it. They are entitled to their position." (Other reasons judges give for not responding to an attack are: no institutional mechanism for responding, respect for the democratic rights of citizens to complain about the government, or that the case was still pending.)

Few of these judges even attempted to respond to a public attack (7 out of 88), and only two of them felt that their response effectively countered the criticism. Those who did respond tried to speak directly to the attacking group to help them understand the legal reasoning behind their decisions, some wrote to the local newspaper, and one judge responded by making speeches on judicial independence to bar and citizens groups.

Very few of the judges who were publicly criticized report that others spoke on their behalf, and most of those speaking up were attorneys. One judge gives an illustration: "I was up for retention . . . and two weeks before the election, a PAC of the local police union, led by one officer I had taken to task, sent out 50,000 fliers and stood on street corners with signs." In response, "friends and lawyers raised $20,000 in two days for radio spots and ads." In the survey, however, only one judge reported that a citizen spoke on his or her behalf, only one judge reported a politician doing so, and only two mentioned the media speaking in support.

Figure 4. Do you feel that these attacks do serious harm to the public's opinion of the judiciary?

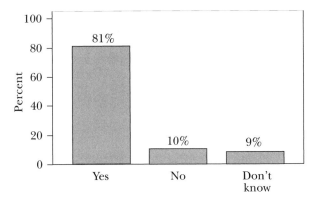

A skeptical public

Unanswered public criticism of judges may diminish the public's confidence in courts. Of those judges responding in the survey that knew of issue-oriented attacks on judges, 81 percent felt that these attacks did serious harm to the public's opinion of the judiciary (see Figure 4). The vast majority of judges responding to the survey feel that citizens are not aware of ethical constraints that prohibit judges from commenting on active cases (85 percent), or of the mechanisms in place for enforcing standards of judicial conduct (84 percent).

In addition, a large majority of responding judges, 87 percent, either agree or strongly agree with the statement that they are under increasing pressure to be directly accountable to public opinion (see Figure 5). Public pressure can affect the independent decision making not only of elected state judges, but even of the life-tenured federal judiciary. Professor Gerald Rosenberg, for instance, in his 1992 *Review of Politics* article titled "Judicial Independence and the Reality of Political Power," shows how anti-court national election campaigns historically have constrained the U.S. Supreme Court's judicial discretion. This is a concern because the role of judges in our government is to decide cases based on existing law and individual rights rather than the prevailing opinion of the day.

These statistics suggest a relatively bleak picture for courts. Judges feel that they are under pressure to be accountable to public opinion, and they perceive that public and issue-oriented criticism of judicial decisions are harming the public's confidence in courts. More and more, courts are feeling pressure from an increasingly skeptical public.

Figure 5. Within the last five years, judges are under more pressure to be directly accountable to public opinion.

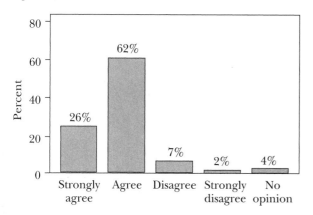

Public outreach efforts

The survey results underscore the need for courts and judges to engage in their own public outreach efforts. The vast majority of the responding judges (84 percent) feel that courts should devote more resources to public relations. One judge wrote that courts need to "educate the public concerning the functions and purposes of the judicial branch of government and how these functions and purposes differ from the legislative and executive branches."

When courts come to rely on third parties to represent their workings to the public, they have few means to respond to criticisms as they arise. When citizens better understand the role of the judicial branch, they are more likely to put criticisms in proper perspective. The earlier-mentioned article in *Justice System Journal,* for example, found that "the more attentive and knowledgeable the public becomes, the more they are able to balance the competing demands of [judicial] independence and accountability." Public outreach efforts give courts the opportunity to explain their role outside of the context of an attack on a specific decision or of a contested election, and in addition help courts remain in touch with local social values.

At the AJS Midwest Conference on State-Federal Judicial Relationships, held in the fall of 1997, judges and court staff from 13 Midwest states endorsed the need for improved public outreach efforts and issued policy recommendations for promoting an independent judiciary. Each delegation listed improved media relations and public outreach as top priorities for courts in their state, and most made public outreach the top recommendation.

Media relations. A recent Federal Judicial Center publication states that "Judicial leadership at both the state and federal level now recognize that improved public relations skills are critical for the courts to maintain a high level of public confidence." Courts are increasingly using public relations specialists, often called public information officers, to help educate reporters and editors about the courts. These officers not only respond to press inquiries, they also can develop consumer information packets and provide training for judges and court staff on how to communicate with the media. In addition, bench-bar-media committees help improve courts' relations with the media. They not only enable judges and reporters to exchange information and views outside of the context of a controversial case or disputed decision, they also give judges and reporters an opportunity to develop guidelines for covering legal matters. These committees in addition provide a forum for resolving "fair trial, free press" disputes as they arise. One of the delegations at the AJS Midwest Conference made recommendations to "establish a program of continuing legal education for the press, designate a media contact in each court (e.g. presiding or chief judge), and communicate standards of reporting on courts and the legal process to editors."

Reaching out to the public. Many court systems have established programs that directly reach out to educate the public. The Wisconsin state court system, which has a variety of public and educational outreach programs, notes in an informational brochure for the public that its efforts "are built on the notion that the courts need to work every day to strengthen their relationship with the communities they serve." Some of these programs, such as the traveling courtroom, classroom programs, and the Supreme Court's web page, seek to educate the public and provide information on how courts work. This information helps give citizens perspective when, for example, they hear criticism that focuses on the outcome rather than the substance of a particular judicial decision.

When courts reach out to the community to better involve citizens in their judicial system, they are doing more than simply educating citizens about what courts do. Public outreach efforts also give courts continuing contact with their community, and this helps them learn the community's enduring norms, standards, and perceptions of fairness. To be in contact with the community helps judges to bring a community perspective to their basic approach to decision making.

Jack Weinstein, a senior federal trial judge in New York, argued in a 1994 *Judicature* article that judges should balance judicial restraints on speaking against their ethical obligations to participate in the community and to speak on judicial matters. In this spirit, one Midwest Conference delegation suggested that: "state and federal courts should take the responsibility to educate the general public about the court system, by including them in . . . programs, and through speaking engagements and explanatory remarks in opinions and the daily work of the courts."

Public "inreach" programs, such as volunteer programs or legislative relation programs, are a particularly effective way to bring judges and court personnel into direct contact with citizens in the community. These efforts enable judges to inform their general decision making in light of local values, and can help generate feedback that enables courts to find ways to better serve the public in their policies, procedures, and the organization of facilities. As one conference delegation wrote, "Opening a two-way communication between citizens and courts can result in a win-win situation for all. The public will perceive the courts as more accessible and courts may receive information which could cause them to re-examine and improve the way they do business."

Outreach and independence

The debate between judicial independence and accountability—that independence and accountability are at odds or involve a tradeoff between fairness and responsiveness—is a product of an implicit assumption that judicial independence simply follows from judicial isolation from the community. Both sides in this debate assume that independence comes at the cost of courts' responsiveness to the local community. Judges reinforce this image in interpreting the judicial speech components of the Code of Judicial Conduct to mean that judges should not speak publicly, should shun the media, and should not actively seek advice and input from lay citizens.

The apparent tension between judicial independence and accountability implies a circular institutional logic. Courts' legitimacy rests on their independence and fairness in applying law to facts, since following majority sentiment is to predetermine the outcome in individual cases. At the same time, simply asserting the importance of judicial independence in response to a specific criticism rings hollow given democratic expectations for accountability. Judicial independence itself is vulnerable to the claim that judges are "out of touch." The problem of public criticism of courts exposes this circularity—that judicial independence rests on judicial legitimacy and vice versa—and implies that courts' best institutional response is to promote both responsiveness and independence simultaneously through greater involvement in the community, and through public education and outreach efforts.

Note

This article originally appeared in Volume 82, Number 3, November–December 1998, pages 112–118. It is based on *Judicial Independence, Public Confidence in Courts, and State-Federal Cooperation in the Midwest: A Research Report on the Midwest Regional Conference on State-Federal Judicial Relationships*, which was published by the American Judicature Society under a grant from the State Justice Institute (#SJI-97-20J-E-021). The State Justice Institute bears no responsibility for the results, analysis, or interpretations.

The Courts and Their Publics

Courts, Congress, and the Presidency

The judicial recruitment process is the most public setting for carrying out of the relationship between the courts, Congress, and the presidency. Perspectives on this interface are offered in several articles in this section. It is important to recognize, however, that there are many other matters that are of shared importance to the courts and to other institutions of American government. For example, judicial decisions based on constitutional or statutory interpretation may be the start of continuing and often heated substantive dialogue between the Court and Congress that can be marked by legislative initiatives, public posturing by legislators, and additional decisions by the courts. In the areas of greatest controversy, Congress may even use its constitutionally defined jurisdictional powers to initiate measures to alter the nature of the cases that federal courts can hear. Matters such as these are the subject of the first two selections in this section of readings.

In "Interactions between legislatures and courts," Mark Miller examines the broad parameters of the multifaceted relationship between the legislature and the judiciary. He notes at the outset that the fundamental reality is that "courts and legislatures have different institutional cultures and different institutional wills" that lead to the conclusion that "some of the difficulties in court-legislative interactions arise because each institution misunderstands the needs, the views, and the institutional realities of the other." Specifically, Miller asserts, "legislatures want courts to do justice in individual cases and to uphold the constitutionality of their legislative enactments."

The potential disconnect between divergent goals has been manifested in recent years, according to the author, by increased tensions between legislatures and the courts. Miller's article focuses on numerous facets of the interinstitutional relationship in which such tension may be felt, including legislative reactions that are critical of rulings; legislative reluctance to raise judicial salaries or provide enhanced operating budgets for courts; and legislative initiatives to overturn decisions, propose constitutional amendments, alter a court's jurisdiction or, in the most drastic scenario, pursue efforts to impeach judges. Miller paints a portrait of considerable and growing conflict that reflects "the different institutional cultures and different institutional wills that the two branches of government have."

While the possibility does exist that a legislature will react to a disagreeable ruling by pursuing legislation to overturn it, such a prospect is unlikely to occur unless the ruling is a very public, very unpopular one coming down from the U.S. Supreme Court. Given the relatively small number of cases the Supreme Court decides each year, however, and the definitive nature of the vast majority of the much more numerous decisions rendered by U.S. courts of appeals, what can be said of legislative reactions to these lower court decisions? This is the subject of Stefanie Lindquist and David Yalof's article, "Congressional responses to federal circuit court decisions." Lindquist and Yalof take note of the clear import of the circuit courts' labor. "Beyond just the overall frequency of statutory interpretation, the actual power that federal courts wield through the interpretive process should not be underestimated. When interpreting statutes in the context of individual disputes, judges can shift the focus of statutory language, nullify or frustrate congressional intent or purpose, or expand the impact of statutory provisions."

To the extent that interpretive statutory rulings from the circuit courts are both numerous and, for the most part, relatively invisible, the congressional oversight of and reaction to them cannot truly serve a policing function. Rather, as Lindquist and Yalof's empirical data suggest, Congress utilizes a "fire-alarm monitoring system" approach. Such an approach in the realm of the bureaucracy "depends on complaints ('alarms') by lobbyists for organized groups to trigger oversight of agency activities." The relative rarity of congressional responses to interpretative appeals court rulings suggests that such an alarm mechanism is at work, with Congress responding sporadically to put "out fires as quickly as possible as they arise." In such a setting, the ultimate policy authority of the circuit courts remains quite substantial.

It should be evident that the judicial selection process is a prime focal point for the president and the Senate to interface with the federal courts, often amid great controversy. In "The Senate's confirmation role in Supreme Court nominations and the politics of ideology versus impartiality," Albert Melone offers a historically driven account of the confirmation process, taking the position that it is perfectly legitimate for senators to ask questions of judicial nominees that explore their ideological preferences. Such questioning, according to Melone, has considerable precedent and was envisioned by the Constitution's framers. He concludes that, "In brief, senators should have a good idea about how future judges and justices will behave."

William Bradford Reynolds, an assistant attorney general who played a central role in judicial selection processes during the Reagan years, takes issue with and responds to Melone's analysis in "The confirmation process: too much advice and too little consent." Reynolds sees the Senate's advice and consent role as a much more constrained one than does Melone, claiming that, "The argument fashioned by Professor Melone and his like-minded academic colleagues is but an intellectual fig leaf for the senators to hide behind." Some readers may find this comment somewhat ironic, given that it comes from an individual who participated in judicial selection processes during a presidential administration often critiqued for the utilization of an ideological litmus test in the vetting of candidates for the federal bench. Perhaps an even greater irony in Reynolds's response to Melone is that it was written in the context of the pending nomination hearings for Clarence Thomas. In the author's view, Thomas was an "exceptionally well-qualified judge" who could only generate opposition for "political" reasons. Events during the Thomas hearings ultimately raised a number of concerns about his candidacy that went well beyond partisan politics, and his eventual confirmation was by the narrowest of margins and was among the most contentious in the Court's history.

As Clarence Thomas's nomination clearly demonstrated, the most public manifestation of senatorial behavior regarding advice and consent, particularly in the Supreme Court confirmation process, takes place in the setting of public Senate hearings. In "Supreme Court confirmation hearings: a view from the Senate," George Watson and John Stookey offer a broad view of the functions of such hearings and stress that even those that lack great controversy warrant public interest and attention. Based on interview data and public records of the confirmation hearings of Justices Sandra Day O'Connor and Antonin Scalia and Chief Justice William Rehnquist, the authors demonstrate that senators pursue numerous roles (evaluator, validator, partisan, educator, and advertiser) in both controversial and noncontroversial hearings, although different

roles predominate in different settings. In an addendum on the confirmation process of the Bork nomination, Watson and Stookey develop and illustrate a model of Senate hearings that is based on each hearing's degree of situational and nominee controversy and that helps to make sense of the outcomes of the Bork and other nomination battles.

The analyses of Melone, Reynolds, and Watson and Stookey hold a good deal more than historic interest. It is clear that the lower court nomination battles during the Clinton and the George W. Bush administrations ratcheted up the tensions in the advice and consent arena. During the shelf life of this edition of *Judicial Politics,* several Supreme Court vacancies are almost inevitable, as is the continued prospect of a closely divided Senate. In such a setting, the questions raised in these articles about the appropriate nature of advice and consent processes and the scenarios likely to be fraught with both situational and nominee controversy will likely remain at center stage.

This section of readings closes with two pieces that underscore the inflamed relationships between the Clinton and the George W. Bush administrations and the Senate regarding the filling of lower federal court judgeships. In "The judicial confirmation process and the blue slip," Brannon Denning offers a fascinating and detailed account of a historical but not formally codified Senate norm that has, in the past, allowed individual senators of either party to hold up and, at times, block the confirmation of lower federal court judges appointed from their states. The history presented demonstrates how the impact of a home state senator delaying or killing a candidacy by not returning a blue slip has varied under different chairs of the Senate's Judiciary Committee. Writing early in George W. Bush's first administration in the relatively brief period of Democratic control of the Judiciary Committee, Denning raises several concerns about recent uses of the blue slip system to kill, not foster, consultation on a judicial candidacy. He was hopeful that the time was then ripe to end the norm, alter it, or codify it in some form. Denning admits, however, that, "initial indications, alas, are not encouraging."

Events somewhat overtook Denning's analysis. The Democrats did not "seize the moment" as he had hoped and, since the Republican return to majority status in the Senate, there have been several instances in which blue slip "vetoes" of Bush's nominees have not been honored by the Republican leadership. Some candidates have had their nominations go through

Judiciary Committee hearings and to the Senate floor for a confirmation vote with blue slip opposition. In some instances, disruptive and highly unusual (and inflammatory) filibusters have been mounted by the Democrats to block these appointments. At bottom, at the time of this writing, lower court confirmation processes and the blue slip system examined by Denning are in a murkier and even more unsettled state than he describes.

The final piece in this section is Sheldon Goldman's effort at "Assessing the Senate confirmation process: the index of obstruction and delay." In an area dominated by charges, countercharges, and a great many rhetorical (and highly partisan) flourishes regarding who is to blame for the highly conflictual state of contemporary judicial selection processes Goldman presents a series of objective measures that allow readers to draw their own conclusions. Goldman documents that "major obstruct and delay tactics for judicial nominations started with the 100th Congress, which was the only Congress during Reagan's presidency with the Senate controlled by the Democrats." While this suggests that the Democrats planted the seeds for the judicial selection relationships during the Clinton years "with the situation reversed with a Democrat in the White House and the Republicans in control of the Senate, the evidence clearly shows that the Republicans ratcheted up obstruction and delay, with all-time records for the district and appeals courts." Goldman's obstruction and delay index also rises during presidential selection years, which suggests that while both parties have a degree of responsibility for where we are today, there are important institutional factors that come into play as well.

Interactions between legislatures and courts

Mark Miller

I think that the interactions between legislatures and courts are a vital part of the governing and lawmaking processes at both the state and federal levels. As a political scientist I approach this question from an institutional perspective, building a little bit on what we heard earlier, because I believe the courts and legislatures have different institutional cultures and different institutional wills. Thus, I believe that some of the difficulties in court-legislative interactions arise because each institution misunderstands the needs, the views, and the institutional realities of the other.

Professor Judith Resnik, who will be talking this afternoon, reminds us that the interactions between courts and legislatures can be both cooperative and conflictual. And as political scientist and now Judge Robert Katzmann of the U.S. Court of Appeals for the Second Circuit notes, "Governance is premised on each institution's respect for and knowledge of the others and on a continuing dialogue that produces shared understanding and comity." However, I feel that institutional misunderstanding is more often the norm, especially when studying the interactions between the Congress and the federal courts.

As political scientists Roger Davidson and Walter Oleszek argue, "Communications between Congress and the federal courts are less than perfect. Neither branch understands the workings of the other very well."

Different cultures

Let's take a minute to think about these different institutional perspectives or institutional cultures. And, again, these differences apply at both the state and federal level. In general, I think the courts seek an environment that is respectful of their independence. Judges clearly see themselves as part of a coequal third branch of government that deserves proper funding and proper respect.

On the other hand, legislatures want courts to do justice in individual cases and to uphold the constitutionality of their legislative enactments. Legislators may view judges as offering just one more political input into what are often highly complex political decisions.

The two institutions also approach communication very differently. About a month ago I was at a panel here in Washington where three federal judges, including [U.S. Supreme Court] Justice Stephen Breyer and two members of the U.S. Congress, as well as a law professor, discussed interactions between the Congress and the courts. I was struck by the legislators who really wanted the judges to pick up the phone and call them to talk about the issues of the day. The judges took a much less partisan, a much less political, if you will a more judicial approach. They were wary of communicating with political officials directly in many cases. And I was struck by this clear institutional difference in styles of communication.

Growing tensions

I think those institutional differences pervade some of the interactions among legislatures, courts, and the executive branch. Recently, in my opinion, it seems the tensions are growing between courts and legislatures nationwide. In fact, over the last several years, some of the justices of the U.S. Supreme Court have been highly critical of the U.S. Congress. In his last several annual reports and in other ways, Chief Justice William Rehnquist has criticized Congress for:

1) delaying the confirmation of federal judges;

2) federalizing too many crimes that he feels are better left to the states;

3) monitoring how individual federal judges deviate from the federal sentencing guidelines;

4) refusing to provide adequate salaries for federal judges; and

5) not enacting the full annual budget request for the federal judiciary.

In addition, Justice Antonin Scalia said in an April 2000 speech that Congress is "increasingly abdicating its independent responsibility to be sure that it is being faithful to the Constitution." Justice Scalia continued, "My Court is fond of saying that acts of Congress come to the Court with the presumption of constitutionality.

Judicature Volume 87, Number 5, pp. 213–216

But if Congress is going to take the attitude that it will do anything it can get away with and then let the Supreme Court worry about the Constitution, then perhaps that presumption is unwarranted."

Justice Scalia, of course, has also been a vocal critic of using legislative history material such as floor statements, committee reports, or conference reports to help courts determine the intent of Congress when interpreting congressional statutes.

On the other hand, for their part, some federal and state legislators have also been vocal critics of courts and of judges, and, of course, of specific judicial decisions. Some Republicans in the U.S. House are so upset with what they perceive as liberal activist judges that they have created a new House caucus on judicial accountability. According to a press release issued by the new caucus, called The House Working Group on Judicial Accountability, this group will educate members of Congress and the public about judicial abuses. Based on early meetings of the group House Majority Leader Tom DeLay, Republican of Texas, stated, "When it comes to judicial abuses, we are going to take no prisoners."

Attack on the courts

Ever since the beginning of our constitutional system of government, legislators have felt free to criticize specific court decisions with which they disagree. These attacks on the courts and on specific decisions of the courts were especially strong in the 1820s, the 1830s, and in the period before the Civil War.

As we heard earlier, in the 1910s and 1920s, Progressives attacked mostly the federal courts for their perceived conservative activism in promoting laissez-faire economic policies. For example, Progressive Senator Robert LaFollette was said to characterize all federal judges as "petty tyrants and arrogant despots."

In the 1930s the New Dealers and certainly President Roosevelt bitterly attacked the U.S. Supreme Court for failing to uphold the New Deal. This led, of course, to Roosevelt's proposal to pack the U.S. Supreme Court, increasing its size so that President Roosevelt would be able to appoint members of the Court who were more sympathetic to his cause.

In the 1950s and 60s conservative legislators frequently attacked decisions of the federal courts that they felt were too liberal. For example, during a debate on a bill that would have attempted to overturn a variety of Supreme Court decisions concerning the rights of criminal defendants, Senator McClellan charged that the Supreme Court wanted to, "protect and liber-

ate guilty criminals to pursue and repeat their nefarious crimes."

In 1980, Ronald Reagan ran for president, in part, on a platform that he would never appoint liberal activist judges to the federal bench. And today some conservative legislators are beginning to criticize both federal and state judges for such things as citing international precedents in their decisions.

On the other hand, lately a series of U.S. Supreme Court decisions regarding Congress's constitutional power to regulate interstate commerce and other federalism issues has brought forth pointed attacks against conservative activist judges from liberal legislators. Just as they did in the 1930s, liberals are now complaining about the evils of "conservative judicial activism."

Reactions to decisions

This new judicial activism has certainly created some disdain for some federal court rulings among liberals in Congress and has led to claims that the U.S. Supreme Court does not understand the institutional needs of Congress, nor Congress' constitutional responsibilities. As legal scholars Lewis Fisher and Neal Devins described the situation in 2001, "The Rehnquist Court may be poised to enter into a battle royale with Congress." Thus some commentators have said that this line of conservative rulings "has roots, in part, in the Court's mistrust of the national legislative process and its sense of institutional competition with Congress." Many legislators were outraged at the Court's conservative activist decisions, and in 2000 journalist Tony Mauro offered his opinion that, "The Supreme Court has declared constitutional war on Congress."

But from the other end of the political spectrum, conservative politicians have created a political firestorm over the U.S. Court of Appeals for the Ninth Circuit's decision that the Pledge of Allegiance is unconstitutional if required to be recited in public schools because it includes the phrase "under God." Conservatives were even able to get an amendment passed in the U.S. House of Representatives to prevent any federal funds from being used to enforce that court's decision. Also in response to the Ninth Circuit's controversial decision in this case, some legislators have again called for the Ninth Circuit to be split into several new circuits in order to combat the liberal tendencies that they perceive from that court.

In addition to the verbal attacks on specific court decisions and on the courts in general, legislators certainly have other tools at their disposal when they are upset about specific court decisions or perceived trends in the judiciary. For instance, of course, there can be delays in creating new judgeships to handle case backlogs, or delays in confirming judges when vacancies occur. Today we are seeing a new period of filibusters in the U.S. Senate against appointees to the lower federal courts. We have seen filibusters on Supreme Court nominees occasionally, but never have we seen filibusters before on lower federal court nominations.

Another area of legislative concern, of course, is a possible attempt to limit salary increases or money for new courthouse construction, for technology improvements, for new staff, etc. Always a major point of contention between the legislative branch and the judicial branch has been budgets for the judiciary, including of course, judicial salaries.

In 1964 the Congress was so upset with the Supreme Court that they increased salaries for lower federal judges by $7,500 per year, but only increased the salaries for Supreme Court justices by $4,500. As two political scientists writing at the time wrote, "The $3,000 differential clearly reflected a direct congressional reprimand to the Supreme Court. This crude rebuff clearly stemmed from congressional dissatisfaction with several controversial decisions rendered by the Court."

These tensions over budget issues are not new and are certainly not confined to the federal level. But in 1969, then Chief Justice Earl Warren publicly criticized Congress for ignoring the budgetary needs of the federal courts. He stated, "It is next to impossible for the courts to get something from Congress."

And as I stated earlier, Chief Justice Rehnquist has used many of his annual year-end reports on the state of the judiciary to scold Congress for not approving sufficient funds for the federal courts. Congress, on the other hand, tends to see the courts as just one more federal agency begging for money. And as former Representative Neal Smith, a longtime chair of the House Appropriations Subcommittee with jurisdiction over the judiciary's budget, has explained,

> The courts do not have many advocates in Congress. They do not have a constituency. Congress continues to pass more and more laws that require the courts to assume jurisdiction of more cases and add to their workload. Congress is eager to authorize more judges, but when it comes to paying for them, the members of Congress do not think that is a very high priority.

There are other ways, more dramatic ways, that Congress can react to court decisions. Legislators are free to pass legislation to overturn statutory decisions with which they disagree. And both state legislators and the U.S. Congress are quite likely to do that when they disagree with statutory interpretation decisions.

Legislative bodies will also pass constitutional amendments to overturn constitutionally based decisions. We have seen that at the federal level, and in my home state of Massachusetts we see the legislature debating whether they're going to enact a constitutional amendment to attempt to overturn the state supreme court's decision on same-sex marriages.

Legislators may also attempt to influence judicial decisions in more traditional, legalistic ways like sending amicus briefs to state and federal appellate courts. The legislatures are also free to enact structural changes like Roosevelt's court-packing plan, or proposals to split up the Ninth Circuit. Again in my home state of Massachusetts, in part in reaction to the state supreme court's decision on same-sex marriage, some legislators are supporting a constitutional amendment that would elect our state judges, replacing the current system of gubernatorial appointment for life terms.

Drastic measures

So legislatures clearly have ways that they can influence decisions and complain about decisions they don't like. More drastic measures include proposals to strip the courts of jurisdiction over certain cases. We've seen federal legislation introduced to prevent the courts from hearing cases on school prayer, abortion, and bussing as a remedy to school segregation, and I believe there's a new proposal to prevent the federal courts from hearing things regarding religion.

Even though there have been many bills introduced in Congress to strip the courts of jurisdiction, Congress has been very reluctant to ever enact such legislation. Legislators attack the courts, but making drastic structural change has been incredibly rare in American history.

An even more drastic proposal, I suppose, would be for legislators to impeach judges for their views or decisions. In the 1950s, after the Supreme Court decision in *Brown v. Board of Education,* we all know that many cars throughout the south and the country had "Impeach Earl Warren" bumper stickers. And more recently in 1997, then House Majority Whip Tom DeLay called for the impeachment of all federal judges who upheld affirmative action decisions.

Finally, state legislative members can certainly work to defeat elected state judges facing regular or retention elections. We've seen many states where legislatures have actively called for electoral defeats of judges. I grew up in Ohio and with its elected judges and its elected legislature, we see many times where state supreme court decisions became key political issues in races for both the judiciary and the legislature.

So I see the interactions between legislatures and courts as often being conflictual. But I don't think we should overlook the many areas in which that relationship is cooperative, however. Courts and legislatures can get along very, very well, but there are times when there are real flash points of difference. I believe that these differences, again, come down to the different institutional cultures and different institutional wills that the two different branches of government have.

There's clearly need for each branch of government to understand the needs and reality of the other branches. And I think there's more need for communication among legislators, judges, and the executive branch, both at the federal and state levels.

Note

This article originally appeared in Volume 87, Number 5, March–April 2004, pages 213–216. It was adapted from remarks made at the 2004 American Judicature Society mid-year meeting program titled "The Courts, the Legislature, and the Executive: Separate and Equal?"

Congressional responses to federal circuit court decisions

Stefanie A. Lindquist and David A. Yalof

Although Congress can counter courts' interpretations of statutes by enacting amendments to preserve or enforce legislative intent, it in fact responds with limited frequency to appeals court decisions.

Scholars, legislators, and judges have long lamented the communications gulf that exists between the United States Congress and the federal judiciary. As federal appeals court judge Robert Katzmann—a leading scholar on the subject—has explained, "legislators and staff are often not aware of relevant appellate statutory opinions, they tend not to take courts into account when writing legislation, and judges may not even be conscious of the effects of their work on congressional decision-making." [1] Still, the two institutions remain functionally dependent on one another, and each has the power to affect the other's activities.

Congress affects the federal courts' business when, for example, it passes legislation that generates increased litigation, fails to address vacancies on the federal bench, or creates new judgeships that relieve crowded dockets. Congress may also impose resource restrictions on the judiciary, whether as a reaction to legitimate overall budget concerns, or in an outright attempt to exercise leverage over a recalcitrant judiciary.[2] These issues have been discussed at length in past issues of *Judicature*, and the American Judicature Society has sponsored round tables to address the growing tensions between the two branches in recent decades.[3]

This article focuses on an equally critical facet of this interbranch relationship that often escapes the public's attention: congressional responses to the courts' various interpretations of federal statutes, particularly at levels below the U.S. Supreme Court. When interpreting statutes, federal courts directly influence the formation of federal policy in a significant way; congressional reaction to those rulings may go far in determining both branches' influence over policy making.

This statutory interpretation dialogue must be analyzed on its own merits, apart from other forms of conversation between Congress and the courts. Certainly a federal court's exercise of judicial review may represent its most dramatic and visible means of influencing

federal policy. But in truth, such instances of judicial activism occur rarely. For example, according to the Congressional Research Service, between 1941 and 1998 the Supreme Court overturned just 76 acts of Congress in whole or in part.[4] By contrast, during that same period federal judges decided literally thousands of cases involving federal statutes, injecting their own interpretation of statutory language whenever the words of the statute itself were ambiguous.

Beyond just the overall frequency of statutory interpretation, the actual power that federal courts wield through the interpretative process should not be underestimated. When interpreting statutes in the context of individual disputes, judges can shift the focus of statutory language, nullify or frustrate congressional intent or purpose, or expand the impact of statutory provisions. In this area, Oliver Wendell Holmes' astute observation that the law is "what the courts will do in fact" [5] appears particularly apt. Moreover, despite recent efforts by Congress to expedite the process of correcting "mistakes" or gaps in legislation,[6] ambiguities remain in nearly every statute on the books. Thus the meaning of statutes can be largely (if not almost entirely) shaped through the process of judicial interpretation.

Judges, practitioners, and legal scholars alike regularly lament just how difficult it is to discern congressional intent in a wide range of cases (see "For further reading," page 528). On occasion, frustrated judges may even go so far as to "invite" Congress to reverse these statutory decisions.[7] Accordingly, scholars have recently shown an increased interest in exploring the process of statutory interpretation by adjudication, as they seek to understand both whether principles of statutory construction can be developed to guide courts in the interpretive process, and whether policy-oriented judges act strategically so as to shield their interpretations from reversal by Congress.[8]

Assumptions

Both of the above areas of inquiry assume that Congress is apt to respond to courts' interpretations of federal statutes by enacting amendments to preserve or enforce legislative intent concerning the statutes' application. For example, the textualist theory of statutory interpretation advocated by Justice Antonin Scalia and Judge Frank Easterbrook suggests that judges should consult only the words within the four corners of the statute itself and eschew legislative history. According to one scholar, this textualist approach rests on the following assumption:

In the event that a statute [interpreted in strict accordance with its text] produced an absurd result, the courts would simply rule in accordance with the statute. The bad result would prod Congress into action and in the next case, clear amended statutory language would produce a more pleasing result.[9]

While this textualist position may seem intuitively reasonable, it rests on certain premises that require some empirical verification. In particular, the textualist position assumes at the outset that members of Congress are able to monitor court decisions effectively, and identify those that fail to comport with congressional preferences. In the case of Supreme Court precedents, which receive relatively full media coverage, such an assumption may be somewhat justified. But members of Congress are much less likely to stay informed about the thousands of statutory decisions rendered by the lower federal courts—most of which are never reviewed by the Supreme Court.

In addition, this theoretical position assumes that, once Congress discovers that a court's interpretation has failed to comport with congressional intent, it can generally amend such legislation quickly enough to avoid unjust results in future cases. Yet even if Congress is able to respond by passing legislation to correct an erroneous interpretation, impediments inherent to the legislative process may delay passage. And during that time the "erroneous" interpretation will continue to be followed, compounding its impact. Clearly, these empirical assumptions underlying the interpretative theory of textualism must be explored before the theory's merits can be fully assessed.

Strategic accounts of judicial decision making may also rest on some potentially flawed empirical assumptions, especially if they are applied to the courts of appeals. For example, strategic models of judicial behavior often rely on the assumption that judges may

seek to shield their decisions from legislative reversal by anticipating adverse congressional reactions. If members of Congress are generally unaware or unlikely to respond to court interpretations of federal statutes, however, it seems highly improbable that judges would take congressional reactions into account when construing federal statutes. Indeed, a fundamental assumption underlying some strategic models of judicial decision making is that Congress actually monitors and tracks unfavorable judicial decisions, since otherwise the technical threat of override would be hollow.

Theories of statutory interpretation and strategic judicial behavior thus rest on critical empirical assumptions and expectations about the relations between Congress and the federal courts. Unfortunately, little systematic research explores the extent of interaction that takes place, particularly with regard to the relationship between Congress and the lower federal courts. In fact, all previous studies of congressional responsiveness to judicial decisions focused essentially on legislative initiatives addressing Supreme Court decisions only.[10]

Certainly Congress tends not to be as aware of lower court decisions, and thus overrides a smaller percentage of them. Nevertheless, circuit court decisions interpreting statutes far exceed Supreme Court decisions both in number and in the scope of issues covered. And in some substantive areas where the Supreme Court rarely grants review, such as cases involving technical bankruptcy issues or benefits claims, the federal appeals courts enjoy the final say on most—if not all—issues of statutory interpretation. Studies of the Supreme Court's agenda-setting process indicate that the Court is less likely to take cases in certain issue areas except when necessary to resolve a circuit court conflict—particularly those that do not involve a constitutional question.[11] For these reasons, congressional responses to courts of appeals decisions often rise to the same level of significance as legislative initiatives involving Supreme Court decisions.

Congressional responses

In addition to limiting their inquiry to reactions to Supreme Court decisions, most existing studies of the cross-institutional dialogue also restrict analysis to congressional *overrides* of court decisions.[12] An override is not the only course of action available to Congress in the face of statutory construction by the courts, however. Congress may also react to judicial decisions by amending a statute to clarify an ambiguity, or it may react positively by adopting or "codifying" judicial interpretations in statutory amendments. These alternatives are especially relevant when considering decisions by the courts of appeals. If the Supreme Court's statutory interpretation is favored by Congress, the legislature has little incentive to amend the legislation, since the Court's word is final and national in scope. At the appeals court level, however, one circuit's interpretation may differ from another's, creating a conflict. In that situation, Congress may decide to amend the statute to incorporate its favored interpretation and thus avoid the potential "cacophony" of judicial pronouncements that could otherwise result.

In light of these theoretical and methodological considerations, this study explores the scope and nature of congressional efforts to override, clarify, or codify statutory decisions made at the circuit court level, based on a comprehensive review of all bills reported out of committee over the nine-year period 1990–1998. In so doing, it develops basic empirical information necessary to assess theories and models of statutory interpretation and strategic judicial behavior.

From a broader perspective, a more complete description of congressional activities in response to appellate court decision making contributes to our understanding of the policy-making process. How wide is the chasm between the courts and Congress? How much power do courts really wield in our democratic system? This study sheds light on the extent to which courts at the appellate level really do represent "the last word" on issues of national policy. In doing so, it may also influence future debates over the appropriate method of interpretation courts should use in our system of separated powers.

Data

The data for this study is derived from reports accompanying all bills reported out of Committee (Senate, House or Conference) from 1990–1998. Bills reported out of committee—unlike the larger pool of bills "introduced" or "enacted"—are most likely to reflect those congressional initiatives "that received serious consideration by the primary power brokers in Congress, the committees, and therefore represent an institutional response." [13] Since the full text of Committee Reports issued in 1990 are available through LEXIS-NEXIS Congressional Universe, a computer search was formulated to identify all instances in which a congressional committee reported on legislation responding favorably or unfavorably to a particular appeals court deci-

sion, or where it resolved a split in the circuits on a particular issue. [14]

The initial search yielded 966 Committee Reports, which were reviewed on-line. We sought to code only those references to a circuit court decision that constituted attempts to override, clarify, or codify a court of appeals decision. A legislative provision was coded as an "override" if the report indicated a specific intent to reverse the court holding; it was coded as a "clarification" if the report indicated that the committee did not desire a direct reversal, but rather expressed a need to clarify (in whole or in part) the statutory language in light of an unclear or contradictory court rulings. And a provision was coded as a "codification" where the report expressly mentioned the intent to codify the language in the opinion. For each codeable reference, we also gathered data about whether the legislature was reacting to a circuit court conflict; the subject area of the decision and proposed legislation; and whether the relevant provision was ultimately enacted.

Not all references to court of appeals decisions fit into one of our three categories of congressional "response"; counsel for the various committees and subcommittees often pepper these reports with multiple citations to cases, even though the report itself expresses no thoughts (positive or negative) about the point of law covered within. Thus from the initial pool of references we culled congressional responses to 187 individual federal appeals court decisions, whether in the form of a bill or provision in a bill reported out of committee during the period under study. Often, a bill or provision in a bill was drafted to respond to two or more actual decisions. (Thus, the number of distinct bills or bill provisions identified in the final tally was 120.)

Findings

Examination of the individual cases revealed that Congress cast its net widely; it responded to statutory cases decided by every circuit, as Table 1 demonstrates. Naturally, Congress responded to more cases from some circuits than others. The D.C. and Ninth Circuits are responded to relatively frequently. In the nine-year period studied, Congress responded to 34 decisions of the D.C. Circuit, and 28 decisions from the Ninth Circuit. This is not surprising. Although the D.C. Circuit has among the lowest caseloads of all the circuits, it renders most of its decisions in regulatory matters of central concern to important legislative programs. And the Ninth Circuit, as the largest circuit with the

Table 1. Frequency and type of congressional responses to decisions of the United States courts of appeals, 1990–1998

Circuit	Percent	Override (n)	Clarify (n)	Codify (n)	Caseload†	Rank (mean)
D.C.	18%	18	5	11	12	(742)
First	5%	6	1	3	11	(782)
Second	9%	10	3	4	8	(1774)
Third	7%	8	2	3	7	(1927)
Fourth	4%	2	1	4	4	(2567)
Fifth	8%	9	0	6	2	(3576)
Sixth	5%	4	2	4	5	(2216)
Seventh	9%	6	1	9	10	(1681)
Eighth	5%	6	0	4	6	(2080)
Ninth	15%	21	1	6	1	(4440)
Tenth	4%	4	1	3	9	(1701)
Eleventh	4%	4	2	2	3	(2846)
Federal	6%	8	2	1	—	
Totals	99%	106 (56.6%)	21 (11.2%)	60 (32%)	—	

N = 187 appeals court cases. Percents do not add to 100 due to rounding.
† Caseload mean is calculated based on average merits terminations over five-year period, 1992–1996.
Source: *Federal Court Management Statistics, 1997* (Administrative Office of the U.S. Courts).

heaviest caseload, renders the most decisions of any circuit court. Simply by virtue of the volume of its decisions, the Ninth Circuit should be more likely to provoke congressional reactions. In addition, however, the Ninth Circuit has generated much interest of late for some controversial decisions, and it has been shown that decisions of the Ninth Circuit are more likely to be reviewed by the Supreme Court in recent terms.[15] Of the remaining circuits, no pattern of response is discernible on the basis of caseload. For example, although the Fifth Circuit has the second highest caseload, Congress responded to fewer decisions rendered in that circuit than to opinions in the Second Circuit, with a much lighter caseload.

Table 1 also indicates that Congress is more likely to respond to statutory interpretation decisions rendered in the courts of appeals by seeking to override their decisions than by clarifying statutory language or codifying a court holding. More than 50 percent of the cases were responded to by a legislative initiative expressly overruling the judicial holding(s).

Congress also responded to appeals court decisions involving a wide range of issue areas. Unlike congressional responses to statutory decisions of the Supreme Court from 1967 to 1990, which were most prevalent in the area of criminal procedure, civil rights, and antitrust, congressional responses to circuit court decisions came most often in the economic regulatory

area, with more than 55 percent of all cases falling in this broad category (see Table 2).

Within the general economic category, a large percentage of cases involved the interpretation of bankruptcy and environmental statutes, highly technical statutes that generate considerable numbers of case decisions and legislative initiatives for reform each year. Moreover, in both the bankruptcy and environmental areas, a highly specialized bar exists that may play an important role in the process of statutory

Table 2. Subject matter of cases generating congressional response, 1990–1998

Issue area	Frequency	(N/%)
Criminal	16	(8.6%)
Civil rights	9	(5%)
First Amendment, due process, privacy	8	(4%)
Labor	12	(6.5%)
Judicial power	20	(11%)
Federalism	6	(3%)
Federal tax	11	(6%)
Economic activity: environment	17	(9%)
Economic activity: bankruptcy	32	(17%)
Other economic activity	55	(29.5%)

N=186. Case categories mirror those used in the Spaeth U.S. Supreme Court Database (ICPSR 9422). In one case, issue area was too ambiguous to code accurately.

Table 3. Age of circuit court decisions generating a
congressional response, 1990–1998

Age of circuit	Override (column percent)	Clarify/codify court decision (column percent)
0–2 Years	50 (47%)	32 (39.5%)
3–5 Years	36 (34%)	18 (22%)
6–10 Year	17 (16%)	19 (23%)
> 10 Years	3 (3%)	12 (15%)
Total	106	81

N=187.

reform. And in the environmental area in particular, active interest groups such as the Sierra Club and the Natural Resources Defense Council actively lobby both Congress and the courts. As a result, they may be more likely to bring adverse court decisions to the attention of members of Congress.

The data also reveal that Congress tends to respond to appeals court statutory decisions with alacrity, particularly when it intends to override those decisions. As Table 3 indicates, almost 50 percent of all congressional initiatives to override statutory decisions were reported out of committee within two years of the court decision date. And 81 percent are responded to within five years of the decision. These decisions are generally younger than Supreme Court decisions considered for override by the Judiciary Committee between 1979 and 1988, as revealed by Eskridge's 1991 study.[16] When Congress considers whether to override a federal appeals court decision, it does so quickly. On the other hand, when Congress responds neutrally or positively to a court's interpretation of a statute (i.e., by clarifying or codifying that particular holding), it tends to do so at a more relaxed pace—with 38 percent of decisions responded to even after five years had passed.

In our initial discussion, we suggested that Congress may act to resolve conflicts among the circuits, since the existence of a circuit court conflict over the interpretation of federal law undermines the uniformity of federal statutes at the national level. This phenomenon has been noted by Arthur Hellman in his work on intercircuit conflicts.[17] In recent years, the Supreme Court has been criticized for failing to grant certiorari so as to resolve existing conflicts, and Congress even commissioned a study to evaluate the scope of the problem.[18]

Of course, the Supreme Court is not the only institution that takes some responsibility to resolve circuit court conflicts. During the period we studied, Congress sought to amend existing statutes or to pass new legislation to resolve at least 19 instances of conflict among the circuits. Of the 187 appeals court cases that comprise our sample, 66 were specifically identified in the context of legislation to resolve 26 intercircuit conflicts. Table 4 presents a list of the proposed bills, the circuit court conflicts each was drafted to resolve (at least in part), and whether the bill was eventually enacted into law. This data reveals that Congress adopts some role in ensuring that its statutes are applied uniformly throughout the country, although Congress is not nearly as active as the Supreme Court in this area.[19]

Clearly Congress has assumed some role for itself as resolver of conflicts among the federal circuits, whether it does so before an interested Supreme Court seizes on that opportunity or (as is most often the case) because the Supreme Court itself shows no interest in doing so. Not surprisingly, when Congress resolves conflicts over highly technical provisions that are part of a larger regulatory scheme (e.g., federal bankruptcy provisions, federal tax provisions, etc.), its efforts go largely unnoticed—except of course by those parties with a direct interest in the provision itself. Still, Congress's role as resolver of circuit court conflicts may occasionally receive greater attention in the media and elsewhere. For example, on October 7, 1996, President Clinton signed into law the "Carjacking Correction Act of 1996," a piece of legislation whose simple purpose was to ensure that a rape perpetrated in connection with a carjacking fell within the definition of "serious bodily injury" under the statute. Why all the fuss? The Court of Appeals for the First Circuit had recently established itself to be an outlier among the circuits, holding that a rape did *not* constitute such a form of injury and thus freeing the perpetrator from enhanced penalties under the statute.

The Carjacking Correction Act represents a fairly visible example of the interbranch phenomenon. Other examples are less visible, but similarly important. Another conflict resolved by Congress considered the question whether U.S. Bankruptcy Courts had the constitutional and statutory authority to conduct jury trials in core bankruptcy proceedings. The issue initially created a conflict between the Second and Tenth Circuits, but the Supreme Court denied certiorari on a petition to resolve the conflict, even though urged by the Solicitor General to take the case. After the circuits continued to divide on the issue, Congress stepped in to resolve the conflict by amending the Bankruptcy

Table 4. Congressional efforts to resolve circuit court conflicts, 1990–1998

Bill	Congress	Bill No.	Pub. L. No.†	Circuits cited‡
Bill to Amend OSHA	105	HR 2873	—	D.C., 7, 11
IRS Restructuring and Reform Act	105	HR 2676	105-206	5, 8
Consumer Bankruptcy Reforms Act	105	S 1301	—	4, 8
Treatment of Pre-78 Sound Recordings	105	HR 1967	—	2, 9
Citizens Fair Hearing Act	105	HR 752	—	8, 9
Civil Assets Forfeiture Reform Act	105	HR 1965	—	2, 3, 4, 5, 8, 9
Continued Participation of Senior Judges in En Banc Proceedings	104	S 531	104-175	5, 7
Carjacking Correction Act	104	HR 3676	104-217	1
Common Sense Legal Reforms Act	104	HR 10	—	7
Private Securities Litigation Reform Act	104	S 240, HR 1058	104-67	2
False Statements Accountability Act	104	HR 3166	104-292	1, 2
Regulatory Fair Warning Act	104	S 343, HR 3307	—	3, 5, 7, 9
Federal Employees Fairness Act	103	HR 2721	—	2, 6
Consumer Reporting Reform Act	103	S 783	—	9
Bankruptcy Reform Act	103	HR 5116	103-394	3, 7
Bankruptcy Reform Act	103	HR 5116	103-394	3, 5, 6, 9
Bankruptcy Reform Act	103	HR 5116	103-394	2, 4, 6, 7, 8, 10
Bankruptcy Reform Act	103	HR 5116	103-394	3, 6, 7
Comprehensive Deposit Insurance Reform and Taxpayer Protection Act	102	S 543	102-242	9, 11
Insurance Competitive Pricing Act	102	HR 9	—	D.C., 2, 6
Bankruptcy Amendments	102	HR 6020	—	2, 3, 5, 9
Revenue Act	102	HR 11	—	7, 8
Revenue Act	102	HR 11	—	9, 11
False Claims Amendment Act	102	HR 4563	—	1, 9, 11
Omnibus Reconciliation Act	101	HR 3299	101-239	6, 9
Antitrust Amendments Act	101	HR 29	101-588	9, 10

† No Public Law No. cited if bill was not passed or was vetoed.

‡ Although the Report may only cite one circuit as an example, we coded the bill as resolving a conflict when the Report otherwise indicated in text that the issue had raised a conflict among multiple circuits.

Code to allow bankruptcy courts to conduct jury trials. Unlike the carjacking cases, these bankruptcy disputes were not prominent news. But given the critical role juries play in our justice system, congressional resolution of this conflict was significant.

Theoretical framework

Congress reacts to statutory decisions of a federal appeals court either by overturning, clarifying, or endorsing individual court holdings. What theoretical framework might explain these patterns of response? Several recent studies sought to construct broader theories of congressional motivation to reverse court decisions. Perhaps the most prominent theoretical perspective now offered to explain cross-institutional interactions between the Supreme Court and Congress is grounded in Positive Political Theory, which presents a strategic picture of the interdependence between court decisions and legislative response. In brief, this theory

suggests that policy-driven political actors anticipate the responses of other relevant political actors when making decisions. Thus, Supreme Court justices will interpret statutes as consistent with their own ideological preferences as possible without being overturned by Congress. And Congress will override the Supreme Court's statutory interpretations only when the median legislators in the House and the Senate prefer to change the status quo created by the Court's opinion and enjoy (at the least) a veto-proof majority.

In contrast to congressional responses to the Supreme Court, however, strategic accounts of legislative responses to appeals court decisions must accommodate a far more complex and multidimensional world. Indeed, in the case of appellate court decisions interpreting federal statutes, Congress is faced with thousands of decisions each year of potential relevance, in contrast to yearly consideration of less than 100 Supreme Court decisions in recent terms. Any theory of congressional responses to appeals court decisions, therefore, must assume a considerable information deficit on the part of Congress.

How does Congress monitor the often critical but exceedingly numerous decisions made by the courts of appeals that affect the implementation of federal programs? Scholars of the bureaucracy have proposed a theory of congressional oversight that provides one possible explanation. McCubbins and Schwartz sought to determine "whether, to what extent, and in what way Congress attempts to detect and remedy executive-branch violations of legislative goals." [20] Exactly the same question could be posed vis-à-vis judicial interpretations of federal statutes that similarly "violate or undermine legislative goals." In the context of bureaucratic politics, McCubbins and Schwartz argue that Congress does not neglect its agency oversight responsibility, but rather demonstrates a rational preference for one form of oversight ("fire-alarm oversight") over another ("police patrol oversight").

Police patrol oversight features the active and systematic surveying or sampling of all agency decisions. Given the enormity of such a task, however, McCubbins and Schwartz suggest that Congress often relies on a fire-alarm monitoring system which depends on complaints ("alarms") by lobbyists for organized groups to trigger oversight of agency activities. Finally, under a fire alarm system of oversight, Congress puts out fires as quickly as possible as they arise, rather than waiting for the issue to develop (or "percolate") fully in the legal forum. Given the mixed frequency but considerable speed with which Congress appears to act in response to appeals court decisions, the "fire-alarm oversight" model seems on the whole most applicable to analysis of congressional responses to circuit courts' interpretations of federal statutes.

The roll of professionals and experts in the process of statutory reform must also be noted. In a recent book on the bankruptcy law reform process, Carruthers and Halliday describe a theory of statutory reform based on the influence of professionals and experts (such as lawyers, judges, and administrators) in the implementation process. "Statutory reform begins for many reasons, but chief among them is the belief among reformers that law and practice diverge too much (and thus that professional creativity has been too successful)." [21]

This disjuncture between law-on-the-books and law-in-practice may come to light through the process of adjudication, as lawyers persuade judges to follow a particular interpretation that may diverge from the original or current legislative intent. Carruthers and Halliday's emphasis on the role of professionals in both the implementation and reform process suggests that statutory reform is most likely to take place in issue areas involving a highly professionalized environment and an active bar. Their hypothesis appears to be confirmed by our own findings: highly specialized regulatory schemes such as bankruptcy and superfund legislation draw disproportionate attention from Congress, at least at the courts of appeals level.

Finally, our findings shed some light on the debate regarding theories of statutory interpretation. Table 1 confirms the suspicions of many that Congress responds to only a minute percentage of cases decided by the courts of appeals, even though the majority of appeals court decisions involve the application of federal statutes. Of the responses to 187 specific cases, provisions involving only 65 cases were actually enacted (three bills were vetoed). Of course, one possible explanation is that Congress is generally happy with judicial interpretations. But since our study also incorporated codifications and clarifications, it appears that Congress may simply be unaware of appeals court decisions, a conclusion that has been suggested by others as well.[22] Thus, any textualist theory of statutory interpretation suggesting that Congress will respond to absurd or incorrect judicial interpretations has little empirical foundation, at least in the courts of appeals. The judiciary cannot "discipline" Congress into writing clearer statutes if Congress is unaware of the disciplinary action.

Raising questions

This study raises questions about applying strategic models of legislative-judicial interactions to the congressional reactions to the courts of appeals, particularly to the extent such models assume that members of Congress have the time, resources, and information necessary to monitor comprehensively the statutory interpretation decisions that emanate from the federal courts of appeals, and then to respond to those decisions efficiently and effectively. Scholars infer from such models that courts need to be wary of Congress's potentially adverse reaction to the exercise of statutory interpretation. Yet our analysis reveals that Congress in fact responds with extremely limited frequency to appeals court decisions, and often does so merely to ensure the uniformity of federal law. In addition, the analysis suggests that when Congress seeks to override a court interpretation, it does so quickly—typically within five years of the court's decision. On the other hand, it tends to respond favorably to court decisions (through codification, for example), at a somewhat more measured pace.

A number of research questions remain. First, the nature of the circuit court decisions that triggered the congressional reaction must be explored, including the involvement of interest groups and the existence of dissenting opinions. From the standpoint of statutory interpretation, the court decisions themselves must be examined to identify the method of statutory interpretation followed by the court. As mentioned above, some scholars advocate a textualist approach to interpretation so as to compel Congress to draft statutes more carefully. Yet if Congress consistently overrides decisions rendered without recourse to legislative history, it may be sending a message that courts should not ignore legislative intent. And such an inquiry may also reveal how or why courts misunderstand legislative intent if they are overridden after seeking to understand the legislature's underlying purpose. Indeed, federal judges may invite congressional response in the face of confusion over congressional intent. Finally, it is imperative to explore the extent to which ideology shapes contours of the cross-institutional dialogue. Positive political theory highlights the importance of ideology as the triggering mechanism for congressional response. Yet many of the legislative initiatives coded for this database had no clear ideological direction. An examination of the actual appeals court decisions themselves may reveal that dimension more clearly.

Notes

This article originally appeared in Volume 85, Number 2, September–October 2001, pages 60–68.

1. Katzmann, *Courts and Congress* (Washington D.C.: Brookings Institution Press, 1997), 80.

2. Congress may respond to judicial decision making in other ways as well. For example, it may react to the courts through the passage of jurisdiction-curbing legislation that eliminates judicial influence in a particular policy area. *See* Jackson, "Introduction: Congressional Control of Jurisdiction and the Future of the Federal Courts—Opposition, Agreement and Hierarchy," *Georgetown L. J.* 86 (1998), 2445; Resnick, "The Federal Courts and Congress: Additional Sources, Alternative Texts, and Altered Aspirations," *Georgetown L. J.* 86 (1998), 2589. Congress may also tailor the scope of judicial review in order to minimize (or maximize) courts' involvement in the implementation of certain legislative programs. *See, e.g.,* Shipan, *Designing*

Judicial Review (Ann Arbor: University of Michigan Press, 1997).

3. Katzmann, "Perspectives on Court-Congress Relations: The View from the Hill and the Federal Bench," *Judicature* 79 (1996), 303; Katzmann, "Building Bridges Instead of Walls: Fostering Communication Between Judges and Legislators," *Judicature* 75 (1991), 167.

4. "The Constitution of the United States of America: Analysis and Interpretation," *S. Doc. No.* 103–106 (1992 and Supp. 1998).

5. Holmes, "The Path of the Law," *Harv. L. Rev.* 10 (1897), 457, 461.

6. In early 1995, House Speaker Newt Gingrich (R-Ga.) proposed the regular scheduling of a day on which the House would enact legislation designed to correct statutory mistakes. Nagle, "Corrections Day," *U.C.L.A. L. Rev.* 43 (1996), 1267. The procedures offered Congress the opportunity to revisit and revise statutes "at a much smaller institutional cost than the existing mechanisms for congressional action." Ibid. at 1319.

7. *E.g.* Hausegger and Baum, "Inviting Congressional Action: A Study of Supreme Court Motivations in Statutory Interpretation," *Am. J. Pol. Sci.* 43 (1999), 162.

8. Scalia, *A Matter of Interpretation* (Princeton: Princeton University Press, 1997); Eskridge, "Post-Enactment Legislative Signals," *Law and Contemp. Prob.* 57 (1994), 75; Segal, "Serparation of Powers Games in the Positive Theory of Congress and the Court," *Am. Pol. Sci. Rev.* 91 (1997), 28; Spiller and Gely, "Congressional Control or Judicial Independence: The Determinants of U.S. Supreme Court Labor-Relations Decisions, 1949–1988," *Rand J. of Econ.* 23 (1992), 463.

9. Stearns, ed., *Public Choice and Public Law: Readings and Commentary* (Cincinnati, Ohio: Anderson Press, 1997), 721.

10. In his 1991 study, Eskridge did explore incidents of congressional overrides of lower court decisions from 1967 to 1990 (including appeals court, district court, bankruptcy court, etc.), but he did so incidentally as part of his larger study of congressional overrides of Supreme Court decisions. Eskridge, "Overriding Supreme Court Statutory Interpretation Decisions," *Yale L. J.* 101 (1991), 331, 337 n.12.

11. Pacelle, *The Transformation of the Supreme Court's Agenda: From the New Deal to the Reagan Administration* (Boulder Colo.: Westview Press, 1991).

12. For one notable exception, *see* Henschen, "Statutory Interpretations of the Supreme Court: Congressional Response," *Am. Pol. Q.* 11 (1983), 441, although the scope of her study was limited to two issue areas before the Supreme Court: labor and antitrust.

13. Igagni and Meernik, "Explaining Congressional Attempts to Reverse Supreme Court Decisions," *Pol. Res. Q.* 47 (1994), 353, 364.

14. Several reports on bills introduced in 1989 were available through the LEXIS-NEXIS database used for this study, presumably because the reports were eventually issued in 1990; we used these few reports in our data collection effort. For the most part, however, bills reported out of the 101st Congress during its first session (1989) were not available in the LEXIS-NEXIS database. The following search was constructed: (divide or split or conflict or overrule! or overturn! or override! or reverse! or clarify! or codify! or adopt or intent! or purpose or interpret!) w/100 (f.2d or f.3d or circuit or "courts of appeals" or "court of appeals" or "appeals court"). This same search was used in the Westlaw Legislative History database to ensure accuracy and to serve as a reliability check.

15. Farris, "The Ninth Circuit—Most Maligned Circuit in the Country—Fact or Fiction?" *Ohio St. L. J.* 58 (1997), 1465; Wasby, "The Ninth Circuit and the Supreme Court: Relations Between Higher and Lower Courts," Paper presented at the Annual Meeting of the American Political Science Association, Boston (1998).

16. *Supra* n. 10.

17. Hellman, "Light on a Darkling Plain: Intercircuit Conflicts in the Perspective of Time and Experience," *1998 Sup. Ct. Rev.* (1999), 247.

18. *See* Tiberi, "Comment: Supreme Court Denials of Certiorari in Conflicts Cases: Percolation or Procrastination?" *U. Pitt. L. Rev.* 54 (1993), 861; Hellman, *Unresolved Conflicts: The Nature and Scope of the Problem, Final Report: Phase I* (Washington D.C.: Federal Judicial Center, 1991).

19. For example, in the 1989 to 1991 Terms, the Supreme Court resolved some 95 instances of conflicts among the circuits. Lindquist, "The Judiciary as Organized Anarchy: Intercircuit Conflicts in the Federal Appellate Courts." Paper presented at the Midwest Political Science Association, Chicago, IL (2000).

20. McCubbins and Schwartz, "Congressional Oversight Overlooked: Police Patrols and Fire Alarms," *Am. J. Pol. Sci.* 28 (1984), 165.

21. Carruthers and Halliday, *Rescuing Business; The Making of Corporate Bankruptcy Law in England and the United States* (Oxford: Clarendon Press, 1998), 54.

22. *See* Katzmann, *supra* n. 1.

For further reading: judicial perspectives on court-congress relations

Friendly, Henry J. "The Gap in Lawmaking—Judges Who Can't and Legislators Who Won't," *Columbia L. Rev.* 63 (1963), 787.

Ginsburg, Ruth Bader, "A Plea for Legislative Review," *S. Cal. L. Rev.* 60 (1987), 995.

Ginsburg, Ruth Bader, and Peter W. Huber, "The Intercircuit Committee," *Harv. L. Rev.* 100 (1987), 1417.

McGowan, Carl. "The View from an Inferior Court," *San Diego L. Rev.* 19 (1982), 659.

The Senate's confirmation role in Supreme Court nominations and the politics of ideology versus impartiality

Albert P. Melone

Nothing in the Constitution, historical experience, political practice, ethical norms, or statutory enactments prohibits senators from asking questions that reveal judicial nominees' views on political and ideological issues.

Controversy surrounds the appropriate role of the United States Senate in exercising its constitutional responsibility of advice and consent. Conservative thinkers and propagandists, right-wing politicians, and others question whether the Senate should rightly concern itself with anything more than the professional qualifications of judicial nominees. The Senate's rejection of Judge Robert Bork's nomination to the Supreme Court is touted as a particularly egregious example of the Senate exceeding its constitutional responsibility.[1] Senator Orrin Hatch of Utah termed the Bork hearing an "... ideological inquisition."[2] Iowa's Senator Charles Grassley charged that Bork's critics "... prefer judges who will act as some kind of super legislature who will give them victories in the courts when they lose in the legislature."[3] Senator Gordon Humphrey of New Hampshire said that the charges against Bork are "pure political poppycock, 99.9 percent pure, so pure it floats."[4]

Nominees are not passive targets of ideological interrogation. They often refuse to answer questions designed to illicit answers about their judicial attitudes. They do so by appealing to the often misunderstood but powerful norm of judicial impartiality. They state that if they reveal their attitudes today about a case that may come before them tomorrow as sitting jurists they will be unable to participate fairly in decision making. Disqualification and recusation is the only honorable course in such a situation, so goes the refrain. Silence, it is believed, is a better course than failing to decide at all.[5]

It is my view that senators may reasonably inquire into and base their final decision to confirm or reject presidential choices on factors other than the nominees' personal and professional qualifications. Senators may legitimately ask nominees about their political and judicial ideology as it may manifest itself in judicial decision making. I base this conclusion upon an analysis of three related factors.

First, the constitutional framers did not intend the Senate to be a rubber stamp for presidential appointments. The advice and consent clause of the Constitution justifies an independent scrutiny of nominees by members of the Senate.

Second, the historical record reveals that from the beginning of the Republic the Senate has rejected nominees for reasons other than personal and professional qualifications. In one fashion or another, political considerations, including evaluations of the ideological soundness of nominees, influence Senate advice and consent decisions.

Finally, I will clarify the claim that nominees should not give answers to questions that may bring into question their impartiality. Nominees may conduct themselves before Senate hearing panels with honor and probity while at the same time providing vital political information. Properly understood, statutory and ethical norms do not prohibit nominees from revealing their views on the great issues of the day.

The meaning of advice and consent

The plain words of the Constitution suggest that the framers contemplated a sharing of responsibility between the executive and legislative branches. Yet a striking feature of this sharing arrangement is the placement of the appointment and confirmation functions in Article II—the executive article—not Article I—the legislative article. Section 2 of Article II provides that the president shall have the power to nominate by and with the consent of the Senate. Clearly, the president may select the persons he or she wants to nominate. The Senate may advise the chief executive on the initial selection, but it may not select particular nominees. Through its consent function, the Senate has the power to accept or reject presidential choices. Therefore, it is erroneous to conclude, as Richard Nixon once did, that the president may name whomever he pleases without senatorial checks.[6] Indeed, a literal interpretation of the Constitution does not indicate any boundaries for senatorial consent. The Constitution's plain words do not prescribe or dictate justification for confirming or rejecting nominees. Moreover, because the Constitution is a document limiting the use of power that derives its authority from the consent of the governed, and since the advice and consent provision of Article II does not impose any limit to its discretion, it is fair to conclude that the Senate may use its constitutional authority as it sees fit. It may do so for whatever reason, be it professional qualifications, personal integrity, or political and ideological considerations.

Investigating beyond literal interpretation to the framers' probable intent reinforces the shared responsibility view. However, historical evidence introduces ambiguity otherwise not present with the more simplistic literalism approach.

The records of the Philadelphia Convention reveal that the shared responsibility feature of the nomination process was the result of compromise,[7] as is the explanation for many other constitutional provisions.[8] Choices presented by the competing Virginia and New Jersey plans framed many of the debates held in Philadelphia. The original Virginia Plan, the basic proposal supported by the large states, sought to locate the appointment of judges in the two legislative chambers. On at least two occasions, however, James Madison expressed the fear that members of the more numerous branch would be ill-suited to evaluate prospective judges. He thought they might select judicial candidates for the poor reason that they were particularly talented legislators or because the aspirants had assisted ignorant legislative members in their own businesses or those of their constituents. On the other hand, the Senate, being an unelected body and therefore a more select group of persons, would be better qualified to evaluate the abilities of candidates with a higher regard for qualifications.[9] William Paterson, the author of the small state plan called the New Jersey Plan, and James Wilson argued for appointment by the executive alone.[10]

Alexander Hamilton informally suggested what finally emerged as the convention's final recommendation, and the one ultimately ratified by the states. In their initial voting, convention delegates rejected both the plan granting advice and consent to the Senate and a proposal to place the appointing authority in the president alone. Instead, what survived until the final days of the convention was a provision granting the appointing power to the Senate alone. Then, finally, in the last days of the convention, there emerged from the Committee of Eleven the present system: nomination by the president, and advice and consent of the Senate.[11]

As is often the case when attempting to identify the framers' original intention, the precise reasons for the compromise are unknown. However, James E. Gauch, the author of a recent and carefully conducted study, reasonably concludes that the framers were concerned with three related issues: the ability to evaluate potential nominee qualifications; the matter of corruption and intrigue in the nomination process; and finally the matter of small versus large state interests.[12] The import of Gauch's finding is that the framers' concerns went beyond good character and professional qualifications of future judicial office-holders. In one form or another, politics entered their thinking.

Analyzing the ratification debates adds somewhat to our total understanding of the framers' intent. But reading too much into a few paragraphs may result in overstating the case. Alexander Hamilton's *The Federalist* 66 and 76 are the authoritative source for evidence of the framers' intent as expressed during the ratification debate.[13]

Without question, Hamilton reinforces a plain meaning interpretation of the advice and consent provision. To that end, the Senate's role is properly confined to the confirmation or rejection of presidential nominees. *The Federalist* 66 reads:[14]

> There will, of course, be no exertion of choice on the part of the Senate. They may defeat one choice of the Executive and oblige him to make another; but they cannot themselves choose—they can only ratify or reject the choice of the President.

The Senate, then, is a major player in the selection drama. However, the chief executive plays a leading role because he or she is in the position of submitting the names of only those persons thought desirable. For what reason then require senatorial consent? Hamilton's answer is instructive. He writes:

> I answer, that the necessity of their concurrence would have a powerful, though, in general a silent operation. It would be an excellent check upon the spirit or favoritism in the President, and would tend greatly to prevent the appointment of unfit characters from state prejudice, from family connection, from personal attachment or from a view to popularity.[15]

Thus, at the very least, the Senate must act as a check against a president who might appoint persons of unfit character. Further, the Senate is in a position to embarrass a chief executive for such attempts. The Senate's institutional leverage will deter presidents from such conduct. Hamilton makes this point by writing:

> ... It will readily be comprehended, that a man who had himself the sole disposition of offices, would be governed much more by his private inclinations and interests than when he was bound to submit the propriety of his choice to the discussion and determination of a different and independent body. . . .[16]

Wrong reasons

Hamilton contributes two major points to our understanding. First, he reinforces the literal understanding of the advice and consent clause; namely, the appointment power is a shared responsibility between the president and the Senate. Second, upper house concurrence is a requisite because the chief executive might otherwise appoint persons for the wrong reasons. Hamilton indicates four wrong reasons for appointment. These are: the appointment of unfit characters "from state prejudice," "from family connection," "from personal attachment," or "from a view to popularity." Do these four justifications for senatorial denial of presidential choices pertain to ideological tests for office? The probable answer is yes.

First and paramount, Hamilton's words commit senators to inquire beyond personal and professional qualifications. It requires the Senate to ascertain whether nominees are associated with the president in any of the four ways. If they are, it does not necessarily mean that the nominees are unqualified to serve. It means that the relationship between the president and the nominees bears scrutiny.

Second, each of the four points have ideological elements. In the context of the eighteenth century, "state prejudice" meant more than good will toward one's neighbors. It also signified common points of view or shared consciousness about the political order. Carolinians two centuries ago, as they do even today, had a different perspective on political events than, for example, do New Yorkers. Indeed, these differences, that are easily describable as ideological, were a source of political disagreement current at the Philadelphia Convention. Appointing persons "from family connection" and "from personal attachment" likewise have ideological dimensions. Conventional wisdom and mod-

ern social science informs us that the family is a strong socializing agent, inculcating attitudes and beliefs including those concerning politics.[17] Further, persons often choose friends who share basic values and attitudes. Finally, appointing persons "from a view to popularity" reasonably entails situations wherein presidents appoint persons meeting with popular approval. Persons with ideological views consistent with those of either elite decision-making bodies, such as the Senate or wider publics, are likely to be popular. The president may then be applauded for his outstanding choices, thereby increasing the value of his political currency.

Third, by his words Hamilton does not exclude any of the four unacceptable reasons as factors in a president's or senator's nomination or a confirmation calculation. He objects to persons named to the judiciary who have "*no other merit than* . . . coming from the same State . . . or being in some way or other personally allied to him, or of possessing the necessary insignificance and pliancy to render them the obsequious instruments of his pleasure."[18] It is perfectly acceptable, therefore, for a president to nominate an individual of personal and professional qualifications who also comes from a preferable state or region, has family connections, is well-liked by the president, and enjoys widespread popularity.

It is conceivable and probable that each of the four reasons for Senate concern contain non-ideological components. However, understood within the context of the time, Hamilton's words leave little doubt that ideology as a belief system, and as reflected in one's character, renders legitimate Senate inquiries into matters other than narrowly conceived personal and professional qualifications.

James E. Gauch suggests that Hamilton's reference to the Senate having a responsibility to explore the "propriety" of executive choices commits senators to look beyond the professional and personal qualifications of the nominees.[19] However, it is unclear to me that Hamilton uses the word "propriety" to mean anything more than a summary term for the four unacceptable reasons for solely nominating persons to the bench: cronyism, family connections, favoring one state over others, or responding to the popular will regardless of qualifications. If this is true, then the word "propriety" is a redundancy and little more than a convenient use of language.

The search for intention is an interesting exercise. Although others have come to conclusions different from the one found here, the weight of the evidence tends to justify Senate inquiries into nominees' ideology. However, the search for original intention in this case does not render other interpretations incorrect. There is no evidence that the framers explicitly debated in the eighteenth century what is today a central concern. Unless an issue is explicitly discussed and a record of that debate is available, what the framers really intended remains a matter of intellectual speculation and curiosity.

I suspect there was no full debate and discussion of the appropriate reasons for rejecting nominees, including an explicit analysis of the proper place for ideological inquiries, because it did not occur to the framers that future judges and justices would be asked to perform anything more than traditional judicial tasks. Surely the framers did not anticipate the considerable institutional authority courts now enjoy. There is considerable doubt the framers envisaged courts with the power to strike down acts of Congress: statutes and administrative acts unrelated to the jurisdiction of the Supreme Court.[20] They could not have imagined an institution as central to the American political system as the contemporary Supreme Court has become.

However, given the framers' clear preference for checks on power, and the institutional importance played by the judiciary today, it seems reasonable that they would consider, as do many contemporary senators, the ideology of unelected and unaccountable lawmakers as appropriate objects of inquiry by a popularly elected body. Senators must respond to the constitutional facts of life as they find them. The living constitution requires the responsible evaluation of potential judicial lawmakers whose eighteenth-century counterparts enjoyed a different kind of status.

Nominee bashing: the historical record

An examination of past Senate practices reveals the considerable extent to which judicial nominees are evaluated on political and ideological grounds. Otherwise well-qualified persons are rejected for a variety of political reasons. Further, contrary to the supposition of some commentators,[21] nominations preceding the 1987 Robert Bork debacle were marked by questions and speculations concerning the ideological fitness of presidential nominees. Judge Bork's case is dramatic because the nominee himself was more than willing to enter into intellectual discourse, thereby revealing his controversial policy inclinations. The existing literature contains several different classification schemes defining the various reasons judicial nominees are rejected by the Sen-

ate. Depending upon the purpose, the adoption of one scheme over another can be important. What is pertinent to note, however, is that all the schemes point out that past nominees were evaluated on political grounds unrelated to professional qualifications.[22]

During the first decade after the adoption of the 1789 Constitution, the Senate rejected a person for reasons unrelated to professional competence. An extremely well-qualified justice of the South Carolina Supreme Court was rejected because he angered powerful Federalist politicians with his vigorous denunciation of the controversial Jay Treaty.[23] Most Federalists viewed support for the treaty as a true indicator of party loyalty, while Republicans thought the treaty an unnecessary concession to British might. The vote to reject John Rutledge was 14 to 10; it was a party vote with 13 Federalists voting against, and only three voting for confirmation. The remaining votes to confirm came from Anti-Federalists.[24] The Rutledge episode is an early example of how politicians mask their real political reasons for opposing candidates by attacking nominees' personal and professional qualifications. Historians point out that Rutledge was attacked falsely as mentally unsound, and therefore unfit for Supreme Court service. The Federalist press employed this malicious tactic rather than stating the true reason for Federalist opposition. They realized that the Jay Treaty was so unpopular that to publicly attack Rutledge for his opposition to it would cause a political backfire.[25]

There are many other examples of nominee-bashing for reasons unrelated to professional competence. The Senate defeat of President James Madison's nomination of Alexander Wolcott was due in large part to the nominee's opposition to the enforcement of embargo and intercourse acts when he was U.S. collector of customs in Connecticut. Federalist senators and the press opposed him for this reason, although, in fairness, there were authentic questions raised about Wolcott's judicial qualifications.[26] An otherwise well-qualified Grant appointee, Ebenezer R. Hoar, suffered rejection because as attorney general he championed the merit system in government. He also drew fire from radical Republicans because of his earlier opposition to the impeachment of President Andrew Johnson.[27]

Harlan Stone's 1925 appointment is the first time a nominee appeared before the Senate Judiciary Committee to explain himself. Senators questioned his qualifications because of his prosecution as attorney general of a senator for participation in an oil and land fraud deal.

There was vigorous Senate floor debate when his nomination came before the entire body; the nomination was recommitted for further consideration to the Senate Judiciary Committee. Unfortunately, transcripts of that appearance are unavailable, but a biographer describes it as an impressive performance that served to vindicate Stone's nomination.[28]

Nominees have been rejected by the Senate for local political reasons having little if anything to do with their professional ability. Senators concerning themselves with their political power bases have invoked senatorial courtesy to block confirmation of presidential nominees. The Senate's rejection of President Polk's 1845 nomination of George Woodward resulted in large part because of home state opposition. A year earlier, in 1844, senatorial courtesy was invoked and was a lesser factor in the defeat of President Tyler's nomination of Reuben H. Walworth. President Cleveland had two nominations defeated when in each case the Senate would not confirm a nominee who was opposed by the senior senator in the president's party from the nominee's state.[29] There are many more instances of its invocation for lower federal court judges, but the point is indisputable.

The twentieth century

The matter of evaluating nominees primarily on ideological grounds is better documented for the present century than for the previous one. There are at least two interrelated explanations. First, in the twentieth century the Senate has become more responsive to popular control. In a recent paper, Charles R. Epp points out that by 1913 the Seventeenth Amendment had shifted the Senate's electoral base from the state legislatures that had theretofore named senators to the popular electorate. This institutional shift in accountability may have made senators more sensitive to interest-group and grassroots awareness of judicial policy making.[30] Second, it may be that judicial ideology played a more limited and ordinarily a less-obvious role during the first century of the Republic than it does today. During the first 100 years of the Republic, only 17 acts of Congress were declared unconstitutional, but in the next 90 years the Court struck down 87 more, an increase of more than 400 percent.[31]

In the nineteenth century there were fewer controversial Supreme Court opinions. Then the full scope of the Court's real and potential ability to affect public policy was not fully understood. However, late in that century and in the first third of this century, the Court's role in policy making became a matter of considerable debate. It became clear that Supreme Court justices exercise their discretion in dramatic ways, including striking down popular congressional acts and state laws. The Court had become a bastion of conservative ideology.[32] By the mid-1960s, it became equally clear that the Court had again become a policy maker; this time, however, it was a vehicle for liberal causes, and once again, many of its decisions were unpopular.[33] In short, because the stakes are high, the judicial philosophy and ideology of potential jurists have become a subject of close scrutiny.

President Wilson's appointment of Louis Brandeis is an early twentieth-century example of how ideology has had a probable impact on the selection process. Wilson attempted to name the brilliant Brandeis as attorney general but met considerable opposition from the elitist Boston bar. When that appointment failed, Wilson pledged to name Brandeis to the next important vacancy. That position turned out to be the Supreme Court. The Brandeis appointment was put off for months as the Senate took volumes of testimony. Much of the opposition was due to the liberal crusader's so-called radical views and his sociological jurisprudence. There is also evidence of an unhealthy dose of antisemitism. But many, including William Howard Taft, were opposed to Brandeis for other reasons, including his views in support of the working classes and his alleged animosity toward big business.[34]

Ideology was a factor in 1930 with the nominations of two otherwise well-qualified persons. Charles Evans Hughes was attacked because, among other reasons, he was regarded by liberal senators as a tool of corporate power, and conservative southerners opposed him as a city slicker who stood against states' rights.[35] The Senate rejected John J. Parker on a close vote due in large measure to opposition generated by the American Federation of Labor and the National Association for the Advancement of Colored People. Parker was thought unfriendly to labor, and he was under attack, probably erroneously, as a racist. There would be no other Senate rejection of a presidential Supreme Court nominee for 40 years.[36]

New Deal opposition to the High Court was transparently ideological. There was an attempt to disguise the ideological source for the conflict by appealing to another motive. President Roosevelt presented his ill-fated Court-Packing plan as a way to relieve elderly justices from a heavy workload. This obvious attempt by the president to change the decision-making composition of the Court by increasing the number of justices was not lost even among the most casual observers. The plan failed to receive congressional approval, but not because members revered the Court and wanted to protect it from institutional attack. As Schmidhauser and Berg point out, an ideologically conservative coalition existed in Congress before FDR introduced his plan. It coalesced before and functioned after the 1937 Court-Packing congressional vote. The purpose of this coalition was to put the brakes on the New Deal.[37] Though the Court-Packing episode did not involve the confirmation of particular justices, it demonstrates that members of Congress viewed the Court in ideological terms. They did not want to give Roosevelt an opportunity to appoint to the Court a sufficient number of persons who would vote to support New Deal programs and goals. Roosevelt ultimately got his way when the Supreme Court began to uphold New Deal initiatives to save the nation's economy from ruin. The lesson is clear. Ideology has been a prominent factor in inter-branch governmental conflicts.[38]

The Warren Court Era (1952–1969) was another period in this century when the Supreme Court came under severe attack. Decisions concerning such matters as segregation, internal security, school prayer, and criminal justice precipitated hostile reaction in and out of Congress. Many of these issues remain hotly contested into the 1990s, and so does the proper role of the Supreme Court.

Warren Court opponents used the occasion of Thurgood Marshall's 1967 nomination to attack the Court's decisions. Southern senators on the Judiciary Committee, including John McClellan, Samuel Ervin, and Strom Thurmond, questioned Marshall, a former solicitor general and then federal appeals court judge, about matters other than his professional qualifications. They also grilled him on his judicial philosophy. For example, Senator McClellan said he could not vote to confirm Marshall's nomination without an answer to his question: "Do you subscribe to the philosophy that the Fifth Amendment right to assistance of counsel requires that counsel be present at a police lineup?"[39] Marshall weathered the storm by employing the now-familiar retort that a number of cases were pending before the Court and therefore he should not respond.[40]

About a year later, in 1968, Abe Fortas became the convenient target for those opposed to the Warren Court when President Lyndon Johnson attempted unsuccessfully to promote his old friend and advisor from associate to chief justice.[41] Senator Strom Thurmond vigorously attacked Fortas by harping on the ill effects of the Court's 1957 decision in *Mallory v. United States*.[42] Significantly, Fortas was not on the Court at the time that this decision was handed down. Besides ideology, Fortas was charged with judicial impropriety by informally advising the president on a variety of policy matters, and also for accepting large lecture fees during the summer of 1968. Further, the nomination of Homer Thornberry as associate justice, a Texas crony of the president, to fill the empty seat upon the elevation of Fortas, was another negative factor.[43] In the end, the president was forced to withdraw the name of the liberal jurist as chief justice when a motion to invoke cloture failed by a 14-vote margin.[44] Because the 1968 presidential election was near at hand, and since the election of a president from the other political party was thought a distinct possibility, the defeat of Fortas is an outward and visible sign of partisan and ideological politics in the modern battle over the struggle for control of the Supreme Court. Richard Nixon ran on an anti-Warren Court platform, and the selection of justices with "strict constructionist" sentiments was part of his winning strategy.[45]

In politics, what goes around comes around. Nixon's 1968 campaign invited intense scrutiny of judicial nominees who might exhibit any professional or personal weaknesses. As part of his "Southern Strategy" to gain grassroots support for the Republican Party in that region of the nation, Nixon sought to appoint to the Court southerners with a "strict constructionist" perspective. The code words fooled no one. This was not simply a matter of choosing for the Court persons who would exercise judicial self-restraint. Nixon wanted to reverse the liberal trend of the Warren Court. Then, as is the case today, arguments about the proper judicial function and role of justices in interpreting statutes and the Constitution are really debates about judicial outcomes.

Factors involving professional conduct and qualifications played important roles in the defeat of two Nixon nominees. South Carolinian Judge Clement Haynsworth was thought by organized labor and its Senate supporters to be anti-labor.[46] Floridian Judge Harold Carswell was painted as a racist. Haynsworth was ostensibly rejected for failing to recuse himself in a few cases involving personal financial gain, and Carswell was portrayed as mediocre.[47] But it is difficult to believe that the underlying causes for their rejections did not involve politics and concerns about the ideological direction of the Court.

Other Nixon and, later, Reagan appointees were subjected to ideological interrogation of one sort or another. However, the 1987 confirmation hearings on the nomination of Judge Robert Bork to the Supreme Court is the clearest case to date of the Senate concerning itself with the ideological characteristics and probable future judicial behavior of a High Court nominee. Those hearings taught Americans that questioning nominees about their judicial philosophy will not bring down the legal edifice. It is possible to probe nominees' attitudes without exacting promises or compromising judicial neutrality toward present or future litigants. In large measure, learning this lesson took place because the nominee himself wanted his views aired. Ironically, it was the ventilation of his own views that contributed directly to Judge Bork's 42-to-58 vote Senate rejection.[48] Bork felt compelled to present his views and fully answer most questions because he felt that his many published articles on constitutional subjects could be misinterpreted, and therefore, his views may be misrepresented.[49] He did so without invoking the oft-heard disarming refrain that discussion of constitutional matters may prejudice cases coming before the High Court.

Some senators conducted themselves with distinction. Senator Arlen Specter, in particular, displayed intelligence and courage in defying his president and his party. During and after the Senate hearings, the Pennsylvania Republican asserted that the Supreme Court confirmation hearings will never be the same.[50] Subsequent Senate confirmation hearings held for the nominations of Judges Kennedy and Souter were not as revealing as the Bork hearings. However, in both cases, senators attempted to probe, albeit with limited success, the nominees' fundamental values and attitudes toward judicial law-making. The hearings for both nominees were relatively brief, lasting only a few days.[51]

Available empirical research indicates that senatorial attitudes are affected by nominees. Controversial nominations stimulate the ideological proclivities of senators, thereby subjecting some nominees to negative votes. The extent to which ideology may adversely affect particular nominee confirmation chances depends upon the direction and intensity of that sentiment.[52] It is little wonder, therefore, why most nominees refrain from full disclosure of their attitudes and beliefs.

In summary, there is ample evidence supporting the working supposition that the judicial ideology of presidential nominees is a factor that senators probe when deciding whether to confirm or reject candidates. This practice did not start with Robert Bork as has been argued.[53] By the early part of this century, as the Supreme Court became a more visible policy-making institution, the matter of nominee ideology became a more salient concern.

The issue of impartiality

The oft-heard justification for failing to answer certain questions put by senators during confirmation hearings is that to do so will violate professional norms of impartiality. Nominees protest that to answer particular queries may at the very least lead to the appearance that their minds are closed on specific legal issues, and therefore, litigants may feel they cannot get a fair hearing in court. Sandra Day O'Connor and Antonin Scalia have been the least cooperative. Robert Bork was the most forthcoming, although he refused to answer some questions. Yet nominees before and after Bork have used the impartiality argument to deflect questions.[54] Their reticence has frustrated attempts by senators to obtain pertinent information useful in evaluating nominee suitability. Complicating the matter is the existence of a federal disqualification statute, and ethical standards of conduct gleaned from the American Bar Association Model Code of Judicial Conduct. However, neither constitute sufficient justification for failing to answer queries aimed at ascertaining nominees' general legal and philosophical perspectives.

Section 455 of Title 28 of the United States Code is a revision of a law first enacted in 1911. Section 24 of Title 28, U.S.C., 1940 edition, contains the amended basic law making it applicable to all justices and judges of the United States. The law was amended in 1974 and again in 1978.[55] Most of section 455 applies unambiguously to disqualifications due to personal biases arising out of private financial or fiduciary interests, previous relationships in law practice or government employment, and being a material witness in a case. Section 455(a) raises the most difficulty. It reads: "Any justice, judge, or magistrate of the United States shall disqualify himself in any proceeding in which his impartiality might reasonably be questioned."

Canon 3C(1) of the Model Code of Judicial Conduct adopted by the American Bar Association in 1972 recommends a judge's disqualification when impartiality is an issue because of personal bias or prejudice toward a party involved in litigation.[56] However, Canon 4 permits judges to ". . . speak, write, lecture, teach, and participate . . ."[57] in matters impacting the legal system. Jeffrey M. Shaman, Steven Lubet, and James J.

Alfini, the authors of a recent treatise on judicial ethics, point out Canon 4 applies to the broader circumstance of quasi-judicial activities where judges speak or write in settings such as public hearings. The normative proscription applies to "*any issue* and not to *pending or impending* judicial proceedings that may come before the judge." [58] The ABA's 1990 version of the Model Code opts for greater expression of opinion. Yet these or any other statutory or ethical provisions do not directly address the matter of nominees revealing their ideological viewpoint. Nor do they require justices to recuse themselves for public comments they might have made prior to their accession to the High Court.

The statutory subject matter found in 28 U.S.C. section 455 deals specifically with appropriate recusal behavior. In the main, the Model Code of Judicial Conduct focuses more broadly upon ethical conduct involving both those situations inviting recusal and those that do not. Although the Code was raised as an issue in recent nomination hearings, no one has invoked any section of it in refusing to answer questions during oral testimony. Sandra Day O'Connor did, however, refuse to answer a written question posed by then-Senator Gordon Humphrey of New Hampshire, citing the Code as the basis for her decision. In several other instances the Code was raised as an issue, but the nominees did not rely on it as a basis for refusing to answer questions. [59]

The ABA Code of Judicial Conduct was first approved in 1972, and in August, 1990, the association's House of Delegates adopted a revised one. It will take some time before the 1990 version is promulgated in the various jurisdictions. Until then, the 1972 Code remains in effect in 47 states and applies to all judges in those jurisdictions. Within the federal system, the District of Columbia and the Judicial Conference of the United States have approved the 1972 Code, applying its provisions to all judges of the United States district courts, the United States courts of appeals, the Court of Claims, the Court of Customs and Patent Appeals, the Customs Court, and to all bankruptcy judges and United States magistrates. Significantly, the Code does not apply to justices of the United States Supreme Court. [60] Technically, then, sitting justices do not fall under the Code's ethical prohibitions and mandates. This also applies to nominees who are not sitting on any bench at the time of their confirmation hearings. However, most recent nominees have been sitting federal judges, and one was a state appellate judge at the time of nomination. Since the 1972

issuance, only two nominees, William Rehnquist and Lewis Powell, have not fallen under the purview of the Code. [61]

Grounds for disqualification

William Rehnquist is the author of the only United States Supreme Court opinion on the subject of recusal. [62] His written opinion was in response to a motion for recusal by the plaintiffs in a class action suit challenging the constitutionality of a program of the federal government for surveillance of civilians. The plaintiffs in *Laird v. Tatum,* (409 U.S. 1 [1972]), wanted Associate Justice Rehnquist to recuse himself because while he was a deputy attorney general he appeared before the Senate Judiciary Committee in support of a program of civilian surveillance, and he also made comments in another public forum concerning the subject.

Although a reasonable case is made that he should have recused himself in *Laird v. Tatum,* [63] Rehnquist's memorandum in defense of his decision not to disqualify himself is instructive. Among other arguments, he points out that other justices have not disqualified themselves in cases involving points of law with which they had expressed an opinion before coming to the High Court. Justices Black, Frankfurter, Jackson, and Hughes are prime examples. [64] However, because other justices may have done the wrong thing does not make it proper for Rehnquist to do the same. Yet the fact that these distinguished jurists did not recuse themselves could mean that they reject the view that because persons don judicial robes they become intellectual and political eunuchs. For these justices, disqualification applies to the more narrow matter of bias toward the litigants, not impartiality toward the great issues of the day. Rehnquist's major point is summarized in one eloquent paragraph. He wrote:

> Since most Justices come to this bench no earlier than their middle years, it would be unusual if they had not by that time formulated at least some tentative notions which would influence them in their interpretation of the sweeping clauses of the Constitution and their interaction with one another. It would be not merely unusual, but extraordinary, if they had not at least given opinions as to constitutional issues in their previous legal careers. Proof that a Justice's mind at the time he joined the Court was a complete tabula rasa in the area of constitutional adjudication would be evidence of lack of qualification, not lack of bias. [65]

The history of the subject is also revealing. Before the establishment of the court system in the United States, English common law judges were disqualified for only the reason of financial interests. Even finding themselves sitting in cases involving relatives was not a cause for recusal. Personal bias was unacceptable grounds for disqualification.[66] The American practice was broadened by adding relationships and bias to financial interests. Not only are cases involving relatives cause for disqualification, but so are relationships with the attorney or party to the suit.[67] The 1974 amendment to 28 U.S.C. section 455 requires disqualification of any justice or judge who ". . . has been of counsel, is or has been a material witness, or is so related to or connected with any party or his attorney as to render it improper, in his opinion, for him to sit on the trial, appeal, or other proceeding therein." [68]

Modern practice recognizes the possibility that past associations with colleagues in law firms or government agencies may make it difficult for judges to always behave impartially. Sitting in a case involving former clients is such a circumstance. However, it is unclear how much time should pass between serving a client as counsel and sitting on the bench in a case involving that client.

In the past, some justices did not feel restrained to occupy the bench in disputes involving former clients. This is also true for those cases where they were indirect parties, or in cases in which they personally were similarly situated at one time. Both Justices Horace Lurton and Willis Van Devanter heard cases involving former railroad clients.[69] Chief Justice John Marshall was the secretary of state who affixed the seal of the United States to the judicial commission, but failed to deliver the midnight appointment to the intended recipient, John Marbury. Fellow Federalist John Marshall then wrote the opinion declaring that Marbury had a right to the commission, but then went on to deny the remedy sought.[70] Besides the case of *Marbury v. Madison* (1803), John Marshall failed to recuse himself in *Fletcher v. Peck* (1810), a landmark decision involving the infamous Yazoo land fraud and state confiscation that was similar to a situation where Marshall was likewise a victim.[71] Further, years earlier, as a congressmen from Virginia, Marshall voted to compensate those who lost money in the Yazoo land fraud scandal.[72]

Today's standards are considerably higher. Justice Robert Jackson publicly criticized Justice Hugo Black for participating in *Jewell Ridge Coal Corp. v. Local No. 6167* (325 U.S. 161, 897 [1945]). The case was argued by Crampton Harris, who had practiced law with Hugo Black some 19 years earlier for a brief two-year period.[73] More recently, Justice Byron White felt compelled to disqualify himself from a Denver school desegregation case. Thirteen years earlier his old law firm had once been the bond counsel for the Denver School District. Justice Lewis Powell disqualified himself in a 1972 case involving a court-ordered city-suburb merger of the Richmond School District. From 1952 to 1961, he was chairman of the district's school board.[74] Finally, unlike his questionable conduct in *Laird v. Tatum*,[75] Justice Rehnquist's conduct in the Watergate case, *Nixon v. United States*, (418 U.S. 683 [1974]), is beyond doubt an example of proper recusal. Rehnquist disqualified himself in the case because, as a United States Department of Justice official, he worked closely with the president's men in drafting Richard Nixon's original position on executive privilege.

There may be a need for stronger laws requiring recusal in a variety of compromising situations.[76] Nevertheless, it is a mistake to suggest that because candidates for judicial posts have formed attitudes, values, and beliefs about legal and constitutional questions they should be prohibited from rendering judgments. It is reasonable and compelling to expect from jurists a lack of personal favoritism, prejudice, or bias toward particular litigants coming before them. Judges can and should be impartial toward the litigants. However, an expectation that they be neutral toward the great issues of the day is an unreasonable one. While attempting to appear more virtuous than Caesar's wife, prospective judges and justices may fall into twin traps. First, they may fail to perform their fundamental responsibility to decide cases once on the bench. As members of a collegial body they should participate in its deliberations and carry their fair share of the workload. And second, by not answering questions concerning their ideology, nominees withhold important political information from senators. These constitutional office-holders have a duty to discharge reasonably their advice and consent function.

Canon 4 of the 1972 Model Code of Judicial Conduct provides that judges may appear at "a public hearing before an executive or legislative body or official on matters concerning the law, the legal system, and the administration of justice, and he may otherwise consult with an executive or legislative body or official, but only on matters concerning the administration of justice." [77] Thus, in the first instance there is no ethical problem giving testimony before the Senate Judiciary Committee. Why voluntarily appear if one is obliged to remain mute? The answer, of course, is that nominee-judges may speak and exchange ideas with those asking the questions. However, Canon 4 requires that when judges do so they do not raise doubts about their "... capacity to decide impartially any issue that may come before ... them." [78] This creates no insurmountable problem for judicial nominees. They must make it clear that they are open to persuasion on the legal issue, and that the facts of particular cases vary widely and are important in deciding whether general rules might apply. As Professor Shaman and his colleagues rightly conclude, Canon 4 is violated only when nominees display a clear intention to decide a forthcoming case in a certain way without the benefit of hearing the arguments within the controlled setting of the courtroom. [79]

The use of the word *impartiality* found in Canon 3C(1) of the 1972 Code of Judicial Conduct is also a source of confusion. It instructs judges to disqualify themselves in proceedings where their impartiality might be reasonably questioned, [80] but it fails to give a precise definition of the word, "impartially." However, the term cannot mean the absence of preexisting values, attitudes, and opinions. That we know already from elementary logic. Furthermore, subsections (a), (b), (c), and (d) of 3C(1) all relate to personal knowledge of the parties or third-party relationships. The Canon does not reference preexisting attitudes about issues raised in particular cases.

Canon 3A(6) is a major source of ambiguity. It counsels that a "judge should abstain from public comment about a pending or impending proceeding in any court." [81] Note that 3A(6) does not forbid general analysis and discussion of the great legal issues of the day. Rather, it applies to *pending or impending* proceedings. As legal ethics experts Shaman, Lubet, and Alfini argue, these words must mean pretrial, trial, appellate activity, and litigation poised for litigation. [82] Consequently, "Canon 3A(6) applies only to comment on actual cases or controversies in law and in equity and not general issues of law and philosophy. If nominee testimony does not reach actual fact situations that involve real issues begging for a legal resolution, then the canon is inapplicable." [83]

Months before the Senate confirmation hearings on the Judge David Souter nomination, the American Bar Association revised its Model Code of Judicial Conduct. The August 1990 revision affirms a freedom of speech approach to public comment. The ABA Standing Committee proposed a number of significant changes in the Code. Twenty-five amendments to the committee's document were proposed, but all were defeated. They sought to keep a number of prohibitions, including that dealing with public comment on pending or impending legislation. [84] Canon 3A(6) is now Canon 3B(9) in the 1990 revision and it reads: "A judge shall not, while a proceeding is pending or impending in any court, make any public comment that might reasonably be expected to affect its outcome or impair its fairness or make any nonpublic comment that might substantially interfere with a fair trial or hearing." [85] The addition of the words "reasonably be expected to affect its outcome or impair its fairness" represents an important recognition that not all public comment may make it difficult for judges to render justice impartially.

There can be little doubt that under the terms of the 1990 Model Code judges may comment publicly on court decisions, provided their remarks do not influence the outcome or impair the fairness of litigation currently pending or impending. Michael Franck, a member of the ABA Standing Committee on Ethics and Professional Responsibility, reportedly said: "We ought to allow speech when it serves a legitimate purpose." [86] Further, George Kuhlman, ethics counsel for the ABA's Center for Professional Responsibility is quoted as saying: "Until a genuine conflict occurs, there's no reason to infringe the First Amendment rights a judge should have." [87] Nominee responses to questions of United States senators designed to understand ideological propensities are appropriate if constitutional responsibility and accountability are to have meaning. Consequently, those who argued in the past that the Code of Judicial Ethics constrained nominee behavior before the Senate Judiciary Committee now have even less justification to do so today.

Neither statute nor ethical norms prohibit nominees from discussing the great constitutional questions of the day with United States senators or others. There are no compelling reasons why, at the very least, nominees' general views should not be known in advance of Court service. Expressing one's view today will not make it impossible or difficult to change that view tomorrow. As the venerable Senator Sam Ervin of North Carolina argued—why should it? After carefully considering the established facts in a case, reviewing the law, reading the briefs, hearing oral arguments, and consulting with colleagues, justices may very well change their minds or at least modify their general views to fit the specific facts before the Court and the desired result.[88] In fact, judges tell us that this happens to them. Good arguments, they insist, can convince them.[89]

A positive feature of the common law tradition is its postulate that we can learn from past lessons. The law is a great laboratory wherein rules and regulations are regarded as testable propositions requiring, from time to time, re-examination. Persons who are ill-disposed to uncertainty make poor judges. Those who are not open to persuasion and do not understand the logic of fact analysis to produce welcome and unwelcome precedents misunderstand the nature of the judicial process, and therefore should not, in any event, become members of the Supreme Court. Nominees only need to avoid answering questions about identifiable cases that may be extant in the legal process system or are pending in an immediate sense. Otherwise, they have a responsibility to cooperate fully with constitutional officers to answer questions pertinent to the office they seek.

Conclusions

Senators should feel free to ask questions that may reveal judicial nominees' views on past, present, or future constitutional issues. There is no statutory or ethical justification for secrecy in such matters, save the exception of commenting on pending or impending actual cases or controversies in law and in equity, and then, only when public comment may affect the fairness or outcome of deliberations.

Despite nominee Antonin Scalia's protestations to the contrary,[90] querying nominees about their attitudes concerning past court decisions is consistent with statutory and ethical norms. There is no reason senators may not ask nominees about how they envision the future shape of the law both in general and specific terms. In brief, senators should have a good idea about how future judges and justices will behave. Yet, they should do so with the knowledge that specific facts of particular cases can impact how jurists will behave, and once on the bench the force of argument may persuade the judges and justices to change their minds.

Although asking questions about particular cases and rules of law are pertinent and possess considerable appeal, senators may also gain considerable insight into the minds and possible future behavior of nominees by employing social science knowledge more broadly. Research in political jurisprudence and judi-

cial behavior establishes the explanatory power of inquiries into the social, economic, political, and judicial philosophies of judicial nominees.[91]

Ideology is the summary term describing the set of attitudes and values that are particularly relevant to the performance of the judicial function. The object of the inquiry is to ascertain probable nominee impact upon the policy-making output of the judiciary. Queries may center on the nominees' past political and judicial decision making, and upon their likely short- and long-term future impact upon the Court's decision making.

Existing knowledge is based on aggregate data and does not hold true in all instances. But there is solid social science evidence that values and attitudes are stable. This is particularly true of judges and justices.[92] Persons acquire attitudes toward political objects or issues through a lifetime of experience, learning, and interaction. Furthermore, attitudes direct actions. Hence, if past, present, and future situations are sufficiently similar, there is every justification to assume that persons will behave in the present and future as they did in the past. It is true that attitudes of adults can change,[93] but it is the exception, not the rule.

Judicial nominees are usually in their middle years of life. Because they often have previous political and judicial experience, there is a record of public decision making. Lawyers as an occupational group have a propensity to write down ideas in the course of conducting their professional activities. This makes the task of gathering attitudinal information less difficult than it otherwise might be.

For instance, senators might ask former criminal prosecutors about the policy of their office toward capital punishment, sentencing policy, the exclusionary rule, or other matters that may help to establish the nominees' past and present attitude toward criminal justice matters. Did a nominee participate in political campaigns as a worker or candidate, and what were the ideological positions at stake in those campaigns? If a nominee has had a private law practice, what was the style of that practice? Did the nominee have for clients Fortune 500 corporations or did he or she devote much of his or her professional life to aiding America's poor and underrepresented?

Depending on the number, studying the published opinions of nominees with prior judicial experience may reveal consistent attitude patterns. Wherever possible and practical, Judiciary Committee staff could construct Guttman-type scales on a variety of issue dimensions to ascertain ideological consistency and relative scale position of those judges sitting in collegial settings.[94] Asking sitting judges informed questions about particularly controversial cases in which they cast votes and wrote opinions can serve to uncover not only policy views, but also nominees' conceptions of the proper judicial role.

Contrary to what some believe, however, prior judicial experience is not a good predictor of a commitment to stare decisis.[95] Finally, culling through and questioning nominees about their publications, including law review and other writings, can serve to reveal a wealth of attitudinal information. Much of the Senate Judiciary Committee's interrogation of Robert Bork centered on his prolific writings. Bork felt compelled to explain his writings, and in the process the nation was treated to a splendid constitutional law seminar. Ironically, it may be that President Bush chose David Souter as his first Supreme Court nominee because of the lack of a paper trail, and consequently, senators had one less indicator of nominee ideology.

There was a period when researchers assumed that newly appointed justices take several years before they settle into their new job. The neophytes were said to exhibit signs of bewilderment by their new duties and responsibilities. Being awed by their new surroundings they need several years to become psychologically adjusted. Attempting to ease newly appointed justices into the demands of the job, senior justices do not assign their junior colleagues an equal share of opinion writing. Finally, freshmen fail to align immediately with the Court's existing voting blocs.[96] Recent research findings, however, reject the freshmen-effect hypothesis.

Findings for the Reagan appointees indicate the period of bewilderment is short, if it exists at all. Although freshmen justices write fewer opinions during their first term on the Court, by the end of the second term they no longer write the fewest number of opinions. Even so, freshmen author important opinions during their initial terms signifying early integration into the work group. Finally, freshmen are not timid about joining preexisting voting blocs.[97]

The importance of the freshmen-effect research is that it highlights the importance of considering the near term consequences newly appointed justices may have on Supreme Court decision making. They can have an immediate impact that senators must consider seriously.

It is untrue that justices today are appointed without considering their immediate impact upon the Court.

Particularly during the Reagan administration, nominees were carefully screened by the president or his advisors for their ideological commitment to a judicial agenda, including a view of the judicial function that in the contemporary context is supportive of conservative ideals. The Reagan appointees did not need time to figure out positions on the great legal and constitutional issues of the day. They were chosen for their ideological correctness. The Bush administration also carefully chose judicial nominees with ideology as a general concern.[98] Because today the U.S. Supreme Court deals mostly with matters affecting statutory and constitutional law and because a good number of constitutional law topics are controversial, it makes good political sense to discover nominee attitudes about these subjects.

In summary, senators need not ask the kinds of questions that require nominees to promise how they will vote in future cases. There is no need to do so. Nominee attitudes and values are discernible and may serve as indicators of likely future behavior. The constitutional framers contemplated an inquisitive and active role in confirming presidential appointments. The advice and consent clause of the Constitution justifies an independent scrutiny of nominees by members of the Senate. The historical record reveals that from the beginning of the new republic the Senate has rejected nominees for reasons other than personal and professional qualifications. In one fashion or another, political considerations, including evaluations of the ideological soundness of nominees, influence Senate advice and consent decisions. Properly understood, statutory and ethical norms do not prohibit nominees from revealing their views on the great issues of the day. Nominees may conduct themselves before Senate hearing panels with honor and probity while at the same time providing vital political information.

Briefly stated, nothing in the Constitution, our historical experience, our political practice, ethical norms, nor statutory enactments prohibits senators from asking judicial nominees pertinent ideological questions. Nominees owe an obligation to the nation to be forthcoming if the advice and consent provision of the Constitution is to have real meaning.

Notes

This article originally appeared in Volume 75, Number 2, August–September 1991, pages 68–79.

The author wishes to acknowledge with deep appreciation the devoted effort of research assistants Alan Arwine, Alan Morris, and Marc George Pufong.

1. Fein, "Commentary: A Circumscribed Senate Confirmation Role," *Harv. L. Rev.* 102 (1989), 687; Bork, *The Tempting of America: The Political Seduction of the Law* (New York: Simon and Schuster, 1990), 298–299; "Were the Bork Hearings Fair?" [Bork Nomination], *A.B.A. J.* December 1987, at 42–43; Carter, "The Confirmation Mess," *Harv. L. Rev.* 101 (1988), 1185; Ackerman, "Transformative Appointments," *Harv. L. Rev.* 101 (1988), 1164; Griffin, "Politics and the Supreme Court: The Case of the Bork Nomination," *J. L. & Pol.* 5 (Spring 1989), 551; Curran, "Bork's Credentials Beyond Challenge: Opponents Use Political Standards," *N.Y. L. J.* Sept. 23, 1987, at 2, col. 7; Kooper and Lloyd, "Judge Bork Should Be Confirmed," *N.Y. L. J.* Sept. 30, 1987, at 2, col. 3; McLaughlin, "For Confirmation," *N.Y. L. J.* Oct. 7, 1987, at 2, col. 3.

2. Bork, Ibid.

3. Ibid.

4. Ibid.

5. U.S. Congress, Senate, Committee on the Judiciary, "Nomination of Thurgood Marshall, of New York, to be an Associate Justice of the United States," Ninetieth Congress, First Session, 1967, p. 9; U.S. Congress, Senate, Committee on the Judiciary, "Nomination of William H. Rehnquist, of Arizona, and Lewis F. Powell, Jr., of Virginia, to be an Associate Justice of the Supreme Court of the United States," Ninety-Seventh Congress, First Session, 1981, p. 56; U.S. Congress, Senate, Committee on the Judiciary, "Nomination of Judge Sandra Day O'Connor of Arizona, to be an Associate Justice of the Supreme Court of the United States," Ninety-Seventh Congress, First Session, 1981, p. 199; U.S. Congress, Senate, Committee on the Judiciary, "Nomination of Judge Antonin Scalia, to be an Associate Justice of the Supreme Court of the United States," Ninety-Ninth Congress, Second Session, 1986, p. 33; U.S. Congress, Senate, Committee on the Judiciary, "Nomination of Anthony M. Kennedy to be an Associate Justice of the Supreme Court of the United States," One-Hundredth Congress, First Session, 1987, p. 164.

6. Abraham, *Justices and Presidents: A Political History of Appointments to the Supreme Court,* 2nd ed. (New York: Oxford University Press, 1985), 18–19.

7. Gauch, "The Intended Role of the Senate in Supreme Court Appointments," *U. Chi. L. Rev.* 5 (1989), 341–347.

8. Swisher, *American Constitutional Development* (Boston: Houghton Mifflin, 1954), 28–45; Kelly and Harbinson, *The American Constitution: Its Origins and Development* (New York: Norton Press, 1955), 114–167.

9. Farand (ed.), *The Records of the Federal Convention of 1787,* vol. 1 (1966), 120, 232–234.

10. Gauch, *supra* n. 7, at 341 (note 23).

11. Ibid. at 341–342.

12. Ibid. at 342–347.

13. Ibid. at 347–458; Slotnick, "Reforms in Judicial Selection: Will they Affect the Senate's Role?," *Judicature* 64 (1980), 62; Jilson, *Constitution Making: Conflict and Consensus in the Federal Convention of 1787* (New York: Agathon, 1988), 80–81, 170–171.

14. Hamilton, *The Federalist,* No. 66 at 405 (New American Library ed., 1961).

15. Hamilton, *The Federalist,* No. 76 at 457 (New American Library ed., 1961).

16. Ibid.

17. Jennings, *Generations and Politics: A Panel Study of Young Adults and Their Parents* (Princeton: Princeton University Press, 1981).

18. Ibid. at 458. Italics added.

19. Gauch, *supra* n. 7, at 352.

20. Melone and Mace, *Judicial Review and American Democracy* (Iowa State Univ. Press, 1988), 120–144.

21. Fein, *supra* n. 1 at 672; Ewing, *The Judges of the Supreme Court, 1789–1937* (Minneapolis: University of Minnesota Press, 1938).

22. Sulfridge, "Ideology as a Factor in Senate Consideration of Supreme Court Nominations," *J. Pol.* 42 (1980), 562. Slotnick, *supra* n. 13, at 63–65. *See more generally,* Chemerinsky, "Ideology, Judicial Selection and Judicial Ethics," *Geo. J. Legal Ethics* 2 (1989), 644–646; Abraham, *supra* n. 6, at 3–12.

23. Abraham, *supra* n. 6, at 41.

24. Gauch, *supra* n. 7, at 359–360.

25. Ibid. at 359–361.

26. Abraham, *supra* n. 6, at 41, 88.

27. Ibid. at 42.

28. Mason, *Harlan Fiske Stone: Pillar of the Law* (New York: Viking Press, 1956), 181–200.

29. Abraham, *supra* n. 6, at 27–28.

30. "The Brandeis and Bork Battles: A Systematic Comparison" (Paper Delivered at the 1991 Annual Meeting of the Midwest Political Science Association, Chicago, April 18–20, 1991).

31. Witt (ed.), *The Supreme Court: Justice and the Law* (Washington, D.C.: Congressional Quarterly Books, 1977), 168; and Clinton, *From Precedent to Myth:* Marbury v. Madison *and The History of Judicial Review in America* (Lawrence: University Press of Kansas, 1989), 209.

32. Melone and Mace, *supra* n. 20; see also, Rodell, *Nine Men: A Political History of the Supreme Court from 1790–1955* (New York: Random House, 1955), 187–189.

33. Melone and Mace, Ibid.

34. Abraham, *supra* n. 6, at 178–181.

35. Ibid. at 198–199.

36. Ibid. at 42–43.

37. Schmidhauser and Berg, *The Supreme Court and Congress: Conflict and Interaction 1945–1968* (New York: The Free Press, 1972), 136–142.

38. The saliency of ideology is further illustrated even after FDR began to appoint justices to the Supreme Court. Hugo Black, Franklin Roosevelt's first appointee, encountered serious difficulties after his confirmation. He felt compelled to go on national radio to account for his prior membership in the Ku Klux Klan. *See,* Abraham, *supra* n. 6, at 212–213.

39. U.S. Congress, Senate, Committee on the Judiciary, "Nomination of Thurgood Marshall," *supra* n. 5, at 14.

40. Ibid.

41. Schmidhauser and Berg, *supra* n. 37, at 111.

42. Ibid. at 129.

43. Abraham, *supra* n. 6, at 286–287.

44. Congressional Quarterly Service, *Congressional Quarterly Almanac,* vol. 24, s.v. "Nomination of Abe Fortas," at 531.

45. Funston, *Constitutional Counterrevolution? The Warren and the Burger Courts: Judicial Policy Making in Modern America* (New York: Halsted Press, 1977); Blasi, *The Burger Court: The Counter-Revolution that Wasn't* (Boston: Atlantic–Little, Brown, 1986).

46. Abraham, *supra* n. 6, at 15.

47. Ibid. at 16–17; Frank, "Disqualification of Judges: In Support of The Bayh Bill," *Law & Contem. Prob.* 35 (1970), 52–62.

48. Congressional Quarterly Service, *The Congressional Quarterly Almanac,* vol. 43 s.v. "Bork Nomination," at 271.

49. Bork, *supra* n. 1, at 300–301.

50. Bork, *supra* n. 1, at 301; U.S. Congress, Senate, Committee on the Judiciary, "Nomination of Robert H. Bork to be Associate Justice of the Supreme Court of the United States," One Hundredth Congress, First Session, 1987, p. 75–76; Noble, "Four Key Senators Say They Will Vote Against Bork," *New York Times,* 2 October, 1987, at A17.

51. The Bork hearings took 12 days to complete, and the hearings totaled 6,511 pages. On the other hand, Kennedy's hearings lasted only three days and the total pages for the hearings were only 1,119. Beginning with Thurgood Marshall and extending through Kennedy, the average number of days to conduct the hearings is only 3.6. The average number of pages of hearings for those same hearings is only 577.

52. Sulfridge, *supra* n. 22, at 560; Melone, "The Senate's Confirmation Role in Supreme Court Nominations: Politics, Ideology and Impartiality" (Paper Delivered at the 49th Annual Meeting of the Midwest Political Science Association, April 18–20, 1991), at 21–29.

53. Fein, *supra* n. 1.

54. Shaman, Lubet, and Alfini, *Judicial Conduct and Ethics* (Charlottesville, Va.: The Michie Company, 1990), 361, 362, 369.

55. 28 U.S.C.S. section 455 (Law, Co-op. 1986).

56. Ross, "The Questioning of Supreme Court Nominees at Senate Confirmation Hearings: Proposals for Accommodating the Needs of the Senate and Ameliorating the Fears of Nominees," *Tulane L. Rev.* 62 (1987), 113; *see* American Bar Association, *Code of Judicial Conduct* (Chicago: American Bar Association, 1972), 14 [hereinafter cited as "1972 Code of Judicial Conduct"].

57. "1972 Code of Judicial Conduct," at 18.

58. Shaman, Lubet, and Alfini, *supra* n. 54, at 372. Italics added.

59. Ibid. at 363–364, footnote 7.

60. Ibid. at 364.

61. Ibid. at 365. This includes Justice David Souter who was first an associate justice of the New Hampshire Supreme Court, and then for a short period a judge of the U.S. Court of Appeals for the First Circuit.

62. Memorandum on Motion to Recuse, *Laird v. Tatum,* 490 U.S. 824; 334 L. Ed. 2d 50; 93 S.Ct. 7 (1972).

63. Stempel, "Rehnquist, Recusal, and Reform," *Brooklyn L. Rev.* 53 (1987), 589–667.

64. Memorandum on Motion to Recuse, *Laird v. Tatum,* 490 U.S. 824; 334 L. Ed. 2d 57 (1972).

65. Ibid. at 59.

66. Frank, "Disqualification of Judges," *Yale L. J.* 56 (1947), 609–612.

67. Ibid. at 615–616.

68. 28 U.S.C. Section 458 at 578.

69. Frank, *supra* n. 66, at 623, footnote 32.

70. Melone and Mace, *supra* n. 20, at 37–54.

71. Magrath, *Yazoo: The Case of* Fletcher v. Peck (New York: W. W. Norton and Company, 1966), 73–74.

72. Ibid. at 34.

73. Frank, *supra* n. 66, at 605–606, footnote 2.

74. Melone, "A Political Scientist Writes in Defense of the Brethren," *Judicature* 64 (1980), 142.

75. Stempel, *supra* n. 63.

76. Ibid.

77. "1972 Code of Judicial Conduct," at 18.

78. Ibid.

79. Shaman, Lubet, and Alfini, *supra* n. 54, at 373.

80. "1972 Code of Judicial Conduct," at 14–15.

81. Ibid. at 12.

82. Shaman, Lubet, and Alfini, *supra* n. 54, at 368.

83. Ibid. at 370–371.

84. Guccione, "ABA Adopts a New Code for Judiciary: Jurists Allowed to Comment on Court Proceedings, Now Reflects Reality," *Los Angeles Daily Journal,* August 8, 1990, at 1, 11.

85. American Bar Association, Standing Committee on Ethics and Professional Responsibility, "Code of Judicial Conduct (1990): as submitted for consideration at the 1990 Annual Meeting of the House of Delegates of the American Bar Association" (Chicago: American Bar Asso-

ciation, 1990), 15. For comments of committee members see, Appendix D, at 13–14.

86. Guccione, *supra* n. 84.

87. Shoop, "ABA Revises Judicial Conduct Code," *Trial* (Nov. 1990), at 107.

88. U.S. Congress, Senate, Committee on the Judiciary, "Nomination of Thurgood Marshall," *supra* n. 5, at 13.

89. U.S. Congress, Senate, Committee on the Judiciary, "Nomination of Robert H. Bork," *supra* n. 50, at 152, 153, 155, 716, 718, 720.

90. U.S. Congress, Senate, Committee on the Judiciary, "Nomination of Antonin Scalia," *supra* n. 5, at 33, 37–38, 45, 58, 86.

91. Stumpf (ed.), "Whither Political Jurisprudence: A Symposium," *W. Pol. Q.* 36 (1983), 533–570.

92. Spaeth, "The Attitudes and Values of Supreme Court Justices," in Ulmer (ed.), *Courts, Law, and Judicial Processes* (New York: The Free Press, Macmillan Publishing Co., 1981), 287–388.

93. Melone and Jones, "Constitutional Convention Delegates and Interest Groups: A Panel Study of Elite Socialization," *J. Pol.* 44 (1982), 183–192.

94. Ulmer, "Scaling Judicial Cases: A Methodological Note," *Behavioral Scientist* 4 (April 1961), 31–34; Schubert, *The Judicial Mind* (Evanston, Ill.: Northwestern University Press, 1965).

95. Schmidhauser, "Stare Decisis, Dissent, and the Background of the Justices of the Supreme Court of the United States," *U. Toronto L. J.* 4 (May 1962), 192–212.

96. *See* Snyder, "The Supreme Court as a Small Group," *Soc. Forces* 36 (1958), 232; Howard, "Mr. Justice Murphy: The Freshman Years," *Vand. L. Rev.* 18 (1965), 473.

97. Scheb and Ailshie, "Justice Sandra Day O'Connor and the 'Freshman Effect,' " *Judicature* 69 (1985), 9; Rubin and Melone, "Justice Antonin Scalia: A First Year Freshman Effect?" *Judicature* 72 (1988), 98–102; Melone, "Revisiting the Freshman Effect Hypothesis: The First Two Terms of Justice Anthony Kennedy," *Judicature* 74 (1990), 6–13.

98. Goldman, "The Bush Imprint on the Judiciary: Carrying on a Tradition," *Judicature* 74 (1991), 297.

The confirmation process: too much advice and too little consent

Wm. Bradford Reynolds

The Senate's "advice and consent" role under the Constitution was understood by the framers in modest terms—as a guard against the president's naming a justice of "unfit" character, or one without professional "merit." Yet the Senate believes it has the authority to do "as it sees fit."

Editor's note: Although Albert Melone's article, "The Senate's confirmation role in Supreme Court nominations and the politics of ideology versus impartiality," was prepared prior to the resignation of Justice Thurgood Marshall, it became quite timely with the confirmation hearings on Judge Clarence Thomas. In order to provide another perspective on the process, particularly as it might apply to Judge Thomas, *Judicature* invited Wm. Bradford Reynolds, who during his tenure as assistant attorney general in the Justice Department was involved in selecting federal judges, to prepare the following commentary.

With the announcement of Justice Thurgood Marshall's resignation from the United States Supreme Court, the stage is set once again for Senate confirmation hearings to fill a vacancy on the High Court. The president nominated an exceptionally well-qualified judge on the District of Columbia Circuit Court, Judge Clarence Thomas, to fill the seat.

Almost immediately, the political battle lines were drawn, and interest groups on both sides began their all-too-familiar refrains. Their objective, ultimately, is to convince a majority of senators to support (or oppose) Judge Thomas because he agrees (or disagrees)—or is perceived to agree (or disagree)—with a particular ideology they endorse. The fine art of confirmation by litmus test, as developed and honed during and after the confirmation hearings of Judge Robert Bork for the Supreme Court, seems to be here to stay.

The question of whether the Senate should rise above the fray and exercise its "advice and consent" responsibility untainted by the political haranguing of special-interest agitators is no longer seriously asked or answered. Rather, as Professor Melone's heavily footnoted article makes clear, the debate has shifted. The legitimacy of politicizing the confirmation process is no longer open for discussion. That other nominees have been mistreated over the past 200 years—even if only a

relatively few—apparently justifies the crudest of tactics in the present environment. The criticism, it is argued, should not be heaped on the senators for seeking politically correct answers, but on the nominee for declining to respond (whatever his or her reason) or, in responding, failing the standard of political correctness.

I continue to be of the school that believes the Senate's "advice and consent" role under Article II, Section 2, cl. 2 of the U.S. Constitution was understood by the framers in far more modest terms. Professor Melone does an adequate job with the historical compromise that placed in the Executive the power to nominate and in the Senate a check on that power to guard against the president's naming of a justice of "unfit" character, or one without professional "merit." *

He stumbles badly, however, in extrapolating (albeit somewhat tentatively) from the framers' debates that the door was unwittingly opened for the Senate to inquire as well into "nominees' ideology." Nor does even that shaky premise sustain the penultimate of the professor's thesis (which we have come to expect from academic circles when the historical analysis fails to produce the desired result), to wit: it is, after all, a "living constitution," which permits the Senate essentially "to use its constitutional authority as it sees fit."

So much for original intent. Not that it makes much practical difference. The argument fashioned by Professor Melone and his like-minded academic colleagues is but an intellectual fig leaf for the senators to hide behind. Senators Biden and Specter wore it rather well to cultivate at least a public perception that their opposition to Judge Bork was reasoned, not political. Senators Heflin and Leahy were far less convincing, while Senators Kennedy and Metzenbaum cast aside all pretexts, seemingly unashamed by the public exposure of their crass political campaign that did not take the measure of the man and his credentials, but instead subjected him and the process to a most unfor-

Judicature Volume 75, Number 2, pp. 80–82

giving liberal litmus test. Whether one agrees or disagrees with my view that such senatorial gracelessness mocks that body's "advice and consent" responsibility is, I would submit, quite beside the point. The reality is that Professor Melone summed things up about right: the senators will do as they damn well please in the confirmation jousting over a nominee for the High Court—even as they pretend to be more deliberative.

Thus, we can expect the inquiry to move sharply away from the topics of judicial qualifications, philosophy, and temperament—all legitimate areas to probe—and, sadly, toward an issues-oriented game of chicken, focused on decisional outcomes, not the methodology a nominee employs to get there. If abortion happens to be the political "hot button" at the time of hearings, whether the candidate is or is not pro-life becomes the litmus test for confirmation. The same holds true for "affirmative action," capital punishment, the exclusionary rule, flag burning, and a host of other issues that make up the grist of the Supreme Court's jurisprudence.

There is, of course, nothing wrong with senators seeking to determine *how* a nominee would approach and go about deciding any or all of these issues. Whether or not historical context is deemed important, what source materials are considered authoritative, the degree of deference (if any) that attaches to Court precedents, and the analytical framework generally followed—these are all appropriate inquiries. But to go beyond methodology and insist on a statement of *what* the nominee's decision will be in any particular case makes political correctness the yardstick for confirmation, not juridical competence.

The correct stand

Refusing to answer the *what* question—except, as with Judge Bork for example, where a thoughtful response had previously been given in writings or opinions—has yet to defeat a nomination. Justice David Souter adopted what seems to me to be the unquestionably correct stand. He demonstrated his general knowledge of competing considerations, identified relevant precedents, even in some instances made reference to learned commentary bearing on the subject raised; he noted that his decision, ultimately, would turn on a careful analysis of the matters he touched upon, the briefs filed by counsel and discussions with his colleagues on the Court. That is, of course, precisely how a Supreme Court justice should approach each issue when first presented to him or her for decision. The demand in confirmation hearings for snap judgments to be offered

in response to invariably poorly crafted questions (which all too frequently do not even ask what the senator *thinks* he is asking) encourages highly injudicious behavior. Resisting such pressure is properly judicious.

A case in point involves the law of privacy. Virtually all the senators—with the notable exception of Senator Hatch—have demonstrated repeatedly and emphatically in the last six Supreme Court confirmation hearings—stretching back to Justice Sandra Day O'Connor in 1982—that their grasp of the issue of constitutional privacy is untutored and inexpert. Judge Thomas, too, will soon be subjected to the ordeal of trying, politely, to answer the predictably inept inquiries from Judiciary Committee members about his views on the "law of privacy" (we all know they really mean "abortion"). He would, in my view, be well advised to give the Souter response if, as I suspect, he has not yet had occasion to sort through the constitutional complexities that attend the issue and have divided learned scholars and jurists for years. Such an answer has the virtue of avoiding the litmus test trap set by those senators intent on securing advance commitments on substantive issues—besides which, it happens to be honest.

This does not suggest that Judge Thomas need equivocate on his *personal* views in the pro-life debate *if* he has heretofore shared them publicly with others. Should the question be asked on that level, I would hope the nominee would make the point that his personal views (whatever they may be) are wholly irrelevant to his constitutional analysis; they then should have no bearing on the confirmation deliberations. Nor do I agree with Governor L. Douglas Wilder's misguided observation (later fuzzily recanted) that Judge Thomas' Catholic upbringing serves to disqualify him—any more than the same religious affiliation undid Justice Kennedy or, at the executive level, stood in the way of John F. Kennedy's bid for the presidency.

To be sure, on issues where he has been outspoken, a more intense probe of that nominee's stated positions can be expected, and properly so. Judge Thomas has not been bashful about his views on "affirmative action," for example. The Senate can properly challenge, and the nominee had better be prepared to defend. The search, however, should be not for areas of personal agreement or disagreement, but for the reasoned explanation. Judge Thomas has Supreme Court precedent and Justices William O. Douglas and Lewis Powell among the reasoned advocates on his side of the debate. His open stand against government policies that promote uneven treatment of individuals because of racial, gender, or ethnic differences—oxymoronically labelled "affirmative"—commands the respect of a majority of today's sitting justices, as well as many judges on the federal appellate and district courts. That reality predictably counts for little among the *political* opposition. Among those for whom intellectual honesty still has value, on the other hand, it is the full answer to critics who seek to miscast this nominee as a "radical thinker" or "outside the mainstream."

Bases for consent

Will Judge Thomas be confirmed? By any objective measure, he should be—overwhelmingly. The framers' nod to the Senate—to give its "advice and consent"— left to the president (and the president alone) the task of nominating. Not surprisingly, George Bush's choices for the Supreme Court are going to be the same as Michael Dukakis'. So long as the persons proposed are of high moral character, strong legal training and experience, and in good physical health, Senate "consent" should not be withheld because conservative credentials shine through.

Fidelity to the written law and disdain for judicial improvisation is a philosophy of judging that undoubtedly dismays liberal senators weaned on a Warren Court openly disdainful of the written law and known best for judicial improvisations. Yet, it is a philosophy that returns to the legislative branch its constitutional responsibility of framing the law, to the executive branch its constitutional responsibility of administering the law, and to the judicial branch its constitutional responsibility of interpreting the law.

If such conservative thinking is all that stands in the way of confirmation by a liberal Senate—because it is regarded as not politically correct—the worst fears of what mischief could come out of Judge Bork's mishandled confirmation hearings will have been realized. The judiciary will no longer be able to lay claim to independence from the other two branches, having become captive to a highly charged and overly politicized selection process that demands from nominees advance commitments to particular policy results being pressed by a senator or favored "interest group."

The Senate Judiciary Committee's scrutiny of Judge Thomas thus bears close viewing. Not only does the future of the nominee hang in the balance, but so, too, does the very character of the Supreme Court. Regrettably, the fate of both the man and the institution will be determined with little senatorial respect for the constitutional role that assigns that body an "advice and consent" responsibility more modest than it is prepared to wield.

Notes

This article originally appeared in Volume 75, Number 2, August–September 1991, pages 80–82.

* *See* Hamilton, *The Federalist* No. 76, at 513.

Supreme Court confirmation hearings: a view from the Senate

George Watson and John Stookey

Through the adoption of certain roles, senators pursue distinct goals throughout Supreme Court confirmation hearings, one of which includes influencing future nominations.

Editor's note. The following article was prepared prior to the nomination and subsequent defeat by the Senate of Judge Robert Bork. The authors discuss the unique nature of the Bork hearing in "The Bork hearing: rocks and roles," page 557.

With the exception of the initial announcement of a nominee's name by the president, public attention to the Supreme Court nomination process is focused mostly on the Senate confirmation hearings. They represent the most visible and formal evaluation of the nominee's suitability and qualifications. With the consideration of Justices Rehnquist and Scalia behind us and with the expectation of others to come in the not too distant future, it is a good time to examine the role of such hearings in the nomination process.

Drama or theatrics

At a common-sense level the significance of a confirmation hearing depends upon how controversial the nomination is. For example, in a relatively controversial nomination, like that of Justice Rehnquist, the hearings of the Judiciary Committee often rate as high drama in the media and are considered a significant part of the confirmation process. Conversely, the hearings in noncontroversial nominations are often dismissed as theatrics, a mere formality of going through the motions.

The conclusion that the high degree of confirmation certainty associated with a noncontroversial nominee precludes interesting and important questions about the hearing process, however, is uninformed. It is based on the limited views that these hearings are worthy of attention only if the voting is expected to be close or if a significant proportion of the legislators are playing what might be called an "evaluator role," namely, seeking information at the hearings to help them decide whether to support or oppose the nominee. From this perspective, the hearings of two of the last three nominees (O'Connor and Scalia) can be ignored as inconsequential, mere theatrical events devoid of any genuine drama or substantive value to judicial or legislative scholars. There was little doubt the decisions to confirm O'Connor or Scalia were assured before the hearings.[1] Nor are such hearings uncommon, as reflected by two scholars who noted that the hearings are "... essentially a pro-forma part of the decision process." [2]

Among the last three hearings, only the Rehnquist one provided the drama that attracts public and scholarly attention. Such interest springs primarily from the uncertainty of the outcome, which derives from a division of opinion among the senators or from an apparent indecision by senators concerning which way to vote. Because scholars have focused primarily on the outcome of hearings, their attention has been on variation in voting behavior and the factors that affect vote decision. While outcome is clearly a significant concern, we believe that a more complete understanding of the confirmation process is desirable. A perspective that helps to make sense of both controversial and noncontroversial nomination hearings is both possible and fruitful.

Such an alternative perspective focuses not on how controversial the nomination is, nor on the impact of the hearings on the outcome, but rather on the individual perceptions and goals of the senators involved. What is each senator trying to accomplish, and how does the configuration of the senators' goals change depending upon the level of controversy involved? Rather than a filter that determines whether the hearings are even worth our attention, level of controversy becomes a variable that affects the goals and behaviors of the senators involved.

Senatorial roles

The concept of legislative role has a long tradition. For example, representation roles, such as delegate and trustee, are often discussed by political scientists.[3] A delegate is a legislator who sees his role as reflecting the wishes of his or her district. On the other hand, the trustee role suggests that the legislator should rely on his or her own judgment about issues, rather than attempt to directly reflect home district opinion on each vote.

These generic types of roles are useful in explaining the behavior of a legislator in the confirmation setting, as well as other legislative decision making. For our discussion here, however, the term "role" is used as a convenient and common sense label to describe what a legislator is trying to accomplish in a given setting. We call these purposive situational roles, because they reveal the purpose or intent of the senator, and they are specific to a particular setting or situation, in this instance, a confirmation hearing. For example, in a Supreme Court confirmation hearing, a senator seeking to gather information and insight concerning the nominee in order to decide about his vote is playing the role of evaluator. The evaluator role provides the normative model of the open-minded senator who uses the hearings to gather and evaluate information in making a decision on how to vote.[4] It is the nature of virtually all nominations, however, that this role is assumed by a distinct minority of the committee membership, whether the nomination be controversial or noncontroversial. The question arises, then, what other roles are adopted by senators in these nomination hearings? If their vote is not at stake, just what *is* happening at these hearings?

Our effort to establish the various roles that senators may play during confirmation hearings, as well as the factors that affect role selection, began with the O'Connor hearings in September 1981. For this initial effort, it seemed important to gather information concerning role selection contemporaneous with the hearing itself. The narrow time frame available, however, provided an obvious problem of access to the senators. As an alternative, we suspected and confirmed that the key people to interview in the attempt to identify roles were the staff members responsible to the various senators for developing information and formulating statements and questions for the hearings.[5] Each senator assigned this responsibility to his chief staff member serving on the Judiciary Committee or, more often, on one of the Judiciary subcommittees.

While the use of staff to measure senator role conceptions may be second-best to interviewing each senator directly, it seems that little measurement error

occurs. This is due to the fact that the interaction between senator and staff member actually produces an articulation of role conception as the senator directs staff members to develop an opening statement and subsequent questions that will reflect the objectives sought by the senator. In those four instances in which both senators and staff were interviewed separately, we found no difference in the role conceptions articulated by the senator and his staff member. In the O'Connor nomination, interviews were conducted with the appropriate staff members for 16 of the 18 senators.[6] One senator was not included in the analysis because of his virtual absence from the proceedings. We were unsuccessful in repeated efforts to gain interviews with staff members for another senator.

In the Rehnquist and Scalia hearings, a different approach was used. Although motivations and behaviors are best understood by talking with the senators or with the staff members responsible for developing the opening statements and questions, such opportunities for "insider information" are rare. Since one purpose of this article is to provide insight that would permit outside observers to interpret the behavior and actions of the senators, we decided to examine the Rehnquist and Scalia hearings by analyzing only the information that would be available to any careful observer, namely, normal press coverage along with the opening statements and subsequent questioning by the senators.

News accounts serve to provide an understanding of the political milieu and an assessment of the nominee's qualification, background, and ideology. They also may serve to provide some sense about senatorial reaction to the nomination. Moreover, we observed a reasonably close adherence in the O'Connor hearings between what senators and staff told us in private and the comments made in the opening statements by these senators in the confirmation hearings. These statements often provide a clue to the senators' intentions and role predispositions.

On the basis of this combination of interviews in the O'Connor hearings, along with the opening statements from all three hearings, we identified various roles that appear to characterize the intentions and goals of senators during these Senate confirmation hearings. The behaviors determined by these roles are the questions and statements made by the senators during the question-and-answer part of the hearings. A specification of these roles and examples of behaviors they engender should prove most helpful in providing insight to the significance of these Senate confirmation hearings.

The prelude to role selection

The fact that many or most senators do not play an evaluator role in Supreme Court nomination hearings is perhaps more easily understood if one realizes that the hearings represent not the first, but the fourth step of the information gathering process for the Judiciary Committee members. Moreover, senatorial role selections are affected by the political environment in which the hearings occur, as well as the personal attitudes and attributes of the senators.

The information gathering process. The first step involves the collection of information by each senator's staff once the nominee is known. Each staff member becomes an independent collector of considerable printed material concerning the nominee and the nomination, in addition to letters and calls that come into the senator's office. At the same time, staffers make telephone calls to friends and associates of the senator in the nominee's home state and elsewhere in an effort to secure overviews and evaluations of the nominee. Almost without exception, special attention is paid to any known liabilities or problems concerning the nominee, such as past memberships in segregated clubs or suspect financial dealings. Because of some presumption by the senators in favor of the president's choice,[7] attention focuses on any negative factors that might alter that presumption. In fact, Wayne Sulfridge posits as virtually a necessary condition for opposition to a nominee "strong emotional issues which can excite the public imagination." [8]

The second step in this process is the collection of information from official sources. FBI reports on nominees, once considered provocative, are now commonplace, but access to them is strictly limited to the senator only, not his staff. The chief counsel, with cooperation from the minority counsel, is responsible for gathering information for the committee as a whole. A questionnaire submitted to the nominee gathers basic biographical information, financial data, conflict of interest statements, and responses to some general interest questions. In the cases of these three justices, questions asked their response to a short criticism of "judicial activism" and to specify actions in their professional and personal lives that demonstrated their concern for "equal justice under the law."

The third part of the pre-hearing process involves a private meeting with the nominee by each of the senators on the committee. This is an important part of the process for both the nominee and the senator. From the nominee and administration's perspective, it provides insights into the concerns of the committee members and permits a preview of questions that are likely to be put to the nominee during the formal hearings. Each senator, in turn, is able to evaluate various aspects of the nominee and check out certain reservations he may possess.

By the time of the hearings, senators have acquired and evaluated substantial information concerning the nominee. They tend to assume that the information gathered is fairly exhaustive and that the nominee's strong and weak points have been identified. Since the senators presume that any important negative information concerning the nominee will be discovered before the hearings, it is further assumed that those who will testify against the confirmation will reveal no startling new information that will alter their assessment of the nominee.

The political and personal environment. While the information gathering process is critical to the individual decisions of senators concerning their vote, there are also many political and personal factors that structure the nature of the hearings. In turn, we may distinguish between those political factors that deal with the political situation in which the nomination occurs and those that involve the specific nominee to the Court. Among those situational variables of importance are presidential power and popularity; partisan and ideological distribution in the Senate; the president's party and ideology; the current make-up of the Court with respect to ideology, race, sex, and other dimensions; and public opinion. Characteristics of the nominee that may assume prominence are ideology, race or ethnicity, sex, religion, character, experience, and other such factors. For an individual senator, factors include, but are not limited to, his general legislative role orientation, sense of loyalty to party and president, personality, constituency consideration, and personal agenda in the Senate.

While any one or more of these factors may play a significant role in one nomination or another, there are two factors, more than any others, that serve to structure the hearings of the modern era: the presumption in favor of the president's nominee and political ideology. As articulated by Senator Simpson in the Rehnquist hearings:

> President Reagan was elected by a large majority. . . . He has the right and the obligation to nominate qualified men and women who share the philosophy of this president.[9]

This presumption exists not from respect for the president's wisdom, although there is an assumption that some initial screening will have produced a nominee without severe moral, ethical, or legal liabilities; rather, the presumption is a recognition of his power. A president willing to "go to the wall" on an issue is a formidable opponent indeed. When that power is augmented by a compatible Senate Judiciary Committee and/or Senate, then the minority must conserve its effort for those situations in which it can appeal beyond ideology. Senator Biden's attempt to place the burden of proof on the supporters of Justice Rehnquist to the contrary,[10] Grossman and Wasby have correctly noted that

> . . . the confirmation process has been based on the assumption that the president should be allowed to make any reasonable choice and that the "burden of proof" as to a nominee's lack of qualifications must be sustained by the opposition.[11]

As Biden's effort demonstrates, however, such a presumption is less likely to be respected by those in ideological opposition to the nominee. There seems little doubt that the ideological match between senator and nominee serves as the primary source of a senator's disposition concerning the nomination. Where ideological congruence exists, the qualifications and background of the nominee are simply less important. The positive elements emerge as great strengths and the negative elements as relatively minor problems. However, where the ideologies of senator and nominee are in conflict, a very careful scrutiny of the qualifications and background is typically pursued by the senator. Positive elements tend to be reduced to a presumptive minimum, and negative items assume considerable prominence.

The significance of ideology on predispositions to the nominees is clearly evident in Table 1. Support for the three Reagan nominees was explicitly forthcoming from committee conservatives in their opening statements in all but four instances. In one of those four, Simpson engaged in a rambling, introspective presentation in which his support for Scalia seemed apparent, but which avoided an explicit statement of it.[12] The other three, occurring in the O'Connor nomination, actually reinforce the importance of ideological congruence rather than refute it. For senators East, Grassley, and Denton, the so-called "right-to-life" principle was a critical component of their conservative ideology. O'Connor's stand on this dimension was unclear. In other words, ideological congruence was precisely the question here. To the extent that they found her in step with them, their support would be forthcoming. On the other hand, to find her in ideological opposition on this principle would likely prompt their opposition.

Examination of the moderates and liberals on the committee confirms that those not in ideological "sync" with the nominees were more likely to withhold support. There are two exceptions. Senator DeConcini qualifies as a moderate based on his voting record, yet he explicitly supported all three nominees. His is an unusual case, however, because of his position as home state senator for both O'Connor and Rehnquist. For DeConcini, the political milieu and his own agenda as an Arizona senator seem to have played a role in his explicit support. The other exception comes in the explicit support for O'Connor from three of the five committee liberals and implicit support from a fourth. Once again, however, the apparent exception to the importance of ideology is actually in accord with it. There is no doubt that O'Connor's status as the first female appointee to the Court overshadowed the concerns of liberals and moderates about her conservative ideology. Committee liberals could hardly place themselves in a position of opposing the first woman, especially in the absence of any considerable negative factors about her. In a real sense, liberal opposition to O'Connor was pre-empted by the liberals' own claims in support of women's rights.

The presumption of confirmation clearly worked to the benefit of nominees O'Connor and Scalia, both of whom were perceived as politically conservative nominees. In the absence of negative findings in any of the pre-hearing information, no opposition emerged. O'Connor's status as the first female nominee overcame questions of experience and competence. Scalia, on the other hand, was unable to win over his ideological adversaries in advance of the hearings. However, the normal presumption in favor of the nominee was augmented in his case by the fact that his hearings came immediately on the heels of Justice Rehnquist's.

Table 1. Political ideology and pre-hearing commitment to the nominee

Senator	Party	Ideology	O'Connor	Rehnquist	Scalia
Thurmond	Rep.	Conservative	ex. sup.	ex. sup.	ex. sup.
Mathias	Rep.	Moderate	ex. sup.	noncom.	im. sup.
Laxalt	Rep.	Conservative	ex. sup.	ex. sup.	ex. sup.
Hatch	Rep.	Conservative	ex. sup.	ex. sup.	ex. sup.
Dole	Rep.	Conservative	ex. sup.	ex. sup.	ex. sup.
Simpson	Rep.	Conservative	ex. sup.	ex. sup.	im. sup.
East	Rep.	Conservative	noncom.	n.a.	n.a.
Grassley	Rep.	Conservative	mixed	ex. sup.	ex. sup.
Denton	Rep.	Conservative	uncertain	ex. sup.	ex. sup.
Specter	Rep.	Moderate	noncom.	noncom.	im. sup.
McConnell	Rep.	Conservative	n.a.	ex. sup.	ex. sup.
Broyhill	Rep.	Conservative	n.a.	ex. sup.	ex. sup.
Biden	Dem.	Liberal	im. sup.	uncertain	noncom.
Kennedy	Dem.	Liberal	ex. sup.	ex. opp.	mixed
Metzenbaum	Dem.	Liberal	ex. sup.	uncertain	mixed
DeConcini	Dem.	Moderate	ex. sup.	ex. sup.	ex. sup.
Leahy	Dem.	Liberal	ex. sup.	uncertain	noncom.
Baucus	Dem.	Liberal	noncom.	n.a.	n.a.
Heflin	Dem.	Conservative	ex. sup.	ex. sup.	ex. sup.
Simon	Dem.	Liberal	n.a.	uncertain	im. sup.

1. The levels of commitment for the last three columns in this table use the following labels: ex. sup.—support for the nominee was stated in the senator's opening remarks: im. sup.—support for the nominee seemed apparent from the senator's positive statements, but a specific commitment of support was not given; uncertain—indecision concerning how one might vote was explicitly stated; noncom.—statement was noncommittal, containing no positive or negative statements concerning the nominee nor any statement of indecision; mixed—both positive traits and negative bases for concern were mentioned, but no explicit support nor opposition was provided; ex. opp.—opposition to rather than support for the nominee was indicated; n.a.—not applicable, the senator was not on the committee for those particular hearings.

2. Political ideology was established using the ratings of the Conservative Caucus and Americans for Democratic Action. Scores between 25 and 75 were assigned a "moderate rating" while scores of 75 and above or 25 and below were assigned the appropriate "conservative" or "liberal" label. The 1981 scores were drawn from the "Congressional Voting Scores" data file made available by the Interuniversity Consortium for Political and Social Research. The 1986 scores were assessed from the November 15th and 22nd issues of *Congressional Quarterly Weekly Report*, 1986. Of course, neither the ICPSR nor *Congressional Quarterly* bears responsibility for the interpretation of the data.

3. With pre-hearing commitment reduced to three categories—support; uncertain/mixed/noncommittal; and opposition—gamma=.80, P<.01, indicating a relationship between ideological congruence and support for the nominee.

4. Denton abstained in the Committee vote on O'Connor. All others voted "Yes." For Rehnquist, the vote was 13–5. The "No" votes came from Biden, Kennedy, Metzenbaum, Leahy and Simon. The Scalia vote was a unanimous "Yes" one.

Opposition from the liberal minority to both of these back-to-back nominations surely seemed unwise, so Justice Rehnquist was targeted as the more vulnerable of the two, precisely because of the presence of certain negative factors on which to base an opposition.[13] Thus, while Scalia failed to gain the prior support of the liberal faction, he at least avoided their opposition.

While one might consider that Justice Rehnquist had a double presumption in his favor, being a sitting justice as well as the president's choice, Justice Fortas' problems in a similar setting in 1968 demonstrate the potential difficulty with being a sitting justice. There is no doubt that Rehnquist's record of conservative judgments bothered committee liberals. While Scalia appeared to be as conservative as Rehnquist in many areas, there were simply no negative emotional issues

associated with Scalia over which the ideological opposition could muster an attack. With Rehnquist, however, there seemed to be several, none of which by itself constituted a sufficient cause, but the cumulative effect of which just might. As we shall see, this ultimately laid the foundation for certain role selections by various senators.

Role types

Given the amount of pre-hearing information and the usual context of the political and personal milieu, it is hardly surprising that by the time of the hearings most senators have already made up their minds and therefore do not pursue an evaluator role. Our concern here is with what alternative roles might be played by the non-evaluators. In these three hearings, we isolated four additional distinct situationally specific roles: validator, partisan, advertiser, and educator.

Each of these roles is a function of the senator's certainty of support for or opposition to the nominee, strategic considerations in light of the senator's political agenda and personal predispositions to act in a certain way. Thus, one who is uncertain about the nominee will almost surely pursue an evaluator role. On the other hand, strategic considerations are significant for those who are certain about their votes. The hearings may be expected to be controversial by virtue of a close or uncertain voting outcome or by a conscious decision by opponents to stir up controversy over the nominee; then the likelihood of a "certain" supporter playing a partisan role to help ensure approval is much more likely. Noncontroversial nominations permit a wider choice of roles. In the absence of uncertainty, which promotes the evaluator role, and controversy, which stimulates partisan roles, senators pursue other objectives. Some of these will become manifest as we describe each of the roles in turn.

The evaluator. The evaluator role is one designed to help a senator make up his mind concerning his vote on the nominee. The archetypal evaluator is probably one who carefully evaluates the nominee's responses to all questions, listens to all the evidence, and poses carefully framed questions designed to determine the fitness of the nominee. In reality, the evaluator is more likely to be one who is uncertain or unsettled about the nominee on some one or just a few issues. It is also likely that any such issue is pivotal, virtually a necessary condition for the senator's consent or opposition to the nomination. The pivotal nature of such an issue usually means that it is a very prominent issue or that it strikes at that senator's "core requirements" for a Supreme Court justice. The evaluator is best characterized as one who will ask serious questions of the nominee that are designed to resolve those doubts in the senator's mind. Such a role is exemplified by the opening statement of Denton to Judge O'Connor:

> Your answers at this hearing . . . will determine my estimate of your position. . . . It is my earnest hope that your responses will be neither broad nor bland, because I will base my single vote on those responses.[14]

Evaluators do not appear to be all that common in confirmation hearings, because so many of the factors that affect the voting decision have already made their impact. Evaluators are often recognizable, however, because of their forthrightness in an opening statement, as with Denton above. However, alternative opening styles for an evaluator are the noncommittal approach, used by East, which often simply notes the significance of the occasion, and the mixed approach of Grassley, who both praised and expressed reservations concerning nominee O'Connor.

Since the evaluator seeks to resolve doubts of a particular nature, he typically displays a very direct style of questioning that relates to those issues deemed so pertinent. For two of the three evaluators we observed in the O'Connor hearings, the issue of abortion was clearly pivotal. East asked eight questions during the hearings, seven of which dealt specifically with abortion. Denton managed 23 questions, 17 of which dealt specifically with abortion, two of which dealt with parents' rights concerning a young daughter's abortion and three of which concerned the role of women in the military. The abortion issue presented precisely the type of strong emotional issue Sulfridge asserts as essential for opposition to a nominee.[15] Had O'Connor given responses that indicated a pro-abortion stance, there seems little doubt that opposition would have resulted.

What makes life particularly difficult for an evaluator in a Supreme Court nomination hearing is the problem of getting straightforward answers from the nominee on any particular issue. Nominees typically are unwilling to comment on particular cases that have come before the Supreme Court or on specific issues that could conceivably come before the Court. After two dozen or so questions dealing with abortion, Denton lamented, "I do not feel I have made any progress personally in determining where you stand on the issue of abortion. . . ."[16] When asked by the chair whether another 15 minutes to question the nominee would be helpful, Denton responded, "I do not know whether another month would do, Mr. Chairman."[17]

Grassley did not pursue the same line of questioning on abortion as the other two, although his questions did support their efforts. His initial round of questions for the most part did not deal with substantive questions designed to assist his evaluation of O'Connor. Rather he attempted to surmount O'Connor's earlier evasiveness with East's questions on abortion and her refusal to comment on *Roe v. Wade* on the grounds that it was an issue that might again confront the Court.[18] The nature of his questioning reminds us that there is more to the evaluator's role than just asking substantive questions with respect to the issues of concern. There may also be "sparring time" in which the evaluator must try to elicit responses from the nominee with an acceptable degree of specificity.

The validator. The validator role is often played by a senator who has made a preliminary decision on the nominee and who wishes to use the hearings to confirm or validate that opinion. Typically, such a role involves one who is inclined to vote "yes" on the confirmation, but who remains sufficiently open-minded to change his mind in the event that some serious shortcoming or flaw in the nominee arises. Such a position was expressed by Senator Metzenbaum in his opening statement in the Scalia hearings, in which he praised the nominee's integrity but proceeded to note that he retained an "open mind on this nomination." [19]

Empirically, we observed no validators who were leaning against the confirmation in any of the three nominations, and it seems probable that an individual leaning in opposition is likely to pursue a more active role in revealing the negative aspects of the nominee's credentials, a role different from that of validator. This assumption stems from the premise of the presumption in favor of the nominee. Since those who oppose carry the burden of establishing the nominee's "unfitness," those who lean in opposition must pursue the negative traits of the nominee to establish certainty of opinion in functionally the same way a negative partisan might carry the battle.

While the evaluator seeks to resolve for himself some very fundamental concerns regarding the fitness of the nominee to serve, the validator usually has resolved such basic questions. There is no need, then, for the validator to ask questions that will reveal the position of the nominee on a fundamental issue that relates to the necessary conditions of fitness for the senator. More commonly expressed is a desire to evaluate the quality of the nominee's mind and to assess the nominee's ability to function in pressure situations. The validator's goal, in effect, is to reassure himself concerning his vote, as exemplified by Biden's "relief" when Scalia affirmed that free speech can encompass physical actions and his overall "feeling better" about Scalia at the conclusion of his questioning.[20]

An analogy to doctoral dissertation defenses comes to mind here. Just as professors engage a doctoral student in mental gymnastics, the validating senator seeks to gain insight into the mental capacities of the nominee. It is conceivable that questions posed by the doctoral committee may reveal an unanticipated weakness that leads to failure of the exam. However, the norm is that the exam is passed, just as it is also the norm that validating senators do indeed validate their prior notions concerning the nominee.

The types of questions that provide such insight will vary widely, according to the knowledge, experience, and characteristics of each individual senator, as well as the order in which the senator is permitted to question. A staff member of one junior senator noted the problem of assuring that the senator would have good questions to ask even after his 15 colleagues had preceded him. Thus, Senator Baucus' so-called "tombstone question" ("How do you want to be remembered?") is an effort to be creative, clever and, at the same time, provide some psychological insight into the nominee.

More often than not, the validator assumes a somewhat benign approach in his questioning. Just as in a dissertation defense, however, senators will not hesitate to pursue certain points where the nominee betrays a weakness. For example, O'Connor responded inadequately on a question dealing with *Brown v. Board,* which prompted further probing by two validating senators on the Republican side.[21] Also similar to dissertation defenses in which the basic subject and approach of the dissertation is accepted, questions tend to focus on procedural matters and questions of interpretation. Among the 100 questions asked O'Connor by presumably validating senators, 85 percent dealt with legal principles and procedures as opposed to substantive policy issues like abortion or school prayer. Thus, O'Connor was quizzed on *stare decisis,* federal-state jurisdictions, federal court jurisdiction, legislative-judicial relationships, constitutional revision, and other topics of judicial relevance, but not on topics one would think sufficient to prompt a negative decision concerning the nominee.

Partisan. A partisan is one who has already decided how to vote on the nominee and uses the hearings to press the partisan view. A partisan may be either positive or negative toward the nominee. The positive partisan will use the hearings as an opportunity to assist the nominee. This is done through praise of the nominee, by posing questions that permit the nominee to look as good as possible and by defending the nominee against attacks of opponents. On the other hand, the negative partisan will use the hearings to call the fitness of the nominee into question.

Senator Thurmond provides an interesting profile of a positive partisan for the Reagan nominations and, by way of contrast, a negative partisan in the Thurgood Marshall and Abe Fortas (nomination to be chief justice) hearings. In the O'Connor, Rehnquist, and Scalia hearings, Thurmond's opening statements were supportive of the nominees. His lead-off questions to each of the justices provided them with the opportunity to confront major issues of their nominations in a relatively unthreatening way. As the initial interrogator, Thurmond was able to pose questions in a very open-ended fashion that dealt with what was perceived to be the concern of potential opponents. In this way the nominee was able to make initial statements about these issues in a nonconfrontational way. This is exemplified by the following questions to O'Connor, each of which was not followed with further probes by Thurmond, but was simply dropped after O'Connor made what appeared to be virtually a prepared statement.

> . . . would you state your views on the proper role of the Supreme Court in our system of government?[22]
>
> Would you discuss your philosophy on abortion, both personal and judicial, and explain your actions as a state senator in Arizona on certain specific matters?[23]

In more controversial nominations, the positive partisan may find it necessary to play a more vigorous role in defense of the nominee and in counter-attacking the negative partisans. In the Rehnquist hearings, Senator Hatch displayed this vigorous aspect of the positive partisan. For example, he defended Rehnquist's lone dissent in the "Bob Jones" case, arguing there were legitimately two sides to the question involved and that Rehnquist's dissent was indeed rational and not a function of racial prejudice. He presented detailed data concerning the frequency of Rehnquist's dissents to demonstrate how his tendency to dissent on his own had declined in more recent years. Even though the Scalia nomination was less controversial, Hatch pursued the positive partisan role there as well, defending certain decisions by Scalia to allay fears that he might be anti-press with respect to the First Amendment.

For negative partisans, the hope is to persuade others to oppose the nomination and to make the nominee look bad. In the Abe Fortas hearings, Thurmond also played the partisan role with cunning and vigor, but in that instance as a negative partisan. His questions were of a type that Fortas, as would have most any other nominee, refused to answer as inappropriate. However, whereas Thurmond invited O'Connor to decline to answer if she felt her answers ". . . would impinge upon (her) responsibilities as an Associate Justice of the Supreme Court . . . ,"[24] Thurmond rifled question after question at Fortas, chiding each refusal to answer with ". . . and you refuse to answer that?"[25] In the Marshall hearings, Thurmond took the nominee through questions of legal technicalities and historical occurrences that proved difficult to answer in an effort to embarrass the nominee and perhaps gain support for the opposition effort.[26]

In the Rehnquist hearings, some Democrats tried to make Rehnquist look bad with respect to certain legal, moral, and ethical questions. For example, they raised questions concerning Rehnquist's accession to restrictive housing covenants, whether he had participated in intimidating minority voters, whether he supported maintaining the "separate but equal" doctrine at the time of *Brown v. Board,* and other issues. They argued that his frequency of lone dissents placed him out of the mainstream of legal thought in the country. In the absence of a single major negative issue, the opponents tried to construct a basis for opposition on an accumulation of negative elements over a period of 32 years. In the end, their failure to rally enough opposition may have been due in part to the absence of a sufficiently strong emotional issue, and certainly in part to the fact that political liberals constituted a distinct minority of senators both on the committee and in the Senate.

Educator. Senators who have made up their minds before the hearings have the most flexibility in their role selection. Unencumbered by a need to establish information on which their decision will be based, they are free to pursue a wide range of objectives. This is particularly true in a noncontroversial nomination in which the role of partisan seems relatively unnecessary. One additional role that surfaced in the O'Connor and Scalia hearings is that of "educator." This is a broad role that may have different targets for educational improvement. Senators may wish to educate the nominee, fellow committee members, fellow senators, the president, the public, and perhaps specific population subgroups as well. The educator, then, is one who wishes to use the hearings as an opportunity to inform and perhaps influence one or more of these targets.

In the Scalia hearing, Senator Kennedy was explicit about his role as he expressed in his opening statement the ". . . hope that, as a result of these hearings . . . he (Scalia) will look with greater sensitivity on (the) critical issues . . ." of race discrimination and women's rights.[27] While it might seem futile to "educate" the nominee, more than one senator thought it worth the effort. As Metzenbaum, an educator in the O'Connor hearings told us, "You just might get her to think or re-think about points that you have made and, at some point down the line, perhaps something positive will happen." Biden also played the educator with nominee O'Connor as the target:

> Would it be, in your opinion, inappropriate for you as the first and only woman at this point on the Supreme Court . . . to for example be involved in national efforts to promote the ERA?
>
> It is your right, if it were your desire, to go out and campaign like the devil for the ERA. It is your right to go out and make speeches across the country about inequality for women, if you believe it. Don't wall your-self off.[28]

Other targets of the educator also surfaced. One Democratic senator commented privately on the need to educate the president to the fact that he should be concerned with more than pleasing conservative Republicans by his appointments, that liberal senators in both parties were concerned about and would scru-tinize the views of Supreme Court nominees. Another senator commented on the opportunity provided by the hearings to raise an issue concerning legislation that he was backing and to obtain publicity for it, tar-geted at both senatorial colleagues and the general public. In one such instance, a senator proceeded to describe the legislation that was pending, provide his justification for the legislation, and secure the nomi-nee's somewhat passive assent that the legislation prob-ably posed no constitutional problems.[29]

Advertiser. Closely akin to the role of educator is that of advertiser. Like the educator, the advertiser may have a variety of targets. Behaviorally, the difference between trying to educate and simply advertise is rather obscure, at best. At this initial stage of inquiry, however, we think there is an important conceptual distinction that relates to the intentions of senators. The intent of the educator is to develop the target's mind and perhaps to persuade to some point of view, while the intent of the advertiser is to inform or publicize some point without the devel-opmental or persuasive component. One example of advertiser behavior is the line of questioning pursued by Kennedy in the O'Connor hearing.

> From your own knowledge and perception how would you characterize the level of discrimination on the basis of sex today?[30]

I wonder if you briefly would discuss your perception of the degree to which black Americans or Hispanic Americans are denied equality in our society.[31]

Such a line of questioning could come from either an educator or an advertiser. This illustrates the inap-propriateness of trying to classify role type from the behavioral enactment of that role. Our interview with Kennedy's staff during the O'Connor hearing led us to conclude that he wished to use this opportunity to demonstrate his concern about what he believed to be the persistent discrimination in our society.

In still other instances, questions asked by the adver-tiser may not differ much from questions asked by an evaluator, to the extent that both may be reflecting con-cerns that are relevant to their constituents. For exam-ple, Senator Dole's question concerning O'Connor's interpretation of the term "strict constructionist" and whether or not she felt that concept described her might come from an evaluator who thought the concept was particularly pertinent. In this case, however, it came form a senator who perceived a home constituency would be reassured by the nominee's anticipated answer. He sought to advertise to his constituency that she was a "strict constructionist" and he was safeguard-ing the Court by making that determination. These examples suggest that, quite often, the advertising sena-tor is also advertising himself by advertising an issue.

Conclusion

With respect to Supreme Court nomination hear-ings, it seems a fact of political and scholarly life that only controversial nominations offer any interest and insight regarding the confirmation process. Such a view tends to focus only on the outcome of the nom-ination as being significant. From that perspective, the most recent three hearings were merely theatrics. As Table 1 shows, the vast majority of senators in each of the three hearings had already made up their minds how to vote even before the hearings had begun. Table 1 reveals that those who expressed "uncertainty" con-cerning their votes ended up opposing the nominee in committee. On the other hand, those whose state-ments were best characterized as "mixed" or "noncom-mittal" always favored the nominee in the committee vote. If one is interested only in outcome, the hearings offered little in drama or significance.

It is our contention, however, that outcome is not the only relevant question for hearings. Senators pursue important goals in both controversial and noncontroversial nominations, as reflected by the efforts of negative partisans, educators and advertisers. Not the least of these goals is to influence the next nomination even before it is made. We do hope that our discussion of several situationally specific roles, along with an explanation of factors that foster these roles, will contribute not only to an understanding of the last three confirmation hearings, but will enhance our comprehension of future hearings—controversial or noncontroversial.

Notes

This article originally appeared in Volume 71, Number 4, December–January 1988, pages 186–196.

1. In the O'Connor nomination, 13 of the 18 committee members made opening statements that voiced satisfaction with the nominee, while only three explicitly expressed any reservations. *Nomination of Sandra Day O'Connor: Hearings Before Congress, First Session* Serial No. J-97-51, 1-31, 34-36, *passim.* (Washington, D.C.: U.S. Government Printing Office, 1982). For Scalia, 13 of the 18 also voiced satisfaction in opening statements, while none of the Senators expressed explicit reservations. *Transcript of Proceedings; United States Senate; Committee on the Judiciary; Nomination of Antonin Scalia, to be Associate Justice of the Supreme Court* (Washington, D.C.: Miller Reporting Co., 1986), 2–3, 11–64, *passim.*

2. Grossman and Wasby, "The Senate and Supreme Court Nominations," *Duke L. J.* (1972), 563.

3. Jewell, "Attitudinal Determinants of Legislative Behavior: The Utility of Role Analysis," in Kornberg and Musolf, (eds.), *Legislatures in Developmental Perspective* (Durham: Duke University Press, 1970), 491.

4. The myth of the hearings as a meeting of open-minded senators seeking information for their decisions is poignantly illustrated during the testimony of Reverand Carl McIntire in the O'Connor hearing. In providing testimony against nominee O'Connor, the Rev. McIntire finds himself addressing only the chair, Senator Thurmond. All other senators are absent. "Senator, I want to protest it. I want to protest coming down to the end of this hearing and only having you to talk to. I sat here and listened at every Senator here on the bench . . . and a majority have already said they are going to vote for her. . . ." *O'Connor Hearings, supra n. 1,* at 345.

5. The role of the staff in interacting with and preparing senators for their committee presentations is noted in Jones and Woll, *The Private World of Congress* (New York: Free Press, 1979), 154–171; and in Mackenzie, *The Politics of Presidential Appointments* (New York: Free Press, 1981), 182.

6. The research design is best described as field research involving an unstructured interview, but one that consistently sought answers to a basic set of concerns, namely:

- the criteria considered important in Supreme Court nominations;
- the techniques and sources for gathering information concerning the nominee;
- the sources of efforts to influence a senator's decision regarding the confirmation;
- the importance of the nominee's gender in this particular nomination;
- the purposes or functions of the senator's questions during the hearings.

7. Grossman and Wasby, *supra* n. 2, at 588.

8. Sulfridge, "Ideology as a Factor in Senate Consideration of Supreme Court Nominations," *J. of Pol.* 42 (May 1980), 566.

9. *Rehnquist Hearings* (C-Span televised hearings, July 30, 1986).

10. In his opening statement of the Rehnquist hearings, Senator Biden, the ranking Democratic member of the committee, asserted that ". . . as the framers of the Constitution intended, the burden is upon the nominee and his proponents to make the case for confirmation of Chief Justice." *Rehnquist Hearings, supra* n. 9.

11. Grossman and Wasby, *supra* n. 2, at 588.

12. *Scalia Proceedings, supra* n. 1, at 36–40.

13. For newspaper coverage of Rehnquist, see especially, the *New York Times* July 27, 1986, at A18, and July 29, 1986, at A14. For a report on Scalia, see the *New York Times,* August 6, 1986, at A13.

14. *O'Connor Hearings, supra* n. 1, at 29.

15. Sulfridge, *supra* n. 8, at 566.

16. *O'Connor Hearings, supra* n. 1, at 249.

17. Ibid. at 248.

18. Ibid. at 116–118.

19. *Scalia Hearings, supra* n. 1, at 29.

20. Ibid. at 118, 121.

21. *O'Connor Hearings, supra* n. 1, at 102–103, 131–132.

22. Ibid. at 60.

23. Ibid. at 60.

24. Ibid. at 132.

25. *Nominations of Abe Fortas and Homer Thornberry; Hearings Before the Committee of the Judiciary, United States Senate, Ninetieth Congress, Second Session* (Washington, D.C.: U.S. Government Printing Office, 1968), 183–184.

26. *Nomination of Thurgood Marshall; Hearings Before the Committee of the Judiciary, United States Senate, Ninetieth Congress, First Session* (Washington, D.C.: U.S. Government Printing Office, 1968), 183–184.

27. *Scalia Proceedings, supra* n. 1, at 25.

28. The written transcript deviates somewhat from Biden's actual comments as revealed by a videotape playback. We provide a quote from the videotape.

29. *O'Connor Hearings, supra* n. 1, at 153–154.

30. Ibid. at 76.

31. Ibid. at 77.

The Bork hearing: rocks and roles

From the day the president nominated Robert Bork, it was apparent this hearing would be different from those of Reagan's other three nominations. Senator Kennedy sounded immediate opposition that grew to include the five liberal Democrats pitted in a partisan battle against the five conservative Republicans[1] for the hearts and votes of the committee moderates (Specter, DeConcini, Byrd) and the conservative Democrat Heflin. As undecided decision makers, these latter four would pursue evaluator roles in an effort to make up their respective minds concerning their votes. Given the uncertainty of the outcome, no one had the luxury of pursuing the validator, educator, and advertiser roles discussed in our accompanying article.

Not only was the configuration of role playing different from the previous hearings, the level of hostility was considerably greater. Partisans on both sides hurled verbal rocks at each other, the president, various groups and individuals lobbying the hearing, and the nominee himself. These differences from previous hearings stimulated our interest in two directions. First, we wanted to see if our approach in the accompanying article could help make sense of these events. Second, we wanted to determine if a more generalized model of the role playing process could be suggested to incorporate the different hearings of the four Reagan nominees.

Hearing controversy

Clearly, what was different about the Bork hearings was their level of controversy. The O'Connor and Scalia hearings lacked any real drama. The Rehnquist elevation to chief justice had stirred some controversy because the relatively small group of Democratic liberals on the Judiciary Committee chose to play negative partisan roles. The Bork nomination added the essential defining characteristic of a controversial nomination, namely, the potential for actually defeating the nomination. For the first time among the Reagan nominees, the outcome was genuinely in doubt.

The controversy stemmed from two of the basic components that structure the nature of the hearings: the political situation at the time of the nomination and the nominee himself.[2] Three aspects of the political situation seem especially significant:

First, the partisan and ideological opposition to the nominee no longer constituted a distinct minority who faced certain defeat. The 1986 election produced a substantial Democratic majority (54 to 46) to replace the Republican majority that had considered the president's previous nominees. On the Judiciary Committee, the Republican majority of 11 members, containing 9 conservatives, was reduced to only 5 conservatives (plus the moderate Specter). On the other hand, the Democrats retained their five liberals, two moderates, and one conservative (see Table 2).

Second, the president's power had waned. Combined with the electoral resurgence of the Democratic opposition in 1986 were the facts that the president had now entered the "lame duck" period, the last two years in office, and had suffered prestige and credibility drops due to the Iran-contra hearings and other political setbacks. At the time of the Rehnquist and Scalia hearings, the president's approval rating hovered around 67 percent. When the Bork hearings took place, these ratings had dropped to about 52 percent.[3] The presumption in favor of a president's nominee, based on the president's power, was seriously eroded.

Third, the ideological balance of the Court seemed to be at stake. The retiring Justice Powell had been on the winning side of more 5 to 4 decisions than any other justice.[4] His apparently pivotal role on the Court upped the ante for this particular nomination.

In addition to the inherently controversial situation, Bork proved to be a nominee who provided several negative emotional issues around which to rally an opposition. In prior nominations, negative emotional issues more commonly involved questions of ethics, incompetence, or racism. The nomination of Bork, an academician with nearly impeccable ethical and intellectual

(Box continues on next page)

The Bork hearing: rocks and roles *(continued)*

Table 2. Political ideology and pre-hearing commitment to Judge Bork

Senator	Party	Ideology[1]	Pre-hearing commitment
Biden	Dem.	liberal	explicit opposition
Kennedy	Dem.	liberal	explicit opposition
Byrd	Dem.	moderate	uncertain
Metzenbaum	Dem.	liberal	explicit opposition
DeConcini	Dem.	moderate	uncertain
Leahy	Dem.	liberal	explicit opposition
Heflin	Dem.	conservative	uncertain
Simon	Dem.	liberal	implicit opposition
Thurmond	Rep.	conservative	explicit support
Hatch	Rep.	conservative	explicit support
Simpson	Rep.	conservative	explicit support
Grassley[2]	Rep.	moderate	explicit support
Specter	Rep.	moderate	uncertain
Humphrey	Rep.	conservative	explicit support

1. Political ideology was established by averaging the ratings of the Conservative Coalition and Americans for Democratic Action (ADA). Scores between 25 and 75 were assigned a "moderate" rating, while scores of 75 and above and 25 and below were assigned the appropriate "conservative" or "liberal" label. The ADA scores were drawn from the *Congressional Quarterly Weekly Report*, August 22, 1987, at 1968. The Conservative Coalition scores were kindly provided by the *Congressional Quarterly* research staff (Michael Amin and Andrew Taylor) and covered 23 votes in 1987 up to the August recess.

2. Senator Grassley's classification reflects a departure from previous, more conservative ratings. With scores of 30 on the ADA index and 61 on the Conservative Coalition, he remains closer to his conservative colleagues than to the other moderates. Given his initial support for Bork and his consistent conservative stance in the Reagan nominations, we have continued to characterize him in the text as one of the five conservative Republicans on the committee.

credentials, might normally have provoked little excitement. Instead the hearings provided a rare sight in judicial nomination proceedings, a controversy stirred by emotions about legal concepts. It was Bork's own intellectual passion, as represented in a career of provocative conservative writings, that roused the opposition, which articulated concerns over the nominee's apparent lack of commitment to a variety of civil rights and liberties.

Controversy, it seems, can arise as a result of an interplay of factors that constitute the political situation or as a result of factors that relate to an individual nominee; however, these are not independent factors. Whether the nominee's sex, ethnicity, religion, or ideology are potentially controversial matters depends, in part, on the political atmosphere of the times. In turn, these factors may help structure the political situation.

In Justice O'Connor's case, gender played a major role in creating a noncontroversial nomination. In Judge Bork's case, his ideology, portrayed by opponents and even some supporters as an ardent, almost reactionary, conservatism, assured his status as a controversial nominee to liberals and eventually to moderates and southern Democratic conservatives as well. Of course, Justice Rehnquist attained a certain controversiality among liberals by virtue of his conservative record. Yet his initial nomination and his more recent elevation to chief justice did not reach the level of controversy surrounding the Bork nomination. Why?

The answer lies with those aspects of the political system and environment in which Judge Bork found himself, as highlighted by the three factors specified at the beginning of this note. In short, the situation was highly charged. Contrast this with Scalia and Rehnquist, both of whom were

Figure 1. Interplay of situation and nominee controversy in the Reagan nominations

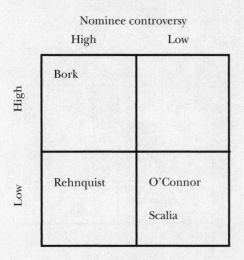

Figure 1 models the interplay of these two areas. We place the O'Connor and Scalia nominations in the cell that denotes a relatively low level of controversy with respect to both the nominee and the situation. Rehnquist presents a controversial nominee, but in a political situation devoid of so many of the potential conflicts that beset Bork. Of course, Bork falls in the cell of high controversy for both situation and nominee, which helps to visualize why the hearings were so controversial. We shall return to this model later to discuss some implications that derive from it.

Controversy and role playing

Given the controversy surrounding the Bork nomination, we may ask whether the types of roles differed from those played in the less controversial hearings of the three previous nominees. Implicit in our article is a model of individual role selection, presented in Figure 2.

We have identified a considerable number of situational, nominee, and personal factors that affect whether or not a senator will make a decision concerning his vote by the commencement of the hearings.[5] These factors determine the level of controversy surrounding the nomination and they affect the pre-hearing disposition of the senator's confirmation decision. The model

perceived as quite conservative nominees. Those hearings, however, occurred with a stronger president, prior to the next congressional election, with a more conservative dominated Republican majority in the Senate, and at a time when the ideological make-up of the Court did not rest in the balance. Conservative Scalia replaced the equally conservative Burger. Rehnquist, of course, was already on the Court.

Figure 2. A model of individual role selection

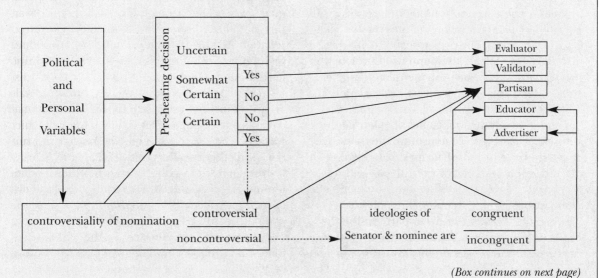

(Box continues on next page)

The Bork hearing: rocks and roles *(continued)*

also suggests that the level of controversy may influence a senator's pre-hearing decision status. For example, it is our perception that controversy tends to reduce the likelihood of a "somewhat certain" position. Controversy is partly generated by firmly held opposing opinions, which, in turn, induces those holding less firm opinions into one or another of the two camps.

The role adopted by a senator at the hearings will depend most directly on his pre-hearing disposition. The model asserts that those senators who are uncertain about their vote will pursue an evaluator role. They must ask questions designed to address their uncertainties. In the Bork nomination senators Specter, DeConcini, and Heflin seem to have done just that.[6] All other votes on the committee were already certain, as evidenced by pre-hearing and/or opening statements. Because the opposition carries the burden of establishing the unfitness of the nominee, they tend to adopt partisan roles in an aggressive effort to discredit the nominee. The "certain Yes" senators can pursue a variety of strategies unless the nomination is controversial. In such circumstances, they too must pursue a partisan role in an effort to combat the opposition. This clearly occurred in the Bork hearing, with the partisan efforts reaching spectacular heights (or depths) that were, in turn, deplored by both sides.

In less controversial hearings, those who still are uncertain about the nominee as the hearings begin will adopt the evaluator role. We are also likely to see the re-emergence of a few who are somewhat certain supporters, in which case the validator role will be pursued. Any opposition will play the negative partisan role[7] The biggest change in less controversial hearings is that those whose votes are certain for confirmation are free to pursue the educator and advertiser roles, as well as a somewhat less intense positive partisan role.

Implications

The two models and the ensuing discussions have implications for assessing the character of future hearings, the individual roles that are pursued in those hearings, and even the outcome. The

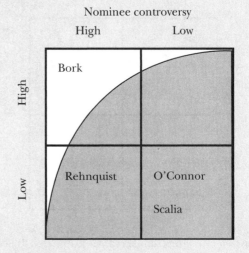

Figure 3. Interplay of situation and nominee controversy on committee confirmation

▓ Committee recomends confirmation
☐ Committee recommends against confirmation

model of situation/nominee controversy provides one way of characterizing hearings. In conjunction with the individual role selection model, one may seek the presence, absence, or predominance of certain roles in particular types of hearings. Thus, partisan and evaluator roles are most likely in instances of high situation and high nominee controversy. Conversely, in a nomination that is low on both dimensions of controversy, senators are able to play educator, advertiser, and validator roles, in addition to the evaluator and partisan ones.

In mixed nominations, where there is controversy on one dimension but not on the other, the partisan and evaluator roles are also quite likely to surface. The other roles may be played as well, but predicting their appearance depends in part on the degrees of controversy presented by the nominee or situation. We save a fuller exploration of such specification for another time.

Another interesting aspect of the situation/nominee controversy model is the implication for predicting outcome. For example, in instances of low situation and low nominee controversy, confirmation is a certainty. Where either the situation or nominee is controversial, but not both, the odds still favor confirmation, depending on the location of the nominee in that particular cell. Finally, in highly charged situations with a controversial nominee, the outcome can go either way. These implications are diagrammed in Figure 3.

An interesting aspect of this model is an implication that, had the Bork and Scalia nominations been reversed in order, both would likely have gained seats on the Court. A Bork nomination in a less controversial situation should have succeeded. Scalia's noncontroversial status as an individual presumably would have produced confirmation even in a more volatile political situation.

Whether the failure of the Bork nomination serves to defuse an inherently controversial political situation remains to be seen at this writing. That seemed clearly to be the administration's strategy in pursuing the Bork nomination to a Senate vote. We think a more certain route towards confirmation is another strategy offered by the model. A simple appointment of a noncontroversial individual, even if quite conservative, can still gain confirmation to the Court.

—John Stookey and George Watson

Notes

This article originally appeared in Volume 71, Number 4, December–January 1988, pages 194–196.

1. See note 2 in Table 1.

2. Watson and Stookey, "Supreme Court confirmation hearings: a view from the Senate," *Judicature* 71 (1988), 188–189.

3. As communicated to us by Richard Morin, polling editor, *Washington Post,* from data collected through the ABC/*Washington Post* surveys of September 1986, and September 1987, respectively.

4. Goldman, *Constitutional Law: Cases and Essays* (New York: Harper and Row, 1987), 157.

5. Watson and Stookey, *supra* n. 2, at 188–189.

6. Senator Byrd did not participate fully in asking questions due to his other commitments as majority leader. While he did exhibit uncertainty in his opening statement of the Bork hearing, his diminished or lack of participation in all of the Reagan nominee hearings has led us to omit him from the analysis.

7. Watson and Stookey, *supra* n. 2, at 191–192.

The judicial confirmation process and the blue slip

Brannon P. Denning

Many senators defend the blue slip as necessary to encourage the president to respect what they see as a constitutional obligation to seek senatorial advice, but in fact it has been used with increasing frequency to defeat nominees.

If there is any bright side to the un-believably rancorous confirmation battles that marked the Clinton years, and which are now occurring in the Bush administration, it is that they have exposed to public scrutiny customs and practices that enable individual senators to wield a *de facto* veto over presidential nominees (and the defensive measures available to presidents). After 1994, for example, when Republicans regained control of the House and Senate, senators used the power of committee chairs and the "hold" to kill nominations for cabinet positions, department heads, ambassadorships, and judgeships on what seemed to be an unprecedented scale. For this, Republicans faced intense criticism. Now, recent controversies over President George W. Bush's judicial appointments have brought to light another obscure Senate custom, the blue slip.

The emotional aftermath of the 2000 election meant that confirmation for Bush's nominees, his judicial nominees in particular, would be rough going. Some commentators even called on the Senate not to confirm *any* Supreme Court nominees, exhorting Senate Democrats to oppose vigorously "judicial ideologues intent on a revolutionary agenda." [1] For their part, Democrats in the then-evenly-divided Senate were demanding that the President respect the blue slip procedure by agreeing to consult Democratic senators prior to nominating persons from their state to judgeships. Democrats on the Judiciary Committee were angered by then-Chairman Orrin Hatch's plan to require *both* home-state senators to withhold slips before sinking a nomination, which Democrats alleged was an abrupt change in the way Hatch had treated blue slips during the Clinton administration.

The issue became so contentious that Democrats, furious at Republican refusals to adhere to past practices, threatened either to place holds on or filibuster Bush judicial nominations unless they were assured that Democrats in states whose delegations were split would have the opportunity to blue-slip judicial nominees to whom they objected. Democrats thus hoped to ensure that the administration would have an incentive to consult with Democrats before formally announcing nominations.

A few days after control switched to the Democrats, the blue slip again made the news when California Senator Barbara Boxer announced her intent to use her prerogative to nix the nomination of California Representative Christopher Cox to the Ninth Circuit Court of Appeals. As a result, Cox asked President Bush to withdraw his name from consideration. Paul Gigot and William Safire criticized Boxer's move, and criticized the blue slip process, likening it to a "blackball" and a "burial shroud" for nominees. [2]

Whether or not the non-return of a blue slip would be the death knell for judicial nominees became one of the most hotly contested issues confronting the Senate as it set about reorganizing following the assumption of control by the Democrats. Republicans demanded floor votes on all of the President's judicial nominees, regardless of whether they received a favorable vote in committee; Democrats refused such blanket assurances, claiming that such a move would undermine the Senate's "advice and consent" role. In the end, Democrats only assured Republicans that they would follow the "tradition of bringing Supreme Court nominees to the Senate floor but stopped short of any iron-clad commitments." [3] Republicans, however, did get an agreement that all blue slips would be made public. [4]

News coverage of the spat raised the visibility of the blue slip, and also exposed it to criticism. In general, editorial commentary was uniformly negative, with many newspapers calling for its abolition. At least, many editorials argued, blue slips should be made public, as they eventually were under the Senate's reorganization plan. However, the coverage did not do much to explain its origins or past practice; some coverage seemed to confuse it with the "hold." Reporters for the *Washington Post* described it only as a custom

Judicature Volume 85, Number 5, pp. 218–226

that "dates back several decades and is rooted in the tradition of 'senatorial courtesy,' which traces its roots to the presidency of George Washington." [5] It was also unclear from published reports whether a senator's failure to return a blue slip was a death blow to a nomination, as Democrats claimed; or, as Senator Hatch argued, "not an absolute bar to proceeding with a nomination. . . ."

History of the blue slip

The blue slip is the result of the institutionalization of "senatorial courtesy." [6] When a judicial nomination is made, the chair of the Senate Judiciary Committee sends "blue slips" (so called because of the color of paper used) to the senators of the nominee's home state. If even one senator declines to return the slip, then the nomination is dead in the water, or further action will be extremely difficult, depending on which practice the chair decides to follow. The blue slip procedure is only employed by the Judiciary Committee for federal judges. Other nominees, however, can be stopped by senators who put a "hold" on a nominee, or by chairs of committees who refuse to hold confirmation hearings. The Senate majority leader too can halt a nomination by refusing to schedule an up-or-down vote. [7]

The blue slip's origins are somewhat obscure. The last extensive debate on its use was in the late 1970s, when Senator Ted Kennedy, then chairman of the Judiciary Committee, announced that withholding blue slips would no longer automatically be fatal to a nominee's chances. [8] Kennedy's position was significant because of the creation of more than 100 district and circuit court vacancies under the Omnibus Judgeship Act in 1978, and by President Jimmy Carter's decision to rely on nominating commissions to select candidates by merit.

According to a memorandum prepared by the Judiciary Committee staff in 1979, the blue slip procedure had been around for more than 25 years. [9] It represented an effort by the committee to institutionalize the "senatorial courtesy" owed to fellow senators' objections to nominees from their home state. A couple of interesting facts emerged from the committee staff's description of the blue slip procedure. On the blue slip itself was written the following: "Under a rule of the Committee, unless a reply is received from you within a week from this date, it will be assumed that you have no objection to this nomination." But the staff memorandum reported that, as of 1979, "at least for a decade there has been no 'rule of the Committee' on the subject"—meaning that there is no formal basis in the Committee's rules for the procedure. This is still true today. [10] Second, as the blue slip literally read, failure to return it meant *no* objection, which is precisely the opposite of how the procedure works. As the staff memorandum noted, "[n]o hearing has been scheduled on a nominee in the absence of a returned blue slip" rendering it "an automatic and mechanical one-member veto over nominees."

The staff noted that presidents "can ignore a senator's personal opposition and attempt to have his nomination confirmed by the Senate"; but the memorandum also hit upon the power of the blue slip—and what makes it so difficult to study. "Generally," continued the memo, "conflicts are resolved *before* a name is submitted. In other cases, the nomination may die in committee without any record on whether a withheld blue slip was responsible."

In his opening statement to the 1979 hearings on filling vacancies created by the Omnibus Judgeship Act, Senator Kennedy stated that he would not "unilaterally table a nomination simply because a blue slip is not returned by a colleague." He conceded, however, that he could not "discard cavalierly the tradition of senatorial courtesy, exception-riddled and outdated as it may be." Therefore, in the absence of a blue slip, he proposed to bring the nomination before the committee for a vote on whether or not to proceed, "rather than letting the nomination die. . . ." Thus, said Kennedy, "[t]he committee, and ultimately the Senate, can work its will."

The "will," however, that his colleagues—particularly those in the minority party—seemed inclined to "work" was not necessarily in concert with Kennedy's reforming spirit. In his opening statement, which was read by Senator Paul Laxalt, Strom Thurmond "presume[d] that the committee will honor the blue-slip system that has worked so well in the past." Not only was this "a matter of senatorial courtesy," but was also a "means of an effective scrutiny of a candidate. . . ." In his statement, Senator Laxalt agreed:

If we finally get through a selection process and somebody comes down here who is . . . obnoxious or otherwise is not acceptable, I think, as a matter of senatorial responsibility, we should preserve [senators' rights to withhold the blue slip]. I feel strongly about the blue slip process, since it has not been abused, that it should be retained. I hope personally that I never have to utilize it, but I never want to foreclose myself or any of my colleagues in the right case from being able to do that.

That responsibility "to call these tough shots within our States," he added, was "why we are here. . . ."

The only other extensive treatment of the blue slip, and senators' attitudes toward it, is found in an excellent article by political scientist Elliott Slotnick, published in *Judicature* around the same time as the Senate hearings. Drawing upon interviews with senators and their staffers, Slotnick acknowledged that the blue slip process "created a sort of 'pocket veto' of judicial nominees for home state senators of both parties," and that it had become "a major target for the reform groups." But Slotnick's research suggested that it had not been used that often, and had not been abused by senators: "Surprisingly . . . 88 per cent of our respondents indicated that they had *never* used the blue slip process for *any* purpose other than signing off or commenting favorably on a nominee." Of the six respondents that had withheld blue slips, only two did not eventually return it. This suggested to Slotnick that "withholding the blue slip was a delaying tactic which allowed [senators] to make further inquiry and to negotiate on the vacancy—the 'classic' use of the blue slip." [11]

The most interesting aspect of Slotnick's research was the "blue slip for me, but not for thee" attitude of many senators. While a majority of the senators he surveyed favored retention of the blue slip process, a larger majority indicated that their decision to support a nominee or not would *not* be dictated by a colleague's decision to withhold the blue slip. Even among those senators who *favored* retaining the process, 39 percent would not defer to colleagues exercising their blue slip prerogative. [12] To Slotnick, this signaled a degradation of certain cherished Senate norms, like reciprocity and courtesy. He might have added that, if forced to choose, most senators would evidently support their colleagues only to ensure that *their* exercise of the prerogative would be supported in the future.

If so much distrust surrounded the procedure, then why had it been retained? For some senators, wrote Slotnick, tradition was enough. Others suggested that the blue slip preserved consensus and harmony among senators by offering an "early warning" system of sorts that could help avoid embarrassing and acrimonious controversies from occurring either in committee or on the Senate floor. Still other senators invoked the historic reason for deferring to senators' wishes regarding

nominees: home state senators are in the best position to evaluate a nominee and provide unique insights.

One obvious reason for retaining the custom is that it forces an administration—even if of a different party from the senator—to deal directly with that senator on judicial nominations, thus enhancing her prestige. Perhaps even more important is the fact that it ensures that senators of the minority party can play a significant role in the nomination process. Not surprisingly, 94 percent of Republicans responding to Slotnick's study favored retaining the blue slip process. "The minority party," he concluded, "will apparently do whatever is necessary to maintain a meaningful role in the judicial recruitment process."

Still, despite the controversy generated by the process, Slotnick was able to conclude in 1980 that "the blue slip system is rarely used and it often serves some other purpose than defeat of a nominee. Its major function seems to be to delay, not defeat, a nomination." It is instructive to compare the blue slip process circa 2001 with the process as described by Slotnick above. Though the secrecy shrouding the process—which has only recently been lifted—makes it difficult to say for sure, it appears that over the past 10 years the fears of the blue slip's critics have been realized.

If Senator Helms's continued obstruction of any North Carolina nominees to the Fourth Circuit, and Senator Boxer's treatment of Christopher Cox are at all representative, the blue slip is now seen as a means to defeat, not merely delay, a nominee; and perhaps prevent the nomination from being made in the first place. Nor is this use without precedent among the Senate's other unwritten customs: witness the hold's evolution from an accommodation to members who can't be present for a debate to a blue slip process writ large, in which legislation *and* nominees can be held up by any senator, for any reason, as long as the leadership decides to honor the hold. That she chose to threaten withholding her blue slip on ideological grounds, as opposed to any other manifest unfitness for office, suggests that Senator Boxer was taking advantage of an established practice. That is, in none of the news reports was she criticized by her colleagues for breaking with tradition. While conservative pundits criticized her action, they seemed to take it only as a symptom of the problem with the custom itself.

Moreover, the withdrawal of Cox from consideration demonstrates the real power of the blue slip: a senator need not use it in a direct confrontation with the administration over a nominee. Just making known that the senator is opposed and would, if the person is nominated, withhold the blue slip, sends a powerful signal that trouble is in the offing. Then the administration must decide whether or not it wants to pick a fight. With judicial nominations, then, the Senate has created an effective procedure for ensuring that its "advice" is sought by the president prior to the announcement of a nomination, despite suggestions that that function has been "short-circuited."[13]

Is it constitutional?

Slotnick noted that the blue slip process was inconsistent with a "minimalist" view of the confirmation process. To be sure, its presence represents a rather more complicated picture of nomination and confirmation than that suggested by Article II. But is it—and the obstacles for nominees that it produces—unconstitutional? Article II, section 2 grants presidents the power to nominate judges, who are appointed when they obtain the "advice and consent" of the Senate. Defending the system in *The Federalist*, Hamilton praised it for its transparency and its clear allocation of responsibility.[14] With the roles clearly assigned, and the matter conducted with publicity, Hamilton wrote, "[t]he blame of a bad nomination would fall upon the President singly and absolutely. The censure of rejecting a good one would lie entirely at the door of the Senate. . . ." Hamilton contrasted the appointment mechanism of the Constitution with New York's Council of Appointment, where, because it was unclear what part anyone played in proposing or approving nominations, and because of the secrecy in which the Council operated, "all idea of responsibility is lost."[15]

One might say the same about the blue slip process. First, it dilutes the power of the executive to appoint whomever he wishes. Knowing of the blue slip process, and of senators' expectations that the president will appoint their people for certain posts, can we assign unqualified responsibility to the president for those appointments? Second, the secrecy with which the blue slip operates (or operated, if the present agreement holds) also diffuses responsibility and reduces transparency in the process. If a senator can withhold a blue slip, give no reasons, and the public knows nothing about it, what is the check upon extreme abuses? But the most serious constitutional objection is that it allows *individuals* to exert what is supposed to be an *institutional* check. A single senator withholding con-

sent, and depriving the Senate as a body from voting a nominee up or down, is difficult to square with the Constitution, which specifies that it is the *Senate* (not "senators") that is to provide "advice and consent."[16] While the Constitution authorizes the Senate to make its own rules, recall that there has not been a formal rule from the Judiciary Committee authorizing the blue slip for nearly a half century.

On the other hand, the Senate is not only expected to "consent" to nominations, but also to give "advice" regarding them. The Constitution does not explicitly set forth an advice-giving mechanism, but the text seems to anticipate more than a rubberstamp role for the Senate. The Constitution establishes an expectation that the president will actively seek the guidance of senators in making appointments. But, there is no mention of *how*, exactly, he is supposed to obtain the advice of the Senate,[17] thus there is no way to assure that he will do so. Moreover, because he alone is vested with the power to appoint, it is unlikely that the Senate could ever persuade a court to invalidate a presidential nomination on the grounds that it was made without sufficient advice from the Senate.

Thus, in the absence of an effective legal sanction, the Senate had to create a sanction that would penalize a president's refusal to seek Senate advice. The Senate decided to "encourage" him to consult with them by creating a way to sanction him if he does not—the blue slip. (Another objection may be lodged: that the blue slip procedure makes no allowance for a president who, in good faith, seeks to comply with the advice norm—as President Clinton is said to have done—but does not take the advice, which he is not required to do. One might argue that the blue slip permits an individual senator to exact an asymmetical penalty. This is a serious objection; one that suggests that reform is needed.)

The blue slip as sanction

Institutional norms and their enforcement. There is a growing body of literature that uses law-and-economics analysis to describe how and why people cooperate in the absence of legal sanction and how non-legal "norms" are derived and enforced in communities. Though even among the specialists in this area there is no one agreed-upon definition for a "norm" most agree that it is a behavioral expectation, deviation from which may call down a sanction from the community in which the norm is operative.

As Michael Gerhardt has recently demonstrated, one might extend norm theory to an institutional relationship, like that of the president to the Senate in the confirmation process.[18] I suggest that the blue slip process is the sanction that a president faces for violating the norm of senatorial courtesy in the judicial appointment process.

One of the most important norms enforced by the Senate is that the president feel obligated to seek senators' advice when the position is located within their state; or, more recently, when the potential nominee is from their state. This is one aspect of "senatorial courtesy"—and one with deep historical roots. When President George Washington failed to seek advice from the Georgia senate delegation regarding a nomination for a federal position in Savannah, Washington was forced to withdraw the nomination in favor of the person recommended by the senators.

While Article II's failure to provide any formal advice-giving process has led some to the erroneous conclusion that "advice and consent" was merely a term of art and not to be understood literally, or that the "advice" component has fallen into desuetude, the persistence of the courtesy norm and the evolution of the blue slip suggest the opposite. One could see the Georgia senators' move against Washington's nominee as a reaction to a violation of the expectation, created by the language of Article II itself, that the president would consult the senators prior to making formal nominations. As Harold Chase has observed, other senators were willing to support their colleagues' in their opposition to the president's choice because it was "easy for senators to see that if they joined together against the president to protect their individual interests in appointments, they could to a large degree assure that the president could only make such appointments as would be palatable to them as individuals." [19]

Both the decision to oppose Washington's appointment and the other senators' decision to support their colleagues in standing against the president were signals. To the president, the senators signaled an intention to regard pre-nomination consultation as a norm of the confirmation process. The other senators signaled to their Georgia colleagues that they could be counted on to support them in their decision, and, consequently, that *they* would be worthy of similar support in the future. The president, on the other hand, by withdrawing the nomination, clearly signaled to the whole Senate that he recognized the validity of the advice norm, and would abide by it.

The evolution of the advice norm as an aspect of senatorial courtesy. Though early presidents resisted, an expectation eventually emerged that presidents would, in fact, consider names for certain governmental posts from the senators and representatives in whose states or districts those persons would serve. While respecting this norm necessarily involved surrendering some of the executive power to nominate, its observance was essential because of the increase in the number of federal offices by the mid-nineteenth century and the inability of the president to evaluate candidates for those positions. By the twentieth century, as one commentator noted:

> [T]he custom of Congressional "advice" was thoroughly systematized by the Republicans. Not only were the Senators recognized as the "referees" in the case of statewide positions; but if there were two administration Senators, and especially if they were not harmonious, they made formal agreements dividing the patronage [in the state].[20]

This norm was considered firmly established by the mid-twentieth century, but was not *static*. For example, prior to the 1950s, Joseph Harris described the custom as follows:

> Under the custom any member of the Senate may block the confirmation of a nomination by stating that the nominee is "personally obnoxious" or offensive to him. In the past, it has not been necessary for the senator to do more than merely indicate his opposition to a nomination, and repeat the customary formula. An objection to a nomination does not mean that the nominee is actually "personally obnoxious" to the objecting senator; it frequently involves no animus whatever, but merely indicates that the senator has another candidate. Formerly it was not necessary or expected that the objecting senator give any reasons to support his objection . . . Usually he advised the chairman of the committee to which the nomination had been referred, and the nomination was not reported to the Senate.

Harris noted, however, that "in recent years the objecting senator has been expected to state his reasons so that the Senate can judge whether they are sufficient." [21] In several cases he described, senators gave as the reason for opposition the fact that the president had ignored (or at least not actively sought) senators' advice on the nominees.

In one particular case, Georgia Senator Richard Russell asked the Senate to oppose a judicial nomination made by President Harry Truman for which Russell preferred another candidate, stating that senators "have a right to believe if the man they recommend is qualified the recommendation will be followed." Otherwise, Russell warned, "the constitutional power of the Senate to advise and consent to a nomination means nothing; it has no significance."[22] The president's nomination, he continued, was "contrary to custom, and in defiance of the constitutional powers of the Senate." The Senate responded to Russell's entreaties by defeating Truman's nominee without a roll call vote.

The Senate's support of Senator Russell and others came after a short period of time in which stating personal opposition was not sufficient to block a confirmation—reasons needed to accompany the charge of "obnoxiousness" so that the Senate could evaluate them.[23]

Contrasting the courtesy norm and the blue slip. Thus, the advice norm clearly preceded the blue slip, and was enforced through the support of colleagues on which objecting senators might count as an aspect of the Senate's courtesy. It is interesting, however, to note a few differences between the courtesy norm and the blue slip. In his classic article on the norm, Joseph Harris noted that the contests usually arose "between the President and members of the Senate . . . when the President declines to nominate the candidate proposed by a senator of his party, ordinarily on the ground that the . . . nominee is not qualified."

A more common objection at the time Harris was writing (1952) was the so-called "personal" objection "entered when the objecting senator concedes that a nominee is fully qualified" but whom the senator nevertheless opposes, often because "the nominee is a political opponent of the [objecting] senator. . . ." The point is that *ideological* opposition did not play a large role, or at least workaday "political" concerns were more often the root source of controversies.

The advice norm was strongest when the president and the objecting senator were of the same political party. Senators of the minority party, wrote Harris, "may enter a personal objection to a nominee, and "some had been sustained, though the custom was that any objection should be based on purely personal grounds;" though, as he admits, "in practice it is frequently difficult to distinguish between personal and political objections." (But again, "political" here means

that the nominee is a political rival of the senator, and not a reference to ideological objections.) Presently, though, the blue slip is available to *all* members of the Senate. Moreover, senators are extremely sensitive about diluting the power of the mechanism by requiring opposition from *both* senators.

Another interesting feature of the courtesy norm circa 1950 is that senators were somewhat limited in the *offices* to which they could object. For example, when Senator Theodore Bilbo of Mississippi objected to a court of appeals nominee, he was forced to lodge a personal objection to the nominee since "the judicial circuit included five or six states, a senator from any one of the states could not claim the right to name the person to be appointed to the vacancy. . . ." Harris also commented that objections "against nominees to national offices by a senator from the state of residence of the nominee" is "uncommon"; "courtesy is ordinarily invoked only against appointments to offices located within the state of the objecting senator." Not so the blue slip, which is available for all judicial nominations—except those to the United States Supreme Court.

Summary. The blue slip is the formal vehicle for sanctioning a president's failure to abide by senators' expectations of consultation prior to making judicial nominations from their states. Prior to the mid-1950s, the sanction was largely available only to senators of the president's own party who either objected to a president's consideration of a nominee to an office inside that senator's state who was a political rival or who simply was not the senator's preferred candidate. Moreover, an objecting senator had to make his objection publicly, and was sometimes even required to state his objections with some specificity, which his colleagues would then weigh.

Under the blue slip regime, on the other hand, senators of either party are entitled to indicate their disapproval of a judicial nominee from their state by withholding a slip of paper distributed to them by the Judiciary Committee. According to Senate custom, if even one senator from a state withholds the slip, the nomination will not go forward. While formerly used primarily to delay candidates, the blue slip has been used with increasing frequency to defeat nominees. Until a new agreement was reached between Republicans and Democrats on the Judiciary Committee last summer, the identity of the senator withholding the blue slip was secret.

Like the arguments employed on behalf of the courtesy norms of which Joseph Harris wrote, many senators defend the blue slip process as necessary to encourage the executive branch to respect what senators see as a constitutional obligation to seek advice from senators prior to making certain judicial nominations. For its part, members of the executive branch have, in candid moments, admitted that without the blue slip presidents would have little incentive to vet nominees with home state senators. Despite its lack of explicit sanction in the Constitution, the mechanism is an outgrowth of norms that are not only suggested by the Constitution (*i.e.,* the Senate is supposed to render "*advice* and consent," not just "consent"), but also are those that have existed since the Washington administration.

One final observation about the blue slip is appropriate here. Just because the blue slip can be characterized as "not unconstitutional" does not mean that the senators who have sustained and used it have done so without a thought to partisan political concerns. Yet, as in other constitutional controversies between the Congress and the president, the protection of constitutionally assigned prerogatives—even if driven somewhat by partisan considerations—does not exclude the possibility that principle, too, plays a role.

Possibilities for reform

As Judge Richard Posner correctly observes, "Norms, like laws, can be bad. . . ." Even if they happen to be "efficient within the group in which they are binding, they may be dysfunctional for society as a whole. . . ."[24] Thus, what norms are operative in the confirmation process and whether those norms are good ones are separate questions. Despite the difficulty one has pronouncing the process *unconstitutional,* the blue slip is clearly at odds with the advertised benefits of dividing responsibility for nomination and confirmation between the president and the Senate. Moreover, recent evidence suggests that, like the hold, changes in the Senate itself have allowed the blue slip to evolve into an offensive, not a defensive, weapon; and possible internal norms that once checked abuses have degraded.[25]

The question then arises, "Can the norm be altered?" Could the blue slip process be scrapped? Or at least replaced with something else? The answer is yes, but the alteration of or destruction of norms, or a norm-enforcement mechanism—particularly one with deep historic roots—can be quite difficult. Professor Gerhardt has argued that uncertainty surrounding the scope of a norm ("norm ambiguation") and the willingness of political actors actively to seek the creation of new norms ("norm entrepreneurship") may "create . . . context[s] in which the development of a new norm is possible."[26]

The early Georgia senators, for example acted as norm entrepreneurs by creating the advice norm that resulted in Washington's withdrawal of his nominee for the post in Savannah. Similarly, President Carter's norm entrepreneurship demonstrated by the creation of nominating committees to fill judicial vacancies temporarily resulted in a period of norm ambiguation, which Senator Kennedy then tried to exploit by modifying the existing blue slip procedure. And, before the Jeffords defection, Senate Republicans attempted to engage in norm entrepreneurship by requiring both senators to withhold blue slips to scuttle a nomination, after years of permitting only one senator to halt a nominee.

Keeping in mind the difficulties inherent in changing a norm or creating a new one, there are some indications that reform may be possible now that power in the Senate has changed hands. First, the Senate itself will soon experience significant personnel changes; specifically, the retirements of Strom Thurmond and Jesse Helms. Senator Thurmond was a vociferous supporter of the blue slip; Senator Helms often took advantage of the procedure to stop unwanted judicial nominations from seeing the light of day. Recall that Slotnick, in his survey of senators' attitudes towards the blue slip, found that seniority and majority/minority status were often significant factors in a senator's favoring the retention of the procedure. The older a senator, the more likely he was to support the blue slip; support among minority senators for the procedure was nearly unanimous. Now, however, some of the blue slip's most ardent proponents have retired, or will retire soon. Unless other, younger senators approach the issue with the passion of the older senators, that alone may make it easier to effect change.

Further contributing to the possible destabilization of the norm and its enforcement mechanism may be the unfavorable press coverage the blue slip has recently received. Reaction to the blue slip by national and regional commentators was universally negative. The idea that a single senator could, because of mere partisan pique, disqualify an otherwise qualified nominee from a judicial position without a good reason strikes most as absurdly unfair. The public reaction following revelations of other individual abuses of power in the Senate, like the filibuster or the hold, was similar.

The return of the Democrats to power in the Senate may also affect the future of the blue slip. After years of complaining that scores of Clinton judges were held hostage to members' whims, Democrats will be under pressure not to pay Republicans back, lest they look like rank hypocrites. But what on the surface appears to be a frustrating restraint on a power that Republicans wielded lustily against Democratic judicial nominees may actually be a golden opportunity for Democrats to serve as norm entrepreneurs in changing the blue slip process.

Because of public pressure not to appear to be giving as good as they got at the hands of Republicans, Democrats may be inhibited in the full exercise of their blue slip power. If so, then perhaps they are in the best position to effect reform. Reforming the blue slip process would enable Democrats to respond to negative public opinion about the blue slip procedure, thus allowing them to claim the progressive, reformist mantel and mark opponents as hidebound protectors of undemocratic privilege, and possibly ease the way for the judicial nominations of a future Democratic president, even if reform inured to the immediate benefit of President Bush and his nominees. (Democrats could always muster support to defeat a truly unacceptable nomination, but having Bush's nominees reap the short-term benefits means that Republicans in the Senate may be more likely to go along.)

Assuming that the possibility of reforming the blue slip process exists, what types of reforms should be attempted? One possibility is that the Senate could "end it, not mend it"; but given senators' perceptions that they have a constitutional role to play in the giving of advice (which has been reinforced through the years), total abandonment is unlikely.

One reform that would help to make the blue slip more consistent with the Constitution's division of power between the president and the Senate—a division that was expected to ensure accountability and transparency in the process—would be to memorialize the custom in a Senate, or at least a Judiciary Committee, rule. Apparently some rule did exist at one time. At a minimum, such a rule should specify that the withholding of a blue slip will be made public by the chair of the Judiciary Committee, even if the chair is the one doing the withholding. Second, senators should be required to communicate their objections to the chair or to the White House. Further, consistent with past practice, the withholding of a blue slip should be a signal that the administration needs to confer with a senator, and not an automatic death sentence for the nominee, especially if the senator is in the minority party. Therefore, some time limit on how long a blue slip

could be withheld should be considered. After a reasonable period of time to resolve differences with the White House, a senator should be required to make her case to her colleagues, indicate her objections to the nominee, ask for their support, and have the Senate decide, as a body, whether or not it wishes to go along.

****

Will Democrats seize the moment and reform the blue slip? Initial indications, alas, are not encouraging. As of late March 2002, the Bush administration had 56 nominations pending. While 42 new judges have been confirmed, 96 judicial vacancies remain unfilled. According to the Department of Justice's website, Democratic senators have not returned blue slips for nominees to the Fourth and Ninth Circuits.[27] Moreover, lingering bitterness over the treatment of President Clinton's nominees to the Sixth Circuit—now operating at nearly half strength—has created a stalemate between the White House and Michigan's two Democratic senators, Carl Levin and Debbie Stabenow. They have refused to consent to four Sixth Circuit nominations from Michigan, and have threatened to put a hold on the rest, until the matter of two Clinton nominees who never received hearings is resolved.

While Democrats have reason to hold a grudge against Republican treatment of Clinton nominees, they are now in control of the Senate and thus have the opportunity to restore some sanity to a process that has become positively toxic over the last several years. If they do not wisely use their power, they will not only become part of the problem, but they will also be ensuring that future Democratic presidents will, as President Clinton was, be forced to seek advice and consent from angry Republicans eager for payback. In the end, overworked judges and litigants forced to endure unconscionable delays will pay the price for partisan intransigence.

Notes

This article originally appeared in Volume 85, Number 5, March–April 2002, pages 218–226.

1. Ackerman, "Foil Bush's Maneuvers for Packing the Court," *L.A. Times*, April 26, 2001, at www.latimes.com/news/comment/20010426/t000035062.htm.
2. Gigot, "Blue Slip," *Wall St. J.*, May 9, 2001; Safire, "Battle of the Blue Slips," *N.Y. Times*, May 10, 2001, at www.ny times.com/2001/05/10/opinions/10SAFLhtml. ("In olden times, the nomination ... died [if a senator failed to return a blue slip]. No hearing; no vote; the unre-

turned blue slip was a form of burial shroud."). Safire went on to describe how "[i]n the 80's, under the chairmanship of Ted Kennedy and later Joe Biden, a little wiggle room was allowed: a nominee, despite being blue-slipped by the home-state senator, could theoretically get a hearing provided the president begged the senator's permission in advance." Ibid.

3. Dewar, "Senate Reorganization Finalized," *Wash. Post,* June 30, 2001, at A11.

4. Boyer, "Senate Concurs on Reorganization; GOP Fails to Win Pledge on Judges," *Wash. Times,* June 30, 2001, at A4; Dewar, *supra* n. 3.

5. Dewar, *supra* n. 3.

6. "Senatorial courtesy" itself is a term that requires some unpacking:

"Traditionally, the term *senatorial courtesy* has referred to the deference the president owes to the recommendation of senators from his own political party on the particular people whom he should nominate to federal offices in the senators' respective states. A second form of senatorial courtesy is the deference a member of Congress, particularly a senator, expects to get from his or her Senate colleagues (or, in the case of a representative, from his Senate counterparts) with respect to his or her own nomination to a confirmable post. Yet another form of senatorial courtesy is the expectation that senators (usually from the president's political party) will confer or consult with the president prior to his nominating people to fill confirmable posts in their fields of expertise . . . or people from their respective states to fill national offices."

Gerhardt, *The Federal Appointments Process* (2001), 143–144; *see also* Chase, *Federal Judges: The Appointing Process* (1972), 7–13; Harris, "The Courtesy of the Senate," *Pol. Sci. Q.* 67 (1952), 36.

7. Means other than the blue slip were used extensively to block nominations during the Clinton administration and have been employed to prevent votes on some Bush appointees. A comparative analysis of the hold and other methods of blocking nominations and the blue slip is beyond the scope of this essay, but are discussed at length in Denning, "Reforming the New Confirmation Process: Replacing 'Despise and Resent' with 'Advice and Consent'," *Admin. L. Rev.* 53 (2001), 1, 20–22.

8. *See* "Selection and Confirmation of Federal Judges: Hearing Before the Senate Committee on the Judiciary," Part I, 96th Cong., 1st Sess. (1979) [hereinafter "Senate Hearing"]; Slotnick, "Reforms in Judicial Selection: Will They Affect the Senate's Role?" (pt. 1), *Judicature* 64 (1980), 60, 69–73; *see also* Fowler, "A Comparison of Initial Recommendation Procedures: Judicial Selection Under Reagan and Carter," *Yale L. & Pol'y Rev.* 1 (1983), 299, 328–330.

9. *See* Memorandum from Senate Judiciary Committee Staff to Senator Edward M. Kennedy, Chair, Senate Judiciary Committee, Jan. 22, 1979, *reprinted in* "Senate Hearing," *supra* n. 8, at 118, 119.

10. No mention of blue slips is made in the rules posted on the Judiciary Committee's website. *See* www.senate.gov/~judiciary/rules.htm (last visited August 6, 2001).

11. Slotnick, *supra* n. 8, at 60, 62–63, 69.

12. Ibid. at 70 ("A majority [57 per cent] favored the continued existence of the blue slip process; 32 per cent thought that the process should be eliminated or the Kennedy reform initiative should be supported"; but 62 percent "also indicated that they would *not* defer as a matter of course to their colleagues' attempt to block a nomination by withholding a blue slip.").

13. Black, "A Note on Senatorial Consideration of Supreme Court Nominees," *Yale L. J.* (1969) 79, 657, 659.

14. See *The Federalist* No. 77, at 432, 433 (Isaac Kramnick ed., 1987) (hereinafter all citations are to this edition). ("[In the Constitution], the power of nomination is unequivocally vested in the executive. And as there would be necessity for submitting each nomination to the judgment of an entire branch of the legislature, *the circumstances attending an appointment, from the mode of conducting it, would naturally become matters of notoriety, and the public would be at no loss to determine what part had been performed by different actors".*) (emphasis added).

15. *The Federalist* No. 76, *supra* n. 14, at 434.

16. Of course, the Senate can't act but through its members; the point is that allowing 2 out of 100 to scuttle a nomination doesn't square with the majority rule requirement implied by Article II.

17. *Compare* U.S. Const., art. II, § 2, cl. 1 ("The President . . . may require the Opinion, in writing, of the principal Officer in each of the executive Departments, upon any Subject relating to the Duties of their respective Offices. . . .").

18. *See,* "Norm Theory and the Future of the Federal Appointments Process," *Duke L. J.* 50 (2001), 1687.

19. *Supra* n. 6, at 7.

20. Fowler, *supra* n. 8, at 49–50.

21. Harris, *supra* n. 6, at 39, 40.

22. Ibid. (quoting Russell).

23. Ibid. at 62 ("For a period it appeared that the Senate would limit the use of the rule by requiring objecting senators to state their reasons, and sustain the objections only if they were found sufficient, but in the last several years the trend has been in the opposite direction.").

24. Posner, *Frontiers of Legal Theory* (2001), 289, 293.

25. For more on these changes in the Senate itself, see Denning, "Reforming the New Confirmation Process," *supra* n. 7, at 14–25.

26. *Supra* n. 18, at 1696, 1710–1714.

27. *See* www.usdoj.gov/olp/blueslips1.htm (last visited Jan. 14, 2002).

Assessing the Senate judicial confirmation process: the index of obstruction and delay

Sheldon Goldman

A summary index offers a simple new way to measure objectively the phenomenon of obstruction and delay in confirming federal judges.

Obstruction and delay by the U.S. Senate of the confirmation of nominations to the two principal lower federal courts is a subject of ongoing debate. But how extensive is such obstruction and delay? Is there an objective way to measure this phenomenon? This article suggests a summary index that can help us do so.[1]

A dramatic, relatively recent example of confirmation delay concerned Judge William A. Fletcher of the U.S. Court of Appeals for the Ninth Circuit. Fletcher was first nominated by President Bill Clinton on April 25, 1995 and had his first hearing on December 19, 1995. On May 21, 1996, he was favorably reported by the Senate Judiciary Committee to the Senate but no floor vote was taken by the end of the 104th Congress.

Fletcher was renominated on January 7, 1997, and a second hearing was held on April 29, 1998. Once again he was favorably reported—this time the following May 21. He was finally confirmed on October 8, 1998, about three and one-half years after he first was nominated. For the courts of appeals during the last six years of Bill Clinton's presidency when Republicans controlled the Senate, eight nominees took more than one year from nomination to confirmation. Another 36 nominees never made it to confirmation—28 of whom did not even have hearings.

Susan Mollway was nominated by President Clinton to the U.S. District Court for Hawaii on December 21, 1995. Her first hearing was on March 27, 1996. She was favorably reported by the Senate Judiciary Committee on April 25, 1996 but no floor vote was taken and the nomination died. She was renominated on January 7, 1997, and had a second hearing on February 4, 1998. Once again she was favorably reported (on April 30) and was eventually confirmed on June 22, 1998, about two and one- half years after first being nominated. For the district courts during Clinton's last six years in office, 14 nominees took more than one year from nomination to confirmation; 64 never made it through confirmation, indeed, 48 of them had no hearings.

Obstruction and delay continued into the George W. Bush presidency with Democrats in control of the Senate for much of the 107th Congress. It took on average more than nine months to confirm the appeals court nominees and 12 did not even receive hearings. For the district courts it took in excess of six months for 16 nominees to be confirmed—and another 15 received no hearings.

Since 1997, Chief Justice William H. Rehnquist, in his annual Report on the Federal Judiciary, has been concerned with confirmation delay and he has criticized both the Republican- and Democratic-controlled Senate.[2] In his 2002 Report, released early in 2003, the Chief Justice recognized that the congressional election returned unified government with the same party controlling the White House and the Senate, but he warned "there will come a time when that is not the case and the judiciary will again suffer the delays of a drawn-out confirmation process."[3] He urged the President and the Senate "to work together to fix the underlying problems that have bogged down the nomination and confirmation process for so many years." As for who was responsible for the underlying problems, Republicans and Democrats in the Senate blamed each other.[4]

Empirical dimensions of delay

The empirical contours of the confirmation process over the last 25 years and the emergence of obstruction and delay are suggested by Tables 1-4. Table 1 for the district courts and Table 2 for the appeals courts show the number and percentage of nominees who received hearings, the average number of days from the time the nomination was received to the date of the hearing, the average number of days from the hearing to the date the nomination was reported, and the number and percentage of nominees confirmed by the full Senate.

The proportion of district court nominees who received hearings was at a high point for the 95th Con-

Judicature Volume 86, Number 5, pp. 251–257

Table 1. District court nominees at the committee stage

Congress	Number and percentage of nominees who received hearings	Average number of days from time nomination received to date of hearing	Average number of days from hearing to date nomination reported	Number and percentage of nominees confirmed by full Senate
95th (1977–1978)	49/49 100%	25.9	13.4	48/49 97.9%
96th (1979–1980)	161/168 95.8%	57.7	21.0	154/168 91.7%
97th (1981–1982)	68/69 98.6%	20.8	11.1	68/69 98.6%
98th (1983–1984)	69/75 92.0%	18.0	10.5	61/75 81.3%
99th (1985–1986)	98/100 98.0%	37.9	26.1	95/100 95.0%
100th (1987–1988)	74/78 94.9%	94.1	28.3	66/78 84.6%
101st (1989–1990)	48/50 96.0%	59.9	14.8	48/50 96.0%
102nd (1991–1992)	100/143 69.9%	92.1	16.4	100/143 69.9%
103rd (1993–1994)	109/118 92.4%	58.5	13.3	107/118 90.7%
104th (1995–1996)	70/85 82.4%	85.5	13.2	62/85 72.9%
105th (1997–1998)	85/94 90.4%	164.7	18.6	79/94 84.0%
106th (1999–2000)	60/83 72.3%	103.9	19.7	57/83 68.7%
107th (2001–2002)	83/98 84.7%	96.3	16.5	83/98 84.7%

Note: The 100th, 101st, 102nd, 104th, 105th, 106th, and 107th Congresses were in a divided government situation with one party controlling the Senate and the other the presidency.
Table includes nominations to lifetime appointments to the district courts. Territorial district courts with set terms are excluded.

Source: Statistics derived from data reported in Committee on the Judiciary, United States Senate, Legislative and Executive Calendars or other committee documents.

gress when all nominees had hearings and for the 97th and 99th Congresses when 98 percent or more of the nominees received hearings. For the courts of appeals, during the 95th, 97th, and 99th Congresses all nominees received hearings. In those three Congresses, the same party controlled the Senate and the White House. The low points for the district courts were the 102nd and the 106th Congresses, with about 70 percent of the nominees receiving hearings. For the appeals courts the low point was about 47 percent during the 106th

Table 2. Courts of appeals nominees at the committee stage

Congress	Number and percentage of nominees who received hearings	Average number of days from time nomination received to date of hearing	Average number of days from hearing to date nomination reported	Number and percentage of nominees confirmed by full Senate
95th (1977–1978)	12/12 100%	21.2	8.9	12/12 100%
96th (1979–1980)	47/48 97.9%	47.7	25.2	44/48 91.7%
97th (1981–1982)	19/19 100%	25.8	6.2	19/19 100%
98th (1983–1984)	14/15 93.3%	14.8	29.7	12/15 80.0%
99th (1985–1986)	32/32 100%	40.8	12.2	32/32 100%
100th (1987–1988)	17/23 73.9%	90.9	41.5	15/23 65.2%
101st (1989–1990)	18/19 94.7%	63.7	14.5	18/19 94.7%
102nd (1991–1992)	21/30 70.0%	80.8	19.6	19/30 63.3%
103rd (1993–1994)	19/21 90.5%	77.4	17	18/21 85.7%
104th (1995–1996)	14/19 73.7%	79	37	11/19 57.9%
105th (1997–1998)	22/28 78.6%	230.9	41.4	19/28 67.9%
106th (1999–2000)	15/32 46.9%	235.3	52.2	13/32 40.6%
107th (2001–2002)	19/31 54.8%	238.4	40.6	16/31 51.6%

Note: The 100th, 101st, 102nd, 104th, 105th, 106th, and 107th Congresses were in a divided government situation with one party controlling the Senate and the other the presidency.

Table includes nominations to courts of appeals of general jurisdiction. This means that the U.S. Court of Appeals for the Federal Circuit is excluded.

Source: Statistics derived from data reported in Committee on the Judiciary, United States Senate, Legislative and Executive Calendars or other committee documents.

Congress. Both the 102nd and 106th Congresses had different parties controlling the Senate and the White House.

The proportion of nominees confirmed has fluctuated. For the district courts, the low points were the 102nd and 106th Congresses at about 70 percent. For the appeals courts the 95th, 97th and 99th Congresses had a high of a 100 percent confirmation rate while the low point was for the 106th Congress at about 41 percent.

In general, Congresses that included a presidential election year (the even numbered Congresses) had a lower proportion of confirmations than Congresses that did not. The same was true for Congresses with divided government, with the exception of the 101st Congress. The findings in Tables 1 and 2 hint that major obstruct and delay tactics for judicial nominations started with the 100th Congress, which was the only Congress during Reagan's presidency with the Senate controlled by the Democrats. Subsequent Congresses on the whole show increases in the average number of days from the time of nomination to hearing and from the date the nomination was reported out of committee and sent to the floor of the Senate, although with some fluctuations.

Hints of the obstruct and delay phenomena are even more apparent with the findings in Table 3 for the district courts and Table 4 for the appeals courts. What once was a routine process when a nomination was favorably reported out of committee and sent to the floor of the Senate—with significant proportions of nominees confirmed the same day reported or one day after—has now become an obstacle course for some nominees. The average number of days from the date the nomination was reported to the date of confirmation ranged from a low of 1.8 days for the 97th Congress for district court appointees and 1.9 days for the appeals court appointees to 38.3 days for district court appointees for the 105th Congress and 68.5 days for appeals court appointees for the 106th. The proportion of district court nominees confirmed the same day reported or one day after fluctuated sharply but showed major decreases during the last three Congresses, reaching low points of less than 4 percent during the 105th and 107th Congresses. For the appeals courts, the high was about 78 percent in the 101st Congress to the single digits with the 104th through the 106th Congresses.

The proportion of district court nominees favorably reported who received confirmation floor votes was below 100 percent for 5 of the 13 Congresses and the proportion of appeals court nominees favorably reported who received confirmation floor votes was below 100 percent for 4 of the 13 Congresses.

The index

The various indicators of obstruct and delay suggested in Tables 1 through 4 are subject to varying interpretations as there are some fluctuations depending on the indicator. It is also unclear whether one measure of those employed in these tables best captures the obstruct and delay phenomenon. Most of these measures utilize averages, which of course can be affected by extreme cases. The usefulness of having one objective summary indicator of obstruct and delay is thus apparent. A simple Index of Obstruction and Delay in the confirmation process for the 95th through the 107th Congresses is offered in Table 5 for the district courts and Table 6 for the appeals courts.

Obstruction is evident when no action is taken on a nomination to confirm or reject. Delay is evident when it takes more than 180 days from the date of nomination to a confirmation vote. The Index of Obstruction and Delay is determined by the number of nominees who remained unconfirmed at the end of the Congress added to the number for whom the confirmation process took in excess of 180 days, which is then divided by the total number of nominees for that Congress.[5] The Index is calculated to four places to the right of the decimal point and thus ranges from 0.0000, which indicates an absence of obstruction and delay, to 1.0000, which indicates the maximum level.

For the district courts, there were low levels of obstruction and delay until the 100th Congress and that was followed by a further increase in the 102nd Congress. The same was true for the appeals courts during the 100th and 102nd Congresses, whose indexes were even higher than those for the district courts. Since the Senate of these Congresses was controlled by the Democrats with a Republican in the White House, the Republican's charge that the Democrats were responsible for initiating the obstruction and delay phenomenon is supported by the objective evidence. But with the situation reversed with a Democrat in the White House and the Republicans in control of the Senate, the evidence clearly shows that the Republicans ratcheted up obstruction and delay, with all-time records for the district and appeals courts, including the then unprecedented index of 0.7931 for appeals court nominees by the 106th Congress. Also, it should be noted that in every even numbered Congress (with one exception for the district courts for the 106th Congress) which always overlaps a presidential election year, the Index was higher than for the previous non-presidential year Congress.

The Democrats assumed control of the Senate after the first five months of the 107th Congress and the Index for the appeals courts reached an even new high of 0.8387. However, the Index for the district courts dropped significantly from the 104th-106th Congresses and was even lower than that for the 102nd Congress. This appeared to reflect a decision of the Democrats to

Table 3. District court nominees on the Senate floor

Congress	Average number of days from date nomination reported to date of confirmation	Proportion of nominees reported who were confirmed the day reported or one day after	Percentage of nominations reported favorably that were confirmed
95th (1977–1978)	2.7	52.1%	100%
96th (1979–1980)	4.6	40.0%	100%
97th (1981–1982)	1.8	61.8%	100%
98th (1983–1984)	7.8	32.8%	92.4%
99th (1985–1986)	8.1	41.7%	100%
100th (1987–1988)	9.8	17.9%	98.5%
101st (1989–1990)	6.2	64.6%	100%
102nd (1991–1992)	3.3	80.0%	100%
103rd (1993–1994)	4.6	31.8%	100%
104th (1995–1996)	34.8	11.3%	95.4%
105th (1997–1998)	38.3	3.7%	96.3%
106th (1999–2000)	25.6	12.3%	98.3%
107th (2001–2002)	24.8	3.6%	100%

Note: The 100th, 101st, 102nd, 104th, 105th, 106th, and 107th Congresses were in a divided government situation with one party controlling the Senate and the other the presidency.
Table includes nominations to lifetime appointments to the district courts. Territorial district courts with set terms are excluded.

Source: Statistics derived from data reported in Committee on the Judiciary, United States Senate, Legislative and Executive Calendars or other committee documents.

focus their attention on the appeals courts and to readily approve Bush's district court nominees.

****

The findings suggest that both parties are responsible for obstruction and delay but also, given the higher indexes for presidential years, that the problem may be an institutional one. The Index has generally been creeping upwards since the 97th Congress whether there has been divided or unified government. Although it is anticipated that with Republican control of the 108th Congress the Index for the district and

Table 4. Courts of appeals nominees on the Senate floor

Congress	Average number of days from date nomination reported to date of confirmation	Proportion of nominees reported who were confirmed the day reported or one day after	Percentage of nominations reported favorably that were confirmed
95th (1977–78)	3.2 days	25.0%	100%
96th (1979–1980)	5.2 days	34.1%	100%
97th (1981–191982)	1.9 days	52.6%	100%
98th (1983–1984)	21.3 days	13.3%	92.3%
99th (1985–1986)	13.3 days	40.6%	100%
100th (1987–1988)	21.5 days	33.3%	93.8%
101st (1989–1990)	2.5 days	77.8%	100%
102nd (1991–1992)	14.4 days	63.2%	100%
103rd (1993–1994)	6.7 days	38.9%	100%
104th (1995–1996)	33.5 days	8.3%	84.6%
105th (1997–1998)	40.7 days	5.3%	95.0%
106th (1999–2000)	68.5 days	7.7%	100%
107th (2001–2002)	26.4 days	20.0%	100%

Note: The 100th, 101st, 102nd, 104th, 105th, 106th, and 107th Congresses were in a divided government situation with one party controlling the Senate and the other the presidency.

Table includes nominations to courts of appeals of general jurisdiction. This means that the U.S. Court of Appeals for the Federal Circuit is excluded.

Source: Statistics derived from data reported in Committee on the Judiciary, United States Senate, Legislative and Executive Calendars or other committee documents.

appeals courts will fall substantially, the problem of obstruct and delay could resurface with the return of divided government. Having an objective summary indicator of the phenomenon is a convenient and comprehensible way of assessing the confirmation process.

Notes

This article originally appeared in Volume 86, Number 5, March–April 2003, pages 251–257.

I would like to thank the Law and Social Science program of the National Science Foundation (NSF grant SBR-

Table 5. Index of obstruction and delay in the Senate processing of district court nominees

Congress	Index	Congress	Index
95th (1977–1978)	0.0000	102nd (1991–1992)	0.3465
96th (1979–1980)	0.0750	103rd (1993–1994)	0.0375
97th (1981–1982)	0.0000	104th (1995–1996)	0.3780
98th (1983–1984)	0.0545	105th (1997–1998)	0.5000
99th (1985–1986)	0.1364	106th (1999–2000)	0.4722
100th (1987–1988)	0.2800	107th (2001–2002)	0.2432
101st (1989–1990)	0.0488		

Note: The 100th, 101st, 102nd, 104th, 105th, 106th, and 107th Congresses were in a divided government situation with one party controlling the Senate and the other the presidency. The Index is only for nominations to lifetime appointments to the district courts. Territorial district courts with set terms are excluded.

Index is calculated as the number of nominations unconfirmed plus the number of nominations that took more than 180 days from nomination to confirmation. It ranges from 0.0000, which indicates the complete absence of obstruction and/or delay, to 1.0000, which indicates complete obstruction and/or delay. Nominations made after July 1 of the second session of each Congress are excluded from the Index.

Table 6. Index of obstruction and delay in the Senate processing of courts of appeals nominees

Congress	Index	Congress	Index
95th (1977–1978)	0.0000	102nd (1991–1992)	0.5000
96th (1979–1980)	0.0682	103rd (1993–1994)	0.0625
97th (1981–1982)	0.0000	104th (1995–1996)	0.5263
98th (1983–1984)	0.1429	105th (1997–1998)	0.6932
99th (1985–1986)	0.0690	106th (1999–2000)	0.7931
100th (1987–1988)	0.4762	107th (2001–2002)	0.8387
101st (1989–1990)	0.0625		

Note: The 100th, 101st, 102nd, 104th, 105th, 106th, and 107th Congresses were in a divided government situation with one party controlling the Senate and the other the presidency. The Index is only for nominations to courts of appeals of general jurisdiction. This means that the U.S. Court of Appeals for the Federal Circuit is excluded. The Index for the 107th Congress excludes the nominations made by President Clinton shortly before leaving office that were subsequently withdrawn by President Bush.

Index is calculated as the number of nominations unconfirmed plus the number of nominations that took more than 180 days from nomination to confirmation. It ranges from 0.0000, which indicates the complete absence of obstruction and/or delay, to 1.0000, which indicates complete obstruction and/or delay. Nominations made after July 1 of the second session of each Congress are excluded from the Index.

9810838), which supported in part the gathering of some of the data for this article. The NSF bears no responsibility for the conclusions drawn herein. I am also grateful to Commonwealth College of the University of Massachusetts at Amherst for providing research assistance. Michael Conlow has my great appreciation for all his help. Note that much of this article draws heavily from portions of my article "Unpicking Pickering in 2002: Some Thoughts on the Politics of Lower Federal Court Selection and Confirmation," *U.C. Davis L. Rev.* 36 (2003), 695.

1. There is no attempt here either to analyze systematically by way of a statistical model of the correlates of obstruction and delay or to provide any detailed discussion of its political context. Others have ably done this. See Bell, *Warring Factions: Interest Groups, Money, and the New Politics of Senate Confirmation* (Columbus: The Ohio State University Press, 2002); Hartley and Holmes, "The In-

creasing Senate Scrutiny of Lower Federal Court Nominees," *Pol. Sci. Q.* 117 (2002), 259; Binder and Maltzman, "Senatorial Delay in Confirming Federal Judges, 1947–1998," *Am. J. Pol. Sci.* 46 (2002), 190; Martinek, Kemper, and Van Winkle, "To Advise and Consent: The Senate and Lower Federal Court Nominations, 1977–1998," *J. Pol.* 64 (2002), 337; Schraufnagel, "The Decline of Comity in Congress and Delay in the Confirmation of Federal Judges, 1977–2000" (April 2002), (unpublished paper presented at the Annual Meeting of the Midwest Political Science Association); Nixon and Goss, "Confirmation Delay for Vacancies on the Circuit Courts of Appeals," *Am. Pol. Res.* 29 (2001), 246; Hartley, "Senate Delay of Minority Judicial Nominees," *Judicature* 84 (2001), 191; Hartley and Holmes, "Increasing Senate Scrutiny of Lower Federal Court Nominees," *Judicature* 80 (1997), 274; Goldman, "The Judicial Confirmation Crisis and the Clinton Presidency," *Presidential Stud. Q.* 28 (1998), 838; and Allison,

"Delay in the Senate Confirmation of Federal Judicial Nominees," *Judicature* 80 (1996), 8.

2. *See* the news story covering his 2001 report, Greenhouse, "Rehnquist Sees a Loss of Prospective Judges," *New York Times,* January 1, 2002 at A14 ("On the pace of confirmation for judicial nominees, Chief Justice Rehnquist noted that in past years he had criticized a Republican-controlled Senate for delays in considering President Bill Clinton's nominees. 'Now the political situation is exactly the reverse, but the same situation obtains,' he said, noting that the Senate confirmed 28 judges during 2001 and adjourned without acting on 37 nominations. 'The Senate is not, of course, obliged to confirm any particular nominee,' he said. 'But it ought to act on each nominee and to do so within a reasonable time.' ").

3. *The Third Branch* 35, vol. 1 (2003) at 2.

4. The Democrats fumed that Republican senators had for several years obstructed consideration of Clinton nominees to some circuits and were now seeking to benefit from their obstructionist tactics. For example, Senator Patrick Leahy noted on the Senate floor: "Large numbers of vacancies continue to exist on many Courts of Appeals, in large measure because the recent Republican majority was not willing to hold hearings or vote on more than half—56 per-cent—of President Clinton's Courts of Appeals nominees in 1999 and 2000 and was not willing to confirm a single judge to the Courts of Appeals during the 1996 session." *Cong Rec.,* July 18, 2002, at S7017. On the other hand Senator Orrin Hatch assailed the Democrats while playing down the record under the Republican control of the Senate. *See,* for example, Senator Hatch's remarks at the July 11, 2002, business meeting of the committee: "Some try to blame Republicans for the current vacancy crisis. That is pure bunk . . . I know that some try to justify wholesale delays as payback for the past. That is just sleight of hand. . . ." Committee Business, Senate Committee on the Judiciary, Transcript of Proceedings, July 11, 2002, at 9, 11.

5. Note that when the Senate remained in control by the same party in the subsequent Congress, a nominee who was renominated had as the date of nomination the original nomination date not the renomination date and that was counted in the calculation of delay. Also note that nominations made after July 1 of the second session of each Congress are not included in the calculations. This is done so as not to inflate the Index artificially on account of end-of-second-session nominations that realistically could not move through the process under an approximately 180 days or less time frame.

The Courts and Their Publics

States and State Courts

The United States is a federal system. National supremacy was definitively established over the state governments by the U.S. Constitution and John Marshall's interpretation of that document in the classic Supreme Court case *McCulloch v. Maryland* in 1819. The American judiciary also is organized on a federal model, with federal courts coexisting with their state court counterparts. The development of constitutional law has established federal judicial supremacy as the rule for the relationships among American courts. Consequently, when examining the relationships between the Supreme Court and its "publics," much attention must be paid to the interface of the federal courts, the states, and state courts.

This section begins with long-serving Wisconsin State Supreme Court Chief Justice Shirley Abrahamson offering a snapshot assessment of "The state of state courts." Abrahamson documents the existence of fifty varied state court systems, staffed by highly qualified benches and handling about 95 percent of the country's judicial business, including varied caseloads of considerable interest. The state courts are shown to be definitive in most matters, since the U.S. Supreme Court's caseload is so small. Still, Abrahamson laments the lack of public support for and trust in the government in general and the courts in particular. She expresses concern for judicial independence in state systems characterized by low interest and for low visibility judicial elections driven by expensive electoral campaigns. More generally, recent state fiscal crises continue to bode poorly for state courts. Abrahamson closes on an optimistic, forward-looking note, however, highlighting the potential for courts in the states, the laboratories of democracy, to play innovative roles in the dispensing of justice.

One innovation is the development of experimental problem-solving courts in state court systems, a phenomenon examined by Greg Berman and John Feinblatt in "Problem-solving justice: a quiet revolution." In these courts, innovative judges "are united by a common belief: rather than complain that society's problems are being dumped in their laps, judges have an obligation to attempt to solve the problems that bring people to court, whether it be as victims, defendants, litigants, or witnesses."

Other voices have been calling for the active pursuit of "new judicial federalism," especially in the wake of the

conservatism in the area of rights and liberties found during the Burger and Rehnquist courts. Under new judicial federalism, state courts rely increasingly on their own laws and constitutions to decide cases whenever possible. It was hoped by many that such an approach to adjudication would protect and perhaps expand upon the rights and liberties legacy of the Warren Court. Shirley Abrahamson and Diane Gutmann offer a view of this topic in "The new federalism: state constitutions and state courts." The article develops the historical foundation of the relationship between federal and state courts while emphasizing the greater role that the state courts could play following the Supreme Court's 1983 decision in *Michigan v. Long*. In that case Justice O'Connor stated for the Court's majority that, "State courts will be presumed to be acting as 'federal forums,' unless they plainly state that they are not so acting . . . If a state court plainly says that it is relying on state law, the Supreme Court will not review its decision."

Abrahamson and Gutmann's analysis of *Michigan v. Long* emphasizes the case's potential for giving state courts "substantial freedom in determining the extent of their autonomy as long as their decisions do not violate federal law." If this suggests, however, that such freedom and the new judicial federalism have led to the widespread expansion of citizens' rights, Michael Esler's study of "State supreme court commitment to state law" offers a cautionary note. Esler demonstrates that despite the rhetoric of the new judicial federalism, "State supreme courts rely on federal law in the vast majority of their decisions." He expands upon this finding by noting that, "The conservatism of most state political systems and entrenched legal and institutional barriers work against widespread development of state constitutional law." In essence, predictions of an increasing liberalism emerging from state court systems as they interpret their own state constitutions generally fall before the realities of the political climate in which most state court systems operate.

Both Abrahamson and Gutmann and Esler underline the fact that federalism is a dynamic process in the American political system. A process that is always in a state of "becoming." This has been made amply clear in Supreme Court decisions in recent years. It is equally clear that federalism issues and the relationship among the Supreme Court, the states, and state courts will remain high on the list of the American judiciary's concerns for years to come.

The state of the state courts

Shirley S. Abrahamson

For state courts, it is the best of times and it is the worst of times.

Editor's note: This article is adapted from Wisconsin Chief Justice Abrahamson's informal remarks at the Midyear Meeting dinner of the American Judicature Society on February 27, 2004.

I am going to talk about the state of the state courts, and I am going to organize my presentation into three clichés. The first cliché is that this is the best of times. The second is that it's the worst of times. The third is that there's a silver lining.

The best of times

It's the best of times because it's well recognized, at least within judicial and legal circles, that more than 95 percent of the legal business of this country is in the state courts. The people of this country are in the state courts from traffic tickets to murder, from small claims through major civil actions.

In prior years we talked a lot about parity of judges. That is, we wanted to bring state court judges up to the qualifications of the federal judges. It's now generally recognized that state court judges do have qualification parity with federal judges. Indeed, a significant percent of federal judges come from the state court bench.

Some of us have declined to go on the federal bench with a life-time tenure, without having to face election, even though the pay might be better, and even though retirement benefits may be better. And the reason we stay in the state court system, with all due respect, is that we have a much more interesting docket.

I prefer to be an appellate judge so I didn't move on to the federal district court. And when opportunities arose to go on the Seventh Circuit, I carefully looked at the dockets, and the docket for the Wisconsin Supreme Court is much more interesting than the docket for the Seventh Circuit. Our docket is, with many exceptions, a common-law docket, which gives us great opportunity to develop common law. We have a variety of cases and in addition we select the cases we hear. We are a court of final jurisdiction except to be reviewed by the U.S. Supreme Court, which is not likely when it is taking only 80 to 100 cases a year. So as to

federal questions, for most of them that come to us, we are the final word.

Why else is it the best of worlds now? We have a number of institutions that are working with and for the state courts that are very influential at the local level and at the national level. For example, we have the National Center for State Courts, which was founded with the great help and assistance of former Chief Justice Warren Burger. It does research work for and with state courts, funds various pilot projects, and draws the state courts together so they have cohesive programs and cohesive approaches to common problems.

We also have the Conference of Chief Justices, which has become more and more active as the years have progressed. We have a Conference of State Court Administrators that assists in the management of the courts. The state courts have worked much more closely as a unit with the federal judiciary. The Judicial Conference of the United States sends representatives to various state conferences. We work in conjunction with the Federal Judicial Center on educational programs. This type of cooperation makes for a stronger state court system and a stronger federal system. Thus I conclude that this is the best of times for the state courts, and we're perched to do better work both within the 50 states and the territories and as a national unit.

The worst of times

But it is also the worst of times. Why? Well for one thing, all courts, federal and state, face a basic problem of an apparent lack of public trust and confidence in government; whether it be federal government or state government, whether it be the legislative or the executive, or the judicial branch.

It's hard for the public to distinguish between what the legislature does and what the executive does, or doesn't do, and what a court does or doesn't do. And to the extent that any branch of government, federal or state, is in disrepute, the fallout is on all of us.

At least from the polls and from what our questionnaires show, the judiciary is still held in high regard. It is very important that we maintain that public trust and confidence. Without public trust and confidence, all government, but especially the judicial branch, is in deep trouble. We really depend on the public for acceptance of our orders and obedience thereto. We are without the power of the sword or the pocket book.

It's also the worst of times because polls show that people think you do better in the courts if you have money. And too many people think that you get a good shot or you don't get a good shot in court depending on your race, and less so now, your gender.

In addition there's the issue of judicial independence. At the federal level we've given to judges, I think, everything a government can give to get judicial independence: appointment, life tenure for good behavior, no salary decreases. In state court systems judges don't have all of these protections. It depends on the state. I come from a state where judges stand for nonpartisan election with six- to ten-year terms.

The difficulty about elections is threefold. First is apathy—less than 25 percent of the people in Wisconsin vote in judicial elections. If you ask the people in Wisconsin if they want to stop electing judges and have them appointed, probably 75 to 95 percent want to stay with elections. They don't vote, but they won't give it up either.

Second, you've got a problem with money. Although the code of conduct says judges can't personally raise money, and I don't think we do, the problem is that people have to contribute to your campaign. It's a widely held view by the public that if a lawyer contributes to the campaign, that lawyer is more apt to win the case. Whether true or not, that is the perception.

Isn't it preferable to take money from lawyers than from nonlawyers? The lawyer doesn't know which end of a case he or she is going to be on most of the time. For the most part, at least in a state like Wisconsin, they're going to be on either side and they're going to want a judge who is not going to be in anyone's pocket. When nonlawyers give money, the chances are they are litigants, or potential litigants, with a vested interest. But it's very hard to persuade anybody that lawyers aren't courting favor in a judicial campaign.

So you've got apathy, you've got dollars, and then you've got speech. I think *Republican Party of Minnesota v. White* was not a very good decision, with all due respect. The decision may affect the appointed judiciary as well as the elected judiciary. I think we're going to see more and more attacks on individual judges to disqualify themselves for some perceived or actual biases resulting from judicial speech or relationships.

Even in a medium-sized state like Wisconsin we know many lawyers and if you start saying, "Oh, you know them, you can't sit on the case," I can't sit on very much, and that goes for my colleagues too. So those are problems about speech and recusal. I know the AJS has looked at and will continue to explore these issues.

It is the worst of times because of states' fiscal crises. Court funding raises its own separation of powers problems: who should control court funding and how should the legislature get money for funding the courts. Raising fees and imposing surcharges on people who come to court raises revenue but creates a problem of access of justice. Courts are collecting fees, forfeitures, and fines. We ought to collect them, but it may mean in some states that we are collection agents for the executive or legislative branches of government, and that may not be the best use of a court's time.

And state courts have problems regarding sentencing similar to those at the federal level. State legislatures tend to follow Congress and adopt some of its ways. So we have prisoner litigation being limited and we have various sentencing mandates. The whole issue of taking away judicial discretion is a significant one.

Silver linings

But I do not want to end on these depressing notes. There are silver linings. First, the state courts are doing a tremendous amount of work of informing each other about the good things that are happening in the states so that each of us does not have to reinvent the wheel. We are using the web and e-mail discussion centers.

States are also doing a great deal of work on access to justice and fairness through the Conference of Chief Justices, and we have a tremendous outreach program all over the country that federal judges are now joining. We have to reach out and persuade everyone that judicial independence is not for judges and is not for the lawyers—it's for the people. Now, everybody wants a judge that's going to rule in their favor. The problem is, you don't know if he or she will. You can't count on a partial judge, so forget it! So really the best judge is an impartial judge. We have to persuade people to support judges, even if you disagree with them, even if you think they're not always right. We must support judges if they're hard-working, well-educated, and qualified judges. It will take years of effort but we are working on it. And I think that is a marvelous silver lining for state court judges.

We are also working long and hard on self-representation. In small claims court self-representation is expected, but in family court, which is the major part of state court business, 40–60 percent of the people are not represented by counsel. It's not a big-state phenomenon. It is universal across this country. Our court system is not set up for self-represented people, but people have a constitutional right to represent themselves, and we have to be sure that they get justice. And we have to also assist the judges. Judges will tell you, if there is a self-represented person it takes at least twice as long to do that case. And so we're working across the country on pro bono activities for the bar and providing self-represented people with forms and other types of assistance.

We are working towards problem-solving courts. Problem-solving courts recognize that judges do more than just move people through the system only to see them return. So you're seeing drug courts; you're seeing courts for the mentally ill, and I think this trend will continue. These courts are expensive, and they need a different kind of judge, but we have to explore these options.

State courts are in a better position than they ever have been to face the changes in practice and to face changes in society. So I look forward to the future. State courts will be in very good shape to handle the future. Let me close by paraphrasing Garrison Keillor, our friend from Minnesota who is on radio on Prairie Home Companion. I summarize the state of the state courts as follows: All the men lawyers are handsome, all the female lawyers are strong, and all of our state court judges are above average.

Note

This article originally appeared in Volume 87, Number 5, March–April 2004, pages 241–242.

Problem-solving justice: a quiet revolution

Greg Berman and John Feinblatt

More and more judges across the country are realizing they have an obligation to attempt to solve the problems that bring people to court.

Alexander Hamilton once wrote that the judicial system is the "least dangerous" branch of government because it lacks power over the sword or the purse. Indeed, judicial authority derives from something much harder to quantify, but no less real: the trust and respect of the American people.

Given this reality, it makes sense every now and then to ask: how does the public feel about the job that judges and courts are doing? By some measures, the news is good. There's an old saying that people vote with their feet. If that's the case, then public confidence in the courts has never been stronger. More and more people are turning to the courts to resolve their disputes and solve their problems. Case filings in state courts hit an all-time high of 91.5 million in 1998. As these numbers suggest, each day our judges are called upon to handle a caseload of staggering complexity—everything from the intimate affairs of troubled families to the intricate dealings of multi-national corporations. By and large they dispense their duties with compassion, precision, and fairness.

But that's not the end of the story. While there is much to be proud of—after all, the independence and integrity of the American judiciary is the envy of much of the world—there are troubling signs of public dissatisfaction with courts that we cannot afford to ignore. As an experiment, go to your corner bar and ask a few people what they think of their local courts. Chances are, you'll find that most people don't know a whole lot about how courts work and have only the vaguest sense of what judges and attorneys do all day. And if you are lucky enough to happen upon someone who does know a thing or two about courts, you're likely to hear a long list of complaints—the courts are too slow, judges are out of touch, the same offenders keep cycling through the system again and again.

In recent years, an innovative group of judges and attorneys has decided to do something about this situation. They have begun to test new ways of doing justice, re-engineering the way that courts address such everyday problems as mental illness, quality-of-life crime, drugs, and child neglect. These innovators are united by a common belief: rather than complain that society's problems are being dumped in their laps, judges have an obligation to attempt to solve the problems that bring people to court, whether it be as victims, defendants, litigants, or witnesses. There's a name for this new kind of thinking: it's called problem-solving justice.

What does a "problem-solving" court look like? Take a typical case involving a defendant arrested for felony possession of drugs. In most such cases, the defendant is not a big-time dealer with a violent history, but rather a hardcore addict caught feeding his or her habit. How should the courts respond? Many judges feel as though they have only two choices: jail or nothing. Neither one feels like a perfect fit for non-violent substance abusers because in neither case does the court get to the underlying problem: the offender's addiction.

The heart of the matter

But in a problem-solving court, addressing addiction isn't an afterthought, it's the heart of the matter. All of the major players in the courtroom—judge, prosecutor, and defense attorney—explicitly acknowledge that the goal is to move offenders from addiction to sobriety (and from crime to law-abiding behavior). In pursuit of this goal, a problem-solving judge uses a broad array of possible sanctions, including drug treatment, mental health counseling, job training, and community restitution projects. And to ensure accountability, problem-solving judges require offenders to return to court frequently—to report on their progress in treatment, to submit to urine tests, and to demonstrate their compliance with court orders.

The bottom line is that problem-solving courts combine punishment and help in an effort both to improve public safety and prevent recidivism. Everybody wins when this happens. The offender wins because he or she breaks the cycle of drugs-crime-jail. The court wins because it no longer has to spend scarce resources on the same offender again and again. But most important, society wins because its streets are safer and its families stronger.

This isn't some sort of judicial fantasy—it's actually happening day after day in thousands of courtrooms across the country. These aren't your grandfather's courts. They include specialized drug courts, community courts, mental health courts, domestic violence courts, and others. And while these problem-solving experiments are still relatively new, there is a growing body of evidence that they are making a real difference. Research indicates that drug courts have reduced drug use and recidivism among program participants while saving the system considerable money. And a recent study of a community court in midtown Manhattan revealed that the court had helped reduce neighborhood street prostitution by as much as 50 percent.

How quiet?

Despite these kinds of statistics, problem-solving courts have generated relatively little attention in the mainstream media. In effect, a quiet revolution is taking place in the courts.

Or maybe it's not so quiet. Last year, the Center for Court Innovation—in partnership with the Open Society Institute and the University of Maryland's Survey Research Center—surveyed more than 500 state court judges nationwide about their attitudes toward problem-solving methods and ideas. What we found was that more than 90 percent of judges believed that they should be involved in addressing social problems like drug addiction, domestic violence, and mental illness. A similar percentage favored treatment over jail for nonviolent drug addicts or mentally ill individuals arrested

for petty crime. And two-thirds said that they should be more involved with community groups in addressing neighborhood safety and quality-of-life concerns.

It's not just judges who are starting to embrace the idea of problem-solving courts. A recent survey conducted by the National Center for State Courts found that a solid majority of the public backs the new court and judicial roles associated with problem solving. For example, more than 80 percent of all respondents expressed support for such problem-solving hallmarks as bringing offenders back to the judge to monitor compliance, coordinating with community agencies, and using the knowledge of psychologists and doctors in the courtroom. Numbers were even higher among Blacks and Latinos, traditionally among the groups most disaffected with courts. The report concludes that the public believes that "courts are able to make an important contribution to solving some of our most difficult social problems."

Are problem-solving courts a magical elixir that will cure all that ails our justice system? Of course not. Is there a need for more research and reflection about their costs and their impacts? You bet. But it's time to admit that there's real potential here. If problem-solving courts don't have judges and citizens on the same page yet, they at least have them reading from the same book. And for those who care about bolstering public confidence in justice, that's good news indeed.

Note

This article originally appeared in Volume 86, Number 4, January–February 2003, pages 182, 213.

The new federalism: state constitutions and state courts

Shirley S. Abrahamson and Diane S. Gutmann

The "perplexing" idea of federalism has a long and complex history in the United States; jurists and commentators have grappled with its application to the state and federal court systems. The U.S. Supreme Court's Michigan v. Long *decision has opened up a new chapter in this struggle.*

In 1984, Judge John Minor Wisdom, senior judge, U.S. Court of Appeals for the Fifth Circuit, commented, "It is striking indeed that so many . . . [who] write on the subject of 'Civil Rights and Federalism' have focused on the growing role of the *states* in protecting civil rights, in some cases going beyond Supreme Court guidelines." [1]

For a long time, few people seemed aware that protection of individual liberties could lie in the state constitution—and not solely in the U.S. Constitution. In the 1970s, state courts gradually reawakened to their legitimate authority to construe the rights that their state constitutions provide independently of the U.S. Supreme Court's construction of analogous rights in the federal Constitution. When a state court construes the state constitution in the same way that the U.S. Supreme Court construes the federal Constitution, or when a state court goes beyond the Supreme Court in the protection of human rights, there is no inherent conflict between nation and state. Conflict does arise when state standards fall short of federal standards.

Federal court of appeals Senior Judge J. Skelly Wright recently declared himself an "enthusiastic new convert to 'federalism' " and applauded "state judges who have resumed their historic role as the primary defenders of civil liberties and equal rights." [2]

Federalism has been a perplexing idea from its very inception. At the Constitutional Convention one of the framers expressed his confusion with the as yet not fully developed idea of federalism when he said, "I cannot conceive of a government in which there exist two supremes." [3] Although the Constitution explicitly makes the federal government supreme, the idea that the states remain in some sense sovereign or autonomous has retained vitality throughout our history.

As James Madison recognized in *Federalist 37*, no mathematical formula can tell us how to allocate power between the national government and the state governments. History shows that the allocation of authority between the states and the national government shifts over time. The tension between pressures for state autonomy and pressures for national supremacy is fundamental to federalism. This tension has led at times to conflict and at other times to dialogue and accommodation.

Some commentators use the term *new federalism* to refer to a new relationship between federal and state courts and between the federal and state constitutions. New federalism refers to the renewed willingness of state courts to rely on their own law, especially state constitutional law, in order to decide questions involving individual rights. In new federalism, the federal Constitution establishes minimum rather than maximum guarantees of individual rights, and the state courts determine, according to their own law (generally their own state constitutions), the nature of the protection against state government. New federalism also includes the potential for greater deference by federal courts to state court proceedings and decisions.

Federal and state courts work out their relationship with each other as they work out the relationship between the federal and state constitutions. The balance between state autonomy and national supremacy is vividly illustrated in the context of the protection of civil liberties.

In this article we examine, first, the historical background of the relationship between federal and state courts. Then, we turn to the experience of both court systems in the protection of civil liberties. Finally, we attempt to assess the impact on both court systems of incorporation, that is, applying many portions of the federal Bill of Rights to the states through the Fourteenth Amendment. We look at the U.S. Supreme Court reaction in *Michigan v. Long* (1983)[4] to the increased role of the state courts in the interpretation and application of the state and federal bills of rights.

Dual governments

The states predate the Constitution and its predecessor, the Articles of Confederation. Before the Declaration of Independence, members of the Continental

Congress suggested that each colony form an independent state government. During the months preceding independence, colonists debated the uniformity of state constitutions but rejected such uniformity in favor of each state's calling a convention to draw up a constitution of its own. This individuality reflected a political reality that manifested itself in such incidents as the response of New Jersey soldiers to George Washington's attempt to get them to swear allegiance to the United States: "New Jersey is our country." [5]

At the time of the Constitutional Convention of 1787 in Philadelphia, the states were an independent and somewhat fractious lot loosely bound together by a central "government" backed only by the force of persuasion. Protective of state autonomy, the people waited nervously for the results of the convention, unaware that the delegates were laboring over an entirely new Constitution in apparent disregard of the mandate to meet "for the sole and express purpose of revising the Articles of Confederation."

The idea of unqualified state "sovereignty" lost some of its luster under the Articles of Confederation, but state sovereignty was to survive—albeit somewhat redefined—the framing and ratification of the Constitution.

A proposal at the convention that the existing governmental foundations be swept away in favor of a purely national government was not well received. The framers built the Constitution on the foundation of the states, rather than attempting to lay an entirely new foundation. The Constitution assumes the existence of states (mentioning them at least 50 times), state judiciaries (at least three times), and state constitutions (at least once). In structure and conception, the Constitution drew heavily on the constitutions of the states. As John Adams declared, "What is the Constitution of the United States, but that of Massachusetts, New York, and Maryland! There is not a feature in it which cannot be found in one or the other." [6]

Thus the document that emerged at Philadelphia presupposed two levels of government, each with its own constitution and governmental structure, each existing simultaneously in the same geographic territory, and each deriving its powers from and governing the same people. The states remained autonomous entities under the Constitution, instead of being reduced to mere administrative subdivisions of the central government. Like the people, the states retained whatever powers were not delegated to the central government. James Madison wrote in *Federalist* 45:

The powers delegated by the proposed Constitution to the federal government are few and defined. Those which are to remain in the State governments are numerous and indefinite. . . . The powers reserved to the several States will extend to all the objects which, in the ordinary course of affairs, concern the lives, liberties, and properties of the people, and the internal order, improvement, and prosperity of the State.

Although the states retained autonomous status, the United States was constituted as more than a federation, more than a league or an alliance between nations. The government established by the new Constitution acted on the people directly as well as on the states, in contrast to the Articles of Confederation, which were concerned only with relations between the states.

As Madison described it, the Constitution "is, in strictness, neither a national nor a federal Constitution, but a composition of both." [7] Alexis de Tocqueville put it aptly many years later: "Evidently this is no longer a federal government, but an incomplete national government, which is neither exactly national nor exactly federal; but the new word which ought to express this novel thing does not yet exist." [8] The Constitution established a hybrid national-federal government in which the national government was not to swallow up the states and the states were not to undermine the national government. The Constitution encased two political communities within one system, creating the potential for conflict as well as the potential for fruitful collaboration and dialogue.

A classic description of our federalism in this century comes from Justice Hugo Black. He described it as "a proper respect for state functions, a recognition of the fact that the entire country is made up of a Union of separate state governments, and a continuance of the belief that the National Government will fare best if the States and their institutions are left free to perform their separate functions in their separate ways." [9] The concept of federalism, observed Justice Black, requires neither "blind deference to States' Rights" nor the centralization of control over every important issue. Rather, each government must be sensitive to the legitimate interests of the other. Anxious though the national government may be to vindicate and protect national rights and national interests, it must do so in ways that will not impede legitimate state activities.

Federalism and individual rights have been intertwined in American constitutional history from the very beginning. The framers strove to bestow upon the national government authority to deal with national problems, while safeguarding state autonomy and individual liberty. As Madison wrote in *Federalist* 51, "In the compound republic of America, the power surrendered by the people is first divided between two distinct governments, and then the portion allotted to each subdivided among distinct and separate departments. Hence, a double security arises to the rights of the people. The different governments will control each other, at the same time that each will be controlled by itself."

With the division of powers between the national and state governments and the separation of powers, the framers of the Constitution, according to John Quincy Adams, gave us "the most complicated government on the face of the globe." [10]

Dual courts

In attempting to tell the story of the dual court system in condensed form, we begin with the ending. This country has two independent but interrelated judicial schemes: state and federal. The framers and Congress provided for a complex and intricate system of two sets of courts with overlapping jurisdiction. They did not attempt to simplify the dual judicial scheme by apportioning federal adjudicative powers solely to the federal courts and state adjudicative powers solely to the state courts. Rather, both the federal and state courts apply federal and state law.

Before exploring the interaction between state and federal courts as an aspect of our federalism, we will trace the origins of the dual system of courts. The dual judicial system grows out of the tension between two contending principles: national supremacy and state autonomy.

The federal judiciary seems so natural and inevitable now that it may be difficult to imagine a time when its establishment and existence were controversial. We have been schooled to think of constitutional governments as necessarily composed of three branches: the legislative, the executive, and the judicial. Our government would seem unbalanced without a judiciary.

Yet in order to comprehend the original understanding of the role of the federal judiciary, we must realize that a federal judiciary was not at all inevitable. There was no national judiciary under the Articles of Confederation. While not very controversial during the drafting process, the establishment of a federal judiciary became intensely controversial during the ratification process. The establishment of the federal judiciary was perceived as a threat to state autonomy. The resistance to this perceived threat did not succeed in block-

ing the establishment of a federal judiciary, but it did succeed in influencing its structure and jurisdiction.

The cornerstones of the present-day federal judicial system are Article III of the Constitution and the Judiciary Act of 1789.

The convention: Article III. If we were to look to the records of the Constitutional Convention for information on the original understanding of the role of the federal judiciary and its relationship to the states, we would find surprisingly little on the subject. What controversy there was concerning the federal judiciary centered on the form it would take, not on whether it should exist at all.

The convention quickly decided to establish a federal judiciary separate from the existing state judicial systems, adopting Edmund Randolph's resolution "that a National Judiciary be established." The reason for this quick assent, Alexander Hamilton later explained, was that the framers were convinced that a national judiciary was an essential part of a government. This conviction must have rested in part on the belief that all properly formed governments have three branches. The national government would rely on the national judicial system to uphold federal laws (especially when the national and local policy were at variance) and to provide a more uniform system of justice than the state courts could. As Tocqueville later put it, "The object of creating a Federal tribunal was to prevent the state courts from deciding, each after its own fashion, questions affecting the national interests, and so to form a uniform body of jurisprudence for the interpretation of the laws of the Union." [11]

Although the framers were willing to limit state autonomy in order to ensure that the laws and the Constitution of the national government would be fairly and uniformly applied, they balked at setting up any federal courts other than the Supreme Court. Many feared that lower federal tribunals would unacceptably infringe on state autonomy and the integrity of the state judicial system. John Rutledge urged that "the State tribunals might and ought to be left in all cases to decide in the first instance, the right of appeal to the supreme national tribunal being sufficient to secure national rights & uniformity of Judgments: that it was making an unnecessary encroachment on the jurisdiction of the States and creating unnecessary obstacles to their adoption of the new system." [12] Some delegates viewed creating a national system of courts as expensive and as a possible impediment to the states' ratification of the Constitution if the states feared that lower federal courts would encroach on the jurisdiction of the state courts. Madison and other delegates, however, favored a provision in the Constitution creating lower federal courts with final jurisdiction.

After Rutledge's motion against lower federal courts carried, James Wilson and Madison urged that "there is a distinction between establishing such tribunals absolutely and giving a discretion to the Legislature to establish or not establish them." [13] They proposed the compromise that the convention adopted: The national legislature would be empowered to institute lower federal courts. Thus, because the framers were unable to reach a conclusion on the issue of lower federal courts, they decided to leave the matter to Congress.

To summarize what emerged from the convention concerning the judiciary, Article III of the Constitution expressly provides that the federal judicial power encompasses both the states and individuals as litigants. Furthermore, the federal judicial power, like the legislative and executive powers, is an enumerated power. The listed categories of cases that federal courts could hear may be viewed as restrictions on federal invasion of state judicial power. The federal judicial power of the United States extends to "all cases in law and equity arising under the Constitution," a broadly worded grant of jurisdiction, and to laws of the United States and to diversity jurisdiction, that is, to suits between citizens of different states.[14] Diversity jurisdiction was accepted without debate at the convention and without explanation of its purpose, although debate on this provision was extensive during ratification and has been intermittent ever since. Hamilton explained in *The Federalist* that because state courts could not be supposed to be impartial in cases pitting a citizen of their state against a citizen of another state, diversity jurisdiction was properly in the federal courts.[15]

The text of the Constitution clearly evinces concern for the independence of the federal judiciary, perhaps because the framers were aware that many state judges depended on state legislatures. This concern is evident in the method of judicial appointment (the president with the advice and consent of the Senate), the protection of judicial tenure (during good behavior), and the prohibition on diminishing judicial salary during continuance in office.

One issue the Constitution did not address directly, however, is the relation of the federal courts to the state courts.

The supremacy clause. A mechanism was needed to settle disputes over the respective spheres of state and federal judicial power, i.e., to ensure that the states did not undermine the national government and that the national government did not usurp state powers. To address that need, the framers adopted Article VI of the Constitution, the supremacy clause. The supremacy clause provides that the Constitution, laws, and treaties of the United States are the supreme law of the land, superior to state constitutions and state laws. State judges are bound by oath to support the Constitution and are "bound [by the Constitution], any thing in the Constitution or Laws of any State to the Contrary notwithstanding." The supremacy clause makes the Constitution enforceable in all the courts in the land.

Madison, in *Federalist* 44, vividly portrayed the need for the supremacy clause, stating that without it, "the world would have seen, for the first time, a system of government founded on an inversion of the fundamental principles of all government; it would have seen the authority of the whole society everywhere subordinate to the authority of the parts; it would have seen a monster, in which the head was under the direction of the members." In contrast to the constitutional mechanism to prevent the states from undermining the national government, the Constitution did not expressly provide a mechanism to thwart a central government's "natural tendency" to destroy state governments. Although scholars still debate the original understanding of the framers, the federal judiciary has had this power since *Marbury v. Madison* (1803).[16]

The framers did not try to resolve with finality the tension they had set up between national supremacy and state autonomy in the judicial sphere. Future generations would have to work that out by adjusting and readjusting the relationship between state and federal courts. As Hamilton said in *Federalist* 82, "Time only can mature and perfect so compound a system, liquidate the meaning of all the parts, and adjust them to each other in a harmonious and consistent WHOLE."

Ratification. The need for a federal judiciary, which had seemed so self-evident to the framers at the convention, became the center of controversy during the ratification debates. Some antifederalists feared the breadth of federal judicial power and argued that state courts were adequate. In fact, the antifederalists prophesied the demise of the state tribunals should the Constitution be ratified. According to George Mason, "the Judiciary of the United States is so constructed and extended, as to absorb and destroy the Judiciaries of the several States." [17]

In contrast to the gloomy picture painted by the antifederalists, some passages of *The Federalist Papers* paint a rosy picture in which the state and federal courts function as kindred systems and parts of a whole. Hamilton interpreted the Constitution as permitting state and federal courts concurrent jurisdiction, with both state courts and federal courts deciding questions of state and federal law arising in cases within their respective judicial powers.

According to Hamilton, the state courts would retain the jurisdiction they had, except where state jurisdiction was expressly prohibited. The state courts were not, according to Hamilton, divested of their "primitive jurisdiction" except for appeals.[18] Furthermore, except where expressly prohibited, the state courts would have concurrent jurisdiction in all cases arising under the laws of the union. Hamilton reasoned that the supremacy clause demonstrates the framers' assumption that state courts could adjudicate issues of federal law.

Hamilton concluded, however, that in instances of concurrent jurisdiction, the Supreme Court's appellate jurisdiction would extend to decisions of the state courts as well as the federal courts. Indeed, Hamilton saw a need for federal appellate jurisdiction over state courts. He claimed in *Federalist* 81 that state judges could not be "relied upon for an inflexible execution of national laws" because, in all states, judges were to some degree dependent on the state legislatures through selection, salary, or term, and might not stand up to them. Hamilton found no impediment to permitting appeals from state courts to inferior federal courts. "The evident aim of the plan of the convention is," wrote Hamilton, "that all the causes of the specific classes shall, for weighty public reasons, receive their original *or* final determination in the courts of the union."

The prospect of a national court with ultimate authority to determine the final meaning of the supremacy clause was a frightening one for the antifederalists. Not only was the federal government deemed supreme, it was also empowered to decide what this supremacy meant. Federal courts were charged with the important responsibility of limiting the supremacy of the federal government and protecting state autonomy.

The Judiciary Act of 1789. Article III was not self-executing, and on September 24, 1789, the first Congress adopted "An Act to establish the Judicial Courts of the United States." The Judiciary Act of 1789 is weighty evidence of the true meaning of the Constitution, according to the U.S. Supreme Court, because it was passed by the first Congress assembled under the Constitution, many of whose members had taken part in the convention. Furthermore, the act set forth, to a large extent, the basic structure of the federal courts as we know it.

The Judiciary Act of 1789 established the Supreme Court, which has existed continuously ever since, although the number of associate justices has changed. More significantly, the act resolved the controversy over lower courts: Congress approved them. After a vigorous debate reminiscent of ratification, Congress decided that federal trial courts were necessary. The act set up two tiers of trial courts: district courts (at least one per state) and three circuit courts. The circuit courts, composed of two Supreme Court justices and one district court judge, were the weak spots in the system and were later abolished; separately constituted circuit courts of appeals were ultimately established.

Congress did not confer on the federal courts the full judicial power granted by the Constitution. Surprisingly, the act did not grant the federal trial courts jurisdiction over "federal question cases," that is, cases arising under the Constitution or laws of the United States in private civil litigation. The prevailing view was that state courts were the appropriate forum for the enforcement of federal law and that federal courts should be available to citizens who might be victims of bias in sister state courts. Accordingly, Congress granted diversity jurisdiction to the lower courts, concurrent with state courts, and authorized the removal of diversity actions from state court to federal court.

Federal district courts did not obtain "federal question" jurisdiction until 1875. Until that time, federal question cases, in the absence of diversity jurisdiction, could only be brought in state courts.

To ensure state court autonomy and a final determination by a federal court for all cases raising federal issues, the 1789 act provided for Supreme Court review of state courts' final judgments or decrees in matters of federal concern in three categories of cases in which the state court held *against* a federal claim:

- where the validity of a treaty, statute, or authority of the United States is drawn into question, and the state court decides against its validity;

- where the validity of a state statute or authority is challenged on the basis of federal law, and the state court decides in favor of the validity of the state statutory authority;

- where a state court construes the U.S. Constitution, a U.S. treaty, statute, or commission and decides against a title, right, privilege, or exemption under any of them.[19]

The Supreme Court could not review state court decisions favorable to a claim of federal right until 1914, when Congress granted this review power to the Supreme Court. This amendment was prompted largely by a New York Court of Appeals decision holding a state workers' compensation law in conflict with the due process guarantees of both the federal and state constitutions.

During Reconstruction and thereafter, Congress broadened federal jurisdiction largely at the expense of state courts. Federal removal jurisdiction was expanded. The writ of *habeas corpus* empowered lower federal courts to test the legality of confinements by reviewing the judgments of state courts, even after they had been affirmed by the state's highest court. Thus, state criminal defendants could challenge their convictions in lower federal court and ultimately in the U.S. Supreme Court. Within this scheme, federal courts have a significant impact on state courts and cases.

The United States still has the dual system of courts it had initially. State courts retain the authority they possessed before the Constitution, plus the power to hear questions of federal law. In the Constitution and the Judiciary Act, the state courts appeared to be the primary guarantors of federal constitutional rights and in many instances actually have been the ultimate ones. Congress gave federal courts, existing side by side with their state counterparts, limited jurisdiction. The ability of federal courts to decide matters of state law was restricted to state law issues arising in cases in which federal jurisdiction was independently established. Thus, only the basic outline of the relationship between federal and state courts was set by the Constitution and the Judiciary Act. Much was left to be worked out in practice.

Protection of liberties

Although it initially lacked a bill of rights, the Constitution did not ignore the subject of individual liberties altogether. It guaranteed jury trial in criminal cases, freedom from both federal and state *ex post facto* laws and bills of attainder, and freedom from state laws impairing the obligation of contract. Missing, however, were the traditional clauses of a bill of rights, found in many state constitutions, protecting such individual liberties as freedom of religion, freedom of speech and press, and freedom from unreasonable searches and seizures or compulsory self-incrimination. Thomas Jefferson viewed the absence of a bill of rights securing the people's liberties against governmental power as a major obstacle to the acceptance of the Constitution. The champions of ratification, recognizing their political error, promised to amend the Constitution. The first session of the first Congress drafted a bill of rights in the form of a series of amendments, 10 of which were approved by the required number of states by December 15, 1791.

The federal Bill of Rights now protects individual liberties against the federal and state governments, while the state constitutions protect against the state government and sometimes against action by private persons. It has not always been so.

The federal Bill of Rights. Despite the presence of bills of rights in so many state constitutions, the delegates, with the notable exception of George Mason, seemed uninterested in appending a bill of rights to the Constitution. Mason objected: "There is no Declaration of Rights, and the laws of the general government being paramount to the laws and constitution[s] of the several states, the Declaration of Rights in the separate states are no security."[20] Until Mason raised it, James Wilson said, the issue of a bill of rights had never "struck the minds" of the delegates.[21]

To many of the delegates, the guarantees of individual liberty in the state constitutions appeared to be enough, in part because the Constitution, unlike the state constitutions, was a government of limited, enumerated powers. Roger Sherman apparently expressed the consensus of the convention when, in response to a question about the need to preserve the right to trial by jury, he said, "The State Declarations of Rights are not repealed by the Constitution; and being in force are sufficient."[22] Sherman's argument was that the Constitution could not be interpreted to authorize the federal government to violate rights that the states could not violate.

During the ratification process, the people were unpersuaded by federalist arguments against inclusion of a federal bill of rights in the Constitution: the state declarations of rights would adequately protect individual liberty; the state declarations of rights would wither away if a federal bill of rights were established;

and the enumeration of rights in a federal declaration of rights might prejudice those rights not enumerated. The popular clamor for a bill of rights was so great that several states agreed to ratify the Constitution only on the understanding that a bill of rights would be added. The Constitution was ratified without a bill of rights, but Congress immediately took up the issue.

Abiding by promises made during ratification, James Madison, initially a staunch opponent of a federal bill of rights, supported the Bill of Rights in Congress. Arguing before Congress that fundamental rights should not depend on the "too uncertain" hope that the limited powers of the national government enumerated in the Constitution would be interpreted to protect individual liberties, Madison claimed that state declarations of rights would not be sufficient. Echoing Mason's argument at the convention, Madison noted that while a state bill of rights might protect an individual's rights from state interference, it might not prevent the national government from interfering with those same rights. Besides, some states had no bill of rights and bills of other states were defective.[23]

Although Madison's arguments in favor of a bill of rights restraining the national government prevailed, his proposal to have the federal bill of rights impose specific restraints on the state governments failed. Madison's proposed amendment no. XIV provided: "No State shall infringe the right of trial by Jury in criminal cases, nor the right of conscience, nor the freedom of speech or of the press." Although some states had no bill of rights, and although Madison reasonably argued that "if there were any reason to restrain the Government of the United States from infringing upon these essential rights, it was equally necessary that they should be secured against the State Governments," [24] amendment no. XIV did not pass. A federal constitutional protection against state infringement of individual rights would have to wait until well after the adoption of the Fourteenth Amendment after the Civil War.

Separate and distinct spheres. The challenge after the ratification of the Bill of Rights was to reconcile its existence with the existence of state bills of rights. The Supreme Court responded to this challenge by confining the Bill of Rights to national governmental action. In *Barron v. Baltimore* (1833),[25] an owner of a wharf sought compensation from the City of Baltimore under the Fifth Amendment to the Constitution for destroying the commercial use of his property in making street improvements. The Supreme Court con-

cluded that the owner had no Fifth Amendment protection, calling the issue a matter "of great importance, but not of much difficulty."

Overlapping spheres of the two constitutions. Reconstruction dramatically changed the scope of the Bill of Rights and changed the relations between the court systems. Adopted in 1868, the Fourteenth Amendment expressly limits states' interference with civil liberties. It is reminiscent of Madison's proposed amendment no. XIV, but Madison's proposal was restricted to certain specific rights; the language of the Fourteenth Amendment is more open-textured.

Section 1 of the Fourteenth Amendment prohibits the state from making or enforcing any law that abridges the privileges or immunities of citizens of the United States; deprives any person of life, liberty, or property without due process of law; or denies any person within its jurisdiction the equal protection of law. The last section of the amendment empowers Congress to enforce the amendment by appropriate legislation.

Between 1866 and 1877 Congress took steps to enforce the Fourteenth Amendment by adopting several major civil rights statutes that created new federal rights and remedies modifying existing state law. Congress also increased federal judicial jurisdiction. It opened the lower federal courts to civil rights claims, and, in 1875, to all cases founded on federal law. Thus, litigants could bypass state courts in federal question cases. Finally, Congress authorized the lower federal courts—as opposed only to the Supreme Court—to supervise or supersede the state courts in their implementation of federal law by *habeas corpus*, removal, and injunction.

The first test of the limits of the postwar restructuring of federal-state relationships came in the *Slaughterhouse Cases* (1873).[26] The Fourteenth Amendment provides that no state shall abridge "the privileges and immunities" of citizens of the United States. In the *Slaughterhouse Cases* a group of butchers challenged as a denial of one of the protected privileges and immunities a Louisiana statute granting a monopoly of the slaughtering trade to a private corporation. The Court declared that the claim was not a federal right or privilege but rather a state right or privilege not within the ambit of the Fourteenth Amendment.

The Supreme Court construed the Fourteenth Amendment as extending against the states only those rights that were national in character: the right to travel, the right to petition for redress of grievances, the right to use the navigable waters of the United States, and other similar rights. This list of national rights remained short, because the Supreme Court refused to hold that the other guarantees enumerated in the Bill of Rights were among the privileges and immunities of citizens of the United States.

Although the Supreme Court read the privileges and immunities clause of the Fourteenth Amendment narrowly in the *Slaughterhouse Cases,* the Court later applied many of the first eight amendments to the states through the Fourteenth Amendment's due process clause, rather than the privileges or immunities clause. This application of the first eight amendments to the states through the Fourteenth Amendment is known as incorporation.

In 1897, the Court held that the Fourteenth Amendment proscribed the taking of private property for public use without payment of just compensation.[27] It was not until 1925, in *Gitlow v. New York,*[28] that the Court suggested in *dictum* that the rights guaranteed by the First Amendment are among the fundamental personal rights and liberties protected by the due process clause of the Fourteenth Amendment against the state government.

Thus, from 1787 to 1925, the Bill of Rights offered individuals little or no protection in their relations with state and local governments. The state constitutions provided those protection. During that period, however, the states' records in preserving individual rights were uneven within a state and among the states. For example, the states' records were good in appointing counsel for indigent criminal defendants at public expense. In 1859, the Wisconsin Supreme Court, as a matter of its own state constitutional law, required counties to appoint counsel for indigent felony defendants at county expense. It was not until 1963, 104 years after the Wisconsin Supreme Court had acted, that the U.S. Supreme Court required states, as a matter of Fourteenth Amendment due process, to provide counsel in state felony trials. By the time the U.S. Supreme Court imposed this requirement, most states appointed counsel at public expense, as called for by state constitutions, state laws, or state practice. In *Gideon v. Wainwright* (1963)[29] the U.S. Supreme Court brought only a few laggard states into line.

In other areas of individual rights, the states' records were poor. Many have argued that the failure of the states to provide better protection for individual rights created a void—one that the Supreme Court felt compelled to fill.

Incorporation after 1925. After 1925, the incorporation of the enumerated guarantees of the first eight amendments into the Fourteenth gained momentum, and the pace accelerated during the 1960s. The incorporation doctrine partly nationalized individual liberties and the doctrine coincided with technological, economic, and social changes that tended also toward nationalization.

Because many of the first eight amendments deal with the criminal process, the incorporation doctrine involves, to a large extent but not exclusively, a defendant's criminal procedural rights. The Fourteenth Amendment, for instance, now applies to the states the guarantees of the Sixth Amendment, including the rights to obtain a speedy trial, to have a public trial, to have an impartial jury, to confront one's accusers, to have compulsory process for obtaining witnesses in one's behalf, and to have the assistance of counsel. The Fourth Amendment right of freedom from unreasonable searches and seizures, including the federal exclusionary rule, which since 1914 has required federal judges to exclude illegally seized evidence from the trial, has been fully binding on the states since 1961. The Court made the Fifth Amendment prohibition of double jeopardy and the rule against compulsory self-incrimination fully binding upon the states as well. This privilege against self-incrimination became the basis of *Miranda v. Arizona* (1966),[30] requiring police to give warnings before custodial interrogation. Those rights in the federal Bill of Rights that are not incorporated in the Fourteenth Amendment remain dependent on state law.

The Supreme Court also expanded certain rights afforded by the Constitution as it was extending them against the states through the Fourteenth Amendment. The Court expanded not only the procedural rights of the criminal defendants but also other civil liberties. For example, several decisions of the 1960s expanded First Amendment protections, thereby barring state-required prayers in public schools and limiting the extent to which public officials and public figures could avail themselves of state libel laws.

The incorporation doctrine gave prominence to the Constitution as a protection against invasions of individual liberties by either the state or national government. The combination of incorporation and expansion of rights increased state judges' obligations to apply federal law in state cases.

State courts, of course, were not total strangers to federal law. The two systems have always influenced each other, both directly and indirectly. Federal courts had always applied and developed state law, and state courts had always applied and developed federal law. As Justice John Harlan wrote in the 1884 *Robb v. Connolly* decision, "Upon the State courts, equally with the courts of the Union, rests the obligation to guard, enforce, and protect every right granted by the Constitution of the United States . . ." [31]

Nevertheless, the incorporation of much of the Bill of Rights through the Fourteenth Amendment, as well as the extension of the reach of federal law in general, made the state courts partners with the federal courts in the enforcement of federal law to an unprecedented extent. Working out the terms of this new partnership is one of the main challenges in adjusting federal-state court relations in the post-incorporation period.

Independent state grounds

The U.S. Supreme Court does not have a responsibility to review a state court interpretation of state law and will not do so unless an interpretation somehow implicates issues of federal law. In other words, if a state judgment rests on adequate and independent state grounds, the Supreme Court will not reach either the state or the federal issues in the case. While some commentators assert that neither the Constitution nor federal statutes requires this position, the adequate and independent state grounds doctrine is the generally accepted and traditional test for reconciling the respective claims of the state for independence of state law and of the national government for review of interpretations of federal law.

The genesis of the adequate and independent state grounds test as a way of determining which state court decisions are subject to Supreme Court review lies in *Murdock v. City of Memphis* (1875).[32] Seventy years later, the Supreme Court more clearly explained its position in *Herb v. Pitcairn* (1945).[33] The doctrine is premised on the Court's respect for the independence of state courts and the Court's desire to avoid issuing advisory opinions, that is, opinions that discuss and answer legal questions unnecessary to the resolution of the case. The Court explained:

> This Court from the time of its foundation has adhered to the principle that it will not review judgments of state courts that rest on adequate and independent state grounds. The reason is so obvious that it has rarely been thought to warrant statement. It is found in the partitioning of power between the state and federal

judicial systems and in the limitations of our own jurisdiction. Our only power over state judgments is to correct them to the extent that they incorrectly adjudge federal rights. And our power is to correct wrong judgments, not to revise opinions. We are not permitted to render an advisory opinion, and if the same judgment would be rendered by the state court after we corrected its views of federal laws, our review could amount to nothing more than an advisory opinion.[34]

Complications arise when the state court opinion is ambiguous about whether the court relied on federal or state law. Determining whether an independent and adequate state ground exists is no easy task. Until 1983, when presented with an ambiguous state court decision, the Supreme Court could exercise one of several options. It could dismiss the case. It could vacate the decision and send the case back to the state court to clarify the grounds. It could order a continuance and direct the petitioner to obtain clarification from the state court. Finally, the Court itself could determine which constitution the state court relied upon.

In 1983, in *Michigan v. Long*, the Court admitted that it "had not developed a satisfying and consistent approach for resolving this vexing issue" and adopted a new approach to the independent and adequate state grounds test, concluding that its prior "ad hoc method of dealing with cases that involve possible adequate and independent state grounds is antithetical to the doctrinal consistency that is required when sensitive issues of federal-state relations are involved."

Michigan v. Long

Michigan v. Long involved the constitutionality of a protective police search of an automobile for weapons. During the search of the trunk, the police found 75 pounds of marijuana; the defendant moved to suppress the evidence. Citing the Michigan Constitution twice, but otherwise relying exclusively on federal law, the Michigan Supreme Court held "that the deputies' search of the vehicle was proscribed by the Fourth Amendment to the United States Constitution and art. I, sec. 11 of the Michigan Constitution." [35]

Writing for the five-member majority, Justice Sandra Day O'Connor stated that the Court was unconvinced that the Michigan decision rested upon independent state grounds. More important, the Court announced a new approach to its use of the adequate and independent state grounds doctrine in state cases in which the grounds for the decision are ambiguous. The

Court would "accept as the most reasonable explanation that the state court decided the case the way it did because it believed that federal law required it to do so."

In other words, the Court set forth a presumption that the state decision rested on federal grounds. If the state court wanted to avoid this presumption, it

> need only make clear by a plain statement in its judgment or opinion that the federal cases are being used only for the purpose of guidance, and do not themselves compel the result that the court has reached. . . . If the state court decision indicates clearly and expressly that it is alternatively based on bona fide separate, adequate, and independent grounds, we, of course, will not undertake to review the decision.[36]

The Court's justification for imposing the plain statement requirement was to protect the integrity of both federal and state law making. To the extent that a state court decision is based on federal law, federal review is required for doctrinal coherence, and for uniformity of federal constitutional law. State court systems and the federal courts develop and interpret federal constitutional law. Indeed, state courts turn out a larger body of criminal law cases than the federal courts. Justice O'Connor viewed the mixed federal-state opinions as threatening the federal system with a deluge of unauthoritative elaboration on federal law. The *Michigan v. Long* rule promotes uniformity by enabling the Court to review more state court decisions, because the Court now reviews decisions that are or *may* be based on federal law. The Supreme Court thus fulfills its role as the final arbiter of federal constitutional law.

Commentators assert that the *Michigan v. Long* presumption apparently rests on the Court's belief that the Constitution is the primary law in the state courts for protecting civil liberties. They say that the presumption relegates state constitutional law to a marginal role such that state judges may ignore it altogether and render judgment exclusively under federal law. The effect of the presumption is that the U.S. Supreme Court treats state courts as functional equivalents of federal courts unless the state courts expressly deny equivalency in a particular case.

In this sense, *Michigan v. Long* nationalizes state courts when their decisions are based on federal and state grounds. The Court will presume that state court decisions resolving federal and state issues rest on the resolution of the federal issues in the case. State courts will be presumed to be acting as "federal forums," unless they plainly state that they are not so acting.

In summary, in the interests of "efficiency," "uniformity," and "justice," and out of "respect for independence of state courts," the Court requires that state court opinions contain a "plain statement" that their judgments rest on adequate and independent state grounds if they do not wish to invite Supreme Court review. The judicial presumption, therefore, is that a state court's decision does *not* rest on adequate and independent state grounds, and a state court must clearly rebut that presumption if it wishes to insulate its decision from federal review.

Michigan v. Long also seeks to protect the integrity of the state. If a state court plainly says that it is relying on state law, the Supreme Court will not review its decision. The Court reaffirms the state court's opportunity to be the final arbiter of its own law and to divest the U.S. Supreme Court of jurisdiction to review. As Justice O'Connor explained in a speech, a state determines whether to "grant or withhold jurisdiction to the Supreme Court by the choice and articulation of the grounds for the state court decisions." [37] Furthermore, *Michigan v. Long* appears to encourage state courts to function more effectively by considering separately their functions as "federal courts" and as state courts. As author of the majority opinion, Justice O'Connor stated the goal as facilitating justice and judicial administration, not thwarting state constitutional development.

One effect of *Michigan v. Long*, therefore, is to shift the burden to the state courts to decide just how far they are going to be nationalized. If a state court feels it important to assert the state's autonomy by interpreting its constitution independently—not necessarily differently, just independently—then the court itself must ensure that its decisions are based on adequate and independent state grounds. Essentially, state courts must begin to develop their own philosophy of federalism from the state perspective.

Nonreviewability is the U.S. Supreme Court's acknowledgment of state autonomy. Reviewability is the affirmation of national supremacy.

The dissent

Justice John Paul Stevens viewed the case as raising "profoundly significant questions concerning the relationship between two sovereigns—the State of Michigan and the United States of America." He argued that historically the presumption was that adequate state grounds are independent unless it clearly appears otherwise. He favored retaining this policy of federal judicial restraint, thereby husbanding the limited resources of the Supreme Court. Justice Stevens expressed the belief that "a policy of judicial restraint—one that allows other decisional bodies to have the last word in legal interpretation until it is truly necessary for this Court to intervene—enables this Court to make its most effective contribution to our federal system of government."

Moreover, Justice Stevens reasoned, the Court has an interest in a case only when state standards fall short of federal standards and an individual has been deprived of a federal right. He believed the Court should not be concerned when the state court interprets federal rights too broadly and overprotects the individual. Justice Stevens complained of a "docket swollen with requests by States to reverse judgments that their courts have rendered in favor of their citizens."

Some commentators take issue with Stevens' contention that the majority's presumption of reviewability is not supported by any significant federal interest. They point out that cases that grant rights to the citizen against the state government affect important government functions that protect all of us and that Supreme Court review ensures that state courts will not hamper state officials by imposing erroneous federal constitutional requirements on them. Other commentators assert that the majority's presumption serves the federal interest in having effectively functioning states, because it eliminates a "dysfunction" caused by incorporation.[38] According to this dysfunction viewpoint, where a state court decision that erroneously relies on federal law to restrain state action goes unreviewed, because a state ground was also cited for the decision, there would be an error in the system that everyone would seem powerless to correct. The Supreme Court could not correct it because it could not review it. It would be beyond the reach of the state legislature as well.

The majority and dissent in *Michigan v. Long* agree that state courts may constitutionally develop an independent body of civil liberties law and that if no federally guaranteed rights are abridged in the process, state courts may apply state law to the exclusion of federal law. *Michigan v. Long* does not signal a change in the rule that state constitutions may provide more protections for the individual than those provided in the federal Constitution. It does remind the states that when they act like federal courts and interpret federal rights, they are potentially subject to review as a federal court.

The disagreement between Justice Stevens and Justice O'Connor is thus not whether to adopt a clear rule for determining whether a state decision is independent, but what that rule should be.

The aftermath

Michigan v. Long has engendered a large body of literature that ranges from praise for the decision to condemnation of the "plain statement" rule to questioning the constitutional, theoretical, and functional bases of the adequate and independent state grounds doctrine. The proponents of the decision support it as a workable, practical way for handling state decisions that fail to state clearly whether they rest on federal grounds or independent and adequate state grounds. They conclude that the U.S. Supreme Court ought to promote its federal lawmaking role and ought not to renounce its power to interpret federal law in favor of the nonauthoritative state court readings of federal law. They view *Michigan v. Long* as promoting the U.S. Supreme Court's maintaining uniformity and supremacy of federal law.

To its admirers, *Michigan v. Long* furthers federalism because it delineates clearly the respective spheres of state and federal law and possibly enhances the ability of state courts to experiment in developing principles of constitutional law suitable for that state's constitution and that state's people. They see the case as attempting to encourage states to construct their own inviolable sphere of state law. Some commentators conclude that the plain statement will be a burden only to those state courts that were purposely ambiguous in grounding their decision in federal and state law to evade Supreme Court review and to insulate the decision from the state political process.

Other commentators are more skeptical. They question whether *Michigan v. Long*, which was decided in the name of federalism, really encourages federal judicial interference with state courts' constitutional discretion. The detractors of *Michigan v. Long* view it as an artificial attempt to impose federal law on state courts. They suspect the case is not based on a natural principle of federalism but rather is a means of constraining civil liberties protection. They view *Michigan v. Long* as masking the Court's substantive goal of keeping state courts from interpreting their constitutions generously.

These commentators conclude that although, in theory, *Michigan v. Long* preserves the state court's ability to interpret its own constitution, in the real world the decision hinders state courts from developing state law. These writers argue that the state political climate might prevent state judges from interpreting state law more broadly than federal law. They say that a state court opinion that benefits a minority or runs against majoritarian preferences places a state judge, who is often an elected official, at risk. The detractors reason that a state judge who holds that state and federal law together compel an unpopular result is taking a safer political course than a judge who holds that state law gives greater rights than federal law. Moreover, these commentators point out that the people of the state can respond to an unpopular state court interpretation by amending the state constitution. Indeed, some states have amended their constitutions to require state courts to harmonize their interpretation of the state constitution with federal precedents. Putting a new twist on the old fear that state judges are "dependent" rather than independent and are not on a par with federal judges, some argue that state courts whose interpretations of the state constitutions will be subject to review by state legislators and the electorate will not be as receptive to claims that a constitutional right has been denied as would be a federal court that is independent from other branches of government and from the electorate at large. Thus, the argument goes, state courts will either interpret their constitutions restrictively or risk Supreme Court review so that the Court will take the blame for the increased protection of civil liberties.

Regardless of which view one takes of *Michigan v. Long*, the U.S. Supreme Court has itself made a plain statement. If a state court wishes to insulate its decision from Supreme Court review, it must express clearly the state law grounds for its decision and must, of course, not deny any federal right.

The advent of incorporation has required a readjustment of the relations between federal and state courts. Incorporation affects each system. It threatens the federal system with a loss of control over federal law, and it threatens the state system with nationalization. In *Michigan v. Long*, the Supreme Court apparently tried to stave off both these threats. The measure of its success will be seen in future state and federal court decisions involving civil liberties.

The impact

Michigan v. Long will be felt in federal district courts and circuit courts of appeals as well as in state courts. As we said earlier, federal courts may apply state law

and thus function as state courts. In *City of Mesquite v. Aladdin's Castle, Inc.* (1982),[39] for example, the U.S. Supreme Court remanded a case to the Fifth Circuit to decide whether its opinion declaring a city ordinance violative of the constitutional guarantees of due process and equal protection rested on Texas law or federal law. The Supreme Court held that it would not decide this novel federal constitutional question if Texas law provided independent support for the courts of appeals judgment.

Similarly, in 1985 the Ninth Circuit set aside a city ordinance prohibiting the solicitation of donations in public areas used by a municipal stadium. The court began its analysis by stating that the challenge was based on both the federal and California constitutions and that if the California Constitution provides independent support for the claim, there is no need for a decision of the federal issue. There is no certification procedure in California for the federal court to ask the state supreme court to declare the state law issue. The Ninth Circuit decided the state law question, holding the ordinance violative of the California Constitution, and did not reach the federal question.

It is too early to judge the long-term impact of *Michigan v. Long* on state and federal courts. We can say, however, that many state courts remain unaffected by *Michigan v. Long*, and their decisions are like their pre-1983 decisions. Many still do not refer to state constitutions. Those that do often make no effort to separate the state and federal grounds upon which the decision is based. At the same time, a growing number of state high courts have been relying on their own constitutions. If a state court adopts federal interpretations as the interpretation of the state constitution, however, the state ground may not be sufficiently independent of federal law to insulate the decision from review.

If federal and state courts respond to *Michigan v. Long* in the future by increased reliance on state law, the number of cases in which the Court can articulate its views of federal constitutional law may be decreased. In this eventuality, *Michigan v. Long* may achieve disparity between federal and state interpretations of similar constitutional provisions.

Michigan v. Long does not mandate any particular approach to federal and state constitutional claims, although scholars are divided on whether Justice O'Connor's and Justice Stevens's opinions represent a debate over the interstitial and primacy approaches, which in turn represent different views toward federalism. For the present, however, hopes and fears will abound with regard to *Michigan v. Long*. Some will continue to fear that federal review of state court decisions that do not make clear whether they rest on federal or state grounds will become "advisory" in a new sense—that the U.S. Supreme Court will be advising the states how to construe their state constitutions. Such advice is not unprecedented. In a case predating *Michigan v. Long*, Chief Justice Burger criticized the Florida Supreme Court's construction of the Florida Constitution, saying that it was not rational law enforcement and suggesting that the people amend the state's laws or constitution to override state court opinions that extend individual rights.

Others will continue to hope that the presumption of reviewability will force state courts to make clear the grounds of their decisions and interpret their state constitutions. In that case, the Supreme Court may also receive some unsolicited commentary, favorable or unfavorable, on its own opinions, such as that found in some recent state court opinions.

Perhaps such spirited mutual advice is not totally unwelcome in a federal system of which one of the chief virtues is the dialogue between the national and the state governments.

Conclusion

Federalism will continue to mean different things to different people. From the time the framers adopted the term *federalism,* there was confusion and disagreement about what the term meant. Deriving from *foedus,* meaning treaty or alliance, the term *federal* was, some assert, coopted by the proponents of the Constitution to refer to their quasi-national form of government. As Garry Wills puts it, "By a kind of pre-emptive verbal strike, the centralizers seized the word and cast the original federalists in the role of antifederalists." [40]

The term was born through a process of redefinition, and it has been continually redefined since that time. The genus federalism already includes a wide variety of species: dual federalism, cooperative federalism, interactive federalism, classical federalism, and dialectical federalism, to name just a few. We will not attempt to classify "new federalism" within any of these categories.

New federalism represents an attempt to reinvigorate the idea of federalism by reviewing the idea of state autonomy, an idea that some had declared dead during the incorporation period. The meaning of state autonomy and the proper role for states remain unset-

tled: state courts, among other institutions, will play a role in resolving these unsettled issues as they decide whether and how to apply the protections of civil liberties in their state constitutions. In this respect, new federalism is a return to the preference of the framers for a monolithic system tempered by pluralism.

New federalism is not an attempt to return to the nullificationist vision of the role of states. The proponents of new federalism do not suggest that state courts be the sole guardians of individual liberty or that the U.S. Supreme Court retreat from applying the Bill of Rights to state action. As Justice Brennan said, "One of the strengths of our federal system is that it provides a double source of protection for the rights of our citizens. Federalism is not served when the federal half of that protection is crippled." [41] The difficulty is to work out a system in which federal and state protections can coexist. The fundamental puzzle, as Professor Paul Bator notes, is to determine what the appropriate criteria are for deciding which questions the federal Constitution should be deemed to have made a matter of uniform national policy. [42]

State court approaches to the questions of when and how to interpret their state bills of rights will also tend to define their relationship with the federal courts. As *Michigan v. Long* seems to indicate, state courts will have substantial freedom in determining the extent of their autonomy as long as their decisions do not violate federal law. Thus, the great challenge for state courts in the post-incorporation era is to ground their decisions both in the protection of individual liberties and in the principles of federalism.

Notes

This article originally appeared in Volume 71, Number 2, August–September 1987, pages 88–99. It is adapted from a paper presented at the 73rd American Assembly, Arden House, Harriman, New York, April 23–26, 1987, and which appears in its entirety in *A Workable Government?: The Constitution After 200 Years* (New York: W. W. Norton, 1987).

The authors wish to thank Diana Balio, Sharon Ruhly, and Joel R. Wells for their assistance in the preparation of the manuscript.

1. Wisdom, "Foreword: The Ever-Whirling Wheels of American Federalism," *Notre Dame L. Rev.* 59 (1984), 1063, 1076.

2. Wright, "In Praise of State Courts: Confessions of a Federal Judge," *Hastings Const. L. Q.* 11 (1984), 165, 188.

3. Gouverneur Morris, quoted in Bowen, *Miracle at Philadelphia* (1966), 40.

4. 463 U.S. 1032 (1983).

5. Bowen, *supra* n. 3, at 7.

6. Ibid. at 199.

7. *The Federalist Papers,* No. 39.

8. De Tocqueville, *Democracy in America* (Henry Reeve text as revised by Francis Bowen, 1945), 164.

9. *Younger v. Harris,* 401 U.S. 37, 44 (1971).

10. John Quincy Adams, "Jubilee of the Constitution: A Discourse Delivered at the Request of the New York Historical Society in the City of New York on Tuesday, the 30th of April, 1839, Being the Fiftieth Anniversary of the Inauguration of George Washington as President of the United States on Thursday, the 30th of April, 1789," p. 115 (1839).

11. De Tocqueville, *supra* n. 8, at 148.

12. 1 Farrand, *The Records of the Federal Convention of 1787,* (1966), 124.

13. Ibid. at 125.

14. Art. III, Sec. 2, U.S. Const.

15. *The Federalist Papers* No. 80.

16. 1 Cranch 137, 2 L.Ed. 60 (1803).

17. 2 Farrand, *The Records of the Federal Convention of 1787,* (1966), 638.

18. *The Federalist Papers* No. 82.

19. Act of Sept. 24, 1789, 1 Stat. 73.

20. 2 Farrand, *supra* n. 17, at 637.

21. Wood, *The Creation of the American Republic* (1969), 536.

22. 2 Farrand, *supra* n. 17, at 588.

23. 1 Kurland & Lerner, *The Founders' Constitution* (1987), 479–484.

24. Ibid. at 492.

25. 32 U.S. (7 Pet.) 243 (1833).

26. 83 U.S. (16 Wall.) 36 (1873).

27. *Chicago B. & Q.R.R. v. Chicago,* 166 U.S. 226, 241 (1897).

28. 268 U.S. 652 (1928).

29. 372 U.S. 335 (1963).

30. 384 U.S. 436 (1966).

31. 111 U.S. 624 (1884).

32. 87 U.S. (20 Wall.) 590 (1875).

33. 324 U.S. 117 (1945).

34. Ibid. at 125–126 [citations omitted].

35. *People v. Long,* 413 Mich. 461, 320 N.W.2d 866, 870 (1982).

36. 463 U.S. 1032, at 1041 (1983).

37. O'Connor, "Our Judicial Federalism," *Case West Res. L. Rev. 35* (1984–1985), 1, 5.

38. Althouse, "How to Build a Separate Sphere: Federal Courts and State Power," *Harv. L. Rev.* 100 (1987), 1485.

39. 455 U.S. 100, 283 (1982).

40. Wills, *Explaining America: The Federalist* (1981), 169.

41. Brennan, "State Constitutions and the Protection of Individual Liberties," *Harv. L. Rev.* 90 (1977), 489, 503.

42. Bator, "Some Thoughts on Applied Federalism," *Harv. J. L. & Pub. Pol'y* 6 (1982), 51, 58.

State supreme court commitment to state law

Michael Esler

Despite promotion of the New Judicial Federalism, state high courts continue to rely on federal law for most of their decisions.

For the last two decades, much interest has been paid to the development and use of state constitutions for protecting civil liberties and rights. While there are good reasons to believe that reliance on state law has grown in recent years, empirical evidence shows that the extent to which state courts rely on their own constitutions has been greatly overstated. One reason is that the predominant focus has been on case outcomes rather than on the decision-making process, often leaving questions about the actual level of reliance on state law unexamined.

Moreover, research that has examined the "use" question specifically is often misleading. Typically, this approach primarily examines decisions and courts that exemplify use of state law. The problem with this leading cases approach is that it ignores the much greater number of decisions based on federal law.

This article reports findings indicating that, at least through the first decade and a half of what has come to be called the New Judicial Federalism, state supreme courts rely on federal law in the vast majority of their decisions. Further, even state courts that base their decisions on state law usually do not do so in ways that will lead to the state law's development as a viable alternative to federal law. The results are best explained by the political, legal, and institutional barriers that limit the willingness of state courts to develop their own constitutions for issues that already have been decided by federal law.

The new judicial federalism

The essence of the New Judicial Federalism is the development of state constitutional law for deciding issues with parallel provisions in state and federal law. Most attention, however, has been directed toward the outcomes of decisions that rely on state law. This emphasis on outcomes corresponds to the perception that federal courts are no longer as committed to protecting individual rights as they were during the Warren Court era.[1] Many advocates of the New Judicial Federalism thus urge greater reliance on state law as a

way to expand rights protections beyond the level required by federal law.[2] The legal means are provided by the independent and adequate state grounds doctrine, which obligates state courts to recognize rights established under federal law, but frees them to establish greater levels of protection as a matter of their own state law.[3]

Not surprisingly, most empirical research about the New Judicial Federalism has analyzed whether state courts have followed the advice of the advocates, and why some courts have been more willing than others to use state law for expanding liberties and rights. Generally, this research has not systematically compared significant numbers of decisions based on state law that both expand and decline to expand rights beyond the level required by federal law.

Many of these problems were avoided in a recent study by Latzer,[4] which is an improvement precisely because it accounts for decisions by all 50 state supreme courts and, more importantly, a full range of decisional outcomes based on state law. Latzer analyzed virtually every state high court criminal procedure decision based on state law from the late 1960s through 1989. He found that only about a third of the decisions based on state law expanded rights beyond the level required by federal law.[5]

This overall pattern of results corresponded to a state-by-state analysis. Here, Latzer found that only four state high courts (Alaska, California, Florida, and Massachusetts) consistently rejected U.S. Supreme Court doctrines in favor of more expansive rights protections on the basis of state law. Of the four, two (California and Florida) did so only until state constitutional amendments compelled conformity with federal law.[6] Thus, all but a small number of state high courts consistently adopted Supreme Court doctrines even when basing decisions on their own constitutions. Latzer presents compelling evidence that, in most cases, state high court decisions do not use state law to further criminal defendant rights beyond the level required by the U.S. Supreme Court. Moreover, very few state high courts

Judicature Volume 78, Number 1, pp. 25–32

consistently interpret their state law in such an expansive manner.

While considerable attention has been directed toward the outcomes of court decisions based on state grounds, relatively little scholarship has focused on what is arguably a more fundamental question: the frequency with which state courts base their decisions on state law. Most research on state court use of state law has involved studies of leading cases,[7] courts,[8] or a simple counting of the number of decisions based on state law for a selected area of law.[9] These approaches are useful for identifying exemplars among state courts, the justifications they provide for relying on state law, and a sense of the changes in absolute numbers of decisions based on state law for a given set of issues. Yet they do not account for the extent to which state courts rely on state law relative to the total number of decisions they make.[10]

Latzer's study is typical of most research. His data consisted solely of decisions based on state law. While this might be appropriate for his main interest—investigating the frequency with which state supreme courts use state law to expand criminal defendant rights beyond federal requirements—it says nothing about the extensiveness of state court reliance on state law. As a result, Latzer could only assume that reliance on state law is generally extensive.[11]

Turning his attention to individual states, Latzer ranked each state supreme court on the basis of its commitment to developing its own law. He did so, however, by simply counting the decisions each court grounded in state law.[12] This method of ranking the "activism" of individual state supreme courts could not account for the number of decisions each court grounded in federal law. Consequently, it is impossible to tell if the most active courts are truly more committed to developing their own constitutions, or whether their ranking is just a function of the number of cases they hear.

The main objective of Latzer's study was to assess the extent to which state high courts use their constitutions to extend rights protections beyond the level required by federal law. His research is important for pointing out the limitations of much of the result-oriented literature as well as for providing a valid assessment of the results of state supreme court decisions.[13] Latzer's criticisms of the result-oriented research can be extended to much of the research that has examined the extent to which state courts rely on their own constitutions.

Measuring reliance on state law

The extent to which state courts rely on their own law can be measured by analyzing judicial decisions based on both state and federal law. The study reported here examined a set of issues related to the right against self-incrimination that were decided by all 50 state supreme courts.[14] Limiting the study to a common set of issues provided some assurance that the courts reacted to similar kinds of legal stimuli. This helped control for the influence of varying legal factors that combine to shape decisions in other cases.

Issues involving questions of self-incrimination were selected for a number of reasons. First, they were frequently litigated before the state high courts. On average, about 27 courts decided each issue. In all, 249 cases were analyzed. These issues also were selected because analogues exist to the Fifth Amendment's protection against self-incrimination in all but two state constitutions.[15] Consequently, state courts for these issues are free to base their decisions on either state or federal law.

Moreover, decisions by the post-Warren Supreme Court arguably have encouraged state high courts to rely on their own constitutions when deciding cases raising these issues. For each of these issues, the post-Warren Court has been less sympathetic to criminal defendant claims than its predecessor. This provides an incentive for state courts that favor more expansive protections for criminal defendants to ground their decisions in state law. State courts also are more inclined to turn to their own law when federal doctrines are undergoing transformation, regardless of the outcomes these courts might favor. Finally, previous research suggests that claims based on state law are more likely to occur in the area of criminal procedure.[16] Focusing on these issues, then, maximized the possibility of finding decisions based on state law.

The time frame of the study, 1981 to 1986, covers the early years of the New Judicial Federalism. This is a likely time for state courts to have turned to their own law when deciding self-incrimination issues. The U.S. Supreme Court decisions that signaled the post-Warren Court's retreat from more protective self-incrimination standards for each of the issues in this study were handed down between 1971 and 1982. The majority of these doctrinal shifts occurred in the years just prior to the period examined. As a consequence of these changes, large numbers of cases raising these issues were brought before the state high courts between 1981 and 1986. Given the unsettled legal status of these issues during this time, state courts had both the incentive and opportunity to base significant numbers of decisions on state law.

Further, this period generally has been identified as a time when state supreme courts began turning to their own constitutions for deciding a range of issues. For instance, research by Collins, Galie, and Kincaid indicates that between 1950 and 1986, the period of greatest reliance on state law by state supreme courts occurred from 1980 to 1986.[17] Much of the literature on the New Judicial Federalism similarly identifies this period as the time when state high courts first began to rely on their own law in significant numbers.[18] The nature of these issues and the time frame involved provide a generous test of the extent to which state courts rely on state law.

Methods

Each majority opinion was coded to measure two aspects of state court commitment to state law. The first was the extent to which state courts rely on state law in their opinions. The second, which focused specifically on the decisions based on state law, measured the strength of state court commitment to developing state law as a viable alternative to federal law.

Coding the reliance of state courts on state law was potentially problematic in that, in the majority of cases (64 percent), both state and federal law were considered in the opinions. Ambiguously worded opinions by state courts is not a problem faced only by scholars. It also creates problems for the U.S. Supreme Court when it grapples with jurisdictional questions. The Court's decision in *Michigan v. Long*[19] was prompted partly by the failure of state courts to explicitly provide the legal bases of their decisions. In *Long*, the Court ruled that it would assume that ambiguously worded decisions were based on federal law unless state courts explicitly declared that their decisions rested on independent and adequate state grounds.

Scholars have used similar criteria when their research has required them to draw the same types of distinctions. For instance, Latzer defined a decision as grounded in state law, and thus selected it for his analysis, only if the majority opinion included a "plain statement" that it was based on state law, or an "exclusive citation to a state constitutional provision, or a citation to a state case which itself clearly rested upon a state provision. . . ."[20] Similarly, Fino coded a decision as

based on state law only if it referred exclusively to state law, unless the reference to federal law was for purely rhetorical purposes or when the federal approach was discussed only to reject it.[21]

This study used similar, if less demanding, criteria for determining whether a decision rested on state law. Even if a decision discussed both state and federal law, it was coded as based on state law if a clear majority of the relevant part of the opinion was devoted to analysis of state law and the opinion otherwise indicated that federal law was not controlling. If it was unclear whether the decision rested on state or federal grounds, it was eliminated from further analysis. This approach was designed to maximize the possibility of finding decisions based on state law.

When a decision met the criteria for being defined as grounded in state law, it was further analyzed before it was finally coded as based on state law. If the opinion cited a state court precedent as the authority for the decision, the precedent, and any other state cases the precedent cited, were analyzed to determine their legal foundation. If any of the state court precedents ultimately were rooted in federal law, the decision was coded as based on federal law. This strategy revealed the ultimate basis of state court decisions, including those that preceded the starting point of this study.

Each majority opinion also was coded for the strength of state court commitment to developing state law as an alternative to federal law. State courts may base their decisions on state law, but nevertheless lack the commitment to developing it in ways that would enable other courts in the state to use and build upon it as a viable alternative to federal law.

A useful measure for distinguishing different levels of state court commitment to developing state law involves the types of law state courts cite as the authority for their opinions. Decisions that rely on state court precedents typically cite the relevant cases without elaboration. Moreover, they rarely express any intent to develop state law as an alternative to federal law.

On the other hand, decisions based on provisions of state constitutions, statutes, or common law doctrines usually involve carefully developed analyses of the requirements of state law and how they are similar to or different from the requirements of federal law. As a result, they establish a foundation and provide a record for other courts in the state to build upon. In this sense, state court decisions based on provisions of state constitutions, statutes, or common law doctrines reflect a commitment to establishing state law as an alternative to federal law that is deeper than decisions authorized by state court precedents.

Three limitations of this study should be noted. First, since this study analyzed the commitment of state supreme courts to developing state law, the primary focus was on the type of law (state or federal) on which these courts base their decisions. The study, however, did not reach the important questions concerning the various state and federal legal influences that may have shaped these laws. Ultimately, both state and federal doctrines are the product of a complex set of relationships between state and federal law.

Second, the data include only decisions by high courts. Since 37 states have intermediate appeals courts, the study does not provide a complete picture of current constitutional law in the states. Still, these courts play a decidedly secondary role to high courts in creating legal doctrine. Therefore, focusing on state high courts provides a reasonably accurate account of legal policy in the states.

A final limitation is the study's focus on one relatively narrow set of legal issues dealing with self-incrimination. It could be that the results drawn from these data are not applicable to other areas of state constitutional law. However, these issues probably are representative of criminal justice cases in general, which constitute the "overwhelming, everyday mass of all constitutional claims."[22] Moreover, the results of this study generally are consistent with the results of several other studies that analyzed different issues. Taken together, these studies cast serious doubt on the commitment of state supreme courts to the development of their own constitutions, at least through the early years of the New Judicial Federalism.

Results

Table 1 shows that state supreme courts based relatively few of the examined decisions on their own state law. Only slightly more than one in five decisions (22 percent) ultimately rely on state law, leaving the vast majority grounded in federal law. Of these decisions, virtually all (98 percent) defer to precedents established by the U.S. Supreme Court.

Table 1 also indicates that, even when they based their decisions on state law, state high courts seldom developed their states' law in ways that would establish it as a viable alternative to federal law. Of the decisions that rest on state law, 70 percent rely only on state court precedents. That is, fewer than a third of these deci-

Table 1. Legal bases for decisions

	N	Percent of state law	Percent of total
State law	54		22%
State precedent	38	70%	15
State constitution	10	19	4
State statute	5	9	2
Common law doctrines	1	2	1

	N	Percent of federal law	Percent of total
Federal law	195		78%
Federal precedent	192*	98%	77
Federal constitution	3	2	1

* Includes 26 cases that originally cited state law but whose decisions ultimately were traced to U.S. Supreme Court precedent.

sions (or about 7 percent of all decisions) are based on state constitutions, statutes, or common law doctrines. Thus, focusing solely on the extensiveness of state supreme court reliance on state law actually overstates the commitment of high courts to developing their states' law, even though the data hardly indicate a strong commitment according to that measure. In short, both measures indicate that state supreme courts are not committed to developing state law, at least through the early years of the New Judicial Federalism.

These findings are consistent with the results of the three other studies, encompassing other issues, that have investigated the extent to which state supreme courts rely on state law. Fino analyzed all the decisions of six state high courts for the year 1975.[23] She found that 17 percent of all cases that raised constitutional issues were decided on the basis of state law.[24] The percentage dropped to 8 percent for constitutional issues that involved questions of criminal procedure.[25] In a separate study of cases involving constitutional issues that raised equal protection claims before the 50 state supreme courts between 1975 and 1984, Fino found that fewer than 7 percent of all cases were decided on the basis of state law (fewer than 5 percent for criminal cases that raised equal protection claims).[26] Finally, Emmert and Traut found that, between 1981 and 1985, about 16 percent of all state supreme court cases that involved challenges to state statutes were decided on the basis of state law (about 18 percent for criminal cases).[27] Although the actual figures vary, the studies that have analyzed the extent to which state courts rely on state law are consistent in showing that, across a

Table 2. State supreme court commitment to use of state law

Level of commitment	Court		Percent of all states
High (At least half of decisions based on state law)	Alaska Arkansas Florida New Jersey	New York South Dakota Tennessee Texas	16%
Moderate (At least one-fourth of decisions based on state law)	California Georgia Illinois Michigan Montana Nebraska	New Hampshire New Mexico Oregon Utah Wyoming	22
Low (At least one decision based on state law)	Alabama Colorado Connecticut Idaho Indiana Iowa Louisiana Maine Massachusetts	Minnesota Mississippi Missouri North Carolina Pennsylvania Vermont Virginia West Virginia	34
Zero	Arizona Delaware Hawaii Kansas Kentucky Maryland Nevada	North Dakota Ohio Oklahoma Rhode Island South Carolina Washington Wisconsin	28

range of issues, a relatively low percentage of all decisions are based on state law.[28]

A state-by-state analysis yielded results that support these general findings. Table 2 groups the 50 state supreme courts into four categories according to the percentage of their decisions grounded in federal law. "High support" courts are those that based at least half their decisions on state law. Only eight state supreme courts (or 16 percent of the total) are in this category. "Moderate support" courts based more than one-fourth, but fewer than half, of their decisions on state law. Eleven courts (22 percent of the total) may be described as providing moderate support for reliance on state law. "Low support" courts based at least one decision, but no more than one-fourth of their decisions, on state law. Seventeen courts (34 percent of the total) are in this category. Finally, the 14 courts (28 percent of the total) that did not base any of their decisions on state law are described as "zero support" courts. Clearly, most state supreme courts based a low

percentage, if any, of their decisions on state law. On the other hand, only a small number of state high courts based as many as half their decisions on state law.

The state supreme courts that were most consistent in their use of state law included several courts, such as those of Alaska, New Jersey, and New York, that are often mentioned as leaders of the New Judicial Federalism. However, courts that usually are not considered leaders in the use of state law, such as those of Texas, South Dakota, Tennessee, Florida, and Arkansas, also based at least half the examined decisions on state law. The courts of California, Oregon, and Washington, usually recognized as leaders, fell short of basing a majority of the examined decisions on state law.

It is noteworthy that the few studies that took account of the relative mix of decisions grounded in state and federal law present an image of the New Judicial Federalism quite different from studies that did not consider a full range of decisions. Even the decisions based on state law reflect a general indifference toward establishing state law as a viable alternative to federal law. The data in this study not only raise questions about the overall commitment of state courts to the development of state law, but about the number of state supreme courts that are actively committed to developing their own constitutions, at least during the first decade and a half of the New Judicial Federalism.

Reliance on federal law

For more than a decade, legal scholars, attorneys, and judges have championed the New Judicial Federalism. Advocates have called for increased reliance on state law both for result-oriented purposes and for ends that are unrelated to political outcomes. Despite the advocacy and a number of notable examples from some state courts, commitment to developing state law is still exceptional. While there is no single explanation for this state of affairs, a number of political, legal, and institutional theories of judicial decision making explain why state courts continue to look to federal law for guidance for the vast majority of their decisions.

As Latzer and others have shown, state supreme courts generally do not support the expansion of constitutional rights in their decisions.[29] Leaving aside the justices' own usually conservative attitudes,[30] groups such as prosecutors, police, corrections administrators, law-and-order legislators, and executives represent strong, organized voices for tougher standards for dealing with the accused.[31] The interests of criminal defendants rarely enjoy the same level of organized support. Electoral pressures and the proximity of state court judges to their constituents also sensitize them to prevailing opinion, which is generally conservative[32] and almost uniformly unsympathetic when it comes to the rights of the accused.[33] Not coincidentally, law enforcement has been the main theme of judicial campaigns for the last 20 years.[34]

Given the reality of state politics, it is hardly surprising that state courts have not been more active in expanding criminal defendant rights. It is one thing for state supreme courts to acknowledge criminal defendant rights when mandated by federal law. It is quite another for them to initiate the expansion of liberties and rights under state law. Judges who forget this fact of political life need only consider several highly publicized cases where the public has rebuked state courts that have used state law to promote the rights of the accused. The defeat of Chief Justice Rose Bird and Associate Justices Cruz Reynoso and Joseph Grodin in Cali-fornia sent a message to all state judges about the consequences of straying too far from prevailing opinion.[35]

Voters in California, Massachusetts, Pennsylvania, and Florida have used alternative, but no less clear, means to express displeasure with their high courts' liberal use of state law. In these states, voters used the power of the initiative to amend their constitutions to overturn defendants' rights decisions. Chief Justice Warren Burger even applauded the action of Florida voters in a 1983 opinion and encouraged voters in other states to overturn state court decisions with which they disagreed.[36] State legislatures also have proposed constitutional amendments, as well as exercised other powers they hold over the courts, when they have been displeased with liberal judicial decisions.[37] To the extent that political forces shape judicial decisions, conservative influences are usually decisive.[38] Since conservative results can be reached on the basis of federal law, state courts that are motivated by political goals have little incentive to base their decisions on state law.

Even courts that are not pursuing a particular political agenda or, for that matter, courts favoring a liberal agenda might also be dissuaded from basing decisions on state law. This follows from the perception that the primary reason for state courts to base their decisions on state law is to achieve liberal outcomes. Governor George Deukmejian promoted this idea when he was California's attorney general. In a widely circulated article, he criticized use of state constitutional law without sufficient theoretical justification. The message for many judges was to question the legitimacy of ever relying on state grounds.[39]

The perception that courts usually base decisions on state law to effect liberal results is shared by many scholars, even those who favor the development of state law for reasons that are not result-oriented.[40] Ironically, overemphasis by advocates of the New Judicial Federalism on the result-oriented uses of state law has contributed to the reluctance of even conservative state courts to develop and use their own law.

The U.S. Supreme Court also has played a role in discouraging development of state law. In several decisions, it has narrowed the definition of what constitutes an "adequate" and "independent" basis for state courts to claim their decisions are grounded in state law.[41] For instance, there has been speculation that the effect of the Court's decision in *Michigan v. Long* has been to make it more difficult for state courts to claim their decisions rest on independent state grounds.[42] By requiring them to issue a "plain statement" that their decisions are grounded in state law, the Court forced state courts to face potential criticism from conservative forces that see reliance on state law as a pretext for liberal activism.[43] In this sense, U.S. Supreme Court decisions play a role in the reluctance of state courts to base decisions on state law.

Few political incentives exist for state courts to develop and use their own constitutions. State court judges who are driven by political considerations are likely to be conservative as a result of their own attitudes and in response to the dominance of conservative pressures that characterize most states. For these courts there is nothing to gain politically from relying on state law when federal law will do. The politics of using state law also are shaped by the mere perception that the purpose of using state law is to effect liberal results. Thus, even courts that might otherwise have an interest in developing their own state law might be reluctant to risk the potential political consequences that go with it.

Dominance of federal law

Politics are not all that work against reliance on state law. Legal and institutional factors also provide important reasons for why state courts continue to rely on federal law for the majority of their decisions. The development and expansion of the incorporation doctrine throughout this century has transformed federal judicial relations in a fundamental way. As the number of incorporated provisions in the U.S. Bill of Rights reached its peak during the Warren years, the dominance of federal law became practically complete.[44]

After decades of looking no further than federal requirements, state court reliance on federal law remains deeply entrenched. State courts continue to view federal law as the primary source for settling individual rights cases.[45] Deference to the rule of precedent is decisive for many state courts. The sheer weight of years of U.S. Supreme Court decisions is reason enough to look no further than federal law. To depart from federal precedent could create uncertainty about legal issues that had been thought to be settled.[46]

Moreover, many state court judges are unwilling to expend the resources, time, and effort to develop state law when an established body of federal law already exists. And, after so many years of neglect, some state courts lack the self-confidence to embark on an independent interpretation of their own law.[47] As a result,

most state court judges view the appropriate role of state law as "reactive" or "supplemental." [48] Federal law is construed first, and state law is consulted only if federal law is found to be inadequate or when there are other reasons to justify turning to state law.[49]

Textual similarities between the federal and state bills of rights also work against independent and innovative interpretations of state law. State court judges often feel they must justify interpreting identically worded provisions in state constitutions differently from their federal analogues.[50] To do so could seem to undermine the idea that written law matters.

Some scholars have expressed concern that excessive concentration on state law could even retard development of federal law. It might "dampen the lively interaction between state and federal interpretations of the federal Bill of Rights . . . and thereby decrease the ability of the United States Supreme Court to select from a wide variety of innovative and well-considered interpretations of the federal charter." [51] Along these lines, a state-centered approach might call into question the meaning and importance of federal law.

State courts especially are unlikely to turn to state law in the area of criminal procedure. Given the relative complexity of criminal law, state courts often find it difficult enough to apply standards mandated by federal law. If state courts were to turn to standards based on state law, their problems could multiply. Prosecutors and police especially might find it difficult to operate under an array of state and federal rules. At least one prosecutor called it "an open invitation to confusion-and-error on the enforcement front." [52]

Federal and state law enforcement officers often work together on the same cases. When this occurs, state officials usually prefer to prosecute under federal laws because they are generally tougher on criminal defendants. Sometimes state prosecutors are even deputized by federal officials so that they can more effectively pursue their cases.[53] State courts may be reluctant to threaten these relationships by basing decisions on state law.

The powerful effect of decades of federal dominance retards development of state law in still another way. Even when state supreme courts are otherwise receptive to basing decisions on state grounds, institutional factors largely beyond their control often present significant obstacles to the development of state law. The general lack of historical records on the events and forces that shaped state constitutions creates problems for judges who wish to develop state law.[54] Moreover, the paucity of precedents grounded in state law and the federal bias that characterizes the legal training of their clerks often means that judges will be presented only with federal cases when writing opinions.[55]

Another factor is that attorneys often do not argue state grounds before state courts. When state grounds are not presented in legal arguments, it is difficult for judges to base their decisions on state law, since to do so they must develop their reasoning without benefit of counsels' briefs. However, there is an even more fundamental reason why the failure to raise state grounds often results in the underdevelopment of state law. Most state supreme courts refuse to base their decisions on legal grounds *sua sponte,* as a matter of principle.[56] Thus, the type of arguments that attorneys present to state courts plays a central role in the relatively low level of development of state law. Indeed, the failure of attorneys to raise state legal grounds is arguably as great a factor in the failure to develop state constitutional law as any lack of will on the part of judges.

Some judges have criticized the failure of attorneys to raise state grounds. Oregon Supreme Court Justice Robert E. Jones has gone as far as stating that any defense lawyer who relies solely on federal grounds when arguing constitutional issues before state courts should be found guilty of legal malpractice.[57] Placing the entire blame on attorneys, however, ignores the role of legal education in this process. Law schools focus scant attention on state law, much less offer courses in state constitutional law.[58] Without training in the substance and procedures of state constitutional law, newly minted lawyers hardly can be expected to present adequate state legal arguments.

For their part, law schools may be forgiven for not including courses in state constitutional law in light of its lack of development by state courts in recent decades. State courts must share some of the blame for generally failing to demand that attorneys raise state claims. Thus, the failure of state courts to develop state constitutional law is part of a self-perpetuating cycle. The typical law school curriculum produces lawyers who are not versed in raising claims under state constitutional law, which means that state grounds often are not presented in court. The result is that judges usually refuse to base their decisions on state law, which in turn discourages law schools from taking state law seriously. This cycle is the basis for what Gardner recently described as the "poverty of state constitutional discourse." [59] This is the idea that state constitutional law

lacks the basic language, conventions, and meanings that are required for participants to make intelligible claims to one another and thus build the foundation for its development.

In the final analysis, the powerful pull of precedent, the history of federal judicial dominance, and the interrelationship of many state and federal practices in the area of criminal law make it likely that state courts will look to federal law first. Given that many issues facing state courts already are settled as a matter of federal law; that constraints of time, resources, and energy confront all courts; and that institutional impediments stand as a barrier to its development, there is little wonder that state constitutional law remains relatively undeveloped. In combination with the potentially high political costs of invoking state law, legal and institutional factors work against the development of state constitutional law for issues that have been decided as a matter of federal law.

Conclusion

The literature on the New Judicial Federalism posits two types of motivations for state court judges to develop state law. One is to avoid conservative federal judicial rulings in pursuit of liberal outcomes. The other is to promote a more balanced system of judicial federalism without regard to substantive results. However, the conservatism of most state political systems and entrenched legal and institutional barriers work against widespread development of state constitutional law. The finding that state supreme courts rely on federal law for almost four of every five decisions is testimony to the importance of these three factors in shaping their behavior, at least through the first decade and a half of the New Judicial Federalism.

The movement toward increased development and reliance on state constitutions is still young, and advocates of the New Judicial Federalism have reason to be optimistic for the future. Although established legal and institutional barriers do not fall easily, they are not immutable. As law journals and other scholarly publications promote the idea of the New Judicial Federalism, law schools could begin to produce attorneys who are well versed in the principles of state constitutional law. As leading courts continue to render pathbreaking decisions while insisting that attorneys argue state grounds in the cases they present, other state courts could follow the lead. As courts within particular states base greater numbers of decisions on state law, they could invite more claims to be brought on the basis of state law. In short, institutional pressures could play the decisive role in establishing doctrines that are rooted in carefully developed principles of state constitutional law.

It is unlikely, however, that any movement toward greater reliance on state law will be associated with liberal outcomes any time soon. Unless the level of federal protection falls below a threshold that state courts are not willing to go, they are unlikely to rush toward advancing new rights under the auspices of state law. Given the current political conditions of state politics, attempts to expand protections for criminal defendants represents too great a risk for most courts.

Notes

This article originally appeared in Volume 78, Number 1, July–August 1994, pages 25–32.

1. Latzer, "The hidden conservatism of the state court 'revolution' " *Judicature* 74 (1991), 195.

2. *See, e.g.,* Brennan, "State Constitutions and the Protection of Individual Rights," *Harv. L. Rev.* 90 (1977), 489. *See, also,* his dissent, joined by Marshall, in *Michigan v. Mosely,* 423 U.S. 96 (1975) and their concurring opinion in *Oregon v. Kennedy,* 456 U.S. 667, 680–681 (1982).

3. *See, e.g.,* Latzer, *State Constitutions and Criminal Justice* (1991), chap. 1; *State Constitutional Law: Cases and Materials* (1990), 93–103; Greenhalgh, "Independent and Adequate State Grounds: The Long and Short of It," in McGraw, ed., *Developments in State Constitutional Law* (1985), 219; and Friedelbaum, "Independent State Grounds: Contemporary Invitations to Judicial Activism," in Porter and Tarr, eds., *State Supreme Courts: Policymakers in the Federal System* (1982).

4. *Supra* n. 1. *See, also,* Latzer, *supra* n. 3.

5. Ibid. at 190, 192.

6. Ibid. at 193–194.

7. *See, e.g.,* Tarr, "State Constitutionalism and First Amendment Rights" in Friedelbaum, ed., *Human Rights in the States* (1988), 21–48; Levinson, "Freedom of Speech and Right of Access to Private Property Under State Constitutional Law" in *Developments in State Constitutional Law, supra* n. 3, at 51–70; Neuborne, "State Constitutional Protection of Free Speech and Establishment Clause Values" in Bamberger, ed., *Recent Developments in State Constitutional Law* (1985), 205–230; Crosby, "Rights of Privacy" in *Recent Developments in State Constitutional Law,* Ibid. at 231–236; Porter with O'Neill, "Personal Autonomy and the Limits of State Authority" in Friedelbaum, ed., *Human Rights in the States,* Ibid. at 73–96; Davis, "Gender Issues in the States: The Private Sphere and the Search for Equality" in *Human Rights in the States,* Ibid. at 49–72; Williams, "Equality and State Constitutional Law" in *Developments in State Constitu-*

tional Law, supra n. 3, at 71–93; Galie, "Social Services and Egalitarian Activism" in *Human Rights in the States,* Ibid. at 97–120; Fino, "Remnants of the Past: Economic Due Process in the States" in *Human Rights in the States,* Ibid. at 145–162; Wilkes, "The New Federalism in Criminal Procedure in 1984: Death of the Phoenix?" in *Developments in State Constitutional Law, supra* n. 3, at 166–200; Kramer, "Reactions of State Courts to Pro-Prosecution Burger Court Decisions" in *Human Rights in the States,* Ibid. at 121–144. Friedelbaum, *supra* n. 3, at 25–31.

8. Galie, "State Constitutional Guarantees and Protection of Defendants' Rights: The Case of New York, 1960–1978," *Buffalo L. Rev.* 28 (1978), 157–194. Kramer and Riga, "The New York Court of Appeals and the U.S. Supreme Court, 1960–1978" in Porter and Tarr, *supra* n. 3, at 175–200. Porter, "State Supreme Courts and the Legacy of the Warren Court: Some Old Inquiries for a New Situation" in Porter and Tarr, Ibid. at 3–22. Tarr and Porter, *State Supreme Courts in State and Nation* (1988).

9. *See, e.g.,* Collins and Galie, "State Constitutional Rights Decisions," *National Law Journal,* Sept. 29, 1986, at S-8-S-19. Actually, their count includes only decisions that are based on state law that expand rights. Yet it is often cited as evidence of increased reliance on state law, more generally.

10. Only a few studies account for a range of decisions that are based on both state and federal law. *See* Fino, *The Role of State Supreme Courts in the New Judicial Federalism* (1987), 70; Fino, "Judicial Federalism and Equality Guarantees in State Supreme Courts," *Publius* 17 (1987), 53; and Emmert and Traut, "State Supreme Courts, State Constitutions, and Judicial Policymaking," *Just. Sys. J.* 16 (1982), 44, Table 2. However, even these studies do not focus specifically on the "use" question. Rather, as is typical of the literature on the New Judicial Federalism, the main focus is on analyzing the results of court decisions. Consequently, discussion about the extent to which state court decisions rely on state law is minimal. The possible exception here is Fino, in *Publius* at 66. These studies are valuable, however, for providing data on the extent to which state courts rely on state law for a range of legal issues.

11. For instance, Latzer refers to a "major upsurge in state court decisions predicated upon state . . . constitutional law," a "sizable and growing body of case law interpreting state constitutional provisions, especially the state bills of rights . . ." and an "extraordinary output" of state constitutional rulings over the last two decades. *Supra* n. 1, at 190, 197.

12. *Supra* n. 1, at 193, Tables 2 and 3.

13. Ibid. at 190.

14. The issues are: (1) using silence to impeach credibility when *Miranda* warnings have not been read; (2) using silence to impeach when *Miranda* warnings have

been read; (3) refusal to stop interrogation; (4) denying counsel access to client; (5) errors in *Miranda* warnings; (6) when rights must be read; (7) using coercion to compel confessions; (8) using inadmissible statements to impeach credibility; (9) informing suspect about nature of the crime.

15. The two states are Iowa and New Jersey. Both states, however, have statutes that provide similar protections.

16. Collins, Galie, and Kincaid, "State High Courts, State Constitutions, and Individual Rights," *Publius* 16 (1986), 153. But see *State v. Earl,* 716 P.2d 803 (1986).

17. *Supra* n. 16, at 142.

18. *Supra* n. 7 and 8.

19. 463 U.S. 1032 (1983).

20. *Supra* n. 1, at 192, n. 8.

21. Fino, *The Role of State Supreme Courts,* and *Publius* at 53, *supra* n. 10.

22. Linde, "Does the 'New Federalism' Have a Future?," *Emerging Issues in State Constitutional Law* 4 (1991), 251.

23. Included were the supreme courts of Arizona, Kentucky, California, Michigan, Nebraska, and New Jersey.

24. Fino, *The Role of State Supreme Courts, supra* n. 10, at 142.

25. Ibid. at 141.

26. Fino, *Publius, supra* n. 10, at 6.

27. Emmert and Traut, *supra* n. 10, at 44, Table 2.

28. Analysis of a sample of state supreme court opinions for issues involving self-incrimination claims that were decided between 1987 and 1992 indicates results consistent with these findings. Moreover, recent comments by two state supreme court judges who have been actively involved in promoting the New Judicial Federalism support the claim that state high court reliance on federal law in recent years is not significantly greater than during the earlier years of the movement. *See* Linde, *supra* n. 22; Utter, "The Practice of Principled Decision-Making in State Constitutionalism: Washington's Experience," *Temple L. Rev.* 65 (1992), 1153.

29. *Supra* n. 1, at 190, 192.

30. Baum, "State Supreme Courts: Activism and Accountability," in Van Horn, ed., *The State of the States* (1989), 110.

31. *Supra* n. 1, at 197. Generally on the concept of intrastate pressures, see Tarr and Porter, *supra* n. 8, at 41–63.

32. A majority of citizens in all but one of the 48 contiguous states consider themselves to be more conservative than liberal. Wright, Erikson, and McIver, "Measuring State Partisanship and Ideology with Survey Data," *J. Pol.* 47 (1985), 469–489.

33. Baum, *supra* n. 30, at 120; Fino, *Publius, supra* n. 10, at 67.

34. Linde, *supra* n. 22, at 257.

35. Stumpf and Culver, *The Politics of State Courts* (1992), 150.

36. *Florida v. Casal,* 462 U.S. 637 (1983). *See also,* Kincaid, "State Constitutions in the Federal System," *Annals* 496 (1988), 18–20.

37. Baum, *supra* n. 30, at 115, 120–121.

38. Not all judicial decisions are shaped by political forces. However, it is well established that at least some judges hold "broad role conceptions." That is, they allow their decisions to be influenced by extra-legal factors such as their attitudes and the political forces in their environments. *See, e.g.,* Gibson, "Judges' Role Orientations, Attitudes, and Decisions," *Am. Pol. Sci. Rev.* 72 (1978), 911–924.

39. Deukmejian and Thompson, "All Sail and No Anchor—Judicial Review under the California Constitution," *Hastings Const. L. Q.* 6 (1979), 975–1010. *See also* Utter, "Don't Make a Constitutional Case Out of it, Unless You Must," *Judicature* 73 (1989), 147.

40. *See, e.g.,* Collins and Galie, "Models of Post-Incorporation Judicial Review: 1985 Survey of State Constitutional Individual Rights Decisions," *Publius* 16 (1986), 117–118.

41. *Henry v. Mississippi,* 379 U.S. 443 (1965), *Delaware v. Prouse,* 440 U.S. 648 (1979), *Michigan v. Long,* 463 U.S. 1032 (1983). *See also,* Latzer, *supra* n. 3, at 20–26.

42. *Supra* n. 3. *But see,* Abrahamson and Gutmann, "The New Federalism: State Constitutions and State Courts," *Judicature* 71 (1987), 88, 97.

43. Ibid. at 98.

44. Utter, *supra* n. 28, at 1155. *See also,* Abraham, *Freedom and the Court* (1988), 107.

45. Linde, "E Pluribus—Constitutional Theory and State Courts," 8 *Ga. L. Rev.* 1 (1984), 173–174; "Developments in the Law—The Interpretation of State Constitutional Rights," *Harv. L. Rev.* 95 (1982), 1356–1357.

46. Frohnmayer, "AGs' Mixed Emotions," *National Law Journal* (Sept. 29, 1986), at S-4.

47. Tarr, "State Constitutionalism and 'First Amendment' Rights," in Friedelbaum, ed., *supra* n. 7, at 39.

48. *Supra* n. 40, at 117.

49. *See, e.g.,* Williams, "In the Supreme Court's Shadow: Legitimacy of State Rejection of Supreme Court Reasoning and Result,"x *S.C. L. Rev.* 95 (1984), 385–388.

50. *Supra* n. 22, at 258.

51. Although it is not his own, this viewpoint is discussed in Utter, "Freedom and Diversity in a Federal System: Perspectives on State Constitutions and the Washington Declaration of Rights," in McGraw, ed., *supra* n. 3, at 248.

52. *Supra* n. 46.

53. Comments of Kaufman in "Judicial Federalism: Don't Make a Federal Case Out of it . . . or Should You?," *Judicature* 73 (1989), 153.

54. Utter, *supra* n. 28, at 1156.

55. Linde, *supra* n. 22, at 259.

56. Collins, Galie, and Kincaid, *supra* n. 16, at 144–145, 154–156. *See also* Emmert and Traut, *supra* n. 10, at 42.

57. *State v. Lowry,* 295 Or. 337, 365 (1983) (Jones concurring).

58. Linde, *supra* n. 22, at 261. A search of The AALS Directory of Law Teachers reveals that only 22 of approximately 177 law schools in the United States offer courses in state constitutional law.

59. Gardner, "The Failed Discourse of State Constitutionalism," *Mich. L. Rev.* 90 (1992), 766.

Alternatives to Traditional Litigation

Not all that many years ago, the consideration of alternatives to traditional litigation would have been a frontier concern not worthy of inclusion in a course examining the workings of the American legal system. Such options, including Alternative Dispute Resolution, or ADR, have not displaced courts as mechanisms for resolving civil disputes by any means; however, multifaceted ADR processes and other nontraditional modes of processing legal claims are here to stay and constitute an important component of the American system of justice. Indeed, situations now exist in which ADR mechanisms are not just vehicles for voluntary settlement but are ordered by courts to seek, in the words of John Cooley, "swift, inexpensive, simple justice." ADR has clearly become, over time, a more accepted means of dealing with court delay and case management problems in a highly litigious society.

In the first article of this section, "Arbitration vs. mediation—explaining the differences," John Cooley examines two ADR approaches. He demonstrates how the techniques are utilized in different types of disputes and settings. Arbitration involves a third-party decision maker, whereas mediation utilizes a facilitator to foster agreement, reconciliation, or both among disputants. In this sense, arbitration proceedings may be pictured as analogous to a trial, while mediation more closely resembles a settlement conference.

In "ADR problems and prospects: looking to the future," Stephen Goldberg, Eric Green, and Frank Sander offer a critical assessment of Alternative Dispute Resolution and ask why ADR has not spread more rapidly given its apparent success when used. Among the impediments to ADR that the authors examine are the lack of public knowledge about and acceptance of alternatives to litigation and the constraining role of lawyers for whom litigation is often the path of least and most profitable resistance. Critiques of ADR, particularly the "second-class justice" argument often attached to it, are explored, as is the emerging concern about the professionalization and institutionalization of ADR mechanisms. The authors are wary of some facets of professional institutionalization, although they are supportive of the certification and training that serves ADR consumers. They do, however, oppose licensure, which in their view only serves professional self-interest.

Much of this article is speculative in tone and clearly underlines the need for additional research in the ADR domain. Indeed, as Goldberg, Green, and Sander conclude:

> What we need now is a multi-pronged effort to expand our limited present understanding of the field. This will require continued experimentation and research . . . . It will necessitate enhanced public education about the benefits to be derived from alternative modes of dispute settlement . . . . Above all, if the movement is to hold any significant promise of gaining a permanent foothold on the American scene, it will require the broadened involvement and support not only of the legal and legal education establishment but also the society at large.

Arbitration vs. mediation—explaining the differences

John W. Cooley

An amazing number of lawyers and business professionals are unaware of the difference between arbitration and mediation. Their confusion is excusable.

In the early development of the English language, the two words were used interchangeably. The *Oxford English Dictionary* provides as one historical definition of arbitration: "to act as formal arbitrator or umpire, to mediate (in a dispute between contending parties)." The Statutes of Edward III (1606) referring to what today obviously would be called a commercial *arbitration* panel, provided: "And two Englishmen, two of Lombardie and two of Almaigne shall (be) chosen to be mediators of questions between sellers and buyers." [1]

Modern labor relations statutes tend to perpetuate this confusion. As one commentator has observed:

> Some statutes, referring to a process as "mediation" describe formal hearings, with witnesses testifying under oath and transcripts made, require reports and recommendations for settlement to be made by the neutral within fixed periods, and either state or imply the finality of the "mediator's recommendations." In one statute the neutral third parties are called, interchangeably, mediators, arbitrators and impasse panels. [2]

The Federal Mediation and Conciliation Service (note the absence of "arbitration" in its title) performs a basic arbitration function by maintaining a roster from which the service can nominate arbitrators to the parties and suggest "certain procedures and guides that [the service believes] will enhance the acceptability of arbitration." [3]

The National *Mediation* Board (emphasis added) performs important functions in the promotion of arbitration and the selection of arbitrators for the railroad and airline industries. [4]

Libraries also assist in perpetuating the arbitration/mediation definitional charade. Search under "mediation" and you will invariably be referred to "arbitration." In the midst of this confusion—even among congressional draftsmen—it is time to explain the differences between the processes.

The most basic difference between the two is that arbitration involves a *decision* by an intervening third party or "neutral"; mediation does not.

Another way to distinguish the two is by describing the processes in terms of the neutral's mental functions. In arbitration, the neutral employs mostly "left brain" or "rational" mental processes—analytical, mathematical, logical, technical, administrative; in mediation, the neutral employs mostly "right brain" or "creative" mental processes—conceptual, intuitive, artistic, holistic, symbolic, emotional.

The arbitrator deals largely with the objective; the mediator, the subjective. The arbitrator is generally a passive functionary who determines right or wrong; the mediator is generally an active functionary who attempts to move the parties to reconciliation and agreement, regardless of who or what is right or wrong.

Because the role of the mediator involves instinctive reactions, intuition, keen interpersonal skills, the ability to perceive subtle psychological and behavioral indicators, in addition to logic and rational thinking, it is much more difficult than the arbitrator's role to perform effectively. [5] It is fair to say that while most mediators can effectively perform the arbitrator's function, the converse is not necessarily true.

Besides these differences the two processes are generally employed to resolve two different types of disputes. Mediation is used where there is a reasonable likelihood that the parties will be able to reach an agreement with the assistance of a neutral. Usually, mediation is used when parties will have an ongoing relationship after resolution of the conflict. Arbitration, on the other hand, is generally appropriate for use when two conditions exist: there is no reasonable likelihood of a negotiated settlement, and there will not be a continuing relationship after resolution. [6]

If the two processes are to be used in sequence, mediation occurs first, and if unsuccessful, resort is made to arbitration. [7] Viewed in terms of the judicial process, arbitration is comparable to a trial and mediation is akin to a judicial settlement conference. They are as different as night and day.[8] The differences can best be understood by discussing them in terms of the processes of arbitration and mediation.

The arbitration process

Arbitration has had a long history in this country, going back to procedures carried over into the colonies from mercantile England. George Washington put an arbitration clause in his last will and testament to resolve disputes among his heirs. Abraham Lincoln urged lawyers to keep their clients out of court and himself arbitrated a boundary dispute between two farmers. Today, arbitration is being used more broadly for dispute settlement both in labor-management relations and in commercial transactions.

Aside from its well-known use in resolving labor disputes, arbitration is now becoming widely used to settle intercompany disputes in various industries, including textile, construction, life and casualty insurance, canning, livestock, air transport, grain and feed, and securities.[9]

Simply defined, arbitration is a process in which a dispute is submitted to a third party or neutral (or sometimes a panel of three arbitrators) to hear arguments, review evidence, and render a decision.[10] Court-annexed arbitration, a relatively new development, is a process in which judges refer civil suits to arbitrators to render prompt, nonbinding decisions. If a particular decision is not accepted by a losing party, a trial *de novo* may be held in the court system. However, adverse decisions sometimes lead to further negotiation and pretrial settlement.[11]

The arbitration process, court-annexed or otherwise, normally consists of six stages: initiation, preparation, prehearing conferences, hearing, decision making, and award.

Initiation. The initiation stage of arbitration consists of two substages: initiating the proceeding, and selecting the arbitrator. An arbitration proceeding may be initiated either by: submission; "demand" or "notice;" or, in the case of a court-annexed proceeding, court rule or court order.

A submission must be signed by both parties and is used where there is no previous agreement to arbitrate. It often names the arbitrator (or method of appointment), contains considerable detail regarding the arbitrator's authority, the procedure to be used at the hearing, statement of the matter in dispute, the

amount of money in controversy, the remedy sought, and other matters.

On the other hand, where the description of a dispute is contained in an agreement and the parties have agreed in advance to arbitrate it, arbitration may be initiated unilaterally by one party serving upon the other a written "demand" or "notice" to arbitrate.

However, even where an agreement contains a "demand" or "notice" arbitration clause, parties sometimes choose also to execute a submission after the dispute has materialized. In the court-annexed situation, a lawsuit is mandatorily referred to an arbitration track and the parties must select an arbitrator from a court-maintained roster or otherwise by mutual agreement.[12]

Several types of tribunals and methods of selecting their membership are available to parties who wish to arbitrate. Parties may choose between the use of a "temporary" or "permanent" arbitrator. They can also choose to have single or multiple arbitrators. Since success of the arbitration process often hinges on the expertise of the tribunal, parties generally select a tribunal whose members possess impartiality, integrity, ability and experience in the field in which the dispute arises. Legal training is often helpful but not indispensable.

Information concerning the qualifications of some of the more active arbitrators is contained in the *Directory of Arbitrators,* prepared by the Bureau of National Affairs, Inc., and in *Who's Who* (of arbitrators) published by Prentice-Hall, Inc. Also, the Federal Mediation and Conciliation Service (FMCS), the National Mediation Board (NMB), and the American Arbitration Association (AAA) provide biographical data on arbitrators.[13]

Preparation. The parties must thoroughly prepare cases for arbitration. Obviously, a party must fully understand its own case to communicate effectively to the arbitrator. Depending on the nature of the case, prehearing discovery may be necessary, and its permissible extent is usually determined by the arbitrator. The advantages of simplicity and utility of the arbitration mode normally weigh against extensive discovery. During this stage, the parties also enter into fact stipulations where possible.[14]

Ordinarily, most or all of the arbitrator's knowledge and understanding of a case is based upon evidence and arguments presented at the arbitration hearing. However, the arbitrator does have some "preparation" functions. Generally, where no tribunal administrator (such as AAA) is involved, the arbitrator, after accepting the office, designates the time and place of the hearing, by mutual agreement of the parties if possible. The arbitrator also signs an oath, if required in the particular jurisdiction, and determines whether the parties will have representation, legal or otherwise, at the hearing.[15]

Prehearing conferences. Depending on the complexity of the matter involved, the arbitrator may wish to schedule a prehearing conference, which is normally administrative in nature.[16] Briefing schedules, if necessary, are set on motions attacking the validity of claims or of the proceeding. But generally, briefing is minimized to preserve the efficiency of the process. Discussion of the underlying merits of claims or defenses of the parties are avoided during a prehearing conference. *Ex parte* conferences between the arbitrator and a party are not permitted.[17]

The hearing. Parties may waive oral hearing and have the controversy determined on the basis of documents only. However, an evidentiary-type hearing in the presence of the arbitrator is deemed imperative in virtually all cases. Since arbitration is a private proceeding, the hearing is not open to the public as a rule but all persons having a direct interest in the case are ordinarily entitled to attend.

A formal written record of the hearing is not always necessary; use of a reporter is the exception rather than the general practice. A party requiring an interpreter has the duty to arrange for one. Witnesses testifying at the hearing may also be required to take an oath if required by law, if ordered by the arbitrator, or on demand of any party.[18]

Opening statements are made orally by each party in a brief, generalized format. They are designed to acquaint the arbitrator with each party's view of what the dispute is about and what the party expects to prove by the evidence. Sometimes an arbitrator requests each party to provide a short written opening statement and issue statement prior to the hearing. Occasionally, a respondent opts for making an opening statement immediately prior to presenting initial evidence.[19]

There is no set order by which parties present their cases in arbitration, although in practice the complaining party normally presents evidence first. The parties may offer any evidence they choose, including personal testimony and affidavits of witnesses. They may be required to produce additional evidence the arbitrator deems necessary to determine the dispute. The arbitrator, when authorized by law, may subpoena witnesses or documents upon his or her own initiative or by request of a party. The arbitrator also decides the relevancy and materiality of all evidence offered. Conformity to legal rules of evidence is unnecessary. The arbitrator has a right to make a physical inspection of premises.[20]

The parties make closing arguments, usually limited in duration. Occasionally, the arbitrator requests post-hearing briefs. When this occurs, the parties usually waive oral closing arguments.[21]

Decision making. When the issues are not complex, an arbitrator may render an immediate decision. However, when the evidence presented is voluminous and/or time is needed for the members of an arbitration panel to confer, it might require several weeks to make a decision.

The award is the arbitrator's decision. It may be given orally but is normally written and signed by the arbitrator(s). Awards are normally short, definite, certain, and final as to all matters under submission. Occasionally, they are accompanied by a short, well-reasoned opinion. The award is usually issued no later than 30 days from the closing date of the hearing. When a party fails to appear, a default award may be entered.[22] Depending on the nature of the award (i.e., binding), it may be judicially enforceable and, to some extent, reviewable. The losing party in a court-annexed arbitration is entitled to trial *de novo* in court.

The mediation process

Mediation is a process in which an impartial intervenor assists the disputants to reach a voluntary settlement of their differences through an agreement that defines their future behavior.[23] The process generally consists of eight stages: initiation, preparation, introduction, problem statement, problem clarification, generation and evaluation of alternatives, selection of alternative(s), and agreement.[24]

Initiation. The mediation process may be initiated in two principal ways: parties submit the matter to a public or private dispute resolution organization or to a private neutral; or the dispute is referred to mediation by court order or rule in a court-annexed mediation program.

In the first instance, counsel for one of the parties or, if unrepresented, the party may contact the neutral organization or individual and the neutral will contact the opposing counsel or party (as the case may be) to see if there is interest in attempting to mediate the dispute.

Preparation. As in arbitration, it is of paramount importance that the parties to a dispute in mediation be as well informed as possible on the background of the dispute, the claims or defenses and the remedies they seek. The parties should seek legal advice if necessary, and although a party's lawyer might attend a typical nonjudicial mediation, he or she normally does not take an adversary role but is rather available to render legal advice as needed.

The mediator should also be well-informed about the parties and the features of their dispute and know something about:

- the balance of power;

- the primary sources of pressure exerted on the parties;

- the pressures motivating them toward agreement as well as pressures blocking agreement;

- the economics of the industry or particular company involved;

- political and personal conflicts within and between the parties;

- the extent of the settlement authority of each of the parties.

The mediator sets the date, time and place for the hearing at everyone's convenience.[25]

Introduction. In the mediation process, the introductory stage may be the most important.[26] It is in that phase, particularly the first joint session, that the mediator establishes his or her acceptability, integrity, credibility, and neutrality. The mediator usually has several objectives to achieve initially. They are: establish control of the process; determine issues and positions of the parties; get the agreement-forging process started; and encourage continuation of direct negotiations.[27]

Unlike a judge in a settlement conference or an arbitrator who wields the clout of a decision, a mediator does not, by virtue of position, ordinarily command the parties' immediate trust and respect; the mediator earns them through a carefully orchestrated and deli-

cately executed ritual of rapport-building. Every competent mediator has a personal style. The content of the mediator's opening remarks is generally crucial to establishing rapport with the parties and the respectability of the mediator and the process.

Opening remarks focus on: identifying the mediator and the parties; explaining the procedures to be followed (including caucusing),[28] describing the mediation function (if appropriate) and emphasizing the continued decision-making responsibility of the parties; and reinforcing the confidentiality and integrity of the process.[29] When appropriate, the mediator might invoke the community and public interest in having the dispute resolved quickly and emphasize the interests of the constituents in the successful conclusion of the negotiations.[30]

Finally, the mediator must assess the parties' competence to participate in the process. If either party has severe emotional, drinking, drug, or health problems, the mediator may postpone the proceeding. If the parties are extremely hostile and verbally abusive, the mediator must endeavor to calm them, by preliminary caucusing if necessary.[31]

Problem statement. There are essentially two ways to open a discussion of the dispute by the parties: Both parties give their positions and discuss each issue as it is raised; or all the issues are first briefly identified, with detailed exposition of positions reserved until all the issues have been identified. The second procedure is preferred; the first approach often leads to tedious time-consuming rambling about insignificant matters, sometimes causing the parties to become more entrenched in their positions.[32]

Generally, the complaining party tells his or her "story" first. It may be the first time that the adverse party has heard the full basis for the complaint. The mediator actively and empathically listens, taking notes if helpful, using listening techniques such as restatement, echo and nonverbal responses. Listening is the mediator's most important dispute-resolving tool.[33]

The mediator also:

- asks open-ended and closed-ended questions at the appropriate time and in a neutral fashion;

- obtains important "signals" from the behavior and body movements of the parties;

- calms a party, as necessary;

- clarifies the narration by focused questions;

- objectively summarizes the first party's story;

- defuses tensions by omitting disparaging comments from the summary;

- determines whether the second party understands the first party's story;

- thanks the first party for his or her contribution.

The process is repeated with the second party.[34]

Problem clarification. It is in this stage that the mediator culls out the true underlying issues in the dispute. Often the parties to a dispute intentionally obfuscate the core issues. The mediator pierces this cloud cover through separate caucuses in which he or she asks direct, probing questions to elicit information that one party would not disclose in the presence of the other party. In a subsequent joint session, the mediator summarizes areas of agreement or disagreement, being careful not to disclose matters that the parties shared with the mediator in confidence. They are assisted in grouping and prioritizing issues and demands.[35]

Generation and evaluation of alternatives. In this stage, the mediator employs two fundamental principles of effective mediation: creating doubt in the minds of the parties as to the validity of their positions on issues; and suggesting alternative approaches that may facilitate agreement.[36] These are two functions that parties to a dispute are very often unable to perform by themselves. To carry out these functions, the mediator has the parties separately brainstorm to produce alternatives or options; discusses the workability of each option; encourages the parties by noting the probability of success, where appropriate; suggests alternatives not raised by the parties, and then repeats the three previous steps.[37]

Selection of alternative(s). The mediator may compliment the parties on their progress and use humor, when appropriate, to relieve tensions; assist the parties in eliminating the unworkable options; and help the parties determine which of the remaining workable solutions will produce the optimum results with which each can live.[38]

Agreement. Before the mediation is terminated, the mediator summarizes and clarifies, as necessary, the terms of the agreement reached and secures the assent of each party to those terms; sets a follow-up date, if necessary; and congratulates the parties on their reasonableness.

The mediator does not usually become involved in drafting a settlement agreement. This task is left to the parties themselves or their counsel. The agreement is the parties', not the mediator's.[39]

A mediator's patience, flexibility, and creativity throughout this entire process are necessary keys to a successful resolution.

The "neutral's" functions

To fully appreciate the differences (or the similarities) between the two processs, and to evaluate the appropriate use of either process, it is instructive to focus on considerations that exist at their interface—the function and power of the "neutral." This is a particularly important exercise to acquire a realistic expectation of the result to be obtained from each process.

The arbitrator's function is quasi-judicial in nature and, because of this, an arbitrator is generally exempt from civil liability for failure to exercise care or skill in performing the arbitral function.[40] As a quasi-judicial officer, the arbitrator is guided by ethical norms in the performance of duties. For example, an arbitrator must refrain from having any private (*ex parte*) consultations with a party or with an attorney representing a party without the consent of the opposing party or counsel.[41]

Moreover, unless the parties agree otherwise, the arbitration proceedings are private and arbitrators must take appropriate measures to maintain the confidentiality of the proceedings.[42] It has generally been held that an arbitrator may not testify as to the meaning and construction of the written award.[43]

In contrast, a mediator is not normally considered to be quasi-judicial, unless he or she is appointed by the court as, for example, a special master. Some courts have extended the doctrine of immunity to persons termed "quasi-arbitrators"—persons empowered by agreement of the parties to resolve disputes arising between them.[44] Although the law is far from clear on this point, a very persuasive argument may be advanced that mediators are generally immune from lawsuits relating to the performance of their mediation duties where the agreement under which they perform contains a hold-harmless provision or its equivalent.

In absence of such contractual provision, it would appear that a functionary such as a mediator, selected by parties to perform skilled or professional services, would not ordinarily be immune from charges of negligence but rather is required to work with the same skill and care exercised by an average person engaged in the trade or profession involved.[45]

Of course, weighing heavily against a finding of negligence on the part of a mediator is the intrinsic nature, if not the essence, of the mediation process which invests the parties with the complete power over their destiny; it also guarantees any party the right to withdraw from the process and even to eject the mediator during any pre-agreement stage.[46]

Also, in contrast to arbitrators, certain ethical restrictions do not apply to mediators. Mediators are permitted to have *ex parte* conferences with the parties or counsel. Indeed, such caucuses, as they are called, are the mediator's stock-in-trade. Furthermore, while one of the principal advantages of a privately-conducted mediation is the nonpublic or confidential nature of the proceedings, and although Rule 408 of the Federal Rules of Evidence and public policy considerations argue in favor of confidentiality, the current state of the law does not provide a guarantee of such confidentiality.[47] However, in most cases a strong argument can be made that the injury from disclosure of a confidential settlement proceeding is greater than the benefit to be gained by the public from nondisclosure.[48]

Finally, unlike the arbitrator, the performance of whose function may be enhanced by knowledge, skill, or ability in a particular field or industry, the mediator need not be an expert in the field that encompasses the subject of the dispute. Expertise may, in fact, be a handicap, if the parties look wrongly to the mediator as an advice-giver or adjudicator.[49]

Comparative power

The arbitrator derives power from many sources. The person may be highly respected in a particular field of expertise or widely renowned for fairness. But aside from these attributes, which emanate from personal talents or characteristics, the arbitrator operates within a procedural and enforcement framework that affords considerable power, at least from the perspective of the disputants. Under certain circumstances, arbitrators may possess broad remedy powers, including the power, though rare, to grant injunctive relief.[50] They normally have subpoena power, and generally they have no obligation to anyone, not even "to the court to give reasons for an award."[51]

In general, a valid arbitration award constitutes a full and final adjustment of the controversy.[52] It has all the force and effect of an adjudication, and effectively precludes the parties from again litigating the same subject.[53] The award can be challenged in court only on very narrow grounds. In some states the grounds related to partiality of the arbitrator or to misconduct in the proceedings, such as refusal to allow the production of evidence or to grant postponements, as well as to other misbehavior in conducting the hearings so as to prejudice the interests of a party.[54]

A further ground for challenge in some states is the failure of the arbitrator to observe the limits of authority as fixed by the parties' agreement—such as determining unsubmitted matters or by not dealing definitely and finally with submitted issues.[55] In Illinois, as in most states, a judgment entered on an arbitration award is enforceable "as any other judgment."[56] Thus, from a systemic perspective, the arbitrator is invested with a substantial amount of power.

In striking contrast, with the exception of a special master appointed by the court or a neutral appointed by some governmental body, the mediator has little if any systemic-based power. Most if not all of a mediator's power is derived from experience, demonstrated skills and abilities, and a reputation for successful settlements.

Any particular mediator may wield power by adopting a particular role on what might be described as a continuum representing the range of strengths of intervention: from virtual passivity, to "chairman," to "enunciator," to "prompter," to "leader," to virtual arbitrator.[57] The mediator who can adopt different roles on this continuum, changing strategies to fit changing circumstances and requirements of both the disputants and himself, is inevitably more effective in accumulating and wielding power that is real, yet often not consciously perceptible by the disputants themselves.[58]

Since, in the ordinary case, the result of the mediation process is an agreement or contract not reduced to a court judgment,[59] the result is binding on the parties only to the extent that the law of contracts in the particular jurisdiction requires. And to the same extent, the result is enforceable by one party against another. As a practical matter, where a party breaches an agreement or contract that is the product of mediation and the agreement is not salvageable, prudence would seem to dictate that in most cases the underlying dispute—and not the breach of agreement—should be litigated.

Summary

It is clear that both the functions and the levels of power of arbitrators and mediators are dramatically different.

Table 1. A comparison of arbitration/mediation processes

Arbitration	Mediation
1. Initiation Submission Demand or notice Court rules or order Selection of arbitrator	**1. Initiation** Submission Court rule or order Assignment or selection of mediator
2. Preparation Discovery Prehearing conference Motions Stipulations Arbitrator's oath Arbitrator's administrative duties Arbitrator does not seek out information about parties or dispute	**2. Preparation** Usually, no discovery Parties obtain background information on claims, defenses, remedies Mediator obtains information on parties and history of dispute Usually, no mediator oath
3. Prehearing conference Administrative Scheduling No discussion of underlying merits of claims or defenses No *ex parte* conference	**3. Introduction** Mediator: Conduct *ex parte* conferences, if necessary, for calming Gives opening descriptive remarks Develops trust and respect Emphasizes importance of successful negotiations Helps parties separate the people from the problem

4. Hearing
Not generally open to public
Written record, optional
Witnesses and parties testify under oath
  Opening statement
  Made orally
  Sometimes also in writing
  Order of proceedings and evidence
  Complaining party usually presents evidence first
  Arbitrator may subpoena witnesses
  Evidence rules relaxed
  Arbitrator rules on objections to evidence; may reject evidence
  Closing arguments
  Oral arguments normally permitted for clarification and synthesis
  Post-hearing briefs sometimes permitted
	4. Problem statement
	Confidential proceeding, no written record
	Parties do not speak under oath
	Issues identified
	Issues discussed separately, stories told
	Mediator listens; takes notes
	Mediator asks questions; reads behavioral signals
	Mediator calms parties; summarizes stories; defuses tensions
	Mediator determines whether parties understand stories
	Mediator usually has no subpoena power

	5. Problem clarification Mediator: Culls out core issues in caucus Asks direct, probing questions Summarizes areas of agreement and disagreement Assists parties in grouping and prioritizing issues and demands Helps parties focus on interests, not positions
5. Decision making If issues non-complex, arbitrator can issue an immediate decision If issues complex, or panel has three members, extra time may be required	**6. Generation and evaluation of alternatives** Mediator: Creates doubts in parties' minds as to validity of their positions Invents options for facilitating agreement Leads "brainstorming;" discusses workability; notes probability of success of options
	7. Selection of alternative(s) Mediator: Compliments parties on progress Assists parties in eliminating unworkable options Helps parties to use objective criteria Helps parties determine which solution will produce optimum results
6. Award Normally in writing, signed by arbitrator(s) Short, definite, certain and final, as to all matters under submission Occasionally a short opinion accompanies award Award may be judicially enforceable or reviewable	**8. Agreement** Mediator: Summarizes and clarifies agreement terms Sets follow-up date, if appropriate Congratulates parties on their reasonableness Usually does not draft or assist in drafting agreement Agreement is enforceable as a contract and subject to later modification by agreement

Counsel must assess the nature of the dispute and the personalities of the disputants prior to determining which process, arbitration or mediation, has the best chance to achieve a successful resolution of the particular conflict.

For example, arbitration would probably prove to be the better dispute resolution choice where the dispute involves highly technical matters; a long-standing feud between the disputants; irrational and high-strung personalities; and no necessity of a continued relationship after resolution of the conflict.

On the other hand, mediation may prove to be the most effective choice where disputants are stubborn but basically sensible; have much to gain from a continued relationship with one another; and conflict resolution is time-critical.

Arbitration and mediation are two separate and distinct processes having a similar overall goal (terminating a dispute), while using totally different methods to obtain dissimilar (decisional vs. contractual) results. These differences are best understood by viewing the processes side-by-side in Table 1.

The benefits of arbitration and mediation to litigants, in terms of cost and time savings, are just beginning to be recognized by lawyers and business professionals alike. It is hoped that this discussion of the arbitration and mediation processes and their differences will help lawyers feel more comfortable with these two methods of dispute resolution and to use them to their clients' advantage in their joint pursuit of swift, inexpensive, simple justice.

Notes

This article originally appeared in Volume 69, Number 5, February–March 1986, pages 263–269. It is adapted from a version that appeared in the *Chicago Bar Record* (January–February, 1985).

1. Robins, *A Guide for Labor Mediators* (Honolulu: University Press of Hawaii, 1976), 6.

2. Ibid.

3. Elkouri and Elkouri, *How Arbitration Works,* 3rd ed. (Washington, D.C.: BNA, 1973), 24.

4. Ibid. at 25.

5. As one American professional mediator put it, the mediator "has no science of navigation, no fund inherited from the experience of others. He is a solitary artist recognizing, at most, a few guiding stars and depending mainly on his personal power of divination." Meyer, "Function of the Mediator in Collective Bargaining," *Indus. & Lab. Rel. Rev.* 13 (1960), 159.

6. In labor relations arbitration, of course, condition (2) is normally not present. Labor disputes are generally divided into two categories: rights disputes and interest disputes. Disputes as to "rights" involve the interpretation or application of existing laws, agreements, or customary practices; disputes as to "interests" involve controversies over the formation of collective agreements or efforts to secure them where no such agreement is yet in existence. Elkouri and Elkouri, *supra* n. 3, at 47.

7. Because of ethical considerations, the arbitrator and mediator normally are different persons. It should also be noted that mediation is frequently effective when it is attempted, with the concurrence of the parties, during the course of an arbitration with a neutral other than the arbitrator serving as the mediator. Often the unfolding of the opponent's evidence during arbitration leads to a better appreciation of the merits of their respective positions and hence an atmosphere conducive to settlement discussions.

8. The stark distinction between mediation and arbitration was well made by a professional mediator who became chairman of the New York State Mediation Board: "Mediation and arbitration . . . have conceptually nothing in common. The one [mediation] involves helping people to decide for themselves, the other involves helping people by deciding for them." Meyer, *supra* n. 5, at 164, as quoted in Gulliver, *Disputes and Negotiations, A Cross-Cultural Perspective* (New York: Academic Press, 1979), 210.

9. Cooley, "Arbitration as an Alternative to Federal Litigation in the Seventh Circuit," *Report of the Subcommittee on Alternatives to the Present Federal Court System, Seventh Circuit Ad Hoc Committee to Study the High Cost of Litigation* (July 13, 1978), 2.

10. "Paths to Justice: Major Public Policy Issues of Dispute Resolution," *Report of the Ad Hoc Panel on Dispute Resolution and Public Policy* (Washington, D.C.: National Institute for Dispute Resolution, October, 1983), Appendix 2.

11. Ibid. See also *Evaluation of Court-Annexed Arbitration in Three Federal District Courts* (Washington, D.C.: Federal Judicial Center, 1981).

12. Cooley, *supra* n. 9, at 4, Elkouri and Elkouri, *supra* n. 3, at 183–186. Domke on Commercial Arbitration. §§14:00–14:05 (rev. ed. 1984). Arbitrators, if chosen from a list maintained by an arbitration organization or court-maintained roster, are normally compensated at the daily rate fixed by the organization or the court. Arbitrators selected independently by the parties are compensated at the daily or hourly rate at which they mutually agree. In such cases, the parties equally share the expense of the arbitrator's services.

13. Elkouri and Elkouri, *supra* n. 3, at 24–25.

14. Elkouri and Elkouri, *supra* n. 3, at 197; (for preparation checklist *see* pp. 198–199); Domke, *supra* n. 12, §§24:01 and 27:01.

15. Ibid.

16. Some of the matters that might be discussed at a prehearing conference are: whether discovery is needed and, if so, scheduling of same; motions that need to be filed and briefed or orally argued; and the setting of firm oral argument and hearing dates.

17. Cooley, *supra* n. 9, at 4–5; Elkouri and Elkouri, *supra* n. 3, at 186–190.

18. Cooley, *supra* n. 9, at 5.

19. Elkouri and Elkouri, *supra* n. 3, at 224–225.

20. Cooley, *supra* n. 9, at 5; Elkouri and Elkouri, *supra* n. 3, at 223–228.

21. Elkouri and Elkouri, *supra* n. 3, at 225.

22. Cooley, *supra* n. 9, at 6.

23. Salem, "Mediation—The Concept and the Process," in *Instructors Manual for Teaching Critical Issues* (1984, unpublished). *See generally* Simkin, *Mediation and the Dynamics of Collective Bargaining* (Washington, D.C.: BNA, 1971), 25. Court-annexed mediation is a process in which judges refer civil cases to a neutral (mediator or master) for settlement purposes. It also includes in-court programs in which judges perform the settlement function full-time.

24. *See generally* Ray, "The Alternative Dispute Resolution Movement," *Peace and Change* 8 (Summer 1982), 117. The process of mediation and the roles and strategies of mediators have been generally neglected in studies of negotiation. As one author remarked, "Mediation still remains a poorly understood process." Gulliver, *supra* n. 8.

25. Meagher, "Mediation Procedures and Techniques," 18–19 (unpublished paper on file in the Office of the General Counsel, FMCS, Washington, D.C.). Mr. Meagher is a former commissioner of FMCS.

26. The success of the introductory stage is directly related to two critical factors: (1) the appropriate timing of the mediator's intervention, and (2) the opportunity for mediator preparation. A mediator's sense of timing is the ability to judge the psychological readiness of an individual or group to respond in the desired way to a particular idea, suggestion, or proposal. Meagher, *supra* n. 25, at 5, *see also* Maggiolo, *Techniques of Mediation in Labor Disputes* (Dobbs Ferry, N.Y.: Oceana Publications, 1971), 62. The kinds of preparatory information needed by the mediator are discussed in the text *supra*. In many instances, such information is not available prior to intervention and thus it must be delicately elicited by the mediator during the introductory stage.

27. Meagher, *supra* n. 25, at 26–27. Wall, "Mediation, An Analysis, Review and Proposed Research," *J. Conflict Res.* 25 (1981), 157, 161.

28. Caucusing is an *ex parte* conference between a mediator and a party.

29. Meagher, *supra* n. 25, at 28; Maggiolo, *supra* n. 26, at 42–44.

30. Ibid.

31. Ray, *supra* n. 24, at 121; Maggiolo, *supra* n. 26, at 52–54.

32. Meagher, *supra* n. 25, at 30; Maggiolo, *supra* n. 26, at 47.

33. Ray, *supra* n. 24, at 121; Salem, *supra* n. 23, at 4–5; Robins, *supra* n. 1, at 27; Maggiolo, *supra* n. 26, at 48–49.

34. Ray, *supra* n. 24, at 121.

35. Ibid. at 121–122; Meagher, *supra* n. 25, at 57–58; Robins, *supra* n. 1, at 43–44; Maggiolo, *supra* n. 26, at 49–50.

36. Maggiolo, *supra* n. 26, at 12. Other basic negotiation principles that some mediators use to advantage throughout the mediation process are found in Fisher and Ury, *Getting to Yes* (New York: Penguin Books, 1983). Those principles are: (1) separate the people from the problem; (2) focus on interests, not positions; (3) invent options of mutual gain; (4) insist on using objective criteria.

37. Ray, *supra* n. 24, at 122. Meagher, *supra* n. 25, at 48–49, describes additional techniques of "planting seeds," "conditioning," and "influencing expectations."

38. Ray, *supra* n. 24, at 122.

39. Ibid.

40. Domke, *supra* n. 12, §23:01, at 351–353.

41. Ibid. §24:05, at 380.

42. Ibid.

43. Ibid. §23:02, at 355.

44. See *Craviolini v. Scholer & Fuller Associated Architects,* Ariz. 24, 357 P.2d 611 (1960), 89, where an architect was deemed to be a "quasi-arbitrator" under an agreement with the parties and therefore entitled to immunity from civil liability in an action brought against him by either party in relation to the architect's dispute-resolving function. Compare *Gammell v. Ernst & Ernst,* 245 Minn. 249, 72 N.W.2d 364 (1955), where certified public accountants, selected for the specific purpose of making an examination and of auditing the books of a corporation to ascertain its earnings, were held not to have acquired the status of arbitrators so as to create immunity for their actions in the performance of such service, simply because the report was to be binding upon the parties.

45. Domke, *supra* n. 12, §23:01, at 352–353.

46. As two professional mediators have commented: "Unlike arbitration and other means of adjudication, the parties retain complete control . . . If they do not like the mediator, they get another one. If they fail to produce results, they may end the mediation at any time." Phillips and Piazza, "How to Use Mediation," *A.B.A. J. of Sect. of Lit.* 10 (Spring 1984), 31.

47. See *Grumman Aerospace Corp. v. Titanium Metals Corp.,* 91 F.R.D. 84 (E.D. N.Y. 1981) (court granted a motion to enforce a subpoena *duces tecum* involving a report prepared by a neutral fact-finder on the effects of certain price-fixing activities). *See generally* Restivo and Mangus, "Alternative Dispute Resolution: Confidential Problem-Solving or Every

Man's Evidence? Alternatives to the High Cost of Litigation,"x *Law & Bus. Inc./Ctr. for Public Resources* 84 (May 1984), 5. Parties can assist the preservation of confidentiality of their mediation proceedings by reducing to writing any expectations or understanding regarding the confidentiality of the proceedings and by being careful to protect against unnecessary disclosure both within their respective constituencies and the outside world, Ibid. at 9.

48. See, e.g., *NLRB v. Joseph Macaluso,* 618 F.2d 51 (9th Cir. 1980); *Pipefitters Local 208 v. Mechanical Contractors Assn. of Colorado,* 90 Lab. Cas. (CCH) ∂12,647 (D. Colo. 1980).

49. Phillips and Piazza, *supra* n. 46, at 33.

50. *In re Ruppert,* 29 LA 775, 777 (N.Y. Ct. App. 1958); *In re Griffin,* 42 LA 511 (N.Y. Sup. Ct. 1964). *See, generally,* Elkouri and Elkouri, *supra* n. 3, at 241–251.

51. Domke, *supra* n. 12, §29:06, at 436.

52. *Donoghue v. Kohlmeyer & Co.,* 63 Ill. App. 3d 979, 380 N.E.2d 1003, 20 Ill. Dec. 794 (1978).

53. *Borg, Inc. v. Morris Middle School Dist. No. 54,* 3 Ill. App. 3d 913, 278 N.E.2d 818 (1972).

54. Domke, *supra* n. 12, §33:00, 463.

55. Ibid. In Illinois, the court's power to vacate or modify arbitration awards is narrowly circumscribed. See *Ill. Rev. Stat.* chap. 10, §§112, 113 (1981).

56. *Ill. Rev. Stat.* chap. 10, §114 (1981).

57. Gulliver, *supra* n. 8, at 220.

58. Ibid. at 226.

59. Where a settlement agreement is reduced to a judgment, for example, through intervention and assistance of a special master, the "consent judgment" is generally enforceable, if necessary, before the court in which the consent judgment is entered.

ADR problems and prospects: looking to the future

Stephen B. Goldberg, Eric D. Green, and Frank E. A. Sander

The alternative dispute resolution movement is at a critical turn in the road. What is needed now is a multipronged effort to expand understanding and promote increased involvement and support among all members of society.

If alternative dispute resolution is an idea whose time has come, why has it not spread more rapidly and widely? Why is it that, although the users of neighborhood justice centers appear satisfied with the process, many of these centers are starving for business? Why is there such an abundance of individuals who want to provide mediation services, yet so few customers? In this article we will explore some of these questions, as well as possible answers. It should be noted at the outset, however, that much of our discussion will be based on speculation, for there is a dearth of reliable data concerning alternative dispute resolution mechanisms. Indeed, the absence of such data is itself a deterrent to the use of alternative processes.

Impediments to ADR use

The reason most frequently given for the failure of disputants to make greater use of mediation and other alternatives to the courts is that they don't know about their existence. Despite increasing publicity given to alternatives, we suspect that if a Gallup poll were taken today asking what an individual should do if he had a dispute with his neighbor which they could not resolve, most citizens would say "go to court" or "see your lawyer," rather than "visit your local neighborhood justice center." The emphasis given to courts and lawyers as the paradigm dispute resolvers in American society is simply too pervasive to be easily disturbed. One need only consider, by way of example, the consistent message conveyed by television—"People's Court," "Miller's Court," and "Perry Mason." We have no programs entitled Perry Mediator, Miller's Neighborhood Justice Center, or People's Ombudsman.

Even if potential disputants are aware of alternatives to the court and live in a community where such mechanisms are available, it is often difficult to locate them because they have not been publicly institutionalized. This segregation of alternatives from the judicial process also has other adverse consequences, such as

the common absence of public funding, which sometimes requires disputants to pay for alternative dispute resolution services even as the judicial ones are provided free. More subtle discouragement derives from the distrust that often accompanies processes that are new and unfamiliar and that appear to be unaccompanied by the legal protections that disputants have been taught over the years to value so highly. A related deterrent may be the absence of mechanisms for ensuring high standards in the provision of alternatives.

Psychological factors may also play a part in the gravitational pull of disputants toward the courts. Over 100 years ago de Tocqueville commented on the tendency in the United States of most social problems to devolve eventually into legal problems. Many disputants go to court because they want to challenge their adversaries rather than come to terms with them. In 20th century United States, lawsuits are the socially acceptable form of fighting.

In addition to these general explanations, special considerations may come into play in particular sectors of the disputing universe. For example, large institutional litigants may want a binding precedent to guide future disputes, which they can only get from a court. In bureaucratic organizations, such as the government, there is also the tendency towards following the path of least resistance and minimal risk. This means taking the tried-and-true route of dumping the problem into the court's lap, rather than risking criticism that might come from what some superior views as an unwise settlement.

The role of lawyers

No discussion of the impediments to the use of alternative dispute resolution processes would be complete without considering the role played by lawyers. For all the reasons alluded to above, most disputes that cannot be resolved by the disputants themselves are today presented to lawyers. In most instances, the client will, we suspect, be unaware of the existence of alternative dispute resolution processes. Hence, if such processes are to be utilized, it will typically be as a result of the lawyer's suggestion and encouragement.[1] The fact that alternative dispute resolution processes have not been more widely used suggests that lawyers have not been actively encouraging their use. Why not?

Initially, some of the factors that deter disputants from using alternative processes also deter lawyers from recommending them. While lawyers are more likely than their clients to be aware of the existence of alternatives, a surprising number of lawyers know very little about them, frequently confusing mediation and arbitration.[2] Hence, they are reluctant to suggest their use. The lack of institutionalization also has a deterrent effect. If a lawyer takes a case to court, she knows what she will find—a procedure that is specified by rules and that is familiar in every respect. If she opts for an alternative process, she frequently must decide what rules she wishes to apply and then obtain opposing counsel's agreement to those rules. The path of least resistance is to litigate. Finally, the lawyer is apt to have in common with her client the view that adversary combat in a judicial arena is the normal, socially acceptable, and psychologically satisfying method of resolving disputes. Indeed, most legal education is premised on an adversarial approach to dispute resolution.[3]

There are also psychological factors that discourage an enthusiastic acceptance of alternative processes by lawyers. Like most other professionals, lawyers frequently exert considerable control over their clients, which derives from the lawyer's ability to utilize a complex set of technical rules. This dominance is jeopardized by the use of dispute resolution methods like negotiation and mediation that place greater emphasis on client control over the outcome. These methods contemplate at times a diminished role for lawyers (e.g., as non-participating advisers in a divorce mediation) and at other times a different conceptualization of their role (e.g., as process facilitators who enable the parties themselves to arrive at the best possible solution). While these new roles may represent an exciting challenge to younger lawyers seeking to integrate their personal values with their professional training, they are regarded as threatening by many older lawyers who have become accustomed to the dominance and control inherent in much traditional legal practice.

Economic considerations may also constitute a significant impediment to the greater use of alternatives. Over the past decade, law firms have built up immense litigation departments. Even though some of the leading litigation practitioners are prominent in the alternatives movement because they see the advantages of accommodative problem-solving in many situations, the very existence of these expanding litigation empires constitutes a self-reinforcing movement towards more and more litigation.

Aside from these institutional forces, there are elements of the typical attorney compensation structure that militate against greater use of alternatives. The lawyer who gets paid on an hourly basis has no short-run economic interest in faster methods of dispute resolution. The plaintiff's lawyer who is paid on a contingent fee basis might, unless he will receive a higher proportion of a jury verdict than of a settlement. Under these circumstances, processes that encourage settlement may not be welcome.

Alternatives may also have an impact on future fees. If mediation, as advertised, deters future disputes so that people do not have to go to a lawyer as often, then lawyers may see the alternatives movement as disadvantageous to their economic interest. On the other hand, lawyers must be concerned about their competitive position vis-à-vis other lawyers; once clients become aware of the benefits of alternatives, they may bring pressure on their attorneys to use these methods or threaten to take their business elsewhere. Inasmuch as attorneys can buttress the case against the use of alternatives by the uncertain results and the absence of legal protections inherent in those processes, it may be only the client with considerable sophistication who will be capable of withstanding the countervailing pressures and insist upon the use of alternatives.

Even those attorneys who support alternative processes in principle, and would encourage their use in specific cases, may encounter difficulties. For example, some lawyers believe that a suggestion to opposing counsel that alternatives to litigation be explored may be taken as a sign of weakness (fear of litigation), which will negatively affect the lawyer's negotiating position. It is also possible that the Code of Professional Responsibility's emphasis on "zealous representation" deters some lawyers from proposing what has been called "a warmer way of disputing."[4] Furthermore, the lawyer who would not only advocate, but engage in, the provision of dispute resolution services must be concerned with the vague prohibitions of the Code against dual representation, which, to some uncertain extent, preclude lawyers from acting in a mediatory role.

There are also barriers to the provision of alternative dispute resolution services by those who are not lawyers. They must first acquire the necessary skills—no easy task at a time when the state of the art is still fairly primitive. Then they must turn these skills into a marketable career, which brings them up against the impediments earlier alluded to—a minimal demand compounded by the absence of institutional structures and public funding. Finally, there is the risk that in providing dispute resolution services they will run afoul of the prohibitions on the unauthorized practice of law. Indeed, there have already been a number of instances in which such prohibitions have been invoked against divorce mediators. To be sure, the extent to which non-lawyers should be free to provide dispute resolution services presents difficult issues. For present purposes, however, the point is that the unauthorized practice rules deter the provision of dispute resolution services by nonlawyers, and thereby to some extent discourage their use.

Needless to say, these barriers to the use of alternatives have crosscutting and interlocking effects. For example, one reason for the shortage of empirical data is the shortage of research funds, but the shortage of persuasive research data in turn makes more difficult the procurement of additional funds to facilitate the enhanced institutionalization of alternative mechanisms.

In subsequent sections of this article, we will explore further some of these barriers and ways of ameliorating them. As regards the overriding goal of the need for enhanced education with respect to alternatives, perhaps the most promising efforts along these lines are presently being made through inclusion of conflict resolution units in the public school curriculum.[5] Only if people learn at an early age about the varied ways of resolving conflict can the prevailing emphasis on adversary dispute settlement be significantly moderated.

Critiques of mediation

The principal thrust of recent criticism of ADR has been aimed primarily at mediation, perhaps because that process blends third-party facilitation with disputant control of outcome, and hence is inherently imprecise and manipulable. In theory, mediation is a voluntary process whereby two or more disputants arrive at a mutually acceptable solution with the help of a neutral third party. In fact, some of these features are often lacking. Because of the not uncommon reluctance of one party to participate in mediation, overt or covert pressure is brought against the reluctant party.

As regards the element of coercion, a distinction should be drawn between coercion "into" and coercion "in" mediation. Although ideally a disputant should be able to make a knowing choice between going to mediation and going to court, a bit of a push towards mediation does not seem too serious, given the general ignorance of that process, as long as the disputants are free to choose any outcome they wish *in* the mediation proceeding.

In a recent piece, Professor Owen Fiss of Yale Law School launched a ringing attack on one of the fundamental premises of the alternatives movement—that settlement as a general rule is a social good.[6] Fiss contends that settlement necessarily involves a compromise of legal entitlements, which is of particular concern when there is a sharp power disparity between the parties.

The case against mediating disputes of the disadvantaged has been articulated with particular fervor by radical critics of the legal system, for they see the alternatives movement as a calculated effort by the establishment to discourage the disadvantaged from asserting their legal rights[7] and hence as simply another form of social control. By way of factual support, these critics point out that the three Neighborhood Justice Centers that were set up by the United States Department of Justice in the late seventies were in fact used predominantly by lower income disputants.[8]

Another argument raised on behalf of the lower income users of alternatives is that they are relegated to "second class" justice while the rich preempt the courts. Like most slogans, the term "second class" justice requires closer analysis. It appears to consist of three distinct ideas.

The first is that the thrust of the mediation process is towards a surrender of legal rights; its goal is settlement, not assertion of principle. This is the thesis that is so forcefully asserted by Fiss, not only from the perspective of the individual disputant but also in terms of the potential harm to society where socially important issues are at stake. To take a common example, if a consumer who has been victimized by a merchant sues in small claims court and then is referred to mediation, the case may be settled by having the vendor make some modest payment, without the consumer ever being apprised of his right to get treble damages under the applicable consumer protection act.

The second concern is that mediation lacks the legal protections associated with the adjudicatory process. Lawyers rarely participate in mediation, there are no evidentiary rules to prevent the introduction of unreliable or even prejudicial evidence, and in criminal-type cases no provision is made for the assertion of constitutional rights, such as the privilege against self-incrimination. In short, there is no guarantee of due process in mediation.

The assumption that underlies both preceding arguments—that many persons "relegated" to alternative processes would prefer to go to court—is dubious at best. When the disputants have an ongoing relationship, or the dispute is polycentric,[9] mediation may be far more responsive to the needs of the disputants than adjudication. Consider, for example, sexual harassment in the work place. While adjudication, if successful, would provide vindication, it might also create such tension that a continuation of the employment relationship might, as a practical matter, be extremely difficult. In such a situation, employees might well prefer mediation to adjudication.

Another assumption of the "second-class" justice argument is that if lower-income disputants were not relegated to alternative processes, they would receive the procedural protections and full-blown trial inherent in the phrase "first-class" justice. In actuality, however, most "minor" disputes are shunted aside or mass-processed by the judicial system in a way that provides very little of the deliberative flavor that is the advertised hallmark of adjudication. Hence, the real choice may often be between mediation and surrogates for true adjudication. In this connection it is crucial to draw a sharp distinction between complex and path-breaking litigation (such as a desegregation case that receives a disproportionate amount of judicial attention) and run-of-the-mill civil or criminal cases that are far more likely to be thoughtfully considered in the alternative processes.

A third implication of the "second-class" justice argument is that mediation, by focusing on accommodative resolutions of individual disputes, prevents aggregate solutions. For example, using the previous consumer fraud example, if a manufacturer has committed flagrant violations of the consumer protection laws, these wrongs will not be effectively redressed if the perpetrator is allowed to "buy off" individual complainants through settlements that do not address directly the legality of the underlying practice.

Here again the assumption that the asserted deficiency is necessarily avoided in court is open to question. To be sure, a class action may be brought, or an individual case may create a binding precedent, but the vast preponderance of cases in court are settled without addressing any broader recurring issue that may be involved. This is particularly true of the high volume lower-level courts where most of these cases are brought. Hence what may be best is a mechanism (such as a consumer protection bureau in an attorney general's office) that effectively blends redress of individual grievances (perhaps through mediation) with aggregate relief through adjudication for "pattern and practice" violations.

In the final analysis, the question is how best to bring about change by individual or by institutional defendants. Sometimes lawsuits represent the most promising way; at other times, institutional change is brought about best from within, through accommodative processes such as mediation.[10]

A need for empirical research

Notable progress has been made in demonstrating empirically some of the claimed advantages of alternative methods of dispute resolution, such as the greater satisfaction of disputants with mediation.[11] Most of the mediation research, however, has been carried out with disputants who mediated voluntarily. The obvious risk is that those disputants who were willing to mediate were particularly susceptible to a mediatory approach, and that if mediation were compulsory, as may be necessary to bring about its widespread use, its apparent advantages would disappear. For example, settlement rates, compliance, and participant satisfaction might all diminish if mediation were compulsory.

Another risk of compulsory mediation is that disputants who would otherwise resolve their disputes through direct negotiation might take advantage of the easy accessibility of mediation, each hoping to do better in mediation than in negotiation. If that would occur in a substantial proportion of cases, mediation would, as a practical matter, be a substitute for negotiation, and should be compared to it, not adjudication. Hence, research on the effects of compulsory mediation on settlements by negotiation is called for, as is research comparing compulsory mediation with adjudication.

The data on compulsory mediation are slim. McEwen and Maiman found that in the mediation of small claims, neither settlement rates nor compliance varied according to whether mediation was voluntary or compulsory.[12] However, their findings are weakened by the fact that in the small claims courts they studied, the assignment of cases to mediation was not random. Judges in some courts ordered disputants to mediation, while others made mediation voluntary. It is not clear whether those judges who imposed mediation did so in all cases, or only in those cases in which they thought the parties were susceptible to a mediatory approach. If the latter procedure were followed, the data regarding the effectiveness of compulsory mediation would be weakened.[13] A subsequent study, however, in which a six-month period of voluntary mediation of grievances arising under a collective bargaining contract was followed by a six-month period of compulsory mediation, found that settlement rates at mediation were not affected by whether mediation was voluntary or compulsory. The same study found compulsory mediation associated with a decrease in directly negotiated settlements, although the existence of a causal relationship could not be determined.[14]

Considerably more research on the effects of compulsory participation in alternatives to litigation is needed. One opportunity for such research in the mediation context is presented by California's recent change from voluntary to compulsory mediation of child custody disputes. Data comparing mandatory mediation to voluntary mediation or adjudication of child custody disputes on each of the criteria discussed by Pearson would be extremely useful.[15] Obviously, any such study would have to be replicated in other contexts before we could generalize from it.

The spread of compulsory court-annexed arbitration provides ample opportunity for testing the extent to which this process is capable of resolving disputes more satisfactorily than they would be resolved by the traditional route of settlement negotiations followed by trial for those cases that do not settle. It is, of course, important in collecting data on this question that courts which are experimenting with arbitration do so in a truly experimental mode, assigning cases randomly to the arbitration route and the traditional route. Only then will we have a clear comparison of the two approaches. One problem with such research, however, is that it is unclear whether random assignment would constitute constitutionally impermissible disparate treatment.[16]

If the alternatives to adjudication have all the advantages claimed for them, why are they not more widely used? The answers to this question remain a matter of controversy. It is, however, an exceedingly important question. For, until we know why voluntary alternatives

are not more used, any response to their underutilization will necessarily be based on speculation, with all the false starts and inefficient expenditure of resources that entails.

Researches have already determined what proportion of disputes result in court filings by tracking disputes from their origin to their final disposition.[17] However, that research does not disclose why those disputants who went to court did not utilize one of the alternatives to litigation. To answer the latter question, one might offer disputants their choice of adjudication or mediation. Those who chose adjudication rather than mediation could be questioned concerning their reasons. Additionally, the characteristics of those who chose mediation could be compared with those who chose adjudication. In conducting research of this type with individuals who accepted and rejected mediation of child custody disputes, Pearson, Thoennes, and Vanderkooi found that the lawyers' attitude toward mediation was the key factor in the choice of processes.[18] Similar research could be conducted in conjunction with the multidoor courthouse experiments described by Finkelstein elsewhere in this issue.[19]

Lack of knowledge

It is frequently asserted that a major reason for the failure to use alternatives to adjudication is lack of knowledge. One recent study, however, casts doubt upon this assertion. According to Merry and Silbey, who studied attitudes and behaviors of disputing in three neighborhoods, disputants do not use alternatives to the extent hoped for by their proponents because by the time they are willing to turn to an outsider for help, they do not want what alternatives have to offer.[20] They no longer wish to settle the dispute by discussion and negotiation; rather each wants vindication, protection of his or her rights, an advocate to help in the battle, or a third party who will declare the other party wrong.

Another approach to testing the hypothesis that lack of knowledge is a major barrier to the use of alternatives would be to compare the number of cases submitted to the judicial system and to, for example, the neighborhood justice center, in two closely matched communities, preceding and following an extensive education program, using both the media and the schools in one of those communities. Any significant difference in the proportion of cases submitted to the neighborhood justice center in the "educated" community compared with the control community could (absent other intervening variables) be attributed to the educational campaign; any significant increase in the total volume of cases presented to the neighborhood justice center and the courts combined in the "educated" community compared with the control community might also indicate that an effect of the education campaign was to reduce the frequency of "lumping it" or avoidance as a means of dispute resolution.[21]

Another means to determine the extent to which lack of knowledge regarding alternatives explains their limited use is to provide such knowledge, together with encouragement to try an alternative in appropriate cases, and facilitate access to the alternatives. That is the approach being taken by the multi-door courthouse experiments.

What can research accomplish?

Can we develop a satisfactory taxonomy of dispute resolution processes, matching disputes to appropriate dispute resolution processes? To some extent, the success of the multidoor courthouse will depend on the capacity of its staff to direct disputants to a process that is appropriate for their dispute. However, to the best of our knowledge, there are no empirical data on this question. To generate such data, a laboratory experiment might be conducted in which the same dispute was dealt with in a variety of dispute resolution processes. Measures could then be taken of settlement rate, cost, speed, participant satisfaction with process and outcome, and other relevant variables. If such an experiment were conducted with a number of different types of disputes, varying in such criteria as subject matter, amount at issue, presence or absence of a continuing relationship, presence or absence of a substantial power disparity, etc., one would begin to develop some empirical basis for suggesting that a particular type of dispute might be best handled in a particular process. Laboratory experiments of this nature, in which the same dispute has been subjected to a variety of dispute resolution processes, and participant satisfaction measured in each, have been conducted by Thibaut and Walker, LaTour, et al. and Brett.[22]

Can we develop a sophisticated cost-benefit analysis for the various dispute resolution processes? Doing so presents substantial questions of measurement. Some items can be measured in financial terms, some in psychological terms, some not at all. For example, many of the costs to both the public and the parties of resolving a dispute in one process or another—attorneys' fees,

dispute resolvers' salaries—are easily measurable in financial terms. Similarly, some benefits, such as increased compliance and deterrence of future disputes, can be translated into financial terms.

There are, however, some items, such as participant satisfaction, that can be measured only in psychological terms, and others that cannot be measured at all. What, for example, is the cost to the justice system or the parties of a dispute being settled in mediation, but no precedent being set, as it would be in adjudication?[23] Another problem of cost-benefit analysis in this context is the difficulty in determining the appropriate unit of measurement. If mediation does, indeed, lead to greater compliance and deterrence of future disputes, its benefits extend beyond the individual case in which it is used, and treating the case as the appropriate unit of measurement would be misleading. In sum, the most that research may be able to accomplish in this context is to provide a variety of measures on which to compare some of the costs and benefits of the various dispute resolution processes. Still, even those data, limited as they are, are preferable to sheer impressionism as a means for allocating limited funds among these processes.

Is there a danger that in our preoccupation with finding the appropriate dispute resolution *process,* we will lose sight of the need for fair outcomes? While one cannot engage in empirical research bearing directly on this speculative question, it is possible to design research with the aim of minimizing the danger that the need for fair outcomes will be overlooked. For example, in doing the research necessary to develop a taxonomy of dispute resolution processes, one could include among the measures to be examined both objective criteria such as the efficiency of the outcome (the extent to which joint gains have been maximized) and subjective criteria such as the parties' satisfaction with outcome, as distinguished from process. Indeed, considerable research has already been done on participant satisfaction. That research suggests that satisfaction with process is related to satisfaction with outcome—disputants who believe that a dispute resolution process was fair tend also to believe that the outcome was fair.

Is there a danger that the availability of alternatives will shunt low- and middle-income disputants to a form of second-class justice, consisting primarily of semi-coerced compromise settlements, while the so-called first-class justice offered by the courts becomes available only to the rich and powerful? To some extent, this question presents an issue of definition. What is first-class justice? If it is defined as a method of resolving disputes that includes legal representation, formal rules of procedure, and a resolution based upon law, then those alternatives that are mediatory in nature will inevitably be labeled second-class, and the central question essentially answers itself. If, however, first-class justice is defined as that dispute resolution process which most satisfies the participants, research can be conducted by surveying the users of the alternative processes concerning their satisfaction with them, and comparing their responses with those of the users of the courts. Much of that research has been done, and uniformly concludes that participants in the alternative processes are as satisfied or more satisfied with those processes than are participants in court adjudication.[24]

There are undoubtedly other questions not mentioned here that are important for the future of the dispute resolution movement as a whole or for particular processes. The crucial point is that as such questions are identified they should be scrutinized to determine the extent to which they are susceptible to empirical research. Such research may, to be sure, have a limited effect on the resolution of the underlying legal and policy questions, a phenomenon frequently noted (and bemoaned) by social science researchers.[25] Still, empirical data can be influential in changing policy, particularly to the extent that existing policy is based on factual misconceptions. In a field as comparatively new as dispute resolution, such misconceptions are certain to abound. Hence, the opportunity exists for empirical researchers to make a significant contribution to removing at least some of the impediments to the expanded use of alternative dispute resolution processes.[26]

Creating a coherent scheme

It is implicit in the preceding discussion that dispute resolution mechanisms are dispersed all through the social fabric. Sometimes they are private; sometimes they are public. Sometimes they are mandatory; at other times they are optional. Wherever disputes arise between individuals and organizations, a complex network of possible grievance mechanisms appears to be available for the venting of these grievances.[27]

The question naturally arises what, if any, relationship there should be between the different types of

mechanisms. This question assumes importance not only for the disputant who might benefit from some guidance concerning where to take any particular dispute but also from the point of view of society seeking to provide a coherent response to these requests.

One can certainly envision a system in which there is some kind of hierarchy and structure within the formal public dispute resolution system, but where that system is complemented in some vague way by a vast and ill-understood network of indigenous dispute mechanisms. Indeed, that, in essence, is our present system. Disputants may first try to utilize the vast array of informal mechanisms that are provided in the particular universe where the dispute arises, and then, as a last resort, take the dispute to the public forum, the court.[28] At least that is the paradigm. In fact, of course, informal private mechanisms often are not available, or if they are, they are not resorted to, and the typically American habit of taking the case immediately to court often becomes the prevailing practice. The net effect is that many disputes presented to court are not appropriate for court adjudication and could be better handled by some other mechanism.[29]

This situation led to a suggestion by one of the authors in a paper delivered at the Pound Conference in 1976[30] that, in lieu of the courthouse as we now know it, we might envision in years ahead a more comprehensive and diverse mechanism known as a Dispute Resolution Center, which would seek to provide a variety of dispute resolution processes, according to the needs of the particular dispute. Someone subsequently dubbed this concept "the multidoor courthouse."

The multidoor courthouse

What would such an institution look like? A provisional first-step type of multidoor courthouse could consist essentially of a screening and referral clerk who would seek to diagnose incoming cases and refer them to the most suitable process. Depending on the available mechanisms in the particular community, referrals might be made to mediation, arbitration, court adjudication, fact finding, malpractice screening, a media action line, or an ombudsman.[31]

One of the fringe benefits of such an institution is that it would provide an opportunity to learn more about what process is most appropriate for what kinds of disputes; it would also give helpful feedback concerning what "doors" were missing or not working effectively. That information could then be utilized to refine the model.

The potential benefits of such an approach are enhanced responsiveness and effectiveness, possible time and cost savings, and the legitimization of various alternative dispute resolution processes. What should result is less frustration among the populace in dealing with the vagaries of the legal system. An additional benefit would come from a better understanding of the peculiar advantages and disadvantages of particular processes for specific types of disputes.

There are also potential pitfalls. Not only will the success of a multidoor courthouse largely depend on the skill of the intake official, there is also a real danger—as with all administrative innovations—that it will become the genesis of a new bureaucracy that will result in Kafkaesque shunting of individuals from one "door" to another without any genuine effort to address the problems presented. In addition, there are some difficult questions that must be addressed such as whether the multidoor courthouse should be a centralized institution under one roof, or more akin to a wheel, with a core operation at the center, supplemented by satellite intake and referral offices. Another critical question—whether the referral should be mandatory or voluntary—is discussed below.

Institutionalization

It should be recognized that the multidoor courthouse is but one form of publicly provided alternative dispute resolution. The issues surrounding the public institutionalization of alternatives, or their private provision through public funding, are vital issues that warrant further discussion.

The case for public institutionalization of alternatives rests on a number of propositions. Since courts are publicly provided, why should an alternative process that might be more effective in particular cases not be publicly provided? Unless it is, society creates a financial disincentive to the use of the more effective process. Moreover, for better or worse, the courthouse is where most American citizens ultimately go if they cannot otherwise resolve their disputes. Hence, from the point of view of public education and exposure, as well as enhanced credibility, governmental provision of alternatives in the courthouse itself may be essential.

The question of mandatory use of alternatives raises different issues depending in large part on the effect to be given to the mandated process. As indicated earlier,

coercion *into* mediation does not seem objectionable, as long as there is no coercion *in* mediation to accept a particular outcome, and as long as unsuccessful mediation does not serve as a barrier to adjudication. Similarly, we perceive no persuasive objection to mandating nonbinding arbitration as a precondition to litigation for small or middle-size money claims. If, however, participation in mandatory mediation or arbitration were to bar access to the courts, serious constitutional questions would be presented. Inasmuch, however, as no program for the mandatory use of alternatives has this effect, the more realistic question concerns the extent to which the outcome of a mandatory alternative should be allowed to affect the adjudication process (e.g., by financial preconditions on resort to court or use in court of the noncourt result).

Public institutionalization of alternatives involves their public funding; that is a powerful additional argument put forward by the proponents of institutionalization, who are all too mindful of the fact that private foundations are constantly searching for novel experiments, and are usually not interested in facilitating the continuation of successful pilot programs.[32]

But public funding does not necessarily imply public provision of dispute resolution services. Governments might make grants to private organizations; this is the path taken by New York State, which supports more than 30 privately operated community dispute resolution programs in the state. Texas, meanwhile, has developed a novel path for raising public funds for alternative dispute resolution; it has authorized counties to add a surcharge to the civil filing fee, with the accumulated funds to be used to fund alternative programs. The possibility of federal funding for dispute resolution programs was at least temporarily aborted when the Dispute Resolution Act of 1980 was not funded.

Institutionalization, whether public or private, carries with it potent dangers. Any attempt to make an experiment permanent and larger in scale is likely to result in increasing bureaucratization.[33] As the proportion of volunteers declines, the exuberance and excitement that initially pervaded the project may give way to routinization and burnout. Particularly where public funds are involved, bureaucratic job requirements are likely to be imposed, and political influences may come into play. Whether an innovative program can withstand "success" by effectively making the transition to institutionalization may well be the ultimate test of the program.

A final question concerns the competing claims of alternatives and the courts for limited public funds. Ideally, the funds should go to that system which is more cost effective or qualitatively superior. But, as was noted earlier, we are only beginning to accumulate adequate sophisticated data to help make that judgment. Pending obtaining that data, we need to hedge our bets by encouraging experimentation with alternatives, coupled with careful research to determine their effectiveness.

Professionalization

As the practice of dispute resolution outside the courts expands, the question arises how to ensure high standards of practice and ethical behavior. A related question is how prospective users can find high-quality dispute resolution services suited to their needs.

These questions urgently require answers. In recent years, the number of persons and organizations offering mediation and other dispute resolution services has increased significantly. In addition to a dozen or more national and regional organizations that offer a broad range of dispute resolution services,[34] there are over 180 local mediation programs.[35] Further, both lawyers and other professionals are more often offering mediation as one of their services.

Ensuring high standards is also important at this time because the alternatives movement is in the early stages of professional development. According to Wilensky's[36] typology of the steps through which "occupations" pass on the way to becoming "professions," the alternatives movement is in the stage of professionalization in which people work at the occupation full-time, practitioners press for the establishment of training schools, enthusiastic leaders emerge who are the protagonists of some new technique, and activists engage in much soul searching on "whether the occupation is a profession, what the professional tasks are, how to raise the quality of recruits, and so on." As this occurs, there is "a self-conscious effort to define and redefine the core tasks of the occupation," [37] and a struggle often ensues over whether the occupation will become fully professionalized with specialized degree programs and exclusionary licensing.

There are vigorous advocates of professionalization of mediation. Robert Coulson, president of the American Arbitration Association, has recently issued a call for "a full-fledged profession of Certified Public Mediator." [38] He visualizes a system in which local courts would regulate mediators as they now regulate lawyers, and litigation could not be undertaken without the assurance by a CPM that mediation had been fully utilized in an effort to avoid litigation. Although most CPMs would be lawyers certified by the court, there would be a role for nonlawyers in specialized substantive areas.[39]

Others oppose efforts to professionalize the alternatives movement. They contend that professionalization is inconsistent with the goal of community building through lay dispute resolution. They are also concerned that replacing volunteer mediators with paid professionals will increase costs and restrict the availability of alternatives.[40]

While at present there is no legal regulation of the private practice of dispute resolution, there is an increasing tendency by public agencies to set minimum education and experience requirements for mediators. The California, Connecticut, Nevada, and Oregon courts, for example, require that family mediators employed by them have a master's degree in counseling, social work, or a related field, as well as substantial experience. Other courts require that mediators working in court-established mediation programs be members of the bar or establish their expertise in the subject of the dispute.[41]

The pros and cons of such standards and of greater regulation of private mediation are discussed by Folberg and Taylor.[42] As they point out, some commentators argue that minimum education and experience requirements and licensure of practitioners are necessary to protect an unknowing public from incompetents and charlatans. These commentators point out that the quality of services cannot easily be judged by the results obtained, and that most clients will have little or no experience against which to evaluate the performance of a mediator or other dispute resolution practitioner. Further, the generally private, informal, and interdisciplinary nature of dispute resolution practice increases the danger that "bad" or unfair practices will occur and go undetected.

Codes and standards

A logical conclusion of this reasoning is not only to set minimum educational and experience requirements, but also to establish standards of practice that will enable clients to judge the quality of the services they receive. Such standards can serve as a set of expectations and minimally acceptable common practices for the service offered, thereby protecting both the client and the provider by defining what is "reasonable care." [43] Others, however, argue that alternative dispute resolution is still such a new field that it is difficult if not impossible to set standards of practice with any degree of confidence. In lieu of standards of practice, they would do no more than articulate basic ethical precepts, derived from fundamental notions of fairness, decency, and morality.

We doubt whether this distinction between standards of practice and ethical limitations—between "do's" and "don'ts" in Folberg and Taylor's terminology[44]—is easy to apply in practice or serves much purpose. Codes of ethics for arbitrators have been promulgated by the American Arbitration Association and other arbitration associations.[45] Standards of practice and codes of ethics have also been promulgated by interested and responsible groups in the fields of family and labor mediation. Others will undoubtedly follow. The real question is what use is to be made of such standards and codes. If they are used to educate novice practitioners and inform the public of what is generally considered good practice, and to serve as guidelines for agencies and courts when judging whether a practitioner has used reasonable care, then careful and flexible use of such standards will be beneficial. If, however, they are applied rigidly or for the purpose of protecting the turf of a particular group, then such standards are likely to retard desirable experimentation and growth.

It is therefore important to consider how standards might be enforced. There are four traditional options:

- regulation and licensing by government;

- self-regulation and licensing by a trade or professional organization with expulsion the ultimate sanction;

- liability principles, i.e., suits for malpractice or negligence;

- public disclosure and the operation of the marketplace, coupled, perhaps, with certification of expertise or education.

These options are not mutually exclusive. In most professions (e.g., law, medicine) standards of practice and ethical behavior are enforced in all of these ways. But these professions tend to be well-established, cohesive, and highly developed, as opposed to the emerging dispute resolution profession.

Moreover, even in the older, established professions, critics contend that professionalization, when coupled with standards and licensure, serve more to protect the turf of the powerful than the interests of the public. The tendency of professionals to create a monopoly by employing licensing standards in an economically self-interested manner is well documented.[46] Indeed, the "higher" stages of professionalization are characterized by this development and by the conflicts within the developing profession and with outsiders that this inevitably generates. According to Wilensky[47] and Pipkin and Rifkin,[48] a pecking order emerges that stratifies practitioners and creates conflict and internecine struggles between new and old cohorts of practitioners, and between practitioners of the new occupation and other occupations who claim the same territory. These final stages of professional development typically involve the formation of associations which seek the support of law to impose licensure restrictions on practitioners and thus protect the territory from outsiders and exclude the unqualified and unscrupulous. At some point in this process, the profession codifies its rules of ethics as a basis for self-regulation.

If the alternatives movement develops in the direction of licensure, the impetus is likely to come from public agencies that employ mediators and which must decide, in making employment decisions, who is qualified to be a mediator. California and other states with publicly supported mediation programs chose to specify formal training and degrees. Rather than specify the kind of degree a person had to have to be a mediator—an approach that is bound to engage the agency in a highly charged and broad-based turf battle between lawyers and those in the healing professions—Michigan chose instead to specify the *skills* that a mediator had to possess.

This approach may only serve to camouflage the conflict by specifying skills that go with a certain kind of education. Moreover, the likely result of specifying skills is the establishment of an industry offering to provide eager practitioners with such skills. There is still the problem of ensuring that practitioners actually possess the skills that their degrees advertise for them. Thus, either the teachers that train practitioners in these skills (or their schools) may have to be licensed (the same old problem), or practitioners will have to be tested. This raises the difficult question of whether it is possible at this time to do skills testing of dispute resolution practitioners.

We believe that it is possible to devise and administer a skills test that could effectively screen for basic mediator competency and ethics. Any such test would have to be carefully pretested and administered with flexibility, however, so as not to exclude practitioners on the basis of legitimate differences of theory or style.

Certification and training

A compromise between full-scale professionalization with licensure and no professionalization at all would be the establishment of certification and training programs for dispute resolution practitioners. Certification would indicate that the certified individual met the criteria established by the certifying organization, and so provide potentially useful information to users, but would not bar practice by noncertified persons. Although the same problems of defining good practice and skills testing exist with certification as with licensure, the absence of any occupational exclusionary power minimizes the problem. Many flowers can bloom and the public may learn to identify the flowers and choose among them. This appears to be the approach favored by the Ethics Committee of the Society of Professionals in Dispute Resolution, although the committee took no formal position on licensure, certification, or training.[49]

A form of certification program for arbitrators, pursuant to which lists of arbitrators certified as meeting minimum criteria are made available on request, is currently administered by the American Arbitration Association and the Federal Mediation and Conciliation Service. Similarly, the Center for Public Resources and the American Arbitration Association provide lists of prominent mediators and private judges. But certification or listing by these organizations is based essentially on recommendations or number of cases handled. There is no attempt at testing, and no effort to train those certified or to monitor their performance. Only a serious violation of ethical rules will cause a listed arbitrator to be removed from the AAA or FMCS lists.

A different approach to certification is offered by educational programs that offer training in dispute resolution skills, and certification based on that training. Some of these programs are university-based, others are free-standing. Some last as long as a year, others no longer than a weekend. Many of these programs do not attempt to evaluate the competency of participants, and others certify everyone who completes the program. Hence, there is apt to be little correlation between possessing a certificate from some of these programs and possessing the certified skills.

Despite those shortcomings, certification, together with the operation of market forces and legal liability for malpractice, appears to be a better approach than licensure for the dispute resolution field at the present time. Notwithstanding problems at the edges in defining standards of good practice and ethical limitations, and in ensuring quality training and monitoring of certified practitioners, certification by responsible organizations and well-established and operated training programs may be of some help to the inexperienced consumer. Licensure, on the other hand, adds little to certification in the way of consumer protection, and creates the very real danger that in enforcing licensing rules, professional self-interest will predominate over consumer protection. Whichever approach is taken, given the conceptual ferment in this field, it is important that standards and norms not be viewed as immutable precepts, but as subject to experience, debate, and modification.

Conclusion

The alternative dispute resolution movement is at a critical turn in the road. After 10 years or so of scholarly inquiry and practical experimentation, our knowledge of the field has been substantially enhanced and there is a far greater awareness, both among the general public and in the legal community, of the promise of alternative dispute settlement.

What we need now is a multipronged effort to expand our limited present understanding of the field. This will require continued experimentation and research, as well as further attempts to conceptualize the field. It will necessitate enhanced public education about the benefits to be derived from alternative modes of dispute settlement. Ways must be found to develop career paths and employment opportunities for talented individuals who wish to devote their lives to providing alternative dispute resolution services. This will probably require, at least in the short run, some infusion of public financing. Above all, if the movement is to hold any significant promise of gaining a permanent foothold on the American scene, it will require the broadened involvement and support not only of the legal education establishments but also of the society at large.

Notes

This article originally appeared in Volume 69, Number 5, February–March 1986, pages 291–299. An initial version was presented by Professor Sander as a paper at a conference at Harvard Law School in October 1982. Portions of the revised paper are adapted from Goldberg, Green, and Sander, *Dispute Resolution* (Little, Brown, 1985).

1. Pearson, Thoennes, and Vanderkooi, "The Decision to Mediate: Profiles of Individuals Who Accept and Reject the Opportunity to Mediate Contested Child Custody and Visitation Issues," *J. Divorce* 6 (1982), 17.

2. *See* Cooley, "Arbitration vs. mediation: explaining the differences," *Judicature* 69 (1986), 263.

3. Riskin, "Mediation and Lawyers," *Ohio St. L. J.* 43 (1982), 29.

4. Smith, "A Warmer Way of Disputing: Mediation and Conciliation," *Am. J. Comp. L.* 26 (Supp.) (1978), 205.

5. Davis, "Justice Without Judges," *Update on Law-Related Education* (Chicago: American Bar Association Special Committee on Youth Education For Citizenship, 1984).

6. Fiss, "Against Settlement," *Yale L. J.* 93 (1984), 1987.

7. Abel, "The Contradictions of Informal Justice," in Abel, ed., *The Politics of Informal Justice: The American Experience* (New York: Academic Press, 1982), 1; Auerbach, *Justice Without Law?* (New York: Oxford, 1983).

8. Cook, Roehl, and Shepard, *Neighborhood Justice Center Field Test: Final Evaluation Report* (Washington, D.C.: U.S. Government Printing Office, 1980).

9. Fuller, "The Forms and Limits of Adjudication," *Harv. L. Rev.* 92 (1979), 353.

10. Singer, "Nonjudicial Dispute Resolution Mechanisms: The Effects on Justice for the Poor," *Clearinghouse Rev.* 13 (1979), 569; Rowe, "Predicting the Effects of Attorney Fee Shifting," *Law and Contemp. Probs.* 47 (1984), 139.

11. Pearson, "An Evaluation of Alternatives to Court Adjudication," *Just. Sys. J.* 7 (1982), 420.

12. McEwen and Maiman, "Small Claims Mediation in Maine: An Empirical Assessment," *Me. L. Rev.* 33 (1981), 237.

13. But *see* McEwen and Maiman, "Mediation in Small Claims Court: Achieving Compliance Through Consent," *Law & Soc'y Rev.* 18 (1984), 11, 22–28.

14. Brett and Goldberg, "Grievance Mediation in the Coal Industry," *Indus. and Lab. Rel. Rev.* 37 (1983), 49, 56, 59–60.

15. Pearson, *supra* n. 11.

16. Federal Judicial Center, *Experimentation in the Law: Report of the Federal Judicial Center Advisory Committee on Experimentation in the Law* (Washington, DC: U.S. Government Printing Office, 1981).

17. Miller and Sarat, "Grievances, Claims and Disputes: Assessing the Adversary Culture," *Law and Soc'y Rev.* 15 (1981), 525.

18. Pearson, Thoennes, and Vanderkooi, *supra* n. 1.

19. Finkelstein, "The D.C. multi-door courthouse," *Judicature* 69 (1986), 305.

20. Merry and Silbey, "What Do Plaintiffs Want? Reexamining the Concept of Dispute," *Just. Sys. J.* 9 (1984), 151.

21. Felsteiner, Abel, and Sarat, "The Emergence and Transformation of Disputes: Naming, Blaming, Claiming," *Law and Soc'y Rev.* 15 (1981), 631.

22. Thibaut and Walker, *Procedural Justice: A Psychological Analysis* (Hillsdale, N.J.: Lawrence Erlbaum, 1975); LaTour, Houlden, Walker, and Thibaut, "Procedure: Transnational Perspectives and Preferences," *Yale L. J.* 86 (1976), 258; Brett, "Procedural Justice in Symposium," *Justice: Beyond Equity Theory* (Academy of Management Convention, 1983).

23. Fiss, *supra* n. 6.

24. Pearson, *supra* n. 11.

25. Weiss, *Using Social Science Research in Public Policy Making* (Lexington, Mass.: Lexington Books, 1977); Lindblom and Cohen, *Usable Knowledge* (New Haven: Yale University Press, 1979).

26. The need for additional empirical data is equaled by the need for careful analysis of both existing and newly-collected data. Galanter, "Reading the Landscape of Disputes: What We Know and Don't Know (and Think We Know) About Our Allegedly Contentious and Litigious Society," *U.C.L.A. L. Rev.* 31 (1983), 4.

27. Galanter, "Justice in Many Rooms," *J. of Leg. Pluralism* 19 (1981), 1.

28. "At present, it is almost accidental if community members find their way to an appropriate forum other than the regular courts. Several other modes of dispute resolution already are available in many communities. Still, since they are operated by a hodge-podge of local government agencies, neighborhood organizations, and trade associations, citizens must be very knowledgeable about community resources to locate the right forum for their particular dispute." Johnson, "Toward a Responsive Justice System" in *State Courts: A Blueprint for the Future* (Williamsburg, Va.: National Center for State Courts, 1978), 122.

29. Sander, "Varieties of Dispute Resolution," *F.R.D.* 19 (1976), 111.

30. Ibid.

31. For a description of the way cases are handled in a multidoor courthouse, see Finkelstein, *supra* n. 19.

32. The National Institute for Dispute Resolution appears to be well aware of the problems of institutionalizing successful programs. Lacking the funds to achieve that goal itself, it has attempted to use its limited resources to leverage public-sector and other private-sector funds.

33. Edelman, "Institutionalizing Dispute Resolution Alternatives," *Just. Sys. J.* 9 (1984), 134.

34. Marks, Johnson, and Szanton, *Dispute Resolution in America: Processes in Evolution* (Washington, D.C.: National Institute for Dispute Resolution, 1984), 69–74.

35. American Bar Association, *Dispute Resolution Program Directory* (Washington, D.C.: American Bar Association, 1983).

36. Wilensky, "The Professionalization of Everyone?," *Am. J. Soc.* 70 (1964), 137.

37. Pipkin and Rifkin, "The Social Organization in Alternative Dispute Resolution: Implications for Professionalization of Mediation," *Just. Sys. J.* 9 (1984), 204, 205–206.

38. Coulson, *Professional Mediation of Civil Disputes* (New York: American Arbitration Association, 1984).

39. Ibid. at 24–25, 32–33.

40. Pipkin and Rifkin, *supra* n. 37, at 207.

41. The issue also arises in connection with confidentiality statutes that seek to limit the individuals who are entitled to the statutory protections. *See e.g.,* Mass. Ann. Laws c. 233, §23c (1985).

42. Folberg and Taylor, *Mediation: A Comprehensive Guide to Resolving Conflicts Without Litigation* (San Francisco, Jossey-Bass, 1984), 244.

43. Ibid. at 250.

44. Ibid.

45. Hay, Carnevale, and Sinicropi, "Professionalization: Selected Ethical Issues in Dispute Resolution," *Just. Sys. J.* 9 (1984), 228, 236.

46. Gellhorn, "Abuse of Occupational Licensing," *U. Chi. L. Rev.* 44 (1976), 6, 39.

47. Wilensky, *supra* n. 36.

48. Pipkin and Rifkin, *supra* n. 37.

49. Hay, Carnevale, and Sinicropi, *supra* n. 45, at 230, 236–240.

Judicial Policy Making and Judicial Independence in the United States

Throughout this anthology, the selections have offered readers a slice of the American judicial process, generally by examining a single topic or facet of the legal system. These articles, viewed collectively, are intended to offer a broad perspective on judicial politics and judicial policymaking and to encourage consideration of the place of the judiciary in the context of the larger fabric of democracy in the United States. Discussions of judicial independence and judicial accountability often take center stage in evaluations and critiques of the judiciary. This is especially true in the context of the controversies that have swirled around American judges in recent years, particularly the vocal condemnation from conservative quarters aimed at perceived judicial activism on the federal branch. These critical concerns are the focus of this final section.

The readings begin with "Reining in the federal judiciary," an essay by Edwin Meese III and Rhett DeHart that is, in many respects, a prototype for broadside critiques of judicial power and judicial independence in America. The authors opine that the role of the courts is to interpret the law and not to make policy, a distinction clearly lost on those who feel that policy is being made in every interpretation of the law. Meese and DeHart believe that the real issue is one of who benefits and who loses from each specific interpretation. A summary of what the authors perceive to be the courts' most egregious activist decisions in the area of rights and liberties is also offered for consideration. The article suggests a number of concrete steps that a Congress and, indeed, a country could take to rein in judicial policymaking. These include confirming only "nonactivist" judges, diminishing the power of the organized bar in the confirmation process, limiting federal court jurisdiction, and allowing states to act without Congress to amend the Constitution.

Meese and DeHart have written a wide-ranging attack on activist judicial policymaking and judicial independence. In "Judicial decision making and the impact of election year rhetoric," Jennifer Segal zeroes in on an isolated case decided by a single federal district court judge. Through this detailed case study of the decision in *U.S. v. Bayless* and its aftermath, Segal adds an empirical component to what, all too often, is simply a rhetorical attack on judicial decisions by those who oppose them. The *Bayless* drama centered around

the decision of Clinton appointee, Judge Harold Baer, to exclude evidence in a drug case because police had violated the Fourth Amendment's prohibition of "unreasonable searches and seizures." Judge Baer's decision was met with great outcry from many quarters, partly because of the inflammatory language he used in reference to the police.

The decision became national news when then Republican presidential candidate Bob Dole asserted that the election was "between a candidate who will appoint conservative judges . . . and a candidate who appoints liberal judges who bend the laws to let drug dealers free." The Clinton administration wavered, at one point hinting through the White House press secretary that Baer's resignation might be sought. Prominent public figures, including New York City police commissioner William J. Bratton; New York City mayor Rudolph Giuliani; Senator Daniel Patrick Moynihan, D-N.Y.; Senator Orrin Hatch, R-Utah; and then Speaker of the House Newt Gingrich, R-Ga., made statements critical of the judge and the decision. Baer ultimately granted a rehearing based on the presence of new evidence and, in fact, reversed his earlier decision. This led to concerns that he had been intimidated by the criticism and that judicial independence was the big loser in the case's outcome.

Segal's article discusses the case in great detail but leaves the question of what caused the judge's change of heart open to interpretation. The piece explores how Baer's actions came to represent those of all Clinton appointees and of liberal activism in general and how the decision was elevated into an issue in electoral politics. The author adds an interesting empirical element by noting that Baer's decision making across all criminal cases was actually strongly pro-prosecution— as was that of virtually all of the judges in the Southern District of New York, regardless of who appointed them to the bench. Criticism of Baer and the *Bayless* decision can be viewed on a broad level as an attack on judicial independence. In this instance, Segal concludes, "it is clear that election year politics overshadowed an important and legitimate debate about law when the focus of discussion turned from the constitutional issues in a single district court case to the political issues in a presidential campaign, and the *Bayless* ruling and Baer himself became instruments in both

Democratic and Republican campaigns for the White House."

Segal's piece, like Meese and DeHart's, provides the popular conservative critique of judicial activism and the problems associated with judicial independence. Stephen Wasby offers a thoughtful counterpoint to the activist critique in "Arrogation of power or accountability: 'judicial imperialism' revisited." Wasby responds to the criticism that the judiciary has become an "imperial" branch of American government that all too often intervenes in American life and policy formation. In the author's view, judges exercise powers that have been granted to them legitimately, and they are held publicly and governmentally accountable in many ways. He also asserts that judges have the capacity to deal with policy matters and that they perform comparatively well when held to the standard of other policymakers in our system.

In asking the question, "Why should we care about independent and accountable judges?" the seemingly unlikely duo of Bruce Fein, a conservative legal commentator who served in Ronald Reagan's Justice Department, and Burt Neuborne, former national legal director of the American Civil Liberties Union, offer a useful complement to Wasby's analysis. Lowering the rhetorical temperature, Fein and Neuborne note that, "judicial independence does not mean rule by platonic guardians who presume omniscience in fashioning enlightened government. It assumes an important element of accountability." Numerous "legitimate" interpretative theories exist in American law and "a judge is often free to choose among several generally accepted alternatives." In this sense, judicial independence does not mean "capricious rule by judges." Instead, it is bounded decision making into which an element of lawmaking has crept, something inevitable in "hard cases."

Like Wasby, Fein and Neuborne note that, "judges are subject to much more accountability than is customarily recognized by critics." Constitutional amendments and, at times, simple legislation are two means by which judges can be held in check. The "political question" doctrine insulates some highly charged issues from judicial review. Beyond such formal and legal constraints on the range of judicial choice "are mortality and orthodoxy." Judges die and retire and "their replacements are appointed by a popularly elected president and confirmed by popularly elected senators. . . . This constant replenishment of 'new blood' on the judiciary insures against decisions that substantially deviate from popular sentiments." Fein and Neuborne assess the current dangers to judicial independence and warn against adoption of any of several suggested initiatives aimed at curbing judicial power. In direct contradiction to Meese and DeHart, they conclude, "the idea that judges are running the country is a figment of vivid imaginations, although many of their decisions are justifiably vulnerable to informed and trenchant criticism, which should be encouraged. That is how judicial error can be corrected without undermining judicial independence."

What is perhaps most interesting about efforts to curb the courts is the fact that, historically, they have pretty much failed to be adopted. This section of readings and this anthology close with Barry Friedman's analysis of "Attacks on judges: why they fail." Friedman notes that judges have been attacked for their decisions for more than two hundred years and that such attacks are invariably driven and motivated by politics and almost always lack popular support. Ultimately, he defines a political attack as one in which, "no matter what members of Congress or the executive branch have said about why they are threatening judicial independence, they are doing it because they do not like the way judges are deciding particular cases."

According to the author, the controls that—in the words of Meese and DeHart—are necessary to "rein in" the judiciary are already part and parcel of the "ordinary" processes of American governance and are working just as they are supposed to. For example, Friedman points to the hierarchical structure of American courts and the normal consequences of appellate processes in which aberrant decisions will be overturned as they work their way up through the judicial system. He also underscores the moderating tendencies of the appointment and confirmation processes that judges go through as well as the noted tendency of Supreme Court justices to not be out of step too far or for too long from the American public.

Certainly several of the articles presented in this final section are advocacy efforts in their tone and provocative in their content. They cannot "solve" for readers the critical dilemmas that they address; however, they do offer considerable food for thought and debate about the role of the courts in the American democracy, an appropriate place to both begin and end a consideration of judicial politics.

Reining in the federal judiciary

Edwin Meese III and Rhett DeHart

Federal judges have strayed far beyond their proper functions of interpreting and clarifying the law by reading their personal views and prejudices into the Constitution.

America's founders created a democratic republic in which elected representatives were to decide the important issues of the day. In the framers' view, the role of the judiciary, although crucial, was to interpret and clarify the law—not to make law. The framers recognized the necessity of judicial restraint and the dangers of judicial activism. James Madison wrote in *The Federalist Papers* that to combine judicial power with executive and legislative authority was "the very definition of tyranny." Thomas Jefferson believed that "[i]t is a very dangerous doctrine to consider the judges as the ultimate arbiters of all constitutional questions. It is one which would place us under the despotism of an oligarchy."

Unfortunately, the federal judiciary has strayed far beyond its proper functions, in many ways validating Jefferson's warnings about judicial power. In no other democracy in the world do unelected judges decide as many vital political issues as they do in America. Supreme Court decisions based on the Constitution cannot be reversed or altered, except by a constitutional amendment. Such decisions are virtually immune from presidential vetoes or congressional legislation. Abraham Lincoln warned of this in his first inaugural address when he wrote:

> [T]he candid citizen must confess that if the policy of the government, upon vital questions, affecting the whole people, is to be irrevocably fixed by decisions of the Supreme Court . . . the people will have ceased to be their own rulers, having, to that extent, practically resigned their government into the hands of that eminent tribunal.

When the most important social and moral issues are removed from the democratic process, citizenship suffers because people lose the political experience and moral education that come from resolving difficult issues and reaching a social consensus. At the swearing-in ceremonies for Chief Justice William Rehnquist and Associate Justice Antonin Scalia, President Reagan explained how judicial activism is incompatible with popular government:

The founding fathers were clear on this issue. For them, the question involved in judicial restraint was not—as it is not—will we have liberal courts or conservative courts? They knew that the courts, like the Constitution itself, must not be liberal or conservative. The question was and is, will we have government by the people?

Judicial excesses

When federal judges exceed their proper interpretive role, the result is not only infidelity to the Constitution, but very often poor public policy. Numerous cases illustrate the consequences of judicial activism and the harm it has caused our society. Activist court decisions have undermined nearly every aspect of public policy. Among the most egregious examples:

Allowing racial preferences and quotas. In *United Steelworkers of America v. Weber* (1979), the Supreme Court held for the first time that the Civil Rights Act of 1964 permits private employers to establish racial preferences and quotas in employment, despite the clear language of the statute that states: "It shall be an unlawful employment practice for any employer . . . to discriminate against any individual because of his race, color, religion, sex, or national origin. . . ." The *Weber* decision is a classic example of how unelected government regulators and federal judges have distorted our civil rights laws from a colorblind ideal to a complex and unfair system of racial and ethnic preferences and quotas that perpetuate bias and discrimination.

Creating a right to public welfare assistance. In *Goldberg v. Kelly* (1970), the Supreme Court sanctioned the idea that welfare entitlements are a form of property under the Fourteenth Amendment. The Court's conclusion: Before a government can terminate benefits on the grounds that the recipient is not eligible, the recipient is entitled to an extensive and costly appeals process akin to a trial. Thanks to the Court, welfare recipients now have a right to receive benefits fraudulently throughout lengthy legal proceedings, and they do not need to reimburse the government if their ineligibility is confirmed. The decision has tied up thousands of welfare workers in judicial hearings and deprived the truly needy of benefits. By 1974, for example, New York City alone needed a staff of 3,000 to conduct *Goldberg* hearings.

Hampering criminal prosecution. In *Mapp v. Ohio* (1961), the Supreme Court began a revolution in criminal procedure by requiring state courts to exclude from criminal cases any evidence found during an "unreasonable" search or seizure. In so holding, the Court overruled a previous case, *Wolf v. Colorado* (1949), which had allowed each state to devise its own methods for deterring unreasonable searches and seizures. The Supreme Court in effect acted like a legislature rather than a judicial body. As a dissenting justice noted, the *Mapp* decision unjustifiably infringed upon the states' sovereign judicial systems and forced them to adopt a uniform, federal procedural remedy ill-suited to serve states with "their own peculiar problems in criminal law enforcement."

In fact, nothing in the Fourth Amendment or any other provision of the Constitution mentions the exclusion of evidence, nor does the legislative history of the Constitution indicate that the framers intended to require such exclusion. We should explore remedies that will deter police misconduct without acquitting criminals, such as civil lawsuits against reckless government officials and internal police sanctions such as fines and demotions.

In *Miranda v. Arizona*, the Supreme Court determined the rules for the admissibility of police interrogations in all criminal trials and radically changed the criminal procedure of every state and the federal government. The Court held that the Fifth Amendment requires what have become known as Miranda warnings whenever a witness in custody is subject to police questioning. Failure to deliver the warnings and obtain the suspect's consent automatically bars the use at trial of the suspect's statements, regardless of whether the suspect confessed or otherwise provided reliable information to authorities. In effect, the Court invented an absolute right for criminal suspects not to be questioned.

Not surprisingly, the costs of *Miranda* have been staggering. In a comprehensive study of the impact of *Miranda* in a 1996 *Northwestern Law Review* article, Professor Paul Cassell estimates that each year *Miranda* results in approximately 28,000 cases of violent crime and 79,000 cases of serious property crime that cannot be prosecuted successfully because of this decision.

Lowering hiring standards. In *Griggs v. Duke Power Co.* (1971), a plaintiff challenged a company's requirement that job applicants possess a high-school diploma and pass a general aptitude test as a condition of employment. The lawsuit argued that because the diploma and test requirements disqualified a disproportionate number of minorities, those requirements were unlawful under the Civil Rights Act of 1964 unless shown to be related to the job in question.

The Court ruled that under the act, employment requirements that disproportionately exclude minorities must be shown to be related to job performance, and it rejected the employer's argument that the diploma and testing requirements were implemented to improve the overall quality of its work force. Moreover, the Court held that "Congress has placed on the employer the burden of showing that any given requirement must have a manifest relationship to the employment in question."

In fact, the act explicitly authorizes an employer to use aptitude tests like the one challenged in *Griggs*. This insidious Court decision has lowered the quality of the U.S. workforce by making it difficult for employers to require high-school diplomas and other neutral job requirements. It also forced employers to adopt racial quotas in order to avoid the expense of defending hiring practices that happen to produce disparate outcomes for different ethnic groups.

Discovering a right to abortion. In *Roe v. Wade* (1973), the Supreme Court considered the constitutionality of a Texas statute that prohibited abortion except to save the life of the mother. Although the Court acknowledged that the Constitution does not explicitly mention a right of privacy, it held that the Constitution protects rights "implicit in the concept of ordered liberty." The Court ruled that "the right of personal privacy includes the abortion decision," and it struck down the Texas statute under the due process clause of the Fourteenth Amendment. The Court then went on, in a blatantly legislative fashion, to proclaim a precise framework limiting the states' ability to regulate abortion.

The dissenting opinion in *Roe* pointed out that, in order to justify its ruling, the majority had to somehow find within the Fourteenth Amendment a right that was unknown to the drafters of the amendment. When the Fourteenth Amendment was adopted in 1868, there were at least 36 state or territorial laws limiting abortion, and the passage of the amendment raised no questions at the time about the validity of those laws. "The only conclusion possible from this history," wrote the dissenting justices, "is that the Drafters did not intend to have the Fourteenth Amendment withdraw from the States the power to legislate with respect to this matter."

One of the most pernicious aspects of the *Roe* decision is that it removed one of the most profound social and moral issues from the democratic process without any constitutional authority. For the first 197 years of America's existence, the abortion issue was decided by state legislatures, with substantially less violence and conflict than has attended the issue since the *Roe* decision. No matter what one's view may be about abortion, it is clear that the founders did not establish the United States as a democratic republic to have unelected judges decide the most important issues of the day.

Overturning state referenda. In *Romer v. Evans* (1996), the Supreme Court actually negated a direct vote of the people. This case concerned an amendment to the Colorado constitution enacted in 1992 by a statewide referendum. "Amendment 2" prohibited the state or any of its political subdivisions from adopting any policy that grants homosexuals "any minority status, quota preference, protected status, or claim of discrimination." The Court ruled that the amendment was unconstitutional, claiming that Amendment 2 did not bear a "rational relationship" to a legitimate government purpose and thus violated the Equal Protection Clause of the Fourteenth Amendment.

The state of Colorado contended that this amendment protected freedom of association, particularly for landlords and employers who have religious objections to homosexuality, and that it only prohibited preferential treatment for homosexuals. The Court, however, rejected these arguments and offered its own interpretation of what motivated the citizens of Colorado, claiming that "laws of the kind now before us raise the inevitable inference that the disadvantage imposed is born of animosity toward the class of persons affected."

The dissenting opinion argued that Amendment 2 denied equal treatment only in the sense that homosexuals may not obtain "preferential treatment without amending the state constitution." The Court's decision, the dissent charged, "is an act not of judicial judgment, but of political will."

Critics argue that the *Romer* decision is the pinnacle of judicial arrogance because six appointed justices struck down a law approved by 54 percent of a state's voters in a direct election, the most democratic of all

procedures. In one of the most egregious usurpations of power in constitutional history, the Supreme Court not only desecrated the principle of self-government, but set itself up as the moral arbiter of the nation's values.

Although this representative sample of Supreme Court decisions demonstrates the widespread impact of judicial activism, other federal courts have usurped executive and legislative functions within their jurisdictions. In nearly every state, district and appellate courts are substituting their judgment for that of local officials and are trying to manage everything from prisons and mental hospitals to grammar schools and athletic leagues. Often they are aided and abetted by extremist lawyers, funded at taxpayers' expense, who bring the cases that serve as the vehicles for judicial activism.

Turning the tide

Fortunately, Congress has a number of strategies at its disposal to confine the judiciary to its proper constitutional role:

The Senate should use its confirmation authority to block the appointment of activist federal judges.

When a president appoints judges who exceed their constitutional authority and usurp the other branches of government, the Senate can properly restrain the judiciary by carefully exercising its responsibilities under the "advise and consent" clause of Article II, Section 2 of the Constitution.

Unfortunately, the confirmation process in recent years has been relatively perfunctory. The Senate has been reluctant to closely question a nominee to ascertain the candidate's understanding of the proper role of the judiciary. The Senate Judiciary Committee hearing provides an excellent opportunity to discern a judicial candidate's understanding of a constitutionally limited judiciary.

Senators, in carrying out this important responsibility, should ascertain a prospective judge's commitment to a philosophy of judicial restraint and constitutional fidelity. In doing so, they should review carefully all the opinions, legal articles, and other materials authored by the candidate; the report of the background investigation conducted by the Federal Bureau of Investigation; and information obtained from judges and other attorneys who have had opportunities to view a candidate's work.

In the name of efficiency, the full Senate sometimes votes to confirm judicial nominees in bundles. This practice should cease. Senators should vote on each nominee individually, in order to remind the prospective judge and the public of the awesome responsibility of each new member of the judiciary and to hold themselves accountable for every judge they confirm to the federal bench.

Congress should strip the American Bar Association of its special role in the judicial selection process.

The American Bar Association has shown itself to be a special-interest group, every bit as politicized as the American Civil Liberties Union or the National Rifle Association. In recent years, for example, the ABA officially supported federal funding for abortion services for the poor, racial and ethnic preferences, and a ban on assault weapons. Moreover, it opposed a ban on flag-burning, reform of the exclusionary rule and of death-penalty appeals, and a proposal to restrict AFDC payments for welfare mothers who have additional children. Hence it should be removed from any official role in evaluating judicial nominees. The ABA should still be free to testify before the Senate Judiciary Committee concerning the potential judge, but it should not have any special status or authority.

The Senate will always need the impartial assessment of judges and lawyers who have a detailed knowledge of the work and background of a judicial candidate. In place of the ABA, the Senate should appoint a special fact-finding committee in each of the 94 federal judicial districts. Members would be selected for their objectivity, ideological neutrality, and understanding of the constitutional role of the judiciary. They would obtain the detailed information the Senate needs to evaluate a candidate and would give that information directly to the Judiciary Committee without subjective comments or evaluation.

Congress should exercise its power to limit the jurisdiction of the federal courts.

Congress has great control over the jurisdiction of the lower federal courts. Article III, Section 1, of the Constitution provides that "[t]he judicial power of the United States, shall be vested in one supreme Court, and in such inferior Courts as the Congress may from time to time ordain and establish." It is well-established that since Congress has total discretion over whether to create the lower federal courts, it also has great discretion over the jurisdiction of those courts it chooses to create. In fact, Congress has in the past withdrawn jurisdiction from the lower federal courts when it became dissatisfied with their performance or concluded that state courts were the better forum for certain types of cases. The Supreme Court has repeatedly upheld Congress's power to do so.

Congress also has some authority to limit the jurisdiction of the Supreme Court and to regulate its activities. Article III, Section 2, of the Constitution states that the Supreme Court "shall have appellate jurisdiction, both as to law and fact, with such Exceptions, and under such Regulations as the Congress shall make." Although we recognize that the scope of Congress's power to regulate and restrict the Supreme Court's jurisdiction over particular types of cases is under debate, there is a constitutional basis for this authority.

In the only case that directly addressed this issue, the Supreme Court upheld Congress's power to restrict the Court's appellate jurisdiction. In *Ex Parte McCardle* (1869), the Court unanimously upheld Congress's power to limits its jurisdiction, stating:

> We are not at liberty to inquire into the motives of the legislature. We can only examine into its power under the Constitution; *and the power to make exceptions to the appellate jurisdiction of this court is given by express words* What, then, is the effect of the repealing act upon the case before us? We cannot doubt as to this. Without jurisdiction, the court cannot proceed at all in any case. [Emphasis added.]

Although some respected constitutional scholars argue that Congress cannot restrict the Supreme Court's jurisdiction to the extent that it intrudes upon the Court's "core functions," there is no question that Congress has more authority under the Constitution to act than it has recently exercised.

The 104th Congress displayed an encouraging willingness to assert its authority over the jurisdiction of the lower federal courts. For example, the Prison Litigation Reform Act of 1995 reduced the discretion of the federal courts to micromanage state prisons and to force the early release of prisoners. The act also makes it more difficult for prisoners to file frivolous lawsuits. (An incredible 63,550 prisoner lawsuits were filed in federal court in 1995 alone.) Congress also passed the Effective Death Penalty Act of 1995. This act limited the power of the federal courts to entertain endless habeas corpus appeals filed by prisoners in death row, significantly expediting the death-penalty process.

Other issues are due for some congressional muscle-flexing to restrain an activist judiciary:

Private-school choice. Some radical groups like the American Civil Liberties Union argue that the government would violate the First Amendment's establishment clause if it gave a tuition voucher to a family that uses it at a religious school. Under current Supreme Court precedents, school vouchers are almost certainly constitutional. Nevertheless, some federal judges have indicated they would invalidate private-school choice plans under the establishment clause. Moreover, if more activist justices are named to the Supreme Court, a liberal majority could crush one of the most promising educational initiatives in recent years by judicial fiat. To ensure that the issue of private-school choice is decided through the democratic process, Congress should consider restricting the Court's jurisdiction over this issue.

Judicial taxation. "Judicial taxation" refers to federal court orders that require a state or local government to make significant expenditures to pay for court-ordered injunctions. For example, one federal judge ordered the state of Missouri to pay for approximately $2.6 billion in capital improvements and other costs to "desegregate" the school districts of St. Louis and Kansas City, which in recent years had lost many white students. To attract white students back into the system, a federal judge required Kansas City to maintain the most lavish schools in the nation, and actually ordered the city to raise property taxes to pay for his court-ordered remedies.

There is a name for tax increases imposed by appointed, life-tenured federal judges: taxation without representation. Under the Constitution, only Congress can lay and collect taxes; our founders would be appalled at the thought of federal judges doing so. Congress should consider restricting the federal courts' authority to order any government at any level to raise taxes under any circumstance.

Use of special masters. Federal judges sometimes appoint special masters to micromanage prisons, mental hospitals, and school districts. In the past, these special masters have been appointed to carry out the illegitimate excursions of judges into the province of the legislative and executive branches. Moreover, the use of special masters has been a form of taxation, in that state and local governments are required to pay their salaries and expenses—which have often been extravagant. In some cases, special masters have hired large staffs to help execute the court order. Congress should outlaw special masters; without them, federal judges would be constrained by the limits on their time and resources from managing prisons or other institutions.

Same-sex marriage. No area of the law has been more firmly reserved to the states than domestic relations.

Nevertheless, the Court's absurd reasoning in *Romer v. Evans* suggests the possibility that some federal judges will discover a constitutional right to homosexual marriage, and thus remove the issue from the democratic process.

The Hawaii Supreme Court recently indicated that it would soon recognize homosexual marriages, which all other states would then have to recognize under the full faith and credit clause of the Constitution (Article IV). This possibility motivated Congress to pass the Defense of Marriage Act, which authorized any state to refuse to recognize a same-sex marriage performed in another state. The act does not, however, prevent the federal judiciary from usurping this issue. Congress should consider going one step further to remove the jurisdiction of the lower federal courts over same-sex marriages to ensure that this cultural issue is decided by the legislative process in each state.

The states should press Congress to amend the Constitution in a way that will allow the states to ratify constitutional amendments in the future without the approval of Congress.

One reason judicial activism is so dangerous and undemocratic is that reversing or amending federal court decisions is so difficult. When a decision by the Supreme Court or a lower federal court is based on the Constitution, the decision cannot be reversed or altered except by a constitutional amendment. Such constitutional decisions are immune from presidential vetoes or congressional legislation.

The existing means of amending the Constitution, however, are seldom effective in halting judicial activism. The amendment procedure set forth in Article V of the Constitution is difficult and lengthy for good reason: to avoid hasty changes spurred by the passions of the moment. But history has shown that even the most egregious court decisions—particularly those that affect the balance of power between the national government and the states—have been impervious to correction by constitutional amendment. One reason for this is that Congress, which must initiate such amendments, is loath to give up federal power.

The amendment procedure of the U.S. Constitution led Lord Bryce to conclude in his 1888 study, *The American Commonwealth*, that "[t]he Constitution which is the most difficult to change is that of the United States." This difficulty has encouraged judicial activism and allowed the unelected federal courts to "twist and shape" the Constitution, as Jefferson predicted, as an "artist shapes a ball of wax." The reason that the difficult amendment procedure encourages judicial activism is simple: Life-tenured judges are less likely to show restraint when the possibility that their rulings will be rejected is slight.

Consequently, one strategy to reign in the federal judiciary is to revise the amendment procedure in Article V of the Constitution to allow the states to amend the Constitution without Congress's approval and without a constitutional convention.

Here is how it would work: When two-thirds of state legislatures pass resolutions in support of a proposed amendment to the Constitution, Congress would have to submit it to all the states for ratification. The proposal would then become part of the Constitution once the legislatures of three-fourths of the states ratify it. Congress's role would be purely ministerial. This process would give the states equal power with Congress to initiate an amendment and would further check the power of the federal courts and of Congress.

Congress should stop the federalization of crime and the expansion of litigation in federal court.

Whenever Congress enacts a new federal criminal statute or a statute creating a cause of action in federal court, it enlarges the power and authority of the federal courts and provides more opportunities for judicial activism. At the same time, the federalization of crimes that have traditionally concerned state and local governments upsets the balance between the national government and the states. The following steps can help reduce the federalization of the law and once again restore balance to the federal-state relationship.

Recodify the U.S. Code. In the present federal criminal code, important offenses like treason are commingled with insignificant offenses like the unauthorized interstate transport of water hyacinths. The Federal Courts Study Committee found that the current federal code is "hard to find, hard to understand, redundant, and conflicting." Ideally, Congress would start with a blank slate, recodifying only those offenses that truly belong under federal jurisdiction. Due to the highly political nature of crime, such an undertaking might require the creation of an independent commission, modeled after the recent commission for closing unneeded military bases.

Require a "federalism assessment" for legislation. This idea would require that all federal legislation offer a justification for a national solution to the issue in question, acknowledge any efforts the states have taken to address the problem, explain the legislation's effect on state experimentation, and cite Congress's constitutional authority to enact the proposed legislation.

Create a federalism subcommittee within the judiciary committees of the House and Senate. First proposed by President Reagan's Working Group on Federalism, federalism subcommittees would attempt to ensure compliance with federalism principles in all proposed legislation.

*****

The framers of the Constitution intended that the federal judiciary play a vital role in America's representative democracy. None of the above material should be interpreted as an assault on the very existence of the judiciary. It is important to remember, however, that in no other democracy in the world do unelected judges decide as many vital political issues as they do in the United States. When viewed objectively, this is actually a nonpartisan issue. The "conservative" activist Supreme Court of the 1920s and 1930s, which struck down as unconstitutional minimum wage and other mild labor reforms, was as repugnant to constitutional democracy as the "liberal" activist Warren Court.

In recent decades, the legislative and executive branches have been very meek in responding to activist federal judges. As a result, perhaps no issue is more in need of attention and effort than restoring the judiciary's non-ideological role as interpreter and clarifier of the law. The strategies listed above illustrate some ways in which the judiciary can be restrained in a proper and constitutional manner. These and other strategies must be used to rein in the activist federal judiciary and return it to its rightful place in our democracy.

Note

This article originally appeared in Volume 80, Number 4, January–February 1997, pages 178–183. It is adapted from *Mandate for Leadership IV*, published by the Heritage Foundation in January 1997.

Judicial decision making and the impact of election year rhetoric

Jennifer A. Segal

The example of Judge Harold Baer and U. S. v. Bayless *illustrates the dramatic consequences of election year rhetoric—particularly inaccurate rhetoric—on the third branch of government.*

In January 1996, federal district court judge Harold Baer of the Southern District of New York captured the attention of national and local politicians and news media when he ruled in *U.S. v. Bayless* that incriminating evidence in a drug case should be excluded because police officers violated the defendant's Fourth Amendment protection against unlawful search and seizure. That decision triggered a series of events, the most notable of which was Baer's reversal of his own decision. The primary stimulus of these events appears to have been presidential electoral politics, led by Republican Speaker of the House Newt Gingrich and presidential candidate Bob Dole, and perpetuated by Democratic President Bill Clinton, who appointed Baer to the federal bench.

There are a number of politically and legally significant dimensions to this story, not the least of which is its implications for the independence of the federal judiciary. Baer's reversal stimulated great discussion and debate about the complex normative questions related to judicial independence, but an important component of this discussion has not been systematically examined.

Whether one believes that judges and courts *should* be separate and unaffected by the pressures of politics or not, it is useful to ask questions about the political pressures themselves that may affect judicial behavior. Even someone who believes that judges should not be isolated might still believe that some political influences are more legitimate than others. For example, the argument that judges should be accountable for the decisions they make may also accommodate the belief that the criticism judges face for unpopular decisions should be based at least on some minimal amount of empirical evidence—that the claims made against them, the political pressure to change their rulings to accommodate the public's will, should be reasonably accurate.

Most of the political criticism of Baer was based on the claim that he (and Clinton's appointees to the federal bench, more generally) is soft on crime, interested primarily in preserving the rights of criminal defendants at the expense of victims and the safety of the community, and generally responsible for "why we are losing our civilization." [1]

The political power of such rhetoric is obvious, particularly in a presidential election year, so it was not surprising (albeit disconcerting perhaps) that Clinton jumped on the bandwagon to criticize his own nominee. Importantly, though, these critiques, by both Republicans and Democrats alike, were unsubstantiated. Indeed, even after the White House suggested that a full review of Baer's record should be completed before an evaluation of him could be made, and while other observers made note of Baer's history as a prosecutor and the moderate nature of Clinton's judges, not a single piece of empirical evidence was presented (at least in public statements) to buttress these claims. While this may not be particularly surprising or unique in American politics, it is troublesome, especially in the context of the extraordinary events surrounding *Bayless* and subsequent discussions about judicial independence.

This article examines Baer's record on crime and the records of his Democratic and Republican colleagues in the Southern District of New York. The data indicate a pattern of pro-prosecution decision making from the judges of both parties. These results are buttressed by the decisions made by other Clinton appointees to the federal district courts across the country. In the final analysis, it appears that the critiques of Baer (and other Clinton appointees) are without empirical support. Despite the legitimate differences in opinion on the merits of judicial independence, the example of Harold Baer and *Bayless* illustrates the dramatic, and perhaps devastating, consequences of election year rhetoric—particularly inaccurate rhetoric—on the third branch of government.

U.S. v. Bayless

On October 1, 1998, one of the most controversial criminal cases of the last several years came to an end in the Southern District of New York when Carol Bayless, arrested in 1995 on suspicion of drug possession with intent to distribute, was sentenced to four and one-half years in prison. The events leading up to the sentencing began in the early morning hours of April 21, 1995. According to the testimony of one of the arresting officers (Officer Carroll) at the suppression hearing, a car driven by Bayless (who was the sole occupant) was seen in Washington Heights, a neighborhood in New York City with a reputation for drug activity.[2] From their own unmarked vehicle, Carroll and his partner (Sergeant Bentley) saw Bayless double-park her car and watched as it was approached by four men who appeared to be waiting for it (Carroll claimed that the men emerged from behind parked cars across the street).

The trunk of Bayless' car was unlocked, presumably from the inside by Bayless; one of the four men proceeded to open the trunk, two others put two large black duffel bags into the trunk, and the last man closed the trunk. According to Carroll, there was no conversation and the entire event took only seconds. Bayless then drove the car to the intersection and stopped for a red light. The police car followed, stopping behind her car while the police officers stared at the four men, who were now walking down the street on the sidewalk. When the men noticed the cops, they dispersed, moving away from the cops and each other quickly; according to Carroll's testimony, one of the men ran when he reached the street corner. The officers made no effort to stop them.

When the traffic light turned green, Bayless drove through the intersection at a normal speed (again, according to Carroll's testimony). Carroll and Bentley followed, radioing for assistance in checking Bayless's license plate (Michigan tags were on the car, which was a rental, unbeknownst to the officers). Before receiving a reply and before they knew the car was rented, the cops followed for a couple more blocks, then turned on their siren and pulled Bayless over.

They pulled her over, according to Carroll, because Bentley was concerned that she would merge onto the highway, which was straight ahead. Additionally, Carroll testified, Bayless was pulled over because her tags were out-of-state, because the actions of the four men were odd (walking in a single file line across the street,

engaging in no conversation with Bayless, and running when they saw the officers), and because of the large duffel bags the cops had seen placed in her trunk. The officers asked Bayless for her license, registration, and proof of insurance (all of which she provided), but did not tell her why she had been pulled over or why they wanted to look in her trunk. After examining the contents of her trunk, Bayless was arrested for drug possession and she gave written and videotaped statements.

Bayless's videotaped testimony provided a number of discrepancies with Carroll's testimony. She testified that she had driven from Michigan with another person, a man who was involved in the drug exchange; that they caravanned with another vehicle, a van with three other men in it; and that it was these men who were responsible for putting five duffel bags of money into the trunk of her car before they departed for New York City and for removing the bags to an apartment in front of which she had double-parked when Carroll and Bentley saw her from their car. According to Bayless, when the police officers pulled her over, they asked her what was in the trunk of the car, to which she replied that she did not know. She then handed over her keys to the officers, and was arrested after the drugs were found in the trunk.

Based on the testimony of Bayless after she was in custody, and the testimony of Officer Carroll at the suppression hearing nine months after the arrest (Sergeant Bentley was not called by the prosecution as a witness), Judge Baer granted Bayless's motion to suppress the drugs and her videotaped confession. He argued that the officers had no reasonable suspicion (the operating standard for searches related to traffic stops) that Bayless had been involved in a crime and so they had no reason to pull her over. As a consequence, their search of her car was unconstitutional, and any evidence seized from that search was inadmissible.

In response to Carroll's testimony, Judge Baer stated very firmly that none of the officers' observations, even considered together, was compelling enough to meet the standard of reasonable suspicion of Bayless. Not only did he not find out-of-state tags, double-parking in the city, or black duffel bags intrinsically suspicious, Baer also noted that in the absence of formal, sanctioned surveillance by the officers or a traffic violation by the defendant, there appeared to be no reason to pull Bayless over or search her trunk.

Furthermore, he argued, the behavior of the men involved was particularly NOT suspicious; indeed, given the turbulent and sometimes violent history between the police and the people living in the Washington Heights community, it was not at all surprising for the young black men to hurry away (or run) when they noticed cops in the vicinity. Referencing the 1994 investigation of an anti-crime unit operating in Washington Heights (in which he played a role as a member of the investigating commission), Baer stated that "... residents in this neighborhood [have] tended to regard police officers as corrupt, abusive and violent. After the attendant publicity surrounding [the investigation], had the men not run when the cops began to stare at them, it would have been unusual."

Finally, in light of the contemporaneous testimony of the defendant and the several discrepancies between Carroll's and Bayless's stories, and without corroborating testimony by Sergeant Bentley, Baer simply did not believe Carroll. "The testimony offered by Office Carroll about how the events of April 21st unfolded when juxtaposed with the defendant's full fledged videotaped confession suggest that Officer Carroll's testimony is at best suspect."

The aftermath

Immediately following this ruling and for months thereafter, Baer was criticized for his decision. Particularly, his political critics and the media focused on his statements disparaging the police officers. It is not surprising, then, that much of the criticism came from people like Police Commissioner William Bratton, who stated that Judge Baer should no longer hear cases involving police officers.[3] But the most damning criticism came from politicians of *both* parties, many of whom were involved in Baer's appointment to the district court bench; these included Mayor Rudolph Giuliani, an old friend and former colleague of Baer's in the U.S. Attorney's Office, who called the ruling "mind-boggling" and "very, very disturbing" and Senator Daniel Patrick Moynihan, who had recommended Baer to President Clinton for the district court bench.[4]

And, even after Baer granted a rehearing to the prosecution (which had petitioned the court with the new evidence of Sergeant Bentley's testimony), calls for his resignation began. Newt Gingrich led the charge with the statement, "This is the kind of pro-drug-dealer, pro-crime, anti-police and anti-law enforcement attitude that makes it so hard for us to win the war on drugs,"[5] which buttressed statements made by Orrin Hatch, chairman of the Senate Judiciary Committee, who

claimed that President Clinton was intent on putting pro-defendant judges on the federal bench.[6] One hundred and fifty members of the House followed with a letter to the President, requesting that he call for Baer to resign. And, in a campaign speech, Bob Dole told his audience that the presidential election was a contest "between a candidate who will appoint conservative judges to the court and a candidate who appoints liberal judges who bend the laws to let drug dealers free."[7]

Immediately, the administration jumped on the bandwagon as the President's press secretary, Mike McCurry, responded with a warning of sorts to Baer: if the *Bayless* ruling was not reversed, the President might ask for his resignation. While tempering this statement by acknowledging that an evaluation of Baer should be based on his whole judicial record and expressing support for an independent federal judiciary, McCurry indicated that the White House was watching to see how Baer would rule in the rehearing. Not to be outdone, the White House also reminded Republicans that conservative judges had also been known to make decisions that appeared antithetical to the public's concern with crime. Given the White House's response to the calls for Baer's resignation, it is not at all clear whether a full evaluation of Baer's record would have been initiated.

As it turns out, the point became moot because soon thereafter Baer overturned his original ruling. Basing his revised decision largely on the new testimony provided by the previously silent Sergeant Bentley and the courtroom testimony of Bayless, Baer vacated his previous ruling and denied Bayless's motion to suppress evidence.[8] He argued that witness credibility, the cornerstone of suppression hearings, shifted from Bayless to the officers with the corroborating testimony of Bentley and the contradictions between Bayless's videotaped testimony (used in the first hearing) and her subsequent court testimony (in the second). Additionally, in a move that surely indicated an awareness of the political critiques of his first ruling, Baer addressed "the hyperbole" in his first decision, which "regretfully may have demeaned the law-abiding men and women who make Washington Heights their home and the vast majority of the dedicated men and women in blue who patrol the streets of our great City."

In response to Baer's reversal, there was immediate legal and political reaction. Many legal experts argued that Baer's original decision had been based on legitimate interpretations of the Fourth Amendment's protection against unreasonable search and seizure and relevant precedent. Furthermore, they questioned the revised opinion, arguing that it ignored an important discrepancy between the written arrest report submitted by Bentley and the verbal testimony of both officers—the report contained no mention of the men running away when they saw the police, yet the testimony in court claimed they did. Overall, much of the legal response to Baer's change centered on concern that this federal judge had caved to political pressure, putting the independence of the federal judiciary in jeopardy.

Not surprisingly, the political response was quite different. A Dole spokesperson said, "Maybe the best that can be said about Judge Baer's ruling is better late than never." [9] And, President Clinton made an about-face, claiming that he did not regret appointing Judge Baer to the bench. And while he defended the right to criticize the rulings of federal judges, Clinton warned Republicans "that it's important not to get into the business of characterizing judges based on one decision they make." [10]

Soft on crime?

There are many important questions about the two decisions and the course of events that led to the settlement of *Bayless*, particularly as observers bring their own political prejudices to bear. We are unlikely to resolve the largely normative questions about the appropriate jurisprudence for federal judges or interpretations of the Fourth Amendment, or the appropriate degree of independence for the federal judiciary. However, we can, and we should, evaluate the veracity of information that is provided to us by political officials, particularly during a presidential election year. After all, the consequences of such information have been made patently clear by the turn of events surrounding *Bayless*—and they continue, as the claims made about Baer have been made also about other Democratic appointees to the federal bench, and have contributed to the years-long conflict between the Senate and the White House over judicial appointments.

To test the validity of claims that Baer and other Clinton appointees are particularly soft on crime, their records in criminal justice cases were examined. There are two sets of data used in this analysis. The first includes cases decided between January 1994 and July 1997 by Baer and his colleagues in the Southern District of New York. The politics that surrounded *Bayless* suggested that this data collection focus on criminal justice issues broadly defined to include a variety of cases that have required judges to make choices between the "good guys" (the police, the wardens, or other government officials involved in the cases) and the alleged "bad guys" (the criminal defendants, arrestees, or other individuals involved). In the court of public and political opinion, the *appearance* of such a choice, regardless of whether it is made in a case involving strictly criminal issues or not, is perhaps more significant than the *actual* choices with which a judge is faced. A search for these cases[11] among those published in the *Federal Supplement* revealed 230 in which conflicts between the good guys and the bad guys were heard by these district court judges. They include, but are not limited to, writs of habeas corpus; motions to suppress evidence, change counsel, reduce and vacate sentences, and expunge records; motions to dismiss (based often on the Speedy Trial Act); and civil rights actions based on violations of the Fourth, Fifth and Eighth Amendments.

The second set of data was collected originally for a different project, which focuses on the published decisions of a subset of Clinton's appointees to the federal district courts from 1993 to 1999. The political context of that research also led to a broad definition of criminal justice issues, one that includes cases requiring judges to make choices between the bad guys and the good guys. More specifically, the 227 cases included in this data set are coded as criminal because they involve claims made by alleged criminals, including due process, equal protection and other civil liberties claims, petitions for writs of habeas corpus, a variety of Fourth, Fifth, Sixth and Eighth Amendment claims, and some statutory issues regarding disclosure rules and rules of evidence.[12]

For the analysis of both sets of data, judicial decisions made in favor of the good guys are categorized as pro-prosecution and decisions made in favor of the bad guys are categorized as pro-defendant. Such labels may not be technically accurate for many of the cases (e.g., civil cases), but they do reflect the political labels that tend to be applied to decisions made in cases involving alleged criminals. Using these labels establishes congruity between the discussion of judicial behavior presented here and the popular discourse about this same decision making.

Table 1 identifies the criminal justice cases heard by Judge Baer from his appointment on August 9, 1994 through July 31, 1997. With the exception of the first

Published vs. unpublished decisions

Most research on federal district courts focuses on decisions published by the *Federal Supplement*. However, in light of judicial control over the publication process and the fact that many decisions are unpublished (either sent to West for release but not official publication, or not sent to West and maintained only at the court), the possibility that district court research may be affected by a nonrandom set of cases is not trivial. It is certainly possible that judges (especially those considered liberal and activist) may choose not to publish decisions that may reveal their political proclivities. There is reason to believe, though, that such strategic publishing is not a problem for this study.

First, published decisions are those that can be used as precedent by the legal community and that are available for political and public scrutiny. In the context of a study stimulated by the political criticism of judicial decision making, these cases are the most interesting and relevant for examination, *even if* they are not a random sample of all criminal justice decisions made by these judges. Second, studies suggest that published decisions are those that involve judicial discretion, value judgments, and policy making*—in the context of the research presented in this article, these are exactly the type of criminal justice cases that liberal, activist judges are alleged to make by their critics.

Finally, if this evidence is accurate, it should not be surprising to see few, if any, unpublished decisions in this area of law. And, in fact, a Westlaw search for unpublished criminal justice decisions by the judges included in both data sets, using the same parameters as the search for published decisions (see note 11 in the main text) revealed no unpublished decisions, in the relevant time period. To further test these results, an additional search on a sample of the judges was conducted using different parameters (a change in the date or case issue). This search revealed that there are indeed unpublished decisions for the judges in these data sets that Westlaw has made available—however, there are simply no unpublished decisions for the criminal justice parameters relevant to this study. This is not to say conclusively that these judges have not made any other decisions in cases involving criminal justice issues during the relevant time period than those included in the examination presented here. If such cases do exist, then it appears they may be accessible only through the judges' district courts.

Jennifer Segal

---

* *See e.g.* Rowland and Carp, *Politics & Judgment in Federal District Courts* (Lawrence: University Press of Kansas, 1996); but *also see* Siegelman and Donohue, "Studying the Iceberg From Its Tip: A Comparison of Published and Unpublished Employment Discrimination Cases," *Law & Soc'y Rev.* 24 (1990), 1133 and Songer, "Nonpublication in the United States District Courts: Official Criteria Versus Inferences from Appellate Review," *J. Pol.* 50 (1988), 206, who suggest that some of these decisions can be found among the unpublished decisions as well.

Table 1.   Judge Baer's rulings in criminal cases, August 1994–July 1997

Case	Disposition	Date of ruling
U.S. v. Love	Pro-prosecution	November 15, 1994
U.S. v. Garcia-Montalvo	Pro-prosecution	May 5, 1995
U.S. v. Ghafoor	Pro-prosecution	July 21, 1995
Garcia v. Kuhlmann	Pro-prosecution	July 21, 1995
U.S. v. Bayless	Pro-defendant	January 22, 1996
U.S. v. Bayless	Pro-prosecution	April 1, 1996
U.S. v. Damblu	Pro-prosecution	November 18, 1996
Harris v. Lord	Pro-prosecution	March 7, 1997

Table 2.   Disposition of criminal cases by judges in the Southern District of New York, by appointing president, January 1994–July 1997 (percentages in parentheses)

Judge	Appointing president	Number of pro-defendant decisions	Number of pro-prosecution decisions
Baer, Harold	Clinton	1 (12.5)	7 (87.5)
Batts, Deborah	Clinton	1 (11.1)	8 (88.9)
Brieant, Charles	Nixon	2 (33.3)	4 (66.7)
Carter, Robert	Nixon	0	0
Casey, Richard	Clinton	0 (0.0)	1 (100.0)
Cedarbaum, Miriam	Reagan	5 (55.6)	4 (44.4)
Chin, Denny	Clinton	3 (42.9)	4 (57.1)
Conner, William	Nixon	2 (50.0)	2 (50.0)
Cote, Denise	Clinton	0	0
Duffy, Kevin	Nixon	0	5 (100.0)
Edelstein, David	Truman	0	12 (100.0)
Gagliardi, Lee	Nixon	0	0
Griesa, Thomas	Nixon	0	0
Haight, Charles	Ford	2 (28.6)	5 (71.4)
Jones, Barbara	Clinton	0	0
Kaplan, Lewis	Clinton	1 (7.7)	12 (92.3)
Keenan, John	Reagan	1 (100.0)	0
Knapp, Whitman	Nixon	0	1 (100.0)
Koeltl, John	Clinton	4 (23.5)	13 (76.5)
Kram, Shirley	Reagan	2 (33.3)	4 (66.7)
Leisure, Peter	Reagan	2 (14.3)	12 (85.7)
Lowe, Mary	Carter	0	2 (100.0)
Martin, John	Bush	0	1 (100.0)
McKenna, Lawrence	Bush	0	4 (100.0)
Motley, Constance	Johnson	0	0
Mukasey, Michael	Reagan	1 (10.0)	9 (90.0)
Owen, Richard	Nixon	0	0
Parker, Barrington	Clinton	0	3 (100.0)
Patterson, Robert	Reagan	0	2 (100.0)
Pollack, Milton	Johnson	0	2 (100.0)
Preska, Loretta	Bush	1 (33.3)	2 (66.7)
Rakoff, Jed	Clinton	0	1 (100.0)
Sand, Leonard	Carter	1 (50.0)	1 (50.0)
Schiendlin, Shira	Clinton	9 (64.3)	5 (35.7)
Schwartz, Allen	Clinton	0	3 (100.0)
Sotomayor, Sonia	Bush	0	4 (100.0)
Sprizzo, John	Reagan	2 (6.5)	29 (93.5)
Stanton, Louis	Reagan	3 (42.9)	4 (57.1)
Stein, Sidney	Clinton	0	2 (100.0)
Sweet, Robert	Carter	4 (40.0)	6 (60.0)
Ward, Robert	Nixon	1 (100.0)	0
Wood, Kimba	Reagan	3 (37.5)	5 (62.5)
Totals		51 (22.2)	179 (77.8)

Bayless case, it is readily apparent that Baer ruled against the defendant in criminal cases every time. These cases involved serious crimes and important issues of criminal justice for which Baer found in favor of the government; they include a case involving drug and gun crimes in which the defendant argued for a continuance under the Speedy Trial Act (*U.S. v. Love*, 1994), a case involving cocaine possession in which the defendant moved to exclude evidence of a prior conviction (*U.S. v. Garcia-Montalvo*, 1995), a case in which the defendant moved to suppress his post-arrest statements because his English was not good enough to understand the Miranda warning (*U.S. v. Ghafoor,* 1995), a murder case in which the defendant petitioned for a writ of habeas corpus based in part on ineffective counsel and inappropriate jury instructions (*Garcia v. Kuhlmann,* 1995), a case in which the defendant moved for a new trial based on new evidence that government testimony was perjured (*U.S. v. Damblu,* 1996), and a case in which the defendant claimed that his access to mental health treatment in prison was denied in violation of the Eighth and Fourteenth Amendments (*Harris v. Lord,* 1997).

Notably, four of the eight criminal decisions Baer made during this time came before the first *Bayless* case—these were the only cases upon which a judgment of Baer could have been legitimately made at the time, and they defuse potential criticism that his subsequent pro-prosecution decisions were a consequence of the *Bayless* experience.

These data indicate, then, that allegations of Baer's pro-defendant tendencies were unfounded. Nevertheless, in the context of election year politics, Baer and *Bayless* were useful components of a larger campaign against President Clinton and his appointees to the federal courts. Despite the claims that they are liberal activists who are pro-drug dealer and pro-crime, however, the evidence suggests that the opposite is true.

An examination of Baer's colleagues in the Southern District of New York—judges appointed by both Republican and Democratic presidents—indicates plainly that Democratic appointees are not more likely than Republican appointees to rule in favor of criminal defendants. Table 2 identifies the judges who sit in the Southern District of New York and their voting records in the criminal justice cases decided between January 1994 and July 1997. As even a cursory glance illustrates, very few pro-defendant decisions were made by *any* of these judges sitting in this district during these three-and-one-half years.[13] Additionally, as the totals indicate, these judges as a group were overwhelmingly pro-prosecution.

When the data are grouped by each appointing president and the president's ideology, this pattern is even more obvious. While there is variation among judges appointed by different presidents, the most meaningful comparison is between Clinton's 11 appointees and Reagan's 9 appointees—despite their ideological differences, these two presidents appointed judges to this bench who are remarkably similar in their disposition of criminal cases (Table 3). As Table 4 further clarifies, personal politics and the extent to which attitudes affect legal judgments seem to have little impact on

Table 3. Disposition of criminal cases, by appointing president, Southern District of New York (percentages in parentheses)

Appointing president	Pro-defendant decision	Pro-prosecution decision	Total number of criminal decisions
Bush	1 (8.3)	11 (91.7)	12 (100.0)
Carter	5 (35.7)	9 (64.3)	14 (100.0)
Clinton	19 (24.4)	59 (75.6)	78 (100.0)
Ford	2 (28.6)	5 (71.4)	7 (100.0)
Johnson	0	2 (100)	2 (100.0)
Nixon	5 (29.4)	12 (70.6)	17 (100.0)
Reagan	19 (21.6)	69 (78.4)	88 (100.0)
Truman	0	12 (100)	12 (100.0)
Totals	51 (22.2)	179 (77.8)	230 (100.0)

Table 4. Disposition of criminal cases, by appointing president's ideology, Southern District of New York (percentages in parentheses)

Appointing president's ideology	Pro-defendant decision	Pro-prosecution decision	Total number of criminal decisions
Republican/conservative	27 (21.8)	97 (78.2)	124 (100.0)
Democratic/liberal	24 (22.6)	80 (77.4)	104 (100.0)
Totals	51 (22.2)	179 (77.8)	230 (100.0)

Table 5.   Disposition of criminal cases, select Clinton district court appointees, by district and judge, 1993–1999 (percentages in parentheses)

State (district)	Judge	Pro-defendant decisions	Pro-prosecution decisions
California (Southern)	Moskowitz	1 (100)	0
Colorado	Daniel	3 (37.5)	5 (62.5)
	Miller	1 (50.0)	1 (50.0)
Connecticut	Chatigny	0	11 (100.0)
	Thompson	1 (100)	0
Florida (Southern)	Ferguson	2 (100)	0
Georgia (Northern)	Cooper	1 (100)	0
	Hunt	1 (100)	0
	Sands	1 (100)	0
Illinois (Northern)	Bucklo	8 (21.6)	29 (78.4)
	Gettleman	9 (34.6)	17 (65.4)
	Manning	1 (20.0)	4 (80.0)
Louisiana (Eastern)	Berrigan	4 (66.7)	2 (33.3)
	Fallon	0	3 (100.0)
	Jones	0	6 (100.0)
	Porteous	0	1 (100.0)
	Vance	0	4 (100)
Maryland	Messitte	3 (37.5)	5 (62.5)
	Williams	0	3 (100.0)
Massachusetts	Lindsay	4 (30.8)	9 (69.2)
	Saris	3 (18.8)	13 (81.3)
	Stearns	0	3 (100.0)
Minnesota	Davis	2 (50.0)	2 (50.0)
	Tunheim	3 (60.0)	2 (40.0)
Missouri	Perry	1 (33.3)	2 (66.7)
New Jersey	Orlofsky	7 (33.3)	14 (66.7)
	Walls	0	2 (100.0)
Ohio (Northern)	Carr	5 (45.5)	6 (54.5)
	Economus	1 (25.0)	3 (75.0)
	Nugent	0	10 (100)
	O'Malley	1 (20.0)	4 (80.0)
	Oliver	0	1 (100.0)
	Wells	1 (25.0)	3 (75.0)
Ohio (Southern)	Dlott	1 (33.3)	2 (66.7)
	Sargus	0	3 (100.0)
Pennsylvania (Western)	Ambrose	0	1 (100.0)
	Cindrich	1 (33.3)	2 (66.7)
	Lancaster	1 (100)	0
Texas (Southern)	Gilmore	2 (50.0)	2 (50.0)
	Jack	1 (100)	0
Totals		69 (30.4)	158 (69.6)

these judges' rulings in criminal cases. The judges who sit in the Southern District of New York appear similarly tough on crime.

Finally, a survey of the other Clinton appointees to federal district courts suggests consistent results.[14] It is evident from Table 5 that most of these judges, who sit in a variety of districts across the country, are not more lenient in criminal cases than their Democratic and Republican colleagues in the Southern District of New York. Over two-thirds of all of their rulings are pro-prosecution—a tendency that is particularly notable in Colorado, Connecticut, Illinois, Massachusetts, and Ohio.

Concluding thoughts

With the arrest of Carol Bayless in 1995 began a series of politically-driven events that led a federal district court judge to overrule himself in an important criminal rights case. Critiques leveled largely by politicians of both parties in the context of a presidential election campaign were at the heart of the events that led to this extraordinary and controversial reversal. The critical question of the validity of the claims against Baer went unanswered at the time, but as the evidence presented here suggests, the statements made by Gingrich and Dole were invalid in their description of Judge Baer and Clinton's other judicial appointees.

The data indicate that not only is Baer no friend to defendants, neither are his Democratic colleagues in the Southern District of New York. Had the White House carried out its examination of Baer's record in criminal justice cases, or had anyone else been interested in a valid interpretation of Baer's decision making in this area of law, they would have found the process to be relatively straightforward and quite enlightening. Instead, it is clear that election year politics overshadowed an important and legitimate debate about law when the focus of discussion turned from the constitutional issues in a single district court case to the political issues in a presidential campaign, and the *Bayless* ruling and Baer himself became instruments in both the Democratic and Republican campaigns for the White House.

Notes

This article originally appeared in Volume 84, Number 1, July–August 2000, pages 26–33.

The author thanks Brad Canon and Elliot Slotnick for their insightful comments on earlier drafts, and Barbara Irwin for her invaluable research assistance.

1. Newt Gingrich, quoted in Mitchell, "Clinton Defends His Criticism of a New York Judge's Ruling," *New York Times*, April 3, 1996, at A12.

2. Unless otherwise indicated, this material comes from *U.S. v. Bayless* (1996) 913 F. Supp. 232.

3. Krauss, "Giuliani and Bratton Assail U.S. Judge's Ruling in Drug Case," *New York Times*, January 27, 1996, at 25.

4. Van Natta, "Judge Finds Wit Tested by Criticism," *New York Times*, February 7, 1996, at B1.

5. Fisher, "Gingrich Asks Judge's Ouster For Ruling Out Drug Evidence," *New York Times*, March 7, 1996, at B4.

6. Mitchell, "Clinton Pressing Judge to Relent," *New York Times*, March 22, 1996, at A1.

7. Ibid.

8. *U.S. v. Bayless* (1996) 921 F. Supp 211.

9. Van Natta, "Under Pressure Federal Judge Reverses Decision in Drug Case," *New York Times*, April 2, 1996, at A1.

10. Mitchell, *supra*. n. 1.

11. This was a Westlaw search that used West's key number system to select for criminal law cases (#110).

12. More information about this project and data can be obtained from the author.

13. For several of Clinton's appointees on this bench, criminal justice data is available through March 1999. These data buttress the results presented in Table 2. Judge Baer ruled for the defendant in 3 additional cases and for the prosecution in 20 additional cases; Judge Batts ruled 2 and 1; Judge Cote ruled 1 and 9; Judge Jones ruled 0 and 5; Judge Parker ruled 5 and 22; Judge Rakoff ruled 3 and 16; Judge Schiendlin ruled 8 and 18, and Judge Stein ruled 0 and 4; for the defendant and for the prosecution, respectively.

14. As noted previously, these judges, including a few who sit in the Southern District of New York, were selected as part of a different research project, and do not represent a random sample of the remaining Clinton appointees to the federal district courts. However, they provide at least a preliminary comparison for the data collected from the Southern District of New York.

Arrogation of power or accountability: "judicial imperialism" revisited

Stephen L. Wasby

The "imperial judiciary" is an illusion. Judges only exercise power given them by others and remain accountable both to professional interests and the public.

In the last half-dozen years it has become increasingly popular to argue that judges, particularly federal judges, have become an "imperial judiciary" improperly intervening in American life. Both an intellectual argument, made most notably by Nathan Glazer and Raoul Berger,[1] and political efforts have developed to restrict courts' power, with the former used to bolster the latter. Proposed constitutional amendments would limit federal judges to a single 10-year term[2] or would directly overturn Supreme Court abortion and school desegregation rulings thought to result from improper activism. Methods for reversing the courts' invalidation of federal or state laws have also been proposed.[3]

Complaints come from within as well as outside the judiciary. Justice Rehnquist has asserted that "It is basically unhealthy to have so much authority concentrated in a small group of lawyers who have been appointed to the Supreme Court and enjoy virtual life tenure." And Justice Powell has characterized the lower courts' orders in the 1979 school desegregation cases as "wholesale substitution of judicial legislation for the judgments of elected officials and professional educators" and "social engineering that hardly is appropriate for the federal judiciary."[4]

One can certainly make a strong, but hardly new, case that courts play a large role in American policy making. The question is whether a critic is engaging in dispassionate treatment of judicial policy making capacity or simply arguing against such policy making on the basis of disliked results. As noted by Cavanagh and Sarat, "However cast, arguments about failures of competence or capacity tend to be political statements about the desirability of particular court decisions or aspects of legal doctrine."[5] In short, dislike of substantive results fully pervades the discussion of "judicial imperialism" and lack of judicial capacity, both explicitly as in Glazer's work or somewhat more thinly veiled as in Horowitz's oft-cited study.[6]

Arguments supporting a limited role for the judiciary are part of a long, honorable tradition of *normative* argument. Among several legitimate normative positions on the place of judges in the system, however, critics of "judicial imperialism" seem to recognize only passivity—at least when convenient to applaud it. (At other times, they often wish judges to retain a strong hand, for example, so that regulators can be restrained or so that some of their own substantive goals can be attained.)

In the social climate of the last decade, with reduced support for civil rights and endemic disaffection with the social programs of the 1960s, crossing over into result-oriented advocacy is especially easy. Arguments like those by Glazer and Horowitz are certainly legitimate social *criticism*, but one should be cautious about accepting them as neutral or objective accounts. "Judicial imperialism" is a useful rhetorical device, but the assertions accompanying it are seldom supported by hard analysis. As Monti notes, "Critics of judicial activism have not posed their arguments in a way that anticipates, much less permits, the introduction of information that could qualify or contradict their positions."[7]

In this essay, I raise questions about the "judicial imperialism" argument as rhetoric and ideology, maintaining that the argument that judges have arrogated power to themselves is seriously defective. Critics of the "imperial judiciary" ignore the genesis of judicial rulings and blame the messenger—the courts—for others' acts or omissions. Instead, judges exercise power given them by others and are accountable in many ways both to professional interests and the larger political system. Furthermore, despite claims often made along with attacks on "judicial imperialism," judges are not incapable of dealing with policy issues presented to them and, when compared with other institutions, do so well.

Judicial imperialism and incapacity

The "imperial judiciary" argument gives disproportionate attention to certain types of cases, reinforced by result-oriented selection of examples; fails to exam-

Judicature Volume 65, Number 4, pp. 209–219

ine closely the causes of litigation, leading to a strong tendency to blame the messenger rather than the source; lacks systematic *comparative* examination of the capacity of courts and other political institutions to resolve policy disputes; and fails to examine ways in which judges, instead of arrogating power, are both potentially and actually accountable.

Selectivity of cases

The general tone of the "judicial imperialism" argument is set by the critics' selectivity in choosing types of cases to support their argument. Horowitz even dismisses the question of whether the cases in his study are representative by asserting—not showing—that they are not "aberrational" and by arguing that "frequency is not an issue in this study." [8] Yet how is one to know whether cases are "aberrational" without some baseline or idea of the frequency with which they occur?

Repeated emphasis on Judge Garrity's Boston school desegregation rulings and Judge Frank Johnson's Alabama prison and mental hospital decisions, with the former often misrepresented, has led many to expect incorrectly that those decisions are the norm. However, most judges are not "activist" but instead are "narrow-minded lawyers with little stomach for being creative or for second-guessing other government officers." [9]

With respect to school desegregation cases, on which critics often focus, "it is not at all clear that the courts are prepared to assume the responsibility of directing a far-reaching program of institutional reform in the public schools." [10] Concerning prison cases, Justice Brennan has pointed out that "no one familiar with litigation in this area could suggest that the courts have been over-eager to usurp the task of running prisons." [11] More generally, "Even in an era in which 'landmark' decisions with broad social implications dominate much of the debate over the role of courts, most court decisions present no arguable infringement on legislative, executive, or electoral prerogatives." [12]

The selectivity of those arguing against "judicial imperialism" extends even further. The pejorative "judicial activism" is applied only to Warren Court decisions and not those of the Burger Court. But certainly, promises to appoint "strict constructionist" judges has not meant that President Nixon's appointees have acted in a consistently "self-restrained" manner when faced with legislation running counter to deeply-held values.

Nor have critics of activism showed concern when judges have acted imperiously in the absence of some large social issue. The critics' concerns would have been more heartening if they had joined dissent from the Supreme Court's ruling in *Stump v. Sparkman* that judges were immune from suit if acting within what appears to be formal jurisdiction. [13] Justice Stewart, objecting to immunity for actions judges have no constitutional or statutory authority to take, certainly has the better of the argument: "A judge is not free, like a loose cannon, to inflict indiscriminate damage whenever he announces that he is acting in his judicial capacity." [14]

Clearly, critics are unable to penetrate the rhetoric of "strict construction," "judicial policy making," an "unaccountable" judiciary, or "judicial imperialism." Certainly political scientists have raised serious questions about accepting at face value a judge's rhetoric on self-restraint; [15] those writing more recently can legitimately be expected to exercise more care in their use of labels. But the critics' inability—or unwillingness—raises the question of how the events leading to 1937, which certainly should have taught us that the courts are policy makers, ever occurred. If "judicial policy making" may still be used pejoratively, chances for serious public discussion of courts' operation are slim. Such a difficulty clearly infects *The Brethren*, [16] where the authors' breathless discussion of bargaining within the Court suggests a failure to accept the Court's role as a policy maker. What else would we expect from a major policy making institution but bargaining and compromise?

An aspect of the critics' biased selectivity is their lack of historical perspective. "Social policy" issues have long been placed in the courts' hands. Contemporary commentators forget that "commercial interests in diversity jurisdiction dominated circuit dockets in the beginning [of the U.S. Courts of Appeals, while] the Great Depression and World War II brought into court continuing relations with powerful social aggregates concerned with labor relations, taxation, and public regulation of basic industries" [17]—all definitely "social policy" matters. Perhaps what discomforts the neoconservatives is that "the deprived have joined the advantaged as users of [the judicial] route of grievance redress." [18] Whatever the reason, the critics confuse differences in substantive content—the presence on the docket of, for example, environmental issues—with differences in procedure and remedy, thus exaggerating changes in the latter.

The "imperial judiciary" critics also demonstrate a lack of historical perspective by failing to remind us of earlier judicial "activism"—interference with governmental regulation of the economy in the 1930s and earlier. Those earlier decisions, in aid of a conservative ideology, are conveniently not seen as activist. Moreover, the critics fail to deal with Dahl's argument that the Supreme Court has seldom been out of line with the nation's dominant political interest.[19] The Court, Dahl argued, has been able to do little without support from Congress and the president, although it could maneuver when the other branches were in disagreement. Neither his posture that the Court conferred legitimacy on the policies developed by the other branches, nor his critics' view that elites legitimize the Court rather than the reverse, support a view of judicial overreaching.[20]

Causes of judicial actions

Although some judicial rulings said to indicate an "imperial judiciary" are based on broad constitutional provisions concerning "equal protection" and "cruel and unusual punishment," many challenged decisions stem from interpretation and enforcement of statutes. Vague and ambiguous constitutional clauses and statutory provisions may allow judges to project their values into decisions. However, the judges are not to blame for either the existence of the provisions or their lack of clarity.

Justice Powell has reminded us that "Congress' failure to make policy judgments can distort our system of separation of powers by encouraging other branches to make essentially legislative decisions."[21] Yet the critics find it easier to blame courts for decisions based on statutes than to question the legislative action itself. Similarly, it is not the plethora of administrative regulations based on those statutes that are attacked but the greater judicial action necessary to resolve disputes stemming from the regulations.[22]

Critics forget that if judges misread congressional intent, Congress has the power to right the situation, just as it can scrutinize the regulations designed to implement its own statutes. Yet critics seldom question Congress' failure to review such regulations and to strike down those that it disapproves. Failing to acknowledge that oversight has often meant *overlook*, critics continue to attack the courts, not the Congress, for not exercising its responsibilities and delegating substantial policy making authority to the executive.[23]

Decisions attracting critics' particular attention restrain officials or require them to improve substantially the conditions in the facilities they direct. It is, however, the judges' actions rather than events leading to their rulings that are criticized. Perhaps the best example is the attention given Judge Garrity's schools desegregation rulings in Boston rather than the Boston School Board's adamant refusal to obey clear state law. Similarly, rulings ordering improvement in prison conditions get attention, not state officials' unwillingness to correct long-standing, appalling and clearly unconstitutional conditions. Wishing to make judges accountable, critics of judicial imperialism ignore institutional officials' desire to remain unaccountable or to criticize legislators and senior political executives for not keeping the officials accountable.

Intent on ignoring the causes of allegedly unprecedented and improper judicial actions, the critics imply that judges are imposing particular views concerning the prisons or schools rather than responding to complaints brought by others, often as a last resort. It is, after all, the litigants, not the courts, who have the "power to initiate legal action," so that "litigants, not judges, set court agendas."[24] People need not turn to courts to satisfy their claims. Perhaps their doing so is in part a reflection of larger social or cultural trends or of "the oft-noted litigiousness of the American people."[25] Perhaps it is because plaintiffs find the legislature or executive unresponsive and are not content to be denied their due. Such use of the courts "belies the assessment of the courts as somehow being immune to the vagaries of the political process"[26] and indeed shows not their imperious isolation but their *connectedness* to the political process.

The critics also do not realize that most judges act only when conditions have become so atrocious that even the most conservative among them are horrified. Such judicial hesitation results from deference paid the expertise of those administering the institutions, part of the older "hands-off" policy now revived and thoroughly ensconced in the Supreme Court's prisoners' rights rulings.[27] Similarly ignored is the fact that more severe judicial orders are provoked by state resistance to initial judicial action; the critics instead make further complaints about later orders, forgetting that intransigent parties have always had to be forced to comply with decrees.[28]

In any event, when judges do act, dire predictions about the potential consequences of their rulings seldom are borne out.[29] Officials' authority is *not* invariably destroyed by judicially-established monitoring of their activities and judicial action does lead defendant officials to undertake seriously their responsibilities, with resulting improvements in institutional conditions.

Critics of the judiciary also conveniently ignore the fact that some decrees are not judicially written or imposed but are consent decrees to which the executive branch agrees. If the state later does not fully assume responsibility for the decree,[30] who is to blame if plaintiffs return to court and the judge orders implementation? It is also important to note that administrators may find it politically useful to be hauled into court, so they have a reason for agreeing to carry out politically unpopular actions.[31] As professionals, they may share plaintiffs' standards about proper conditions. More generally, "the interests of officials with direct operating responsibility—for example, institutional superintendents and their deputies—often overlap substantially with those of the plaintiffs." [32] Perhaps all this is but another piece of evidence for the proposition that litigation is not only an end in itself but is part of a continuing disputing process and a wedge to negotiation when nothing else will attract the other side's serious attention. Indeed, "extended impact litigation does not displace negotiation and compromise but is frequently an essential precondition to it." [33]

The foregoing reinforces the point that judges are embedded in the governmental system, not external to it. Nor is this unusual. Shapiro points out that judging is "an integral part of the mainstream of political authority rather than . . . a separate entity." [34]

What, then, of the norm of "judicial independence" so highly touted in the American political system and so strongly adhered to because of the belief that the costs of a judiciary directly subservient to the political powers-that-be are much too great? At one level it refers to judges not being dependent on one of the parties to a lawsuit; at another level, it entails an institutional separation so that judges are not attached to the same part of the government with whom an individual may be having a dispute.[35] Such a separation, with the judiciary expected to check and balance the other branches, may result in the judiciary acquiring "substantial lawmaking and administering capabilities." [36]

An "independent judiciary" does not, however, mean one completely separate from the political system, and may well indicate a system serving certain broad societal interests, historically the "upper class and nationalizing interests rather than dominant local interests." [37] Among the interests the American federal judiciary has at times served has been the cause of minority rights. The critics forget that the judiciary's very task is to protect civil liberties, a task that, despite public perceptions created by Warren Court decisions, the courts have not often fulfilled. Without such action or "activism," there would be even further erosion of our liberties, "because of the substantial political and bureaucratic obstacles that hinder the implementation of the Court's decisions and blunt their impact." Put differently, "because the statements in the Bill of Rights are only rights in theory, they need all the help they can get if they are to survive in fact" because "pressures in the real world" against them are "substantial"—a consideration favoring the view that courts "lean harder in the direction of emphasizing our nation's constitutional ideals." [38]

Beyond rulings on the merits, judges must also attend to implementation of decrees. Without such "intrusive" implementation, judicial orders are likely to be ineffective, remaining "merely a paper victory for the plaintiffs." [39] If neoconservatives showed greater concern for alternative modes of securing the rights sought and implemented through the courts in this way, their criticism of judicial "activism" would carry more weight. Yet one hears only the criticism, not suggestions of alternative methods of resolving societal disputes.

Judicial incapacity

A last important element of the attack on "judicial imperialism" is the argument that courts lack the capacity to resolve complex social policy issues. (This argument is separate from the position that, regardless of competence, courts in a democracy should not be making decisions about complex social issues.) In making their argument, critics often suffer from indecision about whether to focus only on courts or to compare courts with the other branches of government. They usually settle for the former, taking cheap pot-shots at the courts while ignoring the possibility that the other branches suffer from some of the same defects claimed to affect or infect the judiciary.

An example of the faulty analysis by those claiming judicial incapacity is Horowitz's argument that courts "carve up and . . . treat as separate" related transactions when those transactions "are intertwined in social life." [40] We are also told that judges are preoccupied with individual cases, and thus do not think about whether the cases before them represent a typical situation, from which precedent for later cases might be properly derived, or are extremes and thus to be confined to their facts. Furthermore, attention to individual cases is said to produce piecemeal policy making.

Incremental decision making does characterize the judiciary, but it also characterizes *all* governmental policy making,[41] despite occasional instances of "speculative augmentation." [42] Administrative agencies as well as courts have long been criticized for predominant reliance on a case-by-case approach instead of using rule making—although rule making is also criticized when it produces disliked results.

Nor does reliance on a case-by-case approach always entail ad hoc decision making, as the critics appear to assume. Legislators, administrators, and judges generally begin policy making with a problem presented by particular instances or cases. However, all contemplate to some degree other situations to which their rulings would apply. In particular, courts have regularly grouped cases involving common issues so as not to base decisions too narrowly on the specifics of an individual case. If courts are not self-starters, having to wait for cases to be filed or appealed, we must also remember that most legislative action does not commence until after a series of constituent or interest group complaints.

We are also told that courts cannot effectively make advance estimates of the magnitude or direction of the effects of their decisions. We are not told, of course, that legislatures and executives similarly fail to predict effectively. Judicial correction of policy is said to be intermittent. Yet it is equally the case that agencies charged with enforcing legislation do not continuously monitor many matters under their jurisdiction. The critics also do not recognize that, whatever the courts' difficulties with new subject-matter, other governmental institutions also have trouble processing new material effectively; however, for all institutions, courts included, time and preparation can overcome the problem.

To argue that judges are not prepared by training and experience to supervise administrative agencies like mental health and corrections departments or even to select appropriate masters whose work the judges are to supervise ignores the fact that legislators are generalists sharing problems "of being adequately informed about disputes and in their relations with experts," [43] as well as in selecting specialist staff. Judges' supervision of agencies can be facilitated by requiring periodic reports and by reliance on complainants' attorneys to return to court if something is amiss. Beyond that, judicial appointment of masters can "compensate for judges' lack of familiarity with organizational routines and procedures in defendant institutions," and their use may be essential in securing compliance with judicial decrees. [44]

To engage in serious analysis of courts' capacity to resolve matters requires a set of well-defined criteria;

Carter provides us with one. An institution's policy, to be effective, must "accord with fundamental, widely shared beliefs about acceptable governmental action" and must "carry some plausible hope of alleviating the problem." Moreover, the promulgation and implementation of the policy must not "destroy the position and authority of the position's source." [45] The criteria Carter suggests include technical competence, effective information processing, and political accountability:

(1) *familiarity* with the language in which a policy problem is articulated and an *understanding* about "cause and effect beliefs that define the existence of a problem in the first place";[46]

(2) *reliable access to information* bearing on the problem's causes, on all solutions proposed and their direct and indirect consequences, on targets, and on implementation strategies;

(3) the *ability to reformulate policy* when new information is obtained; and

(4) once there is agreement that a problem exists and on perceptions of the problem, the *public's belief* that the institution's authority and competence match the problem.

Once an institution (legislative, executive, or judicial) is seen to satisfy any one of these criteria, the question arises whether,

> regardless of the skill of members of a given policy making institution (PMI), any other PMI is equally or better prepared to proceed, and whether alternative policy sources, even if they may be better equipped technically to proceed, will in fact do so.[47]

Use of the criteria and of this comparative formulation will produce different answers at different times as to the appropriateness of judicial action. What is important is that, by insisting that the second question be asked, Carter has properly focused attention on *comparative* capacity as well as on the crucial *will to proceed*, neither of which is addressed seriously by the "imperial judiciary" critics.

Judicial accountability

Advocates of the "judicial imperialism" position ignore ways in which the judiciary *is* accountable. To remedy this omission, it helps to stress not arrogation of power but accountability, defined to mean "keeping an institution's decisions in line with community political and social values and otherwise imposing constraints on the courts' exercise of discretion." [48] Means of judicial accountability may appear to be few or at times less than fully effective, but that does not mean there is no accountability.

For one thing, despite American emphasis on judicial independence, courts are not fully independent or autonomous institutions. Their structure, jurisdiction, and resources, including their budget and personnel, are determined by the other branches of government. Courts are initially established, and often reorganized, by the legislature. And, as indicated by current debate over limiting the Supreme Court's appellate jurisdiction—or the jurisdiction of all federal courts—the legislature can limit what the courts hear.

Ironically, discussion of judicial imperialism, both by those attacking the judiciary and defenders, has itself contributed to accountability by producing more intellectual soul-searching by judges. In general, accountability of judges is of two principal types—within the legal system and to the broader political system. The former includes judges' socialization; precedent and the public nature of judicial action; reversal of lower court judges' decisions; and constraints imposed by courts' organizational needs. Political accountability derives from selection and removal of judges (also part of accountability within the legal community); the role of public opinion; and resistance to judges' decisions.

The socialization of judges

Given the limited amount of *formal* training of judges as judges, judges' most extensive socialization has been to their earlier role as lawyers. This includes socialization to the norm of judicial independence, the idea that judges ought not be accountable to the other branches of government. Thus, we find judges, as lawyers, socialized to norms about accountability itself. The lack of formal training for judges means that the most important direct socialization of judges is through contact with other judges; reliance on each other is reinforced by norms against consultation with those who are not judges and especially with nonlawyers. All this reinforces accountability within the judicial profession rather than to others.

Part of lawyers' socialization is to precedent. Lawyers also learn that, even when precedent is lacking, they should look to "the law," not popular feelings, as the source of their decisions. Precedent affects the process by which judges arrive at reasoned decisions:

"We contain our judges by method, and demand justification of their results by reason." [49] In particular, we wish judges' rulings to be characterized by *formality*. The requirement of written opinions is part of the process of producing accountability. Believers in role theory will agree that judges' beliefs that they *should* follow precedent and that their decisional process *ought* to be a reasoned one, even if the true bases of their decisions are not in fact presented, will affect judges' actions.

Socialization to precedent can lead judges away from legislative and executive branches and toward their own colleagues. That has helped produce a consensus on how to decide many cases. That such a consensus exists in the Supreme Court is evident from the high degree of unanimity on which cases are appropriate for review and on the disposition of many other cases. [50] Such consensus suggests that "judicial role," not personal values about preferred policy goals, drives much judicial activity, although variations exist in the degree to which values and judicial role reinforce or crosscut each other.

Other forms of accountability

Coupled with precedent is the openness of the judicial decision process, at least at the result stage. Although most trial court opinions are not written or published, and despite federal appellate courts' increased use of not-for-publication opinions, people expect that judges will justify their rulings in published (or at least public) documents. However, serving to reduce accountability is the fact that judges' deliberations are private. Moreover, some courts have been slow to explain even their operating procedures, and Freedom of Information Act (FOIA) provisions do not extend to internal court documents. A penchant for secrecy seems apparent in the Administrative Office of the U.S. Courts' practice of masking judges' identities so that they cannot be matched with particular decisions.

If precedent and openness help produce accountability, so does the sanction of reversal by higher courts for not following precedent or for not viewing the law as the higher court does. Higher courts thus limit lower courts' freedom of action. However, appellate court review of lower court decisions is limited in several ways. Not all trial court decisions are appealed, because the decision to appeal is in lawyers', not judges', hands. Moreover, the absence of controlling precedent also reduces appellate courts' ability to control lower courts, particularly in novel or changing areas of law. Similarly, the Supreme Court and other courts with discretionary jurisdiction cannot take all cases. Because of the limited number of cases they decide, they cannot establish controlling doctrine for all issues faced by lower courts.[51] Even lower appellate courts hearing a higher volume of cases may be hard pressed to issue controlling precedents for the trial courts.

Certain judicially-established standards—the "abuse of discretion" doctrine, for example—also limit higher courts' propensity to overturn lower courts. Not only are those tests flexible and work to affirm the lower courts' rulings, but high courts also cannot afford to antagonize the lower courts, on which they must rely if their precedential rulings are to be implemented. Frequency of reversal is thus not high, so that the *fear* of reversal—its symbolic effect—must be more important than actual reversal in achieving accountability. And, indeed, most judges do follow law developed by higher courts; at least they "go along" because higher court rulings on most topics fall within their "zone of indifference." [52]

Attention to the criminal trial courts has recently revealed another aspect of judicial accountability—lateral or horizontal accountability to norms of the "courtroom workgroup." [53] Organizational dynamics control many dispositions reached or recorded in the trial courts. Values shared by trial judges, prosecutors, defense attorneys and other court personnel often limit the effect of higher court rulings, particularly in crisis situations, such as major civil disturbances when some judges seem to suspend independent judgment almost completely.

Selection and public opinion

Methods of judicial selection may also help achieve judicial accountability. Although judges, once chosen, might go their own ways, continuing accountability would be less necessary if accountability were "built in" through selection of judges with characteristics and values thought appropriate by those to whom the judges were to be accountable. Which groups play a dominant role in judicial selection is thus quite important, because it is to the values of those groups that accountability will run. Thus the "merit system," in which lawyers play an explicit role, would increase accountability of judges within the legal system, while partisan election systems would increase accountability to political parties and the values represented by party leaders, that is, "political accountability."

Elections, whether in the merit system, which has led to non-retention (removal) of very few judges,[54] or in nonpartisan or partisan elections, do not substantially increase judicial accountability. Use of nonpartisan ballots makes it difficult for voters to tell "good" candidates from "bad" ones, particularly if the candidates lack previous public identity. Moreover, the norm that one should not run against sitting judges often leaves candidates unopposed. Stiff competition occurs infrequently, and voting in judicial elections is generally reduced by comparison with turnout in elections for other positions.[55]

The difficulty of holding judges accountable through methods of selection, coupled with accounts of improper personal or judicial behavior, has led most states to implement methods for judicial discipline, including removal.[56] Serious discussion of means short of impeachment for handling such problems at the federal level has led to proposals for a separate discipline court and to legislation, enacted in 1980, strengthening the role of the circuit councils in the discipline process, but leaving impeachment as the only means of removing a federal judge from office.[57]

Political accountability may also be achieved through public opinion. Despite the high value placed on judicial independence, public opinion does appear to affect judges. Judges politically active before becoming judges had both become familiar with public opinion and accustomed to responding to it. Although judges do differ in how strongly they adhere to local values, the continuing pull of constituency can be seen in numerous cases, for example, in the race relations area.[58]

Public opinion may, however, be less effective in promoting judicial accountability than it is in the legislative arena because the public, accepting the norm of judicial independence, generally leaves judges alone. At least until recently, negative public opinion about judicial decisions has seldom shown up as more than negative responses in public opinion surveys. More recently, however, "single-issue" interest groups have been pressing effectively for legislation to overturn especially disliked decisions or to remove the courts' jurisdiction over controversial areas. However, even without such activity and even in the absence of a high degree of public knowledge about the decisions, public opinion can affect judicial action. The absence of specific mechanisms for transmitting public opinion to the courts indicates not the absence of an effect of public opinion but only the presence of a noncoercive linkage between public opinion and judicial decisions.

If quiescence most often characterizes even negative reaction to the courts' ruling, there *are* notable instances in which the public resists judicial action. Such resistance, while not making judges directly accountable, certainly lessens the claimed effects of "judicial imperialism." Not only are rulings appealed, with reversal or modification producing some accountability, but, more important, they are at times ignored, resisted, attacked, and overturned in other arenas. Such action, whatever it may say about the presence of a "government of laws," is certainly an effective means of holding courts accountable to views of important segments of the public. This is true even if noncompliance may have received attention disproportionate to its occurrence.[59]

In all of this, however, we should be careful not to overestimate the effect of public opinion on judicial accountability. For one thing, as noted above, public knowledge of judicial decisions is limited. For another, if public opinion can produce accountability when it is clear and unidirectional, at many times opinion is confused, fragmented, and weak, thus providing courts considerable room in which to maneuver. When the public's view differs from views held by the organized bar, judges have freedom to choose between competing audiences.

As the above suggests the two basic types of accountability must be seen together. Those mechanisms providing accountability within the legal system and those providing political accountability at times seem to diverge. Within the legal system, judicial accountability is primarily to lawyers or to other judges, while political accountability propels judges toward the broader public or at least the more attentive members of the public. Despite these potentially divergent strains, some overlap exists because lawyers simultaneously play a large role in judicial selection and are members of the political elite.

Perhaps particularly important is that the values and attitudes of the elite constitute a large part of the environment in which judges function. Appellate judges developing legal doctrine base decisions in part on the political environment or "democratic subculture."[60] Lower court judges expected to follow appellate rulings will have absorbed values from that same political and legal culture before taking the bench and will continue to draw from it because of their greater exposure to the local community. This would suggest that, over the long run, important conjoint legal and political system constraints can operate to limit judges' discretion and thus to hold them accountable.

The burden of this essay has been that the "judicial imperialism" and "judicial incapacity" arguments are defective in a number of important ways. One is a failure to use terminology carefully; another is a lack of historical perspective, coupled with a biased selectivity in examples critics choose to make their case. Perhaps most serious is the critics' sole focus on selected judicial acts rather than on the sources of judicial action—in statutes and administrative regulations. Examination of judicial capacity solely in terms of the judiciary rather than through a comparison of differential institutional capacity is another serious weakness in the critics' argument. So is their attention solely to what they see as lack of judicial accountability without attention to the numerous important ways in which judges are accountable.

More, of course, is necessary than a critique of the critics' arguments. These arguments have, however, been so readily accepted that their defects must be exposed. The possibility for evenhanded analysis of the problems of judicial action in a political system and for thorough comparative analysis of institutional capacity has also been pointed to here, but it remains for others to carry such work forward.

Notes

This article originally appeared in Volume 65, Number 4, October 1981, pages 209–219.

An earlier version of this article was presented at the American Political Science Association meeting in New York on September 4, 1981.

1. Glazer, "Toward an Imperial Judiciary," *Pub. Int.* 40 (Fall 1975), 104–123, and "Should Judges Administer Social Services?," *Pub. Int.* 50 (Winter 1980), 64–80; Berger, *Government by Judiciary: The Transformation of the Fourteenth Amendment* (Cambridge: Harvard University Press, 1977).

For other, rather different positions on judicial review, *see* Choper, *Judicial Review and the National Political Process: A Functional Reconsideration of the Role of the Supreme Court* (Chicago: University of Chicago Press, 1980); and Ely, *Democracy and Distrust: A Theory of Judicial Review* (Cambridge: Harvard University Press, 1980).

2. S.J. Res. 24, 97th Cong. 1st Sess., *Cong. Rec.* (Jan. 29, 1981) S 787 (Rep. Dornan).

3. H.R. 4111, 96th Cong. 1st Sess., *Cong. Rec.* (Oct. 10, 1979), E 4953 (Rep. Dornan).

4. *Richmond Newspapers v. Virginia*, 100 S.Ct. 2814, 2843 (1980); *Columbus Bd. of Educ. v. Penick*, 443 u.s. 229 (1979).

5. Cavanagh and Sarat, "Thinking About Courts: Toward and Beyond a Jurisprudence of Judicial Competence," *Law & Soc'y Rev.* 14 (Winter 1980), 371, 386.

6. Glazer, *supra* n. 1, and, particularly, *Affirmative Discrimination: Ethnic Inequality and Public Policy* (New York: Basic Books, 1975), Horowitz, *The Courts and Social Policy* (Washington, D.C.: Brookings Institution, 1977).

7. Monti, "Administrative Foxes in Educational Chicken Coops: An Examination of the Critique of Judicial Activism in School Desegregation Cases," *Law & Pol'y Q.* 2 (April 1980), 233, 242.

8. Horowitz, *supra* n. 6, at 63.

9. Miller, "For Judicial Activism," *N.Y. Times,* Nov. 10, 1979.

10. Monti, *supra* n. 7, at 252–253.

11. *Rhodes v. Chapman,* 101 S.Ct. 2392, 2403 (1981).

12. Cavanagh and Sarat, *supra* n. 5, at 372.

13. 435 U.S. 439 (1978). *See* Way, "A call for limits to judicial immunity: must judges be kings in their courts?," *Judicature* 64 (April 1981), 390.

14. 435 U.S., at 367.

15. *See, e.g.,* Grossman, "Role-Playing and the Analysis of Judicial Behavior: The Case of Mr. Justice Frankfurter," *J. Pub. L.* 11 (1962), 285.

16. Woodward and Armstrong, *The Brethren* (New York: Simon and Schuster, 1979).

17. Howard, *Courts of Appeals in the Federal Judicial System: A Study of the Second, Fifth, and District of Columbia Circuits* (Princeton: Princeton University Press, 1981), 17.

18. Monti, *supra* n. 7, at 236.

19. Dahl, "Decision-Making in a Democracy: The Role of the Supreme Court as a National Policy-Maker," *J. Pub. L.* 6 (Fall 1957), 279.

20. Adamany, "Legitimacy, Realigning Elections, and the Supreme Court," *Wisc. L. Rev.* (1973), 790.

21. *Schweiker v. Wilson,* 101 S.Ct. 1074, 1088 (1981).

22. *See* Greanias and Windsor, "Is judicial restraint possible in an administrative society?," *Judicature* 64 (April 1981), 400, 401.

23. Ibid. at 410–411.

24. Howard, *supra* n. 17, at 13.

25. Ibid. at 17.

26. Monti, *supra* n. 7, at 235–236.

27. *Bell v. Wolfish,* 99 S.Ct. 1861 (1979); *Jones v. North Carolina Prisoners' Labor Union,* 433 U.S. 119 (1977).

28. Eisenberg and Yeazell, "The Ordinary and the Extraordinary in Institutional Litigation," *Harv. L. Rev.* 93 (January 1980), 465, 476–481, 492.

29. Harris and Spiller, *After Decision: Implementation of Judicial Decrees in Correctional Settings* (Washington, D.C.: LEAA, 1977), p. 21, quoted in *Rhodes v. Chapman, supra* n. 11, at 2405 (Justice Brennan).

30. Hansen, "Willowbrook: Try, Try Again," *Soc. Pol'y* 10 (November/December 1979), 41.

31. "Even prison officials have acknowledged that judicial intervention has helped them to obtain support for needed reform." *Rhodes v. Chapman, supra* n. 11, at 2406 (Justice Brennan).

32. Diver, "The Judge as Political Power Broker: Superintending Change in Public Institutions," *Va. L. Rev.* 65 (February 1979), 43, 71.

33. Cavanagh and Sarat, *supra* n. 5, at 405.

34. Shapiro, *Courts: A Comparative and Political Analysis* (Chicago: University of Chicago Press, 1981), 20.

35. Ibid. at 19, 27.

36. Ibid. at 31–32.

37. Ibid. at 24.

38. Wasby, *Continuity and Change: From the Warren Court to the Burger Court* (Pacific Palisades, Calif.: Goodyear, 1976), 210–211.

39. Special Project, "The Remedial Process in Institutional Reform Litigation," *Colum. L. Rev.* 78 (May 1978), 785, 815. *See also* Monti, *supra* n. 7, at 238, 241; Cavanagh and Sarat, *supra* n. 5, at 408; *Rhodes v. Chapman, supra* n. 11, at 2402.

40. Horowitz, *supra* n. 6, at 260.

41. Shapiro, "Stability and Change in Judicial Decision-Making: Incrementalism and Stare Decisis," *Law in Trans. Q.* 78 (1965), 134–157; *see* Lindblom, "The Science of 'Muddling Through'," *Pub. Ad. Rev.* 19 (1959), 79.

42. *See* Jones, "Speculative Augmentation in Federal Air Pollution Policy-Making," *J. Pol.* 36 (May 1974), 438; Schulman, "Nonincremental Policy Making: Notes Toward an Alternative Paradigm," *Am. Pol. Sci. Rev.* 69 (December 1975), 1354.

43. Howard, "Adjudication Considered as a Process of Conflict Resolution: A Variation on the Separation of Powers," *J. Pub. L.* 69 (1969), 339, 350.

44. Cavanagh and Sarat, *supra* n. 5, at 406; *see also* Nathan, "The Use of Masters in Institutional Reform Litigation," *Toledo L. Rev.* 10 (Winter 1979), 419, and Special Project, *supra* n. 39, at 805–809.

45. Carter, "When Courts Should Make Policy: An Institutional Approach," in Gardiner (ed.), *Public Law and Public Policy* (New York: Praeger, 1977), 145.

46. Ibid.

47. Ibid. at 146.

48. Wasby, "Accountability of the Courts", in Greer et al. (eds.), *Accountability in Urban Society* (Beverly Hills: Sage, 1978), 145. The following material draws on that article.

49. Dixon, "The 'New' Substantive Due Process and the Democratic Ethic," *B.Y.U.L. Rev.* (1977), 43, 73 n. 134.

50. Provine, *Case Selection in the United States Supreme Court* (Chicago: University of Chicago Press, 1980).

51. *See* Howard, *supra* n. 17, at 41, 56.

52. Baum, "Lower-Court Response to Supreme Court Decisions: Reconsidering a Negative Picture," *Just Sys. J.* 3 (Spring 1978), 208, 216.

53. See Eisenstein and Jacob, *Felony Justice: An Organizational Analysis of the Criminal Courts* (Boston: Little, Brown, 1977).

54. Carbon, "Judicial retention elections: are they serving their intended purpose?" *Judicature* 64 (November 1980), 210.

55. Dubois, *From Ballot to Bench—Judicial Elections and the Quest for Accountability* (Austin: University of Texas Press, 1980); Dubois, "Public Participation in Trial Court Elections," *L. & Polc'y. Q.* 2 (April 1980), 133.

56. Hoelzel, "No easy answers: a report on the national conference for judicial conduct organizations," *Judicature* 64 (December–January 1981), 279.

57. For a discussion of the new law, *see* Neisser, "The New Federal Judicial Discipline Act: Some Questions Congress Didn't Answer," *Judicature* 65 (September 1981), 142.

58. *See* Peltason, *Fifty-Eight Lonely Men* (New York: Harcourt, Brace and World, 1961); Vines, "Southern State Supreme Courts and Race Relations," *West Pol. Q.* 13 (March 1965), 5; Hamilton, *The Bench and the Ballot: Southern Federal Judges and Black Voters* (New York: Oxford University Press, 1973).

59. Baum, *supra* n. 52.

60. Richardson and Vines, *The Politics of the Federal Courts* (Boston: Little, Brown, 1970).

Why should we care about independent and accountable judges?

Bruce Fein and Burt Neuborne

Judicial independence in the U.S. has proved superior to any alternative form of discharging the judicial function. It would be folly to squander this priceless constitutional gift to placate political partisans.

The rule of law depends on judges. Judges ensure that neither partisan majorities nor overzealous officials violate our constitutional rights. Judges give concrete meaning to statutes and regulations whose texts are frequently ambiguous. State judges make "common law" that, unless modified by statute, governs enormously important day-to-day issues like legal responsibility for harms associated with guns, tobacco, or alcohol.

The difficult legal problems that judges confront often do not yield a single correct answer. No consensus has emerged among judges, scholars, or the broader legal community about the best way to interpret ambiguous language in the Constitution, statutes, and administrative regulations, or how exuberantly judges should employ their common law powers to create judge-made law.

When interpreting the Constitution or a statute, some champion a theory of "original meaning or intent." Others argue in favor of reading ambiguous text in harmony with evolving standards of decency or morality. Yet others insist on an interventionist approach when addressing individual rights implicating civil liberties, but urge extreme deference in economic matters. In sum, a Babel of interpretive theories that will affect the outcome of many controversial cases are available to American judges, lawyers, and law professors.

That is why politicians and interest groups care so deeply about who gets to be a judge, and about how judges perform in office. Interest groups lobby vigorously for the selection of judges they believe will vote to decide cases favorable to their cause, whether the cause is pro-life, pro-choice, pro-labor, pro-affirmative action, pro-federalism, pro-property rights, pro-business, pro-law enforcement, pro-environment, pro-free speech, or pro-capital punishment. They excoriate judicial opinions they dislike, without paying much attention to a judge's reasoning.

There is, of course, nothing wrong with caring about who gets to be a judge, and criticizing a judge's behavior in office. Both activities are protected by the First Amendment. Criticism of judges is pivotal to saving them—and us—from the delusion that judges are infallible. But everything in civilized life is a matter of degree. Allowing for both the accountability of judges to popular opinion in discharging their crucial tasks, and judicial independence from politics, is no exception.

It is troublesome that a growing array of voices seem to measure judicial appointments and performance by applying outcome-determinative litmus tests. Judges who decide (or who would decide) cases one way receive high marks. Everyone else receives failing grades. Whether a judge has interpreted, or will interpret, the law in a legitimate, responsible, and reasonable manner is irrelevant. Law, for such strident voices, is simply partisan politics by other means. Some even argue that a litmus test on outcomes should be used when the President selects federal judges, including members of the Supreme Court. Presidential candidates have promised to reject any prospective nominee that refuses to promise to overrule *Roe v. Wade* (1973), the landmark abortion decision. Pro-choice interest groups insist that no one can be a judge unless he or she pledges allegiance to *Roe v. Wade*.

In the years since the contentious confirmation hearings that resulted in the rejection of Judge Robert H. Bork, it has become common practice for senators to seek to extract commitments from nominees to the federal bench about how they would vote on particular issues. Forcing a prospective judge to pre-commit to a particular outcome in a future case is destructive of judicial independence. It strips the judicial process of its most important attribute—a neutral arbiter willing and able to listen to arguments from both sides before making a decision. Once a judicial nominee has been forced, under oath, to voice an opinion regarding the correctness of a Supreme Court precedent on national television, both the appearance and reality of judicial independence has been compromised.

Recently, some members of Congress have gone far beyond healthy and informed criticism of court rulings to demand impeachment of federal judges whose decisions they dislike, more often because of political calculation than because of deficient reasoning. Nothing could be more damaging to the rule of law than for judges to fear that if they rule against the prevailing political winds, they may be removed from office. The Founders provided for a written Constitution, a Bill of Rights, and federal judges with life tenure to safeguard against majoritarian tyranny. Allowing politicians to threaten to remove federal judges whose rulings displease them strikes directly at the Founders' efforts.

The meaning of independence

Judicial independence does not mean rule by Platonic guardians who presume omniscience in fashioning enlightened government. It assumes an important element of accountability. Since vigorous disputes exist over which theory of interpretation is best, a judge is often free to choose among several generally accepted alternatives. A judge is not free, however, to invent an idiosyncratic theory of interpretation with no roots in our judicial traditions or to decide cases according to personal whim.

In fact, American judges have almost never adopted untenable theories of interpretation to advance personal agendas. During recent congressional hearings on alleged "activist" jurists, harsh critics were unable to cite a single judicial decision over several decades out of the hundreds of thousands delivered annually that adopted a theory of interpretation that fell outside the bounds of general acceptance.

Thus, judicial independence emphatically does not mean capricious rule by judges. Rather, it means promoting a judicial culture and cast of mind that approaches the interpretive task as guided by principles that rise above personal or partisan likes or dislikes, and are anchored to one of a number of theories that the American people have come to accept as a legitimate part of judging.

Are current attacks novel?

Judicial independence has been under attack from the inception of the Constitution. Thomas Jefferson sought to impeach and remove Justice Samuel Chase because of Chase's enthusiasm for enforcing the Sedition Act. Congress even suspended the 1802 Term of the Supreme Court, hoping to foil the Court's ruling in *Marbury v. Madison,* the first case in which the Court comprehensively explained the parameters of its power of judicial review. The Civil War Congress manipulated the size of the Supreme Court to ensure a favorable ruling on wartime Legal Tender legislation, and took away the Court's jurisdiction in a pending case after the war to avoid a constitutional challenge to Reconstruction legislation.

More recently, "Progressives" argued for a popular veto of Court rulings, and for super-majorities on the Supreme Court to invalidate statutes. President Franklin D. Roosevelt tried to increase the size of the Supreme Court so that he could "pack" it with hand-picked appointees to prevent decisions hostile to the New Deal. The unpopularity of many of the Warren Court's civil rights and criminal justice decrees sparked rancorous demands for the impeachment and removal of Chief Justice Earl Warren.

Yet previous attacks on judicial independence have failed. Most Americans respect the courts and the rule of law, in large part because they believe in judicial independence. Deeply controversial decisions in highly polarizing areas like abortion, prayer in school, affirmative action, and the death penalty are widely obeyed because the outcomes are not "rigged," but are the result of a principled process in which independent judges do their best to interpret the law in accordance with their understanding of the correct interpretive philosophy.

So, why worry about this generation's attack on judicial independence? Won't it fail, as have the earlier efforts to undermine the courts? Complacency would be dangerous, however. What is new to this generation of court-bashers is an increasingly widespread willingness to treat judges as if they were merely politicians in black robes who do not deserve to be independent. As Edmund Burke taught, all that is necessary for the triumph of evil is for good men to do nothing. Judicial independence is too important to the welfare of the nation and the rule of law to leave to happenstance.

Interpreting or making law?

Do judges make more law than they interpret? Emphatically "No." Most legal issues that arise in daily life do not raise difficult questions of interpretation. In many settings, the law is so clear that a consensus exists about what a judge would say the law is, whatever the prevailing judicial philosophy. Such "easy" legal questions never enter the courthouse because they fall within that broad universe of judicial consensus about cornerstone canons of construction that substantially limit latitude in deciding concrete cases: precedent should not be lightly overruled; the language and purpose of a law should be honored; deference should be given to longstanding administrative interpretations or practices; and, the essence of judging is like interior decoration of a house that the Constitution or legislatures have built, not remodeling. Even in the Supreme Court, which reviews only the most vexing legal issues, typically 50 percent or more of the cases are decided unanimously by nine justices sporting varied philosophies of interpretation.

It would be wrong, however, to suggest that judges do not also make law occasionally, even highly important and controversial law, especially in matters of constitutional interpretation where proper rules of interpretation have been hotly disputed from the outset. The ambiguous constitutional text seldom offers definitive answers. For example, the enumerated powers of Congress include the creation of an army or navy, but not an air force. Charles Lindbergh was not within the realm of prophecy in 1787. Does that mean that an air force is unconstitutional? Certainly not, since Congress also enjoys powers "necessary and proper" to promote its enumerated powers, and few if any would dispute that an air force complements the defense mission of the army and navy.

Other constitutional ambiguities are much more difficult. The Fourth Amendment prohibits unreasonable searches and seizures. Does the unreasonableness standard apply to wiretapping or electronic bugging that captures conversations? The language is not conclusive, and the Supreme Court has changed its mind on whether to treat wiretapping as a "search." The First Amendment precludes Congress from enacting laws that abridge the freedom of speech. Does that mean laws punishing incitements to riot, or conspiracies to violate the antitrust laws are unconstitutional just because speech is involved? Of course not. The First Amendment cannot be read literally. But that means that judges must decide what fits into "the freedom of speech" without clear guidance from the constitutional text.

In sum, to believe that judges can interpret the Constitution or laws without at times resorting to values and policy preferences is to indulge in delusion. In hard cases, a degree of judicial "law making" is inevitable because there is no universal consensus about how to resolve textual ambiguities among judges, lawyers, professors, scholars, or politicians. Several approaches command legitimacy in our legal culture and traditions.

One interpretive theory, championed by Justice Antonin Scalia, gives pivotal importance to the "original meaning" of the framers of the Constitution or the statute in question. In other words, the judge should interpret the text according to the meaning it held for its originators.

A competing theory gives substantial weight to the underlying purpose of the constitutional provision at issue in giving contemporary meaning to ambiguous language in the Constitution. Former Supreme Court Justice William Brennan was the foremost champion of the purposive theory of interpretation, and it retains a substantial block of adherents.

Some theories insist on a preferred constitutional position for First Amendment rights and special protection for politically weak discrete and insular minorities, while relegating property rights to the caboose on a constitutional locomotive. Others view property rights as the cornerstone of a system of ordered liberty.

Since predictability in the law is valuable, universal agreement on a judicial theory of interpretation would be desirable. Uncertainty and litigation would be reduced (although not eliminated because every theory requires some judgment in application); and, litigants would not be treated differently depending on the luck of the judicial draw. But there is no likelihood that interpretive unanimity, or even close to unanimity, will ever be achieved. No commanding consensus dictates that one interpretive theory is unarguably superior to all others. Rankings turn largely on personal values, a judges' world-view, and beliefs regarding the proper role of the judiciary in policing, complementing, and confining majoritarian politics.

American political and legal culture has come to accept disputes between and among judges about which interpretive theory is best without attempting to enshrine one particular theory as the only acceptable approach. It is not thought unjudicial or heretical for a judge to choose among the dominant theories, like voting Republican rather than Democratic, or vice versa. They are all sufficiently similar as practiced to yield a jurisprudence with a tolerable level of uncertainty and coherence.

Popular control?

If judges make law, at least in some cases, shouldn't they be subject to popular control just like other political actors? The answer seems a categorical "No!" A central point of our Constitution is to limit the power of the political branches of government by deputing independent judges to decide on the constitutionality of laws or executive action in concrete cases. In other words, the Founders did not always desire popular majorities to prevail, recognizing that tyranny by the majority is tyranny nonetheless. If federal judges were mere mouthpieces of popular sentiment, cherished constitutional limitations would largely vanish.

Self-interested majorities are not likely to believe their actions unconstitutional. They are driven overwhelmingly by partisan, parochial, and short-term visions that could destroy ordered liberty both for the living and for those yet to be born. Think of Robespierre, Danton, and the Jacobins of the French Revolution and their oppressive popular tribunals. Remember also the Federalist Party in the United States Congress, which both applauded the First Amendment and soon undermined freedom of speech in the Sedition Act of 1798 to muzzle their Republican rivals.

In sum, everything we know about human nature and political ambition discredits the idea that Congress or the presidency could responsibly be entrusted with adjudicating the constitutionality of their own action or that of the rival branch. Does anyone seriously believe that Congress would have decided the landmark 1974 "Nixon tapes" case fairly, or resolved the parade of cases stemming from the Independent Counsel's investigation of President Clinton evenhandedly?

Judges in the United States, in stark contrast to members of Congress and the executive branch, live in a culture that treasures intellectual honesty and principles that rise above the political moment. That culture is not ordained by law, but it is a critical fact nonetheless. It is what largely inspires the public to comply voluntarily with the countless judicial decisions rendered daily. The judicial process is fair and evenhanded in most cases. Decisions are usually recognized as non-partisan. The past political party attachments of judges are generally recognized by lawyers as marginal to the outcome of most litigation. What is vastly more significant is judicial philosophy, which transcends party lines. Justice John Paul Stevens, thought by many to be a "liberal" judge, was appointed by a Republican President, Gerald Ford; many Republicans, however, regularly disagree with his votes and opinions.

Like judicial decrees, laws enacted by Congress and Executive Orders of the President also command general obedience. But judicial decrees tend to be accepted ungrudgingly as legitimate and fair because of the openness and impartiality of the judicial process and because of the reasoned analyses that are the signature of judicial opinion. By contrast, when Congress holds hearings in anticipation of laws, witness lists are customarily stacked to favor one outcome over another, legislative compromises are regularly brokered in the dark, justifications for the law are often thin and counterfactual, and votes are characteristically cast for partisan rather than principled reasons. In spite of the less than ideal character of the workings of the legislative process, however, laws are obeyed by the American people because Congress itself is established by the Constitution. (Indeed, as the subject of Article I of the Constitution, it is given pride of place.) But the obedience often comes at the price of individual resentment or bitterness that may ultimately find expression in antisocial behavior or political extremism.

In other political and judicial cultures, these observations may not obtain. In Great Britain, for instance, it is arguable that laws enacted by Parliament may be received with greater popular legitimacy than judicial rulings. In other words, judicial independence in the United States may be more compelling than elsewhere. There is nothing inherent in judging, per se, that makes the process superior on the legitimacy scale than legislation.

How accountable are judges?

Judges are subject to much more popular accountability than is customarily recognized by critics. The constitutional rulings of the Supreme Court can be overridden by constitutional amendment, which explains the Eleventh, Fourteenth, Sixteenth, Nineteenth, and Twenty-Sixth Amendments relating to federal jurisdiction, citizenship, income taxation, and the suffrage, respectively.

Statutory and common law rulings can be overcome by simple legislation. The Supreme Court's "political question" doctrine leaves the majority of foreign policy and national security decisions of the Congress and the President beyond judicial review, like the constitutionality of wars or legislative involvement in the revocation of treaties. During wartime, the High Court has uniformly bowed to the political branches in the choice of measures needed to promote victory, including the dubious Sedition Act prosecutions in World War I and the disgraceful relocation and incarceration of Japanese American citizens in World War II.

The Constitution, furthermore, excludes the judiciary from interfering in highly charged political issues. Thus, Congress is entrusted with judging the elections, returns, and qualifications of its own members under Article I, section 5. And issues relating to impeachment and the trial of impeachments are reserved for the House and Senate. In 1876, when disputes arose over 20 electoral votes for the President, Congress decided the questions by creating a 15-member commission to investigate and decide subject to overruling if both the House and Senate disagreed.

Even more important than these formal restraints on the power of judges to defy popular sentiments are mortality and the influence of orthodoxy. Life tenure for federal judges does not confer immortality. All die, and most retire. Their replacements are appointed by a popularly elected President and confirmed by popularly elected senators. Their judicial philosophies will ordinarily echo that of their political benefactors. This constant replenishment of "new blood" on the judiciary insures against decisions that substantially deviate from popular sentiments. That is not academic theorizing; it is the actual experience of the United States, whether in areas of crime, church-state relations, civil rights, abortion, obscenity, privacy, or states' rights.

The United States Supreme Court and lower federal and state judges have never for long blocked policies coveted by the majority, including President Franklin D. Roosevelt's controversial "New Deal." He was able to refashion the High Court without his ill-conceived "court packing" legislation through vacancies created by customary retirements. His New Deal policies ultimately passed muster and grew from an acorn to a giant oak tree in the United States Code.

Intellectual orthodoxy is as potent as the appointment process in keeping judicial decisions within the political mainstream. Justice Benjamin Cardozo described the phenomenon this way in *The Nature of the Judicial Process:* "The great tides and currents which engulf the rest of men, do not turn aside in their course, and pass the judges by." In other words, the majority of judges, despite their life tenures, are influenced in their decisions by prevailing intellectual fashions. Thus, during the heyday of laissez-faire capitalism from the Gilded Age to the Great Depression, the High Court regularly invalidated legislative manipulations of free market forces. When that thinking became discredited and was displaced by "Keynesian" economics

in the 1930s, the most drastic government marketplace interventions were sustained, including federal regulation of the home consumption of wheat! And the dramatic change in judicial attitude came before President Roosevelt made his first Supreme Court appointment.

In addition, one constant in American culture is a deep devotion to majority rule. It is daily indoctrinated, either expressly or tacitly, in group decisions, whether in the family, in the classroom, or in social or other clubs. The majority view is customarily accepted as the right standard. That idea is contained in the strong egalitarian strain in American life deftly portrayed by Alexis de Tocqueville in *Democracy in America:* every person ought to count equally in matters of importance since the law recognizes only first-class citizenship.

Judges do not shed these egalitarian doctrines when they put on robes. Most are instinctively reluctant to challenge popular will, even though that is a staple of constitutional litigation. Even the staunchly independent Justice Oliver Wendell Holmes trumpeted that "the legislatures are ultimate guardians of the liberties and welfare of the people in quite as great degree as the courts."

Finally, direct and informed criticism of judicial decisions also strengthens popular accountability. Chief Justice William Howard Taft lectured:

> Nothing tends more to render judges careful in their decisions and anxiously solicitous to do exact justice than the consciousness that every act of theirs is to be subject to the intelligent scrutiny of their fellow men, and to their candid criticism. . . . In the case of judges having a life tenure, indeed, their very independence makes the right freely to comment on their decisions of greater importance, because it is the only practical and available instrument in the hands of a free people to keep such judges alive to the reasonable demands of those they serve.

While Taft's general point is valid, he neglects constitutional and statutory amendments and the appointment process as equally if not more pivotal than criticism in preventing a life-tenured judiciary from morphing into Platonic guardians. Associate Justice Felix Frankfurter, in a letter to a former law clerk, also underscored the influence of Court criticism:

> I can assure you that explicit analysis and criticism of the way the Court is doing its business really gets under their skin, just as the praise of their constituencies, the so-called liberal journals and well-known liberal

approvers, only fortifies them in their present result-oriented jurisprudence.

All of these varied elements of judicial accountability fully substantiate Alexander Hamilton's characterization of the judicial branch as "the least dangerous to the political rights of the Constitution." The idea that judges are running the country is a figment of vivid imaginations, although many of their decisions are justifiably vulnerable to informed and trenchant criticism, which should be encouraged. That is how judicial errors can be corrected without undermining judicial independence.

The current dangers

The inestimable value of judicial independence is its centrality to the rule of law, that is, a set of rules that govern private behavior and the exercise of government power and whose application in litigation is predictable and evenhanded no matter what the popular politics of the case. Judicial independence also promotes domestic tranquility and harmony by ensuring disputants of a fair day in court and reasoned and careful responses to their claims, a form of catharses when passions are aroused. Losers who feel they received a fair procedural deal will not ordinarily leave the courthouse embittered or angered.

It would be unsustainable to assert, however, that all our cherished freedom and liberties would crumble by even the slightest inroad on judicial independence. A deep and nationwide consensus that has emerged over two centuries would keep a large portion undisturbed even without any institutionalized judicial check on Congress or the President. Judge Learned Hand in "The Contribution of an Independent Judiciary to Civilization" warned against exaggerating the importance of the judicial branch in these words:

> This much I think I do know that a society so riven that the spirit of moderation is gone, no court can save; that a society where that spirit flourishes, no court need save; that in a society which evades its responsibility by thrusting upon the courts the nurture of that spirit, that spirit in the end will perish.

But even small increments of liberty and justice are hard to come by, and thus judicial independence should be jealously guarded against either witting or unwitting subversion. In the contemporary political climate, that means vocal denunciation of the idea of impeaching and removing federal judges for making

decisions that are disliked. Such a political Sword of Damocles would create at least the appearance that federal judges are more beholden to political patrons than the law, and thus undermine the popular legitimacy of the judicial branch. Further, most judges are not second editions of Sir Thomas More (who was executed for his fidelity to the law) and might compromise their intellectual integrity to remain in office.

Case-specific litmus tests for Supreme Court and subordinate federal court appointments should be likewise assailed. Whether the test is applied by the President in searching for a nominee or by senators in the confirmation process, it is a dagger at judicial independence. Supreme Court candidates of ordinary ambition will shade their views in order to pass political muster, and become intellectually "locked in" on a battery of controversial issues before they arise in actual cases and controversies where all sides are heard and debate ensues among the nine justices.

In sum, case-specific questioning of would-be or actual nominees is tantamount to political arm twisting to dictate the outcome of constitutional questions by the judicial branch. Thus, the President should issue an order to the Attorney General prohibiting any such interrogation of potential judicial nominees, and the Senate Judiciary Committee should adopt a companion rule to govern its members during confirmation hearings or face-to-face meetings with nominees.

Questions about judicial philosophy, unlike case-specific litmus tests, have a legitimate place in presidential or senatorial inquiries. Philosophy may give a hint as to how an appointee would decide a particular case, but it is a very inexact proxy. As Justice Holmes quipped, general principles do not decide concrete cases. Associate Justices David Souter and Clarence Thomas were both appointed by President George Bush, but regularly vote diametrically opposite in major constitutional cases. A nominee's philosophy can therefore be scrutinized closely without fostering the damaging appearance that politics, rather than legal reasoning, determines judicial decisions. As long as varied judicial philosophies are accepted as constitutionally legitimate, there is nothing wrong or worrisome to an independent judiciary about a president endorsing one over another in making appointments.

Equally ill-conceived as case-specific intellectual extortion are legislative initiatives to manipulate the jurisdiction of the federal courts in order to circumvent interpretations some politicians disdain. One example are bills that would absolutely prohibit judges from ordering local or state governments to levy taxes even in the absence of less drastic alternatives for remedying a constitutional violation, such as closing all public schools to preserve segregated education via private schooling. The legitimate way for Congress directly to overcome what it believes are Supreme Court constitutional errors is through proposing amendments by two-thirds majorities as stipulated in Article 5 of the Constitution. It speaks volumes about an alleged rogue judiciary that Congress has never sent proposed amendments to the states for ratification that concern abortion, prayer in school, affirmative action, political reapportionment, or flag burning. Such complacency does not mean that the Supreme Court has never erred in these divisive areas of constitutional law; it does mean that whatever errors have been committed have been within a broad mainstream of popular thinking or sentiments and thus at worst only modestly counter-majoritarian.

****

Judicial independence in the United States strengthens ordered liberty, domestic tranquility, the rule of law, and democratic ideals. At least in our political culture, it has proved superior to any alternative form of discharging the judicial function that has ever been tried or conceived. It would be folly to squander this priceless constitutional gift to placate the clamors of benighted political partisans.

Note

This article originally appeared in Volume 84, Number 2, September–October 2000, pages 58–63.

Attacks on judges: why they fail

Barry Friedman

In testimony last summer before a U.S. Senate subcommittee, the author recounts that the American people consistently reject challenges to an independent federal judiciary.

Why are judges attacked at some times, but not others, as interfering with the popular will? The answer is not as obvious as one might think. Judges have been attacked often throughout history, but the complaint has not always been (as it is now) that judges are interfering with the proper workings of democracy.

To answer this question, I have spent the last three years studying the history of popular attacks on the judiciary. Rather than confining myself to academic tomes, my research materials have been newspapers, magazines, books written for the general public, congressional speeches and debates, cartoons, correspondence and speeches of political figures, and letters to the editor by ordinary citizens—in short, anything that would tell me as best as I could discern the state of public opinion about judges.

Attacks on the courts have occurred for some 200 years. My subject matter has been the Jeffersonian attacks on the Federalist judiciary, many similar attacks during the period of Jacksonian democracy, the vilification of the *Dred Scott* decision, challenges to judicial authority during Reconstruction, the large public outcry surrounding the *Legal Tender* decisions, the long period of Populist-Progressive attacks on the courts reaching from the late 1800s to the 1920s, the New Deal and the Court-packing controversy, challenges to the decisions of the Warren Court (such as *Brown v. Board of Education*, decisions favoring communists, and the controversial reapportionment or school prayer decisions), and, finally, some more recent controversies such as that surrounding the Supreme Court's decision in *Roe v. Wade*.

From 200 years of challenges to judicial independence, some fairly clear lessons have emerged. First, attacks on the judiciary throughout history are inevitably political. By this I mean they are launched to express dissatisfaction with the content of particular judicial decisions. Second, those attacks have come from every point on the ideological spectrum. Third, virtually every technique one might think of to limit judicial decision making has already been suggested or tried. Finally, and most important, almost invariably challenges to judicial independence fail, because the public does not support them. Once the citizens of this country pay attention to the debate, they are approving of judicial independence and disapproving of attacks on it. Unquestionably this popular sentiment has grown over the course of the more than two centuries of attacks on the federal judiciary. In the rare instances in which Congress has taken steps to influence judicial decision making, the almost invariable public response has been regret.

Attacks are political

The first lesson is that attacks on the judiciary are invariably political. Note that I say political, and not partisan, though the attacks often (but not always) are partisan as well. By political I mean that no matter what members of Congress or the executive branch have said about why they are threatening judicial independence, they are doing it because they do not like the way judges are deciding particular cases.

Sometimes there is a great deal of candor on the subject, but sometimes political actors try to wrap their motives in something their constituents might find a bit more palatable. The need for sugar coating seems to have increased in this century, as the public increasingly has become uncomfortable with attacks on judges.

An example of candor occurred in the early 1800s, when President Thomas Jefferson's Democrat-Republicans tried to impeach Supreme Court Justice Samuel Chase. This was the first and last time—until recently—that we have seriously considered impeaching federal judges because of unhappiness with the decisions rendered.

Chase, by almost any standard, was fit material for impeachment. He regularly engaged in partisan harangues, he browbeat witnesses and counsel, and he even refused to hear the legal arguments of counsel in some cases. But Chase's impeachment failed, largely because of the Democrat-Republicans' admission that they sought impeachment on the basis of the justice's

Judicature Volume 81, Number 4, pp. 150–155

views on the merits. As John Quincy Adams reported in his memoirs concerning the views of Representative William Branch Giles, one of the prime movers in the impeachment effort, "removal by impeachment was nothing more than a declaration by Congress to this effect: You hold dangerous opinions, and if you are suffered to carry them into effect you will work the destruction of the nation. *We want your offices,* for the purpose of giving them to men who will fill them better."

In contrast, when Franklin Roosevelt launched his attack on the federal judiciary with his now-infamous Court-packing plan, he felt forced to provide a non-ideological cover for what was nonetheless obvious to all. Incidentally, this was not the first, but was assuredly the last, high-profile attempt to "pack" the membership of a federal court to achieve a desired result. When Roosevelt announced the plan on February 5, 1937, he justified it in terms of workload and judicial efficiency. For this he was attacked from all quarters as being disingenuous, and for having dictatorial tendencies. Newspapers around the country questioned Roosevelt's motives. Finally, Roosevelt had no choice but to be candid about his motives, which he did in a March 9 "fireside chat":

> Last Thursday I described the American form of government as a three-horse team provided by the Constitution to the American people so that their field might be plowed. The three horses are, of course, the three branches of government—the Congress, the executive, and the courts. Two of the horses are pulling in unison today; the third is not.

Conservatives and liberals

History teaches that challenges to judicial independence have come from liberals as well as conservatives. It is easy to forget this, because in recent years complaints about judges generally have come from conservatives, concerned about what they perceive as liberal decisions. In the first half of this century, however, it was exactly the opposite. Perhaps it is for this very reason that Americans have developed a deep-seated caution about those attacks, concerned about creating a precedent that might come back to haunt them. Today it might be a liberal judicial ox that is gored, but tomorrow it might be a conservative one.

The issues confronting the United States in its first century were very different from what they are today. In the early 1800s, and again in the 1820s, the Supreme Court was attacked for its nationalizing tendencies. The causes for concern were often Supreme Court decisions that required the states to adhere to the policies of a national Congress and national Constitution. *Dred Scott,* of course, was attacked by Republicans for its pro-slavery outcome, and the notable instance of jurisdiction-stripping during Reconstruction represented a Radical and Republican attack on the Court, which—it was feared—would invalidate Reconstruction.

In this century the ideology is much more familiar. For the first half of this century it was Progressives and liberals who were attacking an entrenched conservative Court. Between the late 1800s and 1937, the Supreme Court invalidated the income tax, upheld the use of injunctions against the labor movement, and struck down numerous laws to protect worker safety, prohibit child labor, and regulate the hours and minimum wages of all employees. Then, of course, there was invalidation of many New Deal measures such as the Agricultural Adjustment Act.

Indeed, it is fair to say that during this century until the late 1950s defenders of judicial independence almost always were conservatives. Generally speaking, we did not really have a Supreme Court of liberal bent in this country until the 1950s. For most of history, conservatives defended the judiciary on the ground that it was the judiciary's job to protect constitutional values against rampant majorities. From the perspective of a constitutional historian, it is more than a little odd to see conservatives attacking the Supreme Court in the name of the people. When the courts were attacked by progressives for interfering with popular will, conservative response was simply to point out that that was the Court's function—to trump popular will in the name of the Constitution. Perhaps it is well to remember the election of 1924, in which Progressive party candidate Robert LaFollette gave a speech to a packed Madison Square Garden, arguing:

> Either the court must be the final arbiter of what the law is, or else some means must be found to correct its decisions. If the court is the final and conclusive authority to determine what laws Congress may pass, then, obviously, the court is the real ruler of the country, exactly the same as the most absolute king would be.

Who was the judiciary's chief defender at the time? The Republican who won the presidential election in which judicial independence was a chief issue: Calvin Coolidge.

A road often traveled

Almost any imaginable technique to control the federal judiciary has been proposed. At times there were very serious efforts to implement such proposals, the vast majority of which failed. As we have proceeded through our 200-plus years of history, the American people seem to have ruled out the candidates one by one.

During the Jeffersonian Era, Congress took two direct swipes at the federal judiciary, one of which was the attempted impeachment of federal judges. First, it repealed the Circuit Judges Act of 1801, which had created numerous judgeships the Federalists rapidly filled before the Democrat-Republicans took office. The legislation, incidentally, was challenged on constitutional grounds and upheld by the Supreme Court. Second, there was the failed campaign to impeach federal judges.

One popular technique for dealing with unpopular decisions has been defiance. During Andrew Jackson's presidency, the states sometimes defied Supreme Court decisions, such as when Georgia went through with the execution by hanging of a Cherokee named Corn Tassels in the face of a Supreme Court order not to do so. Jackson was thought to lack the will to enforce federal court mandates. In another Cherokee controversy with Georgia, Jackson reputedly said, "John Marshall has made his decree, now let him enforce it." As one newspaper aptly reported, "We are sick of such talks [of defiance]. If there is not power in the Constitution to preserve itself—it is not worth keeping." It is notable, however, that when John Calhoun launched the nullification movement, Jackson made it clear he stood behind the Court. The last widespread attempt at defiance was in response to *Brown v. Board of Education,* not a chapter in our history of which anyone today is especially proud.

Attempting to strip the courts of jurisdiction also has been popular. During Reconstruction, Congress succeeded in the only successful attempt to strip the Supreme Court of jurisdiction, passing legislation over a veto by President Andrew Johnson that deprived the Court of jurisdiction to hear *Ex parte McCardle,* in which, it was feared, the Court would strike down Reconstruction. Another attempt shortly thereafter to limit the Court's jurisdiction for similar reason failed, and the only other close attempt was in 1957, in response to Supreme Court decisions that seemed to protect communists. The Jenner-Butler bill, which aimed to strip the Court's power in many cases involving communists, was watered down to almost nothing and still failed. Since then numerous proposals have been made to strip the courts of power over busing, abortion, or school prayer decisions, none of which have gone anywhere.

Court packing also had its day. I already have discussed FDR's failed attempt to pack the New Deal Court, the last serious attempt to do so in our history. The only arguably successful Court-packing occurred on the heels of Reconstruction, when President Ulysses Grant put two new justices on the Supreme Court, thereby rapidly changing the result in the *Legal Tender* cases. I say arguably, because history suggests the appointments may simply have been fortuitous.

Although these are the most frequently used techniques to control the federal courts, numerous others have been proposed. Many of these proposals were made during the Populist-Progressive era, and many have resurfaced recently. Examples include requiring a unanimous or a two-thirds vote for the Supreme Court to overturn laws, limiting the jurisdiction of the lower courts to overturn laws, recall of judges, limited terms of judges, and reversal of judicial decisions by the Senate. About the only thing not seriously proposed has been the rack, although vituperative popular sentiment has been expressed, including burning Supreme Court justices in effigy during the New Deal.

Support for existing system

As the history related thus far suggests, almost every attempt to interfere with judicial independence has failed. There is a reason for this—the public has chosen regularly to support the system we have, warts and all. Often it takes time for the public to focus its attention fully on what is happening in Washington, D.C., and attempts to limit judicial independence have gone quite far before being derailed. But for the most part derailed is what they have been. Interestingly, those politicians who suggested aggressive treatment of the courts sometimes watched their political futures fail along with their proposals.

The only successful attempts to interfere with judicial independence met with subsequent popular unhappiness. Those "successes" were the stripping of the Supreme Court's jurisdiction to hear the *McCardle* case, and the arguable packing of the Court that heard the second *Legal Tender* decision. As noted above, a subsequent attempt to strip jurisdiction failed; the legislation was a matter of tremendous controversy, with many Republicans splitting off and opposing the measure. Similarly, even though the first *Legal Tender* decision— partially invalidating the government's printing of money during the Civil War—was met with widespread unhappiness, when the Court changed its mind in response to new membership, the second *Legal Tender* decision was met with even more widespread derision. It was one of the Supreme Court's lowest moments.

From the early days of the Republic until after the Civil War, judicial supremacy was not established. Once it was established in the minds of the American people, politicians tried varying techniques to control that supremacy. Some of the early attempts succeeded, but gradually over time the citizenry has expressed its view that the ordinary processes of judicial decision making and judicial attrition should run their course.

Although there is loud public clamoring at times to do something about judges, when push comes to shove and calmer minds prevail, the public has always stepped away from the abyss. In the meantime, some politicians have fallen into it. FDR, elected in one of history's largest popular mandates, fell quickly to his lowest approval when he proposed the Court-packing plan. Matters were so bad Republicans stepped aside and permitted Democrats to take the lead in challenging the president, who might not have recovered his popularity absent a world war. Other examples include Teddy Roosevelt, whose broad attacks on federal judges and his Progressive attempts to regain the presidency both failed, as did those of Robert LaFollette.

Ordinary processes work

What final lesson can be drawn from all this? Perhaps that when all is said and done, the American people have come to feel that the ordinary processes for controlling judges and the judiciary should prevail.

What are these ordinary processes? The first, and most relevant to today's debates, is the normal appellate process. Today's complaints seem for the most part to be about the decisions of individual judges, not about the judiciary as a whole. That is why the word impeachment has been uttered so regularly. But why is this necessary? No one judge decides any important case. In the federal system at least a three judge appellate panel, and perhaps an en banc court, reviews any case that is important. And truly significant cases are almost certainly going to be heard by the Supreme Court.

Indeed, it is because of the availability of Supreme Court review—a likelihood in landmark cases—that today's debate is so unfathomable to some of us that watch from the sidelines. Of the nine members of the Supreme Court, seven were appointed by Republican presidents. It is hardly a radical Court, and certainly not a radically liberal one. After all, for the first time since the New Deal we are seeing a resurgence in federalism. The right to abortion, while still existent, has been narrowed. The Court recently lowered the wall between church and state somewhat. Many death sentences are being enforced. It is difficult to see what the concern is for individual decisions, when the mechanism to overturn any aberrant ones appears to be in good health.

Second, there is the ordinary appointment and confirmation process of federal judges. If there was any lesson from the failed Court-packing plan, it was the general public's sense that natural attrition was the correct constitutional way to influence the federal judiciary. It has worked reasonably well—about as well as any system in our government—for almost 200 years. The truly conservative course would seem to be reluctance in tinkering with it.

Indeed, it does seem that much of what is currently occurring reflects anxiety about the number of appointments to the federal bench President Clinton may make. But this too is unseemly and a bit incomprehensible. Historically, it reeks of the same motives that caused the Federalists to pack the judiciary before Jefferson took office. In more recent history, 12 years of Republican presidential leadership placed a majority of Republican judges on the bench. Now, President Clinton's appointments must be approved by a Republican Senate, and given the case backlog and numerous vacancies, one can only hope that nominations will be forthcoming and confirmations will occur at a reasonable pace after that. But by any measure reported in the popular press or academic journals, President Clinton's appointments have been quite moderate in their decision making. It is hard to see, again, what the fuss is about.

The third process is one seldom discussed, but plainly evident. It is, in large part, a function of the appointment process, as well as the fact that federal judges are American citizens like the rest of us, having grown up in the same culture. The result of this process, if one may call it that, is that federal judicial decisions rarely fall out of line with popular sentiment for very long. Political scientist Robert Dahl observed this 40 years ago at the height of the Warren Court controversy, and numerous other academics have made similar observations. Surely that is the case today. The courts have "moderated" (if that is the right word) their views on abortion, the death penalty, the rights of

Delving deeper

Senator John Ashcroft (R-Missouri), chairman of the Judiciary Committee's Subcommittee on the Constitution, Federalism, and Property Rights, and Senator Strom Thurmond (R-South Carolina) followed up on Professor Friedman's testimony with a letter containing additional questions. The following is an edited version of the professor's written response:

Would you agree that, as a general matter, it is a proper function for Congress to examine the proper allocation of jurisdiction between state and federal courts?

In general, the answer is yes. You undoubtedly are familiar with the "Madisonian Compromise," in which the framers of the Constitution gave Congress the power to create lower federal courts, but left it to Congress to decide whether to do so. Generally speaking, that power has been interpreted to give Congress leeway in deciding which lower courts to create and what jurisdiction to bestow upon them. Thus, as a practical matter Congress regularly decides whether to have federal courts hear specific causes of action, or whether to leave them in the hands of the state courts.

The simplicity of this general answer, however, betrays another question of great complexity regarding the extent to which the Constitution imposes limitations on Congress's power to control the jurisdiction of the federal courts. This is one of the most mooted questions in the academic literature, with scholars of great ability coming to very different answers. Some would accord Congress great authority, perhaps even to remove jurisdiction from the federal courts over virtually any question. Others advance varying theories that would limit Congress's power.[*] My own position is that the Constitution is unclear on this question, for better or for worse, and that answers will be worked out as a matter of repeated interaction among the branches of the federal government.

Which brings me to history, once again. Although the question is much-mooted, it tends to be an academic debate simply because Congress rarely has sought to exercise the power. The only "successful" example of jurisdiction stripping occurred when the Republican Congress—in an effort to fend off a decision regarding the constitutionality of Reconstruction—stripped the Supreme Court of its statutory authority to hear certain habeas corpus cases. I put the word "successful" in quotation marks because although the Supreme Court acquiesced in this removal of its jurisdiction, it hinted that other means of review were available, a state of affairs that quickly proved itself to be correct. I also put "successful" in quotations because even the Republican Congress resisted subsequent efforts to strip jurisdiction, necessary though they appeared to be to avoid a decision on Reconstruction. Moderate Republicans (and much of the public) were so put off by the shenanigans that led to the original withdrawal of jurisdiction that they recoiled from further attempts.

The latest major attempt to strip the Supreme Court of jurisdiction was in response to several decisions in 1957 that seemed pro-communist. The bill that was the subject of attention was the Jenner-Butler bill, ironic because in an earlier era Senator Butler had sought to amend the Constitution to protect the Supreme Court from any such incursions on its constitutional role. This only serves to reinforce the point I made in my original testimony: attacks on the Court tend to come when people disagree with the substantive content of judicial decisions. The Jenner-Butler bill attracted wide national attention. In its original form the bill would have stripped jurisdiction over a number of areas, such as state bar admissions. In response to criticism, the original legislation was watered down thoroughly. Nonetheless, it still was defeated in a close and closely watched debate in the Senate. Supreme Court opponents could not even muster the votes to overturn a Supreme Court decision holding that the federal sedition law preempted similar state laws.

The point we can glean from history is that it is important to distinguish between Congress's general power to see that jurisdiction is allocated in sensible fashion between the state and federal courts, and jurisdiction-stripping legislation enacted by Congress simply to reverse the trend of decisions with which it disagrees. I believe no one disputes the necessity of Congress exercising the former function, although they may have strong opinions as to whether Congress is doing a good job or not, as we have seen during recent debates over congressional legislation federalizing crime. On the other hand, historical precedent would discount Congress's power to strike out at the federal courts in response to the substance of decisions. And for good reason. In all these cases the concern was that the independence of federal judges would be threatened.

During my testimony, you questioned whether the removal of jurisdiction over specific sorts of cases necessarily would threaten judicial independence, suggesting that judges would remain free to decide cases in any fashion they wished in the areas left open to them. I understand the logic of your position, but would disagree with its application in practice. I think my central point finds support in the very distinction I draw above. If Congress merely is doing its housekeeping job of allocating jurisdiction, I do not believe independence would be, or would seem to be, threatened. But stripping jurisdiction out of unhappiness with substantive outcomes makes it patent to judges and to the general public that if judges do not toe the line Congress would like to see followed, the judges simply will be removed from the picture. History suggests the public has seen such attempts for precisely what they are, as attacks on judicial independence, and such attacks have been resisted.

One historical example of a successful legislative reaction to perceived judicial activism is the Norris-La Guardia Act, which limits the ability of federal courts to issue injunctions against labor organizations. Do you consider that act to be an illegitimate intrusion on judicial independence?

This question raises a narrower issue than the question above, namely whether Congress has the power to remove a particular remedial tool from the federal courts. My answer turns on the principle widely accepted in this country and made plain by Chief Justice John Marshall in *Marbury v. Madison* that "[t]he very essence of civil liberty certainly consists in the right of every individual to claim the protection of the laws, whenever he receives an injury."

Generally speaking, I do not believe the remedial power of the federal courts can be limited to such an extent that those courts cannot act effectively to

remedy constitutional violations. There is good reason for this. If federal courts lack the power to provide an effective remedy for violations of the citizenry's constitutional rights by the other branches of government, then our entire system of constitutional government is threatened.

The seminal case on the labor injunction provisions of the Norris-La Guardia Act is the Supreme Court's 1938 decision in *Lauf v. E.G. Shinner & Co.* As Professor Gordon Young made clear in a law review article (*A Critical Reassessment of the Case Law Bearing on Congress's Power to Restrict the Jurisdiction of the Lower Federal Courts*, 54 Md. L.Rev. 132 (1995)), some read the *Lauf* decision as approving of Congress's broad power to limit the federal courts' jurisdiction.

I believe, in agreement with Professor Young, that *Lauf* stands for a narrower principle, one consistent with the general principle I advanced above. The injunction provision challenged in *Lauf* did not forbid labor injunctions entirely; it merely curtailed their use unless specific (albeit stringent) conditions were met. To the extent that those conditions themselves permitted federal courts to issue injunctions when the Constitution required them, the decision is unproblematic. Moreover, there is every reason to suspect that at the time *Lauf* was decided, this was the case. *Lauf* was decided right after the Supreme Court famously switched direction on the question of economic rights. The employers' constitutional "right" to a labor injunction depended on substantive due process protection of property rights that by 1938 there was every reason to doubt the courts would afford. If this were the case, no constitutional right was threatened by the provisions of the Norris-La Guardia Act at issue, and the limitation on the remedy was unproblematic as well.

You state in your prepared testimony that "no one judge decides any important case." How do you respond to the concern that, as a practical matter, litigants often may not appeal activist decisions?

In answering this question, I would like to distinguish between the decision of a particular dispute between parties, and the resolution of a broader legal issue by the courts. The distinction is an important one, because in our society any important and

(Box continues on next page)

Delving deeper *(continued)*

controversial legal question is likely to arise in more than one case. Generally speaking, important questions tend to filter their way through the state and federal courts to the Supreme Court, gleaning the wisdom of many judges, rendered in disputes presented in adversarial fashion by several sets of lawyers.

As for the impact of a decision in any single case, however, I adhere completely to my view, which is that such a decision can be appealed. Appeal is of right, of course, to at least a three-judge panel of the court of appeals. After that, en banc review and review by the Supreme Court are available on a discretionary basis.

As litigants, some governments choose not to appeal. This, of course, is their decision. A government might decide to forego an appeal because the district court decision is persuasive, because it appears the weight of the law is against it, or even because the government's position is politically unpopular. It is difficult to hold the federal courts accountable for these governmental decisions. Indeed, because these governments are accountable to their citizens, it is difficult to complain about a government's decision not to appeal on the ground that the unappealed decision interferes with popular will.

It is possible that governments decide not to appeal because of the expense of litigation, a point which deserves response. This economic decision is one that every litigant faces. It is resolved by considering the cost of litigation, available resources, the importance of the case, and the likelihood of prevailing. These are the difficult decisions governments face every day. My own suspicion is that in the vast majority of cases that truly are of importance to a government, in which there is any chance of ultimate success, an appeal is taken.

Moreover, it is inaccurate to portray governments as standing alone in facing the resource question of whether to take an appeal. There are many organizations that assist governments in this regard. For example, I serve on the advisory board to the State and Local Legal Center, an organization that files briefs before the Supreme Court in matters of interest to state and local government.

I hope these answers are helpful to the subcommittee's further deliberations.

Note

* My own views are set out in Friedman, "A Different Dialogue: The Supreme Court, Congress and Federal Jurisdiction," *Nw. U. L. Rev.* 85 (1990), 1, which also contains a summary of the diversity of opinion on the subject.

---

criminal defendants, and the wall between church and state.

It is hard to see many issues on which today's federal judiciary is far outside the mainstream of public opinion. There may be a few, but then that is what living under a Constitution is all about. My sense is that they are undoubtedly very few, so few that those who are suggesting otherwise might check their premises. And yes, there are going to be decisions with which many of us disagree, even bitterly. Some decisions will seem very, very wrong. But we do have a way of correcting those problems, and that system has worked powerfully well for a long time. History suggests attempts to tamper with it are not, even in the short run, met with much success or public approval.

Note

This article originally appeared in Volume 81, Number 4, January–February 1998, pages 150–155. It was adapted from the author's testimony before the U.S. Senate Judiciary Committee's Subcommittee on the Constitution, Federalism, and Property Rights, July 14, 1997.